Contents

Preface

This new edition of the Oxford–Duden German Minidictionary reflects the changes to the spelling of German ratified by the governments of Germany, Austria, and Switzerland in July 1996.

It provides a handy and comprehensive reference work for tourists and business people, and covers the needs of the student for GCSE.

G. P. & J. S.

Introduction

The text of this new edition reflects recent changes to the spelling of German ratified in July 1996. The symbol (NEW) has been introduced to refer from the old spelling to the new, preferred one:

As *nt* **-ses, -se** (NEW) **Ass**

Diät *f* -,-en (*Med*) diet; **D~ leben** be on a diet. **d~** *adv* **d~ leben** (NEW) **D~ leben**, *s.* **Diät**.

absein† *vi sep* (*sein*) (NEW) **ab sein**, *s.* **ab**

schneuzen (sich) *vr* (NEW) **schnäuzen (sich)**

Rolladen *m* (NEW) **Rollladen**

When the two forms follow each other alphabetically or are used in phrases, the old form is shown in brackets after the new, preferred one:

Abfluss (Abfluß) *m* drainage; (*Öffnung*) drain. **A~rohr** *nt* drain-pipe

arm *a* (**ärmer, ärmst**) poor; **Arm und Reich (arm und reich)** rich and poor

Where both the old and new forms are valid, an equals sign = is used to refer to the preferred form:

aufwändig *a* = **aufwendig**

Tunfisch *m* = **Thunfisch**

Rand *m* . . . **zu R~e kommen mit** = **zurande kommen mit**, *s.* **zurande**

Stand *m* . . . **in S~ halten/setzen** = **instand halten/setzen**, *s.* **instand** . . .

Oxford University Press, Great Clarendon Street, Oxford OX2 6DP

Oxford New York
Athens Auckland Bangkok Bogota Bombay
Buenos Aires Calcutta Cape Town Dar es Salaam
Delhi Florence Hong Kong Istanbul Karachi
Kuala Lumpur Madras Madrid Melbourne
Mexico City Nairobi Paris Singapore
Taipei Tokyo Toronto Warsaw

and associated companies in
Berlin Ibadan

First published 1997

British Library Cataloguing in Publication Data

Data available

Library of Congress Cataloging in Publication Data

Data available

ISBN 0-19-860108-5

10 9 8 7 6 5 4 3 2 1

Typeset in Monotype Nimrod and Arial by
Latimer Trend & Company Ltd.

Printed in Great Britain by
Charles Letts (Scotland) Ltd.
Dalkeith, Scotland

The Oxford–Duden German Minidictionary

Second Edition

GERMAN–ENGLISH
ENGLISH–GERMAN

DEUTSCH–ENGLISCH
ENGLISCH–DEUTSCH

Gunhild Prowe
Jill Schneider

Oxford New York
OXFORD UNIVERSITY PRESS
1997

When such forms follow each other alphabetically, they are given with commas, with the preferred form in first place:

Pạnther, Pạnter *m* -s, - panther

In phrases, *od* (oder) is used:

. . . **deine(r,s)** *poss pron* yours; **die D~en** *od* **d~en** *pl* your family *sg*

. . . **seine(r,s)** *poss pron* his; **das S~e** *od* **s~e tun** do one's share

On the English–German side, only the preferred German form is given.

- A swung dash ~ represents the headword or that part of the headword preceding a vertical bar |. The initial letter of a German headword is given to show whether or not it is a capital.
- The vertical bar | follows the part of the headword which is not repeated in compounds or derivatives.
- Square brackets [ ] are used for optional material.
- Angled brackets < > are used after a verb translation to indicate the object; before a verb translation to indicate the subject; before an adjective to indicate a typical noun which it qualifies.
- Round brackets ( ) are used for field or style labels (see list on page vii) and for explanatory matter.
- A box □ indicates a new part of speech within an entry.
- *od* (oder) and *or* denote that words or portions of a phrase are synonymous. An oblique stroke / is used where there is a difference in usage or meaning.
- ≈ is used where no exact equivalent exists in the other language.
- A dagger † indicates that a German verb is irregular and that the parts can be found in the verb table on page 705. Compound verbs are not listed there as they follow the pattern of the basic verb.

- The stressed vowel is marked in a German headword by - (long) or · (short). A phonetic transcription is only given for words which do not follow the normal rules of pronunciation. These rules can be found on page 703.
- Phonetics are given for all English headwords and for derivatives where there is a change of pronunciation or stress. In blocks of compounds, if no stress is shown, it falls on the first element.
- A change in pronunciation or stress shown within a block of compounds applies only to that particular word (subsequent entries revert to the pronunciation and stress of the headword).
- German headword nouns are followed by the gender and, with the exception of compound nouns, by the genitive and plural. These are only given at compound nouns if they present some difficulty. Otherwise the user should refer to the final element.
- Nouns that decline like adjectives are entered as follows: **-e(r)** *m/f*, **-e(s)** *nt*.
- Adjectives which have no undeclined form are entered in the feminine form with the masculine and neuter in brackets **-e(r,s)**.
- The reflexive pronoun **sich** is accusative unless marked (*dat*).

Proprietary terms

This dictionary includes some words which are, or are asserted to be, proprietary names or trademarks. Their inclusion does not imply that they have acquired for legal purposes a non-proprietary or general significance, nor is any other judgement implied concerning their legal status. In cases where the editor has some evidence that a word is used as a proprietary name or trademark this is indicated by the letter (P), but no judgement concerning the legal status of such words is made or implied thereby.

Abbreviations / Abkürzungen

adjective	a	Adjektiv
abbreviation	abbr	Abkürzung
accusative	acc	Akkusativ
Administration	Admin	Administration
adverb	adv	Adverb
American	Amer	amerikanisch
Anatomy	Anat	Anatomie
Archaeology	Archaeol	Archäologie
Architecture	Archit	Architektur
Astronomy	Astr	Astronomie
attributive	attrib	attributiv
Austrian	Aust	österreichisch
Motor vehicles	Auto	Automobil
Aviation	Aviat	Luftfahrt
Biology	Biol	Biologie
Botany	Bot	Botanik
Chemistry	Chem	Chemie
collective	coll	Kollektivum
Commerce	Comm	Handel
conjunction	conj	Konjunktion
Cookery	Culin	Kochkunst
dative	dat	Dativ
definite article	def art	bestimmter Artikel
demonstrative	dem	Demonstrativ-
dialect	dial	Dialekt
Electricity	Electr	Elektrizität
something	etw	etwas
feminine	f	Femininum
familiar	fam	familiär
figurative	fig	figurativ
genitive	gen	Genitiv
Geography	Geog	Geographie
Geology	Geol	Geologie
Geometry	Geom	Geometrie

Grammar	Gram	Grammatik
Horticulture	Hort	Gartenbau
impersonal	impers	unpersönlich
indefinite article	indef art	unbestimmter Artikel
indefinite pronoun	indef pron	unbestimmtes Pronomen
infinitive	inf	Infinitiv
inseparable	insep	untrennbar
interjection	int	Interjektion
invariable	inv	unveränderlich
irregular	irreg	unregelmäßig
someone	jd	jemand
someone	jdm	jemandem
someone	jdn	jemanden
someone's	jds	jemandes
Journalism	Journ	Journalismus
Law	Jur	Jura
Language	Lang	Sprache
literary	liter	dichterisch
masculine	m	Maskulinum
Mathematics	Math	Mathematik
Medicine	Med	Medizin
Meteorology	Meteorol	Meteorologie
Military	Mil	Militär
Mineralogy	Miner	Mineralogie
Music	Mus	Musik
noun	n	Substantiv
Nautical	Naut	nautisch
North German	N Ger	Norddeutsch
nominative	nom	Nominativ
neuter	nt	Neutrum
or	od	oder
Proprietary term	P	Warenzeichen
pejorative	pej	abwertend
Photography	Phot	Fotografie
Physics	Phys	Physik
plural	pl	Plural
Politics	Pol	Politik

Pronunciation of the alphabet
Aussprache des Alphabets

English/Englisch		*German/Deutsch*
eɪ	a	a:
bi:	b	be:
si:	c	t͜se:
di:	d	de:
i:	e	e:
ef	f	ɛf
dʒi:	g	ge:
eɪtʃ	h	ha:
aɪ	i	i:
dʒeɪ	j	jɔt
keɪ	k	ka:
el	l	ɛl
em	m	ɛm
en	n	ɛn
əʊ	o	o:
pi:	p	pe:
kju:	q	ku:
a:(r)	r	ɛr
es	s	ɛs
ti:	t	te:
ju:	u	u:
vi:	v	fa͜u
'dʌblju:	w	ve:
eks	x	ɪks
waɪ	y	'ʏpsilɔn
zed	z	t͜sɛt
eɪ umlaut	ä	ɛ:
əʊ umlaut	ö	ø:
ju: umlaut	ü	y:
es'zed	ß	ɛs't͜sɛt

possessive	poss	Possessiv-
past participle	pp	zweites Partizip
predicative	pred	prädikativ
prefix	pref	Präfix
preposition	prep	Präposition
present	pres	Präsens
present participle	pres p	erstes Partizip
pronoun	pron	Pronomen
Psychology	Psych	Psychologie
past tense	pt	Präteritum
Railway	Rail	Eisenbahn
reflexive	refl	reflexiv
regular	reg	regelmäßig
relative	rel	Relativ-
Religion	Relig	Religion
see	s.	siehe
School	Sch	Schule
separable	sep	trennbar
singular	sg	Singular
South German	S Ger	Süddeutsch
slang	sl	Slang
someone	s.o.	jemand
something	sth	etwas
Technical	Techn	Technik
Telephone	Teleph	Telefon
Textiles	Tex	Textilien
Theatre	Theat	Theater
Television	TV	Fernsehen
Typography	Typ	Typographie
University	Univ	Universität
auxiliary verb	v aux	Hilfsverb
intransitive verb	vi	intransitives Verb
reflexive verb	vr	reflexives Verb
transitive verb	vt	transitives Verb
vulgar	vulg	vulgär
Zoology	Zool	Zoologie

A

Aal *m* **-[e]s,-e** eel. **a~en (sich)** *vr* laze; (*ausgestreckt*) stretch out

Aas *nt* **-es** carrion; (*sl*) swine

ab *prep* (+ *dat*) from; **ab Montag** from Monday □ *adv* off; (*weg*) away; (*auf Fahrplan*) departs; **ab sein** (*fam*) have come off; (*erschöpft*) be worn out; **von jetzt ab** from now on; **ab und zu** now and then; **auf und ab** up and down

abändern *vt sep* alter; (*abwandeln*) modify

abarbeiten *vt sep* work off; **sich a~** slave away

Abart *f* variety. **a~ig** *a* abnormal

Abbau *m* dismantling; (*Kohlen-*) mining; (*fig*) reduction. **a~en** *vt sep* dismantle; mine ⟨*Kohle*⟩; (*fig*) reduce, cut

abbeißen† *vt sep* bite off

abbeizen *vt sep* strip

abberufen† *vt sep* recall

abbestellen *vt sep* cancel; **jdn a~** put s.o. off

abbiegen† *vi sep* (*sein*) turn off; **[nach] links a~** turn left

Abbild *nt* image. **a~en** *vt sep* depict, portray. **A~ung** *f* **-,-en** illustration

Abbitte *f* **A~ leisten** apologize

abblättern *vi sep* (*sein*) flake off

abblend|en *vt/i sep* (*haben*) **[die Scheinwerfer] a~en** dip one's headlights. **A~licht** *nt* dipped headlights *pl*

abbrechen† *v sep* □ *vt* break off; (*abreißen*) demolish □ *vi* (*sein/haben*) break off

abbrennen† *v sep* □ *vt* burn off; (*niederbrennen*) burn down; let off ⟨*Feuerwerkskörper*⟩ □ *vi* (*sein*) burn down

abbringen† *vt sep* dissuade (**von** from)

Abbruch *m* demolition; (*Beenden*) breaking off; **etw** (*dat*) **keinen A~ tun** do no harm to sth

abbuchen *vt sep* debit

abbürsten *vt sep* brush down; (*entfernen*) brush off

abdank|en *vi sep* (*haben*) resign; ⟨*Herrscher:*⟩ abdicate. **A~ung** *f* **-,-en** resignation; abdication

abdecken *vt sep* uncover; (*abnehmen*) take off; (*zudecken*) cover; **den Tisch a~** clear the table

abdichten *vt sep* seal

abdrehen *vt sep* turn off

Abdruck *m* (*pl* ⸚e) impression; (*Finger-*) print; (*Nachdruck*) reprint. **a~en** *vt sep* print

abdrücken *vt/i sep* (*haben*) fire; **sich a~** leave an impression

Abend *m* **-s,-e** evening; **am A~** in the evening; **heute A~** this evening, tonight; **gestern A~** yesterday evening, last night. **a~** *adv* **heute/gestern a~** (NEW) **heute/gestern A~**, *s.* **Abend**. **A~brot** *nt* supper. **A~essen** *nt* dinner; (*einfacher*) supper. **A~kurs[us]** *m* evening class. **A~mahl** *nt* (*Relig*) [Holy] Communion. **a~s** *adv* in the evening

Abenteuer *nt* **-s,-** adventure; (*Liebes-*) affair. **a~lich** *a* fantastic; (*gefährlich*) hazardous

Abenteurer *m* **-s,-** adventurer

aber *conj* but; **oder a~** or else □ *adv* (*wirklich*) really; **a~ ja!** but of course! **Tausende und a~ Tausende** thousands upon thousands

Aber|glaube *m* superstition. **a~-gläubisch** *a* superstitious
aber|mals *adv* once again. **A~-tausende, a~tausende** *pl* thousands upon thousands
abfahr|en† *v sep* □ *vi* (*sein*) leave; ⟨*Auto:*⟩ drive off □ *vt* take away; (*entlangfahren*) drive along; use ⟨*Fahrkarte*⟩; **abgefahrene Reifen** worn tyres. **A~t** *f* departure; (*Talfahrt*) descent; (*Piste*) run; (*Ausfahrt*) exit
Abfall *m* refuse, rubbish, (*Amer*) garbage; (*auf der Straße*) litter; (*Industrie-*) waste. **A~eimer** *m* rubbish-bin; litter-bin
abfallen† *vi sep* (*sein*) drop, fall; (*übrig bleiben*) be left (**für** for); (*sich neigen*) slope away; (*fig*) compare badly (**gegen** with); **vom Glauben a~** renounce one's faith. **a~d** *a* sloping
Abfallhaufen *m* rubbish-dump
abfällig *a* disparaging, *adv* -ly
abfangen† *vt sep* intercept; (*beherrschen*) bring under control
abfärben *vi sep* (*haben*) ⟨*Farbe:*⟩ run; ⟨*Stoff:*⟩ not be colour-fast; **a~ auf** (+ *acc*) (*fig*) rub off on
abfassen *vt sep* draft
abfertigen *vt sep* attend to; (*zollamtlich*) clear; **jdn kurz a~** (*fam*) give s.o. short shrift
abfeuern *vt sep* fire
abfind|en† *vt sep* pay off; (*entschädigen*) compensate; **sich a~en mit** come to terms with. **A~ung** *f* -,-**en** compensation
abflauen *vi sep* (*sein*) decrease
abfliegen† *vi sep* (*sein*) fly off; (*Aviat*) take off
abfließen† *vi sep* (*sein*) drain *or* run away
Abflug *m* (*Aviat*) departure
Abfluss (**Abfluß**) *m* drainage; (*Öffnung*) drain. **A~rohr** *nt* drain-pipe
abfragen *vt sep* **jdn** *od* **jdm Vokabeln a~** test s.o. on vocabulary
Abfuhr *f* - removal; (*fig*) rebuff
abführ|en *vt sep* take *or* lead away. **a~end** *a* laxative. **A~mittel** *nt* laxative
abfüllen *vt sep* **auf** *od* **in Flaschen a~** bottle
Abgabe *f* handing in; (*Verkauf*) sale; (*Fußball*) pass; (*Steuer*) tax
Abgang *m* departure; (*Theat*) exit; (*Schul-*) leaving
Abgase *ntpl* exhaust fumes
abgeben† *vt sep* hand in; (*abliefern*) deliver; (*verkaufen*) sell; (*zur Aufbewahrung*) leave; (*Fußball*) pass; (*ausströmen*) give off; (*abfeuern*) fire; (*verlauten lassen*) give; cast ⟨*Stimme*⟩; **jdm etw a~** give s.o. a share of sth; **sich a~ mit** occupy oneself with
abgedroschen *a* hackneyed
abgehen† *v sep* □ *vi* (*sein*) leave; (*Theat*) exit; (*sich lösen*) come off; (*abgezogen werden*) be deducted; (*abbiegen*) turn off; (*verlaufen*) go off; **ihr geht jeglicher Humor ab** she totally lacks a sense of humour □ *vt* walk along
abgehetzt *a* harassed. **abgelegen** *a* remote. **abgeneigt** *a* **etw** (*dat*) **nicht abgeneigt sein** not be averse to sth. **abgenutzt** *a* worn.
Abgeordnete(r) *m/f* deputy; (*Pol*) Member of Parliament. **abgepackt** *a* pre-packed. **abgerissen** *a* ragged
abgeschieden *a* secluded. **A~heit** *f* - seclusion
abgeschlossen *a* (*fig*) complete; ⟨*Wohnung*⟩ self-contained. **abgeschmackt** *a* (*fig*) tasteless. **abgesehen** *prep* apart (from **von**). **abgespannt** *a* exhausted. **abgestanden** *a* stale. **abgestorben** *a* dead; ⟨*Glied*⟩ numb. **abgetragen** *a* worn. **abgewetzt** *a* threadbare
abgewinnen† *vt sep* win (**jdm** from s.o.); **etw** (*dat*) **Geschmack a~** get a taste for sth
abgewöhnen *vt sep* **jdm/sich das Rauchen a~** cure s.o. of/give up smoking
abgezehrt *a* emaciated

abgießen† *vt sep* pour off; drain ⟨*Gemüse*⟩
abgleiten† *vi sep (sein)* slip
Abgott *m* idol
abgöttisch *adv* **a~ lieben** idolize
abgrenz|en *vt sep* divide off; *(fig)* define. **A~ung** *f* - demarcation
Abgrund *m* abyss; *(fig)* depths *pl*
abgucken *vt sep (fam)* copy
Abguss (**Abguß**) *m* cast
abhacken *vt sep* chop off
abhaken *vt sep* tick off
abhalten† *vt sep* keep off; *(hindern)* keep, prevent (**von** from); *(veranstalten)* hold
abhanden *adv* **a~ kommen** get lost
Abhandlung *f* treatise
Abhang *m* slope
abhängen¹ *vt sep (reg)* take down; *(abkuppeln)* uncouple
abhäng|en²† *vi sep (haben)* depend (**von** on). **a~ig** *a* dependent (**von** on). **A~igkeit** *f* - dependence
abhärten *vt sep* toughen up
abhauen† *v sep* □ *vt* chop off □ *vi (sein) (fam)* clear off
abheben† *v sep* □ *vt* take off; *(vom Konto)* withdraw; **sich a~** stand out (**gegen** against) □ *vi (haben) (Cards)* cut [the cards]; *(Aviat)* take off; ⟨*Rakete:*⟩ lift off
abheften *vt sep* file
abhelfen† *vt sep (+ dat)* remedy
Abhilfe *f* remedy; **A~ schaffen** take [remedial] action
abholen *vt sep* collect; call for ⟨*Person*⟩; **jdn am Bahnhof a~** meet s.o. at the station
abhorchen *vt sep (Med)* sound
abhör|en *vt sep* listen to; *(überwachen)* tap; **jdn** *od* **jdm Vokabeln a~en** test s.o. on vocabulary. **A~gerät** *nt* bugging device
Abitur *nt* **-s** ≈ A levels *pl.* **A~ient(in)** *m* **-en,-en** *(f* **-,-nen**) pupil taking the '*Abitur*'
abkanzeln *vt sep (fam)* reprimand
abkaufen *vt sep* buy (*dat* from)
abkehren (sich) *vr sep* turn away
abkette[l]n *vt/i sep (haben)* cast off
abklingen† *vi sep (sein)* die away; *(nachlassen)* subside
abkochen *vt sep* boil
abkommen† *vi sep (sein)* **a~ von** stray from; *(aufgeben)* give up; **vom Thema a~** digress. **A~** *nt* **-s,-** agreement
abkömmlich *a* available
Abkömmling *m* **-s,-e** descendant
abkratzen *v sep* □ *vt* scrape off □ *vi (sein) (sl)* die
abkühlen *vt/i sep (sein)* cool; **sich a~** cool [down]; ⟨*Wetter:*⟩ turn cooler
Abkunft *f* - origin
abkuppeln *vt sep* uncouple
abkürz|en *vt sep* shorten; abbreviate ⟨*Wort*⟩. **A~ung** *f* short cut; *(Wort)* abbreviation
abladen† *vt sep* unload
Ablage *f* shelf; *(für Akten)* tray
ablager|n *vt sep* deposit; **sich a~n** be deposited. **A~ung** *f* **-,-en** deposit
ablassen† *v sep* □ *vt* drain [off]; let off ⟨*Dampf*⟩; *(vom Preis)* knock off □ *vi (haben)* **a~ von** give up; **von jdm a~** leave s.o. alone
Ablauf *m* drain; *(Verlauf)* course; *(Ende)* end; *(einer Frist)* expiry. **a~en**† *v sep* □ *vi (sein)* run *or* drain off; *(verlaufen)* go off; *(enden)* expire; ⟨*Zeit:*⟩ run out; ⟨*Uhrwerk:*⟩ run down □ *vt* walk along; *(absuchen)* scour (**nach** for); *(abnutzen)* wear down
ableg|en *v sep* □ *vt* put down; discard ⟨*Karte*⟩; *(abheften)* file; *(ausziehen)* take off; *(aufgeben)* give up; sit, take ⟨*Prüfung*⟩; **abgelegte Kleidung** cast-offs *pl* □ *vi (haben)* take off one's coat; *(Naut)* cast off. **A~er** *m* **-s,-** *(Bot)* cutting; *(Schössling)* shoot

ablehn|en *vt sep* refuse; (*missbilligen*) reject. **A~ung** *f* -,-en refusal; rejection
ableit|en *vt sep* divert; **sich a~en** be derived (**von/aus** from). **A~ung** *f* derivation; (*Wort*) derivative
ablenk|en *vt sep* deflect; divert ⟨*Aufmerksamkeit*⟩; (*zerstreuen*) distract. **A~ung** *f* -,-en distraction
ablesen† *vt sep* read; (*absuchen*) pick off
ableugnen *vt sep* deny
ablicht|en *vt sep* photocopy. **A~ung** *f* photocopy
abliefern *vt sep* deliver
ablös|en *vt sep* detach; (*abwechseln*) relieve; **sich a~en** come off; (*sich abwechseln*) take turns. **A~ung** *f* relief
abmach|en *vt sep* remove; (*ausmachen*) arrange; (*vereinbaren*) agree; **abgemacht!** agreed! **A~ung** *f* -,-en agreement
abmager|n *vi sep* (*sein*) lose weight. **A~ungskur** *f* slimming diet
abmarschieren *vi sep* (*sein*) march off
abmelden *vt sep* cancel ⟨*Zeitung*⟩; **sich a~** report that one is leaving; (*im Hotel*) check out
abmess|en† *vt sep* measure. **A~ungen** *fpl* measurements
abmühen (sich) *vr sep* struggle
abnäh|en *vt sep* take in. **A~er** *m* -s,- dart
Abnahme *f* - removal; (*Kauf*) purchase; (*Verminderung*) decrease
abnehm|en† *v sep* □ *vt* take off, remove; pick up ⟨*Hörer*⟩; **jdm etw a~en** take/(*kaufen*) buy sth from s.o. □ *vi* (*haben*) decrease; (*nachlassen*) decline; ⟨*Person:*⟩ lose weight; ⟨*Mond:*⟩ wane. **A~er** *m* -s,- buyer
Abneigung *f* dislike (**gegen** of)
abnorm *a* abnormal, *adv* -ly
abnutz|en *vt sep* wear out; **sich a~en** wear out. **A~ung** *f* - wear [and tear]
Abon|nement /abɔnəˈmã:/ *nt* -s,-s subscription. **A~nent** *m* -en,-en subscriber. **a~nieren** *vt* take out a subscription to
Abordnung *f* -,-en deputation
abpassen *vt sep* wait for; **gut a~** time well
abprallen *vi sep* (*sein*) rebound; ⟨*Geschoss:*⟩ ricochet
abraten† *vi sep* (*haben*) **jdm von etw a~** advise s.o. against sth
abräumen *vt/i* (*haben*) clear away; clear ⟨*Tisch*⟩
abrechn|en *v sep* □ *vt* deduct □ *vi* (*haben*) settle up; (*fig*) get even. **A~ung** *f* settlement [of accounts]; (*Rechnung*) account
Abreise *f* departure. **a~n** *vi sep* (*sein*) leave
abreißen† *v sep* □ *vt* tear off; (*demolieren*) pull down □ *vi* (*sein*) come off; (*fig*) break off
abrichten *vt sep* train
abriegeln *vt sep* bolt; (*absperren*) seal off
Abriss (Abriß) *m* demolition; (*Übersicht*) summary
abrufen† *vt sep* call away; (*Computer*) retrieve
abrunden *vt sep* round off; **nach unten/oben a~** round down/up
abrupt *a* abrupt, *adv* -ly
abrüst|en *vi sep* (*haben*) disarm. **A~ung** *f* disarmament
abrutschen *vi sep* (*sein*) slip
Absage *f* -,-n cancellation; (*Ablehnung*) refusal. **a~n** *v sep* □ *vt* cancel □ *vi* (*haben*) **[jdm] a~n** cancel an appointment [with s.o.]; (*auf Einladung*) refuse [s.o.'s invitation]
absägen *vt sep* saw off; (*fam*) sack
Absatz *m* heel; (*Abschnitt*) paragraph; (*Verkauf*) sale
abschaff|en *vt sep* abolish; get rid of ⟨*Auto, Hund*⟩. **A~ung** *f* abolition

abschalten *vt/i sep (haben)* switch off
abschätzig *a* disparaging, *adv* -ly
Abschaum *m (fig)* scum
Abscheu *m* - revulsion
abscheulich *a* revolting; *(fam)* horrible, *adv* -bly
abschicken *vt sep* send off
Abschied *m* **-[e]s,-e** farewell; *(Trennung)* parting; **A~ nehmen** say goodbye (**von** to)
abschießen† *vt sep* shoot down; *(abtrennen)* shoot off; *(abfeuern)* fire; launch ⟨*Rakete*⟩
abschirmen *vt sep* shield
abschlagen† *vt sep* knock off; *(verweigern)* refuse; *(abwehren)* repel
abschlägig *a* negative; **a~e Antwort** refusal
Abschlepp|dienst *m* breakdown service. **a~en** *vt sep* tow away. **A~seil** *nt* tow-rope. **A~wagen** *m* breakdown vehicle
abschließen† *v sep* □ *vt* lock; *(beenden, abmachen)* conclude; make ⟨*Wette*⟩; balance ⟨*Bücher*⟩; **sich a~** *(fig)* cut oneself off □ *vi (haben)* lock up; *(enden)* end. **a~d** *adv* in conclusion
Abschluss (Abschluß) *m* conclusion. **A~prüfung** *f* final examination. **A~zeugnis** *nt* diploma
abschmecken *vt sep* season
abschmieren *vt sep* lubricate
abschneiden† *v sep* □ *vt* cut off; **den Weg a~** take a short cut □ *vi (haben)* **gut/schlecht a~** do well/badly
Abschnitt *m* section; *(Stadium)* stage; *(Absatz)* paragraph; *(Kontroll-)* counterfoil
abschöpfen *vt sep* skim off
abschrauben *vt sep* unscrew
abschreck|en *vt sep* deter; *(Culin)* put in cold water ⟨*Ei*⟩. **a~end** *a* repulsive, *adv* -ly; **a~endes Beispiel** warning. **A~ungsmittel** *nt* deterrent
abschreib|en† *v sep* □ *vt* copy; *(Comm & fig)* write off □ *vi (haben)* copy. **A~ung** *f (Comm)* depreciation
Abschrift *f* copy
Abschuss (Abschuß) *m* shooting down; *(Abfeuern)* firing; *(Raketen-)* launch
abschüssig *a* sloping; *(steil)* steep
abschwächen *vt sep* lessen; **sich a~** lessen; *(schwächer werden)* weaken
abschweifen *vi sep (sein)* digress
abschwellen† *vi sep (sein)* go down
abschwören† *vi sep (haben)* (+ *dat*) renounce
abseh|bar *a* **in a~barer Zeit** in the foreseeable future. **a~en**† *vt/i sep (haben)* copy; *(voraussehen)* foresee; **a~en von** disregard; *(aufgeben)* refrain from; **es abgesehen haben auf** (+ *acc*) have one's eye on; *(schikanieren)* have it in for
abseìn† *vi sep (sein)* (NEW) **ab sein**, *s.* **ab**
abseits *adv* apart; *(Sport)* offside □ *prep* (+ *gen*) away from. **A~** *nt* - *(Sport)* offside
absend|en† *vt sep* send off. **A~er** *m* sender
absetzen *v sep* □ *vt* put *or* set down; *(ablagern)* deposit; *(abnehmen)* take off; *(absagen)* cancel; *(abbrechen)* stop; *(entlassen)* dismiss; *(verkaufen)* sell; *(abziehen)* deduct; **sich a~** be deposited; *(fliehen)* flee □ *vi (haben)* pause
Absicht *f* **-,-en** intention; **mit A~** intentionally, on purpose
absichtlich *a* intentional, *adv* -ly, deliberate, *adv* -ly
absitzen† *v sep* □ *vi (sein)* dismount □ *vt (fam)* serve ⟨*Strafe*⟩
absolut *a* absolute, *adv* -ly
Absolution /-ˈtsi̯oːn/ *f* - absolution
absolvieren *vt* complete; *(bestehen)* pass

absonderlich *a* odd
absonder|n *vt sep* separate; (*ausscheiden*) secrete; **sich a~n** keep apart (**von** from). **A~ung** *f* -,-en secretion
absor|bieren *vt* absorb. **A~ption** /-'tsjo:n/ *f* - absorption
abspeisen *vt sep* fob off (**mit** with)
abspenstig *a* **a~ machen** take (**jdm** from s.o.)
absperr|en *vt sep* cordon off; (*abstellen*) turn off; (*SGer*) lock. **A~ung** *f* -,-en barrier
abspielen *vt sep* play; (*Fußball*) pass; **sich a~** take place
Absprache *f* agreement
absprechen† *vt sep* arrange; **sich a~** agree; **jdm etw a~** deny s.o. sth
abspringen† *vi sep* (*sein*) jump off; (*mit Fallschirm*) parachute; (*abgehen*) come off; (*fam; zurücktreten*) back out
Absprung *m* jump
abspülen *vt sep* rinse; (*entfernen*) rinse off
abstamm|en *vi sep* (*haben*) be descended (**von** from). **A~ung** *f* - descent
Abstand *m* distance; (*zeitlich*) interval; **A~ halten** keep one's distance; **A~ nehmen von** (*fig*) refrain from
abstatten *vt sep* **jdm einen Besuch a~** pay s.o. a visit
abstauben *vt sep* dust
abstech|en† *vi sep* (*haben*) stand out. **A~er** *m* -s,- detour
abstehen† *vi sep* (*haben*) stick out; **a~ von** be away from
absteigen† *vi sep* (*sein*) dismount; (*niedersteigen*) descend; (*Fußball*) be relegated
abstell|en *vt sep* put down; (*lagern*) store; (*parken*) park; (*abschalten*) turn off; (*fig: beheben*) remedy. **A~gleis** *nt* siding. **A~raum** *m* box-room
absterben† *vi sep* (*sein*) die; (*gefühllos werden*) go numb
Abstieg *m* -[e]s,-e descent; (*Fußball*) relegation
abstimm|en *v sep* □ *vi* (*haben*) vote (**über** + *acc* on) □ *vt* coordinate (**auf** + *acc* with). **A~ung** *f* vote
Abstinenz /-st-/ *f* - abstinence. **A~ler** *m* -s,- teetotaller
abstoßen† *vt sep* knock off; (*abschieben*) push off; (*verkaufen*) sell; (*fig: ekeln*) repel. **a~d** *a* repulsive, *adv* -ly
abstrakt /-st-/ *a* abstract
abstreifen *vt sep* remove; slip off ⟨*Kleidungsstück, Schuhe*⟩
abstreiten† *vt sep* deny
Abstrich *m* (*Med*) smear; (*Kürzung*) cut
abstufen *vt sep* grade
Absturz *m* fall; (*Aviat*) crash
abstürzen *vi sep* (*sein*) fall; (*Aviat*) crash
absuchen *vt sep* search; (*ablesen*) pick off
absurd *a* absurd
Abszess *m* -es,-e (**Abszeß** *m* -sses,-sse) abscess
Abt *m* -[e]s,-̈e abbot
abtasten *vt sep* feel; (*Techn*) scan
abtauen *vt/i sep* (*sein*) thaw; (*entfrosten*) defrost
Abtei *f* -,-en abbey
Abteil *nt* compartment
abteilen *vt sep* divide off
Abteilung *f* -,-en section; (*Admin, Comm*) department
abtragen† *vt sep* clear; (*einebnen*) level; (*abnutzen*) wear out; (*abzahlen*) pay off
abträglich *a* detrimental (*dat* to)
abtreib|en† *v sep* □ *vt* (*Naut*) drive off course; **ein Kind a~en lassen** have an abortion □ *vi* (*sein*) drift off course. **A~ung** *f* -,-en abortion
abtrennen *vt sep* detach; (*abteilen*) divide off
abtret|en† *v sep* □ *vt* cede (**an** + *acc* to); **sich** (*dat*) **die Füße a~en** wipe one's feet □ *vi* (*sein*) (*Theat*)

exit; (*fig*) resign. **A∼er** *m* **-s,-** doormat

abtrocknen *vt/i sep* (*haben*) dry; **sich a∼** dry oneself

abtropfen *vi sep* (*sein*) drain

abtrünnig *a* renegade; **a∼ werden** (+ *dat*) desert

abtun† *vt sep* (*fig*) dismiss

abverlangen *vt sep* demand (*dat* from)

abwägen† *vt sep* (*fig*) weigh

abwandeln *vt sep* modify

abwandern *vi sep* (*sein*) move away

abwarten *v sep* □ *vt* wait for □ *vi* (*haben*) wait [and see]

abwärts *adv* down[wards]

Abwasch *m* **-[e]s** washing-up; (*Geschirr*) dirty dishes *pl*. **a∼en**† *v sep* □ *vt* wash; wash up ⟨*Geschirr*⟩; (*entfernen*) wash off □ *vi* (*haben*) wash up. **A∼lappen** *m* dishcloth

Abwasser *nt* **-s,¨** sewage. **A∼kanal** *m* sewer

abwechseln *vi/r sep* (*haben*) **[sich] a∼** alternate; ⟨*Personen:*⟩ take turns. **a∼d** *a* alternate, *adv* -ly

Abwechslung *f* **-,-en** change; **zur A∼** for a change. **a∼sreich** *a* varied

Abweg *m* **auf A∼e geraten** (*fig*) go astray. **a∼ig** *a* absurd

Abwehr *f* - defence; (*Widerstand*) resistance; (*Pol*) counter-espionage. **a∼en** *vt sep* ward off; (*Mil*) repel; (*zurückweisen*) dismiss. **A∼system** *nt* immune system

abweich|en† *vi sep* (*sein*) deviate/(*von Regel*) depart (**von** from); (*sich unterscheiden*) differ (**von** from). **a∼end** *a* divergent; (*verschieden*) different. **A∼ung** *f* **-,-en** deviation; difference

abweis|en† *vt sep* turn down; turn away ⟨*Person*⟩; (*abwehren*) repel. **a∼end** *a* unfriendly. **A∼ung** *f* rejection; (*Abfuhr*) rebuff

abwenden† *vt sep* turn away; (*verhindern*) avert; **sich a∼** turn away; **den Blick a∼** look away

abwerfen† *vt sep* throw off; throw ⟨*Reiter*⟩; (*Aviat*) drop; (*Kartenspiel*) discard; shed ⟨*Haut, Blätter*⟩; yield ⟨*Gewinn*⟩

abwert|en *vt sep* devalue. **a∼end** *a* pejorative, *adv* -ly. **A∼ung** *f* **-,-en** devaluation

abwesen|d *a* absent; (*zerstreut*) absent-minded. **A∼heit** *f* - absence; absent-mindedness

abwickeln *vt sep* unwind; (*erledigen*) settle

abwischen *vt sep* wipe; (*entfernen*) wipe off

abwürgen *vt sep* stall ⟨*Motor*⟩

abzahlen *vt sep* pay off

abzählen *vt sep* count

Abzahlung *f* instalment

abzapfen *vt sep* draw

Abzeichen *nt* badge

abzeichnen *vt sep* copy; (*unterzeichnen*) initial; **sich a∼** stand out

Abzieh|bild *nt* transfer. **a∼en**† *v sep* □ *vt* pull off; take off ⟨*Laken*⟩; strip ⟨*Bett*⟩; (*häuten*) skin; (*Phot*) print; run off ⟨*Kopien*⟩; (*zurückziehen*) withdraw; (*abrechnen*) deduct □ *vi* (*sein*) go away, ⟨*Rauch:*⟩ escape

abzielen *vi sep* (*haben*) **a∼ auf** (+ *acc*) (*fig*) be aimed at

Abzug *m* withdrawal; (*Abrechnung*) deduction; (*Phot*) print; (*Korrektur-*) proof; (*am Gewehr*) trigger; (*A∼söffnung*) vent; **A¨∼e** *pl* deductions

abzüglich *prep* (+ *gen*) less

Abzugshaube *f* [cooker] hood

abzweig|en *v sep* □ *vi* (*sein*) branch off □ *vt* divert. **A∼ung** *f* **-,-en** junction; (*Gabelung*) fork

ach *int* oh; **a∼ je!** oh dear! **a∼ so** I see; **mit A∼ und Krach** (*fam*) by the skin of one's teeth

Achse *f* **-,-n** axis; (*Rad-*) axle

Achsel *f* -,-n shoulder; **die A~n zucken** shrug one's shoulders. **A~höhle** *f* armpit. **A~zucken** *nt* -s shrug

acht[1] *inv a*, **A~**[1] *f* -,-en eight; **heute in a~ Tagen** a week today

acht[2] **außer a~ lassen/sich in a~ nehmen** (NEW) **außer Acht lassen/sich in Acht nehmen**, *s.* **Acht**[2]

Acht[2] *f* **A~ geben** be careful; **A~ geben auf** (+ *acc*) look after; **außer A~ lassen** disregard; **sich in A~ nehmen** be careful

acht|e(r,s) *a* eighth. **a~eckig** *a* octagonal. **a~el** *inv a* eighth. **A~el** *nt* -s,- eighth. **A~elnote** *f* quaver, (*Amer*) eighth note

achten *vt* respect □ *vi* (*haben*) **a~ auf** (+ *acc*) pay attention to; (*aufpassen*) look after; **darauf a~, dass** take care that

ächten *vt* ban; ostracize ⟨*Person*⟩

Achter|bahn *f* roller-coaster. **a~n** *adv* (*Naut*) aft

achtgeben† *vi sep* (*haben*) (NEW) **Acht geben**, *s.* **Acht**[2]

achtlos *a* careless, *adv* -ly

achtsam *a* careful, *adv* -ly

Achtung *f* - respect (**vor** + *dat* for); **A~!** look out! (*Mil*) attention! '**A~ Stufe**' 'mind the step'

acht|zehn *inv a* eighteen. **a~zehnte(r,s)** *a* eighteenth. **a~zig** *a inv* eighty. **a~zigste(r,s)** *a* eightieth

ächzen *vi* (*haben*) groan

Acker *m* -s,⸚ field. **A~bau** *m* agriculture. **A~land** *nt* arable land

addieren *vt/i* (*haben*) add; (*zusammenzählen*) add up

Addition /'tsi̯o:n/ *f* -,-en addition

ade *int* goodbye

Adel *m* -s nobility

Ader *f* -,-n vein; **künstlerische A~** artistic bent

Adjektiv *nt* -s,-e adjective

Adler *m* -s,- eagle

adlig *a* noble. **A~e(r)** *m* nobleman

Administration /-'tsi̯o:n/ *f* - administration

Admiral *m* -s,⸚e admiral

adop|tieren *vt* adopt. **A~tion** /-'tsi̯o:n/ *f* -,-en adoption. **A~tiveltern** *pl* adoptive parents. **A~tivkind** *nt* adopted child

Adrenalin *nt* -s adrenalin

Adres|se *f* -,-n address. **a~sieren** *vt* address

adrett *a* neat, *adv* -ly

Adria *f* - Adriatic

Advent *m* -s Advent. **A~skranz** *m* Advent wreath

Adverb *nt* -s,-ien /-i̯ən/ adverb

Affäre *f* -,-n affair

Affe *m* -n,-n monkey; (*Menschen-*) ape

Affekt *m* -[e]s,-e **im A~** in the heat of the moment

affektiert *a* affected. **A~heit** *f* - affectation

affig *a* affected; (*eitel*) vain

Afrika *nt* -s Africa

Afrikan|er(in) *m* -s,- (*f* -,-nen) African. **a~isch** *a* African

After *m* -s,- anus

Agen|t(in) *m* -en,-en (*f* -,-nen) agent. **A~tur** *f* -,-en agency

Aggres|sion *f* -,-en aggression. **a~siv** *a* aggressive, *adv* -ly. **A~sivität** *f* - aggressiveness

Agitation /-'tsi̯o:n/ *f* - agitation

Agnostiker *m* -s,- agnostic

Ägypt|en /ɛ'gʏptən/ *nt* -s Egypt. **Ä~er(in)** *m* -s,- (*f* -,-nen) Egyptian. **ä~isch** *a* Egyptian

ähneln *vi* (*haben*) (+ *dat*) resemble; **sich ä~** be alike

ahnen *vt* have a presentiment of; (*vermuten*) suspect

Ahnen *mpl* ancestors. **A~forschung** *f* genealogy. **A~tafel** *f* family tree

ähnlich *a* similar, *adv* -ly; **jdm ä~ sehen** resemble s.o.; (*typisch sein*) be just like s.o. **Ä~keit** *f* -,-en similarity; resemblance

Ahnung *f* -,-en premonition; (*Vermutung*) idea, hunch; **keine**

A~ (*fam*) no idea. **a~slos** *a* unsuspecting
Ahorn *m* **-s,-e** maple
Ähre *f* **-,-n** ear [of corn]
Aids /e:ts/ *nt* - Aids
Akademie *f* **-,-n** academy
Akademiker(in) *m* **-s,-** (*f* **-,-nen**) university graduate. **a~isch** *a* academic, *adv* -ally
akklimatisieren (sich) *vr* become acclimatized
Akkord *m* **-[e]s,-e** (*Mus*) chord; **im A~ arbeiten** be on piece-work. **A~arbeit** *f* piece-work
Akkordeon *nt* **-s,-s** accordion
Akkumulator *m* **-s,-en** /-'to:rən/ (*Electr*) accumulator
Akkusativ *m* **-s,-e** accusative. **A~objekt** *nt* direct object
Akrobat|(in) *m* **-en,-en** (*f* **-,-nen**) acrobat. **a~isch** *a* acrobatic
Akt *m* **-[e]s,-e** act; (*Kunst*) nude
Akte *f* **-,-n** file; **A~n** documents. **A~ndeckel** *m* folder. **A~nkoffer** *m* attaché case. **A~nschrank** *m* filing cabinet. **A~ntasche** *f* briefcase
Aktie /'aktsiə/ *f* **-,-n** (*Comm*) share. **A~ngesellschaft** *f* joint-stock company
Aktion /ak'tsio:n/ *f* **-,-en** action; (*Kampagne*) campaign. **A~är** *m* **-s,-e** shareholder
aktiv *a* active, *adv* -ly. **a~ieren** *vt* activate. **A~ität** *f* **-,-en** activity
Aktualität *f* **-,-en** topicality; **A~en** current events
aktuell *a* topical; (*gegenwärtig*) current; **nicht mehr a~** no longer relevant
Akupunktur *f* - acupuncture
Akustik *f* - acoustics *pl*. **a~isch** *a* acoustic, *adv* -ally
akut *a* acute
Akzent *m* **-[e]s,-e** accent
akzept|abel *a* acceptable. **a~ieren** *vt* accept
Alarm *m* **-s** alarm; (*Mil*) alert; **A~schlagen** raise the alarm. **a~ieren** *vt* alert; (*beunruhigen*) alarm. **a~ierend** *a* alarming
Albdruck *m* = **Alpdruck**
albern *a* silly □ *adv* in a silly way □ *vi* (*haben*) play the fool
Albtraum *m* = **Alptraum**
Album *nt* **-s,-ben** album
Algebra *f* - algebra
Algen *fpl* algae
Algerien /-iən/ *nt* **-s** Algeria
Alibi *nt* **-s,-s** alibi
Alimente *pl* maintenance *sg*
Alkohol *m* **-s** alcohol. **a~frei** *a* non-alcoholic
Alkoholiker(in) *m* **-s,-** (*f* **-,-nen**) alcoholic. **a~isch** *a* alcoholic. **A~ismus** *m* - alcoholism
all *inv pron* **all das/mein Geld** all the/my money; **all dies** all this
All *nt* **-s** universe
alle *pred a* finished, (*fam*) all gone; **a~ machen** finish up
all|e(r,s) *pron* all; (*jeder*) every; **a~es** everything, all; (*alle Leute*) everyone; **a~e** *pl* all; **a~es Geld** all the money; **a~e meine Freunde** all my friends; **a~e beide** both [of them/us]; **wir a~e** we all; **a~e Tage** every day; **a~e drei Jahre** every three years; **in a~er Unschuld** in all innocence; **ohne a~en Grund** without any reason; **vor a~em** above all; **a~es in a~em** all in all; **a~es aussteigen!** all change! **a~edem** *pron* **bei/trotz a~edem** with/despite all that
Allee *f* **-,-n** avenue
Alleg|orie *f* **-,-n** allegory. **a~orisch** *a* allegorical
allein *adv* alone; (*nur*) only; **a~stehend** single; **a~ der Gedanke** the mere thought; **von a~[e]** of its/⟨*Person*⟩ one's own accord; (*automatisch*) automatically; **einzig und a~** solely □ *conj* but. **A~erziehende(r)** *m/f* single parent. **a~ig** *a* sole. **a~stehend** *a* (NEW) **a~ stehend**, *s.* **allein**. **A~stehende** *pl* single people

allemal *adv* every time; (*gewiss*) certainly; **ein für a~** (NEW) **ein für alle Mal**, *s.* **Mal**
allenfalls *adv* at most; (*eventuell*) possibly
aller|beste(r,s) *a* very best; **am a~besten** best of all. **a~dings** *adv* indeed; (*zwar*) admittedly. **a~erste(r,s)** *a* very first
Allergie *f* -,-n allergy
allergisch *a* allergic (**gegen** to)
aller|hand *inv a* all sorts of □ *pron* all sorts of things; **das ist a~hand!** that's quite something! (*empört*) that's a bit much! **A~heiligen** *nt* **-s** All Saints Day. **a~höchstens** *adv* at the very most. **a~lei** *inv a* all sorts of □ *pron* all sorts of things. **a~letzte(r,s)** *a* very last. **a~liebst** *a* enchanting. **a~liebste(r,s)** *a* favourite □ *adv* **am a~liebsten** for preference; **am a~liebsten haben** like best of all. **a~meiste(r,s)** *a* most □ *adv* **am a~meisten** most of all. **A~seelen** *nt* **-s** All Souls Day. **a~seits** *adv* generally; **guten Morgen a~seits!** good morning everyone! **a~wenigste(r,s)** *a* very least □ *adv* **am a~wenigsten** least of all
alle|s *s.* **alle(r,s)**. **a~samt** *adv* all. **A~swisser** *m* **-s,-** (*fam*) know-all
allgemein *a* general, *adv* -ly; **im A~en (a~en)** in general. **A~heit** *f* - community; (*Öffentlichkeit*) general public
Allheilmittel *nt* panacea
Allianz *f* -,-en alliance
Alligator *m* **-s,-en** /-ˈtoːrən/ alligator
alliiert *a* allied; **die A~en** *pl* the Allies
all|jährlich *a* annual, *adv* -ly. **a~mächtig** *a* almighty; **der A~mächtige** the Almighty. **a~mählich** *a* gradual, *adv* -ly
Alltag *m* working day; **der A~** (*fig*) everyday life
alltäglich *a* daily; (*gewöhnlich*) everyday; ⟨*Mensch*⟩ ordinary □ *adv* daily
alltags *adv* on weekdays
allzu *adv* [far] too; **a~ bald/oft** all too soon/often; **a~ sehr/viel** far too much; **a~ vorsichtig** over-cautious. **a~bald** *adv* (NEW) **a~ bald**, *s.* **allzu**. **a~oft** *adv* (NEW) **a~ oft**, *s.* **allzu**. **a~sehr** *adv* (NEW) **a~ sehr**, *s.* **allzu**. **a~viel** *adv* (NEW) **a~ viel**, *s.* **allzu**
Alm *f* -,-en alpine pasture
Almosen *ntpl* alms
Alpdruck *m* nightmare
Alpen *pl* Alps. **A~veilchen** *nt* cyclamen
Alphabet *nt* **-[e]s,-e** alphabet. **a~isch** *a* alphabetical, *adv* -ly
Alptraum *m* nightmare
als *conj* as; (*zeitlich*) when; (*mit Komparativ*) than; **nichts als** nothing but; **als ob** as if *or* though; **so tun als ob** (*fam*) pretend
also *adv & conj* so; **a~ gut** all right then; **na a~!** there you are!
alt *a* (**älter, ältest**) old; (*gebraucht*) second-hand; (*ehemalig*) former; **alt werden** grow old; **alles beim A~en (a~en) lassen** leave things as they are
Alt *m* **-s** (*Mus*) contralto
Altar *m* **-s,⸚e** altar
Alt|e(r) *m/f* old man/woman; **die A~en** old people. **A~eisen** *nt* scrap iron. **A~enheim** *nt* old people's home
Alter *nt* **-s,-** age; (*Bejahrtheit*) old age; **im A~ von** at the age of; **im A~** in old age
älter *a* older; **mein ä~er Bruder** my elder brother
altern *vi* (*sein*) age
Alternative *f* -,-n alternative
Alters|grenze *f* age limit. **A~heim** *nt* old people's home. **A~rente** *f* old-age pension. **a~schwach** *a* old and infirm; ⟨*Ding*⟩ decrepit

Alter|tum *nt* **-s,¨-er** antiquity. **a∼tümlich** *a* old; (*altmodisch*) old-fashioned

ältest|e(r,s) *a* oldest; **der ä∼e Sohn** the eldest son

althergebracht *a* traditional

altklug *a* precocious, *adv* -ly

ältlich *a* elderly

alt|modisch old-fashioned □ *adv* in an old-fashioned way. **A∼papier** *nt* waste paper. **A∼stadt** *f* old [part of a] town. **A∼warenhändler** *m* second-hand dealer. **A∼weibermärchen** *nt* old wives' tale. **A∼weibersommer** *m* Indian summer; (*Spinnfäden*) gossamer

Alufolie *f* [aluminium] foil

Aluminium *nt* **-s** aluminium, (*Amer*) aluminum

am *prep* = **an dem; am Montag** on Monday; **am Morgen** in the morning; **am besten/meisten** [the] best/most; **am teuersten sein** be the most expensive

Amateur /-'tø:ɐ̯/ *m* **-s,-e** amateur

Ambition /-'tsi̯o:n/ *f* **-,-en** ambition

Amboss *m* **-es,-e** (**Amboß** *m* **-sses,-sse**) anvil

ambulan|t *a* out-patient . . . □ *adv* **a∼t behandeln** treat as an out-patient. **A∼z** *f* **-,-en** out-patients' department; (*Krankenwagen*) ambulance

Ameise *f* **-,-n** ant

amen *int*, **A∼** *nt* **-s** amen

Amerika *nt* -s America

Amerikan|er(in) *m* **-s,-** (*f* **-,-nen**) American. **a∼isch** *a* American

Ami *m* **-s,-s** (*fam*) Yank

Ammoniak *nt* **-s** ammonia

Amnestie *f* **-,-n** amnesty

amoralisch *a* amoral

Ampel *f* **-,-n** traffic lights *pl*; (*Blumen-*) hanging basket

Amphib|ie /-i̯ə/ *f* **-,-n** amphibian. **a∼isch** *a* amphibious

Amphitheater *nt* amphitheatre

Amput|ation /-'tsi̯o:n/ *f* **-,-en** amputation. **a∼ieren** *vt* amputate

Amsel *f* **-,-n** blackbird

Amt *nt* **-[e]s,¨-er** office; (*Aufgabe*) task; (*Teleph*) exchange. **a∼ieren** *vi* (*haben*) hold office; **a∼ierend** acting. **a∼lich** *a* official, *adv* -ly. **A∼szeichen** *nt* dialling tone

Amulett *nt* **-[e]s,-e** [lucky] charm

amüs|ant *a* amusing, *adv* -ly. **a∼ieren** *vt* amuse; **sich a∼ieren** be amused (**über** + *acc* at); (*sich vergnügen*) enjoy oneself

an *prep* (+ *dat/acc*) at; (*haftend, berührend*) on; (*gegen*) against; (+ *acc*) ⟨*schicken*⟩ to; **an der/die Universität** at/to university; **an dem Tag** on that day; **es ist an mir** it is up to me; **an [und für] sich** actually; **die Arbeit an sich** the work as such □ *adv* (*angeschaltet*) on; (*auf Fahrplan*) arriving; **an die zwanzig Mark/Leute** about twenty marks/people; **von heute an** from today

analog *a* analogous; (*Computer*) analog. **A∼ie** *f* **-,-n** analogy

Analphabet *m* **-en,-en** illiterate person. **A∼entum** *nt* **-s** illiteracy

Analy|se *f* **-,-n** analysis. **a∼sieren** *vt* analyse. **A∼tiker** *m* **-s,-** analyst. **a∼tisch** *a* analytical

Anämie *f* **-** anaemia

Ananas *f* **-,-[se]** pineapple

Anarch|ie *f* **-** anarchy. **A∼ist** *m* **-en,-en** anarchist

Anat|omie *f* **-** anatomy. **a∼omisch** *a* anatomical, *adv* -ly

anbahnen (sich) *vr sep* develop

Anbau *m* cultivation; (*Gebäude*) extension. **a∼en** *vt sep* build on; (*anpflanzen*) cultivate, grow

anbehalten† *vt sep* keep on

anbei *adv* enclosed

anbeißen† *v sep* □ *vt* take a bite of □ *vi* (*haben*) ⟨*Fisch:*⟩ bite; (*fig*) take the bait

anbelangen *vt sep* = **anbetreffen**

anbellen *vt sep* bark at
anbeten *vt sep* worship
Anbetracht *m* **in A~** (+ *gen*) in view of
anbetreffen† *vt sep* **was mich/das anbetrifft** as far as I am/that is concerned
Anbetung *f* - worship
anbiedern (sich) *vr sep* ingratiate oneself (**bei** with)
anbieten† *vt sep* offer; **sich a~** offer (**zu** to)
anbinden† *vt sep* tie up
Anblick *m* sight. **a~en** *vt sep* look at
anbrechen† *v sep* □ *vt* start on; break into ⟨*Vorräte*⟩ □ *vi* (*sein*) begin; ⟨*Tag:*⟩ break; ⟨*Nacht:*⟩ fall
anbrennen† *v sep* □ *vt* light □ *vi* (*sein*) burn; (*Feuer fangen*) catch fire
anbringen† *vt sep* bring [along]; (*befestigen*) fix
Anbruch *m* (*fig*) dawn; **bei A~ des Tages/der Nacht** at daybreak/nightfall
anbrüllen *vt sep* (*fam*) bellow at
Andacht *f* -,-**en** reverence; (*Gottesdienst*) prayers *pl*
andächtig *a* reverent, *adv* -ly; (*fig*) rapt, *adv* -ly
andauern *vi sep* (*haben*) last; (*anhalten*) continue. **a~d** *a* persistent, *adv* -ly; (*ständig*) constant, *adv* -ly
Andenken *nt* **-s,-** memory; (*Souvenir*) souvenir; **zum A~ an** (+ *acc*) in memory of
ander|e(r,s) *a* other; (*verschieden*) different; (*nächste*) next; **ein a~er, eine a~e** another □ *pron* **der a~e/die a~en** the other/others; **ein a~er** another [one]; (*Person*) someone else; **kein a~er** no one else; **einer nach dem a~en** one after the other; **alles a~e/nichts a~es** everything/nothing else; **etwas ganz a~es** something quite different; **alles a~e als** anything but; **unter a~em** among other things. **a~enfalls** *adv* otherwise. **a~erseits** *adv* on the other hand. **a~mal** *adv* **ein a~mal** another time
ändern *vt* alter; (*wechseln*) change; **sich ä~** change
andernfalls *adv* otherwise
anders *pred a* different; **a~ werden** change □ *adv* differently; ⟨*riechen, schmecken*⟩ different; (*sonst*) else; **jemand/niemand/irgendwo a~** someone/no one/somewhere else
anderseits *adv* on the other hand
anders|herum *adv* the other way round. **a~wo** *adv* (*fam*) somewhere else
anderthalb *inv a* one and a half; **a~ Stunden** an hour and a half
Änderung *f* -,-**en** alteration; (*Wechsel*) change
anderweitig *a* other □ *adv* otherwise; (*anderswo*) elsewhere
andeut|en *vt sep* indicate; (*anspielen*) hint at. **A~ung** *f* -,-**en** indication; hint
andicken *vt sep* (*Culin*) thicken
Andrang *m* rush (**nach** for); (*Gedränge*) crush
andre *a & pron* = **andere**
andrehen *vt sep* turn on; **jdm etw a~** (*fam*) palm sth off on s.o.
andrerseits *adv* = **andererseits**
androhen *vt sep* **jdm etw a~** threaten s.o. with sth
aneignen *vt sep* **sich** (*dat*) **a~** appropriate; (*lernen*) learn
aneinander *adv & pref* together; ⟨*denken*⟩ of one another; **a~ vorbei** past one another; **a~ geraten** quarrel. **a~geraten†** *vi sep* (*sein*) (NEW) **a~ geraten**, *s.* **aneinander**
Anekdote *f* -,-**n** anecdote
anekeln *vt sep* nauseate
anerkannt *a* acknowledged
anerkenn|en† *vt sep* acknowledge, recognize; (*würdigen*) appreciate. **a~end** *a* approving,

adv -ly. **A~ung** *f* - acknowledgement, recognition; appreciation

anfahren† *v sep* □ *vt* deliver; (*streifen*) hit; (*schimpfen*) snap at □ *vi* (*sein*) start; **angefahren kommen** drive up

Anfall *m* fit, attack. **a~en**† *v sep* □ *vt* attack □ *vi* (*sein*) arise; ⟨*Zinsen:*⟩ accrue

anfällig *a* susceptible (**für** to); (*zart*) delicate. **A~keit** *f* - susceptibility (**für** to)

Anfang *m* **-s,¨e** beginning, start; **zu** *od* **am A~** at the beginning; (*anfangs*) at first. **a~en**† *vt/i sep* (*haben*) begin, start; (*tun*) do

Anfäng|er(in) *m* **-s,-** (*f* **-,-nen**) beginner. **a~lich** *a* initial, *adv* -ly

anfangs *adv* at first. **A~buchstabe** *m* initial letter. **A~gehalt** *nt* starting salary. **A~gründe** *mpl* rudiments

anfassen *v sep* □ *vt* touch; (*behandeln*) treat; tackle ⟨*Arbeit*⟩; **jdn a~** take s.o.'s hand; **sich a~** hold hands; **sich weich a~** feel soft □ *vi* (*haben*) **mit a~** lend a hand

anfechten† *vt sep* contest; (*fig: beunruhigen*) trouble

anfeinden *vt sep* be hostile to

anfertigen *vt sep* make

anfeuchten *vt sep* moisten

anfeuern *vt sep* spur on

anflehen *vt sep* implore, beg

Anflug *m* (*Avia*) approach; (*fig: Spur*) trace

anforder|n *vt sep* demand; (*Comm*) order. **A~ung** *f* demand

Anfrage *f* enquiry. **a~n** *vi sep* (*haben*) enquire, ask

anfreunden (sich) *vr sep* make friends (**mit** with); (*miteinander*) become friends

anfügen *vt sep* add

anfühlen *vt sep* feel; **sich weich a~** feel soft

anführ|en *vt sep* lead; (*zitieren*) quote; (*angeben*) give; **jdn a~en** (*fam*) have s.o. on. **A~er** *m* leader. **A~ungszeichen** *ntpl* quotation marks

Angabe *f* statement; (*Anweisung*) instruction; (*Tennis*) service; (*fam; Angeberei*) showing-off; **nähere A~n** particulars

angeb|en† *v sep* □ *vt* state; give ⟨*Namen, Grund*⟩; (*anzeigen*) indicate; set ⟨*Tempo*⟩ □ *vi* (*haben*) (*Tennis*) serve; (*fam; protzen*) show off. **A~er(in)** *m* **-s,-** (*f* **-,-nen**) (*fam*) show-off. **A~erei** *f* - (*fam*) showing-off

angeblich *a* alleged, *adv* -ly

angeboren *a* innate; (*Med*) congenital

Angebot *nt* offer; (*Auswahl*) range; **A~ und Nachfrage** supply and demand

angebracht *a* appropriate

angebunden *a* **kurz a~** curt

angegriffen *a* worn out; ⟨*Gesundheit*⟩ poor

angeheiratet *a* ⟨*Onkel, Tante*⟩ by marriage

angeheitert *a* (*fam*) tipsy

angehen† *v sep* □ *vi* (*sein*) begin, start; ⟨*Licht, Radio:*⟩ come on; (*anwachsen*) take root; **a~ gegen** fight □ *vt* attack; tackle ⟨*Arbeit*⟩; (*bitten*) ask (**um** for); (*betreffen*) concern; **das geht dich nichts an** it's none of your business. **a~d** *a* future; ⟨*Künstler*⟩ budding

angehör|en *vi sep* (*haben*) (+ *dat*) belong to. **A~ige(r)** *m/f* relative; (*Mitglied*) member

Angeklagte(r) *m/f* accused

Angel *f* **-,-n** fishing-rod; (*Tür-*) hinge

Angelegenheit *f* matter; **auswärtige A~en** foreign affairs

Angel|haken *m* fish-hook. **a~n** *vi* (*haben*) fish (**nach** for); **a~n gehen** go fishing □ *vt* (*fangen*) catch. **A~rute** *f* fishing-rod

angelsächsisch *a* Anglo-Saxon

angemessen *a* commensurate (*dat* with); (*passend*) appropriate, *adv* -ly

angenehm *a* pleasant, *adv* -ly; (*bei Vorstellung*) **a~!** delighted to meet you!

angenommen *a* ⟨*Kind*⟩ adopted; ⟨*Name*⟩ assumed

angeregt *a* animated, *adv* -ly

angesehen *a* respected; ⟨*Firma*⟩ reputable

angesichts *prep* (+ *gen*) in view of

angespannt *a* intent, *adv* -ly; ⟨*Lage*⟩ tense

Angestellte(r) *m/f* employee

angetan *a* **a~ sein von** be taken with

angetrunken *a* slightly drunk

angewandt *a* applied

angewiesen *a* dependent (**auf** + *acc* on); **auf sich selbst a~** on one's own

angewöhnen *vt sep* **jdm etw a~** get s.o. used to sth; **sich** (*dat*) **etw a~** get into the habit of doing sth

Angewohnheit *f* habit

Angina *f* - tonsillitis

angleichen† *vt sep* adjust (*dat* to)

Angler *m* **-s,-** angler

anglikanisch *a* Anglican

Anglistik *f* - English [language and literature]

Angorakatze *f* Persian cat

angreif|en† *vt sep* attack; tackle ⟨*Arbeit*⟩; (*schädigen*) damage; (*anbrechen*) break into; (*anfassen*) touch. **A~er** *m* **-s,-** attacker; (*Pol*) aggressor

angrenzen *vi sep* (*haben*) adjoin (**an etw** *acc* sth). **a~d** *a* adjoining

Angriff *m* attack; **in A~ nehmen** tackle. **a~slustig** *a* aggressive

Angst *f* **-,̈e** fear; (*Psych*) anxiety; (*Sorge*) worry (**um** about); **A~ haben** be afraid (**vor** + *dat* of); (*sich sorgen*) be worried (**um** about); **jdm A~ machen** frighten s.o. □ **mir ist a~** I am frightened; I am worried (**um** about); **jdm a~ machen** (NEW) **jdm A~ machen**

ängstigen *vt* frighten; (*Sorge machen*) worry; **sich ä~** be frightened; be worried (**um** about)

ängstlich *a* nervous, *adv* -ly; (*scheu*) timid, *adv* -ly; (*verängstigt*) frightened, scared; (*besorgt*) anxious, *adv* -ly; **Ä~keit** *f* - nervousness; timidity; anxiety

angstvoll *a* anxious, *adv* -ly; (*verängstigt*) frightened

angucken *vt sep* (*fam*) look at

angurten (sich) *vr sep* fasten one's seat-belt

anhaben† *vt sep* have on; **er/es kann mir nichts a~** (*fig*) he/it cannot hurt me

anhalt|en† *v sep* □ *vt* stop; hold ⟨*Atem*⟩; **jdn zur Arbeit/Ordnung a~en** urge s.o. to work/be tidy □ *vi* (*haben*) stop; (*andauern*) continue. **a~end** *a* persistent, *adv* -ly; ⟨*Beifall*⟩ prolonged. **A~er(in)** *m* **-s,-** (*f* **-,-nen**) hitchhiker; **per A~er fahren** hitchhike. **A~spunkt** *m* clue

anhand *prep* (+ *gen*) with the aid of

Anhang *m* appendix; (*fam: Angehörige*) family

anhängen[1] *vt sep* (*reg*) hang up; (*befestigen*) attach; (*hinzufügen*) add

anhäng|en[2]† *vi* (*haben*) be a follower of. **A~er** *m* **-s,-** follower; (*Auto*) trailer; (*Schild*) [tie-on] label; (*Schmuck*) pendant; (*Aufhänger*) loop. **A~erin** *f* **-,-nen** follower. **A~erschaft** *f* - following, followers *pl*. **a~lich** *a* affectionate. **A~sel** *nt* **-s,-** appendage

anhäufen *vt sep* pile up; **sich a~** pile up, accumulate

anheben† *vt sep* lift; (*erhöhen*) raise

Anhieb *m* **auf A~** straight away

Anhöhe *f* hill

anhören *vt sep* listen to; **mit a~** overhear; **sich gut a~** sound good

animieren *vt* encourage (**zu** to)
Anis *m* **-es** aniseed
Anker *m* **-s,-** anchor; **vor A~ gehen** drop anchor. **a~n** *vi* (*haben*) anchor; (*liegen*) be anchored
anketten *vt sep* chain up
Anklage *f* accusation; (*Jur*) charge; (*Ankläger*) prosecution. **A~bank** *f* dock. **a~n** *vt sep* accuse (*gen* of); (*Jur*) charge (*gen* with)
Ankläger *m* accuser; (*Jur*) prosecutor
anklammern *vt sep* clip on; peg on the line ⟨*Wäsche*⟩; **sich a~** cling (**an** + *acc* to)
Anklang *m* **bei jdm A~ finden** meet with s.o.'s approval
ankleben *v sep* □ *vt* stick on □ *vi* (*sein*) stick (**an** + *dat* to)
Ankleide|kabine *f* changing cubicle; (*zur Anprobe*) fitting-room. **a~n** *vt sep* dress; **sich a~n** dress
anklopfen *vi sep* (*haben*) knock
anknipsen *vt sep* (*fam*) switch on
anknüpfen *v sep* □ *vt* tie on; (*fig*) enter into ⟨*Gespräch, Beziehung*⟩ □ *vi* (*haben*) refer (**an** + *acc* to)
ankommen† *vi sep* (*sein*) arrive; (*sich nähern*) approach; **gut a~** arrive safely; (*fig*) go down well (**bei** with); **nicht a~ gegen** (*fig*) be no match for; **a~ auf** (+ *acc*) depend on; **es a~ lassen auf** (+ *acc*) risk; **das kommt darauf an** it [all] depends
ankreuzen *vt sep* mark with a cross
ankündig|en *vt sep* announce. **A~ung** *f* announcement
Ankunft *f* - arrival
ankurbeln *vt sep* (*fig*) boost
anlächeln *vt sep* smile at
anlachen *vt sep* smile at
Anlage *f* **-,-n** installation; (*Industrie-*) plant; (*Komplex*) complex; (*Geld-*) investment; (*Plan*) layout; (*Beilage*) enclosure; (*Veranlagung*) aptitude; (*Neigung*) predisposition; **[öffentliche] A~n** [public] gardens; **als A~** enclosed
Anlass *m* **-es,⸚e** (**Anlaß** *m* **-sses, ⸚sse**) reason; (*Gelegenheit*) occasion; **A~ geben zu** give cause for
anlass|en† *vt sep* (*Auto*) start; (*fam*) leave on ⟨*Licht*⟩; keep on ⟨*Mantel*⟩; **sich gut/schlecht a~en** start off well/badly. **A~er** *m* **-s,-** starter
anlässlich (**anläßlich**) *prep* (+ *gen*) on the occasion of
Anlauf *m* (*Sport*) run-up; (*fig*) attempt. **a~en†** *v sep* □ *vi* (*sein*) start; (*beschlagen*) mist up; ⟨*Metall:*⟩ tarnish; **rot a~en** go red; (*erröten*) blush; **angelaufen kommen** come running up □ *vt* (*Naut*) call at
anlegen *v sep* □ *vt* put (**an** + *acc* against); put on ⟨*Kleidung, Verband*⟩; lay back ⟨*Ohren*⟩; aim ⟨*Gewehr*⟩; (*investieren*) invest; (*ausgeben*) spend (**für** on); (*erstellen*) build; (*gestalten*) lay out; draw up ⟨*Liste*⟩; **[mit] Hand a~** lend a hand; **es darauf a~** (*fig*) aim (**zu** to); **sich a~ mit** quarrel with □ *vi* (*haben*) ⟨*Schiff:*⟩ moor; **a~ auf** (+ *acc*) aim at
anlehnen *vt sep* lean (**an** + *acc* against); **sich a~** lean (**an** + *acc* on); **eine Tür angelehnt lassen** leave a door ajar
Anleihe *f* **-,-n** loan
anleinen *vt sep* put on a lead
anleit|en *vt sep* instruct. **A~ung** *f* instructions *pl*
anlernen *vt sep* train
Anliegen *nt* **-s,-** request; (*Wunsch*) desire
anlieg|en† *vi sep* (*haben*) **[eng] a~en** fit closely; **[eng] a~end** close-fitting. **A~er** *mpl* residents; **'A~er frei'** 'access for residents only'
anlocken *vt sep* attract
anlügen† *vt sep* lie to

anmachen *vt sep (fam)* fix; *(anschalten)* turn on; *(anzünden)* light; *(Culin)* dress ⟨*Salat*⟩
anmalen *vt sep* paint
Anmarsch *m (Mil)* approach
anmaß|en *vt sep* **sich** *(dat)* **a~en** presume (**zu** to); **sich** *(dat)* **ein Recht a~en** claim a right. **a~end** *a* presumptuous, *adv* -ly; *(arrogant)* arrogant, *adv* -ly. **A~ung** *f* - presumption; arrogance
anmeld|en *vt sep* announce; *(Admin)* register; **sich a~en** say that one is coming; *(Admin)* register; *(Sch)* enrol; *(im Hotel)* check in; *(beim Arzt)* make an appointment. **A~ung** *f* announcement; *(Admin)* registration; *(Sch)* enrolment; *(Termin)* appointment
anmerk|en *vt sep* mark; **sich** *(dat)* **etw a~en lassen** show sth. **A~ung** *f* -,-**en** note
Anmut *f* - grace; *(Charme)* charm
anmuten *vt sep* **es mutet mich seltsam/vertraut an** it seems odd/familiar to me
anmutig *a* graceful, *adv* -ly; *(lieblich)* charming, *adv* -ly
annähen *vt sep* sew on
annäher|nd *a* approximate, *adv* -ly. **A~ungsversuche** *mpl* advances
Annahme *f* -,-**n** acceptance; *(Adoption)* adoption; *(Vermutung)* assumption
annehm|bar *a* acceptable. **a~en**† *vt sep* accept; *(adoptieren)* adopt; acquire ⟨*Gewohnheit*⟩; *(sich zulegen, vermuten)* assume; **sich a~en** (+ *gen*) take care of; **angenommen, dass** assuming that. **A~lichkeiten** *fpl* comforts
annektieren *vt* annex
Anno *adv* **A~ 1920** in the year 1920
Annon|ce /a'nõ:sə/ *f* -,-**n** advertisement. **a~cieren** /-'si:-/ *vt/i* *(haben)* advertise
annullieren *vt* annul; cancel ⟨*Flug*⟩
anöden *vt sep (fam)* bore
Anomalie *f* -,-**n** anomaly
anonym *a* anonymous, *adv* -ly
Anorak *m* -**s**,-**s** anorak
anordn|en *vt sep* arrange; *(befehlen)* order. **A~ung** *f* arrangement; order
anorganisch *a* inorganic
anormal *a* abnormal
anpacken *v sep* □ *vt* grasp; tackle ⟨*Arbeit, Problem*⟩ □ *vi (haben)* **mit a~** lend a hand
anpass|en *vt sep* try on; *(angleichen)* adapt (*dat* to); **sich a~** adapt (*dat* to). **A~ung** *f* - adaptation. **a~ungsfähig** *a* adaptable. **A~ungsfähigkeit** *f* adaptability
Anpfiff *m (Sport)* kick-off; *(fam: Rüge)* reprimand
anpflanzen *vt sep* plant; *(anbauen)* grow
Anprall *m* -**[e]s** impact. **a~en** *vi sep (sein)* strike (**an etw** *acc* sth)
anprangern *vt sep* denounce
anpreisen† *vt sep* commend
Anprob|e *f* fitting. **a~ieren** *vt sep* try on
anrechnen *vt sep* count (**als** as); *(berechnen)* charge for; *(verrechnen)* allow ⟨*Summe*⟩; **ich rechne ihm seine Hilfe hoch an** I very much appreciate his help
Anrecht *nt* right (**auf** + *acc* to)
Anrede *f* [form of] address. **a~n** *vt sep* address; *(ansprechen)* speak to
anreg|en *vt sep* stimulate; *(ermuntern)* encourage (**zu** to); *(vorschlagen)* suggest. **a~end** *a* stimulating. **A~ung** *f* stimulation; *(Vorschlag)* suggestion
anreichern *vt sep* enrich
Anreise *f* journey; *(Ankunft)* arrival. **a~n** *vi sep (sein)* arrive
Anreiz *m* incentive
anrempeln *vt sep* jostle
Anrichte *f* -,-**n** sideboard. **a~n** *vt sep (Culin)* prepare; *(garnieren)*

garnish (**mit** with); (*verursachen*) cause

anrüchig *a* disreputable

Anruf *m* call. **A~beantworter** *m* **-s,-** answering machine. **a~en**† *v sep* □ *vt* call to; (*bitten*) call on (**um** for); (*Teleph*) ring □ *vi* (*haben*) ring (**bei jdm** s.o.)

anrühren *vt sep* touch; (*verrühren*) mix

ans *prep* = **an das**

Ansage *f* announcement. **a~n** *vt sep* announce; **sich a~n** say that one is coming. **A~r(in)** *m* **-s,-** (*f* **-,-nen**) announcer

ansamm|eln *vt sep* collect; (*anhäufen*) accumulate; **sich a~eln** collect; (*sich häufen*) accumulate; ⟨*Leute:*⟩ gather. **A~lung** *f* collection; (*Menschen-*) crowd

ansässig *a* resident

Ansatz *m* beginning; (*Haar-*) hairline; (*Versuch*) attempt; (*Techn*) extension

anschaff|en *vt sep* [**sich** *dat*] **etw a~en** acquire/(*kaufen*) buy sth. **A~ung** *f* **-,-en** acquisition; (*Kauf*) purchase

anschalten *vt sep* switch on

anschau|en *vt sep* look at. **a~lich** *a* vivid, *adv* -ly. **A~ung** *f* **-,-en** (*fig*) view

Anschein *m* appearance; **den A~ haben** seem. **a~end** *adv* apparently

anschicken (sich) *vr sep* be about (**zu** to)

anschirren *vt sep* harness

Anschlag *m* notice; (*Vor-*) estimate; (*Überfall*) attack (**auf** + *acc* on); (*Mus*) touch; (*Techn*) stop; **240 A~e in der Minute** ≈ 50 words per minute. **A~brett** *nt* notice board. **a~en**† *v sep* □ *vt* put up ⟨*Aushang*⟩; strike ⟨*Note, Taste*⟩; cast on ⟨*Masche*⟩; (*beschädigen*) chip □ *vi* (*haben*) strike/(*stoßen*) knock (**an** + *acc* against); ⟨*Hund:*⟩ bark; (*wirken*) be effective □ *vi* (*sein*) knock (**an** + *acc* against); **mit dem Kopf a~en** hit one's head. **A~zettel** *m* notice

anschließen† *v sep* □ *vt* connect (**an** + *acc* to); (*zufügen*) add; **sich a~ an** (+ *acc*) (*anstoßen*) adjoin; (*folgen*) follow; (*sich anfreunden*) become friendly with; **sich jdm a~** join s.o. □ *vi* (*haben*) **a~an** (+ *acc*) adjoin; (*folgen*) follow. **a~d** *a* adjoining; (*zeitlich*) following □ *adv* afterwards; **a~d an** (+ *acc*) after

Anschluss (Anschluß) *m* connection; (*Kontakt*) contact; **A~ finden** make friends; **im A~ an** (+ *acc*) after

anschmieg|en (sich) *vr sep* snuggle up/⟨*Kleid:*⟩ cling (**an** + *acc* to). **a~sam** *a* affectionate

anschmieren *vt sep* smear; (*fam: täuschen*) cheat

anschnallen *vt sep* strap on; **sich a~** fasten one's seat-belt

anschneiden† *vt sep* cut into; broach ⟨*Thema*⟩

anschreiben† *vt sep* write (**an** + *acc* on); (*Comm*) put on s.o.'s account; (*sich wenden*) write to; **bei jdm gut/schlecht angeschrieben sein** be in s.o.'s good/bad books

anschreien† *vt sep* shout at

Anschrift *f* address

anschuldig|en *vt sep* accuse. **A~ung** *f* **-,-en** accusation

anschwellen† *vi sep* (*sein*) swell

anschwemmen *vt sep* wash up

anschwindeln *vt sep* (*fam*) lie to

ansehen† *vt sep* look at; (*einschätzen*) regard (**als** as); [**sich** *dat*] **etw a~** look at sth; (*TV*) watch sth. **A~** *nt* **-s** respect; (*Ruf*) reputation

ansehnlich *a* considerable

ansetzen *v sep* □ *vt* join (**an** + *acc* to); (*festsetzen*) fix; (*veranschlagen*) estimate; **Rost a~** get rusty; **sich a~** form □ *vi* (*haben*) (*anbrennen*) burn; **zum Sprung a~** get ready to jump

Ansicht *f* view; **meiner A~ nach** in my view; **zur A~** (*Comm*) on approval. **A~s[post]karte** *f* picture postcard. **A~ssache** *f* matter of opinion

ansiedeln (sich) *vr sep* settle

ansonsten *adv* apart from that

anspannen *vt sep* hitch up; (*anstrengen*) strain; tense ⟨*Muskel*⟩

anspiel|en *vi sep* (*haben*) **a~en auf** (+ *acc*) allude to; (*versteckt*) hint at. **A~ung** *f* -,-en allusion; hint

Anspitzer *m* -s,- pencil-sharpener

Ansporn *m* (*fig*) incentive. **a~en** *vt sep* spur on

Ansprache *f* address

ansprechen† *v sep* □ *vt* speak to; (*fig*) appeal to □ *vi* (*haben*) respond (**auf** + *acc* to). **a~d** *a* attractive

anspringen† *v sep* □ *vt* jump at □ *vi* (*sein*) (*Auto*) start

Anspruch *m* claim/(*Recht*) right (**auf** + *acc* to); **A~ haben** be entitled (**auf** + *acc* to); **in A~ nehmen** make use of; (*erfordern*) demand; take up ⟨*Zeit*⟩; occupy ⟨*Person*⟩; **hohe A~e stellen** be very demanding. **a~slos** *a* undemanding; (*bescheiden*) unpretentious. **a~svoll** *a* demanding; (*kritisch*) discriminating; (*vornehm*) up-market

anspucken *vt sep* spit at

anstacheln *vt sep* (*fig*) spur on

Anstalt *f* -,-en institution; **A~en/keine A~en machen** prepare/make no move (**zu** to)

Anstand *m* decency; (*Benehmen*) [good] manners *pl*

anständig *a* decent, *adv* -ly; (*ehrbar*) respectable, *adv* -bly; (*fam: beträchtlich*) considerable, *adv* -bly; (*richtig*) proper, *adv* -ly

Anstands|dame *f* chaperon. **a~los** *adv* without any trouble; (*bedenkenlos*) without hesitation

anstarren *vt sep* stare at

anstatt *conj & prep* (+ *gen*) instead of; **a~ zu arbeiten** instead of working

anstechen† *vt sep* tap ⟨*Fass*⟩

ansteck|en *v sep* □ *vt* pin (**an** + *acc* to/on); put on ⟨*Ring*⟩; (*anzünden*) light; (*in Brand stecken*) set fire to; (*Med*) infect; **sich a~en** catch an infection (**bei** from) □ *vi* (*haben*) be infectious. **a~end** *a* infectious, (*fam*) catching. **A~ung** *f* -,-en infection

anstehen† *vi sep* (*haben*) queue, (*Amer*) stand in line

ansteigen† *vi sep* (*sein*) climb; ⟨*Gelände, Preise:*⟩ rise

anstelle *prep* (+ *gen*) instead of

anstell|en *vt sep* put, stand (**an** + *acc* against); (*einstellen*) employ; (*anschalten*) turn on; (*tun*) do; **sich a~en** queue [up], (*Amer*) stand in line; (*sich haben*) make a fuss. **A~ung** *f* employment; (*Stelle*) job

Anstieg *m* -[e]s,-e climb; (*fig*) rise

anstifte|n *vt sep* cause; (*anzetteln*) instigate; **jdn a~n** put s.o. up (**zu** to). **A~r** *m* instigator

Anstoß *m* (*Anregung*) impetus; (*Stoß*) knock; (*Fußball*) kick-off; **A~ erregen/nehmen** give/take offence (**an** + *dat* at). **a~en†** *v sep* □ *vt* knock; (*mit dem Ellbogen*) nudge □ *vi* (*sein*) knock (**an** + *acc* against) □ *vi* (*haben*) adjoin (**an etw** *acc* sth); **[mit den Gläsern] a~en** clink glasses; **a~en auf** (+ *acc*) drink to; **mit der Zunge a~en** lisp

anstößig *a* offensive, *adv* -ly

anstrahlen *vt sep* floodlight; (*anlachen*) beam at

anstreiche|n† *vt sep* paint; (*anmerken*) mark. **A~r** *m* -s,- painter

anstreng|en *vt sep* strain; (*ermüden*) tire; **sich a~en** exert oneself; (*sich bemühen*) make an effort (**zu** to). **a~end** *a* strenuous; (*ermüdend*) tiring. **A~ung** *f* -,-en strain; (*Mühe*) effort

Anstrich *m* coat [of paint]
Ansturm *m* rush; (*Mil*) assault
Ansuchen *nt* **-s,-** request
Antagonismus *m* - antagonism
Antarktis *f* - Antarctic
Anteil *m* share; **A~ nehmen** take an interest (**an** + *dat* in); (*mitfühlen*) sympathize. **A~nahme** *f* - interest (**an** + *dat* in); (*Mitgefühl*) sympathy
Antenne *f* -,-**n** aerial
Anthologie *f* -,-**n** anthology
Anthropologie *f* - anthropology
Anti|alkoholiker *m* teetotaller. **A~biotikum** *nt* **-s,-ka** antibiotic
antik *a* antique. **A~e** *f* - [classical] antiquity
Antikörper *m* antibody
Antilope *f* -,-**n** antelope
Antipathie *f* - antipathy
Anti|quariat *nt* **-[e]s,-e** antiquarian bookshop. **a~quarisch** *a & adv* second-hand
Antiquitäten *fpl* antiques. **A~händler** *m* antique dealer
Antisemitismus *m* - anti-Semitism
Antisept|ikum *nt* **-s,-ka** antiseptic. **a~isch** *a* antiseptic
Antrag *m* **-[e]s,¨e** proposal; (*Pol*) motion; (*Gesuch*) application. **A~steller** *m* **-s,-** applicant
antreffen† *vt sep* find
antreiben† *v sep* □ *vt* urge on; (*Techn*) drive; (*anschwemmen*) wash up □ *vi* (*sein*) be washed up
antreten† *v sep* □ *vt* start; take up ⟨*Amt*⟩ □ *vi* (*sein*) line up; (*Mil*) fall in
Antrieb *m* urge; (*Techn*) drive; **aus eigenem A~** of one's own accord
antrinken† *vt sep* **sich** (*dat*) **einen Rausch a~** get drunk; **sich** (*dat*) **Mut a~** give oneself Dutch courage
Antritt *m* start; **bei A~ eines Amtes** when taking office. **A~srede** *f* inaugural address
antun† *vt sep* **jdm etw a~** do sth to s.o.; **sich** (*dat*) **etwas a~** take one's own life; **es jdm angetan haben** appeal to s.o.
Antwort *f* -,-**en** answer, reply (**auf** + *acc* to). **a~en** *vt/i* (*haben*) answer (**jdm** s.o.)
anvertrauen *vt sep* entrust/(*mitteilen*) confide (**jdm** to s.o.); **sich jdm a~** confide in s.o.
anwachsen† *vi sep* (*sein*) take root; (*zunehmen*) grow
Anwalt *m* **-[e]s,¨e, Anwältin** *f* -,-**nen** lawyer; (*vor Gericht*) counsel
Anwandlung *f* -,-**en** fit (**von** of)
Anwärter(in) *m(f)* candidate
anweis|en† *vt sep* assign (*dat* to); (*beauftragen*) instruct. **A~ung** *f* instruction; (*Geld-*) money order
anwend|en *vt sep* apply (**auf** + *acc* to); (*gebrauchen*) use. **A~ung** *f* application; use
anwerben† *vt sep* recruit
Anwesen *nt* **-s,-** property
anwesen|d *a* present (**bei** at); **die A~den** those present. **A~heit** *f* - presence
anwidern *vt sep* disgust
Anwohner *mpl* residents
Anzahl *f* number
anzahl|en *vt sep* pay a deposit on; pay on account ⟨*Summe*⟩. **A~ung** *f* deposit
anzapfen *vt sep* tap
Anzeichen *nt* sign
Anzeige *f* -,-**n** announcement; (*Inserat*) advertisement; **A~ erstatten gegen jdn** report s.o. to the police. **a~n** *vt sep* announce; (*inserieren*) advertise; (*melden*) report [to the police]; (*angeben*) indicate, show. **A~r** *m* indicator
anzieh|en† *vt sep* □ *vt* attract; (*festziehen*) tighten; put on ⟨*Kleider, Bremse*⟩; draw up ⟨*Beine*⟩; (*ankleiden*) dress; **sich a~en** get dressed; **was soll ich a~en?** what shall I wear? **gut angezogen** well-dressed □ *vi* (*haben*) start pulling; ⟨*Preise:*⟩ go up.

a~end *a* attractive. **A~ung** *f* - attraction. **A~ungskraft** *f* attraction; (*Phys*) gravity
Anzug *m* suit; **im A~ sein** (*fig*) be imminent
anzüglich *a* suggestive; ⟨*Bemerkung*⟩ personal
anzünden *vt sep* light; (*in Brand stecken*) set fire to
anzweifeln *vt sep* question
apart *a* striking, *adv* -ly
Apathie *f* - apathy
apathisch *a* apathetic, *adv* -ally
Aperitif *m* -s,-s aperitif
Apfel *m* -s,¨ apple. **A~mus** *nt* apple purée
Apfelsine *f* -,-n orange
Apostel *m* -s,- apostle
Apostroph *m* -s,-e apostrophe
Apothek|e *f* -,-n pharmacy. **A~er(in)** *m* -s,- (*f* -,-nen) pharmacist, [dispensing] chemist
Apparat *m* -[e]s,-e device; (*Phot*) camera; (*Radio, TV*) set; (*Teleph*) telephone; **am A~!** speaking! **A~ur** *f* -,-en apparatus
Appell *m* -s,-e appeal; (*Mil*) roll-call. **a~ieren** *vi* (*haben*) appeal (**an** + *acc* to)
Appetit *m* -s appetite; **guten A~!** enjoy your meal! **a~lich** *a* appetizing, *adv* -ly
applaudieren *vi* (*haben*) applaud
Applaus *m* -es applause
Aprikose *f* -,-n apricot
April *m* -[s] April; **in den A~schicken** (*fam*) make an April fool of
Aquarell *nt* -s,-e water-colour
Aquarium *nt* -s,-ien aquarium
Äquator *m* -s equator
Ära *f* - era
Araber(in) *m* -s,- (*f* -,-nen) Arab
arabisch *a* Arab; (*Geog*) Arabian; ⟨*Ziffer*⟩ Arabic
Arbeit *f* -,-en work; (*Anstellung*) employment, job; (*Aufgabe*) task; (*Sch*) [written] test; (*Abhandlung*) treatise; (*Qualität*) workmanship; **bei der A~** at work; **zur A~ gehen** go to work; **an die A~ gehen, sich an die A~ machen** set to work; **sich** (*dat*) **viel A~ machen** go to a lot of trouble. **a~en** *v sep* □ *vi* (*haben*) work (**an** + *dat* on) □ *vt* make; **einen Anzug a~en lassen** have a suit made; **sich durch etw a~en** work one's way through sth. **A~er(in)** *m* -s,- (*f* -,-nen) worker; (*Land-, Hilfs-*) labourer. **A~erklasse** *f* working class
Arbeit|geber *m* -s,- employer. **A~nehmer** *m* -s,- employee. **a~sam** *a* industrious
Arbeits|amt *nt* employment exchange. **A~erlaubnis, A~genehmigung** *f* work permit. **A~kraft** *f* worker; **Mangel an A~kräften** shortage of labour. **a~los** *a* unemployed; **~los sein** be out of work. **A~lose(r)** *m/f* unemployed person; **die A~losen** the unemployed *pl*. **A~losenunterstützung** *f* unemployment benefit. **A~losigkeit** *f* - unemployment
arbeitsparend *a* labour-saving
Arbeits|platz *m* job. **A~tag** *m* working day. **A~zimmer** *nt* study
Archäo|loge *m* -n,-n archaeologist. **A~logie** *f* - archaeology. **a~logisch** *a* archaeological
Arche *f* - **die A~ Noah** Noah's Ark
Architek|t(in) *m* -en,-en (*f* -,-nen) architect. **a~tonisch** *a* architectural. **A~tur** *f* - architecture
Archiv *nt* -s,-e archives *pl*
Arena *f* -,-nen arena
arg *a* (**ärger, ärgst**) bad; (*groß*) terrible; **sein ärgster Feind** his worst enemy □ *adv* badly; (*sehr*) terribly
Argentin|ien /-iən/ *nt* -s Argentina. **a~isch** *a* Argentinian
Ärger *m* -s annoyance; (*Unannehmlichkeit*) trouble. **ä~lich** *a* annoyed; (*leidig*) annoying;

ä~lich sein be annoyed. **ä~n** *vt* annoy; (*necken*) tease; **sich ä~n** get annoyed (**über jdn/etw** with s.o./ about sth). **Ä~nis** *nt* **-ses, -se** annoyance; **öffentliches Ä~nis** public nuisance

Arglist *f* - malice. **a~ig** *a* malicious, *adv* -ly

arglos *a* unsuspecting; (*unschuldig*) innocent, *adv* -ly

Argument *nt* **-[e]s,-e** argument. **a~ieren** *vi* (*haben*) argue (**dass** that)

Argwohn *m* **-s** suspicion

argwöhn|en *vt* suspect. **a~isch** *a* suspicious, *adv* -ly

Arie /ˈa:ri̯ə/ *f* **-,-n** aria

Aristo|krat *m* **-en,-en** aristocrat. **A~kratie** *f* - aristocracy. **a~kratisch** *a* aristocratic

Arithmetik *f* - arithmetic

Arkt|is *f* - Arctic. **a~isch** *a* Arctic

arm *a* (**ärmer, ärmst**) poor; **Arm und Reich (arm und reich)** rich and poor

Arm *m* **-[e]s,-e** arm; **jdn auf den Arm nehmen** (*fam*) pull s.o.'s leg

Armaturenbrett *nt* instrument panel; (*Auto*) dashboard

Armband *nt* (*pl* **-bänder**) bracelet; (*Uhr-*) watch-strap. **A~uhr** *f* wrist-watch

Arm|e(r) *m/f* poor man/woman; **die A~en** the poor *pl*; **du A~e** *od* **Ärmste!** you poor thing!

Armee *f* **-,-n** army

Ärmel *m* **-s,-** sleeve. **Ä~kanal** *m* [English] Channel. **ä~los** *a* sleeveless

Arm|lehne *f* arm. **A~leuchter** *m* candelabra

ärmlich *a* poor, *adv* -ly; (*elend*) miserable, *adv* -bly

armselig *a* miserable, *adv* -bly

Armut *f* - poverty

Arom|a *nt* **-s,-men** & **-mas** aroma; (*Culin*) essence. **a~atisch** *a* aromatic

Arran|gement /arãʒəˈmã:/ *nt* **-s,-s** arrangement. **a~gieren** /-ˈʒi:rən/ *vt* arrange; **sich a~gieren** come to an arrangement

Arrest *m* **-[e]s** (*Mil*) detention

arrogan|t *a* arrogant, *adv* -ly. **A~z** *f* - arrogance

Arsch *m* **-[e]s,¨e** (*vulg*) arse

Arsen *nt* **-s** arsenic

Art *f* **-,-en** manner; (*Weise*) way; (*Natur*) nature; (*Sorte*) kind; (*Biol*) species; **auf diese Art** in this way. **a~en** *vi* (*sein*) **a~en nach** take after

Arterie /-i̯ə/ *f* **-,-n** artery

Arthritis *f* - arthritis

artig *a* well-behaved; (*höflich*) polite, *adv* -ly; **sei a~!** be good!

Artikel *m* **-s,-** article

Artillerie *f* - artillery

Artischocke *f* **-,-n** artichoke

Artist(in) *m* **-en,-en** (*f* **-,-nen**) [circus] artiste

Arznei *f* **-,-en** medicine. **A~mittel** *nt* drug

Arzt *m* **-[e]s,¨e** doctor

Ärzt|in *f* **-,-nen** [woman] doctor. **ä~lich** *a* medical

As *nt* **-ses,-se** (NEW) **Ass**

Asbest *m* **-[e]s** asbestos

Asche *f* - ash. **A~nbecher** *m* ashtray. **A~rmittwoch** *m* Ash Wednesday

Asiat|(in) *m* **-en,-en** (*f* **-,-nen**) Asian. **a~isch** *a* Asian

Asien /ˈa:zi̯ən/ *nt* **-s** Asia

asozial *a* antisocial

Aspekt *m* **-[e]s,-e** aspect

Asphalt *m* **-[e]s** asphalt. **a~ieren** *vt* asphalt

Ass *nt* **-es,-e** ace

Assistent(in) *m* **-en,-en** (*f* **-,-nen**) assistant

Ast *m* **-[e]s,¨e** branch

ästhetisch *a* aesthetic

Asth|ma *nt* **-s** asthma. **a~matisch** *a* asthmatic

Astro|loge *m* **-n,-n** astrologer. **A~logie** *f* - astrology. **A~naut** *m* **-en,-en** astronaut. **A~nom** *m*

-**en,-en** astronomer. **A~nomie** *f* - astronomy. **a~nomisch** *a* astronomical

Asyl *nt* **-s,-e** home; (*Pol*) asylum. **A~ant** *m* **-en,-en** asylum-seeker

Atelier /-'lie:/ *nt* **-s,-s** studio

Atem *m* **-s** breath; **tief A~ holen** take a deep breath. **a~beraubend** *a* breath-taking. **a~los** *a* breathless, *adv* -ly. **A~pause** *f* breather. **A~zug** *m* breath

Atheist *m* **-en,-en** atheist

Äther *m* **-s** ether

Äthiopien /-iən/ *nt* **-s** Ethiopia

Athlet|(in) *m* **-en,-en** (*f* **-,-nen**) athlete. **a~isch** *a* athletic

Atlant|ik *m* **-s** Atlantic. **a~isch** *a* Atlantic; **der A~ische Ozean** the Atlantic Ocean

Atlas *m* **-lasses,-lanten** atlas

atmen *vt/i* (*haben*) breathe

Atmosphär|e *f* **-,-n** atmosphere. **a~isch** *a* atmospheric

Atmung *f* - breathing

Atom *nt* **-s,-e** atom. **a~ar** *a* atomic. **A~bombe** *f* atom bomb. **A~krieg** *m* nuclear war

Atten|tat *nt* **-[e]s,-e** assassination attempt. **A~täter** *m* [would-be] assassin

Attest *nt* **-[e]s,-e** certificate

Attrak|tion /-'tsio:n/ *f* **-,-en** attraction. **a~tiv** *a* attractive, *adv* -ly

Attrappe *f* **-,-n** dummy

Attribut *nt* **-[e]s,-e** attribute. **a~iv** *a* attributive, *adv* -ly

ätzen *vt* corrode; (*Med*) cauterize; (*Kunst*) etch. **ä~d** *a* corrosive; ⟨*Spott*⟩ caustic

au *int* ouch; **au fein!** oh good!

Aubergine /obɛr'ʒi:nə/ *f* **-,-n** aubergine

auch *adv & conj* also, too; (*außerdem*) what's more; (*selbst*) even; **a~ wenn** even if; **ich mag ihn—ich a~** I like him—so do I; **ich bin nicht müde—ich a~ nicht** I'm not tired—nor *or* neither am I; **sie weiß es a~ nicht** she doesn't know either; **wer/wie/was a~ immer** whoever/however/whatever; **ist das a~ wahr?** is that really true?

Audienz *f* **-,-en** audience

audiovisuell *a* audio-visual

Auditorium *nt* **-s,-ien** (*Univ*) lecture hall

auf *prep* (+ *dat*) on; (+ *acc*) on [to]; (*bis*) until, till; (*Proportion*) to; **auf Deutsch/Englisch** in German/English; **auf einer/eine Party** at/to a party; **auf der Straße** in the street; **auf seinem Zimmer** in one's room; **auf einem Ohr taub** deaf in one ear; **auf einen Stuhl steigen** climb on [to] a chair; **auf die Toilette gehen** go to the toilet; **auf ein paar Tage verreisen** go away for a few days; **auf 10 Kilometer zu sehen** visible for 10 kilometres □ *adv* open; (*in die Höhe*) up; **auf sein** be open; ⟨*Person:*⟩ be up; **auf und ab** up and down; **sich auf und davon machen** make off; **Tür auf!** open the door!

aufarbeiten *vt sep* do up; **Rückstände a~** clear arrears [of work]

aufatmen *vi sep* (*haben*) heave a sigh of relief

aufbahren *vt sep* lay out

Aufbau *m* construction; (*Struktur*) structure. **a~en** *v sep* □ *vt* construct, build; (*errichten*) erect; (*schaffen*) build up; (*arrangieren*) arrange; **wieder a~en** reconstruct; **sich a~en** (*fig*) be based (**auf** + *dat* on) □ *vi* (*haben*) be based (**auf** + *dat* on)

aufbäumen (sich) *vr sep* rear [up]; (*fig*) rebel

aufbauschen *vt sep* puff out; (*fig*) exaggerate

aufbehalten† *vt sep* keep on

aufbekommen† *vt sep* get open; (*Sch*) be given [as homework]

aufbessern *vt sep* improve; (*erhöhen*) increase

aufbewahr|en *vt sep* keep; (*lagern*) store. **A~ung** *f* - safe keeping; storage; (*Gepäck-*) left-luggage office
aufbieten† *vt sep* mobilize; (*fig*) summon up
aufblas|bar *a* inflatable. **a~en**† *vt sep* inflate; **sich a~en** (*fig*) give oneself airs
aufbleiben† *vi sep* (*sein*) stay open; ⟨*Person:*⟩ stay up
aufblenden *vt/i sep* (*haben*) (*Auto*) switch to full beam
aufblicken *vi sep* (*haben*) look up (**zu** at/(*fig*) to)
aufblühen *vi sep* (*sein*) flower; ⟨*Knospe:*⟩ open
aufbocken *vt sep* jack up
aufbraten† *vt sep* fry up
aufbrauchen *vt sep* use up
aufbrausen *vi sep* (*sein*) (*fig*) flare up. **a~d** *a* quick-tempered
aufbrechen† *v sep* □ *vt* break open □ *vi* (*sein*) ⟨*Knospe:*⟩ open; (*sich aufmachen*) set out, start
aufbringen† *vt sep* raise ⟨*Geld*⟩; find ⟨*Kraft*⟩; (*wütend machen*) infuriate
Aufbruch *m* start, departure
aufbrühen *vt sep* make ⟨*Tee*⟩
aufbürden *vt sep* **jdm etw a~** (*fig*) burden s.o. with sth
aufdecken *vt sep* (*auflegen*) put on; (*abdecken*) uncover; (*fig*) expose
aufdrängen *vt sep* force (*dat* on); **sich jdm a~** force one's company on s.o.
aufdrehen *vt sep* turn on
aufdringlich *a* persistent
aufeinander *adv* one on top of the other; ⟨*schießen*⟩ at each other; ⟨*warten*⟩ for each other; **a~ folgen** follow one another; **a~ folgend** successive; ⟨*Tage*⟩ consecutive. **a~folgen** *vi sep* (*sein*) (NEW) **a~ folgen**, *s.* **aufeinander**. **a~folgend** *a* (NEW) **a~ folgend**, *s.* **aufeinander**

Aufenthalt *m* stay; **10 Minuten A~ haben** ⟨*Zug:*⟩ stop for 10 minutes. **A~serlaubnis, A~sgenehmigung** *f* residence permit. **A~sraum** *m* recreation room; (*im Hotel*) lounge
auferlegen *vt sep* impose (*dat* on)
aufersteh|en† *vi sep* (*sein*) rise from the dead. **A~ung** *f* - resurrection
aufessen† *vt sep* eat up
auffahr|en† *vi sep* (*sein*) drive up; (*aufprallen*) crash, run (**auf** + *acc* into); (*aufschrecken*) start up; (*aufbrausen*) flare up. **A~t** *f* drive; (*Autobahn-*) access road, slip road; (*Bergfahrt*) ascent
auffallen† *vi sep* (*sein*) be conspicuous; **unangenehm a~** make a bad impression; **jdm a~** strike s.o. **a~d** *a* striking, *adv* -ly
auffällig *a* conspicuous, *adv* -ly; (*grell*) gaudy, *adv* -ily
auffangen† *vt sep* catch; pick up ⟨*Funkspruch*⟩
auffass|en *vt sep* understand; (*deuten*) take; **falsch a~en** misunderstand. **A~ung** *f* understanding; (*Ansicht*) view. **A~ungsgabe** *f* grasp
aufforder|n *vt sep* ask; (*einladen*) invite; **jdn zum Tanz a~n** ask s.o. to dance. **A~ung** *f* request; invitation
auffrischen *v sep* □ *vt* freshen up; revive ⟨*Erinnerung*⟩; **seine Englischkenntnisse a~** brush up one's English
aufführ|en *vt sep* perform; (*angeben*) list; **sich a~en** behave. **A~ung** *f* performance
auffüllen *vt sep* fill up; **[wieder] a~** replenish
Aufgabe *f* task; (*Rechen-*) problem; (*Verzicht*) giving up; **A~n** (*Sch*) homework *sg*
Aufgang *m* way up; (*Treppe*) stairs *pl*; (*Astr*) rise
aufgeben† *v sep* □ *vt* give up; post ⟨*Brief*⟩; send ⟨*Telegramm*⟩; place ⟨*Bestellung*⟩; register ⟨*Gepäck*⟩;

put in the paper ⟨*Annonce*⟩; **jdm eine Aufgabe/ein Rätsel a~** set s.o. a task/a riddle; **jdm Suppe a~** serve s.o. with soup □ *vi* (*haben*) give up

aufgeblasen *a* (*fig*) conceited

Aufgebot *nt* contingent (**an** + *dat* of); (*Relig*) banns *pl*; **unter A~ aller Kräfte** with all one's strength

aufgebracht *a* (*fam*) angry

aufgedunsen *a* bloated

aufgehen† *vi sep* (*sein*) open; (*sich lösen*) come undone; ⟨*Teig, Sonne:*⟩ rise; ⟨*Saat:*⟩ come up; (*Math*) come out exactly; **in Flammen a~** go up in flames; **in etw** (*dat*) **a~** (*fig*) be wrapped up in sth; **ihm ging auf** (*fam*) he realized (**dass** that)

aufgelegt *a* **a~ sein zu** be in the mood for; **gut/schlecht a~ sein** be in a good/bad mood

aufgelöst *a* (*fig*) distraught; **in Tränen a~** in floods of tears

aufgeregt *a* excited, *adv* -ly; (*erregt*) agitated, *adv* -ly

aufgeschlossen *a* (*fig*) open-minded

aufgesprungen *a* chapped

aufgeweckt *a* (*fig*) bright

aufgießen† *vt sep* pour on; (*aufbrühen*) make ⟨*Tee*⟩

aufgreifen† *vt sep* pick up; take up ⟨*Vorschlag, Thema*⟩

aufgrund *prep* (+ *gen*) on the strength of

Aufguss (**Aufguß**) *m* infusion

aufhaben† *v sep* □ *vt* have on; **den Mund a~** have one's mouth open; **viel a~** (*Sch*) have a lot of homework □ *vi* (*haben*) be open

aufhalsen *vt sep* (*fam*) saddle with

aufhalten† *vt sep* hold up; (*anhalten*) stop; (*abhalten*) keep, detain; (*offenhalten*) hold open; hold out ⟨*Hand*⟩; **sich a~** stay; (*sich befassen*) spend one's time (**mit** on)

aufhäng|en *vt/i sep* (*haben*) hang up; (*henken*) hang; **sich a~en** hang oneself. **A~er** *m* **-s,-** loop. **A~ung** *f* **-** (*Auto*) suspension

aufheben† *vt sep* pick up; (*hochheben*) raise; (*aufbewahren*) keep; (*beenden*) end; (*rückgängig machen*) lift; (*abschaffen*) abolish; (*Jur*) quash ⟨*Urteil*⟩; repeal ⟨*Gesetz*⟩; (*ausgleichen*) cancel out; **sich a~** cancel each other out; **gut aufgehoben sein** be well looked after. **A~** *nt* **-s viel A~s machen** make a great fuss (**von** about)

aufheitern *vt sep* cheer up; **sich a~** ⟨*Wetter:*⟩ brighten up

aufhellen *vt sep* lighten; **sich a~** ⟨*Himmel:*⟩ brighten

aufhetzen *vt sep* incite

aufholen *v sep* □ *vt* make up □ *vi* (*haben*) catch up; (*zeitlich*) make up time

aufhorchen *vi sep* (*haben*) prick up one's ears

aufhören *vi sep* (*haben*) stop; **mit der Arbeit a~, a~ zu arbeiten** stop working

aufklappen *vt/i sep* (*sein*) open

aufklär|en *vt sep* solve; **jdn a~en** enlighten s.o.; (*sexuell*) tell s.o. the facts of life; **sich a~en** be solved; ⟨*Wetter:*⟩ clear up. **A~ung** *f* solution; enlightenment; (*Mil*) reconnaissance; **sexuelle A~ung** sex education

aufkleb|en *vt sep* stick on. **A~er** *m* **-s,-** sticker

aufknöpfen *vt sep* unbutton

aufkochen *v sep* □ *vt* bring to the boil □ *vi* (*sein*) come to the boil

aufkommen† *vi sep* (*sein*) start; ⟨*Wind:*⟩ spring up; ⟨*Mode:*⟩ come in; **a~ für** pay for

aufkrempeln *vt sep* roll up

aufladen† *vt sep* load; (*Electr*) charge

Auflage *f* impression; (*Ausgabe*) edition; (*Zeitungs-*) circulation; (*Bedingung*) condition; (*Überzug*) coating

auflassen† *vt sep* leave open; leave on ⟨*Hut*⟩
auflauern *vi sep* (*haben*) **jdm a~** lie in wait for s.o.
Auflauf *m* crowd; (*Culin*) ≈ soufflé. **a~en**† *vi sep* (*sein*) (*Naut*) run aground
auflegen *v sep* □ *vt* apply (**auf** + *acc* to); put down ⟨*Hörer*⟩; **neu a~** reprint □ *vi* (*haben*) ring off
auflehn|en (sich) *vr sep* (*fig*) rebel. **A~ung** *f* - rebellion
auflesen† *vt sep* pick up
aufleuchten *vi sep* (*haben*) light up
aufliegen† *vi sep* (*haben*) rest (**auf** + *dat* on)
auflisten *vt sep* list
auflockern *vt sep* break up; (*entspannen*) relax; (*fig*) liven up
auflös|en *vt sep* dissolve; close ⟨*Konto*⟩; **sich a~en** dissolve; ⟨*Nebel:*⟩ clear. **A~ung** dissolution; (*Lösung*) solution
aufmach|en *v sep* □ *vt* open; (*lösen*) undo; **sich a~en** set out (**nach** for); (*sich schminken*) make oneself up □ *vi* (*haben*) open; **jdm a~en** open the door to s.o. **A~ung** *f* -,-**en** get-up; (*Comm*) presentation
aufmerksam *a* attentive, *adv* -ly; **a~ werden auf** (+ *acc*) notice; **jdn a~ machen auf** (+ *acc*) draw s.o.'s attention to. **A~keit** *f* -,-**en** attention; (*Höflichkeit*) courtesy
aufmucken *vi sep* (*haben*) rebel
aufmuntern *vt sep* cheer up
Aufnahme *f* -,-**n** acceptance; (*Empfang*) reception; (*in Klub, Krankenhaus*) admission; (*Einbeziehung*) inclusion; (*Beginn*) start; (*Foto*) photograph; (*Film-*) shot; (*Mus*) recording; (*Band-*) tape recording. **a~fähig** a receptive. **A~prüfung** *f* entrance examination
aufnehmen† *vt sep* pick up; (*absorbieren*) absorb; take ⟨*Nahrung, Foto*⟩; (*fassen*) hold; (*annehmen*) accept; (*leihen*) borrow; (*empfangen*) receive; (*in Klub, Krankenhaus*) admit; (*beherbergen, geistig erfassen*) take in; (*einbeziehen*) include; (*beginnen*) take up; (*niederschreiben*) take down; (*filmen*) film, shoot; (*Mus*) record; **auf Band a~** tape[-record]; **etw gelassen a~** take sth calmly; **es a~ können mit** (*fig*) be a match for
aufopfer|n *vt sep* sacrifice; **sich a~n** sacrifice oneself. **a~nd** *a* devoted, *adv* -ly. **A~ung** *f* self-sacrifice
aufpassen *vi sep* (*haben*) pay attention; (*sich vorsehen*) take care; **a~auf** (+ *acc*) look after
aufpflanzen (sich) *vr sep* (*fam*) plant oneself
aufplatzen *vi sep* (*sein*) split open
aufplustern (sich) *vr sep* ⟨*Vogel:*⟩ ruffle up its feathers
Aufprall *m* -**[e]s** impact. **a~en** *vi sep* (*sein*) **a~en auf** (+ *acc*) hit
aufpumpen *vt sep* pump up, inflate
aufputsch|en *vt sep* incite; **sich a~en** take stimulants. **A~mittel** *nt* stimulant
aufquellen† *vi sep* (*sein*) swell
aufraffen *vt sep* pick up; **sich a~** pick oneself up; (*fig*) pull oneself together; (*sich aufschwingen*) find the energy (**zu** for)
aufragen *vi sep* (*sein*) rise [up]
aufräumen *vt/i sep* (*haben*) tidy up; (*wegräumen*) put away; **a~ mit** (*fig*) get rid of
aufrecht *a & adv* upright. **a~erhalten**† *vt sep* (*fig*) maintain
aufreg|en *vt* excite; (*beunruhigen*) upset; (*ärgern*) annoy; **sich a~en** get excited; (*sich erregen*) get worked up. **a~end** *a* exciting. **A~ung** *f* excitement
aufreiben† *vt sep* chafe; (*fig*) wear down; **sich a~** wear oneself out. **a~d** *a* trying, wearing
aufreißen† *v sep* □ *vt* tear open; dig up ⟨*Straße*⟩; open wide

〈*Augen, Mund*〉 □ *vi* (*sein*) split open
aufreizend *a* provocative, *adv* -ly
aufrichten *vt sep* erect; (*fig: trösten*) comfort; **sich a~** straighten up; (*sich setzen*) sit up
aufrichtig *a* sincere, *adv* -ly. **A~keit** *f* - sincerity
aufriegeln *vt sep* unbolt
aufrollen *vt sep* roll up; (*entrollen*) unroll
aufrücken *vi sep* (*sein*) move up; (*fig*) be promoted
Aufruf *m* appeal (**an** + *dat* to); **a~en**† *vt sep* call out 〈*Namen*〉; **jdn a~en** call s.o.'s name; (*fig*) call on s.o. (**zu** to)
Aufruhr *m* **-s,-e** turmoil; (*Empörung*) revolt
aufrühr|en *vt sep* stir up. **A~er** *m* **-s,-** rebel. **a~erisch** *a* inflammatory; (*rebellisch*) rebellious
aufrunden *vt sep* round up
aufrüsten *vi sep* (*haben*) arm
aufs *prep* = **auf das**
aufsagen *vt sep* recite
aufsammeln *vt sep* gather up
aufsässig *a* rebellious
Aufsatz *m* top; (*Sch*) essay
aufsaugen† *vt sep* soak up
aufschauen *vi sep* (*haben*) look up (**zu** at/(*fig*) to)
aufschichten *vt sep* stack up
aufschieben† *vt sep* slide open; (*verschieben*) put off, postpone
Aufschlag *m* impact; (*Tennis*) service; (*Hosen-*) turn-up; (*Ärmel-*) upturned cuff; (*Revers*) lapel; (*Comm*) surcharge. **a~en**† *v sep* □ *vt* open; crack 〈*Ei*〉; (*hochschlagen*) turn up; (*errichten*) put up; (*erhöhen*) increase; cast on 〈*Masche*〉; **sich** (*dat*) **das Knie a~en** cut [open] one's knee □ *vi* (*haben*) hit (**auf etw** *acc/dat* sth); (*Tennis*) serve; (*teurer werden*) go up
aufschließen† *v sep* □ *vt* unlock □ *vi* (*haben*) unlock the door
aufschlitzen *vt sep* slit open
Aufschluss (**Aufschluß**) *m* **A~ geben** give information (**über** + *acc* on). **a~reich** *a* revealing; (*lehrreich*) informative
aufschneid|en† *v sep* □ *vt* cut open; (*in Scheiben*) slice; carve 〈*Braten*〉 □ *vi* (*haben*) (*fam*) exaggerate. **A~er** *m* **-s,-** (*fam*) showoff
Aufschnitt *m* sliced sausage, cold meat [and cheese]
aufschrauben *vt sep* screw on; (*abschrauben*) unscrew
aufschrecken *v sep* □ *vt* startle □ *vi*† (*sein*) start up; **aus dem Schlaf a~** wake up with a start
Aufschrei *m* [sudden] cry
aufschreiben† *vt sep* write down; (*fam: verschreiben*) prescribe; **jdn a~** 〈*Polizist:*〉 book s.o.
aufschreien† *vi sep* (*haben*) cry out
Aufschrift *f* inscription; (*Etikett*) label
Aufschub *m* delay; (*Frist*) grace
aufschürfen *vt sep* **sich** (*dat*) **das Knie a~** graze one's knee
aufschwatzen *vt sep* **jdm etw a~** talk s.o. into buying sth
aufschwingen† **(sich)** *vr sep* find the energy (**zu** for)
Aufschwung *m* (*fig*) upturn
aufsehen† *vi sep* (*haben*) look up (**zu** at/(*fig*) to). **A~** *nt* **-s A~ erregen** cause a sensation; **A~ erregend** sensational. **a~erregend** *a* (NEW) **A~ erregend**, *s.* **Aufsehen**
Aufseher(in) *m* **-s,-** (*f* **-,-nen**) supervisor; (*Gefängnis-*) warder
aufsein† *vi sep* (*sein*) (NEW) **auf sein**, *s.* **auf**
aufsetzen *vt sep* put on; (*verfassen*) draw up; (*entwerfen*) draft; **sich a~** sit up
Aufsicht *f* supervision; (*Person*) supervisor. **A~srat** *m* board of directors
aufsitzen† *vi sep* (*sein*) mount
aufspannen *vt sep* put up
aufsparen *vt sep* save, keep

aufsperren *vt sep* open wide
aufspielen *v sep* □ *vi* (*haben*) play □ *vr* **sich a~** show off; **sich als Held a~** play the hero
aufspießen *vt sep* spear
aufspringen† *vi sep* (*sein*) jump up; (*aufprallen*) bounce; (*sich öffnen*) burst open; ⟨*Haut:*⟩ become chapped; **a~ auf** (+ *acc*) jump on
aufspüren *vt sep* track down
aufstacheln *vt sep* incite
aufstampfen *vi sep* (*haben*) **mit dem Fuß a~** stamp one's foot
Aufstand *m* uprising, rebellion
aufständisch *a* rebellious. **A~e(r)** *m* rebel, insurgent
aufstapeln *vt sep* stack up
aufstauen *vt sep* dam [up]
aufstehen† *vi sep* (*sein*) get up; (*offen sein*) be open; (*fig*) rise up
aufsteigen† *vi sep* (*sein*) get on; ⟨*Reiter:*⟩ mount; ⟨*Bergsteiger:*⟩ climb up; (*hochsteigen*) rise [up]; (*fig: befördert werden*) rise (**zu** to); (*Sport*) be promoted
aufstell|en *vt sep* put up; (*Culin*) put on; (*postieren*) post; (*in einer Reihe*) line up; (*nominieren*) nominate; (*Sport*) select ⟨*Mannschaft*⟩; make out ⟨*Liste*⟩; lay down ⟨*Regel*⟩; make ⟨*Behauptung*⟩; set up ⟨*Rekord*⟩; **sich a~en** rise [up]; (*in einer Reihe*) line up. **A~ung** *f* nomination; (*Liste*) list
Aufstieg *m* **-[e]s, -e** ascent; (*fig*) rise; (*Sport*) promotion
aufstöbern *vt sep* flush out; (*fig*) track down
aufstoßen† *v sep* □ *vt* push open □ *vi* (*haben*) burp; **a~ auf** (+ *acc*) strike. **A~** *nt* **-s** burping
aufstrebend *a* (*fig*) ambitious
Aufstrich *m* [sandwich] spread
aufstützen *vt sep* rest (**auf** + *acc* on); **sich a~** lean (**auf** + *acc* on)
aufsuchen *vt sep* look for; (*besuchen*) go to see
Auftakt *m* (*fig*) start
auftauchen *vi sep* (*sein*) emerge; ⟨*U-Boot:*⟩ surface; (*fig*) turn up; ⟨*Frage:*⟩ crop up
auftauen *vt/i sep* (*sein*) thaw
aufteil|en *vt sep* divide [up]. **A~ung** *f* division
auftischen *vt sep* serve [up]
Auftrag *m* **-[e]s,¨e** task; (*Kunst*) commission; (*Comm*) order; **im A~** (+ *gen*) on behalf of. **a~en**† *v sep* □ *vt* apply; (*servieren*) serve; (*abtragen*) wear out; **jdm a~en** instruct s.o. (**zu** to) □ *vi* (*haben*) **dick a~en** (*fam*) exaggerate. **A~geber** *m* **-s,-** client
auftreiben† *vt sep* distend; (*fam: beschaffen*) get hold of
auftrennen *vt sep* unpick, undo
auftreten† *v sep* □ *vi* (*sein*) tread; (*sich benehmen*) behave, act; (*Theat*) appear; (*die Bühne betreten*) enter; (*vorkommen*) occur □ *vt* kick open. **A~** *nt* **-s** occurrence; (*Benehmen*) manner
Auftrieb *m* buoyancy; (*fig*) boost
Auftritt *m* (*Theat*) appearance; (*auf die Bühne*) entrance; (*Szene*) scene
auftun† *vt sep* **jdm Suppe a~** serve s.o. with soup; **sich** (*dat*) **etw a~** help oneself to sth; **sich a~** open
aufwachen *vi sep* (*sein*) wake up
aufwachsen† *vi sep* (*sein*) grow up
Aufwand *m* **-[e]s** expenditure; (*Luxus*) extravagance; (*Mühe*) trouble; **A~ treiben** be extravagant
aufwändig *a* = **aufwendig**
aufwärmen *vt sep* heat up; (*fig*) rake up; **sich a~** warm oneself; (*Sport*) warm up
Aufwartefrau *f* cleaner
aufwärts *adv* upwards; (*bergauf*) uphill; **es geht a~ mit jdm/etw** s.o./sth is improving. **a~gehen**† *vi sep* (*sein*) (NEW) **a~ gehen**, *s.* **aufwärts**
Aufwartung *f* **-** cleaner; **jdm seine A~ machen** call on s.o.

aufwaschen† *vt/i sep (haben)* wash up
aufwecken *vt sep* wake up
aufweichen *v sep* □ *vt* soften □ *vi (sein)* become soft
aufweisen† *vt sep* have, show
aufwend|en† *vt sep* spend; **Mühe a∼en** take pains. **a∼ig** *a* lavish, *adv* -ly; *(teuer)* expensive, *adv* -ly
aufwerfen† *vt sep (fig)* raise
aufwert|en *vt sep* revalue. **A∼ung** *f* revaluation
aufwickeln *vt sep* roll up; *(auswickeln)* unwrap
aufwiegeln *vt sep* stir up
aufwiegen† *vt sep* compensate for
Aufwiegler *m* **-s,-** agitator
aufwirbeln *vt sep* **Staub a∼** stir up dust; *(fig)* cause a stir
aufwisch|en *vt sep* wipe up; wash ⟨*Fußboden*⟩. **A∼lappen** *m* floorcloth
aufwühlen *vt sep* churn up; *(fig)* stir up
aufzähl|en *vt sep* enumerate, list. **A∼ung** *f* list
aufzeichn|en *vt sep* record; *(zeichnen)* draw. **A∼ung** *f* recording; **A∼ungen** notes
aufziehen† *v sep* □ *vt* pull up; hoist ⟨*Segel*⟩; *(öffnen)* open; draw ⟨*Vorhang*⟩; *(auftrennen)* undo; *(großziehen)* bring up; rear ⟨*Tier*⟩; mount ⟨*Bild*⟩; thread ⟨*Perlen*⟩; wind up ⟨*Uhr*⟩; *(arrangieren)* organize; *(fam: necken)* tease □ *vi (sein)* approach
Aufzucht *f* rearing
Aufzug *m* hoist; *(Fahrstuhl)* lift, *(Amer)* elevator; *(Prozession)* procession; *(Theat)* act; *(fam: Aufmachung)* get-up
Augapfel *m* eyeball
Auge *nt* **-s,-n** eye; *(Punkt)* spot; **vier A∼n werfen** throw a four; **gute A∼n** good eyesight; **unter vier A∼n** in private; **aus den A∼n verlieren** lose sight of; **im A∼ behalten** keep in sight; *(fig)* bear in mind

Augenblick *m* moment; **im/jeden A∼** at the/at any moment; **A∼!** just a moment! **a∼lich** *a* immediate; *(derzeitig)* present □ *adv* immediately; *(derzeit)* at present
Augen|braue *f* eyebrow. **A∼höhle** *f* eye socket. **A∼licht** *nt* sight. **A∼lid** *nt* eyelid. **A∼schein** *m* **in A∼schein nehmen** inspect. **A∼zeuge** *m* eyewitness
August *m* **-[s]** August
Auktion /ˈtsi̯oːn/ *f* **-,-en** auction. **A∼ator** *m* **-s,-en** /-ˈtoːrən/ auctioneer
Aula *f* **-,-len** *(Sch)* [assembly] hall
Aupairmädchen, Au-pair-Mädchen /oˈpɛːr-/ *nt* au pair
aus *prep (+ dat)* out of; *(von)* from; *(bestehend)* [made] of; **aus Angst** from *or* out of fear; **aus Spaß** for fun □ *adv* out; ⟨*Licht, Radio*⟩ off; **aus sein** be out; ⟨*Licht, Radio:*⟩ be off; *(zu Ende sein)* be over; **aus sein auf** *(+ acc)* be after; **mit ihm ist es aus** he's had it; **aus und ein** in and out; **nicht mehr aus noch ein wissen** be at one's wits' end; **von ... aus** from ...; **von sich aus** of one's own accord; **von mir aus** as far as I'm concerned
ausarbeiten *vt sep* work out
ausarten *vi sep (sein)* degenerate **(in** *+ acc* into)
ausatmen *vt/i sep (haben)* breathe out
ausbaggern *vt sep* excavate; dredge ⟨*Fluss*⟩
ausbauen *vt sep* remove; *(vergrößern)* extend; *(fig)* expand
ausbedingen† *vt sep* **sich** *(dat)* **a∼** insist on; *(zur Bedingung machen)* stipulate
ausbesser|n *vt sep* mend, repair. **A∼ung** *f* repair
ausbeulen *vt sep* remove the dents from; *(dehnen)* make baggy
Ausbeut|e *f* yield. **a∼en** *vt sep* exploit. **A∼ung** *f* exploitation
ausbild|en *vt sep* train; *(formen)* form; *(entwickeln)* develop; **sich**

a~en train (**als/zu** as); (*entstehen*) develop. **A~er** *m* **-s,-** instructor. **A~ung** *f* training; (*Sch*) education

ausbitten† *vt sep* **sich** (*dat*) **a~** ask for; (*verlangen*) insist on

ausblasen† *vt sep* blow out

ausbleiben† *vi sep* (*sein*) fail to appear/ ⟨*Erfolg:*⟩ materialize; (*nicht heimkommen*) stay out; **es konnte nicht a~** it was inevitable. **A~** *nt* **-s** absence

Ausblick *m* view

ausbrech|en† *vi sep* (*sein*) break out; ⟨*Vulkan:*⟩ erupt; (*fliehen*) escape; **in Tränen a~en** burst into tears. **A~er** *m* runaway

ausbreit|en *vt sep* spread [out]; **sich a~en** spread. **A~ung** *f* spread

ausbrennen† *v sep* □ *vt* cauterize □ *vi* (*sein*) burn out; ⟨*Haus:*⟩ be gutted [by fire]

Ausbruch *m* outbreak; (*Vulkan-*) eruption; (*Wut-*) outburst; (*Flucht*) escape, break-out

ausbrüten *vt sep* hatch

Ausbund *m* **A~der Tugend** paragon of virtue

ausbürsten *vt sep* brush; (*entfernen*) brush out

Ausdauer *f* perseverance; (*körperlich*) stamina. **a~nd** a persevering; (*unermüdlich*) untiring; (*Bot*) perennial □ *adv* with perseverance; untiringly

ausdehn|en *vt sep* stretch; (*fig*) extend; **sich a~en** stretch; (*Phys & fig*) expand; (*dauern*) last. **A~ung** *f* expansion; (*Umfang*) extent

ausdenken† *vt sep* **sich** (*dat*) **a~** think up; (*sich vorstellen*) imagine

ausdrehen *vt sep* turn off

Ausdruck *m* expression; (*Fach-*) term; (*Computer*) printout. **a~en** *vt sep* print

ausdrück|en *vt sep* squeeze out; squeeze ⟨*Zitrone*⟩; stub out ⟨*Zigarette*⟩; (*äußern*) express; **sich a~en** express oneself. **a~lich** *a* express, *adv -ly*

ausdrucks|los *a* expressionless. **a~voll** *a* expressive

auseinander *adv* apart; (*entzwei*) in pieces; **a~ falten** unfold; **a~ gehen** part; ⟨*Linien, Meinungen:*⟩ diverge; ⟨*Menge:*⟩ disperse; ⟨*Ehe:*⟩ break up; (*entzweigehen*) come apart; **a~ halten** tell apart; **a~ nehmen** take apart *or* to pieces; **a~ setzen** place apart; (*erklären*) explain (**jdm** to s.o.); **sich a~ setzen** sit apart; (*sich aussprechen*) have it out (**mit jdm** with s.o.); come to grips (**mit einem Problem** with a problem). **a~falten** *vt sep* (NEW) **a~ falten**, *s.* **auseinander**. **a~gehen**† *vi sep* (*sein*) (NEW) **a~ gehen**, *s.* **auseinander**. **a~halten**† *vt sep* (NEW) **a~ halten**, *s.* **auseinander**. **a~nehmen**† *vt sep* (NEW) **a~ nehmen**, *s.* **auseinander**. **a~setzen** *vt sep* (NEW) **a~ setzen**, *s.* **auseinander**. **A~setzung** *f* **-,-en** discussion; (*Streit*) argument

auserlesen *a* select, choice

ausfahr|en† *v sep* □ *vt* take for a drive; take out ⟨*Baby*⟩ [in the pram] □ *vi* (*sein*) go for a drive. **A~t** *f* drive; (*Autobahn-, Garagen-*) exit

Ausfall *m* failure; (*Absage*) cancellation; (*Comm*) loss. **a~en**† *vi sep* (*sein*) fall out; (*versagen*) fail; (*abgesagt werden*) be cancelled; **gut/schlecht a~en** turn out to be good/poor

ausfallend, **ausfällig** *a* abusive

ausfertig|en *vt sep* make out. **A~ung** *f* **-,-en in doppelter/ dreifacher A~ung** in duplicate/ triplicate

ausfindig *a* **a~ machen** find

ausflippen *vi* (*sein*) freak out

Ausflucht *f* **-,-e** excuse

Ausflug *m* excursion, outing

Ausflügler *m* **-s,-** [day-]tripper

Ausfluss (**Ausfluß**) *m* outlet; (*Abfluss*) drain; (*Med*) discharge

ausfragen *vt sep* question
ausfransen *vi sep* (*sein*) fray
Ausfuhr *f* **-,-en** (*Comm*) export
ausführ|en *vt sep* take out; (*Comm*) export; (*durchführen*) carry out; (*erklären*) explain. **a~lich** *a* detailed □ *adv* in detail. **A~ung** *f* execution; (*Comm*) version; (*äußere*) finish; (*Qualität*) workmanship; (*Erklärung*) explanation
Ausgabe *f* issue; (*Buch-*) edition; (*Comm*) version
Ausgang *m* way out, exit; (*Flugsteig*) gate; (*Ende*) end; (*Ergebnis*) outcome, result; **A~ haben** have time off. **A~spunkt** *m* starting-point. **A~ssperre** *f* curfew
ausgeben† *vt sep* hand out; issue ⟨*Fahrkarten*⟩; spend ⟨*Geld*⟩; buy ⟨*Runde Bier*⟩; **sich a~ als** pretend to be
ausgebeult *a* baggy
ausgebildet *a* trained
ausgebucht *a* fully booked; ⟨*Vorstellung*⟩ sold out
ausgedehnt *a* extensive; (*lang*) long
ausgedient *a* worn out; ⟨*Person*⟩ retired
ausgefallen *a* unusual
ausgefranst *a* frayed
ausgeglichen *a* [well-]balanced; (*gelassen*) even-tempered
ausgeh|en† *vi sep* (*sein*) go out; ⟨*Haare:*⟩ fall out; ⟨*Vorräte, Geld:*⟩ run out; (*verblassen*) fade; (*herrühren*) come (**von** from); (*abzielen*) aim (**auf** + *acc* at); **gut/schlecht a~en** end well/badly; **leer a~en** come away empty-handed; **davon a~en, dass** assume that. **A~verbot** *nt* curfew
ausgelassen *a* high-spirited; **a~ sein** be in high spirits
ausgelernt *a* [fully] trained
ausgemacht *a* agreed; (*fam: vollkommen*) utter
ausgenommen *conj* except; **a~ wenn** unless
ausgeprägt *a* marked
ausgerechnet *adv* **a~ heute** today of all days; **a~er/Rom** he of all people/Rome of all places
ausgeschlossen *pred a* out of the question
ausgeschnitten *a* low-cut
ausgesprochen *a* marked □ *adv* decidedly
ausgestorben *a* extinct; **[wie] a~** ⟨*Straße:*⟩ deserted
Ausgestoßene(r) *m/f* outcast
ausgewachsen *a* fully-grown
ausgewogen *a* [well-]balanced
ausgezeichnet *a* excellent, *adv* -ly
ausgiebig *a* extensive, *adv* -ly; (*ausgedehnt*) long; **a~ Gebrauch machen von** make full use of; **a~ frühstücken** have a really good breakfast
ausgießen† *vt sep* pour out; (*leeren*) empty
Ausgleich *m* **-[e]s** balance; (*Entschädigung*) compensation. **a~en**† *v sep* □ *vt* balance; even out ⟨*Höhe*⟩; (*wettmachen*) compensate for; **sich a~en** balance out □ *vi* (*haben*) (*Sport*) equalize. **A~sgymnastik** *f* keep-fit exercises *pl*. **A~streffer** *m* equalizer
ausgleiten† *vi sep* (*sein*) slip
ausgrab|en† *vt sep* dig up; (*Archaeol*) excavate. **A~ung** *f* **-,-en** excavation
Ausguck *m* **-[e]s,-e** look-out post; (*Person*) look-out
Ausguss (**Ausguß**) *m* [kitchen] sink
aushaben† *vt sep* have finished ⟨*Buch*⟩; **wann habt ihr Schule aus?** when do you finish school?
aushalten† *v sep* □ *vt* bear, stand; hold ⟨*Note*⟩; (*Unterhalt zahlen für*) keep; **nicht auszuhalten, nicht zum A~** unbearable □ *vi* (*haben*) hold out
aushandeln *vt sep* negotiate

aushändigen *vt sep* hand over
Aushang *m* [public] notice
aushängen[1] *vt sep (reg)* display; take off its hinges ⟨*Tür*⟩
aushäng|en[2]† *vi sep (haben)* be displayed. **A~eschild** *nt* sign
ausharren *vi sep (haben)* hold out
ausheben† *vt sep* excavate; take off its hinges ⟨*Tür*⟩
aushecken *vt sep (fig)* hatch
aushelfen† *vi sep (haben)* help out **(jdm** s.o.)
Aushilf|e *f* [temporary] assistant; **zur A~e** to help out. **A~skraft** *f* temporary worker. **a~sweise** *adv* temporarily
aushöhlen *vt sep* hollow out
ausholen *vi sep (haben)* **[zum Schlag] a~** raise one's arm [ready to strike]
aushorchen *vt sep* sound out
auskennen† **(sich)** *vr sep* know one's way around; **sich mit/in etw** *(dat)* **a~** know all about sth
auskleiden *vt sep* undress; *(Techn)* line; **sich a~** undress
ausknipsen *vi sep* switch off
auskommen† *vi sep (sein)* manage **(mit/ohne** with/without); *(sich vertragen)* get on **(gut** well). **A~** *nt* **-s sein A~/ein gutes A~ haben** get by/be well off
auskosten *vt sep* enjoy [to the full]
auskugeln *vt sep* **sich** *(dat)* **den Arm a~** dislocate one's shoulder
auskühlen *vt/i sep (sein)* cool
auskundschaften *vt sep* spy out; *(erfahren)* find out
Auskunft *f* **-,¨e** information; *(A~sstelle)* information desk/ *(Büro)* bureau; *(Teleph)* enquiries *pl*; **eine A~** a piece of information. **A~sbüro** *nt* information bureau
auslachen *vt sep* laugh at
ausladen† *vt sep* unload; *(fam: absagen)* put off ⟨*Gast*⟩. **a~d** *a* projecting
Auslage *f* [window] display; **A~n** expenses
Ausland *nt* **im/ins A~** abroad
Ausländ|er(in) *m* **-s,-** *(f* **-,-nen)** foreigner. **a~isch** *a* foreign
Auslandsgespräch *nt* international call
auslass|en† *vt sep* let out; let down ⟨*Saum*⟩; *(weglassen)* leave out; *(versäumen)* miss; *(Culin)* melt; *(fig)* vent ⟨*Ärger*⟩ **(an** + *dat* on); **sich a~en über** (+ *acc*) go on about. **A~ungszeichen** *nt* apostrophe
Auslauf *m* run. **a~en**† *vi sep (sein)* run out; ⟨*Farbe:*⟩ run; *(Naut)* put to sea; *(leerlaufen)* run dry; *(enden)* end; ⟨*Modell:*⟩ be discontinued
Ausläufer *m (Geog)* spur; *(Bot)* runner, sucker
ausleeren *vt sep* empty [out]
ausleg|en *vt sep* lay out; display ⟨*Waren*⟩; *(bedecken)* cover/ *(auskleiden)* line **(mit** with); *(bezahlen)* pay; *(deuten)* interpret. **A~ung** *f* **-,-en** interpretation
ausleihen† *vt sep* lend; **sich** *(dat)* **a~** borrow
auslernen *vi sep (haben)* finish one's training
Auslese *f* **-** selection; *(fig)* pick; *(Elite)* elite. **a~n**† *vt sep* finish reading ⟨*Buch*⟩; *(auswählen)* pick out, select
ausliefer|n *vt sep* hand over; *(Jur)* extradite; **ausgeliefert sein** (+ *dat*) be at the mercy of. **A~ung** *f* handing over; *(Jur)* extradition; *(Comm)* distribution
ausliegen† *vi sep (haben)* be on display
auslöschen *vt sep* extinguish; *(abwischen)* wipe off; *(fig)* erase
auslosen *vt sep* draw lots for
auslös|en *vt sep* set off, trigger; *(fig)* cause; arouse ⟨*Begeisterung*⟩; *(einlösen)* redeem; pay a ransom for ⟨*Gefangene*⟩. **A~er** *m* **-s,-** trigger; *(Phot)* shutter release
Auslosung *f* draw
auslüften *vt/i sep (haben)* air

ausmachen *vt sep* put out; (*abschalten*) turn off; (*abmachen*) arrange; (*erkennen*) make out; (*betragen*) amount to; (*darstellen*) represent; (*wichtig sein*) matter; **das macht mir nichts aus** I don't mind

ausmalen *vt sep* paint; (*fig*) describe; **sich** (*dat*) **a∼** imagine

Ausmaß *nt* extent; **A∼e** dimensions

ausmerzen *vt sep* eliminate

ausmessen† *vt sep* measure

Ausnahm|e *f* -,-n exception. **A∼ezustand** *m* state of emergency. **a∼slos** *adv* without exception. **a∼sweise** *adv* as an exception

ausnehmen† *vt sep* take out; gut ⟨*Fisch*⟩; draw ⟨*Huhn*⟩; (*ausschließen*) exclude; (*fam: schröpfen*) fleece; **sich gut a∼** look good. **a∼d** *adv* exceptionally

ausnutz|en, ausnütz|en *vt sep* exploit; make the most of ⟨*Gelegenheit*⟩. **A∼ung** *f* exploitation

auspacken *v sep* □ *vt* unpack; (*auswickeln*) unwrap □ *vi* (*haben*) (*fam*) talk

auspeitschen *vt sep* flog

auspfeifen *vt sep* whistle and boo

ausplaudern *vt sep* let out, blab

ausplündern *vt sep* loot; rob ⟨*Person*⟩

ausprobieren *vt sep* try out

Auspuff *m* -s exhaust [system]. **A∼gase** *ntpl* exhaust fumes. **A∼rohr** *nt* exhaust pipe

auspusten *vt sep* blow out

ausradieren *vt sep* rub out

ausrangieren *vt sep* (*fam*) discard

ausrauben *vt sep* rob

ausräuchern *vt sep* smoke out; fumigate ⟨*Zimmer*⟩

ausräumen *vt sep* clear out

ausrechnen *vt sep* work out, calculate

Ausrede *f* excuse. **a∼n** *v sep* □ *vi* (*haben*) finish speaking; **lass mich a∼n!** let me finish! □ *vt* **jdm etw a∼n** talk s.o. out of sth

ausreichen *vi sep* (*haben*) be enough; **a∼ mit** have enough. **a∼d** a adequate, *adv* -ly; (*Sch*) ≈ pass

Ausreise *f* departure [from a country]. **a∼n** *vi sep* (*sein*) leave the country. **A∼visum** *nt* exit visa

ausreiß|en† *v sep* □ *vt* pull *or* tear out □ *vi* (*sein*) (*fam*) run away. **A∼er** *m* (*fam*) runaway

ausrenken *vt sep* dislocate; **sich** (*dat*) **den Arm a∼** dislocate one's shoulder

ausrichten *vt sep* align; (*bestellen*) deliver; (*erreichen*) achieve; **jdm a∼** tell s.o. (**dass** that); **kann ich etwas a∼?** can I take a message? **ich soll Ihnen Grüße von X a∼** X sends [you] his regards

ausrotten *vt sep* exterminate; (*fig*) eradicate

ausrücken *vi sep* (*sein*) (*Mil*) march off; (*fam*) run away

Ausruf *m* exclamation. **a∼en**† *vt sep* exclaim; call out ⟨*Namen*⟩; (*verkünden*) proclaim; call ⟨*Streik*⟩; **jdn a∼en lassen** have s.o. paged. **A∼ezeichen** *nt* exclamation mark

ausruhen *vt/i sep* (*haben*) rest; **sich a∼** have a rest

ausrüst|en *vt sep* equip. **A∼ung** *f* equipment; (*Mil*) kit

ausrutschen *vi sep* (*sein*) slip

Aussage *f* -,-n statement; (*Jur*) testimony, evidence; (*Gram*) predicate. **a∼n** *vt/i sep* (*haben*) state; (*Jur*) give evidence, testify

Aussatz *m* leprosy

Aussätzige(r) *m/f* leper

ausschachten *vt sep* excavate

ausschalten *vt sep* switch *or* turn off; (*fig*) eliminate

Ausschank *m* sale of alcoholic drinks; (*Bar*) bar

Ausschau *f* - **A∼ halten nach** look out for. **a∼en** *vi sep* (*haben*)

(*SGer*) look; **a~en nach** look out for

ausscheiden† *v sep* □ *vi* (*sein*) leave; (*Sport*) drop out; (*nicht in Frage kommen*) be excluded; **aus dem Dienst a~** retire □ *vt* eliminate; (*Med*) excrete

ausschenken *vt sep* pour out; (*verkaufen*) sell

ausscheren *vi sep* (*sein*) (*Auto*) pull out

ausschildern *vt sep* signpost

ausschimpfen *vt sep* tell off

ausschlachten *vt sep* (*fig*) exploit

ausschlafen† *v sep* □ *vi/r* (*haben*) **[sich] a~** get enough sleep; (*morgens*) sleep late; **nicht ausgeschlafen haben** *od* **sein** be still tired □ *vt* sleep off ⟨*Rausch*⟩

Ausschlag *m* (*Med*) rash; **den A~ geben** (*fig*) tip the balance. **a~en**† *v sep* □ *vi* (*haben*) kick [out]; (*Bot*) sprout; ⟨*Baum:*⟩ come into leaf □ *vt* knock out; (*auskleiden*) line; (*ablehnen*) refuse. **a~gebend** *a* decisive

ausschließ|en† *vt sep* lock out; (*fig*) exclude; (*entfernen*) expel. **a~lich** *a* exclusive, *adv* -ly

ausschlüpfen *vi sep* (*sein*) hatch

Ausschluss (**Ausschluß**) *m* exclusion; expulsion; **unter A~ der Öffentlichkeit** in camera

ausschmücken *vt sep* decorate; (*fig*) embellish

ausschneiden† *vt sep* cut out

Ausschnitt *m* excerpt, extract; (*Zeitungs-*) cutting; (*Hals-*) neckline

ausschöpfen *vt sep* ladle out; (*Naut*) bail out; exhaust ⟨*Möglichkeiten*⟩

ausschreiben† *vt sep* write out; (*ausstellen*) make out; (*bekanntgeben*) announce; put out to tender ⟨*Auftrag*⟩

Ausschreitungen *fpl* riots; (*Exzesse*) excesses

Ausschuss (**Ausschuß**) *m* committee; (*Comm*) rejects *pl*

ausschütten *vt sep* tip out; (*verschütten*) spill; (*leeren*) empty; **sich vor Lachen a~** (*fam*) be in stitches

ausschweif|end *a* dissolute. **A~ung** *f* -,-en debauchery; **A~ungen** excesses

ausschwenken *vt sep* rinse [out]

aussehen† *vi sep* (*haben*) look; **es sieht nach Regen aus** it looks like rain; **wie sieht er/es aus?** what does he/it look like? **ein gut a~der Mann** a good-looking man. **A~** *nt* **-s** appearance

aussein† *vi sep* (*sein*) (NEW) **aus sein**, *s.* **aus**

außen *adv* [on the] outside; **nach a~** outwards. **A~bordmotor** *m* outboard motor. **A~handel** *m* foreign trade. **A~minister** *m* Foreign Minister. **A~politik** *f* foreign policy. **A~seite** *f* outside. **A~seiter** *m* **-s,-** outsider; (*fig*) misfit. **A~stände** *mpl* outstanding debts. **A~stehende(r)** *m/f* outsider

außer *prep* (+ *dat*) except [for], apart from; (*außerhalb*) out of; **a~ Atem/Sicht** out of breath/sight; **a~ sich** (*fig*) beside oneself □ *conj* except; **a~ wenn** unless. **a~dem** *adv* in addition, as well □ *conj* moreover

äußer|e(r,s) *a* external; ⟨*Teil, Schicht*⟩ outer. **Ä~e(s)** *nt* exterior; (*Aussehen*) appearance

außer|ehelich *a* extramarital. **a~gewöhnlich** *a* exceptional, *adv* -ly. **a~halb** *prep* (+ *gen*) outside □ *adv* **a~halb wohnen** live outside town

äußer|lich *a* external, *adv* -ly; (*fig*) outward, *adv* -ly. **ä~n** *vt* express; **sich ä~n** comment; (*sich zeigen*) manifest itself

außerordentlich *a* extraordinary, *adv* -ily; (*außergewöhnlich*) exceptional, *adv* -ly

äußerst *adv* extremely

außerstande *adv* unable (**zu** to)

äußerste|(r,s) *a* outermost; (*weiteste*) furthest; (*höchste*) utmost, extreme; (*letzte*) last; (*schlimmste*) worst; **am ä~n Ende** at the very end; **aufs ä~ = aufs Ä~**, *s.* **Äußerste(s). Ä~(s)** *nt* **das Ä~** the limit; (*Schlimmste*) the worst; **sein Ä~s tun** do one's utmost; **aufs Ä~** extremely

Äußerung *f* **-,-en** comment; (*Bemerkung*) remark

aussetzen *v sep* □ *vt* expose (*dat* to); abandon ⟨*Kind, Hund*⟩; launch ⟨*Boot*⟩; offer ⟨*Belohnung*⟩; **etwas auszusetzen haben an** (+ *dat*) find fault with □ *vi* (*haben*) stop; ⟨*Motor:*⟩ cut out

Aussicht *f* **-,-en** view/(*fig*) prospect (**auf** + *acc* of); **in A~ stellen** promise; **weitere A~en** (*Meteorol*) further outlook *sg.* **a~slos** *a* hopeless, *adv* -ly. **a~sreich** *a* promising

aussöhnen *vt sep* reconcile; **sich a~** become reconciled

aussortieren *vt sep* pick out; (*ausscheiden*) eliminate

ausspann|en *v sep* □ *vt* spread out; unhitch ⟨*Pferd*⟩; (*fam: wegnehmen*) take (*dat* from) □ *vi* (*haben*) rest. **A~ung** *f* rest

aussperr|en *vt sep* lock out. **A~ung** *f* **-,-en** lock-out

ausspielen *v sep* □ *vt* play ⟨*Karte*⟩; (*fig*) play off (**gegen** against) □ *vi* (*haben*) (*Kartenspiel*) lead

Aussprache *f* pronunciation; (*Sprechweise*) diction; (*Gespräch*) talk

aussprechen† *v sep* □ *vt* pronounce; (*äußern*) express; **sich a~** talk; come out (**für/gegen** in favour of/against) □ *vi* (*haben*) finish [speaking]

Ausspruch *m* saying

ausspucken *v sep* □ *vt* spit out □ *vi* (*haben*) spit

ausspülen *vt sep* rinse out

ausstaffieren *vt sep* (*fam*) kit out

Ausstand *m* strike; **in den A~ treten** go on strike

ausstatt|en *vt sep* equip; **mit Möbeln a~en** furnish. **A~ung** *f* **-,-en** equipment; (*Innen-*) furnishings *pl*; (*Theat*) scenery and costumes *pl*; (*Aufmachung*) get-up

ausstehen† *v sep* □ *vt* suffer; **Angst a~** be frightened; **ich kann sie nicht a~** I can't stand her □ *vi* (*haben*) be outstanding

aussteig|en† *vi sep* (*sein*) get out; (*aus Bus, Zug*) get off; (*fam: ausscheiden*) opt out; (*aus einem Geschäft*) back out; **alles a~en!** all change! **A~er(in)** *m* **-s,-** (*f* **-,-nen**) (*fam*) drop-out

ausstell|en *vt sep* exhibit; (*Comm*) display; (*ausfertigen*) make out; issue ⟨*Pass*⟩. **A~er** *m* **-s,-** exhibitor. **A~ung** *f* exhibition; (*Comm*) display. **A~ungsstück** *nt* exhibit

aussterben† *vi sep* (*sein*) die out; (*Biol*) become extinct. **A~** *nt* **-s** extinction

Aussteuer *f* trousseau

Ausstieg *m* **-[e]s,-e** exit

ausstopfen *vt sep* stuff

ausstoßen† *vt sep* emit; utter ⟨*Fluch*⟩; heave ⟨*Seufzer*⟩; (*ausschließen*) expel

ausstrahl|en *vt/i sep* (*sein*) radiate, emit; (*Radio, TV*) broadcast. **A~ung** *f* radiation; (*fig*) charisma

ausstrecken *vt sep* stretch out; put out ⟨*Hand*⟩; **sich a~** stretch out

ausstreichen† *vt sep* cross out

ausstreuen *vt sep* scatter; spread ⟨*Gerüchte*⟩

ausströmen *v sep* □ *vi* (*sein*) pour out; (*entweichen*) escape □ *vt* emit; (*ausstrahlen*) radiate

aussuchen *vt sep* pick, choose

Austausch *m* exchange. **a~bar** *a* interchangeable. **a~en** *vt sep* exchange; (*auswechseln*) replace

austeilen *vt sep* distribute; (*ausgeben*) hand out

Auster *f* **-,-n** oyster

austoben (sich) *vr sep* ⟨*Sturm:*⟩ rage; ⟨*Person:*⟩ let off steam; ⟨*Kinder:*⟩ romp about
austragen† *vt sep* deliver; hold ⟨*Wettkampf*⟩; play ⟨*Spiel*⟩
Australlien /-iən/ *nt* **-s** Australia. **A~ier(in)** *m* **-s,-** (*f* **-,-nen**) Australian. **a~isch** *a* Australian
austreiben† *v sep* □ *vt* drive out; (*Relig*) exorcize □ *vi* (*haben*) (*Bot*) sprout
austreten† *v sep* □ *vt* stamp out; (*abnutzen*) wear down □ *vi* (*sein*) come out; (*ausscheiden*) leave **(aus etw** sth); **[mal] a~** (*fam*) go to the loo; (*Sch*) be excused
austrinken† *vt/i sep* (*haben*) drink up; (*leeren*) drain
Austritt *m* resignation
austrocknen *vt/i sep* (*sein*) dry out
ausüben *vt sep* practise; carry on ⟨*Handwerk*⟩; exercise ⟨*Recht*⟩; exert ⟨*Druck, Einfluss*⟩; have ⟨*Wirkung*⟩
Ausverkauf *m* [clearance] sale. **a~t** *a* sold out; **a~tes Haus** full house
auswachsen† *vt sep* outgrow
Auswahl *f* choice, selection; (*Comm*) range; (*Sport*) team
auswählen *vt sep* choose, select
Auswanderler *m* emigrant. **a~n** *vi sep* (*sein*) emigrate. **A~ung** *f* emigration
auswärtlig *a* non-local; (*ausländisch*) foreign. **a~s** *adv* outwards; (*Sport*) away; **a~s essen** eat out; **a~s arbeiten** not work locally. **A~ spiel** *nt* away game
auswaschen† *vt sep* wash out
auswechseln *vt sep* change; (*ersetzen*) replace; (*Sport*) substitute
Ausweg *m* (*fig*) way out. **a~los** *a* (*fig*) hopeless
ausweichlen† *vi sep* (*sein*) get out of the way; **jdm/etw a~en** avoid/ (*sich entziehen*) evade s.o./sth. **a~end** *a* evasive, *adv* -ly
ausweinen *vt sep* **sich** (*dat*) **die Augen a~** cry one's eyes out; **sich a~** have a good cry
Ausweis *m* **-es,-e** pass; (*Mitglieds-, Studenten-*) card. **a~en**† *vt sep* deport; **sich a~en** prove one's identity. **A~papiere** *ntpl* identification papers. **A~ung** *f* deportation
ausweiten *vt sep* stretch; (*fig*) expand
auswendig *adv* by heart
auswerten *vt sep* evaluate; (*nutzen*) utilize
auswickeln *vt sep* unwrap
auswirklen (sich) *vr sep* have an effect **(auf** + *acc* on). **A~ung** *f* effect; (*Folge*) consequence
auswischen *vt sep* wipe out; **jdm eins a~** (*fam*) play a nasty trick on s.o.
auswringen *vt sep* wring out
Auswuchs *m* excrescence; **Auswüchse** (*fig*) excesses
auszahlen *vt sep* pay out; (*entlohnen*) pay off; (*abfinden*) buy out; **sich a~** (*fig*) pay off
auszählen *vt sep* count; (*Boxen*) count out
Auszahlung *f* payment
auszeichnlen *vt sep* (*Comm*) price; (*ehren*) honour; (*mit einem Preis*) award a prize to; (*Mil*) decorate; **sich a~en** distinguish oneself. **A~ung** *f* honour; (*Preis*) award; (*Mil*) decoration; (*Sch*) distinction
ausziehen† *v sep* □ *vt* pull out; (*auskleiden*) undress; take off ⟨*Mantel, Schuhe*⟩; **sich a~** take off one's coat; (*sich entkleiden*) undress □ *vi* (*sein*) move out; (*sich aufmachen*) set out
Auszubildende(r) *m/f* trainee
Auszug *m* departure; (*Umzug*) move; (*Ausschnitt*) extract, excerpt; (*Bank-*) statement
authentisch *a* authentic
Auto *nt* **-s,-s** car; **A~ fahren** drive; (*mitfahren*) go in the car.

A~bahn *f* motorway, (*Amer*) freeway
Autobiographie *f* autobiography
Auto|bus *m* bus. **A~fähre** *f* car ferry. **A~fahrer(in)** *m(f)* driver, motorist. **A~fahrt** *f* drive
Autogramm *nt* **-s,-e** autograph
autokratisch *a* autocratic
Automat *m* **-en,-en** automatic device; (*Münz-*) slot-machine; (*Verkaufs-*) vending-machine; (*Fahrkarten-*) machine; (*Techn*) robot. **A~ik** *f* **-** automatic mechanism; (*Auto*) automatic transmission
Auto|mation /-'tsio:n/ *f* **-** automation. **a~matisch** *a* automatic, *adv* -ally
autonom *a* autonomous. **A~ie** *f* **-** autonomy
Autonummer *f* registration number
Autopsie *f* **-,-n** autopsy
Autor *m* **-s,-en** /-'to:rən/ author
Auto|reisezug *m* Motorail. **A~rennen** *nt* motor race
Autorin *f* **-,-nen** author[ess]
Autori|sation /-'tsio:n/ *f* **-** authorization. **a~sieren** *vt* authorize. **a~tär** *a* authoritarian. **A~tät** *f* **-,-en** authority
Auto|schlosser *m* motor mechanic. **A~skooter** /-sku:tɐ/ *m* **-s,-** dodgem. **A~stopp** *m* **-s per A~stopp fahren** hitch-hike. **A~verleih** *m* car hire [firm]. **A~waschanlage** *f* car wash
autsch *int* ouch
Aversion *f* **-,-en** aversion (**gegen** to)
Axt *f* **-,¨e** axe

B

B, b /be:/ *nt* **-** (*Mus*) B flat
Baby /'be:bi/ *nt* **-s,-s** baby. **B~ausstattung** *f* layette. **B~sitter** /-sɪtɐ/ *m* **-s,-** babysitter
Bach *m* **-[e]s,¨e** stream
Backbord *nt* **-[e]s** port [side]
Backe *f* **-,-n** cheek
backen *v* □ *vt/i*† (*haben*) bake; (*braten*) fry □ *vi* (*reg*) (*haben*) (*kleben*) stick (**an** + *dat* to)
Backenzahn *m* molar
Bäcker *m* **-s,-** baker. **B~ei** *f* **-,-en, B~laden** *m* baker's shop
Back|form *f* baking tin. **B~obst** *nt* dried fruit. **B~ofen** *m* oven. **B~pfeife** *f* (*fam*) slap in the face. **B~pflaume** *f* prune. **B~pulver** *nt* baking-powder. **B~rohr** *nt* oven. **B~stein** *m* brick. **B~werk** *nt* cakes and pastries *pl*
Bad *nt* **-[e]s,¨er** bath; (*im Meer*) bathe; (*Zimmer*) bathroom; (*Schwimm-*) pool; (*Ort*) spa
Bade|anstalt *f* swimming baths *pl*. **B~anzug** *m* swim-suit. **B~hose** *f* swimming trunks *pl*. **B~kappe** *f* bathing-cap. **B~mantel** *m* bathrobe. **B~matte** *f* bath-mat. **B~mütze** *f* bathing-cap. **b~n** *vi* (*haben*) have a bath; (*im Meer*) bathe □ *vt* bath; (*waschen*) bathe. **B~ort** *m* seaside resort; (*Kurort*) spa. **B~tuch** *nt* bath-towel. **B~wanne** *f* bath. **B~zimmer** *nt* bathroom
Bagatelle *f* **-,-n** trifle; (*Mus*) bagatelle
Bagger *m* **-s,-** excavator; (*Nass-*) dredger. **b~n** *vt/i* (*haben*) excavate; dredge. **B~see** *m* flooded gravel-pit
Bahn *f* **-,-en** path; (*Astr*) orbit; (*Sport*) track; (*einzelne*) lane; (*Rodel-*) run; (*Stoff-, Papier-*) width; (*Rock-*) panel; (*Eisen-*) railway; (*Zug*) train; (*Straßen-*) tram; **auf die schiefe B~ kommen** (*fig*) get into bad ways. **b~brechend** *a* (*fig*) pioneering. **b~en** *vt* **sich** (*dat*) **einen Weg b~en** clear a way (**durch** through). **B~hof** *m* [railway] station. **B~steig** *m* **-[e]s,-e** platform. **B~übergang** *m* level crossing, (*Amer*) grade crossing

permission. **B~gerüst** *nt* scaffolding. **B~jahr** *nt* year of construction; **B~jahr 1985** (*Auto*) 1985 model. **B~kasten** *m* box of building bricks; (*Modell-*) model kit. **B~klotz** *m* building brick. **B~kunst** *f* architecture. **b~lich** *a* structural, *adv* -ly. **B~lichkeiten** *fpl* buildings

Baum *m* **-[e]s, Bäume** tree

baumeln *vi* (*haben*) dangle; **die Beine b~ lassen** dangle one's legs

bäumen (sich) *vr* rear [up]

Baum|schule *f* [tree] nursery. **B~stamm** *m* tree-trunk. **B~wolle** *f* cotton. **b~wollen** *a* cotton

Bauplatz *m* building plot

bäurisch *a* rustic; (*plump*) uncouth

Bausch *m* **-[e]s, Bäusche** wad; **in B~ und Bogen** (*fig*) wholesale. **b~en** *vt* puff out; **sich b~en** billow [out]. **b~ig** *a* puffed [out]; 〈*Ärmel*〉 full

Bau|sparkasse *f* building society. **B~stein** *m* building brick; (*fig*) element. **B~stelle** *f* building site; (*Straßen-*) roadworks *pl*. **B~unternehmer** *m* building contractor. **B~werk** *nt* building. **B~zaun** *m* hoarding

Bayer|(in) *m* **-s,-n** (*f* **-,-nen**) Bavarian. **B~n** *nt* **-s** Bavaria

bay[e]risch *a* Bavarian

Bazillus *m* **-,-len** bacillus; (*fam: Keim*) germ

beabsichtig|en *vt* intend. **b~t** *a* intended; (*absichtlich*) intentional

beacht|en *vt* take notice of; (*einhalten*) observe; (*folgen*) follow; **nicht b~en** ignore. **b~lich** *a* considerable. **B~ung** *f* - observance; **etw** (*dat*) **keine B~ung schenken** take no notice of sth

Beamte(r) *m*, **Beamtin** *f* **-,-nen** official; (*Staats-*) civil servant; (*Schalter-*) clerk

beängstigend *a* alarming

beanspruchen *vt* claim; (*erfordern*) demand; (*brauchen*) take up; (*Techn*) stress; **die Arbeit beansprucht ihn sehr** his work is very demanding

beanstand|en *vt* find fault with; (*Comm*) make a complaint about. **B~ung** *f* **-,-en** complaint

beantragen *vt* apply for

beantworten *vt* answer

bearbeiten *vt* work; (*weiter-*) process; (*behandeln*) treat (**mit** with); (*Admin*) deal with; (*redigieren*) edit; (*Theat*) adapt; (*Mus*) arrange; (*fam: bedrängen*) pester; (*fam: schlagen*) pummel

Beatmung *f* **künstliche B~** artificial respiration. **B~sgerät** *nt* ventilator

beaufsichtig|en *vt* supervise. **B~ung** *f* - supervision

beauftrag|en *vt* instruct; commission 〈*Künstler*〉; **jdn mit einer Arbeit b~en** assign a task to s.o. **B~te(r)** *m/f* representative

bebauen *vt* build on; (*bestellen*) cultivate

beben *vi* (*haben*) tremble

bebildert *a* illustrated

Becher *m* **-s,-** beaker; (*Henkel-*) mug; (*Joghurt-, Sahne-*) carton

Becken *nt* **-s,-** basin; (*Schwimm-*) pool; (*Mus*) cymbals *pl*; (*Anat*) pelvis

bedacht *a* careful; **b~ auf** (+ *acc*) concerned about; **darauf b~** anxious (**zu** to)

bedächtig *a* careful, *adv* -ly; (*langsam*) slow, *adv* -ly

bedanken (sich) *vr* thank (**bei jdm** s.o.)

Bedarf *m* **-s** need/(*Comm*) demand (**an** + *dat* for); **bei B~** if required. **B~sartikel** *mpl* requisites. **B~shaltestelle** *f* request stop

bedauer|lich *a* regrettable. **b~licherweise** *adv* unfortunately. **b~n** *vt* regret; (*bemitleiden*) feel sorry for; **bedaure!**

sorry! **B~n** *nt* **-s** regret; (*Mitgefühl*) sympathy. **b~nswert** *a* pitiful; (*bedauerlich*) regrettable

bedeck|en *vt* cover; **sich b~en** (*Himmel:*) cloud over. **b~t** *a* covered; (*Himmel*) overcast

bedenken† *vt* consider; (*überlegen*) think over; **jdn b~** give s.o. a present; **sich b~** consider. **B~** *pl* misgivings; **ohne B~** without hesitation. **b~los** *a* unhesitating, *adv* -ly

bedenklich *a* doubtful; (*verdächtig*) dubious; (*bedrohlich*) worrying; (*ernst*) serious

bedeut|en *vi* (*haben*) mean; **jdm viel/nichts b~en** mean a lot/nothing to s.o.; **es hat nichts zu b~en** it is of no significance. **b~end** *a* important; (*beträchtlich*) considerable. **b~sam** *a* = **b~ungsvoll. B~ung** *f* -,-en meaning; (*Wichtigkeit*) importance. **b~ungslos** *a* meaningless; (*unwichtig*) unimportant. **b~ungsvoll** *a* significant; (*vielsagend*) meaningful, *adv* -ly

bedien|en *vt* serve; (*betätigen*) operate; **sich [selbst] b~en** help oneself. **B~ung** *f* -,-en service; (*Betätigung*) operation; (*Kellner*) waiter; (*Kellnerin*) waitress. **B~ungsgeld** *nt*, **B~ungszuschlag** *m* service charge

bedingt *a* conditional; (*eingeschränkt*) qualified

Bedingung *f* -,-en condition; **B~en** conditions; (*Comm*) terms. **b~slos** *a* unconditional, *adv* -ly; (*unbedingt*) unquestioning, *adv* -ly

bedrängen *vt* press; (*belästigen*) pester

bedroh|en *vt* threaten. **b~lich** *a* threatening. **B~ung** *f* threat

bedrück|en *vt* depress. **b~end** *a* depressing. **b~t** *a* depressed

bedruckt *a* printed

bedürf|en† *vi* (*haben*) (+ *gen*) need. **B~nis** *nt* **-ses,-se** need. **B~nisanstalt** *f* public convenience. **b~tig** *a* needy

Beefsteak /ˈbi:fste:k/ *nt* **-s,-s** steak; **deutsches B~** hamburger

beeilen (sich) *vr* hurry; hasten (**zu** to); **beeilt euch!** hurry up!

beeindrucken *vt* impress

beeinflussen *vt* influence

beeinträchtigen *vt* mar; (*schädigen*) impair

beend[ig]en *vt* end

beengen *vt* restrict; **beengt wohnen** live in cramped conditions

beerben *vt* **jdn b~** inherit s.o.'s property

beerdig|en *vt* bury. **B~ung** *f* -,-en funeral

Beere *f* -,-n berry

Beet *nt* **-[e]s,-e** (*Hort*) bed

Beete *f* -,-n **rote B~** beetroot

befähig|en *vt* enable; (*qualifizieren*) qualify. **B~ung** *f* - qualification; (*Fähigkeit*) ability

befahr|bar *a* passable. **b~en†** *vt* drive along; **stark b~ene Straße** busy road

befallen† *vt* attack; (*Angst:*) seize

befangen *a* shy; (*gehemmt*) self-conscious; (*Jur*) biased. **B~heit** *f* - shyness; self-consciousness; bias

befassen (sich) *vr* concern oneself/(*behandeln*) deal (**mit** with)

Befehl *m* **-[e]s,-e** order; (*Leitung*) command (**über** + *acc* of). **b~en†** *vt* **jdm etw b~en** order s.o. to do sth □ *vi* (*haben*) give the orders. **b~igen** *vt* (*Mil*) command. **B~sform** *f* (*Gram*) imperative. **B~shaber** *m* **-s,-** commander

befestig|en *vt* fasten (**an** + *dat* to); (*stärken*) strengthen; (*Mil*) fortify. **B~ung** *f* -,-en fastening; (*Mil*) fortification

befeuchten *vt* moisten

befinden† (sich) *vr* be. **B~** *nt* **-s** [state of] health

beflecken *vt* stain

beflissen *a* assiduous, *adv* -ly

befolgen *vt* follow

beförder|n *vt* transport; (*im Rang*) promote. **B~ung** *f* -,-en transport; promotion

befragen *vt* question

befrei|en *vt* free; (*räumen*) clear (**von** of); (*freistellen*) exempt (**von** from); **sich b~en** free oneself. **B~er** *m* -s,- liberator. **b~t** *a* (*erleichtert*) relieved. **B~ung** *f* - liberation; exemption

befremd|en *vt* disconcert. **B~en** *nt* -s surprise. **b~lich** *a* strange

befreunden (sich) *vr* make friends; **befreundet sein** be friends

befriedig|en *vt* satisfy. **b~end** *a* satisfying; (*zufrieden stellend*) satisfactory. **B~ung** *f* - satisfaction

befrucht|en *vt* fertilize. **B~ung** *f* - fertilization; **künstliche B~ung** artificial insemination

Befug|nis *f* -,-se authority. **b~t** *a* authorized

Befund *m* result

befürcht|en *vt* fear. **B~ung** *f* -,-en fear

befürworten *vt* support

begab|t *a* gifted. **B~ung** *f* -,-en gift, talent

begatten (sich) *vr* mate

begeben† (sich) *vr* go; (*liter: geschehen*) happen; **sich in Gefahr b~** expose oneself to danger. **B~heit** *f* -,-en incident

begegn|en *vi* (*sein*) **jdm/etw b~en** meet s.o./sth; **sich b~en** meet. **B~ung** *f* -,-en meeting; (*Sport*) encounter

begehen† *vt* walk along; (*verüben*) commit; (*feiern*) celebrate

begehr|en *vt* desire. **b~enswert** *a* desirable. **b~t** *a* sought-after

begeister|n *vt* **jdn b~n** arouse s.o.'s enthusiasm; **sich b~n** be enthusiastic (**für** about). **b~t** *a* enthusiastic, *adv* -ally; (*eifrig*) keen. **B~ung** *f* - enthusiasm

Begier|de *f* -,-n desire. **b~ig** *a* eager (**auf** + *acc* for)

begießen† *vt* water; (*Culin*) baste; (*fam: feiern*) celebrate

Beginn *m* -s beginning; **zu B~** at the beginning. **b~en†** *vt/i* (*haben*) start, begin; (*anstellen*) do

beglaubigen *vt* authenticate

begleichen† *vt* settle

begleit|en *vt* accompany. **B~er** *m* -s,-, **B~erin** *f* -,-nen companion; (*Mus*) accompanist. **B~ung** *f* -,-en company; (*Gefolge*) entourage; (*Mus*) accompaniment

beglück|en *vt* make happy. **b~t** *a* happy. **b~wünschen** *vt* congratulate (**zu** on)

begnadig|en *vt* (*Jur*) pardon. **B~ung** *f* -,-en (*Jur*) pardon

begnügen (sich) *vr* content oneself (**mit** with)

Begonie /-jə/ *f* -,-n begonia

begraben† *vt* bury

Begräbnis *n* -ses,-se burial; (*Feier*) funeral

begreif|en† *vt* understand; **nicht zu b~en** incomprehensible. **b~lich** *a* understandable; **jdm etw b~lich machen** make s.o. understand sth. **b~licherweise** *adv* understandably

begrenz|en *vt* form the boundary of; (*beschränken*) restrict. **b~t** *a* limited. **B~ung** *f* -,-en restriction; (*Grenze*) boundary

Begriff *m* -[e]s,-e concept; (*Ausdruck*) term; (*Vorstellung*) idea; **für meine B~e** to my mind; **im B~sein** *od* **stehen** be about (**zu** to); **schwer von B~** (*fam*) slow on the uptake. **b~sstutzig** *a* obtuse

begründ|en *vt* give one's reason for; (*gründen*) establish. **b~et** *a* justified. **B~ung** *f* -,-en reason

begrüß|en *vt* greet; (*billigen*) welcome. **b~enswert** *a* welcome. **B~ung** *f* - greeting; welcome

begünstigen *vt* favour; (*fördern*) encourage

begutachten *vt* give an opinion on; (*fam: ansehen*) look at
begütert *a* wealthy
begütigen *vt* placate
behaart *a* hairy
behäbig *a* portly; (*gemütlich*) comfortable, *adv* -bly
behag|en *vi* (*haben*) please (**jdm** s.o.). **B~en** *nt* **-s** contentment; (*Genuss*) enjoyment. **b~lich** *a* comfortable, *adv* -bly. **B~lichkeit** *f* - comfort
behalten† *vt* keep; (*sich merken*) remember; **etw für sich b~** (*verschweigen*) keep sth to oneself
Behälter *m* **-s,-** container
behände *a* nimble, *adv* -bly
behand|eln *vt* treat; (*sich befassen*) deal with. **B~lung** *f* treatment
beharr|en *vi* (*haben*) persist (**auf** + *dat* in). **b~lich** *a* persistent, *adv* -ly; (*hartnäckig*) dogged, *adv* -ly. **B~lichkeit** *f* - persistence
behaupt|en *vt* maintain; (*vorgeben*) claim; (*sagen*) say; (*bewahren*) retain; **sich b~en** hold one's own. **B~ung** *f* -,-**en** assertion; claim; (*Äußerung*) statement
beheben† *vt* remedy; (*beseitigen*) remove
behelf|en† **(sich)** *vr* make do (**mit** with). **b~smäßig** *a* make-shift □ *adv* provisionally
behelligen *vt* bother
behende *a* (NEW) **behände**
beherbergen *vt* put up
beherrsch|en *vt* rule over; (*dominieren*) dominate; (*meistern, zügeln*) control; (*können*) know; **sich b~en** control oneself. **b~t** *a* self-controlled. **B~ung** *f* - control; (*Selbst-*) self-control; (*Können*) mastery
beherz|igen *vt* heed. **b~t** *a* courageous, *adv* -ly
behilflich *a* **jdm b~ sein** help s.o.
behinder|n *vt* hinder; (*blockieren*) obstruct. **b~t** *a* handicapped; (*schwer*) disabled. **B~te(r)** *m/f* handicapped/disabled person. **B~ung** *f* -,-**en** obstruction; (*Med*) handicap; disability
Behörde *f* -,-**n** [public] authority
behüte|n *vt* protect; **Gott behüte!** heaven forbid! **b~t** *a* sheltered
behutsam *a* careful, *adv* -ly; (*zart*) gentle, *adv* -ly
bei *prep* (+ *dat*) near; (*dicht*) by; at ⟨*Firma, Veranstaltung*⟩; **bei der Hand nehmen** take by the hand; **bei sich haben** have with one; **bei mir** at my place; (*in meinem Fall*) in my case; **Herr X bei Meyer** Mr X c/o Meyer; **bei Regen** when/(*falls*) if it rains; **bei Feuer** in case of fire; **bei Tag/Nacht** by day/night; **bei der Ankunft** on arrival; **bei Tisch/der Arbeit** at table/work; **bei guter Gesundheit** in good health; **bei der hohen Miete** [what] with the high rent; **bei all seiner Klugheit** for all his cleverness
beibehalten† *vt sep* keep
beibringen† *vt sep* **jdm etw b~** teach s.o. sth; (*mitteilen*) break sth to s.o.; (*zufügen*) inflict sth on s.o.
Beicht|e *f* -,-**n** confession. **b~en** *vt/i* (*haben*) confess. **B~stuhl** *m* confessional
beide *a & pron* both; **die b~n Brüder** the two brothers; **b~s** both; **dreißig b~** (*Tennis*) thirty all. **b~rseitig** *a* mutual. **b~rseits** *adv & prep* (+ *gen*) on both sides (of)
beidrehen *vi sep* (*haben*) heave to
beieinander *adv* together
Beifahrer|(in) *m(f)* [front-seat] passenger; (*Lkw*) driver's mate; (*Motorrad*) pillion passenger. **B~sitz** *m* passenger seat
Beifall *m* -**[e]s** applause; (*Billigung*) approval; **B~ klatschen** applaud
beifällig *a* approving, *adv* -ly
beifügen *vt sep* add; (*beilegen*) enclose

beige /bɛːʒ/ *inv a* beige
beigeben† *v sep* □ *vt* add □ *vi* (*haben*) **klein b~** give in
Beigeschmack *m* [slight] taste
Beihilfe *f* financial aid; (*Studien-*) grant; (*Jur*) aiding and abetting
beikommen† *vi sep* (*sein*) **jdm b~** get the better of s.o.
Beil *nt* **-[e]s,-e** hatchet, axe
Beilage *f* supplement; (*Gemüse*) vegetable; **als B~ Reis** (*Culin*) served with rice
beiläufig *a* casual, *adv* -ly
beilegen *vt sep* enclose; (*schlichten*) settle
beileibe *adv* **b~ nicht** by no means
Beileid *nt* condolences *pl*. **B~sbrief** *m* letter of condolence
beiliegend *a* enclosed
beim *prep* = **bei dem; b~ Militär** in the army; **b~ Frühstück** at breakfast; **b~ Lesen** when reading; **b~ Lesen sein** be reading
beimessen† *vt sep* (*fig*) attach (*dat* to)
Bein *nt* **-[e]s,-e** leg; **jdm ein B~ stellen** trip s.o. up
beinah[e] *adv* nearly, almost
Beiname *m* epithet
beipflichten *vi sep* (*haben*) agree (*dat* with)
Beirat *m* advisory committee
beirren *vt* **sich nicht b~ lassen** not let oneself be put off
beisammen *adv* together; **b~ sein** be together. **b~sein**† *vi sep* (*sein*) (NEW) **b~ sein**, *s*. **beisammen**. **B~sein** *nt* **-s** get-together
Beisein *nt* presence
beiseite *adv* aside; (*abseits*) apart; **b~ legen** put aside; (*sparen*) put by; **Spaß** *od* **Scherz b~** joking apart
beisetz|en *vt sep* bury. **B~ung** *f* **-,-en** funeral
Beispiel *nt* example; **zum B~** for example. **b~haft** *a* exemplary. **b~los** *a* unprecedented. **b~sweise** *adv* for example
beispringen† *vi sep* (*sein*) **jdm b~** come to s.o.'s aid
beiß|en† *vt/i* (*haben*) bite; (*brennen*) sting; **sich b~en** ⟨*Farben:*⟩ clash. **b~end** *a* (*fig*) biting; ⟨*Bemerkung*⟩ caustic. **B~zange** *f* pliers *pl*
Bei|stand *m* **-[e]s** help; **jdm B~stand leisten** help s.o. **b~stehen**† *vi sep* (*haben*) **jdm b~stehen** help s.o.
beisteuern *vt sep* contribute
beistimmen *vi sep* (*haben*) agree
Beistrich *m* comma
Beitrag *m* **-[e]s,¨-e** contribution; (*Mitglieds-*) subscription; (*Versicherungs-*) premium; (*Zeitungs-*) article. **b~en**† *vt/i sep* (*haben*) contribute
bei|treten† *vi sep* (*sein*) (+ *dat*) join. **B~tritt** *m* joining
beiwohnen *vi sep* (*haben*) (+ *dat*) be present at
Beize *f* **-,-n** (*Holz-*) stain; (*Culin*) marinade
beizeiten *adv* in good time
beizen *vt* stain ⟨*Holz*⟩
bejahen *vt* answer in the affirmative; (*billigen*) approve of
bejahrt *a* aged, old
bejubeln *vt* cheer
bekämpf|en *vt* fight. **B~ung** *f* - fight (*gen* against)
bekannt *a* well-known; (*vertraut*) familiar; **jdm b~ sein** be known to s.o.; **jdn b~ machen** introduce s.o.; **etw b~ machen** *od* **geben** announce sth; **b~ werden** become known. **B~e(r)** *m/f* acquaintance; (*Freund*) friend. **B~gabe** *f* announcement. **b~geben**† *vt sep* (NEW) **b~ geben**, *s*. **bekannt**. **b~lich** *adv* as is well known. **b~machen** *vt sep* (NEW) **b~ machen**, *s*. **bekannt**. **B~machung** *f* **-,-en** announcement; (*Anschlag*) notice. **B~schaft** *f* - acquaintance; (*Leute*) acquaintances *pl*; (*Freunde*) friends *pl*. **b~werden**†

vi sep (sein) (NEW) **b~ werden**, *s.* **bekannt**

bekehr|en *vt* convert; **sich b~en** become converted. **B~ung** *f* **-,-en** conversion

bekenn|en† *vt* confess, profess ⟨*Glauben*⟩; **sich [für] schuldig b~en** admit one's guilt; **sich b~en zu** confess to ⟨*Tat*⟩; profess ⟨*Glauben*⟩; *(stehen zu)* stand by. **B~tnis** *nt* **-ses,-se** confession; *(Konfession)* denomination

beklag|en *vt* lament; *(bedauern)* deplore; **sich b~en** complain. **b~enswert** *a* unfortunate. **B~te(r)** *m/f (Jur)* defendant

beklatschen *vt* applaud

bekleid|en *vt* hold ⟨*Amt*⟩. **b~et** *a* dressed (**mit** in). **B~ung** *f* clothing

Beklemmung *f* **-,-en** feeling of oppression

beklommen *a* uneasy; *(ängstlich)* anxious, *adv* -ly

bekommen† *vt* get; have ⟨*Baby*⟩; catch ⟨*Erkältung*⟩; **Angst/Hunger b~** get frightened/hungry; **etw geliehen b~** be lent sth □ *vi (sein)* **jdm gut b~** do s.o. good; ⟨*Essen:*⟩ agree with s.o.

bekömmlich *a* digestible

beköstig|en *vt* feed; **sich selbst b~en** cater for oneself. **B~ung** *f* - board; *(Essen)* food

bekräftigen *vt* reaffirm; *(bestätigen)* confirm

bekreuzigen (sich) *vr* cross oneself

bekümmert *a* troubled; *(besorgt)* worried

bekunden *vt* show; *(bezeugen)* testify

belächeln *vt* laugh at

beladen† *vt* load □ *a* laden

Belag *m* **-[e]s,¨e** coating; *(Fußboden-)* covering; *(Brot-)* topping; *(Zahn-)* tartar; *(Brems-)* lining

belager|n *vt* besiege. **B~ung** *f* **-,-en** siege

Belang *m* **von/ohne B~** of/of no importance; **B~e** *pl* interests. **b~en** *vt (Jur)* sue. **b~los** *a* irrelevant; *(unwichtig)* trivial. **B~losigkeit** *f* **-,-en** triviality

belassen† *vt* leave; **es dabei b~** leave it at that

belasten *vt* load; *(fig)* burden; *(beanspruchen)* put a strain on; *(Comm)* debit; *(Jur)* incriminate

belästigen *vt* bother; *(bedrängen)* pester; *(unsittlich)* molest

Belastung *f* **-,-en** load; *(fig)* strain; *(Last)* burden; *(Comm)* debit. **B~smaterial** *nt* incriminating evidence. **B~szeuge** *m* prosecution witness

belaufen† (sich) *vr* amount **(auf** + *acc* to)

belauschen *vt* eavesdrop on

beleb|en *vt (fig)* revive; *(lebhaft machen)* enliven; **wieder b~en** *(Med)* revive, resuscitate; *(fig)* revive ⟨*Handel*⟩; **sich b~en** revive; ⟨*Stadt:*⟩ come to life. **b~t** *a* lively; ⟨*Straße*⟩ busy

Beleg *m* **-[e]s,-e** evidence; *(Beispiel)* instance (**für** of); *(Quittung)* receipt. **b~en** *vt* cover/ *(garnieren)* garnish (**mit** with); *(besetzen)* reserve; *(Univ)* enrol for; *(nachweisen)* provide evidence for; **den ersten Platz b~en** *(Sport)* take first place. **B~schaft** *f* **-,-en** work-force. **b~t** *a* occupied; ⟨*Zunge*⟩ coated; ⟨*Stimme*⟩ husky; **b~te Brote** open sandwiches; **der Platz ist b~t** this seat is taken

belehren *vt* instruct; *(aufklären)* inform

beleibt *a* corpulent

beleidig|en *vt* offend; *(absichtlich)* insult. **B~ung** *f* **-,-en** insult

belesen *a* well-read

beleucht|en *vt* light; *(anleuchten)* illuminate. **B~ung** *f* **-,-en** illumination; *(elektrisch)* lighting; *(Licht)* light

Belg|ien /-i̯ən/ *nt* **-s** Belgium. **B~ier(in)** *m* **-s,-** (*f* **-,-nen**) Belgian. **b~isch** *a* Belgian
belicht|en *vt* (*Phot*) expose. **B~ung** *f* - exposure
Belieb|en *nt* **-s nach B~en** [just] as one likes; (*Culin*) if liked. **b~ig** *a* **eine b~ige Zahl/Farbe** any number/colour you like □ *adv* **b~ig lange/oft** as long/often as one likes. **b~t** *a* popular. **B~theit** *f* - popularity
beliefern *vt* supply (**mit** with)
bellen *vi* (*haben*) bark
belohn|en *vt* reward. **B~ung** *f* **-,-en** reward
belüften *vt* ventilate
belügen† *vt* lie to; **sich [selbst] b~** deceive oneself
belustig|en *vt* amuse. **B~ung** *f* **-,-en** amusement
bemächtigen (sich) *vr* (+ *gen*) seize
bemalen *vt* paint
bemängeln *vt* criticize
bemannt *a* manned
bemerk|bar *a* **sich b~bar machen** attract attention; (*Ding:*) become noticeable. **b~en** *vt* notice; (*äußern*) remark. **b~enswert** *a* remarkable, *adv* -bly. **B~ung** *f* **-,-en** remark
bemitleiden *vt* pity
bemittelt *a* well-to-do
bemüh|en *vt* trouble; **sich b~en** try (**zu** to; **um etw** to get sth); (*sich kümmern*) attend (**um** to); **b~t sein** endeavour (**zu** to). **B~ung** *f* **-,-en** effort; (*Mühe*) trouble
bemuttern *vt* mother
benachbart *a* neighbouring
benachrichtig|en *vt* inform; (*amtlich*) notify. **B~ung** *f* **-,-en** notification
benachteilig|en *vt* discriminate against; (*ungerecht sein*) treat unfairly. **B~ung** *f* **-,-en** discrimination (*gen* against)
benehmen† **(sich)** *vr* behave. **B~** *nt* **-s** behaviour
beneiden *vt* envy (**um etw** sth). **b~swert** *a* enviable
Bengel *m* **-s,-** boy; (*Rüpel*) lout
benommen *a* dazed
benötigen *vt* need
benutz|en, (*SGer*) **benütz|en** *vt* use; take (*Bahn*). **B~er** *m* **-s,-** user. **b~erfreundlich** *a* user-friendly. **B~ung** *f* use
Benzin *nt* **-s** petrol, (*Amer*) gasoline. **B~tank** *m* petrol tank
beobacht|en *vt* observe. **B~er** *m* **-s,-** observer. **B~ung** *f* **-,-en** observation
bepacken *vt* load (**mit** with)
bepflanzen *vt* plant (**mit** with)
bequem *a* comfortable, *adv* -bly; (*mühelos*) easy, *adv* -ily; (*faul*) lazy. **b~en (sich)** *vr* deign (**zu** to). **B~lichkeit** *f* **-,-en** comfort; (*Faulheit*) laziness
berat|en† *vt* advise; (*überlegen*) discuss; **sich b~en** confer; **sich b~en lassen** get advice □ *vi* (*haben*) discuss (**über etw** *acc* sth); (*beratschlagen*) confer. **B~er(in)** *m* **-s,-** (*f* **-,-nen**) adviser. **b~schlagen** *vi* (*haben*) confer. **B~ung** *f* **-,-en** guidance; (*Rat*) advice; (*Besprechung*) discussion; (*Med, Jur*) consultation. **B~ungsstelle** *f* advice centre
berauben *vt* rob (*gen* of)
berauschen *vt* intoxicate. **b~d** *a* intoxicating, heady
berechn|en *vt* calculate; (*anrechnen*) charge for; (*abfordern*) charge. **b~end** *a* (*fig*) calculating. **B~ung** *f* calculation
berechtig|en *vt* entitle; (*befugen*) authorize; (*fig*) justify. **b~t** *a* justified, justifiable. **B~ung** *f* **-,-en** authorization; (*Recht*) right; (*Rechtmäßigkeit*) justification
bered|en *vt* talk about; (*klatschen*) gossip about; (*überreden*) talk round; **sich b~en** talk. **B~samkeit** *f* - eloquence
beredt *a* eloquent, *adv* -ly

Bereich *m* **-[e]s,-e** area; (*fig*) realm; (*Fach-*) field

bereichern *vt* enrich; **sich b~** grow rich (**an** + *dat* on)

Bereifung *f* - tyres *pl*

bereinigen *vt* (*fig*) settle

bereit *a* ready. **b~en** *vt* prepare; (*verursachen*) cause; give (*Überraschung*). **b~halten**† *vt sep* have/(*ständig*) keep ready. **b~legen** *vt sep* put out [ready]. **b~machen** *vt sep* get ready; **sich b~machen** get ready. **b~s** *adv* already

Bereitschaft *f* -,-**en** readiness; (*Einheit*) squad. **B~sdienst** *m* **B~sdienst haben** (*Mil*) be on stand-by; (*Arzt:*) be on call; (*Apotheke:*) be open for out-of-hours dispensing. **B~spolizei** *f* riot police

bereit|stehen† *vi sep* (*haben*) be ready. **b~stellen** *vt sep* put out ready; (*verfügbar machen*) make available. **B~ung** *f* - preparation. **b~willig** *a* willing, *adv* -ly. **B~willigkeit** *f* - willingness

bereuen *vt* regret

Berg *m* **-[e]s,-e** mountain; (*Anhöhe*) hill; **in den B~en** in the mountains. **b~ab** *adv* downhill. **b~an** *adv* uphill. **B~arbeiter** *m* miner. **b~auf** *adv* uphill; **es geht b~auf** (*fig*) things are looking up. **B~bau** *m* **-[e]s** mining

bergen† *vt* recover; (*Naut*) salvage; (*retten*) rescue

Berg|führer *m* mountain guide. **b~ig** *a* mountainous. **B~kette** *f* mountain range. **B~mann** *m* (*pl* **-leute**) miner. **B~steigen** *nt* **-s** mountaineering. **B~steiger(in)** *m* **-s,-** (*f* **-,-nen**) mountaineer, climber. **B~-und-Talbahn** *f* roller-coaster

Bergung *f* - recovery; (*Naut*) salvage; (*Rettung*) rescue

Berg|wacht *f* mountain rescue service. **B~werk** *nt* mine

Bericht *m* **-[e]s,-e** report; (*Reise-*) account; **B~ erstatten** report (**über** + *acc* on). **b~en** *vt/i* (*haben*) report; (*erzählen*) tell (**von** of). **B~erstatter(in)** *m* **-s,-** (*f* **-,-nen**) reporter; (*Korrespondent*) correspondent

berichtig|en *vt* correct. **B~ung** *f* -,-**en** correction

beriesel|n *vt* irrigate. **B~ungsanlage** *f* sprinkler system

beritten *a* (*Polizei*) mounted

Berlin *nt* **-s** Berlin. **B~er** *m* **-s,-** Berliner; (*Culin*) doughnut □ *a* Berlin . . .

Bernhardiner *m* **-s,-** St Bernard

Bernstein *m* amber

bersten† *vi* (*sein*) burst

berüchtigt *a* notorious

berückend *a* entrancing

berücksichtig|en *vt* take into consideration. **B~ung** *f* - consideration

Beruf *m* profession; (*Tätigkeit*) occupation; (*Handwerk*) trade. **b~en**† *vt* appoint; **sich b~en** refer (**auf** + *acc* to); (*vorgeben*) plead (**auf etw** *acc* sth) □ *a* competent; **b~en sein** be destined (**zu** to). **b~lich** *a* professional; (*Ausbildung*) vocational □ *adv* professionally; **b~lich tätig sein** work, have a job. **B~saussichten** *fpl* career prospects. **B~sberater(in)** *m(f)* careers officer. **B~sberatung** *f* vocational guidance. **b~smäßig** *adv* professionally. **B~sschule** *f* vocational school. **B~ssoldat** *m* regular soldier. **b~stätig** *a* working; **b~stätig sein** work, have a job. **B~stätige(r)** *m/f* working man/woman. **B~sverkehr** *m* rush-hour traffic. **B~ung** *f* -,-**en** appointment; (*Bestimmung*) vocation; (*Jur*) appeal; **B~ung einlegen** appeal. **B~ungsgericht** *nt* appeal court

beruhen *vi* (*haben*) be based (**auf** + *dat* on); **eine Sache auf sich b~ lassen** let a matter rest

beruhig|en *vt* calm [down]; (*zuversichtlich machen*) reassure;

sich b~en calm down. **b~end** *a* calming; (*tröstend*) reassuring; (*Med*) sedative. **B~ung** *f* - calming; reassurance; (*Med*) sedation. **B~ungsmittel** *nt* sedative; (*bei Psychosen*) tranquillizer

berühmt *a* famous. **B~heit** *f* -,-en fame; (*Person*) celebrity

berühr|en *vt* touch; (*erwähnen*) touch on; (*beeindrucken*) affect; **sich b~en** touch. **B~ung** *f* -,-en touch; (*Kontakt*) contact

besag|en *vt* say; (*bedeuten*) mean. **b~t** *a* [afore]said

besänftigen *vt* soothe; **sich b~** calm down

Besatz *m* **-es,¨e** trimming

Besatzung *f* **-,-en** crew; (*Mil*) occupying force

besaufen† **(sich)** *vr* (*sl*) get drunk

beschädig|en *vt* damage. **B~ung** *f* **-,-en** damage

beschaffen *vt* obtain, get □ *a* **so b~ sein, dass** be such that; **wie ist es b~ mit?** what about? **B~heit** *f* - consistency; (*Art*) nature

beschäftig|en *vt* occupy; ⟨*Arbeitgeber:*⟩ employ; **sich b~en** occupy oneself. **b~t** *a* busy; (*angestellt*) employed (**bei** at). **B~te(r)** *m/f* employee. **B~ung** *f* **-,-en** occupation; (*Anstellung*) employment. **b~ungslos** *a* unemployed. **B~ungstherapie** *f* occupational therapy

beschäm|en *vt* make ashamed. **b~end** *a* shameful; (*demütigend*) humiliating. **b~t** *a* ashamed; (*verlegen*) embarrassed

beschatten *vt* shade; (*überwachen*) shadow

beschau|en *vt* (*SGer*) [**sich** (*dat*)] **etw b~en** look at sth. **b~lich** *a* tranquil; (*Relig*) contemplative

Bescheid *m* **-[e]s** information; **jdm B~ sagen** *od* **geben** let s.o. know; **B~ wissen** know

bescheiden *a* modest, *adv* -ly. **B~heit** *f* - modesty

bescheinen† *vt* shine on; **von der Sonne beschienen** sunlit

bescheinig|en *vt* certify. **B~ung** *f* **-,-en** [written] confirmation; (*Schein*) certificate

beschenken *vt* give a present/presents to

bescher|en *vt* **jdn b~en** give s.o. presents; **jdm etw b~en** give s.o. sth. **B~ung** *f* **-,-en** distribution of Christmas presents; (*fam: Schlamassel*) mess

beschießen† *vt* fire at; (*mit Artillerie*) shell, bombard

beschildern *vt* signpost

beschimpf|en *vt* abuse, swear at. **B~ung** *f* **-,-en** abuse

beschirmen *vt* protect

Beschlag *m* **in B~ nehmen, mit B~ belegen** monopolize. **b~en†** *vt* shoe □ *vi* (*sein*) steam *or* mist up □ *a* steamed *or* misted up; (*erfahren*) knowledgeable (**in** + *dat* about). **B~nahme** *f* **-,-n** confiscation; (*Jur*) seizure. **b~nahmen** *vt* confiscate; (*Jur*) seize; (*fam*) monopolize

beschleunig|en *vt* hasten; (*schneller machen*) speed up; quicken ⟨*Schritt, Tempo*⟩; **sich b~en** speed up; quicken □ *vi* (*haben*) accelerate. **B~ung** *f* - acceleration

beschließen† *vt* decide; (*beenden*) end □ *vi* (*haben*) decide (**über** + *acc* about)

Beschluss (**Beschluß**) *m* decision

beschmieren *vt* smear/(*bestreichen*) spread (**mit** with)

beschmutzen *vt* make dirty; **sich b~** get [oneself] dirty

beschneid|en† *vt* trim; (*Hort*) prune; (*fig: kürzen*) cut back; (*Relig*) circumcise. **B~ung** *f* - circumcision

beschneit *a* snow-covered

beschnüffeln, beschnuppern *vt* sniff at

beschönigen *vt* (*fig*) gloss over

beschränken *vt* limit, restrict; **sich b~auf** (+ *acc*) confine oneself to; ⟨*Sache:*⟩ be limited to
beschrankt *a* ⟨*Bahnübergang*⟩ with barrier[s]
beschränk|t *a* limited; (*geistig*) dull-witted; (*borniert*) narrow-minded. **B~ung** *f* **-,-en** limitation, restriction
beschreib|en† *vt* describe; (*schreiben*) write on. **B~ung** *f* **-,-en** description
beschuldig|en *vt* accuse. **B~ung** *f* **-,-en** accusation
beschummeln *vt* (*fam*) cheat
Beschuss (**Beschuß**) *m* (*Mil*) fire; (*Artillerie-*) shelling
beschütz|en *vt* protect. **B~er** *m* **-s,-** protector
Beschwer|de *f* **-,-n** complaint; **B~den** (*Med*) trouble *sg*. **b~en** *vt* weight down; **sich b~en** complain. **b~lich** *a* difficult
beschwichtigen *vt* placate
beschwindeln *vt* cheat (**um** out of); (*belügen*) lie to
beschwingt *a* elated; (*munter*) lively
beschwipst *a* (*fam*) tipsy
beschwören† *vt* swear to; (*anflehen*) implore; (*herauf-*) invoke
besehen† *vt* look at
beseitig|en *vt* remove. **B~ung** *f* - removal
Besen *m* **-s,-** broom. **B~ginster** *m* (*Bot*) broom. **B~stiel** *m* broomstick
besessen *a* obsessed (**von** by)
besetz|en *vt* occupy; fill ⟨*Posten*⟩; (*Theat*) cast ⟨*Rolle*⟩; (*verzieren*) trim (**mit** with). **b~t** *a* occupied; ⟨*Toilette, Leitung*⟩ engaged; ⟨*Zug, Bus*⟩ full up; **der Platz ist b~t** this seat is taken; **mit Perlen b~t** set with pearls. **B~tzeichen** *nt* engaged tone. **B~ung** *f* **-,-en** occupation; (*Theat*) cast
besichtig|en *vt* look round ⟨*Stadt, Museum*⟩; (*prüfen*) inspect; (*besuchen*) visit. **B~ung** *f* **-,-en** visit; (*Prüfung*) inspection; (*Stadt-*) sightseeing
besiedelt *a* **dünn/dicht b~** sparsely/densely populated
besiegeln *vt* (*fig*) seal
besieg|en *vt* defeat; (*fig*) overcome. **B~te(r)** *m/f* loser
besinn|en† (**sich**) *vr* think, reflect; (*sich erinnern*) remember (**auf jdn/etw** s.o./sth); **sich anders b~en** change one's mind. **b~lich** *a* contemplative; (*nachdenklich*) thoughtful. **B~ung** *f* - reflection; (*Bewusstsein*) consciousness; **bei/ohne B~ung** conscious/unconscious; **zur B~ung kommen** regain consciousness; (*fig*) come to one's senses. **b~ungslos** *a* unconscious
Besitz *m* possession; (*Eigentum, Land-*) property; (*Gut*) estate. **b~anzeigend** *a* (*Gram*) possessive. **b~en†** *vt* own, possess; (*haben*) have. **B~er(in)** *m* **-s,-** (*f* **-,-nen**) owner; (*Comm*) proprietor. **B~ung** *f* **-,-en** [landed] property; (*Gut*) estate
besoffen *a* (*sl*) drunken; **b~ sein** be drunk
besohlen *vt* sole
besold|en *vt* pay. **B~ung** *f* - pay
besonder|e(r,s) *a* special; (*bestimmt*) particular; (*gesondert*) separate; **nichts B~es** nothing special. **B~heit** *f* **-,-en** peculiarity. **b~s** *adv* [e]specially, particularly; (*gesondert*) separately
besonnen *a* calm, *adv* -ly
besorg|en *vt* get; (*kaufen*) buy; (*erledigen*) attend to; (*versorgen*) look after. **B~nis** *f* **-,-se** anxiety; (*Sorge*) worry. **b~niserregend** *a* worrying. **b~t** *a* worried/(*bedacht*) concerned (**um** about). **B~ung** *f* **-,-en** errand; **B~ungen machen** do shopping
bespielt *a* recorded
bespitzeln *vt* spy on
besprech|en† *vt* discuss; (*rezensieren*) review; **sich b~en** confer;

ein Tonband b~en make a tape recording. **B~ung** *f* **-,-en** discussion; review; (*Konferenz*) meeting

bespritzen *vt* splash

besser *a & adv* better. **b~n** *vt* improve; **sich b~n** get better, improve. **B~ung** *f* **-** improvement; **gute B~ung!** get well soon! **B~wisser** *m* **-s,-** know-all

Bestand *m* **-[e]s,¨e** existence; (*Vorrat*) stock (**an** + *dat* of); **B~haben, von B~ sein** last

beständig *a* constant, *adv* -ly; ⟨*Wetter*⟩ settled; **b~ gegen** resistant to

Bestand|saufnahme *f* stocktaking. **B~teil** *m* part

bestärken *vt* (*fig*) strengthen

bestätig|en *vt* confirm; acknowledge ⟨*Empfang*⟩; **sich b~en** prove to be true. **B~ung** *f* **-,-en** confirmation

bestatt|en *vt* bury. **B~ung** *f* **-,-en** funeral. **B~ungsinstitut** *nt* [firm of] undertakers *pl*, (*Amer*) funeral home

bestäuben *vt* pollinate

bestaubt *a* dusty

Bestäubung *f* **-** pollination

bestaunen *vt* gaze at in amazement; (*bewundern*) admire

best|e(r,s) *a* best; **b~en Dank!** many thanks! **am b~en sein** be best; **zum b~en geben/halten** (NEW) **zum B~en geben/halten**, *s.* **Beste(r,s)**. **B~e(r,s)** *m/f/nt* best; **sein B~es tun** do one's best; **zum B~en der Armen** for the benefit of the poor; **zum B~n geben** recite ⟨*Gedicht*⟩; tell ⟨*Geschichte, Witz*⟩; sing ⟨*Lied*⟩; **jdn zum B~n halten** (*fam*) pull s.o.'s leg

bestech|en† *vt* bribe; (*bezaubern*) captivate. **b~end** *a* captivating. **b~lich** *a* corruptible. **B~ung** *f* **-** bribery. **B~ungsgeld** *nt* bribe

Besteck *nt* **-[e]s,-e** [set of] knife, fork and spoon; (*coll*) cutlery

bestehen† *vi* (*haben*) exist; (*fortdauern*) last; (*bei Prüfung*) pass; **~ aus** consist/(*gemacht sein*) be made of; **~ auf** (+ *dat*) insist on □ *vt* pass ⟨*Prüfung*⟩. **B~** *nt* **-s** existence

bestehlen† *vt* rob

besteig|en† *vt* climb; (*einsteigen*) board; (*aufsteigen*) mount; ascend ⟨*Thron*⟩. **B~ung** *f* ascent

bestell|en *vt* order; (*vor-*) book; (*ernennen*) appoint; (*bebauen*) cultivate; (*aurichten*) tell; **zu sich b~en** send for; **b~t sein** have an appointment; **kann ich etwas b~en?** can I take a message? **b~en Sie Ihrer Frau Grüße von mir** give my regards to your wife. **B~schein** *m* order form. **B~ung** *f* order; (*Botschaft*) message; (*Bebauung*) cultivation

besten|falls *adv* at best. **b~s** *adv* very well

besteuer|n *vt* tax. **B~ung** *f* **-** taxation

bestialisch /-st-/ *a* bestial

Bestie /ˈbɛstjə/ *f* **-,-n** beast

bestimm|en *vt* fix; (*entscheiden*) decide; (*vorsehen*) intend; (*ernennen*) appoint; (*ermitteln*) determine; (*definieren*) define; (*Gram*) qualify □ *vi* (*haben*) be in charge (**über** + *acc* of). **~t** *a* definite, *adv* -ly; (*gewiss*) certain, *adv* -ly; (*fest*) firm, *adv* -ly. **B~theit** *f* **-** firmness; **mit B~theit** for certain. **B~ung** *f* fixing; (*Vorschrift*) regulation; (*Ermittlung*) determination; (*Definition*) definition; (*Zweck*) purpose; (*Schicksal*) destiny. **B~ungsort** *m* destination

Bestleistung *f* (*Sport*) record

bestraf|en *vt* punish. **B~ung** *f* **-,-en** punishment

bestrahl|en *vt* shine on; (*Med*) treat with radiotherapy; irradiate ⟨*Lebensmittel*⟩. **B~ung** *f* radiotherapy

Bestreb|en *nt* **-s** endeavour; (*Absicht*) aim. **b~t** *a* **b~t sein** endeavour (**zu** to). **B~ung** *f* **-,-en** effort

bestreichen† *vt* spread (**mit** with)

bestreikt *a* strike-hit

bestreiten† *vt* dispute; (*leugnen*) deny; (*bezahlen*) pay for

bestreuen *vt* sprinkle (**mit** with)

bestürmen *vt* (*fig*) besiege

bestürz|t *a* dismayed; (*erschüttert*) stunned. **B~ung** *f* **-** dismay, consternation

Bestzeit *f* (*Sport*) record [time]

Besuch *m* **-[e]s,-e** visit; (*kurz*) call; (*Schul-*) attendance; (*Gast*) visitor; (*Gäste*) visitors *pl*; **B~ haben** have a visitor/visitors; **bei jdm zu** *od* **auf B~ sein** be staying with s.o. **~en** *vt* visit; (*kurz*) call on; (*teilnehmen*) attend; go to ⟨*Schule, Ausstellung*⟩; **gut b~t** well attended. **B~er(in)** *m* **-s,-** (*f* **-,-nen**) visitor; caller; (*Theat*) patron. **B~szeit** *f* visiting hours *pl*

betagt *a* aged, old

betasten *vt* feel

betätig|en *vt* operate; **sich b~en** work (**als** as); **sich politisch b~en** engage in politics. **B~ung** *f* **-,-en** operation; (*Tätigkeit*) activity

betäub|en *vt* stun; ⟨*Lärm:*⟩ deafen; (*Med*) anaesthetize; (*lindern*) ease; deaden ⟨*Schmerz*⟩; **wie b~t** dazed. **B~ung** *f* **-** daze; (*Med*) anaesthesia; **unter örtlicher B~ung** under local anaesthetic. **B~ungsmittel** *nt* anaesthetic

Bete *f* **-,-n rote B~** beetroot

beteilig|en *vt* give a share to; **sich b~en** take part (**an** + *dat* in); (*beitragen*) contribute (**an** + *dat* to). **b~t** *a* **b~t sein** take part/(*an Unfall*) be involved/(*Comm*) have a share (**an** + *dat* in); **alle B~ten** all those involved. **B~ung** *f* **-,-en** participation; involvement; (*Anteil*) share

beten *vi* (*haben*) pray; (*bei Tisch*) say grace □ *vt* say

beteuer|n *vt* protest. **B~ung** *f* **-,-en** protestation

Beton /be'tɔŋ/ *m* **-s** concrete

betonen *vt* stressed, emphasize

betonieren *vt* concrete

beton|t *a* stressed; (*fig*) pointed, *adv* -ly. **B~ung** *f* **-,-en** stress, emphasis

betören *vt* bewitch

betr., **Betr.** *abbr* (**betreffs**) re

Betracht *m* **in B~ ziehen** consider; **außer B~ lassen** disregard; **nicht in B~ kommen** be out of the question. **b~en** *vt* look at; (*fig*) regard (**als** as)

beträchtlich *a* considerable, *adv* -bly

Betrachtung *f* **-,-en** contemplation; (*Überlegung*) reflection

Betrag *m* **-[e]s,⸚e** amount. **b~en**† *vt* amount to; **sich b~en** behave. **B~en** *nt* **-s** behaviour; (*Sch*) conduct

betrauen *vt* entrust (**mit** with)

betrauern *vt* mourn

betreff|en† *vt* affect; (*angehen*) concern; **was mich betrifft** as far as I am concerned. **b~end** *a* relevant; **der b~ende Brief** the letter in question. **b~s** *prep* (+ *gen*) concerning

betreiben† *vt* (*leiten*) run; (*ausüben*) carry on; (*vorantreiben*) pursue; (*antreiben*) run (**mit** on)

betreten† *vt* step on; (*eintreten*) enter; '**B~ verboten**' 'no entry'; (*bei Rasen*) 'keep off [the grass]' □ *a* embarrassed □ *adv* in embarrassment

betreu|en *vt* look after. **B~er(in)** *m* **-s,-** (*f* **-,-nen**) helper; (*Kranken-*) nurse. **B~ung** *f* **-** care

Betrieb *m* business; (*Firma*) firm; (*Treiben*) activity; (*Verkehr*) traffic; **in B~** working; (*in Gebrauch*) in use; **außer B~** not in use; (*defekt*) out of order

Betriebs|anleitung, **B~anweisung** *f* operating instructions *pl*. **B~ferien** *pl* firm's holiday; '**B~ferien**' 'closed for the holidays'. **B~leitung** *f* management. **B~rat** *m* works committee. **B~ruhe** *f* '**montags B~ruhe**' 'closed on Mondays'. **B~störung** *f* breakdown

betrinken† (sich) *vr* get drunk

betroffen *a* disconcerted; **b~ sein** be affected (**von** by); **die B~en** those affected □ *adv* in consternation

betrüb|en *vt* sadden. **b~lich** *a* sad. **b~t** *a* sad, *adv* -ly

Betrug *m* **-[e]s** deception; (*Jur*) fraud

betrüg|en† *vt* cheat, swindle; (*Jur*) defraud; (*in der Ehe*) be unfaithful to; **sich selbst b~en** deceive oneself. **B~er(in)** *m* **-s,-** (*f* **-,-nen**) swindler. **B~erei** *f* **-,-en** fraud. **b~erisch** *a* fraudulent; ⟨*Person*⟩ deceitful

betrunken *a* drunken; **b~ sein** be drunk. **B~e(r)** *m* drunk

Bett *nt* **-[e]s,-en** bed; **im B~** in bed; **ins** *od* **zu B~ gehen** go to bed. **B~couch** *f* sofa-bed. **B~decke** *f* blanket; (*Tages-*) bedspread

bettel|arm *a* destitute. **B~ei** *f* **-** begging. **b~n** *vi* (*haben*) beg

bett|en *vt* lay, put; **sich b~en** lie down. **b~lägerig** *a* bedridden. **B~laken** *nt* sheet

Bettler(in) *m* **-s,-** (*f* **-,-nen**) beggar

Bettpfanne *f* bedpan

Betttuch (**Bettuch**) *nt* sheet

Bett|vorleger *m* bedside rug. **B~wäsche** *f* bed linen. **B~zeug** *nt* bedding

betupfen *vt* dab (**mit** with)

beug|en *vt* bend; (*Gram*) decline; conjugate ⟨*Verb*⟩; **sich b~en** bend; (*lehnen*) lean; (*sich fügen*) submit (*dat* to). **B~ung** *f* **-,-en** (*Gram*) declension; conjugation

Beule *f* **-,-n** bump; (*Delle*) dent

beunruhig|en *vt* worry; **sich b~en** worry. **B~ung** *f* **-** worry

beurlauben *vt* give leave to; (*des Dienstes entheben*) suspend

beurteil|en *vt* judge. **B~ung** *f* **-,-en** judgement; (*Ansicht*) opinion

Beute *f* **-** booty, haul; (*Jagd-*) bag; (*B~tier*) quarry; (*eines Raubtiers*) prey

Beutel *m* **-s,-** bag; (*Geld-*) purse; (*Tabak- & Zool*) pouch. **B~tier** *nt* marsupial

bevölker|n *vt* populate. **B~ung** *f* **-,-en** population

bevollmächtig|en *vt* authorize. **B~te(r)** *m/f* [authorized] agent

bevor *conj* before; **b~ nicht** until

bevormunden *vt* treat like a child

bevorstehen† *vi sep* (*haben*) approach; (*unmittelbar*) be imminent; **jdm b~** be in store for s.o. **b~d** *a* approaching, forthcoming; **unmittelbar b~d** imminent

bevorzug|en *vt* prefer; (*begünstigen*) favour. **b~t** *a* privileged; ⟨*Behandlung*⟩ preferential; (*beliebt*) favoured

bewachen *vt* guard; **bewachter Parkplatz** car park with an attendant

bewachsen *a* covered (**mit** with)

Bewachung *f* **-** guard; **unter B~** under guard

bewaffn|en *vt* arm. **b~et** *a* armed. **B~ung** *f* **-** armament; (*Waffen*) arms *pl*

bewahren *vt* protect (**vor** + *dat* from); (*behalten*) keep; **die Ruhe b~** keep calm; **Gott bewahre!** heaven forbid!

bewähren (sich) *vr* prove one's/⟨*Ding:*⟩ its worth; (*erfolgreich sein*) prove a success

bewahrheiten (sich) *vr* prove to be true

bewähr|t *a* reliable; (*erprobt*) proven. **B~ung** *f* **-** (*Jur*) probation. **B~ungsfrist** *f* [period of] probation. **B~ungsprobe** *f* (*fig*) test

bewaldet *a* wooded

bewältigen *vt* cope with; (*überwinden*) overcome; (*schaffen*) manage
bewandert *a* knowledgeable
bewässer|n *vt* irrigate. **B~ung** *f* - irrigation
bewegen[1] *vt* (*reg*) move; **sich b~** move; (*körperlich*) take exercise
bewegen†[2] *vt* **jdn dazu b~, etw zu tun** induce s.o. to do sth
Beweg|grund *m* motive. **b~lich** *a* movable, mobile; (*wendig*) agile. **B~lichkeit** *f* - mobility; agility. **b~t** *a* moved; (*ereignisreich*) eventful; ⟨*See*⟩ rough. **B~ung** *f* -,-**en** movement; (*Phys*) motion; (*Rührung*) emotion; (*Gruppe*) movement; **körperliche B~ung** physical exercise; **sich in B~ung setzen** [start to] move. **B~ungsfreiheit** *f* freedom of movement/(*fig*) of action. **b~ungslos** *a* motionless
beweinen *vt* mourn
Beweis *m* **-es,-e** proof; (*Zeichen*) token; **B~e** evidence *sg*. **b~en**† *vt* prove; (*zeigen*) show; **sich b~en** prove oneself/⟨*Ding:*⟩ itself. **B~material** *nt* evidence
bewenden *vi* **es dabei b~lassen** leave it at that
bewerb|en† **(sich)** *vr* apply (**um** for; **bei** to). **B~er(in)** *m* **-s,-** (*f* -,-**nen**) applicant. **B~ung** *f* -,-**en** application
bewerkstelligen *vt* manage
bewerten *vt* value; (*einschätzen*) rate; (*Sch*) mark, grade
bewilligen *vt* grant
bewirken *vt* cause; (*herbeiführen*) bring about; (*erreichen*) achieve
bewirt|en *vt* entertain. **B~ung** *f* - hospitality
bewohn|bar *a* habitable. **b~en** *vt* inhabit, live in. **B~er(in)** *m* **-s,-** (*f* **-,-nen**) resident, occupant; (*Einwohner*) inhabitant
bewölk|en (sich) *vr* cloud over; **b~t** cloudy. **B~ung** *f* - clouds *pl*
bewunder|n *vt* admire. **b~nswert** *a* admirable. **B~ung** *f* - admiration
bewusst (bewußt) *a* conscious (*gen* of); (*absichtlich*) deliberate, *adv* -ly; (*besagt*) said; **sich** (*dat*) **etw** (*gen*) **b~ sein/werden** be/become aware of sth. **b~los** *a* unconscious. **B~losigkeit** *f* - unconsciousness; **B~sein** *n* **-s** consciousness; (*Gewissheit*) awareness; **bei [vollem] B~sein** [fully] conscious; **mir kam zum B~sein** I realized (**dass** that)
bez. *abbr* (**bezahlt**) paid; (**bezüglich**) re
bezahl|en *vt/i* (*haben*) pay; pay for ⟨*Ware, Essen*⟩; **gut b~te Arbeit** well-paid work; **sich b~t machen** (*fig*) pay off. **B~ung** *f* - payment; (*Lohn*) pay
bezähmen *vt* control; (*zügeln*) restrain; **sich b~** restrain oneself
bezaubern *vt* enchant. **b~d** *a* enchanting
bezeichn|en *vt* mark; (*bedeuten*) denote; (*beschreiben, nennen*) describe (**als** as). **b~end** *a* typical. **B~ung** *f* marking; (*Beschreibung*) description (**als** as); (*Ausdruck*) term; (*Name*) name
bezeugen *vt* testify to
bezichtigen *vt* accuse (*gen* of)
bezieh|en† *vt* cover; (*einziehen*) move into; (*beschaffen*) obtain; (*erhalten*) get, receive; take ⟨*Zeitung*⟩; (*in Verbindung bringen*) relate (**auf** + *acc* to); **sich b~en** (*bewölken*) cloud over; **sich b~en auf** (+ *acc*) refer to; **das Bett frisch b~en** put clean sheets on the bed. **B~ung** *f* -,-**en** relation; (*Verhältnis*) relationship; (*Bezug*) respect; **in dieser B~ung** in this respect; **[gute] B~ungen haben** have [good] connections. **b~ungsweise** *adv* respectively; (*vielmehr*) or rather
beziffern (sich) *vr* amount (**auf** + *acc* to)
Bezirk *m* **-[e]s,-e** district

Bezug *m* cover; (*Kissen-*) case; (*Beschaffung*) obtaining; (*Kauf*) purchase; (*Zusammenhang*) reference; **B~e** *pl* earnings; **B~ nehmen** refer (**auf** + *acc* to); **in B~ (b~) auf** (+ *acc*) regarding, concerning

bezüglich *prep* (+ *gen*) regarding, concerning □ *a* relating (**auf** + *acc* to); (*Gram*) relative

bezwecken *vt* (*fig*) aim at

bezweifeln *vt* doubt

bezwingen† *vt* conquer

BH /be:'ha:/ *m* **-[s],-[s]** bra

bibbern *vi* (*haben*) tremble; (*vor Kälte*) shiver

Bibel *f* **-,-n** Bible

Biber[1] *m* **-s,-** beaver

Biber[2] *m & nt* **-s** flannelette

Biblio|graphie, **B~grafie** *f* **-,-n** bibliography. **B~thek** *f* **-,-en** library. **B~thekar(in)** *m* **-s,-** (*f* **-,-nen**) librarian

biblisch *a* biblical

bieder *a* honest, upright; (*ehrenwert*) worthy; (*einfach*) simple

bieg|en† *vt* bend; **sich b~en** bend; **sich vor Lachen b~en** (*fam*) double up with laughter □ *vi* (*sein*) curve (**nach** to); **um die Ecke b~en** turn the corner. **b~sam** *a* flexible, supple. **B~ung** *f* **-,-en** bend

Biene *f* **-,-n** bee. **B~nhonig** *m* natural honey. **B~nstock** *m* beehive. **B~nwabe** *f* honey-comb

Bier *nt* **-s,-e** beer. **B~deckel** *m* beer-mat. **B~krug** *m* beer-mug

Biest *nt* **-[e]s,-er** (*fam*) beast

bieten† *vt* offer; (*bei Auktion*) bid; (*zeigen*) present; **das lasse ich mir nicht b~** I won't stand for that

Bifokalbrille *f* bifocals *pl*

Biga|mie *f* **-** bigamy. **B~ mist** *m* **-en,-en** bigamist

bigott *a* over-pious

Bikini *m* **-s,-s** bikini

Bilanz *f* **-,-en** balance sheet; (*fig*) result; **die B~ ziehen** (*fig*) draw conclusions (**aus** from)

Bild *nt* **-[e]s,-er** picture; (*Theat*) scene; **jdn ins B~ setzen** put s.o. in the picture

bilden *vt* form; (*sein*) be; (*erziehen*) educate; **sich b~** form; (*geistig*) educate oneself

Bild|erbuch *nt* picture-book. **B~ergalerie** *f* picture gallery. **B~fläche** *f* screen; **von der B~fläche verschwinden** disappear from the scene. **B~hauer** *m* **-s,-** sculptor. **B~hauerei** *f* **-** sculpture. **b~hübsch** *a* very pretty. **b~lich** *a* pictorial; (*figurativ*) figurative, *adv* -ly. **B~nis** *nt* **-ses,-se** portrait. **B~schirm** *m* (*TV*) screen. **B~schirmgerät** *nt* visual display unit, VDU. **b~schön** *a* very beautiful

Bildung *f* **-** formation; (*Erziehung*) education; (*Kultur*) culture

Billard /'bɪljart/ *nt* **-s** billiards *sg*. **B~tisch** *m* billiard table

Billett /bɪl'jɛt/ *nt* **-[e]s,-e & -s** ticket

Billiarde *f* **-,-n** thousand million million

billig *a* cheap, *adv* -ly; (*dürftig*) poor; (*gerecht*) just; **recht und b~** right and proper. **b~en** *vt* approve. **B~ung** *f* **-** approval

Billion /bɪlio:n/ *f* **-,-en** million million, billion

bimmeln *vi* (*haben*) tinkle

Bimsstein *m* pumice stone

bin *s.* **sein; ich bin** I am

Binde *f* **-,-n** band; (*Verband*) bandage; (*Damen-*) sanitary towel. **B~hautentzündung** *f* conjunctivitis. **b~n**† *vt* tie (**an** + *acc* to); make ⟨*Strauß*⟩; bind ⟨*Buch*⟩; (*fesseln*) tie up; (*Culin*) thicken; **sich b~n** commit oneself. **b~nd** *a* (*fig*) binding. **B~strich** *m* hyphen. **B~wort** *nt* (*pl* **-wörter**) (*Gram*) conjunction

Bind|faden *m* string; **ein B~faden** a piece of string. **B~ung** *f* -,-**en** (*fig*) tie, bond; (*Beziehung*) relationship; (*Verpflichtung*) commitment; (*Ski-*) binding; (*Tex*) weave

binnen *prep* (+ *dat*) within; **b~kurzem** shortly. **B~handel** *m* home trade

Binse *f* -,-**n** (*Bot*) rush. **B~nwahrheit, B~nweisheit** *f* truism

Bio- *pref* organic

Bio|chemie *f* biochemistry. **b~dynamisch** *m* organic. **B~graphie, B~grafie** *f* -,-**n** biography

Bio|hof *m* organic farm. **B~laden** *m* health-food store

Biolog|e *m* -**n**,-**n** biologist. **B~ie** *f* - biology. **b~isch** *a* biological, *adv* -ly; **b~ischer Anbau** organic farming; **b~isch angebaut** organically grown

Birke *f* -,-**n** birch [tree]

Birm|a *nt* -**s** Burma. **b~anisch** *a* Burmese

Birn|baum *m* pear-tree. **B~e** *f* -,-**n** pear; (*Electr*) bulb

bis *prep* (+ *acc*) as far as, [up] to; (*zeitlich*) until, till; (*spätestens*) by; **bis zu** up to; **bis jetzt** up to now, so far; **bis dahin** until/(*spätestens*) by then; **bis auf** (+ *acc*) (*einschließlich*) [down] to; (*ausgenommen*) except [for]; **drei bis vier Mark** three to four marks; **bis morgen!** see you tomorrow! □ *conj* until

Bischof *m* -**s**,**¨e** bishop

bisher *adv* so far, up to now. **b~ig** *attrib a* ⟨*Präsident*⟩ outgoing; **meine b~igen Erfahrungen** my experiences so far

Biskuit|rolle /bɪsˈkviːt-/ *f* Swiss roll. **B~teig** *m* sponge mixture

bislang *adv* so far, up to now

Biss *m* -**es**,-**e** (**Biß** *m* -**sses**,-**sse**) bite

bisschen (**bißchen**) *inv pron* **ein b~** a bit, a little; **ein b~ Brot** a bit of bread; **kein b~** not a bit

Biss|en *m* -**s**,- bite, mouthful. **b~ig** *a* vicious; (*fig*) caustic

bist *s.* **sein; du b~** you are

Bistum *nt* -**s**,**¨er** diocese, see

bisweilen *adv* from time to time

bitt|e *adv* please; (*nach Klopfen*) come in; (*als Antwort auf 'danke'*) don't mention it, you're welcome; **wie b~e?** pardon? (*empört*) I beg your pardon? **möchten Sie Kaffee?—ja b~e** would you like some coffee?—yes please. **B~e** *f* -,-**n** request/(*dringend*) plea (**um** for). **b~en**† *vt/i* (*haben*) ask/(*dringend*) beg (**um** for); (*einladen*) invite, ask; **ich b~e dich!** I beg [of] you! (*empört*) I ask you! **b~end** *a* pleading, *adv* -ly

bitter *a* bitter, *adv* -ly. **B~keit** *f* - bitterness. **b~lich** *adv* bitterly

Bittschrift *f* petition

bizarr *a* bizarre, *adv* -ly

bläh|en *vt* swell; puff out ⟨*Vorhang*⟩; **sich b~en** swell; ⟨*Vorhang, Segel:*⟩ billow □ *vi* (*haben*) cause flatulence. **B~ungen** *fpl* flatulence *sg*, (*fam*) wind *sg*

Blamage /blaˈmaːʒə/ *f* -,-**n** humiliation; (*Schande*) disgrace

blamieren *vt* disgrace; **sich b~** disgrace oneself; (*sich lächerlich machen*) make a fool of oneself

blanchieren /blãˈʃiːrən/ *vt* (*Culin*) blanch

blank *a* shiny; (*nackt*) bare; **b~sein** (*fam*) be broke. **B~oscheck** *m* blank cheque

Blase *f* -,-**n** bubble; (*Med*) blister; (*Anat*) bladder. **B~balg** *m* -**[e]s**,**¨e** bellows *pl*. **b~n**† *vt/i* (*haben*) blow; play ⟨*Flöte*⟩. **B~nentzündung** *f* cystitis

Bläser *m* -**s**,- (*Mus*) wind player; **die B~** the wind section *sg*

blasiert *a* blasé

Blas|instrument *nt* wind instrument. **B~kapelle** *f* brass band

Blasphemie *f* - blasphemy

blass (**blaß**) *a* (**blasser, blassest**) pale; (*schwach*) faint; **b~ werden** turn pale

Blässe *f* - pallor

Blatt *nt* **-[e]s,¨er** (*Bot*) leaf; (*Papier*) sheet; (*Zeitung*) paper; **kein B~ vor den Mund nehmen** (*fig*) not mince one's words

blätter|n *vi* (*haben*) **b~n in** (+ *dat*) leaf through. **B~teig** *m* puff pastry

Blattlaus *f* greenfly

blau *a*, **B~** *nt* **-s,-** blue; **b~er Fleck** bruise; **b~es Auge** black eye; **b~ sein** (*fam*) be tight; **Fahrt ins B~e** mystery tour. **B~beere** *f* bilberry. **B~licht** *nt* blue flashing light. **b~machen** *vi sep* (*haben*) (*fam*) skive off work

Blech *nt* **-[e]s,-e** sheet metal; (*Weiß-*) tin; (*Platte*) metal sheet; (*Back-*) baking sheet; (*Mus*) brass; (*fam: Unsinn*) rubbish. **b~en** *vt/i* (*haben*) (*fam*) pay. **B~[blas]instrument** *nt* brass instrument. **B~schaden** *m* (*Auto*) damage to the bodywork

Blei *nt* **-[e]s** lead

Bleibe *f* - place to stay. **b~n†** *vi* (*sein*) remain, stay; (*übrig-*) be left; **ruhig b~n** keep calm; **bei etw b~n** (*fig*) stick to sth; **b~n Sie am Apparat** hold the line; **etw b~n lassen** not do sth.; (*aufhören*) stop doing sth. **b~nd** *a* permanent; (*anhaltend*) lasting. **b~nlassen†** *vt sep* (NEW) **b~n lassen**, *s.* **bleiben**

bleich *a* pale. **b~en†** *vi* (*sein*) bleach; (*ver-*) fade □ *vt* (*reg*) bleach. **B~mittel** *nt* bleach

blei|ern *a* leaden. **b~frei** *a* unleaded. **B~stift** *m* pencil. **B~stiftabsatz** *m* stiletto heel. **B~stiftspitzer** *m* **-s,-** pencil-sharpener

Blende *f* **-,-n** shade, shield; (*Sonnen-*) [sun] visor; (*Phot*) diaphragm; (*Öffnung*) aperture; (*an Kleid*) facing. **b~n** *vt* dazzle, blind. **b~nd** *a* (*fig*) dazzling; (*prima*) marvellous, *adv* -ly

Blick *m* **-[e]s,-e** look; (*kurz*) glance; (*Aussicht*) view; **auf den ersten B~** at first sight; **einen B~ für etw haben** (*fig*) have an eye for sth. **b~en** *vi* (*haben*) look/(*kurz*) glance (**auf** + *acc* at). **B~punkt** *m* (*fig*) point of view

blind *a* blind; (*trübe*) dull; **b~er Alarm** false alarm; **b~er Passagier** stowaway. **B~darm** *m* appendix. **B~darmentzündung** *f* appendicitis. **B~e(r)** *m/f* blind man/woman; **die B~en** the blind *pl.* **B~enhund** *m* guidedog. **B~enschrift** *f* braille. **B~gänger** *m* **-s,-** (*Mil*) dud. **B~heit** *f* - blindness. **b~lings** *adv* (*fig*) blindly

blink|en *vi* (*haben*) flash; (*funkeln*) gleam; (*Auto*) indicate. **B~er** *m* **-s,-** (*Auto*) indicator. **B~licht** *nt* flashing light

blinzeln *vi* (*haben*) blink

Blitz *m* **-es,-e** [flash of] lightning; (*Phot*) flash; **ein B~ aus heiterem Himmel** (*fig*) a bolt from the blue. **B~ableiter** *m* lightning-conductor. **b~artig** *a* lightning ... □ *adv* like lightning. **B~birne** *f* flashbulb. **b~en** *vi* (*haben*) flash; (*funkeln*) sparkle; **es hat geblitzt** there was a flash of lightning. **B~gerät** *nt* flash [unit]. **B~licht** *nt* (*Phot*) flash. **b~sauber** *a* spick and span. **b~schnell** *a* lightning ... □ *adv* like lightning. **B~strahl** *m* flash of lightning

Block *m* **-[e]s,¨e** block □ **-[e]s,-s** & **¨e** (*Schreib-*) [note-]pad; (*Häuser-*) block; (*Pol*) bloc

Blockade *f* **-,-n** blockade

Blockflöte *f* recorder

blockieren *vt* block; (*Mil*) blockade

Blockschrift *f* block letters *pl*

blöd[e] *a* feeble-minded; (*dumm*) stupid, *adv* -ly

Blödsinn *m* **-[e]s** idiocy; (*Unsinn*) nonsense. **b~ig** *a* feeble-minded; (*verrückt*) idiotic

blöken *vi* (*haben*) bleat

blond *a* fair-haired; ⟨*Haar*⟩ fair. **B~ine** *f* -,-n blonde

bloß *a* bare; (*alleinig*) mere; **mit b~em Auge** with the naked eye □ *adv* only, just; **was mache ich b~?** whatever shall I do?

Blöße *f* -,-n nakedness; **sich** (*dat*) **eine B~ geben** (*fig*) show a weakness

bloß|legen *vt sep* uncover. **b~stellen** *vt sep* compromise; **sich b~stellen** show oneself up

Bluff *m* **-s,-s** bluff. **b~en** *vt/i* (*haben*) bluff

blühen *vi* (*haben*) flower; (*fig*) flourish. **b~d** *a* flowering; (*fig*) flourishing, thriving; ⟨*Phantasie*⟩ fertile

Blume *f* -,-n flower; (*vom Wein*) bouquet. **B~nbeet** *n* flower-bed. **B~ngeschäft** *nt* flower-shop, florist's [shop]. **B~nkohl** *m* cauliflower. **B~nmuster** *nt* floral design. **B~nstrauß** *m* bunch of flowers. **B~ntopf** *m* flowerpot; (*Pflanze*) [flowering] pot plant. **B~nzwiebel** *f* bulb

blumig *a* (*fig*) flowery

Bluse *f* -,-n blouse

Blut *nt* **-[e]s** blood. **b~arm** *a* anaemic. **B~bahn** *f* blood-stream. **b~befleckt** *a* blood-stained. **B~bild** *nt* blood count. **B~buche** *f* copper beech. **B~druck** *m* blood pressure. **b~dürstig** *a* bloodthirsty

Blüte *f* -,-n flower, bloom; (*vom Baum*) blossom; (*B~zeit*) flowering period; (*Baum-*) blossom time; (*fig*) flowering; (*Höhepunkt*) peak, prime; (*fam: Banknote*) forged note, (*fam*) dud

Blut|egel *m* **-s,-** leech. **b~en** *vi* (*haben*) bleed

Blüten|blatt *nt* petal. **B~staub** *m* pollen

Blut|er *m* **-s,-** haemophiliac. **B~erguss (B~erguß)** *m* bruise. **B~gefäß** *nt* blood-vessel. **B~gruppe** *f* blood group. **B~hund** *m* bloodhound. **b~ig** *a* bloody. **b~jung** *a* very young. **B~körperchen** *nt* **-s,-** [blood] corpuscle. **B~probe** *f* blood test. **b~rünstig** *a* (*fig*) bloody, gory; ⟨*Person*⟩ blood-thirsty. **B~schande** *f* incest. **B~spender** *m* blood donor. **B~sturz** *m* haemorrhage. **B~sverwandte(r)** *m/f* blood relation. **B~transfusion, B~übertragung** *f* blood transfusion. **B~ung** *f* -,-en bleeding; (*Med*) haemorrhage; (*Regel-*) period. **b~unterlaufen** *a* bruised; ⟨*Auge*⟩ bloodshot. **B~vergießen** *nt* **-s** bloodshed. **B~vergiftung** *f* blood-poisoning. **B~wurst** *f* black pudding

Bö *f* -,-en gust; (*Regen-*) squall

Bob *m* **-s,-s** bob[-sleigh]

Bock *m* **-[e]s,¨e** buck; (*Ziege*) billy goat; (*Schaf*) ram; (*Gestell*) support; **einen B~ schießen** (*fam*) make a blunder. **b~en** *vi* (*haben*) ⟨*Pferd:*⟩ buck; ⟨*Kind:*⟩ be stubborn. **b~ig** *a* (*fam*) stubborn. **B~springen** *nt* leap-frog

Boden *m* **-s,¨** ground; (*Erde*) soil; (*Fuß-*) floor; (*Grundfläche*) bottom; (*Dach-*) loft, attic. **B~kammer** *f* attic [room]. **b~los** *a* bottomless; (*fam*) incredible. **B~satz** *m* sediment. **B~schätze** *mpl* mineral deposits. **B~see (der)** Lake Constance

Bogen *m* **-s,- &** ¨ curve; (*Geom*) arc; (*beim Skilauf*) turn; (*Archit*) arch; (*Waffe, Geigen-*) bow; (*Papier*) sheet; **einen großen B~ um jdn/etw machen** (*fam*) give s.o./sth a wide berth. **B~gang** *m* arcade. **B~schießen** *nt* archery

Bohle *f* -,-n [thick] plank

Böhm|en *nt* **-s** Bohemia. **b~isch** *a* Bohemian

Bohne *f* -,-n bean; **grüne B~n** French beans. **B~nkaffee** *m* real coffee

bohner|n *vt* polish. **B~wachs** *nt* floor-polish

bohr|en *vt/i* (*haben*) drill (**nach** for); drive ⟨*Tunnel*⟩; sink ⟨*Brunnen*⟩; ⟨*Insekt:*⟩ bore; **in der Nase b~en** pick one's nose. **B~er** *m* **-s,-** drill. **B~insel** *f* [offshore] drilling rig. **B~maschine** *f* electric drill. **B~turm** *m* derrick

Boje *f* **-,-n** buoy

Böllerschuss *m* gun salute

Bolzen *m* **-s,-** bolt; (*Stift*) pin

bombardieren *vt* bomb; (*fig*) bombard (**mit** with)

bombastisch *a* bombastic

Bombe *f* **-,-n** bomb. **B~nangriff** *m* bombing raid. **B~nerfolg** *m* huge success. **B~r** *m* **-s,-** (*Aviat*) bomber

Bon /bɔŋ/ *m* **-s,-s** voucher; (*Kassen-*) receipt

Bonbon /bɔŋˈbɔŋ/ *m & nt* **-s,-s** sweet

Bonus *m* **-[sses],-[sse]** bonus

Boot *nt* **-[e]s,-e** boat. **B~ssteg** *m* landing-stage

Bord1 *nt* **-[e]s,-e** shelf

Bord2 *m* (*Naut*) **an B~** aboard, on board; **über B~** overboard. **B~buch** *nt* log[-book]

Bordell *nt* **-s,-e** brothel

Bord|karte *f* boarding-pass. **B~stein** *m* kerb

borgen *vt* borrow; **jdm etw b~** lend s.o. sth

Borke *f* **-,-n** bark

borniert *a* narrow-minded

Börse *f* **-,-n** purse; (*Comm*) stock exchange. **B~nmakler** *m* stockbroker

Borst|e *f* **-,-n** bristle. **b~ig** *a* bristly

Borte *f* **-,-n** braid

bösartig *a* vicious; (*Med*) malignant

Böschung *f* **-,-en** embankment; (*Hang*) slope

böse *a* wicked, evil; (*unartig*) naughty; (*schlimm*) bad, *adv* -ly; (*zornig*) cross; **jdm** *od* **auf jdn b~ sein** be cross with s.o. **B~wicht** *m* **-[e]s,-e** villain; (*Schlingel*) rascal

bos|haft *a* malicious, *adv* -ly; (*gehässig*) spiteful, *adv* -ly. **B~heit** *f* **-,-en** malice; spite; (*Handlung*) spiteful act/(*Bemerkung*) remark

böswillig *a* malicious, *adv* -ly. **B~keit** *f* **-** malice

Botani|k *f* **-** botany. **B~ker(in)** *m* **-s,-** (*f* **-,-nen**) botanist. **b~sch** *a* botanical

Bot|e *m* **-n,-n** messenger. **B~engang** *m* errand. **B~schaft** *f* **-,-en** message; (*Pol*) embassy. **B~schafter** *m* **-s,-** ambassador

Bottich *m* **-[e]s,-e** vat; (*Wasch-*) tub

Bouillon /bʊlˈjɔŋ/ *f* **-,-s** clear soup. **B~würfel** *m* stock cube

Bowle /ˈboːlə/ *f* **-,-n** punch

box|en *vi* (*haben*) box □ *vt* punch. **B~en** *nt* **-s** boxing. **B~er** *m* **-s,-** boxer. **B~kampf** *m* boxing match; (*Boxen*) boxing

Boykott *m* **-[e]s,-s** boycott. **b~ieren** *vt* boycott; (*Comm*) black

brachliegen† *vi sep* (*haben*) lie fallow

Branche /ˈbrãːʃə/ *f* **-,-n** [line of] business. **B~nverzeichnis** *nt* (*Teleph*) classified directory

Brand *m* **-[e]s,¨e** fire; (*Med*) gangrene; (*Bot*) blight; **in B~ geraten** catch fire; **in B~ setzen** *od* **stecken** set on fire. **B~bombe** *f* incendiary bomb

branden *vi* (*haben*) surge; (*sich brechen*) break

Brand|geruch *m* smell of burning. **b~marken** *vt* (*fig*) brand. **B~stifter** *m* arsonist. **B~stiftung** *f* arson

Brandung *f* **-** surf. **B~sreiten** *nt* surfing

Brand|wunde *f* burn. **B~zeichen** *nt* brand

Branntwein *m* spirit; (*coll*) spirits *pl*. **B~brennerei** *f* distillery

bras|ilianisch *a* Brazilian. **B~ilien** /-iən/ *nt* **-s** Brazil

Brat|apfel *m* baked apple. **b~en**† *vt/i* (*haben*) roast; (*in der Pfanne*) fry. **B~en** *m* **-s,-** roast; (*B~stück*) joint. **B~ensoße** *f* gravy. **b~fertig** *a* oven-ready. **B~hähnchen, B~huhn** *nt* roast/(*zum Braten*) roasting chicken. **B~kartoffeln** *fpl* fried potatoes. **B~klops** *m* rissole. **B~pfanne** *f* frying-pan

Bratsche *f* **-,-n** (*Mus*) viola

Brat|spieß *m* spit. **B~wurst** *f* sausage for frying; (*gebraten*) fried sausage

Brauch *m* **-[e]s,Bräuche** custom. **b~bar** *a* usable; (*nützlich*) useful. **b~en** *vt* need; (*ge-, verbrauchen*) use; take ⟨*Zeit*⟩; **er b~t es nur zu sagen** he only has to say; **du b~st nicht zu gehen** you needn't go

Braue *f* **-,-n** eyebrow

brau|en *vt* brew. **B~er** *m* **-s,-** brewer. **B~erei** *f* **-,-en** brewery

braun *a*, **B~** *nt* **-s,-** brown; **b~ werden** ⟨*Person:*⟩ get a tan; **b~ [gebrannt] sein** be [sun-]tanned

Bräune *f* **-** [sun-]tan. **b~n** *vt/i* (*haben*) brown; (*in der Sonne*) tan

braungebrannt *a* (NEW) **braun gebrannt**, *s.* **braun**

Braunschweig *nt* **-s** Brunswick

Brause *f* **-,-n** (*Dusche*) shower; (*an Gießkanne*) rose; (*B~limonade*) fizzy drink. **b~n** *vi* (*haben*) roar; (*duschen*) shower □ *vi* (*sein*) rush [along] □ *vr* **sich b~n** shower. **b~nd** *a* roaring; (*sprudelnd*) effervescent

Braut *f* **-,¨e** bride; (*Verlobte*) fiancée

Bräutigam *m* **-s,-e** bridegroom; (*Verlobter*) fiancé

Brautkleid *nt* wedding dress

bräutlich *a* bridal

Brautpaar *nt* bridal couple; (*Verlobte*) engaged couple

brav *a* good, well-behaved; (*redlich*) honest □ *adv* dutifully; (*redlich*) honestly

bravo *int* bravo!

BRD *abbr* (**Bundesrepublik Deutschland**) FRG

Brech|eisen *nt* jemmy; (*B~stange*) crowbar. **b~en**† *vt* break; (*Phys*) refract ⟨*Licht*⟩; (*erbrechen*) vomit; **sich b~en** ⟨*Wellen:*⟩ break; ⟨*Licht:*⟩ be refracted; **sich** (*dat*) **den Arm b~en** break one's arm □ *vi* (*sein*) break □ *vi* (*haben*) vomit, be sick; **mit jdm b~en** (*fig*) break with s.o. **B~er** *m* **-s,-** breaker. **B~reiz** *m* nausea. **B~stange** *f* crowbar

Brei *m* **-[e]s,-e** paste; (*Culin*) purée; (*Grieß-*) pudding; (*Hafer-*) porridge. **b~ig** *a* mushy

breit *a* wide; ⟨*Schultern, Grinsen*⟩ broad □ *adv* **b~ grinsen** grin broadly. **b~beinig** *a & adv* with legs apart. **B~e** *f* **-,-n** width; breadth; (*Geog*) latitude. **b~en** *vt* spread (**über** + *acc* over). **B~engrad** *m* [degree of] latitude. **B~enkreis** *m* parallel. **B~seite** *f* long side; (*Naut*) broadside

Bremse[1] *f* **-,-n** horsefly

Bremse[2] *f* **-,-n** brake. **b~n** *vt* slow down; (*fig*) restrain □ *vi* (*haben*) brake

Bremslicht *nt* brake-light

brenn|bar *a* combustible; **leicht b~bar** highly [in]flammable. **b~en**† *vi* (*haben*) burn; ⟨*Licht:*⟩ be on; ⟨*Zigarette:*⟩ be alight; (*weh tun*) smart, sting; **es b~t in X** there's a fire in X; **darauf b~en, etw zu tun** be dying to do sth □ *vt* burn; (*rösten*) roast; (*im Brennofen*) fire; (*destillieren*) distil. **b~end** *a* burning; (*angezündet*) lighted; (*fig*) fervent □ *adv* **ich würde b~end gern ...** I'd love to ... **B~erei** *f* **-,-en** distillery

Brennessel *f* (NEW) **Brennnessel**

Brenn|holz *nt* firewood. **B~nessel** *f* stinging nettle. **B~ofen** *m* kiln. **B~punkt** *m* (*Phys*) focus;

im B~punkt des Interesses stehen be the focus of attention. **B~spiritus** *m* methylated spirits. **B~stoff** *m* fuel

brenzlig *a* (*fam*) risky; **b~er Geruch** smell of burning

Bresche *f* -,-n (*fig*) breach

Bretagne /bre'tanjə/ **(die)** - Brittany

Brett *nt* **-[e]s,-er** board; (*im Regal*) shelf; **schwarzes B~** notice board. **B~chen** *nt* **-s,-** slat; (*Frühstücks-*) small board (*used as plate*). **B~spiel** *nt* board game

Brezel *f* -,-n pretzel

Bridge /brɪtʃ/ *nt* - (*Spiel*) bridge

Brief *m* **-[e]s,-e** letter. **B~beschwerer** *m* **-s,-** paperweight. **B~block** *m* writing pad. **B~freund(in)** *m(f)* pen-friend. **B~kasten** *m* letter-box, (*Amer*) mailbox. **B~kopf** *m* letter-head. **b~lich** *a & adv* by letter. **B~marke** *f* [postage] stamp. **B~öffner** *m* paper-knife. **B~papier** *nt* notepaper. **B~porto** *nt* letter rate. **B~tasche** *f* wallet. **B~träger** *m* postman, (*Amer*) mailman. **B~umschlag** *m* envelope. **B~wahl** *f* postal vote. **B~wechsel** *m* correspondence

Brigade *f* -,-n brigade

Brikett *nt* **-s,-s** briquette

brillan|t /brɪl'jant/ *a* brilliant, *adv* -ly. **B~t** *m* **-en,-en** [cut] diamond. **B~z** *f* - brilliance

Brille *f* -,-n glasses *pl*, spectacles *pl*; (*Schutz-*) goggles *pl*; (*Klosett-*) toilet seat

bringen† *vt* bring; (*fort-*) take; (*ein-*) yield; (*veröffentlichen*) publish; (*im Radio*) broadcast; show ⟨*Film*⟩; **ins Bett b~** put to bed; **jdn nach Hause b~** take/(*begleiten*) see s.o. home; **an sich** (*acc*) **b~** get possession of; **mit sich b~** entail; **um etw b~** deprive of sth; **etw hinter sich** (*acc*) **b~** get sth over [and done] with; **jdn dazu b~, etw zu tun** get s.o. to do sth; **es weit b~** (*fig*) go far

brisant *a* explosive

Brise *f* -,-n breeze

Brit|e *m* **-n,-n, B~in** *f* **-,-nen** Briton. **b~isch** *a* British

Bröck|chen *nt* **-s,-** (*Culin*) crouton. **b~elig** *a* crumbly; ⟨*Gestein*⟩ friable. **b~eln** *vt/i* (*haben/sein*) crumble

Brocken *m* **-s,-** chunk; (*Erde, Kohle*) lump; **ein paar B~ Englisch** (*fam*) a smattering of English

Brokat *m* **-[e]s,-e** brocade

Brokkoli *pl* broccoli *sg*

Brombeer|e *f* blackberry. **B~strauch** *m* bramble [bush]

Bronchitis *f* - bronchitis

Bronze /'brõ:sə/ *f* **-,-n** bronze

Brosch|e *f* -,-n brooch. **b~iert** *a* paperback. **B~üre** *f* **-,-n** brochure; (*Heft*) booklet

Brösel *mpl* (*Culin*) breadcrumbs

Brot *n* **-[e]s,-e** bread; **ein B~** a loaf [of bread]; (*Scheibe*) a slice of bread; **sein B~ verdienen** (*fig*) earn one's living (**mit** by)

Brötchen *n* **-s,-** [bread] roll

Brot|krümel *m* breadcrumb. **B~verdiener** *m* breadwinner

Bruch *m* **-[e]s,⸚e** break; (*Brechen*) breaking; (*Rohr-*) burst; (*Med*) fracture; (*Eingeweide-*) rupture, hernia; (*Math*) fraction; (*fig*) breach; (*in Beziehung*) break-up

brüchig *a* brittle

Bruch|landung *f* crash-landing. **B~rechnung** *f* fractions *pl*. **B~stück** *nt* fragment. **b~stückhaft** *a* fragmentary. **B~teil** *m* fraction

Brücke *f* **-,-n** bridge; (*Teppich*) rug

Bruder *m* **-s,⸚** brother

brüderlich *a* brotherly, fraternal

Brügge *nt* **-s** Bruges

Brüh|e *f* **-,-n** broth; (*Knochen-*) stock; **klare B~e** clear soup. **b~en** *vt* scald; (*auf-*) make

⟨*Kaffee*⟩. **B~würfel** *m* stock cube
brüllen *vt/i* (*haben*) roar; ⟨*Kuh:*⟩ moo; (*fam: schreien*) bawl
brumm|eln *vt/i* (*haben*) mumble. **b~en** *vi* (*haben*) ⟨*Insekt:*⟩ buzz; ⟨*Bär:*⟩ growl; ⟨*Motor:*⟩ hum; (*murren*) grumble □ *vt* mutter. **B~er** *m* **-s,-** (*fam*) bluebottle. **b~ig** *a* (*fam*) grumpy, *adv* -ily
brünett *a* dark-haired. **B~e** *f* **-,-n** brunette
Brunnen *m* **-s,-** well; (*Spring-*) fountain; (*Heil-*) spa water. **B~kresse** *f* watercress
brüsk *a* brusque, *adv* -ly. **b~ieren** *vt* snub
Brüssel *nt* **-s** Brussels
Brust *f* **-,¨e** chest; (*weibliche, Culin: B~stück*) breast. **B~bein** *nt* breastbone. **B~beutel** *m* purse worn round the neck
brüsten (sich) *vr* boast
Brust|fellentzündung *f* pleurisy. **B~schwimmen** *nt* breaststroke
Brüstung *f* **-,-en** parapet
Brustwarze *f* nipple
Brut *f* **-,-en** incubation; (*Junge*) brood; (*Fisch-*) fry
brutal *a* brutal, *adv* -ly. **B~ität** *f* **-,-en** brutality
brüten *vi* (*haben*) sit (*on eggs*); (*fig*) ponder (**über** + *dat* over); **b~de Hitze** oppressive heat
Brutkasten *m* (*Med*) incubator
brutto *adv*, **B~-** *pref* gross
brutzeln *vi* (*haben*) sizzle □ *vt* fry
Bub *m* **-en,-en** (*SGer*) boy. **B~e** *m* **-n,-n** (*Karte*) jack, knave
Bubikopf *m* bob
Buch *nt* **-[e]s,¨er** book; **B~ führen** keep a record (**über** + *acc* of); **die B~er führen** keep the accounts. **B~drucker** *m* printer
Buche *f* **-,-n** beech
buchen *vt* book; (*Comm*) enter
Bücher|bord, **B~brett** *nt* bookshelf. **B~ei** *f* **-,-en** library. **B~regal** *nt* bookcase, bookshelves *pl*.
B~schrank *m* bookcase. **B~wurm** *m* bookworm
Buchfink *m* chaffinch
Buch|führung *f* bookkeeping. **B~halter(in)** *m* **-s,-** (*f* **-,-nen**) bookkeeper, accountant. **B~haltung** *f* bookkeeping, accountancy; (*Abteilung*) accounts department. **B~händler(in)** *m(f)* bookseller. **B~handlung** *f* bookshop. **B~macher** *m* **-s,-** bookmaker. **B~prüfer** *m* auditor
Büchse *f* **-,-n** box; (*Konserven-*) tin, can; (*Gewehr*) [sporting] gun. **B~nmilch** *f* evaporated milk. **B~nöffner** *m* tin *or* can opener
Buch|stabe *m* **-n,-n** letter. **b~stabieren** *vt* spell [out]. **b~stäblich** *adv* literally
Buchstützen *fpl* book-ends
Bucht *f* **-,-en** (*Geog*) bay
Buchung *f* **-,-en** booking, reservation; (*Comm*) entry
Buckel *m* **-s,-** hump; (*Beule*) bump; (*Hügel*) hillock; **einen B~ machen** ⟨*Katze:*⟩ arch its back
bücken (sich) *vr* bend down
bucklig *a* hunchbacked. **B~e(r)** *m/f* hunchback
Bückling *m* **-s,-e** smoked herring; (*fam: Verbeugung*) bow
buddeln *vt/i* (*haben*) (*fam*) dig
Buddhis|mus *m* **-** Buddhism. **B~t(in)** *m* **-en,-en** (*f* **-,-nen**) Buddhist. **b~tisch** *a* Buddhist
Bude *f* **-,-n** hut; (*Kiosk*) kiosk; (*Markt-*) stall; (*fam: Zimmer*) room; (*Studenten-*) digs *pl*
Budget /bʏˈdʒeː/ *nt* **-s,-s** budget
Büfett *nt* **-[e]s,-e** sideboard; (*Theke*) bar; **kaltes B~** cold buffet
Büffel *m* **-s,-** buffalo. **b~n** *vt/i* (*haben*) (*fam*) swot
Bug *m* **-[e]s,-e** (*Naut*) bow[s *pl*]
Bügel *m* **-s,-** frame; (*Kleider-*) coathanger; (*Steig-*) stirrup; (*Brillen-*) sidepiece. **B~brett** *nt*

ironing-board. **B~eisen** *nt* iron. **B~falte** *f* crease. **b~frei** *a* non-iron. **b~n** *vt/i* (*haben*) iron

bugsieren *vt* (*fam*) manœuvre

buhen *vi* (*haben*) (*fam*) boo

Buhne *f* -,-n breakwater

Bühne *f* -,-n stage. **B~nbild** *nt* set. **B~neingang** *m* stage door

Buhrufe *mpl* boos

Bukett *nt* -[e]s,-e bouquet

Bulette *f* -,-n [meat] rissole

Bulgarien /-iən/ *nt* -s Bulgaria

Bull|auge *nt* (*Naut*) porthole. **B~dogge** *f* bulldog. **B~dozer** /-do:zɐ/ *m* -s,- bulldozer. **B~e** *m* -n,-n bull; (*sl: Polizist*) cop

Bumme|l *m* -s,- (*fam*) stroll. **B~lant** *m* -en,-en (*fam*) dawdler; (*Faulenzer*) loafer. **B~lei** *f* - (*fam*) dawdling; (*Nachlässigkeit*) carelessness

bummel|ig *a* (*fam*) slow; (*nachlässig*) careless. **b~n** *vi* (*sein*) (*fam*) stroll □ *vi* (*haben*) (*fam*) dawdle. **B~streik** *m* go-slow. **B~zug** *m* (*fam*) slow train

Bums *m* -es,-e (*fam*) bump, thump

Bund[1] *nt* -[e]s,-e bunch; (*Stroh-*) bundle

Bund[2] *m* -[e]s,¨e association; (*Bündnis*) alliance; (*Pol*) federation; (*Rock-, Hosen-*) waistband; **im B~e sein** be in league (**mit** with); **der B~** the Federal Government; (*fam: Bundeswehr*) the [German] Army

Bündel *nt* -s,- bundle. **b~n** *vt* bundle [up]

Bundes|- *pref* Federal. **B~genosse** *m* ally. **B~kanzler** *m* Federal Chancellor. **B~land** *nt* [federal] state; (*Aust*) province. **B~liga** *f* German national league. **B~rat** *m* Upper House of Parliament. **B~regierung** *f* Federal Government. **B~republik** *f* **die B~republik Deutschland** the Federal Republic of Germany. **B~straße** *f* ≈ A road. **B~tag** *m* Lower House of Parliament. **B~wehr** *f* [Federal German] Army

bünd|ig *a & adv* **kurz und b~ig** short and to the point. **B~nis** *nt* -sses,-sse alliance

Bunker *m* -s,- bunker; (*Luftschutz-*) shelter

bunt *a* coloured; (*farbenfroh*) colourful; (*grell*) gaudy; (*gemischt*) varied; (*wirr*) confused; **b~er Abend** social evening; **b~e Platte** assorted cold meats □ *adv* **b~ durcheinander** higgledy-piggledy; **es zu b~ treiben** (*fam*) go too far. **B~stift** *m* crayon

Bürde *f* -,-n (*fig*) burden

Burg *f* -,-en castle

Bürge *m* -n,-n guarantor. **b~n** *vi* (*haben*) **b~n für** vouch for; (*fig*) guarantee

Bürger|(in) *m* -s,- (*f* -,-nen) citizen. **B~krieg** *m* civil war. **b~lich** *a* civil; (*Pflicht*) civic; (*mittelständisch*) middle-class; **b~liche Küche** plain cooking. **B~liche(r)** *m/f* commoner. **B~meister** *m* mayor. **B~rechte** *npl* civil rights. **B~steig** *m* -[e]s, -e pavement, (*Amer*) sidewalk

Burggraben *m* moat

Bürgschaft *f* -,-en surety; **B~ leisten** stand surety

Burgunder *m* -s,- (*Wein*) Burgundy

Burleske *f* -,-n burlesque

Büro *nt* -s,-s office. **B~angestellte(r)** *m/f* office-worker. **B~klammer** *f* paper-clip. **B~krat** *m* -en,-en bureaucrat. **B~kratie** *f* -,-n bureaucracy. **b~kratisch** *a* bureaucratic

Bursch|e *m* -n,-n lad, youth; (*fam: Kerl*) fellow. **b~ikos** *a* hearty; (*männlich*) mannish

Bürste *f* -,-n brush. **b~n** *vt* brush. **B~nschnitt** *m* crew cut

Bus *m* -ses,-se bus; (*Reise-*) coach. **B~bahnhof** *m* bus and coach station

Busch *m* -[e]s,¨e bush

Büschel *nt* -s,- tuft

buschig *a* bushy
Busen *m* **-s,-** bosom
Bussard *m* **-s,-e** buzzard
Buße *f* **-,-n** penance; (*Jur*) fine
büßen *vt/i* (*haben*) **[für] etw b~** atone for sth; (*fig: bezahlen*) pay for sth
buß|fertig *a* penitent. **B~geld** *nt* (*Jur*) fine
Büste *f* **-,-n** bust; (*Schneider-*) dummy. **B~nhalter** *m* **-s,-** bra
Butter *f* **-** butter. **B~blume** *f* buttercup. **B~brot** *nt* slice of bread and butter. **B~brotpapier** *nt* grease-proof paper. **B~fass (B~faß)** *nt* churn. **B~milch** *f* buttermilk. **b~n** *vi* (*haben*) make butter □ *vt* butter
b.w. *abbr* (**bitte wenden**) P.T.O.
bzgl. *abbr s.* **bezüglich**
bzw. *abbr s.* **beziehungsweise**

C

ca. *abbr* (**circa**) about
Café /ka'fe:/ *nt* **-s,-s** café
Cafeteria /kafete'ri:a/ *f* **-,-s** cafeteria
camp|en /'kɛmpən/ *vi* (*haben*) go camping. **C~ing** *nt* **-s** camping. **C~ingplatz** *m* campsite
Cape /ke:p/ *nt* **-s,-s** cape
Caravan /'ka[:]ravan/ *m* **-s,-s** (*Auto*) caravan; (*Kombi*) estate car
Cassette /ka'sɛtə/ *f* **-,-n** cassette. **C~nrecorder** /-rekɔrdɐ/ *m* **-s,-** cassette recorder
CD /tse:'de:/ *f* **-,-s** compact disc, CD
Cell|ist(in) /tʃɛ'lɪst(ɪn)/ *m* **-en,-en** (*f* **-,-nen**) cellist. **C~o** /'tʃɛlo/ *nt* **-,-los** & **-li** cello
Celsius /'tsɛlziʊs/ *inv* Celsius, centigrade
Cembalo /'tʃɛmbalo/ *nt* **-s,-los** & **-li** harpsichord

Champagner /ʃam'panjɐ/ *m* **-s** champagne
Champignon /'ʃampɪnjɔŋ/ *m* **-s,-s** [field] mushroom
Chance /'ʃã:s[ə]/ *f* **-,-n** chance
Chaos /'ka:ɔs/ *nt* **-** chaos
chaotisch /ka'o:tɪʃ/ *a* chaotic
Charakter /ka'raktɐ/ *m* **-s,-e** /-'te:rə/ character. **c~isieren** *vt* characterize. **c~istisch** *a* characteristic (**für** of), *adv* -ally
Charism|a /ka'rɪsma/ *nt* **-s** charisma. **c~atisch** *a* charismatic
charm|ant /ʃar'mant/ *a* charming, *adv* -ly. **C~e** /ʃarm/ *m* **-s** charm
Charter|flug /'tʃ-, 'ʃartɐ-/ *m* charter flight. **c~n** *vt* charter
Chassis /ʃa'si:/ *nt* **-,-** /-'si:[s], -'si:s/ chassis
Chauffeur /ʃɔ'fø:ɐ̯/ *m* **-s,-e** chauffeur; (*Taxi-*) driver
Chauvinis|mus /ʃovi'nɪsmʊs/ *m* **-** chauvinism. **C~t** *m* **-en,-en** chauvinist
Chef /ʃɛf/ *m* **-s,-s** head; (*fam*) boss
Chem|ie /çe'mi:/ *f* **-** chemistry. **C~ikalien** /-i̯ən/ *fpl* chemicals
Chem|iker(in) /'çe:-/ *m* **-s,-** (*f* **-,-nen**) chemist. **c~isch** *a* chemical, *adv* -ly; **c~ische Reinigung** dry-cleaning; (*Geschäft*) dry-cleaner's
Chicorée /'ʃɪkore:/ *m* **-s** chicory
Chiffr|e /'ʃɪfɐ, 'ʃɪfrə/ *f* **-,-n** cipher; (*bei Annonce*) box number. **c~iert** *a* coded
Chile /'çi:le/ *nt* **-s** Chile
Chin|a /'çi:na/ *nt* **-s** China. **C~ese** *m* **-n,-n**, **C~esin** *f* **-,-nen** Chinese. **c~esisch** *a* Chinese. **C~esisch** *nt* **-[s]** (*Lang*) Chinese
Chip /tʃɪp/ *m* **-s,-s** [micro]chip. **C~s** *pl* crisps, (*Amer*) chips
Chirurg /çi'rʊrk/ *m* **-en,-en** surgeon. **C~ie** /-'gi:/ *f* **-** surgery. **c~isch** /-g-/ *a* surgical, *adv* -ly
Chlor /klo:ɐ̯/ *nt* **-s** chlorine. **C~oform** /kloro'fɔrm/ *nt* **-s** chloroform

Choke /tʃo:k/ *m* **-s,-s** (*Auto*) choke
Cholera /ˈko:lera/ *f* - cholera
cholerisch /koˈle:rɪʃ/ *a* irascible
Cholesterin /ço-, kolɛsteˈri:n/ *nt* **-s** cholesterol
Chor /ko:ɐ̯/ *m* **-[e]s,¨e** choir; (*Theat*) chorus; **im C~** in chorus
Choral /koˈra:l/ *m* **-[e]s,¨e** chorale
Choreographie, **Choreografie** /koreograˈfi:/ *f* **-,-n** choreography
Chor|knabe /ˈko:ɐ̯-/ *m* choirboy. **C~musik** *f* choral music
Christ /krɪst/ *m* **-en,-en** Christian. **C~baum** *m* Christmas tree. **C~entum** *nt* **-s** Christianity. **C~in** *f* **-,-nen** Christian. **C~kind** *nt* Christ-child; (*als Geschenkbringer*) ≈ Father Christmas. **c~lich** *a* Christian
Christus /ˈkrɪstʊs/ *m* **-ti** Christ
Chrom /kro:m/ *nt* **-s** chromium
Chromosom /kromoˈzo:m/ *nt* **-s,-en** chromosome
Chronik /ˈkro:nɪk/ *f* **-,-en** chronicle
chron|isch /ˈkro:nɪʃ/ *a* chronic, *adv* -ally. **c~ologisch** *a* chronological, *adv* -ly
Chrysantheme /krʏzanˈte:mə/ *f* **-,-n** chrysanthemum
circa /ˈtsɪrka/ *adv* about
Clique /ˈklɪkə/ *f* **-,-n** clique
Clou /klu:/ *m* **-s,-s** highlight, (*fam*) high spot
Clown /klaun/ *m* **-s,-s** clown. **c~en** *vi* (*haben*) clown
Club /klʊp/ *m* **-s,-s** club
Cocktail /ˈkɔkte:l/ *m* **-s,-s** cocktail
Code /ˈko:t/ *m* **-s,-s** code
Cola /ˈko:la/ *f* **-,-** (*fam*) Coke (P)
Comic-Heft /ˈkɔmɪk-/ *nt* comic
Computer /kɔmˈpju:tɐ/ *m* **-s,-** computer. **c~isieren** *vt* computerize
Conférencier /kõˈferãˈsi̯e:/ *m* **-s,-** compère
Cord /kɔrt/ *m* **-s**, **C~samt** *m* corduroy. **C~[samt]hose** *f* cords *pl*
Couch /kautʃ/ *f* **-,-es** settee. **C~tisch** *m* coffee-table
Coupon /kuˈpõ:/ *m* **-s,-s** = **Kupon**
Cousin /kuˈzɛ̃:/ *m* **-s,-s** [male] cousin. **C~e** /-ˈzi:nə/ *f* **-,-n** [female] cousin
Crem|e /kre:m/ *f* **-s,-s** cream; (*Speise*) cream dessert. **c~efarben** *a* cream. **c~ig** *a* creamy
Curry /ˈkari, ˈkœri/ *nt & m* **-s** curry powder □ *nt* **-s,-s** (*Gericht*) curry

D

da *adv* there; (*hier*) here; (*zeitlich*) then; (*in dem Fall*) in that case; **von da an** from then on; **da sein** be there/(*hier*) here; (*existieren*) exist; **wieder da sein** be back; **noch nie da gewesen** unprecedented □ *conj* as, since
dabehalten† *vt sep* keep there
dabei (*emphatic*: **dabei**) *adv* nearby; (*daran*) with it; (*eingeschlossen*) included; (*hinsichtlich*) about it; (*währenddem*) during this; (*gleichzeitig*) at the same time; (*doch*) and yet; **dicht d~** close by; **d~ sein** be present; (*mitmachen*) be involved; **d~ sein, etw zu tun** be just doing sth; **d~ bleiben** (*fig*) remain adamant; **was ist denn d~?** (*fam*) so what? **d~sein**† *vi sep* (*sein*) (NEW) **d~ sein**, *s.* **dabei**
dableiben† *vi sep* (*sein*) stay there
Dach *nt* **-[e]s,¨er** roof. **D~boden** *m* loft. **D~gepäckträger** *m* roof-rack. **D~kammer** *f* attic room. **D~luke** *f* skylight. **D~rinne** *f* gutter
Dachs *m* **-es,-e** badger

Dach|sparren *m* **-s,-** rafter. **D~ziegel** *m* [roofing] tile
Dackel *m* **-s,-** dachshund
dadurch (*emphatic:* **dadurch**) *adv* through it/them; (*Ursache*) by it; (*deshalb*) because of that; **d~, dass** because
dafür (*emphatic:* **dafür**) *adv* for it/them; (*anstatt*) instead; (*als Ausgleich*) but [on the other hand]; **d~, dass** considering that; **ich kann nichts dafür** it's not my fault. **d~können†** *vi sep* (*haben*) (NEW) **d~ können**, *s.* **dafür**
dagegen (*emphatic:* **dagegen**) *adv* against it/them; (*Mittel, Tausch*) for it; (*verglichen damit*) by comparison; (*jedoch*) however; **hast du was d~?** do you mind? **d~halten†** *vt sep* argue **(dass** that)
daheim *adv* at home
daher (*emphatic:* **daher**) *adv* from there; (*deshalb*) for that reason; **das kommt d~, weil** that's because; **d~ meine Eile** hence my hurry □ *conj* that is why
dahin (*emphatic:* **dahin**) *adv* there; **bis d~** up to there; (*bis dann*) until/(*Zukunft*) by then; **jdn d~bringen, dass er etw tut** get s.o. to do sth; **d~sein** (*fam*) be gone. **d~gehen†** *vi sep* (*sein*) walk along; ⟨*Zeit:*⟩ pass. **d~gestellt** *a* **d~gestellt lassen** (*fig*) leave open; **das bleibt d~gestellt** that remains to be seen
dahinten *adv* back there
dahinter (*emphatic:* **dahinter**) *adv* behind it/them; **d~ kommen** (*fig*) get to the bottom of it. **d~kommen†** *vi sep* (*sein*) (NEW) **d~ kommen**, *s.* **dahinter**
Dahlie /-i̯ə/ *f* **-,-n** dahlia
dalassen† *vt sep* leave there
daliegen† *vi sep* (*haben*) lie there
damalig *a* at that time; **der d~e Minister** the then minister
damals *adv* at that time
Damast *m* **-es,-e** damask

Dame *f* **-,-n** lady; (*Karte, Schach*) queen; (*D~spiel*) draughts *sg*, (*Amer*) checkers *sg*; (*Doppelstein*) king. **D~n-** *pref* ladies'/lady's ... **d~nhaft** *a* ladylike
damit (*emphatic:* **damit**) *adv* with it/them; (*dadurch*) by it; **hör auf d~!** stop it! □ *conj* so that
dämlich *a* (*fam*) stupid, *adv* -ly
Damm *m* **-[e]s,¨e** dam; (*Insel-*) causeway; **nicht auf dem D~** (*fam*) under the weather
dämmer|ig *a* dim; **es wird d~ig** dusk is falling. **D~licht** *nt* twilight. **d~n** *vi* ⟨*haben*⟩ ⟨*Morgen:*⟩ dawn; **der Abend d~t** dusk is falling; **es d~t** it is getting light/(*abends*) dark. **D~ung** *f* dawn; (*Abend-*) dusk
Dämon *m* **-s,-en** /-ˈmo:nən/ demon
Dampf *m* **-es,¨e** steam; (*Chem*) vapour. **d~en** *vi* (*haben*) steam
dämpfen *vt* (*Culin*) steam; (*fig*) muffle ⟨*Ton*⟩; lower ⟨*Stimme*⟩; dampen ⟨*Enthusiasmus*⟩
Dampf|er *m* **-s,-** steamer. **D~kochtopf** *m* pressure-cooker. **D~maschine** *f* steam engine. **D~walze** *f* steamroller
Damwild *nt* fallow deer *pl*
danach (*emphatic:* **danach**) *adv* after it/them; ⟨*suchen*⟩ for it/them; ⟨*riechen*⟩ of it; (*später*) afterwards; (*entsprechend*) accordingly; **es sieht d~ aus** it looks like it
Däne *m* **-n,-n** Dane
daneben (*emphatic:* **daneben**) *adv* beside it/them; (*außerdem*) in addition; (*verglichen damit*) by comparison. **d~gehen†** *vi sep* (*sein*) miss; (*scheitern*) fail
Dän|emark *nt* **-s** Denmark. **D~in** *f* **-,-nen** Dane. **d~isch** *a* Danish
Dank *m* **-es** thanks *pl*; **vielen D~!** thank you very much! **d~** *prep* (+ *dat or gen*) thanks to. **d~bar** *a* grateful, *adv* -ly; (*erleichtert*)

thankful, *adv* -ly; (*lohnend*) rewarding. **D~barkeit** *f* - gratitude. **d~e** *adv* **d~e [schön** *od* **sehr]!** thank you [very much]! **[nein] d~e!** no thank you! **d~en** *vi* (*haben*) thank (**jdm** s.o.); (*ablehnen*) decline; **ich d~e!** no thank you! **nichts zu d~en!** don't mention it!

dann *adv* then; **d~ und wann** now and then; **nur/selbst d~, wenn** only/even if

daran (*emphatic:* **daran**) *adv* on it/them; at it/them; 〈*denken*〉 of it; **nahe d~** on the point (**etw zu tun** of doing sth); **denkt d~!** remember! **d~gehen**† *vi sep* (*sein*), **d~machen (sich)** *vr sep* set about (**etw zu tun** doing sth). **d~setzen** *vt sep* **alles d~setzen** do one's utmost (**zu** to)

darauf (*emphatic:* **darauf**) *adv* on it/them; 〈*warten*〉 for it; 〈*antworten*〉 to it; (*danach*) after that; (*d~hin*) as a result; **am Tag d~** the day after; **am d~ folgenden Tag** the following *or* next day. **d~folgend** *a* (NEW) **d~ folgend**, *s.* **darauf. d~hin** *adv* as a result

daraus (*emphatic:* **daraus**) *adv* out of *or* from it/them; **er macht sich nichts d~** he doesn't care for it; **was ist d~ geworden?** what has become of it?

Darbietung *f* -,-en performance; (*Nummer*) item

darin (*emphatic:* **darin**) *adv* in it/them

darlegen *vt sep* expound; (*erklären*) explain

Darlehen *nt* **-s,-** loan

Darm *m* **-[e]s,¨e** intestine; (*Wurst-*) skin. **D~grippe** *f* gastric flu

darstell|en *vt sep* represent; (*bildlich*) portray; (*Theat*) interpret; (*spielen*) play; (*schildern*) describe. **D~er** *m* **-s,-** actor. **D~erin** *f* **-,-nen** actress. **D~ung** *f* representation; interpretation; description; (*Bericht*) account

darüber (*emphatic:* **darüber**) *adv* over it/them; (*höher*) above it/them; 〈*sprechen, lachen, sich freuen*〉 about it; (*mehr*) more; (*inzwischen*) in the meantime; **d~hinaus** beyond [it]; (*dazu*) on top of that

darum (*emphatic:* **darum**) *adv* round it/them; 〈*bitten, kämpfen*〉 for it; (*deshalb*) that is why; **d~, weil** because

darunter (*emphatic:* **darunter**) *adv* under it/them; (*tiefer*) below it/them; (*weniger*) less; (*dazwischen*) among them

das *def art & pron s.* **der**

dasein† *vi sep* (*sein*) (NEW) **da sein**, *s.* **da. D~** *nt* **-s** existence

dasitzen† *vi sep* (*haben*) sit there

dasjenige *pron s.* **derjenige**

dass (**daß**) *conj* that; **d~ du nicht fällst!** mind you don't fall!

dasselbe *pron s.* **derselbe**

dastehen† *vi sep* (*haben*) stand there; **allein d~** (*fig*) be alone

Daten|sichtgerät *nt* visual display unit, VDU. **D~verarbeitung** *f* data processing

datieren *vt/i* (*haben*) date

Dativ *m* **-s,-e** dative. **D~objekt** *nt* indirect object

Dattel *f* **-,-n** date

Datum *nt* **s,-ten** date; **Daten** dates; (*Angaben*) data

Dauer *f* - duration, length; (*Jur*) term; **von D~** lasting; **auf die D~** in the long run. **D~auftrag** *m* standing order. **d~haft** *a* lasting, enduring; (*fest*) durable. **D~karte** *f* season ticket. **D~lauf** *m* **im D~lauf** at a jog. **D~milch** *f* long-life milk. **d~n** *vi* (*haben*) last; **lange d~n** take a long time. **d~nd** *a* lasting; (*ständig*) constant, *adv* -ly; **d~nd fragen** keep asking. **D~stellung** *f* permanent position. **D~welle** *f* perm. **D~wurst** *f* salami-type sausage

Daumen *m* **-s,-** thumb; **jdm den D~drücken** *od* **halten** keep one's fingers crossed for s.o.

Daunen *fpl* down *sg*. **D~decke** *f* [down-filled] duvet

davon (*emphatic:* **davon**) *adv* from it/them; (*dadurch*) by it; (*damit*) with it/them; (*darüber*) about it; (*Menge*) of it/them; **die Hälfte d~** half of it/them; **das kommt d~!** it serves you right! **d~kommen†** *vi sep* (*sein*) escape (**mit dem Leben** with one's life). **d~laufen†** *vi sep* (*sein*) run away. **d~machen** (**sich**) *vr sep* (*fam*) make off. **d~tragen†** *vt sep* carry off; (*erleiden*) suffer; (*gewinnen*) win

davor (*emphatic:* **davor**) *adv* in front of it/them; ⟨*sich fürchten*⟩ of it; (*zeitlich*) before it/them

dazu (*emphatic:* **dazu**) *adv* to it/them; (*damit*) with it/them; (*dafür*) for it; **noch d~** in addition to that; **jdn d~bringen, etw zu tun** get s.o. to do sth; **ich kam nicht d~** I didn't get round to [doing] it. **d~gehören** *vi sep* (*haben*) belong to it/them; **alles, was d~gehört** everything that goes with it. **d~kommen†** *vi sep* (*sein*) arrive [on the scene]; (*hinzukommen*) be added; **d~ kommt, dass er krank ist** on top of that he is ill. **d~rechnen** *vt sep* add to it/them

dazwischen (*emphatic:* **dazwischen**) *adv* between them; in between; (*darunter*) among them. **d~fahren†** *vi sep* (*sein*) (*fig*) intervene. **d~kommen†** *vi sep* (*sein*) (*fig*) crop up; **wenn nichts d~kommt** if all goes well. **d~reden** *vi sep* (*haben*) interrupt. **d~treten†** *vi sep* (*sein*) (*fig*) intervene

DDR *f* - *abbr* (**Deutsche Demokratische Republik**) GDR

Debat|te *f* **-,-n** debate; **zur D~te stehen** be at issue. **d~tieren** *vt/i* (*haben*) debate

Debüt /de'by:/ *nt* **-s,-s** début

dechiffrieren /deʃɪ'fri:rən/ *vt* decipher

Deck *nt* **-[e]s,-s** (*Naut*) deck; **an D~** on deck. **D~bett** *nt* duvet

Decke *f* **-,-n** cover; (*Tisch-*) tablecloth; (*Bett-*) blanket; (*Reise-*) rug; (*Zimmer-*) ceiling; **unter einer D~stecken** (*fam*) be in league

Deckel *m* **-s,-** lid; (*Flaschen-*) top; (*Buch-*) cover

decken *vt* cover; tile ⟨*Dach*⟩; lay ⟨*Tisch*⟩; (*schützen*) shield; (*Sport*) mark; meet ⟨*Bedarf*⟩; **jdn d~** (*fig*) cover up for s.o.; **sich d~** (*fig*) cover oneself (**gegen** against); (*übereinstimmen*) coincide

Deck|mantel *m* (*fig*) pretence. **D~name** *m* pseudonym

Deckung *f* - (*Mil*) cover; (*Sport*) defence; (*Mann-*) marking; (*Boxen*) guard; (*Sicherheit*) security; **in D~gehen** take cover

Defekt *m* **-[e]s,-e** defect. **d~** *a* defective

defensiv *a* defensive. **D~e** *f* - defensive

defilieren *vi* (*sein/haben*) file past

defin|ieren *vt* define. **D~ition** /-'tsi̯o:n/ *f* **-,-en** definition. **d~itiv** *a* definite, *adv* -ly

Defizit *nt* **-s,-e** deficit

Deflation /-'tsi̯o:n/ *f* - deflation

deformiert *a* deformed

deftig *a* (*fam*) ⟨*Mahlzeit*⟩ hearty; ⟨*Witz*⟩ coarse

Degen *m* **-s,-** sword; (*Fecht-*) épée

degenerier|en *vi* (*sein*) degenerate. **d~t** *a* (*fig*) degenerate

degradieren *vt* (*Mil*) demote; (*fig*) degrade

dehn|bar *a* elastic. **d~en** *vt* stretch; lengthen ⟨*Vokal*⟩; **sich d~en** stretch

Deich *m* **-[e]s,-e** dike

Deichsel *f* **-,-n** pole; (*Gabel-*) shafts *pl*

dein *poss pron* your. **d~e(r,s)** *poss pron* yours; **die D~en** *od* **d~en** *pl* your family *sg*. **d~erseits** *adv* for your part. **d~etwegen** *adv* for your sake; (*wegen dir*) because of you, on your account. **d~etwillen** *adv* **um d~etwillen** for your sake. **d~ige** *poss pron* **der/die/das d~ige** yours. **d~s** *poss pron* yours

Deka *nt* **-[s],-** (*Aust*) = **Dekagramm**

dekaden|t *a* decadent. **D~z** *f* - decadence

Dekagramm *nt* (*Aust*) 10 grams; **10 D~** 100 grams

Dekan *m* **-s,-e** dean

Deklin|ation /-'tsi̯o:n/ *f* **-,-en** declension. **d~ieren** *vt* decline

Dekolleté, Dekolletee /dekɔl'te:/ *nt* **-s,-s** low neckline

Dekor *m & nt* **-s** decoration. **D~ateur** /-'tø:ɐ̯/ *m* **-s,-e** interior decorator; (*Schaufenster-*) window-dresser. **D~ation** /-'tsi̯o:n/ *f* **-,-en** decoration; (*Schaufenster-*) window-dressing; (*Auslage*) display; **D~ationen** (*Theat*) scenery *sg*. **d~ativ** *a* decorative. **d~ieren** *vt* decorate; dress ⟨*Schaufenster*⟩

Deleg|ation /-'tsi̯o:n/ *f* **-,-en** delegation. **d~ieren** *vt* delegate. **D~ierte(r)** *m/f* delegate

Delfin *m* **-s,-e** = **Delphin**

delikat *a* delicate; (*lecker*) delicious; (*taktvoll*) tactful, *adv* -ly. **D~esse** *f* **-,-n** delicacy. **D~essengeschäft** *nt* delicatessen

Delikt *nt* **-[e]s,-e** offence

Delinquent *m* **-en,-en** offender

Delirium *nt* **-s** delirium

Delle *f* **-,-n** dent

Delphin *m* **-s,-e** dolphin

Delta *nt* **-s,-s** delta

dem *def art & pron s.* **der**

Dement|i *nt* **-s,-s** denial. **d~ieren** *vt* deny

dem|entsprechend *a* corresponding; (*passend*) appropriate □ *adv* accordingly; (*passend*) appropriately. **d~gemäß** *adv* accordingly. **d~nach** *adv* according to that; (*folglich*) consequently. **d~nächst** *adv* soon; (*in Kürze*) shortly

Demokrat *m* **-en,-en** democrat. **D~ie** *f* **-,-n** democracy. **d~isch** *a* democratic, *adv* -ally

demolieren *vt* wreck

Demonstr|ant *m* **-en,-en** demonstrator. **D~ation** /-'tsi̯o:n/ *f* **-,-en** demonstration. **d~ativ** *a* pointed, *adv* -ly; (*Gram*) demonstrative. **D~ativpronomen** *nt* demonstrative pronoun. **d~ieren** *vt/i* (*haben*) demonstrate

demontieren *vt* dismantle

demoralisieren *vt* demoralize

Demoskopie *f* - opinion research

Demut *f* - humility

demütig *a* humble, *adv* -bly. **d~en** *vt* humiliate; **sich d~en** humble oneself. **D~ung** *f* **-,-en** humiliation

demzufolge *adv* = **demnach**

den *def art & pron s.* **der. d~en** *pron s.* **der**

denk|bar *a* conceivable. **d~en**† *vt/i* (*haben*) think (**an** + *acc* of); (*sich erinnern*) remember (**an etw** *acc* sth); **für jdn gedacht** meant for s.o.; **das kann ich mir d~en** I can imagine [that]; **ich d~e nicht daran** I have no intention of doing it; **d~t daran!** don't forget! **D~mal** *nt* memorial; (*Monument*) monument. **d~würdig** *a* memorable. **D~zettel** *m* **jdm einen D~zettel geben** (*fam*) teach s.o. a lesson

denn *conj* for; **besser/mehr d~je** better/more than ever □ *adv* **wie/wo d~?** but how/where? **warum d~ nicht?** why ever not? **es sei d~ [, dass]** unless

dennoch *adv* nevertheless

Denunz|iant *m* **-en,-en** informer. **d~ieren** *vt* denounce

Deodorant *nt* **-s,-s** deodorant

deplaciert, deplatziert (deplaziert) /-'tsi:ɐ̯t/ *a* (*fig*) out of place

Deponie *f* **-,-n** dump. **d~ren** *vt* deposit
deportieren *vt* deport
Depot /de'po:/ *nt* **-s,-s** depot; (*Lager*) warehouse; (*Bank-*) safe deposit
Depression *f* **-,-en** depression
deprimieren *vt* depress. **d~d** *a* depressing
Deputation /-'tsi̯o:n/ *f* **-,-en** deputation
der, die, das, *pl* **die** *def art* (*acc* **den, die, das,** *pl* **die**; *gen* **des, der, des,** *pl* **der**; *dat* **dem, der, dem,** *pl* **den**) the; **der Mensch** man; **die Natur** nature; **das Leben** life; **das Lesen/Tanzen** reading/dancing; **sich** (*dat*) **das Gesicht/die Hände waschen** wash one's face/hands; **5 Mark das Pfund** 5 marks a pound □ *pron* (*acc* **den, die, das,** *pl* **die**; *gen* **dessen, deren, dessen,** *pl* **deren**; *dat* **dem, der, dem,** *pl* **denen**) □ *dem pron* that; (*pl*) those; (*substantivisch*) he, she, it; (*Ding*) it; (*betont*) that; (*d~jenige*) the one; (*pl*) they, those; (*Dinge*) those; (*diejenigen*) the ones; **der und der** such and such; **um die und die Zeit** at such and such a time; **das waren Zeiten!** those were the days! □ *rel pron* who; (*Ding*) which, that
derart *adv* so; (*so sehr*) so much. **d~ig** *a* such □ *adv* = **derart**
derb *a* tough; (*kräftig*) strong; (*grob*) coarse, *adv* -ly; (*unsanft*) rough, *adv* -ly
deren *pron s.* **der**
dergleichen *inv a* such □ *pron* such a thing/such things; **nichts d~** nothing of the kind; **und d~** and the like
der-/die-/dasjenige, *pl* **diejenigen** *pron* the one; (*Person*) he, she; (*Ding*) it; (*pl*) those, the ones
dermaßen *adv* = **derart**
der-/die-/dasselbe, *pl* **dieselben** *pron* the same; **ein- und dasselbe** one and the same thing
derzeit *adv* at present
des *def art s.* **der**
Desert|eur /-'tø:ɐ̯/ *m* **-s,-e** deserter. **d~ieren** *vi* (*sein/haben*) desert
desgleichen *adv* likewise □ *pron* the like
deshalb *adv* for this reason; (*also*) therefore
Designer(in) /di'zai̯nɐ, -nərɪn/ *m* **-s,-** (*f*, **-,-nen**) designer
Desin|fektion /dɛsˀɪnfɛk'tsi̯o:n/ *f* disinfecting. **D~fektionsmittel** *nt* disinfectant. **d~fizieren** *vt* disinfect
Desodorant *nt* **-s,-s** deodorant
Despot *m* **-en,-en** despot
dessen *pron s.* **der**
Dessert /dɛ'se:ɐ̯/ *nt* **-s,-s** dessert, sweet. **D~löffel** *m* dessertspoon
Destill|ation /-'tsi̯o:n/ *f* **-** distillation. **d~ieren** *vt* distil
desto *adv* **je mehr/eher, d~besser** the more/sooner the better
destruktiv *a* (*fig*) destructive
deswegen *adv* = **deshalb**
Detail /de'tai̯/ *nt* **-s,-s** detail
Detektiv *m* **-s,-e** detective. **D~roman** *m* detective story
Deton|ation /-'tsi̯o:n/ *f* **-,-en** explosion. **d~ieren** *vi* (*sein*) explode
deut|en *vt* interpret; predict ⟨*Zukunft*⟩ □ *vi* (*haben*) point (**auf** + *acc* at/(*fig*) to). **d~lich** *a* clear, *adv* -ly; (*eindeutig*) plain, *adv* -ly. **D~lichkeit** *f* **-** clarity
deutsch *a* German; **auf d~** (NEW) **auf D~**, *s.* **Deutsch**. **D~** *nt* **-[s]** (*Lang*) German; **auf D~** in German. **D~e(r)** *m/f* German. **D~land** *nt* **-s** Germany
Deutung *f* **-,-en** interpretation
Devise *f* **-,-n** motto. **D~n** *pl* foreign currency *or* exchange *sg*
Dezember *m* **-s,-** December
dezent *a* unobtrusive, *adv* -ly; (*diskret*) discreet, *adv* -ly

Dezernat *nt* **-[e]s,-e** department
Dezimal|system *nt* decimal system. **D~zahl** *f* decimal
dezimieren *vt* decimate
dgl. *abbr s.* **dergleichen**
d.h. *abbr* (*das heißt*) i.e.
Dia *nt* **-s,-s** (*Phot*) slide
Diabet|es *m* - diabetes. **D~iker** *m* **-s,-** diabetic
Diadem *nt* **-s,-e** tiara
Diagnos|e *f* **-,-n** diagnosis. **d~tizieren** *vt* diagnose
diagonal *a* diagonal, *adv* -ly. **D~e** *f* **-,-n** diagonal
Diagramm *nt* **-s,-e** diagram; (*Kurven-*) graph
Diakon *m* **-s,-e** deacon
Dialekt *m* **-[e]s,-e** dialect
Dialog *m* **-[e]s,-e** dialogue
Diamant *m* **-en,-en** diamond
Diameter *m* **-s,-** diameter
Diapositiv *nt* **-s,-e** (*Phot*) slide
Diaprojektor *m* slide projector
Diät *f* **-,-en** (*Med*) diet; **D~ leben** be on a diet. **d~** *adv* **d~ leben** (NEW) **D~ leben**, *s.* **Diät. D~assistent(in)** *m(f)* dietician
dich *pron* (*acc of* **du**) you; (*refl*) yourself
dicht *a* dense; (*dick*) thick; (*undurchlässig*) airtight; (*wasser-*) watertight □ *adv* densely; thickly; (*nahe*) close (**bei** to). **D~e** *f* density. **d~en**[1] *vt* make watertight; (*ab-*) seal
dicht|en[2] *vi* (*haben*) write poetry. □ *vt* write, compose. **D~er(in)** *m* **-s,-** (*f* **-,-en**) poet. **d~erisch** *a* poetic. **D~ung**[1] *f* **-,-en** poetry; (*Gedicht*) poem
Dichtung[2] *f* **-,-en** seal; (*Ring*) washer; (*Auto*) gasket
dick *a* thick, *adv* -ly; (*beleibt*) fat; (*geschwollen*) swollen; (*fam; eng*) close; **d~ werden** get fat; **d~ machen** be fattening; **ein d~es Fell haben** (*fam*) be thick-skinned. **D~e** *f* **-,-n** thickness; (*D~leibigkeit*) fatness. **d~fellig** *a* (*fam*) thick-skinned. **d~flüssig** *a* thick; (*Phys*) viscous. **D~kopf** *m* (*fam*) stubborn person; **einen D~kopf haben** be stubborn. **d~köpfig** *a* (*fam*) stubborn
didaktisch *a* didactic
die *def art & pron s.* **der**
Dieb|(in) *m* **-[e]s,-e** (*f* **-,-nen**) thief. **d~isch** *a* thieving; ⟨*Freude*⟩ malicious. **D~stahl** *m* **-[e]s,¨e** theft; (*geistig*) plagiarism
diejenige *pron s.* **derjenige**
Diele *f* **-,-n** floorboard; (*Flur*) hall
dien|en *vi* (*haben*) serve. **D~er** *m* **-s,-** servant; (*Verbeugung*) bow. **D~erin** *f* **-,-nen** maid, servant. **d~lich** *a* helpful
Dienst *m* **-[e]s,-e** service; (*Arbeit*) work; (*Amtsausübung*) duty; **außer D~** off duty; (*pensioniert*) retired; **D~ haben** work; ⟨*Soldat, Arzt:*⟩ be on duty; **der D~ habende Arzt** the duty doctor; **jdm einen schlechten D~ erweisen** do s.o. a disservice
Dienstag *m* Tuesday. **d~s** *adv* on Tuesdays
Dienst|alter *nt* seniority. **d~bereit** *a* obliging; ⟨*Apotheke*⟩ open. **D~bote** *m* servant. **d~eifrig** *a* zealous, *adv* -ly. **d~frei** *a* **d~freier Tag** day off; **d~frei haben** have time off; ⟨*Soldat, Arzt:*⟩ be off duty. **D~grad** *m* rank. **d~habend** *a* (NEW) **D~ habend**, *s.* **Dienst. D~leistung** *f* service. **d~lich** *a* official □ *adv* **d~lich verreist** away on business. **D~mädchen** *nt* maid. **D~reise** *f* business trip. **D~stelle** *f* office. **D~stunden** *fpl* office hours. **D~weg** *m* official channels *pl*
dies *inv pron* this. **d~bezüglich** *a* relevant □ *adv* regarding this matter. **d~e(r,s)** *pron* this; (*pl*) these; (*substantivisch*) this [one]; (*pl*) these; **d~e Nacht** tonight; (*letzte*) last night
Diesel *m* **-[s],-** (*fam*) diesel
dieselbe *pron s.* **derselbe**
Diesel|kraftstoff *m* diesel [oil]. **D~motor** *m* diesel engine

diesig *a* hazy, misty
dies|mal *adv* this time. **d~seits** *adv & prep* (+ *gen*) this side (of)
Dietrich *m* **-s,-e** skeleton key
Diffam|ation /-'tsio:n/ *f* - defamation. **d~ierend** *a* defamatory
Differential /-'tsia:l/ *nt* **-s,-e** (NEW) **Differenzial**
Differenz *f* **-,-en** difference. **D~ial** *nt* **-s,-e** differential. **d~ieren** *vt/i* (*haben*) differentiate (**zwischen** + *dat* between)
Digital- *pref* digital. **D~uhr** *f* digital clock/watch
Dikt|at *nt* **-[e]s,-e** dictation. **D~ator** *m* **-s,-en** /-'to:rən/ dictator. **d~atorisch** *a* dictatorial. **D~atur** *f* **-,-en** dictatorship. **d~ieren** *vt/i* (*haben*) dictate
Dilemma *nt* **-s,-s** dilemma
Dilettant|(in) *m* **-en,-en** (*f* **-,-nen**) dilettante. **d~isch** *a* amateurish
Dill *m* **-s** dill
Dimension *f* **-,-en** dimension
Ding *nt* **-[e]s,-e** & (*fam*) **-er** thing; **guter D~e sein** be cheerful; **vor allen D~en** above all
Dinghi /'dɪŋgi/ *nt* **-s,-s** dinghy
Dinosaurier /-iɐ/ *m* **-s,-** dinosaur
Diözese *f* **-,-n** diocese
Diphtherie *f* - diphtheria
Diplom *nt* **-s,-e** diploma; (*Univ*) degree
Diplomat *m* **-en,-en** diplomat. **D~ie** *f* - diplomacy. **d~isch** *a* diplomatic, *adv* -ally
dir *pron* (*dat of* **du**) [to] you; (*refl*) yourself; **ein Freund von dir** a friend of yours
direkt *a* direct □ *adv* directly; (*wirklich*) really. **D~ion** /-'tsio:n/ *f* - management; (*Vorstand*) board of directors. **D~or** *m* **-s, -en** /-'to:rən/, **D~orin** *f* **-,-nen** director; (*Bank-, Theater-*) manager; (*Sch*) head; (*Gefängnis*) governor. **D~übertragung** *f* live transmission
Dirig|ent *m* **-en,-en** (*Mus*) conductor. **d~ieren** *vt* direct; (*Mus*) conduct

Dirndl *nt* **-s,-** dirndl [dress]
Dirne *f* **-,-n** prostitute
Diskant *m* **-s,-e** (*Mus*) treble
Diskette *f* **-,-n** floppy disc
Disko *f* **-,-s** (*fam*) disco. **D~thek** *f* **-,-en** discothèque
Diskrepanz *f* **-,-en** discrepancy
diskret *a* discreet, *adv* -ly. **D~ion** /-'tsio:n/ *f* - discretion
diskriminier|en *vt* discriminate against. **D~ung** *f* - discrimination
Diskus *m* **-,-se & Disken** discus
Disku|ssion *f* **-,-en** discussion. **d~tieren** *vt/i* (*haben*) discuss
disponieren *vi* (*haben*) make arrangements; **d~ [können] über** (+ *acc*) have at one's disposal
Disput *m* **-[e]s,-e** dispute
Disqualifi|kation /-'tsio:n/ *f* disqualification. **d~zieren** *vt* disqualify
Dissertation /-'tsio:n/ *f* **-,-en** dissertation
Dissident *m* **-en,-en** dissident
Dissonanz *f* **-,-en** dissonance
Distanz *f* **-,-en** distance. **d~ieren (sich)** *vr* dissociate oneself (**von** from). **d~iert** *a* aloof
Distel *f* **-,-n** thistle
distinguiert /dɪstɪŋ'gi:ɐt/ *a* distinguished
Disziplin *f* **-,-en** discipline. **d~arisch** *a* disciplinary. **d~iert** *a* disciplined
dito *adv* ditto
diverse *attrib a pl* various
Divid|ende *f* **-,-en** dividend. **d~ieren** *vt* divide (**durch** by)
Division *f* **-,-en** division
DJH *abbr* (**Deutsche Jugendherberge**) [German] youth hostel
DM *abbr* (**Deutsche Mark**) DM
doch *conj & adv* but; (*dennoch*) yet; (*trotzdem*) after all; **wenn d~** ...! if only ...! **nicht d~!** don't [do that]! **er kommt d~?** he is coming, isn't he? **kommst du nicht?—d~!** aren't you coming? —yes, I am!

Docht *m* **-[e]s,-e** wick
Dock *nt* **-s,-s** dock. **d~en** *vt/i* (*haben*) dock
Dogge *f* **-,-n** Great Dane
Dogm|a *nt* **-s,-men** dogma. **d~atisch** *a* dogmatic, *adv* -ally
Dohle *f* **-,-n** jackdaw
Doktor *m* **-s,-en** /-ˈto:rən/ doctor. **D~arbeit** *f* [doctoral] thesis. **D~würde** *f* doctorate
Doktrin *f* **-,-en** doctrine
Dokument *nt* **-[e]s,-e** document. **D~arbericht** *m* documentary. **D~arfilm** *m* documentary film
Dolch *m* **-[e]s,-e** dagger
doll *a* (*fam*) fantastic; (*schlimm*) awful □ *adv* beautifully; (*sehr*) very; (*schlimm*) badly
Dollar *m* **-s,-** dollar
dolmetsch|en *vt/i* (*haben*) interpret. **D~er(in)** *m* **-s,-** (*f* **-,-nen**) interpreter
Dom *m* **-[e]s,-e** cathedral
domin|ant *a* dominant. **d~ieren** *vi* (*haben*) dominate; (*vorherrschen*) predominate
Domino *nt* **-s,-s** dominoes *sg*. **D~stein** *m* domino
Dompfaff *m* **-en,-en** bullfinch
Donau *f* **-** Danube
Donner *m* **-s** thunder. **d~n** *vi* (*haben*) thunder
Donnerstag *m* Thursday. **d~s** *adv* on Thursdays
Donnerwetter *nt* (*fam*) telling-off; (*Krach*) row □ *int* /ˈ--ˈ--/ wow! (*Fluch*) damn it!
doof *a* (*fam*) stupid, *adv* -ly
Doppel *nt* **-s,-** duplicate; (*Tennis*) doubles *pl*. **D~bett** *nt* double bed. **D~decker** *m* **-s,-** double-decker [bus]. **d~deutig** *a* ambiguous. **D~gänger** *m* **-s,-** double. **D~kinn** *nt* double chin. **D~name** *m* double-barrelled name. **D~punkt** *m* (*Gram*) colon. **D~schnitte** *f* sandwich. **d~sinnig** *a* ambiguous. **D~stecker** *m* two-way adaptor. **d~t** *a* double; ⟨*Boden*⟩ false; **in d~ter Ausfertigung** in duplicate; **die d~te Menge** twice the amount □ *adv* doubly; (*zweimal*) twice; **d~t so viel** twice as much. **D~zimmer** *nt* double room
Dorf *nt* **-[e]s,¨er** village. **D~bewohner** *m* villager
dörflich *a* rural
Dorn *m* **-[e]s,-en** thorn. **d~ig** *a* thorny
Dörrobst *nt* dried fruit
Dorsch *m* **-[e]s,-e** cod
dort *adv* there; **d~ drüben** over there. **d~her** *adv* **[von] d~her** from there. **d~hin** *adv* there. **d~ig** *a* local
Dose *f* **-,-n** tin, can; (*Schmuck-*) box
dösen *vi* (*haben*) doze
Dosen|milch *f* evaporated milk. **D~öffner** *m* tin *or* can opener
dosieren *vt* measure out
Dosis *f* **-, Dosen** dose
Dotter *m & nt* **-s,-** [egg] yolk
Dozent(in) *m* **-en,-en** (*f* **-,-nen**) (*Univ*) lecturer
Dr. *abbr* (**Doktor**) Dr
Drache *m* **-n,-n** dragon. **D~n** *m* **-s,-** kite; (*fam: Frau*) dragon. **D~nfliegen** *nt* hang-gliding. **D~nflieger** *m* hang-glider
Draht *m* **-[e]s,¨e** wire; **auf D~** (*fam*) on the ball. **d~ig** *a* (*fig*) wiry. **D~seilbahn** *f* cable railway
drall *a* plump; ⟨*Frau*⟩ buxom
Dram|a *nt* **-s,-men** drama. **D~atik** *f* **-** drama. **D~atiker** *m* **-s,-** dramatist. **d~atisch** *a* dramatic, *adv* -ally. **d~atisieren** *vt* dramatize
dran *adv* (*fam*) = **daran; gut/schlecht d~ sein** be well off/in a bad way; **ich bin d~** it's my turn
Dränage /-ˈna:ʒə/ *f* **-** drainage
Drang *m* **-[e]s** urge; (*Druck*) pressure
drängeln *vt/i* (*haben*) push; (*bedrängen*) pester. **d~en** *vt* push;

(*bedrängen*) urge; **sich d~en** crowd (**um** round) □ *vi* (*haben*) push; (*eilen*) be urgent; ⟨*Zeit:*⟩ press; **d~en auf** (+ *acc*) press for
dran|halten† (**sich**) *vr sep* hurry. **d~kommen†** *vi sep* (*sein*) have one's turn; **wer kommt dran?** whose turn is it?
drapieren *vt* drape
drastisch *a* drastic, *adv* -ally
drauf *adv* (*fam*) = **darauf**; **d~und dran sein** be on the point (**etw zu tun** of doing sth). **D~gänger** *m* **-s,-** daredevil. **d~gängerisch** *a* reckless
draus *adv* (*fam*) = **daraus**
draußen *adv* outside; (*im Freien*) out of doors
drechseln *vt* (*Techn*) turn
Dreck *m* **-s** dirt; (*Morast*) mud; (*fam: Kleinigkeit*) trifle; **in den D~ziehen** (*fig*) denigrate. **d~ig** *a* dirty; muddy
Dreh *m* **-s** (*fam*) knack; **den D~ heraushaben** have got the hang of it. **D~bank** *f* lathe. **D~bleistift** *m* propelling pencil. **D~buch** *nt* screenplay, script. **d~en** *vt* turn; (*im Kreis*) rotate; (*verschlingen*) twist; roll ⟨*Zigarette*⟩; shoot ⟨*Film*⟩; **lauter/leiser d~en** turn up/down; **sich d~en** turn; (*im Kreis*) rotate; (*schnell*) spin; ⟨*Wind:*⟩ change; **sich d~en um** revolve around; (*sich handeln*) be about □ *vi* (*haben*) turn; ⟨*Wind:*⟩ change; **an etw** (*dat*) **d~en** turn sth. **D~orgel** *f* barrel organ. **D~stuhl** *m* swivel chair. **D~tür** *f* revolving door. **D~ung** *f* **-,-en** turn; (*im Kreis*) rotation. **D~zahl** *f* number of revolutions
drei *inv a*, **D~** *f* **-,-en** three; (*Sch*) ≈ pass. **D~eck** *nt* **-[e]s,-e** triangle. **d~eckig** *a* triangular. **D~einigkeit** *f* **- die [Heilige] D~einigkeit** the [Holy] Trinity. **d~erlei** *inv* a three kinds of □ *pron* three things. **d~fach** *a* triple; **in d~facher Ausfertigung** in triplicate. **D~faltigkeit** *f* **-** = **D~einigkeit. d~mal** *adv* three times. **D~rad** *nt* tricycle
dreißig *inv a* thirty. **d~ste(r,s)** *a* thirtieth
dreist *a* impudent, *adv* -ly; (*verwegen*) audacious, *adv* -ly. **D~igkeit** *f* - impudence; audacity
dreiviertel *inv a* (NEW) **drei viertel**, *s.* **viertel**. **D~stunde** *f* three-quarters of an hour
dreizehn *inv a* thirteen **d~te(r,s)** *a* thirteenth
dreschen† *vt* thresh
dress|ieren *vt* train. **D~ur** *f* - training
dribbeln *vi* (*haben*) dribble
Drill *m* **-[e]s** (*Mil*) drill. **d~en** *vt* drill
Drillinge *mpl* triplets
drin *adv* (*fam*) = **darin**; (*drinnen*) inside
dring|en† *vi* (*sein*) penetrate (**in** + *acc* into; **durch etw** sth); (*heraus-*) come (**aus** out of); **d~en auf** (+ *acc*) insist on. **d~end** *a* urgent, *adv* -ly. **d~lich** *a* urgent. **D~lichkeit** *f* - urgency
Drink *m* **-[s],-s** [alcoholic] drink
drinnen *adv* inside; (*im Haus*) indoors
dritt *adv* **zu d~** in threes; **wir waren zu d~** there were three of us. **d~e(r,s)** *a* third; **ein D~er** a third person. **d~el** *inv a* third; **ein d~el Apfel** a third of an apple. **D~el** *nt* **-s,-** third. **d~ens** *adv* thirdly. **d~rangig** *a* third-rate
Drog|e *f* **-,-n** drug. **D~enabhängige(r)** *m/f* drug addict. **D~erie** *f* **-,-n** chemist's shop, (*Amer*) drugstore. **D~ist** *m* **-en,-en** chemist
drohen *vi* (*haben*) threaten (**jdm** s.o.). **d~d** *a* threatening; ⟨*Gefahr*⟩ imminent
dröhnen *vi* (*haben*) resound; (*tönen*) boom
Drohung *f* **-,-en** threat

drollig *a* funny; (*seltsam*) odd
Drops *m* -,- [fruit] drop
Droschke *f* -,-n cab
Drossel *f* -,-n thrush
drosseln *vt* (*Techn*) throttle; (*fig*) cut back
drüb|en *adv* over there. **d~er** *adv* (*fam*) = darüber
Druck[1] *m* -[e]s,¨e pressure; **unter D~setzen** (*fig*) pressurize
Druck[2] *m* -[e]s,-e printing; (*Schrift, Reproduktion*) print. **D~buchstabe** *m* block letter
Drückeberger *m* -s,- shirker
drucken *vt* print
drücken *vt/i* (*haben*) press; (*aus*-) squeeze; ⟨*Schuh:*⟩ pinch; (*umarmen*) hug; (*fig: belasten*) weigh down; **Preise d~** force down prices; (*an Tür*) **d~push**; **sich d~** (*fam*) make oneself scarce; **sich d~ vor** (+ *dat*) (*fam*) shirk. **d~d** *a* heavy; (*schwül*) oppressive
Drucker *m* -s,- printer
Drücker *m* -s,- push-button; (*Tür*-) door knob
Druckerei *f* -,-en printing works
Druck|fehler *m* misprint. **D~knopf** *m* press-stud; (*Drücker*) push-button. **D~luft** *f* compressed air. **D~sache** *f* printed matter. **D~schrift** *f* type; (*Veröffentlichung*) publication; **in D~schrift** in block letters *pl*
drucksen *vi* (*haben*) hum and haw
Druck|stelle *f* bruise. **D~taste** *f* push-button. **D~topf** *m* pressure-cooker
drum *adv* (*fam*) = **darum**
drunter *adv* (*fam*) = **darunter; alles geht d~ und drüber** (*fam*) everything is topsy-turvy
Drüse *f* -,-n (*Anat*) gland
Dschungel *m* -s,- jungle
du *pron* (*familiar address*) you; **auf Du und Du** (**auf du und du**) on familiar terms
Dübel *m* -s,- plug
duck|en *vt* duck; (*fig: demütigen*) humiliate; **sich~en** duck; (*fig*) cringe. **D~mäuser** *m* -s,- moral coward
Dudelsack *m* bagpipes *pl*
Duell *nt* -s,-e duel
Duett *nt* -s,-e [vocal] duet
Duft *m* -[e]s,¨e fragrance, scent; (*Aroma*) aroma. **d~en** *vi* (*haben*) smell (**nach** of). **d~ig** *a* fine; (*zart*) delicate
duld|en *vt* tolerate; (*erleiden*) suffer □ *vi* (*haben*) suffer. **d~sam** *a* tolerant
dumm *a* (**dümmer, dümmst**) stupid, *adv* -ly; (*unklug*) foolish, *adv* -ly; (*fam: lästig*) awkward; **wie d~!** what a nuisance! **der D~e sein** (*fig*) be the loser. **d~erweise** *adv* stupidly; (*leider*) unfortunately. **D~heit** *f* -,-en stupidity; (*Torheit*) foolishness; (*Handlung*) folly. **D~kopf** *m* (*fam*) fool.
dumpf *a* dull, *adv* -y; (*muffig*) musty. **d~ig** *a* musty
Düne *f* -,-n dune
Dung *m* -s manure
Düng|emittel *nt* fertilizer. **d~en** *vt* fertilize. **D~er** *m* -s,- fertilizer
dunk|el *a* dark; (*vage*) vague, *adv* -ly; (*fragwürdig*) shady; **d~les Bier** brown ale; **im D~eln** in the dark
Dünkel *m* -s conceit
dunkel|blau *a* dark blue. **d~braun** *a* dark brown
dünkelhaft *a* conceited
Dunkel|heit *f* - darkness. **D~kammer** *f* dark-room. **d~n** *vi* (*haben*) get dark. **d~rot** *a* dark red
dünn *a* thin, *adv* -ly; ⟨*Buch*⟩ slim; (*spärlich*) sparse; (*schwach*) weak
Dunst *m* -es,¨e mist, haze; (*Dampf*) vapour
dünsten *vt* steam
dunstig *a* misty, hazy
Dünung *f* - swell
Duo *nt* -s,-s [instrumental] duet

Duplikat *nt* **-[e]s,-e** duplicate
Dur *nt* - (*Mus*) major [key]; **in A-Dur** in A major
durch *prep* (+ *acc*) through; (*mittels*) by; **[geteilt] d~** (*Math*) divided by □ *adv* **die Nacht d~** throughout the night; **sechs Uhr d~** (*fam*) gone six o'clock; **d~und d~ nass** wet through
durcharbeiten *vt sep* work through; **sich d~** work one's way through
durchaus *adv* absolutely; **d~nicht** by no means
durchbeißen† *vt sep* bite through
durchblättern *vt sep* leaf through
durchblicken *vi sep* (*haben*) look through; **d~ lassen** (*fig*) hint at
Durchblutung *f* circulation
durchbohren *vt insep* pierce
durchbrechen†[1] *vt/i sep* (*haben*) break [in two]
durchbrechen†[2] *vt insep* break through; break ⟨*Schallmauer*⟩
durchbrennen† *vi sep* (*sein*) burn through; ⟨*Sicherung:*⟩ blow; (*fam: weglaufen*) run away
durchbringen† *vt sep* get through; (*verschwenden*) squander; (*versorgen*) support; **sich d~ mit** make a living by
Durchbruch *m* breakthrough
durchdacht *a* **gut d~** well thought out
durchdrehen *v sep* □ *vt* mince □ *vi* (*haben/sein*) (*fam*) go crazy
durchdringen†[1] *vt insep* penetrate
durchdringen†[2] *vi sep* (*sein*) penetrate; (*sich durchsetzen*) get one's way. **d~d** *a* penetrating; ⟨*Schrei*⟩ piercing
durcheinander *adv* in a muddle; ⟨*Person*⟩ confused; **d~ bringen** muddle [up]; confuse ⟨*Person*⟩; **d~ geraten** get mixed up; **d~ reden** all talk at once. **D~** *nt* **-s** muddle. **d~bringen**† *vt sep* (NEW) **d~ bringen**, *s.* **durcheinander**. **d~geraten**† *vi sep* (*sein*) (NEW) **d~ geraten**, *s.* **durcheinander**. **d~reden** *vi sep* (*haben*) (NEW) **d~ reden**, *s.* **durcheinander**
durchfahren[1] *vi sep* (*sein*) drive through; ⟨*Zug:*⟩ go through
durchfahren†[2] *vt insep* drive/go through; **jdn d~** ⟨*Gedanke:*⟩ flash through s.o.'s mind
Durchfahrt *f* journey/drive through; **auf der D~** passing through; **'D~ verboten'** 'no thoroughfare'
Durchfall *m* diarrhoea; (*fam: Versagen*) flop. **d~en**/ *vi sep* (*sein*) fall through; (*fam: versagen*) flop; (*bei Prüfung*) fail
durchfliegen†[1] *vi sep* (*sein*) fly through; (*fam: durchfallen*) fail
durchfliegen†[2] *vt insep* fly through; (*lesen*) skim through
durchfroren *a* frozen
Durchfuhr *f* - (*Comm*) transit
durchführ|bar *a* feasible. **d~en** *vt sep* carry out
Durchgang *m* passage; (*Sport*) round; **'D~ verboten'** 'no entry'. **D~sverkehr** *m* through traffic
durchgeben† *vt sep* pass through; (*übermitteln*) transmit; (*Radio, TV*) broadcast
durchgebraten *a* **gut d~** well done
durchgehen† *v sep* □ *vi* (*sein*) go through; (*davonlaufen*) run away; ⟨*Pferd:*⟩ bolt; **jdm etw d~ lassen** let s.o. get away with sth □ *vt* go through. **d~d a continuous**, *adv* -ly; **d~d geöffnet** open all day; **d~der Wagen/Zug** through carriage/train
durchgreifen† *vi sep* (*haben*) reach through; (*vorgehen*) take drastic action. **d~d** *a* drastic
durchhalte|n† *v sep* (*fig*) □ *vi* (*haben*) hold out □ *vt* keep up. **D~vermögen** *nt* stamina
durchhängen† *vi sep* (*haben*) sag

durchkommen† *vi sep (sein)* come through; *(gelangen, am Telefon)* get through; *(bestehen)* pass; *(überleben)* pull through; *(finanziell)* get by (**mit** on)

durchkreuzen *vt insep* thwart

durchlassen† *vt sep* let through

durchlässig *a* permeable; *(undicht)* leaky

durchlaufen†[1] *v sep* □ *vi (sein)* run through □ *vt* wear out

durchlaufen†[2] *vt insep* pass through

Durchlauferhitzer *m* **-s,-** geyser

durchleben *vt insep* live through

durchlesen† *vt sep* read through

durchleuchten *vt insep* X-ray

durchlöchert *a* riddled with holes

durchmachen *vt sep* go through; *(erleiden)* undergo; have ⟨*Krankheit*⟩

Durchmesser *m* **-s,-** diameter

durchnässt (durchnäßt) *a* wet through

durchnehmen† *vt sep (Sch)* do

durchnummeriert (durchnumeriert) *a* numbered consecutively

durchpausen *vt sep* trace

durchqueren *vt insep* cross

Durchreiche *f* **-,-n** [serving] hatch. **d~n** *vt sep* pass through

Durchreise *f* journey through; **auf der D~** passing through. **d~n** *vi sep (sein)* pass through

durchreißen† *vt/i sep (sein)* tear

durchs *adv* = **durch das**

Durchsage *f* **-,-n** announcement. **d~n** *vt sep* announce

durchschauen *vt insep (fig)* see through

durchscheinend *a* translucent

Durchschlag *m* carbon copy; *(Culin)* colander. **d~en**[1]† *v sep* □ *vt (Culin)* rub through a sieve; **sich d~en** *(fig)* struggle through □ *vi (sein)* ⟨*Sicherung:*⟩ blow

durchschlagen†[2] *vt insep* smash

durchschlagend *a (fig)* effective; ⟨*Erfolg*⟩ resounding

durchschneiden† *vt sep* cut

Durchschnitt *m* average; **im D~** on average. **d~lich** *a* average □ *adv* on average. **D~s-** *pref* average

Durchschrift *f* carbon copy

durchsehen† *v sep* □ *vi (haben)* see through □ *vt* look through

durchseihen *vt sep* strain

durchsetzen[1] *vt sep* force through; **sich d~** assert oneself; ⟨*Mode:*⟩ catch on

durchsetzen[2] *vt insep* intersperse; *(infiltrieren)* infiltrate

Durchsicht *f* check

durchsichtig *a* transparent

durchsickern *vi sep (sein)* seep through; ⟨*Neuigkeit:*⟩ leak out

durchsprechen† *vt sep* discuss

durchstehen† *vt sep (fig)* come through

durchstreichen† *vt sep* cross out

durchsuch|en *vt insep* search. **D~ung** *f* **-,-en** search

durchtrieben *a* cunning

durchwachsen *a* ⟨*Speck*⟩ streaky; *(fam: gemischt)* mixed

durchwacht *a* sleepless ⟨*Nacht*⟩

durchwählen *vi sep (haben) (Teleph)* dial direct

durchweg *adv* without exception

durchweicht *a* soggy

durchwühlen *vt insep* rummage through; ransack ⟨*Haus*⟩

durchziehen† *v sep* □ *vt* pull through □ *vi (sein)* pass through

durchzucken *vt insep (fig)* shoot through; **jdn d~** ⟨*Gedanke:*⟩ flash through s.o.'s mind

Durchzug *m* through draught

dürfen† *vt & v aux* **etw [tun] d~** be allowed to do sth; **darf ich?** may I? **sie darf es nicht sehen** she must not see it; **ich hätte es nicht tun/sagen d~** I ought not to have done/said it; **das dürfte nicht allzu schwer sein** that should not be too difficult

dürftig *a* poor; ⟨*Mahlzeit*⟩ scanty

dürr *a* dry; ⟨*Boden*⟩ arid; (*mager*) skinny. **D∼e** *f* -,-n drought

Durst *m* -[e]s thirst; **D∼haben** be thirsty. **d∼en** *vi* (*haben*) be thirsty. **d∼ig** *a* thirsty

Dusche *f* -,-n shower. **d∼n** *vi/r* (*haben*) **[sich] d∼n** have a shower

Düse *f* -,-n nozzle. **D∼nflugzeug** *nt* jet

düster *a* gloomy, *adv* -ily; (*dunkel*) dark

Dutzend *nt* -s,-e dozen. **d∼weise** *adv* by the dozen

duzen *vt* **jdn d∼** call s.o. 'du'

Dynam|ik *f* - dynamics *sg*; (*fig*) dynamism. **d∼isch** *a* dynamic; ⟨*Rente*⟩ index-linked

Dynamit *nt* -es dynamite

Dynamo *m* -s,-s dynamo

Dynastie *f* -,-n dynasty

D-Zug /'de:-/ *m* express [train]

E

Ebbe *f* -,-n low tide

eben *a* level; (*glatt*) smooth; **zu e∼er Erde** on the ground floor □ *adv* just; (*genau*) exactly; **e∼ noch** only just; (*gerade vorhin*) just now; **das ist es e∼!** that's just it! **[na] e∼** exactly! **E∼bild** *nt* image. **e∼bürtig** *a* equal; **jdm e∼bürtig sein** be s.o.'s equal

Ebene *f* -,-n (*Geog*) plain; (*Geom*) plane; (*fig: Niveau*) level

eben|falls *adv* also; **danke, e∼falls** thank you, [the] same to you. **E∼holz** *nt* ebony. **e∼mäßig** *a* regular, *adv* -ly. **e∼so** *adv* just the same; (*ebenso sehr*) just as much; **e∼so schön/teuer** just as beautiful/expensive; **e∼so gut** just as good; *adv* just as well; **e∼so sehr** just as much; **e∼so viel** just as much/many; **e∼so wenig** just as little/few; (*noch*) no more. **e∼sogut** *adv* (NEW) **e∼so gut**, *s.* **ebenso**. **e∼sosehr** *adv* (NEW) **e∼so sehr**, *s.* **ebenso**. **e∼soviel** *adv* (NEW) **e∼so viel**, *s.* **ebenso**. **e∼sowenig** *adv* (NEW) **e∼so wenig**, *s.* **ebenso**

Eber *m* -s,- boar. **E∼esche** *f* rowan

ebnen *vt* level; (*fig*) smooth

Echo *nt* -s,-s echo. **e∼en** *vt/i* (*haben*) echo

echt *a* genuine, real; (*authentisch*) authentic; ⟨*Farbe*⟩ fast; (*typisch*) typical □ *adv* (*fam*) really; typically. **E∼heit** *f* - authenticity

Eck|ball *m* (*Sport*) corner. **E∼e** *f* -,-n corner; **um die E∼e bringen** (*fam*) bump off. **e∼ig** *a* angular; ⟨*Klammern*⟩ square; (*unbeholfen*) awkward. **E∼stein** *m* cornerstone. **E∼stoß** *m* = **E∼ball**. **E∼zahn** *m* canine tooth

Ecu, ECU /e'ky:/ *m* -[s],-[s] ecu

edel *a* noble, *adv* -bly; (*wertvoll*) precious; (*fein*) fine. **E∼mann** *m* (*pl* -leute) nobleman. **E∼mut** *m* magnanimity. **e∼mütig** *a* magnanimous, *adv* -ly. **E∼stahl** *m* stainless steel. **E∼stein** *m* precious stone

Efeu *m* -s ivy

Effekt *m* -[e]s,-e effect. **E∼en** *pl* securities. **e∼iv** *a* actual, *adv* -ly; (*wirksam*) effective, *adv* -ly. **e∼voll** *a* effective

EG *f* - *abbr* (**Europäische Gemeinschaft**) EC

egal *a* **das ist mir e∼** (*fam*) it's all the same to me □ *adv* **e∼ wie/wo** no matter how/where. **e∼itär** *a* egalitarian

Egge *f* -,-n harrow

Ego|ismus *m* - selfishness. **E∼ist(in)** *m* -en,-en (*f* -,-nen) egoist. **e∼istisch** *a* selfish, *adv* -ly. **e∼zentrisch** *a* egocentric

eh *adv* (*Aust fam*) anyway; **seit eh und je** from time immemorial

ehe *conj* before; **ehe nicht** until

Ehe *f* -,-n marriage. **E∼bett** *nt* double bed. **E∼bruch** *m* adultery. **E∼frau** *f* wife. **E∼leute** *pl* married couple *sg*. **e~lich** *a* marital; ⟨*Recht*⟩ conjugal; ⟨*Kind*⟩ legitimate

ehemal|ig *a* former. **e~s** *adv* formerly

Ehe|mann *m* (*pl* **-männer**) husband. **E~paar** *nt* married couple

eher *adv* earlier, sooner; (*lieber, vielmehr*) rather; (*mehr*) more

Ehering *m* wedding ring

ehr|bar *a* respectable. **E~e** *f* **-,-n** honour; **jdm E~e machen** do credit to s.o. **e~en** *vt* honour. **e~enamtlich** *a* honorary □ *adv* in an honorary capacity. **E~endoktorat** *nt* honorary doctorate **E~engast** *m* guest of honour. **e~enhaft** *a* honourable, *adv* -bly. **E~enmann** *m* (*pl* **-männer**) man of honour. **E~enmitglied** *nt* honorary member. **e~enrührig** *a* defamatory. **E~enrunde** *f* lap of honour. **E~ensache** *f* point of honour. **e~enwert** *a* honourable. **E~enwort** *nt* word of honour. **e~erbietig** *a* deferential, *adv* -ly. **E~erbietung** *f* - deference. **E~furcht** *f* reverence; (*Scheu*) awe. **e~fürchtig** *a* reverent, *adv* -ly. **E~gefühl** *nt* sense of honour. **E~geiz** *m* ambition. **e~geizig** *a* ambitious. **e~lich** *a* honest, *adv* -ly; **e~lich gesagt** to be honest. **E~lichkeit** *f* - honesty. **e~los** *a* dishonourable. **e~sam** *a* respectable. **e~würdig** *a* venerable; (*als Anrede*) Reverend

Ei *nt* **-[e]s,-er** egg

Eibe *f* **-,-n** yew

Eiche *f* **-,-n** oak. **E~l** *f* **-,-n** acorn. **E~lhäher** *m* **-s,-** jay

eichen *vt* standardize

Eichhörnchen *nt* **-s,-** squirrel

Eid *m* **-[e]s,-e** oath

Eidechse *f* **-,-n** lizard

eidlich *a* sworn □ *adv* on oath

Eidotter *m & nt* egg yolk

Eier|becher *m* egg-cup. **E~kuchen** *m* pancake; (*Omelett*) omelette. **E~schale** *f* eggshell. **E~schnee** *m* beaten egg-white. **E~stock** *m* ovary. **E~uhr** *f* egg-timer

Eifer *m* **-s** eagerness; (*Streben*) zeal. **E~sucht** *f* jealousy. **e~süchtig** *a* jealous, *adv* -ly

eiförmig *a* egg-shaped; (*oval*) oval

eifrig *a* eager, *adv* -ly; (*begeistert*) keen, *adv* -ly

Eigelb *nt* **-[e]s,-e** [egg] yolk

eigen *a* own; (*typisch*) characteristic (*dat* of); (*seltsam*) odd, *adv* -ly; (*genau*) particular. **E~art** *f* peculiarity. **e~artig** *a* peculiar, *adv* -ly; (*seltsam*) odd, **E~brötler** *m* **-s,-** crank. **e~händig** *a* personal, *adv* -ly; ⟨*Unterschrift*⟩ own. **E~heit** *f* **-,-en** peculiarity. **e~mächtig** *a* high-handed; (*unbefugt*) unauthorized □ *adv* high-handedly; without authority. **E~name** *m* proper name. **E~nutz** *m* self-interest. **e~nützig** *a* selfish, *adv* -ly. **e~s** *adv* specially. **E~schaft** *f* **-,-en** quality; (*Phys*) property; (*Merkmal*) characteristic; (*Funktion*) capacity. **E~schaftswort** *nt* (*pl* **-wörter**) adjective. **E~sinn** *m* obstinacy. **e~sinnig** *a* obstinate, *adv* -ly

eigentlich *a* actual, real; (*wahr*) true □ *adv* actually, really; (*streng genommen*) strictly speaking; **wie geht es ihm e~?** by the way, how is he?

Eigen|tor *nt* own goal. **E~tum** *nt* **-s** property. **E~tümer(in)** *m* **-s,-** (*f* **-,-nen**) owner. **e~tümlich** *a* odd, *adv* -ly; (*typisch*) characteristic. **E~tumswohnung** *f* freehold flat. **e~willig** *a* self-willed; ⟨*Stil*⟩ highly individual

eign|en (sich) *vr* be suitable. **E~ung** *f* - suitability

Eil|brief *m* express letter. **E~e** *f* - hurry; **E~e haben** be in a hurry; ⟨*Sache:*⟩ be urgent. **e~en** *vi* (*sein*) hurry □ (*haben*) (*drängen*) be urgent. **e~ends** *adv* hurriedly. **e~ig** *a* hurried, *adv* -ly; (*dringend*) urgent, *adv* -ly; **es e~ig**

haben be in a hurry. **E~zug** *m* semi-fast train

Eimer *m* **-s,-** bucket; (*Abfall-*) bin

ein[1] *adj* one; **e~es Tages/ Abends** one day/evening; **mit jdm in einem Zimmer schlafen** sleep in the same room as s.o. □ *indef art* a, (*vor Vokal*) an; **so ein** such a; **was für ein** (*Frage*) what kind of a? (*Ausruf*) what a!

ein[2] *adv* **ein und aus** in and out; **nicht mehr ein noch aus wissen** (*fam*) be at one's wits' end

einander *pron* one another

einarbeiten *vt sep* train

einäscher|n *vt sep* reduce to ashes; cremate ⟨*Leiche*⟩. **E~ung** *f* **-,-en** cremation

einatmen *vt/i sep* (*haben*) inhale, breathe in

ein|äugig *a* one-eyed. **E~bahnstraße** *f* one-way street

einbalsamieren *vt sep* embalm

Einband *m* binding

Einbau *m* installation; (*Montage*) fitting. **e~en** *vt sep* install; (*montieren*) fit. **E~küche** *f* fitted kitchen

einbegriffen *pred a* included

einberuf|en† *vt sep* convene; (*Mil*) call up, (*Amer*) draft. **E~ung** *f* call-up, (*Amer*) draft

Einbettzimmer *nt* single room

einbeulen *vt sep* dent

einbeziehen† *vt sep* **[mit] e~** include; (*berücksichtigen*) take into account

einbiegen† *vi sep* (*sein*) turn

einbild|en *vt sep* **sich** (*dat*) **etw e~en** imagine sth; **sich** (*dat*) **viel e~en** be conceited. **E~ung** *f* imagination; (*Dünkel*) conceit. **E~ungskraft** *f* imagination

einbläuen *vt sep* **jdm etw e~** (*fam*) drum sth into s.o.

einblenden *vt sep* fade in

einbleuen *vt sep* (NEW) **einbläuen**

Einblick *m* insight

einbrech|en† *vi sep* (*haben/sein*) break in; **bei uns ist eingebrochen worden** we have been burgled □ (*sein*) set in; ⟨*Nacht:*⟩ fall. **E~er** *m* burglar

einbring|en† *vt sep* get in; bring in ⟨*Geld*⟩; **das bringt nichts ein** it's not worth while. **e~lich** *a* profitable

Einbruch *m* burglary; **bei E~ der Nacht** at nightfall

einbürger|n *vt sep* naturalize; **sich e~n** become established. **E~ung** *f* - naturalization

Ein|buße *f* loss (**an** + *dat* of). **e~büßen** *vt sep* lose

einchecken /-tʃɛkən/ *vt/i sep* (*haben*) check in

eindecken (sich) *vr sep* stock up

eindeutig *a* unambiguous; (*deutlich*) clear, *adv* -ly

eindicken *vt sep* (*Culin*) thicken

eindring|en† *vi sep* (*sein*) **e~en in** (+ *acc*) penetrate into; (*mit Gewalt*) force one's/⟨*Wasser:*⟩ its way into; (*Mil*) invade; **auf jdn e~en** (*fig*) press s.o.; (*bittend*) plead with s.o. **e~lich** *a* urgent, *adv* -ly. **E~ling** *m* **-s,-e** intruder

Eindruck *m* impression; **E~ machen** impress (**auf jdn** s.o.)

eindrücken *vt sep* crush

eindrucksvoll *a* impressive

ein|e(r,s) *pron* one; (*jemand*) someone; (*man*) one, you; **e~er von uns** one of us; **es macht e~en müde** it makes you tired

einebnen *vt sep* level

eineiig *a* ⟨*Zwillinge*⟩ identical

eineinhalb *inv a* one and a half; **e~ Stunden** an hour and a half

Einelternfamilie *f* one-parent family

einengen *vt sep* restrict

Einer *m* **-s,-** (*Math*) unit. **e~** *pron s.* **eine(r,s)**. **e~lei** *inv a* □ *attrib a* one kind of; (*eintönig, einheitlich*) the same □ *pred a* (*fam*) immaterial; **es ist mir e~lei** it's all the same to me. **E~lei** *nt* **-s** monotony. **e~seits** *adv* on the one hand

einfach *a* simple, *adv* -ly; ⟨*Essen*⟩ plain; ⟨*Faden, Fahrt, Fahrkarte*⟩ single; **e~er Soldat** private. **E~heit** *f* - simplicity

einfädeln *vt sep* thread; (*fig; arrangieren*) arrange; **sich e~** (*Auto*) filter in

einfahr|en† *v sep* □ *vi* (*sein*) arrive; ⟨*Zug:*⟩ pull in □ *vt* (*Auto*) run in; **die Ernte e~en** get in the harvest. **E~t** *f* arrival; (*Eingang*) entrance, way in; (*Auffahrt*) drive; (*Autobahn-*) access road; **keine E~t** no entry

Einfall *m* idea; (*Mil*) invasion. **e~en**† *vi sep* (*sein*) collapse; (*eindringen*) invade; (*einstimmen*) join in; **jdm e~en** occur to s.o.; **sein Name fällt mir nicht ein** I can't think of his name; **was fällt ihm ein!** what does he think he is doing! **e~sreich** *a* imaginative

Einfalt *f* - naïvety

einfältig *a* simple; (*naiv*) naïve

Einfaltspinsel *m* simpleton

einfangen† *vt sep* catch

einfarbig *a* of one colour; ⟨*Stoff, Kleid*⟩ plain

einfass|en *vt sep* edge; set ⟨*Edelstein*⟩. **E~ung** *f* border, edging

einfetten *vt sep* grease

einfinden† **(sich)** *vr sep* turn up

einfließen† *vi sep* (*sein*) flow in

einflößen *vt sep* **jdm etw e~** give s.o. sips of sth; **jdm Angst e~** (*fig*) frighten s.o.

Einfluss (**Einfluß**) *m* influence. **e~reich** *a* influential

einförmig *a* monotonous, *adv* -ly. **E~keit** *f* - monotony

einfried[ig]|en *vt sep* enclose. **E~ung** *f* -,-**en** enclosure

einfrieren† *vt/i sep* (*sein*) freeze

einfügen *vt sep* insert; (*einschieben*) interpolate; **sich e~** fit in

einfühl|en (sich) *vr sep* empathize (**in** + *acc* with). **e~sam** *a* sensitive

Einfuhr *f* -,-**en** import

einführ|en *vt sep* introduce; (*einstecken*) insert; (*einweisen*) initiate; (*Comm*) import. **e~end** *a* introductory. **E~ung** *f* introduction; (*Einweisung*) initiation

Eingabe *f* petition; (*Computer*) input

Eingang *m* entrance, way in; (*Ankunft*) arrival

eingebaut *a* built-in; ⟨*Schrank*⟩ fitted

eingeben† *vt sep* hand in; (*einflößen*) give (**jdm** s.o.); (*Computer*) feed in

eingebildet *a* imaginary; (*überheblich*) conceited

Eingeborene(r) *m/f* native

Eingebung *f* -,-**en** inspiration

eingedenk *prep* (+ *gen*) mindful of

eingefleischt *a* **e~er Junggeselle** confirmed bachelor

eingehakt *adv* arm in arm

eingehen† *v sep* □ *vi* (*sein*) come in; (*ankommen*) arrive; (*einlaufen*) shrink; (*sterben*) die; ⟨*Zeitung, Firma:*⟩ fold; **auf etw** (*acc*) **e~** go into sth; (*annehmen*) agree to sth □ *vt* enter into; contract ⟨*Ehe*⟩; make ⟨*Wette*⟩; take ⟨*Risiko*⟩. **e~d** *a* detailed; (*gründlich*) thorough, *adv* -ly

eingelegt *a* inlaid; (*Culin*) pickled; (*mariniert*) marinaded

eingemacht *a* (*Culin*) bottled

eingenommen *pred a* (*fig*) taken (**von** with); prejudiced (**gegen** against); **von sich e~** conceited

eingeschneit *a* snowbound

eingeschrieben *a* registered

Einge|ständnis *nt* admission. **e~stehen**† *vt sep* admit

eingetragen *a* registered

Eingeweide *pl* bowels, entrails

eingewöhnen (sich) *vr sep* settle in

eingießen† *vt sep* pour in; (*einschenken*) pour

eingleisig *a* single-track

eingliederln *vt sep* integrate. **E~ung** *f* integration

eingraben† *vt sep* bury

eingravieren *vt sep* engrave

eingreifen† *vi sep (haben)* intervene. **E~** *nt* **-s** intervention

Eingriff *m* intervention; *(Med)* operation

einhaken *vt/r sep* **jdn e~** *od* **sich bei jdm e~** take s.o.'s arm

einhalten† *v sep* □ *vt* keep; *(befolgen)* observe □ *vi (haben)* stop

einhändigen *vt sep* hand in

einhängen *v sep* □ *vt* hang; put down ⟨*Hörer*⟩; **sich bei jdm e~** take s.o.'s arm □ *vi (haben)* hang up

einheimisch *a* local; *(eines Landes)* native; *(Comm)* homeproduced. **E~e(r)** *m/f* local native

Einheit *f* **-,-en** unity; *(Maß-, Mil)* unit. **e~lich** *a* uniform, *adv* -ly; *(vereinheitlicht)* standard. **E~spreis** *m* standard price; *(Fahrpreis)* flat fare

einhellig *a* unanimous, *adv* -ly

einholen *vt sep* catch up with; *(aufholen)* make up for; *(erbitten)* seek; *(einkaufen)* buy; **e~ gehen** go shopping

einhüllen *vt sep* wrap

einhundert *inv a* one hundred

einig *a* united; **[sich** *(dat)***] e~ werden/sein** come to an/be in agreement

einigle(r,s) *pron* some; *(ziemlich viel)* quite a lot of; *(substantivisch)* **e~e** *pl* some; *(mehrere)* several; *(ziemlich viele)* quite a lot; **e~es** *sg* some things; **vor e~er Zeit** some time ago. **e~emal** *adv* (NEW) **e~e Mal**, *s.* **Mal**

einigen *vt* unite; unify ⟨*Land*⟩; **sich e~** come to an agreement; *(ausmachen)* agree (**auf** + *acc* on)

einigermaßen *adv* to some extent; *(ziemlich)* fairly; *(ziemlich gut)* fairly well

Einiglkeit *f* - unity; *(Übereinstimmung)* agreement. **E~ung** *f* - unification; *(Übereinkunft)* agreement

einjährig *a* one-year-old; *(ein Jahr dauernd)* one year's . . .; **e~e Pflanze** annual

einkalkulieren *vt sep* take into account

einkassieren *vt sep* collect

Einkauf *m* purchase; *(Einkaufen)* shopping; **Einkäufe machen** do some shopping. **e~en** *vt sep* buy; **e~en gehen** go shopping. **E~skorb** *m* shopping/*(im Geschäft)* wire basket. **E~stasche** *f* shopping bag. **E~swagen** *m* shopping trolley. **E~szentrum** *nt* shopping centre

einkehren *vi sep (sein)* **[in einem Lokal] e~** stop for a meal/drink [at an inn]

einklammern *vt sep* bracket

Einklang *m* harmony; **in E~ stehen** be in accord (**mit** with)

einkleben *vt sep* stick in

einkleiden *vt sep* fit out

einklemmen *vt sep* clamp; **sich** *(dat)* **den Finger in der Tür e~** catch one's finger in the door

einkochen *v sep* □ *vi (sein)* boil down □ *vt* preserve, bottle

Einkommen *nt* **-s** income. **E~[s]steuer** *f* income tax

einkreisen *vt sep* encircle; **rot e~** ring in red

Einkünfte *pl* income *sg*; *(Einnahmen)* revenue *sg*

einladlen† *vt sep* load; *(auffordern)* invite; *(bezahlen für)* treat. **e~end** *a* inviting. **E~ung** *f* invitation

Einlage *f* enclosure; *(Schuh-)* arch support; *(Zahn-)* temporary filling; *(Programm-)* interlude; *(Comm)* investment; *(Bank-)* deposit; **Suppe mit E~** soup with noodles/dumplings

Einllass *m* **-es** (**Einlaß** *m* **-sses**) admittance. **e~lassen**† *vt sep* let in; run ⟨*Bad, Wasser*⟩; **sich auf**

etw (*acc*)/**mit jdm e~lassen** get involved in sth/with s.o.

einlaufen† *vi sep* (*sein*) come in; (*ankommen*) arrive; ⟨*Wasser*:⟩ run in; (*schrumpfen*) shrink; **[in den Hafen] e~** enter port

einleben (sich) *vr sep* settle in

Einlege|arbeit *f* inlaid work. **e~n** *vt sep* put in; lay in ⟨*Vorrat*⟩; lodge ⟨*Protest, Berufung*⟩; (*einfügen*) insert; (*Auto*) engage ⟨*Gang*⟩; (*verzieren*) inlay; (*Culin*) pickle; (*marinieren*) marinade; **eine Pause e~n** have a break. **E~sohle** *f* insole

einleit|en *vt sep* initiate; (*eröffnen*) begin. **e~end** *a* introductory. **E~ung** *f* introduction

einlenken *vi sep* (*haben*) (*fig*) relent

einleuchten *vi sep* (*haben*) be clear (*dat* to). **e~d** *a* convincing

einliefer|n *vt sep* take (**ins Krankenhaus** to hospital). **E~ung** *f* admission

einlösen *vt sep* cash ⟨*Scheck*⟩; redeem ⟨*Pfand*⟩; (*fig*) keep

einmachen *vt sep* preserve

einmal *adv* once; (*eines Tages*) one *or* some day; **noch/schon e~** again/before; **noch e~ so teuer** twice as expensive; **auf e~** at the same time; (*plötzlich*) suddenly; **nicht e~** not even; **es geht nun e~ nicht** it's just not possible. **E~eins** *nt* - [multiplication] tables *pl*. **e~ig** *a* single; (*einzigartig*) unique; (*fam: großartig*) fantastic, *adv* -ally

einmarschieren *vi sep* (*sein*) march in

einmisch|en (sich) *vr sep* interfere. **E~ung** *f* interference

einmütig *a* unanimous, *adv* -ly

Einnahme *f* -,-**n** taking; (*Mil*) capture; **E~n** *pl* income *sg*; (*Einkünfte*) revenue *sg*; (*Comm*) receipts; (*eines Ladens*) takings

einnehmen† *vt sep* take; have ⟨*Mahlzeit*⟩; (*Mil*) capture; take up ⟨*Platz*⟩; (*fig*) prejudice (**gegen** against); **jdn für sich e~** win s.o. over. **e~d** *a* engaging

einnicken *vi sep* (*sein*) nod off

Einöde *f* wilderness

einordnen *vt sep* put in its proper place; (*klassifizieren*) classify; **sich e~** fit in; (*Auto*) get in lane

einpacken *vt sep* pack; (*einhüllen*) wrap

einparken *vt sep* park

einpauken *vt sep* **jdm etw e~** (*fam*) drum sth into s.o.

einpflanzen *vt sep* plant; implant ⟨*Organ*⟩

einplanen *vt sep* allow for

einpräg|en *vt sep* impress (**jdm** [up]on s.o.); **sich** (*dat*) **etw e~en** memorize sth. **e~sam** *a* easy to remember; ⟨*Melodie*⟩ catchy

einquartieren *vt sep* (*Mil*) billet (**bei** on); **sich in einem Hotel e~** put up at a hotel

einrahmen *vt sep* frame

einrasten *vi sep* (*sein*) engage

einräumen *vt sep* put away; (*zugeben*) admit; (*zugestehen*) grant

einrechnen *vt sep* include

einreden *v sep* □ *vt* **jdm/sich** (*dat*) **etw e~** persuade s.o./oneself of sth □ *vi* (*haben*) **auf jdn e~** talk insistently to s.o.

einreib|en† *vt sep* rub (**mit** with). **E~mittel** *nt* liniment

einreichen *vt sep* submit; **die Scheidung e~** file for divorce

Einreih|er *m* -**s**,- single-breasted suit. **e~ig** *a* single-breasted

Einreise *f* entry. **e~n** *vi sep* (*sein*) enter (**nach Irland** Ireland). **E~visum** *nt* entry visa

einreißen† *v sep* □ *vt* tear; (*abreißen*) pull down □ *vi* (*sein*) tear; ⟨*Sitte*:⟩ become a habit

einrenken *vt sep* (*Med*) set

einricht|en *vt sep* fit out; (*möblieren*) furnish; (*anordnen*) arrange; (*Med*) set ⟨*Bruch*⟩; (*eröffnen*) set up; **sich e~en** furnish one's home; (*sich einschränken*) economize; (*sich *vorbereiten*) prepare (**auf** + *acc* for). **E~ung** *f* furnishing; (*Möbel*) furnishings *pl*; (*Techn*) equipment; (*Vorrichtung*) device; (*Eröffnung*) setting up; (*Institution*) institution; (*Gewohnheit*) practice. **E~ungsgegenstand** *m* piece of equipment/(*Möbelstück*) furniture

einrollen *vt sep* roll up; put in rollers ⟨*Haare*⟩

einrosten *vi sep* (*sein*) rust; (*fig*) get rusty

einrücken *v sep* □ *vi* (*sein*) (*Mil*) be called up; (*einmarschieren*) move in □ *vt* indent

eins *inv a & pron* one; **noch e~** one other thing; **mir ist alles e~** (*fam*) it's all the same to me. **E~** *f* -,-en one; (*Sch*) ≈ A

einsam *a* lonely; (*allein*) solitary; (*abgelegen*) isolated. **E~keit** *f* - loneliness; solitude; isolation

einsammeln *vt sep* collect

Einsatz *m* use; (*Mil*) mission; (*Wett-*) stake; (*E~teil*) insert; **im E~** in action. **e~bereit** *a* ready for action

einschalt|en *vt sep* switch on; (*einschieben*) interpolate; (*fig: beteiligen*) call in; **sich e~en** (*fig*) intervene. **E~quote** *f* (*TV*) viewing figures *pl*; ≈ ratings *pl*

einschärfen *vt sep* **jdm etw e~** impress sth [up]on s.o.

einschätz|en *vt sep* assess; (*bewerten*) rate. **E~ung** *f* assessment; estimation

einschenken *vt sep* pour

einscheren *vi sep* (*sein*) pull in

einschicken *vt sep* send in

einschieben† *vt sep* push in; (*einfügen*) insert; (*fig*) interpolate

einschiff|en (sich) *vr sep* embark. **E~ung** *f* - embarkation

einschlafen† *vi sep* (*sein*) go to sleep; (*aufhören*) peter out

einschläfern *vt sep* lull to sleep; (*betäuben*) put out; (*töten*) put to sleep. **e~d** *a* soporific

Einschlag *m* impact; (*fig: Beimischung*) element. **e~en**† *v sep* □ *vt* knock in; (*zerschlagen*) smash; (*einwickeln*) wrap; (*falten*) turn up; (*drehen*) turn; take ⟨*Weg*⟩; take up ⟨*Laufbahn*⟩ □ *vi* (*haben*) hit/⟨*Blitz:*⟩ strike (**in etw** *acc* sth); (*zustimmen*) shake hands [on a deal]; (*Erfolg haben*) be a hit; **auf jdn e~en** beat s.o.

einschlägig *a* relevant

einschleusen *vt sep* infiltrate

einschließ|en† *vt sep* lock in; (*umgeben*) enclose; (*einkreisen*) surround; (*einbeziehen*) include; **sich e~en** lock oneself in; **Bedienung eingeschlossen** service included. **e~lich** *adv* inclusive □ *prep* (+ *gen*) including

einschmeicheln (sich) *vr sep* ingratiate oneself (**bei** with)

einschnappen *vi sep* (*sein*) click shut; **eingeschnappt sein** (*fam*) be in a huff

einschneiden† *vt/i sep* (*haben*) **[in] etw** *acc* **e~** cut into sth. **e~d** *a* (*fig*) drastic, *adv* -ally

Einschnitt *m* cut; (*Med*) incision; (*Lücke*) gap; (*fig*) decisive event

einschränk|en *vt sep* restrict; (*reduzieren*) cut back; **sich e~en** economize. **E~ung** *f* -,-en restriction; (*Reduzierung*) reduction; (*Vorbehalt*) reservation

Einschreib|[e]brief *m* registered letter. **e~en**† *vt sep* enter; register ⟨*Brief*⟩; **sich e~en** put one's name down; (*sich anmelden*) enrol. **E~en** *nt* registered letter/packet; **als** *od* **per E~en** by registered post

einschreiten† *vi sep* (*sein*) intervene

einschüchter|n *vt sep* intimidate. **E~ung** *f* - intimidation

einsegn|en *vt sep* (*Relig*) confirm. **E~ung** *f* -,-en confirmation

einsehen† *vt sep* inspect; (*lesen*) consult; (*begreifen*) see. **E~** *nt* -s

ein E~ haben show some understanding; (*vernünftig sein*) see reason

einseitig *a* one-sided; (*Pol*) unilateral □ *adv* on one side; (*fig*) one-sidedly; (*Pol*) unilaterally

einsenden† *vt sep* send in

einsetzen *v sep* □ *vt* put in; (*einfügen*) insert; (*verwenden*) use; put on ⟨*Zug*⟩; call out ⟨*Truppen*⟩; (*Mil*) deploy; (*ernennen*) appoint; (*wetten*) stake; (*riskieren*) risk; **sich e~ für** support □ *vi* (*haben*) start; ⟨*Winter, Regen:*⟩ set in

Einsicht *f* insight; (*Verständnis*) understanding; (*Vernunft*) reason; **zur E~ kommen** see reason. **e~ig** *a* understanding; (*vernünftig*) sensible

Einsiedler *m* hermit

einsilbig *a* monosyllabic; ⟨*Person*⟩ taciturn

einsinken† *vi sep* (*sein*) sink in

einspannen *vt sep* harness; **jdn e~** (*fam*) rope s.o. in; **sehr eingespannt** (*fam*) very busy

einsparen *vt sep* save

einsperren *vt sep* shut/(*im Gefängnis*) lock up

einspielen (sich) *vr sep* warm up; **gut aufeinander eingespielt sein** work well together

einsprachig *a* monolingual

einspringen† *vi sep* (*sein*) step in (**für** for)

einspritzen *vt sep* inject

Einspruch *m* objection; **E~ erheben** object; (*Jur*) appeal

einspurig *a* single-track; (*Auto*) single-lane

einst *adv* once; (*Zukunft*) one day

Einstand *m* (*Tennis*) deuce

einstecken *vt sep* put in; post ⟨*Brief*⟩; (*Electr*) plug in; (*fam: behalten*) pocket; (*fam: hinnehmen*) take; suffer ⟨*Niederlage*⟩; **etw e~** put sth in one's pocket

einstehen† *vi sep* (*haben*) **e~ für** vouch for; answer for ⟨*Folgen*⟩

einsteigen† *vi sep* (*sein*) get in; (*in Bus/Zug*) get on

einstell|en *vt sep* put in; (*anstellen*) employ; (*aufhören*) stop; (*regulieren*) adjust, set; (*Optik*) focus; tune ⟨*Motor, Zündung*⟩; tune to ⟨*Sender*⟩; **sich e~en** turn up; (*ankommen*) arrive; (*eintreten*) occur; ⟨*Schwierigkeiten:*⟩ arise; **sich e~en auf** (+ *acc*) adjust to; (*sich vorbereiten*) prepare for. **E~ung** *f* employment; (*Aufhören*) cessation; (*Regulierung*) adjustment; (*Optik*) focusing; (*TV, Auto*) tuning; (*Haltung*) attitude

Einstieg *m* **-[e]s,-e** entrance

einstig *a* former

einstimmen *vi sep* (*haben*) join in

einstimmig *a* unanimous, *adv* -ly. **E~keit** *f* - unanimity

einstöckig *a* single-storey

einstudieren *vt sep* rehearse

einstufen *vt sep* classify

Ein|sturz *m* collapse. **e~stürzen** *vi sep* (*sein*) collapse

einstweil|en *adv* for the time being; (*inzwischen*) meanwhile. **e~ig** *a* temporary

eintasten *vt sep* key in

eintauchen *vt/i sep* (*sein*) dip in; (*heftiger*) plunge in

eintauschen *vt sep* exchange

eintausend *inv a* one thousand

einteil|en *vt sep* divide (**in** + *acc* into); (*Biol*) classify; **sich** (*dat*) **seine Zeit gut e~en** organize one's time well. **e~ig** *a* one piece. **E~ung** *f* division; classification

eintönig *a* monotonous, *adv* -ly. **E~keit** *f* - monotony

Eintopf *m*, **E~gericht** *nt* stew

Ein|tracht *f* - harmony. **e~trächtig** *a* harmonious □ *adv* in harmony

Eintrag *m* **-[e]s,¨e** entry. **e~en**† *vt sep* enter; (*Admin*) register; (*einbringen*) bring in; **sich e~en** put one's name down

einträglich *a* profitable

Eintragung *f* **-,-en** registration; (*Eintrag*) entry
eintreffen† *vi sep* (*sein*) arrive; (*fig*) come true; (*geschehen*) happen. **E~** *nt* **-s** arrival
eintreiben† *vt sep* drive in; (*einziehen*) collect
eintreten† *v sep* □ *vi* (*sein*) enter; (*geschehen*) occur; **in einen Klub e~** join a club; **e~ für** (*fig*) stand up for □ *vt* kick in
Eintritt *m* entrance; (*zu Veranstaltung*) admission; (*Beitritt*) joining; (*Beginn*) beginning. **E~skarte** *f* [admission] ticket
eintrocknen *vi sep* (*sein*) dry up
einüben *vt sep* practise
einundachtzig *inv a* eighty-one
einverleiben *vt sep* incorporate (*dat* into); **sich** (*dat*) **etw e~** (*fam*) consume sth
Einvernehmen *nt* **-s** understanding; (*Übereinstimmung*) agreement; **in bestem E~** on the best of terms
einverstanden *a* **e~ sein** agree
Einverständnis *nt* agreement; (*Zustimmung*) consent
Einwand *m* **-[e]s,¨e** objection
Einwander|er *m* immigrant. **e~n** *vi sep* (*sein*) immigrate. **E~ung** *f* immigration
einwandfrei *a* perfect, *adv* -ly; (*untadelig*) impeccable, *adv* -bly; (*eindeutig*) indisputable, *adv* -bly
einwärts *adv* inwards
einwechseln *vt sep* change
einwecken *vt sep* preserve, bottle
Einweg- *pref* non-returnable; (*Feuerzeug*) throw-away
einweichen *vt sep* soak
einweih|en *vt sep* inaugurate; (*Relig*) consecrate; (*einführen*) initiate; (*fam*) use for the first time; **in ein Geheimnis e~en** let into a secret. **E~ung** *f* **-,-en** inauguration; consecration; initiation
einweisen† *vt sep* direct; (*einführen*) initiate; **ins Krankenhaus e~** send to hospital
einwenden† *vt sep* **etwas e~** object (**gegen** to); **dagegen hätte ich nichts einzuwenden** (*fam*) I wouldn't say no
einwerfen† *vt sep* insert; post (*Brief*); (*Sport*) throw in; (*vorbringen*) interject; (*zertrümmern*) smash
einwickeln *vt sep* wrap [up]
einwillig|en *vi sep* (*haben*) consent, agree (**in** + *acc* to). **E~ung** *f* - consent
einwirken *vi sep* (*haben*) **e~ auf** (+ *acc*) have an effect on; (*beeinflussen*) influence
Einwohner|(in) *m* **-s,-** (*f* **-,-nen**) inhabitant. **E~zahl** *f* population
Einwurf *m* interjection; (*Einwand*) objection; (*Sport*) throw-in; (*Münz-*) slot
Einzahl *f* (*Gram*) singular
einzahl|en *vt sep* pay in. **E~ung** *f* payment; (*Einlage*) deposit
einzäunen *vt sep* fence in
Einzel *nt* **-s,-** (*Tennis*) singles *pl*. **E~bett** *nt* single bed. **E~fall** *m* individual/(*Sonderfall*) isolated case. **E~gänger** *m* **-s,-** loner. **E~haft** *f* solitary confinement. **E~handel** *m* retail trade. **E~händler** *m* retailer. **E~haus** *nt* detached house. **E~heit** *f* **-,-en** detail. **E~karte** *f* single ticket. **E~kind** *nt* only child
einzeln *a* single, *adv* -gly; (*individuell*) individual, *adv* -ly; (*gesondert*) separate, *adv* -ly; odd (*Handschuh, Socken*); **e~e Fälle** some cases. **E~e(r,s)** (**e~e(r,s)**) *pron* **der/die E~e** (**e~e**) the individual; **ein E~er** (**e~er**) a single one; (*Person*) one individual; **jeder E~e** (**e~e**) every single one; (*Person*) each individual; **E~e** (**e~e**) *pl* some; **im E~en** (**e~en**) in detail; **ins E~e** (**e~e**) **gehen** go into detail
Einzel|person *f* single person. **E~teil** *nt* [component] part. **E~zimmer** *nt* single room

einziehen† *v sep* □ *vt* pull in; draw in ⟨*Atem, Krallen*⟩; (*Zool, Techn*) retract; indent ⟨*Zeile*⟩; (*aus dem Verkehr ziehen*) withdraw; (*beschlagnahmen*) confiscate; (*eintreiben*) collect; make ⟨*Erkundigungen*⟩; (*Mil*) call up; (*einfügen*) insert; (*einbauen*) put in; **den Kopf e~** duck [one's head] □ *vi* (*sein*) enter; (*umziehen*) move in; (*eindringen*) penetrate

einzig *a* only; (*einmalig*) unique; **eine/keine e~e Frage** a/not a single question; **ein e~es Mal** only once □ *adv* only; **e~ und allein** solely. **e~artig** *a* unique; (*unvergleichlich*) unparalleled. **E~e(r,s) (e~e(r,s))** *pron* **der/die/das E~e (e~e)** the only one; **ein/kein E~er (e~er)** a/not a single one; **das E~e (e~e), was mich stört** the only thing that bothers me

Einzug *m* entry; (*Umzug*) move (**in** + *acc* into). **E~sgebiet** *nt* catchment area

Eis *nt* **-es** ice; (*Speise-*) ice-cream; **Eis am Stiel** ice lolly; **Eis laufen** skate. **E~bahn** *f* ice rink. **E~bär** *m* polar bear. **E~becher** *m* ice-cream sundae. **E~bein** *nt* (*Culin*) knuckle of pork. **E~berg** *m* iceberg. **E~diele** *f* ice-cream parlour

Eisen *nt* **-s,-** iron. **E~bahn** *f* railway. **E~bahner** *m* **-s,-** railwayman

eisern *a* iron; (*fest*) resolute, *adv* -ly; **e~er Vorhang** (*Theat*) safety curtain; (*Pol*) Iron Curtain

Eis|fach *nt* freezer compartment. **e~gekühlt** *a* chilled. **e~ig** *a* icy. **E~kaffee** *m* iced coffee. **e~kalt** *a* ice cold; (*fig*) icy, *adv* -ily. **E~kunstlauf** *m* figure skating. **E~lauf** *m* skating. **e~laufen**† *vi sep* (*sein*) (NEW) **Eis laufen**, *s.* **Eis**. **E~läufer(in)** *m(f)* skater. **E~pickel** *m* ice-axe. **E~scholle** *f* ice-floe. **E~schrank** *m* refrigerator. **E~vogel** *m* kingfisher. **E~würfel** *m* icecube. **E~zapfen** *m* icicle. **E~zeit** *f* ice age

eitel *a* vain; (*rein*) pure. **E~keit** *f* - vanity

Eiter *m* **-s** pus. **e~n** *vi* (*haben*) discharge pus

Eiweiß *nt* **-es,-e** egg-white; (*Chem*) protein

Ekel[1] *m* **-s** disgust; (*Widerwille*) revulsion

Ekel[2] *nt* **-s,-** (*fam*) beast

ekel|erregend *a* nauseating. **e~haft** *a* nauseating; (*widerlich*) repulsive. **e~n** *vt/i* (*haben*) **mich** *od* **mir e~t [es] davor** it makes me feel sick □ *vr* **sich e~n vor** (+ *dat*) find repulsive

eklig *a* disgusting, repulsive

Eksta|se *f* - ecstasy. **e~tisch** *a* ecstatic, *adv* -ally

Ekzem *nt* **-s,-e** eczema

elasti|sch *a* elastic; (*federnd*) springy; (*fig*) flexible. **E~zität** *f* - elasticity; flexibility

Elch *m* **-[e]s,-e** elk

Elefant *m* **-en,-en** elephant

elegan|t *a* elegant, *adv* -ly. **E~z** *f* - elegance

elektrifizieren *vt* electrify

Elektri|ker *m* **-s,-** electrician. **e~sch** *a* electric, *adv* -ally

elektrisieren *vt* electrify; **sich e~** get an electric shock

Elektrizität *f* - electricity. **E~swerk** *nt* power station

Elektr|oartikel *mpl* electrical appliances. **E~ode** *f* **-,-n** electrode. **E~oherd** *m* electric cooker. **E~on** *nt* **-s,-en** /-'tro:nən/ electron. **E~onik** *f* - electronics *sg*. **e~onisch** *a* electronic

Element *nt* **-[e]s,-e** element; (*Anbau-*) unit. **e~ar** *a* elementary

Elend *nt* **-s** misery; (*Armut*) poverty. **e~** *a* miserable, *adv* -bly, wretched, *adv* -ly; (*krank*) poorly; (*gemein*) contemptible; (*fam:*

schrecklich) dreadful, *adv* -ly. **E~sviertel** *nt* slum
elf *inv a*, **E~** *f* -,-en eleven
Elfe *f* -,-n fairy
Elfenbein *nt* ivory
Elfmeter *m* (*Fußball*) penalty
elfte(r,s) *a* eleventh
eliminieren *vt* eliminate
Elite *f* -,-n élite
Elixier *nt* -s,-e elixir
Ell[en]bogen *m* elbow
Ellip|se *f* -,-n ellipse. **e~tisch** *a* elliptical
Elsass (Elsaß) *nt* - Alsace
elsässisch *a* Alsatian
Elster *f* -,-n magpie
elter|lich *a* parental. **E~n** *pl* parents. **E~nhaus** *nt* [parental] home. **e~nlos** *a* orphaned. **E~nteil** *m* parent
Email /e'maj/ *nt* -s,-s, **E~le** /e'maljə/ *f* -,-n enamel. **e~lieren** /ema[l]'ji:rən/ *vt* enamel
Emanzi|pation /-'tsi̯o:n/ *f* - emancipation. **e~piert** *a* emancipated
Embargo *nt* -s,-s embargo
Emblem *nt* -s,-e emblem
Embryo *m* -s,-s embryo
Emigr|ant(in) *m* -en,-en (*f* -,-nen) emigrant. **E~ation** /-'tsi̯o:n/ *f* - emigration. **e~ieren** *vi* (*sein*) emigrate
eminent *a* eminent, *adv* -ly
Emission *f* -,-en emission; (*Comm*) issue
Emotion /-'tsi̯o:n/ *f* -,-en emotion. **e~al** *a* emotional
Empfang *m* -[e]s,¨e reception; (*Erhalt*) receipt; **in E~ nehmen** receive; (*annehmen*) accept. **e~en**† *vt* receive; (*Biol*) conceive
Empfäng|er *m* -s,- recipient; (*Post-*) addressee; (*Zahlungs-*) payee; (*Radio, TV*) receiver. **e~lich** *a* receptive/(*Med*) susceptible (**für** to). **E~nis** *f* - (*Biol*) conception
Empfängnisverhütung *f* contraception. **E~smittel** *nt* contraceptive
Empfangs|bestätigung *f* receipt. **E~chef** *m* reception manager. **E~dame** *f* receptionist. **E~halle** *f* [hotel] foyer
empfehl|en† *vt* recommend; **sich e~en** be advisable; (*verabschieden*) take one's leave. **e~enswert** *a* to be recommended; (*ratsam*) advisable. **E~ung** *f* -,-en recommendation; (*Gruß*) regards *pl*
empfind|en† *vt* feel. **e~lich** *a* sensitive (**gegen** to); (*zart*) delicate; (*wund*) tender; (*reizbar*) touchy; (*hart*) severe, *adv* -ly. **E~lichkeit** *f* - sensitivity; delicacy; tenderness; touchiness. **e~sam** *a* sensitive; (*sentimental*) sentimental. **E~ung** *f* -,-en sensation; (*Regung*) feeling
emphatisch *a* emphatic, *adv* -ally
empor *adv* (*liter*) up[wards]
empören *vt* incense; **sich e~** be indignant; (*sich auflehnen*) rebel. **e~d** *a* outrageous
Empor|kömmling *m* -s,-e upstart. **e~ragen** *vi sep* (*haben*) rise [up]
empör|t *a* indignant, *adv* -ly. **E~ung** *f* - indignation; (*Auflehnung*) rebellion
emsig *a* busy, *adv* -ily
Ende *nt* -s,-n end; (*eines Films, Romans*) ending; (*fam: Stück*) bit; **E~ Mai** at the end of May; **zu E~sein/gehen** be finished/come to an end; **etw zu E~ schreiben** finish writing sth; **am E~** at the end; (*schließlich*) in the end; (*fam: vielleicht*) perhaps; (*fam: erschöpft*) at the end of one's tether
end|en *vi* (*haben*) end. **e~gültig** *a* final, *adv* -ly; (*bestimmt*) definite, *adv* -ly
Endivie /-i̯ə/ *f* -,-n endive
end|lich *adv* at last, finally; (*schließlich*) in the end. **e~los** *a* endless, *adv* -ly. **E~resultat** *nt* final result. **E~spiel** *nt* final. **E~spurt** *m* -[e]s final

spurt. **E~station** *f* terminus. **E~ung** *f* -,-en (*Gram*) ending

Energie *f* - energy

energisch *a* resolute, *adv* -ly; (*nachdrücklich*) vigorous, *adv* -ly; **e~werden** put one's foot down

eng *a* narrow; (*beengt*) cramped; (*anliegend*) tight; (*nah*) close, *adv* -ly; **e~ anliegend** tight-fitting

Enga|gement /ãgaʒə'mã:/ *nt* **-s,-s** (*Theat*) engagement; (*fig*) commitment. **e~gieren** /-'ʒi:rən/ *vt* (*Theat*) engage; **sich e~gieren** become involved; **e~giert** committed

eng|anliegend *a* (NEW) **e~ anliegend**, *s.* **eng. E~e** *f* - narrowness; **in die E~e treiben** (*fig*) drive into a corner

Engel *m* **-s,-** angel. **e~haft** *a* angelic

engherzig *a* petty

England *nt* **-s** England

Engländer *m* **-s,-** Englishman; (*Techn*) monkey-wrench; **die E~** the English *pl*. **E~in** *f* **-,-nen** Englishwoman

englisch *a* English; **auf e~** (NEW) **auf E~**, *s.* **Englisch. E~** *nt* **-[s]** (*Lang*) English; **auf E~** in English

Engpass (**Engpaß**) *m* (*fig*) bottleneck

en gros /ã'gro:/ *adv* wholesale

engstirnig *a* (*fig*) narrowminded

Enkel *m* **-s,-** grandson; **E~** *pl* grandchildren. **E~in** *f* **-,-nen** granddaughter. **E~kind** *nt* grandchild. **E~sohn** *m* grandson. **E~tochter** *f* granddaughter

enorm *a* enormous, *adv* -ly; (*fam: großartig*) fantastic

Ensemble /ã'sã:bəl/ *nt* **-s,-s** ensemble; (*Theat*) company

entart|en *vi* (*sein*) degenerate. **e~et** *a* degenerate

entbehr|en *vt* do without; (*vermissen*) miss. **e~lich** *a* dispensable; (*überflüssig*) superfluous. **E~ung** *f* **-,-en** privation

entbind|en† *vt* release (**von** from); (*Med*) deliver (**von** of) □ *vi* (*haben*) give birth. **E~ung** *f* delivery. **E~ungsstation** *f* maternity ward

entblöß|en *vt* bare. **e~t** *a* bare

entdeck|en *vt* discover. **E~er** *m* **-s,-** discoverer; (*Forscher*) explorer. **E~ung** *f* **-,-en** discovery

Ente *f* **-,-n** duck

entehren *vt* dishonour

enteignen *vt* dispossess; expropriate ⟨*Eigentum*⟩

enterben *vt* disinherit

Enterich *m* **-s,-e** drake

entfachen *vt* kindle

entfallen† *vi* (*sein*) not apply; **jdm e~** slip from s.o.'s hand; (*aus dem Gedächtnis*) slip s.o.'s mind; **auf jdn e~** be s.o.'s share

entfalt|en *vt* unfold; (*entwickeln*) develop; (*zeigen*) display; **sich e~en** unfold; develop. **E~ung** *f* - development

entfern|en *vt* remove; **sich e~en** leave. **e~t** *a* distant; (*schwach*) vague, *adv* -ly; **2 Kilometer e~t** 2 kilometres away; **e~t verwandt** distantly related; **nicht im E~testen** (**e~testen**) not in the least. **E~ung** *f* **-,-en** removal; (*Abstand*) distance; (*Reichweite*) range. **E~ungsmesser** *m* rangefinder

entfesseln *vt* (*fig*) unleash

entfliehen† *vi* (*sein*) escape

entfremd|en *vt* alienate. **E~ung** *f* - alienation

entfrosten *vt* defrost

entführ|en *vt* abduct, kidnap; hijack ⟨*Flugzeug*⟩. **E~er** *m* abductor, kidnapper; hijacker. **E~ung** *f* abduction, kidnapping; hijacking

entgegen *adv* towards □ *prep* (+ *dat*) contrary to. **e~gehen**† *vi sep* (*sein*) (+ *dat*) go to meet; (*fig*) be heading for. **e~gesetzt** *a* opposite; (*gegensätzlich*) opposing. **e~halten**† *vt sep* (*fig*) object. **e~kommen**† *vi sep* (*sein*) (+ *dat*) come to meet; (*zukommen auf*) come towards; (*fig*) oblige. **E~kommen** *nt* **-s** helpfulness; (*Zugeständnis*) concession. **e~kommend** *a* approaching; ⟨*Verkehr*⟩ oncoming; (*fig*) obliging. **e~nehmen†** *vt sep* accept. **e~sehen†** *vi sep* (*haben*) (+ *dat*) (*fig*) await; (*freudig*) look forward to. **e~setzen** *vt sep* **Widerstand e~setzen** (+ *dat*) resist. **e~treten†** *vi sep* (*sein*) (+ *dat*) (*fig*) confront; (*bekämpfen*) fight. **e~wirken** *vi sep* (*haben*) (+ *dat*) counteract; (*fig*) oppose

entgegn|en *vt* reply (**auf** + *acc* to). **E~ung** *f* **-,-en** reply

entgehen† *vi sep* (*sein*) (+ *dat*) escape; **jdm e~** (*unbemerkt bleiben*) escape s.o.'s notice; **sich** (*dat*) **etw e~ lassen** miss sth

entgeistert *a* flabbergasted

Entgelt *nt* **-[e]s** payment; **gegen E~** for money. **e~en** *vt* **jdn etw e~en lassen** (*fig*) make s.o. pay for sth

entgleis|en *vi* (*sein*) be derailed; (*fig*) make a gaffe. **E~ung** *f* **-,-en** derailment; (*fig*) gaffe

entgleiten† *vi* (*sein*) **jdm e~** slip from s.o.'s grasp

entgräten *vt* fillet, bone

Enthaarungsmittel *nt* depilatory

enthalt|en† *vt* contain; **in etw** (*dat*) **e~en sein** be contained/ (*eingeschlossen*) included in sth; **sich der Stimme e~en** (*Pol*) abstain. **e~sam** *a* abstemious. **E~samkeit** *f* - abstinence. **E~ung** *f* (*Pol*) abstention

enthaupten *vt* behead

entheben† *vt* **jdn seines Amtes e~** relieve s.o. of his post

enthüll|en *vt* unveil; (*fig*) reveal. **E~ung** *f* **-,-en** revelation

Enthusias|mus *m* - enthusiast. **E~t** *m* **-en,-en** enthusiast. **e~tisch** *a* enthusiastic, *adv* -ally

entkernen *vt* stone; core ⟨*Apfel*⟩

entkleid|en *vt* undress; **sich e~en** undress. **E~ungsnummer** *f* strip-tease [act]

entkommen† *vi* (*sein*) escape

entkorken *vt* uncork

entkräft|en *vt* weaken; (*fig*) invalidate. **E~ung** *f* - debility

entkrampfen *vt* relax; **sich e~** relax

entladen† *vt* unload; (*Electr*) discharge; **sich e~** discharge; ⟨*Gewitter:*⟩ break; ⟨*Zorn:*⟩ explode

entlang *adv & prep* (+ *preceding acc or following dat*) along; **die Straße e~, e~ der Straße** along the road; **an etw** (*dat*) **e~** along sth. **e~fahren†** *vi sep* (*sein*) drive along. **e~gehen†** *vi sep* (*sein*) walk along

entlarven *vt* unmask

entlass|en† *vt* dismiss; (*aus Krankenhaus*) discharge; (*aus der Haft*) release; **aus der Schule e~en werden** leave school. **E~ung** *f* **-,-en** dismissal; discharge; release

entlast|en *vt* relieve the strain on; ease ⟨*Gewissen, Verkehr*⟩; relieve (**von** of); (*Jur*) exonerate. **E~ung** *f* - relief; exoneration. **E~ungszug** *m* relief train

entlaufen† *vi* (*sein*) run away

entledigen (sich) *vr* (+ *gen*) rid oneself of; (*ausziehen*) take off; (*erfüllen*) discharge

entleeren *vt* empty

entlegen *a* remote

entleihen† *vt* borrow (**von** from)

entlocken *vt* coax (*dat* from)

entlohnen *vt* pay

entlüft|en *vt* ventilate. **E~er** *m* **-s,-** extractor fan. **E~ung** *f* ventilation

entmündigen *vt* declare incapable of managing his own affairs

entmutigen *vt* discourage

entnehmen† *vt* take (*dat* from); (*schließen*) gather (*dat* from)

Entomologie *f* - entomology

entpuppen (sich) *vr* (*fig*) turn out (**als etw** to be sth)
entrahmt *a* skimmed
entreißen† *vt* snatch (*dat* from)
entrichten *vt* pay
entrinnen† *vi* (*sein*) escape
entrollen *vt* unroll; unfurl ⟨*Fahne*⟩; **sich e~** unroll; unfurl
entrüst|en *vt* fill with indignation; **sich e~en** be indignant (**über** + *acc* at). **e~et** *a* indignant, *adv* -ly. **E~ung** *f* - indignation
entsaft|en *vt* extract the juice from. **E~er** *m* **-s,-** juice extractor
entsag|en *vi* (*haben*) (+ *dat*) renounce. **E~ung** *f* - renunciation
entschädig|en *vt* compensate. **E~ung** *f* **-,-en** compensation
entschärfen *vt* defuse
entscheid|en† *vt/i* (*haben*) decide; **sich e~en** decide; ⟨*Sache:*⟩ be decided. **e~end** *a* decisive, *adv* -ly; (*kritisch*) crucial. **E~ung** *f* decision
entschieden *a* decided, *adv* -ly; (*fest*) firm, *adv* -ly
entschlafen† *vi* (*sein*) (*liter*) pass away
entschließen† **(sich)** *vr* decide, make up one's mind; **sich anders e~** change one's mind
entschlossen *a* determined; (*energisch*) resolute, *adv* -ly, **kurz e~** without hesitation; (*spontan*) on the spur of the moment. **E~heit** *f* - determination
Entschluss (**Entschluß**) *m* decision; **einen E~ fassen** make a decision
entschlüsseln *vt* decode
entschuld|bar *a* excusable. **e~igen** *vt* excuse; **sich e~igen** apologize (**bei** to); **e~igen Sie [bitte]!** sorry! (*bei Frage*) excuse me. **E~igung** *f* **-,-en** apology; (*Ausrede*) excuse; **[jdn] um E~igung bitten** apologize [to s.o.]; **E~igung!** sorry! (*bei Frage*) excuse me
entsetz|en *vt* horrify. **E~en** *nt* **-s** horror. **e~lich** *a* horrible, *adv* -bly, (*schrecklich*) terrible, *adv* -bly. **e~t** *a* horrified
entsinnen† **(sich)** *vr* (+ *gen*) remember
Entsorgung *f* - waste disposal
entspann|en *vt* relax; **sich e~en** relax; ⟨*Lage:*⟩ ease. **E~ung** *f* - relaxation; easing; (*Pol*) détente
entsprech|en† *vi* (*haben*) (+ *dat*) correspond to; (*übereinstimmen*) agree with; (*nachkommen*) comply with. **e~end** *a* corresponding; (*angemessen*) appropriate; (*zuständig*) relevant □ *adv* correspondingly; appropriately; (*demgemäß*) accordingly □ *prep* (+ *dat*) in accordance with. **E~ung** *f* **-,-en** equivalent
entspringen† *vi* (*sein*) ⟨*Fluss:*⟩ rise; (*fig*) arise, spring (*dat* from); (*entfliehen*) escape
entstammen *vi* (*sein*) come/(*abstammen*) be descended (*dat* from)
entsteh|en† *vi* (*sein*) come into being; (*sich bilden*) form; (*sich entwickeln*) develop; ⟨*Brand:*⟩ start; (*stammen*) originate/(*sich ergeben*) result (**aus** from). **E~ung** *f* - origin; formation; development; (*fig*) birth
entsteinen *vt* stone
entstell|en *vt* disfigure; (*verzerren*) distort. **E~ung** *f* disfigurement; distortion
entstört *a* (*Electr*) suppressed
enttäusch|en *vt* disappoint. **E~ung** *f* disappointment
entvölkern *vt* depopulate
entwaffnen *vt* disarm. **e~d** *a* (*fig*) disarming
Entwarnung *f* all-clear [signal]
entwässer|n *vt* drain. **E~ung** *f* - drainage
entweder *conj & adv* either
entweichen† *vi* (*sein*) escape
entweih|en *vt* desecrate. **E~ung** *f* - desecration

entwenden *vt* steal (*dat* from)
entwerfen† *vt* design; (*aufsetzen*) draft; (*skizzieren*) sketch
entwert|en *vt* devalue; (*ungültig machen*) cancel. **E~er** *m* **-s,-** ticket-cancelling machine. **E~ung** *f* devaluation; cancelling
entwick|eln *vt* develop; **sich e~eln** develop. **E~lung** *f* **-,-en** development; (*Biol*) evolution. **E~lungsland** *nt* developing country
entwinden† *vt* wrench (*dat* from)
entwirren *vt* disentangle; (*fig*) unravel
entwischen *vi* (*sein*) **jdm e~** (*fam*) give s.o. the slip
entwöhnen *vt* wean (*gen* from); cure ⟨*Süchtige*⟩
entwürdigend *a* degrading
Entwurf *m* design; (*Konzept*) draft; (*Skizze*) sketch
entwurzeln *vt* uproot
entzie|hen† *vt* take away (*dat* from); **jdm den Führerschein e~hen** disqualify s.o. from driving; **sich e~hen** (+ *dat*) withdraw from; (*entgehen*) evade. **E~hungskur** *f* treatment for drug/alcohol addiction
entziffern *vt* decipher
entzücken *vt* delight. **E~** *nt* **-s** delight. **e~d** *a* delightful
Entzug *m* withdrawal; (*Vorenthaltung*) deprivation. **E~serscheinungen** *fpl* withdrawal symptoms
entzünd|en *vt* ignite; (*anstecken*) light; (*fig: erregen*) inflame; **sich e~en** ignite; (*Med*) become inflamed. **e~et** *a* (*Med*) inflamed. **e~lich** *a* inflammable. **E~ung** *f* (*Med*) inflammation
entzwei *a* broken. **e~en (sich)** *vr* quarrel. **e~gehen**† *vi sep* (*sein*) break
Enzian *m* **-s,-e** gentian
Enzyklo|pädie *f* **-,-en** encyclopaedia. **e~pädisch** *a* encyclopaedic
Enzym *nt* **-s,-e** enzyme
Epidemie *f* **-,-n** epidemic
Epi|lepsie *f* **-** epilepsy. **E~leptiker(in)** *m* **-s,-** (*f* **-,-nen**) epileptic. **e~leptisch** *a* epileptic
Epilog *m* **-s,-e** epilogue
episch *a* epic
Episode *f* **-,-n** episode
Epitaph *nt* **-s,-e** epitaph
Epoche *f* **-,-n** epoch. **e~machend** *a* epoch-making
Epos *nt* **-/Epen** epic
er *pron* he; (*Ding, Tier*) it
erachten *vt* consider **(für nötig** necessary). **E~** *nt* **-s meines E~s** in my opinion
erbarmen (sich) *vr* have pity/ ⟨*Gott:*⟩ mercy (*gen* on). **E~** *nt* **-s** pity; mercy
erbärmlich *a* wretched, *adv* -ly (*stark*) terrible, *adv* -bly
erbarmungslos *a* merciless, *adv* -ly
erbau|en *vt* build; (*fig*) edify; **sich e~en** be edified **(an** + *dat* by); **nicht e~t von** (*fam*) not pleased about. **e~lich** *a* edifying
Erbe[1] *m* **-n,-n** heir
Erbe[2] *nt* **-s** inheritance; (*fig*) heritage. **e~n** *vt* inherit
erbeuten *vt* get; (*Mil*) capture
Erbfolge *f* (*Jur*) succession
erbieten† **(sich)** *vr* offer **(zu** to)
Erbin *f* **-,-nen** heiress
erbitten† *vt* ask for
erbittert *a* bitter; (*heftig*) fierce, *adv* -ly
erblassen *vi* (*sein*) turn pale
erblich *a* hereditary
erblicken *vt* catch sight of
erblinden *vi* (*sein*) go blind
erbost *a* angry, *adv* -ily
erbrechen† *vt* vomit □ *vi/r* **[sich] e~** vomit. **E~** *nt* **-s** vomiting
Erbschaft *f* **-,-en** inheritance
Erbse *f* **-,-n** pea
Erb|stück *nt* heirloom. **E~teil** *nt* inheritance

Erd|apfel *m* (*Aust*) potato. **E~beben** *nt* **-s,-** earthquake. **E~beere** *f* strawberry. **E~boden** *m* ground

Erde *f* **-,-n** earth; (*Erdboden*) ground; (*Fußboden*) floor; **auf der E~** on earth; (*auf dem Boden*) on the ground/floor. **e~n** *vt* (*Electr*) earth

erdenklich *a* imaginable

Erd|gas *nt* natural gas. **E~geschoss (E~geschoß)** *nt* ground floor, (*Amer*) first floor. **e~ig** *a* earthy. **E~kugel** *f* globe. **E~kunde** *f* geography. **E~nuss (E~nuß)** *f* peanut. **E~öl** *nt* [mineral] oil. **E~reich** *nt* soil

erdreisten (sich) *vr* have the audacity (**zu** to)

erdrosseln *vt* strangle

erdrücken *vt* crush to death. **e~d** *a* (*fig*) overwhelming

Erd|rutsch *m* landslide. **E~teil** *m* continent

erdulden *vt* endure

ereifern (sich) *vr* get worked up

ereignen (sich) *vr* happen

Ereignis *nt* **-ses,-se** event. **e~los** *a* uneventful. **e~reich** *a* eventful

Eremit *m* **-en,-en** hermit

ererbt *a* inherited

erfahr|en† *vt* learn, hear; (*erleben*) experience □ *a* experienced. **E~ung** *f* **-,-en** experience; **in E~ung bringen** find out

erfassen *vt* seize; (*begreifen*) grasp; (*einbeziehen*) include; (*aufzeichnen*) record; **von einem Auto erfasst werden** be struck by a car

erfind|en† *vt* invent. **E~er** *m* **-s,-** inventor. **e~erisch** *a* inventive. **E~ung** *f* **-,-en** invention

Erfolg *m* **-[e]s,-e** success; (*Folge*) result; **E~ haben** be successful; **E~ versprechend** promising. **e~en** *vi* (*sein*) take place; (*geschehen*) happen. **e~los** *a* unsuccessful, *adv* -ly. **e~reich** *a* successful, *adv* -ly. **e~versprechend** *a* (NEW) **E~ versprechend**, *s.* **Erfolg**

erforder|lich *a* required, necessary. **e~n** *vt* require, demand. **E~nis** *nt* **-ses,-se** requirement

erforsch|en *vt* explore; (*untersuchen*) investigate. **E~ung** *f* exploration; investigation

erfreu|en *vt* please; **sich guter Gesundheit e~en** enjoy good health. **e~lich** *a* pleasing, gratifying; (*willkommen*) welcome. **e~licherweise** *adv* happily. **e~t** *a* pleased

erfrier|en† *vi* (*sein*) freeze to death; ⟨*Glied:*⟩ become frostbitten; ⟨*Pflanze:*⟩ be killed by the frost. **E~ung** *f* **-,-en** frostbite

erfrisch|en *vt* refresh; **sich e~en** refresh onself. **e~end** *a* refreshing. **E~ung** *f* **-,-en** refreshment

erfüll|en *vt* fill; (*nachkommen*) fulfil; serve ⟨*Zweck*⟩; discharge ⟨*Pflicht:*⟩ **sich e~en** come true. **E~ung** *f* fulfilment; **in E~ung gehen** come true

erfunden invented; (*fiktiv*) fictitious

ergänz|en *vt* complement; (*nachtragen*) supplement; (*auffüllen*) replenish; (*vervollständigen*) complete; (*hinzufügen*) add; **sich e~en** complement each other. **E~ung** *f* complement; supplement; (*Zusatz*) addition. **E~ungsband** *m* supplement

ergeb|en† *vt* produce; (*zeigen*) show, establish; **sich e~en** result; ⟨*Schwierigkeit:*⟩ arise; (*kapitulieren*) surrender; (*sich fügen*) submit; **es ergab sich** it turned out (**dass** that) □ *a* devoted, *adv* -ly; (*resigniert*) resigned, *adv* -ly. **E~enheit** *f* - devotion

Ergebnis *nt* **-ses,-se** result. **e~los** *a* fruitless, *adv* -ly

ergehen† *vi* (*sein*) be issued; **etw über sich** (*acc*) **e~ lassen** submit to sth; **wie ist es dir ergangen?**

how did you get on? □ *vr* **sich e∼in** (+ *dat*) indulge in
ergiebig *a* productive; (*fig*) rich
ergötzen *vt* amuse
ergreifen† *vt* seize; take ⟨*Maßnahme, Gelegenheit*⟩; take up ⟨*Beruf*⟩; (*rühren*) move; **die Flucht e∼** flee. **e∼d** *a* moving
ergriffen *a* deeply moved. **E∼heit** *f* - emotion
ergründen *vt* (*fig*) get to the bottom of
erhaben *a* raised; (*fig*) sublime; **über etw** (*acc*) **e∼ sein** (*fig*) be above sth
Erhalt *m* **-[e]s** receipt. **e∼en**† *vt* receive, get; (*gewinnen*) obtain; (*bewahren*) preserve, keep; (*instand halten*) maintain; (*unterhalten*) support; **am Leben e∼en** keep alive □ *a* **gut/schlecht e∼en** in good/bad condition; **e∼en bleiben** survive
erhältlich *a* obtainable
Erhaltung *f* - (s. **erhalten**) preservation; maintenance
erhängen (sich) *vr* hang oneself
erhärten *vt* (*fig*) substantiate
erheb|en† *vt* raise; levy ⟨*Steuer*⟩; charge ⟨*Gebühr*⟩; **Anspruch e∼en** lay claim (**auf** + *acc* to); **Protest e∼en** protest; **sich e∼en** rise; ⟨*Frage:*⟩ arise; (*sich empören*) rise up. **e∼lich** *a* considerable, *adv* -bly. **E∼ung** *f* -,-**en** elevation; (*Anhöhe*) rise; (*Aufstand*) uprising; (*Ermittlung*) survey
erheiter|n *vt* amuse. **E∼ung** *f* - amusement
erhitzen *vt* heat; **sich e∼** get hot; (*fig*) get heated
erhoffen *vt* **sich** (*dat*) **etw e∼** hope for sth
erhöh|en *vt* raise; (*fig*) increase; **sich e∼en** rise, increase. **E∼ung** *f* -,-**en** increase. **E∼ungszeichen** *nt* (*Mus*) sharp
erhol|en (sich) *vr* recover (**von** from); (*nach Krankheit*) convalesce, recuperate; (*sich ausruhen*) have a rest. **e∼sam** *a* restful. **E∼ung** *f* - recovery; convalescence; (*Ruhe*) rest. **E∼ungsheim** *nt* convalescent home
erhören *vt* (*fig*) answer
erinner|n *vt* remind (**an** + *acc* of); **sich e∼n** remember (**an jdn/etw** s.o./sth). **E∼ung** *f* -,-**en** memory; (*Andenken*) souvenir
erkält|en (sich) *vr* catch a cold; **e∼et sein** have a cold. **E∼ung** *f* -,-**en** cold
erkenn|bar *a* recognizable; (*sichtbar*) visible. **e∼en**† *vt* recognize; (*wahrnehmen*) distinguish; (*einsehen*) realize. **e∼tlich** *a* **sich e∼tlich zeigen** show one's appreciation. **E∼tnis** *f* -,-**se** recognition; realization; (*Wissen*) knowledge; **die neuesten E∼tnisse** the latest findings
Erker *m* **-s,-** bay
erklär|en *vt* declare; (*erläutern*) explain; **sich bereit e∼en** agree (**zu** to); **ich kann es mir nicht e∼en** I can't explain it. **e∼end** *a* explanatory. **e∼lich** *a* explicable; (*verständlich*) understandable. **e∼licherweise** *adv* understandably. **e∼t** *attrib a* declared. **E∼ung** *f* -,-**en** declaration; explanation; **öffentliche E∼ung** public statement
erklingen† *vi* (*sein*) ring out
erkrank|en *vi* (*sein*) fall ill; be taken ill (**an** + *dat* with). **E∼ung** *f* -,-**en** illness
erkunden *vt* explore; (*Mil*) reconnoitre
erkundig|en (sich) *vr* enquire (**nach jdm/etw** after s.o./about sth). **E∼ung** *f* -,-**en** enquiry
erlahmen *vi* (*sein*) tire; ⟨*Kraft, Eifer:*⟩ flag
erlangen *vt* attain, get
Erlass *m* **-es,¨-e** (**Erlaß** *m* **-sses, ¨-sse**) (*Admin*) decree; (*Befreiung*) exemption; (*Straf-*) remission
erlassen† *vt* (*Admin*) issue; **jdm etw e∼** exempt s.o. from sth; let s.o. off ⟨*Strafe*⟩

erlauben *vt* allow, permit; **sich e∼, etw zu tun** take the liberty of doing sth; **ich kann es mir nicht e∼** I can't afford it

Erlaubnis *f* - permission. **E∼schein** *m* permit

erläuter|n *vt* explain. **E∼ung** *f* -,-**en** explanation

Erle *f* -,-**n** alder

erleb|en *vt* experience; (*mit-*) see; have ⟨*Überraschung, Enttäuschung*⟩; **etw nicht mehr e∼en** not live to see sth. **E∼nis** *nt* -**ses,-se** experience

erledig|en *vt* do; (*sich befassen mit*) deal with; (*beenden*) finish; (*entscheiden*) settle; (*töten*) kill; **e∼t sein** be done/settled/(*fam: müde*) worn out/(*fam: ruiniert*) finished

erleichter|n *vt* lighten; (*vereinfachen*) make easier; (*befreien*) relieve; (*lindern*) ease; **sich e∼n** (*fig*) unburden oneself. **e∼t** *a* relieved. **E∼ung** *f* - relief

erleiden† *vt* suffer

erlernen *vt* learn

erlesen *a* exquisite; (*auserlesen*) choice, select

erleucht|en *vt* illuminate; **hell e∼et** brightly lit. **E∼ung** *f* -,-**en** (*fig*) inspiration

erliegen† *vi* (*sein*) succumb (*dat* to); **seinen Verletzungen e∼** die of one's injuries

erlogen *a* untrue, false

Erlös *m* -**es** proceeds *pl*

erlöschen† *vi* (*sein*) go out; (*vergehen*) die; (*aussterben*) die out; (*ungültig werden*) expire; **erloschener Vulkan** extinct volcano

erlös|en *vt* save; (*befreien*) release (**von** from); (*Relig*) redeem. **e∼t** *a* relieved. **E∼ung** *f* release; (*Erleichterung*) relief; (*Relig*) redemption

ermächtig|en *vt* authorize. **E∼ung** *f* -,-**en** authorization

ermahn|en *vt* exhort; (*zurechtweisen*) admonish. **E∼ung** *f* exhortation; admonition

ermäßig|en *vt* reduce. **E∼ung** *f* -,-**en** reduction

ermatt|en *vi* (*sein*) grow weary □ *vt* weary. **E∼ung** *f* - weariness

ermessen† *vt* judge; (*begreifen*) appreciate. **E∼** *nt* -**s** discretion; (*Urteil*) judgement; **nach eigenem E∼** at one's own discretion

ermitt|eln *vt* establish; (*herausfinden*) find out □ *vi* (*haben*) investigate (**gegen jdn** s.o.). **E∼lungen** *fpl* investigations. **E∼lungsverfahren** *nt* (*Jur*) preliminary inquiry

ermöglichen *vt* make possible

ermord|en *vt* murder. **E∼ung** *f* -,-**en** murder

ermüd|en *vt* tire □ *vi* (*sein*) get tired. **E∼ung** *f* - tiredness

ermunter|n *vt* encourage; **sich e∼n** rouse oneself. **E∼ung** *f* - encouragement

ermutigen *vt* encourage. **e∼d** *a* encouraging

ernähr|en *vt* feed; (*unterhalten*) support, keep; **sich e∼en von** live/⟨*Tier:*⟩ feed on. **E∼er** *m* -**s,-** breadwinner. **E∼ung** *f* - nourishment; nutrition; (*Kost*) diet

ernenn|en† *vt* appoint. **E∼ung** *f* -,-**en** appointment

erneu|ern *vt* renew; (*auswechseln*) replace; change ⟨*Verband*⟩; (*renovieren*) renovate. **E∼erung** *f* renewal; replacement; renovation. **e∼t** *a* renewed; (*neu*) new □ *adv* again

erniedrig|en *vt* degrade; **sich e∼en** lower oneself **e∼end** *a* degrading. **E∼ungszeichen** *nt* (*Mus*) flat

ernst *a* serious, *adv* -ly; **e∼ nehmen** take seriously. **E∼** *m* -**es** seriousness; **im E∼** seriously; **mit einer Drohung E∼ machen** carry out a threat; **ist das dein E∼?** are you serious? **E∼fall** *m* **im E∼fall** when the real thing

happens. **e~haft** *a* serious, *adv* -ly. **e~lich** *a* serious, *adv* -ly
Ernte *f* **-,-n** harvest; (*Ertrag*) crop. **E~dankfest** *nt* harvest festival. **e~n** *vt* harvest; (*fig*) reap, win
ernüchter|n *vt* sober up; (*fig*) bring down to earth; (*enttäuschen*) disillusion. **e~nd** *a* (*fig*) sobering. **E~ung** *f* - disillusionment
Erober|er *m* **-s,-** conqueror. **e~n** *vt* conquer. **E~ung** *f* **-,-en** conquest
eröffn|en *vt* open; **jdm etw e~en** announce sth to s.o.; **sich jdm e~en** ⟨*Aussicht:*⟩ present itself to s.o. **E~ung** *f* opening; (*Mitteilung*) announcement. **E~ungsansprache** *f* opening address
erörter|n *vt* discuss. **E~ung** *f* **-,-en** discussion
Erosion *f* **-,-en** erosion
Erot|ik *f* - eroticism. **e~isch** *a* erotic
Erpel *m* **-s,-** drake
erpicht *a* **e~auf** (+ *acc*) keen on
erpress|en *vt* extort; blackmail ⟨*Person*⟩. **E~er** *m* **-s,-** blackmailer. **E~ung** *f* - extortion; blackmail
erprob|en *vt* test. **e~t** *a* proven
erquicken *vt* refresh
erraten† *vt* guess
erreg|bar *a* excitable. **e~en** *vt* excite; (*hervorrufen*) arouse; **sich e~en** get worked up. **e~end** *a* exciting. **E~er** *m* **-s,-** (*Med*) germ. **e~t** *a* agitated; (*hitzig*) heated. **E~ung** *f* - excitement; (*Erregtheit*) agitation
erreich|bar *a* within reach; ⟨*Ziel*⟩ attainable; ⟨*Person*⟩ available. **e~en** *vt* reach; catch ⟨*Zug*⟩; live to ⟨*Alter*⟩; (*durchsetzen*) achieve
erretten *vt* save
errichten *vt* erect
erringen† *vt* gain, win
erröten *vi* (*sein*) blush
Errungenschaft *f* **-,-en** achievement; (*fam: Anschaffung*) acquisition; **E~en der Technik** technical advances
Ersatz *m* **-es** replacement, substitute; (*Entschädigung*) compensation. **E~dienst** *m* = **Zivildienst. E~reifen** *m* spare tyre. **E~spieler(in)** *m(f)* substitute. **E~teil** *nt* spare part
ersäufen *vt* drown
erschaffen† *vt* create
erschallen† *vi* (*sein*) ring out
erschein|en† *vi* (*sein*) appear; ⟨*Buch:*⟩ be published; **jdm merkwürdig e~en** seem odd to s.o. **E~en** *nt* **-s** appearance; publication. **E~ung** *f* **-,-en** appearance; (*Person*) figure; (*Phänomen*) phenomenon; (*Symptom*) symptom; (*Geist*) apparition
erschieß|en† *vt* shoot [dead]. **E~ungskommando** *nt* firing squad
erschlaffen *vi* (*sein*) go limp; ⟨*Haut, Muskeln:*⟩ become flabby
erschlagen† *vt* beat to death; (*tödlich treffen*) strike dead; **vom Blitz e~ werden** be killed by lightning □ *a* (*fam*) (*erschöpft*) worn out; (*fassungslos*) stunned
erschließen† *vt* develop; (*zugänglich machen*) open up; (*nutzbar machen*) tap
erschöpf|en *vt* exhaust. **e~end** *a* exhausting; (*fig: vollständig*) exhaustive. **e~t** *a* exhausted. **E~ung** *f* - exhaustion
erschreck|en† *vi* (*sein*) get a fright □ *vt* (*reg*) startle; (*beunruhigen*) alarm; **du hast mich e~t** you gave me a fright □ *vr* (*reg & irreg*) **sich e~en** get a fright. **e~end** *a* alarming, *adv* -ly
erschrocken *a* frightened; (*erschreckt*) startled; (*bestürzt*) dismayed
erschütter|n *vt* shake; (*ergreifen*) upset deeply. **E~ung** *f* **-,-en** shock

erschweren *vt* make more difficult
erschwinglich *a* affordable
ersehen† *vt* (*fig*) see (**aus** from)
ersetzen *vt* replace; make good ⟨*Schaden*⟩; refund ⟨*Kosten*⟩; **jdm etw e∼** compensate s.o. for sth
ersichtlich *a* obvious, apparent
erspar|en *vt* save; **jdm etw e∼en** save/(*fernhalten*) spare s.o. sth. **E∼nis** *f* **-,-se** saving; **E∼nisse** savings
erst *adv* (*zuerst*) first; (*noch nicht mehr als*) only; (*nicht vor*) not until; **e∼ dann** only then; **eben** *od* **gerade e∼** [only] just; **das machte ihn e∼ recht wütend** it made him all the more angry
erstarren *vi* (*sein*) solidify; (*gefrieren*) freeze; (*steif werden*) go stiff; (*vor Schreck*) be paralysed
erstatten *vt* (*zurück-*) refund; **Bericht e∼** report (**jdm** to s.o.)
Erstaufführung *f* first performance, première
erstaun|en *vt* amaze, astonish. **E∼en** *nt* amazement, astonishment. **e∼lich** *a* amazing, *adv* -ly. **e∼licherweise** *adv* amazingly
Erst|ausgabe *f* first edition. **e∼e(r,s)** *a* first; (*beste*) best; **e∼e (E∼e) Hilfe** first aid; **der e∼e Beste (beste)** the first one to come along; (*fam*) any Tom, Dick or Harry; **als e∼es/fürs e∼e** (NEW) **als E∼es/fürs E∼e**, *s.* **Erste(r,s). E∼e(r)** *m/f* first; (*Beste*) best; **fürs E∼e** for the time being; **als E∼es** first of all; **er kam als E∼er** he arrived first; **er ist der/sie ist die E∼e in Latein** he/she is top in Latin
erstechen† *vt* stab to death
erstehen† *vt* buy
ersteigern *vt* buy at an auction
erst|emal *adv* **das e∼emal/zum e∼enmal** (NEW) **das erste Mal/zum ersten Mal**, *s.* **Mal**[1]. **e∼ens** *adv* firstly, in the first place. **e∼ere(r,s)** *a* the former; **der/die/das E∼ere (e∼ere)** the former
ersticken *vt* suffocate; smother ⟨*Flammen*⟩; (*unterdrücken*) suppress □ *vi* (*sein*) suffocate. **E∼** *nt* **-s** suffocation; **zum E∼** stifling
erst|klassig *a* first-class. **e∼mals** *adv* for the first time
erstreben *vt* strive for. **e∼swert** *a* desirable
erstrecken (sich) *vr* stretch; **sich e∼auf** (+ *acc*) (*fig*) apply to
ersuchen *vt* ask, request. **E∼** *nt* **-s** request
ertappen *vt* (*fam*) catch
erteilen *vt* give (**jdm** s.o.)
ertönen *vi* (*sein*) sound; (*erschallen*) ring out
Ertrag *m* **-[e]s,⸚e** yield. **e∼en**† *vt* bear
erträglich *a* bearable; (*leidlich*) tolerable
ertränken *vt* drown
ertrinken† *vi* (*sein*) drown
erübrigen (sich) *vr* be unnecessary
erwachen *vi* (*sein*) awake
erwachsen *a* grown-up. **E∼e(r)** *m/f* adult, grown-up
erwäg|en† *vt* consider. **E∼ung** *f* **-,-en** consideration; **in E∼ung ziehen** consider
erwähn|en *vt* mention. **E∼ung** *f* **-,-en** mention
erwärmen *vt* warm; **sich e∼** warm up; (*fig*) warm (**für** to)
erwart|en *vt* expect; (*warten auf*) wait for. **E∼ung** *f* **-,-en** expectation. **e∼ungsvoll** *a* expectant, *adv* -ly
erwecken *vt* (*fig*) arouse; give ⟨*Anschein*⟩
erweichen *vt* soften; (*fig*) move; **sich e∼ lassen** (*fig*) relent
erweisen† *vt* prove; (*bezeigen*) do ⟨*Gefallen, Dienst, Ehre*⟩; **sich e∼ als** prove to be
erweitern *vt* widen; dilate ⟨*Pupille*⟩; (*fig*) extend, expand
Erwerb *m* **-[e]s** acquisition; (*Kauf*) purchase; (*Brot-*) livelihood; (*Verdienst*) earnings *pl.*

e~en† *vt* acquire; (*kaufen*) purchase; (*fig: erlangen*) gain. **e~slos** *a* unemployed. **e~stätig** *a* [gainfully] employed. **E~ung** *f* **-,-en** acquisition
erwider|n *vt* reply; return ⟨*Besuch, Gruß*⟩. **E~ung** *f* -,-**en** reply
erwirken *vt* obtain
erwischen *vt* (*fam*) catch
erwünscht *a* desired
erwürgen *vt* strangle
Erz *nt* **-es,-e** ore
erzähl|en *vt* tell (**jdm** s.o.) □ *vi* (*haben*) talk (**von** about). **E~er** *m* **-s,-** narrator. **E~ung** *f* **-,-en** story, tale
Erzbischof *m* archbishop
erzeug|en *vt* produce; (*Electr*) generate; (*fig*) create. **E~er** *m* **-s,-** producer; (*Vater*) father. **E~nis** *nt* **-ses,-se** product; **landwirtschaftliche E~nisse** farm produce *sg*. **E~ung** *f* - production; generation
Erz|feind *m* arch-enemy. **E~herzog** *m* archduke
erzieh|en† *vt* bring up; (*Sch*) educate. **E~er** *m* **-s,-** [private] tutor. **E~erin** *f* **-,-nen** governess. **E~ung** *f* - upbringing; education
erzielen *vt* achieve; score ⟨*Tor*⟩
erzogen *a* **gut/schlecht e~** well/badly brought up
erzürnt *a* angry
erzwingen† *vt* force
es *pron* it; (*Mädchen*) she; (*acc*) her; *impers* **es regnet** it is raining; **es gibt** there is/(*pl*) are; **ich hoffe es** I hope so
Esche *f* **-,-n** ash
Esel *m* **-s,-** donkey; (*fam: Person*) ass. **E~sohr** *nt* **E~sohren haben** ⟨*Buch:*⟩ be dog-eared
Eskal|ation /-'tsio:n/ *f* - escalation. **e~ieren** *vt/i* (*haben*) escalate
Eskimo *m* **-[s],-[s]** Eskimo
Eskort|e *f* **-,-n** (*Mil*) escort. **e~ieren** *vt* escort
essbar (**eßbar**) *a* edible. **Essecke** (**Eßecke**) *f* dining area
essen† *vt/i* (*haben*) eat; **zu Mittag Abend e~** have lunch/supper; **[auswärts] e~ gehen** eat out; **chinesisch e~** have a Chinese meal. **E~** *nt* **-s,-** food; (*Mahl*) meal; (*festlich*) dinner
Essenz *f* **-,-en** essence
Esser(in) *m* **-s,-** (*f* **-,-nen**) eater
Essig *m* **-s** vinegar. **E~gurke** *f* [pickled] gherkin
Esskastanie (**Eßkastanie**) *f* sweet chestnut. **Esslöffel** (**Eßlöffel**) *m* ≈ dessertspoon. **Essstäbchen** (**Eßstäbchen**) *ntpl* chopsticks. **Esstisch** (**Eßtisch**) *m* dining-table. **Esswaren** (**Eßwaren**) *fpl* food *sg*; (*Vorräte*) provisions. **Esszimmer** (**Eßzimmer**) *nt* dining-room
Estland *nt* **-s** Estonia
Estragon *m* **-s** tarragon
etablieren (sich) *vr* establish oneself/⟨*Geschäft:*⟩ itself
Etage /e'ta:ʒə/ *f* **-,-n** storey. **E~nbett** *nt* bunk-beds *pl*. **E~nwohnung** *f* flat, (*Amer*) apartment
Etappe *f* **-,-n** stage
Etat /e'ta:/ *m* **-s,-s** budget
etepetete *a* (*fam*) fussy
Eth|ik *f* - ethic; (*Sittenlehre*) ethics *sg*. **e~isch** *a* ethical
Etikett *nt* **-[e]s,-e[n]** label; (*Preis-*) tag. **E~e** *f* **-,-n** etiquette; (*Aust*) = **Etikett. e~ieren** *vt* label
etlich|e(r,s) *pron* some; (*mehrere*) several; **e~e Mal** several times; **e~es** a number of things; (*ziemlich viel*) quite a lot. **e~emal** *adv* (NEW) **e~e Mal**, *s.* **etliche(r,s)**
Etui /e'tvi:/ *nt* **-s,-s** case
etwa *adv* (*ungefähr*) about; (*zum Beispiel*) for instance; (*womöglich*) perhaps; **nicht e~, dass** ... not that ...; **denkt nicht e~** ... don't imagine ...; **du hast doch nicht e~ Angst?** you're not afraid, are you? **e~ig** *a* possible

etwas *pron* something; (*fragend/verneint*) anything; (*ein bisschen*) some, a little; **ohne e~ zu sagen** without saying anything; **sonst noch e~?** anything else? **noch e~ Tee?** some more tea? **so e~ Ärgerliches!** what a nuisance! □ *adv* a bit

Etymologie *f* - etymology

euch *pron* (*acc of* **ihr** *pl*) you; (*dat*) [to] you; (*refl*) yourselves; (*einander*) each other; **ein Freund von e~** a friend of yours

euer *poss pron pl* your. **e~e, e~t-** *s.* **eure, euret-**

Eule *f* -,-**n** owl

Euphorie *f* - euphoria

eur|e *poss pron pl* your. **e~e(r,s)** *poss pron* yours. **e~erseits** *adv* for your part. **e~etwegen** *adv* for your sake; (*wegen euch*) because of you, on your account. **e~etwillen** *adv* **um e~etwillen** for your sake. **e~ige** *poss pron* **der/die/das e~ige** yours

Euro *m* -**[s]/-[s]** Euro. **E~-** *pref* Euro-

Europa *nt* -**s** Europe. **E~-** *pref* European

Europä|er(in) *m* -**s,-** (*f* -,-**nen**) European. **e~isch** *a* European; **E~ische Gemeinschaft** European Community

Euro|paß *m* Europassport. **E~scheck** *m* Eurocheque

Euter *nt* -**s,-** udder

evakuier|en *vt* evacuate. **E~ung** *f* - evacuation

evan|gelisch *a* Protestant. **E~gelist** *m* -**en,-en** evangelist. **E~gelium** *nt* -**s,-ien** gospel

evaporieren *vt/i* (*sein*) evaporate

Eventu|alität *f* -,-**en** eventuality. **e~ell** *a* possible □ *adv* possibly; (*vielleicht*) perhaps

Evolution /-'tsio:n/ *f* - evolution

evtl. *abbr s.* **eventuell**

ewig *a* eternal, *adv* -ly; (*fam: ständig*) constant, *adv* -ly; (*endlos*) never-ending; **e~ dauern** (*fam*) take ages. **E~keit** *f* - eternity; **eine E~keit** (*fam*) ages

exakt *a* exact, *adv* -ly. **E~heit** *f* - exactitude

Examen *nt* -**s,-** & -**mina** (*Sch*) examination

Exekutive *f* - (*Pol*) executive

Exempel *nt* -**s,-** example; **ein E~ an jdm statuieren** make an example of s.o.

Exemplar *nt* -**s,-e** specimen; (*Buch*) copy. **e~isch** *a* exemplary

exerzieren *vt/i* (*haben*) (*Mil*) drill; (*üben*) practise

exhumieren *vt* exhume

Exil *nt* -**s** exile

Existenz *f* -,-**en** existence; (*Lebensgrundlage*) livelihood; (*pej: Person*) individual

existieren *vi* (*haben*) exist

exklusiv *a* exclusive. **e~e** *prep* (+ *gen*) excluding

exkommunizieren *vt* excommunicate

Exkremente *npl* excrement *sg*

exotisch *a* exotic

expan|dieren *vt/i* (*haben*) expand. **E~sion** *f* - expansion

Expedition /-'tsio:n/ *f* -,-**en** expedition

Experiment *nt* -**[e]s,-e** experiment. **e~ell** *a* experimental. **e~ieren** *vi* (*haben*) experiment

Experte *m* -**n,-n** expert

explo|dieren *vi* (*sein*) explode. **E~sion** *f* -,-**en** explosion. **e~siv** *a* explosive

Expor|t *m* -**[e]s,-e** export. **E~teur** /-'tø:ɐ̯/ *m* -**s,-e** exporter. **e~tieren** *vt* export

Express *m* -**es,-e** (**Expreß** *m* -**sses,-sse**) express

extra *adv* separately; (*zusätzlich*) extra; (*eigens*) specially; (*fam: absichtlich*) on purpose

Extrakt *m* -**[e]s,-e** extract

Extras *npl* (*Auto*) extras

extravagan|t *a* flamboyant, *adv* -ly; (*übertrieben*) extravagant. **E~z** *f* -,-**en** flamboyance; extravagance; (*Überspanntheit*) folly

extravertiert *a* extrovert

extrem *a* extreme, *adv* -ly. **E~** *nt* **-s,-e** extreme. **E~ist** *m* **-en,-en** extremist. **E~itäten** *fpl* extremities

Exzellenz *f* - (*title*) Excellency

Exzentr|iker *m* **-s,-** eccentric. **e~isch** *a* eccentric

Exzess *m* **-es,-e** (**Exzeß** *m* **-sses, -sse**) excess

F

Fabel *f* **-,-n** fable. **f~haft** *a* (*fam*) fantastic, *adv* -ally

Fabrik *f* **-,-en** factory. **F~ant** *m* **-en,-en** manufacturer. **F~at** *nt* **-[e]s,-e** product; (*Marke*) make. **F~ation** /-ˈtsi̯oːn/ *f* - manufacture

Facette /faˈsɛtə/ *f* **-,-n** facet

Fach *nt* **-[e]s,¨er** compartment; (*Schub-*) drawer; (*Gebiet*) field; (*Sch*) subject. **F~arbeiter** *m* skilled worker. **F~arzt** *m*, **F~ärztin** *f* specialist. **F~ausdruck** *m* technical term

fäch|eln (sich) *vr* fan oneself. **F~er** *m* **-s,-** fan

Fach|gebiet *nt* field. **f~gemäß, f~gerecht** *a* expert, *adv* -ly. **F~hochschule** *f* ≈ technical university. **f~kundig** *a* expert, *adv* -ly. **f~lich** *a* technical, *adv* -ly; (*beruflich*) professional. **F~mann** *m* (*pl* **-leute**) expert. **f~männisch** *a* expert, *adv* -ly. **F~schule** *f* technical college. **f~simpeln** *vi* (*haben*) (*fam*) talk shop. **F~werkhaus** *nt* half-timbered house. **F~wort** *nt* (*pl* **-wörter**) technical term

Fackel *f* **-,-n** torch. **F~zug** *m* torchlight procession

fade *a* insipid; (*langweilig*) dull

Faden *m* **-s,¨** thread; (*Bohnen-*) string; (*Naut*) fathom. **f~scheinig** *a* threadbare; ⟨*Grund*⟩ flimsy

Fagott *nt* **-[e]s,-e** bassoon

fähig *a* capable (**zu**/*gen* of); (*tüchtig*) able, competent. **F~keit** *f* **-,-en** ability; competence

fahl *a* pale

fahnd|en *vi* (*haben*) search (**nach** for). **F~ung** *f* **-,-en** search

Fahne *f* **-,-n** flag; (*Druck-*) galley [proof]; **eine F~ haben** (*fam*) reek of alcohol. **F~nflucht** *f* desertion. **f~nflüchtig** *a* **f~nflüchtig werden** desert

Fahr|ausweis *m* ticket. **F~bahn** *f* carriageway; (*Straße*) road. **f~bar** *a* mobile

Fähre *f* **-,-n** ferry

fahr|en† *vi* (*sein*) go, travel; ⟨*Fahrer:*⟩ drive; ⟨*Radfahrer:*⟩ ride; (*verkehren*) run, (*ab-*) leave; ⟨*Schiff:*⟩ sail; **mit dem Auto/Zug f~en** go by car/train; **in die Höhe f~en** start up; **in die Kleider f~en** throw on one's clothes; **mit der Hand über etw** (*acc*) **f~en** run one's hand over sth; **was ist in ihn gefahren?** (*fam*) what has got into him? □ *vt* drive; ride ⟨*Fahrrad*⟩; take ⟨*Kurve*⟩. **f~end** *a* moving; (*f~bar*) mobile; (*nicht sesshaft*) travelling, itinerant. **F~er** *m* **-s,-** driver. **F~erflucht** *f* failure to stop after an accident. **F~erhaus** *nt* driver's cab. **F~erin** *f* **-,-nen** woman driver. **F~gast** *m* passenger; (*im Taxi*) fare. **F~geld** *nt* fare. **F~gestell** *nt* chassis; (*Aviat*) undercarriage. **f~ig** *a* nervy; (*zerstreut*) distracted. **F~karte** *f* ticket. **F~kartenausgabe** *f*, **F~kartenschalter** *m* ticket office. **f~lässig** *a* negligent, *adv* -ly. **F~lässigkeit** *f* - negligence. **F~lehrer** *m* driving instructor. **F~plan** *m* timetable. **f~planmäßig** *a* scheduled □ *adv* according to/(*pünktlich*) on schedule. **F~preis** *m* fare. **F~prüfung** *f* driving test. **F~rad** *nt* bicycle. **F~schein** *m* ticket

Fährschiff *nt* ferry

Fahr|schule *f* driving school. **F~schüler(in)** *m(f)* learner driver. **F~spur** *f* [traffic] lane. **F~stuhl** *m* lift, (*Amer*) elevator. **F~stunde** *f* driving lesson

Fahrt *f* -,-en journey; (*Auto*) drive; (*Ausflug*) trip; (*Tempo*) speed; **in voller F~** at full speed. **F~ausweis** *m* ticket

Fährte *f* -,-n track; (*Witterung*) scent; **auf der falschen F~** (*fig*) on the wrong track

Fahr|tkosten *pl* travelling expenses. **F~werk** *nt* undercarriage. **F~zeug** *nt* -[e]s,-e vehicle; (*Wasser-*) craft, vessel

fair /fɛːɐ̯/ *a* fair, *adv* -ly. **F~ness** (**F~neß**) *f* - fairness

Fakten *pl* facts

Faktor *m* -s,-en /-ˈtoːrən/ factor

Fakul|tät *f* -,-en faculty. **f~tativ** *a* optional

Falke *m* -n,-n falcon

Fall *m* -[e]s,¨e fall; (*Jur, Med, Gram*) case; **im F~[e]** in case (*gen* of); **auf jeden F~, auf alle F¨~e** in any case; (*bestimmt*) definitely; **für alle F¨~e** just in case; **auf keinen F~** on no account

Falle *f* -,-n trap; **eine F~ stellen** set a trap (*dat* for)

fallen† *vi* (*sein*) fall; (*sinken*) go down; **[im Krieg] f~** be killed in the war; **f~ lassen** drop ⟨*etw, fig: Plan, jdn*⟩; make ⟨*Bemerkung*⟩

fällen *vt* fell; (*fig*) pass ⟨*Urteil*⟩; make ⟨*Entscheidung*⟩

fallenlassen† *vt sep* (NEW) **fallen lassen**, *s.* **fallen**

fällig *a* due; ⟨*Wechsel*⟩ mature; **längst f~** long overdue. **F~keit** *f* - (*Comm*) maturity

Fallobst *nt* windfalls *pl*

falls *conj* in case; (*wenn*) if

Fallschirm *m* parachute. **F~jäger** *m* paratrooper. **F~springer** *m* parachutist

Falltür *f* trapdoor

falsch *a* wrong; (*nicht echt, unaufrichtig*) false; (*gefälscht*) forged; ⟨*Geld*⟩ counterfeit; ⟨*Schmuck*⟩ fake □ *adv* wrongly; falsely; ⟨*singen*⟩ out of tune; **f~ gehen** ⟨*Uhr:*⟩ be wrong

fälsch|en *vt* forge, fake. **F~er** *m* -s,- forger

Falsch|geld *nt* counterfeit money. **F~heit** *f* - falseness

fälschlich *a* wrong, *adv* -ly; (*irrtümlich*) mistaken, *adv* -ly. **f~erweise** *adv* by mistake

Falsch|meldung *f* false report; (*absichtlich*) hoax report. **F~münzer** *m* -s,- counterfeiter

Fälschung *f* -,-en forgery, fake; (*Fälschen*) forging

Falte *f* -,-n fold; (*Rock-*) pleat; (*Knitter-*) crease; (*im Gesicht*) line; (*Runzel*) wrinkle

falten *vt* fold; **sich f~** ⟨*Haut:*⟩ wrinkle. **F~rock** *m* pleated skirt

Falter *m* -s,- butterfly; (*Nacht-*) moth

faltig *a* creased; ⟨*Gesicht*⟩ lined; (*runzlig*) wrinkled

familiär *a* family ...; (*vertraut, zudringlich*) familiar; (*zwanglos*) informal

Familie /-i̯ə/ *f* -,-n family. **F~nanschluss** (**F~nanschluß**) *m* **F~nanschluss haben** live as one of the family. **F~nforschung** *f* genealogy. **F~nleben** *nt* family life. **F~nname** *m* surname. **F~nplanung** *f* family planning. **F~nstand** *m* marital status

Fan /fɛn/ *m* -s,-s fan

Fana|tiker *m* -s,- fanatic. **f~tisch** *a* fanatical, *adv* -ly. **F~tismus** *m* - fanaticism

Fanfare *f* -,-n trumpet; (*Signal*) fanfare

Fang *m* -[e]s,¨e capture; (*Beute*) catch; **F¨~e** (*Krallen*) talons; (*Zähne*) fangs. **F~arm** *m* tentacle. **f~en**† *vt* catch; (*ein-*) capture; **sich f~en** get caught (**in** + *dat* in); (*fig*) regain one's balance/ (*seelisch*) composure; **gefangen**

nehmen take prisoner; **gefangen halten** hold prisoner; keep in captivity ⟨*Tier*⟩. **F~en** *nt* **-s F~en spielen** play tag. **F~frage** *f* catch question. **F~zahn** *m* fang
Fantasie *f* -,-n = **Phantasie**
fantastisch *a* = **phantastisch**
Farb|aufnahme *f* colour photograph. **F~band** *nt* (*pl* **-bänder**) typewriter ribbon. **F~e** *f* -,-n colour; (*Maler-*) paint; (*zum Färben*) dye; (*Karten*) suit. **f~echt** *a* colour-fast
färben *vt* colour; dye ⟨*Textilien, Haare*⟩; (*fig*) slant ⟨*Bericht*⟩; **sich [rot] f~** turn [red] □ *vi* (*haben*) not be colour-fast
farb|enblind *a* colour-blind. **f~enfroh** *a* colourful. **F~fernsehen** *nt* colour television. **F~film** *m* colour film. **F~foto** *nt* colour photo. **f~ig** *a* coloured □ *adv* in colour. **F~ige(r)** *m/f* coloured man/woman. **F~kasten** *m* box of paints. **f~los** *a* colourless. **F~stift** *m* crayon. **F~stoff** *m* dye; (*Lebensmittel-*) colouring. **F~ton** *m* shade
Färbung *f* -,-en colouring; (*fig: Anstrich*) bias
Farce /'farsə/ *f* -,-n farce; (*Culin*) stuffing
Farn *m* **-[e]s,-e, F~kraut** *nt* fern
Färse *f* -,-n heifer
Fasan *m* **-[e]s,-e[n]** pheasant
Faschierte(s) *nt* (*Aust*) mince
Fasching *m* -s (*SGer*) carnival
Faschis|mus *m* - fascism. **F~t** *m* **-en,-en** fascist. **f~tisch** *a* fascist
faseln *vt/i* (*haben*) (*fam*) **[Unsinn] f~** talk nonsense
Faser *f* -,-n fibre. **f~n** *vi* (*haben*) fray
Fass *nt* **-es,⸚er** (**Faß** *nt* **-sses,⸚sser**) barrel, cask; **Bier vom F~** draught beer; **F~ ohne Boden** (*fig*) bottomless pit
Fassade *f* -,-n façade
fassbar (**faßbar**) *a* comprehensible; (*greifbar*) tangible
fassen *vt* take [hold of], grasp; (*ergreifen*) seize; (*fangen*) catch; (*ein-*) set; (*enthalten*) hold; (*fig: begreifen*) take in, grasp; conceive ⟨*Plan*⟩; make ⟨*Entschluss*⟩; **sich f~** compose oneself; **sich kurz/in Geduld f~** be brief/patient; **in Worte f~** put into words; **nicht zu f~** (*fig*) unbelievable □ *vi* (*haben*) **f~ an** (+ *acc*) touch; **f~ nach** reach for
fasslich (**faßlich**) *a* comprehensible
Fasson /fa'sõ:/ *f* - style; (*Form*) shape; (*Weise*) way
Fassung *f* -,-en mount; (*Edelstein-*) setting; (*Electr*) socket; (*Version*) version; (*Beherrschung*) composure; **aus der F~ bringen** disconcert. **f~slos** *a* shaken; (*erstaunt*) flabbergasted. **F~svermögen** *nt* capacity
fast *adv* almost, nearly; **f~ nie** hardly ever
fast|en *vi* (*haben*) fast. **F~enzeit** *f* Lent. **F~nacht** *f* Shrovetide; (*Karneval*) carnival. **F~nachtsdienstag** *m* Shrove Tuesday. **F~tag** *m* fast-day
Faszin|ation /-'tsio:n/ *f* - fascination. **f~ieren** *vt* fascinate; **f~ierend** fascinating
fatal *a* fatal; (*peinlich*) embarrassing. **F~ismus** *m* - fatalism. **F~ist** *m* **-en,-en** fatalist
Fata Morgana *f* --, --nen mirage
fauchen *vi* (*haben*) spit, hiss □ *vt* snarl
faul *a* lazy; (*verdorben*) rotten, bad; ⟨*Ausrede*⟩ lame; (*zweifelhaft*) bad; (*verdächtig*) fishy
Fäule *f* - decay
faul|en *vi* (*sein*) rot; ⟨*Zahn:*⟩ decay; (*verwesen*) putrefy. **f~enzen** *vi* (*haben*) be lazy. **F~enzer** *m* **-s,-** lazy-bones *sg*. **F~heit** *f* - laziness. **f~ig** *a* rotting; ⟨*Geruch*⟩ putrid
Fäulnis *f* - decay

Faulpelz *m* (*fam*) lazy-bones *sg*
Fauna *f* - fauna
Faust *f* -,**Fäuste** fist; **auf eigene F~** (*fig*) off one's own bat. **F~handschuh** *m* mitten. **F~schlag** *m* punch
Fauxpas /fo'pa/ *m* -,- /-[s],-s/ gaffe
Favorit(in) /favo'ri:t(ɪn)/ *m* **-en, -en** (*f* -,**-nen**) (*Sport*) favourite
Fax *nt* -,-[e] fax. **f~en** *vt* fax
Faxen *fpl* (*fam*) antics; **F~ machen** fool about; **F~ schneiden** pull faces
Faxgerät *nt* fax machine
Feber *m* **-s,-** (*Aust*) February
Februar *m* **-s,-e** February
fecht|en† *vi* (*haben*) fence. **F~er** *m* **-s,-** fencer
Feder *f* -,**-n** feather; (*Schreib-*) pen; (*Spitze*) nib; (*Techn*) spring. **F~ball** *m* shuttlecock; (*Spiel*) badminton. **F~busch** *m* plume. **f~leicht** *a* as light as a feather. **F~messer** *nt* penknife. **f~nd** *vi* (*haben*) be springy; (*nachgeben*) give; (*hoch-*) bounce. **f~nd** *a* springy; (*elastisch*) elastic. **F~ung** *f* - (*Techn*) springs *pl*; (*Auto*) suspension
Fee *f* -,**-n** fairy
Fegefeuer *nt* purgatory
fegen *vt* sweep □ *vi* (*sein*) (*rasen*) tear
Fehde *f* -,**-n** feud
fehl *a* **f~ am Platze** out of place. **F~betrag** *m* deficit. **f~en** *vi* (*haben*) be missing/(*Sch*) absent; (*mangeln*) be lacking; **es f~t an** (+ *dat*) there is a shortage of; **mir f~t die Zeit** I haven't got the time; **sie/es f~t mir sehr** I miss her/it very much; **was f~t ihm?** what's the matter with him? **es f~te nicht viel und er** ... he very nearly ...; **das hat uns noch gefehlt!** that's all we need! **f~end** *a* missing; (*Sch*) absent
Fehler *m* **-s,-** mistake, error; (*Sport & fig*) fault; (*Makel*) flaw. **f~frei** *a* faultless, *adv* -ly. **f~haft** *a* faulty. **f~los** *a* flawless, *adv* -ly
Fehl|geburt *f* miscarriage. **f~gehen**† *vi sep* (*sein*) go wrong; ⟨*Schuss:*⟩ miss; (*fig*) be mistaken. **F~griff** *m* mistake. **F~kalkulation** *f* miscalculation. **F~schlag** *m* failure. **f~schlagen**† *vi sep* (*sein*) fail. **F~start** *m* (*Sport*) false start. **F~tritt** *m* false step; (*fig*) [moral] lapse. **F~zündung** *f* (*Auto*) misfire
Feier *f* -,**-n** celebration; (*Zeremonie*) ceremony; (*Party*) party. **F~abend** *m* end of the working day; **F~abend machen** stop work, (*fam*) knock off; **nach F~abend** after work. **f~lich** *a* solemn, *adv* -ly. (*förmlich*) formal, *adv* -ly. **F~lichkeit** *f* -,**-en** solemnity; **F~lichkeiten** festivities. **f~n** *vt* celebrate; hold ⟨*Fest*⟩; (*ehren*) fête □ *vi* (*haben*) celebrate; (*lustig sein*) make merry. **F~tag** *m* [public] holiday; (*kirchlicher*) feast-day; **erster/zweiter F~tag** Christmas Day / Boxing Day. **f~tags** *adv* on public holidays
feige *a* cowardly; **f~ sein** be a coward □ *adv* in a cowardly way
Feige *f* -,**-n** fig. **F~nbaum** *m* fig tree
Feig|heit *f* - cowardice. **F~ling** *m* **-s,-e** coward
Feile *f* -,**-n** file. **f~n** *vt/i* (*haben*) file
feilschen *vi* (*haben*) haggle
Feilspäne *mpl* filings
fein *a* fine, *adv* -ly; (*zart*) delicate, *adv* -ly; ⟨*Strümpfe*⟩ sheer; ⟨*Unterschied*⟩ subtle; (*scharf*) keen; (*vornehm*) refined; (*elegant*) elegant; (*prima*) great; **sich f~ machen** dress up. **F~arbeit** *f* precision work
feind *a* **jdm f~ sein** (NEW) **jdm F~ sein**, *s.* **Feind**. **F~(in)** *m* **-es,-e** (*f* -,**-nen**) enemy; **jdm F~ sein** be hostile towards s.o. **f~lich** *a* enemy; (*f~selig*) hostile.

F~schaft *f* **-,-en** enmity. **f~selig** *a* hostile. **F~seligkeit** *f* **-,-en** hostility

fein|fühlig *a* sensitive. **F~gefühl** *nt* sensitivity; (*Takt*) delicacy. **F~heit** *f* **-,-en** (*s.* **fein**) fineness; delicacy; subtlety; keenness; refinement; **F~heiten** subtleties. **F~kostgeschäft** *nt* delicatessen [shop]. **F~schmecker** *m* **-s,-** gourmet

feist *a* fat

feixen *vi* (*haben*) smirk

Feld *nt* **-[e]s,-er** field; (*Fläche*) ground; (*Sport*) pitch; (*Schach-*) square; (*auf Formular*) box. **F~bau** *m* agriculture. **F~bett** *nt* camp-bed, (*Amer*) cot. **F~forschung** *f* fieldwork. **F~herr** *m* commander. **F~marschall** *m* Field Marshal. **F~stecher** *m* **-s,-** field-glasses *pl*. **F~webel** *m* **-s,-** (*Mil*) sergeant. **F~zug** *m* campaign

Felge *f* **-,-n** [wheel] rim

Fell *nt* **-[e]s,-e** (*Zool*) coat; (*Pelz*) fur; (*abgezogen*) skin, pelt; **ein dickes F~ haben** (*fam*) be thick-skinned

Fels *m* **-en,-en** rock. **F~block** *m* boulder. **F~en** *m* **-s,-** rock. **f~enfest** *a* (*fig*) firm, *adv* -ly. **f~ig** *a* rocky

feminin *a* feminine; (*weibisch*) effeminate

Femininum *nt* **-s,-na** (*Gram*) feminine

Feminist|(in) *m* **-en,-en** (*f* **-,-nen**) feminist. **f~isch** *a* feminist

Fenchel *m* **-s** fennel

Fenster *nt* **-s,-** window. **F~brett** *nt* window-sill. **F~laden** *m* [window] shutter. **F~leder** *nt* chamois[-leather]. **F~putzer** *m* **-s,-** window-cleaner. **F~scheibe** *f* [window-]pane

Ferien /'fe:rjən/ *pl* holidays; (*Univ*) vacation *sg*; **F~ haben** be on holiday. **F~ort** *m* holiday resort

Ferkel *nt* **-s,-** piglet

fern *a* distant; **der F~e Osten** the Far East; **f~ halten** keep away; **sich f~ halten** keep away □ *adv* far away; **von f~** from a distance □ *prep* (+ *dat*) far [away] from. **F~bedienung** *f* remote control. **f~bleiben**† *vi sep* (*sein*) stay away (*dat* from). **F~e** *f* - distance; **in/aus der F~e** in the/from a distance; **in weiter F~e** far away; (*zeitlich*) in the distant future. **f~er** *a* further □ *adv* (*außerdem*) furthermore; (*in Zukunft*) in future. **f~gelenkt** *a* remote-controlled; ⟨*Rakete*⟩ guided. **F~gespräch** *nt* long-distance call. **f~gesteuert** *a* = **f~gelenkt**. **F~glas** *nt* binoculars *pl*. **f~halten**† *vt sep* (NEW) **f~ halten**, *s.* **fern**. **F~kopierer** *m* **-s,-** fax machine. **F~kurs[us]** *m* correspondence course. **F~lenkung** *f* remote control. **F~licht** *nt* (*Auto*) full beam. **F~meldewesen** *nt* telecommunications *pl*. **F~rohr** *nt* telescope. **F~schreiben** *nt* telex. **F~schreiber** *m* **-s,-** telex [machine]

Fernseh|apparat *m* television set. **f~en**† *vi sep* (*haben*) watch television. **F~en** *nt* **-s** television. **F~er** *m* **-s,-** [television] viewer; (*Gerät*) television set. **F~gerät** *nt* television set

Fernsprech|amt *nt* telephone exchange, (*Amer*) central. **F~er** *m* telephone. **F~nummer** *f* telephone number. **F~zelle** *f* telephone box

Fernsteuerung *f* remote control

Ferse *f* **-,-n** heel. **F~ngeld** *nt* **F~ngeld geben** (*fam*) take to one's heels

fertig *a* finished; (*bereit*) ready; (*Comm*) ready-made; ⟨*Gericht*⟩ ready-to-serve; **f~ werden mit** finish; (*bewältigen*) cope with; **f~ sein** have finished; (*fig*) be through (**mit jdm** with s.o.); (*fam: erschöpft*) be all in/(*seelisch*) shattered; **etw f~ bringen**

od (*fam*) **kriegen** manage to do sth; (*beenden*) finish sth; **ich bringe** *od* (*fam*) **kriege es nicht f~** I can't bring myself to do it; **etw/jdn f~ machen** finish sth; (*bereitmachen*) get sth/s.o. ready; (*fam: erschöpfen*) wear s.o. out; (*seelisch*) shatter s.o.; (*fam: abkanzeln*) carpet s.o.; **sich f~ machen** get ready; **etw f~ stellen** complete sth □ *adv* **f~ essen/lesen** finish eating/reading. **F~bau** *m* (*pl* **-bauten**) prefabricated building. **f~bringen**† *vt sep* (NEW) **f~ bringen**, *s.* **fertig**. **f~en** *vt* make. **F~gericht** *nt* ready-to-serve meal. **F~haus** *nt* prefabricated house. **F~keit** *f* **-,-en** skill. **f~kriegen** *vt sep* (*fam*) (NEW) **f~ kriegen**, *s.* **fertig**. **f~machen** *vt sep* (NEW) **f~ machen**, *s.* **fertig**. **f~stellen** *vt sep* (NEW) **f~ stellen**, *s.* **fertig**. **F~stellung** *f* completion. **F~ung** *f* **-** manufacture

fesch *a* (*fam*) attractive; (*flott*) smart; (*Aust: nett*) kind

Fessel *f* **-,-n** ankle

fesseln *vt* tie up; tie (**an** + *acc* to); (*fig*) fascinate; **ans Bett gefesselt** confined to bed. **F~** *fpl* bonds. **f~d** *a* (*fig*) fascinating; (*packend*) absorbing

fest *a* firm; (*nicht flüssig*) solid; (*erstarrt*) set; (*haltbar*) strong; (*nicht locker*) tight; (*feststehend*) fixed; (*ständig*) steady; ⟨*Anstellung*⟩ permanent; ⟨*Schlaf*⟩ sound; ⟨*Blick, Stimme*⟩ steady; **f~ werden** harden; ⟨*Gelee:*⟩ set; **f~e Nahrung** solids *pl* □ *adv* firmly; tightly; steadily; soundly; (*kräftig, tüchtig*) hard; **f~ schlafen** be fast asleep; **f~ angestellt** permanent

Fest *nt* **-[e]s,-e** celebration; (*Party*) party; (*Relig*) festival; **frohes F~!** happy Christmas!

fest|angestellt *a* (NEW) **f~ angestellt**, *s.* **fest**. **f~binden**† *vt sep* tie (**an** + *dat* to). **f~bleiben**† *vi sep* (*sein*) (*fig*) remain firm. **f~e** *adv* (*fam*) hard. **F~essen** *nt* = **F~mahl**. **f~fahren**† *vi/r sep* (*sein*) **[sich] f~fahren** get stuck; ⟨*Verhandlungen:*⟩ reach deadlock. **f~halten**† *v sep* □ *vt* hold on to; (*aufzeichnen*) record; **sich f~halten** hold on □ *vi* (*haben*) **f~halten an** (+ *dat*) (*fig*) stick to; cling to ⟨*Tradition*⟩. **f~igen** *vt* strengthen; **sich f~igen** grow stronger. **F~iger** *m* **-s,-** styling lotion/(*Schaum-*) mousse. **F~igkeit** *f* **-** (*s.* **fest**) firmness; solidity; strength; steadiness. **f~klammern** *vt sep* clip (**an** + *dat* to); **sich f~klammern** cling (**an** + *dat* to). **F~land** *nt* mainland; (*Kontinent*) continent. **f~legen** *vt sep* (*fig*) fix, settle; lay down ⟨*Regeln*⟩; tie up ⟨*Geld*⟩; **sich f~legen** commit oneself

festlich *a* festive, *adv* -ly. **F~keiten** *fpl* festivities

fest|liegen† *vi sep* (*haben*) be fixed, settled. **f~machen** *v sep* □ *vt* fasten/(*binden*) tie (**an** + *dat* to); (*f~legen*) fix, settle □ *vi* (*haben*) (*Naut*) moor. **F~mahl** *nt* feast; (*Bankett*) banquet. **F~nahme** *f* **-,-n** arrest. **f~nehmen**† *vt sep* arrest. **F~ordner** *m* steward. **f~setzen** *vt sep* fix, settle; (*inhaftieren*) gaol; **sich f~setzen** collect. **f~sitzen**† *vi sep* (*haben*) be firm/⟨*Schraube:*⟩ tight; (*haften*) stick; (*nicht weiterkommen*) be stuck. **F~spiele** *npl* festival *sg*. **f~stehen**† *vi sep* (*haben*) be certain. **f~stellen** *vt sep* fix; (*ermitteln*) establish; (*bemerken*) notice; (*sagen*) state. **F~stellung** *f* establishment; (*Aussage*) statement; (*Erkenntnis*) realization. **F~tag** *m* special day

Festung *f* **-,-en** fortress

Fest|zelt *nt* marquee. **f~ziehen**† *vt sep* pull tight. **F~zug** *m* [grand] procession

Fete /ˈfeːtə, ˈfɛːtə/ *f* **-,-n** party

fẹtt *a* fat; (*f~reich*) fatty; (*fettig*) greasy; (*üppig*) rich; 〈*Druck*〉 bold; **f~ gedruckt** bold. **F~** *nt* **-[e]s,-e** fat; (*flüssig*) grease. **f~arm** *a* low-fat. **f~en** *vt* grease □ *vi* (*haben*) be greasy. **F~fleck** *m* grease mark. **f~ig** *a* greasy. **f~leibig** *a* obese. **F~näpfchen** *nt* **ins F~näpfchen treten** (*fam*) put one's foot in it

Fẹtzen *m* **-s,-** scrap; (*Stoff*) rag; **in F~** in shreds

feucht *a* damp, moist; 〈*Luft*〉 humid. **f~heiß** *a* humid. **F~igkeit** *f* **-** dampness; (*Nässe*) moisture; (*Luft-*) humidity. **F~igkeitscreme** *f* moisturizer

feudal *a* (*fam: vornehm*) sumptuous, *adv* -ly. **F~ịsmus** *m* **-** feudalism

Feuer *nt* **-s,-** fire; (*für Zigarette*) light; (*Begeisterung*) passion; **F~ machen** light a fire; **F~ fangen** catch fire; (*fam: sich verlieben*) be smitten; **jdm F~ geben** give s.o. a light; **F~ speiender Berg** volcano. **F~alarm** *m* fire alarm. **F~bestattung** *f* cremation. **f~gefährlich** *a* [in]flammable. **F~leiter** *f* fire-escape. **F~löscher** *m* **-s,-** fire extinguisher. **F~melder** *m* **-s,-** fire alarm. **f~n** *vi* (*haben*) fire (**auf** + *acc* on) □ *vt* (*fam*) (*schleudern*) fling; (*entlassen*) fire. **F~probe** *f* (*fig*) test. **f~rot** *a* crimson. **f~speiend** *a* (NEW) **F~ speiend**, *s.* **Feuer**. **F~stein** *m* flint. **F~stelle** *f* hearth. **F~treppe** *f* fire-escape. **F~wache** *f* fire station. **F~waffe** *f* firearm. **F~wehr** *f* **-,-en** fire brigade. **F~wehrauto** *nt* fire-engine. **F~wehrmann** *m* (*pl* **-männer** & **-leute**) fireman. **F~werk** *nt* firework display, fireworks *pl*. **F~werkskörper** *m* firework. **F~zeug** *nt* lighter

feurig *a* fiery; (*fig*) passionate

Fiạker *m* **-s,-** (*Aust*) horse-drawn cab

Fịchte *f* **-,-n** spruce

fidel *a* cheerful

Fieber *nt* **-s** [raised] temperature; **F~ haben** have a temperature. **f~haft** *a* (*fig*) feverish, *adv* -ly. **f~n** *vi* (*haben*) be feverish. **F~thermometer** *nt* thermometer

fiebrig *a* feverish

fies *a* (*fam*) nasty, *adv* -ily

Figur *f* **-,-en** figure; (*Roman-, Film-*) character; (*Schach-*) piece

Fik|tion /-'tsi̯o:n/ *f* **-,-en** fiction. **f~tịv** *a* fictitious

Filet /fi'le:/ *nt* **-s,-s** fillet

Filial|e *f* **-,-n,** **F~geschäft** *nt* (*Comm*) branch

Filigran *nt* **-s** filigree

Fịlm *m* **-[e]s,-e** film; (*Kino-*) film, (*Amer*) movie; (*Schicht*) coating. **f~en** *vt/i* (*haben*) film. **F~kamera** *f* cine/(*für Kinofilm*) film camera

Fịlt|er *m* & (*Techn*) *nt* **-s,-** filter; (*Zigaretten-*) filter-tip. **f~ern** *vt* filter. **F~erzigarette** *f* filter-tipped cigarette. **f~rieren** *vt* filter

Fịlz *m* **-es** felt. **f~en** *vi* (*haben*) become matted □ *vt* (*fam*) (*durchsuchen*) frisk; (*stehlen*) steal. **F~schreiber** *m* **-s,-**, **F~stift** *m* felt-tipped pen

Fịmmel *m* **-s,-** (*fam*) obsession

Fina|le *nt* **-s,-** (*Mus*) finale; (*Sport*) final. **F~lịst(in)** *m* **-en,-en** (*f* **-,-nen**) finalist

Finạnz *f* **-,-en** finance. **F~amt** *nt* tax office. **f~iẹll** *a* financial, *adv* -ly. **f~ieren** *vt* finance. **F~minister** *m* minister of finance

fịnd|en† *vt* find; (*meinen*) think; **den Tod f~en** meet one's death; **wie f~est du das?** what do you think of that? **f~est du?** do you think so? **es wird sich f~en** it'll turn up; (*fig*) it'll be all right □ *vi* (*haben*) find one's way. **F~er** *m* **-s,-** finder. **F~erlohn** *m* reward.

f~ig *a* resourceful. **F~ling** *m* **-s,-e** boulder
Finesse *f* **-,-n** (*Kniff*) trick; **F~n** (*Techn*) refinements
Finger *m* **-s,-** finger; **die F~ lassen von** (*fam*) leave alone; **etw im kleinen F~ haben** (*fam*) have sth at one's fingertips. **F~abdruck** *m* finger-mark; (*Admin*) fingerprint. **F~hut** *m* thimble. **F~nagel** *m* finger-nail. **F~ring** *m* ring. **F~spitze** *f* finger-tip. **F~zeig** *m* **-[e]s,-e** hint
fingier|en *vt* fake. **f~t** *a* fictitious
Fink *m* **-en,-en** finch
Finn|e *m* **-n,-n, F~in** *f* **-,-nen** Finn. **f~isch** *a* Finnish. **F~land** *nt* **-s** Finland
finster *a* dark; (*düster*) gloomy; (*unheildrohend*) sinister; **im F~n** in the dark. **F~nis** *f* **-** darkness; (*Astr*) eclipse
Finte *f* **-,-n** trick; (*Boxen*) feint
Firma *f* **-,-men** firm, company
firmen *vt* (*Relig*) confirm
Firmen|wagen *m* company car. **F~zeichen** *nt* trade mark, logo
Firmung *f* **-,-en** (*Relig*) confirmation
Firnis *m* **-ses,-se** varnish. **f~sen** *vt* varnish
First *m* **-[e]s,-e** [roof] ridge
Fisch *m* **-[e]s,-e** fish; **F~e** (*Astr*) Pisces. **F~dampfer** *m* trawler. **f~en** *vt/i* (*haben*) fish; **aus dem Wasser f~en** (*fam*) fish out of the water. **F~er** *m* **-s,-** fisherman. **F~erei** *f* **-**, **F~fang** *m* fishing. **F~gräte** *f* fishbone. **F~händler** *m* fishmonger. **F~otter** *m* otter. **F~reiher** *m* heron. **F~stäbchen** *nt* **-s,-** fish finger. **F~teich** *m* fishpond
Fiskus *m* **- der F~** the Treasury
Fisole *f* **-,-n** (*Aust*) French bean
fit *a* fit. **Fitness (Fitneß)** *f* **-** fitness
fix *a* (*fam*) quick, *adv* -ly; (*geistig*) bright; **f~e Idee** obsession; **fix und fertig** all finished; (*bereit*) all ready; (*fam: erschöpft*) shattered. **F~er** *m* **-s,-** (*sl*) junkie
fixieren *vt* stare at; (*Phot*) fix
Fjord *m* **-[e]s,-e** fiord
FKK *abbr* (**Freikörperkultur**) naturism
flach *a* flat; (*eben*) level; (*niedrig*) low; (*nicht tief*) shallow; **f~er Teller** dinner plate; **die f~e Hand** the flat of the hand
Fläche *f* **-,-n** area; (*Ober-*) surface; (*Seite*) face. **F~nmaß** *nt* square measure
Flachs *m* **-es** flax. **f~blond** *a* flaxen-haired; 〈*Haar*〉 flaxen
flackern *vi* (*haben*) flicker
Flagge *f* **-,-n** flag
flagrant *a* flagrant
Flair /flɛ:ɐ̯/ *nt* **-s** air, aura
Flak *f* **-,-[s]** anti-aircraft artillery/(*Geschütz*) gun
flämisch *a* Flemish
Flamme *f* **-,-n** flame; (*Koch-*) burner; **in F~n** in flames
Flanell *m* **-s** (*Tex*) flannel
Flank|e *f* **-,-n** flank. **f~ieren** *vt* flank
Flasche *f* **-,-n** bottle. **F~nbier** *nt* bottled beer. **F~nöffner** *m* bottle-opener
flatter|haft *a* fickle. **f~n** *vi* (*sein/haben*) flutter; 〈*Segel:*〉 flap
flau *a* (*schwach*) faint; (*Comm*) slack; **mir ist f~** I feel faint
Flaum *m* **-[e]s** down. **f~ig** *a* downy; **f~ig rühren** (*Aust Culin*) cream
flauschig *a* fleecy; 〈*Spielzeug*〉 fluffy
Flausen *fpl* (*fam*) silly ideas; (*Ausflüchte*) silly excuses
Flaute *f* **-,-n** (*Naut*) calm; (*Comm*) slack period; (*Schwäche*) low
fläzen (sich) *vr* (*fam*) sprawl
Flechte *f* **-,-n** (*Med*) eczema; (*Bot*) lichen; (*Zopf*) plait. **f~n**† *vt* plait; weave 〈*Korb*〉
Fleck *m* **-[e]s,-e[n]** spot; (*größer*) patch; (*Schmutz-*) stain, mark; **blauer F~** bruise; **nicht vom F~kommen** (*fam*) make no progress. **f~en** *vi* (*haben*) stain.

F~en *m* **-s,-** = **Fleck**; (*Ortschaft*) small town. **f~enlos** *a* spotless. **F~entferner** *m* **-s,-** stain remover. **f~ig** *a* stained; ⟨*Haut*⟩ blotchy
Fledermaus *f* bat
Flegel *m* **-s,-** lout. **f~haft** *a* loutish. **F~jahre** *npl* (*fam*) awkward age *sg*. **f~n (sich)** *vr* loll
flehen *vi* (*haben*) beg (**um** for). **f~tlich** *a* pleading, *adv* -ly
Fleisch *nt* **-[e]s** flesh; (*Culin*) meat; (*Frucht-*) pulp; **F~ fressend** carnivorous. **F~er** *m* **-s,-** butcher. **F~erei** *f* **-,-en, F~erladen** *m* butcher's shop. **f~fressend** *a* (NEW) **F~ fressend**, *s.* **Fleisch. F~fresser** *m* **-s,-** carnivore. **F~hauer** *m* **-s,-** (*Aust*) butcher. **f~ig** *a* fleshy. **f~lich** *a* carnal. **F~wolf** *m* mincer. **F~wunde** *f* flesh-wound
Fleiß *m* **-es** diligence; **mit F~** diligently; (*absichtlich*) on purpose. **f~ig** *a* diligent, *adv* -ly; (*arbeitsam*) industrious, *adv* -ly
flektieren *vt* (*Gram*) inflect
fletschen *vt* **die Zähne f~** ⟨*Tier:*⟩ bare its teeth
flex|ibel *a* flexible; ⟨*Einband*⟩ limp. **F~ibilität** *f* - flexibility. **F~ion** *f* **-,-en** (*Gram*) inflexion
flicken *vt* mend; (*mit Flicken*) patch. **F~** *m* **-s,-** patch
Flieder *m* **-s** lilac. **f~farben** *a* lilac
Fliege *f* **-,-n** fly; (*Schleife*) bow-tie; **zwei F~n mit einer Klappe schlagen** kill two birds with one stone. **f~n**† *vi* (*sein*) fly; (*geworfen werden*) be thrown; (*fam: fallen*) fall; (*fam: entlassen werden*) be fired/(*von der Schule*) expelled; **in die Luft f~n** blow up □ *vt* fly. **f~nd** *a* flying; ⟨*Händler*⟩ itinerant; **in f~nder Eile** in great haste. **F~r** *m* **-s,-** airman; (*Pilot*); pilot; (*fam: Flugzeug*) plane. **F~rangriff** *m* air raid
flieh|en† *vi* (*sein*) flee (**vor** + *dat* from); (*entweichen*) escape □ *vt* shun. **f~end** *a* fleeing; ⟨*Kinn, Stirn*⟩ receding. **F~kraft** *f* centrifugal force
Fliese *f* **-,-n** tile
Fließ|band *nt* assembly line. **f~en**† *vi* (*sein*) flow; (*aus Wasserhahn*) run. **f~end** *a* flowing; ⟨*Wasser*⟩ running; ⟨*Verkehr*⟩ moving; (*geläufig*) fluent, *adv* -ly. **F~heck** *nt* fastback. **F~wasser** *nt* running water
flimmern *vi* (*haben*) shimmer; (*TV*) flicker; **es flimmert mir vor den Augen** everything is dancing in front of my eyes
flink *a* nimble, *adv* -bly; (*schnell*) quick, *adv* -ly
Flinte *f* **-,-n** shotgun
Flirt /flœrt/ *m* **-s,-s** flirtation. **f~en** *vi* (*haben*) flirt
Flitter *m* **-s** sequins *pl*; (*F~schmuck*) tinsel. **F~wochen** *fpl* honeymoon *sg*
flitzen *vi* (*sein*) (*fam*) dash; ⟨*Auto:*⟩ whizz
Flock|e *f* **-,-n** flake; (*Wolle*) tuft. **f~ig** *a* fluffy
Floh *m* **-[e]s,⸚e** flea. **F~markt** *m* flea market. **F~spiel** *nt* tiddlywinks *sg*
Flor *m* **-s** gauze; (*Trauer-*) crape; (*Samt-, Teppich-*) pile
Flora *f* - flora
Florett *nt* **-[e]s,-e** foil
florieren *vi* (*haben*) flourish
Floskel *f* **-,-n** [empty] phrase
Floß *nt* **-es,⸚e** raft
Flosse *f* **-,-n** fin; (*Seehund-, Gummi-*) flipper; (*sl: Hand*) paw
Flöt|e *f* **-,-n** flute; (*Block-*) recorder. **f~en** *vi* (*haben*) play the flute/recorder; (*fam: pfeifen*) whistle □ *vt* play on the flute/recorder. **F~ist(in)** *m* **-en,-en** (*f* **-,-nen**) flautist
flott *a* quick, *adv* -ly; (*lebhaft*) lively; (*schick*) smart, *adv* -ly; **f~leben** live it up
Flotte *f* **-,-n** fleet

flottmachen *vt sep* **wieder f~** (*Naut*) refloat; get going again ⟨*Auto*⟩; put back on its feet ⟨*Unternehmen*⟩
Flöz *nt* **-es,-e** [coal] seam
Fluch *m* **-[e]s,⸚e** curse. **f~en** *vi* (*haben*) curse, swear
Flucht[1] *f* **-,-en** (*Reihe*) line; (*Zimmer-*) suite
Flucht[2] *f* **-** flight; (*Entweichen*) escape; **die F~ ergreifen** take flight. **f~artig** *a* hasty, *adv* -ily
flücht|en *vi* (*sein*) flee (**vor** + *dat* from); (*entweichen*) escape □ *vr* **sich f~en** take refuge. **f~ig** *a* fugitive; (*kurz*) brief, *adv* -ly; ⟨*Blick, Gedanke*⟩ fleeting; ⟨*Bekanntschaft*⟩ passing; (*oberflächlich*) cursory, *adv* -ily; (*nicht sorgfältig*) careless, *adv* -ly; (*Chem*) volatile; **f~ig sein** be on the run; **f~ig kennen** know slightly. **F~igkeitsfehler** *m* slip. **F~ling** *m* **-s,-e** fugitive; (*Pol*) refugee
Fluchwort *nt* (*pl* **-wörter**) swear-word
Flug *m* **-[e]s,⸚e** flight. **F~abwehr** *f* anti-aircraft defence. **F~ball** *m* (*Tennis*) volley. **F~blatt** *nt* pamphlet
Flügel *m* **-s,-** wing; (*Fenster-*) casement; (*Mus*) grand piano
Fluggast *m* [air] passenger
flügge *a* fully-fledged
Flug|gesellschaft *f* airline. **F~hafen** *m* airport. **F~lotse** *m* air-traffic controller. **F~platz** *m* airport; (*klein*) airfield. **F~preis** *m* air fare. **F~schein** *m* air ticket. **F~schneise** *f* flight path. **F~schreiber** *m* **-s,-** flight recorder. **F~schrift** *f* pamphlet. **F~steig** *m* **-[e]s,-e** gate. **F~wesen** *nt* aviation. **F~zeug** *nt* **-[e]s,-e** aircraft, plane
Fluidum *nt* **-s** aura
Flunder *f* **-,-n** flounder
flunkern *vi* (*haben*) (*fam*) tell fibs; (*aufschneiden*) tell tall stories
Flunsch *m* **-[e]s,-e** pout
fluoreszierend *a* fluorescent
Flur *m* **-[e]s,-e** [entrance] hall; (*Gang*) corridor
Flusen *fpl* fluff *sg*
Fluss *m* **-es,⸚e** (**Fluß** *m* **-sses,⸚sse**) river; (*Fließen*) flow; **im F~** (*fig*) in a state of flux. **f~abwärts** *adv* down-stream. **f~aufwärts** *adv* up-stream. **F~bett** *nt* river-bed
flüssig *a* liquid; ⟨*Lava*⟩ molten; (*fließend*) fluent, *adv* -ly; ⟨*Verkehr*⟩ freely moving. **F~keit** *f* **-,-en** liquid; (*Anat*) fluid
Flusspferd (**Flußpferd**) *nt* hippopotamus
flüstern *vt/i* (*haben*) whisper
Flut *f* **-,-en** high tide; (*fig*) flood; **F~en** waters. **F~licht** *nt* floodlight. **F~welle** *f* tidal wave
Föderation /-ˈt̮sio:n/ *f* **-,-en** federation
Fohlen *nt* **-s,-** foal
Föhn *m* **-s** föhn [wind]; (*Haartrockner*) hair-drier. **f~en** *vt* [blow-]dry
Folg|e *f* **-,-n** consequence; (*Reihe*) succession; (*Fortsetzung*) instalment; (*Teil*) part; **F~e leisten** (+ *dat*) accept ⟨*Einladung*⟩; obey ⟨*Befehl*⟩. **f~en** *vi* (*sein*) follow (**jdm/etw** s.o./sth); (*zuhören*) listen (*dat* to); **daraus f~t, dass** it follows that; **wie f~t** as follows □ (*haben*) (*gehorchen*) obey (**jdm** s.o.). **f~end** *a* following; **F~endes** (**f~endes**) the following. **f~endermaßen** *adv* as follows
folger|n *vt* conclude (**aus** from). **F~ung** *f* **-,-en** conclusion
folg|lich *adv* consequently. **f~sam** *a* obedient, *adv* -ly
Folie /ˈfo:li̯ə/ *f* **-,-n** foil; (*Plastik-*) film
Folklore *f* **-** folklore
Folter *f* **-,-n** torture; **auf die F~ spannen** (*fig*) keep on tenterhooks. **f~n** *vt* torture
Fön (P) *m* **-s,-e** hair-drier
Fonds /fõ:/ *m* **-,-** /-[s],-s/ fund

fönen *vt* (NEW) **föhnen**
Fontäne *f* **-,-n** jet; (*Brunnen*) fountain
Förder|band *nt* (*pl* **-bänder**) conveyor belt. **f~lich** *a* beneficial
fordern *vt* demand; (*beanspruchen*) claim; (*zum Kampf*) challenge; **gefordert werden** (*fig*) be stretched
fördern *vt* promote; (*unterstützen*) encourage; (*finanziell*) sponsor; (*gewinnen*) extract
Forderung *f* **-,-en** demand; (*Anspruch*) claim
Förderung *f* **-** (*s.* **fördern**) promotion; encouragement; (*Techn*) production
Forelle *f* **-,-n** trout
Form *f* **-,-en** form; (*Gestalt*) shape; (*Culin, Techn*) mould; (*Back-*) tin; **[gut] in F~** in good form
Formalität *f* **-,-en** formality
Format *nt* **-[e]s,-e** format; (*Größe*) size; (*fig: Bedeutung*) stature
Formation /-ˈt͡sjo:n/ *f* **-,-en** formation
Formel *f* **-,-n** formula
formell *a* formal, *adv* -ly
formen *vt* shape, mould; (*bilden*) form; **sich f~** take shape
förmlich *a* formal, *adv* -ly; (*regelrecht*) virtual, *adv* -ly. **F~keit** *f* **-,-en** formality
form|los *a* shapeless; (*zwanglos*) informal, *adv* -ly. **F~sache** *f* formality
Formular *nt* **-s,-e** [printed] form
formulier|en *vt* formulate, word. **F~ung** *f* **-,-en** wording
forsch *a* brisk, *adv* -ly; (*schneidig*) dashing, *adv* -ly
forsch|en *vi* (*haben*) search (**nach** for). **f~end** *a* searching. **F~er** *m* **-s,-** research scientist; (*Reisender*) explorer. **F~ung** *f* **-,-en** research. **F~ungsreisende(r)** *m* explorer
Forst *m* **-[e]s,-e** forest
Förster *m* **-s,-** forester
Forstwirtschaft *f* forestry
Forsythie /-t͡sjə/ *f* **-,-n** forsythia
Fort *nt* **-s,-s** (*Mil*) fort
fort *adv* away; **f~ sein** be away; (*gegangen/verschwunden*) have gone; **und so f~** and so on; **in einem f~** continuously. **f~bewegen** *vt sep* move; **sich f~bewegen** move. **F~bewegung** *f* locomotion. **F~bildung** *f* further education/training. **f~bleiben**† *vi sep* (*sein*) stay away. **f~bringen**† *vt sep* take away. **f~fahren**† *vi sep* (*sein*) go away □ (*haben/sein*) continue (**zu** to). **f~fallen**† *vi sep* (*sein*) be dropped/(*ausgelassen*) omitted; (*entfallen*) no longer apply; (*aufhören*) cease. **f~führen** *vt sep* continue. **F~gang** *m* departure; (*Verlauf*) progress. **f~gehen**† *vi sep* (*sein*) leave, go away; (*ausgehen*) go out; (*andauern*) go on. **f~geschritten** *a* advanced; (*spät*) late. **F~geschrittene(r)** *m/f* advanced student. **f~gesetzt** *a* constant, *adv* -ly. **f~jagen** *vt sep* chase away. **f~lassen**† *vt sep* let go; (*auslassen*) omit. **f~laufen**† *vi sep* (*sein*) run away; (*sich f~setzen*) continue. **f~laufend** *a* consecutive, *adv* -ly. **f~nehmen**† *vt sep* take away. **f~pflanzen (sich)** *vr sep* reproduce; ⟨*Ton, Licht:*⟩ travel. **F~pflanzung** *f* **-** reproduction. **F~pflanzungsorgan** *nt* reproductive organ. **f~reißen**† *vt sep* carry away; (*entreißen*) tear away. **f~schaffen** *vt sep* take away. **f~schicken** *vt sep* send away; (*abschicken*) send off. **f~schreiten**† *vi sep* (*sein*) continue; (*Fortschritte machen*) progress, advance. **f~schreitend** *a* progressive; ⟨*Alter*⟩ advancing. **F~schritt** *m* progress; **F~schritte machen** make progress. **f~schrittlich** *a* progressive. **f~setzen** *vt sep* continue; **sich f~setzen** continue. **F~setzung** *f* **-,-en** continuation; (*Folge*) instalment; **F~setzung folgt** to

be continued. **F~setzungsroman** *m* serialized novel, serial. **f~während** *a* constant, *adv* -ly. **f~werfen**† *vt sep* throw away. **f~ziehen**† *v sep* □ *vt* pull away □ *vi* (*sein*) move away

Fossil *nt* -s,-ien /-jən/ fossil

Foto *nt* -s,-s photo. **F~apparat** *m* camera. **f~gen** *a* photogenic

Fotograf|(in) *m* -en,-en (*f* -,-nen) photographer. **F~ie** *f* -,-n photography; (*Bild*) photograph. **f~ieren** *vt* take a photo[graph] of; **sich f~ieren lassen** have one's photo[graph] taken □ *vi* (*haben*) take photographs. **f~isch** *a* photographic

Fotokopie *f* photocopy. **f~ren** *vt* photocopy. **F~rgerät** *nt* photocopier

Fötus *m* -,-ten foetus

Foul /faul/ *nt* -s,-s (*Sport*) foul. **f~en** *vt* foul

Foyer /foa'je:/ *nt* -s,-s foyer

Fracht *f* -,-en freight. **F~er** *m* -s,- freighter. **F~gut** *nt* freight. **F~schiff** *nt* cargo boat

Frack *m* -[e]s,⁻e & -s tailcoat; **im F~** in tails *pl*

Frage *f* -,-n question; **ohne F~** undoubtedly; **eine F~ stellen** ask a question; **etw in F~ stellen = etw infrage stellen**, *s.* **infrage**; **nicht in F~ kommen = nicht infrage kommen**, *s.* **infrage**. **F~bogen** *m* questionnaire. **f~n** *vt* (*haben*) ask; **sich f~n** wonder (**ob** whether). **f~nd** *a* questioning, *adv* -ly; (*Gram*) interrogative. **F~zeichen** *nt* question mark

frag|lich *a* doubtful; ⟨*Person, Sache*⟩ in question. **f~los** *adv* undoubtedly

Fragment *nt* -[e]s,-e fragment. **f~arisch** *a* fragmentary

fragwürdig *a* questionable; (*verdächtig*) dubious

fraisefarben /'frɛ:s-/ *a* strawberry-pink

Fraktion /-'tsio:n/ *f* -,-en parliamentary party

Franken[1] *m* -s,- (*Swiss*) franc

Franken[2] *nt* -s Franconia

Frankfurter *f* -,- frankfurter

frankieren *vt* stamp, frank

Frankreich *nt* -s France

Fransen *fpl* fringe *sg*

Franz|ose *m* -n,-n Frenchman; **die F~osen** the French *pl*. **F~ösin** *f* -,-nen Frenchwoman. **f~ösisch** *a* French. **F~ösisch** *nt* -[s] (*Lang*) French

frapp|ant *a* striking. **f~ieren** *vt* (*fig*) strike; **f~ierend** striking

fräsen *vt* (*Techn*) mill

Fraß *m* -es feed; (*pej: Essen*) muck

Fratze *f* -,-n grotesque face; (*Grimasse*) grimace; (*pej: Gesicht*) face; **F~n schneiden** pull faces

Frau *f* -,-en woman; (*Ehe-*) wife; **F~ Thomas** Mrs/(*unverheiratet*) Miss/(*Admin*) Ms Thomas; **Unsere Liebe F~** (*Relig*) Our Lady. **F~chen** *nt* -s,- mistress

Frauen|arzt *m*, **F~ärztin** *f* gynaecologist. **F~rechtlerin** *f* -,-nen feminist. **F~zimmer** *nt* woman

Fräulein *nt* -s,- single woman; (*jung*) young lady; (*Anrede*) Miss

fraulich *a* womanly

frech *a* cheeky, *adv* -ily; (*unverschämt*) impudent, *adv* -ly. **F~dachs** *m* (*fam*) cheeky monkey. **F~heit** *f* -,-en cheekiness; impudence; (*Äußerung, Handlung*) impertinence

frei *a* free; (*freischaffend*) freelance; ⟨*Künstler*⟩ independent; (*nicht besetzt*) vacant; (*offen*) open; (*bloß*) bare; **f~er Tag** day off; **sich** (*dat*) **f~ nehmen** take time off; **f~ machen** (*räumen*) clear; vacate ⟨*Platz*⟩; (*befreien*) liberate; **f~ lassen** leave free; **jdm f~e Hand lassen** give s.o. a free hand; **ist dieser Platz f~?** is this seat taken? '**Zimmer f~**' 'vacancies' □ *adv* freely; (*ohne*

Notizen) without notes; (*umsonst*) free

Frei|bad *nt* open-air swimming pool. **f∼bekommen**† *vt sep* get released; **einen Tag f∼bekommen** get a day off. **f∼beruflich** *a & adv* freelance. **F∼e** *nt* **im F∼en** in the open air, out of doors. **F∼frau** *f* baroness. **F∼gabe** *f* release. **f∼geben**† *v sep* □ *vt* release; (*eröffnen*) open; **jdm einen Tag f∼geben** give s.o. a day off □ *vi* (*haben*) **jdm f∼geben** give s.o. time off. **f∼gebig** *a* generous, *adv* -ly. **F∼gebigkeit** *f* - generosity. **f∼haben**† *v sep* □ *vt* **eine Stunde f∼haben** have an hour off; (*Sch*) have a free period □ *vi* (*haben*) be off work/(*Sch*) school; (*beurlaubt sein*) have time off. **f∼halten**† *vt sep* keep clear; (*belegen*) keep; **einen Tag/sich f∼halten** keep a day/oneself free; **jdn f∼halten** treat s.o. [to a meal/drink]. **F∼handelszone** *f* free-trade area. **f∼händig** *adv* without holding on

Freiheit *f* -,-**en** freedom, liberty; **sich** (*dat*) **F∼en erlauben** take liberties. **F∼sstrafe** *f* prison sentence

freiheraus *adv* frankly

Frei|herr *m* baron. **F∼karte** *f* free ticket. **F∼körperkultur** *f* naturism. **f∼lassen**† *vt sep* release, set free. **F∼lassung** *f* - release. **F∼lauf** *m* free-wheel. **f∼legen** *vt sep* expose. **f∼lich** *adv* admittedly; (*natürlich*) of course. **F∼lichttheater** *nt* open-air theatre. **f∼machen** *v sep* □ *vt* (*frankieren*) frank; (*entkleiden*) bare; **einen Tag f∼machen** take a day off □ *vi/r* (*haben*) **[sich] f∼machen** take time off. **F∼marke** *f* [postage] stamp. **F∼maurer** *m* Freemason. **f∼mütig** *a* candid, *adv* -ly. **F∼platz** *m* free seat; (*Sch*) free place. **f∼schaffend** *a* freelance. **f∼schwimmen**† **(sich)** *v sep* pass one's swimming test. **f∼setzen** *vt sep* release; (*entlassen*) make redundant. **f∼sprechen**† *vt sep* acquit. **F∼spruch** *m* acquittal. **f∼stehen**† *vi sep* (*haben*) stand empty; **es steht ihm f∼** (*fig*) he is free (**zu** to). **f∼stellen** *vt sep* exempt (**von** from); **jdm etw f∼stellen** leave sth up to s.o. **f∼stempeln** *vt sep* frank. **F∼stil** *m* freestyle. **F∼stoß** *m* free kick. **F∼stunde** *f* (*Sch*) free period

Freitag *m* Friday. **f∼s** *adv* on Fridays

Frei|tod *m* suicide. **F∼übungen** *fpl* [physical] exercises. **F∼umschlag** *m* stamped envelope. **f∼weg** *adv* freely; (*offen*) openly. **f∼willig** *a* voluntary, *adv* -ily. **F∼willige(r)** *m/f* volunteer. **F∼zeichen** *nt* ringing tone; (*Rufzeichen*) dialling tone. **F∼zeit** *f* free *or* spare time; (*Muße*) leisure; (*Tagung*) [weekend/holiday] course. **F∼zeit-** *pref* leisure ... **F∼zeitbekleidung** *f* casual wear. **f∼zügig** *a* unrestricted; (*großzügig*) liberal; (*moralisch*) permissive

fremd *a* foreign; (*unbekannt, ungewohnt*) strange; (*nicht das eigene*) other people's; **ein f∼er Mann** a stranger; **f∼e Leute** strangers; **unter f∼em Namen** under an assumed name; **jdm f∼sein** be unknown/(*wesens-*) alien to s.o.; **ich bin hier f∼** I'm a stranger here. **f∼artig** *a* strange, *adv* -ly; (*exotisch*) exotic. **F∼e** *f* - **in der F∼e** away from home; (*im Ausland*) in a foreign country. **F∼e(r)** *m/f* stranger; (*Ausländer*) foreigner; (*Tourist*) tourist. **F∼enführer** *m* [tourist] guide. **F∼enverkehr** *m* tourism. **F∼enzimmer** *nt* room [to let]; (*Gäste-*) guest room. **f∼gehen**† *vi sep* (*sein*) (*fam*) be unfaithful. **F∼körper** *m* foreign body.

f~ländisch *a* foreign; (*exotisch*) exotic. **F~ling** *m* **-s,-e** stranger. **F~sprache** *f* foreign language. **F~wort** *nt* (*pl* **-wörter**) foreign word

frenetisch *a* frenzied

frequ|entieren *vt* frequent. **F~enz** *f* **-,-en** frequency

Freske *f* **-,-n, Fresko** *nt* **-s,-ken** fresco

Fresse *f* **-,-n** (*sl*) (*Mund*) gob; (*Gesicht*) mug; **halt die F~!** shut your trap! **f~n†** *vt/i* (*haben*) eat. **F~n** *nt* **-s** feed; (*sl: Essen*) grub

Fressnapf (**Freßnapf**) *m* feeding bowl

Freud|e *f* **-,-n** pleasure; (*innere*) joy; **mit F~en** with pleasure; **jdm eine F~e machen** please s.o. **f~ig** *a* joyful, *adv* -ly; **f~iges Ereignis** (*fig*) happy event. **f~los** *a* cheerless; (*traurig*) sad

freuen *vt* please; **sich f~** be pleased (**über** + *acc* about); **sich f~ auf** (+ *acc*) look forward to; **es freut mich, ich freue mich** I'm glad *or* pleased (**dass** that)

Freund *m* **-es,-e** friend; (*Verehrer*) boyfriend; (*Anhänger*) lover (*gen* of). **F~in** *f* **-,-nen** friend; (*Liebste*) girlfriend; (*Anhängerin*) lover (*gen* of). **f~lich** *a* kind, *adv* -ly; (*umgänglich*) friendly; (*angenehm*) pleasant; **wären Sie so f~lich?** would you be so kind? **f~licherweise** *adv* kindly. **F~lichkeit** *f* **-,-en** kindness; friendliness; pleasantness

Freundschaft *f* **-,-en** friendship; **F~ schließen** become friends. **f~lich** *a* friendly

Frevel /ˈfreːfəl/ *m* **-s,-** (*liter*) outrage. **f~haft** *a* (*liter*) wicked

Frieden *m* **-s** peace; **F~ schließen** make peace; **im F~** in peace-time; **laß mich in F~!** leave me alone! **F~srichter** *m* ≈ magistrate. **F~svertrag** *m* peace treaty

fried|fertig *a* peaceable. **F~hof** *m* cemetery. **f~lich** *a* peaceful, *adv* -ly; (*verträglich*) peaceable. **f~liebend** *a* peace-loving

frieren† *vi* (*haben*) (*Person:*) be cold; *impers* **es friert/hat gefroren** it is freezing/there has been a frost; **frierst du? friert [es] dich?** are you cold? □ (*sein*) (*gefrieren*) freeze

Fries *m* **-es,-e** frieze

Frikadelle *f* **-,-n** [meat] rissole

frisch *a* fresh; (*sauber*) clean; (*leuchtend*) bright; (*munter*) lively; (*rüstig*) fit; **sich f~ machen** freshen up □ *adv* freshly, newly; **f~ gelegte Eier** new-laid eggs; **ein Bett f~ beziehen** put clean sheets on a bed; **f~ gestrichen!** wet paint! **F~e** *f* - freshness; brightness; liveliness; fitness. **F~haltepackung** *f* vacuum pack. **F~käse** *m* ≈ cottage cheese. **f~weg** *adv* freely

Fri|seur /friˈzøːɐ̯/ *m* **-s,-e** hairdresser; (*Herren-*) barber. **F~seursalon** *m* hairdressing salon. **F~seuse** /-ˈzøːzə/ *f* **-,-n** hairdresser

frisier|en *vt* **jdn/sich f~en** do s.o.'s/one's hair; **die Bilanz/einen Motor f~en** (*fam*) fiddle the accounts/soup up an engine. **F~kommode** *f* dressing-table. **F~salon** *m* = **Friseursalon. F~tisch** *m* dressing-table

Frisör *m* **-s,-e** = **Friseur**

Frist *f* **-,-en** period; (*Termin*) deadline; (*Aufschub*) time; **drei Tage F~** three days' grace. **f~en** *vt* **sein Leben f~en** eke out an existence. **f~los** *a* instant, *adv* -ly

Frisur *f* **-,-en** hairstyle

frittieren (**fritieren**) *vt* deep-fry

frivol /friˈvoːl/ *a* frivolous, *adv* -ly; (*schlüpfrig*) smutty

froh *a* happy; (*freudig*) joyful; (*erleichtert*) glad; **f~e Ostern!** happy Easter!

fröhlich *a* cheerful, *adv* -ly; (*vergnügt*) merry, *adv* -ily; **f~e Weihnachten!** merry Christmas!

F~keit *f* - cheerfulness; merriment
frohlocken *vi* (*haben*) rejoice; (*schadenfroh*) gloat
Frohsinn *m* - cheerfulness
fromm *a* (**frömmer, frömmst**) devout, *adv* -ly; (*gutartig*) docile, *adv* -ly; **f~er Wunsch** idle wish
Frömm|igkeit *f* - devoutness, piety. **f~lerisch** *a* sanctimonious, *adv* -ly
frönen *vi* (*haben*) indulge (*dat* in)
Fronleichnam *m* Corpus Christi
Front *f* -,-en front. **f~al** *a* frontal; ⟨*Zusammenstoß*⟩ head-on □ *adv* from the front; ⟨*zusammenstoßen*⟩ head-on. **F~alzusammenstoß** *m* head-on collision
Frosch *m* -[e]s,¨e frog. **F~laich** *m* frog-spawn. **F~mann** *m* (*pl* -**männer**) frogman
Frost *m* -[e]s,¨e frost. **F~beule** *f* chilblain
frösteln *vi* (*haben*) shiver; **mich fröstelte [es]** I shivered/(*fror*) felt chilly
frost|ig *a* frosty, *adv* -ily. **F~schutzmittel** *nt* antifreeze
Frottee *nt* & *m* -**s** towelling
frottier|en *vt* rub down. **F~[hand]tuch** *nt* terry towel
frotzeln *vt/i* (*haben*) **[über] jdn f~** make fun of s.o.
Frucht *f* -,¨e fruit; **F~tragen** bear fruit. **f~bar** *a* fertile; (*fig*) fruitful. **F~barkeit** *f* - fertility. **f~en** *vi* (*haben*) **wenig/nichts f~en** have little/no effect. **f~ig** *a* fruity. **f~los** *a* fruitless, *adv* -ly. **F~saft** *m* fruit juice
frugal *a* frugal, *adv* -ly
früh *a* early □ *adv* early; (*morgens*) in the morning; **heute/gestern/morgen f~** this/yesterday/tomorrow morning; **von f~an** *od* **auf** from an early age. **f~auf** *adv* **von f~auf** (NEW) **von f~ auf**, *s.* **früh**. **F~aufsteher** *m* -**s**,- early riser. **F~e** *f* - **in aller F~e** bright and early; **in der F~e** (*SGer*) in the morning.
f~er *adv* earlier; (*eher*) sooner; (*ehemals*) formerly; (*vor langer Zeit*) in the old days; **f~er oder später** sooner or later; **ich wohnte f~er in X** I used to live in X. **f~ere(r,s)** *a* earlier; (*ehemalig*) former; (*vorige*) previous; **in f~eren Zeiten** in former times. **f~estens** *adv* at the earliest. **F~geburt** *f* premature birth/(*Kind*) baby. **F~jahr** *nt* spring. **F~jahrsputz** *m* spring-cleaning. **F~kartoffeln** *fpl* new potatoes. **F~ling** *m* -**s**,-**e** spring. **f~morgens** *adv* early in the morning. **f~reif** *a* precocious
Frühstück *nt* breakfast. **f~en** *vi* (*haben*) have breakfast
frühzeitig *a* & *adv* early; (*vorzeitig*) premature, *adv* -ly
Frustr|ation /-ˈtsi̯o:n/ *f* -,-**en** frustration. **f~ieren** *vt* frustrate; **f~ierend** frustrating
Fuchs *m* -**es**,¨**e** fox; (*Pferd*) chestnut. **f~en** *vt* (*fam*) annoy
Füchsin *f* -,-**nen** vixen
fuchteln *vi* (*haben*) **mit etw f~** (*fam*) wave sth about
Fuder *nt* -**s**,- cart-load
Fuge[1] *f* -,-**n** joint; **aus den F~n gehen** fall apart
Fuge[2] *f* -,-**n** (*Mus*) fugue
füg|en *vt* fit (**in** + *acc* into); (*an-*) join (**an** + *acc* on to); (*dazu-*) add (**zu** to); (*fig: bewirken*) ordain; **sich f~en** fit (**in** + *acc* into); adjoin/(*folgen*) follow (**an etw** *acc* sth); (*fig: gehorchen*) submit (*dat* to); **sich in sein Schicksal f~en** resign oneself to one's fate; **es f~te sich** it so happened (**dass** that). **f~sam** *a* obedient, *adv* -ly. **F~ung** *f* -,-**en eine F~ung des Schicksals** a stroke of fate
fühl|bar *a* noticeable. **f~en** *vt/i* (*haben*) feel; **sich f~en** feel (**krank/einsam** ill/lonely); (*fam: stolz sein*) fancy oneself; **sich [nicht] wohl f~en** [not] feel well. **F~er** *m* -**s**,- feeler. **F~ung**

f - contact; **F~ung aufnehmen** get in touch

Fuhre *f* -,-**n** load

führ|en *vt* lead; guide ⟨*Tourist*⟩; (*geleiten*) take; (*leiten*) run; (*befehligen*) command; (*verkaufen*) stock; bear ⟨*Namen, Titel*⟩; keep ⟨*Liste, Bücher, Tagebuch*⟩; **bei** *od* **mit sich f~en** carry; **sich gut/schlecht f~en** conduct oneself well/badly □ *vi* (*haben*) lead; (*verlaufen*) go, run; **zu etw f~en** lead to sth. **f~end** *a* leading. **F~er** *m* **-s,-** leader; (*Fremden-*) guide; (*Buch*) guide[book]. **F~erhaus** *nt* driver's cab. **F~erschein** *m* driving licence; **den F~erschein machen** take one's driving test. **F~erscheinentzug** *m* disqualification from driving. **F~ung** *f* -,-**en** leadership; (*Leitung*) management; (*Mil*) command; (*Betragen*) conduct; (*Besichtigung*) guided tour; (*Vorsprung*) lead; **in F~ung gehen** go into the lead

Fuhr|unternehmer *m* haulage contractor. **F~werk** *nt* cart

Fülle *f* -,-**n** abundance, wealth (**an** + *dat* of); (*Körper-*) plumpness. **f~n** *vt* fill; (*Culin*) stuff; **sich f~n** fill [up]

Füllen *nt* **-s,-** foal

Füll|er *m* **-s,-** (*fam*), **F~federhalter** *m* fountain pen. **f~ig** *a* plump; ⟨*Busen*⟩ ample. **F~ung** *f* -,-**en** filling; (*Kissen-, Braten-*) stuffing; (*Pralinen-*) centre

fummeln *vi* (*haben*) fumble (**an** + *dat* with)

Fund *m* **-[e]s,-e** find

Fundament *nt* **-[e]s,-e** foundations *pl*. **f~al** *a* fundamental

Fund|büro *nt* lost-property office. **F~grube** *f* (*fig*) treasure trove. **F~sachen** *fpl* lost property *sg*

fünf *inv a*, **F~** *f* -,-**en** five; (*Sch*) ≈ fail mark. **F~linge** *mpl* quintuplets. **f~te(r,s)** *a* fifth. **f~zehn** *inv a* fifteen. **f~zehnte(r,s)** *a* fifteenth. **f~zig** *inv a* fifty. **F~ziger** *m* **-s,-** man in his fifties; (*Münze*) 50-pfennig piece. **f~zigste(r,s)** *a* fiftieth

fungieren *vi* (*haben*) act (**als** as)

Funk *m* **-s** radio; **über F~** over the radio. **F~e** *m* **-n,-n** spark. **f~eln** *vi* (*haben*) sparkle; ⟨*Stern:*⟩ twinkle. **f~elnagelneu** *a* (*fam*) brand-new. **F~en** *m* **-s,-** spark. **f~en** *vt* radio. **F~er** *m* **-s,-** radio operator. **F~sprechgerät** *nt* walkie-talkie. **F~spruch** *m* radio message. **F~streife** *f* [police] radio patrol

Funktion /-'tsi̯o:n/ *f* -,-**en** function; (*Stellung*) position; (*Funktionieren*) working; **außer F~** out of action. **F~är** *m* **-s,-e** official. **f~ieren** *vi* (*haben*) work

für *prep* (+ *acc*) for; **Schritt für Schritt** step by step; **was für [ein]** what [a]! (*fragend*) what sort of [a]? **für sich** by oneself/⟨*Ding:*⟩ itself. **Für** *nt* **das Für und Wider** the pros and cons *pl*. **F~bitte** *f* intercession

Furche *f* -,-**n** furrow

Furcht *f* - fear (**vor** + *dat* of); **F~erregend** terrifying. **f~bar** *a* terrible, *adv* -bly

fürcht|en *vt/i* (*haben*) fear; **sich f~en** be afraid (**vor** + *dat* of); **ich f~e, das geht nicht** I'm afraid that's impossible. **f~erlich** *a* dreadful, *adv* -ly

furcht|erregend *a* (NEW) **F~ erregend**, *s.* **Furcht**. **f~los** *a* fearless, *adv* -ly. **f~sam** *a* timid. *adv* -ly

füreinander *adv* for each other

Furnier *nt* **-s,-e** veneer. **f~t** *a* veneered

fürs *prep* = **für das**

Fürsorg|e *f* care; (*Admin*) welfare; (*fam: Geld*) ≈ social security. **F~er(in)** *m* **-s,-** (*f* -,-**nen**) social worker. **f~lich** *a* solicitous

Fürsprache *f* intercession; **F~ einlegen** intercede

Fürsprecher *m* (*fig*) advocate

Fürst *m* **-en,-en** prince. **F~entum** *nt* **-s,¨er** principality. **F~in** *f* **-,-nen** princess. **f~lich** *a* princely; (*üppig*) lavish, *adv* -ly
Furt *f* **-,-en** ford
Furunkel *m* **-s,-** (*Med*) boil
Fürwort *nt* (*pl* **-wörter**) pronoun
Furz *m* **-es,-e** (*vulg*) fart. **f~en** *vi* (*haben*) (*vulg*) fart
Fusion *f* **-,-en** fusion; (*Comm*) merger. **f~ieren** *vi* (*haben*) (*Comm*) merge
Fuß *m* **-es,¨e** foot; (*Aust: Bein*) leg; (*Lampen-*) base; (*von Weinglas*) stem; **zu Fuß** on foot; **zu Fuß gehen** walk; **auf freiem Fuß** free; **auf freundschaftlichem/großem Fuß** on friendly terms/in grand style. **F~abdruck** *m* footprint. **F~abtreter** *m* **-s,-** doormat. **F~bad** *nt* footbath. **F~ball** *m* football. **F~ballspieler** *m* footballer. **F~balltoto** *nt* football pools *pl*. **F~bank** *f* footstool. **F~boden** *m* floor. **F~bremse** *f* footbrake
Fussel *f* **-,-n** & *m* **-s,-[n]** piece of fluff; **F~n** fluff *sg*. **f~n** *vi* (*haben*) shed fluff
fuß|en *vi* (*haben*) be based (**auf** + *dat* on). **F~ende** *nt* foot
Fußgänger|(in) *m* **-s,-** (*f* **-,-nen**) pedestrian. **F~brücke** *f* footbridge. **F~überweg** *m* pedestrian crossing. **F~zone** *f* pedestrian precinct
Fuß|geher *m* **-s,-** (*Aust*) = **F~gänger. F~gelenk** *nt* ankle. **F~hebel** *m* pedal. **F~nagel** *m* toenail. **F~note** *f* footnote. **F~pflege** *f* chiropody. **F~pfleger(in)** *m*(*f*) chiropodist. **F~rücken** *m* instep. **F~sohle** *f* sole of the foot. **F~stapfen** *pl* **in jds F~stapfen treten** (*fig*) follow in s.o.'s footsteps. **F~tritt** *m* kick. **F~weg** *m* footpath; **eine Stunde F~weg** an hour's walk
futsch *pred a* (*fam*) gone
Futter[1] *nt* **-s** feed; (*Trocken-*) fodder
Futter[2] *nt* **-s,-** (*Kleider-*) lining
Futteral *nt* **-s,-e** case
füttern[1] *vt* feed
füttern[2] *vt* line
Futur *nt* **-s** (*Gram*) future; **zweites F~** future perfect. **f~istisch** *a* futuristic

G

Gabe *f* **-,-n** gift; (*Dosis*) dose
Gabel *f* **-,-n** fork. **g~n (sich)** *vr* fork. **G~stapler** *m* **-s,-** fork-lift truck. **G~ung** *f* **-,-en** fork
gackern *vi* (*haben*) cackle
gaffen *vi* (*haben*) gape, stare
Gag /gɛk/ *m* **-s,-s** (*Theat*) gag
Gage /ˈga:ʒə/ *f* **-,-n** (*Theat*) fee
gähnen *vi* (*haben*) yawn. **G~** *nt* **-s** yawn; (*wiederholt*) yawning
Gala *f* **-** ceremonial dress
galant *a* gallant, *adv* -ly
Galavorstellung *f* gala performance
Galerie *f* **-,-n** gallery
Galgen *m* **-s,-** gallows *sg*. **G~frist** *f* (*fam*) reprieve
Galionsfigur *f* figurehead
Galle *f* **-** bile; (*G~nblase*) gall-bladder. **G~nblase** *f* gall-bladder. **G~nstein** *m* gallstone
Gallert *nt* **-[e]s,-e, Gallerte** *f* **-,-n** [meat] jelly
Galopp *m* **-s** gallop; **im G~** at a gallop. **g~ieren** *vi* (*sein*) gallop
galvanisieren *vt* galvanize
gamm|eln *vi* (*haben*) (*fam*) loaf around. **G~ler(in)** *m* **-s,-** (*f* **-,-nen**) drop-out
Gams *f* **-,-en** (*Aust*) chamois
Gämse *f* **-,-n** chamois
gang *pred a* **g~ und gäbe** quite usual
Gang *m* **-[e]s,¨e** walk; (*G~art*) gait; (*Boten-*) errand; (*Funktionieren*) running; (*Verlauf, Culin*) course; (*Durch-*) passage; (*Korridor*) corridor; (*zwischen

Sitzreihen) aisle, gangway; (*Anat*) duct; (*Auto*) gear; **in G~ bringen/halten** get/keep going; **in G~ kommen** get going/(*fig*) under way; **im G~e/in vollem G~e sein** be in progress/in full swing; **Essen mit vier G~en** four-course meal. **G~art** *f* gait

gängig *a* common; (*Comm*) popular

Gangschaltung *f* gear change

Gangster /'gɛŋstɐ/ *m* **-s,-** gangster

Gangway /'gɛŋwe:/ *f* **-,-s** gangway

Ganove *m* **-n,-n** (*fam*) crook

Gans *f* **-,¨e** goose

Gänse|blümchen *nt* **-s,-** daisy. **G~füßchen** *ntpl* inverted commas. **G~haut** *f* goose-pimples *pl*. **G~marsch** *m* **im G~marsch** in single file. **G~rich** *m* **-s,-e** gander

ganz *a* whole, entire; (*vollständig*) complete; (*fam: heil*) undamaged, intact; **die g~e Zeit** all the time, the whole time; **eine g~e Weile/Menge** quite a while/lot; **g~e zehn Mark** all of ten marks; **meine g~en Bücher** all my books; *inv* **g~ Deutschland** the whole of Germany; **g~ bleiben** (*fam*) remain intact; **wieder g~ machen** (*fam*) mend; **im G~en (g~en)** in all, altogether; **im Großen und G~en (im großen und g~en)** on the whole □ *adv* quite; (*völlig*) completely, entirely; (*sehr*) very; **nicht g~** not quite; **g~ allein** all on one's own; **ein g~ alter Mann** a very old man; **g~ wie du willst** just as you like; **es war g~ nett** it was quite nice; **g~ und gar** completely, totally; **g~ und gar nicht** not at all. **G~e(s)** *nt* whole; **es geht ums G~e** it's all or nothing. **g~jährig** *adv* all the year round

gänzlich *adv* completely, entirely

ganz|tägig *a & adv* full-time; ⟨*geöffnet*⟩ all day. **g~tags** *adv* all day; ⟨*arbeiten*⟩ full-time

gar[1] *a* done, cooked

gar[2] *adv* **gar nicht/nichts/niemand** not/nothing/no one at all; **oder gar** or even

Garage /ga'ra:ʒə/ *f* **-,-n** garage

Garantie *f* **-,-n** guarantee. **g~ren** *vt/i* (*haben*) **[für] etw g~ren** guarantee sth; **er kommt g~rt zu spät** (*fam*) he's sure to be late. **G~schein** *m* guarantee

Garbe *f* **-,-n** sheaf

Garderobe *f* **-,-n** (*Kleider*) wardrobe; (*Ablage*) cloakroom, (*Amer*) checkroom; (*Flur-*) coat-rack; (*Künstler-*) dressing-room. **G~nfrau** *f* cloakroom attendant

Gardine *f* **-,-n** curtain. **G~nstange** *f* curtain rail

garen *vt/i* (*haben*) cook

gären† *vi* (*haben*) ferment; (*fig*) seethe

Garn *nt* **-[e]s,-e** yarn; (*Näh-*) cotton

Garnele *f* **-,-n** shrimp; (*rote*) prawn

garnieren *vt* decorate; (*Culin*) garnish

Garnison *f* **-,-en** garrison

Garnitur *f* **-,-en** set; (*Wäsche*) set of matching underwear; (*Möbel-*) suite; **erste/zweite G~ sein** (*fam*) be first-rate/second best

garstig *a* nasty

Garten *m* **-s,¨** garden; **botanischer G~** botanical gardens *pl*. **G~arbeit** *f* gardening. **G~bau** *m* horticulture. **G~haus** *nt*, **G~laube** *f* summerhouse. **G~lokal** *nt* open-air café. **G~schere** *f* secateurs *pl*

Gärtner|(in) *m* **-s,-** (*f* **-,-nen**) gardener. **G~ei** *f* **-,-en** nursery; (*fam: Gartenarbeit*) gardening

Gärung *f* **-** fermentation

Gas *nt* **-es,-e** gas; **Gas geben** (*fam*) accelerate. **G~herd** *m* gas cooker. **G~maske** *f* gas mask. **G~pedal** *nt* (*Auto*) accelerator

Gasse *f* **-,-n** alley; (*Aust*) street

Gast *m* **-[e]s,⸚e** guest; (*Hotel-, Urlaubs-*) visitor; (*im Lokal*) patron; **zum Mittag G⸚e haben** have people to lunch; **bei jdm zu G~ sein** be staying with s.o. **G~arbeiter** *m* foreign worker. **G~bett** *nt* spare bed

Gäste|bett *nt* spare bed. **G~buch** *nt* visitors' book. **G~zimmer** *nt* [hotel] room; (*privat*) spare room; (*Aufenthaltsraum*) residents' lounge

gast|frei, g~freundlich *a* hospitable, *adv* -bly. **G~freundschaft** *f* hospitality. **G~geber** *m* **-s,-** host. **G~geberin** *f* **-,-nen** hostess. **G~haus** *nt*, **G~hof** *m* inn, hotel

gastieren *vi* (*haben*) make a guest appearance; ⟨*Truppe, Zirkus:*⟩ perform (**in** + *dat* in)

gastlich *a* hospitable, *adv* -bly. **G~keit** *f* - hospitality

Gastro|nomie *f* - gastronomy. **g~nomisch** *a* gastronomic

Gast|spiel *nt* guest performance. **G~spielreise** *f* (*Theat*) tour. **G~stätte** *f* restaurant. **G~stube** *f* bar; (*Restaurant*) restaurant. **G~wirt** *m* landlord. **G~wirtin** *f* landlady. **G~wirtschaft** *f* restaurant

Gas|werk *nt* gasworks *sg*. **G~zähler** *m* gas-meter

Gatte *m* **-n,-n** husband

Gatter *nt* **-s,-** gate; (*Gehege*) pen

Gattin *f* **-,-nen** wife

Gattung *f* **-,-en** kind; (*Biol*) genus; (*Kunst*) genre. **G~sbegriff** *m* generic term

Gaudi *f* - (*Aust, fam*) fun

Gaul *m* **-[e]s, Gäule** [old] nag

Gaumen *m* **-s,-** palate

Gauner *m* **-s,-** crook, swindler. **G~ei** *f* **-,-en** swindle

Gaze /ˈgaːzə/ *f* - gauze

Gazelle *f* **-,-n** gazelle

geachtet *a* respected

geädert *a* veined

geartet *a* **gut g~** good-natured; **anders g~** different

Gebäck *nt* **-s** [cakes and] pastries *pl*; (*Kekse*) biscuits *pl*

Gebälk *nt* **-s** timbers *pl*

geballt *a* ⟨*Faust*⟩ clenched

Gebärde *f* **-,-n** gesture. **g~n (sich)** *vr* behave (**wie** like)

Gebaren *nt* **-s** behaviour

gebär|en† *vt* give birth to, bear; **geboren werden** be born. **G~mutter** *f* womb, uterus

Gebäude *nt* **-s,-** building

Gebeine *ntpl* [mortal] remains

Gebell *nt* **-s** barking

geben† *vt* give; (*tun, bringen*) put; (*Karten*) deal; (*aufführen*) perform; (*unterrichten*) teach; **etw verloren g~** give sth up as lost; **von sich g~** utter; (*fam: erbrechen*) bring up; **viel/wenig g~ auf** (+ *acc*) set great/little store by; **sich g~** (*nachlassen*) wear off; (*besser werden*) get better; (*sich verhalten*) behave; **sich geschlagen g~** admit defeat □ *impers* **es gibt** there is/are; **was gibt es Neues/zum Mittag/im Kino?** what's the news/for lunch/on at the cinema? **es wird Regen g~** it's going to rain; **das gibt es nicht** there's no such thing □ *vi* (*haben*) (*Karten*) deal

Gebet *nt* **-[e]s,-e** prayer

Gebiet *nt* **-[e]s,-e** area; (*Hoheits-*) territory; (*Sach-*) field

gebiet|en† *vt* command; (*erfordern*) demand □ *vi* (*haben*) rule. **G~er** *m* **-s,-** master; (*Herrscher*) ruler. **g~erisch** *a* imperious, *adv* -ly; ⟨*Ton*⟩ peremptory

Gebilde *nt* **-s,-** structure

gebildet *a* educated; (*kultiviert*) cultured

Gebirg|e *nt* **-s,-** mountains *pl*. **g~ig** *a* mountainous

Gebiss *nt* **-es,-e (Gebiß** *nt* **-sses, -sse)** teeth *pl*; (*künstliches*) false teeth *pl*, dentures *pl*; (*des Zaumes*) bit

geblümt *a* floral, flowered
gebogen *a* curved
geboren *a* born; **g~er Deutscher** German by birth; **Frau X, g~e Y** Mrs X, née Y
geborgen *a* safe, secure. **G~heit** *f* - security
Gebot *nt* **-[e]s,-e** rule; (*Relig*) commandment; (*bei Auktion*) bid
gebraten *a* fried
Gebrauch *m* use; (*Sprach-*) usage; **Gebräuche** customs; **in G~** in use; **G~ machen von** make use of. **g~en** *vt* use; **ich kann es nicht/gut g~en** I have no use for/can make good use of it; **zu nichts zu g~en** useless
gebräuchlich *a* common; ⟨*Wort*⟩ in common use
Gebrauch|sanleitung, G~s-anweisung *f* directions *pl* for use. **g~t** *a* used; (*Comm*) secondhand. **G~twagen** *m* used car
gebrechlich *a* frail, infirm
gebrochen *a* broken □ *adv* **g~Englisch sprechen** speak broken English
Gebrüll *nt* **-s** roaring; (*fam: Schreien*) bawling
Gebrumm *nt* **-s** buzzing; (*Motoren-*) humming
Gebühr *f* **-,-en** charge, fee; **über G~** excessively. **g~en** *vi* (*haben*) **ihm g~t Respekt** he deserves respect; **wie es sich g~t** as is right and proper. **g~end** *a* due, *adv* duly; (*geziemend*) proper, *adv* -ly. **g~enfrei** *a* free □ *adv* free of charge. **g~enpflichtig** *a* & *adv* subject to a charge; **g~enpflichtige Straße** toll road
gebunden *a* bound; ⟨*Suppe*⟩ thickened
Geburt *f* **-,-en** birth; **von G~** by birth. **G~enkontrolle, G~enregelung** *f* birth-control. **G~enziffer** *f* birth-rate
gebürtig *a* native (**aus** of); **g~er Deutscher** German by birth
Geburts|datum *nt* date of birth. **G~helfer** *m* obstetrician. **G~hilfe** *f* obstetrics *sg*. **G~ort** *m* place of birth. **G~tag** *m* birthday. **G~urkunde** *f* birth certificate
Gebüsch *nt* **-[e]s,-e** bushes *pl*
Gedächtnis *nt* **-ses** memory; **aus dem G~** from memory
gedämpft *a* ⟨*Ton*⟩ muffled; ⟨*Stimme*⟩ hushed; ⟨*Musik*⟩ soft; ⟨*Licht, Stimmung*⟩ subdued
Gedanke *m* **-ns,n-** thought (**an** + *acc* of); (*Idee*) idea; **sich** (*dat*) **G~n machen** worry (**über** + *acc* about). **G~nblitz** *m* brainwave. **g~nlos** *a* thoughtless, *adv* -ly; (*zerstreut*) absent-minded, *adv* -ly. **G~nstrich** *m* dash. **G~nübertragung** *f* telepathy. **g~nvoll** *a* pensive, *adv* -ly
Gedärme *ntpl* intestines; (*Tier-*) entrails
Gedeck *nt* **-[e]s,-e** place setting; (*auf Speisekarte*) set meal; **ein G~auflegen** set a place. **g~t** *a* covered; ⟨*Farbe*⟩ muted
gedeihen† *vi* (*sein*) thrive, flourish
gedenken† *vi* (*haben*) propose (**etw zu tun** to do sth); **jds/etw g~** remember s.o./sth. **G~** *nt* **-s** memory; **zum G~ an** (+ *acc*) in memory of
Gedenk|feier *f* commemoration. **G~gottesdienst** *m* memorial service. **G~stätte** *f* memorial. **G~tafel** *f* commemorative plaque. **G~tag** *m* day of remembrance; (*Jahrestag*) anniversary
Gedicht *nt* **-[e]s,-e** poem
gediegen *a* quality ...; (*solide*) well-made; ⟨*Charakter*⟩ upright; ⟨*Gold*⟩ pure □ *adv* **g~ gebaut** well built
Gedräng|e *nt* **-s** crush, crowd. **g~t** *a* (*knapp*) concise □ *adv* **g~t voll** packed
gedrückt *a* depressed
gedrungen *a* stocky

Geduld *f* - patience; **G~ haben** be patient. **g~en (sich)** *vr* be patient. **g~ig** *a* patient, *adv* -ly. **G~[s]spiel** *nt* puzzle
gedunsen *a* bloated
geehrt *a* honoured; **Sehr g~er Herr X** Dear Mr X
geeignet *a* suitable; **im g~en Moment** at the right moment
Gefahr *f* -,-en danger; **in/außer G~** in/out of danger; **auf eigene G~** at one's own risk; **G~ laufen** run the risk (**etw zu tun** of doing sth)
gefähr|den *vt* endanger; (*fig*) jeopardize. **g~lich** *a* dangerous, *adv* -ly; (*riskant*) risky
gefahrlos *a* safe
Gefährt *nt* **-[e]s,-e** vehicle
Gefährte *m* **-n,-n, Gefährtin** *f* **-,-nen** companion
gefahrvoll *a* dangerous, perilous
Gefälle *nt* **-s,-** slope; (*Straßen-*) gradient
gefallen† *vi* (*haben*) **jdm g~** please s.o.; **er/es gefällt mir** I like him/it; **sich** (*dat*) **etw g~ lassen** put up with sth
Gefallen[1] *m* **-s,-** favour
Gefallen[2] *nt* **-s** pleasure (**an** + *dat* in); **G~ finden an** (+ *dat*) like; **dir zu G~** to please you
Gefallene(r) *m* soldier killed in the war
gefällig *a* pleasing; (*hübsch*) attractive, *adv* -ly; (*hilfsbereit*) obliging; **jdm g~ sein** do s.o. a good turn; **[sonst] noch etwas g~?** will there be anything else? **G~keit** *f* -,-en favour; (*Freundlichkeit*) kindness. **g~st** *adv* (*fam*) kindly
Gefangen|e(r) *m/f* prisoner. **g~halten**† *vt sep* (NEW) **g~ halten**, *s.* **fangen**. **G~nahme** *f* - capture. **g~nehmen**† *vt sep* (NEW) **g~ nehmen**, *s.* **fangen**. **G~schaft** *f* - captivity; **in G~schaft geraten** be taken prisoner
Gefängnis *nt* **-ses,-se** prison; (*Strafe*) imprisonment. **G~strafe** *f* imprisonment; (*Urteil*) prison sentence. **G~wärter** *m* [prison] warder, (*Amer*) guard
Gefäß *nt* **-es,-e** container, receptacle; (*Blut-*) vessel
gefasst (gefaßt) *a* composed; (*ruhig*) calm, *adv* -ly; **g~ sein auf** (+ *acc*) be prepared for
Gefecht *nt* **-[e]s,-e** fight; (*Mil*) engagement; **außer G~ setzen** put out of action
gefedert *a* sprung
gefeiert *a* celebrated
Gefieder *nt* **-s** plumage. **g~t** *a* feathered
Geflecht *nt* **-[e]s,-e** network; (*Gewirr*) tangle; (*Korb-*) wicker-work
gefleckt *a* spotted
geflissentlich *adv* studiously
Geflügel *nt* **-s** poultry. **G~klein** *nt* **-s** giblets *pl*. **g~t** *a* winged; **g~tes Wort** familiar quotation
Geflüster *nt* **-s** whispering
Gefolg|e *nt* **-s** retinue, entourage. **G~schaft** *f* - followers *pl*, following; (*Treue*) allegiance
gefragt *a* popular; **g~ sein** be in demand
gefräßig *a* voracious; (*Mensch*) greedy
Gefreite(r) *m* lance-corporal
gefrier|en† *vi* (*sein*) freeze. **G~fach** *nt* freezer compartment. **G~punkt** *m* freezing point. **G~schrank** *m* upright freezer. **G~truhe** *f* chest freezer
gefroren *a* frozen. **G~e(s)** *nt* (*Aust*) ice-cream
Gefüge *nt* **-s,-** structure; (*fig*) fabric
gefügig *a* compliant; (*gehorsam*) obedient
Gefühl *nt* **-[e]s,-e** feeling; (*Empfindung*) sensation; (*G~sregung*) emotion; **im G~ haben** know instinctively. **g~los** *a* insensitive; (*herzlos*) unfeeling;

(*taub*) numb. **g~sbetont** *a* emotional. **g~skalt** *a* (*fig*) cold. **g~smäßig** *a* emotional, *adv* -ly; (*instinktiv*) instinctive, *adv* -ly. **G~sregung** *f* emotion. **g~svoll** *a* sensitive, *adv* -ly; (*sentimental*) sentimental, *adv* -ly

gefüllt *a* filled; (*voll*) full; (*Bot*) double; (*Culin*) stuffed; ⟨*Schokolade*⟩ with a filling

gefürchtet *a* feared, dreaded

gefüttert *a* lined

gegeben *a* given; (*bestehend*) present; (*passend*) appropriate; **zu g~er Zeit** at the proper time. **g~enfalls** *adv* if need be. **G~heiten** *fpl* realities, facts

gegen *prep* (+ *acc*) against; (*Sport*) versus; (*g~über*) to[wards]; (*Vergleich*) compared with; (*Richtung, Zeit*) towards; (*ungefähr*) around; **ein Mittel g~** a remedy for □ *adv* **g~ 100 Leute** about 100 people. **G~angriff** *m* counter-attack

Gegend *f* -,-en area, region; (*Umgebung*) neighbourhood

gegeneinander *adv* against/(*gegenüber*) towards one another

Gegen|fahrbahn *f* opposite carriageway. **G~gift** *nt* antidote. **G~leistung** *f* **als G~leistung** in return. **G~maßnahme** *f* countermeasure. **G~satz** *m* contrast; (*Widerspruch*) contradiction; (*G~teil*) opposite; **im G~satz zu** unlike. **g~sätzlich** *a* contrasting; (*widersprüchlich*) opposing. **g~seitig** *a* mutual, *adv* -ly; **sich g~seitig hassen** hate one another. **G~spieler** *m* opponent. **G~sprechanlage** *f* intercom. **G~stand** *m* object; (*Gram, Gesprächs-*) subject. **g~standslos** *a* unfounded; (*überflüssig*) irrelevant; (*abstrakt*) abstract. **G~stück** *nt* counterpart; (*G~teil*) opposite. **G~teil** *nt* opposite, contrary; **im G~teil** on the contrary. **g~teilig** *a* opposite

gegenüber *prep* (+ *dat*) opposite; (*Vergleich*) compared with; **jdm g~ höflich sein** be polite to s.o. □ *adv* opposite. **G~** *nt* -s person opposite. **g~liegen†** *vi sep* (*haben*) be opposite (**etw** *dat* sth). **g~liegend** *a* opposite. **g~stehen†** *vi sep* (*haben*) (+ *dat*) face; **feindlich g~stehen** (+ *dat*) be hostile to. **g~stellen** *vt sep* confront; (*vergleichen*) compare. **g~treten†** *vi sep* (*sein*) (+ *dat*) face

Gegen|verkehr *m* oncoming traffic. **G~vorschlag** *m* counter-proposal. **G~wart** *f* - present; (*Anwesenheit*) presence. **g~wärtig** *a* present □ *adv* at present. **G~wehr** *f* - resistance. **G~wert** *m* equivalent. **G~wind** *m* head wind. **g~zeichnen** *vt sep* countersign

geglückt *a* successful

Gegner|(in) *m* -s,- (*f* -,-nen) opponent. **g~isch** *a* opposing

Gehabe *nt* -s affected behaviour

Gehackte(s) *nt* mince, (*Amer*) ground meat

Gehalt[1] *m* -[e]s content

Gehalt[2] *nt* -[e]s,¨er salary. **G~serhöhung** *f* rise, (*Amer*) raise

gehaltvoll *a* nourishing

gehässig *a* spiteful, *adv* -ly

gehäuft *a* heaped

Gehäuse *nt* -s,- case; (*TV, Radio*) cabinet; (*Schnecken-*) shell; (*Kern-*) core

Gehege *nt* -s,- enclosure

geheim *a* secret; **g~ halten** keep secret; **im g~en** secretly. **G~dienst** *m* Secret Service. **g~halten†** *vt sep* (NEW) **g~ halten**, *s.* **geheim**. **G~nis** *nt* -ses,-se secret. **g~nisvoll** *a* mysterious, *adv* -ly. **G~polizei** *f* secret police

gehemmt *a* (*fig*) inhibited

gehen† *vi* (*sein*) go; (*zu Fuß*) walk; (*fort-*) leave; (*funktionieren*) work; ⟨*Teig:*⟩ rise; **tanzen/einkaufen g~** go dancing/shopping; **an die Arbeit g~** set to work; **in Schwarz [gekleidet] g~** dress in black; **nach Norden g~** ⟨*Fenster:*⟩ face north; **wenn es nach mir ginge** if I had my way; **über die Straße g~** cross the road; **was geht hier vor sich?** what is going on here? **das geht zu weit** (*fam*) that's going too far; *impers* **wie geht es [Ihnen]?** how are you? **es geht ihm gut/besser/schlecht** he is well/better/not well; (*geschäftlich*) he is doing well/better/badly; **ein gut g~des Geschäft** a flourishing *or* thriving business; **es geht nicht/nicht anders** it's impossible/there is no other way; **es ging ganz schnell** it was very quick; **es geht um** it concerns; **es geht ihr nur ums Geld** she is only interested in the money; **es geht [so]** (*fam*) not too bad; **sich g~ lassen** lose one's self-control; (*sich vernachlässigen*) let oneself go □ *vt* walk. **g~lassen†** **(sich)** *vr sep* (NEW) **g~ lassen (sich)**, *s.* **gehen**

geheuer *a* **nicht g~** eerie; (*verdächtig*) suspicious; **mir ist nicht g~** I feel uneasy

Geheul *nt* **-s** howling

Gehilfe *m* **-n,-n, Gehilfin** *f* **-,-nen** trainee; (*Helfer*) assistant

Gehirn *nt* **-s** brain; (*Verstand*) brains *pl* **G~erschütterung** *f* concussion. **G~hautentzündung** *f* meningitis. **G~wäsche** *f* brainwashing

gehoben *a* (*fig*) superior; ⟨*Sprache*⟩ elevated

Gehöft *nt* **-[e]s,-e** farm

Gehölz *nt* **-es,-e** coppice, copse

Gehör *nt* **-s** hearing; **G~ schenken** (+ *dat*) listen to

gehorchen *vi* (*haben*) (+ *dat*) obey

gehören *vi* (*haben*) belong (*dat* to); **zu den Besten g~** be one of the best; **dazu gehört Mut** that takes courage; **sich g~** be [right and] proper; **es gehört sich nicht** it isn't done

gehörig *a* proper, *adv* -ly; **jdn g~ verprügeln** give s.o. a good hiding

gehörlos *a* deaf

Gehörn *nt* **-s,-e** horns *pl*; (*Geweih*) antlers *pl*

gehorsam *a* obedient, *adv* -ly. **G~** *m* **-s** obedience

Geh|steig *m* **-[e]s,-e** pavement, (*Amer*) sidewalk. **G~weg** *m* = **Gehsteig;** (*Fußweg*) footpath

Geier *m* **-s,-** vulture

Geig|e *f* **-,-n** violin. **g~en** *vi* (*haben*) play the violin □ *vt* play on the violin. **G~er(in)** *m* **-s,-** (*f* **-,-nen**) violinist

geil *a* lecherous; (*fam*) randy; (*fam: toll*) great

Geisel *f* **-,-n** hostage

Geiß *f* **-,-en** (*SGer*) [nanny-]goat. **G~blatt** *nt* honeysuckle

Geißel *f* **-,-n** scourge

Geist *m* **-[e]s,-er** mind; (*Witz*) wit; (*Gesinnung*) spirit; (*Gespenst*) ghost; **der Heilige G~** the Holy Ghost *or* Spirit; **im G~** in one's mind. **g~erhaft** *a* ghostly

geistes|abwesend *a* absent-minded, *adv* -ly. **G~blitz** *m* brainwave. **G~gegenwart** *f* presence of mind. **g~gegenwärtig** *adv* with great presence of mind. **g~gestört** *a* [mentally] deranged. **g~krank** *a* mentally ill. **G~krankheit** *f* mental illness. **G~wissenschaften** *fpl* arts. **G~zustand** *m* mental state

geist|ig *a* mental, *adv* -ly; (*intellektuell*) intellectual, *adv* -ly; **g~ige Getränke** spirits. **g~lich** *a* spiritual, *adv* -ly; (*religiös*) religious; ⟨*Musik*⟩ sacred; ⟨*Tracht*⟩ clerical. **G~liche(r)** *m* clergyman. **G~lichkeit** *f* **-** clergy. **g~los** *a* uninspired. **g~reich** *a* clever; (*witzig*) witty

Geiz *m* **-es** meanness. **g~en** *vi* (*haben*) be mean (**mit** with). **G~hals** *m* (*fam*) miser. **g~ig** *a* mean, miserly. **G~kragen** *m* (*fam*) miser
Gekicher *nt* **-s** giggling
geknickt *a* (*fam*) dejected, *adv* -ly
gekonnt *a* accomplished □ *adv* expertly
Gekrakel *nt* **-s** scrawl
gekränkt *a* offended, hurt
Gekritzel *nt* **-s** scribble
gekünstelt *a* affected, *adv* -ly
Gelächter *nt* **-s** laughter
geladen *a* loaded; (*fam: wütend*) furious
Gelage *nt* **-s,-** feast
gelähmt *a* paralysed
Gelände *nt* **-s,-** terrain; (*Grundstück*) site. **G~lauf** *m* cross-country run
Geländer *nt* **-s,-** railings *pl*; (*Treppen-*) banisters *pl*; (*Brücken-*) parapet
gelangen *vi* (*sein*) reach/(*fig*) attain (**zu etw/an etw** *acc* sth); **in jds Besitz g~** come into s.o.'s possession
gelassen *a* composed; (*ruhig*) calm, *adv* -ly. **G~heit** *f* - equanimity; (*Fassung*) composure
Gelatine /ʒela-/ *f* - gelatine
geläufig *a* common, current; (*fließend*) fluent, *adv* -ly; **jdm g~ sein** be familiar to s.o.
gelaunt *a* **gut/schlecht g~e Leute** good-humoured/bad-tempered people; **gut/schlecht g~ sein** be in a good/bad mood
gelb *a* yellow; (*bei Ampel*) amber; **g~e Rübe** (*SGer*) carrot; **das G~e vom Ei** the yolk of the egg. **G~** *nt* **-s,-** yellow; **bei G~** (*Auto*) on [the] amber. **g~lich** *a* yellowish. **G~sucht** *f* jaundice
Geld *nt* **-es,-er** money; **öffentliche G~er** public funds. **G~beutel** *m*, **G~börse** *f* purse. **G~geber** *m* **-s,-** backer. **g~lich** *a* financial, *adv* -ly. **G~mittel** *ntpl* funds. **G~schein** *m* banknote. **G~schrank** *m* safe. **G~strafe** *f* fine. **G~stück** *nt* coin
Gelee /ʒe'le:/ *nt* **-s,-s** jelly
gelegen *a* situated; (*passend*) convenient; **jdm sehr g~ sein** *od* **kommen** suit s.o. well; **mir ist viel/wenig daran g~** I'm very/not keen on it; (*es ist wichtig*) it matters a lot/little to me
Gelegenheit *f* **-,-en** opportunity, chance; (*Anlass*) occasion; (*Comm*) bargain; **bei G~** some time. **G~sarbeit** *f* casual work. **G~sarbeiter** *m* casual worker. **G~skauf** *m* bargain
gelegentlich *a* occasional □ *adv* occasionally; (*bei Gelegenheit*) some time □ *prep* (+ *gen*) on the occasion of
gelehrt *a* learned. **G~e(r)** *m/f* scholar
Geleise *nt* **-s,-** = **Gleis**
Geleit *nt* **-[e]s** escort; **freies G~** safe conduct. **g~en** *vt* escort. **G~zug** *m* (*Naut*) convoy
Gelenk *nt* **-[e]s,-e** joint. **g~ig** *a* supple; (*Techn*) flexible
gelernt *a* skilled
Geliebte(r) *m/f* lover; (*liter*) beloved
gelieren /ʒe-/ *vi* (*haben*) set
gelinde *a* mild, *adv* -ly; **g~ gesagt** to put it mildly
gelingen† *vi* (*sein*) succeed, be successful; **es gelang ihm, zu entkommen** he succeeded in escaping. **G~** *nt* **-s** success
gell *int* (*SGer*) = **gelt**
gellend *a* shrill, *adv* -y
geloben *vt* promise [solemnly]; **sich** (*dat*) **g~** vow (**zu** to); **das Gelobte Land** the Promised Land
Gelöbnis *nt* **-ses,-se** vow
gelöst *a* (*fig*) relaxed
Gelse *f* **-,-n** (*Aust*) mosquito
gelt *nt* (*SGer*) **das ist schön, g~?** it's nice, isn't it? **ihr kommt**

doch, g~? you are coming, aren't you?
gelten† *vi (haben)* be valid; ⟨*Regel:*⟩ apply; **g~ als** be regarded as; **etw nicht g~ lassen** not accept sth; **wenig/viel g~** be worth/*(fig)* count for little/a lot; **jdm g~** be meant for s.o.; **das gilt nicht** that doesn't count. **g~d** *a* valid; ⟨*Preise*⟩ current; ⟨*Meinung*⟩ prevailing; **g~d machen** assert ⟨*Recht, Forderung*⟩; bring to bear ⟨*Einfluss*⟩
Geltung *f* - validity; *(Ansehen)* prestige; **G~ haben** be valid; **zur G~ bringen/kommen** set off/show to advantage
Gelübde *nt* **-s,-** vow
gelungen *a* successful
Gelüst *nt* **-[e]s,-e** desire/*(stark)* craving (**nach** for)
gemächlich *a* leisurely □ *adv* in a leisurely manner
Gemahl *m* **-s,-e** husband. **G~in** *f* **-,-nen** wife
Gemälde *nt* **-s,-** painting. **G~galerie** *f* picture gallery
gemäß *prep* (+ *dat*) in accordance with □ *a* **etw** (*dat*) **g~ sein** be in keeping with sth
gemäßigt *a* moderate; ⟨*Klima*⟩ temperate
gemein *a* common; *(unanständig)* vulgar; *(niederträchtig)* mean; **g~er Soldat** private; **etw g~ haben** have sth in common □ *adv* shabbily; *(fam: schrecklich)* terribly
Gemeinde *f* **-,-n** [local] community; *(Admin)* borough; *(Pfarr-)* parish; *(bei Gottesdienst)* congregation. **G~rat** *m* local council/*(Person)* councillor. **G~wahlen** *fpl* local elections
gemein|gefährlich *a* dangerous. **G~heit** *f* **-,-en** (*s.* **gemein**) commonness; vulgarity; meanness; *(Bemerkung, Handlung)* mean thing [to say/do]; **so eine G~heit!** how mean! *(wie ärgerlich)* what a nuisance! **G~kosten** *pl* overheads. **g~nützig** *a* charitable. **G~platz** *m* platitude. **g~sam** *a* common; **etw g~sam haben** have sth in common □ *adv* together
Gemeinschaft *f* **-,-en** community. **g~lich** *a* joint; ⟨*Besitz*⟩ communal □ *adv* jointly; *(zusammen)* together. **G~sarbeit** *f* team-work
Gemenge *nt* **-s,-** mixture
gemessen *a* measured; *(würdevoll)* dignified
Gemetzel *nt* **-s,-** carnage
Gemisch *nt* **-[e]s,-e** mixture. **g~t** *a* mixed
Gemme *f* **-,-n** engraved gem
Gemse *f* **-,-n** (NEW) **Gämse**
Gemurmel *nt* **-s** murmuring
Gemüse *nt* **-s,-** vegetable; *(coll)* vegetables *pl*. **G~händler** *m* greengrocer
gemustert *a* patterned
Gemüt *nt* **-[e]s,-er** nature, disposition; *(Gefühl)* feelings *pl*; *(Person)* soul
gemütlich *a* cosy; *(gemächlich)* leisurely; *(zwanglos)* informal; ⟨*Person*⟩ genial; **es sich** (*dat*) **g~ machen** make oneself comfortable □ *adv* cosily; in a leisurely manner; informally. **G~keit** *f* - cosiness; leisureliness
Gemüts|art *f* nature, disposition. **G~mensch** *m* *(fam)* placid person. **G~ruhe** *f* **in aller G~ruhe** *(fam)* calmly. **G~verfassung** *f* frame of mind
Gen *nt* **-s,-e** gene
genau *a* exact, *adv* -ly, precise, *adv* -ly; ⟨*Waage, Messung*⟩ accurate, *adv* -ly; *(sorgfältig)* meticulous, *adv* -ly; *(ausführlich)* detailed; **nichts G~es wissen** not know any details; **es nicht so g~ nehmen** not be too particular; **g~ genommen** strictly speaking; **g~!** exactly! **g~genommen** *adv* (NEW) **g~ genommen**, *s.* **genau**. **G~igkeit** *f* -

exactitude; precision; accuracy; meticulousness

genauso *adv* just the same; (*g~sehr*) just as much; **g~ schön/teuer** just as beautiful/ expensive; **g~ gut** just as good; *adv* just as well; **g~ sehr** just as much; **g~ viel** just as much/ many; **g~ wenig** just as little/ few; (*noch*) no more. **g~gut** *adv* (NEW) **g~ gut**, *s.* **genauso**. **g~sehr** *adv* (NEW) **g~ sehr**, *s.* **genauso**. **g~viel** *adv* (NEW) **g~ viel**, *s.* **genauso**. **g~wenig** *adv* (NEW) **g~ wenig**, *s.* **genauso**

Gendarm /ʒã'darm/ *m* **-en,-en** (*Aust*) policeman

Genealogie *f* - genealogy

genehmig|en *vt* grant; approve ⟨*Plan*⟩. **G~ung** *f* **-,-en** permission; (*Schein*) permit

geneigt *a* sloping, inclined; (*fig*) well-disposed (*dat* towards); **[nicht] g~ sein** (*fig*) [not] feel inclined (**zu** to)

General *m* **-s,¨e** general. **G~direktor** *m* managing director. **g~isieren** *vi* (*haben*) generalize. **G~probe** *f* dress rehearsal. **G~streik** *m* general strike. **g~überholen** *vt insep* (*inf & pp only*) completely overhaul

Generation /-'tsi̯o:n/ *f* **-,-en** generation

Generator *m* **-s,-en** /-'to:rən/ generator

generell *a* general, *adv* -ly

genes|en† *vi* (*sein*) recover. **G~ung** *f* - recovery; (*Erholung*) convalescence

Genet|ik *f* - genetics *sg*. **g~isch** *a* genetic, *adv* -ally

Genf *nt* **-s** Geneva. **G~er** *a* Geneva ...; **G~er See** Lake Geneva

genial *a* brilliant, *adv* -ly; **ein g~er Mann** a man of genius. **G~ität** *f* - genius

Genick *nt* **-s,-e** [back of the] neck; **sich** (*dat*) **das G~ brechen** break one's neck

Genie /ʒe'ni:/ *nt* **-s,-s** genius

genieren /ʒe'ni:rən/ *vt* embarrass; **sich g~** feel *or* be embarrassed

genieß|bar *a* fit to eat/drink. **g~en**† *vt* enjoy; (*verzehren*) eat/ drink. **G~er** *m* **-s,-** gourmet. **g~erisch** *a* appreciative □ *adv* with relish

Genitiv *m* **-s,-e** genitive

Genosse *m* **-n,-n** (*Pol*) comrade. **G~nschaft** *f* **-,-en** cooperative

Genre /'ʒã:rə/ *nt* **-s,-s** genre

Gentechnologie *f* genetic engineering

genug *inv a & adv* enough

Genüge *f* **zur G~** sufficiently. **g~n** *vi* (*haben*) be enough; **jds Anforderungen g~n** meet s.o.'s requirements. **g~nd** *inv a* sufficient, enough; (*Sch*) fair □ *adv* sufficiently, enough

genügsam *a* frugal, *adv* -ly; (*bescheiden*) modest, *adv* -ly

Genugtuung *f* - satisfaction

Genuss *m* **-es,¨e** (**Genuß** *m* **-sses, ¨sse**) enjoyment; (*Vergnügen*) pleasure; (*Verzehr*) consumption

genüsslich (**genüßlich**) *a* pleasurable □ *adv* with relish

geöffnet *a* open

Geo|graphie, **G~grafie** *f* - geography. **g~graphisch**, **g~grafisch** *a* geographical, *adv* -ly. **G~loge** *m* **-n,-n** geologist. **G~logie** *f* - geology. **g~logisch** *a* geological, *adv* -ly. **G~meter** *m* **-s,-** surveyor. **G~metrie** *f* - geometry. **g~metrisch** *a* geometric[al]

geordnet *a* well-ordered; (*stabil*) stable; **alphabetisch g~** in alphabetical order

Gepäck *nt* **-s** luggage, baggage. **G~ablage** *f* luggage-rack. **G~aufbewahrung** *f* left-luggage office. **G~schalter** *m* luggage office. **G~schein** *m* left-luggage ticket; (*Aviat*) baggage check. **G~stück** *nt* piece of luggage. **G~träger** *m* porter;

(*Fahrrad-*) luggage carrier; (*Dach-*) roof-rack. **G~wagen** *m* luggage-van

Gepard *m* **-s,-e** cheetah

gepflegt *a* well-kept; ⟨*Person*⟩ well-groomed; ⟨*Hotel*⟩ first-class

Gepflogenheit *f* **-,-en** practice; (*Brauch*) custom

Gepolter *nt* **-s** [loud] noise

gepunktet *a* spotted

gerade *a* straight; (*direkt*) direct; (*aufrecht*) upright; (*aufrichtig*) straightforward; ⟨*Zahl*⟩ even; **etw g~ biegen** straighten sth; **sich g~ halten** hold oneself straight □ *adv* straight; directly; (*eben*) just; (*genau*) exactly; (*besonders*) especially; **g~ sitzen/stehen** sit/stand [up] straight; **nicht g~ billig** not exactly cheap; **g~ erst** only just; **g~ an dem Tag** on that very day. **G~** *f* **-,-n** straight line. **g~aus** *adv* straight ahead/on

gerade|biegen† *vt sep* (NEW) **g~ biegen**, *s.* **gerade**. **g~halten**† **(sich)** *vr sep* (NEW) **sich g~ halten**, *s.* **gerade**. **g~heraus** *adv* (*fig*) straight out. **g~sitzen**† *vi sep* (*haben*) (NEW) **g~ sitzen**, *s.* **gerade**. **g~so** *adv* just the same; **g~so gut** just as good; *adv* just as well. **g~sogut** *adv* (NEW) **g~so gut**, *s.* **geradeso**. **g~stehen**† *vi sep* (*haben*) (*fig*) accept responsibility **(für** for); (*aufrecht stehen*) (NEW) **g~ stehen**, *s.* **gerade**. **g~wegs** *adv* directly, straight. **g~zu** *adv* virtually; (*wirklich*) absolutely

Geranie /-i̯ə/ *f* **-,-n** geranium

Gerät *nt* **-[e]s,-e** tool; (*Acker-*) implement; (*Küchen-*) utensil; (*Elektro-*) appliance; (*Radio-, Fernseh-*) set; (*Turn-*) piece of apparatus; (*coll*) equipment

geraten† *vi* (*sein*) get; **in Brand g~** catch fire; **in Wut g~** get angry; **in Streit g~** start quarrelling; **gut/schlecht g~** turn out well/badly; **nach jdm g~** take after s.o.

Geratewohl *nt* **aufs G~** at random

geräuchert *a* smoked

geräumig *a* spacious, roomy

Geräusch *nt* **-[e]s,-e** noise. **g~los** *a* noiseless, *adv* -ly. **g~voll** *a* noisy, *adv* -ily

gerben *vt* tan

gerecht *a* just, *adv* -ly; (*fair*) fair, *adv* -ly; **g~ werden** (+ *dat*) do justice to. **g~fertigt** *a* justified. **G~igkeit** *f* - justice; fairness

Gerede *nt* **-s** talk; (*Klatsch*) gossip

geregelt *a* regular

gereift *a* mature

gereizt *a* irritable, *adv* -bly **G~heit** *f* - irritability

gereuen *vt* **es gereut mich nicht** I don't regret it

Geriatrie *f* - geriatrics *sg*

Gericht[1] *nt* **-[e]s,-e** (*Culin*) dish

Gericht[2] *nt* **-[e]s,-e** court [of law]; **vor G~** in court; **das Jüngste G~** the Last Judgement; **mit jdm ins G~ gehen** take s.o. to task. **g~lich** *a* judicial; ⟨*Verfahren*⟩ legal □ *adv* **g~lich vorgehen** take legal action. **G~sbarkeit** *f* - jurisdiction. **G~shof** *m* court of justice. **G~smedizin** *f* forensic medicine. **G~ssaal** *m* courtroom. **G~svollzieher** *m* **-s,-** bailiff

gerieben *a* grated; (*fam: schlau*) crafty

gering *a* small; (*niedrig*) low; (*g~fügig*) slight; **jdn/etw g~ achten** have little regard for s.o./sth; (*verachten*) despise s.o./sth. **g~achten** *vt sep* (NEW) **g~ achten**, *s.* **gering**. **g~fügig** *a* slight, *adv* -ly. **g~schätzig** *a* contemptuous, *adv* -ly; ⟨*Bemerkung*⟩ disparaging. **g~ste(r,s)** *a* least; **nicht im G~sten (g~sten)** not in the least

gerinnen† *vi* (*sein*) curdle; ⟨*Blut:*⟩ clot

Gerippe *nt* **-s,-** skeleton; (*fig*) framework
gerissen *a* (*fam*) crafty
Germ *m* **-[e]s** & (*Aust*) *f* **-** yeast
German|e *m* **-n,-n** [ancient] German. **g~isch** *a* Germanic. **G~ist(in)** *m* **-en,-en** (*f* **-,-nen**) Germanist. **G~istik** *f* **-** German [language and literature]
gern[e] *adv* gladly; **g~ haben** like; (*lieben*) be fond of; **ich tanze/schwimme g~** I like dancing-/swimming; **das kannst du g~ tun** you're welcome to do that; **willst du mit?—g~!** do you want to come?—I'd love to!
gerötet *a* red
Gerste *f* **-** barley. **G~nkorn** *nt* (*Med*) stye
Geruch *m* **-[e]s,⸚e** smell (**von/nach** of). **g~los** *a* odourless. **G~ssinn** *m* sense of smell
Gerücht *nt* **-[e]s,-e** rumour
geruhen *vi* (*haben*) deign (**zu** to)
gerührt *a* (*fig*) moved, touched
Gerümpel *nt* **-s** lumber, junk
Gerüst *nt* **-[e]s,-e** scaffolding; (*fig*) framework
gesalzen *a* salted; (*fam: hoch*) steep
gesammelt *a* collected; (*gefasst*) composed
gesamt *a* entire, whole. **G~ausgabe** *f* complete edition. **G~betrag** *m* total amount. **G~eindruck** *m* overall impression. **G~heit** *f* **-** whole. **G~schule** *f* comprehensive school. **G~summe** *f* total
Gesandte(r) *m/f* envoy
Gesang *m* **-[e]s,⸚e** singing; (*Lied*) song; (*Kirchen-*) hymn. **G~buch** *nt* hymn-book. **G~verein** *m* choral society
Gesäß *nt* **-es** buttocks *pl*. **G~tasche** *f* hip pocket
Geschäft *nt* **-[e]s,-e** business; (*Laden*) shop, (*Amer*) store; (*Transaktion*) deal; (*fam: Büro*) office; **schmutzige G~e** shady dealings; **ein gutes G~ machen** do very well (**mit** out of); **sein G~ verstehen** know one's job. **g~ehalber** *adv* on business. **g~ig** *a* busy, *adv* -ily; ⟨*Treiben*⟩ bustling. **G~igkeit** *f* **-** activity. **g~lich** *a* business ... □ *adv* on business
Geschäfts|brief *m* business letter. **G~führer** *m* manager; (*Vereins-*) secretary. **G~mann** *m* (*pl* **-leute**) businessman. **G~reise** *f* business trip. **G~stelle** *f* office; (*Zweigstelle*) branch. **g~tüchtig** *a* **g~tüchtig sein** be a good businessman/-woman. **G~viertel** *nt* shopping area. **G~zeiten** *fpl* hours of business
geschehen† *vi* (*sein*) happen (*dat* to); **es ist ein Unglück g~** there has been an accident; **es ist um uns g~** we are done for; **das geschieht dir recht!** it serves you right! **gern g~!** you're welcome! **G~** *nt* **-s** events *pl*
gescheit *a* clever; **daraus werde ich nicht g~** I can't make head or tail of it
Geschenk *nt* **-[e]s,-e** present, gift. **G~korb** *m* gift hamper
Geschicht|e *f* **-,-n** history; (*Erzählung*) story; (*fam: Sache*) business. **g~lich** *a* historical, *adv* -ly
Geschick *nt* **-[e]s** fate; (*Talent*) skill; **G~ haben** be good (**zu** at). **G~lichkeit** *f* **-** skilfulness, skill. **g~t** *a* skilful, *adv* -ly; (*klug*) clever, *adv* -ly
geschieden *a* divorced. **G~e(r)** *m/f* divorcee
Geschirr *nt* **-s,-e** (*coll*) crockery; (*Porzellan*) china; (*Service*) service; (*Pferde-*) harness; **schmutziges G~** dirty dishes *pl*. **G~spülmaschine** *f* dishwasher. **G~tuch** *nt* tea-towel
Geschlecht *nt* **-[e]s,-er** sex; (*Gram*) gender; (*Familie*) family; (*Generation*) generation. **g~lich** *a* sexual, *adv* -ly. **G~skrankheit** *f* venereal disease. **G~steile** *ntpl*

genitals. **G~sverkehr** *m* sexual intercourse. **G~swort** *nt* (*pl* **-wörter**) article
geschliffen *a* (*fig*) polished
geschlossen *a* closed □ *adv* unanimously; (*vereint*) in a body
Geschmack *m* **-[e]s,-̈e** taste; (*Aroma*) flavour; (*G~ssinn*) sense of taste; **einen guten G~ haben** (*fig*) have good taste; **G~ finden an** (+ *dat*) acquire a taste for. **g~los** *a* tasteless, *adv* -ly; **g~los sein** (*fig*) be in bad taste. **G~ssache** *f* matter of taste. **g~voll** *a* (*fig*) tasteful, *adv* -ly
geschmeidig *a* supple; (*weich*) soft
Geschöpf *nt* **-[e]s,-e** creature
Geschoss *nt* **-es,-e** (**Geschoß** *nt* **-sses,-sse**) missile; (*Stockwerk*) storey, floor
geschraubt *a* (*fig*) stilted
Geschrei *nt* **-s** screaming; (*fig*) fuss
Geschütz *nt* **-es,-e** gun, cannon
geschützt *a* protected; ⟨*Stelle*⟩ sheltered
Geschwader *nt* **-s,-** squadron
Geschwätz *nt* **-es** talk. **g~ig** *a* garrulous
geschweift *a* curved
geschweige *conj* **g~ denn** let alone
geschwind *a* quick, *adv* -ly
Geschwindigkeit *f* **-,-en** speed; (*Phys*) velocity. **G~sbegrenzung, G~sbeschränkung** *f* speed limit
Geschwister *pl* brother[s] and sister[s]; siblings
geschwollen *a* swollen; (*fig*) pompous, *adv* -ly
Geschworene|(r) *m/f* juror; **die G~n** the jury *sg*
Geschwulst *f* **-,-̈e** swelling; (*Tumor*) tumour
geschwungen *a* curved
Geschwür *nt* **-s,-e** ulcer
Geselle *m* **-n,-n** fellow; (*Handwerks-*) journeyman
gesellig *a* sociable; (*Zool*) gregarious; (*unterhaltsam*) convivial; **g~er Abend** social evening. **G~keit** *f* **-,-en** entertaining; **die G~keit lieben** love company
Gesellschaft *f* **-,-en** company; (*Veranstaltung*) party; **die G~** society; **jdm G~ leisten** keep s.o. company. **g~lich** *a* social, *adv* -ly. **G~sreise** *f* group tour. **G~sspiel** *nt* party game
Gesetz *nt* **-es,-e** law. **G~entwurf** *m* bill. **g~gebend** *a* legislative. **G~gebung** *f* **-** legislation. **g~lich** *a* legal, *adv* -ly. **g~los** *a* lawless. **g~mäßig** *a* lawful, *adv* -ly; (*gesetzlich*) legal, *adv* -ly
gesetzt *a* staid; (*Sport*) seeded □ *conj* **g~ den Fall** supposing
gesetzwidrig *a* illegal, *adv* -ly
gesichert *a* secure
Gesicht *nt* **-[e]s,-er** face; (*Aussehen*) appearance; **zu G~ bekommen** set eyes on. **G~sausdruck** *m* [facial] expression. **G~sfarbe** *f* complexion. **G~spunkt** *m* point of view. **G~szüge** *mpl* features
Gesindel *nt* **-s** riff-raff
gesinnt *a* **gut/übel g~** well/ill disposed (*dat* towards)
Gesinnung *f* **-,-en** mind; (*Einstellung*) attitude; **politische G~** political convictions *pl*
gesittet *a* well-mannered; (*zivilisiert*) civilized
gesondert *a* separate, *adv* -ly
Gespann *nt* **-[e]s,-e** team; (*Wagen*) horse and cart/carriage
gespannt *a* taut; (*fig*) tense, *adv* -ly; ⟨*Beziehungen*⟩ strained; (*neugierig*) eager, *adv* -ly; (*erwartungsvoll*) expectant, *adv* -ly; **g~ sein, ob** wonder whether; **auf etw/jdn g~ sein** look forward eagerly to sth/to seeing s.o.
Gespenst *nt* **-[e]s,-er** ghost. **g~isch** *a* ghostly; (*unheimlich*) eerie

Gespött *nt* **-[e]s** mockery; **zum G~ werden** become a laughing-stock
Gespräch *nt* **-[e]s-e** conversation; (*Telefon-*) call; **ins G~ kommen** get talking; **im G~ sein** be under discussion. **g~ig** *a* talkative. **G~sgegenstand** *m*, **G~sthema** *nt* topic of conversation
gesprenkelt *a* speckled
Gespür *nt* **-s** feeling; (*Instinkt*) instinct
Gestalt *f* **-,-en** figure; (*Form*) shape, form; **G~ annehmen** (*fig*) take shape. **g~en** *vt* shape; (*organisieren*) arrange; (*schaffen*) create; (*entwerfen*) design; **sich g~en** turn out
geständ|ig *a* confessed; **g~ig sein** have confessed. **G~nis** *nt* **-ses,-se** confession
Gestank *m* **-s** stench, [bad] smell
gestatten *vt* allow, permit; **nicht gestattet** prohibited; **g~ Sie?** may I?
Geste /ˈgɛ-, ˈgeːstə/ *f* **-,-n** gesture
Gesteck *nt* **-[e]s,-e** flower arrangement
gestehen† *vt/i* (*haben*) confess; confess to ⟨*Verbrechen*⟩; **offen gestanden** to tell the truth
Gestein *nt* **-[e]s,-e** rock
Gestell *nt* **-[e]s,-e** stand; (*Flaschen-*) rack; (*Rahmen*) frame
gestellt *a* **gut/schlecht g~** well/badly off; **auf sich** (*acc*) **selbst g~ sein** be thrown on one's own resources
gestelzt *a* (*fig*) stilted
gesteppt *a* quilted
gestern *adv* yesterday; **g~ Nacht (nacht)** last night
Gestik /ˈgɛstɪk/ *f* - gestures *pl*. **g~ulieren** *vi* (*haben*) gesticulate
gestrandet *a* stranded
gestreift *a* striped
gestrichelt *a* ⟨*Linie*⟩ dotted
gestrichen *a* **g~er Teelöffel** level teaspoon[ful]
gestrig /ˈgɛstrɪç/ *a* yesterday's; **am g~en Tag** yesterday
Gestrüpp *nt* **-s,-e** undergrowth
Gestüt *nt* **-[e]s,-e** stud [farm]
Gesuch *nt* **-[e]s,-e** request; (*Admin*) application. **g~t** *a* sought-after; (*gekünstelt*) contrived
gesund *a* healthy, *adv* -ily; **g~ sein** be in good health; ⟨*Sport, Getränk:*⟩ be good for one; **wieder g~ werden** get well again
Gesundheit *f* - health; **G~!** (*bei Niesen*) bless you! **g~lich** *a* health ...; **g~licher Zustand** state of health □ *adv* **es geht ihm g~lich gut/schlecht** he is in good/poor health. **g~shalber** *adv* for health reasons. **g~sschädlich** *a* harmful. **G~szustand** *m* state of health
getäfelt *a* panelled
getigert *a* tabby
Getöse *nt* **-s** racket, din
getragen *a* solemn, *adv* -ly
Getränk *nt* **-[e]s,-e** drink. **G~ekarte** *f* wine-list
getrauen *vt* **sich** (*dat*) **etw g~** dare [to] do sth; **sich g~** dare
Getreide *nt* **-s** (*coll*) grain
getrennt *a* separate, *adv* -ly; **g~ leben** live apart; **g~ schreiben** write as two words. **g~schreiben**† *vt sep* (NEW) **g~ schreiben**, *s*. **getrennt**
getreu *a* faithful, *adv* -ly □ *prep* (+ *dat*) true to; **der Wahrheit g~** truthfully. **g~lich** *adv* faithfully
Getriebe *nt* **-s,-** bustle; (*Techn*) gear; (*Auto*) transmission; (*Gehäuse*) gearbox
getrost *adv* with confidence
Getto *nt* **-s,-s** ghetto
Getue *nt* **-s** (*fam*) fuss
Getümmel *nt* **-s** tumult
getüpfelt *a* spotted
geübt *a* skilled; ⟨*Auge, Hand*⟩ practised
Gewächs *nt* **-es,-e** plant; (*Med*) growth

gewachsen *a* **jdm/etw g~ sein** be a match for s.o./be equal to sth
Gewächshaus *nt* greenhouse; (*Treibhaus*) hothouse
gewagt *a* daring
gewählt *a* refined
gewahr *a* **g~ werden** become aware (*acc/gen* of)
Gewähr *f* - guarantee
gewahren *vt* notice
gewähr|en *vt* grant; (*geben*) offer; **jdn g~en lassen** let s.o. have his way. **g~leisten** *vt* guarantee
Gewahrsam *m* **-s** safekeeping; (*Haft*) custody
Gewährsmann *m* (*pl* **-männer & -leute**) informant, source
Gewalt *f* **-,-en** power; (*Kraft*) force; (*Brutalität*) violence; **mit G~** by force; **G~ anwenden** use force; **sich in der G~ haben** be in control of oneself. **G~herrschaft** *f* tyranny. **g~ig** *a* powerful; (*fam: groß*) enormous, *adv* -ly; (*stark*) tremendous, *adv* -ly. **g~sam** *a* forcible, *adv* -bly; ⟨*Tod*⟩ violent. **g~tätig** *a* violent. **G~tätigkeit** *f* **-,-en** violence; (*Handlung*) act of violence
Gewand *nt* **-[e]s,¨er** robe
gewandt *a* skilful, *adv* -ly; (*flink*) nimble, *adv* -bly. **G~heit** *f* - skill; nimbleness
Gewässer *nt* **-s,-** body of water; **G~** *pl* waters
Gewebe *nt* **-s,-** fabric; (*Anat*) tissue
Gewehr *nt* **-s,-e** rifle, gun
Geweih *nt* **-[e]s,-e** antlers *pl*
Gewerb|e *nt* **-s,-** trade. **g~lich** *a* commercial, *adv* -ly. **g~smäßig** *a* professional, *adv* -ly
Gewerkschaft *f* **-,-en** trade union. **G~ler(in)** *m* **-s,-** (*f* **-,-nen**) trade unionist
Gewicht *nt* **-[e]s,-e** weight; (*Bedeutung*) importance. **G~heben** *nt* **-s** weight-lifting. **g~ig** *a* important
gewieft *a* (*fam*) crafty
gewillt *a* **g~ sein** be willing
Gewinde *nt* **-s,-** [screw] thread
Gewinn *m* **-[e]s,-e** profit; (*fig*) gain, benefit; (*beim Spiel*) winnings *pl*; (*Preis*) prize; (*Los*) winning ticket; **G~ bringend** profitable, *adv* -bly. **G~beteiligung** *f* profit-sharing. **g~bringend** *a* (NEW) **G~ bringend**, *s.* **Gewinn**. **g~en**† *vt* win; (*erlangen*) gain; (*fördern*) extract; **jdn für sich g~en** win s.o. over □ *vi* (*haben*) win; **g~en an** (+ *dat*) gain in. **g~end** *a* engaging. **G~er(in)** *m* **-s,-** (*f* **-,-nen**) winner
Gewirr *nt* **-s,-e** tangle; (*Straßen-*) maze; **G~ von Stimmen** hubbub of voices
gewiss (gewiß) *a* **(gewisser, gewissest)** certain, *adv* -ly
Gewissen *nt* **-s,-** conscience. **g~haft** *a* conscientious, *adv* -ly. **g~los** *a* unscrupulous. **G~sbisse** *mpl* pangs of conscience
gewissermaßen *adv* to a certain extent; (*sozusagen*) as it were
Gewissheit (Gewißheit) *f* - certainty
Gewitt|er *nt* **-s,-** thunderstorm. **g~ern** *vi* (*haben*) **es g~ert** it is thundering. **g~rig** *a* thundery
gewogen *a* (*fig*) well-disposed (*dat* towards)
gewöhnen *vt* **jdn/sich g~an** (+ *acc*) get s.o. used to/get used to; **[an] jdn/etw gewöhnt sein** be used to s.o./sth
Gewohnheit *f* **-,-en** habit. **g~smäßig** *a* habitual, *adv* -ly. **G~srecht** *nt* common law
gewöhnlich *a* ordinary, *adv* -ily; (*üblich*) usual, *adv* -ly; (*ordinär*) common
gewohnt *a* customary; (*vertraut*) familiar; (*üblich*) usual; **etw** (*acc*) **g~ sein** be used to sth
Gewöhnung *f* - getting used (**an** + *acc* to); (*Süchtigkeit*) addiction
Gewölb|e *nt* **-s,-** vault. **g~t** *a* curved; (*Archit*) vaulted

gewollt *a* forced
Gewühl *nt* **-[e]s** crush
gewunden *a* winding
gewürfelt *a* check[ed]
Gewürz *nt* **-es,-e** spice. **G~nelke** *f* clove
gezackt *a* serrated
gezähnt *a* serrated; ⟨*Säge*⟩ toothed
Gezeiten *fpl* tides
gezielt *a* specific; ⟨*Frage*⟩ pointed
geziemend *a* proper, *adv* -ly
geziert *a* affected, *adv* -ly
gezwungen *a* forced □ *adv* **g~ lachen** give a forced laugh. **g~ermaßen** *adv* of necessity; **etw g~ermaßen tun** be forced to do sth
Gicht *f* - gout
Giebel *m* **-s,-** gable
Gier *f* - greed (**nach** for). **g~ig** *a* greedy, *adv* -ily
gieß|en† *vt* pour; water ⟨*Blumen, Garten*⟩; (*Techn*) cast □ *v impers* **es g~t** it is pouring [with rain]. **G~erei** *f* **-,-en** foundry. **G~kanne** *f* watering-can
Gift *nt* **-[e]s,-e** poison; (*Schlangen-*) venom; (*Biol, Med*) toxin. **g~ig** *a* poisonous; ⟨*Schlange*⟩ venomous; (*Med, Chem*) toxic; (*fig*) spiteful, *adv* -ly. **G~müll** *m* toxic waste. **G~pilz** *m* poisonous fungus, toadstool. **G~zahn** *m* [poison] fang
gigantisch *a* gigantic
Gilde *f* **-,-n** guild
Gimpel *m* **-s,-** bullfinch; (*fam: Tölpel*) simpleton
Gin /dʒɪn/ *m* **-s** gin
Ginster *m* **-s** (*Bot*) broom
Gipfel *m* **-s,-** summit, top; (*fig*) peak. **G~konferenz** *f* summit conference. **g~n** *vi* (*haben*) culminate (**in** + *dat* in)
Gips *m* **-es** plaster. **G~abguss** (**G~abguß**) *m* plaster cast. **G~er** *m* **-s,-** plasterer. **G~verband** *m* (*Med*) plaster cast
Giraffe *f* **-,-n** giraffe
Girlande *f* **-,-n** garland
Girokonto /ˈʒi:ro-/ *nt* current account
Gischt *m* **-[e]s** & *f* - spray
Gitar|re *f* **-,-n** guitar. **G~rist(in)** *m* **-en,-en** (*f* **-,-nen**) guitarist
Gitter *nt* **-s,-** bars *pl*; (*Rost*) grating, grid; (*Geländer, Zaun*) railings *pl*; (*Fenster-*) grille; (*Draht-*) wire screen; **hinter G~n** (*fam*) behind bars. **G~netz** *nt* grid
Glanz *m* **-es** shine; (*von Farbe, Papier*) gloss; (*Seiden-*) sheen; (*Politur*) polish; (*fig*) brilliance; (*Pracht*) splendour
glänzen *vi* (*haben*) shine. **g~d** *a* shining, bright; ⟨*Papier, Haar*⟩ glossy; (*fig*) brilliant, *adv* -ly
glanz|los *a* dull. **G~stück** *nt* masterpiece; (*einer Sammlung*) showpiece. **g~voll** *a* (*fig*) brilliant, *adv* -ly; (*prachtvoll*) splendid, *adv* -ly. **G~zeit** *f* heyday
Glas *nt* **-es,¨-er** glass; (*Brillen-*) lens; (*Fern-*) binoculars *pl*; (*Marmeladen-*) [glass] jar. **G~er** *m* **-s,-** glazier
gläsern *a* glass ...
Glashaus *nt* greenhouse
glasieren *vt* glaze; ice ⟨*Kuchen*⟩
glas|ig *a* glassy; (*durchsichtig*) transparent. **G~scheibe** *f* pane
Glasur *f* **-,-en** glaze; (*Culin*) icing
glatt *a* smooth; (*eben*) even; ⟨*Haar*⟩ straight; (*rutschig*) slippery; (*einfach*) straightforward; (*eindeutig*) downright; ⟨*Absage*⟩ flat; **g~ streichen** smooth out □ *adv* smoothly; evenly; (*fam: völlig*) completely; (*gerade*) straight; (*leicht*) easily; ⟨*ablehnen*⟩ flatly; **g~ rasiert** clean-shaven; **g~ gehen** *od* **verlaufen** go off smoothly; **das ist g~ gelogen** it's a downright lie
Glätte *f* - smoothness; (*Rutschigkeit*) slipperiness
Glatteis *nt* [black] ice; **aufs G~ führen** (*fam*) take for a ride
glätten *vt* smooth; **sich g~** become smooth; ⟨*Wellen:*⟩ subside

glatt|gehen† *vi sep (sein)* (NEW) **g~ gehen**, *s.* **glatt. g~rasiert** *a* (NEW) **g~ rasiert**, *s.* **glatt. g~streichen**† *vt sep* (NEW) **g~ streichen**, *s.* **glatt. g~weg** *adv* (*fam*) outright

Glatz|e *f* **-,-n** bald patch; (*Voll-*) bald head; **eine G~e bekommen** go bald. **g~köpfig** *a* bald

Glaube *m* **-ns** belief (**an** + *acc* in); (*Relig*) faith; **in gutem G~n** in good faith; **G~n schenken** (+ *dat*) believe. **g~n** *vt/i (haben)* believe (**an** + *acc* in); (*vermuten*) think; **jdm g~n** believe s.o; **nicht zu g~n** unbelievable, incredible. **G~nsbekenntnis** *nt* creed

glaubhaft *a* credible; (*überzeugend*) convincing, *adv* -ly

gläubig *a* religious; (*vertrauend*) trusting, *adv* -ly. **G~e(r)** *m/f* (*Relig*) believer; **die G~en** the faithful. **G~er** *m* **-s,-** (*Comm*) creditor

glaub|lich *a* **kaum g~lich** scarcely believable. **g~würdig** *a* credible; ⟨*Person*⟩ reliable. **G~würdigkeit** *f* **-** credibility; reliability

gleich *a* same; (*identisch*) identical; (*g~wertig*) equal; **g~ bleibend** constant; **2 mal 5 [ist] g~ 10** two times 5 equals 10; **das ist mir g~** it's all the same to me; **ganz g~, wo/wer** no matter where/who □ *adv* equally; (*übereinstimmend*) identically, the same; (*sofort*) immediately; (*in Kürze*) in a minute; (*fast*) nearly; (*direkt*) right; **g~ gesinnt** like-minded; **g~ alt/schwer sein** be the same age/weight. **g~altrig** *a* [of] the same age. **g~artig** *a* similar. **g~bedeutend** *a* synonymous. **g~berechtigt** *a* equal. **G~berechtigung** *f* equality. **g~bleibend** *a* (NEW) **g~ bleibend**, *s.* **gleich**

gleichen† *vi (haben)* **jdm/etw g~** be like *or* resemble s.o./sth; **sich g~** be alike

gleich|ermaßen *adv* equally. **g~falls** *adv* also, likewise; **danke g~falls** thank you, the same to you. **g~förmig** *a* uniform, *adv* -ly; (*eintönig*) monotonous, *adv* -ly. **G~förmigkeit** *f* uniformity; monotony. **g~gesinnt** *a* (NEW) **g~ gesinnt**, *s.* **gleich. G~gewicht** *nt* balance; (*Phys & fig*) equilibrium. **g~gültig** *a* indifferent, *adv* -ly; (*unwichtig*) unimportant. **G~gültigkeit** *f* indifference. **G~heit** *f* **-** equality; (*Ähnlichkeit*) similarity. **g~machen** *vt sep* make equal; **dem Erdboden g~machen** raze to the ground. **g~mäßig** *a* even, *adv* -ly, regular, *adv* -ly; (*beständig*) constant, *adv* -ly; **G~mäßigkeit** *f* **-** regularity. **G~mut** *m* equanimity. **g~mütig** *a* calm, *adv* -ly

Gleichnis *nt* **-ses,-se** parable

gleich|sam *adv* as it were. **G~schritt** *m* **im G~schritt** in step. **g~sehen**† *vi sep (haben)* **jdm g~sehen** look like s.o.; (*fam: typisch sein*) be just like s.o. **g~setzen** *vt sep* equate/(*g~stellen*) place on a par (*dat*/**mit** with). **g~stellen** *vt sep* place on a par (*dat* with). **G~strom** *m* direct current. **g~tun**† *vi sep (haben)* **es jdm g~tun** emulate s.o.

Gleichung *f* **-,-en** equation

gleich|viel *adv* no matter (**ob/wer** whether/who). **g~wertig** *a* of equal value. **g~zeitig** *a* simultaneous, *adv* -ly

Gleis *nt* **-es,-e** track; (*Bahnsteig*) platform; **G~ 5** platform 5

gleiten† *vi (sein)* glide; (*rutschen*) slide. **g~d** *a* sliding; **g~de Arbeitszeit** flexitime

Gleitzeit *f* flexitime

Gletscher *m* **-s,-** glacier. **G~spalte** *f* crevasse

Glied *nt* **-[e]s,-er** limb; (*Teil*) part; (*Ketten-*) link; (*Mitglied*) member; (*Mil*) rank. **g~ern** *vt* arrange;

(*einteilen*) divide; **sich g~ern** be divided (*in* + *acc* into). **G~maßen** *fpl* limbs

glimmen† *vi* (*haben*) glimmer

glimpflich *a* lenient, *adv* -ly; **g~ davonkommen** get off lightly

glitschig *a* slippery

glitzern *vi* (*haben*) glitter

global *a* global, *adv* -ly

Globus *m* - & **-busses,-ben** & **-busse** globe

Glocke *f* **-,-n** bell. **G~nturm** *m* bell-tower, belfry

glorifizieren *vt* glorify

glorreich *a* glorious

Glossar *nt* **-s,-e** glossary

Glosse *f* **-,-n** comment

glotzen *vi* (*haben*) stare

Glück *nt* **-[e]s** [good] luck; (*Zufriedenheit*) happiness; **G~ bringend** lucky; **G~/kein G~ haben** be lucky/unlucky; **zum G~** luckily, fortunately; **auf gut G~** on the off chance; (*wahllos*) at random. **g~bringend** *a* (NEW) **G~ bringend**, *s.* **Glück. g~en** *vi* (*sein*) succeed; **es ist mir geglückt** I succeeded

gluckern *vi* (*haben*) gurgle

glücklich *a* lucky, fortunate; (*zufrieden*) happy; (*sicher*) safe □ *adv* happily; safely; (*fam: endlich*) finally. **g~erweise** *adv* luckily, fortunately

glückselig *a* blissfully happy. **G~keit** *f* bliss

glucksen *vi* (*haben*) gurgle

Glücksspiel *nt* game of chance; (*Spielen*) gambling

Glückwunsch *m* good wishes *pl*; (*Gratulation*) congratulations *pl*; **herzlichen G~!** congratulations! (*zum Geburtstag*) happy birthday! **G~karte** *f* greetings card

Glüh|birne *f* light-bulb. **g~en** *vi* (*haben*) glow. **g~end** *a* glowing; (*rot-*) red-hot; ⟨*Hitze*⟩ scorching; (*leidenschaftlich*) fervent, *adv* -ly. **G~faden** *m* filament. **G~wein** *m* mulled wine. **G~würmchen** *nt* **-s,-** glow-worm

Glukose *f* - glucose

Glut *f* - embers *pl*; (*Röte*) glow; (*Hitze*) heat; (*fig*) ardour

Glyzinie /-jə/ *f* **-,-n** wisteria

GmbH *abbr* (**Gesellschaft mit beschränkter Haftung**) ≈ plc

Gnade *f* - mercy; (*Gunst*) favour; (*Relig*) grace. **G~nfrist** *f* reprieve. **g~nlos** *a* merciless, *adv* -ly

gnädig *a* gracious, *adv* -ly; (*mild*) lenient, *adv* -ly; **g~e Frau** Madam

Gnom *m* **-en,-en** gnome

Gobelin /gobəˈlɛ̃ː/ *m* **-s,-s** tapestry

Gold *nt* **-[e]s** gold. **g~en** *a* gold . . .; (*g~farben*) golden; **g~ene Hochzeit** golden wedding. **G~fisch** *m* goldfish. **G~grube** *f* gold-mine. **g~ig** *a* sweet, lovely. **G~lack** *m* wallflower. **G~regen** *m* laburnum. **G~schmied** *m* goldsmith

Golf[1] *m* **-[e]s,-e** (*Geog*) gulf

Golf[2] *nt* **-s** golf. **G~platz** *m* golf-course. **G~schläger** *m* golf-club. **G~spieler(in)** *m(f)* golfer

Gondel *f* **-,-n** gondola; (*Kabine*) cabin

Gong *m* **-s,-s** gong

gönnen *vt* **jdm etw g~** not begrudge s.o. sth; **jdm etw nicht g~** begrudge s.o. sth; **sie gönnte sich** (*dat*) **keine Ruhe** she allowed herself no rest

Gönner *m* **-s,-** patron. **g~haft** *a* patronizing, *adv* -ly

Gör *nt* **-s,-en, Göre** *f* **-,-n** (*fam*) kid

Gorilla *m* **-s,-s** gorilla

Gosse *f* **-,-n** gutter

Got|ik *f* - Gothic. **g~isch** *a* Gothic

Gott *m* **-[e]s,⸚er** God; (*Myth*) god

Götterspeise *f* jelly

Gottes|dienst *m* service. **g~lästerlich** *a* blasphemous, *adv* -ly. **G~lästerung** *f* blasphemy

Gottheit *f* **-,-en** deity
Göttin *f* **-,-nen** goddess
göttlich *a* divine, *adv* -ly
gott|los *a* ungodly; (*atheistisch*) godless. **g~verlassen** *a* God-forsaken
Götze *m* **-n,-n**, **G~nbild** *nt* idol
Gouver|nante /guvər'nantə/ *f* **-,-n** governess. **G~neur** /-'nø:ɐ̯/ *m* **-s,-e** governor
Grab *nt* **-[e]s,¨-er** grave
graben† *vi* (*haben*) dig
Graben *m* **-s,¨** ditch; (*Mil*) trench
Grab|mal *nt* tomb. **G~stein** *m* gravestone, tombstone
Grad *m* **-[e]s,-e** degree
Graf *m* **-en,-en** count
Grafik *f* **-,-en** graphics *sg*; (*Kunst*) graphic arts *pl*; (*Druck*) print
Gräfin *f* **-,-nen** countess
grafisch *a* graphic; **g~e Darstellung** diagram
Grafschaft *f* **-,-en** county
Gram *m* **-s** grief
grämen (sich) *vr* grieve
grämlich *a* morose, *adv* -ly
Gramm *nt* **-s,-e** gram
Gram|matik *f* **-,-en** grammar. **g~matikalisch, g~matisch** *a* grammatical, *adv* -ly
Granat *m* **-[e]s,-e** (*Miner*) garnet. **G~apfel** *m* pomegranate. **G~e** *f* **-,-n** shell; (*Hand-*) grenade
Granit *m* **-s,-e** granite
Graph|ik *f*, **g~isch** *a* = **Grafik, grafisch**
Gras *nt* **-es,¨-er** grass. **g~en** *vi* (*haben*) graze. **G~hüpfer** *m* **-s,-** grasshopper
grassieren *vi* (*haben*) be rife
grässlich (gräßlich) *a* dreadful, *adv* -ly
Grat *m* **-[e]s,-e** [mountain] ridge
Gräte *f* **-,-n** fishbone
Gratifikation /-'tsi̯o:n/ *f* **-,-en** bonus
gratis *adv* free [of charge]. **G~probe** *f* free sample
Gratu|lant(in) *m* **-en,-en** (*f* **-,-nen**) well-wisher. **G~lation** /-'tsi̯o:n/ *f* **-,-en** congratulations *pl*; (*Glückwünsche*) best wishes *pl*. **g~lieren** *vi* (*haben*) **jdm g~lieren** congratulate s.o. (**zu** on); (*zum Geburtstag*) wish s.o. happy birthday; **[ich] g~liere!** congratulations!
grau *a*, **G~** *nt* **-s,-** grey. **G~brot** *nt* mixed rye and wheat bread
Gräuel *m* **-s,-** horror. **G~tat** *f* atrocity
grauen[1] *vi* (*haben*) **der Morgen** *od* **es graut** dawn is breaking
grauen[2] *v impers* **mir graut [es] davor** I dread it. **G~** *nt* **-s** dread. **g~haft, g~voll** *a* gruesome; (*grässlich*) horrible, *adv* -bly
gräulich[1] *a* greyish
gräulich[2] *a* horrible, *adv* -bly
Graupeln *fpl* soft hail *sg*
grausam *a* cruel, *adv* -ly. **G~keit** *f* **-,-en** cruelty
graus|en *v impers* **mir graust davor** I dread it. **G~en** *nt* **-s** horror, dread. **g~ig** *a* gruesome
gravieren *vt* engrave. **g~d** *a* (*fig*) serious
Grazie /'gra:tsi̯ə/ *f* **-** grace
graziös *a* graceful, *adv* -ly
greifbar *a* tangible; **in g~er Nähe** within reach
greifen† *vt* take hold of; (*fangen*) catch □ *vi* (*haben*) reach (**nach** for); **g~ zu** (*fig*) turn to; **um sich g~** (*fig*) spread. **G~** *nt* **G~ spielen** play tag
Greis *m* **-es,-e** old man. **G~enalter** *nt* extreme old age. **g~enhaft** *a* old. **G~in** *f* **-,-nen** old woman
grell *a* glaring; ⟨*Farbe*⟩ garish; (*schrill*) shrill, *adv* -y
Gremium *nt* **-s,-ien** committee
Grenz|e *f* **-,-n** border; (*Staats-*) frontier; (*Grundstücks-*) boundary; (*fig*) limit. **g~en** *vi* (*haben*) border (**an** + *acc* on). **g~enlos** *a* boundless; (*maßlos*) infinite, *adv* -ly. **G~fall** *m* borderline case
Greu|el *m* **-s,-** (NEW) **Gräuel**. **g~lich** *a* (NEW) **gräulich**[2]

Griech|e *m* **-n,-n** Greek. **G~enland** *nt* **-s** Greece. **G~in** *f* **-,-nen** Greek woman. **g~isch** *a* Greek. **G~isch** *nt* **-[s]** (*Lang*) Greek
griesgrämig *a* (*fam*) grumpy
Grieß *m* **-es** semolina
Griff *m* **-[e]s,-e** grasp, hold; (*Hand-*) movement of the hand; (*Tür-, Messer-*) handle; (*Schwert-*) hilt. **g~bereit** *a* handy
Grill *m* **-s,-s** grill; (*Garten-*) barbecue
Grille *f* **-,-n** (*Zool*) cricket; (*fig: Laune*) whim
grill|en *vt* grill; (*im Freien*) barbecue □ *vi* (*haben*) have a barbecue. **G~fest** *nt* barbecue. **G~gericht** *nt* grill
Grimasse *f* **-,-n** grimace; **G~n schneiden** pull faces
grimmig *a* furious; ⟨*Kälte*⟩ bitter
grinsen *vi* (*haben*) grin. **G~** *nt* **-s** grin
Grippe *f* **-,-n** influenza, (*fam*) flu
grob *a* **(gröber, gröbst)** coarse, *adv* -ly; (*unsanft, ungefähr*) rough, *adv* -ly; (*unhöflich*) rude, *adv* -ly; (*schwer*) gross, *adv* -ly; ⟨*Fehler*⟩ bad; **g~e Arbeit** rough work; **g~ geschätzt** roughly. **G~ian** *m* **-s,-e** brute
gröblich *a* gross, *adv* -ly
grölen *vt/i* (*haben*) bawl
Groll *m* **-[e]s** resentment; **einen G~ gegen jdn hegen** bear s.o. a grudge. **g~en** *vi* (*haben*) be angry (*dat* with); ⟨*Donner:*⟩ rumble
Grönland *nt* **-s** Greenland
Gros[1] *nt* **-ses,-** (*Maß*) gross
Gros[2] /gro:/ *nt* **-** majority, bulk
Groschen *m* **-s,-** (*Aust*) groschen; (*fam*) ten-pfennig piece; **der G~ ist gefallen** (*fam*) the penny's dropped
groß *a* **(größer, größt)** big; ⟨*Anzahl, Summe*⟩ large; (*bedeutend, stark*) great; (*g~artig*) grand; ⟨*Buchstabe*⟩ capital; **g~e Ferien** summer holidays; **g~e Angst haben** be very frightened; **der größte Teil** the majority *or* bulk; **g~ werden** ⟨*Person:*⟩ grow up; **g~ in etw** (*dat*) **sein** be good at sth; **g~ geschrieben werden** (*fig*) be very important (**bei jdm** to s.o.); **G~ und Klein (g~ und klein)** young and old; **im G~en und Ganzen (im g~en und ganzen)** on the whole □ *adv* ⟨*feiern*⟩ in style; (*fam: viel*) much; **jdn g~ ansehen** look at s.o. in amazement
groß|artig *a* magnificent, *adv* -ly. **G~aufnahme** *f* close-up. **G~britannien** *nt* **-s** Great Britain. **G~buchstabe** *m* capital letter. **G~e(r)** *m/f* **unser G~er** our eldest; **die G~en** the grown-ups; (*fig*) the great *pl*
Größe *f* **-,-n** size; (*Ausmaß*) extent; (*Körper-*) height; (*Bedeutsamkeit*) greatness; (*Math*) quantity; (*Person*) great figure
Groß|eltern *pl* grandparents. **g~enteils** *adv* largely
Größenwahnsinn *m* megalomania
Groß|handel *m* wholesale trade. **G~händler** *m* wholesaler. **g~herzig** *a* magnanimous, *adv* -ly. **G~macht** *f* superpower. **G~mut** *f* - magnanimity. **g~mütig** *a* magnanimous, *adv* -ly. **G~mutter** *f* grandmother. **G~onkel** *m* great-uncle. **G~reinemachen** *nt* **-s** spring-clean. **g~schreiben**† *vt sep* write with a capital [initial] letter; **g~geschrieben werden** (*fig*) (NEW) **g~ geschrieben werden**, *s.* **groß**. **G~schreibung** *f* capitalization. **g~sprecherisch** *a* boastful. **g~spurig** *a* pompous, *adv* -ly; (*überheblich*) arrogant, *adv* -ly. **G~stadt** *f* [large] city. **g~städtisch** *a* city ... **G~tante** *f* great-aunt. **G~teil** *m* large proportion; (*Hauptteil*) bulk
größtenteils *adv* for the most part

groß|tun† **(sich)** *vr sep* brag. **G~vater** *m* grandfather. **g~ziehen†** *vt sep* bring up; rear ⟨*Tier*⟩. **g~zügig** *a* generous, *adv* -ly; (*weiträumig*) spacious. **G~zügigkeit** *f* - generosity

grotesk *a* grotesque, *adv* -ly

Grotte *f* -,-n grotto

Grübchen *nt* -s,- dimple

Grube *f* -,-n pit

grübeln *vi* (*haben*) brood

Gruft *f* -,¨e [burial] vault

grün *a* green; **im G~en** out in the country; **die G~en** the Greens. **G~** *nt* -s,- green; (*Laub, Zweige*) greenery

Grund *m* -[e]s,¨e ground; (*Boden*) bottom; (*Hinter-*) background; (*Ursache*) reason; **aus diesem G~e** for this reason; **von G~ auf** (*fig*) radically; **im G~e [genommen]** basically; **auf G~ laufen** (*Naut*) run aground; **auf G~** (+ *gen*) = **aufgrund**; **zu G~e richten/gehen/liegen** = **zugrunde richten/gehen/liegen**, *s.* **zugrunde**. **G~begriffe** *mpl* basics. **G~besitz** *m* landed property. **G~besitzer** *m* landowner

gründ|en *vt* found, set up; start ⟨*Familie*⟩; (*fig*) base (**auf** + *acc* on); **sich g~en** be based (**auf** + *acc* on). **G~er(in)** *m* -s,- (*f* -,-nen) founder

Grund|farbe *f* primary colour. **G~form** *f* (*Gram*) infinitive. **G~gesetz** *nt* (*Pol*) constitution. **G~lage** *f* basis, foundation. **g~legend** *a* fundamental, *adv* -ly

gründlich *a* thorough, *adv* -ly. **G~keit** *f* - thoroughness

grund|los *a* bottomless; (*fig*) groundless □ *adv* without reason. **G~mauern** *fpl* foundations

Gründonnerstag *m* Maundy Thursday

Grund|regel *f* basic rule. **G~riss** (**G~riß**) *m* ground-plan; (*fig*) outline. **G~satz** *m* principle. **g~sätzlich** *a* fundamental, *adv* -ly; (*im Allgemeinen*) in principle; (*prinzipiell*) on principle; **G~schule** *f* primary school. **G~stein** *m* foundation-stone. **G~stück** *nt* plot [of land]

Gründung *f* -,-en foundation

grün|en *vi* (*haben*) become green. **G~gürtel** *m* green belt. **G~span** *m* verdigris. **G~streifen** *m* grass verge; (*Mittel-*) central reservation, (*Amer*) median strip

grunzen *vi* (*haben*) grunt

Gruppe *f* -,-n group; (*Reise-*) party

gruppieren *vt* group; **sich g~** form a group/groups

Grusel|geschichte *f* horror story. **g~ig** *a* creepy

Gruß *m* -es,¨e greeting; (*Mil*) salute; **einen schönen G~ an X** give my regards to X; **viele/herzliche G~e** regards; **Mit freundlichen G~en** Yours sincerely/(*Comm*) faithfully

grüßen *vt/i* (*haben*) say hallo (**jdn** to s.o.); (*Mil*) salute; **g~Sie X von mir** give my regards to X; **jdn g~ lassen** send one's regards to s.o.; **grüß Gott!** (*SGer, Aust*) good morning/afternoon/evening!

guck|en *vi* (*haben*) (*fam*) look. **G~loch** *nt* peep-hole

Guerilla /ge'rɪlja/ *f* - guerrilla warfare. **G~kämpfer** *m* guerrilla

Gulasch *nt & m* -[e]s goulash

gültig *a* valid, *adv* -ly. **G~keit** *f* - validity

Gummi *m & nt* -s,-[s] rubber; (*Harz*) gum. **G~band** *nt* (*pl* **-bänder**) elastic *or* rubber band; (*G~zug*) elastic

gummiert *a* gummed

Gummi|knüppel *m* truncheon. **G~stiefel** *m* gumboot, wellington. **G~zug** *m* elastic

Gunst *f* - favour; **zu jds G~en** in s.o.'s favour; **zu G~** (+ *gen*) = **zugunsten**

günstig *a* favourable, *adv* -bly; (*passend*) convenient, *adv* -ly

Günstling *m* -s,-e favourite

Gurgel *f* **-,-n** throat. **g~n** *vi* (*haben*) gargle. **G~wasser** *nt* gargle

Gurke *f* **-,-n** cucumber; (*Essig-*) gherkin

gurren *vi* (*haben*) coo

Gurt *m* **-[e]s,-e** strap; (*Gürtel*) belt; (*Auto*) safety-belt. **G~band** *nt* (*pl* **-bänder**) waistband

Gürtel *m* **-s,-** belt. **G~linie** *f* waistline. **G~rose** *f* shingles *sg*

GUS *abbr* **(Gemeinschaft Unabhängiger Staaten)** CIS

Guss *m* **-es,¨e (Guß** *m* **-sses,¨sse)** (*Techn*) casting; (*Strom*) stream; (*Regen-*) down-pour; (*Torten-*) icing. **G~eisen** *nt* cast iron. **g~eisern** *a* cast-iron

gut *a* **(besser, best)** good; ⟨*Gewissen*⟩ clear; (*gütig*) kind (**zu** to); **jdm gut sein** be fond of s.o.; **im G~en (g~en)** amicably; **zu g~er Letzt** in the end; **schon gut** that's all right □ *adv* well; ⟨*schmecken, riechen*⟩ good; (*leicht*) easily; **es gut haben** be well off; (*Glück haben*) be lucky; **gut zu sehen** clearly visible; **gut drei Stunden** a good three hours; **du hast gut reden** it's easy for you to talk

Gut *nt* **-[e]s,¨er** possession, property; (*Land-*) estate; **Gut und Böse** good and evil; **Güter** (*Comm*) goods

Gutacht|en *nt* **-s,-** expert's report. **G~er** *m* **-s,-** expert

gut|artig *a* good-natured; (*Med*) benign. **g~aussehend** *a* (NEW) **gut aussehend**, *s.* **aussehen. g~bezahlt** *a* (NEW) **gut bezahlt**, *s.* **bezahlen. G~dünken** *nt* **-s nach eigenem G~dünken** at one's own discretion

Gute|(s) *nt* **etwas/nichts G~s** something/nothing good; **G~s tun** do good; **das G~ daran** the good thing about it all; **alles G~!** all the best!

Güte *f* **-,-n** goodness, kindness; (*Qualität*) quality; **du meine G~!** my goodness!

Güterzug *m* goods/(*Amer*) freight train

gut|gehen† *vi sep* (*sein*) (NEW) **gut gehen**, *s.* **gehen. g~gehend** *a* (NEW) **gut gehend**, *s.* **gehen. g~gemeint** *a* (NEW) **gut gemeint**, *s.* **meinen. g~gläubig** *a* trusting. **g~haben**† *vt sep* **fünfzig Mark g~haben** have fifty marks credit (**bei** with). **G~haben** *nt* **-s,-** [credit] balance; (*Kredit*) credit. **g~heißen**† *vt sep* approve of

gütig *a* kind, *adv* -*ly*

gütlich *a* amicable, *adv* -*bly*

gut|machen *vt sep* make up for; make good ⟨*Schaden*⟩. **g~mütig** *a* good-natured, *adv* -*ly*. **G~mütigkeit** *f* - good nature. **G~schein** *m* credit note; (*Bon*) voucher; (*Geschenk-*) gift token. **g~schreiben**† *vt sep* credit. **G~schrift** *f* credit

Guts|haus *nt* manor house. **G~hof** *m* manor

gut|situiert *a* (NEW) **gut situiert**, *s.* **situiert. g~tun**† *vi sep* (*haben*) (NEW) **gut tun**, *s.* **tun. g~willig** *a* willing, *adv* -ly

Gymnasium *nt* **-s,-ien** ≈ grammar school

Gymnast|ik *f* - [keep-fit] exercises *pl*; (*Turnen*) gymnastics *sg*. **g~isch** *a* **g~ische Übung** exercise

Gynäko|loge *m* **-n,-n** gynaecologist. **G~logie** *f* - gynaecology. **g~logisch** *a* gynaecological

H

H, h /haː/ *nt*, **-,-** (*Mus*) B, b

Haar *nt* **-[e]s,-e** hair; **sich** (*dat*) **die Haare** *od* **das H~ waschen** wash one's hair; **um ein H~** (*fam*) very nearly. **H~bürste** *f* hairbrush. **h~en** *vi* (*haben*) shed hairs; ⟨*Tier:*⟩ moult □ *vr* **sich**

h~en moult. **h~ig** *a* hairy; (*fam*) tricky. **H~klammer, H~klemme** *f* hair-grip. **H~nadel** *f* hairpin. **H~nadelkurve** *f* hairpin bend. **H~schleife** *f* bow. **H~schnitt** *m* haircut. **H~spange** *f* slide. **h~sträubend** *a* hair-raising; (*empörend*) shocking. **H~trockner** *m* **-s,-** hair-drier. **H~waschmittel** *nt* shampoo

Habe *f* - possessions *pl*

haben† *vt* have; **Angst/Hunger/Durst h~** be frightened/hungry/thirsty; **ich hätte gern** I'd like; **sich h~** (*fam*) make a fuss; **es gut/schlecht h~** be well/badly off; **etw gegen jdn h~** have sth against s.o.; **was hat er?** what's the matter with him? □ *v aux* have; **ich habe/hatte geschrieben** I have/had written; **er hätte ihr geholfen** he would have helped her

Habgier *f* greed. **h~ig** *a* greedy

Habicht *m* **-[e]s,-e** hawk

Hab|seligkeiten *fpl* belongings. **H~sucht** *f* = **Habgier**

Hachse *f* **-,-n** (*Culin*) knuckle

Hack|beil *nt* chopper. **H~braten** *m* meat loaf

Hacke[1] *f* **-,-n** hoe; (*Spitz-*) pick

Hacke[2] *f* **-,-n, Hacken** *m* **-s,-** heel

hack|en *vt* hoe; (*schlagen, zerkleinern*) chop; ⟨*Vogel:*⟩ peck; **gehacktes Rindfleisch** minced/(*Amer*) ground beef. **H~fleisch** *nt* mince, (*Amer*) ground meat

Hafen *m* **-s,⸚** harbour; (*See-*) port. **H~arbeiter** *m* docker. **H~damm** *m* mole. **H~stadt** *f* port

Hafer *m* **-s** oats *pl*. **H~flocken** *fpl* [rolled] oats. **H~mehl** *nt* oatmeal

Haft *f* - (*Jur*) custody; (*H~strafe*) imprisonment. **h~bar** *a* (*Jur*) liable. **H~befehl** *m* warrant [of arrest]

haften *vi* (*haben*) cling; (*kleben*) stick; (*bürgen*) vouch/(*Jur*) be liable (**für** for)

Häftling *m* **-s,-e** detainee

Haftpflicht *f* (*Jur*) liability. **H~versicherung** *f* (*Auto*) third-party insurance

Haftstrafe *f* imprisonment

Haftung *f* - (*Jur*) liability

Hagebutte *f* **-,-n** rose-hip

Hagel *m* **-s** hail. **H~korn** *nt* hailstone. **h~n** *vi* (*haben*) hail

hager *a* gaunt

Hahn *m* **-[e]s,⸚e** cock; (*Techn*) tap, (*Amer*) faucet

Hähnchen *nt* **-s,-** (*Culin*) chicken

Hai[fisch] *m* **-[e]s,-e** shark

Häkchen *nt* **-s,-** tick

häkel|n *vt/i* (*haben*) crochet. **H~nadel** *f* crochet-hook

Haken *m* **-s,-** hook; (*Häkchen*) tick; (*fam: Schwierigkeit*) snag. **h~** *vt* hook (**an** + *acc* to). **H~kreuz** *nt* swastika. **H~nase** *f* hooked nose

halb *a* half; **eine h~e Stunde** half an hour; **zum h~en Preis** at half price; **auf h~em Weg** half-way □ *adv* half; **h~drei** half past two; **fünf [Minuten] vor/nach h~vier** twenty-five [minutes] past three/to four; **h~ und h~** half and half; (*fast ganz*) more or less. **H~blut** *nt* half-breed. **H~dunkel** *nt* semi-darkness. **H~e(r,s)** *f/m/nt* half [a litre]

halber *prep* (+ *gen*) for the sake of; **Geschäfte h~** on business

Halb|finale *nt* semifinal. **H~heit** *f* **-,-en** (*fig*) half-measure

halbieren *vt* halve, divide in half; (*Geom*) bisect

Halb|insel *f* peninsula. **H~kreis** *m* semicircle. **H~kugel** *f* hemisphere. **h~laut** *a* low □ *adv* in an undertone. **h~mast** *adv* at half-mast. **H~messer** *m* **-s,-** radius. **H~mond** *m* half moon. **H~pension** *f* half-board. **h~rund** *a* semicircular. **H~schuh** *m* [flat] shoe. **h~stündlich** *a & adv* half-hourly. **h~tags** *adv* [for] half a day; **h~tags arbeiten** ≈ work part-time. **H~ton** *m* semitone.

h~wegs *adv* half-way; (*ziemlich*) more or less. **h~wüchsig** *a* adolescent. **H~zeit** *f* (*Sport*) half-time; (*Spielzeit*) half

Halde *f* **-,-n** dump, tip

Hälfte *f* **-,-n** half; **zur H~** half

Halfter[1] *m & nt* **-s,-** halter

Halfter[2] *f* **-,-n** & *nt* **-s,-** holster

Hall *m* **-[e]s,-e** sound

Halle *f* **-,-n** hall; (*Hotel-*) lobby; (*Bahnhofs-*) station concourse

hallen *vi* (*haben*) resound; (*wider-*) echo

Hallen- *pref* indoor

hallo *int* hallo

Halluzination /-ˈtsi̯oːn/ *f* **-,-en** hallucination

Halm *m* **-[e]s,-e** stalk; (*Gras-*) blade

Hals *m* **-es,⸗e** neck; (*Kehle*) throat; **aus vollem H~e** at the top of one's voice; ⟨*lachen*⟩ out loud. **H~ausschnitt** *m* neckline. **H~band** *nt* (*pl* **-bänder**) collar. **H~kette** *f* necklace. **H~schmerzen** *mpl* sore throat *sg*. **h~starrig** *a* stubborn. **H~tuch** *nt* scarf

halt[1] *adv* (*SGer*) just; **es geht h~ nicht** it's just not possible

halt[2] *int* stop! (*Mil*) halt! (*fam*) wait a minute!

Halt *m* **-[e]s,-e** hold; (*Stütze*) support; (*innerer*) stability; (*Anhalten*) stop; **H~ machen** stop. **h~bar** *a* durable; (*Tex*) hard-wearing; (*fig*) tenable; **h~bar bis** ... (*Comm*) use by ...

halten† *vt* hold; make ⟨*Rede*⟩; give ⟨*Vortrag*⟩; (*einhalten, bewahren*) keep; **[sich** (*dat*)**] etw h~** keep ⟨*Hund*⟩; take ⟨*Zeitung*⟩; run ⟨*Auto*⟩; **warm h~** keep warm; **h~ für** regard as; **viel/nicht viel h~ von** think highly/little of; **sich h~** hold on (**an** + *dat* to); (*fig*) hold out; ⟨*Geschäft:*⟩ keep going; (*haltbar sein*) keep; ⟨*Wetter:*⟩ hold; ⟨*Blumen:*⟩ last; **sich links h~** keep left; **sich gerade h~** hold oneself upright; **sich h~ an** (+ *acc*) (*fig*) keep to □ *vi* (*haben*) hold; (*haltbar sein, bestehen bleiben*) keep; ⟨*Freundschaft, Blumen:*⟩ last; (*Halt machen*) stop; **h~ auf** (+ *acc*) (*fig*) set great store by; **auf sich** (*acc*) **h~** take pride in oneself; **an sich** (*acc*) **h~** contain oneself; **zu jdm h~** be loyal to s.o.

Halter *m* **-s,-** holder

Halte|stelle *f* stop. **H~verbot** *nt* waiting restriction; **'H~verbot'** 'no waiting'

halt|los *a* (*fig*) unstable; (*unbegründet*) unfounded. **h~machen** *vi sep* (*haben*) (NEW) **H~ machen**, *s.* **Halt**

Haltung *f* **-,-en** (*Körper-*) posture; (*Verhalten*) manner; (*Einstellung*) attitude; (*Fassung*) composure; (*Halten*) keeping; **H~ annehmen** (*Mil*) stand to attention

Halunke *m* **-n,-n** scoundrel

Hamburger *m* **-s,-** hamburger

hämisch *a* malicious, *adv* -ly

Hammel *m* **-s,-** ram; (*Culin*) mutton. **H~fleisch** *nt* mutton

Hammer *m* **-s,⸚** hammer

hämmern *vt/i* (*haben*) hammer; ⟨*Herz:*⟩ pound

Hämorrhoiden /hɛmɔroˈiːdən/, **Hämorriden** /hɛmɔˈriːdən/ *fpl* haemorrhoids

Hamster *m* **-s,-** hamster. **h~n** *vt/i* (*fam*) hoard

Hand *f* **-,⸚e** hand; **eine H~ voll Kirschen** a handful of cherries; **jdm die H~ geben** shake hands with s.o.; **rechter/linker H~** on the right/left; **[aus] zweiter H~** second-hand; **unter der H~** unofficially; (*geheim*) secretly; **an H~** (+ *gen*) = **anhand**; **H~ und Fuß haben** (*fig*) be sound. **H~arbeit** *f* manual work; (*handwerklich*) handicraft; (*Nadelarbeit*) needlework; (*Gegenstand*) handmade article. **H~ball** *m* [German] handball. **H~besen** *m* brush. **H~bewegung** *f* gesture.

H~bremse *f* handbrake. **H~buch** *nt* handbook, manual
Händedruck *m* handshake
Handel *m* **-s** trade, commerce; (*Unternehmen*) business; (*Geschäft*) deal; **H~ treiben** trade. **h~n** *vi* (*haben*) act; (*Handel treiben*) trade (**mit** in); **von etw** *od* **über etw** (*acc*) **h~n** deal with sth; **sich h~n um** be about, concern. **H~smarine** *f* merchant navy. **H~sschiff** *nt* merchant vessel. **H~sschule** *f* commercial college. **h~süblich** *a* customary. **H~sware** *f* merchandise
Hand|feger *m* **-s,-** brush. **H~fertigkeit** *f* dexterity. **h~fest** *a* sturdy; (*fig*) solid. **H~fläche** *f* palm. **h~gearbeitet** *a* handmade. **H~gelenk** *nt* wrist. **h~gemacht** *a* handmade. **H~gemenge** *nt* **-s,-** scuffle. **H~gepäck** *nt* hand-luggage. **h~geschrieben** *a* hand-written. **H~granate** *f* hand-grenade. **h~greiflich** *a* tangible; **h~greiflich werden** become violent. **H~griff** *m* handle; **mit einem H~griff** with a flick of the wrist
handhaben *vt insep* (*reg*) handle
Handikap /ˈhɛndikɛp/ *nt* **-s,-s** handicap
Hand|kuss (**Handkuß**) *m* kiss on the hand. **H~lauf** *m* handrail
Händler *m* **-s,-** dealer, trader
handlich *a* handy
Handlung *f* **-,-en** act; (*Handeln*) action; (*Roman-*) plot; (*Geschäft*) shop. **H~sweise** *f* conduct
Hand|schellen *fpl* handcuffs. **H~schlag** *m* handshake. **H~schrift** *f* handwriting; (*Text*) manuscript. **H~schuh** *m* glove. **H~schuhfach** *nt* glove compartment. **H~stand** *m* handstand. **H~tasche** *f* handbag. **H~tuch** *nt* towel. **H~voll** *f* **-,- eine H~voll** (NEW) **eine H~ voll**, *s.* **Hand**
Handwerk *nt* craft, trade; **sein H~ verstehen** know one's job. **H~er** *m* **-s,-** craftsman; (*Arbeiter*) workman
Handy /ˈhɛndi/ *nt* **-s,-s** mobile phone
Hanf *m* **-[e]s** hemp
Hang *m* **-[e]s,-̈e** slope; (*fig*) inclination, tendency
Hänge|brücke *f* suspension bridge. **H~lampe** *f* [light] pendant. **H~matte** *f* hammock
hängen[1] *vt* (*reg*) hang
hängen†[2] *vi* (*haben*) hang; **h~ an** (+ *dat*) (*fig*) be attached to; **h~ bleiben** stick (**an** + *dat* to); (*Kleid:*) catch (**an** + *dat* on); **h~ lassen** leave; **den Kopf h~ lassen** be downcast. **h~bleiben**† *vi sep* (*sein*) (NEW) **h~ bleiben**, *s.* **hängen**. **h~lassen**† *vt sep* (NEW) **h~ lassen**, *s.* **hängen**
Hannover *nt* **-s** Hanover
hänseln *vt* tease
hantieren *vi* (*haben*) busy oneself
hapern *vi* (*haben*) **es hapert** there's a lack (**an** + *dat* of)
Happen *m* **-s,-** mouthful; **einen H~ essen** have a bite to eat
Harfe *f* **-,-n** harp
Harke *f* **-,-n** rake. **h~n** *vt/i* (*haben*) rake
harmlos *a* harmless; (*arglos*) innocent, *adv* -ly. **H~igkeit** *f* - harmlessness; innocence
Harmonie *f* **-,-n** harmony. **h~ren** *vi* (*haben*) harmonize; (*gut auskommen*) get on well
Harmonika *f* **-,-s** accordion; (*Mund-*) mouth-organ
harmonisch *a* harmonious, *adv* -ly
Harn *m* **-[e]s** urine. **H~blase** *f* bladder
Harpune *f* **-,-n** harpoon
hart (**härter, härtest**) *a* hard; (*heftig*) violent; (*streng*) harsh □ *adv* hard; (*streng*) harshly
Härte *f* **-,-n** hardness; (*Strenge*) harshness; (*Not*) hardship. **h~n** *vt* harden

Hart|faserplatte *f* hardboard. **h~gekocht** *a* (NEW) **h~ gekocht**, *s.* **kochen**. **h~herzig** *a* hard-hearted. **h~näckig** *a* stubborn, *adv* -ly; (*ausdauernd*) persistent, *adv* -ly. **H~näckigkeit** *f* - stubbornness; persistence

Harz *nt* **-es,-e** resin

Haschee *nt* **-s,-s** (*Culin*) hash

haschen *vi* (*haben*) **h~ nach** try to catch

Haschisch *nt & m* **-[s]** hashish

Hase *m* **-n,-n** hare; **falscher H~** meat loaf

Hasel *f* **-,-n** hazel. **H~maus** *f* dormouse. **H~nuss** (**H~nuß**) *f* hazel-nut

Hasenfuß *m* (*fam*) coward

Hass *m* **-es** (**Haß** *m* **-sses**) hatred

hassen *vt* hate

hässlich (**häßlich**) *a* ugly; (*unfreundlich*) nasty, *adv* -ily. **H~keit** *f* - ugliness; nastiness

Hast *f* - haste. **h~en** *vi* (*sein*) hasten, hurry. **h~ig** *a* hasty, *adv* -ily, hurried, *adv* -ly

hast, hat, hatte, hätte *s.* **haben**

Haube *f* **-,-n** cap; (*Trocken-*) drier; (*Kühler-*) bonnet, (*Amer*) hood

Hauch *m* **-[e]s** breath; (*Luft-*) breeze; (*Duft*) whiff; (*Spur*) tinge. **h~dünn** *a* very thin; ⟨*Strümpfe*⟩ sheer. **h~en** *vt/i* (*haben*) breathe

Haue *f* **-,-n** pick; (*fam: Prügel*) beating. **h~n**† *vt* beat; (*hämmern*) knock; (*meißeln*) hew; **sich h~n** fight; **übers Ohr h~n** (*fam*) cheat □ *vi* (*haben*) bang (**auf** + *acc* on); **jdm ins Gesicht h~n** hit s.o. in the face

Haufen *m* **-s,-** heap, pile; (*Leute*) crowd

häufen *vt* heap *or* pile [up]; **sich h~** pile up; (*zunehmen*) increase

haufenweise *adv* in large numbers; **h~ Geld** pots of money

häufig *a* frequent, *adv* -ly. **H~keit** *f* - frequency

Haupt *nt* **-[e]s, Häupter** head. **H~bahnhof** *m* main station. **H~darsteller** *m*, **H~darstellerin** *f* male/female lead. **H~fach** *nt* main subject. **H~gericht** *nt* main course. **H~hahn** *m* mains tap; (*Wasser-*) stopcock

Häuptling *m* **-s,-e** chief

Haupt|mahlzeit *f* main meal. **H~mann** *m* (*pl* **-leute**) captain. **H~person** *f* most important person; (*Theat*) principal character. **H~post** *f* main post office. **H~quartier** *nt* headquarters *pl*. **H~rolle** *f* lead; (*fig*) leading role. **H~sache** *f* main thing; **in der H~sache** in the main. **h~sächlich** *a* main, *adv* -ly. **H~satz** *m* main clause. **H~schlüssel** *m* master key. **H~stadt** *f* capital. **H~straße** *f* main street. **H~verkehrsstraße** *f* main road. **H~verkehrszeit** *f* rush-hour. **H~wort** *nt* (*pl* **-wörter**) noun

Haus *nt* **-es, Häuser** house; (*Gebäude*) building; (*Schnecken-*) shell; **zu H~e** at home; **nach H~e** home; **H~ halten** = **haushalten**. **H~angestellte(r)** *m/f* domestic servant. **H~arbeit** *f* housework; (*Sch*) homework. **H~arzt** *m* family doctor. **H~aufgaben** *fpl* homework *sg*. **H~besetzer** *m* **-s,-** squatter. **H~besuch** *m* house-call

hausen *vi* (*haben*) live; (*wüten*) wreak havoc

Haus|frau *f* housewife. **H~gehilfin** *f* domestic help. **h~gemacht** *a* home-made. **H~halt** *m* **-[e]s,-e** household; (*Pol*) budget. **h~halten**† *vi sep* (*haben*) **h~halten mit** manage carefully; conserve ⟨*Kraft*⟩. **H~hälterin** *f* **-,-nen** housekeeper. **H~haltsgeld** *nt* housekeeping [money]. **H~haltsplan** *m* budget. **H~herr** *m* head of the household; (*Gastgeber*) host. **h~hoch** *a* huge; (*fam*) big □ *adv* (*fam*) vastly; (*verlieren*) by a wide margin

hausier|en *vi* (*haben*) **~en mit** hawk. **H~er** *m* **-s,-** hawker
Hauslehrer *m* [private] tutor. **H~in** *f* governess
häuslich *a* domestic, ⟨*Person*⟩ domesticated
Haus|meister *m* caretaker. **H~nummer** *f* house number. **H~ordnung** *f* house rules *pl.* **H~putz** *m* cleaning. **H~rat** *m* **-[e]s** household effects *pl.* **H~schlüssel** *m* front-door key. **H~schuh** *m* slipper. **H~stand** *m* household. **H~suchung** *f* [police] search. **H~suchungsbefehl** *m* search-warrant. **H~tier** *nt* domestic animal; (*Hund, Katze*) pet. **H~tür** *f* front door. **H~wart** *m* **-[e]s,-e** caretaker. **H~wirt** *m* landlord. **H~wirtin** *f* landlady
Haut *f* **-,Häute** skin; (*Tier-*) hide; **aus der H~fahren** (*fam*) fly off the handle. **H~arzt** *m* dermatologist
häuten *vt* skin; **sich h~** moult
haut|eng *a* skin-tight. **H~farbe** *f* colour; (*Teint*) complexion
Haxe *f* **-,-n** = **Hachse**
Hbf. *abbr s.* **Hauptbahnhof**
Hebamme *f* **-,-n** midwife
Hebel *m* **-s,-** lever. **H~kraft, H~wirkung** *f* leverage
heben† *vt* lift; (*hoch-, steigern*) raise; **sich h~** rise; ⟨*Nebel:*⟩ lift; (*sich verbessern*) improve
hebräisch *a* Hebrew
hecheln *vi* (*haben*) pant
Hecht *m* **-[e]s,-e** pike
Heck *nt* **-s,-s** (*Naut*) stern; (*Aviat*) tail; (*Auto*) rear
Hecke *f* **-,-n** hedge. **H~nschütze** *m* sniper
Heck|fenster *nt* rear window. **H~motor** *m* rear engine. **H~tür** *f* hatchback
Heer *nt* **-[e]s,-e** army
Hefe *f* **-** yeast. **H~teig** *m* yeast dough. **H~teilchen** *nt* Danish pastry
Heft[1] *nt* **-[e]s,-e** haft, handle
Heft[2] *nt* **-[e]s,-e** booklet; (*Sch*) exercise book; (*Zeitschrift*) issue. **h~en** *vt* (*nähen*) tack; (*stecken*) pin/(*klammern*) clip/(*mit Heftmaschine*) staple (**an** + *acc* to). **H~er** *m* **-s,-** file
heftig *a* fierce, *adv* -ly, violent, *adv* -ly; ⟨*Schlag, Regen*⟩ heavy, *adv* -ly; ⟨*Schmerz, Gefühl*⟩ intense, *adv* -ly; ⟨*Person*⟩ quick-tempered. **H~keit** *f* **-** fierceness, violence; intensity
Heft|klammer *f* staple; (*Büro-*) paper-clip. **H~maschine** *f* stapler. **H~pflaster** *nt* sticking plaster. **H~zwecke** *f* **-,-n** drawing-pin
hegen *vt* care for; (*fig*) cherish ⟨*Hoffnung*⟩; harbour ⟨*Verdacht*⟩
Hehl *nt* & *m* **kein[en] H~ machen aus** make no secret of. **H~er** *m* **-s,-** receiver, fence
Heide[1] *m* **-n,-n** heathen
Heide[2] *f* **-,-n** heath; (*Bot*) heather. **H~kraut** *nt* heather
Heidelbeere *f* bilberry, (*Amer*) blueberry
Heid|in *f* **-,-nen** heathen. **h~nisch** *a* heathen
heikel *a* difficult, tricky; (*delikat*) delicate; (*dial*) ⟨*Person*⟩ fussy
heil *a* undamaged, intact; ⟨*Person*⟩ unhurt; (*gesund*) well; **mit h~er Haut** (*fam*) unscathed
Heil *nt* **-s** salvation; **sein H~ versuchen** try one's luck
Heiland *m* **-s** (*Relig*) Saviour
Heil|anstalt *f* sanatorium; (*Nerven-*) mental hospital. **H~bad** *nt* spa. **h~bar** *a* curable
Heilbutt *m* **-[e]s,-e** halibut
heilen *vt* cure; heal ⟨*Wunde*⟩ □ *vi* (*sein*) heal
heilfroh *a* (*fam*) very relieved
Heilgymnastik *f* physiotherapy
heilig *a* holy; (*geweiht*) sacred; **der H~e Abend** Christmas Eve; **die h~e Anna** Saint Anne; **h~**

halten hold sacred; keep ⟨*Feiertag*⟩; **h~ sprechen** canonize. **H~abend** *m* Christmas Eve. **H~e(r)** *m/f* saint. **h~en** *vt* keep, observe. **H~enschein** *m* halo. **h~halten**† *vt sep* (NEW) **h~ halten**, *s.* **halten**. **H~keit** *f* - sanctity, holiness. **h~sprechen**† *vt sep* (NEW) **h~ sprechen**, *s.* **heilig**. **H~tum** *nt* **-s,¨er** shrine

heil|kräftig *a* medicinal. **H~kräuter** *ntpl* medicinal herbs. **h~los** *a* unholy. **H~mittel** *nt* remedy. **H~praktiker** *m* **-s,-** practitioner of alternative medicine. **h~sam** *a* (*fig*) salutary. **H~sarmee** *f* Salvation Army. **H~ung** *f* - cure

Heim *nt* **-[e]s,-e** home; (*Studenten-*) hostel. **h~** *adv* home

Heimat *f* **-,-en** home; (*Land*) native land. **H~abend** *m* folk evening. **h~los** *a* homeless. **H~stadt** *f* home town

heim|begleiten *vt sep* see home. **h~bringen**† *vt sep* bring home; (*begleiten*) see home. **H~computer** *m* home computer. **h~fahren**† *v sep* □ *vi* (*sein*) go/drive home □ *vt* take/drive home. **H~fahrt** *f* way home. **h~gehen**† *vi sep* (*sein*) go home; (*sterben*) die

heimisch *a* native, indigenous; (*Pol*) domestic; **h~ sein/sich h~fühlen** be/feel at home

Heim|kehr *f* - return [home]. **h~kehren** *vi sep* (*sein*) return home. **h~kommen**† *vi sep* (*sein*) come home

heimlich *a* secret, *adv* -ly; **h~ tun** be secretive; **etw h~ tun** do sth secretly *or* in secret. **H~keit** *f* **-,-en** secrecy; **H~keiten** secrets. **H~tuerei** *f* - secretiveness

Heim|reise *f* journey home. **h~reisen** *vi sep* (*sein*) go home. **H~spiel** *nt* home game. **h~suchen** *vt sep* afflict. **h~tückisch** *a* treacherous; ⟨*Krankheit*⟩ insidious. **h~wärts** *adv* home. **H~weg** *m* way home. **H~weh** *nt* **-s** homesickness; **H~weh haben** be homesick. **H~werker** *m* **-s,-** [home] handyman. **h~zahlen** *vt sep* **jdm etw h~zahlen** (*fig*) pay s.o. back for sth

Heirat *f* **-,-en** marriage. **h~en** *vt/i* (*haben*) marry. **H~santrag** *m* proposal; **jdm einen H~santrag machen** propose to s.o. **h~sfähig** *a* marriageable

heiser *a* hoarse, *adv* -ly. **H~keit** *f* - hoarseness

heiß *a* hot, *adv* -ly; (*hitzig*) heated; (*leidenschaftlich*) fervent, *adv* -ly; **mein h~ geliebter Sohn** my beloved son; **mir ist h~** I am hot

heißen† *vi* (*haben*) be called; (*bedeuten*) mean; **ich heiße** ... my name is ...; **wie h~ Sie?** what is your name? **wie heißt ... auf Englisch?** what's the English for ...? **es heißt** it says; (*man sagt*) it is said; **das heißt** that is [to say]; **was soll das h~?** what does it mean? (*empört*) what is the meaning of this? □ *vt* call; **jdn etw tun h~** tell s.o. to do sth

heiß|geliebt *a* (NEW) **h~ geliebt**, *s.* **heiß**. **h~hungrig** *a* ravenous. **H~wasserbereiter** *m* **-s,-** water heater

heiter *a* cheerful, *adv* -ly; ⟨*Wetter*⟩ bright; (*amüsant*) amusing; **aus h~em Himmel** (*fig*) out of the blue. **H~keit** *f* - cheerfulness; (*Gelächter*) mirth

Heiz|anlage *f* heating; (*Auto*) heater. **H~decke** *f* electric blanket. **h~en** *vt* heat; light ⟨*Ofen*⟩ □ *vi* (*haben*) put the heating on; ⟨*Ofen:*⟩ give out heat. **H~gerät** *nt* heater. **H~kessel** *m* boiler. **H~körper** *m* radiator. **H~lüfter** *m* **-s,-** fan heater. **H~material** *nt* fuel. **H~ofen** *m* heater. **H~ung** *f* **-,-en** heating; (*Heizkörper*) radiator

Hektar *nt & m* **-s,-** hectare

hektisch *a* hectic

Held *m* **-en,-en** hero. **h~enhaft** *a* heroic, *adv* -ally. **H~enmut** *m* heroism. **h~enmütig** *a* heroic, *adv* -ally. **H~entum** *nt* **-s** heroism. **H~in** *f* **-,-nen** heroine

helf|en† *vi* (*haben*) help (**jdm** s.o.); (*nützen*) be effective; **sich** (*dat*) **nicht zu h~en wissen** not know what to do; **es hilft nichts** it's no use. **H~er(in)** *m* **-s,-** (*f* **-,-nen**) helper, assistant. **H~ershelfer** *m* accomplice.

hell *a* light; (*Licht ausstrahlend, klug*) bright; ⟨*Stimme*⟩ clear; (*fam: völlig*) utter; **h~es Bier** ≈ lager □ *adv* brightly; **h~ begeistert** absolutely delighted. **h~hörig** *a* poorly soundproofed; **h~hörig werden** (*fig*) sit up and take notice

hellicht *a* (NEW) **helllicht**

Hell|igkeit *f* - brightness. **H~seher(in)** *m* **-s,-** (*f* **-,-nen**) clairvoyant. **h~wach** *a* wide awake

helllicht *a* **h~er Tag** broad daylight

Helm *m* **-[e]s,-e** helmet

Hemd *nt* **-[e]s,-en** vest, (*Amer*) undershirt; (*Ober-*) shirt. **H~bluse** *f* shirt

Hemisphäre *f* **-,-n** hemisphere

hemm|en *vt* check; (*verzögern*) impede; (*fig*) inhibit. **H~ung** *f* **-,-en** (*fig*) inhibition; (*Skrupel*) scruple; **H~ungen haben** be inhibited. **h~ungslos** *a* unrestrained, *adv* -ly

Hendl *nt* **-s,-[n]** (*Aust*) chicken

Hengst *m* **-[e]s,-e** stallion. **H~fohlen** *nt* colt

Henkel *m* **-s,-** handle

henken *vt* hang

Henne *f* **-,-n** hen

her *adv* here; (*zeitlich*) ago; **her mit ...!** give me ...! **von oben unten/Norden/weit her** from above/below/the/north/far away; **von der Farbe/vom Thema her** as far as the colour/subject is concerned; **vor/hinter jdm/etw her** in front of/behind s.o./sth; **hinter jdm/etw her sein** be after s.o./sth; **her sein** come (**von** from); **es ist schon lange/drei Tage her** it was a long time/three days ago

herab *adv* down [here]; **von oben h~** from above; (*fig*) condescending, *adv* -ly. **h~blicken** *vi sep* (*haben*) = **h~sehen**

herablass|en† *vt sep* let down; **sich~en** condescend (**zu** to). **h~end** *a* condescending, *adv* -ly. **H~ung** *f* - condescension

herab|sehen† *vi sep* (*haben*) look down (**auf** + *acc* on). **h~setzen** *vt sep* reduce, cut; (*fig*) belittle. **h~setzend** *a* disparaging, *adv* -ly. **h~würdigen** *vt sep* belittle, disparage

Heraldik *f* - heraldry

heran *adv* near; **[bis] h~ an** (+ *acc*) up to. **h~bilden** *vt sep* train. **h~gehen†** *vi sep* (*sein*) **h~gehen an** (+ *acc*) go up to; get down to ⟨*Arbeit*⟩. **h~kommen†** *vi sep* (*sein*) approach; **h~kommen an** (+ *acc*) come up to; (*erreichen*) get at; (*fig*) measure up to. **h~machen (sich)** *vr sep* **sich h~machen an** (+ *acc*) approach; get down to ⟨*Arbeit*⟩. **h~reichen** *vi sep* (*haben*) **h~reichen an** (+ *acc*) reach; (*fig*) measure up to. **h~wachsen†** *vi sep* (*sein*) grow up. **h~ziehen†** *v sep* □ *vt* pull up (**an** + *acc* to); (*züchten*) raise; (*h~bilden*) train; (*hinzuziehen*) call in □ *vi* (*sein*) approach

herauf *adv* up [here]; **die Treppe h~** up the stairs. **h~beschwören** *vt sep* evoke; (*verursachen*) cause. **h~kommen†** *vi sep* (*sein*) come up. **h~setzen** *vt sep* raise, increase

heraus *adv* out (**aus** of); **h~damit** *od* **mit der Sprache!** out with it! **h~ sein** be out; **aus dem Gröbsten h~ sein** be over the worst; **fein h~ sein** be sitting pretty. **h~bekommen†** *vt sep* get out; (*ausfindig machen*) find out;

(*lösen*) solve; **Geld h~bekommen** get change. **h~bringen**† *vt sep* bring out; (*fam*) get out. **h~finden**† *v sep* □ *vt* find out □ *vi* (*haben*) find one's way out. **H~forderer** *m* **-s,-** challenger. **h~fordern** *vt sep* provoke; challenge ⟨*Person*⟩. **H~forderung** *f* provocation; challenge. **H~gabe** *f* handing over; (*Admin*) issue; (*Veröffentlichung*) publication. **h~geben**† *vt sep* hand over; (*Admin*) issue; (*veröffentlichen*) publish; edit ⟨*Zeitschrift*⟩; **jdm Geld h~geben** give s.o. change □ *vi* (*haben*) give change (**auf** + *acc* for). **H~geber** *m* **-s,-** publisher; editor. **h~gehen**† *vi sep* (*sein*) ⟨*Fleck:*⟩ come out; **aus sich h~gehen** (*fig*) come out of one's shell. **h~halten**† **(sich)** *vr sep* (*fig*) keep out (**aus** of). **h~holen** *vt sep* get out. **h~kommen**† *vi sep* (*sein*) come out; (*aus Schwierigkeit, Takt*) get out; **auf eins** *od* **dasselbe h~kommen** (*fam*) come to the same thing. **h~lassen**† *vt sep* let out. **h~machen** *vt sep* get out; **sich gut h~machen** (*fig*) do well. **h~nehmen**† *vt sep* take out; **sich zu viel h~nehmen** (*fig*) take liberties. **h~platzen** *vi sep* (*haben*) (*fam*) burst out laughing. **h~putzen (sich)** *vr sep* doll oneself up. **h~ragen** *vi sep* (*haben*) jut out; (*fig*) stand out. **h~reden (sich)** *vr sep* make excuses. **h~rücken** *v sep* □ *vt* move out; (*hergeben*) hand over □ *vi* (*sein*) **h~rücken mit** hand over; (*fig: sagen*) come out with. **h~rutschen** *vi sep* (*sein*) slip out. **h~schlagen**† *vt sep* knock out; (*fig*) gain. **h~stellen** *vt sep* put out; **sich h~stellen** turn out (**als** to be; **daß** that). **h~suchen** *vt sep* pick out. **h~wollen**† *vi sep* (*haben*) **nicht mit der Sprache h~wollen** hum and haw. **h~ziehen**† *vt sep* pull out

herb *a* sharp; ⟨*Wein*⟩ dry; ⟨*Landschaft*⟩ austere; (*fig*) harsh

herbei *adv* here. **h~führen** *vt sep* (*fig*) bring about. **h~lassen**† **(sich)** *vr sep* condescend (**zu** to). **h~schaffen** *vt sep* get. **h~sehnen** *vt sep* long for

Herberg|e *f* **-,-n** [youth] hostel; (*Unterkunft*) lodging. **H~svater** *m* warden

herbestellen *vt sep* summon

herbitten† *vt sep* ask to come

herbringen† *vt sep* bring [here]

Herbst *m* **-[e]s,-e** autumn. **h~lich** *a* autumnal

Herd *m* **-[e]s,-e** stove, cooker; (*fig*) focus

Herde *f* **-,-n** herd; (*Schaf-*) flock

herein *adv* in [here]; **h~!** come in! **h~bitten**† *vt sep* ask in. **h~brechen**† *vi sep* (*sein*) burst in; (*fig*) set in; ⟨*Nacht:*⟩ fall; **h~brechen über** (+ *acc*) (*fig*) overtake. **h~fallen**† *vi sep* (*sein*) (*fam*) be taken in (**auf** + *acc* by). **h~kommen**† *vi sep* (*sein*) come in. **h~lassen**† *vt sep* let in. **h~legen** *vt sep* (*fam*) take for a ride. **h~rufen**† *vt sep* call in

Herfahrt *f* journey/drive here

herfallen† *vi sep* (*sein*) **~ über** (+ *acc*) attack; fall upon ⟨*Essen*⟩

hergeben† *vt sep* hand over; (*fig*) give up; **sich h~ zu** (*fig*) be a party to

hergebracht *a* traditional

hergehen† *vi sep* (*sein*) **h~ vor/neben/hinter** (+ *dat*) walk along in front of/beside/behind; **es ging lustig her** (*fam*) there was a lot of merriment

herhalten† *vi sep* (*haben*) hold out; **h~ müssen** be the one to suffer

herholen *vt sep* fetch; **weit hergeholt** (*fig*) far-fetched

Hering *m* **-s,-e** herring; (*Zeltpflock*) tent-peg

her|kommen† *vi sep* (*sein*) come here; **wo kommt das her?** where does it come from? **h~kömmlich** *a* traditional. **H~kunft** *f* - origin

herlaufen† *vi sep (sein)* **h~ vor/neben/hinter** (+ *dat*) run/(*gehen*) walk along in front of/beside/behind

herleiten *vt sep* derive

hermachen *vt sep* **viel/wenig h~** be impressive/unimpressive; (*wichtig nehmen*) make a lot of/little fuss (**von** of); **sich h~ über** (+ *acc*) fall upon; tackle ⟨*Arbeit*⟩

Hermelin[1] *nt* **-s,-e** (*Zool*) stoat

Hermelin[2] *m* **-s,-e** (*Pelz*) ermine

hermetisch *a* hermetic, *adv* -ally

Hernie /ˈhɛrniə/ *f* **-,-n** hernia

Heroin *nt* **-s** heroin

heroisch *a* heroic, *adv* -ally

Herr *m* **-n,-en** gentleman; (*Gebieter*) master (**über** + *acc* of); **[Gott,] der H~** the Lord [God]; **H~ Meier** Mr Meier; **Sehr geehrte H~en** Dear Sirs. **H~chen** *nt* **-s,-** master. **H~enhaus** *nt* manor [house]. **h~enlos** *a* ownerless; ⟨*Tier*⟩ stray. **H~ensitz** *m* manor

Herrgott *m* **der H~** the Lord; **H~ [noch mal]!** damn it!

herrichten *vt sep* prepare; **wieder h~** renovate

Herrin *f* **-,-nen** mistress

herrisch *a* imperious, *adv* -ly; ⟨*Ton*⟩ peremptory; (*herrschsüchtig*) overbearing

herrlich *a* marvellous, *adv* -ly; (*großartig*) magnificent, *adv* -ly. **H~keit** *f* **-,-en** splendour

Herrschaft *f* **-,-en** rule; (*Macht*) power; (*Kontrolle*) control; **meine H~en!** ladies and gentlemen!

herrsch|en *vi* (*haben*) rule; (*verbreitet sein*) prevail; **es h~te Stille/große Aufregung** there was silence/great excitement. **H~er(in)** *m* **-s,-** (*f* **-,-nen**) ruler. **h~süchtig** *a* domineering

herrühren *vi sep* (*haben*) stem (**von** from)

hersein† *vi sep (sein)* (NEW) **her sein**, *s.* **her**

herstammen *vi sep* (*haben*) come (**aus/von** from)

herstell|en *vt sep* establish; (*Comm*) manufacture, make. **H~er** *m* **-s,-** manufacturer, maker. **H~ung** *f* - establishment; manufacture

herüber *adv* over [here]. **h~kommen**† *vi sep (sein)* come over [here]

herum *adv* **im Kreis h~** [round] in a circle; **falsch h~** the wrong way round; **um ... h~** round ...; (*ungefähr*) [round] about ...; **h~ sein** be over. **h~albern** *vi sep* (*haben*) fool around. **h~drehen** *vt sep* turn round/(*wenden*) over; turn ⟨*Schlüssel*⟩; **sich h~drehen** turn round/over. **h~gehen**† *vi sep (sein)* walk around; ⟨*Zeit:*⟩ pass; **h~gehen um** go round. **h~kommen**† *vi sep (sein)* get about; **h~kommen um** get round; come round ⟨*Ecke*⟩; **um etw [nicht] h~kommen** (*fig*) [not] get out of sth. **h~kriegen** *vt sep* **jdn h~kriegen** (*fam*) talk s.o. round. **h~liegen**† *vi sep (sein)* lie around. **h~lungern** *vi sep* (*haben*) loiter. **h~schnüffeln** *vi sep* (*haben*) (*fam*) nose about. **h~sitzen**† *vi sep* (*haben*) sit around; **h~sitzen um** sit round. **h~sprechen**† **(sich)** *vr sep* ⟨*Gerücht:*⟩ get about. **h~stehen**† *vi sep* (*haben*) stand around; **h~stehen um** stand round. **h~treiben**† **(sich)** *vr sep* hang around. **h~ziehen**† *vi sep (sein)* move around; (*ziellos*) wander about

herunter *adv* down [here]; **die Treppe h~** down the stairs; **h~ sein** be down; (*körperlich*) be run down. **h~fallen**† *vi* fall off. **h~gehen**† *vi sep (sein)* come down; (*sinken*) go/come down.

h~gekommen *a* (*fig*) run-down; ⟨*Gebäude*⟩ dilapidated; ⟨*Person*⟩ down-at-heel. **h~kommen**† *vi sep* (*sein*) come down; (*fig*) go to rack and ruin; ⟨*Firma, Person:*⟩ go downhill; (*gesundheitlich*) get run down. **h~lassen**† *vt sep* let down, lower. **h~machen** *vt sep* (*fam*) reprimand; (*herabsetzen*) run down. **h~spielen** *vt sep* (*fig*) play down. **h~ziehen**† *vt sep* pull down

hervor *adv* out (**aus** of). **h~bringen**† *vt sep* produce; utter ⟨*Wort*⟩. **h~gehen**† *vi sep* (*sein*) come/(*sich ergeben*) emerge/(*folgen*) follow (**aus** from). **h~heben**† *vt sep* (*fig*) stress, emphasize. **h~quellen**† *vi sep* (*sein*) stream out; (*h~treten*) bulge. **h~ragen** *vi sep* (*haben*) jut out; (*fig*) stand out. **h~ragend** *a* (*fig*) outstanding. **h~rufen**† *vt sep* (*fig*) cause. **h~stehen**† *vi sep* (*haben*) protrude. **h~treten**† *vi sep* (*sein*) protrude, bulge; (*fig*) stand out. **h~tun**† **(sich)** *vr sep* (*fig*) distinguish oneself; (*angeben*) show off

Herweg *m* way here

Herz *nt* **-ens,-en** heart; (*Kartenspiel*) hearts *pl*; **sich** (*dat*) **ein H~ fassen** pluck up courage. **H~anfall** *m* heart attack

herzeigen *vt sep* show

herz|en *vt* hug. **H~enslust** *f* **nach H~enslust** to one's heart's content. **h~haft** *a* hearty, *adv* -ily; (*würzig*) savoury

herziehen† *v sep* □ *vt* **hinter sich** (*dat*) **h~** pull along [behind one] □ *vi* (*sein*) **hinter jdm h~** follow along behind s.o.; **über jdn h~** (*fam*) run s.o. down

herz|ig *a* sweet, adorable. **H~infarkt** *m* heart attack. **H~klopfen** *nt* **-s** palpitations *pl*; **ich hatte H~klopfen** my heart was pounding

herzlich *a* cordial, *adv* -ly; (*warm*) warm, *adv* -ly; (*aufrichtig*) sincere, *adv* -ly; **h~en Dank!** many thanks! **h~e Grüße** kind regards; **h~ wenig** precious little. **H~keit** *f* - cordiality; warmth; sincerity

herzlos *a* heartless

Herzog *m* **-s,¨e** duke. **H~in** *f* **-,-nen** duchess. **H~tum** *nt* **-s,¨er** duchy

Herz|schlag *m* heartbeat; (*Med*) heart failure. **h~zerreißend** *a* heart-breaking

Hessen *nt* **-s** Hesse

heterosexuell *a* heterosexual

Hetze *f* - rush; (*Kampagne*) virulent campaign (**gegen** against). **h~n** *vt* chase; **sich h~n** hurry □ *vi* (*haben*) agitate; (*sich beeilen*) hurry □ *vi* (*sein*) rush

Heu *nt* **-s** hay; **Geld wie Heu haben** (*fam*) have pots of money

Heuchelei *f* - hypocrisy

heuch|eln *vt* feign □ *vi* (*haben*) pretend. **H~ler(in)** *m* **-s,-** (*f* **-,-nen**) hypocrite. **h~lerisch** *a* hypocritical, *adv* -ly

heuer *adv* (*Aust*) this year

Heuer *f* **-,-n** (*Naut*) pay. **h~n** *vt* hire; sign on ⟨*Matrosen*⟩

heulen *vi* (*haben*) howl; (*fam: weinen*) cry; ⟨*Sirene:*⟩ wail

Heurige(r) *m* (*Aust*) new wine

Heu|schnupfen *m* hay fever. **H~schober** *m* **-s,-** haystack. **H~schrecke** *f* **-,-n** grasshopper; (*Wander-*) locust

heut|e *adv* today; (*heutzutage*) nowadays; **h~e früh** *od* **Morgen (morgen)** this morning; **von h~e auf morgen** from one day to the next. **h~ig** *a* today's ...; (*gegenwärtig*) present; **der h~ige Tag** today. **h~zutage** *adv* nowadays

Hexe *f* **-,-n** witch. **h~n** *vi* (*haben*) work magic; **ich kann nicht h~n** (*fam*) I can't perform miracles. **H~njagd** *f* witch-hunt.

H~nschuss (**H~nschuß**) *m* lumbago. **H~rei** *f* - witchcraft

Hieb *m* **-[e]s,-e** blow; (*Peitschen-*) lash; **H~e** hiding *sg*

hier *adv* here; **h~ sein/bleiben/lassen/behalten** be/stay/leave/keep here; **h~ und da** here and there; (*zeitlich*) now and again

Hierarchie /hierar'çi:/ *f* **-,-n** hierarchy

hier|auf *adv* on this/these; (*antworten*) to this; (*zeitlich*) after this. **h~aus** *adv* out of *or* from this/these. **h~behalten**† *vt sep* (NEW) **h~ behalten**, *s.* **hier**. **h~bleiben**† *vi sep* (*sein*) (NEW) **h~ bleiben**, *s.* **hier**. **h~durch** *adv* through this/these; (*Ursache*) as a result of this. **h~für** *adv* for this/these. **h~her** *adv* here. **h~hin** *adv* here. **h~in** *adv* in this/these. **h~lassen**† *vt sep* (NEW) **h~ lassen**, *s.* **hier**. **h~mit** *adv* with this/these; (*Comm*) herewith; (*Admin*) hereby. **h~nach** *adv* after this/these; (*demgemäß*) according to this/these. **h~sein**† *vi sep* (*sein*) (NEW) **h~ sein**, *s.* **hier**. **h~über** *adv* over/(*höher*) above this/these; ⟨*sprechen, streiten*⟩ about this/these. **h~unter** *adv* under/(*tiefer*) below this/these; (*dazwischen*) among these. **h~von** *adv* from this/these; (*h~über*) about this/these; (*Menge*) of this/these. **h~zu** *adv* to this/these; (*h~für*) for this/these. **h~zulande** *adv* here

hiesig *a* local. **H~e(r)** *m/f* local

Hilf|e *f* **-,-n** help, aid; **um H~e rufen** call for help; **jdm zu H~e kommen** come to s.o.'s aid; **mit H~e** (+ *gen*) (NEW) **mithilfe**. **h~los** *a* helpless, *adv* -ly. **H~losigkeit** *f* - helplessness. **h~reich** *a* helpful

Hilfs|arbeiter *m* unskilled labourer. **h~bedürftig** *a* needy; **h~bedürftig sein** be in need of help. **h~bereit** *a* helpful, *adv* -ly. **H~kraft** *f* helper. **H~mittel** *nt* aid. **H~verb, H~zeitwort** *nt* auxiliary verb

Himbeere *f* raspberry

Himmel *m* **-s,-** sky; (*Relig & fig*) heaven; (*Bett-*) canopy; **am H~** in the sky; **unter freiem H~** in the open air. **H~bett** *nt* four-poster [bed]. **H~fahrt** *f* Ascension; **Mariä H~fahrt** Assumption. **h~schreiend** *a* scandalous. **H~srichtung** *f* compass point; **in alle H~srichtungen** in all directions. **h~weit** *a* (*fam*) vast

himmlisch *a* heavenly

hin *adv* there; **hin und her** to and fro; **hin und zurück** there and back; (*Rail*) return; **hin und wieder** now and again; **an** (+ *dat*) . . . **hin** along; **auf** (+ *acc*) . . . **hin** in reply to ⟨*Brief, Anzeige*⟩; on ⟨*jds Rat*⟩; **zu** *od* **nach . . . hin** towards; **vor sich hin reden** talk to oneself; **hin sein** (*fam*) be gone; (*kaputt, tot*) have had it; **[ganz] hin sein von** be overwhelmed by; **es ist noch/nicht mehr lange hin** it's a long time yet/not long to go

hinab *adv* down [there]

hinauf *adv* up [there]; **die Treppe Straße h~** up the stairs/road. **h~gehen**† *vi sep* (*sein*) go up. **h~setzen** *vt sep* raise

hinaus *adv* out [there]; (*nach draußen*) outside; **zur Tür h~** out of the door; **auf Jahre h~** for years to come; **über etw** (*acc*) **h~** beyond sth; (*Menge*) [over and] above sth; **über etw** (*acc*) **h~ sein** (*fig*) be past sth. **h~fliegen**† *v sep* □ *vi* (*sein*) fly out; (*fam*) get the sack □ *vt* out fly out. **h~gehen**† *vi sep* (*sein*) go out; ⟨*Zimmer:*⟩ face (**nach Norden** north); **h~gehen über** (+ *acc*) go beyond, exceed. **h~kommen**† *vi sep* (*sein*) get out; **h~kommen über** (+ *acc*) get beyond. **h~laufen**† *vi sep* (*sein*) run out; **h~laufen auf** (+ *acc*) (*fig*) amount to. **h~lehnen (sich)** *vr sep* lean out. **h~ragen** *vi sep* (*haben*) **h~ragen über** (+ *acc*) project beyond; (*in der Höhe*) rise above; (*fig*) stand out above. **h~schicken** *vt sep* send out. **h~schieben**† *vt sep* push out; (*fig*) put off. **h~sehen**† *vi sep* (*haben*) look out. **h~sein**† *vi sep* (*sein*) (NEW) **h~ sein**, *s.* **hinaus**. **h~werfen**† *vt sep* throw out; (*fam: entlassen*) fire. **h~wollen**† *vi sep* (*haben*) want to go out; **h~wollen auf** (+ *acc*) (*fig*) aim at; **hoch h~wollen** (*fig*) be ambitious. **h~ziehen**† *v sep* □ *vt* pull out; (*in die Länge ziehen*) drag out; (*verzögern*) delay; **sich h~ziehen** drag on; be delayed □ *vi* (*sein*) move out. **h~zögern** *vt* delay; **sich h~zögern** be delayed

Hinblick *m* **im H~ auf** (+ *acc*) in view of; (*hinsichtlich*) regarding

hinbringen† *vt sep* take there; (*verbringen*) spend

hinder|lich *a* awkward; **jdm h~lich sein** hamper s.o. **h~n** *vt* hamper; (*verhindern*) prevent. **H~nis** *nt* **-ses,-se** obstacle. **H~nisrennen** *nt* steeplechase

hindeuten *vi sep* (*haben*) point (**auf** + *acc* to)

Hindu *m* **-s,-s** Hindu. **H~ismus** *m* - Hinduism

hindurch *adv* through it/them; **den Sommer h~** throughout the summer

hinein *adv* in [there]; (*nach drinnen*) inside; **h~ in** (+ *acc*) into. **h~fallen**† *vi sep* (*sein*) fall in. **h~gehen**† *vi sep* (*sein*) go in; **h~gehen in** (+ *acc*) go into. **h~laufen**† *vi sep* (*sein*) run in; **h~laufen in** (+ *acc*) run into. **h~reden** *vi sep* (*haben*) **jdm h~reden** interrupt s.o.; (*sich einmischen*) interfere in s.o.'s affairs. **h~versetzen (sich)** *vr sep* **sich in jds Lage h~versetzen** put oneself in s.o.'s position. **h~ziehen**† *vt sep* pull in; **h~ziehen in** (+ *acc*) pull into; **in etw** (*acc*) **h~gezogen werden** (*fig*) become involved in sth

hin|fahren† *v sep* □ *vi* (*sein*) go/drive there □ *vt* take/drive there. **H~fahrt** *f* journey/drive there; (*Rail*) outward journey. **h~fallen**† *vi sep* (*sein*) fall. **h~fällig** *a* (*gebrechlich*) frail; (*ungültig*) invalid. **h~fliegen**† *v sep* □ *vi* (*sein*) fly there; (*fam*) fall □ *vt* fly there. **H~flug** *m* flight there; (*Admin*) outward flight. **H~gabe** *f* - devotion; (*Eifer*) dedication

hingeb|en† *vt sep* give up; **sich h~en** (*fig*) devote oneself (**einer Aufgabe** to a task); abandon oneself (**dem Vergnügen** to pleasure). **H~ung** *f* - devotion. **h~ungsvoll** *a* devoted, *adv* -ly

hingegen *adv* on the other hand

hingehen† *vi sep* (*sein*) go/(*zu Fuß*) walk there; (*vergehen*) pass; **h~ zu** go up to; **wo gehst du hin?** where are you going? **etw h~ lassen** (*fig*) let sth pass

hingerissen *a* rapt, *adv* -ly; **h~ sein** be carried away (**von** by)

hin|halten† *vt sep* hold out; (*warten lassen*) keep waiting. **h~hocken (sich)** *vr sep* squat down. **h~kauern (sich)** *vr sep* crouch down

hinken *vi* (*haben/sein*) limp

hin|knien (sich) *vr sep* kneel down. **h~kommen**† *vi sep* (*sein*) get there; (*h~gehören*) belong, go; (*fam: auskommen*) manage (**mit** with); (*fam: stimmen*) be right. **h~länglich** *a* adequate, *adv* -ly. **h~laufen**† *vi sep* (*sein*) run/(*gehen*) walk there. **h~legen** *vt sep* lay *or* put down; **sich h~legen** lie down. **h~nehmen**† *vt sep* (*fig*) accept

hinreichen *v sep* □ *vt* hand (*dat* to) □ *vi* (*haben*) extend (**bis** to); (*ausreichen*) be adequate. **h~d** *a* adequate, *adv* -ly

Hinreise *f* journey there; (*Rail*) outward journey
hinreißen† *vt sep* (*fig*) carry away; **sich h~ lassen** get carried away. **h~d** *a* ravishing, *adv* -ly
hinricht|en *vt sep* execute. **H~ung** *f* execution
hinschicken *vt sep* send there
hinschleppen *vt sep* drag there; (*fig*) drag out; **sich h~** drag oneself along; (*fig*) drag on
hinschreiben† *vt sep* write there; (*aufschreiben*) write down
hinsehen† *vi sep* (*haben*) look
hinsein† *vi sep* (*sein*) (*fam*) (NEW) **hin sein**, *s.* **hin**
hinsetzen *vt sep* put down; **sich h~** sit down
Hinsicht *f* - **in dieser/gewisser H~** in this respect/in a certain sense; **in finanzieller H~** financially. **h~lich** *prep* (+ *gen*) regarding
hinstellen *vt sep* put *or* set down; park ⟨*Auto*⟩; (*fig*) make out (**als** to be); **sich h~** stand
hinstrecken *vt sep* hold out; **sich h~** extend
hintan|setzen, **h~stellen** *vt sep* ignore; (*vernachlässigen*) neglect
hinten *adv* at the back; **dort h~** back there; **nach/von h~** to the back/from behind. **h~herum** *adv* round the back; (*fam*) by devious means; ⟨*erfahren*⟩ in a roundabout way
hinter *prep* (+ *dat/acc*) behind; (*nach*) after; **h~ jdm/etw herlaufen** run after s.o./sth; **h~ etw** (*dat*) **stecken** (*fig*) be behind sth; **h~ etw** (*acc*) **kommen** (*fig*) get to the bottom of sth; **etw h~ sich** (*acc*) **bringen** get sth over [and done] with. **H~bein** *nt* hind leg
Hinterbliebene *pl* (*Admin*) surviving dependants; **die H~n** the bereaved family *sg*
hinterbringen† *vt* tell (**jdm** s.o.)
hintere|(r,s) *a* back, rear; **h~s Ende** far end
hintereinander *adv* one behind/(*zeitlich*) after the other; **dreimal h~** three times in succession *or* (*fam*) in a row
Hintergedanke *m* ulterior motive
hintergehen† *vt* deceive
Hinter|grund *m* background. **H~halt** *m* -[e]s,-e ambush; **aus dem H~halt überfallen** ambush. **h~hältig** *a* underhand
hinterher *adv* behind, after; (*zeitlich*) afterwards. **h~gehen**† *vi sep* (*sein*) follow (**jdm** s.o.). **h~kommen**† *vi sep* (*sein*) follow [behind]. **h~laufen**† *vi sep* (*sein*) run after (**jdm** s.o.)
Hinter|hof *m* back yard. **H~kopf** *m* back of the head
hinterlassen† *vt* leave [behind]; (*Jur*) leave, bequeath (*dat* to). **H~schaft** *f* -,-en (*Jur*) estate
hinterlegen *vt* deposit
Hinter|leib *m* (*Zool*) abdomen. **H~list** *f* deceit. **h~listig** *a* deceitful, *adv* -ly. **h~m** *prep* = **hinter dem**. **H~mann** *m* (*pl* **-männer**) person behind. **h~n** *prep* = **hinter den**. **H~n** *m* -s,- (*fam*) bottom, backside. **H~rad** *nt* rear *or* back wheel. **h~rücks** *adv* from behind. **h~s** *prep* = **hinter das**. **h~ste(r,s)** *a* last; **h~ste Reihe** back row. **H~teil** *nt* (*fam*) behind
hintertreiben† *vt* (*fig*) block
Hinter|treppe *f* back stairs *pl*. **H~tür** *f* back door; (*fig*) loophole
hinterziehen† *vt* (*Admin*) evade
Hinterzimmer *nt* back room
hinüber *adv* over *or* across [*there*]; **h~ sein** (*fam: unbrauchbar, tot*) have had it; (*betrunken*) be gone. **h~gehen**† *vi sep* (*sein*) go over *or* across; **h~gehen über** (+ *acc*) *or* cross
hinunter *adv* down [there]; **die Treppe/Straße h~** down the stairs/road. **h~gehen**† *vi sep*

(*sein*) go down. **h~schlucken** *vt sep* swallow

Hinweg *m* way there

hinweg *adv* away, off; **h~ über** (+ *acc*) over; **über eine Zeit h~** over a period. **h~gehen**† *vi sep* (*sein*) **h~gehen über** (+ *acc*) (*fig*) pass over. **h~kommen**† *vt sep* (*sein*) **h~kommen über** (+ *acc*) (*fig*) get over. **h~sehen**† *vi sep* (*haben*) **h~sehen über** (+ *acc*) see over; (*fig*) overlook. **h~setzen** (sich) *vr sep* **sich h~setzen über** (+ *acc*) ignore

Hinweis *m* **-es,-e** reference; (*Andeutung*) hint; (*Anzeichen*) indication; **unter H~ auf** (+ *acc*) with reference to. **h~en**† *v sep* □ *vi* (*haben*) point (**auf** + *acc* to) □ *vt* **jdn auf etw** (*acc*) **h~en** point sth out to s.o. **h~end** *a* (*Gram*) demonstrative

hin|wenden† *vt sep* turn; **sich h~wenden** turn (**zu** to). **h~werfen**† *vt sep* throw down; drop ⟨*Bemerkung*⟩; (*schreiben*) jot down; (*zeichnen*) sketch; (*fam: aufgeben*) pack in

hinwieder *adv* on the other hand

hin|zeigen *vi sep* (*haben*) point (**auf** + *acc* to). **h~ziehen**† *vt sep* pull; (*fig: in die Länge ziehen*) drag out; (*verzögern*) delay; **sich h~ziehen** drag on; be delayed; **sich h~gezogen fühlen zu** (*fig*) feel drawn to

hinzu *adv* in addition. **h~fügen** *vt sep* add. **h~kommen**† *vt sep* (*sein*) be added; (*ankommen*) arrive [on the scene]; join (**zu jdm** s.o.). **h~rechnen** *vt sep* add. **h~ziehen**† *vt sep* call in

Hiobsbotschaft *f* bad news *sg*

Hirn *nt* **-s** brain; (*Culin*) brains *pl*. **H~gespinst** *nt* **-[e]s,-e** figment of the imagination. **H~hautentzündung** *f* meningitis. **h~verbrannt** *a* (*fam*) crazy

Hirsch *m* **-[e]s,-e** deer; (*männlich*) stag; (*Culin*) venison

Hirse *f* - millet

Hirt *m* **-en,-en**, **Hirte** *m* **-n,-n** shepherd

hissen *vt* hoist

Histor|iker *m* **-s,-** historian. **h~isch** *a* historical; (*bedeutend*) historic

Hit *m* **-s,-s** (*Mus*) hit

Hitz|e *f* - heat. **H~ewelle** *f* heatwave. **h~ig** *a* (*fig*) heated, *adv* -ly; ⟨*Person*⟩ hot-headed; (*jähzornig*) hot-tempered. **H~kopf** *m* hothead. **H~schlag** *m* heat-stroke

H-Milch /ˈhaː-/ *f* long-life milk

Hobby *nt* **-s,-s** hobby

Hobel *m* **-s,-** (*Techn*) plane; (*Culin*) slicer. **h~n** *vt/i* (*haben*) plane. **H~späne** *mpl* shavings

hoch *a* (**höher, höchst**; *attrib* **hohe(r,s)**) high; ⟨*Baum, Mast*⟩ tall; ⟨*Offizier*⟩ high-ranking; ⟨*Alter*⟩ great; ⟨*Summe*⟩ large; ⟨*Strafe*⟩ heavy; **hohe Schuhe** ankle boots □ *adv* high; (*sehr*) highly; **h~ gewachsen** tall; **h~ begabt** highly gifted; **h~ gestellte Persönlichkeit** important person; **die Treppe/den Berg h~** up the stairs/hill; **sechs Mann h~** six of us/them. **H~** *nt* **-s,-s** cheer; (*Meteorol*) high

Hoch|achtung *f* high esteem. **H~achtungsvoll** *adv* Yours faithfully. **H~amt** *nt* High Mass. **h~arbeiten (sich)** *vr sep* work one's way up. **h~begabt** *attrib a* (NEW) **h~ begabt**, *s.* **hoch**. **H~betrieb** *m* great activity; **in den Geschäften herrscht H~betrieb** the shops are terribly busy. **H~burg** *f* (*fig*) stronghold. **H~deutsch** *nt* High German. **H~druck** *m* High pressure. **H~ebene** *f* plateau. **h~fahren**† *vi sep* (*sein*) go up; (*auffahren*) start up; (*aufbrausen*) flare up. **h~fliegend** *a* (*fig*) ambitious. **h~gehen**† *vi sep* (*sein*) go up; (*explodieren*) blow up; (*aufbrausen*) flare up. **h~gestellt** *attrib a* ⟨*Zahl*⟩ superior;

(*fig*) (NEW) **h~ gestellt**, *s.* **hoch**. **h~gewachsen** *a* (NEW) **h~ gewachsen**, *s.* **hoch**. **H~glanz** *m* high gloss. **h~gradig** *a* extreme, *adv* -ly. **h~hackig** *a* high-heeled. **h~halten**† *vt sep* hold up; (*fig*) uphold. **H~haus** *nt* high-rise building. **h~heben**† *vt sep* lift up; raise ⟨*Kopf, Hand*⟩. **h~herzig** *a* magnanimous, *adv* -ly. **h~kant** *adv* on end. **h~kommen**† *vi sep* (*sein*) come up; (*aufstehen*) get up; (*fig*) get on [in the world]. **H~konjunktur** *f* boom. **h~krempeln** *vt sep* roll up. **h~leben** *vi sep* (*haben*) **h~leben lassen** give three cheers for; ... **lebe hoch!** three cheers for ...! **H~mut** *m* pride, arrogance. **h~mütig** *a* arrogant, *adv* -ly. **h~näsig** *a* (*fam*) snooty. **h~nehmen**† *vt sep* pick up; (*fam*) tease. **H~ofen** *m* blast-furnace. **h~ragen** *vi sep* rise [up]; ⟨*Turm:*⟩ soar. **H~ruf** *m* cheer. **H~saison** *f* high season. **H~schätzung** *f* high esteem. **h~schlagen**† *vt sep* turn up ⟨*Kragen*⟩. **h~schrecken**† *vi sep* (*sein*) start up. **H~schule** *f* university; (*Musik-, Kunst-*) academy. **h~sehen**† *vi sep* (*haben*) look up. **H~sommer** *m* midsummer. **H~spannung** *f* high/(*fig*) great tension. **h~spielen** *vt sep* (*fig*) magnify. **H~sprache** *f* standard language. **H~sprung** *m* high jump

höchst *adv* extremely, most

Hochstapler *m* **-s,-** confidence trickster

höchst|e(r,s) *a* highest; ⟨*Baum, Turm*⟩ tallest; (*oberste, größte*) top; **es ist h~e Zeit** it is high time. **h~ens** *adv* at most; (*es sei denn*) except perhaps. **H~fall** *m* **im H~fall** at most. **H~geschwindigkeit** *f* top or maximum speed. **H~maß** *nt* maximum. **h~persönlich** *adv* in person. **H~preis** *m* top price. **H~temperatur** *f* maximum temperature. **h~wahrscheinlich** *adv* most probably

hoch|trabend *a* pompous, *adv* -ly. **h~treiben**† *vt sep* push up ⟨*Preis*⟩. **H~verrat** *m* high treason. **H~wasser** *nt* high tide; (*Überschwemmung*) floods *pl.* **H~würden** *m* **-s** Reverend; (*Anrede*) Father

Hochzeit *f* **-,-en** wedding; **H~feiern** get married. **H~skleid** *nt* wedding dress. **H~sreise** *f* honeymoon [trip]. **H~stag** *m* wedding day/(*Jahrestag*) anniversary

hochziehen† *vt sep* pull up; (*hissen*) hoist; raise ⟨*Augenbrauen*⟩

Hocke *f* - **in der H~ sitzen** squat; **in die H~ gehen** squat down. **h~n** *vi* (*haben*) squat □ *vr* **sich h~n** squat down

Hocker *m* **-s,-** stool

Höcker *m* **-s,-** bump; (*Kamel-*) hump

Hockey /hɔki/ *nt* **-s** hockey

Hode *f* **-,-n, Hoden** *m* **-s,-** testicle

Hof *m* **-[e]s,¨e** [court]yard; (*Bauern-*) farm; (*Königs-*) court; (*Schul-*) playground; (*Astr*) halo; **Hof halten** hold court

hoffen *vt/i* (*haben*) hope (**auf** + *acc* for). **h~tlich** *adv* I hope, let us hope; (*als Antwort*) **h~tlich/h~tlich nicht** let's hope so/not

Hoffnung *f* **-,-en** hope. **h~slos** *a* hopeless, *adv* -ly. **h~svoll** *a* hopeful, *adv* -ly

höflich *a* polite, *adv* -ly, courteous, *adv* -ly. **H~keit** *f* **-,-en** politeness, courtesy; (*Äußerung*) civility

hohe(r,s) *a s.* **hoch**

Höhe *f* **-,-n** height; (*Aviat, Geog*) altitude; (*Niveau*) level; (*einer Summe*) size; (*An-*) hill; **in die H~ gehen** rise, go up; **nicht auf der H~** (*fam*) under the weather;

das ist die H~! (*fam*) that's the limit!

Hoheit *f* -,-en (*Staats-*) sovereignty; (*Titel*) Highness. **H~sgebiet** *nt* [sovereign] territory. **H~szeichen** *nt* national emblem

Höhe|nlinie *f* contour line. **H~nsonne** *f* sun-lamp. **H~nzug** *m* mountain range. **H~punkt** *m* (*fig*) climax, peak; (*einer Vorstellung*) highlight. **h~r** *a & adv* higher; **h~re Schule** secondary school

hohl *a* hollow; (*leer*) empty

Höhle *f* -,-n cave; (*Tier-*) den; (*Hohlraum*) cavity; (*Augen-*) socket

Hohl|maß *nt* measure of capacity. **H~raum** *m* cavity

Hohn *m* -s scorn, derision

höhn|en *vt* deride □ *vi* (*haben*) jeer. **h~isch** *a* scornful, *adv* -ly

holen *vt* fetch, get; (*kaufen*) buy; (*nehmen*) take (**aus** from); **h~ lassen** send for; **[tief] Atem** *od* **Luft h~** take a [deep] breath; **sich** (*dat*) **etw h~** get sth; catch ⟨*Erkältung*⟩

Holland *nt* -s Holland

Holländ|er *m* -s,- Dutchman; **die H~er** the Dutch *pl*. **H~erin** *f* -,-nen Dutchwoman. **h~isch** *a* Dutch

Höll|e *f* - hell. **h~isch** *a* infernal; (*schrecklich*) terrible, *adv* -bly

holpern *vi* (*sein*) jolt *or* bump along □ *vi* (*haben*) be bumpy

holp[e]rig *a* bumpy

Holunder *m* -s (*Bot*) elder

Holz *nt* -es,⸚er wood; (*Nutz-*) timber. **H~blasinstrument** *nt* woodwind instrument

hölzern *a* wooden

Holz|hammer *m* mallet. **~ig** *a* woody. **H~kohle** *f* charcoal. **H~schnitt** *m* woodcut. **H~schuh** *m* [wooden] clog. **H~wolle** *f* wood shavings *pl*. **H~wurm** *m* woodworm

homogen *a* homogeneous

Homöopathie *f* - homoeopathy

homosexuell *a* homosexual. **H~e(r)** *m/f* homosexual

Honig *m* -s honey. **H~wabe** *f* honeycomb

Hono|rar *nt* -s,-e fee. **h~rieren** *vt* remunerate; (*fig*) reward

Hopfen *m* -s hops *pl*; (*Bot*) hop

hopsen *vi* (*sein*) jump

Hör|apparat *m* hearing-aid. **h~bar** *a* audible, *adv* -bly

horchen *vi* (*haben*) listen (**auf** + *acc* to); (*heimlich*) eavesdrop

Horde *f* -,-n horde; (*Gestell*) rack

hören *vt* hear; (*an-*) listen to □ *vi* (*haben*) hear; (*horchen*) listen; (*gehorchen*) obey; **h~ auf** (+ *acc*) listen to. **H~sagen** *nt* **vom H~sagen** from hearsay

Hör|er *m* -s,- listener; (*Teleph*) receiver. **H~funk** *m* radio. **H~gerät** *nt* hearing-aid

Horizon|t *m* -[e]s horizon. **h~tal** *a* horizontal, *adv* -ly

Hormon *nt* -s,-e hormone

Horn *nt* -s,⸚er horn. **H~haut** *f* hard skin; (*Augen-*) cornea

Hornisse *f* -,-n hornet

Horoskop *nt* -[e]s,-e horoscope

Hörrohr *nt* stethoscope

Horrorfilm *m* horror film

Hör|saal *m* (*Univ*) lecture hall. **H~spiel** *nt* radio play

Hort *m* -[e]s,-e (*Schatz*) hoard; (*fig*) refuge. **h~en** *vt* hoard

Hortensie /-i̯ə/ *f* -,-n hydrangea

Hörweite *f* **in/außer H~** within/out of earshot

Hose *f* -,-n, **Hosen** *pl* trousers *pl*. **H~nrock** *m* culottes *pl*. **H~nschlitz** *m* fly, flies *pl*. **H~nträger** *mpl* braces, (*Amer*) suspenders

Hostess (**Hosteß**) *f* -,-tessen hostess; (*Aviat*) air hostess

Hostie /ˈhɔsti̯ə/ *f* -,-n (*Relig*) host

Hotel *nt* -s,-s hotel; **H~ garni** /garˈniː/ bed-and-breakfast hotel. **H~ier** /-ˈli̯eː/ *m* -s,-s hotelier

hübsch *a* pretty, *adv* -ily; (*nett*) nice, *adv* -ly; ⟨*Summe*⟩ tidy
Hubschrauber *m* -s,- helicopter
huckepack *adv* **jdn h~ tragen** give s.o. a piggyback
Huf *m* -[e]s,-e hoof. **H~eisen** *nt* horseshoe
Hüft|e *f* -,-n hip. **H~gürtel, H~halter** *m* -s,- girdle
Hügel *m* -s,- hill. **h~ig** *a* hilly
Huhn *nt* -s,¨-er chicken; (*Henne*) hen
Hühn|chen *nt* -s,- chicken. **H~erauge** *nt* corn. **H~erbrühe** *f* chicken broth. **H~erstall** *m* henhouse, chicken-coop
huldig|en *vi* (*haben*) pay homage (*dat* to). **H~ung** *f* - homage
Hülle *f* -,-n cover; (*Verpackung*) wrapping; (*Platten-*) sleeve; **in H~ und Fülle** in abundance. **h~n** *vt* wrap
Hülse *f* -,-n (*Bot*) pod; (*Etui*) case. **H~nfrüchte** *fpl* pulses
human *a* humane, *adv* -ly. **h~itär** *a* humanitarian. **H~ität** *f* - humanity
Hummel *f* -,-n bumble-bee
Hummer *m* -s,- lobster
Hum|or *m* -s humour; **H~or haben** have a sense of humour. **h~oristisch** *a* humorous. **h~orvoll** *a* humorous, *adv* -ly
humpeln *vi* (*sein/haben*) hobble
Humpen *m* -s,- tankard
Hund *m* -[e]s,-e dog; (*Jagd-*) hound. **H~ehalsband** *nt* dog-collar. **H~ehütte** *f* kennel. **H~eleine** *f* dog lead
hundert *inv a* one/a hundred. **H~** *nt* -s,-e hundred; **H~e** *od* **h~e von** hundreds of. **H~jahrfeier** *f* centenary, (*Amer*) centennial. **h~prozentig** *a & adv* one hundred per cent. **h~ste(r,s)** *a* hundredth. **H~stel** *nt* -s,- hundredth
Hündin *f* -,-nen bitch
Hüne *m* -n,-n giant
Hunger *m* -s hunger; **H~ haben** be hungry. **h~n** *vi* (*haben*) starve; **h~n nach** (*fig*) hunger for. **H~snot** *f* famine
hungrig *a* hungry, *adv* -ily
Hupe *f* -,-n (*Auto*) horn. **h~n** *vi* (*haben*) sound one's horn
hüpf|en *vi* (*sein*) skip; ⟨*Vogel, Frosch:*⟩ hop; ⟨*Grashüpfer:*⟩ jump. **H~er** *m* -s,- skip, hop
Hürde *f* -,-n (*Sport & fig*) hurdle; (*Schaf-*) pen, fold
Hure *f* -,-n whore
hurra *int* hurray. **H~** *nt* -s,-s hurray; (*Beifallsruf*) cheer
Husche *f* -,-n [short] shower. **h~n** *vi* (*sein*) slip; ⟨*Eidechse:*⟩ dart; ⟨*Maus:*⟩ scurry; ⟨*Lächeln:*⟩ flit
hüsteln *vi* (*haben*) give a slight cough
husten *vi* (*haben*) cough. **H~** *m* -s cough. **H~saft** *m* cough mixture
Hut[1] *m* -[e]s,¨-e hat; (*Pilz-*) cap
Hut[2] *f* - **auf der H~ sein** be on one's guard (**vor** + *dat* against)
hüten *vt* watch over; tend ⟨*Tiere*⟩; (*aufpassen*) look after; **das Bett h~ müssen** be confined to bed; **sich h~** be on one's guard (**vor** + *dat* against); **sich h~, etw zu tun** take care not to do sth
Hütte *f* -,-n hut; (*Hunde-*) kennel; (*Techn*) iron and steel works. **H~nkäse** *m* cottage cheese. **H~nkunde** *f* metallurgy
Hyäne *f* -,-n hyena
Hybride *f* -,-n hybrid
Hydrant *m* -en,-en hydrant
hydraulisch *a* hydraulic, *adv* -ally
hydroelektrisch /hydroʔeˈlɛktrɪʃ/ *a* hydroelectric
Hygien|e /hyˈgi̯eːnə/ *f* - hygiene. **h~isch** *a* hygienic, *adv* -ally
hypermodern *a* ultra-modern
Hypno|se *f* - hypnosis. **h~tisch** *a* hypnotic. **H~tiseur** /-ˈzøːɐ̯/ *m* -s,-e hypnotist. **h~tisieren** *vt* hypnotize

Hypochonder /hypo'xɔndɐ/ *m* **-s,-** hypochondriac
Hypothek *f* **-,-en** mortgage
Hypothe|se *f* **-,-n** hypothesis. **h~tisch** *a* hypothetical, *adv* -ly
Hys|terie *f* **-** hysteria. **h~terisch** *a* hysterical, *adv* -ly

I

ich *pron* I; **ich bin's** it's me. **Ich** *nt* **-[s],-[s]** self; (*Psych*) ego
IC-Zug /i'tse:-/ *m* inter-city train
ideal *a* ideal. **I~** *nt* **-s,-e** ideal. **i~isieren** *vt* idealize. **I~ismus** *m* **-** idealism. **I~ist(in)** *m* **-en, -en** (*f* **-,-nen**) idealist. **i~istisch** *a* idealistic
Idee *f* **-,-n** idea; **fixe I~** obsession; **eine I~** (*fam: wenig*) a tiny bit
identifizieren *vt* identify
identi|sch *a* identical. **I~tät** *f* **-,-en** identity
Ideo|logie *f* **-,-n** ideology. **i~logisch** *a* ideological
idiomatisch *a* idiomatic
Idiot *m* **-en,-en** idiot. **i~isch** *a* idiotic, *adv* -ally
Idol *nt* **-s,-e** idol
idyllisch /i'dʏlɪʃ/ *a* idyllic
Igel *m* **-s,-** hedgehog
ignorieren *vt* ignore
ihm *pron* (*dat of* **er, es**) [to] him; (*Ding, Tier*) [to] it; **Freunde von ihm** friends of his
ihn *pron* (*acc of* **er**) him; (*Ding, Tier*) it. **i~en** *pron* (*dat of* **sie** *pl*) [to] them; **Freunde von i~en** friends of theirs. **I~en** *pron* (*dat of* **Sie**) [to] you; **Freunde von I~en** friends of yours
ihr *pron* (*2nd pers pl*) you □ (*dat of* **sie** *sg*) [to] her; (*Ding, Tier*) [to] it; **Freunde von ihr** friends of hers □ *poss pron* her; (*Ding, Tier*) its; (*pl*) their. **Ihr** *poss pron* your. **i~e(r,s)** *poss pron* hers; (*pl*) theirs. **I~e(r,s)** *poss pron* yours.
i~erseits *adv* for her/(*pl*) their part. **I~erseits** *adv* on your part. **i~etwegen** *adv* for her/(*Ding, Tier*) its/(*pl*) their sake; (*wegen*) because of her/it/them, on her/its/their account. **I~etwegen** *adv* for your sake; (*wegen*) because of you, on your account. **i~etwillen** *adv* **um i~etwillen** for her/(*Ding, Tier*) its/(*pl*) their sake. **I~etwillen** *adv* **um I~etwillen** for your sake. **i~ige** *poss pron* **der/die/das i~ige** hers; (*pl*) theirs. **I~ige** *poss pron* **der/die/das I~ige** yours. **i~s** *poss pron* hers; (*pl*) theirs. **I~s** *poss pron* yours
Ikone *f* **-,-n** icon
illegal *a* illegal, *adv* -ly
Illus|ion *f* **-,-en** illusion; **sich** (*dat*) **I~ionen machen** delude oneself. **i~orisch** *a* illusory
Illustr|ation /-'tsi̯o:n/ *f* **-,-en** illustration. **i~ieren** *vt* illustrate. **I~ierte** *f* **-n,-[n]** [illustrated] magazine
Iltis *m* **-ses,-se** polecat
im *prep* = **in dem; im Mai** in May; **im Kino** at the cinema
Image /'ɪmɪdʒ/ *nt* **-[s],-s** /-ɪs/ [public] image
Imbiss (Imbiß) *m* snack. **I~halle, I~stube** *f* snack-bar
Imit|ation /-'tsi̯o:n/ *f* **-,-en** imitation. **i~ieren** *vt* imitate
Imker *m* **-s,-** bee-keeper
Immatrikul|ation /-'tsi̯o:n/ *f* **-** (*Univ*) enrolment. **i~ieren** *vt* (*Univ*) enrol; **sich i~ieren** enrol
immer *adv* always; **für i~** for ever; (*endgültig*) for good; **i~ noch** still; **i~ mehr/weniger/wieder** more and more/less and less/again and again; **wer/was [auch] i~** whoever/whatever. **i~fort** *adv* = **i~zu. i~grün** *a* evergreen. **i~hin** *adv* (*wenigstens*) at least; (*trotzdem*) all the same; (*schließlich*) after all. **i~zu** *adv* all the time

Immobilien /-jən/ *pl* real estate *sg.* **I~händler, I~makler** *m* estate agent, (*Amer*) realtor
immun *a* immune (**gegen** to). **i~isieren** *vt* immunize. **I~ität** *f* - immunity
Imperativ *m* **-s,-e** imperative
Imperfekt *nt* **-s,-e** imperfect
Imperialismus *m* - imperialism
impf|en *vt* vaccinate, inoculate. **I~stoff** *m* vaccine. **I~ung** *f* **-,-en** vaccination, inoculation
Implantat *nt* **-[e]s,-e** implant
imponieren *vi* (*haben*) impress (**jdm** s.o.)
Impor|t *m* **-[e]s,-e** import. **I~teur** /-'tø:ɐ̯/ *m* **-s,-e** importer. **i~tieren** *vt* import
imposant *a* imposing
impoten|t *a* (*Med*) impotent. **I~z** *f* - (*Med*) impotence
imprägnieren *vt* waterproof
Impressionismus *m* - impressionism
improvisieren *vt/i* (*haben*) improvise
Impuls *m* **-es,-e** impulse. **i~iv** *a* impulsive, *adv* -ly
imstande *pred a* able (**zu** to); capable (**etw zu tun** of doing sth)
in *prep* (+ *dat*) in; (+ *acc*) into, in; (*bei Bus, Zug*) on; **in der Schule/Oper** at school/the opera; **in die Schule** to school □ *a* **in sein** be in
Inbegriff *m* embodiment. **i~en** *pred a* included
Inbrunst *f* - fervour
inbrünstig *a* fervent, *adv* -ly
indem *conj* (*während*) while; (*dadurch*) by (+ -ing)
Inder(in) *m* **-s,-** (*f* **-,-nen**) Indian
indessen *conj* while □ *adv* (*unterdessen*) meanwhile; (*jedoch*) however
Indian *m* **-s,-e** (*Aust*) turkey
Indian|er(in) *m* **-s,-** (*f* **-,-nen**) (American) Indian. **i~isch** *a* Indian
Indien /'ɪndjən/ *nt* **-s** India
indigniert *a* indignant, *adv* -ly
Indikativ *m* **-s,-e** indicative
indirekt *a* indirect, *adv* -ly
indisch *a* Indian
indiskre|t *a* indiscreet. **I~tion** /-'tsjo:n/ *f* **-,-en** indiscretion
indiskutabel *a* out of the question
indisponiert *a* indisposed
Individu|alist *m* **-en,-en** individualist. **I~alität** *f* - individuality. **i~ell** *a* individual, *adv* -ly. **I~um** /-'vi:duʊm/ *nt* **-s,-duen** individual
Indizienbeweis /ɪn'di:tsjən-/ *m* circumstantial evidence
indoktrinieren *vt* indoctrinate
industr|ialisiert *a* industrialized. **I~ie** *f* **-,-n** industry. **i~iell** *a* industrial. **I~ielle(r)** *m* industrialist
ineinander *adv* in/into one another
Infanterie *f* - infantry
Infektion /-'tsjo:n/ *f* **-,-en** infection. **I~skrankheit** *f* infectious disease
Infinitiv *m* **-s,-e** infinitive
infizieren *vt* infect; **sich i~** become/ ⟨*Person:*⟩ be infected
Inflation /-'tsjo:n/ *f* - inflation. **i~är** *a* inflationary
infolge *prep* (+ *gen*) as a result of. **i~dessen** *adv* consequently
Inform|atik *f* - information science. **I~ation** /-'tsjo:n/ *f* **-,-en** information; **I~ationen** information *sg.* **i~ieren** *vt* inform; **sich i~ieren** find out (**über** + *acc* about)
infrage *adv* **etw i~ stellen** question sth; (*ungewiss machen*) make sth doubtful; **nicht i~ kommen** be out of the question
infrarot *a* infra-red
Ingenieur /ɪnʒe'njø:ɐ̯/ *m* **-s,-e** engineer
Ingwer *m* **-s** ginger
Inhaber(in) *m* **-s,-** (*f* **-,-nen**) holder; (*Besitzer*) proprietor; (*Scheck-*) bearer

inhaftieren *vt* take into custody
inhalieren *vt/i* (*haben*) inhale
Inhalt *m* **-[e]s,-e** contents *pl*; (*Bedeutung, Gehalt*) content; (*Geschichte*) story. **I~sangabe** *f* summary. **I~sverzeichnis** *nt* list/(*in Buch*) table of contents
Initiale /-'tsi̯a:lə/ *f* **-,-n** initial
Initiative /initsi̯a'ti:və/ *f* **-,-n** initiative
Injektion /-'tsi̯o:n/ *f* **-,-en** injection. **injizieren** *vt* inject
inklusive *prep* (+ *gen*) including □ *adv* inclusive
inkognito *adv* incognito
inkonsequen|t *a* inconsistent, *adv* -ly. **I~z** *f* **-,-en** inconsistency
inkorrekt *a* incorrect, *adv* -ly
Inkubationszeit /-'tsi̯o:ns-/ *f* (*Med*) incubation period
Inland *nt* **-[e]s** home country; (*Binnenland*) interior. **I~sgespräch** *nt* inland call
inmitten *prep* (+ *gen*) in the middle of; (*unter*) amongst □ *adv* **i~ von** amongst, amidst
inne|haben† *vt sep* hold, have. **i~halten**† *vi sep* (*haben*) pause
innen *adv* inside; **nach i~** inwards. **I~architekt(in)** *m(f)* interior designer. **I~minister** *m* Minister of the Interior; (*in UK*) Home Secretary. **I~politik** *f* domestic policy. **I~stadt** *f* town centre
inner|e(r,s) *a* inner; (*Med, Pol*) internal. **I~e(s)** *nt* interior; (*Mitte*) centre; (*fig: Seele*) inner being. **I~eien** *fpl* (*Culin*) offal *sg*. **i~halb** *prep* (+ *gen*) inside; (*zeitlich & fig*) within; (*während*) during □ *adv* **i~halb von** within. **i~lich** *a* internal; (*seelisch*) inner; (*besinnlich*) introspective □ *adv* internally; (*im Inneren*) inwardly. **i~ste(r,s)** *a* innermost; **im I~sten** (*fig*) deep down
innig *a* sincere, *adv* -ly; (*tief*) deep, *adv* -ly; (*eng*) intimate, *adv* -ly
Innung *f* **-,-en** guild

inoffiziell *a* unofficial, *adv* -ly
ins *prep* = **in das; ins Kino/Büro** to the cinema/office
Insasse *m* **-n,-n** inmate; (*im Auto*) occupant; (*Passagier*) passenger
insbesondere *adv* especially
Inschrift *f* inscription
Insekt *nt* **-[e]s,-en** insect. **I~envertilgungsmittel** *nt* insecticide
Insel *f* **-,-n** island
Inser|at *nt* **-[e]s,-e** [newspaper] advertisement. **I~ent** *m* **-en,-en** advertiser. **i~ieren** *vt/i* (*haben*) advertise
insge|heim *adv* secretly. **i~samt** *adv* [all] in all
Insignien /-i̯ən/ *pl* insignia
insofern, insoweit *adv* /-'zo:-/ in this respect; **i~ als** in as much as □ *conj* /-zo'fɛrn, -'vai̯t/ **i~ als** in so far as
Insp|ektion /ɪnspɛk'tsi̯o:n/ *f* **-,-en** inspection. **I~ektor** *m* **-en,-en** /-'to:rən/ inspector
Inspir|ation /ɪnspira'tsi̯o:n/ *f* **-,-en** inspiration. **i~ieren** *vt* inspire
inspizieren /-sp-/ *vt* inspect
Install|ateur /ɪnstala'tø:ɐ̯/ *m* **-s,-e** fitter; (*Klempner*) plumber. **i~ieren** *vt* install
instand *adv* **i~ halten** maintain; (*pflegen*) look after; **i~ setzen** restore; (*reparieren*) repair. **I~haltung** *f* - maintenance, upkeep
inständig *a* urgent, *adv* -ly
Instandsetzung *f* - repair
Instant- /'ɪnstənt-/ *pref* instant
Instanz /-st-/ *f* **-,-en** authority
Instinkt /-st-/ *m* **-[e]s,-e** instinct. **i~iv** *a* instinctive, *adv* -ly
Institu|t /-st-/ *nt* **-[e]s,-e** institute. **I~tion** /-'tsi̯o:n/ *f* **-,-en** institution
Instrument /-st-/ *nt* **-[e]s,-e** instrument. **I~almusik** *f* instrumental music
Insulin *nt* **-s** insulin
inszenier|en *vt* (*Theat*) produce. **I~ung** *f* **-,-en** production

Integr|ation /-'tsi̯o:n/ *f* - integration. **i~ieren** *vt* integrate; **sich i~ieren** integrate. **I~ität** *f* - integrity
Intellekt *m* **-[e]s** intellect. **i~uell** *a* intellectual
intelligen|t *a* intelligent, *adv* -ly. **I~z** *f* - intelligence; (*Leute*) intelligentsia
Intendant *m* **-en,-en** director
Intens|ität *f* - intensity. **i~iv** *a* intensive, *adv* -ly. **i~ivieren** *vt* intensify. **I~ivstation** *f* intensive-care unit
inter|essant *a* interesting. **I~esse** *nt* **-s,-n** interest; **I~esse haben** be interested (**an** + *dat* in). **I~essengruppe** *f* pressure group. **I~essent** *m* **-en,-en** interested party; (*Käufer*) prospective buyer. **i~essieren** *vt* interest; **sich i~essieren** be interested (**für** in)
intern *a* (*fig*) internal, *adv* -ly
Inter|nat *nt* **-[e]s,-e** boarding school. **i~national** *a* international, *adv* -ly. **i~nieren** *vt* intern. **I~nierung** *f* - internment. **I~nist** *m* **-en,-en** specialist in internal diseases. **I~pretation** /-'tsi̯o:n/ *f* **-,-en** interpretation. **i~pretieren** *vt* interpret. **I~punktion** /-'tsi̯o:n/ *f* - punctuation. **I~rogativpronomen** *nt* interrogative pronoun. **I~vall** *nt* **-s,-e** interval. **I~vention** /-'tsi̯o:n/ *f* **-,-en** intervention
Interview /'ɪntɐvju:/ *nt* **-s,-s** interview. **i~en** /-'vju:ən/ *vt* interview
intim *a* intimate, *adv* -ly. **I~ität** *f* **-,-en** intimacy
intoleran|t *a* intolerant. **I~z** *f* - intolerance
intransitiv *a* intransitive, *adv* -ly
intravenös *a* intravenous, *adv* -ly
Intrig|e *f* **-,-n** intrigue. **i~ieren** *vi* (*haben*) plot
introvertiert *a* introverted
Intui|tion /-'tsi̯o:n/ *f* **-,-en** intuition. **i~tiv** *a* intuitive, *adv* -ly
Invalidenrente *f* disability pension
Invasion *f* **-,-en** invasion
Inven|tar *nt* **-s,-e** furnishings and fittings *pl*; (*Techn*) equipment; (*Bestand*) stock; (*Liste*) inventory. **I~tur** *f* **-,-en** stock-taking
investieren *vt* invest
inwendig *a & adv* inside
inwie|fern *adv* in what way. **i~weit** *adv* how far, to what extent
Inzest *m* **-[e]s** incest
inzwischen *adv* in the meantime
Irak (der) -[s] Iraq. **i~isch** *a* Iraqi
Iran (der) -[s] Iran. **i~isch** *a* Iranian
irdisch *a* earthly
Ire *m* **-n,-n** Irishman; **die I~n** the Irish *pl*
irgend *adv* **wer/was/wann i~** whoever/whatever/whenever; **wenn i~ möglich** if at all possible; **i~ etwas** (NEW) **i~etwas**; **i~ jemand** (NEW) **i~jemand**. **i~ein** *indef art* some/any; **i~ein anderer** someone/anyone else. **i~eine(r,s)** *pron* any one; (*jemand*) someone/anyone. **i~etwas** *pron* something; (*fragend, verneint*) anything. **i~jemand** *pron* someone; (*fragend, verneint*) anyone. **i~wann** *pron* at some time [or other]/at any time. **i~was** *pron* (*fam*) something [or other]/anything. **i~welche(r,s)** *pron* any. **i~wer** *pron* someone/anyone. **i~wie** *adv* somehow [or other]. **i~wo** *adv* somewhere/anywhere; **i~wo anders** somewhere else
Irin *f* **-,-nen** Irishwoman
Iris *f* **-,-** (*Anat, Bot*) iris
irisch *a* Irish
Irland *nt* **-s** Ireland
Ironie *f* - irony
ironisch *a* ironic, *adv* -ally
irr *a* = **irre**
irrational *a* irrational

irre *a* mad, crazy; (*fam: gewaltig*) incredible, *adv* -bly; **i~ werden** (NEW) **i~werden. I~(r)** *m/f* lunatic. **i~führen** *vt sep* (*fig*) mislead. **i~gehen**† *vi sep* (*sein*) lose one's way; (*sich täuschen*) be wrong

irrelevant *a* irrelevant

irre|machen *vt sep* confuse. **i~n** *vi/r* (*haben*) **[sich] i~n** be mistaken; **wenn ich mich nicht i~** if I am not mistaken □ *vi* (*sein*) wander. **I~nanstalt** *f*, **I~nhaus** *nt* lunatic asylum. **i~reden** *vi sep* (*haben*) ramble. **i~werden**† *vi sep* (*sein*) get confused

Irr|garten *m* maze. **i~ig** *a* erroneous

irritieren *vt* irritate

Irr|sinn *m* madness, lunacy. **i~sinnig** *a* mad; (*fam: gewaltig*) incredible, *adv* -bly. **I~tum** *m* -s,¨er mistake. **i~tümlich** *a* mistaken, *adv* -ly

Ischias *m & nt* - sciatica

Islam (der) -[s] Islam. **islamisch** *a* Islamic

Island *nt* -s Iceland

Isolier|band *nt* insulating tape. **i~en** *vt* isolate; (*Phys, Electr*) insulate; (*gegen Schall*) soundproof. **I~ung** *f* - isolation; insulation; soundproofing

Isra|el /ˈɪsraeːl/ *nt* **-s** Israel. **I~eli** *m* **-[s],-s** & *f* **-,-[s]** Israeli. **i~elisch** *a* Israeli

ist *s.* **sein; er ist** he is

Ital|ien /-i̯ən/ *nt* **-s** Italy. **I~iener(in)** *m* **-s,-** (*f* **-,-nen**) Italian. **i~ienisch** *a* Italian. **I~ienisch** *nt* **-[s]** (*Lang*) Italian

J

ja *adv*, **Ja** *nt* **-[s]** yes; **ich glaube ja** I think so; **ja nicht!** not on any account! **seid ja vorsichtig!** whatever you do, be careful! **da seid ihr ja!** there you are! **das ist es ja** that's just it; **das mag ja wahr sein** that may well be true

Jacht *f* **-,-en** yacht

Jacke *f* **-,-n** jacket; (*Strick-*) cardigan

Jackett /ʒaˈkɛt/ *nt* **-s,-s** jacket

Jade *m* **-[s]** & *f* - jade

Jagd *f* **-,-en** hunt; (*Schießen*) shoot; (*Jagen*) hunting; shooting; (*fig*) pursuit (**nach** of); **auf die J~ gehen** go hunting/shooting. **J~flugzeug** *nt* fighter aircraft. **J~gewehr** *nt* sporting gun. **J~hund** *m* gun-dog: (*Hetzhund*) hound

jagen *vt* hunt; (*schießen*) shoot; (*verfolgen, wegjagen*) chase; (*treiben*) drive; **sich j~** chase each other; **in die Luft j~** blow up □ *vi* (*haben*) hunt, go hunting/shooting; (*fig*) chase (**nach** after) □ *vi* (*sein*) race, dash

Jäger *m* **-s,-** hunter

jäh *a* sudden, *adv* -ly; (*steil*) steep, *adv* -ly

Jahr *nt* **-[e]s,-e** year. **J~buch** *nt* year-book. **j~elang** *adv* for years. **J~estag** *m* anniversary. **J~eszahl** *f* year. **J~eszeit** *f* season. **J~gang** *m* year; (*Wein*) vintage. **J~hundert** *nt* century. **J~hundertfeier** *f* centenary, (*Amer*) centennial

jährlich *a* annual, yearly □ *adv* annually, yearly

Jahr|markt *m* fair. **J~tausend** *nt* millenium. **J~zehnt** *nt* **-[e]s,-e** decade

Jähzorn *m* violent temper. **j~ig** *a* hot-tempered

Jalousie /ʒaluˈziː/ *f* **-,-n** venetian blind

Jammer *m* **-s** misery; (*Klagen*) lamenting; **es ist ein J~** it is a shame

jämmerlich *a* miserable, *adv* -bly; (*Mitleid erregend*) pitiful, *adv* -ly

jammer|n *vi* (*haben*) lament □ *vt* **jdn j~n** arouse s.o.'s pity. **j~schade** *a* **j~schade sein** (*fam*) be a terrible shame

Jänner *m* **-s,-** (*Aust*) January
Januar *m* **-s,-e** January
Jap|an *nt* **-s** Japan. **J~aner(in)** *m* **-s,-** (*f* **-,-nen**) Japanese. **j~anisch** *a* Japanese. **J~anisch** *nt* **-[s]** (*Lang*) Japanese
Jargon /ʒarˈgõ:/ *m* **-s** jargon
jäten *vt/i* (*haben*) weed
jauchzen *vi* (*haben*) (*liter*) exult
jaulen *vi* (*haben*) yelp
Jause *f* **-,-n** (*Aust*) snack
jawohl *adv* yes
Jawort *nt* **jdm sein J~ geben** accept s.o.'s proposal [of marriage]
Jazz /jats, dʒɛs/ *m* **-** jazz
je *adv* (*jemals*) ever; (*jeweils*) each; (*pro*) per; **je nach** according to; **seit eh und je always; besser denn je** better than ever □ *conj* **je mehr, desto** *od* **umso besser** the more the better □ *prep* (+ *acc*) per
Jeans /dʒi:ns/ *pl* jeans
jed|e(r,s) *pron* every; (*j~er Einzelne*) each; (*j~er Beliebige*) any; (*substantivisch*) everyone; each one; anyone; **ohne j~en Grund** without any reason. **j~enfalls** *adv* in any case; (*wenigstens*) at least. **j~ermann** *pron* everyone. **j~erzeit** *adv* at any time. **j~esmal** *adv* (NEW) **jedes Mal**, *s.* **Mal**[1]
jedoch *adv & conj* however
jeher *adv* **von** *od* **seit j~** always
jemals *adv* ever
jemand *pron* someone, somebody; (*fragend, verneint*) anyone, anybody
jen|e(r,s) *pron* that; (*pl*) those; (*substantivisch*) that one; (*pl*) those. **j~seits** *prep* (+ *gen*) [on] the other side of
jetzig *a* present; ⟨*Preis*⟩ current
jetzt *adv* now. **J~zeit** *f* present
jeweil|ig *a* respective. **j~s** *adv* at a time
jiddisch *a*, **J~** *nt* **-[s]** Yiddish
Job /dʒɔp/ *m* **-s,-s** job. **j~ben** *vi* (*haben*) (*fam*) work
Joch *nt* **-[e]s,-e** yoke
Jockei, Jockey /ˈdʒɔki/ *m* **-s,-s** jockey
Jod *nt* **-[e]s** iodine
jodeln *vi* (*haben*) yodel
Joga *m & nt* **-[s]** yoga
jogg|en /ˈdʒɔgən/ *vi* (*haben/sein*) jog. **J~ing** *nt* **-[s]** jogging
Joghurt, Jogurt *m & nt* **-[s]** yoghurt
Johannisbeere *f* redcurrant; **schwarze J~** blackcurrant
johlen *vi* (*haben*) yell; (*empört*) jeer
Joker *m* **-s,-** (*Karte*) joker
Jolle *f* **-,-n** dinghy
Jongl|eur /ʒõˈglø:ɐ̯/ *m* **-s,-e** juggler. **j~ieren** *vi* (*haben*) juggle
Joppe *f* **-,-n** [thick] jacket
Jordanien /-iən/ *nt* **-s** Jordan
Journalis|mus /ʒʊrnaˈlɪsmʊs/ *m* **-** journalism. **J~t(in)** *m* **-en,-en** (*f* **-,-nen**) journalist
Jubel *m* **-s** rejoicing, jubilation. **j~n** *vi* (*haben*) rejoice
Jubil|ar(in) *m* **-s,-e** (*f* **-,-nen**) person celebrating an anniversary. **J~äum** *nt* **-s,-äen** jubilee; (*Jahrestag*) anniversary
juck|en *vi* (*haben*) itch; **sich j~en** scratch; **es j~t mich** I have an itch; (*fam: möchte*) I'm itching (**zu** to). **J~reiz** *m* itch[ing]
Jude *m* **-n,-n** Jew. **J~ntum** *nt* **-s** Judaism; (*Juden*) Jewry
Jüd|in *f* **-,-nen** Jewess. **j~isch** *a* Jewish
Judo *nt* **-[s]** judo
Jugend *f* **-** youth; (*junge Leute*) young people *pl*. **J~herberge** *f* youth hostel. **J~klub** *m* youth club. **J~kriminalität** *f* juvenile delinquency. **j~lich** *a* youthful. **J~liche(r)** *m/f* young man/woman; (*Admin*) juvenile; **J~liche** *pl* young people. **J~stil** *m* art nouveau. **J~zeit** *f* youth
Jugoslaw|ien /-iən/ *nt* **-s** Yugoslavia. **j~isch** *a* Yugoslav
Juli *m* **-[s],-s** July

jung *a* (**jünger, jüngst**) young; ⟨*Wein*⟩ new □*pron* **J~ und Alt** (**j~ und alt**) young and old. **J~e** *m* **-n,-n** boy. **J~e(s)** *nt* young animal/bird; (*Katzen-*) kitten; (*Bären-, Löwen-*) cub; (*Hunde-, Seehund-*) pup; **die J~en** the young *pl*. **j~enhaft** *a* boyish
Jünger *m* **-s,-** disciple
Jungfer *f* **-,-n alte J~** old maid. **J~nfahrt** *f* maiden voyage
Jung|frau *f* virgin; (*Astr*) Virgo. **j~fräulich** *a* virginal. **J~geselle** *m* bachelor
Jüngling *m* **-s,-e** youth
jüngst|e(r,s) *a* youngest; (*neueste*) latest; **in j~er Zeit** recently
Juni *m* **-[s],-s** June
Junior *m* **-s,-en** /-ˈoːrən/ junior
Jura *pl* law *sg*
Jurist|(in) *m* **-en,-en** (*f* **-,-nen**) lawyer. **j~isch** *a* legal, *adv* -ly
Jury /ʒyˈriː/ *f* **-,-s** jury; (*Sport*) judges *pl*
justieren *vt* adjust
Justiz *f* **- die J~** justice. **J~irrtum** *m* miscarriage of justice. **J~minister** *m* Minister of Justice
Juwel *nt* **-s,-en** & (*fig*) **-e** jewel. **J~ier** *m* **-es,-e** jeweller
Jux *m* **-es,-e** (*fam*) joke; **aus Jux** for fun

K

Kabarett *nt* **-s,-s** & **-e** cabaret
kabbelig *a* choppy
Kabel *nt* **-s,-** cable. **K~fernsehen** *nt* cable television
Kabeljau *m* **-s,-e** & **-s** cod
Kabine *f* **-,-n** cabin; (*Umkleide-*) cubicle; (*Telefon-*) booth; (*einer K~nbahn*) car. **K~nbahn** *f* cable-car
Kabinett *nt* **-s,-e** (*Pol*) Cabinet
Kabriolett *nt* **-s,-s** convertible
Kachel *f* **-,-n** tile. **k~n** *vt* tile
Kadaver *m* **-s,-** carcass
Kadenz *f* **-,-en** (*Mus*) cadence; (*für Solisten*) cadenza
Kadett *m* **-en,-en** cadet
Käfer *m* **-s,-** beetle
Kaff *nt* **-s,-s** (*fam*) dump
Kaffee /ˈkafeː, kaˈfeː/ *m* **-s,-s** coffee; (*Mahlzeit*) afternoon coffee. **K~grund** *m* = **K~satz**. **K~kanne** *f* coffee-pot. **K~maschine** *f* coffee-maker. **K~mühle** *f* coffee-grinder. **K~satz** *m* coffee-grounds *pl*
Käfig *m* **-s,-e** cage
kahl *a* bare; (*haarlos*) bald; **k~ geschoren** shaven. **k~geschoren** *a* (NEW) **k~ geschoren**, *s*. **kahl**. **k~köpfig** *a* bald-headed
Kahn *m* **-s,¨-e** boat; (*Last-*) barge
Kai *m* **-s,-s** quay
Kaiser *m* **-s,-** emperor. **K~in** *f* **-,-nen** empress. **k~lich** *a* imperial. **K~reich** *nt* empire. **K~schnitt** *m* Caesarean [section]
Kajüte *f* **-,-n** (*Naut*) cabin
Kakao /kaˈkau̯/ *m* **-s** cocoa
Kakerlak *m* **-s** & **-en,-en** cockroach
Kaktee /kakˈteːə/ *f* **-,-n**, **Kaktus** *m* **-,-teen** /-ˈteːən/ cactus
Kalb *nt* **-[e]s,¨-er** calf. **K~fleisch** *nt* veal
Kalender *m* **-s,-** calendar; (*Taschen-, Termin-*) diary
Kaliber *nt* **-s,-** calibre; (*Gewehr-*) bore
Kalium *nt* **-s** potassium
Kalk *m* **-[e]s,-e** lime; (*Kalzium*) calcium. **k~en** *vt* whitewash. **K~stein** *m* limestone
Kalkul|ation /-ˈt͜si̯oːn/ *f* **-,-en** calculation. **k~ieren** *vt/i* (*haben*) calculate
Kalorie *f* **-,-n** calorie
kalt *a* (**kälter, kältest**) cold; **es ist k~** it is cold; **mir ist k~** I am cold. **k~blütig** *a* cold-blooded, *adv* -ly; (*ruhig*) cool, *adv* -ly
Kälte *f* **-** cold; (*Gefühls-*) coldness; **10 Grad K~** 10 degrees below zero. **K~welle** *f* cold spell

kalt|herzig *a* cold-hearted. **k~schnäuzig** *a* (*fam*) cold, *adv* -ly
Kalzium *nt* **-s** calcium
Kamel *nt* **-s,-e** camel; (*fam: Idiot*) fool
Kamera *f* **-,-s** camera
Kamerad|(in) *m* **-en,-en** (*f* **-,-nen**) companion; (*Freund*) mate; (*Mil, Pol*) comrade. **K~schaft** *f* - comradeship
Kameramann *m* (*pl* **-männer & -leute**) cameraman
Kamille *f* - camomille
Kamin *m* **-s,-e** fireplace; (*SGer: Schornstein*) chimney. **K~feger** *m* **-s,-** (*SGer*) chimney-sweep
Kamm *m* **-[e]s,¨e** comb; (*Berg-*) ridge; (*Zool, Wellen-*) crest
kämmen *vt* comb; **jdn/sich k~** comb s.o.'s/one's hair
Kammer *f* **-,-n** small room; (*Techn, Biol, Pol*) chamber. **K~diener** *m* valet. **K~musik** *f* chamber music
Kammgarn *nt* (*Tex*) worsted
Kampagne /kam'panjə/ *f* **-,-n** (*Pol, Comm*) campaign
Kampf *m* **-es,¨e** fight; (*Schlacht*) battle; (*Wett-*) contest; (*fig*) struggle; **schwere K¨e** heavy fighting *sg*; **den K~ ansagen** (+ *dat*) (*fig*) declare war on
kämpf|en *vi* (*haben*) fight; **sich k~en durch** fight one's way through. **K~er(in)** *m* **-s,-** (*f* **-,-nen**) fighter
kampf|los *adv* without a fight. **K~richter** *m* (*Sport*) judge
kampieren *vi* (*haben*) camp
Kanada *nt* **-s** Canada
Kanad|ier(in) /-i̯ɐ, -i̯ərɪn/ *m* **-s,-** (*f* **-,-nen**) Canadian. **k~isch** *a* Canadian
Kanal *m* **-s,¨e** canal; (*Abfluss-*) drain, sewer; (*Radio, TV*) channel; **der K~** the [English] Channel
Kanalis|ation /-'tsi̯o:n/ *f* - sewerage system, drains *pl*. **k~ieren** *vt* canalize; (*fig: lenken*) channel
Kanarienvogel /-i̯ən-/ *m* canary
Kanarisch *a* **K~e Inseln** Canaries
Kandi|dat(in) *m* **-en,-en** (*f* **-,-nen**) candidate. **k~dieren** *vi* (*haben*) stand (**für** for)
kandiert *a* candied
Känguru (**Känguruh**) *nt* **-s,-s** kangaroo
Kaninchen *nt* **-s,-** rabbit
Kanister *m* **-s,-** canister; (*Benzin-*) can
Kännchen *nt* **-s,-** [small] jug; (*Kaffee-*) pot
Kanne *f* **-,-n** jug; (*Kaffee-, Tee-*) pot; (*Öl-*) can; (*große Milch-*) churn; (*Gieß-*) watering-can
Kannibal|e *m* **-n,-n** cannibal. **K~ismus** *m* - cannibalism
Kanon *m* **-s,-s** canon; (*Lied*) round
Kanone *f* **-,-n** cannon, gun; (*fig: Könner*) ace
kanonisieren *vt* canonize
Kantate *f* **-,-n** cantata
Kante *f* **-,-n** edge; **auf die hohe K~ legen** (*fam*) put by
Kanten *m* **-s,-** crust [of bread]
Kanter *m* **-s,-** canter
kantig *a* angular
Kantine *f* **-,-n** canteen
Kanton *m* **-s,-e** (*Swiss*) canton
Kantor *m* **-s,-en** /-'to:rən/ choirmaster and organist
Kanu *nt* **-s,-s** canoe
Kanzel *f* **-,-n** pulpit; (*Aviat*) cockpit
Kanzleistil *m* officialese
Kanzler *m* **-s,-** chancellor
Kap *nt* **-s,-s** (*Geog*) cape
Kapazität *f* **-,-en** capacity; (*Experte*) authority
Kapelle *f* **-,-n** chapel; (*Mus*) band
Kaper *f* **-,-n** (*Culin*) caper
kapern *vt* (*Naut*) seize
kapieren *vt* (*fam*) understand, (*fam*) get
Kapital *nt* **-s** capital; **K~ schlagen aus** (*fig*) capitalize on. **K~ismus** *m* - capitalism. **K~ist**

m **-en,-en** capitalist. **k~istisch** *a* capitalist
Kapitän *m* **-s,-e** captain
Kapitel *nt* **-s,-** chapter
Kapitul|ation /-'tsio:n/ *f* **-** capitulation. **k~ieren** *vi* (*haben*) capitulate
Kaplan *m* **-s,-e** curate
Kappe *f* **-,-n** cap. **k~n** *vt* cut
Kapsel *f* **-,-n** capsule; (*Flaschen-*) top
kaputt *a* (*fam*) broken; (*zerrissen*) torn; (*defekt*) out of order; (*ruiniert*) ruined; (*erschöpft*) worn out. **k~gehen**† *vi sep* (*sein*) (*fam*) break; (*zerreißen*) tear; (*defekt werden*) pack up; ⟨*Ehe, Freundschaft:*⟩ break up. **k~lachen (sich)** *vr sep* (*fam*) be in stitches. **k~machen** *vt sep* (*fam*) break; (*zerreißen*) tear; (*defekt machen*) put out of order; (*erschöpfen*) wear out; **sich k~machen** wear oneself out
Kapuze *f* **-,-n** hood
Kapuzinerkresse *f* nasturtium
Karaffe *f* **-,-n** carafe; (*mit Stöpsel*) decanter
Karambolage /karambo'la:ʒə/ *f* **-,-n** collision
Karamell (**Karamel**) *m* **-s** caramel. **K~bonbon** *m & nt* ≈ toffee
Karat *nt* **-[e]s,-e** carat
Karawane *f* **-,-n** caravan
Kardinal *m* **-s,-̈e** **cardinal**. **K~zahl** *f* cardinal number
Karfiol *m* **-s** (*Aust*) cauliflower
Karfreitag *m* Good Friday
karg *a* (**kärger, kärgst**) meagre; (*frugal*) frugal; (*spärlich*) sparse; (*unfruchtbar*) barren; (*gering*) scant. **k~en** *vi* (*haben*) be sparing (*mit* with)
kärglich *a* poor, meagre; (*gering*) scant
Karibik *f* **-** Caribbean
kariert *a* check[ed]; ⟨*Papier*⟩ squared; **schottisch k~** tartan
Karik|atur *f* **-,-en** caricature; (*Journ*) cartoon. **k~ieren** *vt* caricature
karitativ *a* charitable
Karneval *m* **-s,-e** & **-s** carnival
Karnickel *nt* **-s,-** (*dial*) rabbit
Kärnten *nt* **-s** Carinthia
Karo *nt* **-s,-s** (*Raute*) diamond; (*Viereck*) square; (*Muster*) check; (*Kartenspiel*) diamonds *pl*. **K~muster** *nt* check
Karosserie *f* **-,-n** bodywork
Karotte *f* **-,-n** carrot
Karpfen *m* **-s,-**, carp
Karre *f* **-,-n** = **Karren**
Karree *nt* **-s,-s**, square; **ums K~** round the block
Karren *m* **-s,-** cart; (*Hand-*) barrow. **k~** *vt* cart
Karriere /ka'rje:rə/ *f* **-,-n** career; **K~ machen** get to the top
Karte *f* **-,-n** card; (*Eintritts-, Fahr-*) ticket; (*Speise-*) menu; (*Land-*) map
Kartei *f* **-,-en** card index. **K~karte** *f* index card
Karten|spiel *nt* card-game; (*Spielkarten*) pack/(*Amer*) deck of cards. **K~vorverkauf** *m* advance booking
Kartoffel *f* **-,-n** potato. **K~brei** *m*, **K~püree** *nt* mashed potatoes *pl*. **K~salat** *m* potato salad
Karton /kar'tɔŋ/ *m* **-s,-s** cardboard; (**Schachtel**) carton, cardboard box
Karussell *nt* **-s,-s** & **-e** roundabout
Karwoche *f* Holy Week
Käse *m* **-s,-** cheese. **K~kuchen** *m* cheesecake
Kaserne *f* **-,-n** barracks *pl*
Kasino *nt* **-s,-s** casino
Kasperle *nt* & *m* **-s,-** Punch. **K~theater** *nt* Punch and Judy show
Kasse *f* **-,-n** till; (*Registrier-*) cash register; (*Zahlstelle*) cash desk; (*im Supermarkt*) check-out; (*Theater-*) box-office; (*Geld*) pool [of money], (*fam*) kitty; (*Kranken-*) health insurance scheme; (*Spar-*) savings bank;

knapp/gut bei K~ sein (*fam*) be short of cash/be flush. **K~npatient** *m* ≈ NHS patient. **K~nschlager** *m* box-office hit. **K~nwart** *m* **-[e]s,-e** treasurer. **K~nzettel** *m* receipt

Kasserolle *f* **-,-n** saucepan [with one handle]

Kassette *f* **-,-n** cassette; (*Film-, Farbband-*) cartridge; (*Geld-*) money-box; (*Schmuck-*) case. **K~nrecorder** /-rəkɔrdɐ/ *m* **-s,-** cassette recorder

kassier|en *vi* (*haben*) collect the money/(*im Bus*) the fares □ *vt* collect. **K~er(in)** *m* **-s,-** (*f* **-,-nen**) cashier

Kastagnetten /kastan'jɛtən/ *pl* castanets

Kastanie /kas'ta:njə/ *f* **-,-n** [horse] chestnut, (*fam*) conker. **k~nbraun** *a* chestnut

Kaste *f* **-,-n** caste

Kasten *m* **-s,⸚** box; (*Brot-*) bin; (*Flaschen-*) crate; (*Brief-*) letter-box; (*Aust: Schrank*) cupboard; (*Kleider-*) wardrobe

kastrieren *vt* castrate; neuter ⟨*Tier*⟩

Kasus *m* **-,-** /-u:s/ (*Gram*) case

Katalog *m* **-[e]s,-e** catalogue. **k~isieren** *vt* catalogue

Katalysator *m* **-s,-en** /-'to:rən/ catalyst; (*Auto*) catalytic converter

Katapult *nt* **-[e]s,-e** catapult. **k~ieren** *vt* catapult

Katarrh, Katarr *m* **-s,-e** catarrh

katastr|ophal *a* catastrophic. **K~ophe** *f* **-,-n** catastrophe

Katechismus *m* **-** catechism

Kateg|orie *f* **-,-n** category. **k~orisch** *a* categorical, *adv* -ly

Kater *m* **-s,-** tom-cat; (*fam: Katzenjammer*) hangover

Katheder *nt* **-s,-** [teacher's] desk

Kathedrale *f* **-,-n** cathedral

Kath|olik(in) *m* **-en,-en** (*f* **-,-nen**) Catholic. **k~olisch** *a* Catholic. **K~olizismus** *m* **-** Catholicism

Kätzchen *nt* **-s,-** kitten; (*Bot*) catkin

Katze *f* **-,-n** cat. **K~njammer** *m* (*fam*) hangover. **K~nsprung** *m* **ein K~nsprung** (*fam*) a stone's throw

Kauderwelsch *nt* **-[s]** gibberish

kauen *vt/i* (*haben*) chew; bite ⟨*Nägel*⟩

kauern *vi* (*haben*) crouch; **sich k~** crouch down

Kauf *m* **-[e]s, Käufe** purchase; **guter K~** bargain; **in K~ nehmen** (*fig*) put up with. **k~en** *vt/i* (*haben*) buy; **k~en bei** shop at

Käufer(in) *m* **-s,-** (*f* **-,-nen**) buyer; (*im Geschäft*) shopper

Kauf|haus *nt* department store. **K~kraft** *f* purchasing power. **K~laden** *m* shop

käuflich *a* saleable; (*bestechlich*) corruptible; **k~ sein** be for sale; **k~ erwerben** buy

Kauf|mann *m* (*pl* **-leute**) businessman; (*Händler*) dealer; (*dial*) grocer. **k~männisch** *a* commercial. **K~preis** *m* purchase price

Kaugummi *m* chewing-gum

Kaulquappe *f* **-,-n** tadpole

kaum *adv* hardly; **k~ glaublich** *od* **zu glauben** hard to believe

kauterisieren *vt* cauterize

Kaution /-'tsjo:n/ *f* **-,-en** surety; (*Jur*) bail; (*Miet-*) deposit

Kautschuk *m* **-s** rubber

Kauz *m* **-es, Käuze** owl; **komischer K~** (*fam*) odd fellow

Kavalier *m* **-s,-e** gentleman

Kavallerie *f* **-** cavalry

Kaviar *m* **-s** caviare

keck *a* bold; (*frech*) cheeky

Kegel *m* **-s,-** skittle; (*Geom*) cone; **mit Kind und K~** (*fam*) with all the family. **K~bahn** *f* skittle-alley. **k~förmig** *a* conical. **k~n** *vi* (*haben*) play skittles

Kehl|e *f* **-,-n** throat; **aus voller K~e** at the top of one's voice; **etw in die falsche K~e bekommen** (*fam*) take sth the wrong way.

K∼kopf *m* larynx. **K∼kopfentzündung** *f* laryngitis

Kehr|e *f* -,-n [hairpin] bend. **k∼en** *vi* (*haben*) (*fegen*) sweep □ *vt* sweep; (*wenden*) turn; **den Rücken k∼en** turn one's back (*dat* on); **sich k∼en** turn; **sich nicht k∼en an** (+ *acc*) not care about. **K∼icht** *m* -[e]s sweepings *pl*. **K∼reim** *m* refrain. **K∼seite** *f* (*fig*) drawback; **die K∼seite der Medaille** the other side of the coin. **k∼tmachen** *vi sep* (*haben*) turn back; (*sich umdrehen*) turn round. **K∼twendung** *f* about-turn; (*fig*) U-turn

keifen *vi* (*haben*) scold

Keil *m* -[e]s,-e wedge

Keile *f* - (*fam*) hiding. **k∼n (sich)** *vr* (*fam*) fight. **K∼rei** *f* -,-en (*fam*) punch-up

Keil|kissen *nt* [wedge-shaped] bolster. **K∼riemen** *m* fan belt

Keim *m* -[e]s,-e (*Bot*) sprout; (*Med*) germ; **im K∼ ersticken** (*fig*) nip in the bud. **k∼en** *vi* (*haben*) germinate; (*austreiben*) sprout. **k∼frei** *a* sterile

kein *pron* no; not a; **auf k∼en Fall** on no account; **k∼e fünf Minuten** less than five minutes. **k∼e(r,s)** *pron* no one, nobody; (*Ding*) none, not one. **k∼esfalls** *adv* on no account. **k∼eswegs** *adv* by no means. **k∼mal** *adv* not once. **k∼s** *pron* none, not one

Keks *m* -[es],-[e] biscuit, (*Amer*) cookie

Kelch *m* -[e]s,-e goblet, cup; (*Relig*) chalice; (*Bot*) calyx

Kelle *f* -,-n ladle; (*Maurer-, Pflanz-*) trowel

Keller *m* -s,- cellar. **K∼ei** *f* -,-en winery. **K∼geschoss** (**K∼geschoß**) *nt* cellar; (*bewohnbar*) basement. **K∼wohnung** *f* basement flat

Kellner *m* -s,- waiter. **K∼in** *f* -,-nen waitress

keltern *vt* press

keltisch *a* Celtic

Kenia *nt* -s Kenya

kenn|en† *vt* know; **k∼en lernen** get to know; (*treffen*) meet; **sich k∼en lernen** meet; (*näher*) get to know one another. **k∼enlernen** *vt sep* (NEW) **k∼en lernen**, *s.* **kennen**. **K∼er** *m* -s,-, **K∼erin** *f* -,-nen connoisseur; (*Experte*) expert. **K∼melodie** *f* signature tune. **k∼tlich** *a* recognizable; **k∼tlich machen** mark. **K∼tnis** *f* -,-se knowledge; **zur K∼tnis nehmen** take note of; **in K∼tnis setzen** inform (**von** of). **K∼wort** *nt* (*pl* **-wörter**) reference; (*geheimes*) password. **K∼zeichen** *nt* distinguishing mark *or* feature; (*Merkmal*) characteristic, (*Markierung*) mark, marking; (*Abzeichen*) badge; (*Auto*) registration. **k∼zeichnen** *vt* distinguish; (*markieren*) mark. **k∼zeichnend** *a* typical (**für** of). **K∼ziffer** *f* reference number

kentern *vi* (*sein*) capsize

Keramik *f* -,-en pottery, ceramics *sg*; (*Gegenstand*) piece of pottery

Kerbe *f* -,-n notch

Kerbholz *nt* **etwas auf dem K∼haben** (*fam*) have a record

Kerker *m* -s,- dungeon; (*Gefängnis*) prison

Kerl *m* -s,-e & -s (*fam*) fellow, bloke

Kern *m* -s,-e pip; (*Kirsch-*) stone; (*Nuss-*) kernel; (*Techn*) core; (*Atom-, Zell- & fig*) nucleus; (*Stadt-*) centre; (*einer Sache*) heart. **K∼energie** *f* nuclear energy. **K∼gehäuse** *nt* core. **k∼gesund** *a* perfectly healthy. **k∼ig** *a* robust; (*Ausspruch*) pithy. **k∼los** *a* seedless. **K∼physik** *f* nuclear physics *sg*

Kerze *f* -,-n candle. **k∼ngerade** *a & adv* straight. **K∼nhalter** *m* -s,- candlestick

kess (**keß**) *a* (**kesser, kessest**) pert

Kessel *m* **-s,-** kettle; (*Heiz-*) boiler. **K~stein** *m* fur

Ketschup (**Ketchup**) /ˈkɛtʃap/ *m* **-[s],-s** ketchup

Kette *f* **-,-n** chain; (*Hals-*) necklace. **k~n** *vt* chain (**an** + *acc* to). **K~nladen** *m* chain store. **K~nraucher** *m* chain-smoker. **K~nreaktion** *f* chain reaction

Ketze|r(in) *m* **-s,-** (*f* **-,-nen**) heretic. **K~rei** *f* - heresy

keuch|en *vi* (*haben*) pant. **K~husten** *m* whooping cough

Keule *f* **-,-n** club; (*Culin*) leg; (*Hühner-*) drumstick

keusch *a* chaste. **K~heit** *f* - chastity

Kfz *abbr s.* **Kraftfahrzeug**

Khaki *nt* - khaki. **k~farben** *a* khaki

kichern *vi* (*haben*) giggle

Kiefer[1] *f* **-,-n** pine[-tree]

Kiefer[2] *m* **-s,-** jaw

Kiel *m* **-s,-e** (*Naut*) keel. **K~wasser** *nt* wake

Kiemen *fpl* gills

Kies *m* **-es** gravel. **K~el** *m* **-s,-**, **K~elstein** *m* pebble. **K~grube** *f* gravel pit

Kilo *nt* **-s,-[s]** kilo. **K~gramm** *nt* kilogram. **K~hertz** *nt* kilohertz. **K~meter** *m* kilometre. **K~meterstand** *m* ≈ mileage. **K~watt** *nt* kilowatt

Kind *nt* **-es,-er** child; **von K~ auf** from childhood

Kinder|arzt *m*, **K~ärztin** *f* paediatrician. **K~bett** *nt* child's cot. **K~ei** *f* **-,-en** childish prank. **K~garten** *m* nursery school. **K~gärtnerin** *f* nursery-school teacher. **K~geld** *nt* child benefit. **K~gottesdienst** *m* Sunday school. **K~lähmung** *f* polio. **k~leicht** *a* very easy. **k~los** *a* childless. **K~mädchen** *nt* nanny. **k~reich** *a* **k~reiche Familie** large family. **K~reim** *m* nursery rhyme. **K~spiel** *nt* children's game; **das ist ein/kein K~spiel** that is dead easy/not easy. **K~tagesstätte** *f* day nursery. **K~teller** *m* children's menu. **K~wagen** *m* pram, (*Amer*) baby carriage. **K~zimmer** *nt* child's/children's room; (*für Baby*) nursery

Kind|heit *f* - childhood. **k~isch** *a* childish, puerile. **k~lich** *a* childlike

kinetisch *a* kinetic

Kinn *nt* **-[e]s,-e** chin. **K~lade** *f* jaw

Kino *nt* **-s,-s** cinema

Kiosk *m* **-[e]s,-e** kiosk

Kippe *f* **-,-n** (*Müll-*) dump; (*fam: Zigaretten-*) fag-end; **auf der K~ stehen** (*fam*) be in a precarious position; (*unsicher sein*) hang in the balance. **k~lig** *a* wobbly. **k~ln** *vi* (*haben*) wobble. **k~n** *vt* tilt; (*schütten*) tip (**in** + *acc* into) □ *vi* (*sein*) topple

Kirch|e *f* **-,-n** church. **K~enbank** *f* pew. **K~endiener** *m* verger. **K~enlied** *nt* hymn. **K~enschiff** *nt* nave. **K~hof** *m* churchyard. **k~lich** *a* church ... □ *adv* **k~lich getraut werden** be married in church. **K~turm** *m* church tower, steeple. **K~weih** *f* **-,-en** [village] fair

Kirmes *f* **-,-sen** = **Kirchweih**

Kirsch|e *f* **-,-n** cherry. **K~wasser** *nt* kirsch

Kissen *nt* **-s,-** cushion; (*Kopf-*) pillow

Kiste *f* **-,-n** crate; (*Zigarren-*) box

Kitsch *m* **-es** sentimental rubbish; (*Kunst*) kitsch. **k~ig** *a* slushy; (*Kunst*) kitschy

Kitt *m* **-s** [adhesive] cement; (*Fenster-*) putty

Kittel *m* **-s,-** overall, smock; (*Arzt-, Labor-*) white coat

kitten *nt* stick; (*fig*) cement

Kitz *nt* **-es,-e** (*Zool*) kid

Kitz|el *m* **-s,-** tickle; (*Nerven-*) thrill. **k~eln** *vt/i* (*haben*) tickle. **k~lig** *a* ticklish

Kladde *f* **-,-n** notebook

klaffen *vi* (*haben*) gape
kläffen *vi* (*haben*) yap
Klage *f* **-,-n** lament; (*Beschwerde*) complaint; (*Jur*) action. **k~n** *vi* (*haben*) lament; (*sich beklagen*) complaint; (*Jur*) sue
Kläger(in) *m* **-s,-** (*f* **-,-nen**) (*Jur*) plaintiff
kläglich *a* pitiful, *adv* -ly; (*erbärmlich*) miserable, *adv* -bly
klamm *a* cold and damp; (*steif*) stiff. **K~** *f* **-,-en** (*Geog*) gorge
Klammer *f* **-,-n** (*Wäsche-*) peg; (*Büro-*) paper-clip; (*Heft-*) staple; (*Haar-*) grip; (*für Zähne*) brace; (*Techn*) clamp; (*Typ*) bracket. **k~n (sich)** *vr* cling (**an** + *acc* to)
Klang *m* **-[e]s,¨e** sound; (*K~farbe*) tone. **k~voll** *a* resonant; (*Stimme*) sonorous
Klapp|bett *nt* folding bed. **K~e** *f* **-,-n** flap; (*fam: Mund*) trap. **k~en** *vt* fold; (*hoch-*) tip up □ *vi* (*haben*) (*fam*) work out. **K~entext** *m* blurb
Klapper *f* **-,-n** rattle. **k~n** *vi* (*haben*) rattle. **K~schlange** rattlesnake
klapp|rig *a* rickety; (*schwach*) decrepit. **K~stuhl** *m* folding chair. **K~tisch** *m* folding table
Klaps *m* **-es,-e** pat; (*strafend*) smack. **k~en** *vt* smack
klar *a* clear; **k~ werden** clear; (*fig*) become clear (**dat** to); **sich** (*dat*) **k~ werden** make up one's mind; (*erkennen*) realize (**dass** that); **sich** (*dat*) **k~** *od* **im K~en (k~en) sein** realize (**dass** that) □ *adv* clearly; (*fam: natürlich*) of course. **K~e(r)** *m* (*fam*) schnapps
klären *vt* clarify; **sich k~** clear; (*fig: sich lösen*) resolve itself
Klarheit *f* **-,-** clarity
Klarinette *f* **-,-n** clarinet
klar|machen *vt sep* make clear (*dat* to); **sich** (*dat*) **etw k~machen** understand sth.
K~sichtfolie *f* transparent/(*haftend*) cling film. **k~stellen** *vt sep* clarify
Klärung *f* **-** clarification
klarwerden† *vi sep* (*sein*) (NEW) **klar werden**, *s.* **klar**
Klasse *f* **-,-n** class; (*Sch*) class, form, (*Amer*) grade; (*Zimmer*) classroom; **erster/zweiter K~ reisen** travel first/second class. **k~** *inv a* (*fam*) super. **K~narbeit** *f* [written] test. **K~nbuch** *nt* ≈ register. **K~nkamerad(in)** *m(f)* class-mate. **K~nkampf** *m* class struggle. **K~nzimmer** *nt* classroom
klassifizier|en *vt* classify. **K~ung** *f* **-,-en** classification
Klass|ik *f* **-** classicism; (*Epoche*) classical period. **K~iker** *m* **-s,-** classical author/(*Mus*) composer. **k~isch** *a* classical; (*mustergültig, typisch*) classic
Klatsch *m* **-[e]s** gossip. **K~base** *f* (*fam*) gossip. **k~en** *vt* slap; **Beifall k~en** applaud □ *vi* (*haben*) make a slapping sound; (*im Wasser*) splash; (*tratschen*) gossip; (*applaudieren*) clap; **[in die Hände] k~en** clap one's hands □ *vi* (*haben/sein*) slap (**gegen** against). **K~maul** *nt* gossip. **k~nass (k~naß)** *a* (*fam*) soaking wet
klauben *vt* pick
Klaue *f* **-,-n** claw; (*fam: Schrift*) scrawl. **k~n** *vt/i* (*haben*) (*fam*) steal
Klausel *f* **-,-n** clause
Klaustrophobie *f* **-** claustrophobia
Klausur *f* **-,-en** (*Univ*) [examination] paper; (*Sch*) written test
Klaviatur *f* **-,-en** keyboard
Klavier *nt* **-s,-e** piano. **K~spieler(in)** *m(f)* pianist
kleb|en *vt* stick/(*mit Klebstoff*) glue (**an** + *acc* to) □ *vi* (*haben*) stick (**an** + *dat* to). **k~rig** *a* sticky. **K~stoff** *m* adhesive, glue. **K~streifen** *m* adhesive tape

kleckern *vi* (*haben*) (*fam*) = **klecksen**
Klecks *m* **-es,-e** stain; (*Tinten-*) blot; (*kleine Menge*) dab. **k~en** *vi* (*haben*) make a mess
Klee *m* **-s** clover. **K~blatt** *nt* clover leaf
Kleid *nt* **-[e]s,-er** dress; **K~er** dresses; (*Kleidung*) clothes. **k~en** *vt* dress; (*gut stehen*) suit; **sich k~en** dress. **K~erbügel** *m* coat-hanger. **K~erbürste** *f* clothes-brush. **K~erhaken** *m* coat-hook. **K~errock** *m* pinafore dress. **K~erschrank** *m* wardrobe, (*Amer*) clothes closet. **k~sam** *a* becoming. **K~ung** *f* - clothes *pl*, clothing. **K~ungsstück** *nt* garment
Kleie *f* - bran
klein *a* small, little; (*von kleinem Wuchs*) short; **k~ hacken/schneiden** chop/cut up small *or* into small pieces; **k~ geschrieben werden** (*fig*) count for very little (**bei jdm** with s.o.); **von k~ auf** from childhood. **K~arbeit** *f* painstaking work. **K~bus** *m* minibus. **K~e(r,s)** *m/f/nt* little one. **K~geld** *nt* [small] change. **k~hacken** *vt sep* (NEW) **k~ hacken**, *s.* **klein**. **K~handel** *m* retail trade. **K~heit** *f* - smallness; (*Wuchs*) short stature. **K~holz** *nt* firewood. **K~igkeit** *f* **-,-en** trifle; (*Mahl*) snack. **K~kind** *nt* infant. **K~kram** *m* (*fam*) odds and ends *pl*; (*Angelegenheiten*) trivia *pl*. **k~laut** *a* subdued. **k~lich** *a* petty. **K~lichkeit** *f* - pettiness. **k~mütig** *a* faint-hearted
Kleinod *nt* **-[e]s,-e** jewel
klein|schneiden† *vt sep* (NEW) **k~ schneiden**, *s.* **klein**. **k~schreiben**† *vt sep* write with a small [initial] letter; **k~geschrieben werden** (*fig*) (NEW) **k~ geschrieben werden**, *s.* **klein**. **K~stadt** *f* small town. **k~städtisch** *a* provincial. **K~wagen** *m* small car
Kleister *m* **-s** paste. **k~n** *vt* paste
Klemme *f* **-,-n** [hair-]grip; **in der K~sitzen** (*fam*) be in a fix. **k~n** *vt* jam; **sich** (*dat*) **den Finger k~n** get one's finger caught □ *vi* (*haben*) jam, stick
Klempner *m* **-s,-** plumber
Klerus (der) - the clergy
Klette *f* **-,-n** burr; **wie eine K~** (*fig*) like a limpet
kletter|n *vi* (*sein*) climb. **K~pflanze** *f* climber. **K~rose** *f* climbing rose
Klettverschluss (**Klettverschluß**) *m* Velcro (P) fastening
klicken *vi* (*haben*) click
Klient(in) /kliˈɛnt(ɪn)/ *m* **-en,-en** (*f* **-,-nen**) (*Jur*) client
Kliff *nt* **-[e]s,-e** cliff
Klima *nt* **-s** climate. **K~anlage** *f* air-conditioning
klimat|isch *a* climatic. **k~isiert** *a* air-conditioned
klimpern *vi* (*haben*) jingle; **k~ auf** (+ *dat*) tinkle on ⟨*Klavier*⟩; strum ⟨*Gitarre*⟩
Klinge *f* **-,-n** blade
Klingel *f* **-,-n** bell. **k~n** *vi* (*haben*) ring; **es k~t** there's a ring at the door
klingen† *vi* (*haben*) sound
Klini|k *f* **-,-en** clinic. **k~sch** *a* clinical, *adv* -ly
Klinke *f* **-,-n** [door] handle
klipp *pred a* **k~ und klar** quite plain, *adv* -ly
Klipp *m* **-s,-s** = **Klips**
Klippe *f* **-,-n** [submerged] rock
Klips *m* **-es,-e** clip; (*Ohr-*) clip-on ear-ring
klirren *vi* (*haben*) rattle; ⟨*Geschirr, Glas:*⟩ chink
Klischee *nt* **-s,-s** cliché
Klo *nt* **-s,-s** (*fam*) loo, (*Amer*) john
klobig *a* clumsy
klönen *vi* (*haben*) (*NGer fam*) chat

klopf|en *vi* (*haben*) knock; (*leicht*) tap; ⟨*Herz:*⟩ pound; **es k~te** there was a knock at the door □ *vt* beat; (*ein-*) knock
Klops *m* **-es,-e** meatball; (*Brat-*) rissole
Klosett *nt* **-s,-s** lavatory
Kloß *m* **-es,⸚e** dumpling; **ein K~ im Hals** (*fam*) a lump in one's throat
Kloster *nt* **-s,⸚** monastery; (*Nonnen-*) convent
klösterlich *a* monastic
Klotz *m* **-es,⸚e** block
Klub *m* **-s,-s** club
Kluft1 *f* **-,⸚e** cleft; (*fig: Gegensatz*) gulf
Kluft2 *f* **-,-en** outfit; (*Uniform*) uniform
klug *a* (**klüger, klügst**) intelligent, *adv* -ly; (*schlau*) clever, *adv* -ly, **nicht k~ werden aus** not understand. **K~heit** *f* - cleverness
Klump|en *m* **-s,-** lump. **k~en** *vi* (*haben*) go lumpy
knabbern *vt/i* (*haben*) nibble
Knabe *m* **-n,-n** boy. **k~nhaft** *a* boyish
Knäckebrot *nt* crispbread
knack|en *vt/i* (*haben*) crack. **K~s** *m* **-es,-e** crack; **einen K~s haben** be cracked/(*fam: verrückt sein*) crackers
Knall *m* **-[e]s,-e** bang. **K~bonbon** *m* cracker. **k~en** *vi* (*haben*) go bang; ⟨*Peitsche:*⟩ crack □ *vt* (*fam: werfen*) chuck; **jdm eine k~en** (*fam*) clout s.o. **k~ig** *a* (*fam*) gaudy. **k~rot** *a* bright red
knapp *a* (*gering*) scant; (*kurz*) short; (*mangelnd*) scarce; (*gerade ausreichend*) bare; (*eng*) tight; **ein k~es Pfund** just under a pound; **jdn k~ halten** (*fam*) keep s.o. short (**mit** of). **k~halten**† *vt sep* (NEW) **k~ halten**, *s.* **knapp**. **K~heit** *f* - scarcity
Knarre *f* **-,-n** rattle. **k~n** *vi* (*haben*) creak
Knast *m* **-[e]s** (*fam*) prison
knattern *vi* (*haben*) crackle; ⟨*Gewehr:*⟩ stutter
Knäuel *m & nt* **-s,-** ball
Knauf *m* **-[e]s, Knäufe** knob
knauser|ig *a* (*fam*) stingy. **k~n** *vi* (*haben*) (*fam*) be stingy
knautschen *vt* (*fam*) crumple □ *vi* (*haben*) crease
Knebel *m* **-s,-** gag. **k~n** *vt* gag
Knecht *m* **-[e]s,-e** farm-hand; (*fig*) slave. **k~en** *vt* (*fig*) enslave. **K~schaft** *f* - (*fig*) slavery
kneif|en† *vt* pinch □ *vi* (*haben*) pinch; (*fam: sich drücken*) chicken out. **K~zange** *f* pincers *pl*
Kneipe *f* **-,-n** (*fam*) pub, (*Amer*) bar
knet|en *vt* knead; (*formen*) mould. **K~masse** *f* Plasticine(P)
Knick *m* **-[e]s,-e** bend; (*im Draht*) kink; (*Kniff*) crease. **k~en** *vt* bend; (*kniffen*) fold; **geknickt sein** (*fam*) be dejected. **k~[e]rig** *a* (*fam*) stingy
Knicks *m* **-es,-e** curtsy. **k~en** *vi* (*haben*) curtsy
Knie *nt* **-s,-** /ˈkniːə/ knee. **K~bundhose** *f* knee-breeches *pl*. **K~kehle** *f* hollow of the knee
knien /ˈkniːən/ *vi* (*haben*) kneel □ *vr* **sich k~** kneel [down]
Knie|scheibe *f* kneecap. **K~strumpf** *m* knee-length sock
Kniff *m* **-[e]s,-e** pinch; (*Falte*) crease; (*fam: Trick*) trick. **k~en** *vt* fold. **k~[e]lig** *a* (*fam*) tricky
knipsen *vt* (*lochen*) punch; (*Phot*) photograph □ *vi* (*haben*) take a photograph/photographs
Knirps *m* **-es,-e** (*fam*) little chap; (**P**) (*Schirm*) telescopic umbrella
knirschen *vi* (*haben*) grate; ⟨*Schnee, Kies:*⟩ crunch; **mit den Zähnen k~** grind one's teeth
knistern *vi* (*haben*) crackle; ⟨*Papier:*⟩ rustle
Knitter|falte *f* crease. **k~frei** *a* crease-resistant. **k~n** *vi* (*haben*) crease

knobeln *vi* (*haben*) toss (**um** for); (*fam: überlegen*) puzzle
Knoblauch *m* **-s** garlic
Knöchel *m* **-s,-** ankle; (*Finger-*) knuckle
Knochen *m* **-s,-** bone. **K~mark** *nt* bone marrow. **k~trocken** *a* bone-dry
knochig *a* bony
Knödel *m* **-s,-** (*SGer*) dumpling
Knoll|e *f* **-,-n** tuber. **k~ig** *a* bulbous
Knopf *m* **-[e]s,¨e** button; (*Kragen-*) stud; (*Griff*) knob
knöpfen *vt* button
Knopfloch *nt* buttonhole
Knorpel *m* **-s** gristle; (*Anat*) cartilage
knorrig *a* gnarled
Knospe *f* bud
Knötchen *nt* **-s,-** nodule
Knoten *m* **-s,-** knot; (*Med*) lump; (*Haar-*) bun, chignon. **k~** *vt* knot. **K~punkt** *m* junction
knotig *a* knotty; ⟨*Hände*⟩ gnarled
knuffen *vt* poke
knüll|en *vt* crumple □ *vi* (*haben*) crease. **K~er** *m* **-s,-** (*fam*) sensation
knüpfen *vt* knot; (*verbinden*) attach (**an** + *acc* to)
Knüppel *m* **-s,-** club; (*Gummi-*) truncheon
knurr|en *vi* (*haben*) growl; ⟨*Magen:*⟩ rumble; (*fam: schimpfen*) grumble. **k~ig** *a* grumpy
knusprig *a* crunchy, crisp
knutschen *vi* (*haben*) (*fam*) smooch
k.o. /ka'ˀo:/ *a* **k.o. schlagen** knock out; **k.o. sein** (*fam*) be worn out. **K.o.** *m* **-s,-s** knock-out
Koalition /koali'tsi̯o:n/ *f* **-,-en** coalition
Kobold *m* **-[e]s,-e** goblin, imp
Koch *m* **-[e]s,¨e** cook; (*im Restaurant*) chef. **K~buch** *nt* cookery book, (*Amer*) cookbook. **k~en** *vt* cook; (*sieden*) boil; make ⟨*Kaffee, Tee*⟩; **hart gekochtes Ei** hard-boiled egg □ *vi* (*haben*) cook; (*sieden*) boil; (*fam*) seethe (**vor** + *dat* with). **K~en** *nt* **-s** cooking; (*Sieden*) boiling; **zum K~n bringen/kommen** bring/come to the boil. **k~end** *a* boiling □ *adv* **k~end heiß** boiling hot. **K~er** *m* **-s,-** cooker. **K~gelegenheit** *f* cooking facilities *pl*. **K~herd** *m* cooker, stove
Köchin *f* **-,-nen** [woman] cook
Koch|kunst *f* cookery. **K~löffel** *m* wooden spoon. **K~nische** *f* kitchenette. **K~platte** *f* hotplate. **K~topf** *m* saucepan
Kode /ko:t/ *m* **-s,-s** code
Köder *m* **-s,-** bait
Koexist|enz /'ko:ˀɛksɪstɛnts/ *f* coexistence. **k~ieren** *vi* (*haben*) coexist
Koffein /kɔfe'i:n/ *nt* **-s** caffeine. **k~frei** *a* decaffeinated
Koffer *m* **-s,-** suitcase. **K~kuli** *m* luggage trolley. **K~radio** *nt* portable radio. **K~raum** *m* (*Auto*) boot, (*Amer*) trunk
Kognak /'kɔnjak/ *m* **-s,-s** brandy
Kohl *m* **-[e]s** cabbage
Kohle *f* **-,-n** coal. **K~[n]hydrat** *nt* **-[e]s,-e** carbohydrate. **K~nbergwerk** *nt* coal-mine, colliery. **K~ndioxid** *nt* carbon dioxide. **K~ngrube** *f* = **K~nbergwerk**. **K~nherd** *m* [kitchen] range. **K~nsäure** *f* carbon dioxide. **K~nstoff** *m* carbon. **K~papier** *nt* carbon paper
Kohl|kopf *m* cabbage. **K~rabi** *m* **-[s],-[s]** kohlrabi. **K~rübe** *f* swede
Koje *f* **-,-n** (*Naut*) bunk
Kokain /koka'i:n/ *nt* **-s** cocaine
kokett *a* flirtatious. **k~ieren** *vi* (*haben*) flirt
Kokon /ko'kõ:/ *m* **-s,-s** cocoon
Kokosnuss (**Kokosnuß**) *f* coconut
Koks *m* **-es** coke
Kolben *m* **-s,-** (*Gewehr-*) butt; (*Mais-*) cob; (*Techn*) piston; (*Chem*) flask

Kolibri *m* **-s,-s** humming-bird
Kolik *f* **-,-en** colic
Kollabora|teur /-'tø:ɐ̯/ *m* **-s,-e** collaborator. **K~tion** /-'tsi̯o:n/ *f* **-** collaboration
Kolleg *nt* **-s,-s & -ien** /-i̯ən/ (*Univ*) course of lectures
Kolleg|e *m* **-n,-n**, **K~in** *f* **-,-nen** colleague. **K~ium** *nt* **-s,-ien** staff
Kollek|te *f* **-,-n** (*Relig*) collection. **K~tion** /-'tsi̯o:n/ *f* **-,-en** collection. **k~tiv** *a* collective. **K~tivum** *nt* **-s,-va** collective noun
kolli|dieren *vi* (*sein*) collide. **K~sion** *f* **-,-en** collision
Köln *nt* **-s** Cologne. **K~ischwasser, K~isch Wasser** *nt* eau-de-Cologne
Kolonialwaren *fpl* groceries
Kolon|ie *f* **-,-n** colony. **k~isieren** *vt* colonize
Kolonne *f* **-,-n** column; (*Mil*) convoy
Koloss *m* **-es,-e** (**Koloß** *m* **-sses,-sse**) giant
kolossal *a* enormous, *adv* -ly
Kolumne *f* **-,-n** (*Journ*) column
Koma *nt* **-s,-s** coma
Kombi *m* **-s,-s** = **K~wagen**. **K~nation** /-'tsi̯o:n/ *f* **-,-en** combination; (*Folgerung*) deduction; (*Kleidung*) co-ordinating outfit. **k~nieren** *vt* combine; (*fig*) reason; (*folgern*) deduce. **K~wagen** *m* estate car, (*Amer*) station-wagon
Kombüse *f* **-,-n** (*Naut*) galley
Komet *m* **-en,-en** comet. **k~enhaft** *a* (*fig*) meteoric
Komfort /kɔm'fo:ɐ̯/ *m* **-s** comfort; (*Luxus*) luxury. **k~abel** /-'ta:bəl/ *a* comfortable, *adv* -bly; (*luxuriös*) luxurious, *adv* -ly
Komik *f* **-** humour. **K~er** *m* **-s,-** comic, comedian
komisch *a* funny; ⟨*Oper*⟩ comic; (*sonderbar*) odd, funny □ *adv* funnily; oddly. **k~erweise** *adv* funnily enough
Komitee *nt* **-s,-s** committee
Komma *nt* **-s,-s & -ta** comma; (*Dezimal-*) decimal point; **drei K~ fünf** three point five
Komman|dant *m* **-en,-en** commanding officer. **K~deur** /-'dø:ɐ̯/ *m* **-s,-e** commander. **k~dieren** *vt* command; (*befehlen*) order; (*fam: herum-*) order about □ *vi* (*haben*) give the orders
Kommando *nt* **-s,-s** order; (*Befehlsgewalt*) command; (*Einheit*) detachment. **K~brücke** *f* bridge
kommen† *vi* (*sein*) come; (*eintreffen*) arrive; (*gelangen*) get (**nach** to); **k~ lassen** send for; **auf/hinter etw** (*acc*) **k~** think of/find out about sth; **um/zu etw k~** lose/acquire sth; **wieder zu sich k~** come round; **wie kommt das?** why is that? **K~** *nt* **-s** coming; **K~und Gehen** coming and going. **k~d** *a* coming; **k~den Montag** next Monday
Kommen|tar *m* **-s,-e** commentary; (*Bemerkung*) comment. **K~tator** *m* **-s,-en** /-'to:rən/ commentator. **k~tieren** *vt* comment on
kommer|zialisieren *vt* commercialize. **k~ziell** *a* commercial, *adv* -ly
Kommili|tone *m* **-n,-n**, **K~tonin** *f* **-,-nen** fellow student
Kommiss *m* **-es** (**Kommiß** *m* **-sses**) (*fam*) army
Kommissar *m* **-s,-e** commissioner; (*Polizei-*) superintendent
Kommission *f* **-,-en** commission; (*Gremium*) committee
Kommode *f* **-,-n** chest of drawers
Kommunalwahlen *fpl* local elections
Kommunikation /-'tsi̯o:n/ *f* **-,-en** communication
Kommunikee /kɔmyni'ke:/ *nt* **-s,-s** = **Kommuniqué**
Kommunion *f* **-,-en** [Holy] Communion
Kommuniqué /kɔmyni'ke:/ *nt* **-s,-s** communiqué

Kommun|ismus *m* - Communism. **K~ist(in)** *m* **-en,-en** (*f* **-,-nen**) Communist. **k~istisch** *a* Communist
kommunizieren *vi* (*haben*) receive [Holy] Communion
Komödie /ko'mø:di̯ə/ *f* **-,-n** comedy
Kompagnon /'kɔmpanjõ:/ *m* **-s,-s** (*Comm*) partner
kompakt *a* compact. **K~schallplatte** *f* compact disc
Kompanie *f* **-,-n** (*Mil*) company
Komparativ *m* **-s,-e** comparative
Komparse *m* **-n,-n** (*Theat*) extra
Kompass *m* **-es,-e** (**Kompaß** *m* **-sses,-sse**) compass
kompatibel *a* compatible
kompeten|t *a* competent. **K~z** *f* **-,-en** competence
komplett *a* complete, *adv* -ly
Komplex *m* **-es,-e** complex. **k~** *a* complex
Komplikation /-'tsi̯o:n/ *f* **-,-en** complication
Kompliment *nt* **-[e]s,-e** compliment
Komplize *m* **-n,-n** accomplice
komplizier|en *vt* complicate. **k~t** *a* complicated
Komplott *nt* **-[e]s,-e** plot
kompo|nieren *vt/i* (*haben*) compose. **K~nist** *m* **-en,-en** composer. **K~sition** /-'tsi̯o:n/ *f* **-,-en** composition
Kompositum *nt* **-s,-ta** compound
Kompost *m* **-[e]s** compost
Kompott *nt* **-[e]s,-e** stewed fruit
Kompresse *f* **-,-n** compress
komprimieren *vt* compress
Kompromiss *m* **-es,-e** (**Kompromiß** *m* **-sses,-sse**) compromise; **einen K~ schließen** compromise. **k~los** *a* uncompromising
kompromittieren *vt* compromise
Konden|sation /-'tsi̯o:n/ *f* - condensation. **k~sieren** *vt* condense
Kondensmilch *f* evaporated/(*gesüßt*) condensed milk
Kondition /-'tsi̯o:n/ *f* - (*Sport*) fitness; **in K~** in form. **K~al** *m* **-s,-e** (*Gram*) conditional
Konditor *m* **-s,-en** /-'to:rən/ confectioner. **K~ei** *f* **-,-en** patisserie
Kondo|lenzbrief *m* letter of condolence. **k~lieren** *vi* (*haben*) express one's condolences
Kondom *nt & m* **-s,-e** condom
Konfekt *nt* **-[e]s** confectionery; (*Pralinen*) chocolates *pl*
Konfektion /-'tsi̯o:n/ *f* - ready-to-wear clothes *pl*
Konferenz *f* **-,-en** conference; (*Besprechung*) meeting
Konfession *f* **-,-en** [religious] denomination. **k~ell** *a* denominational. **k~slos** *a* non-denominational
Konfetti *nt* **-s** confetti
Konfirm|and(in) *m* **-en,-en** (*f* **-,-nen**) candidate for confirmation. **K~ation** /-'tsi̯o:n/ *f* **-,-en** (*Relig*) confirmation. **k~ieren** *vt* (*Relig*) confirm
Konfitüre *f* **-,-n** jam
Konflikt *m* **-[e]s,-e** conflict
Konföderation /-'tsi̯o:n/ *f* confederation
Konfront|ation /-'tsi̯o:n/ *f* **-,-en** confrontation. **k~ieren** *vt* confront
konfus *a* confused
Kongress *m* **-es,-e** (**Kongreß** *m* **-sses,-sse**) congress
König *m* **-s,-e** king. **K~in** *f* **-,-nen** queen. **k~lich** *a* royal, *adv* -ly; (*hoheitsvoll*) regal, *adv* -ly; (*großzügig*) handsome, *adv* -ly; (*fam: groß*) tremendous, *adv* -ly. **K~reich** *nt* kingdom
konisch *a* conical
Konjug|ation /-'tsi̯o:n/ *f* **-,-en** conjugation. **k~ieren** *vt* conjugate
Konjunktion /-'tsi̯o:n/ *f* **-,-en** (*Gram*) conjunction
Konjunktiv *m* **-s,-e** subjunctive

Konjunktur *f* - economic situation; (*Hoch-*) boom
konkav *a* concave
konkret *a* concrete
Konkurren|t(in) *m* **-en,-en** (*f* **-,-nen**) competitor, rival. **K~z** *f* - competition; **jdm K~z machen** compete with s.o. **k~zfähig** *a* (*Comm*) competitive. **K~zkampf** *m* competition, rivalry
konkurrieren *vi* (*haben*) compete
Konkurs *m* **-es,-e** bankruptcy; **K~ machen** go bankrupt
können† *vt/i* (*haben*) **etw k~** be able to do sth; (*beherrschen*) know sth; **k~ Sie Deutsch?** do you know any German? **das kann ich nicht** I can't do that; **er kann nicht mehr** he can't go on; **für etw nichts k~** not be to blame for sth □ *v aux* **lesen/schwimmen k~** be able to read/swim; **er kann/konnte es tun** he can/could do it; **das kann** *od* **könnte [gut] sein** that may [well] be. **K~** *nt* **-s** ability, (*Wissen*) knowledge.
Könner(in) *m* **-s,-** (*f* **-,-nen**) expert
konsequen|t *a* consistent, *adv* -ly; (*logisch*) logical, *adv* -ly. **K~z** *f* **-,-en** consequence
konservativ *a* conservative
Konserv|en *fpl* tinned or canned food *sg*. **K~enbüchse, K~endose** *f* tin, can. **k~ieren** *vt* preserve; (*in Dosen*) tin, can **K~ierungsmittel** *nt* preservative
Konsistenz *f* - consistency
konsolidieren *vt* consolidate
Konsonant *m* **-en,-en** consonant
konsterniert *a* dismayed
Konstitution /-'tsi̯o:n/ *f* **-,-en** constitution. **k~ell** *a* constitutional
konstruieren *vt* construct; (*entwerfen*) design
Konstruk|tion /-'tsi̯o:n/ *f* **-,-en** construction; (*Entwurf*) design. **k~tiv** *a* constructive
Konsul *m* **-s,-n** consul. **K~at** *nt* **-[e]-s,-e** consulate
Konsult|ation /-'tsi̯o:n/ *f* **-,-en** consultation. **k~ieren** *vt* consult
Konsum *m* **-s** consumption. **K~ent** *m* **-en,-en** consumer. **K~güter** *npl* consumer goods
Kontakt *m* **-[e]s,-e** contact. **K~linsen** *fpl* contact lenses. **K~person** *f* contact
kontern *vt/i* (*haben*) counter
Kontinent /'kɔn-, kɔnti'nɛnt/ *m* **-[e]s,-e** continent
Kontingent *nt* **-[e]s,-e** (*Comm*) quota; (*Mil*) contingent
Kontinuität *f* - continuity
Konto *nt* **-s,-s** account. **K~auszug** *m* [bank] statement. **K~nummer** *f* account number. **K~stand** *m* [bank] balance
Kontrabass (**Kontrabaß**) *m* double-bass
Kontrast *m* **-[e]s,-e** contrast
Kontroll|abschnitt *m* counterfoil. **K~e** *f* **-,-n** control; (*Prüfung*) check. **K~eur** /-'lø:ɐ̯/ *m* **-s,-e** [ticket] inspector. **k~ieren** *vt* check; inspect ⟨*Fahrkarten*⟩; (*beherrschen*) control
Kontroverse *f* **-,-n** controversy
Kontur *f* **-,-en** contour
Konvention /-'tsi̯o:n/ *f* **-,-en** convention. **k~ell** *a* conventional, *adv* -ly
Konversation /-'tsi̯o:n/ *f* **-,-en** conversation. **K~slexikon** *nt* encyclopaedia
konvert|ieren *vi* (*haben*) (*Relig*) convert. **K~it** *m* **-en,-en** convert
konvex *a* convex
Konvoi /kɔn'vɔy/ *m* **-s,-s** convoy
Konzentration /-'tsi̯o:n/ *f* **-,-en** concentration. **K~slager** *nt* concentration camp
konzentrieren *vt* concentrate; **sich k~** concentrate (**auf** + *acc* on)
Konzept *nt* **-[e]s,-e** [rough] draft; **jdn aus dem K~bringen** put s.o.

off his stroke. **K~papier** *nt* rough paper

Konzern *m* **-s,-e** (*Comm*) group [of companies]

Konzert *nt* **-[e]s,-e** concert; (*Klavier-, Geigen-*) concerto. **K~meister** *m* leader, (*Amer*) concertmaster

Konzession *f* **-,-en** licence; (*Zugeständnis*) concession

Konzil *nt* **-s,-e** (*Relig*) council

Kooperation /koʔɔpera'tsi̯o:n/ *f* co-operation

Koordin|ation /koʔɔrdina'tsi̯o:n/ *f* - co-ordination. **k~ieren** *vt* co-ordinate

Kopf *m* **-[e]s,¨e** head; **ein K~ Kohl/Salat** a cabbage/lettuce; **aus dem K~** from memory; (*auswendig*) by heart; **auf dem K~** (*verkehrt*) upside down; **K~ an K~** neck and neck; ⟨*stehen*⟩ shoulder to shoulder; **K~ stehen** stand on one's head; **sich** (*dat*) **den K~ waschen** wash one's hair; **sich** (*dat*) **den K~ zerbrechen** rack one's brains. **K~ball** *m* header. **K~bedeckung** *f* head-covering

Köpf|chen *nt* **-s,-** little head; **K~chen haben** (*fam*) be clever. **k~en** *vt* behead; (*Fußball*) head

Kopf|ende *nt* head. **K~haut** *f* scalp. **K~hörer** *m* headphones *pl*. **K~kissen** *nt* pillow. **K~kissenbezug** *m* pillow-case. **k~los** *a* panic-stricken. **K~nicken** *nt* **-s** nod. **K~rechnen** *nt* mental arithmetic. **K~salat** *m* lettuce. **K~schmerzen** *mpl* headache *sg*. **K~schütteln** *nt* **-s** shake of the head. **K~sprung** *m* header, dive. **K~stand** *m* headstand. **K~steinpflaster** *nt nt* cobble-stones *pl*. **K~stütze** *f* head-rest. **K~tuch** *nt* headscarf. **k~über** *adv* head first; (*fig*) headlong. **K~wäsche** *f* shampoo. **K~weh** *nt* headache. **K~zerbrechen** *nt* **-s sich** (*dat*) **K~zerbrechen machen** rack one's brains; (*sich sorgen*) worry

Kopie *f* **-,-n** copy. **k~ren** *vt* copy

Koppel[1] *f* **-,-n** enclosure; (*Pferde-*) paddock

Koppel[2] *nt* **-s,-** (*Mil*) belt. **k~n** *vt* couple

Koralle *f* **-,-n** coral

Korb *m* **-[e]s,¨e** basket; **jdm einen K~ geben** (*fig*) turn s.o. down. **K~ball** *m* [kind of] netball. **K~stuhl** *m* wicker chair

Kord *m* **-s** (*Tex*) corduroy

Kordel *f* **-,-n** cord

Korinthe *f* **-,-n** currant

Kork *m* **-s,-** cork. **K~en** *m* **-s,-** cork. **K~enzieher** *m* **-s,-** corkscrew

Korn[1] *nt* **-[e]s,¨er** grain, (*Samen-*) seed; (*coll: Getreide*) grain, corn; (*am Visier*) front sight

Korn[2] *m* **-[e]s,-** (*fam*) grain schnapps

Körn|chen *nt* **-s,-** granule. **k~ig** *a* granular

Körper *m* **-s,-** body; (*Geom*) solid. **K~bau** *m* build, physique. **k~behindert** *a* physically disabled. **k~lich** *a* physical, *adv* -ly; ⟨*Strafe*⟩ corporal. **K~pflege** *f* personal hygiene. **K~puder** *m* talcum powder. **K~schaft** *f* **-,-en** corporation, body. **K~strafe** *f* corporal punishment. **K~teil** *m* part of the body

Korps /ko:ɐ̯/ *nt* **-,-** /-[s],-s/ corps

korpulent *a* corpulent

korrekt *a* correct, *adv* -ly. **K~or** *m* **-s,-en** /-'to:rən/ proof-reader. **K~ur** *f* **-,-en** correction. **K~urabzug**, **K~urbogen** *m* proof

Korrespon|dent(in) *m* **-en,-en** (*f* **-,-nen**) correspondent. **K~denz** *f* **-,-en** correspondence. **k~dieren** *vi* (*haben*) correspond

Korridor *m* **-s,-e** corridor

korrigieren *vt* correct

Korrosion *f* **-** corrosion

korrumpieren *vt* corrupt

korrup|t *a* corrupt. **K~tion** /-'tsi̯o:n/ *f* - corruption
Korsett *nt* **-[e]s,-e** corset
koscher *a* kosher
Kose|name *m* pet name. **K~wort** *nt* (*pl* **-wörter**) term of endearment
Kosmet|ik *f* - beauty culture. **K~ika** *ntpl* cosmetics. **K~ikerin** *f* **-,-nen** beautician. **k~isch** *a* cosmetic; ⟨*Chirurgie*⟩ plastic
kosm|isch *a* cosmic. **K~onaut(in)** *m* **-en,-en** (*f* **-,-nen**) cosmonaut. **k~opolitisch** *a* cosmopolitan
Kosmos *m* - cosmos
Kost *f* - food; (*Ernährung*) diet; (*Verpflegung*) board
kostbar *a* precious. **K~keit** *f* **-,-en** treasure
kosten¹ *vt/i* (*haben*) **[von] etw k~** taste sth
kosten² *vt* cost; (*brauchen*) take; **wie viel kostet es?** how much is it? **K~** *pl* expense *sg*, cost *sg*; (*Jur*) costs; **auf meine K~** at my expense. **K~[vor]anschlag** *m* estimate. **k~los** *a* free □ *adv* free [of charge]
Kosthappen *m* taste
köstlich *a* delicious; (*entzückend*) delightful. **K~keit** *f* **-,-en** (*fig*) gem; (*Culin*) delicacy
Kost|probe *f* taste; (*fig*) sample. **k~spielig** *a* expensive, costly
Kostüm *nt* **-s,-e** (*Theat*) costume; (*Verkleidung*) fancy dress; (*Schneider-*) suit. **K~fest** *nt* fancy-dress party. **k~iert** *a* **k~iert sein** be in fancy dress
Kot *m* **-[e]s** excrement; (*Schmutz*) dirt
Kotelett /kɔt'lɛt/ *nt* **-s,-s** chop, cutlet. **K~en** *pl* sideburns
Köter *m* **-s,-** (*pej*) dog
Kotflügel *m* (*Auto*) wing, (*Amer*) fender
kotzen *vi* (*haben*) (*sl*) throw up; **es ist zum K~** it makes you sick
Krabbe *f* **-,-n** crab; (*Garnele*) shrimp; (*rote*) prawn
krabbeln *vi* (*sein*) crawl
Krach *m* **-[e]s,⸚e** din, racket; (*Knall*) crash; (*fam: Streit*) row; (*fam: Ruin*) crash. **k~en** *vi* (*haben*) crash; **es hat gekracht** there was a bang/(*fam: Unfall*) a crash □ (*sein*) break, crack; (*auftreffen*) crash (**gegen** into)
krächzen *vi* (*haben*) croak
Kraft *f* **-,⸚e** strength; (*Gewalt*) force; (*Arbeits-*) worker; **in/außer K~** in/no longer in force; **in K~ treten** come into force. **k~** *prep* (+ *gen*) by virtue of. **K~ausdruck** *m* swear-word. **K~fahrer** *m* driver. **K~fahrzeug** *nt* motor vehicle. **K~fahrzeugbrief** *m* [vehicle] registration document
kräftig *a* strong; (*gut entwickelt*) sturdy; (*nahrhaft*) nutritious; (*heftig*) hard □ *adv* strongly; (*heftig*) hard. **k~en** *vt* strengthen
kraft|los *a* weak. **K~post** *f* post bus service. **K~probe** *f* trial of strength. **K~rad** *nt* motorcycle. **K~stoff** *m* (*Auto*) fuel. **k~voll** *a* strong, powerful. **K~wagen** *m* motor car. **K~werk** *nt* power station
Kragen *m* **-s,-** collar
Krähe *f* **-,-n** crow
krähen *vi* (*haben*) crow
krakeln *vt/i* (*haben*) scrawl
Kralle *f* **-,-n** claw. **k~n (sich)** *vr* clutch (**an jdn/etw** s.o./sth); ⟨*Katze:*⟩ dig its claws (**in** + *acc* into)
Kram *m* **-s** (*fam*) things *pl*, (*fam*) stuff; (*Angelegenheiten*) business; **wertloser K~** junk. **k~en** *vi* (*haben*) rummage about (**in** + *dat* in; **nach** for). **K~laden** *m* [small] general store
Krampf *m* **-[e]s,⸚e** cramp. **K~adern** *fpl* varicose veins. **k~haft** *a* convulsive, *adv* -ly; (*verbissen*) desperate, *adv* -ly
Kran *m* **-[e]s,⸚e** (*Techn*) crane

Kranich *m* **-s,-e** (*Zool*) crane
krank *a* (**kränker, kränkst**) sick; ⟨*Knie, Herz*⟩ bad; **k~ sein/werden/machen** be/fall/make ill; **jdn k~ melden/schreiben** NEW **jdn k~melden/k~schreiben**, *s.* **krankmelden, krankschreiben. K~e(r)** *m/f* sick man/woman, invalid; **die K~en** the sick *pl*
kränkeln *vi* (*haben*) be in poor health. **k~d** *a* ailing
kränken *vi* (*haben*) (*fig*) suffer (**an** + *dat* from)
kränken *vt* offend, hurt
Kranken|bett *nt* sick-bed. **K~geld** *nt* sickness benefit. **K~gymnast(in)** *m* **-en,-en** (*f* **-,-nen**) physiotherapist. **K~gymnastik** *f* physiotherapy. **K~haus** *nt* hospital. **K~kasse** *f* health insurance scheme/(*Amt*) office. **K~pflege** *f* nursing. **K~pfleger(in)** *m(f)* nurse. **K~saal** *m* [hospital] ward. **K~schein** *m* certificate of entitlement to medical treatment. **K~schwester** *f* nurse. **K~urlaub** *m* sick-leave. **K~versicherung** *f* health insurance. **K~wagen** *m* ambulance. **K~zimmer** *nt* sick-room
krank|haft *a* morbid; (*pathologisch*) pathological. **K~heit** *f* **-,-en** illness, disease
kränklich *a* sickly
krank|melden *vt sep* **jdn k~melden** report s.o. sick; **sich k~melden** report sick. **k~schreiben**† *vt sep* **jdn k~schreiben** give s.o. a medical certificate; **sich k~schreiben lassen** get a medical certificate
Kränkung *f* **-,-en** slight
Kranz *m* **-es,¨e** wreath; (*Ring*) ring
Krapfen *m* **-s,-** doughnut
krass (kraß) *a* (**krasser, krassest**) glaring; (*offensichtlich*) blatant; (*stark*) gross; rank ⟨*Außenseiter*⟩
Krater *m* **-s,-** crater
kratz|bürstig *a* (*fam*) prickly. **k~en** *vt/i* (*haben*) scratch; **sich k~en** scratch oneself/⟨*Tier:*⟩ itself. **K~er** *m* **-s,-** scratch; (*Werkzeug*) scraper
Kraul *nt* **-s** (*Sport*) crawl. **k~en**[1] *vi* (*haben/sein*) (*Sport*) do the crawl
kraulen[2] *vt* tickle; **sich am Kopf k~** scratch one's head
kraus *a* wrinkled; ⟨*Haar*⟩ frizzy; (*verworren*) muddled; **k~ ziehen** wrinkle. **K~e** *f* **-,-n** frill, ruffle; (*Haar-*) frizziness
kräuseln *vt* wrinkle; frizz ⟨*Haar-*⟩; gather ⟨*Stoff*⟩; ripple ⟨*Wasser*⟩; **sich k~** wrinkle; (*sich kringeln*) curl; ⟨*Haar:*⟩ go frizzy; ⟨*Wasser:*⟩ ripple
krausen *vt* wrinkle; frizz ⟨*Haar*⟩; gather ⟨*Stoff*⟩; **sich k~** wrinkle; ⟨*Haar:*⟩ go frizzy
Kraut *nt* **-[e]s, Kräuter** herb; (*SGer*) cabbage; (*Sauer-*) sauerkraut; **wie K~ und Rüben** (*fam*) higgledy-piggledy
Krawall *m* **-s,-e** riot; (*Lärm*) row
Krawatte *f* **-,-n** [neck]tie
kraxeln *vi* (*sein*) (*fam*) clamber
krea|tiv /krea'ti:f/ *a* creative. **K~tur** *f* **-,-en** creature
Krebs *m* **-es,-e** crayfish; (*Med*) cancer; (*Astr*) Cancer. **k~ig** *a* cancerous
Kredit *m* **-s,-e** credit; (*Darlehen*) loan; **auf K~** on credit. **K~karte** *f* credit card
Kreid|e *f* **-** chalk. **k~ebleich** *a* deathly pale. **k~ig** *a* chalky
kreieren /kre'i:rən/ *vt* create
Kreis *m* **-es,-e** circle; (*Admin*) district
kreischen *vt/i* (*haben*) screech; (*schreien*) shriek

Kreisel *m* **-s,-** [spinning] top; (*fam: Kreisverkehr*) roundabout

kreis|en *vi* (*haben*) circle; revolve (**um** around). **k~förmig** *a* circular. **K~lauf** *m* cycle; (*Med*) circulation. **k~rund** *a* circular. **K~säge** *f* circular saw. **K~verkehr** *m* [traffic] roundabout, (*Amer*) traffic circle

Krem *f* **-,-s** & *m* **-s,-e** cream

Krematorium *nt* **-s,-ien** crematorium

Krempe *f* **-,-n** [hat] brim

Krempel *m* **-s** (*fam*) junk

krempeln *vt* turn (**nach oben** up)

Kren *m* **-[e]s** (*Aust*) horseradish

krepieren *vi* (*sein*) explode; (*sl: sterben*) die

Krepp *m* **-s,-s** & **-e** crêpe

Krepppapier (Kreppapier) *nt* crêpe paper

Kresse *f* **-,-n** cress; (*Kapuziner-*) nasturtium

Kreta *nt* **-s** Crete

Kreuz *nt* **-es,-e** cross; (*Kreuzung*) intersection; (*Mus*) sharp; (*Kartenspiel*) clubs *pl*; (*Anat*) small of the back; **über K~** crosswise; **das K~ schlagen** cross oneself. **k~** *adv* **k~ und quer** in all directions. **k~en** *vt* cross; **sich k~en** cross; ⟨*Straßen:*⟩ intersect; ⟨*Meinungen:*⟩ clash □ *vi* (*haben/sein*) cruise; ⟨*Segelschiff:*⟩ tack. **K~er** *m* **-s,-** cruiser. **K~fahrt** *f* (*Naut*) cruise; (*K~zug*) crusade. **K~feuer** *nt* crossfire. **K~gang** *m* cloister

kreuzig|en *vt* crucify. **K~ung** *f* **-,-en** crucifixion

Kreuz|otter *f* adder, common viper. **K~ung** *f* **-,-en** intersection; (*Straßen-*) crossroads *sg*; (*Hybride*) cross. **K~verhör** *nt* cross-examination; **ins K~verhör nehmen** cross-examine. **K~weg** *m* crossroads *sg*; (*Relig*) Way of the Cross. **k~weise** *adv* crosswise. **K~worträtsel** *nt* crossword [puzzle]. **K~zug** *m* crusade

kribbel|ig *a* (*fam*) edgy. **k~n** *vi* (*haben*) tingle; (*kitzeln*) tickle

kriech|en† *vi* (*sein*) crawl; (*fig*) grovel (**vor** + *dat* to). **k~erisch** *a* grovelling. **K~spur** *f* (*Auto*) crawler lane. **K~tier** *nt* reptile

Krieg *m* **-[e]s,-e** war; **K~ führen** wage war (**gegen** on)

kriegen *vt* (*fam*) get; **ein Kind k~** have a baby

Krieger|denkmal *nt* war memorial. **k~isch** *a* warlike; (*militärisch*) military

kriegs|beschädigt *a* war-disabled. **K~dienstverweigerer** *m* **-s,-** conscientious objector. **K~gefangene(r)** *m* prisoner of war. **K~gefangenschaft** *f* captivity. **K~gericht** *nt* court martial. **K~list** *f* stratagem. **K~rat** *m* council of war. **K~recht** *nt* martial law. **K~schiff** *nt* warship. **K~verbrechen** *nt* war crime

Krimi *m* **-s,-s** (*fam*) crime story/film. **K~nalität** *f* **-** crime; (*Vorkommen*) crime rate. **K~nalpolizei** *f* criminal investigation department. **K~nalroman** *m* crime novel. **k~nell** *a* criminal. **K~nelle(r)** *m* criminal

kringeln (sich) *vr* curl [up]; (*vor Lachen*) fall about

Kripo *f* **-** = **Kriminalpolizei**

Krippe *f* **-,-n** manger; (*Weihnachts-*) crib; (*Kinder-*) crèche. **K~nspiel** *nt* Nativity play

Krise *f* **-,-n** crisis

Kristall[1] *nt* **-s** (*Glas*) crystal; (*geschliffen*) cut glass

Kristall[2] *m* **-s,-e** crystal. **k~isieren** *vi/r* (*haben*) **[sich] k~isieren** crystallize

Kriterium *nt* **-s,-ien** criterion

Kritik *f* **-,-en** criticism; (*Rezension*) review; **unter aller K~** (*fam*) abysmal

Kriti|ker *m* **-s,-** critic; (*Rezensent*) reviewer. **k~sch** *a* critical, *adv* **-ly**. **k~sieren** *vt* criticize; review

kritteln *vi* (*haben*) find fault (**an** + *acc* with)
kritzeln *vt/i* (*haben*) scribble
Krokette *f* -,-**n** (*Culin*) croquette
Krokodil *nt* -**s**,-**e** crocodile
Krokus *m* -,-[**se**] crocus
Krone *f* -,-**n** crown; (*Baum-*) top
krönen *vt* crown
Kron|leuchter *m* chandelier. **K~prinz** *m* crown prince
Krönung *f* -,-**en** coronation; (*fig: Höhepunkt*) crowning event/ (*Leistung*) achievement
Kropf *m* -[**e**]**s**,**¨e** (*Zool*) crop; (*Med*) goitre
Kröte *f* -,-**n** toad
Krücke *f* -,-**n** crutch; (*Stock-*) handle; **an K~n** on crutches
Krug *m* -[**e**]**s**,**¨e** jug; (*Bier-*) tankard
Krume *f* -,-**n** soft part [of loaf]; (*Krümel*) crumb; (*Acker-*) topsoil
Krümel *m* -**s**,- crumb. **k~ig** *a* crumbly. **k~n** *vt* crumble □ *vi* (*haben*) be crumbly; ⟨*Person:*⟩ drop crumbs
krumm *a* crooked; (*gebogen*) curved; (*verbogen*) bent; **etw k~ nehmen** (*fam*) take sth amiss. **k~beinig** *a* bow-legged
krümmen *vt* bend; crook ⟨*Finger*⟩; **sich k~** bend; (*sich winden*) writhe; (*vor Schmerzen/Lachen*) double up
krummnehmen† *vt sep* (NEW) **krumm nehmen**, *s.* **krumm**
Krümmung *f* -,-**en** bend; (*Kurve*) curve
Krüppel *m* -**s**,- cripple
Kruste *f* -,-**n** crust; (*Schorf*) scab
Kruzifix *nt* -**es**,-**e** crucifix
Krypta /ˈkrʏpta/ *f* -,-**ten** crypt
Kub|a *nt* -**s** Cuba. **k~anisch** *a* Cuban
Kübel *m* -**s**,- tub; (*Eimer*) bucket; (*Techn*) skip
Kubik- *pref* cubic. **K~meter** *m* & *nt* cubic metre
Küche *f* -,-**n** kitchen; (*Kochkunst*) cooking; **kalte/warme K~** cold/hot food; **französische K~** French cuisine
Kuchen *m* -**s**,- cake
Küchen|herd *m* cooker, stove. **K~maschine** *f* food processor, mixer. **K~schabe** *f* -,-**n** cockroach. **K~zettel** *m* menu
Kuckuck *m* -**s**,-**e** cuckoo; **zum K~!** (*fam*) hang it! **K~suhr** *f* cuckoo clock
Kufe *f* -,-**n** [sledge] runner
Kugel *f* -,-**n** ball; (*Geom*) sphere; (*Gewehr-*) bullet; (*Sport*) shot. **k~förmig** *a* spherical. **K~lager** *nt* ball-bearing. **k~n** *vt/i* (*haben*) roll; *sich k~n* roll/(*vor Lachen*) fall about. **k~rund** *a* spherical; (*fam: dick*) tubby. **K~schreiber** *m* -**s**,-, ballpoint [pen]. **k~sicher** *a* bullet-proof. **K~stoßen** *nt* -**s** shot-putting
Kuh *f* -,**¨e** cow
kühl *a* cool, *adv* -ly; (*kalt*) chilly. **K~box** *f* -,-**en** cool-box. **K~e** *f* - coolness; chilliness. **k~en** *vt* cool; refrigerate ⟨*Lebensmittel*⟩; chill ⟨*Wein*⟩. **K~er** *m* -**s**,- ice-bucket; (*Auto*) radiator. **K~erhaube** *f* bonnet, (*Amer*) hood. **K~fach** *nt* frozen-food compartment. **K~raum** *m* cold store. **K~schrank** *m* refrigerator. **K~truhe** *f* freezer. **K~ung** *f* - cooling; (*Frische*) coolness. **K~wasser** *nt* [radiator] water
Kuhmilch *f* cow's milk
kühn *a* bold, *adv* -ly; (*wagemutig*) daring. **K~heit** *f* - boldness
Kuhstall *m* cowshed
Küken *nt* -**s**,- chick; (*Enten-*) duckling
Kukuruz *m* -[**es**] (*Aust*) maize
kulant *a* obliging
Kuli *m* -**s**,- (*fam: Kugelschreiber*) ballpoint [pen], Biro (P)
kulinarisch *a* culinary
Kulissen *fpl* (*Theat*) scenery *sg;* (*seitlich*) wings; **hinter den K~** (*fig*) behind the scenes

kullern *vt/i* (*sein*) (*fam*) roll
Kult *m* **-[e]s,-e** cult
kultivier|en *vt* cultivate. **k~t** *a* cultured
Kultur *f* **-,-en** culture; **K~en** plantations. **K~beutel** *m* toiletbag. **k~ell** *a* cultural. **K~film** *m* documentary film
Kultusminister *m* Minister of Education and Arts
Kümmel *m* **-s** caraway; (*Getränk*) kümmel
Kummer *m* **-s** sorrow, grief; (*Sorge*) worry; (*Ärger*) trouble
kümmer|lich *a* puny; (*dürftig*) meagre; (*armselig*) wretched. **k~n** *vt* concern; **sich k~n um** look after; (*sich befassen*) concern oneself with; (*beachten*) take notice of; **ich werde mich darum k~n** I shall see to it; **k~e dich um deine eigenen Angelegenheiten!** mind your own business!
kummervoll *a* sorrowful
Kumpel *m* **-s,-** (*fam*) mate
Kunde *m* **-n,-n** customer. **K~ndienst** *m* [after-sales] service
Kund|gebung *f* **-,-en** (*Pol*) rally. **k~ig** *a* knowledgeable; (*sach-*) expert
kündig|en *vt* cancel ⟨*Vertrag*⟩; give notice of withdrawal for ⟨*Geld*⟩; give notice to quit ⟨*Wohnung*⟩; **seine Stellung k~en** give [in one's] notice □ *vi* (*haben*) give [in one's] notice; **jdm k~en** give s.o. notice [of dismissal/⟨*Vermieter:*⟩ to quit]. **K~ung** *f* **-,-en** cancellation; notice [of withdrawal/dismissal/to quit]; (*Entlassung*) dismissal. **K~ungsfrist** *f* period of notice
Kund|in *f* **-,-nen** [woman] customer. **K~machung** *f* **-,-en** (*Aust*) [public] notice. **K~schaft** *f* - clientele, customers *pl*
künftig *a* future □ *adv* in future
Kunst *f* **-,¨e** art; (*Können*) skill. **K~dünger** *m* artificial fertilizer. **K~faser** *f* synthetic fibre. **k~fertig** *a* skilful. **K~fertigkeit** *f* skill. **K~galerie** *f* art gallery. **k~gerecht** *a* expert, *adv* -ly. **K~geschichte** *f* history of art. **K~gewerbe** *nt* arts and crafts *pl*. **K~griff** *m* trick. **K~händler** *m* art dealer
Künstler *m* **-s,-** artist; (*Könner*) master. **K~in** *f* **-,-nen** [woman] artist. **k~isch** *a* artistic, *adv* -ally. **K~name** *m* pseudonym; (*Theat*) stage name
künstlich *a* artificial, *adv* -ly
kunst|los *a* simple. **K~maler** *m* painter. **K~stoff** *m* plastic. **K~stopfen** *nt* invisible mending. **K~stück** *nt* trick; (*große Leistung*) feat. **k~voll** *a* artistic; (*geschickt*) skilful, *adv* -ly; (*kompliziert*) elaborate, *adv* -ly. **K~werk** *nt* work of art
kunterbunt *a* multicoloured; (*gemischt*) mixed □ *adv* **k~ durcheinander** higgledy-piggledy
Kupfer *nt* **-s** copper. **k~n** *a* copper
kupieren *vt* crop
Kupon /ku'põ:/ *m* **-s,-s** voucher; (*Zins-*) coupon; (*Stoff-*) length
Kuppe *f* **-,-n** [rounded] top; (*Finger-*) end, tip
Kuppel *f* **-,-n** dome
kupp|eln *vt* couple (**an** + *acc* to) □ *vi* (*haben*) (*Auto*) operate the clutch. **K~lung** *f* **-,-en** coupling; (*Auto*) clutch
Kur *f* **-,-en** course of treatment; (*im Kurort*) cure
Kür *f* **-,-en** (*Sport*) free exercise; (*Eislauf*) free programme
Kurbel *f* **-,-n** crank. **k~n** *vt* wind (**nach oben/unten** up/down). **K~welle** *f* crankshaft
Kürbis *m* **-ses,-se** pumpkin; (*Flaschen-*) marrow
Kurgast *m* health-resort visitor
Kurier *m* **-s,-e** courier
kurieren *vt* cure
kurios *a* curious, odd. **K~ität** *f* **-,-en** oddness; (*Objekt*) curiosity; (*Kunst*) curio

Kurort *m* health resort; (*Badeort*) spa. **K~pfuscher** *m* quack
Kurs *m* **-es,-e** course; (*Aktien-*) price. **K~buch** *nt* timetable
kursieren *vi* (*haben*) circulate
kursiv *a* italic □ *adv* in italics. **K~schrift** *f* italics *pl*
Kursus *m* **-,Kurse** course
Kurswagen *m* through carriage
Kurtaxe *f* visitors' tax
Kurve *f* **-,-n** curve; (*Straßen-*) bend
kurz *a* (**kürzer, kürzest**) short; (*knapp*) brief; (*rasch*) quick; (*schroff*) curt; **k~e Hosen** shorts; **vor k~em** a short time ago; **seit k~em** lately; **binnen k~em** shortly; **den Kürzeren (kürzeren) ziehen** get the worst of it □ *adv* briefly; quickly; curtly; **k~ vor/nach** a little way/(*zeitlich*) shortly before/after; **sich k~ fassen** be brief; **k~ und gut** in short; **über k~ oder lang** sooner or later; **zu k~ kommen** get less than one's fair share. **K~arbeit** *f* short-time working. **k~ärmelig** *a* short-sleeved. **k~atmig** *a* **k~atmig sein** be short of breath
Kürze *f* - shortness; (*Knappheit*) brevity; **in K~** shortly. **k~n** *vt* shorten; (*verringern*) cut
kurzerhand *adv* without further ado. **k~fristig** *a* short-term □ *adv* at short notice. **K~geschichte** *f* short story. **k~lebig** *a* short-lived
kürzlich *adv* recently
Kurzmeldung *f* newsflash. **K~nachrichten** *fpl* news headlines. **K~schluss (K~schluß)** *m* short circuit; (*fig*) brainstorm. **K~schrift** *f* shorthand. **k~sichtig** *a* short-sighted. **K~sichtigkeit** *f* - short-sightedness. **K~streckenrakete** *f* short-range missile. **k~um** *adv* in short
Kürzung *f* **-,-en** shortening; (*Verringerung*) cut (*gen* in)
Kurzwaren *fpl* haberdashery *sg*, (*Amer*) notions. **k~weilig** *a* amusing. **K~welle** *f* short wave
kuscheln (sich) *vr* snuggle (**an** + *acc* up to)
Kusine *f* **-,-n** [female] cousin
Kuss *m* **-es,¨-e (Kuß** *m* **-sses,¨-sse)** kiss
küssen *vt/i* (*haben*) kiss; **sich k~** kiss
Küste *f* **-,-n** coast. **K~nwache, K~nwacht** *f* coastguard
Küster *m* **-s,-** verger
Kustos *m* **-,-oden** /-'to:-/ curator
Kutsche *f* **-,-n** [horse-drawn] carriage/(*geschlossen*) coach. **K~er** *m* **-s,-** coachman, driver. **k~ieren** *vt/i* (*haben*) drive
Kutte *f* **-,-n** (*Relig*) habit
Kutter *m* **-s,-** (*Naut*) cutter
Kuvert /ku've:ɐ̯/ *nt* **-s,-s** envelope
KZ /ka:'tsɛt/ *nt* **-[s],-[s]** concentration camp

L

labil *a* unstable
Labor *nt* **-s,-s** & **-e** laboratory. **L~ant(in)** *m* **-en,-en** (*f* **-,-nen**) laboratory assistant. **L~atorium** *nt* **-s,-ien** laboratory
Labyrinth *nt* **-[e]s,-e** maze, labyrinth
Lache *f* **-,-n** puddle; (*Blut-*) pool
lächeln *vi* (*haben*) smile. **L~** *nt* **-s** smile. **l~d** *a* smiling
lachen *vi* (*haben*) laugh. **L~** *nt* **-s** laugh; (*Gelächter*) laughter
lächerlich *a* ridiculous, *adv* -ly; **sich l~ machen** make a fool of oneself. **L~keit** *f* **-,-en** ridiculousness; (*Kleinigkeit*) triviality
lachhaft *a* laughable
Lachs *m* **-es,-e** salmon. **l~farben, l~rosa** *a* salmon-pink
Lack *m* **-[e]s,-e** varnish; (*Japan-*) lacquer; (*Auto*) paint. **l~en** *vt* varnish. **l~ieren** *vt* varnish;

(*spritzen*) spray. **L~schuhe** *mpl* patent-leather shoes

Lade *f* **-,-n** drawer

laden† *vt* load; (*Electr*) charge; (*Jur: vor-*) summons

Laden *m* **-s,¨** shop, (*Amer*) store; (*Fenster-*) shutter. **L~dieb** *m* shop-lifter. **L~diebstahl** *m* shop-lifting. **L~schluss** (**L~schluß**) *m* [shop] closing-time. **L~tisch** *m* counter

Laderaum *m* (*Naut*) hold

lädieren *vt* damage

Ladung *f* **-,-en** load; (*Naut, Aviat*) cargo; (*elektrische, Spreng-*) charge; (*Jur: Vor-*) summons

Lage *f* **-,-n** position; (*Situation*) situation; (*Schicht*) layer; (*fam: Runde*) round; **nicht in der L~ sein** not be in a position (**zu** to)

Lager *nt* **-s,-** camp; (*L~haus*) warehouse; (*Vorrat*) stock; (*Techn*) bearing; (*Erz-, Ruhe-*) bed; (*eines Tieres*) lair; **[nicht] auf L~** [not] in stock. **L~haus** *nt* warehouse. **l~n** *vt* store; (*legen*) lay; **sich l~n** settle; (*sich legen*) lie down □ *vi* (*haben*) camp; (*liegen*) lie; ⟨*Waren:*⟩ be stored. **L~raum** *m* store-room. **L~stätte** *f* (*Geol*) deposit. **L~ung** *f* - storage

Lagune *f* **-,-n** lagoon

lahm *a* lame; **l~ legen** (*fig*) paralyse. **l~en** *vi* (*haben*) be lame

lähmen *vt* paralyse

lahmlegen *vt sep* (NEW) **lahm legen**, *s.* **lahm**

Lähmung *f* **-,-en** paralysis

Laib *m* **-[e]s,-e** loaf

Laich *m* **-[e]s** (*Zool*) spawn. **l~en** *vi* (*haben*) spawn

Laie *m* **-n,-n** layman; (*Theat*) amateur. **l~nhaft** *a* amateurish. **L~nprediger** *m* lay preacher

Lake *f* **-,-n** brine

Laken *nt* **-s,-** sheet

lakonisch *a* laconic, *adv* -ally

Lakritze *f* - liquorice

lallen *vt/i* (*haben*) mumble; ⟨*Baby:*⟩ babble

Lametta *nt* **-s** tinsel

Lamm *nt* **-[e]s,¨er** lamb

Lampe *f* **-,-n** lamp; (*Decken-, Wand-*) light; (*Glüh-*) bulb. **L~nfieber** *nt* stage fright. **L~nschirm** *m* lampshade

Lampion /lam'pi̯ɔŋ/ *m* **-s,-s** Chinese lantern

lancieren /lã'si:rən/ *vt* (*Comm*) launch

Land *nt* **-[e]s,¨er** country; (*Fest-*) land; (*Bundes-*) state, Land; (*Aust*) province; **Stück L~** piece of land; **auf dem L~e** in the country; **an L~ gehen** (*Naut*) go ashore; **hier zu L~e** = **hierzulande**. **L~arbeiter** *m* agricultural worker. **L~ebahn** *f* runway. **l~einwärts** *adv* inland. **l~en** *vt/i* (*sein*) land; (*fam: gelangen*) end up

Ländereien *pl* estates

Länderspiel *nt* international

Landesteg *m* landing-stage

Landesverrat *m* treason

Land|karte *f* map. **l~läufig** *a* popular

ländlich *a* rural

Land|maschinen *fpl* agricultural machinery *sg*. **L~schaft** *f* **-,-en** scenery; (*Geog, Kunst*) landscape; (*Gegend*) country[side]. **l~schaftlich** *a* scenic; (*regional*) regional. **L~smann** *m* (*pl* **-leute**) fellow countryman, compatriot. **L~smännin** *f* **-,-nen** fellow countrywoman. **L~straße** *f* country road; (*Admin*) ≈ B road. **L~streicher** *m* **-s,-** tramp. **L~tag** *m* state/(*Aust*) provincial parliament

Landung *f* **-,-en** landing. **L~sbrücke** *f* landing-stage

Land|vermesser *m* **-s,-** surveyor. **L~weg** *m* country lane; **auf dem L~weg** overland. **L~wirt** *m* farmer. **L~wirtschaft** *f* agriculture; (*Hof*) farm. **l~wirtschaftlich** *a* agricultural

lang[1] *adv & prep* (+ *preceding acc or preceding* **an** + *dat*) along; **den** *od* **am Fluss l~** along the river
lang[2] *a* (**länger, längst**) long; (*groß*) tall; **seit l~em** for a long time □ *adv* **eine Stunde/Woche l~** for an hour/a week; **mein Leben l~** all my life. **l~ärmelig** *a* long-sleeved. **l~atmig** *a* long-winded. **l~e** *adv* a long time; ⟨*schlafen*⟩ late; **wie/zu l~e** how/too long; **schon l~e** [for] a long time; (*zurückliegend*) a long time ago; **so l~e wie möglich** as long as possible; **l~e nicht** not for a long time; (*bei weitem nicht*) nowhere near
Länge *f* -,-n length; (*Geog*) longitude; **der L~nach** lengthways; ⟨*liegen, fallen*⟩ full length
langen *vt* hand (*dat* to) □ *vi* (*haben*) reach (**an etw** *acc* sth; **nach** for); (*genügen*) be enough
Läng|engrad *m* degree of longitude. **L~enmaß** *nt* linear measure. **l~er** *a & adv* longer; (*längere Zeit*) [for] some time
Langeweile *f* - boredom; **L~ haben** be bored
lang|fristig *a* long-term; ⟨*Vorhersage*⟩ long-range. **l~jährig** *a* long-standing; ⟨*Erfahrung*⟩ long. **l~lebig** *a* long-lived
länglich *a* oblong; **l~ rund** oval
langmütig *a* long-suffering
längs *adv & prep* (+ *gen/dat*) along; (*der Länge nach*) lengthways
lang|sam *a* slow, *adv* -ly. **L~samkeit** *f* - slowness. **L~schläfer(in)** *m(f)* (*fam*) late riser. **L~schrift** *f* longhand
längst *adv* **[schon] l~** for a long time; (*zurückliegend*) a long time ago; **l~ nicht** nowhere near
Lang|strecken- *pref* long-distance; (*Mil, Aviat*) long-range. **l~weilen** *vt* bore; **sich l~weilen** be bored. **l~weilig** *a* boring, *adv* -ly. **L~welle** *f* long wave. **l~wierig** *a* lengthy
Lanze *f* -,-n lance
Lappalie /la'pa:li̯ə/ *f* -,-n trifle
Lappen *m* -s,- cloth; (*Anat*) lobe
läppisch *a* silly
Lapsus *m* -,- slip
Lärche *f* -,-n larch
Lärm *m* -s noise. **l~en** *vi* (*haben*) make a noise. **l~end** *a* noisy
Larve /'larfə/ *f* -,-n larva; (*Maske*) mask
lasch *a* listless; (*schlaff*) limp; (*fade*) insipid
Lasche *f* -,-n tab; (*Verschluss-*) flap; (*Zunge*) tongue
Laser /'le:-, 'la:zɐ/ *m* -s,- laser
lassen† *vt* leave; (*zulassen*) let; **jdm etw l~** let s.o. keep sth; **sein Leben l~** lose one's life; **etw [sein** *od* **bleiben] l~** not do sth; (*aufhören*) stop [doing] sth; **lass das!** stop it! **jdn schlafen/gewinnen l~** let s.o. sleep/win; **jdn warten l~** keep s.o. waiting; **etw machen/reparieren l~** have sth done/repaired; **etw verschwinden l~** make sth disappear; **sich [leicht] biegen/öffnen l~** bend/open [easily]; **sich gut waschen l~** wash well; **es lässt sich nicht leugnen** it is undeniable; **lasst uns gehen!** let's go!
lässig *a* casual, *adv* -ly. **L~keit** *f* - casualness
Lasso *nt* -s,-s lasso
Last *f* -,-en load; (*Gewicht*) weight; (*fig*) burden; **L~en** charges; (*Steuern*) taxes; **jdm zur L~ fallen** be a burden on s.o. **L~auto** *nt* lorry. **l~en** *vi* (*haben*) weigh heavily/(*liegen*) rest (**auf** + *dat* on). **L~enaufzug** *m* goods lift
Laster[1] *m* -s,- (*fam*) lorry, (*Amer*) truck
Laster[2] *nt* -s,- vice. **l~haft** *a* depraved; (*zügellos*) dissolute
läster|lich *a* blasphemous. **l~n** *vt* blaspheme □ *vi* (*haben*) make disparaging remarks (**über** + *acc* about). **L~ung** *f* -,-en blasphemy

lästig *a* troublesome; **l~ sein/werden** be/become a nuisance

Last|kahn *m* barge. **L~[kraft]wagen** *m* lorry, (*Amer*) truck. **L~zug** *m* lorry with trailer[s]

Latein *nt* **-[s]** Latin. **L~amerika** *nt* Latin America. **l~isch** *a* Latin

latent *a* latent

Laterne *f* **-,-n** lantern; (*Straßen-*) street lamp. **L~npfahl** *m* lamp-post

latschen *vi* (*sein*) (*fam*) traipse; (*schlurfen*) shuffle

Latte *f* **-,-n** slat; (*Tor-, Hochsprung-*) bar

Latz *m* **-es,¨e** bib

Lätzchen *nt* **-s,-** [baby's] bib

Latzhose *f* dungarees *pl*

lau *a* lukewarm; (*mild*) mild

Laub *nt* **-[e]s** leaves *pl*; (*L~werk*) foliage. **L~baum** *m* deciduous tree

Laube *f* **-,-n** summer-house; (*gewachsen*) arbour. **L~ngang** *m* pergola; (*Archit*) arcades *pl*

Laub|säge *f* fretsaw. **L~wald** *m* deciduous forest

Lauch *m* **-[e]s** leeks *pl*

Lauer *f* **auf der L~ liegen** lie in wait. **l~n** *vi* (*haben*) lurk; **l~n auf** (+ *acc*) lie in wait for

Lauf *m* **-[e]s, Läufe** run; (*Laufen*) running; (*Verlauf*) course; (*Wett-*) race; (*Sport: Durchgang*) heat; (*Gewehr-*) barrel; **im L~[e]** (+ *gen*) in the course of. **L~bahn** *f* career. **l~en**† *vi* (*sein*) run; (*zu Fuß gehen*) walk; (*gelten*) be valid; **Ski/Schlittschuh l~en** ski/skate; **jdn l~en lassen** (*fam*) let s.o. go. **l~end** *a* running; (*gegenwärtig*) current; (*regelmäßig*) regular; **l~ende Nummer** serial number; **auf dem L~enden (l~enden) sein/jdn auf dem L~enden (l~enden) halten** be/keep s.o. up to date □ *adv* continually. **l~enlassen**† *vt sep* (NEW) **l~en lassen**, *s.* **laufen**

Läufer *m* **-s,-** (*Person, Teppich*) runner; (*Schach*) bishop

Lauf|gitter *nt* play-pen. **L~masche** *f* ladder. **L~rolle** *f* castor. **L~schritt** *m* **im L~schritt** at a run; (*Mil*) at the double. **L~stall** *m* play-pen. **L~zettel** *m* circular

Lauge *f* **-,-n** soapy water

Laun|e *f* **-,-n** mood; (*Einfall*) whim; **guter L~e sein, gute L~e haben** be in a good mood. **l~enhaft** *a* capricious. **l~isch** *a* moody

Laus *f* **-,Läuse** louse; (*Blatt-*) greenfly. **L~bub** *m* (*fam*) rascal

lauschen *vi* (*haben*) listen; (*heimlich*) eavesdrop

lausig *a* (*fam*) lousy □ *adv* terribly

laut *a* loud, *adv* -ly; (*geräuschvoll*) noisy, *adv* -ily; **l~ lesen** read aloud; **l~er stellen** turn up □ *prep* (+ *gen/dat*) according to. **L~** *m* **-es,-e** sound

Laute *f* **-,-n** (*Mus*) lute

lauten *vi* (*haben*) ⟨*Text:*⟩ run, read; **auf jds Namen l~** be in s.o.'s name

läuten *vt/i* (*haben*) ring

lauter *a* pure; (*ehrlich*) honest; ⟨*Wahrheit*⟩ plain □ *a inv* sheer; (*nichts als*) nothing but. **L~keit** *f* - integrity

läutern *vt* purify

laut|hals *adv* at the top of one's voice, ⟨*lachen*⟩ out loud. **l~los** *a* silent, *adv* -ly; ⟨*Stille*⟩ hushed. **L~schrift** *f* phonetics *pl*. **L~sprecher** *m* loudspeaker. **l~stark** *a* vociferous, *adv* -ly. **L~stärke** *f* volume

lauwarm *a* lukewarm

Lava *f* **-,-ven** lava

Lavendel *m* **-s** lavender

lavieren *vi* (*haben*) manœuvre

Lawine *f* **-,-n** avalanche

lax *a* lax. **L~heit** *f* - laxity

Lazarett *nt* **-[e]s,-e** military hospital

leasen /ˈliːsən/ *vt* rent

Lebehoch *nt* cheer
leben *vt/i* (*haben*) live (**von** on); **leb wohl!** farewell! **L~** *nt* **-s,-** life, (*Treiben*) bustle; **am L~** alive. **l~d** *a* living
lebendig *a* live; (*lebhaft*) lively; (*anschaulich*) vivid, *adv* -ly; **l~ sein** be alive. **L~keit** *f* - liveliness; vividness
Lebens|abend *m* old age. **L~alter** *nt* age. **L~art** *f* manners *pl*. **l~fähig** *a* viable. **L~gefahr** *f* mortal danger; **in L~gefahr** in mortal danger; ⟨*Patient*⟩ critically ill. **l~gefährlich** *a* extremely dangerous; ⟨*Verletzung*⟩ critical □ *adv* critically. **L~größe** *f* **in L~größe** life-sized. **L~haltungskosten** *pl* cost of living *sg*. **l~lang** *a* lifelong. **l~länglich** *a* life ... □ *adv* for life. **L~lauf** *m* curriculum vitae. **L~mittel** *ntpl* food *sg*. **L~mittelgeschäft** *nt* food shop. **L~mittelhändler** *m* grocer. **l~notwendig** *a* vital. **L~retter** *m* rescuer; (*beim Schwimmen*) life-guard. **L~standard** *m* standard of living. **L~unterhalt** *m* livelihood; **seinen L~unterhalt verdienen** earn one's living. **L~versicherung** *f* life assurance. **L~wandel** *m* conduct. **l~wichtig** *a* vital. **L~zeichen** *nt* sign of life. **L~zeit** *f* **auf L~zeit** for life
Leber *f* **-,-n** liver. **L~fleck** *m* mole. **L~wurst** *f* liver sausage
Lebe|wesen *nt* living being. **L~wohl** *nt* **-s,-s** & **-e** farewell
leb|haft *a* lively; ⟨*Farbe*⟩ vivid. **L~haftigkeit** *f* - liveliness. **L~kuchen** *m* gingerbread. **l~los** *a* lifeless. **L~tag** *m* **mein/dein L~tag** all my/your life. **L~zeiten** *fpl* **zu jds L~zeiten** in s.o.'s lifetime
leck *a* leaking. **L~** *nt* **-s,-s** leak. **l~en**[1] *vi* (*haben*) leak
lecken[2] *vi* (*haben*) lick
lecker *a* tasty. **L~bissen** *m* delicacy. **L~ei** *f* **-,-en** sweet
Leder *nt* **-s,-** leather. **l~n** *a* leather; (*wie Leder*) leathery
ledig *a* single. **l~lich** *adv* merely
Lee *f* & *nt* - **nach Lee** (*Naut*) to leeward
leer *a* empty; (*unbesetzt*) vacant; **l~ laufen** (*Auto*) idle. **L~e** *f* - emptiness; (*leerer Raum*) void. **l~en** *vt* empty; **sich l~en** empty. **L~lauf** *m* (*Auto*) neutral. **L~ung** *f* **-,-en** (*Post*) collection
legal *a* legal, *adv* -ly. **l~isieren** *vt* legalize. **L~ität** *f* - legality
Legas|thenie *f* - dyslexia **L~theniker** *m* **-s,-** dyslexic
legen *vt* put; (*hin-, ver-*) lay; set ⟨*Haare*⟩; **Eier l~** lay eggs; **sich l~** lie down; ⟨*Staub:*⟩ settle; (*nachlassen*) subside
legendär *a* legendary
Legende *f* **-,-n** legend
leger /le'ʒe:ɐ̯/ *a* casual, *adv* -ly
legier|en *vt* alloy; (*Culin*) thicken. **L~ung** *f* **-,-en** alloy
Legion *f* **-,-en** legion
Legislative *f* - legislature
legitim *a* legitimate, *adv* -ly. **l~ieren (sich)** *vr* prove one's identity. **L~ität** *f* - legitimacy
Lehm *m* **-s** clay. **l~ig** *a* clayey
Lehn|e *f* **-,-n** (*Rücken-*) back; (*Arm-*) arm. **l~en** *vt* lean (**an** + *acc* against); **sich l~en** lean (**an** + *acc* against) □ *vi* (*haben*) be leaning (**an** + *acc* against). **L~sessel, L~stuhl** *m* armchair
Lehr|buch *nt* textbook. **L~e** *f* **-,-n** apprenticeship; (*Anschauung*) doctrine; (*Theorie*) theory; (*Wissenschaft*) science; (*Ratschlag*) advice; (*Erfahrung*) lesson; **jdm eine L~e erteilen** (*fig*) teach s.o. a lesson. **l~en** *vt/i* (*haben*) teach. **L~er** *m* **-s,-** teacher; (*Fahr-, Ski-*) instructor. **L~erin** *f* **-,-nen** teacher. **L~erzimmer** *nt* staff-room. **L~fach** *nt* (*Sch*) subject. **L~gang** *m* course.

L~kraft *f* teacher. **L~ling** *m* **-s,-e** apprentice; (*Auszubildender*) trainee. **L~plan** *m* syllabus. **l~reich** *a* instructive. **L~stelle** *f* apprenticeship. **L~stuhl** *m* (*Univ*) chair. **L~zeit** *f* apprenticeship

Leib *m* **-es,-er** body; (*Bauch*) belly. **L~eserziehung** *f* (*Sch*) physical education. **L~eskraft** *f* **aus L~eskräften** as hard/⟨*schreien*⟩ loud as one can. **L~gericht** *nt* favourite dish. **l~haftig** *a* **der l~haftige Satan** the devil incarnate □ *adv* in the flesh. **l~lich** *a* physical; (*blutsverwandt*) real, natural. **L~speise** *f* = **L~gericht. L~wache** *f* (*coll*) bodyguard. **L~wächter** *m* bodyguard. **L~wäsche** *f* underwear

Leiche *f* **-,-n** [dead] body; corpse, **L~nbegängnis** *nt* **-ses,-se** funeral. **L~nbestatter** *m* **-s,-** undertaker. **l~nblass (l~nblaß)** *a* deathly pale. **L~nhalle** *f* mortuary. **L~nwagen** *m* hearse. **L~nzug** *m* funeral procession, cortège

Leichnam *m* **-s,-e** [dead] body

leicht *a* light, *adv* -ly; ⟨*Stoff, Anzug*⟩ lightweight; (*gering*) slight, *adv* -ly; (*mühelos*) easy, *adv* -ily; **jdm l~ fallen** be easy for s.o.; **etw l~ machen** make sth easy (**dat** for); **es sich** (*dat*) **l~ machen** take the easy way out; **etw l~ nehmen** (*fig*) take sth lightly. **L~athletik** *f* [track and field] athletics *sg*. **l~fallen**† *vi sep* (*sein*) (NEW) **l~ fallen**, *s.* **leicht**. **l~fertig** *a* thoughtless, *adv* -ly; (*vorschnell*) rash, *adv* -ly; (*frivol*) frivolous, *adv* -ly. **L~gewicht** *nt* (*Boxen*) lightweight. **l~gläubig** *a* gullible. **l~hin** *adv* casually. **L~igkeit** *f* - lightness; (*Mühelosigkeit*) ease; (*L~sein*) easiness; **mit L~igkeit** with ease. **l~lebig** *a* happy-go-lucky. **l~machen** *vt sep* (NEW) **l~ machen**, *s.* **leicht**. **l~nehmen**† *vt sep* (NEW) **l~ nehmen**, *s.* **leicht**. **L~sinn** *m* carelessness; recklessness; (*Frivolität*) frivolity. **l~sinnig** *a* careless, *adv* -ly; (*unvorsichtig*) reckless, *adv* -ly; (*frivol*) frivolous, *adv* -ly

Leid *nt* **-[e]s** sorrow, grief; (*Böses*) harm; **es tut mir L~** I am sorry; **er tut mir L~** I feel sorry for him; **jdm etw zu L~e tun** = **jdm etw zuleide tun**, *s.* **zuleide**. **l~** *a* **jdn/etw l~ sein/werden** be/get tired of s.o./sth; **jdm l~ tun** (NEW) **jdm L~ tun**, *s.* **Leid**

Leide|form *f* passive. **l~n**† *vt/i* (*haben*) suffer (**an** + *dat* from); **jdn [gut] l~n können** like s.o.; **jdn/etw nicht l~n können** dislike s.o./sth. **L~n** *nt* **-s,-** suffering; (*Med*) complaint; (*Krankheit*) disease. **l~nd** *a* suffering; **l~nd sein** be in poor health. **L~nschaft** *f* **-,-en** passion. **l~nschaftlich** *a* passionate, *adv* -ly

leid|er *adv* unfortunately; **l~er ja/nicht** I'm afraid so/not. **l~ig** *a* wretched. **l~lich** *a* tolerable, *adv* -bly. **L~tragende(r)** *m/f* person who suffers; (*Trauernde*) mourner. **L~wesen** *nt* **zu meinem L~wesen** to my regret

Leier *f* **-,-n die alte L~** (*fam*) the same old story. **L~kasten** *m* barrel-organ. **l~n** *vt/i* (*haben*) wind; (*herunter-*) drone out

Leih|bibliothek, L~bücherei *f* lending library. **L~e** *f* **-,-n** loan. **l~en**† *vt* lend; **sich** (*dat*) **etw l~en** borrow sth. **L~gabe** *f* loan. **L~gebühr** *f* rental; (*für Bücher*) lending charge. **L~haus** *nt* pawnshop. **L~wagen** *m* hire-car. **l~weise** *adv* on loan

Leim *m* **-s** glue. **l~en** *vt* glue

Leine *f* **-,-n** rope; (*Wäsche-*) line; (*Hunde-*) lead, leash

Lein|en *nt* **-s** linen. **l~en** *a* linen. **L~tuch** *nt* sheet. **L~wand** *f* linen; (*Kunst*) canvas; (*Film-*) screen

leise *a* quiet, *adv* -ly; ⟨*Stimme, Musik, Berührung*⟩ soft, *adv* -ly; (*schwach*) faint, *adv* -ly; (*leicht*) light, *adv* -ly; **l~r stellen** turn down

Leiste *f* -,-n strip; (*Holz-*) batten; (*Zier-*) moulding; (*Anat*) groin

Leisten *m* -s,- [shoemaker's] last

leist|en *vt* achieve, accomplish; **sich** (*dat*) **etw l~en** treat oneself to sth; (*fam: anstellen*) get up to sth; **ich kann es mir nicht l~en** I can't afford it. **L~ung** *f* -,-en achievement; (*Sport, Techn*) performance; (*Produktion*) output; (*Zahlung*) payment. **l~ungsfähig** *a* efficient. **L~ungsfähigkeit** *f* efficiency

Leit|artikel *m* leader, editorial. **L~bild** *nt* (*fig*) model. **l~en** *vt* run, manage; (*an-/hinführen*) lead; (*Mus, Techn, Phys*) conduct; (*lenken, schicken*) direct. **l~end** *a* leading; ⟨*Posten*⟩ executive

Leiter[1] *f* -,-n ladder

Leit|er[2] *m* -s,- director; (*Comm*) manager; (*Führer*) leader; (*Sch*) head; (*Mus, Phys*) conductor. **L~erin** *f* -,-nen director; manageress; leader; head. **L~faden** *m* manual. **L~kegel** *m* [traffic] cone. **L~planke** *f* crash barrier. **L~spruch** *m* motto. **L~ung** *f* -,-en (*Führung*) direction; (*Comm*) management; (*Aufsicht*) control; (*Electr: Schnur*) lead, flex; (*Kabel*) cable; (*Telefon-*) line; (*Rohr-*) pipe; (*Haupt-*) main. **L~ungswasser** *nt* tap water

Lektion /-ˈtsi̯oːn/ *f* -,-en lesson

Lekt|or *m* -s,-en /-ˈtoːrən/, **L~orin** *f* -,-nen (*Univ*) assistant lecturer; (*Verlags-*) editor. **L~üre** *f* -,-n reading matter; (*Lesen*) reading

Lende *f* -,-n loin

lenk|bar *a* steerable; (*fügsam*) tractable. **l~en** *vt* guide; (*steuern*) steer; (*Aust*) drive; (*regeln*) control; **jds Aufmerksamkeit auf sich** (*acc*) **l~en** attract s.o.'s attention. **L~er** *m* -s,- driver; (*L~stange*) handlebars *pl*. **L~rad** *nt* steering-wheel. **L~stange** *f* handlebars *pl*. **L~ung** *f* - steering

Leopard *m* -en,-en leopard

Lepra *f* - leprosy

Lerche *f* -,-n lark

lernen *vt/i* (*haben*) learn; (*für die Schule*) study; **schwimmen l~** learn to swim

lesbar *a* readable; (*leserlich*) legible

Lesb|ierin /ˈlɛsbi̯ərɪn/ *f* -,-nen lesbian. **l~isch** *a* lesbian

Lese *f* -,-n harvest. **L~buch** *nt* reader. **l~n**† *vt/i* (*haben*) read; (*Univ*) lecture □ *vt* pick, gather. **L~n** *nt* -s reading. **L~r(in)** *m* -s,- (*f* -,-nen) reader. **L~ratte** *f* (*fam*) bookworm. **l~rlich** *a* legible, *adv* -bly. **L~zeichen** *nt* bookmark

Lesung *f* -,-en reading

lethargisch *a* lethargic, *adv* -ally

Lettland *nt* -s Latvia

letzt|e(r,s) *a* last; (*neueste*) latest; **in l~er Zeit** recently; **l~en Endes** in the end; **er kam als L~er (l~er)** he arrived last. **l~emal** *adv* **das l~emal/zum l~enmal** (NEW) **das l~e Mal/zum l~en Mal**, *s.* **Mal**[1]. **l~ens** *adv* recently; (*zuletzt*) lastly. **l~ere(r,s)** *a* the latter; **der/die/das L~ere (l~ere)** the latter

Leucht|e *f* -,-n light. **l~en** *vi* (*haben*) shine. **l~end** *a* shining. **L~er** *m* -s,- candlestick. **L~feuer** *nt* beacon. **L~kugel, L~rakete** *f* flare. **L~reklame** *f* neon sign. **L~[stoff]röhre** *f* fluorescent tube. **L~turm** *m* lighthouse. **L~zifferblatt** *nt* luminous dial

leugnen *vt* deny

Leukämie *f* - leukaemia

Leumund *m* -s reputation

Leute *pl* people; (*Mil*) men; (*Arbeiter*) workers

Leutnant *m* **-s,-s** second lieutenant
leutselig *a* affable, *adv* -bly
Levkoje /lɛf'ko:jə/ *f* **-,-n** stock
Lexikon *nt* **-s,-ka** encyclopaedia; (*Wörterbuch*) dictionary
Libanon (der) -s Lebanon
Libelle *f* **-,-n** dragonfly; (*Techn*) spirit-level; (*Haarspange*) slide
liberal *a* (*Pol*) Liberal
Libyen *nt* **-s** Libya
Licht *nt* **-[e]s,-er** light; (*Kerze*) candle; **L~ machen** turn on the light; **hinters L~ führen** (*fam*) dupe. **l~** *a* bright; (*Med*) lucid; (*spärlich*) sparse. **L~bild** *nt* [passport] photograph; (*Dia*) slide. **L~bildervortrag** *m* slide lecture. **L~blick** *m* (*fig*) ray of hope. **l~en** *vt* thin out; **den Anker l~en** (*Naut*) weigh anchor; **sich l~en** become less dense; ⟨*Haare:*⟩ thin. **L~hupe** *f* headlight flasher; **die L~hupe betätigen** flash one's headlights. **L~maschine** *f* dynamo. **L~schalter** *m* light-switch. **L~ung** *f* **-,-en** clearing
Lid *nt* **-[e]s,-er** [eye]lid. **L~schatten** *m* eye-shadow
lieb *a* dear; (*nett*) nice; (*artig*) good; **jdn l~ haben** be fond of s.o.; (*lieben*) love s.o.; **jdn l~ gewinnen** grow fond of s.o.; **es ist mir l~** I'm glad (**dass** that); **es wäre mir l~er** I should prefer it (**wenn** if). **l~äugeln** *vi* (*haben*) **l~äugeln mit** fancy; toy with ⟨*Gedanken*⟩
Liebe *f* **-,-n** love. **L~lei** *f* **-,en** flirtation. **l~n** *vt* love; (*mögen*) like; **sich l~n** love each other; (*körperlich*) make love. **l~nd** *a* loving □ *adv* **etw l~nd gern tun** love to do sth. **l~nswert** a lovable. **l~nswürdig** *a* kind. **l~nswürdigerweise** *adv* very kindly. **L~nswürdigkeit** *f* **-,-en** kindness
lieber *adv* rather; (*besser*) better; **l~ mögen** like better; **ich trinke l~ Tee** I prefer tea
Liebes|brief *m* love letter. **L~dienst** *m* favour. **L~geschichte** *f* love story. **L~kummer** *m* heartache; **L~kummer haben** be depressed over an unhappy love-affair. **L~paar** *nt* [pair of] lovers *pl*
lieb|evoll *a* loving, *adv* -ly, (*zärtlich*) affectionate, *adv* -ly. **L~gewinnen**† *vt sep* (NEW) **l~ gewinnen**, *s.* **lieb**; **l~haben**† *vt sep* (NEW) **l~ haben**, *s.* **lieb**. **L~haber** *m* **-s,-** lover; (*Sammler*) collector. **L~haberei** *f* **-,-en** hobby. **l~kosen** *vt* caress. **L~kosung** *f* **-,-en** caress. **l~lich** *a* lovely; (*sanft*) gentle; (*süß*) sweet. **L~ling** *m* **-s,-e** darling; (*Bevorzugte*) favourite. **L~lings-** *pref* favourite. **l~los** *a* loveless; ⟨*Eltern*⟩ uncaring; (*unfreundlich*) unkind □ *adv* unkindly; (*ohne Sorgfalt*) without care. **L~schaft** *f* **-,-en** [love] affair. **l~ste(r,s)** *a* dearest; (*bevorzugt*) favourite □ *adv* **am l~sten** best [of all]; **jdn/etw am l~sten mögen** like s.o./sth best [of all]; **ich hätte am l~sten geweint** I felt like crying. **L~ste(r)** *m/f* beloved; (*Schatz*) sweetheart
Lied *nt* **-[e]s,-er** song
liederlich *a* slovenly; (*unordentlich*) untidy; (*ausschweifend*) dissolute. **L~keit** *f* **-** slovenliness; untidiness; dissoluteness
Lieferant *m* **-en,-en** supplier
liefer|bar *a* (*Comm*) available. **l~n** *vt* supply; (*zustellen*) deliver; (*hervorbringen*) yield. **L~ung** *f* **-,-en** delivery; (*Sendung*) consignment; (*per Schiff*) shipment. **L~wagen** *m* delivery van
Liege *f* **-,-n** couch. **l~n**† *vi* (*haben*) lie; (*gelegen sein*) be situated; **l~n bleiben** remain lying [there]; (*im Bett*) stay in bed; ⟨*Ding:*⟩ be left; ⟨*Schnee:*⟩ settle; ⟨*Arbeit:*⟩ remain

undone; (*zurückgelassen werden*) be left behind; (*Panne haben*) break down; **l~n lassen** leave [lying there]; (*zurücklassen*) leave behind; (*nicht fortführen*) leave undone; **l~n an** (+ *dat*) (*fig*) be due to; (*abhängen*) depend on; **jdm [nicht] l~n** [not] suit s.o.; (*ansprechen*) [not] appeal to s.o.; **mir liegt viel/nicht daran** it is very/ not important to me. **l~nbleiben**† *vi sep* (*sein*) NEW **l~n bleiben**, *s.* **liegen**. **l~nlassen**† *vt sep* NEW **l~ lassen**, *s.* **liegen**. **L~sitz** *m* reclining seat. **L~stuhl** *m* deckchair. **L~stütz** *m* **-es,-e** press-up, (*Amer*) push-up. **L~wagen** *m* couchette car. **L~wiese** *f* lawn for sunbathing

Lift *m* **-[e]s,-e** & **-s** lift, (*Amer*) elevator

Liga *f* **-,-gen** league

Likör *m* **-s,-e** liqueur

lila *inv a* mauve; (*dunkel*) purple

Lilie /ˈli:liə/ *f* **-,-n** lily

Liliputaner(in) *m* **-s,-** (*f* **-,-nen**) dwarf

Limo *f* **-,-[s]** (*fam*), **L~nade** *f* **-,-n** fizzy drink, (*Amer*) soda; (*Zitronen-*) lemonade

Limousine /limuˈzi:nə/ *f* **-,-n** saloon, (*Amer*) sedan; (*mit Trennscheibe*) limousine

lind *a* mild; (*sanft*) gentle

Linde *f* **-,-n** lime tree

linder|n *vt* relieve, ease. **L~ung** *f* **-** relief

Line|al *nt* **-s,-e** ruler. **l~ar** *a* linear

Linguistik *f* **-** linguistics *sg*

Linie /-iə/ *f* **-,-n** line; (*Zweig*) branch; (*Bus-*) route; **L~ 4** number 4 [bus/tram]; **in erster L~** primarily. **L~nflug** *m* scheduled flight. **L~nrichter** *m* linesman

lin[i]iert *a* lined, ruled

Link|e *f* **-n,-n** left side; (*Hand*) left hand; (*Boxen*) left; **die L~e** (*Pol*) the left; **zu meiner L~en** on my left. **l~e(r,s)** *a* left; (*Pol*) leftwing; **l~e Seite** left[-hand] side; (*von Stoff*) wrong side; **l~e Masche** purl. **l~isch** *a* awkward, *adv* -ly

links *adv* on the left; (*bei Stoff*) on the wrong side; (*verkehrt*) inside out; **von/nach l~** from/to the left; **l~stricken** purl. **L~händer(in)** *m* **-s,-** (*f* **-,-nen**) lefthander. **l~händig** *a* & *adv* lefthanded. **L~verkehr** *m* driving on the left

Linoleum /-leʊm/ *nt* **-s** lino, linoleum

Linse *f* **-,-n** lens; (*Bot*) lentil

Lippe *f* **-,-n** lip. **L~nstift** *m* lipstick

Liquid|ation /-ˈtsi̯o:n/ *f* **-,-en** liquidation. **l~ieren** *vt* liquidate

lispeln *vt/i* (*haben*) lisp

List *f* **-,-en** trick, ruse; (*Listigkeit*) cunning

Liste *f* **-,-n** list

listig *a* cunning, crafty

Litanei *f* **-,-en** litany

Litauen *nt* **-s** Lithuania

Liter *m* & *nt* **-s,-** litre

liter|arisch *a* literary. **L~atur** *f* **-** literature

Litfaßsäule *f* advertising pillar

Liturgie *f* **-,-n** liturgy

Litze *f* **-,-n** braid; (*Electr*) flex

live /laif/ *adv* (*Radio, TV*) live

Lizenz *f* **-,-en** licence

Lkw /ɛlkaˈve:/ *m* **-[s],-s** = **Lastkraftwagen**

Lob *nt* **-[e]s** praise

Lobby /ˈlɔbi/ *f* **-** (*Pol*) lobby

loben *vt* praise. **l~swert** *a* praiseworthy, laudable

löblich *a* praiseworthy

Lobrede *f* eulogy

Loch *nt* **-[e]s,⸚er** hole. **l~en** *vt* punch a hole/holes in; punch ⟨*Fahrkarte*⟩. **L~er** *m* **-s,-** punch

löcher|ig *a* full of holes. **l~n** *vt* (*fam*) pester

Locke *f* **-,-n** curl. **l~n**[1] *vt* curl; **sich l~n** curl

locken[2] *vt* lure, entice; (*reizen*) tempt. **l~d** *a* tempting

Lockenwickler *m* **-s,-** curler; (*Rolle*) roller

locker *a* loose, *adv* -ly; ⟨*Seil*⟩ slack; ⟨*Erde, Kuchen*⟩ light; (*zwanglos*) casual; (*zu frei*) lax; (*unmoralisch*) loose. **l~n** *vt* loosen; slacken ⟨*Seil, Zügel*⟩; break up ⟨*Boden*⟩; relax ⟨*Griff*⟩; **sich l~n** become loose; ⟨*Seil:*⟩ slacken; (*sich entspannen*) relax. **L~ungsübungen** *fpl* limbering-up exercises

lockig *a* curly

Lock|mittel *nt* bait. **L~ung** *f* **-,-en** lure; (*Versuchung*) temptation. **L~vogel** *m* decoy

Loden *m* -s (*Tex*) loden

lodern *vi* (*haben*) blaze

Löffel *m* **-s,-** spoon; (*L~ voll*) spoonful. **l~n** *vt* spoon up

Logarithmus *m* **-,-men** logarithm

Logbuch *nt* (*Naut*) log-book

Loge /'lo:ʒə/ *f* **-,-n** lodge; (*Theat*) box

Logierbesuch /lo'ʒi:ɐ̯-/ *m* house guest|guests *pl*

Log|ik *f* - logic. **l~isch** *a* logical, *adv* -ly

Logo *nt* **-s,-s** logo

Lohn *m* **-[e]s,¨e** wages *pl*, pay; (*fig*) reward. **L~empfänger** *m* wage-earner. **l~en** *vi|r* (*haben*) **[sich] l~en** be worth it *or* worth while □ *vt* be worth; **jdm etw l~en** reward s.o. for sth. **l~end** *a* worthwhile; (*befriedigend*) rewarding. **L~erhöhung** *f* [pay] rise; (*Amer*) raise. **L~steuer** *f* income tax

Lok *f* -,-s (*fam*) = **Lokomotive**

Lokal *nt* -s,-e restaurant; (*Trink-*) bar. **l~** *a* local. **l~sieren** *vt* locate; (*begrenzen*) localize

Lokomotiv|e *f* -,-n engine, locomotive. **L~führer** *m* engine driver

London *nt* **-s** London. **L~er** *a* London ... □ *m* **-s,-** Londoner

Lorbeer *m* **-s,-en** laurel; **echter L~** bay. **L~blatt** *nt* (*Culin*) bay-leaf

Lore *f* **-,-n** (*Rail*) truck

Los *nt* **-es,-e** lot; (*Lotterie-*) ticket; (*Schicksal*) fate; **das große Los ziehen** hit the jackpot

los *pred a* **los sein** be loose; **jdn/etw los sein** be rid of s.o./sth; **was ist [mit ihm] los?** what's the matter [with him]? □ *adv* **los!** go on! **Achtung, fertig, los!** ready, steady, go!

lösbar *a* soluble

losbinden† *vt sep* untie

Lösch|blatt *nt* sheet of blotting-paper. **l~**[1] *vt* put out, extinguish; quench ⟨*Durst*⟩; blot ⟨*Tinte*⟩; (*tilgen*) cancel; (*streichen*) delete; erase ⟨*Aufnahme*⟩

löschen[2] *vt* (*Naut*) unload

Lösch|fahrzeug *nt* fire-engine. **L~gerät** *nt* fire extinguisher. **L~papier** *nt* blotting-paper

lose *a* loose, *adv* -ly

Lösegeld *nt* ransom

losen *vt* (*haben*) draw lots **(um** for)

lösen *vt* undo; (*lockern*) loosen; (*entfernen*) detach; (*klären*) solve; (*auflösen*) dissolve; cancel ⟨*Vertrag*⟩; break off ⟨*Beziehung, Verlobung*⟩; (*kaufen*) buy; **sich l~** come off; (*sich trennen*) detach oneself/itself; (*lose werden*) come undone; (*sich entspannen*) relax; (*sich klären*) resolve itself; (*sich auflösen*) dissolve

los|fahren† *vi sep* (*sein*) start; ⟨*Auto:*⟩ drive off; **l~fahren auf** (+ *acc*) head for; (*fig: angreifen*) go for. **l~gehen**† *vi sep* (*sein*) set off; (*fam: anfangen*) start; (*fam: abgehen*) come off; ⟨*Bombe, Gewehr:*⟩ go off; **l~gehen auf** (+ *acc*) head for; (*fig angreifen*) go for. **l~kommen**† *vi sep* (*sein*) get away (**von** from); **l~kommen auf** (+ *acc*) come towards. **l~lachen** *vi sep* (*haben*) burst out laughing. **l~lassen**† *vt sep* let go of; (*freilassen*) release

löslich *a* soluble

los|lösen *vt sep* detach; **sich l~lösen** become detached; (*fig*) break away (**von** from). **l~machen** *vt sep* detach; (*losbinden*) untie; **sich l~machen** free oneself/itself. **l~platzen** *vi sep* (*sein*) (*fam*) burst out laughing. **l~reißen**† *vt sep* tear off; **sich l~reißen** break free; (*fig*) tear oneself away. **l~sagen (sich)** *vr sep* renounce (**von etw** sth). **l~schicken** *vt sep* send off. **l~sprechen**† *vt sep* absolve (**von** from). **l~steuern** *vi sep* (*sein*) head (**auf** + *acc* for)

Losung *f* **-,-en** (*Pol*) slogan; (*Mil*) password

Lösung *f* **-,-en** solution. **L~smittel** *nt* solvent

los|werden† *vt sep* get rid of. **l~ziehen**† *vi sep* (*sein*) set off; **l~ziehen gegen** *od* **über** (+ *acc*) (*beschimpfen*) run down

Lot *nt* **-[e]s,-e** perpendicular; (*Blei-*) plumb[-bob]; **im Lot sein** (*fig*) be all right. **l~en** *vt* plumb

löt|en *vt* solder. **L~lampe** *f* blowlamp, (*Amer*) blowtorch. **L~metall** *nt* solder

lotrecht *a* perpendicular, *adv* -ly

Lotse *m* **-n,-n** (*Naut*) pilot. **l~n** *vt* (*Naut*) pilot; (*fig*) guide

Lotterie *f* **-,-n** lottery

Lotto *nt* **-s,-s** lotto; (*Lotterie*) lottery

Löw|e *m* **-n,-n** lion; (*Astr*) Leo. **L~enanteil** *m* (*fig*) lion's share. **L~enzahn** *m* (*Bot*) dandelion. **L~in** *f* **-,-nen** lioness

loyal /lo̦a'ja:l/ *a* loyal. **L~ität** *f* - loyalty

Luchs *m* **-es,-e** lynx

Lücke *f* **-,-n** gap. **L~nbüßer** *m* **-s,-** stopgap. **l~nhaft** *a* incomplete; ⟨*Wissen*⟩ patchy. **l~nlos** *a* complete; ⟨*Folge*⟩ unbroken

Luder *nt* **-s,-** (*sl*) (*Frau*) bitch; **armes L~** poor wretch

Luft *f* **-,¨e** air; **tief L~ holen** take a deep breath; **in die L~ gehen** explode. **L~angriff** *m* air raid. **L~aufnahme** *f* aerial photograph. **L~ballon** *m* balloon. **L~bild** *nt* aerial photograph. **L~blase** *f* air bubble

Lüftchen *nt* **-s,-** breeze

luft|dicht *a* airtight. **L~druck** *m* atmospheric pressure

lüften *vt* air; raise ⟨*Hut*⟩; reveal ⟨*Geheimnis*⟩

Luft|fahrt *f* aviation. **L~fahrtgesellschaft** *f* airline. **L~gewehr** *nt* airgun. **L~hauch** *m* breath of air. **l~ig** *a* airy; ⟨*Kleid*⟩ light. **L~kissenfahrzeug** *nt* hovercraft. **L~krieg** *m* aerial warfare. **L~kurort** *m* climatic health resort. **l~leer** *a* **l~leerer Raum** vacuum. **L~linie** *f* **100 km L~linie** 100 km as the crow flies. **L~loch** *nt* air-hole; (*Aviat*) air pocket. **L~matratze** *f* airbed, inflatable mattress. **L~pirat** *m* [aircraft] hijacker. **L~post** *f* airmail. **L~pumpe** *f* air pump; (*Fahrrad-*) bicycle-pump. **L~röhre** *f* windpipe. **L~schiff** *nt* airship. **L~schlange** *f* [paper] streamer. **L~schlösser** *ntpl* castles in the air. **L~schutzbunker** *m* air-raid shelter

Lüftung *f* - ventilation

Luft|veränderung *f* change of air. **L~waffe** *f* air force. **L~weg** *m* **auf dem L~weg** by air. **L~zug** *m* draught

Lüg|e *f* **-,-n** lie. **l~en**† *vt/i* (*haben*) lie. **L~ner(in)** *m* **-s,-** (*f* **-,-nen**) liar. **l~nerisch** *a* untrue; ⟨*Person*⟩ untruthful

Luke *f* **-,-n** hatch; (*Dach-*) skylight

Lümmel *m* **-s,-** lout; (*fam: Schelm*) rascal. **l~n (sich)** *vr* loll

Lump *m* **-en,-en** scoundrel. **L~en** *m* **-s,-** rag; **in ~en** in rags. **l~en** *vt* **sich nicht l~en lassen** be generous. **L~engesindel, L~enpack** *nt*

riff-raff. **L~ensammler** *m* rag-and-bone man. **l~ig** *a* mean, shabby; (*gering*) measley

Lunchpacket /ˈlan[t]ʃ-/ *nt* packed lunch

Lunge *f* -,-n lungs *pl*; (*L~nflügel*) lung. **L~nentzündung** *f* pneumonia

lungern *vi* (*haben*) loiter

Lunte *f* **L~ riechen** (*fam*) smell a rat

Lupe *f* -,-n magnifying glass

Lurch *m* -[e]s,-e amphibian

Lust *f* -,¨e pleasure; (*Verlangen*) desire; (*sinnliche Begierde*) lust; **L~ haben** feel like (**auf etw** *acc* sth); **ich habe keine L~** I don't feel like it; (*will nicht*) I don't want to

Lüster *m* -s,- lustre; (*Kronleuchter*) chandelier

lüstern *a* greedy (**auf** + *acc* for); (*sinnlich*) lascivious; (*geil*) lecherous

lustig *a* jolly; (*komisch*) funny; **sich l~ machen über** (+ *acc*) make fun of

Lüstling *m* -s,-e lecher

lust|los *a* listless, *adv* -ly. **L~mörder** *m* sex killer. **L~spiel** *nt* comedy

lutherisch *a* Lutheran

lutsch|en *vt/i* (*haben*) suck. **L~er** *m* -s,- lollipop; (*Schnuller*) dummy, (*Amer*) pacifier

lütt *a* (*NGer*) little

Lüttich *nt* -s Liège

Luv *f* & *nt* - **nach Luv** (*Naut*) to windward

luxuriös *a* luxurious, *adv* -ly

Luxus *m* - luxury. **L~artikel** *m* luxury article. **L~ausgabe** *f* de luxe edition. **L~hotel** *nt* luxury hotel

Lymph|drüse /ˈlʏmf-/ *f*, **L~knoten** *m* lymph gland

lynchen /ˈlʏnçən/ *vt* lynch

Lyr|ik *f* - lyric poetry. **L~iker** *m* -s,- lyric poet. **l~isch** *a* lyrical; ⟨*Dichtung*⟩ lyric

M

Mach|art *f* style. **m~bar** *a* feasible. **m~en** *vt* make; get ⟨*Mahlzeit*⟩; take ⟨*Foto*⟩; (*ausführen, tun, in Ordnung bringen*) do; (*Math: ergeben*) be; (*kosten*) come to, **sich** (*dat*) **etw m~en lassen** have sth made; **was m~st du da?** what are you doing? **was m~t die Arbeit?** how is work? **das m~t 6 Mark [zusammen]** that's 6 marks [altogether]; **das m~t nichts** it doesn't matter; **sich** (*dat*) **wenig/nichts m~en aus** care little/ nothing for □ *vr* **sich m~en** do well; **sich an die Arbeit m~en** get down to work □ *vi* (*haben*) **ins Bett m~en** (*fam*) wet the bed; **schnell m~en** hurry. **M~enschaften** *fpl* machinations

Macht *f* -,¨e power; **mit aller M~** with all one's might. **M~haber** *m* -s,- ruler

mächtig *a* powerful; (*groß*) enormous □ *adv* (*fam*) terribly

macht|los *a* powerless. **M~wort** *nt* **ein M~wort sprechen** put one's foot down

Mädchen *nt* -s,- girl; (*Dienst-*) maid. **m~haft** *a* girlish. **M~name** *m* girl's name; (*vor der Ehe*) maiden name

Made *f* -,-n maggot

Mädel *nt* -s,- girl

madig *a* maggoty; **jdn m~ machen** (*fam*) run s.o. down

Madonna *f* -,-nen madonna

Magazin *nt* -s,-e magazine; (*Lager*) warehouse; (*Raum*) store-room

Magd *f* -,¨e maid

Magen *m* **-s,-** stomach. **M~schmerzen** *mpl* stomach-ache *sg*. **M~verstimmung** *f* stomach upset

mager *a* thin; ⟨*Fleisch*⟩ lean; ⟨*Boden*⟩ poor; (*dürftig*) meagre. **M~keit** *f* - thinness; leanness. **M~sucht** *f* anorexia

Magie *f* - magic

Mag|ier /ˈmaːgi̯ɐ/ *m* **-s,-** magician. **m~isch** *a* magic; (*geheimnisvoll*) magical

Magistrat *m* **-s,-e** city council

Magnesia *f* - magnesia

Magnet *m* **-en & -[e]s,-e** magnet. **m~isch** *a* magnetic. **m~isieren** *vt* magnetize. **M~ismus** *m* - magnetism

Mahagoni *nt* **-s** mahogany

Mäh|drescher *m* **-s,-** combine harvester. **m~en** *vt/i* (*haben*) mow

Mahl *nt* **-[e]s,¨er & -e** meal

mahlen† *vt* grind

Mahlzeit *f* meal; **M~!** enjoy your meal!

Mähne *f* **-,-n** mane

mahn|en *vt/i* (*haben*) remind (**wegen** about); (*ermahnen*) admonish; (*auffordern*) urge (**zu** to); **zur Vorsicht/Eile m~en** urge caution/haste. **M~ung** *f* **-,-en** reminder; admonition; (*Aufforderung*) exhortation

Mai *m* **-[e]s,-e** May; **der Erste Mai** May Day. **M~glöckchen** *nt* **-s,-** lily of the valley. **M~käfer** *m* cockchafer

Mailand *nt* **-s** Milan

Mais *m* **-es** maize, (*Amer*) corn; (*Culin*) sweet corn. **M~kolben** *m* corn-cob

Majestät *f* **-,-en** majesty. **m~isch** *a* majestic, *adv* -ally

Major *m* **-s,-e** major

Majoran *m* **-s** marjoram

Majorität *f* **-,-en** majority

makaber *a* macabre

Makel *m* **-s,-** blemish; (*Defekt*) flaw; (*fig*) stain. **m~los** *a* flawless; (*fig*) unblemished

mäkeln *vi* (*haben*) grumble

Makkaroni *pl* macaroni *sg*

Makler *m* **-s,-** (*Comm*) broker

Makrele *f* **-,-n** mackerel

Makrone *f* **-,-n** macaroon

mal *adv* (*Math*) times; (*bei Maßen*) by; (*fam: einmal*) once; (*eines Tages*) one day; **schon mal** once before; (*jemals*) ever; **nicht mal** not even; **hört/seht mal!** listen!/look!

Mal[1] *nt* **-[e]s,-e** time; **das erste/zweite/letzte/nächste Mal** the first/second/last/next time; **zum ersten/letzten Mal** for the first/last time; **mit einem Mal** all at once; **ein für alle Mal** once and for all; **jedes Mal** every time; **jedes Mal, wenn** whenever; **einige/mehrere Mal** a few/several times

Mal[2] *nt* **-[e]s,-e** mark; (*auf der Haut*) mole; (*Mutter-*) birthmark

Mal|buch *nt* colouring book. **m~en** *vt/i* (*haben*) paint. **M~er** *m* **-s,-** painter. **M~erei** *f* **-,-en** painting. **M~erin** *f* **-,-nen** painter. **m~erisch** *a* picturesque

Malheur /maˈløːɐ̯/ *nt* **-s,-e & -s** (*fam*) mishap; (*Ärger*) trouble

Mallorca /maˈlɔrka, -ˈjɔrka/ *nt* **-s** Majorca

malnehmen† *vt sep* multiply (**mit** by)

Malz *nt* **-es** malt. **M~bier** *nt* malt beer

Mama /ˈmama, maˈmaː/ *f* **-s,-s** mummy

Mammut *nt* **-s,-e & -s** mammoth

mampfen *vt* (*fam*) munch

man *pron* one, you; (*die Leute*) people, they; **man sagt** they say, it is said

Manager /ˈmɛnɪdʒɐ/ *m* **-s,-** manager

manch *inv pron* **m~ ein(e)** many a; **m~ einer/eine** many a man/woman. **m~e(r,s)** *pron* many a; **[so] m~es Mal** many a time;

m~e Leute some people □ (*substantivisch*) **m~er/m~e** many a man/woman; **m~e** *pl* some; (*Leute*) some people; (*viele*) many [people]; **m~es** some things; (*vieles*) many things. **m~erlei** *inv a* various □ *pron* various things

manchmal *adv* sometimes

Mandant(in) *m* **-en,-en** (*f* **-,-nen**) (*Jur*) client

Mandarine *f* **-,-n** mandarin

Mandat *nt* **-[e]s,-e** mandate; (*Jur*) brief; (*Pol*) seat

Mandel *f* **-,-n** almond; (*Anat*) tonsil. **M~entzündung** *f* tonsillitis

Manege /ma'ne:ʒə/ *f* **-,-n** ring; (*Reit-*) arena

Mangel[1] *m* **-s,¨** lack; (*Knappheit*) shortage; (*Med*) deficiency; (*Fehler*) defect; **M~ leiden** go short

Mangel[2] *f* **-,-n** mangle

mangel|haft *a* faulty, defective; (*Sch*) unsatisfactory. **m~n**[1] *vi* (*haben*) **es m~t an** (+ *dat*) there is a lack/(*Knappheit*) shortage of

mangeln[2] *vt* put through the mangle

mangels *prep* (+ *gen*) for lack of

Mango *f* **-,-s** mango

Manie *f* **-,-n** mania; (*Sucht*) obsession

Manier *f* **-,-en** manner; **M~en** manners. **m~lich** *a* well-mannered □ *adv* properly

Manifest *nt* **-[e]s,-e** manifesto. **m~ieren (sich)** *vr* manifest itself

Maniküre *f* **-,-n** manicure; (*Person*) manicurist. **m~n** *vt* manicure

Manipul|ation /-'tsio:n/ *f* **-,-en** manipulation. **m~ieren** *vt* manipulate

Manko *nt* **-s,-s** disadvantage; (*Fehlbetrag*) deficit

Mann *m* **-[e]s,¨er** man; (*Ehe-*) husband

Männchen *nt* **-s,-** little man; (*Zool*) male; **M~ machen** ⟨*Hund:*⟩ sit up

Mannequin /'manəkɛ̃/ *nt* **-s,-s** model

Männerchor *m* male voice choir

Mannes|alter *nt* manhood. **M~kraft** *f* virility

mannhaft *a* manful, *adv* -ly

mannigfaltig *a* manifold; (*verschieden*) diverse

männlich *a* male; (*Gram & fig*) masculine; (*mannhaft*) manly; ⟨*Frau*⟩ mannish. **M~keit** *f* - masculinity; (*fig*) manhood

Mannschaft *f* **-,-en** team; (*Naut*) crew. **M~sgeist** *m* team spirit

Manöv|er *nt* **-s,-** manœuvre; (*Winkelzug*) trick. **m~rieren** *vt/i* (*haben*) manœuvre

Mansarde *f* **-,-n** attic room; (*Wohnung*) attic flat

Manschette *f* **-,-n** cuff; (*Blumentopf-*) paper frill. **M~nknopf** *m* cuff-link

Mantel *m* **-s,¨** coat; (*dick*) overcoat; (*Reifen-*) outer tyre

Manuskript *nt* **-[e]s,-e** manuscript

Mappe *f* **-,-n** folder; (*Akten-*) briefcase; (*Schul-*) bag

Marathon *m* **-s,-s** marathon

Märchen *nt* **-s,-** fairy-tale. **m~haft** *a* fairy-tale . . .; (*phantastisch*) fabulous

Margarine *f* - margarine

Marienkäfer /ma'ri:ən-/ *m* ladybird, (*Amer*) ladybug

Marihuana *nt* **-s** marijuana

Marille *f* **-,-n** (*Aust*) apricot

Marinade *f* **-,-n** marinade

Marine *f* marine; (*Kriegs-*) navy. **m~blau** *a* navy [blue]. **M~infanterist** *m* marine

marinieren *vt* marinade

Marionette *f* **-,-n** puppet, marionette

Mark[1] *f* **-,-** mark; **drei M~** three marks

Mark2 *nt* **-[e]s** (*Knochen-*) marrow (*Bot*)pith; (*Frucht-*) pulp; **bis ins M~ getroffen** (*fig*) cut to the quick
markant *a* striking
Marke *f* **-,-n** token; (*rund*) disc; (*Erkennungs-*) tag; (*Brief-*) stamp; (*Lebensmittel-*) coupon; (*Spiel-*) counter; (*Markierung*) mark; (*Fabrikat*) make; (*Tabak-*) brand. **M~nartikel** *m* branded article
markier|en *vt* mark; (*fam: vortäuschen*) fake. **M~ung** *f* **-,-en** marking
Markise *f* **-,-n** awning
Markstück *nt* one-mark piece
Markt *m* **-[e]s,¨e** market; (*M~platz*) market-place. **M~forschung** *f* market research. **M~platz** *m* market-place
Marmelade *f* **-,-n** jam; (*Orangen-*) marmalade
Marmor *m* **-s** marble
Marokko *nt* **-s** Morocco
Marone *f* **-,-n** [sweet] chestnut
Marotte *f* **-,-n** whim
Marsch1 *f* **-,-en** marsh
Marsch2 *m* **-[e]s,¨e** march. **m~** *int* (*Mil*) march! **m~ ins Bett!** off to bed!
Marschall *m* **-s,¨e** marshal
marschieren *vi* (*sein*) march
Marter *f* **-,-n** torture. **m~n** *vt* torture
Martinshorn *nt* [police] siren
Märtyrer(in) *m* **-s,-** (*f* **-,-nen**) martyr
Martyrium *nt* **-s** martyrdom
Mar|xismus *m* **-** Marxism. **m~xistisch** *a* Marxist
März *m* **-,-e** March
Marzipan *nt* **-s** marzipan
Masche *f* **-,-n** stitch; (*im Netz*) mesh; (*fam: Trick*) dodge. **M~ndraht** *m* wire netting
Maschin|e *f* **-,-n** machine; (*Flugzeug*) plane; (*Schreib-*) typewriter; **M~e schreiben** type. **m~egeschrieben** *a* typewritten, typed. **m~ell** *a* machine . . . □ *adv* by machine. **M~enbau** *m* mechanical engineering. **M~engewehr** *nt* machine-gun. **M~enpistole** *f* sub-machine-gun. **M~erie** *f* **-** machinery. **M~eschreiben** *nt* typing. **M~ist** *m* **-en,-en** machinist; (*Naut*) engineer
Masern *pl* measles *sg*
Maserung *f* **-,-en** [wood] grain
Maske *f* **-,-n** mask; (*Theat*) make-up. **M~rade** *f* **-,-n** disguise; (*fig: Heuchelei*) masquerade
maskieren *vt* mask; **sich m~** dress up (**als** as)
Maskottchen *nt* **-s,-** mascot
maskulin *a* masculine
Maskulinum *nt* **-s,-na** (*Gram*) masculine
Masochis|mus /mazo'xɪsmʊs/ *m* **-** masochism. **M~t** *m* **-en,-en** masochist
Maß1 *nt* **-es,-e** measure; (*Abmessung*) measurement; (*Grad*) degree; (*Mäßigung*) moderation; **Maß halten** exercise moderation; **in** *od* **mit Maß[en]** in moderation; **in hohem Maße** to a high degree
Maß2 *f* **-,-** (*SGer*) litre [of beer]
Massage /ma'sa:ʒə/ *f* **-,-n** massage
Massaker *nt* **-s,-** massacre
Maß|anzug *m* made-to-measure suit. **M~band** *nt* (*pl* **-bänder**) tape-measure
Masse *f* **-,-n** mass; (*Culin*) mixture; (*Menschen-*) crowd; **eine M~ Arbeit** (*fam*) masses of work. **M~nartikel** *m* mass-produced article. **m~nhaft** *adv* in huge quantities. **M~nmedien** *pl* mass media. **M~nproduktion** *f* mass production. **m~nweise** *adv* in huge numbers
Masseu|r /ma'sø:ɐ̯/ *m* **-s,-e** masseur. **M~rin** *f* **-,-nen, M~se** /-'sø:zə/ *f* **-,-n** masseuse
maß|gebend *a* authoritative; (*einflussreich*) influential. **m~geblich** *a* decisive, *adv* -ly.

m~geschneidert *a* made-to-measure. **m~halten†** *vi sep* (*haben*) (NEW) **Maß halten**, *s.* **Maß**[1]
massieren[1] *vt* massage
massieren[2] **(sich)** *vr* mass
massig *a* massive
mäßig *a* moderate, *adv* -ly; (*mittelmäßig*) indifferent. **m~en** *vt* moderate; **sich m~en** moderate; (*sich beherrschen*) restrain oneself. **M~keit** *f* - moderation. **M~ung** *f* - moderation
massiv *a* solid; (*stark*) heavy
Maß|krug *m* beer mug. **m~los** *a* excessive; (*grenzenlos*) boundless; (*äußerst*) extreme, *adv* -ly. **M~nahme** *f* -,-n measure. **m~regeln** *vt* reprimand
Maßstab *m* scale; (*Norm & fig*) standard. **m~sgerecht, m~sgetreu** *a* scale ... □ *adv* to scale
maßvoll *a* moderate
Mast[1] *m* **-[e]s,-en** pole; (*Überland-*) pylon; (*Naut*) mast
Mast[2] *f* - fattening. **M~darm** *m* rectum
mästen *vt* fatten
Masturb|ation /-ˈtsi̯o:n/ *f* - masturbation. **m~ieren** *vi* (*haben*) masturbate
Material *nt* **-s,-ien** /-i̯ən/ material; (*coll*) materials *pl*. **M~ismus** *m* - materialism. **m~istisch** *a* materialistic
Mater|ie /maˈte:ri̯ə/ *f* **-,-n** matter; (*Thema*) subject. **m~iell** *a* material
Mathe *f* - (*fam*) maths *sg*
Mathe|matik *f* - mathematics *sg*. **M~matiker** *m* **-s,-** mathematician. **m~matisch** *a* mathematical
Matinee *f* **-,-n** (*Theat*) morning performance
Matratze *f* **-,-n** mattress
Mätresse *f* **-,-n** mistress
Matrose *m* **-n,-n** sailor
Matsch *m* **-[e]s** mud; (*Schnee-*) slush. **m~ig** *a* muddy; slushy; (*weich*) mushy

matt *a* weak; (*gedämpft*) dim; (*glanzlos*) dull; ⟨*Politur, Farbe*⟩ matt; **jdn m~ setzen** checkmate s.o. **M~** *nt* **-s** (*Schach*) mate
Matte *f* **-,-n** mat
Mattglas *nt* frosted glass
Matt|igkeit *f* - weakness; (*Müdigkeit*) weariness. **M~scheibe** *f* (*fam*) television screen
Matura *f* - (*Aust*) ≈ A levels *pl*
Mauer *f* **-,-n** wall. **m~n** *vt* build □ *vi* (*haben*) lay bricks. **M~werk** *nt* masonry
Maul *nt* **-[e]s, Mäuler** (*Zool*) mouth; **halt's M~!** (*fam*) shut up! **m~en** *vi* (*haben*) (*fam*) grumble. **M~korb** *m* muzzle. **M~tier** *nt* mule. **M~wurf** *m* mole. **M~wurfshaufen, M~wurfshügel** *m* molehill
Maurer *m* **-s,-** bricklayer
Maus *f* **-,Mäuse** mouse. **M~efalle** *f* mousetrap
mausern (sich) *vr* moult; (*fam*) turn **(zu** into)
Maut *f* **-,-en** (*Aust*) toll. **M~straße** *f* toll road
maximal *a* maximum
Maximum *nt* **-s,-ma** maximum
Mayonnaise /majɔˈnɛ:zə/ *f* **-,-n** mayonnaise
Mäzen *m* **-s,-e** patron
Mechan|ik /meˈça:nɪk/ *f* - mechanics *sg*; (*Mechanismus*) mechanism. **M~iker** *m* **-s,-** mechanic. **m~isch** *a* mechanical, *adv* -ly. **m~isieren** *vt* mechanize. **M~ismus** *m* **-,-men** mechanism
meckern *vi* (*haben*) bleat; (*fam: nörgeln*) grumble
Medaill|e /meˈdaljə/ *f* **-,-n** medal. **M~on** /-ˈjõ:/ *nt* **-s,-s** medallion (*Schmuck*) locket
Medikament *nt* **-[e]s,-e** medicine
Medit|ation /-ˈtsi̯o:n/ *f* **-,-en** meditation. **m~ieren** *vi* (*haben*) meditate
Medium *nt* **-s,-ien** medium; **die Medien** the media

Medizin *f* **-,-en** medicine. **M~er** *m* **-s,-** doctor; (*Student*) medical student. **m~isch** *a* medical; (*heilkräftig*) medicinal

Meer *nt* **-[e]s,-e** sea. **M~busen** *m* gulf. **M~enge** *f* strait. **M~esspiegel** *m* sea-level. **M~jungfrau** *f* mermaid. **M~rettich** *m* horseradish. **M~schweinchen** *nt* **-s,-** guinea-pig

Megaphon, Megafon *nt* **-s,-e** megaphone

Mehl *nt* **-[e]s** flour. **m~ig** *a* floury. **M~schwitze** *f* (*Culin*) roux. **M~speise** *f* (*Aust*) dessert; (*Kuchen*) pastry. **M~tau** *m* (*Bot*) mildew

mehr *pron & adv* more; **nicht m~** no more; (*zeitlich*) no longer; **nichts m~** no more; (*nichts weiter*) nothing else; **nie m~** never again. **m~deutig** *a* ambiguous. **m~en** *vt* increase; **sich m~en** increase. **m~ere** *pron* several. **m~eremal** *adv* (NEW) **m~ere Mal,** *s.* **Mal. m~eres** *pron* several things *pl.* **m~fach** *a* multiple; (*mehrmalig*) repeated □ *adv* several times. **M~fahrtenkarte** *f* book of tickets. **m~farbig** *a* [multi]coloured. **M~heit** *f* **-,-en** majority. **m~malig** *a* repeated. **m~mals** *adv* several times. **m~sprachig** *a* multilingual. **m~stimmig** *a* (*Mus*) for several voices □ *adv* **m~stimmig singen** sing in harmony. **M~wertsteuer** *f* value-added tax, VAT. **M~zahl** *f* majority; (*Gram*) plural. **M~zweck-** *pref* multi-purpose

meiden† *vt* avoid, shun

Meierei *f* **-,-en** (*dial*) dairy

Meile *f* **-,-n** mile. **M~nstein** *m* milestone. **m~nweit** *adv* [for] miles

mein *poss pron* my. **m~e(r,s)** *poss pron* mine; **die M~en** *od* **m~en** *pl* my family *sg*

Meineid *m* perjury; **einen M~ leisten** perjure oneself

meinen *vt* mean; (*glauben*) think; (*sagen*) say; **gut gemeinter Rat** wel-meant advice; **es gut m~** mean well

mein|erseits *adv* for my part. **m~etwegen** *adv* for my sake; (*wegen mir*) because of me, on my account; (*fam: von mir aus*) as far as I'm concerned. **m~etwillen** *adv* **um m~etwillen** for my sake. **m~ige** *poss pron* **der/die/das m~ige** mine. **m~s** *poss pron* mine

Meinung *f* **-,-en** opinion; **jdm die M~ sagen** give s.o. a piece of one's mind. **M~sumfrage** *f* opinion poll

Meise *f* **-,-n** (*Zool*) tit

Meißel *m* **-s,-** chisel. **m~n** *vt/i* (*haben*) chisel

meist *adv* mostly; (*gewöhnlich*) usually. **m~e** *a* **der/die/das m~e** most; **die m~en Leute** most people; **die m~e Zeit** most of the time; **am m~en** [the] most □ *pron* **das m~e** most [of it]; **die m~en** most. **m~ens** *adv* mostly; (*gewöhnlich*) usually

Meister *m* **-s,-** master craftsman; (*Könner*) master; (*Sport*) champion. **m~haft** *a* masterly □ *adv* in masterly fashion. **m~n** *vt* master. **M~schaft** *f* **-,-en** mastery; (*Sport*) championship. **M~stück, M~werk** *nt* masterpiece

Melanch|olie /melaŋko'li:/ *f* - melancholy. **m~olisch** *a* melancholy

meld|en *vt* report; (*anmelden*) register; (*ankündigen*) announce; **sich m~en** report (**bei** to); (*zum Militär*) enlist; (*freiwillig*) volunteer; (*Teleph*) answer; (*Sch*) put up one's hand; (*von sich hören lassen*) get in touch (**bei** with); **sich krank m~en** (NEW) **sich krankmelden. M~ung** *f* **-,-en** report; (*Anmeldung*) registration

meliert *a* mottled; **grau m~es Haar** hair flecked with grey

melken† *vt* milk

Melod|ie *f* **-,-n** tune, melody. **m~iös** *a* melodious
melodisch *a* melodic; (*melodiös*) melodious, tuneful
melodramatisch *a* melodramatic, *adv* -ally
Melone *f* **-,-n** melon; **[schwarze] M~** (*fam*) bowler [hat]
Membran *f* **-,-en** membrane
Memoiren /me'moa:rən/ *pl* memoirs
Menge *f* **-,-n** amount, quantity; (*Menschen-*) crowd; (*Math*) set; **eine M~ Geld** a lot of money. **m~n** *vt* mix
Mensa *f* **-,-sen** (*Univ*) refectory
Mensch *m* **-en,-en** human being; **der M~** man; **die M~en** people; **jeder/kein M~** everybody/nobody. **M~enaffe** *m* ape. **M~enfeind** *m* misanthropist. **m~enfeindlich** *a* antisocial. **M~enfresser** *m* **-s,-** cannibal; (*Zool*) man-eater; (*fam*) ogre. **m~enfreundlich** *a* philanthropic. **M~enleben** *nt* human life; (*Lebenszeit*) lifetime. **m~enleer** *a* deserted. **M~enmenge** *f* crowd. **M~enraub** *m* kidnapping. **M~enrechte** *ntpl* human rights. **m~enscheu** *a* unsociable. **M~enskind** *int* (*fam*) good heavens! **M~enverstand** *m* **gesunder M~enverstand** common sense. **m~enwürdig** *a* humane, *adv* -ly. **M~heit** *f* - **die M~heit** mankind, humanity. **m~lich** *a* human; (*human*) humane, *adv* -ly. **M~lichkeit** *f* - humanity
Menstru|ation /-'tsio:n/ *f* - menstruation. **m~ieren** *vi* (*haben*) menstruate
Mentalität *f* **-,-en** mentality
Menü *nt* **-s,-s** menu; (*festes M~*) set meal
Menuett *nt* **-[e]s,-e** minuet
Meridian *m* **-s,-e** meridian
merk|bar *a* noticeable. **M~blatt** *nt* [explanatory] leaflet. **m~en** *vt* notice; **sich** (*dat*) **etw m~en** remember sth. **m~lich** *a* noticeable, *adv* -bly. **M~mal** *nt* feature
merkwürdig *a* odd, *adv* -ly, strange, *adv* -ly. **m~erweise** *adv* oddly enough
mess|bar (**meß|bar**) *a* measurable. **M~becher** *m* (*Culin*) measure
Messe[1] *f* **-,-n** (*Relig*) mass; (*Comm*) [trade] fair
Messe[2] *f* **-,-n** (*Mil*) mess
messen† *vt/i* (*haben*) measure; (*ansehen*) look at; **[bei jdm] Fieber m~** take s.o.'s temperature; **sich m~** compete (**mit** with); **sich mit jdm m~/nicht m~ können** be a/no match for s.o.
Messer *nt* **-s,-** knife
Messias *m* - Messiah
Messing *nt* **-s** brass
Messung *f* **-,-en** measurement
Metabolismus *m* - metabolism
Metall *nt* **-s,-e** metal. **m~en** *a* metal; (*metallisch*) metallic. **m~isch** *a* metallic
Metallurgie *f* - metallurgy
Metamorphose *f* **-,-n** metamorphosis
Metaph|er *f* **-,-n** metaphor. **m~orisch** *a* metaphorical, *adv* -ly
Meteor *m* **-s,-e** meteor. **M~ologe** *m* **-n,-n** meteorologist. **M~ologie** *f* - meteorology. **m~ologisch** *a* meteorological
Meter *m & nt* **-s,-** metre, (*Amer*) meter. **M~maß** *nt* tape-measure
Method|e *f* **-,-n** method. **m~isch** *a* methodical
metrisch *a* metric
Metropole *f* **-,-n** metropolis
metzeln *vt* (*fig*) massacre
Metzger *m* **-s,-** butcher. **M~ei** *f* **-,-en** butcher's shop
Meute *f* **-,-n** pack [of hounds]; (*fig: Menge*) mob
Meuterei *f* **-,-en** mutiny
meutern *vi* (*haben*) mutiny; (*fam: schimpfen*) grumble

Mexikan|er(in) *m* **-s,-** (*f* **-,-nen**) Mexican. **m~isch** *a* Mexican

Mexiko *nt* **-s** Mexico

miauen *vi* (*haben*) mew, miaow

mich *pron* (*acc of* **ich**) me; (*refl*) myself

Mieder *nt* **-s,-** bodice; (*Korsett*) corset

Miene *f* **-,-n** expression; **M~ machen** make as if (**zu** to)

mies *a* (*fam*) lousy; **mir ist m~** I feel rotten

Miet|e *f* **-,-n** rent; (*Mietgebühr*) hire charge; **zur M~e wohnen** live in rented accommodation. **m~en** *vt* rent ⟨*Haus, Zimmer*⟩; hire ⟨*Auto, Boot, Fernseher*⟩. **M~er(in)** *m* **-s,-** (*f* **-,-nen**) tenant. **m~frei** *a & adv* rent-free. **M~shaus** *nt* block of rented flats. **M~vertrag** *m* lease. **M~wagen** *m* hire-car. **M~wohnung** *f* rented flat; (*zu vermieten*) flat to let

Mieze *f* **-,-n** (*fam*) puss[y]

Migräne *f* **-,-n** migraine

Mikrobe *f* **-,-n** microbe

Mikro|chip *m* microchip. **M~computer** *m* microcomputer. **M~film** *m* microfilm

Mikro|fon, M~phon *nt* **-s,-e** microphone. **M~prozessor** *m* **-s,-en** /-ˈsoːrən/ microprocessor. **M~skop** *nt* **-s,-e** microscope. **m~skopisch** *a* microscopic

Mikrowelle *f* microwave. **M~ngerät** *nt*, **M~nherd** *m* microwave oven

Milbe *f* **-,-n** mite

Milch *f* **-** milk. **M~bar** *f* milk bar. **M~geschäft** *nt* dairy. **M~glas** *nt* opal glass. **m~ig** *a* milky. **M~kuh** *f* dairy cow. **M~mann** *m* (*pl* **-männer**) milkman. **M~mixgetränk** *nt* milk shake. **M~straße** *f* Milky Way. **M~zahn** *m* milk tooth

mild *a* mild; (*nachsichtig*) lenient; **m~e Gaben** alms. **M~e** *f* **-** mildness; leniency. **m~ern** *vt* make milder; (*mäßigen*) moderate; (*lindern*) alleviate, ease; **sich m~ern** become milder; (*sich mäßigen*) moderate; (*nachlassen*) abate; ⟨*Schmerz:*⟩ ease; **m~ernde Umstände** mitigating circumstances. **m~tätig** *a* charitable

Milieu /miˈli̯øː/ *nt* **-s,-s** [social] environment

militant *a* militant

Militär *nt* **-s** army; (*Soldaten*) troops *pl*; **beim M~** in the army. **m~isch** *a* military

Miliz *f* **-,-en** militia

Milliarde /mɪˈli̯ardə/ *f* **-,-n** thousand million, billion

Milli|gramm *nt* milligram. **M~meter** *m & nt* millimetre. **M~meterpapier** *nt* graph paper

Million /mɪˈli̯oːn/ *f* **-,-en** million. **M~är** *m* **-s,-e** millionaire. **M~ärin** *f* **-,-nen** millionairess

Milz *f* **-** (*Anat*) spleen

mim|en *vt* (*fam: vortäuschen*) act. **M~ik** *f* **-** [expressive] gestures and facial expressions *pl*

Mimose *f* **-,-n** mimosa

minder *a* lesser □ *adv* less; **mehr oder m~** more or less. **M~heit** *f* **-,-en** minority

minderjährig *a* (*Jur*) under-age; **m~ sein** be under age. **M~e(r)** *m/f* (*Jur*) minor. **M~keit** *f* **-** (*Jur*) minority

minder|n *vt* diminish; decrease ⟨*Tempo*⟩. **M~ung** *f* **-** decrease

minderwertig *a* inferior. **M~keit** *f* **-** inferiority. **M~keitskomplex** *m* inferiority complex

Mindest- *pref* minimum. **m~e** *a & pron* **der/die/das M~e** *od* **m~e** the least; **zum M~en** *od* **m~en** at least; **nicht im M~en** *od* **m~en** not in the least. **m~ens** *adv* at least. **M~lohn** *m* minimum wage. **M~maß** *nt* minimum

Mine *f* **-,-n** mine; (*Bleistift-*) lead; (*Kugelschreiber-*) refill. **M~nfeld** *nt* minefield. **M~nräumboot** *nt* minesweeper

Mineral *nt* **-s,-e & -ien** /-i̯ən/ mineral. **m~isch** *a* mineral. **M~ogie** *f* - mineralogy. **M~wasser** *nt* mineral water

Miniatur *f* **-,-en** miniature

Minigolf *nt* miniature golf

minimal *a* minimal

Minimum *nt* **-s,-ma** minimum

Minirock *m* miniskirt

Minilster *m*, **-s,-** minister. **m~steriell** *a* ministerial. **M~sterium** *nt* **-s,-ien** ministry

Minorität *f* **-,-en** minority

minus *conj, adv & prep* (+ *gen*) minus. **M~** *nt* **-** deficit; (*Nachteil*) disadvantage. **M~zeichen** *nt* minus [sign]

Minute *f* **-,-n** minute

mir *pron* (*dat of* **ich**) [to] me; (*refl*) myself; **mir nichts, dir nichts** without so much as a 'by your leave'

Misch|ehe *f* mixed marriage. **m~en** *vt* mix; blend ⟨*Tee, Kaffee*⟩; toss ⟨*Salat*⟩; shuffle ⟨*Karten*⟩; **sich m~en** mix; ⟨*Person,*⟩ mingle (**unter** + *acc* with); **sich m~en in** (+ *acc*) join in ⟨*Gespräch*⟩; meddle in ⟨*Angelegenheit*⟩ □ *vi* (*haben*) shuffle the cards. **M~ling** *m* **-s,-e** half-caste; (*Hund*) cross. **M~masch** *m* **-[e]s,-e** (*fam*) hotchpotch. **M~ung** *f* **-,-en** mixture; blend

miserabel *a* abominable; (*erbärmlich*) wretched

missachten (**mißachten**) *vt* disregard

Miss|achtung (**Miß|achtung**) *f* disregard. **M~behagen** *nt* [feeling of] unease. **M~bildung** *f* deformity

missbilligen (**mißbilligen**) *vt* disapprove of

Miss|billigung (**Miß|billigung**) *f* disapproval. **M~brauch** *m* abuse; **M~brauch treiben mit** abuse

miss|brauchen (**miß|brauchen**) *vt* abuse; (*vergewaltigen*) rape. **m~deuten** *vt* misinterpret

missen *vt* do without; **ich möchte es nicht m~** I should not like to be without it

Miss|erfolg (**Miß|erfolg**) *m* failure. **M~ernte** *f* crop failure

Misse|tat *f* misdeed. **M~täter** *m* (*fam*) culprit

missfallen† (**mißfallen**†) *vi* (*haben*) displease (**jdm** s.o.)

Miss|fallen (**Miß|fallen**) *nt* **-s** displeasure; (*Missbilligung*) disapproval. **m~gebildet** *a* deformed. **M~geburt** *f* freak; (*fig*) monstrosity. **M~geschick** *nt* mishap; (*Unglück*) misfortune. **m~gestimmt** *a* **m~gestimmt sein** be in a bad mood

miss|glücken (**miß|glücken**) *vi* (*sein*) fail. **m~gönnen** *vt* begrudge

Miss|griff (**Miß|griff**) *m* mistake. **M~gunst** *f* resentment. **m~günstig** *a* resentful

misshandeln (**mißhandeln**) *vt* ill-treat

Miss|handlung (**Miß|handlung**) *f* ill-treatment. **M~helligkeit** *f* **-,-en** disagreement

Mission *f* **-,-en** mission

Missionar(in) *m* **-s,-e** (*f* **-,-nen**) missionary

Miss|klang (**Miß|klang**) *m* discord. **M~kredit** *m* discredit; **in M~kredit bringen** discredit. **m~lich** *a* awkward. **m~liebig** *a* unpopular

misslingen† (**mißlingen**†) *vi* (*sein*) fail; **es misslang ihr** she failed. **M~** *nt* **-s** failure

Missmut (**Mißmut**) *m* ill humour. **m~ig** *a* morose, *adv* *-ly*

missraten† (**mißraten**†) *vi* (*sein*) turn out badly

Miss|stand (**Miß|stand**) *m* abuse; (*Zustand*) undesirable state of affairs. **M~stimmung** *f* discord; (*Laune*) bad mood. **M~ton** *m* discordant note

misstrauen (**mißtrauen**) *vi* (*haben*) **jdm/etw m~** mistrust s.o./sth; (*Argwohn hegen*) distrust s.o./sth

Misstrau|en (**Mißtrau|en**) *nt* **-s** mistrust; (*Argwohn*) distrust. **M~ensvotum** *nt* vote of no confidence. **m~isch** *a* distrustful; (*argwöhnisch*) suspicious

Miss|verhältnis (**Miß|verhältnis**) *nt* disproportion. **M~verständnis** *nt* misunderstanding. **m~verstehen**† *vt* misunderstand. **M~wirtschaft** *f* mismanagement

Mist *m* **-[e]s** manure; (*fam*) rubbish

Mistel *f* **-,-n** mistletoe

Misthaufen *m* dungheap

mit *prep* (+ *dat*) with; ⟨*sprechen*⟩ to; (*mittels*) by; (*inklusive*) including; (*bei*) at; **mit Bleistift** in pencil; **mit lauter Stimme** in a loud voice; **mit drei Jahren** at the age of three □ *adv* (*auch*) as well; **mit anfassen** (*fig*) lend a hand; **es ist mit das ärmste Land der Welt** it is among the poorest countries in the world

Mitarbeit *f* collaboration. **m~en** *vi sep* collaborate (**an** + *dat* on). **M~er(in)** *m(f)* collaborator; (*Kollege*) colleague; (*Betriebsangehörige*) employee

Mitbestimmung *f* co-determination

mitbring|en† *vt sep* bring [along]; **jdm Blumen m~en** bring/ (*hinbringen*) take s.o. flowers. **M~sel** *nt* **-s,-** present (*brought back from holiday etc*)

Mitbürger *m* fellow citizen

miteinander *adv* with each other

miterleben *vt sep* witness

Mitesser *m* (*Med*) blackhead

mitfahren† *vi sep* (*sein*) go/come along; **mit jdm m~** go with s.o.; (*mitgenommen werden*) be given a lift by s.o.

mitfühlen *vi sep* (*haben*) sympathize. **m~d** *a* sympathetic; (*mitleidig*) compassionate

mitgeben† *vt sep* **jdm etw m~** give s.o. sth to take with him

Mitgefühl *nt* sympathy

mitgehen† *vi sep* (*sein*) **mit jdm m~** go with s.o.; **etw m~ lassen** (*fam*) pinch sth

mitgenommen *a* worn; **m~ sein** be in a sorry state; (*erschöpft*) be exhausted

Mitgift *f* **-,-en** dowry

Mitglied *nt* member. **M~schaft** *f* - membership

mithalten† *vi sep* (*haben*) join in; **mit jdm nicht m~ können** not be able to keep up with s.o.

Mithilfe *f* assistance

mithilfe *prep* (+ *gen*) with the aid of

mitkommen† *vi sep* (*sein*) come [along] too; (*fig: folgen können*) keep up; (*verstehen*) follow

Mitlaut *m* consonant

Mitleid *nt* pity, compassion; **M~ erregend** pitiful. **M~enschaft** *f* **in M~enschaft ziehen** affect. **m~erregend** *a* = **M~ erregend**, *s.* **Mitleid**. **m~ig** *a* pitying; (*mitfühlend*) compassionate. **m~slos** *a* pitiless

mitmachen *v sep* □ *vt* take part in; (*erleben*) go through □ *vi* (*haben*) join in

Mitmensch *m* fellow man

mitnehmen† *vt sep* take along; (*mitfahren lassen*) give a lift to; (*fig: schädigen*) affect badly; (*erschöpfen*) exhaust; **'zum M~'** 'to take away', (*Amer*) 'to go'

mitnichten *adv* not at all

mitreden *vi sep* (*haben*) join in [the conversation]; (*mit entscheiden*) have a say (**bei** in)

mitreißen† *vt sep* sweep along; (*fig: begeistern*) carry away; **m~d** rousing

mitsamt *prep* (+ *dat*) together with

mitschneiden† *vt sep* record

mitschreiben† *vt sep* (*haben*) take down

Mitschuld *f* partial blame. **m~ig** *a* **m~ig sein** be partly to blame
Mitschüler(in) *m(f)* fellow pupil
mitspiel|en *vi sep (haben)* join in; *(Theat)* be in the cast; *(beitragen)* play a part; **jdm übel m~en** treat s.o. badly. **M~er** *m* fellow player; *(Mitwirkender)* participant
Mittag *m* midday, noon; *(Mahlzeit)* lunch; *(Pause)* lunch-break; **heute/gestern M~** at lunchtime today/yesterday; **[zu] M~ essen** have lunch. **m~** *adv* **heute/gestern m~** (NEW) **heute/gestern M~**, *s.* **Mittag. M~essen** *nt* lunch. **m~s** *adv* at noon; *(als Mahlzeit)* for lunch; **um 12 Uhr m~s** at noon. **M~spause** *f* lunch-hour; *(Pause)* lunch-break. **M~sschlaf** *m* after-lunch nap. **M~stisch** *m* lunch table; *(Essen)* lunch. **M~szeit** *f* lunch-time
Mittäter|(in) *m(f)* accomplice. **M~schaft** *f* - complicity
Mitte *f* -,-n middle; *(Zentrum)* centre; **die goldene M~** the golden mean; **M~ Mai** in mid-May; **in unserer M~** in our midst
mitteil|en *vt sep* **jdm etw m~en** tell s.o. sth; *(amtlich)* inform s.o. of sth. **m~sam** *a* communicative. **M~ung** *f* -,-en communication; *(Nachricht)* piece of news
Mittel *nt* -s,- means *sg*; *(Heil)* remedy; *(Medikament)* medicine; *(M~wert)* mean; *(Durchschnitt)* average; **M~** *pl (Geld-)* funds, resources. **m~** *pred a* medium; *(m~mäßig)* middling. **M~alter** *nt* Middle Ages *pl*. **m~alterlich** *a* medieval. **m~bar** *a* indirect, *adv* -ly. **M~ding** *nt (fig)* cross. **m~europäisch** *a* Central European. **M~finger** *m* middle finger. **m~groß** *a* medium-sized; *(Person)* of medium height. **M~klasse** *f* middle range. **m~los** *a* destitute. **m~mäßig** *a* middling; **[nur] m~mäßig** mediocre. **M~meer** *nt* Mediterranean. **M~punkt** *m* centre; *(fig)* centre of attention
mittels *prep (+ gen)* by means of
Mittel|schule *f* = **Realschule. M~smann** *m (pl* **-männer**), **M~sperson** *f* intermediary, go-between. **M~stand** *m* middle class. **m~ste(r,s)** *a* middle. **M~streifen** *m (Auto)* central reservation, *(Amer)* median strip. **M~stürmer** *m* centre-forward. **M~weg** *m (fig)* middle course; **goldener M~weg** happy medium. **M~welle** *f* medium wave. **M~wort** *nt (pl* **-wörter**) participle
mitten *adv* **m~ in/auf** *(dat/acc)* in the middle of; **m~ unter** *(dat/acc)* amidst. **m~durch** *adv* [right] through the middle
Mitternacht *f* midnight
mittler|e(r,s) *a* middle; *(Größe, Qualität)* medium; *(durchschnittlich)* mean, average. **m~weile** *adv* meanwhile; *(seitdem)* by now
Mittwoch *m* -s,-e Wednesday. **m~s** *adv* on Wednesdays
mitunter *adv* now and again
mitwirk|en *vi sep (haben)* take part; *(helfen)* contribute. **M~ung** *f* participation
mix|en *vt* mix. **M~er** *m* -s,- *(Culin)* liquidizer, blender. **M~tur** *f* -,-en *(Med)* mixture
Möbel *pl* furniture *sg*. **M~stück** *nt* piece of furniture. **M~tischler** *m* cabinet-maker. **M~wagen** *m* removal van
mobil *a* mobile; *(fam: munter)* lively; *(nach Krankheit)* fit [and well]; **m~machen** mobilize
Mobile *nt* -s,-s mobile
Mobiliar *nt* -s furniture
mobilisier|en *vt* mobilize. **M~ung** *f* - mobilization
Mobil|machung *f* - mobilization. **M~telefon** *nt* mobile phone
möblier|en *vt* furnish; **m~tes Zimmer** furnished room

mochte, möchte *s.* **mögen**
Modalverb *nt* modal auxiliary
Mode *f* -,-n fashion; **M~ sein** be fashionable
Modell *nt* -s,-e model; **M~ stehen** pose (**jdm** for s.o.). **m~ieren** *vt* model
Modenschau *f* fashion show
Mödera|tor *m* -s,-en /-ˈtoːrən/, **M~torin** *f* -,-nen (*TV*) presenter
modern[1] *vi* (*haben*) decay
modern[2] *a* modern; (*modisch*) fashionable. **m~isieren** *vt* modernize
Mode|schmuck *m* costume jewellery. **M~schöpfer** *m* fashion designer
Modifi|kation /-ˈtsi̯oːn/ *f* -,-en modification. **m~zieren** *vt* modify
modisch *a* fashionable
Modistin *f* -,-nen milliner
modrig *a* musty
modulieren *vt* modulate
Mofa *nt* -s,-s moped
mogeln *vi* (*haben*) (*fam*) cheat
mögen† *vt* like; **lieber m~** prefer □*v aux* **ich möchte** I'd like; **möchtest du nach Hause?** do you want to go home? **ich mag nicht mehr** I've had enough; **ich hätte weinen m~** I could have cried; **ich mag mich irren** I may be wrong; **wer/was mag das sein?** whoever/whatever can it be? **wie mag es ihm ergangen sein?** I wonder how he got on; **[das] mag sein** that may well be; **mag kommen, was da will** come what may
möglich *a* possible; **alle m~en** all sorts of; **über alles M~e (m~e) sprechen** talk about all sorts of things; **sein M~stes (m~stes) tun** do one's utmost. **m~erweise** *adv* possibly. **M~keit** *f* -,-en possibility. **M~keitsform** *f* subjunctive. **m~st** *adv* if possible; **m~st viel/früh** as much/early as possible
Mohammedan|er(in) *m* -s,- (*f* -,-nen) Muslim. **m~isch** *a* Muslim
Mohn *m* -s poppy; (*Culin*) poppyseed. **M~blume** *f* poppy
Möhre, Mohrrübe *f* -,-n carrot
mokieren (sich) *vr* make fun (**über** + *acc* of)
Mokka *m* -s mocha; (*Geschmack*) coffee
Molch *m* -[e]s,-e newt
Mole *f* -,-n (*Naut*) mole
Molekül *nt* -s,-e molecule
Molkerei *f* -,-en dairy
Moll *nt* - (*Mus*) minor
mollig *a* cosy; (*warm*) warm; (*rundlich*) plump
Moment *m* -s,-e moment; **im/jeden M~** at the/any moment; **M~[mal]!** just a moment! **m~an** *a* momentary, *adv* -ily; (*gegenwärtig*) at the moment
Momentaufnahme *f* snapshot
Monarch *m* -en,-en monarch. **M~ie** *f* -,-n monarchy
Monat *m* -s,-e month. **m~elang** *adv* for months. **m~lich** *a* & *adv* monthly. **M~skarte** *f* monthly season ticket
Mönch *m* -[e]s,-e monk
Mond *m* -[e]s,-e moon
mondän *a* fashionable, *adv* -bly
Mond|finsternis *f* lunar eclipse. **m~hell** *a* moonlit. **M~sichel** *f* crescent moon. **M~schein** *m* moonlight
monieren *vt* criticize
Monitor *m* -s,-en /-ˈtoːrən/ (*Techn*) monitor
Monogramm *nt* -s,-e monogram
Mono|log *m* -s,-e monologue. **M~pol** *nt* -s,-e monopoly. **m~polisieren** *vt* monopolize. **m~ton** *a* monotonous, *adv* -ly. **M~tonie** *f* - monotony
Monster *nt* -s,- monster
monstr|ös *a* monstrous **M~osität** *f* -,-en monstrosity
Monstrum *nt* -s,-stren monster
Monsun *m* -s,-e monsoon
Montag *m* Monday

Montage /mɔn'ta:ʒə/ *f* **-,-n** fitting; (*Zusammenbau*) assembly; (*Film-*) editing; (*Kunst*) montage
montags *adv* on Mondays
Montanindustrie *f* coal and steel industry
Monteur /mɔn'tø:ɐ̯/ *m* **-s,-e** fitter. **M~anzug** *m* overalls *pl*
montieren *vt* fit; (*zusammenbauen*) assemble
Monument *nt* **-[e]s,-e** monument. **m~al** *a* monumental
Moor *nt* **-[e]s,-e** bog; (*Heide-*) moor
Moos *nt* **es,-e** moss **m~ig** *a* mossy
Mop *m* **-s,-s** (NEW) **Mopp**
Moped *nt* **-s,-s** moped
Mopp *m* **-s,-s** mop
Mops *m* **-s,¨-e** pug [dog]
Moral *f* - morals *pl*, (*Selbstvertrauen*) morale; (*Lehre*) moral. **m~isch** *a* moral, *adv* -ly. **m~isieren** *vi* (*haben*) moralize
Morast *m* **-[e]s,-e** morass; (*Schlamm*) mud
Mord *m* **-[e]s,-e** murder, (*Pol*) assassination. **M~anschlag** *m* murder/assassination attempt. **m~en** *vt/i* (*haben*) murder, kill
Mörder *m* **-s,-** murderer, (*Pol*) assassin. **M~in** *f* **-,-nen** murderess. **m~isch** *a* murderous; (*fam: schlimm*) dreadful
Mords- *pref* (*fam*) terrific. **m~mäßig** *a* (*fam*) frightful, *adv* -ly
morgen *adv* tomorrow; **m~ Abend (abend)/Nachmittag (nachmittag)** tomorrow evening/afternoon; **heute/gestern/Montag m~** (NEW) **heute/gestern/Montag M~**, *s.* **Morgen**
Morgen *m* **-s,-** morning; (*Maß*) ≈ acre; **am M~** in the morning; **heute/gestern/Montag M~** this/yesterday/Monday morning. **M~dämmerung** *f* dawn. **m~dlich** *a* morning ... **M~grauen** *nt* **-s** dawn; **im M~grauen** at dawn. **M~mantel, M~rock** *m* dressing-gown.
M~rot *nt* red sky in the morning. **m~s** *a* in the morning
morgig *a* tomorrow's; **der m~e Tag** tomorrow
Morphium *nt* **-s** morphine
morsch *a* rotten
Morsealphabet *nt* Morse code
Mörtel *m* **-s** mortar
Mosaik /moza'i:k/ *nt* **-s,-e[n]** mosaic
Moschee *f* **-,-n** mosque
Mosel *f* - Moselle. **M~wein** *m* Moselle [wine]
Moskau *nt* **-s** Moscow
Moskito *m* **-s,-s** mosquito
Mos|lem *m* **-s,-s** Muslim. **m~lemisch** *a* Muslim
Most *m* **-[e]s** must; (*Apfel-*) ≈ cider
Mostrich *m* **-s** (*NGer*) mustard
Motel *nt* **-s,-s** motel
Motiv *nt* **-s,-e** motive; (*Kunst*) motif. **M~ation** /-'tsi̯o:n/ *f* - motivation. **m~ieren** *vt* motivate
Motor /'mo:tɔr, mo'to:ɐ̯/ *m* **-s,-en** /-'to:rən/ engine; (*Elektro-*) motor. **M~boot** *nt* motor boat
motorisieren *vt* motorize
Motor|rad *nt* motor cycle. **M~radfahrer** *m* motor-cyclist. **M~roller** *m* motor scooter
Motte *f* **-,-n** moth. **M~nkugel** *f* mothball
Motto *nt* **-s,-s** motto
Möwe *f* **-,-n** gull
Mücke *f* **-,-n** gnat; (*kleine*) midge; (*Stech-*) mosquito
mucksen (sich) *vr* **sich nicht m~** (*fam*) keep quiet
müd|e *a* tired; **nicht m~e werden/es m~e sein** not tire/be tired (**etw zu tun** of doing sth). **M~igkeit** *f* - tiredness
Muff *m* **-s,-e** muff
muffig *a* musty; (*fam: mürrisch*) grumpy
Mühe *f* **-,-n** effort; (*Aufwand*) trouble; **sich** (*dat*) **M~ geben** make an effort; (*sich bemühen*) try; **nicht der M~ wert** not worth

while; mit **M~ und** Not with great difficulty; (*gerade noch*) only just. **m~los** *a* effortless, *adv* -ly

muhen *vi* (*haben*) moo

mühe|n **(sich)** *vr* struggle. **m~voll** *a* laborious; (*anstrengend*) arduous

Mühl|e *f* **-,-n** mill; (*Kaffee-*) grinder. **M~stein** *m* millstone

Müh|sal *f* **-,-e** (*liter*) toil; (*Mühe*) trouble. **m~sam** *a* laborious, *adv* -ly; (*beschwerlich*) difficult, *adv* with difficulty. **m~selig** *a* laborious, *adv* -ly

Mulde *f* **-,-n** hollow

Müll *m* **-s** refuse, (*Amer*) garbage. **M~abfuhr** *f* refuse collection

Mullbinde *f* gauze bandage

Mülleimer *m* waste bin; (*Mülltonne*) dustbin, (*Amer*) garbage can

Müller *m* **-s,-** miller

Müll|halde *f* [rubbish] dump. **M~schlucker** *m* refuse chute. **M~tonne** *f* dustbin, (*Amer*) garbage can. **M~wagen** *m* dustcart, (*Amer*) garbage truck

mulmig *a* (*fam*) dodgy; ⟨*Gefühl*⟩ uneasy; **ihm war m~ zumute** he felt uneasy/(*übel*) queasy

multi|national *a* multinational. **M~plikation** /-'tsio:n/ *f* **-,-en** multiplication. **m~plizieren** *vt* multiply

Mumie /'mu:miə/ *f* **-,-n** mummy

mumifiziert *a* mummified

Mumm *m* **-s** (*fam*) energy

Mumps *m* **-** mumps

Mund *m* **-[e]s,¨er** mouth; **ein M~ voll Suppe** a mouthful of soup; **halt den M~!** be quiet! (*sl*) shut up! **M~art** *f* dialect. **m~artlich** *a* dialect

Mündel *nt & m* **-s,-** (*Jur*) ward. **m~sicher** *a* gilt-edged

münden *vi* (*sein*) flow/⟨*Straße:*⟩ lead (**in** + *acc* into)

mund|faul *a* taciturn. **M~geruch** *m* bad breath. **M~harmonika** *f* mouth-organ

mündig *a* **m~ sein/werden** (*Jur*) be/come of age. **M~keit** *f* **-** (*Jur*) majority

mündlich *a* verbal, *adv* -ly; **m~e Prüfung** oral

Mund|stück *nt* mouthpiece; (*Zigaretten-*) tip. **m~tot** *a* **m~tot machen** (*fig*) gag

Mündung *f* **-,-en** (*Fluss-*) mouth; (*Gewehr-*) muzzle

Mund|voll *m* **-,-** **ein M~voll** (NEW) **ein M~ voll**, *s.* **Mund**. **M~wasser** *nt* mouthwash. **M~werk** *nt* **ein gutes M~werk haben** (*fam*) be very talkative. **M~winkel** *m* corner of the mouth

Munition /-'tsio:n/ *f* **-** ammunition

munkeln *vt/i* (*haben*) talk **(von** of); **es wird gemunkelt** rumour has it **(dass** that)

Münster *nt* **-s,-** cathedral

munter *a* lively; (*heiter*) merry; **m~ sein** (*wach*) **be wide awake**/(*aufgestanden, gesund*) up and about; **gesund und m~** fit and well □ *adv* **[immer] m~** merrily

Münz|e *f* **-,-n** coin; (*M~stätte*) mint. **m~en** *vt* mint; **das war auf dich gemünzt** (*fam*) that was aimed at you. **M~fernsprecher** *m* coin-box telephone, payphone. **M~wäscherei** *f* launderette

mürbe *a* crumbly; ⟨*Obst*⟩ mellow; ⟨*Fleisch*⟩ tender; **jdn m~ machen** (*fig*) wear s.o. down. **M~teig** *m* short pastry

Murmel *f* **-,-n** marble

murmeln *vt/i* (*haben*) murmur; (*undeutlich*) mumble, mutter. **M~** *nt* **-s** murmur

Murmeltier *nt* marmot

murren *vt/i* (*haben*) grumble

mürrisch *a* surly

Mus *nt* **-es** purée

Muschel *f* **-,-n** mussel; (*Schale*) [sea] shell

Museum /mu'ze:ʊm/ *nt* **-s,-seen** /-'ze:ən/ museum

Musik *f* - music. **M~alien** /-iən/ *pl* [printed] music *sg*. **m~alisch** *a* musical

Musikbox *f* juke-box

Musiker(in) *m* **-s,-** (*f* **-,-nen**) musician

Musik|instrument *nt* musical instrument. **M~kapelle** *f* band. **M~pavillon** *m* bandstand

musisch *a* artistic

musizieren *vi* (*haben*) make music

Muskat *m* **-[e]s** nutmeg

Muskel *m* **-s,-n** muscle. **M~kater** *m* stiff and aching muscles *pl*

Musku|latur *f* - muscles *pl*. **m~lös** *a* muscular

Müsli *nt* **-s** muesli

muss (**muß**) *s*. **müssen**. **Muss** (**Muß**) *nt* - **ein M~** a must

Muße *f* - leisure; **mit M~** at leisure

müssen† *v aux* **etw tun m~** have to/(*fam*) have got to do sth; **ich muss jetzt gehen** I have to *or* must go now; **ich musste lachen** I had to laugh; **ich muss es wissen** I need to know; **du müsstest es mal versuchen** you ought to *or* should try it; **muss das sein?** is that necessary?

müßig *a* idle; (*unnütz*) futile. **M~gang** *m* - idleness

musste (**mußte**), **müsste** (**müßte**) *s*. **müssen**

Muster *nt* **-s,-** pattern; (*Probe*) sample; (*Vorbild*) model. **M~beispiel** *nt* typical example; (*Vorbild*) perfect example. **M~betrieb** *m* model factory. **m~gültig, m~haft** *a* exemplary. **m~n** *vt* eye; (*inspizieren*) inspect. **M~schüler(in)** *m(f)* model pupil. **M~ung** *f* **-,-en** inspection; (*Mil*) medical; (*Muster*) pattern

Mut *m* **-[e]s** courage; **jdm Mut machen** encourage s.o.; **zu M~e sein** = **zumute sein**, *s*. **zumute**

Mutation /-ˈtsi̯oːn/ *f* **-,-en** (*Biol*) mutation

mut|ig *a* courageous, *adv* -ly. **m~los** *a* despondent; (*entmutigt*) disheartened

mutmaß|en *vt* presume; (*Vermutungen anstellen*) speculate. **m~lich** *a* probable, *adv* -bly; **der m~liche Täter** the suspect. **M~ung** *f* **-,-en** speculation, conjecture

Mutprobe *f* test of courage

Mutter[1] *f* **-,̈** mother; **werdende M~** mother-to-be

Mutter[2] *f* **-,-n** (*Techn*) nut

Muttergottes *f* **-,-** madonna

Mutter|land *nt* motherland. **M~leib** *m* womb

mütterlich *a* maternal; (*fürsorglich*) motherly. **m~erseits** *adv* on one's/the mother's side

Mutter|mal *nt* birthmark; (*dunkel*) mole. **M~schaft** *f* - motherhood. **m~seelenallein** *a* & *adv* all alone. **M~sprache** *f* mother tongue. **M~tag** *m* Mother's Day

Mutti *f* **-,-s** (*fam*) mummy

Mutwill|e *m* wantonness. **m~ig** *a* wanton, *adv* -ly

Mütze *f* **-,-n** cap; **wollene M~** woolly hat

MwSt. *abbr* (**Mehrwertsteuer**) VAT

mysteriös *a* mysterious, *adv* -ly

Myst|ik /ˈmʏstɪk/ *f* - mysticism. **m~isch** *a* mystical

myth|isch *a* mythical. **M~ologie** *f* - mythology. **M~os** *m* **-,-then** myth

N

na *int* well; **na gut** all right then; **na ja** oh well; **na und?** so what?

Nabe *f* **-,-n** hub

Nabel *m* **-s,-** navel. **N~schnur** *f* umbilical cord

nach *prep* (+ *dat*) after; (*Uhrzeit*) past; (*Richtung*) to; ⟨*greifen, rufen, sich sehnen*⟩ for; (*gemäß*) according to; **meiner Meinung n~** in my opinion; **n~ oben** upwards □ *adv* **n~ und n~** gradually, bit by bit; **n~ wie vor** still
nachäffen *vt sep* mimic
nachahm|en *vt sep* imitate. **N~ung** *f* **-,-en** imitation
nacharbeiten *vt sep* make up for
nacharten *vi sep* (*sein*) **jdm n~** take after s.o.
Nachbar|(in) *m* **-n,-n** (*f* **-,-nen**) neighbour. **N~haus** *nt* house next door. **N~land** *nt* neighbouring country. **n~lich** *a* neighbourly; (*Nachbar-*) neighbouring. **N~schaft** *f* **-** neighbourhood; **gute N~schaft** neighbourliness
nachbestell|en *vt sep* reorder. **N~ung** *f* repeat order
nachbild|en *vt sep* copy, reproduce. **N~ung** *f* copy, reproduction
nachdatieren *vt sep* backdate
nachdem *conj* after; **je n~** it depends
nachdenk|en† *vi sep* (*haben*) think (**über** + *acc* about). **N~en** *nt* **-s** reflection, thought. **n~lich** *a* thoughtful, *adv* -ly
Nachdruck *m* (*pl* **-e**) reproduction; (*unveränderter*) reprint; (*Betonung*) emphasis
nachdrücklich *a* emphatic, *adv* -ally
nacheifern *vi sep* (*haben*) **jdm n~** emulate s.o.
nacheilen *vi sep* (*sein*) (+ *dat*) hurry after
nacheinander *adv* one after the other
Nachfahre *m* **-n,-n** descendant
Nachfolg|e *f* succession. **n~en** *vi sep* (*sein*) (+ *dat*) follow; (*im Amt*) succeed. **N~er(in)** *m* **-s,-** (*f* **-,-nen**) successor
nachforsch|en *vi sep* (*haben*) make enquiries. **N~ung** *f* enquiry; **N~ungen anstellen** make enquiries
Nachfrage *f* (*Comm*) demand. **n~n** *vi sep* (*haben*) enquire
nachfüllen *vt sep* refill ⟨*Behälter*⟩; **Wasser n~** fill up with water
nachgeben† *v sep* □ *vi* (*haben*) give way: (*sich fügen*) give in, yield □ *vt* **jdm Suppe n~** give s.o. more soup
Nachgebühr *f* surcharge
nachgehen† *vi sep* (*sein*) ⟨*Uhr:*⟩ be slow; **jdm/etw n~** follow s.o./sth; follow up ⟨*Spur, Angelegenheit*⟩; pursue ⟨*Angelegenheit, Tätigkeit*⟩; go about ⟨*Arbeit*⟩
nachgeraten† *vi sep* (*sein*) **jdm n~** take after s.o.
Nachgeschmack *m* after-taste
nachgiebig *a* indulgent; (*gefällig*) compliant. **N~keit** *f* **-** indulgence; compliance
nachgrübeln *vi sep* (*haben*) ponder (**über** + *acc* on)
nachhallen *vi sep* (*haben*) reverberate
nachhaltig *a* lasting
nachhause *adv* = **nach Hause**, *s.* **Haus**
nachhelfen† *vi sep* (*haben*) help
nachher *adv* later; (*danach*) afterwards; **bis n~!** see you later!
Nachhilfeunterricht *m* coaching
Nachhinein (nachhinein) *adv* **im N~ (n~)** afterwards
nachhinken *vi sep* (*sein*) (*fig*) lag behind
nachholen *vt sep* (*später holen*) fetch later; (*mehr holen*) get more; (*später machen*) do later; (*aufholen*) catch up on; make up for ⟨*Zeit*⟩
nachjagen *vi sep* (*haben*) (+ *dat*) chase after
Nachkomme *m* **-n,-n** descendant. **n~n**† *vi sep* (*sein*) follow [later], come later; (*Schritt halten*) keep

up; **etw** (*dat*) **N~n** (*fig*) comply with ⟨*Bitte, Wunsch*⟩; carry out ⟨*Versprechen, Pflicht*⟩. **N~nschaft** *f* - descendants *pl*, progeny

Nachkriegszeit *f* post-war period

Nachlass *m* **-es,¨e** (**Nachlaß** *m* **-sses,¨sse**) discount; (*Jur*) [deceased's] estate

nachlassen† *v sep* □ *vi* (*haben*) decrease; ⟨*Regen, Hitze*:⟩ let up; ⟨*Schmerz*:⟩ ease; ⟨*Sturm*:⟩ abate; ⟨*Augen, Kräfte, Leistungen*:⟩ deteriorate; **er ließ nicht nach [mit Fragen]** he persisted [with his questions] □ *vt* **etw vom Preis n~** take sth off the price

nachlässig *a* careless, *adv* -ly; (*leger*) casual, *adv* -ly; (*unordentlich*) sloppy, *adv* -ily. **N~keit** *f* - carelessness; sloppiness

nachlaufen† *vi sep* (*sein*) (+ *dat*) run after

nachlegen *vt sep* **Holz/Kohlen n~** put more wood/coal on the fire

nachlesen† *vt sep* look up

nachlöse|n *vi sep* (*haben*) pay one's fare on the train/on arrival. **N~schalter** *m* excess-fare office

nachmachen *vt sep* (*später machen*) do later; (*imitieren*) imitate, copy; (*fälschen*) forge; **jdm etw n~** copy sth from s.o.; repeat ⟨*Übung*⟩ after s.o.

Nachmittag *m* afternoon; **heute/gestern N~** this/yesterday afternoon. **n~** *adv* **heute/gestern n~** (NEW) **heute/gestern N~**, *s.* **Nachmittag**. **n~s** *adv* in the afternoon

Nachnahme *f* **etw per N~ schicken** send sth cash on delivery *or* COD

Nachname *m* surname

Nachporto *nt* excess postage

nachprüfen *vt sep* check, verify

nachrechnen *vt sep* work out; (*prüfen*) check

Nachrede *f* **üble N~** defamation

Nachricht *f* **-,-en** [piece of] news *sg*; **N~en** news *sg*; **eine N~ hinterlassen** leave a message; **jdm N~ geben** inform, notify s.o. **N~endienst** *m* (*Mil*) intelligence service. **N~ensendung** *f* news bulletin. **N~enwesen** *nt* communications *pl*

nachrücken *vi sep* (*sein*) move up

Nachruf *m* obituary

nachsagen *vt sep* repeat (**jdm** after s.o.); **jdm Schlechtes/Gutes n~** speak ill/well of s.o.; **man sagt ihm nach, dass er geizig ist** he is said to be stingy

Nachsaison *f* late season

Nachsatz *m* postscript

nachschicken *vt sep* (*später schicken*) send later; (*hinterher-*) send after (**jdm** s.o.); send on ⟨*Post*⟩ (**jdm** to s.o.)

nachschlag|en† *v sep* □ *vt* look up □ *vi* (*haben*) **in einem Wörterbuch n~en** consult a dictionary; **jdm n~en** take after s.o. **N~ewerk** *nt* reference book

Nachschlüssel *m* duplicate key

Nachschrift *f* transcript; (*Nachsatz*) postscript

Nachschub *m* (*Mil*) supplies *pl*

nachsehen† *v sep* □ *vt* (*prüfen*) check; (*nachschlagen*) look up; (*hinwegsehen über*) overlook □ *vi* (*haben*) have a look; (*prüfen*) check; **im Wörterbuch n~** consult a dictionary; **jdm/etw n~** gaze after s.o./sth. **N~** *nt* **das N~ haben** (*fam*) go empty-handed

nachsenden† *vt sep* forward ⟨*Post*⟩ (**jdm** to s.o.); '**bitte n~**' 'please forward'

Nachsicht *f* forbearance; (*Milde*) leniency; (*Nachgiebigkeit*) indulgence. **n~ig** *a* forbearing; lenient; indulgent

Nachsilbe *f* suffix

nachsitzen† *vi sep* (*haben*) **n~ müssen** be kept in [after school]; **jdn n~ lassen** give s.o. detention. **N~** *nt* **-s** (*Sch*) detention

Nachspeise *f* dessert, sweet

Nachspiel *nt* (*fig*) sequel
nachspionieren *vi sep* (*haben*) **jdm n~** spy on s.o.
nachsprechen† *vt sep* repeat (**jdm** after s.o.)
nachspülen *vt sep* rinse
nächst /-çst/ *prep* (+ *dat*) next to. **n~beste(r,s)** *a* first [available]; (*zweitbeste*) next best. **n~e(r,s)** *a* next; (*nächstgelegene*) nearest; ⟨*Verwandte*⟩ closest; **n~e Woche** next week; **in n~er Nähe** close by; **am n~en sein** be nearest *or* closest □ *pron* **der/die/das N~e (n~e)** the next; **der N~e (n~e) bitte** next please; **als N~es (n~es)** next; **fürs N~e (n~e)** for the time being. **N~e(r)** *m* fellow man
nachstehend *a* following □ *adv* below
nachstellen *v sep* □ *vt* readjust; put back ⟨*Uhr*⟩ □ *vi* (*haben*) (+ *dat*) pursue
nächst|emal *adv* **das n~emal** (NEW) **das nächste Mal**, *s.* **Mal**[1]. **N~enliebe** *f* charity. **n~ens** *adv* shortly. **n~gelegen** *a* nearest. **n~liegend** *a* most obvious
nachstreben *vi sep* (*haben*) **jdm n~** emulate s.o.
nachsuchen *vi sep* (*haben*) search; **n~ um** request
Nacht *f* -,-̈e night; **über/bei N~** overnight/at night; **Montag/morgen N~** Monday/tomorrow night; **heute N~** tonight; (*letzte Nacht*) last night; **gestern N~** last night; (*vorletzte Nacht*) the night before last. **n~** *adv* **morgen/heute/gestern n~** (NEW) **morgen/heute/gestern N~**, *s.* **Nacht**. **N~dienst** *m* night duty
Nachteil *m* disadvantage; **zum N~** to the detriment (*gen* of). **n~ig** *a* adverse, *adv* -ly
Nacht|essen *nt* (*SGer*) supper. **N~falter** *m* moth. **N~hemd** *nt* night-dress; (*Männer-*) night-shirt
Nachtigall *f* -,-en nightingale
Nachtisch *m* dessert
Nacht|klub *m* night-club. **N~leben** *nt* night-life
nächtlich *a* nocturnal, night ...
Nacht|lokal *nt* night-club. **N~mahl** *nt* (*Aust*) supper
Nachtrag *m* postscript; (*Ergänzung*) supplement. **n~en**† *vt sep* add; **jdm etw n~en** walk behind s.o. carrying sth; (*fig*) bear a grudge against s.o. for sth. **n~end** *a* vindictive; **n~end sein** bear grudges
nachträglich *a* subsequent, later; (*verspätet*) belated □ *adv* later; (*nachher*) afterwards; (*verspätet*) belatedly
nachtrauern *vi sep* (*haben*) (+ *dat*) mourn the loss of
Nacht|ruhe *f* night's rest; **angenehme N~ruhe!** sleep well! **n~s** *adv* at night; **2 Uhr n~s** 2 o'clock in the morning. **N~schicht** *f* night-shift. **N~tisch** *m* bedside table. **N~tischlampe** *f* bedside lamp. **N~topf** *m* chamber-pot. **N~wächter** *m* night-watchman. **N~zeit** *f* night-time
Nachuntersuchung *f* check-up
nachwachsen† *vi sep* (*sein*) grow again
Nachwahl *f* by-election
Nachweis *m* -es,-e proof. **n~bar** *a* demonstrable. **n~en**† *vt sep* prove; (*aufzeigen*) show; (*vermitteln*) give details of; **jdm nichts n~en können** have no proof against s.o. **n~lich** *a* demonstrable, *adv* -bly
Nachwelt *f* posterity
Nachwirkung *f* after-effect
Nachwort *nt* (*pl* -e) epilogue
Nachwuchs *m* new generation; (*fam: Kinder*) offspring. **N~spieler** *m* young player
nachzahlen *vt/i sep* (*haben*) pay extra; (*später zahlen*) pay later; **Steuern n~** pay tax arrears

nachzählen *vt/i sep (haben)* count again; *(prüfen)* check
Nachzahlung *f* extra/later payment; *(Gehalts-)* back-payment
nachzeichnen *vt sep* copy
Nachzügler *m* **-s,-** late-comer; *(Zurückgebliebener)* straggler
Nacken *m* **-s,-** nape *or* back of the neck
nackt *a* naked; *(bloß, kahl)* bare; ⟨*Wahrheit*⟩ plain. **N~baden** *nt* nude bathing. **N~heit** *f* - nakedness, nudity. **N~kultur** *f* nudism. **N~schnecke** *f* slug
Nadel *f* **-,-n** needle; *(Häkel-)* hook; *(Schmuck-, Hut-)* pin. **N~arbeit** *f* needlework. **N~baum** *m* conifer. **N~kissen** *nt* pincushion. **N~stich** *m* stitch; *(fig)* pinprick. **N~wald** *m* coniferous forest
Nagel *m* **-s,¨** nail. **N~bürste** *f* nail-brush. **N~feile** *f* nail-file. **N~haut** *f* cuticle. **N~lack** *m* nail varnish. **n~n** *vt* nail. **n~neu** *a* brand-new. **N~schere** *f* nail scissors *pl*
nagen *vt/i (haben)* gnaw (**an** + *dat* at); **n~d** *(fig)* nagging
Nagetier *nt* rodent
nah *a, adv & prep* = **nahe; von nah und fern** from far and wide
Näharbeit *f* sewing; **eine N~** a piece of sewing
Nahaufnahme *f* close-up
nahe *a* (**näher, nächst**) nearby; *(zeitlich)* imminent; *(eng)* close; **der N~ Osten** the Middle East; **in n~r Zukunft** in the near future; **von n~m** [from] close to; **n~ sein** be close *(dat* to); **den Tränen n~** close to tears □ *adv* near, close; ⟨*verwandt*⟩ closely; **n~ an** (+ *acc/dat*) near [to], close to; **n~ daran sein, etw zu tun** nearly do sth; **n~ liegen** be close; *(fig)* be highly likely; **n~ liegende Lösung** obvious solution; **n~ legen** *(fig)* recommend (**dat** to); **jdm n~ legen, etw zu tun** urge s.o. to do sth; **jdm n~ stehen** *(fig)* be close to s.o.; **etw** *(dat)* **n~ kommen** *(fig)* come close to sth; **jdm n~ kommen** *(fig)* get close to s.o.; **jdm n~ gehen** *(fig)* affect s.o. deeply; **jdm zu n~ treten** *(fig)* offend s.o. □ *prep* (+ *dat*) near [to], close to
Nähe *f* - nearness, proximity; **aus der N~** [from] close to; **in der N~** near *or* close by; **in der N~ der Kirche** near the church
nahebei *adv* near *or* close by
nahe|gehen† *vi sep (sein)* (NEW) **n~ gehen,** *s.* **nahe. n~kommen**† *vi sep (sein)* (NEW) **n~ kommen,** *s.* **nahe. n~legen** *vt sep* (NEW) **n~ legen,** *s.* **nahe. n~liegen**† *vi sep (haben)* (NEW) **n~ liegen,** *s.* **nahe. n~liegend** *a* (NEW) **n~ liegend,** *s.* **nahe**
nahen *vi (sein) (liter)* approach
nähen *vt/i (haben)* sew; *(anfertigen)* make; *(Med)* stitch [up]
näher *a* closer; ⟨*Weg*⟩ shorter; ⟨*Einzelheiten*⟩ further □ *adv* closer; *(genauer)* more closely; **n~ kommen** come closer, approach; *(fig)* get closer (**dat** to); **sich n~ erkundigen** make further enquiries; **n~an** (+ *acc/dat*) nearer [to], closer to □ *prep* (+ *dat*) nearer [to], closer to. **N~e[s]** *nt* [further] details *pl.* **n~kommen**† *vi sep (sein)* (NEW) **n~ kommen,** *s.* **näher. n~n (sich)** *vr* approach
nahestehen† *vi sep (haben)* (NEW) **nahe stehen,** *s.* **nahe**
nahezu *adv* almost
Nähgarn *nt* [sewing] cotton
Nahkampf *m* close combat
Näh|maschine *f* sewing machine. **N~nadel** *f* sewing-needle
nähren *vt* feed; *(fig)* nurture; **sich n~ von** live on □ *vi (haben)* be nutritious
nahrhaft *a* nutritious
Nährstoff *m* nutrient
Nahrung *f* - food, nourishment. **N~smittel** *nt* food
Nährwert *m* nutritional value

Naht *f* -,⸚e seam; (*Med*) suture. **n~los** *a* seamless
Nahverkehr *m* local service. **N~szug** *m* local train
Nähzeug *nt* sewing; (*Zubehör*) sewing kit
naiv /na'i:f/ *a* naïve, *adv* -ly. **N~ität** /-vi'tɛ:t/ *f* - naïvety
Name *m* **-ns,-n** name; **im N~n** (+ *gen*) in the name of; ⟨*handeln*⟩ on behalf of; **das Kind beim rechten N~n nennen** (*fam*) call a spade a spade. **n~nlos** *a* nameless; (*unbekannt*) unknown, anonymous. **n~ns** *adv* by the name of □ *prep* (+ *gen*) on behalf of. **N~nstag** *m* name-day. **N~nsvetter** *m* namesake. **N~nszug** *m* signature. **n~ntlich** *adv* by name; (*besonders*) especially
namhaft *a* noted; (*ansehnlich*) considerable; **n~ machen** name
nämlich *adv* (*und zwar*) namely; (*denn*) because
nanu *int* hallo
Napf *m* **-[e]s,⸚e** bowl
Narbe *f* -,-n scar
Narkose *f* -,-n general anaesthetic. **N~arzt** *m* anaesthetist. **N~mittel** *nt* anaesthetic
Narkot|ikum *nt* **-s,-ka** narcotic; (*Narkosemittel*) anaesthetic. **n~isieren** *vt* anaesthetize
Narr *m* **-en,-en** fool; **zum N~en haben** *od* **halten** make a fool of. **n~en** *vt* fool. **n~ensicher** *a* foolproof. **N~heit** *f* **-,-en** folly
Närr|in *f* **-,-nen** fool. **n~isch** *a* foolish; (*fam: verrückt*) crazy (**auf** + *acc* about)
Narzisse *f* -,-n narcissus; **gelbe N~** daffodil
nasal *a* nasal
nasch|en *vt/i* (*haben*) nibble (**an** + *dat* at); **wer hat vom Kuchen genascht?** who's been at the cake? **n~haft** *a* sweet-toothed
Nase *f* -,-n nose; **an der N~ herumführen** (*fam*) dupe
näseln *vi* (*haben*) speak through one's nose; **n~d** nasal
Nasen|bluten *nt* -s nosebleed. **N~loch** *nt* nostril. **N~rücken** *m* bridge of the nose
Naseweis *m* -es,-e (*fam*) know-all
Nashorn *nt* rhinoceros
nass (**naß**) *a* (**nasser, nassest**) wet
Nässe *f* - wet; (*Nasssein*) wetness. **n~n** *vt* wet
nasskalt (**naßkalt**) *a* cold and wet
Nation /na'tsio:n/ *f* **-,-en** nation. **n~al** *a* national. **N~alhymne** *f* national anthem. **N~alismus** *m* - nationalism. **N~alität** *f* **-,-en** nationality. **N~alsozialismus** *m* National Socialism. **N~alspieler** *m* international
Natrium *nt* -s sodium
Natron *nt* -s **doppeltkohlensaures N~** bicarbonate of soda
Natter *f* -,-n snake; (*Gift-*) viper
Natur *f* **-,-en** nature; **von N~ aus** by nature. **N~alien** /-iən/ *pl* natural produce *sg*. **n~alisieren** *vt* naturalize. **N~alisierung** *f* **-,-en** naturalization
Naturell *nt* -s,-e disposition
Natur|erscheinung *f* natural phenomenon. **n~farben** *a* natural[-coloured]. **N~forscher** *m* naturalist. **N~kunde** *f* natural history. **N~lehrpfad** *m* nature trail
natürlich *a* natural □ *adv* naturally; (*selbstverständlich*) of course. **N~keit** *f* - naturalness
natur|rein *a* pure. **N~schutz** *m* nature conservation; **unter N~schutz stehen** be protected. **N~schutzgebiet** *nt* nature reserve. **N~wissenschaft** *f* [natural] science. **N~wissenschaftler** *m* scientist. **n~wissenschaftlich** *a* scientific; (*Sch*) science ...
nautisch *a* nautical
Navigation /-'tsio:n/ *f* - navigation

Nazi *m* **-s,-s** Nazi
n.Chr. *abbr* (**nach Christus**) AD
Nebel *m* **-s,-** fog; (*leicht*) mist. **n~haft** *a* hazy. **N~horn** *nt* foghorn. **n~ig** *a* = **neblig**
neben *prep* (+ *dat/acc*) next to, beside; (+ *dat*) (*außer*) apart from; **n~ mir** next to me. **n~an** *adv* next door
Neben|anschluss (**Nebenanschluß**) *m* (*Teleph*) extension. **N~ausgaben** *fpl* incidental expenses
nebenbei *adv* in addition; (*beiläufig*) casually; **n~ bemerkt** incidentally
Neben|bemerkung *f* passing remark. **N~beruf** *m* second job. **N~beschäftigung** *f* spare-time occupation. **N~buhler(in)** *m* **-s,-** (*f* **-,-nen**) rival
nebeneinander *adv* next to each other, side by side
Neben|eingang *m* side entrance. **N~fach** *nt* (*Univ*) subsidiary subject. **N~fluss** (**N~fluß**) *m* tributary. **N~gleis** *nt* siding. **N~haus** *nt* house next door
nebenher *adv* in addition. **n~gehen†** *vi sep* (*sein*) walk alongside
nebenhin *adv* casually
Neben|höhle *f* sinus. **N~kosten** *pl* additional costs. **N~mann** *m* (*pl* **-männer**) person next to one. **N~produkt** *nt* by-product. **N~rolle** *f* supporting role; (*Kleine*) minor role; **eine N~rolle spielen** (*fig*) be unimportant. **N~sache** *f* unimportant matter. **n~sächlich** *a* unimportant. **N~satz** *m* subordinate clause. **N~straße** *f* minor road; (*Seiten-*) side street. **N~verdienst** *m* additional earnings *pl*. **N~wirkung** *f* side-effect. **N~zimmer** *nt* room next door
neblig *a* foggy; (*leicht*) misty
nebst *prep* (+ *dat*) [together] with
Necessaire /nesɛ'sɛ:ɐ̯/ *nt* **-s,-s** toilet bag; (*Näh-, Nagel-*) set
neck|en *vt* tease. **N~erei** *f* - teasing. **n~isch** *a* teasing; (*kess*) saucy
nee *adv* (*fam*) no
Neffe *m* **-n,-n** nephew
negativ *a* negative. **N~** *nt* **-s,-e** (*Phot*) negative
Neger *m* **-s,-** Negro
nehmen† *vt* take (*dat* from); **sich** (*dat*) **etw n~** take sth; help oneself to ⟨*Essen*⟩; **jdn zu sich n~** have s.o. to live with one
Neid *m* **-[e]s** envy, jealousy. **n~en** *vt* **jdm den Erfolg n~en** be jealous of s.o.'s success. **n~isch** *a* envious, jealous (**auf** + *acc* of); **auf jdn n~isch sein** envy s.o.
neig|en *vt* incline; (*zur Seite*) tilt; (*beugen*) bend; **sich n~en** incline; ⟨*Boden:*⟩ slope; ⟨*Person:*⟩ bend (**über** + *acc* over) □ *vi* (*haben*) **n~en zu** (*fig*) have a tendency towards; be prone to ⟨*Krankheit*⟩; incline towards ⟨*Ansicht*⟩; **dazu n~en, etw zu tun** tend to do sth. **N~ung** *f* **-,-en** inclination; (*Gefälle*) slope; (*fig*) tendency; (*Hang*) leaning; (*Herzens-*) affection
nein *adv*, **N~** *nt* **-s** no
Nektar *m* **-s** nectar
Nelke *f* **-,-n** carnation; (*Feder-*) pink; (*Culin*) clove
nenn|en† *vt* call; (*taufen*) name; (*angeben*) give; (*erwähnen*) mention; **sich n~en** call oneself. **n~enswert** *a* significant. **N~ung** *f* **-,-en** mention; (*Sport*) entry. **N~wert** *m* face value
Neofaschismus *m* neofascism
Neon *nt* **-s** neon. **N~beleuchtung** *f* fluorescent lighting
neppen *vt* (*fam*) rip off
Nerv *m* **-s,-en** /-fən/ nerve; **die N~en verlieren** lose control of oneself. **n~en** *vt* **jdn n~en** (*sl*) get on s.o.'s nerves. **N~enarzt** *m* neurologist. **n~enaufreibend** *a* nerve-racking. **N~enbündel** *nt*

(*fam*) bundle of nerves. **N~enkitzel** *m* (*fam*) thrill. **N~ensystem** *nt* nervous system. **N~enzusammenbruch** *m* nervous breakdown

nervös *a* nervy, edgy; (*Med*) nervous; **n~ sein** be on edge

Nervosität *f* - nerviness, edginess

Nerz *m* **-es,-e** mink

Nessel *f* **-,-n** nettle

Nessessär *nt* **-s,-s** = **Necessaire**

Nest *nt* **-[e]s,-er** nest; (*fam: Ort*) small place

nesteln *vi* (*haben*) fumble (**an** + *dat* with)

Nesthäkchen *nt* **-s,-** (*fam*) baby of the family

nett *a* nice, *adv* -ly; (*freundlich*) kind, *adv* -ly

netto *adv* net. **N~gewicht** *nt* net weight

Netz *nt* **-es,-e** net; (*Einkaufs-*) string bag; (*Spinnen-*) web; (*auf Landkarte*) grid; (*System*) network; (*Electr*) mains *pl*. **N~haut** *f* retina. **N~karte** *f* area season ticket. **N~werk** *nt* network

neu *a* new; (*modern*) modern; **wie neu** as good as new; **das ist mir neu** it's news to me; **aufs N~e (n~e)** [once] again; **von n~em** all over again □ *adv* newly; (*gerade erst*) only just; (*erneut*) again; **etw neu schreiben/streichen** rewrite/repaint sth; **neu vermähltes Paar** newly-weds *pl*. **N~ankömmling** *m* **-s,-e** newcomer. **N~anschaffung** *f* recent acquisition. **n~artig** *a* new [kind of]. **N~auflage** *f* new edition; (*unverändert*) reprint. **N~bau** *m* (*pl* **-ten**) new house/building

Neu|e(r) *m/f* new person, newcomer; (*Schüler*) new boy/girl. **N~e(s)** *nt* **das N~e** the new; **etwas N~es** something new; (*Neuigkeit*) a piece of news; **was gibt's N~es?** what's the news?

neuer|dings *adv* [just] recently. **n~lich** *a* renewed, new □ *adv* again. **N~ung** *f* **-,-en** innovation

neuest|e(r,s) *a* newest; (*letzte*) latest; **seit n~em** just recently. **N~e** *nt* **das N~e** the latest thing; (*Neuigkeit*) the latest news *sg*

neugeboren *a* newborn

Neugier, Neugierde *f* - curiosity; (*Wissbegierde*) inquisitiveness

neugierig *a* curious (**auf** + *acc* about), *adv* -ly; (*wissbegierig*) inquisitive, *adv* -ly

Neuheit *f* **-,-en** novelty; (*Neusein*) newness; **die letzte N~** the latest thing

Neuigkeit *f* **-,-en** piece of news; **N~en** news *sg*

Neujahr *nt* New Year's Day; **über N~** over the New Year

neulich *adv* the other day

Neu|ling *m* **-s,-e** novice. **n~modisch** *a* newfangled. **N~mond** *m* new moon

neun *inv a*, **N~** *f* **-,-en** nine. **N~malkluge(r)** *m* (*fam*) clever Dick. **n~te(r,s)** *a* ninth. **n~zehn** *inv a* nineteen. **n~zehnte(r,s)** *a* nineteenth. **n~zig** *inv a* ninety. **n~zigste(r,s)** *a* ninetieth

Neuralgie *f* **-,-n** neuralgia

neureich *a* nouveau riche

Neurologe *m* **-n,-n** neurologist

Neuro|se *f* **-,-n** neurosis. **n~tisch** *a* neurotic

Neuschnee *m* fresh snow

Neuseeland *nt* **-s** New Zealand

neuste(r,s) *a* = **neueste(r,s)**

neutral *a* neutral. **n~isieren** *vt* neutralize. **N~ität** *f* - neutrality

Neutrum *nt* **-s,-tra** neuter noun

neu|vermählt *a* (NEW) **n~ vermählt**, *s.* **neu**. **N~zeit** *f* modern times *pl*

nicht *adv* not; **ich kann n~** I cannot *or* can't; **er ist n~ gekommen** he hasn't come; **n~ mehr/besser als** no more/better than; **bitte n~!** please don't! **n~ berühren!** do not touch! **du kommst doch auch, ~ [wahr]?** you are coming too, aren't you? **du kennst ihn doch, n~?** you know him, don't you?

Nichtachtung *f* disregard; (*Geringschätzung*) disdain

Nichte *f* -,-n niece

nichtig *a* trivial; (*Jur*) [null and] void

Nichtraucher *m* non-smoker. **N~abteil** *nt* non-smoking compartment

nichts *pron & a* nothing; **n~ anderes/Besseres** nothing else/better; **n~ mehr** no more; **ich weiß n~** I know nothing *or* don't know anything; **n~ ahnend** unsuspecting; **n~ sagend** meaningless; (*uninteressant*) nondescript. **N~** *nt* - nothingness; (*fig: Leere*) void; (*Person*) nonentity. **n~ahnend** *a* (NEW) **n~ ahnend**, *s.* **nichts**

Nichtschwimmer *m* non-swimmer

nichtsdesto|trotz *adv* all the same. **n~weniger** *adv* nevertheless

nichts|nutzig *a* good-for-nothing; (*fam: unartig*) naughty. **n~sagend** *a* (NEW) **n~ sagend**, *s.* **nichts**. **N~tun** *nt* -s idleness

Nickel *nt* -s nickel

nicken *vi* (*haben*) nod. **N~** *nt* -s nod

Nickerchen *nt* -s,-, (*fam*) nap; **ein N~ machen** have forty winks

nie *adv* never

nieder *a* low □ *adv* down. **n~brennen†** *vt/i sep* (*sein*) burn down. **N~deutsch** *nt* Low German. **N~gang** *m* (*fig*) decline. **n~gedrückt** *a* (*fig*) depressed. **n~gehen†** *vi sep* (*sein*) come down. **n~geschlagen** *a* dejected, despondent. **N~geschlagenheit** *f* - dejection, despondency. **N~kunft** *f* -,¨e confinement. **N~lage** *f* defeat

Niederlande (die) *pl* the Netherlands

Niederländ|er *m* -s,- Dutchman; **die N~er** the Dutch *pl.* **N~erin** *f* -,-nen Dutchwoman. **n~isch** *a* Dutch

nieder|lassen† *vt sep* let down; **sich n~lassen** settle; (*sich setzen*) sit down. **N~lassung** *f* -,-en settlement; (*Zweigstelle*) branch. **n~legen** *vt sep* put *or* lay down; resign ⟨*Amt*⟩; **die Arbeit n~legen** go on strike; **sich n~legen** lie down. **n~machen, n~metzeln** *vt sep* massacre. **n~reißen†** *vt sep* tear down. **N~sachsen** *nt* Lower Saxony. **N~schlag** *m* precipitation; (*Regen*) rainfall; (*radioaktiver*) fallout; (*Boxen*) knock-down; **n~schlagen†** *vt sep* knock down; lower ⟨*Augen*⟩; (*unterdrücken*) crush. **n~schmettern** *vt sep* (*fig*) shatter. **n~schreiben†** *vt sep* write down. **n~schreien†** *vt sep* shout down. **n~setzen** *vt sep* put *or* set down; **sich n~setzen** sit down. **n~strecken** *vt sep* fell; (*durch Schuss*) gun down

niederträchtig *a* base, vile

Niederung *f* -,-en low ground

nieder|walzen *vt sep* flatten. **n~werfen†** *vt sep* throw down; (*unterdrücken*) crush; **sich n~werfen** prostrate oneself

niedlich *a* pretty; (*goldig*) sweet; (*Amer*) cute

niedrig *a* low; (*fig: gemein*) base □ *adv* low

niemals *adv* never

niemand *pron* nobody, no one

Niere *f* -,-n kidney; **künstliche N~** kidney machine

niesel|n *vi* (*haben*) drizzle; **es n~t** it is drizzling. **N~regen** *m* drizzle

niesen *vi* (*haben*) sneeze. **N~** *nt* -s sneezing; (*Nieser*) sneeze

Niet *m & nt* -[e]s,e, **Niete**[1] *f* -,-n rivet; (*an Jeans*) stud

Niete[2] *f* -,-n blank; (*fam*) failure

nieten *vt* rivet

Nikotin *nt* -s nicotine

Nil *m* **-[s]** Nile. **N~pferd** *nt* hippopotamus

nimmer *adv* (*SGer*) not any more; **nie und n~** never. **n~müde** *a* tireless. **n~satt** *a* insatiable. **N~wiedersehen** *nt* **auf N~wiedersehen** (*fam*) for good

nippen *vi* (*haben*) take a sip (**an** + *dat* of)

nirgend|s, n~wo *adv* nowhere

Nische *f* **-,-n** recess, niche

nisten *vi* (*haben*) nest

Nitrat *nt* **-[e]s,-e** nitrate

Niveau /ni'vo:/ *nt* **-s,-s** level; (*geistig, künstlerisch*) standard

nix *adv* (*fam*) nothing

Nixe *f* **-,-n** mermaid

nobel *a* noble; (*fam: luxuriös*) luxurious; (*fam: großzügig*) generous

noch *adv* still; (*zusätzlich*) as well; (*mit Komparativ*) even; **n~ nicht** not yet; **gerade n~** only just; **n~ immer** *od* **immer n~** still; **n~ letzte Woche** only last week; **es ist n~ viel Zeit** there's plenty of time yet; **wer/was/wo n~?** who/what/where else? **n~ jemand/etwas** someone/something else; (*Frage*) anyone/anything else? **n~ einmal** again; **n~ einmal so viel** as much again; **n~ ein Bier** another beer; **n~ größer** even bigger; **n~ so sehr/schön** however much/beautiful □ *conj* **weder ... n~** neither ... nor

nochmal|ig *a* further. **n~s** *adv* again

Nomad|e *m* **-n,-n** nomad. **n~isch** *a* nomadic

Nominativ *m* **-s,-e** nominative

nominell *a* nominal, *adv* -ly

nominier|en *vt* nominate. **N~ung** *f* **-,-en** nomination

nonchalant /nõʃa'lã:/ *a* nonchalant, *adv* -ly

Nonne *f* **-,-n** nun. **N~nkloster** *nt* convent

Nonstopflug *m* direct flight

Nord *m* **-[e]s** north. **N~amerika** *nt* North America. **n~deutsch** *a* North German

Norden *m* **-s** north; **nach N~** north

nordisch *a* Nordic

nördlich *a* northern; ⟨*Richtung*⟩ northerly □ *adv & prep* (+ *gen*) **n~ [von] der Stadt** [to the] north of the town

Nordosten *m* north-east

Nord|pol *m* North Pole. **N~see** *f* **-** North Sea. **n~wärts** *adv* northwards. **N~westen** *m* north-west

Nörgelei *f* **-,-en** grumbling

nörgeln *vi* (*haben*) grumble

Norm *f* **-,-en** norm; (*Techn*) standard; (*Soll*) quota

normal *a* normal, *adv* -ly. **n~erweise** *adv* normally. **n~isieren** *vt* normalize; **sich n~isieren** return to normal

normen, normieren *vt* standardize

Norwe|gen *nt* **-s** Norway. **N~ger(in)** *m* **-s,-** (*f* **-,-nen**) Norwegian. **n~gisch** *a* Norwegian

Nost|algie *f* **-** nostalgia. **n~algisch** *a* nostalgic

Not *f* **-,¨e** need; (*Notwendigkeit*) necessity; (*Entbehrung*) hardship; (*seelisch*) trouble; **Not leiden** be in need, suffer hardship; **Not leidende Menschen** needy people; **mit knapper Not** only just; **zur Not** if need be; (*äußerstenfalls*) at a pinch

Notar *m* **-s,-e** notary public

Not|arzt *m* emergency doctor. **N~ausgang** *m* emergency exit. **N~behelf** *m* **-[e]s,-e** makeshift. **N~bremse** *f* emergency brake. **N~dienst** *m* **N~dienst haben** be on call. **n~dürftig** *a* scant; (*behelfsmäßig*) makeshift

Note *f* **-,-n** note; (*Zensur*) mark; **ganze/halbe N~** (*Mus*) semibreve/minim, (*Amer*) whole/half note; **N~n lesen** read music; **persönliche N~** personal touch. **N~nblatt** *nt* sheet of music. **N~nschlüssel** *m* clef. **N~nständer** *m* music-stand

Notfall *m* emergency; **im N~** in an emergency; (*notfalls*) if need be; **für den N~** just in case. **n~s** *adv* if need be

not|gedrungen *adv* of necessity. **N~groschen** *m* nest-egg

notieren *vt* note down; (*Comm*) quote; **sich** (*dat*) **etw n~** make a note of sth

nötig *a* necessary; **n~ haben** need; **das N~ste** the essentials *pl* □ *adv* urgently. **n~en** *vt* force; (*auffordern*) press; **laßt euch nicht n~en** help yourselves. **n~enfalls** *adv* if need be. **N~ung** *f* - coercion

Notiz *f* -,-en note; (*Zeitungs-*) item; **[keine] N~ nehmen von** take [no] notice of. **N~buch** *nt* notebook. **N~kalender** *m* diary

Not|lage *f* plight. **n~landen** *vi* (*sein*) make a forced landing. **N~landung** *f* forced landing. **n~leidend** *a* (NEW) **Not leidend**, s. **Not**. **N~lösung** *f* stopgap. **N~lüge** *f* white lie

notorisch *a* notorious

Not|ruf *m* emergency call; (*Naut, Aviat*) distress call; (*Nummer*) emergency services number. **N~signal** *nt* distress signal. **N~stand** *m* state of emergency. **N~unterkunft** *f* emergency accommodation. **N~wehr** *f* - (*Jur*) self-defence

notwendig *a* necessary; (*unerlässlich*) essential □ *adv* urgently. **N~keit** *f* -,-en necessity

Notzucht *f* - (*Jur*) rape

Nougat /ˈnu:gat/ *m* & *nt* -s nougat

Novelle *f* -,-n novella; (*Pol*) amendment

November *m* -s,- November

Novität *f* -,-en novelty

Novize *m* -n,-n, **Novizin** *f* -,-nen (*Relig*) novice

Nu *m* **im Nu** (*fam*) in a flash

Nuance /ˈnÿã:sə/ *f* -,-n nuance; (*Spur*) shade

nüchtern *a* sober; (*sachlich*) matter-of-fact; (*schmucklos*) bare; (*ohne Würze*) bland; **auf n~en Magen** on an empty stomach □ *adv* soberly

Nudel *f* -,-n piece of pasta; **N~n** pasta *sg*; (*Band-*) noodles. **N~holz** *nt* rolling-pin

Nudist *m* -en,-en nudist

nuklear *a* nuclear

null *inv a* zero, nought; (*Teleph*) O; (*Sport*) nil; (*Tennis*) love; **n~ Fehler** no mistakes; **n~ und nichtig** (*Jur*) null and void. **N~** *f* -,-en nought, zero; (*fig: Person*) nonentity; **drei Grad unter N~** three degrees below zero. **N~punkt** *m* zero

numerieren *vt* (NEW) **nummerieren**

numerisch *a* numerical

Nummer *f* -,-n number; (*Ausgabe*) issue; (*Darbietung*) item; (*Zirkus-*) act; (*Größe*) size. **n~ieren** *vt* number. **N~nschild** *nt* number-/(*Amer*) license-plate

nun *adv* now; (*na*) well; (*halt*) just; **von nun an** from now on; **nun gut!** very well then! **das Leben ist nun mal so** life's like that

nur *adv* only, just; **wo kann sie nur sein?** wherever can she be? **alles, was ich nur will** everything I could possibly want; **er soll es nur versuchen!** (*drohend*) just let him try! **könnte/hätte ich nur ...!** if only I could/had ...! **nur Geduld!** just be patient!

Nürnberg *nt* -s Nuremberg

nuscheln *vt/i* (*haben*) mumble

Nuss *f* -,¨e (**Nuß** *f* -,¨sse) nut. **N~baum** *m* walnut tree. **N~knacker** *m* -s,- nutcrackers *pl*. **N~schale** *f* nutshell

Nüstern *fpl* nostrils

Nut *f* -,-en, **Nute** *f* -,-n groove

Nutte *f* -,-n (*sl*) tart (*sl*)

Nutz zu N~e machen = **zunutze machen**, *s.* **zunutze**. **n~bar** *a* usable; **n~bar machen** utilize; cultivate ⟨*Boden*⟩. **n~bringend** *a* profitable, *adv* -bly

nütze *a* **zu etwas/nichts n~ sein** be useful/useless

nutzen *vt* use, utilize; (*aus-*) take advantage of □ *vi* (*haben*) = **nützen. N~** *m* **-s** benefit; (*Comm*) profit; **N~ ziehen aus** benefit from; **von N~ sein** be useful

nützen *vi* (*haben*) be useful *or* of use (*dat* to); ⟨*Mittel:*⟩ be effective; **nichts n~** be useless *or* no use; **was nützt mir das?** what good is that to me? □ *vt* = **nutzen**

Nutzholz *nt* timber

nützlich *a* useful; **sich n~ machen** make oneself useful. **N~keit** *f* - usefulness

nutz|los *a* useless; (*vergeblich*) vain. **N~losigkeit** *f* - uselessness. **N~nießer** *m* **-s,-** beneficiary. **N~ung** *f* - use, utilization

Nylon /'nai̯lɔn/ *nt* **-s** nylon

Nymphe /'nʏmfə/ *f* **-,-n** nymph

O

o *int* **o ja/nein!** oh yes/no! **o weh!** oh dear!

Oase *f* **-,-n** oasis

ob *conj* whether; **ob reich, ob arm** rich or poor; **ob sie wohl krank ist?** I wonder whether she is ill; **und ob!** (*fam*) you bet!

Obacht *f* **O~ geben** pay attention; **O~ geben auf** (+ *acc*) look after; **O~!** look out!

Obdach *nt* **-[e]s** shelter. **o~los** *a* homeless. **O~lose(r)** *m/f* homeless person; **die O~losen** the homeless *pl*

Obduktion /-'tsi̯o:n/ *f* **-,-en** postmortem

O-Beine *ntpl* (*fam*) bow-legs, bandy legs. **O-beinig, o-beinig** *a* bandy-legged

oben *adv* at the top; (*auf der Oberseite*) on top; (*eine Treppe hoch*) upstairs; (*im Text*) above; **da o~** up there; **o~ im Norden** up in the north; **siehe o~** see above; **o~ auf** (+ *acc/dat*) on top of; **nach o~** up[wards]; (*die Treppe hinauf*) upstairs; **von o~** from above/upstairs; **von o~ bis unten** from top to bottom/⟨*Person*⟩ to toe; **jdn von o~ bis unten mustern** look s.o. up and down; **o~ erwähnt** *od* **genannt** above-mentioned. **o~an** *adv* at the top. **o~auf** *adv* on top; **o~auf sein** (*fig*) be cheerful. **o~drein** *adv* on top of that. **o~erwähnt, o~genannt** *a* (NEW) **o~ erwähnt** *od* **genannt**, *s.* **oben**. **o~hin** *adv* casually

Ober *m* **-s,-** waiter

Ober|arm *m* upper arm. **O~arzt** *m* ≈ senior registrar. **O~befehlshaber** *m* commander-in-chief. **O~begriff** *m* generic term. **O~deck** *nt* upper deck. **o~e(r,s)** *a* upper; (*höhere*) higher. **O~fläche** *f* surface. **o~flächlich** *a* superficial, *adv* -ly. **O~geschoss** (**O~geschoß**) *nt* upper storey. **o~halb** *adv & prep* (+ *gen*) above; **o~halb vom Dorf** *od* **des Dorfes** above the village. **O~hand** *f* **die O~hand gewinnen** gain the upper hand. **O~haupt** *nt* (*fig*) head. **O~haus** *nt* (*Pol*) upper house; (*in UK*) House of Lords. **O~hemd** *nt* [man's] shirt

Oberin *f* **-,-nen** matron; (*Relig*) mother superior

ober|irdisch *a* surface ... □ *adv* above ground. **O~kellner** *m* head waiter. **O~kiefer** *m* upper jaw. **O~körper** *m* upper part of the body. **O~leutnant** *m* lieutenant. **O~licht** *nt* overhead light; (*Fenster*) skylight; (*über*

Tür) fanlight. **O~lippe** *f* upper lip

Obers *nt* - (*Aust*) cream

Ober|schenkel *m* thigh. **O~schicht** *f* upper class. **O~schule** *f* grammar school. **O~schwester** *f* (*Med*) sister. **O~seite** *f* upper/(*rechte Seite*) right side

Oberst *m* **-en & -s,-en** colonel

oberste(r,s) *a* top; (*höchste*) highest; ⟨*Befehlshaber, Gerichtshof*⟩ supreme; (*wichtigste*) first

Ober|stimme *f* treble. **O~stufe** *f* upper school. **O~teil** *nt* top. **O~weite** *f* chest/(*der Frau*) bust size

obgleich *conj* although

Obhut *f* - care; **in guter O~ sein** be well looked after

obig *a* above

Objekt *nt* **-[e]s,-e** object; (*Haus, Grundstück*) property; **O~ der Forschung** subject of research

Objektiv *nt* **-s,-e** lens. **o~** *a* objective, *adv* -ly. **O~ität** *f* - objectivity

Oblate *f* **-,-n** (*Relig*) wafer

obligat *a* (*fam*) inevitable. **O~tion** /-'tsi̯o:n/ *f* **-,-en** obligation; (*Comm*) bond. **o~torisch** *a* obligatory

Obmann *m* (*pl* **-männer**) [jury] foreman; (*Sport*) referee

Oboe /o'bo:ə/ *f* **-,-n** oboe

Obrigkeit *f* - authorities *pl*

obschon *conj* although

Observatorium *nt* **-s,-ien** observatory

obskur *a* obscure; (*zweifelhaft*) dubious

Obst *nt* **-es** (*coll*) fruit. **O~baum** *m* fruit-tree. **O~garten** *m* orchard. **O~händler** *m* fruiterer. **O~kuchen** *m* fruit flan. **O~salat** *m* fruit salad

obszön *a* obscene. **O~ität** *f* **-,-en** obscenity

O-Bus *m* trolley bus

obwohl *conj* although

Ochse *m* **-n,-n** ox. **o~n** *vi* (*haben*) (*fam*) swot. **O~nschwanzsuppe** *f* oxtail soup

öde *a* desolate; (*unfruchtbar*) barren; (*langweilig*) dull. **Öde** *f* - desolation; barrenness; dullness; (*Gegend*) waste

oder *conj* or; **du kennst ihn doch, o~?** you know him, don't you?

Ofen *m* **-s,⸚** stove; (*Heiz-*) heater; (*Back-*) oven; (*Techn*) furnace

offen *a* open, *adv* -ly; ⟨*Haar*⟩ loose; ⟨*Flamme*⟩ naked; (*o~herzig*) frank, *adv* -ly; (*o~ gezeigt*) overt, *adv* -ly; (*unentschieden*) unsettled; **o~e Stelle** vacancy; **Tag der o~en Tür** open day; **Wein o~ verkaufen** sell wine by the glass; **o~ bleiben** remain open; **o~ halten** hold open ⟨*Tür*⟩; keep open ⟨*Mund, Augen*⟩; **o~ lassen** leave open; leave vacant ⟨*Stelle*⟩; **o~ stehen** be open; ⟨*Rechnung:*⟩ be outstanding; **jdm o~ stehen** (*fig*) be open to s.o.; *adv* **o~ gesagt** *od* **gestanden** to be honest. **o~bar** *a* obvious □ *adv* apparently. **o~baren** *vt* reveal. **O~barung** *f* **-,-en** revelation. **o~bleiben**† *vi sep* (*sein*) (NEW) **o~ bleiben**, *s.* **offen**. **o~halten**† *vt sep* (NEW) **o~ halten**, *s.* **offen**. **O~heit** *f* - frankness, openness. **o~herzig** *a* frank, *adv* -ly. **O~herzigkeit** *f* - frankness. **o~kundig** *a* manifest, *adv* -ly. **o~lassen**† *vt sep* (NEW) **o~ lassen**, *s.* **offen**. **o~sichtlich** *a* obvious, *adv* -ly

offensiv *a* offensive. **O~e** *f* **-,-n** offensive

offenstehen† *vi sep* (*haben*) (NEW) **offen stehen**, *s.* **offen**

öffentlich *a* public, *adv* -ly. **Ö~keit** *f* - public; **an die Ö~keit gelangen** become public; **in aller Ö~keit** in public, publicly

Offerte *f* **-,-n** (*Comm*) offer

offiziell *a* official, *adv* -ly

Offizier *m* **-s,-e** (*Mil*) officer

öffn|en *vt/i* (*haben*) open; **sich ö~en** open. **Ö~er** *m* **-s,-** opener. **Ö~ung** *f* **-,-en** opening. **Ö~ungszeiten** *fpl* opening hours

oft *adv* often

öfter *adv* quite often. **ö~e(r,s)** *a* frequent; **des Ö~en (ö~en)** frequently. **ö~s** *adv* (*fam*) quite often

oftmals *adv* often

oh *int* oh!

ohne *prep* (+ *acc*) without; **o~ mich!** count me out! **oben o~** topless; **nicht o~ sein** (*fam*) be not bad; (*nicht harmlos*) be quite nasty □ *conj* **o~ zu überlegen** without thinking; **o~ dass ich es merkte** without my noticing it. **o~dies** *adv* anyway. **o~gleichen** *pred a* unparalleled; **eine Frechheit o~gleichen** a piece of unprecedented insolence. **o~hin** *adv* anyway

Ohn|macht *f* **-,-en** faint; (*fig*) powerlessness; **in O~macht fallen** faint. **o~mächtig** *a* unconscious; (*fig*) powerless; **o~mächtig werden** faint

Ohr *nt* **-[e]s,-en** ear; **übers Ohr hauen** (*fam*) cheat

Öhr *nt* **-[e]s,-e** eye

ohren|betäubend *a* deafening. **O~schmalz** *nt* ear-wax. **O~schmerzen** *mpl* earache *sg*. **O~sessel** *m* wing-chair. **O~tropfen** *mpl* ear drops

Ohrfeige *f* slap in the face; **jdm eine O~ geben** slap s.o.'s face. **o~n** *vt* **jdn o~n** slap s.o.'s face

Ohr|läppchen *nt* **-s,-** ear-lobe. **O~ring** *m* ear-ring. **O~wurm** *m* earwig

oje *int* oh dear!

okay /o'ke:/ *a & adv* (*fam*) OK

okkult *a* occult

Öko|logie *f* **-** ecology. **ö~logisch** *a* ecological. **Ö~nomie** *f* **-** economy; (*Wissenschaft*) economics *sg*. **ö~nomisch** *a* economic; (*sparsam*) economical

Oktave *f* **-,-n** octave

Oktober *m* **-s,-** October

Okular *nt* **-s,-e** eyepiece

okulieren *vt* graft

ökumenisch *a* ecumenical

Öl *nt* **-[e]s,-e** oil; **in Öl malen** paint in oils. **Ölbaum** *m* olivetree. **ölen** *vt* oil; **wie ein geölter Blitz** (*fam*) like greased lightning. **Ölfarbe** *f* oil-paint. **Ölfeld** *nt* oilfield. **Ölgemälde** *nt* oil-painting. **ölig** *a* oily

Oliv|e *f* **-,-n** olive. **O~enöl** *nt* olive oil. **o~grün** *a* olive[-green]

oll *a* (*fam*) old; (*fam: hässlich*) nasty

Ölmessstab (Ölmeßstab) *m* dipstick. **Ölsardinen** *fpl* sardines in oil. **Ölstand** *m* oil-level. **Öltanker** *m* oil-tanker. **Ölteppich** *m* oil-slick

Olympiade *f* **-,-n** Olympic Games *pl*, Olympics *pl*

Olymp|iasieger(in) /o'lympia-/ *m(f)* Olympic champion. **o~isch** *a* Olympic; **O~ische Spiele** Olympic Games

Ölzeug *nt* oilskins *pl*

Oma *f* **-,-s** (*fam*) granny

Omelett *nt* **-[e]s,-e & -s** omelette

Omen *nt* **-s,-** omen

ominös *a* ominous

Omnibus *m* bus; (*Reise-*) coach

onanieren *vi* (*haben*) masturbate

Onkel *m* **-s,-** uncle

Opa *m* **-s,-s** (*fam*) grandad

Opal *m* **-s,-e** opal

Oper *f* **-,-n** opera

Operation /-'tsio:n/ *f* **-,-en** operation. **O~ssaal** *m* operating theatre

Operette *f* **-,-n** operetta

operieren *vt* operate on ⟨*Patient, Herz*⟩; **sich o~ lassen** have an operation □ *vi* (*haben*) operate

Opern|glas *nt* opera-glasses *pl*. **O~haus** *nt* opera-house. **O~sänger(in)** *m(f)* opera-singer

Opfer *nt* **-s,-** sacrifice; (*eines Unglücks*) victim; **ein O~ bringen** make a sacrifice;

jdm/etw zum O~ fallen fall victim to s.o./sth. **o~n** *vt* sacrifice. **O~ung** *f* **-,-en** sacrifice

Opium *nt* **-s** opium

opponieren *vi* (*haben*) **o~ gegen** oppose

Opportunist *m* **-en,-en** opportunist. **o~isch** *a* opportunist

Opposition /-ˈtsio:n/ *f* - opposition. **O~spartei** *f* opposition party

Optik *f* - optics *sg*, (*fam: Objektiv*) lens. **O~er** *m* **-s,-** optician

optimal *a* optimum

Optimis|mus *m* - optimism. **O~t** *m* **-en,-en** optimist. **o~tisch** *a* optimistic, *adv* -ally

Optimum *nt* **-s,-ma** optimum

Option /ɔpˈtsio:n/ *f* **-,-en** option

optisch *a* optical; ⟨*Eindruck*⟩ visual

Orakel *nt* **-s,-** oracle

Orange /oˈrã:ʒə/ *f* **-,-n** orange. **o~** *inv a* orange. **O~ade** /orãˈʒa:də/ *f* **-,-n** orangeade. **O~nmarmelade** *f* [orange] marmalade. **O~nsaft** *m* orange juice

Oratorium *nt* **-s,-ien** oratorio

Orchest|er /ɔrˈkɛstɐ/ *nt* **-s,-** orchestra. **o~rieren** *vt* orchestrate

Orchidee /ɔrçiˈde:ə/ *f* **-,-n** orchid

Orden *m* **-s,-** (*Ritter-, Kloster-*) order; (*Auszeichnung*) medal, decoration; **jdm einen O~ verleihen** decorate s.o. **O~stracht** *f* (*Relig*) habit

ordentlich *a* neat, tidy; (*anständig*) respectable; (*ordnungsgemäß, fam: richtig*) proper; ⟨*Mitglied, Versammlung*⟩ ordinary; (*fam: gut*) decent; (*fam: gehörig*) good □ *adv* neatly, tidily; respectably; properly; (*fam: gut, gehörig*) well; (*sehr*) very; (*regelrecht*) really

Order *f* **-,-s & -n** order

ordinär *a* common

Ordin|ation /-ˈtsio:n/ *f* **-,-en** (*Relig*) ordination; (*Aust*) surgery. **o~ieren** *vt* (*Relig*) ordain

ordn|en *vt* put in order; (*aufräumen*) tidy; (*an-*) arrange; **sich zum Zug o~en** form a procession. **O~er** *m* **-s,-** steward; (*Akten-*) file

Ordnung *f* - order; **O~ halten** keep order; **O~ machen** tidy up; **in O~ bringen** put in order; (*aufräumen*) tidy; (*reparieren*) mend; (*fig*) put right; **in O~ sein** be in order; (*ordentlich sein*) be tidy; (*fig*) be all right; **ich bin mit dem Magen od mein Magen ist nicht ganz in O~** I have a slight stomach upset; **[geht] in O~!** OK! **o~sgemäß** *a* proper, *adv* -ly. **O~sstrafe** *f* (*Jur*) fine. **o~swidrig** *a* improper, *adv* -ly

Ordonnanz, Ordonanz *f* **-,-en** (*Mil*) orderly

Organ *nt* **-s,-e** organ; (*fam: Stimme*) voice

Organi|sation /-ˈtsio:n/ *f* **-,-en** organization. **O~sator** *m* **-s,-en** /-ˈto:rən/ organizer

organisch *a* organic, *adv* -ally

organisieren *vt* organize; (*fam: beschaffen*) get [hold of]

Organis|mus *m* **-,-men** organism; (*System*) system. **O~t** *m* **-en,-en** organist

Organspenderkarte *f* donor card

Orgasmus *m* **-,-men** orgasm

Orgel *f* **-,-n** (*Mus*) organ. **O~pfeife** *f* organ-pipe

Orgie /ˈɔrgiə/ *f* **-,-n** orgy

Orien|t /ˈo:riɛnt/ *m* **-s** Orient. **o~talisch** *a* Oriental

orientier|en /oriɛnˈti:rən/ *vt* inform (**über** + *acc* about); **sich o~en** get one's bearings, orientate oneself; (*unterrichten*) inform oneself (**über** + *acc* about). **O~ung** *f* - orientation; **die O~ung verlieren** lose one's bearings

original *a* original. **O~** *nt* **-s,-e** original; (*Person*) character. **O~ität** *f* - originality. **O~übertragung** *f* live transmission

originell *a* original; (*eigenartig*) unusual
Orkan *m* -s,-e hurricane
Ornament *nt* -[e]s,-e ornament
Ornat *m* -[e]s,-e robes *pl*
Ornithologie *f* - ornithology
Ort *m* -[e]s,-e place; (*Ortschaft*) [small] town; **am Ort** locally; **am Ort des Verbrechens** at the scene of the crime; **an Ort und Stelle** in the right place; (*sofort*) on the spot. **o~en** *vt* locate
ortho|dox *a* orthodox. **O~graphie**, **O~grafie** *f* - spelling. **o~graphisch**, **o~grafisch** *a* spelling ... **O~päde** *m* -n,-n orthopaedic specialist. **o~pädisch** *a* orthopaedic
örtlich *a* local, *adv* -ly. **Ö~keit** *f* -,-en locality
Ortschaft *f* -,-en [small] town; (*Dorf*) village; **geschlossene O~** (*Auto*) built-up area
orts|fremd *a* **o~fremd sein** be a stranger. **O~gespräch** *nt* (*Teleph*) local call. **O~name** *m* place-name. **O~sinn** *m* sense of direction. **O~verkehr** *m* local traffic. **O~zeit** *f* local time
Öse *f* -,-n eyelet; (*Schlinge*) loop; **Haken und Öse** hook and eye
Ost *m* -[e]s east. **o~deutsch** *a* Eastern/(*Pol*) East German
Osten *m* -s east; **nach O~** east
ostentativ *a* pointed, *adv* -ly
Osteopath *m* -en,-en osteopath
Oster|ei /ˈoːstɐʔai/ *nt* Easter egg. **O~fest** *nt* Easter. **O~glocke** *f* daffodil. **O~montag** *m* Easter Monday. **O~n** *nt* -,- Easter; **frohe O~n!** happy Easter!
Österreich *nt* -s Austria. **Ö~er** *m*, -s,-, **Ö~erin** *f* -,-nen Austrian. **ö~isch** *a* Austrian
östlich *a* eastern; ⟨*Richtung*⟩ easterly □ *adv & prep* (+ *gen*) **ö~ [von] der Stadt** [to the] east of the town
Ost|see *f* Baltic [Sea]. **o~wärts** *adv* eastwards

oszillieren *vi*(*haben*) oscillate
Otter[1] *m* -s,- otter
Otter[2] *f* -,-n adder
Ouverture /uvɛrˈtyːrə/ *f* -,-n overture
oval *a* oval. **O~** *nt* -s,-e oval
Ovation /-ˈtsi̯oːn/ *f* -,-en ovation
Ovulation /-ˈtsi̯oːn/ *f* -,-en ovulation
Oxid, **Oxyd** *nt* -[e]s,-e oxide
Ozean *m* -s,-e ocean
Ozon *nt* -s ozone. **O~loch** *nt* hole in the ozone layer. **O~schicht** *f* ozone layer

P

paar *pron inv* **ein p~** a few; **ein p~ Mal** a few times; **alle p~ Tage** every few days. **P~** *nt* -[e]s,-e pair; (*Ehe-, Liebes-, Tanz-*) couple. **p~en** *vt* mate; (*verbinden*) combine; **sich p~en** mate. **p~mal** *adv* **ein p~mal** (NEW) **ein p~ Mal**, *s.* **paar**. **P~ung** *f* -,-en mating. **p~weise** *adv* in pairs, in twos
Pacht *f* -,-en lease; (*P~summe*) rent. **p~en** *vt* lease
Pächter *m* -s,- lessee; (*eines Hofes*) tenant
Pachtvertrag *m* lease
Pack[1] *m* -[e]s,-e bundle
Pack[2] *nt* -[e]s (*sl*) rabble
Päckchen *nt* -s,- package, small packet
pack|en *vt/i* (*haben*) pack; (*ergreifen*) seize; (*fig: fesseln*) grip; **p~ dich!** (*sl*) beat it! **P~en** *m* -s,- bundle. **p~end** *a* (*fig*) gripping. **P~papier** *nt* [strong] wrapping paper. **P~ung** *f* -,-en packet; (*Med*) pack
Pädagog|e *m* -n,-n educationalist; (*Lehrer*) teacher. **P~ik** *f* - educational science. **p~isch** *a* educational

Paddel *nt* **-s,-** paddle. **P~boot** *nt* canoe. **p~n** *vt/i* (*haben/sein*) paddle. **P~sport** *m* canoeing
Page /'pa:ʒə/ *m* **-n,-n** page
Paillette /paj'jɛtə/ *f* **-,-n** sequin
Paket *nt* **-[e]s,-e** packet; (*Post-*) parcel
Pakist|an *nt* **-s** Pakistan. **P~aner(in)** *m* **-s,-** (*f* **-,-nen**) Pakistani. **p~anisch** *a* Pakistani
Pakt *m* **-[e]s,-e** pact
Palast *m* **-[e]s,⸚e** palace
Paläst|ina *nt* **-s** Palestine. **P~inenser(in)** *m* **-s,-** (*f* **-,-nen**) Palestinian. **p~inensisch** *a* Palestinian
Palette *f* **-,-n** palette
Palm|e *f* **-,-n** palm[-tree]; **jdn auf die P~e bringen** (*fam*) drive s.o. up the wall. **P~sonntag** *m* Palm Sunday
Pampelmuse *f* **-,-n** grapefruit
Panier|mehl *nt* (*Culin*) breadcrumbs *pl*. **p~t** *a* (*Culin*) breaded
Panik *f* **-** panic; **in P~ geraten** panic
panisch *a* **p~e Angst** panic
Panne *f* **-,-n** breakdown; (*Reifen-*) flat tyre; (*Missgeschick*) mishap. **P~ndienst** *m* breakdown service
Panorama *nt* **-s** panorama
panschen *vt* adulterate □ *vi* (*haben*) splash about
Panther, Panter *m* **-s,-** panther
Pantine *f* **-,-n** [wooden] clog
Pantoffel *m* **-s,-n** slipper; (*ohne Ferse*) mule. **P~held** *m* (*fam*) henpecked husband
Pantomime¹ *f* **-,-n** mime
Pantomime² *m* **-n,-n** mime artist
pantschen *vt/i* = **panschen**
Panzer *m* **-s,-** armour; (*Mil*) tank; (*Zool*) shell. **p~n** *vt* armourplate. **P~schrank** *m* safe
Papa /'papa, pa'pa:/ *m* **-s,-s** daddy
Papagei *m* **-s & -en,-en** parrot
Papier *nt* **-[e]s,-e** paper. **P~korb** *m* waste-paper basket. **P~schlange** *f* streamer. **P~waren** *fpl* stationery *sg*
Pappe *f* **-** cardboard; (*dial: Kleister*) glue
Pappel *f* **-,-n** poplar
pappen *vt/i* (*haben*) (*fam*) stick
pappig *a* (*fam*) sticky
Papp|karton *m*, **P~schachtel** *f* cardboard box
Paprika *m* **-s,-[s]** [sweet] pepper; (*Gewürz*) paprika
Papst *m* **-[e]s,⸚e** pope
päpstlich *a* papal
Parade *f* **-,-n** parade
Paradeiser *m* **-s,-** (*Aust*) tomato
Paradies *nt* **-es,-e** paradise. **p~isch** *a* heavenly
Paradox *nt* **-es,-e** paradox. **p~** *a* paradoxical
Paraffin *nt* **-s** paraffin
Paragraph, Paragraf *m* **-en,-en** section
parallel *a & adv* parallel. **P~e** *f* **-,-n** parallel
Paranuss (**Paranuß**) *f* Brazil nut
Parasit *m* **-en,-en** parasite
parat *a* ready
Pärchen *nt* **-s,-** pair; (*Liebes-*) couple
Parcours /par'ku:ɐ̯/ *m* **-,-** /-[s],-s/ (*Sport*) course
Pardon /par'dõ:/ *int* sorry!
Parfüm *nt* **-s,-e & -s** perfume, scent. **p~iert** *a* perfumed, scented
parieren¹ *vt* parry
parieren² *vi* (*haben*) (*fam*) obey
Parität *f* **-** parity; (*in Ausschuss*) equal representation
Park *m* **-s,-s** park. **p~en** *vt/i* (*haben*) park. **P~en** *nt* **-s** parking; **'P~en verboten'** 'no parking'
Parkett *nt* **-[e]s, -e** parquet floor; (*Theat*) stalls *pl*
Park|haus *nt* multi-storey car park. **P~lücke** *f* parking space. **P~platz** *m* car park, (*Amer*)

parking-lot; (*für ein Auto*) parking space; (*Autobahn-*) lay-by. **P~scheibe** *f* parking-disc. **P~schein** *m* car-park ticket. **P~uhr** *f* parking-meter. **P~verbot** *nt* parking ban; **'P~verbot'** 'no parking'

Parlament *nt* **-[e]s,-e** parliament. **p~arisch** *a* parliamentary

Parodie *f* **-,-n** parody. **p~ren** *vt* parody

Parole *f* **-,-n** slogan; (*Mil*) password

Part *m* **-s,-s** (*Theat, Mus*) part

Partei *f* **-,-en** (*Pol, Jur*) party; (*Miet-*) tenant; **für jdn P~ ergreifen** take s.o.'s part. **p~isch** *a* biased. **p~los** *a* independent

Parterre /par'tɛr/ *nt* **-s,-s** ground floor, (*Amer*) first floor; (*Theat*) rear stalls *pl*. **p~** *adv* on the ground floor

Partie *f* **-,-n** part; (*Tennis, Schach*) game; (*Golf*) round; (*Comm*) batch; **eine gute P~ machen** marry well

Partikel[1] *nt* **-s,-** particle

Partikel[2] *f* **-,-n** (*Gram*) particle

Partitur *f* **-,-en** (*Mus*) full score

Partizip *nt* **-s,-ien** /-i̯ən/ participle; **erstes/zweites P~** present/past participle

Partner|(in) *m* **-s,-** (*f* **-,-nen**) partner. **P~schaft** *f* **-,-en** partnership. **P~stadt** *f* twin town

Party /'pa:ɐ̯ti/ *f* **-,-s** party

Parzelle *f* **-,-n** plot [of ground]

Pass *m* **-es,⸚e** (**Paß** *m* **-sses,⸚sse**) passport; (*Geog, Sport*) pass

passabel *a* passable

Passage /pa'sa:ʒə/ *f* **-,-n** passage; (*Einkaufs-*) shopping arcade

Passagier /pasa'ʒi:ɐ̯/ *m* **-s,-e** passenger

Passamt (**Paßamt**) *nt* passport office

Passant(in) *m* **-en,-en** (*f* **-,-nen**) passer-by

Passbild (**Paßbild**) *nt* passport photograph

Passe *f* **-,-n** yoke

passen *vi* (*haben*) fit; (*geeignet sein*) be right (**für** for); (*Sport*) pass the ball; (*aufgeben*) pass; **p~ zu go** [well] with; (*übereinstimmen*) match; **jdm p~** fit s.o.; (*gelegen sein*) suit s.o.; **seine Art passt mir nicht** I don't like his manner; **[ich] passe** pass. **p~d** *a* suitable; (*angemessen*) appropriate; (*günstig*) convenient; (*übereinstimmend*) matching

passier|bar *a* passable. **p~en** *vt* **pass; cross** ⟨*Grenze*⟩; (*Culin*) rub through a sieve □ *vi* (*sein*) happen (**jdm** to s.o.); **es ist ein Unglück p~t** there has been an accident. **P~schein** *m* pass

Passion *f* **-,-en** passion. **p~iert** *a* very keen ⟨*Jäger, Angler*⟩

passiv *a* passive. **P~** *nt* **-s,-e** (*Gram*) passive

Pass|kontrolle (**Paßkontrolle**) *f* passport control. **P~straße** *f* pass

Paste *f* **-,-n** paste

Pastell *nt* **-[e]s,-e** pastel. **P~farbe** *f* pastel colour

Pastet|chen *nt* **-s,-** [individual] pie; (*Königin-*) vol-au-vent. **P~e** *f* **-,-n** pie; (*Gänseleber-*) pâté

pasteurisieren /pastøri'zi:rən/ *vt* pasteurize

Pastille *f* **-,-n** pastille

Pastinake *f* **-,-n** parsnip

Pastor *m* **-s,-en** /-'to:rən/ pastor

Pate *m* **-n,-n** godfather; (*fig*) sponsor; **P~n** godparents. **P~nkind** *nt* godchild. **P~nschaft** *f* **-** sponsorship. **P~nsohn** *m* godson

Patent *nt* **-[e]s,-e** patent; (*Offiziers-*) commission. **p~** *a* (*fam*) clever, *adv* -ly; ⟨*Person*⟩ resourceful. **p~ieren** *vt* patent

Patentochter *f* god-daughter

Pater *m* **-s,-** (*Relig*) Father

pathetisch *a* emotional □ *adv* with emotion

Patholog|e *m* **-n,-n** pathologist. **p~isch** *a* pathological, *adv* -ly

Pathos *nt* - emotion, feeling
Patience /pa'sjã:s/ *f* **-,-n** patience
Patient(in) /pa'tsiɛnt(ɪn)/ *m* **-en, -en** (*f* **-,-nen**) patient
Patin *f* **-,-nen** godmother
Patriot|(in) *m* **-en,-en** (*f* **-,-nen**) patriot. **p~isch** *a* patriotic. **P~ismus** *m* - patriotism
Patrone *f* **-,-n** cartridge
Patrouill|e /pa'trʊljə/ *f* **-,-n** patrol. **p~ieren** /-'ji:rən/ *vi* (*haben/sein*) patrol
Patsch|e *f* **in der P~e sitzen** (*fam*) be in a jam. **p~en** *vi* (*haben/sein*) splash □ *vt* slap. **p~nass (p~naß)** *a* (*fam*) soaking wet
Patt *nt* **-s** stalemate
Patz|er *m* **-s,-** (*fam*) slip. **p~ig** *a* (*fam*) insolent
Pauk|e *f* **-,-n** kettledrum; **auf die P~e hauen** (*fam*) have a good time; (*prahlen*) boast. **p~en** *vt/i* (*haben*) (*fam*) swot. **P~er** *m* **-s,-** (*fam: Lehrer*) teacher
pausbäckig *a* chubby-cheeked
pauschal *a* all-inclusive; (*einheitlich*) flat-rate; (*fig*) sweeping ⟨*Urteil*⟩; **p~e Summe** lump sum □ *adv* in a lump sum; (*fig*) wholesale. **P~e** *f* **-,-n** lump sum. **P~reise** *f* package tour. **P~summe** *f* lump sum
Pause[1] *f* **-,-n** break; (*beim Sprechen*) pause; (*Theat*) interval; (*im Kino*) intermission; (*Mus*) rest; **P~ machen** have a break
Pause[2] *f* **-,-n** tracing. **p~n** *vt* trace
pausenlos *a* incessant, *adv* -ly
pausieren *vi* (*haben*) have a break; (*ausruhen*) rest
Pauspapier *nt* tracing-paper
Pavian *m* **-s,-e** baboon
Pavillon /'pavɪljõ/ *m* **-s,-s** pavilion
Pazifi|k *m* **-s** Pacific [Ocean]. **p~sch** *a* Pacific
Pazifist *m* **-en,-en** pacifist
Pech *nt* **-s** pitch; (*Unglück*) bad luck; **P~ haben** be unlucky. **p~schwarz** *a* pitch-black; ⟨*Haare, Augen*⟩ jet-black. **P~strähne** *f* run of bad luck. **P~vogel** *m* (*fam*) unlucky devil
Pedal *nt* **-s,-e** pedal
Pedant *m* **-en,-en** pedant. **p~isch** *a* pedantic, *adv* -ally
Pediküre *f* **-,-n** pedicure
Pegel *m* **-s,-** level; (*Gerät*) water-level indicator. **P~stand** *m* [water] level
peilen *vt* take a bearing on; **über den Daumen gepeilt** (*fam*) at a rough guess
Pein *f* - (*liter*) torment. **p~igen** *vt* torment
peinlich *a* embarrassing, awkward; (*genau*) scrupulous, *adv* -ly; **es war mir sehr p~** I was very embarrassed
Peitsche *f* **-,-n** whip. **p~n** *vt* whip; (*fig*) lash □ *vi* (*sein*) lash (**an** + *acc* against). **P~nhieb** *m* lash
pekuniär *a* financial, *adv* -ly
Pelikan *m* **-s,-e** pelican
Pell|e *f* **-,-n** skin. **p~en** *vt* peel; shell ⟨*Ei*⟩; **sich p~en** peel. **P~kartoffeln** *fpl* potatoes boiled in their skins
Pelz *m* **-es,-e** fur. **P~mantel** *m* fur coat
Pendel *nt* **-s,-** pendulum. **p~n** *vi* (*haben*) swing □ *vi* (*sein*) commute. **P~verkehr** *m* shuttle-service; (*für Pendler*) commuter traffic
Pendler *m* **-s,-** commuter
penetrant *a* penetrating; (*fig*) obtrusive, *adv* -ly
penibel *a* fastidious, fussy; (*pedantisch*) pedantic
Penis *m* **-,-se** penis
Penne *f* **-,-n** (*fam*) school. **P~n** *vi* (*haben*) (*fam*) sleep. **P~r** *m* **-s,-** (*sl*) tramp
Pension /pã'zio:n/ *f* **-,-en** pension; (*Hotel*) guest-house; **bei voller/halber P~** with full/half board. **P~är(in)** *m* **-s,-e** (*f* **-,-nen**)

pensioner. **P~at** *nt* **-[e]s,-e** boarding-school. **p~ieren** *vt* retire. **p~iert** *a* retired. **P~ierung** *f* - retirement
Pensum *nt* **-s** [allotted] work
Peperoni *f* **-,-** chilli
per *prep* (+ *acc*) by; **per Luftpost** by airmail
perfekt *a* perfect, *adv* -ly; **p~ sein** ⟨*Vertrag:*⟩ be settled
Perfekt *nt* **-s** (*Gram*) perfect
Perfektion /-'tsi̯o:n/ *f* - perfection
perforiert *a* perforated
Pergament *nt* **-[e]s,-e** parchment. **P~papier** *nt* grease-proof paper
Period|e *f* **-,-n** period. **p~isch** *a* periodic, *adv* -ally
Perl|e *f* **-,-n** pearl; (*Glas-, Holz-*) bead; (*Sekt-*) bubble; (*fam: Hilfe*) treasure. **p~en** *vi* (*haben*) bubble. **P~mutt** *nt* **-s**, **P~mutter** *f* - & *nt* **-s** mother-of-pearl
perplex *a* (*fam*) perplexed
Perserkatze *f* Persian cat
Pers|ien /-i̯ən/ *nt* **-s** Persia. **p~isch** *a* Persian
Person *f* **-,-en** person; (*Theat*) character; **ich für meine P~** [I] for my part; **für vier P~en** for four people
Personal *nt* **-s** personnel, staff. **P~ausweis** *m* identity card. **P~chef** *m* personnel manager. **P~ien** /-i̯ən/ *pl* personal particulars. **P~mangel** *m* staff shortage. **P~pronomen** *nt* personal pronoun
Personen|kraftwagen *m* private car. **P~zug** *m* stopping train
personifizieren *vt* personify
persönlich *a* personal □ *adv* personally, in person. **P~keit** *f* **-,-en** personality
Perspektive *f* **-,-n** perspective; (*Zukunfts-*) prospect
Perücke *f* **-,-n** wig
pervers *a* [sexually] perverted. **P~ion** *f* **-,-en** perversion

Pessimis|mus *m* - pessimism. **P~t** *m* **-en,-en** pessimist. **p~tisch** *a* pessimistic, *adv* -ally
Pest *f* - plague
Petersilie /-i̯ə/ *f* - parsley
Petroleum /-leum/ *nt* **-s** paraffin, (*Amer*) kerosene
Petze *f* **-,-n** (*fam*) sneak. **p~n** *vi* (*haben*) (*fam*) sneak
Pfad *m* **-[e]s,-e** path. **P~finder** *m* **-s,-** [Boy] Scout. **P~finderin** *f* **-,-nen** [Girl] Guide
Pfahl *m* **-[e]s,¨-e** stake, post
Pfalz (die) - the Palatinate
Pfand *nt* **-[e]s,¨-er** pledge; (*beim Spiel*) forfeit; (*Flaschen-*) deposit
pfänd|en *vt* (*Jur*) seize. **P~erspiel** *nt* game of forfeits
Pfand|haus *nt* pawnshop. **P~leiher** *m* **-s,-** pawnbroker
Pfändung *f* **-,-en** (*Jur*) seizure
Pfann|e *f* **-,-n** [frying-]pan. **P~kuchen** *m* pancake; **Berliner P~kuchen** doughnut
Pfarr|er *m* **-s,-** vicar, parson; (*katholischer*) priest. **P~haus** *nt* vicarage
Pfau *m* **-s,-en** peacock
Pfeffer *m* **-s** pepper. **P~kuchen** *m* gingerbread. **P~minzbonbon** *m & nt* [pepper]mint. **P~minze** *f* - (*Bot*) peppermint. **P~minztee** *m* [pepper]mint tea. **p~n** *vt* pepper; (*fam: schmeißen*) chuck. **P~streuer** *m* **-s,-** pepperpot
Pfeif|e *f* **-,-n** whistle; (*Tabak-, Orgel-*) pipe. **p~en**† *vt/i* (*haben*) whistle; (*als Signal*) blow the whistle; **ich p~e darauf!** (*fam*) I couldn't care less [about it]!
Pfeil *m* **-[e]s,-e** arrow
Pfeiler *m* **-s,-** pillar; (*Brücken-*) pier
Pfennig *m* **-s,-e** pfennig; **10 P~** 10 pfennigs
Pferch *m* **-[e]s,-e** [sheep] pen. **p~en** *vt* (*fam*) cram (**in** + *acc* into)
Pferd *nt* **-es,-e** horse; **zu P~e** on horseback; **das P~ beim**

Schwanz aufzäumen put the cart before the horse. **P~e-rennen** *nt* horse-race; (*als Sport*) [horse-]racing. **P~eschwanz** *m* horse's tail; (*Frisur*) pony-tail. **P~estall** *m* stable. **P~estärke** *f* horsepower. **P~ewagen** *m* horse-drawn cart

Pfiff *m* **-[e]s,-e** whistle; **P~ haben** (*fam*) have style

Pfifferling *m* **-s,-e** chanterelle

pfiffig *a* smart

Pfingst|en *nt* **-s** Whitsun. **P~montag** *m* Whit Monday. **P~rose** *f* peony

Pfirsich *m* **-s,-e** peach. **p~farben** *a* peach[-coloured]

Pflanz|e *f* **-,-n** plant. **p~en** *vt* plant. **P~enfett** *nt* vegetable fat. **p~lich** *a* vegetable; ⟨*Mittel*⟩ herbal. **P~ung** *f* **-,-en** plantation

Pflaster *nt* **-s,-** pavement; (*Heft-*) plaster. **p~n** *vt* pave. **P~stein** *m* paving-stone

Pflaume *f* **-,-n** plum

Pflege *f* **-** care; (*Kranken-*) nursing; **in P~ nehmen** look after; (*Admin*) foster ⟨*Kind*⟩. **p~bedürftig** *a* in need of care. **P~eltern** *pl* foster-parents. **P~kind** *nt* foster-child. **p~leicht** *a* easy-care. **P~mutter** *f* foster-mother. **p~n** *vt* look after, care for; nurse ⟨*Kranke*⟩; cultivate ⟨*Künste, Freundschaft*⟩. **P~r(in)** *m* **-s,-** (*f* **-,-nen**) nurse; (*Tier-*) keeper

Pflicht *f* **-,-en** duty; (*Sport*) compulsory exercise/routine. **p~bewusst (p~bewußt)** *a* conscientious, *adv* -ly. **p~eifrig** *a* zealous, *adv* -ly. **P~fach** *nt* (*Sch*) compulsory subject. **P~gefühl** *nt* sense of duty. **p~gemäß** *a* due □ *adv* duly

Pflock *m* **-[e]s,-̈e** peg

pflücken *vt* pick

Pflug *m* **-[e]s,-̈e** plough

pflügen *vt/i* (*haben*) plough

Pforte *f* **-,-n** gate

Pförtner *m* **-s,-** porter

Pfosten *m* **-s,-** post

Pfote *f* **-,-n** paw

Pfropfen *m* **-s,-** stopper; (*Korken*) cork. **p~** *vt* graft **(auf** + *acc* on [to]); (*fam: pressen*) cram **(in** + *acc* into)

pfui *int* ugh; **p~ schäm dich!** you should be ashamed of yourself!

Pfund *nt* **-[e]s,-e** & **-** pound

Pfusch|arbeit *f* (*fam*) shoddy work. **p~en** *vi* (*haben*) (*fam*) botch one's work. **P~er** *m* **-s,-** (*fam*) shoddy worker. **P~erei** *f* **-,-en** (*fam*) botch-up

Pfütze *f* **-,-n** puddle

Phänomen *nt* **-s,-e** phenomenon. **p~al** *a* phenomenal

Phantasie *f* **-,-n** imagination; **P~n** fantasies; (*Fieber-*) hallucinations. **p~los** *a* unimaginative. **p~ren** *vi* (*haben*) fantasize; (*im Fieber*) be delirious. **p~voll** *a* imaginative, *adv* -ly

phant|astisch *a* fantastic, *adv* -ally. **P~om** *nt* **-s,-e** phantom

pharma|zeutisch *a* pharmaceutical. **P~zie** *f* **-** pharmacy

Phase *f* **-,-n** phase

Philanthrop *m* **-en,-en** philanthropist. **p~isch** *a* philanthropic

Philolo|ge *m* **-n,-n** teacher/student of language and literature. **P~gie** *f* **-** [study of] language and literature

Philosoph *m* **-en,-en** philosopher. **P~ie** *f* **-,-n** philosophy. **p~ieren** *vi* (*haben*) philosophize

philosophisch *a* philosophical, *adv* -ly

phlegmatisch *a* phlegmatic

Phobie *f* **-,-n** phobia

Phonet|ik *f* **-** phonetics *sg*. **p~isch** *a* phonetic, *adv* -ally

Phonotypistin *f* **-,-nen** audio typist

Phosphor *m* **-s** phosphorus

Photo *nt*, **Photo-** = **Foto, Foto-**

Phrase *f* **-,-n** empty phrase

Physik *f* **-** physics *sg*. **p~alisch** *a* physical

Physiker(in) *m* **-s,-** (*f* **-,-nen**) physicist
Physio|logie *f* - physiology. **P~therapie** *f* physiotherapy
physisch *a* physical, *adv* -ly
Pianist(in) *m* **-en,-en** (*f* **-,-nen**) pianist
Pickel *m* **-s,-** pimple, spot; (*Spitzhacke*) pick. **p~ig** *a* spotty
picken *vt/i* (*haben*) peck (**nach** at); (*fam: nehmen*) pick (**aus** out of); (*Aust fam: kleben*) stick
Picknick *nt* **-s,-s** picnic. **p~en** *vi* (*haben*) picnic
piep[s]|en *vi* (*haben*) ⟨*Vogel:*⟩ cheep; ⟨*Maus:*⟩ squeak; (*Techn*) bleep. **P~er** *m* **-s,-** bleeper
Pier *m* **-s,-e** [harbour] pier
Pietät /pie'tɛ:t/ *f* - reverence. **p~los** *a* irreverent, *adv* -ly
Pigment *nt* **-[e]s,-e** pigment. **P~ierung** *f* - pigmentation
Pik *nt* **-s,-s** (*Karten*) spades *pl*
pikant *a* piquant; (*gewagt*) racy
piken *vt* (*fam*) prick
pikiert *a* offended, hurt
piksen *vt* (*fam*) prick
Pilger|(in) *m* **-s,-** (*f* **-,-nen**) pilgrim. **P~fahrt** *f* pilgrimage. **p~n** *vi* (*sein*) make a pilgrimage
Pille *f* **-,-n** pill
Pilot *m* **-en,-en** pilot
Pilz *m* **-es,-e** fungus; (*essbarer*) mushroom; **wie P~e aus dem Boden schießen** (*fig*) mushroom
pingelig *a* (*fam*) fussy
Pinguin *m* **-s,-e** penguin
Pinie /-iə/ *f* **-,-n** stone-pine
pink *pred a* shocking pink
pinkeln *vi* (*haben*) (*fam*) pee
Pinsel *m* **-s,-** [paint]brush
Pinzette *f* **-,-n** tweezers *pl*
Pionier *m* **-s,-e** (*Mil*) sapper; (*fig*) pioneer. **P~arbeit** *f* pioneering work
Pirat *m* **-en,-en** pirate
pirschen *vi* (*haben*) **p~ auf** (+ *acc*) stalk □ *vr* **sich p~** creep (**an** + *acc* up to)
pissen *vi* (*haben*) (*sl*) piss
Piste *f* **-,-n** (*Ski-*) run, piste; (*Renn-*) track; (*Aviat*) runway
Pistole *f* **-,-n** pistol
pitschnass (**pitschnaß**) *a* (*fam*) soaking wet
pittoresk *a* picturesque
Pizza *f* **-,-s** pizza
Pkw /'pe:kave:/ *m* **-s,-s** (= **Personenkraftwagen**) [private] car
placieren /-'tsi:rən/ *vt* = **platzieren**
Plackerei *f* - (*fam*) drudgery
plädieren *vi* (*haben*) plead (**für** for); **auf Freispruch p~** (*Jur*) ask for an acquittal
Plädoyer /plɛdoa'je:/ *nt* **-s,-s** (*Jur*) closing speech; (*fig*) plea
Plage *f* **-,-n** [hard] labour; (*Mühe*) trouble; (*Belästigung*) nuisance. **p~n** *vt* torment, plague; (*bedrängen*) pester; **sich p~n** struggle; (*arbeiten*) work hard
Plagi|at *nt* **-[e]s,-e** plagiarism. **p~ieren** *vt* plagiarize
Plakat *nt* **-[e]s,-e** poster
Plakette *f* **-,-n** badge
Plan *m* **-[e]s,¨e** plan
Plane *f* **-,-n** tarpaulin; (*Boden-*) groundsheet
planen *vt/i* (*haben*) plan
Planet *m* **-en,-en** planet
planier|en *vt* level. **P~raupe** *f* bulldozer
Planke *f* **-,-n** plank
plan|los *a* unsystematic, *adv* -ally. **p~mäßig** *a* systematic; ⟨*Ankunft*⟩ scheduled □ *adv* systematically; (*nach Plan*) according to plan; ⟨*ankommen*⟩ on schedule
Plansch|becken *nt* paddling pool. **p~en** *vi* (*haben*) splash about
Plantage /plan'ta:ʒə/ *f* **-,-n** plantation
Planung *f* - planning
Plapper|maul *nt* (*fam*) chatterbox. **p~n** *vi* (*haben*) chatter □ *vt* talk ⟨*Unsinn*⟩
plärren *vi* (*haben*) bawl; ⟨*Radio:*⟩ blare

Plasma *nt* **-s** plasma
Plastik[1] *f* **-,-en** sculpture
Plast|ik[2] *nt* **-s** plastic. **p~isch** *a* three-dimensional; (*formbar*) plastic; (*anschaulich*) graphic, *adv* -ally; **p~ische Chirurgie** plastic surgery
Platane *f* **-,-n** plane [tree]
Plateau /pla'to:/ *nt* **-s,-s** plateau
Platin *nt* **-s** platinum
Platitüde *f* **-,-n** (NEW) **Plattitüde**
platonisch *a* platonic
platschen *vi* (*sein*) splash
plätschern *vi* (*haben*) splash; ⟨*Bach:*⟩ babble □ *vi* (*sein*) ⟨*Bach:*⟩ babble along
platt *a & adv* flat; **p~ sein** (*fam*) be flabbergasted. **P~** *nt* **-[s]** (*Lang*) Low German
Plättbrett *nt* ironing-board
Platte *f* **-,-n** slab; (*Druck-*) plate; (*Metall-, Glas-*) sheet; (*Fliese*) tile; (*Koch-*) hotplate; (*Tisch-*) top; (*Auszieh-*) leaf; (*Schall-*) record, disc; (*zum Servieren*) [flat] dish, platter; **kalte P~** assorted cold meats and cheeses *pl*
Plätt|eisen *nt* iron. **p~en** *vt/i* (*haben*) iron
Plattenspieler *m* record-player
Platt|form *f* **-,-en** platform. **P~füße** *mpl* flat feet. **P~heit** *f* **-,-en** platitude
Plattitüde *f* **-,-n** platitude
Platz *m* **-es,¨e** place; (*von Häusern umgeben*) square; (*Sitz-*) seat; (*Sport-*) ground; (*Fußball-*) pitch; (*Tennis-*) court; (*Golf-*) course; (*freier Raum*) room, space; **P~ nehmen** take a seat; **P~ machen/lassen** make/leave room; **vom P~ stellen** (*Sport*) send off. **P~angst** *f* agoraphobia; (*Klaustrophobie*) claustrophobia. **P~anweiserin** *f* **-,-nen** usherette
Plätzchen *nt* **-s,-** spot; (*Culin*) biscuit
platzen *vi* (*sein*) burst; (*auf-*) split; (*fam: scheitern*) fall through; ⟨*Verlobung:*⟩ be off; **vor Neugier p~** be bursting with curiosity
platzieren *vt* place, put; **sich p~** (*Sport*) be placed
Platz|karte *f* seat reservation ticket. **P~konzert** *nt* open-air concert. **P~mangel** *m* lack of space. **P~patrone** *f* blank. **P~regen** *m* downpour. **P~verweis** *m* (*Sport*) sending off. **P~wunde** *f* laceration
Plauderei *f* **-,-en** chat
plaudern *vi* (*haben*) chat
Plausch *m* **-[e]s,-e** (*SGer*) chat. **p~en** *vi* (*haben*) (*SGer*) chat
plausibel *a* plausible
plazieren *vt* (NEW) **platzieren**
pleite *a* (*fam*) **p~ sein** be broke: ⟨*Firma:*⟩ be bankrupt; **p~ gehen** (NEW) **P~ gehen**, *s.* **Pleite**. **P~** *f* **-,-n** (*fam*) bankruptcy; (*Misserfolg*) flop; **P~ gehen** *od* **machen** go bankrupt
plissiert *a* [finely] pleated
Plomb|e *f* **-,-n** seal; (*Zahn-*) filling. **p~ieren** *vt* seal; fill ⟨*Zahn*⟩
plötzlich *a* sudden, *adv* -ly
plump *a* plump; (*ungeschickt*) clumsy, *adv* -ily
plumpsen *vi* (*sein*) (*fam*) fall
Plunder *m* **-s** (*fam*) junk, rubbish
plündern *vt/i* (*haben*) loot
Plunderstück *nt* Danish pastry
Plural *m* **-s,-e** plural
plus *adv, conj & prep* (+ *dat*) plus. **P~** *nt* **-** surplus; (*Gewinn*) profit (*Vorteil*) advantage, plus. **P~punkt** *m* (*Sport*) point; (*fig*) plus. **P~quamperfekt** *nt* pluperfect. **P~zeichen** *nt* plus sign
Po *m* **-s,-s** (*fam*) bottom
Pöbel *m* **-s** mob, rabble. **p~haft** *a* loutish
pochen *vi* (*haben*) knock, ⟨*Herz:*⟩ pound; **p~ auf** (+ *acc*) (*fig*) insist on
pochieren /pɔ'ʃi:rən/ *vt* poach
Pocken *pl* smallpox *sg*
Podest *nt* **-[e]s,-e** rostrum

Podium *nt* **-s,-ien** /-i̯ən/ platform; (*Podest*) rostrum
Poesie /poe'zi:/ *f* **-** poetry
poetisch *a* poetic
Pointe /'pọɛ̃:tə/ *f* **-,-n** point (*of a joke*)
Pokal *m* **-s,-e** goblet; (*Sport*) cup
pökeln *vt* (*Culin*) salt
Poker *nt* **-s** poker
Pol *m* **-s,-e** pole. **p~ar** *a* polar
polarisieren *vt* polarize
Polarstern *m* pole-star
Pole *m*, **-n,-n** Pole. **P~n** *nt* **-s** Poland
Police /po'li:sə/ *f* **-,-n** policy
Polier *m* **-s,-e** foreman
polieren *vt* polish
Polin *f* **-,-nen** Pole
Politesse *f* **-,-n** [woman] traffic warden
Politik *f* **-** politics *sg*; (*Vorgehen, Maßnahme*) policy
Polit|iker(in) *m* **-s,-** (*f*, **-,-nen**) politician. **p~isch** *a* political, *adv* -ly
Politur *f* **-,-en** polish
Polizei *f* **-** police *pl*. **P~beamte(r)** *m* police officer. **p~lich** *a* police ... □ *adv* by the police; ⟨*sich anmelden*⟩ with the police. **P~streife** *f* police patrol. **P~stunde** *f* closing time. **P~wache** *f* police station
Polizist *m* **-en,-en** policeman. **P~in** *f* **-,-nen** policewoman
Pollen *m* **-s** pollen
polnisch *a* Polish
Polohemd *nt* polo shirt
Polster *nt* **-s,-** pad; (*Kissen*) cushion; (*Möbel-*) upholstery; (*fam: Rücklage*) reserves *pl*. **P~er** *m* **-s,-** upholsterer. **P~möbel** *pl* upholstered furniture *sg*. **p~n** *vt* pad; upholster ⟨*Möbel*⟩. **P~ung** *f* **-** padding; upholstery
Polter|abend *m* wedding-eve party. **p~n** *vi* (*haben*) thump bang; (*schelten*) bawl □ *vi* (*sein*) crash down; (*gehen*) clump [along]; (*fahren*) rumble [along]
Polyäthylen *nt* **-s** polythene
Polyester *m* **-s** polyester
Polyp *m* **-en,-en** polyp; (*sl: Polizist*) copper; **P~en** adenoids *pl*
Pomeranze *f* **-,-n** Seville orange
Pommes *pl* (*fam*) French fries
Pommes frites /pɔm'fri:t/ *pl* chips; (*dünner*) French fries
Pomp *m* **-s** pomp
Pompon /põ'põ:/ *m* **-s,-s** pompon
pompös *a* ostentatious, *adv* -ly
Pony¹ *nt* **-s,-s** pony
Pony² *m* **-s,-s** fringe
Pop *m* **-[s]** pop. **P~musik** *f* pop music
Popo *m* **-s,-s** (*fam*) bottom
popul|är *a* popular. **P~arität** *f* **-** popularity
Pore *f* **-,-n** pore
Porno|graphie, **Pornografie** *f* **-** pornography. **p~graphisch**, **p~grafisch** *a* pornographic
porös *a* porous
Porree *m* **-s** leeks *pl*; **eine Stange P~** a leek
Portal *nt* **-s,-e** portal
Portemonnaie /pɔrtmɔ'ne:/ *nt* **-s,-s** purse
Portier /pɔr'ti̯e:/ *m* **-s,-s** doorman, porter
Portion /-'t̮si̯o:n/ *f* **-,-en** helping, portion
Portmonee *nt* **-s,-s** = **Portemonnaie**
Porto *nt* **-s** postage. **p~frei** *adv* post free, post paid
Porträ|t /pɔr'trɛ:/ *nt* **-s,-s** portrait. **p~tieren** *vt* paint a portrait of
Portugal *nt* **-s** Portugal
Portugies|e *m* **-n,-n**, **P~in** *f* **-,-nen** Portuguese. **p~isch** *a* Portuguese
Portwein *m* port
Porzellan *nt* **-s** china, porcelain
Posaune *f* **-,-n** trombone
Pose *f* **-,-n** pose
posieren *vi* (*haben*) pose
Position /-'t̮si̯o:n/ *f* **-,-en** position

positiv *a* positive, *adv* -ly. **P~** *nt* **-s,-e** (*Phot*) positive
Posse *f* **-,-n** (*Theat*) farce. **P~n** *m* **-s,-** prank; **P~n** *pl* tomfoolery *sg*
Possessivpronomen *nt* possessive pronoun
possierlich *a* cute
Post *f* **-** post office; (*Briefe*) mail, post; **mit der P~** by post
postalisch *a* postal
Post|amt *nt* post office. **P~anweisung** *f* postal money order. **P~bote** *m* postman
Posten *m* **-s,-** post; (*Wache*) sentry; (*Waren-*) batch; (*Rechnungs-*) item, entry; **P~ stehen** stand guard; **nicht auf dem P~** (*fam*) under the weather
Poster *nt & m* **-s,-** poster
Postfach *nt* post-office *or* PO box
postieren *vt* post, station; **sich p~** station oneself
Post|karte *f* postcard. **p~lagernd** *adv* poste restante. **P~leitzahl** *f* postcode, (*Amer*) Zip code. **P~scheckkonto** *nt* ≈ National Girobank account. **P~stempel** *m* postmark
postum *a* posthumous, *adv* -ly
post|wendend *adv* by return of post. **P~wertzeichen** *nt* [postage] stamp
Poten|tial /-'tsja:l/ *nt* **-s,-e** = **Potenzial. p~tiell** /-'tsiɛl/ *a* = **potenziell**
Potenz *f* **-,-en** potency; (*Math & fig*) power. **P~ial** *nt* **-s,-e** potential. **p~iell** *a* potential, *adv* -ly
Pracht *f* **-** magnificence, splendour. **P~exemplar** *nt* magnificent specimen
prächtig *a* magnificent, *adv* -ly; (*prima*) splendid, *adv* -ly
prachtvoll *a* magnificent, *adv* -ly
Prädikat *nt* **-[e]s,-e** rating; (*Comm*) grade; (*Gram*) predicate. **p~iv** *a* (*Gram*) predicative, *adv* -ly. **P~swein** *m* high-quality wine
präge|n *vt* stamp (**auf** + *acc* on); emboss ⟨*Leder, Papier*⟩; mint ⟨*Münze*⟩; coin ⟨*Wort, Ausdruck*⟩; (*fig*) shape. **P~stempel** *m* die
pragmatisch *a* pragmatic, *adv* -ally
prägnant *a* succinct, *adv* -ly
prähistorisch *a* prehistoric
prahl|en *vi* (*haben*) boast, brag (**mit** about). **p~erisch** *a* boastful, *adv* -ly
Prakti|k *f* **-,-en** practice. **P~kant(in)** *m* **-en,-en** (*f* **-,-nen**) trainee
Prakti|kum *nt* **-s,-ka** practical training. **p~sch** *a* practical; (*nützlich*) handy; (*tatsächlich*) virtual; **p~scher Arzt** general practitioner □ *adv* practically; virtually; (*in der Praxis*) in practice; **p~sch arbeiten** do practical work. **p~zieren** *vt/i* (*haben*) practise; (*anwenden*) put into practice; (*fam: bekommen*) get
Praline *f* **-,-n** chocolate; **Schachtel P~n** box of chocolates
prall *a* bulging; (*dick*) plump; ⟨*Sonne*⟩ blazing □ *adv* **p~ gefüllt** full to bursting. **p~en** *vi* (*sein*) **p~ auf** (+ *acc*)/**gegen** collide with, hit; ⟨*Sonne:*⟩ blaze down on
Prämie /-jə/ *f* **-,-n** premium; (*Preis*) award
präm[i]ieren *vt* award a prize to
Pranger *m* **-s,-** pillory
Pranke *f* **-,-n** paw
Präpar|at *nt* **-[e]s,-e** preparation. **p~ieren** *vt* prepare; (*zerlegen*) dissect; (*ausstopfen*) stuff
Präposition /-'tsjo:n/ *f* **-,-en** preposition
Präsens *nt* **-** (*Gram*) present
präsentieren *vt* present; **sich p~** present itself/⟨*Person:*⟩ oneself
Präsenz *f* **-** presence
Präservativ *nt* **-s,-e** condom
Präsident|(in) *m* **-en,-en** (*f* **-,-nen**) president. **P~schaft** *f* **-** presidency

Präsidium *nt* **-s** presidency; (*Gremium*) executive committee; (*Polizei-*) headquarters *pl*
prasseln *vi* (*haben*) ⟨*Regen:*⟩ beat down; ⟨*Feuer:*⟩ crackle □ *vi* (*sein*) **p~ auf** (+ *acc*)/**gegen** beat down on/beat against
prassen *vi* (*haben*) live extravagantly; (*schmausen*) feast
Präteritum *nt* **-s** imperfect
präventiv *a* preventive
Praxis *f* **-,-xen** practice; (*Erfahrung*) practical experience; (*Arzt-*) surgery; **in der P~** in practice
Präzedenzfall *m* precedent
präzis[e] *a* precise, *adv* -ly
Präzision *f* **-** precision
predig|en *vt/i* (*haben*) preach. **P~er** *m* **-s,-** preacher. **P~t** *f* **-,-en** sermon
Preis *m* **-es,-e** price; (*Belohnung*) prize; **um jeden/keinen P~** at any/not at any price. **P~ausschreiben** *nt* competition
Preiselbeere *f* (*Bot*) cowberry; (*Culin*) ≈ cranberry
preisen† *vt* praise; **sich glücklich p~** count oneself lucky
preisgeben† *vt sep* abandon (*dat* to); reveal ⟨*Geheimnis*⟩
preis|gekrönt *a* award-winning. **P~gericht** *nt* jury. **p~günstig** *a* reasonably priced □ *adv* at a reasonable price. **P~lage** *f* price range. **p~lich** *a* price ... □ *adv* in price. **P~richter** *m* judge. **P~schild** *nt* price-tag. **P~träger(in)** *m(f)* prize-winner. **p~wert** *a* reasonable, *adv* -bly; (*billig*) inexpensive, *adv* -ly
prekär *a* difficult; (*heikel*) delicate
Prell|bock *m* buffers *pl*. **p~en** *vt* bounce; (*verletzen*) bruise; (*fam: betrügen*) cheat. **P~ung** *f* **-,-en** bruise
Premiere /prəˈmi̯eːrə/ *f* **-,-n** première
Premierminister(in) /prəˈmi̯eː-/ *m(f)* Prime Minister
Presse *f* **-,-n** press. **p~n** *vt* press; **sich p~n** press (**an** + *acc* against)
pressieren *vi* (*haben*) (*SGer*) be urgent
Pressluft (**Preßluft**) *f* compressed air. **P~bohrer** *m* pneumatic drill
Prestige /prɛsˈtiːʒə/ *nt* **-s** prestige
Preuß|en *nt* **-s** Prussia. **p~isch** *a* Prussian
prickeln *vi* (*haben*) tingle
Priester *m* **-s,-** priest
prima *inv* a first-class, first-rate; (*fam: toll*) fantastic, *adv* fantastically well
primär *a* primary, *adv* -ily
Primel *f* **-,-n** primula; (*Garten-*) polyanthus
primitiv *a* primitive
Prinz *m* **-en,-en** prince. **P~essin** *f* **-,-nen** princess
Prinzip *nt* **-s,-ien** /-i̯ən/ principle; **im/aus P~** in/on principle. **p~iell** *a* ⟨*Frage*⟩ of principle □ *adv* on principle; (*im Prinzip*) in principle
Priorität *f* **-,-en** priority
Prise *f* **-,-n P~ Salz** pinch of salt
Prisma *nt* **-s,-men** prism
privat *a* private, *adv* -ly; (*persönlich*) personal. **P~adresse** *f* home address. **p~isieren** *vt* privatize
Privat|leben *nt* private life. **P~lehrer** *m* private tutor. **P~lehrerin** *f* governess. **P~patient(in)** *m(f)* private patient
Privileg *nt* **-[e]s,-ien** /-i̯ən/ privilege. **p~iert** *a* privileged
pro *prep* (+ *dat*) per. **Pro** *nt* **- das Pro und Kontra** the pros and cons *pl*
Probe *f* **-,-n** test, trial; (*Menge, Muster*) sample; (*Theat*) rehearsal; **auf die P~ stellen** put to the test; **ein Auto P~ fahren** test-drive a car. **P~fahrt** *f* test drive. **p~n** *vt/i* (*haben*) (*Theat*) rehearse. **p~weise** *adv* on a trial

basis. **P~zeit** *f* probationary period
probieren *vt/i* (*haben*) try; (*kosten*) taste; (*proben*) rehearse
Problem *nt* **-s,-e** problem. **p~atisch** *a* problematic
problemlos *a* problem-free □ *adv* without any problems
Produkt *nt* **-[e]s,-e** product
Produk|tion /-ˈtsi̯o:n/ *f* **-,-en** production. **p~tiv** *a* productive. **P~tivität** *f* **-** productivity
Produ|zent *m* **-en,-en** producer. **p~zieren** *vt* produce; **sich p~zieren** (*fam*) show off
professionell *a* professional, *adv* -ly
Professor *m* **-s,-en** /-ˈso:rən/ professor
Profi *m* **-s,-s** (*Sport*) professional
Profil *nt* **-s,-e** profile; (*Reifen-*) tread; (*fig*) image. **p~iert** *a* (*fig*) distinguished
Profit *m* **-[e]s,-e** profit. **p~ieren** *vi* (*haben*) profit (**von** from)
Prognose *f* **-,-n** forecast; (*Med*) prognosis
Programm *nt* **-s,-e** programme; (*Computer-*) program; (*TV*) channel; (*Comm: Sortiment*) range. **p~ieren** *vt/i* (*haben*) (*Computer*) program. **P~ierer(in)** *m* **-s,-** (*f* **-,-nen**) [computer] programmer
progressiv *a* progressive
Projekt *nt* **-[e]s,-e** project
Projektor *m* **-s,-en** /-ˈto:rən/ projector
projizieren *vt* project
Proklam|ation /-ˈtsi̯o:n/ *f* **-,-en** proclamation. **p~ieren** *vt* proclaim
Prolet *m* **-en,-en** boor. **P~ariat** *nt* **-[e]s** proletariat. **P~arier** /-i̯ɐ/ *m* **-s,-** proletarian
Prolog *m* **-s,-e** prologue
Promenade *f* **-,-n** promenade. **P~nmischung** *f* (*fam*) mongrel
Promille *pl* (*fam*) alcohol level *sg* in the blood; **zu viel P~ haben** (*fam*) be over the limit
prominen|t *a* prominent. **P~z** *f* **-** prominent figures *pl*
Promiskuität *f* **-** promiscuity
promovieren *vi* (*haben*) obtain one's doctorate
prompt *a* prompt, *adv* -ly; (*fam: natürlich*) of course
Pronomen *nt* **-s,-** pronoun
Propag|anda *f* **-** propaganda; (*Reklame*) publicity. **p~ieren** *vt* propagate
Propeller *m* **-s,-** propeller
Prophet *m* **-en,-en** prophet. **p~isch** *a* prophetic
prophezei|en *vt* prophesy. **P~ung** *f* **-,-en** prophecy
Proportion /-ˈtsi̯o:n/ *f* **-,-en** proportion. **p~al** *a* proportional. **p~iert** *a* **gut p~iert** well proportioned
Prosa *f* **-** prose
prosaisch *a* prosaic, *adv* -ally
prosit *int* cheers!
Prospekt *m* **-[e]s,-e** brochure; (*Comm*) prospectus
prost *int* cheers!
Prostitu|ierte *f* **-n,-n** prostitute. **P~tion** /-ˈtsi̯o:n/ *f* **-** prostitution
Protest *m* **-[e]s,-e** protest
Protestant|(in) *m* **-en,-en** (*f* **-,-nen**) (*Relig*) Protestant. **p~isch** *a* (*Relig*) Protestant
protestieren *vi* (*haben*) protest
Prothese *f* **-,-n** artificial limb; (*Zahn-*) denture
Protokoll *nt* **-s,-e** record; (*Sitzungs-*) minutes *pl*; (*diplomatisches*) protocol; (*Strafzettel*) ticket
Prototyp *m* **-s,-en** prototype
protz|en *vi* (*haben*) show off (**mit** etw sth). **p~ig** *a* ostentatious
Proviant *m* **-s** provisions *pl*
Provinz *f* **-,-en** province. **p~iell** *a* provincial
Provision *f* **-,-en** (*Comm*) commission
provisorisch *a* provisional, *adv* -ly, temporary, *adv* -ily

Provokation /-'tsjo:n/ *f* -,-en provocation
provozieren *vt* provoke. **p~d** *a* provocative, *adv* -ly
Prozedur *f* -,-en [lengthy] business
Prozent *nt* -[e]s,-e & - per cent; 5 **P~** 5 per cent. **P~satz** *m* percentage. **p~ual** *a* percentage ...
Prozess *m* -es,-e (**Prozeß** *m* -sses,-sse) process; (*Jur*) lawsuit; (*Kriminal-*) trial
Prozession *f* -,-en procession
prüde *a* prudish
prüf|en *vt* test/(*über-*) check (**auf** + *acc* for); audit ⟨*Bücher*⟩; (*Sch*) examine; **p~ender Blick** searching look. **P~er** *m* -s,- inspector; (*Buch-*) auditor; (*Sch*) examiner. **P~ling** *m* -s,-e examination candidate. **P~ung** *f* -,-en examination; (*Test*) test; (*Bücher-*) audit; (*fig*) trial
Prügel *m* -s,- cudgel; **P~** *pl* hiding *sg*, beating *sg*. **P~ei** *f* -,-en brawl, fight. **p~n** *vt* beat, thrash; **sich p~n** fight, brawl
Prunk *m* -[e]s magnificence, splendour. **p~en** *vi* (*haben*) show off (**mit etw** sth). **p~voll** *a* magnificent, *adv* -ly
prusten *vi* (*haben*) splutter; (*schnauben*) snort
Psalm *m* -s,-en psalm
Pseudonym *nt* -s,-e pseudonym
pst *int* shush!
Psychi|ater *m* -s,- psychiatrist. **P~atrie** *f* - psychiatry. **p~atrisch** *a* psychiatric
psychisch *a* psychological, *adv* -ly; (*Med*) mental, *adv* -ly
Psycho|analyse *f* psychoanalysis. **P~loge** *m* -n,-n psychologist. **P~logie** *f* - psychology. **p~logisch** *a* psychological, *adv* -ly
Pubertät *f* - puberty
publik *a* **p~ werden/machen** become/make public
Publi|kum *nt* -s public; (*Zuhörer*) audience; (*Zuschauer*) spectators *pl*. **p~zieren** *vt* publish
Pudding *m* -s,-s blancmange; (*im Wasserbad gekocht*) pudding
Pudel *m* -s,- poodle
Puder *m* & (*fam*) *nt* -s,- powder; (*Körper-*) talcum [powder]. **P~dose** *f* [powder] compact. **p~n** *vt* powder. **P~zucker** *m* icing sugar
Puff¹ *m* -[e]s,⸚e push, poke
Puff² *m* & *nt* -s,-s (*sl*) brothel
puffen *vt* (*fam*) poke □ *vi* (*sein*) puff along
Puffer *m* -s,- (*Rail*) buffer; (*Culin*) pancake. **P~zone** *f* buffer zone
Pull|i *m* -s,-s jumper. **P~over** *m* -s,- jumper; (*Herren-*) pullover
Puls *m* -es pulse. **P~ader** *f* artery. **p~ieren** *vi* (*haben*) pulsate
Pult *nt* -[e]s,-e desk; (*Lese-*) lectern
Pulver *nt* -s,- powder. **p~ig** *a* powdery. **p~isieren** *vt* pulverize
Pulver|kaffee *m* instant coffee. **P~schnee** *m* powder snow
pummelig *a* (*fam*) chubby
Pump *m* **auf P~** (*fam*) on tick
Pumpe *f* -,-n pump. **p~n** *vt/i* (*haben*) pump; (*fam: leihen*) lend; [**sich** (*dat*)] **etw p~n** (*fam: borgen*) borrow sth
Pumps /pœmps/ *pl* court shoes
Punkt *m* -[e]s,-e dot; (*Tex*) spot; (*Geom, Sport & fig*) point; (*Gram*) full stop, period; **P~ sechs Uhr** at six o'clock sharp; **nach P~en siegen** win on points. **p~iert** *a* ⟨*Linie, Note*⟩ dotted
pünktlich *a* punctual, *adv* -ly. **P~keit** *f* - punctuality
Punsch *m* -[e]s,-e [hot] punch
Pupille *f* -,-n (*Anat*) pupil
Puppe *f* -,-n doll; (*Marionette*) puppet; (*Schaufenster-, Schneider-*) dummy; (*Zool*) chrysalis
pur *a* pure; (*fam: bloß*) sheer; **Whisky pur** neat whisky

Püree *nt* **-s,-s** purée; (*Kartoffel-*) mashed potatoes *pl*
puritanisch *a* puritanical
purpurrot *a* crimson
Purzel|baum *m* (*fam*) somersault. **p~n** *vi* (*sein*) (*fam*) tumble
pusseln *vi* (*haben*) (*fam*) potter
Puste *f* - (*fam*) breath; **aus der P~** out of breath. **p~n** *vt/i* (*haben*) (*fam*) blow
Pute *f* -,-**n** turkey; (*Henne*) turkey hen. **P~r** *m* **-s,-** turkey cock
Putsch *m* **-[e]s,-e** coup
Putz *m* **-es** plaster; (*Staat*) finery. **p~en** *vt* clean; (*Aust*) dry-clean; (*zieren*) adorn; **sich p~en** dress up; **sich** (*dat*) **die Zähne/Nase p~en** clean one's teeth/blow one's nose. **P~frau** *f* cleaner, charwoman. **p~ig** *a* (*fam*) amusing, cute; (*seltsam*) odd. **P~macherin** *f* -,-**nen** milliner
Puzzlespiel /ˈpazl-/ *nt* jigsaw
Pyramide *f* -,-**n** pyramid

Q

Quacksalber *m* **-s,-** quack
Quadrat *nt* **-[e]s,-e** square. **q~isch** *a* square. **Q~meter** *m & nt* square metre
quaken *vi* (*haben*) quack; ⟨*Frosch:*⟩ croak
quäken *vi* (*haben*) screech; ⟨*Baby:*⟩ whine
Quäker(in) *m* **-s,-** (*f* **-,-nen**) Quaker
Qual *f* **-,-en** torment; (*Schmerz*) agony
quälen *vt* torment; (*foltern*) torture; (*bedrängen*) pester; **sich q~** torment oneself; (*leiden*) suffer; (*sich mühen*) struggle. **q~d** *a* agonizing
Quälerei *f* **-,-en** torture; (*Qual*) agony
Quälgeist *m* (*fam*) pest
Qualifi|kation /-ˈtsi̯oːn/ *f* **-,-en** qualification. **q~zieren** *vt* qualify; **sich q~zieren** qualify. **q~ziert** *a* qualified; (*fähig*) competent; ⟨*Arbeit*⟩ skilled
Qualität *f* **-,-en** quality
Qualle *f* -,-**n** jellyfish
Qualm *m* **-s** [thick] smoke. **q~en** *vi* (*haben*) smoke
qualvoll *a* agonizing
Quantität *f* **-,-en** quantity
Quantum *nt* **-s,-ten** quantity; (*Anteil*) share, quota
Quarantäne *f* - quarantine
Quark *m* **-s** quark, ≈ curd cheese; (*fam: Unsinn*) rubbish
Quartal *nt* **-s,-e** quarter
Quartett *nt* **-[e]s,-e** quartet
Quartier *nt* **-s,-e** accommodation; (*Mil*) quarters *pl*; **ein Q~ suchen** look for accommodation
Quarz *m* **-es** quartz
quasseln *vi* (*haben*) (*fam*) jabber
Quaste *f* -,-**n** tassel
Quatsch *m* **-[e]s** (*fam*) nonsense, rubbish; **Q~ machen** (*Unfug machen*) fool around; (*etw falsch machen*) do a silly thing. **q~en** (*fam*) *vi* (*haben*) talk; (*schwatzen*) natter; ⟨*Wasser, Schlamm:*⟩ squelch □ *vt* talk. **q~nass** (**q~naß**) *a* (*fam*) soaking wet
Quecksilber *nt* mercury
Quelle *f* -,-**n** spring; (*Fluss- & fig*) source. **q~n**† *vi* (*sein*) well [up]/(*fließen*) pour (**aus** from); (*aufquellen*) swell; (*hervortreten*) bulge
quengeln *vi* (*fam*) whine; ⟨*Baby:*⟩ grizzle
quer *adv* across, crosswise; (*schräg*) diagonally; **q~ gestreift** horizontally striped
Quere *f* - **der Q~ nach** across, crosswise; **jdm in die Q~ kommen** get in s.o.'s way
querfeldein *adv* across country
quer|gestreift *a* (NEW) **q~ gestreift**, *s.* **quer**. **q~köpfig** *a* (*fam*) awkward. **Q~latte** *f* cross-

bar. **Q~schiff** *nt* transept. **Q~schnitt** *m* cross-section. **q~schnittsgelähmt** *a* paraplegic. **Q~straße** *f* side-street; **die erste Q~straße links** the first turning on the left. **Q~verweis** *m* cross-reference

quetsch|en *vt* squash; (*drücken*) squeeze; (*zerdrücken*) crush; (*Culin*) mash; **sich q~en in** (+ *acc*) squeeze into; **sich** (*dat*) **den Arm q~en** bruise one's arm. **Q~ung** *f* -,-en, **Q~wunde** *f* bruise

Queue /kø:/ *nt* **-s,-s** cue

quicklebendig *a* very lively

quieken *vi* (*haben*) squeal; ⟨*Maus:*⟩ squeak

quietschen *vi* (*haben*) squeal; ⟨*Tür, Dielen:*⟩ creak

Quintett *nt* **-[e]s,-e** quintet

Quirl *m* **-[e]s,-e** blender with a star-shaped head. **q~en** *vt* mix

quitt *a* **q~ sein** (*fam*) be quits

Quitte *f* **-,-n** quince

quittieren *vt* receipt ⟨*Rechnung*⟩; sign for ⟨*Geldsumme, Sendung*⟩; (*reagieren auf*) greet (**mit** with); **den Dienst q~** resign

Quittung *f* **-,-en** receipt

Quiz /kvɪs/ *nt* **-,-** quiz

Quote *f* **-,-n** proportion

R

Rabatt *m* **-[e]s,-e** discount

Rabatte *f* **-,-n** (*Hort*) border

Rabattmarke *f* trading stamp

Rabbiner *m* **-s,-** rabbi

Rabe *m* **-n,-n** raven. **r~nschwarz** *a* pitch-black

rabiat *a* violent, *adv* -ly; (*wütend*) furious, *adv* -ly

Rache *f* **-** revenge, vengeance

Rachen *m* **-s,-** pharynx; (*Maul*) jaws *pl*

rächen *vt* avenge; **sich r~** take revenge (**an** + *dat* on); ⟨*Fehler, Leichtsinn:*⟩ cost s.o. dear

Racker *m* **-s,-** (*fam*) rascal

Rad *nt* **-[e]s,⸗er** wheel; (*Fahr-*) bicycle, (*fam*) bike; **Rad fahren** cycle

Radar *m & nt* **-s** radar

Radau *m* **-s** (*fam*) din, racket

radebrechen *vt/i* (*haben*) **[Deutsch/Englisch] r~** speak broken German/English

radeln *vi* (*sein*) (*fam*) cycle

Rädelsführer *m* ringleader

radfahr|en† *vi sep* (*sein*) (NEW) **Rad fahren**, *s.* **Rad**. **R~er(in)** *m*(*f*) **-s,-** (*f* **-,-nen**) cyclist

radier|en *vt/i* (*haben*) rub out; (*Kunst*) etch. **R~gummi** *m* eraser, rubber. **R~ung** *f* **-,-en** etching

Radieschen /-ˈdi:sçən/ *nt* **-s,-** radish

radikal *a* radical, *adv* -ly; (*drastisch*) drastic, *adv* -ally. **R~e(r)** *m/f* (*Pol*) radical

Radio *nt* **-s,-s** radio

radioaktiv *a* radioactive. **R~ität** *f* **-** radioactivity

Radioapparat *m* radio [set]

Radius *m* **-,-ien** /-jən/ radius

Rad|kappe *f* hub-cap. **R~ler** *m* **-s,-** cyclist; (*Getränk*) shandy. **R~weg** *m* cycle track

raff|en *vt* grab; (*kräuseln*) gather; (*kürzen*) condense. **r~gierig** *a* avaricious

Raffin|ade *f* **-** refined sugar. **R~erie** *f* **-,-n** refinery. **R~esse** *f* **-,-n** refinement; (*Schlauheit*) cunning. **r~ieren** *vt* refine. **r~iert** *a* ingenious, *adv* -ly; (*durchtrieben*) crafty, *adv* -ily

Rage /ˈra:ʒə/ *f* **-** (*fam*) fury

ragen *vi* (*haben*) rise [up]

Rahm *m* **-s** (*SGer*) cream

rahmen *vt* frame. **R~** *m* **-s,-** frame; (*fig*) framework; (*Grenze*) limits *pl*; (*einer Feier*) setting

Rain *m* **-[e]s,-e** grass verge

räkeln *v* = **rekeln**

Rakete *f* **-,-n** rocket; (*Mil*) missile

Rallye /'rali/ *nt* **-s,-s** rally
rammen *vt* ram
Rampe *f* **-,-n** ramp; (*Theat*) front of the stage. **R~nlicht** *nt* **im R~nlicht stehen** (*fig*) be in the limelight
ramponier|en *vt* (*fam*) damage; (*ruinieren*) ruin; **r~t** battered
Ramsch *m* **-[e]s** junk. **R~laden** *m* junk-shop
ran *adv* = **heran**
Rand *m* **-[e]s,¨er** edge; (*Teller-, Gläser-, Brillen-*) rim; (*Zier-*) border, edging; (*Buch-, Brief-*) margin; (*Stadt-*) outskirts *pl*; (*Ring*) ring; **am R~e des Ruins** on the brink of ruin; **am R~e erwähnen** mention in passing; **zu R~e kommen mit** = **zurande kommen mit**, *s.* **zurande**; **außer R~ und Band** (*fam: ausgelassen*) very boisterous
randalieren *vi* (*haben*) rampage
Rand|bemerkung *f* marginal note. **R~streifen** *m* (*Auto*) hard shoulder
Rang *m* **-[e]s,¨e** rank; (*Theat*) tier; **erster/zweiter R~** (*Theat*) dress/upper circle; **ersten R~es** first-class
rangieren /raŋ'ʒi:rən/ *vt* shunt □ *vi* (*haben*) rank (**vor** + *dat* before); **an erster Stelle r~** come first
Rangordnung *f* order of importance; (*Hierarchie*) hierarchy
Ranke *f* **-,-n** tendril; (*Trieb*) shoot
ranken (sich) *vr* (*Bot*) trail; (*in die Höhe*) climb; **sich r~ um** twine around
Ranzen *m* **-s,-** (*Sch*) satchel
ranzig *a* rancid
Rappe *m* **-n,-n** black horse
rappeln *v* (*fam*) □ *vi* (*haben*) rattle □ *vr* **sich r~** pick oneself up; (*fig*) rally
Raps *m* **-es** (*Bot*) rape
rar *a* rare; **er macht sich rar** (*fam*) we don't see much of him. **R~ität** *f* **-,-en** rarity
rasant *a* fast; (*schnittig, schick*) stylish □ *adv* fast; stylishly
rasch *a* quick, *adv* -ly
rascheln *vi* (*haben*) rustle
Rasen *m* **-s,-** lawn
rasen *vi* (*sein*) tear [along]; ⟨*Puls:*⟩ race; ⟨*Zeit:*⟩ fly; **gegen eine Mauer r~** career into a wall □ *vi* (*haben*) rave; ⟨*Sturm:*⟩ rage; **vor Begeisterung r~** go wild with enthusiasm. **r~d** *a* furious; (*tobend*) raving; ⟨*Sturm, Durst*⟩ raging; ⟨*Schmerz*⟩ excruciating; ⟨*Beifall*⟩ tumultuous □ *adv* terribly
Rasenmäher *m* lawn-mower
Raserei *f* - speeding; (*Toben*) frenzy
Rasier|apparat *m* razor. **r~en** *vt* shave; **sich r~en** shave. **R~klinge** *f* razor blade. **R~pinsel** *m* shaving-brush. **R~wasser** *nt* aftershave [lotion]
Raspel *f* **-,-n** rasp; (*Culin*) grater. **r~n** *vt* grate
Rasse *f* **-,-n** race. **R~hund** *m* pedigree dog
Rassel *f* **-,-n** rattle. **r~n** *vi* (*haben*) rattle; ⟨*Schlüssel:*⟩ jangle; ⟨*Kette:*⟩ clank □ *vi* (*sein*) rattle [along]
Rassen|diskriminierung *f* racial discrimination. **R~trennung** *f* racial segregation
Rassepferd *nt* thoroughbred
rassisch *a* racial
Rassis|mus *m* - racism. **r~tisch** *a* racist
Rast *f* **-,-en** rest. **r~en** *vi* (*haben*) rest. **R~haus** *nt* motorway restaurant. **r~los** *a* restless, *adv* -ly; (*ununterbrochen*) ceaseless, *adv* -ly. **R~platz** *m* picnic area. **R~stätte** *f* motorway restaurant [and services]
Rasur *f* **-,-en** shave
Rat[1] *m* **-[e]s** [piece of] advice; **guter Rat** good advice; **sich** (*dat*) **keinen Rat wissen** not know what to do; **zu Rat[e] ziehen** = **zurate ziehen**, *s.* **zurate**

Rat² *m* **-[e]s,⸚e** (*Admin*) council; (*Person*) councillor

Rate *f* **-,-n** instalment

raten† *vt* guess; (*empfehlen*) advise □ *vi* (*haben*) guess; **jdm r~** advise s.o.

Ratenzahlung *f* payment by instalments

Rat|geber *m* **-s,-** adviser; (*Buch*) guide. **R~haus** *nt* town hall

ratifizier|en *vt* ratify. **R~ung** *f* **-,-en** ratification

Ration /ra'tsi̯o:n/ *f* **-,-en** ration; **eiserne R~** iron rations *pl*. **r~al** *a* rational, *adv* -ly. **r~alisieren** *vt/i* (*haben*) rationalize. **r~ell** *a* efficient, *adv* -ly. **r~ieren** *vt* ration

rat|los *a* helpless, *adv* -ly; **r~los sein** not know what to do. **r~sam** *pred a* advisable; (*klug*) prudent. **R~schlag** *m* piece of advice; **R~schläge** advice *sg*

Rätsel *nt* **-s,-** riddle; (*Kreuzwort-*) puzzle; (*Geheimnis*) mystery. **r~haft** *a* puzzling, mysterious. **r~n** *vi* (*haben*) puzzle

Ratte *f* **-,-n** rat

rattern *vi* (*haben*) rattle □ *vi* (*sein*) rattle [along]

rau *a* rough, *adv* -ly; (*unfreundlich*) gruff, *adv* -ly; ⟨*Klima, Wind*⟩ harsh, raw; ⟨*Landschaft*⟩ rugged; (*heiser*) husky; ⟨*Hals*⟩ sore

Raub *m* **-[e]s** robbery; (*Menschen-*) abduction; (*Beute*) loot, booty. **r~en** *vt* steal; abduct ⟨*Menschen*⟩; **jdm etw r~en** rob s.o. of sth

Räuber *m* **-s,-** robber

Raub|mord *m* robbery with murder. **R~tier** *nt* predator. **R~überfall** *m* robbery. **R~vogel** *m* bird of prey

Rauch *m* **-[e]s** smoke. **r~en** *vt/i* (*haben*) smoke. **R~en** *nt* **-s** smoking; **'R~en verboten'** 'no smoking'. **R~er** *m* **-s,-**smoker. **R~erabteil** *nt* smoking compartment

Räucher|lachs *m* smoked salmon. **r~n** *vt* (*Culin*) smoke

Rauch|fang *m* (*Aust*) chimney. **r~ig** *a* smoky. **R~verbot** *nt* smoking ban

räudig *a* mangy

rauf *adv* = **herauf, hinauf**

rauf|en *vt* pull; **sich** (*dat*) **die Haare r~en** (*fig*) tear one's hair □ *vr/i* (*haben*) **[sich] r~en** fight. **R~erei** *f* **-,-en** fight

rauh *a* (NEW) **rau**

rau|haarig *a* wire-haired. **R~heit** *f* - (*s.* **rau**) roughness; gruffness; harshness; ruggedness

rauh|haarig *a* (NEW) **rauhaarig**. **R~reif** *m* (NEW) **Raureif**

Raum *m* **-[e]s, Räume** room; (*Gebiet*) area; (*Welt-*) space

räumen *vt* clear; vacate ⟨*Wohnung*⟩; evacuate ⟨*Gebäude, Gebiet, (Mil) Stellung*⟩; (*bringen*) put (**in/auf** + *acc* into/on); (*holen*) get (**aus** out of); **beiseite r~** move/put to one side; **aus dem Weg r~** (*fam*) get rid of

Raum|fahrer *m* astronaut. **R~fahrt** *f* space travel. **R~fahrzeug** *nt* spacecraft. **R~flug** *m* space flight. **R~inhalt** *m* volume

räumlich *a* spatial. **R~keiten** *fpl* rooms

Raum|pflegerin *f* cleaner. **R~schiff** *nt* spaceship

Räumung *f* - (*s.* **räumen**) clearing; vacating; evacuation. **R~sverkauf** *m* clearance/closing-down sale

raunen *vt/i* (*haben*) whisper

Raupe *f* **-,-n** caterpillar

Raureif *m* hoar-frost

raus *adv* = **heraus, hinaus**

Rausch *m* **-[e]s, Räusche** intoxication; (*fig*) exhilaration; **einen R~haben** be drunk

rauschen *vi* (*haben*) ⟨*Wasser, Wind:*⟩ rush; ⟨*Bäume Blätter:*⟩ rustle □ *vi* (*sein*) rush [along]; **aus dem Zimmer r~** sweep out of the room. **r～d** *a* rushing; rustling; ⟨*Applaus*⟩ tumultuous

Rauschgift *nt* [narcotic] drug; (*coll*) drugs *pl*. **R～süchtige(r)** *m/f* drug addict

räuspern (sich) *vr* clear one's throat

rausschmeiß|en† *vt sep* (*fam*) throw out; (*entlassen*) sack. **R～er** *m* **-s,-** (*fam*) bouncer

Raute *f* **-,-n** diamond

Razzia *f* **-,-ien** /-i̯ən/ [police] raid

Reagenzglas *nt* test-tube

reagieren *vi* (*haben*) react (**auf** + *acc* to)

Reaktion /-ˈt̮si̯o:n/ *f* **-,-en** reaction. **r～är** *a* reactionary

Reaktor *m* **-s,-en** /-ˈto:rən/ reactor

real *a* real; (*gegenständlich*) tangible; (*realistisch*) realistic, *adv* -ally. **r～isieren** *vt* realize

Realis|mus *m* - realism. **R～t** *m* **-en,-en** realist. **r～tisch** *a* realistic, *adv* -ally

Realität *f* **-,-en** reality

Realschule *f* ≈ secondary modern school

Rebe *f* **-,-n** vine

Rebell *m* **-en,-en** rebel. **r～ieren** *vi* (*haben*) rebel. **R～ion** *f* **-,-en** rebellion

rebellisch *a* rebellious

Rebhuhn *nt* partridge

Rebstock *m* vine

Rechen *m* **-s-** rake. **r～** *vt/i* (*haben*) rake

Rechen|aufgabe *f* arithmetical problem; (*Sch*) sum. **R～fehler** *m* arithmetical error. **R～maschine** *f* calculator

Rechenschaft *f* - **R～ ablegen** give account (**über** + *acc* of); **jdn zur R～ ziehen** call s.o. to account

recherchieren /reʃɛrˈʃi:rən/ *vt/i* (*haben*) investigate; (*Journ*) research

rechnen *vi* (*haben*) do arithmetic; (*schätzen*) reckon; (*zählen*) count (**zu** among; **auf** + *acc* on); **r～ mit** reckon with; (*erwarten*) expect; **gut r～ können** be good at figures □ *vt* calculate, work out; do ⟨*Aufgabe*⟩; (*dazu-*) add (**zu** to); (*fig*) count (**zu** among). **R～** *nt* **-s** arithmetic

Rechner *m* **-s,-** calculator; (*Computer*) computer; **ein guter R～ sein** be good at figures

Rechnung *f* **-,-en** bill, (*Amer*) check; (*Comm*) invoice; (*Berechnung*) calculation; **R～ führen über** (+ *acc*) keep account of; **etw** (*dat*) **R～ tragen** (*fig*) take sth into account. **R～sjahr** *nt* financial year. **R～sprüfer** *m* auditor

Recht *nt* **-[e]s,-e** law; (*Berechtigung*) right (**auf** + *acc* to); **im R～ sein** be in the right; **R～ haben/behalten** be right; **R～ bekommen** be proved right; **jdm R～ geben** agree with s.o.; **mit** *od* **zu R～** rightly; **von R～s wegen** by right; (*eigentlich*) by rights

recht *a* right; (*wirklich*) real; **ich habe keine r～e Lust** I don't really feel like it; **es jdm r～ machen** please s.o.; **jdm r～ sein** be all right with s.o.; **r～ haben/behalten/bekommen** (NEW) **Recht haben/behalten/bekommen**, *s*. **Recht**; **jdm r～ geben** (NEW) **jdm Recht geben**, *s*. **Recht** □ *adv* correctly; (*ziemlich*) quite; (*sehr*) very; **r～ vielen Dank** many thanks

Recht|e *f* **-n,-[n]** right side; (*Hand*) right hand; (*Boxen*) right; **die R～e** (*Pol*) the right; **zu meiner R～en** on my right. **r～e(r,s)** *a* right; (*Pol*) right-wing; **r～e Masche** plain stitch. **R～e(r)** *m/f* **der/die R～e** the right man/woman; **du bist mir der/die R～e!** you're a fine one! **R～e(s)** *nt* **das R～e** the right thing; **etwas R～es lernen** learn something useful; **nach dem**

R~en sehen see that everything is all right
Rechteck *nt* **-[e]s,-e** rectangle. **r~ig** *a* rectangular
rechtfertig|en *vt* justify; **sich r~en** justify oneself. **R~ung** *f* - justification
recht|haberisch *a* opinionated. **r~lich** *a* legal, *adv* -ly. **r~mäßig** *a* legitimate, *adv* -ly.
rechts *adv* on the right; (*bei Stoff*) on the right side; **von/nach r~** from/to the right; **zwei r~, zwei links stricken** knit two, purl two. **R~anwalt** *m*, **R~anwältin** *f* lawyer
rechtschaffen *a* upright; (*ehrlich*) honest, *adv* -ly; **r~ müde** thoroughly tired
rechtschreib|en *vi* (*inf only*) spell correctly. **R~fehler** *m* spelling mistake. **R~ung** *f* - spelling
Rechts|händer(in) *m* **-s,-** (*f* **-,-nen**) right-hander. **r~händig** *a & adv* right-handed **r~kräftig** *a* legal, *adv* -ly. **R~streit** *m* law suit. **R~verkehr** *m* driving on the right. **r~widrig** *a* illegal, *adv* -ly. **R~wissenschaft** *f* jurisprudence
recht|winklig *a* right-angled. **r~zeitig** *a & adv* in time
Reck *nt* **-[e]s,-e** horizontal bar
recken *vt* stretch; **sich r~** stretch; **den Hals r~** crane one's neck
Redakteur /redak'tø:ɐ̯/ *m* **-s,-e** editor; (*Radio, TV*) producer
Redaktion /-'tsio:n/ *f* **-,-en** editing; (*Radio, TV*) production; (*Abteilung*) editorial/production department. **r~ell** *a* editorial
Rede *f* **-,-n** speech; **zur R~stellen** demand an explanation from; **davon ist keine R~** there's no question of it; **nicht der R~ wert** not worth mentioning. **r~gewandt** *a* eloquent, *adv* -ly
reden *vi* (*haben*) talk (**von** about; **mit** to); (*eine Rede halten*) speak □ *vt* talk; speak ⟨*Wahrheit*⟩; **kein Wort r~** not say a word. **R~sart** *f* saying; (*Phrase*) phrase
Redewendung *f* idiom
redigieren *vt* edit
redlich *a* honest, *adv* -ly
Red|ner *m* **-s,-** speaker. **r~selig** *a* talkative
reduzieren *vt* reduce
Reeder *m* **-s,-** shipowner. **R~ei** *f* **-,-en** shipping company
reell *a* real; (*ehrlich*) honest, *adv* -ly; ⟨*Preis, Angebot*⟩ fair
Refer|at *nt* **-[e]s,-e** report; (*Abhandlung*) paper; (*Abteilung*) section. **R~ent(in)** *m* **-en,-en** (*f* **-,-nen**) speaker; (*Sachbearbeiter*) expert. **R~enz** *f* **-,-en** reference. **r~ieren** *vi* (*haben*) deliver a paper; (*berichten*) report (**über** + *acc* on)
reflektieren *vt/i* (*haben*) reflect (**über** + *acc* on)
Reflex *m* **-es,-e** reflex; (*Widerschein*) reflection. **R~ion** *f* **-,-en** reflection. **r~iv** *a* reflexive. **R~ivpronomen** *nt* reflexive pronoun
Reform *f* **-,-en** reform. **R~ation** /-'tsio:n/ *f* - (*Relig*) Reformation
Reform|haus *nt* health-food shop. **r~ieren** *vt* reform
Refrain /rə'frɛ̃:/ *m* **-s,-s** refrain
Regal *nt* **-s,-e** [set of] shelves *pl*
Regatta *f* **-,-ten** regatta
rege *a* active; (*lebhaft*) lively; (*geistig*) alert; ⟨*Handel*⟩ brisk □ *adv* actively
Regel *f* **-,-n** rule; (*Monats-*) period; **in der R~** as a rule. **r~mäßig** *a* regular, *adv* -ly. **r~n** *vt* regulate; direct ⟨*Verkehr*⟩; (*erledigen*) settle. **r~recht** *a* real, proper □ *adv* really. **R~ung** *f* **-,-en** regulation; settlement. **r~widrig** *a* irregular, *adv* -ly
regen *vt* move; **sich r~** move; (*wach werden*) stir
Regen *m* **-s,-** rain. **R~bogen** *m* rainbow. **R~bogenhaut** *f* iris

Regener|ation /-'tsio:n/ *f* - regeneration. **r~ieren** *vt* regenerate; **sich r~ieren** regenerate

Regen|mantel *m* raincoat. **R~schirm** *m* umbrella. **R~tag** *m* rainy day. **R~tropfen** *m* raindrop. **R~wetter** *nt* wet weather. **R~wurm** *m* earthworm

Regie /re'ʒi:/ *f* - direction; **R~ führen** direct

regier|en *vt/i* (*haben*) govern, rule; ⟨*Monarch:*⟩ reign [over]; (*Gram*) take. **r~end** *a* ruling; reigning. **R~ung** *f* -,-**en** government; (*Herrschaft*) rule; (*eines Monarchen*) reign

Regime /re'ʒi:m/ *nt* **-s,-** /-mə/ regime

Regiment1 *nt* **-[e]s,-er** regiment

Regiment2 *nt* **-[e]s,-e** rule

Region *f* **-,-en** region. **r~al** *a* regional, *adv* -ly

Regisseur /reʒɪ'sø:ɐ̯/ *m* **-s,-e** director

Register *nt* **-s,-** register; (*Inhaltsverzeichnis*) index; (*Orgel-*) stop

registrier|en *vt* register; (*Techn*) record. **R~kasse** *f* cash register

Regler *m* **-s,-** regulator

reglos *a & adv* motionless

regn|en *vi* (*haben*) rain; **es r~et** it is raining. **r~erisch** *a* rainy

regul|är *a* normal, *adv* -ly; (*rechtmäßig*) legitimate, *adv* -ly. **r~ieren** *vt* regulate

Regung *f* **-,-en** movement; (*Gefühls-*) emotion. **r~slos** *a & adv* motionless

Reh *nt* **-[e]s,-e** roe-deer; (*Culin*) venison

Rehabilit|ation /-'tsio:n/ *f* - rehabilitation. **r~ieren** *vt* rehabilitate

Rehbock *m* roebuck

Reib|e *f* **-,-n** grater. **r~en**† *vt* rub; (*Culin*) grate; **blank r~en** polish □ *vi* (*haben*) rub. **R~ereien** *fpl* (*fam*) friction *sg*. **R~ung** *f* - friction. **r~ungslos** *a* (*fig*) smooth, *adv* -ly

reich *a* rich (**an** + *dat* in), *adv* -ly; (*r~haltig*) abundant, *adv* -ly; **Arm und R~ (arm und r~)** rich and poor

Reich *nt* **-[e]s,-e** empire; (*König-*) kingdom; (*Bereich*) realm

Reich|e(r) *m/f* rich man/woman; **die R~en** the rich *pl*

reichen *vt* hand; (*anbieten*) offer □ *vi* (*haben*) be enough; (*in der Länge*) be long enough; **r~ bis zu** reach [up to]; (*sich erstrecken*) extend to; **mit dem Geld r~** have enough money; **mir reicht's!** I've had enough!

reich|haltig *a* extensive, large ⟨*Mahlzeit*⟩ substantial. **r~lich** *a* ample; ⟨*Vorrat*⟩ abundant, plentiful; **eine r~liche Stunde** a good hour □ *adv* amply; abundantly; (*fam: sehr*) very. **R~tum** *m* **-s,-tümer** wealth (**an** + *dat* of); **R~tümer** riches. **R~weite** *f* reach; (*Techn, Mil*) range

Reif *m* **-[e]s** [hoar-]frost

reif *a* ripe; (*fig*) mature; **r~ für** ready for. **R~e** *f* - ripeness; (*fig*) maturity. **r~en** *vi* (*sein*) ripen; ⟨*Wein, Käse & fig*⟩ mature

Reifen *m* **-s,-** hoop; (*Arm-*) bangle; (*Auto-*) tyre. **R~druck** *m* tyre pressure. **R~panne** *f* puncture, flat tyre

Reifeprüfung *f* ≈ A levels *pl*

reiflich *a* careful, *adv* -ly

Reihe *f* **-,-n** row; (*Anzahl & Math*) series; **der R~ nach** in turn; **außer der R~** out of turn; **wer ist an der** *od* **kommt an die R~?** whose turn is it? **r~n (sich)** *vr* **sich r~n an** (+ *acc*) follow. **R~nfolge** *f* order. **R~nhaus** *nt* terraced house. **r~nweise** *adv* in rows; (*fam*) in large numbers

Reiher *m* **-s,-** heron

Reim *m* **-[e]s,-e** rhyme. **r~en** *vt* rhyme; **sich r~en** rhyme

rein1 *a* pure; (*sauber*) clean; ⟨*Unsinn, Dummheit*⟩ sheer; **ins R~e (r~e) schreiben** make a fair copy of; **ins R~e (r~e) bringen**

(*fig*) sort out □ *adv* purely; (*fam*) absolutely

rein² *adv* = **herein, hinein**

Reineclaude /rɛ:nə'klo:də/ *f* **-,-n** greengage

Reinfall *m* (*fam*) let-down; (*Misserfolg*) flop. **r~en†** *vi sep* (*sein*) fall in; (*fam*) be taken in (**auf** + *acc* by)

Rein|gewinn *m* net profit. **R~heit** *f* - purity

reinig|en *vt* clean; (*chemisch*) dry-clean. **R~ung** *f* **-,-en** cleaning; (*chemische*) dry-cleaning; (*Geschäft*) dry cleaner's

Reinkarnation /reʔɪnkarna'tsi̯o:n/ *f* **-,-en** reincarnation

reinlegen *vt sep* put in; (*fam*) dupe; (*betrügen*) take for a ride

reinlich *a* clean. **R~keit** *f* - cleanliness

Rein|machefrau *f* cleaner. **R~schrift** *f* fair copy. **r~seiden** *a* pure silk

Reis *m* **-es** rice

Reise *f* **-,-n** journey; (*See-*) voyage; (*Urlaubs-*, *Geschäfts-*) trip. **R~andenken** *nt* souvenir. **R~büro** *nt* travel agency. **R~bus** *m* coach. **R~führer** *m* tourist guide; (*Buch*) guide. **R~gesellschaft** *f* tourist group. **R~leiter(in)** *m*(*f*) courier. **r~n** *vi* (*sein*) travel. **R~nde(r)** *m*/*f* traveller. **R~pass (R~paß)** *m* passport. **R~scheck** *m* traveller's cheque. **R~unternehmer**, **R~veranstalter** *m* **-s,-** tour operator. **R~ziel** *nt* destination

Reisig *nt* **-s** brushwood

Reißaus *m* **R~ nehmen** (*fam*) run away

Reißbrett *nt* drawing-board

reißen† *vt* tear; (*weg-*) snatch; (*töten*) kill; **Witze r~** crack jokes; **aus dem Schlaf r~** awaken rudely; **an sich** (*acc*) **r~** snatch; seize ⟨*Macht*⟩; **mit sich r~** sweep away; **sich r~ um** (*fam*) fight for; (*gern mögen*) be keen on; **hin und her gerissen sein** (*fig*) be torn □ *vi* (*sein*) tear; ⟨*Seil, Faden:*⟩ break □ *vi* (*haben*) **r~ an** (+ *dat*) pull at. **r~d** *a* raging; ⟨*Tier*⟩ ferocious; ⟨*Schmerz*⟩ violent

Reißer *m* **-s,-** (*fam*) thriller; (*Erfolg*) big hit. **r~isch** *a* (*fam*) sensational

Reiß|nagel *m* = **R~zwecke. R~verschluss (R~verschluß)** *m* zip [fastener]. **R~wolf** *m* shredder. **R~zwecke** *f* **-,-n** drawing-pin, (*Amer*) thumbtack

reit|en† *vt*/*i* (*sein*) ride. **R~er(in)** *m* **-s,-** (*f* **-,-nen**) rider. **R~hose** *f* riding breeches *pl*. **R~pferd** *nt* saddle-horse. **R~schule** *f* riding-school. **R~weg** *m* bridle-path

Reiz *m* **-es,-e** stimulus; (*Anziehungskraft*) attraction, appeal; (*Charme*) charm. **r~bar** *a* irritable. **R~barkeit** *f* - irratability. **r~en** *vt* provoke; (*Med*) irritate; (*interessieren, locken*) appeal to, attract; arouse ⟨*Neugier*⟩; (*beim Kartenspiel*) bid. **r~end** *a* charming, *adv* -ly; (*entzückend*) delightful. **R~ung** *f* **-,-en** (*Med*) irritation. **r~voll** *a* attractive

rekapitulieren *vt*/*i* (*haben*) recapitulate

rekeln (sich) *vr* stretch; (*lümmeln*) sprawl

Reklamation /-'tsi̯o:n/ *f* **-,-en** (*Comm*) complaint

Reklam|e *f* **-,-n** advertising, publicity; (*Anzeige*) advertisement; (*TV, Radio*) commercial; **R~e machen** advertise (**für etw** sth). **r~ieren** *vt* complain about; (*fordern*) claim □ *vi* (*haben*) complain

rekonstru|ieren *vt* reconstruct. **R~ktion** /-'tsi̯o:n/ *f* **-,-en** reconstruction

Rekonvaleszenz *f* - convalescence

Rekord *m* **-[e]s,-e** record

Rekrut *m* **-en,-en** recruit. **r~ieren** *vt* recruit

Rek|tor *m* **-s,-en** /-ˈto:rən/ (*Sch*) head[master]; (*Univ*) vice-chancellor. **R~torin** *f* **-,-nen** head, headmistress; vice-chancellor
Relais /rəˈlɛ:/ *nt* **-,-** /-s,-s/ (*Electr*) relay
relativ *a* relative, *adv* -ly. **R~pronomen** *nt* relative pronoun
relevan|t *a* relevant (**für** to). **R~z** *f* - relevance
Relief /rəˈli̯ɛf/ *nt* **-s,-s** relief
Religi|on *f* **-,-en** religion; (*Sch*) religious education. **r~ös** *a* religious
Reling *f* **-,-s** (*Naut*) rail
Reliquie /reˈli:kvi̯ə/ *f* **-,-n** relic
Remouladensoße /remuˈla:dən-/ *f* ≈ tartar sauce
rempeln *vt* jostle; (*stoßen*) push
Ren *nt* **-s,-s** reindeer
Reneklode *f* **-,-n** greengage
Renn|auto *nt* racing car. **R~bahn** *f* race-track; (*Pferde-*) racecourse. **R~boot** *nt* speedboat. **r~en**† *vt/i* (*sein*) run; **um die Wette r~en** have a race. **R~en** *nt* **-s,-** race. **R~pferd** *nt* racehorse. **R~sport** *m* racing. **R~wagen** *m* racing car
renommiert *a* renowned; ⟨*Hotel, Firma*⟩ of repute
renovier|en *vt* renovate; redecorate ⟨*Zimmer*⟩. **R~ung** *f* - renovation; redecoration
rentabel *a* profitable, *adv* -bly
Rente *f* **-,-n** pension; **in R~ gehen** (*fam*) retire. **R~nversicherung** *f* pension scheme
Rentier *nt* reindeer
rentieren (sich) *vr* be profitable; (*sich lohnen*) be worth while
Rentner(in) *m* **-s,-** (*f* **-,-nen**) [old-age] pensioner
Reparatur *f* **-,-en** repair. **R~werkstatt** *f* repair workshop; (*Auto*) garage
reparieren *vt* repair, mend
repatriieren *vt* repatriate
Repertoire /repɛrˈto̯a:ɐ̯/ *nt* **-s,-s** repertoire
Reportage /-ˈta:ʒə/ *f* **-,-n** report
Reporter(in) *m* **-s,-** (*f* **-,-nen**) reporter
repräsent|ativ *a* representative (**für** of); (*eindrucksvoll*) imposing; (*Prestige verleihend*) prestigious. **r~ieren** *vt* represent □ *vi* (*haben*) perform official/social duties
Repress|alie /-li̯ə/ *f* **-,-n** reprisal. **r~iv** *a* repressive
Reprodu|ktion /-ˈtsi̯o:n/ *f* **-,-en** reproduction. **r~zieren** *vt* reproduce
Reptil *nt* **-s,-ien** /-i̯ən/ reptile
Republik *f* **-,-en** republic. **r~anisch** *a* republican
requirieren *vt* (*Mil*) requisition
Requisiten *pl* (*Theat*) properties, (*fam*) props
Reservat *nt* **-[e]s,-e** reservation
Reserve *f* **-,-n** reserve; (*Mil, Sport*) reserves *pl*. **R~rad** *nt* spare wheel. **R~spieler** *m* reserve. **R~tank** *m* reserve tank
reservier|en *vt* reserve; **r~en lassen** book. **r~t** *a* reserved. **R~ung** *f* **-,-en** reservation
Reservoir /rezɛrˈvo̯a:ɐ̯/ *nt* **-s,-s** reservoir
Resid|enz *f* **-,-en** residence. **r~ieren** *vi* (*haben*) reside
Resign|ation /-ˈtsi̯o:n/ *f* - resignation. **r~ieren** *vi* (*haben*) (*fig*) give up. **r~iert** *a* resigned, *adv* -ly
resolut *a* resolute, *adv* -ly
Resolution /-ˈtsi̯o:n/ *f* **-,-en** resolution
Resonanz *f* **-,-en** resonanance; (*fig: Widerhall*) response
Respekt /-sp-, -ʃp-/ *m* **-[e]s** respect (**vor** + *dat* for). **r~abel** *a* respectable. **r~ieren** *vt* respect
respekt|los *a* disrespectful, *adv* -ly. **r~voll** *a* respectful, *adv* -ly
Ressort /rɛˈso:ɐ̯/ *nt* **-s,-s** department

Rest *m* **-[e]s,-e** remainder, rest; **R~e** remains; (*Essens-*) leftovers
Restaurant /rɛsto'rã:/ *nt* **-s,-s** restaurant
Restaur|ation /rɛstaura'tsjo:n/ *f* - restoration. **r~ieren** *vt* restore
Rest|betrag *m* balance. **r~lich** *a* remaining. **r~los** *a* utter, *adv* -ly
Resultat *nt* **-[e]s,-e** result
Retorte *f* **-,-n** (*Chem*) retort. **R~nbaby** *nt* (*fam*) test-tube baby
rett|en *vt* save (**vor** + *dat* from); (*aus Gefahr befreien*) rescue; **sich r~en** save oneself; (*flüchten*) escape. **R~er** *m* **-s,-** rescuer; (*fig*) saviour
Rettich *m* **-s,-e** white radish
Rettung *f* **-,-en** rescue; (*fig*) salvation; **jds letzte R~** s.o.'s last hope. **R~sboot** *nt* lifeboat. **R~sdienst** *m* rescue service. **R~sgürtel** *m* lifebelt. **r~slos** *adv* hopelessly. **R~sring** *m* lifebelt. **R~swagen** *m* ambulance
retuschieren *vt* (*Phot*) retouch
Reu|e *f* - remorse; (*Relig*) repentance. **r~en** *vt* fill with remorse; **es reut mich nicht** I don't regret it. **r~ig** *a* penitent. **r~mütig** *a* contrite, *adv* -ly
Revanch|e /re'vã:ʃə/ *f* **-,-n** revenge; **R~e fordern** (*Sport*) ask for a return match. **r~ieren (sich)** *vr* take revenge; (*sich erkenntlich zeigen*) reciprocate (**mit** with); **sich für eine Einladung r~ieren** return an invitation
Revers /re've:ɐ̯/ *nt* **-,-** /-[s],-s/ lapel
revidieren *vt* revise; (*prüfen*) check
Revier *nt* **-s,-e** district; (*Zool & fig*) territory; (*Polizei-*) [police] station
Revision *f* **-,-en** revision; (*Prüfung*) check; (*Bücher-*) audit; (*Jur*) appeal
Revolte *f* **-,-n** revolt
Revolution /-'tsjo:n/ *f* **-,-en** revolution. **r~är** *a* revolutionary. **r~ieren** *vt* revolutionize
Revolver *m* **-s,-** revolver
Revue /rə'vy:/ *f* **-,-n** revue
Rezen|sent *m* **-en,-en** reviewer. **r~sieren** *vt* review. **R~sion** *f* **-,-en** review
Rezept *nt* **-[e]s,-e** prescription; (*Culin*) recipe
Rezeption /-'tsi̯o:n/ *f* **-,-en** reception
Rezession *f* **-,-en** recession
rezitieren *vt* recite
R-Gespräch *nt* reverse-charge call, (*Amer*) collect call
Rhabarber *m* **-s** rhubarb
Rhapsodie *f* **-,-n** rhapsody
Rhein *m* **-s** Rhine. **R~land** *nt* **-s** Rhineland. **R~wein** *m* hock
Rhetori|k *f* - rhetoric. **r~sch** *a* rhetorical
Rheum|a *nt* **-s** rheumatism. **r~atisch** *a* rheumatic. **R~atismus** *m* - rheumatism
Rhinozeros *nt* **-[ses],-se** rhinoceros
rhyth|misch /'rʏt-/ *a* rhythmic[al], *adv* -ally. **R~mus** *m* **-,-men** rhythm
Ribisel *f* **-,-n** (*Aust*) redcurrant
richten *vt* direct (**auf** + *acc* at); address ⟨*Frage, Briefe*⟩ (**an** + *acc* to); aim, train ⟨*Waffe*⟩ (**auf** + *acc* at); (*einstellen*) set; (*vorbereiten*) prepare; (*reparieren*) mend; (*hinrichten*) execute; (*SGer: ordentlich machen*) tidy; **in die Höhe r~** raise [up]; **das Wort an jdn r~** address s.o.; **sich r~** be directed (**auf** + *acc* at; **gegen** against); ⟨*Blick:*⟩ turn (**auf** + *acc* on); **sich r~ nach** comply with ⟨*Vorschrift, jds Wünschen*⟩; fit in with ⟨*jds Plänen*⟩; (*befolgen*) go by; (*abhängen*) depend on □ *vi* (*haben*) **r~ über** (+ *acc*) judge
Richter *m* **-s,-** judge
Richtfest *nt* topping-out ceremony

richtig *a* right, correct; (*wirklich, echt*) real; **das R~e (r~e)** the right thing □ *adv* correctly; really; **r~ stellen** put right ⟨*Uhr*⟩; (*fig*) correct ⟨*Irrtum*⟩; **die Uhr geht r~** the clock is right. **R~keit** *f* - correctness. **r~stellen** *vt sep* (NEW) **r~ stellen**, *s.* **richtig**
Richtlinien *fpl* guidelines
Richtung *f* -,-en direction; (*fig*) trend
riechen† *vt/i* (*haben*) smell (**nach** of; **an etw** *dat* sth)
Riegel *m* -s,- bolt; (*Seife*) bar
Riemen *m* -s,- strap; (*Ruder*) oar
Riese *m* -n,-n giant
rieseln *vi* (*sein*) trickle; ⟨*Schnee:*⟩ fall lightly
Riesen|erfolg *m* huge success. **r~groß** *a* huge, enormous
riesig *a* huge; (*gewaltig*) enormous □ *adv* (*fam*) terribly
Riff *nt* -[e]s,-e reef
rigoros *a* rigorous, *adv* -ly
Rille *f* -,-n groove
Rind *nt* -es,-er ox; (*Kuh*) cow; (*Stier*) bull; (*R~fleisch*) beef; **R~er** cattle *pl*
Rinde *f* -,-n bark; (*Käse-*) rind; (*Brot-*) crust
Rinderbraten *m* roast beef
Rind|fleisch *nt* beef. **R~vieh** *nt* cattle *pl*; (*fam: Idiot*) idiot
Ring *m* -[e]s,-e ring
ringeln (sich) *vr* curl; ⟨*Schlange:*⟩ coil itself (**um** round)
ring|en† *vi* (*haben*) wrestle; (*fig*) struggle (**um/nach** for) □ *vt* wring ⟨*Hände*⟩. **R~en** *nt* -s wrestling. **R~er** *m* -s,- wrestler. **R~kampf** *m* wrestling match; (*als Sport*) wrestling. **R~richter** *m* referee
rings *adv* **r~ im Kreis** in a circle; **r~ um jdn/etw** all around s.o./sth. **r~herum, r~um** *adv* all around
Rinn|e *f* -,-n channel; (*Dach-*) gutter. **r~en**† *vi* (*sein*) run; ⟨*Sand:*⟩ trickle. **R~stein** *m* gutter
Rippe *f* -,-n rib. **R~nfellentzündung** *f* pleurisy. **R~nstoß** *m* dig in the ribs
Risiko *nt* -s,-s & -ken risk; **ein R~eingehen** take a risk
risk|ant *a* risky. **r~ieren** *vt* risk
Riss *m* -es,-e (**Riß** *m* -sses,-sse) tear; (*Mauer-*) crack; (*fig*) rift
rissig *a* cracked; ⟨*Haut*⟩ chapped
Rist *m* -[e]s,-e instep
Ritt *m* -[e]s,-e ride
Ritter *m* -s,- knight. **r~lich** *a* chivalrous, *adv* -ly. **R~lichkeit** *f* - chivalry
rittlings *adv* astride
Ritu|al *nt* -s,-e ritual. **r~ell** *a* ritual
Ritz *m* -es,-e scratch. **R~e** *f* -,-n crack; (*Fels-*) cleft; (*zwischen Betten, Vorhängen*) gap. **r~en** *vt* scratch
Rival|e *m* -n,-n, **R~in** *f* -,-nen rival. **r~isieren** *vi* (*haben*) compete (**mit** with). **r~isierend** *a* rival ... **R~ität** *f* -,-en rivalry
Robbe *f* -,-n seal. **r~n** *vi* (*sein*) crawl
Robe *f* -,-n gown; (*Talar*) robe
Roboter *m* -s,- robot
robust *a* robust
röcheln *vi* (*haben*) breathe stertorously
Rochen *m* -s,- (*Zool*) ray
Rock[1] *m* -[e]s,⸚e skirt; (*Jacke*) jacket
Rock[2] *m* -[s] (*Mus*) rock
Rodel|bahn *f* toboggan run. **r~n** *vi* (*sein/haben*) toboggan. **R~schlitten** *m* toboggan
roden *vt* clear ⟨*Land*⟩; grub up ⟨*Stumpf*⟩
Rogen *m* -s,- [hard] roe
Roggen *m* -s rye
roh *a* rough; (*ungekocht*) raw; ⟨*Holz*⟩ bare; (*brutal*) brutal; **r~e Gewalt** brute force □ *adv* roughly; brutally. **R~bau** *m* -[e]s,-ten shell. **R~heit** *f* -,-en

brutality. **R∼kost** *f* raw [vegetarian] food. **R∼ling** *m* **-s,-e** brute. **R∼material** *nt* raw material. **R∼öl** *nt* crude oil

Rohr *nt* **-[e]s,-e** pipe; (*Geschütz-*) barrel; (*Bot*) reed; (*Zucker-, Bambus-*) cane

Röhr|chen *nt* **-s,-** [drinking] straw; (*Auto, fam*) breathalyser (P). **R∼e** *f* **-,-n** tube; (*Radio-*) valve; (*Back-*) oven

Rohstoff *m* raw material

Rokoko *nt* **-s** rococo

Rolladen *m* (NEW) **Rollladen**

Rollbahn *f* taxiway; (*Start-/Landebahn*) runaway

Rolle *f* **-,-n** roll; (*Garn-*) reel; (*Draht-*) coil; (*Techn*) roller; (*Seil-*) pulley; (*Wäsche-*) mangle; (*Lauf-*) castor; (*Schrift-*) scroll; (*Theat*) part, role; **das spielt keine R∼** (*fig*) that doesn't matter. **r∼n** *vt* roll; (*auf-*) roll up; roll out ⟨*Teig*⟩; put through the mangle ⟨*Wäsche*⟩; **sich r∼n** roll; (*sich ein-*) curl up □ *vi* (*sein*) roll; ⟨*Flugzeug:*⟩ taxi □ *vi* (*haben*) ⟨*Donner:*⟩ rumble. **R∼r** *m* **-s,-** scooter

Roll|feld *nt* airfield. **R∼kragen** *m* polo-neck. **R∼laden** *m* roller shutter. **R∼mops** *m* rollmop[s] *sg*

Rollo *nt* **-s,-s** [roller] blind

Roll|schuh *m* roller-skate; **R∼schuh laufen** roller-skate. **R∼splitt** *m* **-s** loose chippings *pl*. **R∼stuhl** *m* wheelchair. **R∼treppe** *f* escalator

Rom *nt* **-s** Rome

Roman *m* **-s,-e** novel. **r∼isch** *a* Romanesque; ⟨*Sprache*⟩ Romance. **R∼schriftsteller(in)** *m(f)* novelist

Romant|ik *f* - romanticism. **r∼isch** *a* romantic, *adv* -ally

Romanze *f* **-,-n** romance

Röm|er(in) *m* **-s,-** (*f* **-,-nen**) Roman. **r∼isch** *a* Roman

Rommé, Rommee /ˈrɔme:/ *nt* **-s** rummy

röntgen *vt* X-ray. **R∼aufnahme** *f*, **R∼bild** *nt* X-ray. **R∼strahlen** *mpl* X-rays

rosa *inv a*, **R∼** *nt* **-[s],-** pink

Rose *f* **-,-n** rose. **R∼nkohl** *m* [Brussels] sprouts *pl*. **R∼nkranz** *m* (*Relig*) rosary. **R∼nmontag** *m* Monday before Shrove Tuesday

Rosette *f* **-,-n** rosette

rosig *a* rosy

Rosine *f* **-,-n** raisin

Rosmarin *m* **-s** rosemary

Ross *nt* **-es,¨-er** (**Roß** *nt* **-sses, ¨sser**) horse. **R∼kastanie** *f* horse-chestnut

Rost[1] *m* **-[e]s,-e** grating; (*Kamin-*) grate; (*Brat-*) grill

Rost[2] *m* **-[e]s** rust. **r∼en** *vi* (*haben*) rust; **nicht r∼end** stainless

röst|en *vt* roast; toast ⟨*Brot*⟩. **R∼er** *m* **-s,-** toaster

rostfrei *a* stainless

rostig *a* rusty

rot *a* (**röter, rötest**), **Rot** *nt* **-s,-** red; **rot werden** turn red; (*erröten*) go red, blush

Rotation /-ˈtsi̯o:n/ *f* **-,-en** rotation

Röte *f* - redness; (*Scham-*) blush

Röteln *pl* German measles *sg*

röten *vt* redden; **sich r∼** turn red

rothaarig *a* red-haired

rotieren *vi* (*haben*) rotate

Rot|kehlchen *nt* **-s,-** robin. **R∼kohl** *m* red cabbage

rötlich *a* reddish

Rot|licht *nt* red light. **R∼wein** *m* red wine

Rou|lade /ruˈla:də/ *f* **-,-n** beef olive. **R∼leau** /-ˈlo:/ *nt* **-s,-s** [roller] blind

Route /ˈru:tə/ *f* **-,-n** route

Routin|e /ruˈti:nə/ *f* **-,-n** routine; (*Erfahrung*) experience. **r∼emäßig** *a* routine … □ *adv* routinely. **r∼iert** *a* experienced

Rowdy /ˈrau̯di/ *m* **-s,-s** hooligan

Rübe *f* **-,-n** beet; **rote R∼** beetroot; **gelbe R∼** (*SGer*) carrot

rüber *adv* = **herüber, hinüber**
Rubin *m* **-s,-e** ruby
Rubrik *f* **-,-en** column; (*Kategorie*) category
Ruck *m* **-[e]s,-e** jerk
Rückantwort *f* reply
ruckartig *a* jerky, *adv* -ily
rück|bezüglich *a* (*Gram*) reflexive. **R~blende** *f* flashback. **R~blick** *m* (*fig*) review (**auf** + *acc* of). **r~blickend** *adv* in retrospect. **r~datieren** *vt* (*inf & pp only*) backdate
rücken *vt/i* (*sein/haben*) move; **an etw** (*dat*) **r~** move sth
Rücken *m* **-s,-** back; (*Buch-*) spine; (*Berg-*) ridge. **R~lehne** *f* back. **R~mark** *nt* spinal cord. **R~schwimmen** *nt* backstroke. **R~wind** *m* following wind; (*Aviat*) tail wind
rückerstatten *vt* (*inf & pp only*) refund
Rückfahr|karte *f* return ticket. **R~t** *f* return journey
Rück|fall *m* relapse. **r~fällig** *a* **r~fällig werden** (*Jur*) re-offend. **R~flug** *m* return flight. **R~frage** *f* [further] query. **r~fragen** *vi* (*haben*) (*inf & pp only*) check (**bei** with). **R~gabe** *f* return. **R~gang** *m* decline; (*Preis-*) drop, fall. **r~gängig** *a* **r~gängig machen** cancel; break off ⟨*Verlobung*⟩. **R~grat** *nt* **-[e]s, -e** spine, backbone. **R~halt** *m* (*fig*) support. **R~hand** *f* backhand. **R~kehr** return. **R~lagen** *fpl* reserves. **R~licht** *nt* rear-light. **r~lings** *adv* backwards; (*von hinten*) from behind. **R~reise** *f* return journey
Rucksack *m* rucksack
Rück|schau *f* review. **R~schlag** *m* (*Sport*) return; (*fig*) set-back. **R~schluss** (**R~schluß**) *m* conclusion. **R~schritt** *m* (*fig*) retrograde step. **r~schrittlich** *a* retrograde. **R~seite** *f* back; (*einer Münze*) reverse
Rücksicht *f* **-,-en** consideration; **R~ nehmen auf** (+ *acc*) show consideration for; (*berücksichtigen*) take into consideration. **R~nahme** *f* - consideration. **r~slos** *a* inconsiderate, *adv* -ly; (*schonungslos*) ruthless, *adv* -ly. **r~svoll** *a* considerate, *adv* -ly
Rück|sitz *m* back seat; (*Sozius*) pillion. **R~spiegel** *m* rear-view mirror. **R~spiel** *nt* return match. **R~sprache** *f* consultation; **R~sprache nehmen mit** consult. **R~stand** *m* (*Chem*) residue; (*Arbeits-*) backlog; **R~stände** arrears; **im R~stand sein** be behind. **r~ständig** *a* (*fig*) backward. **R~stau** *m* (*Auto*) tailback. **R~strahler** *m* **-s,-** reflector. **R~tritt** *m* resignation; (*Fahrrad*) back pedalling. **r~vergüten** *vt* (*inf & pp only*) refund. **R~wanderer** *m* repatriate
rückwärt|ig *a* back ..., rear ... **r~s** *adv* backwards. **R~sgang** *m* reverse [gear]
Rückweg *m* way back
ruckweise *adv* jerkily
rück|wirkend *a* retrospective, *adv* -ly. **R~wirkung** *f* retrospective force; **mit R~wirkung vom** backdated to. **R~zahlung** *f* repayment. **R~zug** *m* retreat
Rüde *m* **-n,-n** [male] dog
Rudel *nt* **-s,-** herd; (*Wolfs-*) pack; (*Löwen-*) pride
Ruder *nt* **-s,-** oar; (*Steuer-*) rudder; **am R~** (*Naut & fig*) at the helm. **R~boot** *nt* rowing boat. **R~er** *m* **-s,-** oarsman. **r~n** *vt/i* (*haben/sein*) row
Ruf *m* **-[e]s,-e** call; (*laut*) shout; (*Telefon*) telephone number; (*Ansehen*) reputation; **Künstler von Ruf** artist of repute. **r~en†** *vt/i* (*haben*) call (**nach** for); **r~en lassen** send for
Rüffel *m* **-s,-** (*fam*) telling-off. **r~n** *vt* (*fam*) tell off

Ruf|name *m* forename by which one is known. **R~nummer** *f* telephone number. **R~zeichen** *nt* dialling tone

Rüge *f* -,-n reprimand. **r~n** *vt* reprimand; (*kritisieren*) criticize

Ruhe *f* - rest; (*Stille*) quiet; (*Frieden*) peace; (*innere*) calm; (*Gelassenheit*) composure; **die R~ bewahren** keep calm; **in R~ lassen** leave in peace; **sich zur R~ setzen** retire; **R~ [da]!** quiet! **R~gehalt** *nt* [retirement] pension. **r~los** *a* restless, *adv* -ly. **r~n** *vi* (*haben*) rest (**auf** + *dat* on); ⟨*Arbeit, Verkehr:*⟩ have stopped; **hier ruht ...** here lies ... **R~pause** *f* rest, break. **R~stand** *m* retirement; **in den R~stand treten** retire; **im R~stand** retired. **R~störung** *f* disturbance of the peace. **R~tag** *m* day of rest; **'Montag R~tag'** 'closed on Mondays'

ruhig *a* quiet, *adv* -ly; (*erholsam*) restful; (*friedlich*) peaceful, *adv* -ly; (*unbewegt, gelassen*) calm, *adv* -ly; **r~ bleiben** remain calm; **sehen Sie sich r~ um** you're welcome to look round; **man kann r~ darüber sprechen** there's no harm in talking about it

Ruhm *m* -[e]s fame; (*Ehre*) glory

rühmen *vt* praise; **sich r~** boast (*gen* about)

ruhmreich *a* glorious

Ruhr *f* - (*Med*) dysentery

Rühr|ei *nt* scrambled eggs *pl*. **r~en** *vt* move; (*Culin*) stir; **sich r~en** move; **zu Tränen r~en** move to tears; **r~t euch!** (*Mil*) at ease! □ *vi* (*haben*) stir; **r~en an** (+ *acc*) touch; (*fig*) touch on; **r~en von** (*fig*) come from. **r~end** *a* touching, *adv* -ly

rühr|ig *a* active. **r~selig** *a* sentimental. **R~ung** *f* - emotion

Ruin *m* -s ruin. **R~e** *f* -,-n ruin; ruins *pl* (*gen* of). **r~ieren** *vt* ruin

rülpsen *vi* (*haben*) (*fam*) belch

Rum *m* -s rum

rum *adv* = **herum**

Rumän|ien /-iən/ *nt* -s Romania. **r~isch** *a* Romanian

Rummel *m* -s (*fam*) hustle and bustle; (*Jahrmarkt*) funfair. **R~platz** *m* fairground

rumoren *vi* (*haben*) make a noise; ⟨*Magen:*⟩ rumble

Rumpel|kammer *f* junk-room. **r~n** *vi* (*haben/sein*) rumble

Rumpf *m* -[e]s,¨e body, trunk; (*Schiffs-*) hull; (*Aviat*) fuselage

rümpfen *vt* **die Nase r~** turn up one's nose (**über** + *acc* at)

rund *a* round □ *adv* approximately; **r~ um** [a]round. **R~blick** *m* panoramic view. **R~brief** *m* circular [letter]

Runde *f* -,-n round; (*Kreis*) circle; (*eines Polizisten*) beat; (*beim Rennen*) lap; **eine R~ Bier** a round of beer. **r~n** *vt* round; **sich r~n** become round; ⟨*Backen:*⟩ fill out

Rund|fahrt *f* tour. **R~frage** *f* poll

Rundfunk *m* radio; **im R~** on the radio. **R~gerät** *nt* radio [set]

Rund|gang *m* round; (*Spaziergang*) walk (**durch** round). **r~heraus** *adv* straight out. **r~herum** *adv* all around. **r~lich** *a* rounded; (*mollig*) plump. **R~reise** *f* [circular] tour. **R~schreiben** *nt* circular. **r~um** *adv* all round. **R~ung** *f* -,-en curve. **r~weg** *adv* ⟨*ablehnen*⟩ flatly

runter *adv* = **herunter, hinunter**

Runzel *f* -,-n wrinkle. **r~n** *vt* **die Stirn r~n** frown

runzlig *a* wrinkled

Rüpel *m* -s,- (*fam*) lout. **r~haft** *a* (*fam*) loutish

rupfen *vt* pull out; pluck ⟨*Geflügel*⟩; (*fam: schröpfen*) fleece

ruppig *a* rude, *adv* -ly

Rüsche *f* -,-n frill

Ruß *m* **-es** soot
Russe *m* **-n,-n** Russian
Rüssel *m* **-s,-** (*Zool*) trunk
ruß|en *vi* (*haben*) smoke. **r~ig** *a* sooty
Russ|in *f* **-,-nen** Russian. **r~isch** *a* Russian. **R~isch** *nt* **-[s]** (*Lang*) Russian
Russland (**Rußland**) *nt* **-s** Russia
rüsten *vi* (*haben*) prepare (**zu/für** for) □ *vr* **sich r~** get ready; **gerüstet sein** be ready
rüstig *a* sprightly
rustikal *a* rustic
Rüstung *f* **-,-en** armament; (*Harnisch*) armour. **R~skontrolle** *f* arms control
Rute *f* **-,-n** twig; (*Angel-, Wünschel-*) rod; (*zur Züchtigung*) birch; (*Schwanz*) tail
Rutsch *m* **-[e]s,-e** slide. **R~bahn** *f* slide. **R~e** *f* **-,-n** chute. **r~en** *vt* slide; (*rücken*) move □ *vi* (*sein*) slide; (*aus-, ab-*) slip; (*Auto*) skid; (*rücken*) move [along]. **r~ig** *a* slippery
rütteln *vt* shake □ *vi* (*haben*) **r~ an** (+ *dat*) rattle

S

Saal *m* **-[e]s,Säle** hall; (*Theat*) auditorium; (*Kranken-*) ward
Saat *f* **-,-en** seed; (*Säen*) sowing; (*Gesätes*) crop. **S~gut** *nt* seed
sabbern *vi* (*haben*) (*fam*) slobber; ⟨*Baby:*⟩ dribble; (*reden*) jabber
Säbel *m* **-s,-** sabre
Sabo|tage /zabo'ta:ʒə/ *f* **-** sabotage. **S~teur** /-'tø:ɐ̯/ *m* **-s,-e** saboteur. **s~tieren** *vt* sabotage
Sach|bearbeiter *m* expert. **S~buch** *nt* non-fiction book. **s~dienlich** *a* relevant
Sache *f* **-,-n** matter, business; (*Ding*) thing; (*fig*) cause; **zur S~ kommen** come to the point
Sach|gebiet *nt* (*fig*) area, field. **s~gemäß** *a* proper, *adv* -ly. **S~kenntnis** *f* expertise. **s~kundig** *a* expert, *adv* -ly. **s~lich** *a* factual, *adv* -ly; (*nüchtern*) matter-of-fact, *adv* -ly; (*objektiv*) objective, *adv* -ly; (*schmucklos*) functional
sächlich *a* (*Gram*) neuter
Sachse *m* **-n,-n** Saxon. **S~n** *nt* **-s** Saxony
sächsisch *a* Saxon
sacht *a* gentle, *adv* -ly
Sach|verhalt *m* **-[e]s** facts *pl*. **s~verständig** *a* expert, *adv* -ly. **S~verständige(r)** *mf* expert
Sack *m* **-[e]s,¨e** sack; **mit S~ und Pack** with all one's belongings
sacken *vi* (*sein*) sink; (*zusammen-*) go down; ⟨*Person:*⟩ slump
Sack|gasse *f* cul-de-sac; (*fig*) impasse. **S~leinen** *nt* sacking
Sadis|mus *m* **-** sadism. **S~t** *m* **-en,-en** sadist. **s~tisch** *a* sadistic, *adv* -ally
säen *vt/i* (*haben*) sow
Safe /ze:f/ *m* **-s,-s** safe
Saft *m* **-[e]s,¨e** juice; (*Bot*) sap. **s~ig** *a* juicy; ⟨*Wiese*⟩ lush; ⟨*Preis, Rechnung*⟩ hefty; ⟨*Witz*⟩ coarse. **s~los** *a* dry
Sage *f* **-,-n** legend
Säge *f* **-,-n** saw. **S~mehl** *nt* sawdust
sagen *vt* say; (*mitteilen*) tell; (*bedeuten*) mean; **das hat nichts zu s~** it doesn't mean anything; **ein viel s~der Blick** a meaningful look
sägen *vt/i* (*haben*) saw
sagenhaft *a* legendary; (*fam: unglaublich*) fantastic, *adv* -ally
Säge|späne *mpl* wood shavings. **S~werk** *nt* sawmill
Sahn|e *f* **-** cream. **S~ebonbon** *m* & *nt* ≈ toffee. **s~ig** *a* creamy
Saison /zɛ'zõ:/ *f* **-,-s** season
Saite *f* **-,-n** (*Mus, Sport*) string. **S~ninstrument** *nt* stringed instrument

Sakko *m & nt* **-s,-s** sports jacket
Sakrament *nt* **-[e]s,-e** sacrament
Sakrileg *nt* **-s,-e** sacrilege
Sakrist|an *m* **-s,-e** verger. **S~ei** *f* **-,-en** vestry
Salat *m* **-[e]s,-e** salad; **ein Kopf S~** a lettuce. **S~soße** *f* salad-dressing
Salbe *f* **-,-n** ointment
Salbei *m* **-s** & *f* **-** sage
salben *vt* anoint
Saldo *m* **-s,-dos** & **-den** balance
Salon /za'lõ:/ *m* **-s,-s** salon; (*Naut*) saloon
salopp *a* casual, *adv* -ly; ⟨*Benehmen*⟩ informal, *adv* -ly; ⟨*Ausdruck*⟩ slangy
Salto *m* **-s,-s** somersault
Salut *m* **-[e]s,-e** salute. **s~ieren** *vi* (*haben*) salute
Salve *f* **-,-n** volley; (*Geschütz-*) salvo, (*von Gelächter*) burst
Salz *nt* **-es,-e** salt. **s~en†** *vt* salt. **S~fass** (**S~faß**) *nt* salt-cellar. **s~ig** *a* salty. **S~kartoffeln** *fpl* boiled potatoes. **S~säure** *f* hydrochloric acid
Samen *m* **-s,-** seed; (*Anat*) semen, sperm
sämig *a* (*Culin*) thick
Sämling *m* **-s,-e** seedling
Sammel|becken *nt* reservoir. **S~begriff** *m* collective term. **s~n** *vt/i* (*haben*) collect; (*suchen, versammeln*) gather; **sich s~n** collect; (*sich versammeln*) gather; (*sich fassen*) collect oneself. **S~name** *m* collective noun
Samm|ler(in) *m* **-s,-** (*f* **-,-nen**) collector. **S~lung** *f* **-,-en** collection; (*innere*) composure
Samstag *m* **-s,-e** Saturday. **s~s** *adv* on Saturdays
samt *prep* (+ *dat*) together with □ *adv* **s~ und sonders** without exception
Samt *m* **-[e]s** velvet. **s~ig** *a* velvety
sämtlich *indef pron inv* all. **s~e(r,s)** *indef pron* all the; **s~e Werke** complete works; **meine s~en Bücher** all my books
Sanatorium *nt* **-s,-ien** sanatorium
Sand *m* **-[e]s** sand
Sandal|e *f* **-,-n** sandal. **S~ette** *f* **-,-n** high-heeled sandal
Sand|bank *f* sandbank. **S~burg** *f* sand-castle. **s~ig** *a* sandy. **S~kasten** *m* sand-pit. **S~kuchen** *m* Madeira cake. **S~papier** *nt* sandpaper. **S~stein** *m* sandstone
sanft *a* gentle, *adv* -ly. **s~mütig** *a* meek
Sänger(in) *m* **-s,-**(*f* **-,-nen**) singer
sanieren *vt* clean up; redevelop ⟨*Gebiet*⟩; (*modernisieren*) modernize; make profitable ⟨*Industrie, Firma*⟩; **sich s~** become profitable
sanitär *a* sanitary
Sanität|er *m* **-s,-** first-aid man; (*Fahrer*) ambulance man; (*Mil*) medical orderly. **S~swagen** *m* ambulance
Sanktion /zaŋk'tsio:n/ *f* **-,-en** sanction. **s~ieren** *vt* sanction
Saphir *m* **-s,-e** sapphire
Sardelle *f* **-,-n** anchovy
Sardine *f* **-,-n** sardine
Sarg *m* **-[e]s,¨e** coffin
Sarkas|mus *m* **-** sarcasm. **s~tisch** *a* sarcastic, *adv* -ally
Sat|an *m* **-s** Satan; (*fam: Teufel*) devil. **s~anisch** *a* satanic
Satellit *m* **-en,-en** satellite. **S~enfernsehen** *nt* satellite television
Satin /za'tɛŋ/ *m* **-s** satin
Satir|e *f* **-,-n** satire. **s~isch** *a* **satirical**, *adv* -ly
satt *a* full; ⟨*Farbe*⟩ rich; **s~ sein** have had enough [to eat]; **sich s~ essen** eat as much as one wants; **s~ machen** feed; ⟨*Speise:*⟩ be filling; **etw s~ haben** (*fam*) be fed up with sth
Sattel *m* **-s,¨** saddle. **s~n** *vt* saddle. **S~schlepper** *m* tractor unit. **S~zug** *m* articulated lorry

sättigen *vt* satisfy; (*Chem & fig*) saturate □ *vi* (*haben*) be filling. **s~d** a filling

Satz *m* **-es,⸚e** sentence; (*Teil-*) clause; (*These*) proposition; (*Math*) theorem; (*Mus*) movement; (*Tennis, Zusammengehöriges*) set; (*Boden-*) sediment; (*Kaffee-*) grounds *pl*; (*Steuer-, Zins-*) rate; (*Druck-*) setting; (*Schrift-*) type; (*Sprung*) leap, bound. **S~aussage** *f* predicate. **S~gegenstand** *m* subject. **S~zeichen** *nt* punctuation mark

Sau *f* **-,Säue** sow; (*sl: schmutziger Mensch*) dirty pig

sauber *a* clean; (*ordentlich*) neat, *adv* -ly; (*anständig*) decent, *adv* -ly; (*fam: nicht anständig*) fine; **s~ halten** keep clean; **s~ machen** clean. **s~halten†** *vt sep* (NEW) **s~ halten**, *s.* **sauber**. **S~keit** *f* - cleanliness; neatness; decency

säuberlich *a* neat, *adv* -ly

saubermachen *vt/i sep* (*haben*) (NEW) **sauber machen**, *s.* **sauber**

säuber|n *vt* clean; (*befreien*) rid/ (*Pol*) purge (**von** of). **S~ungsaktion** *f* (*Pol*) purge

Sauce /'zo:sə/ *f* **-,-n** sauce; (*Braten-*) gravy

Saudi-Arabien /-i̯ən/ *nt* **-s** Saudi Arabia

sauer *a* sour; (*Chem*) acid; (*eingelegt*) pickled; (*schwer*) hard; **saurer Regen** acid rain; **s~ sein** (*fam*) be annoyed

Sauerei *f* **-,-en** = **Schweinerei**

Sauerkraut *nt* sauerkraut

säuerlich *a* slightly sour

Sauer|stoff *m* oxygen

saufen† *vt/i* (*haben*) drink; (*sl*) booze

Säufer *m* **-s,-** (*sl*) boozer

saugen† *vt/i* (*haben*) suck; (*staub-*) vacuum, hoover; **sich voll Wasser s~** soak up water

säugen *vt* suckle

Sauger *m* **-s,-** [baby's] dummy, (*Amer*) pacifier; (*Flaschen-*) teat

Säugetier *nt* mammal

saugfähig *a* absorbent

Säugling *m* **-s,-e** infant

Säule *f* **-,-n** column

Saum *m* **-[e]s,Säume** hem; (*Rand*) edge

säumen[1] *vt* hem; (*fig*) line

säum|en[2] *vi* (*haben*) delay. **s~ig** *a* dilatory

Sauna *f* **-,-nas & -nen** sauna

Säure *f* **-,-n** acidity; (*Chem*) acid

säuseln *vi* (*haben*) rustle [softly]

sausen *vi* (*haben*) rush; ⟨*Ohren:*⟩ buzz □ *vi* (*sein*) rush [along]

Sauwetter *nt* (*sl*) lousy weather

Saxophon, Saxofon *nt* **-s,-e** saxophone

SB- /ɛs'be:-/ *pref* (= **Selbstbedienung**) self-service . . .

S-Bahn *f* city and suburban railway

sch *int* shush! (*fort*) shoo!

Schabe *f* **-,-n** cockroach

schaben *vt/i* (*haben*) scrape

schäbig *a* shabby, *adv* -ily

Schablone *f* **-,-n** stencil; (*Muster*) pattern; (*fig*) stereotype

Schach *nt* **-s** chess; **S~!** check! **in S~ halten** (*fig*) keep in check. **S~brett** *nt* chessboard

schachern *vi* (*haben*) haggle

Schachfigur *f* chess-man

schachmatt *a* **s~ setzen** checkmate; **s~!** checkmate!

Schachspiel *nt* game of chess

Schacht *m* **-[e]s,⸚e** shaft

Schachtel *f* **-,-n** box; (*Zigaretten-*) packet

Schachzug *m* move

schade *a* **s~ sein** be a pity *or* shame: **zu s~ für** too good for; **[wie] s~!** [what a] pity *or* shame!

Schädel *m* **-s**, skull. **S~bruch** *m* fractured skull

schaden *vi* (*haben*) (+ *dat*) damage; (*nachteilig sein*) hurt; **das schadet nichts** that doesn't matter. **S~** *m* **-s,⸚** damage; (*Defekt*) defect; *(Nachteil)* disadvantage; **zu S~ kommen** be hurt. **S~ersatz** *m* damages *pl.* **S~freude** *f* malicious glee. **s~froh** *a* gloating

schadhaft *a* defective

schädig|en *vt* damage, harm. **S~ung** *f* -,-en damage

schädlich *a* harmful

Schädling *m* -s,-e pest. **S~sbekämpfungsmittel** *nt* pesticide

Schaf *nt* -[e]s,-e sheep; *(fam: Idiot)* idiot. **S~bock** *m* ram

Schäfchen *nt* -s,- lamb

Schäfer *m* -s,- shepherd. **S~hund** *m* sheepdog; **Deutscher S~hund** German shepherd, alsatian

Schaffell *nt* sheepskin

schaffen†[1] *vt* create; *(herstellen)* establish; make ⟨*Platz*⟩; **wie geschaffen für** made for

schaffen[2] *v (reg)* □ *vt* manage [to do]; pass ⟨*Prüfung*⟩; catch ⟨*Zug*⟩; *(bringen)* take; **jdm zu~ machen** trouble s.o.; **sich** *(dat)* **zu s~ machen** busy oneself (**an** + *dat* with) □ *vi (haben) (SGer: arbeiten)* work. **S~** *nt* -s work

Schaffner *m* -s,- conductor; *(Zug-)* ticket-inspector

Schaffung *f* - creation

Schaft *m* -[e]s,¨e shaft; *(Gewehr-)* stock; *(Stiefel-)* leg. **S~stiefel** *m* high boot

Schal *m* -s,-s scarf

schal *a* insipid; *(abgestanden)* flat; *(fig)* stale

Schale *f* -,-n skin; *(abgeschält)* peel; *(Eier-, Nuss-, Muschel-)* shell; *(Schüssel)* dish

schälen *vt* peel; **sich s~** peel

schalkhaft *a* mischievous, *adv* -ly

Schall *m* -[e]s sound. **S~dämpfer** *m* silencer. **s~dicht** *a* soundproof. **s~en** *vi (haben)* ring out: *(nachhallen)* resound; **s~end lachen** roar with laughter. **S~mauer** *f* sound barrier. **S~platte** *f* record, disc

schalt|en *vt* switch □ *vi (haben)* switch/⟨*Ampel:*⟩ turn (**auf** + *acc* to); *(Auto)* change gear; *(fam: begreifen)* catch on. **S~er** *m* -s,- switch; *(Post-, Bank-)* counter; *(Fahrkarten-)* ticket window. **S~hebel** *m* switch; *(Auto)* gear lever. **S~jahr** *nt* leap year. **S~kreis** *m* circuit. **S~ung** *f* -,-en circuit; *(Auto)* gear change

Scham *f* - shame; *(Anat)* private parts *pl*; **falsche S~** false modesty

schämen (sich) *vr* be ashamed; **schämt euch!** you should be ashamed of yourselves!

scham|haft *a* modest, *adv* -ly; *(schüchtern)* bashful, *adv* -ly. **s~los** *a* shameless, *adv* -ly

Schampon *nt* -s shampoo. **s~ieren** *vt* shampoo

Schande *f* - disgrace, shame; **S~ machen** (+ *dat*) bring shame on; **zu S~n machen/werden** = **zuschanden machen/werden**, *s.* **zuschanden**

schänd|en *vt* dishonour; *(fig)* defile; *(Relig)* desecrate; *(sexuell)* violate. **s~lich** *a* disgraceful, *adv* -ly. **S~ung** *f* -,-en defilement, desecration; violation

Schänke *f* -,-n = **Schenke**

Schanktisch *m* bar

Schanze *f*, -,-n [ski-]jump

Schar *f* -,-en crowd; *(Vogel-)* flock; **in [hellen] S~en** in droves

Scharade *f* -,-n charade

scharen *vt* **um sich s~** gather round one; **sich s~ um** flock round. **s~weise** *adv* in droves

scharf *a* (**schärfer, schärfst**) sharp; *(stark)* strong; *(stark gewürzt)* hot; ⟨*Geruch*⟩ pungent; ⟨*Frost, Wind, Augen, Verstand*⟩ keen; *(streng)* harsh; ⟨*Galopp, Ritt*⟩ hard; ⟨*Munition*⟩ live; ⟨*Hund*⟩ fierce; **s~ einstellen** *(Phot)* focus; **s~ sein** *(Phot)* be in focus; **s~ sein auf** (+ *acc*) *(fam)* be keen on □ *adv* sharply; ⟨*hinsehen, nachdenken, bremsen,*

reiten) hard; (*streng*) harshly; **s~ schießen** fire live ammunition
Scharfblick *m* perspicacity
Schärfe *f* - (*s.* **scharf**) sharpness; strength; hotness; pungency; keenness; harshness. **s~n** *vt* sharpen
scharf|machen *vt sep* (*fam*) incite. **S~richter** *m* executioner. **S~schütze** *m* marksman. **s~sichtig** *a* perspicacious. **S~sinn** *m* astuteness. **s~sinnig** *a* astute, *adv* -ly
Scharlach *m* **-s** scarlet fever
Scharlatan *m* **-s,-e** charlatan
Scharnier *nt* **-s,-e** hinge
Schärpe *f* **-,-n** sash
scharren *vi* (*haben*) scrape; ⟨*Huhn*⟩ scratch; ⟨*Pferd:*⟩ paw the ground □ *vt* scrape
Schart|e *f* **-,-n** nick. **s~ig** *a* jagged
Schaschlik *m & nt* **-s,-s** kebab
Schatten *m* **-s,-** shadow; (*schattige Stelle*) shade; **im S~** in the shade. **s~haft** *a* shadowy. **S~riss** (**S~riß**) *m* silhouette. **S~seite** *f* shady side; (*fig*) disadvantage
schattier|en *vt* shade. **S~ung** *f* **-,-en** shading; (*fig: Variante*) shade
schattig *a* shady
Schatz *m* **-es,¨-e** treasure; (*Freund, Freundin*) sweetheart; (*Anrede*) darling
Schätzchen *nt* **-s,-** darling
schätzen *vt* estimate; (*taxieren*) value; (*achten*) esteem; (*würdigen*) appreciate; (*fam: vermuten*) reckon; **sich glücklich s~** consider oneself lucky
Schätzung *f* **-,-en** estimate; (*Taxierung*) valuation. **s~sweise** *adv* approximately
Schau *f* **-,-en** show; **zur S~ stellen** display. **S~ bild** *nt* diagram
Schauder *m* **-s** shiver; (*vor Abscheu*) shudder. **s~ haft** *a* dreadful, *adv* -ly. **s~n** *vi* (*haben*) shiver; (*vor Abscheu*) shudder; **mich s~te** I shivered/shuddered
schauen *vi* (*haben*) (*SGer, Aust*) look; **s~, dass** make sure that
Schauer *m* **-s,-** shower; (*Schauder*) shiver. **S~geschichte** *f* horror story. **s~lich** *a* ghastly. **s~n** *vi* (*haben*) shiver; **mich s~te** I shivered
Schaufel *f* **-,-n** shovel; (*Kehr-*) dustpan. **s~n** *vt* shovel; (*graben*) dig
Schaufenster *nt* shop-window. **S~bummel** *m* window-shopping. **S~puppe** *f* dummy
Schaukasten *m* display case
Schaukel *f* **-,-n** swing. **s~n** *vt* rock □ *vi* (*haben*) rock; (*auf einer Schaukel*) swing; (*schwanken*) sway. **S~pferd** *nt* rocking-horse. **S~stuhl** *m* rocking-chair
schaulustig *a* curious
Schaum *m* **-[e]s** foam; (*Seifen-*) lather; (*auf Bier*) froth; (*als Frisier-, Rasiermittel*) mousse
schäumen *vi* (*haben*) foam, froth; ⟨*Seife:*⟩ lather
Schaum|gummi *m* foam rubber. **s~ig** *a* frothy; **s~ig rühren** (*Culin*) cream. **S~krone** *f* white crest; (*auf Bier*) head. **S~speise** *f* mousse. **S~stoff** *m* [synthetic] foam. **S~wein** *m* sparkling wine
Schauplatz *m* scene
schaurig *a* dreadful, *adv* -ly; (*unheimlich*) eerie, *adv* eerily
Schauspiel *nt* play; (*Anblick*) spectacle. **S~er** *m* actor. **S~erin** *f* actress. **s~ern** *vi* (*haben*) act; (*sich verstellen*) play-act
Scheck *m* **-s,-s** cheque, (*Amer*) check. **S~buch, S~heft** *nt* cheque-book. **S~karte** *f* cheque card
Scheibe *f* **-,-n** disc; (*Schieß-*) target; (*Glas-*) pane; (*Brot-, Wurst-*) slice. **S~nwaschanlage** *f* windscreen washer. **S~nwischer** *m* **-s,-** windscreen-wiper
Scheich *m* **-s,-e & -s** sheikh

Scheide *f* **-,-n** sheath; (*Anat*) vagina
scheid|en† *vt* separate; (*unterscheiden*) distinguish; dissolve ⟨*Ehe*⟩; **sich s~en lassen** get divorced; **sich s~en** diverge; ⟨*Meinungen*:⟩ differ □ *vi* (*sein*) leave; (*voneinander*) part. **S~ung** *f* **-,-en** divorce
Schein *m* **-[e]s,-e** light; (*Anschein*) appearance; (*Bescheinigung*) certificate; (*Geld-*) note; **etw nur zum S~ tun** only pretend to do sth. **s~bar** *a* apparent, *adv* -ly. **s~en**† *vi* (*haben*) shine; (*den Anschein haben*) seem, appear; **mir s~t** it seems to me
scheinheilig *a* hypocritical, *adv* -ly. **S~keit** *f* hypocrisy
Scheinwerfer *m* **-s,-** floodlight; (*Such-*) searchlight; (*Auto*) headlight; (*Theat*) spotlight
Scheiß-, **scheiß-** *pref* (*vulg*) bloody. **S~e** *f* - (*vulg*) shit. **s~en**† *vi* (*haben*) (*vulg*) shit
Scheit *nt* **-[e]s,-e** log
Scheitel *m* **-s,-** parting. **s~n** *vt* part ⟨*Haar*⟩
scheitern *vi* (*sein*) fail
Schelle *f* **-,-n** bell. **s~n** *vi* (*haben*) ring
Schellfisch *m* haddock
Schelm *m* **-s,-e** rogue. **s~isch** *a* mischievous, *adv* -ly
Schelte *f* - scolding. **s~n**† *vi* (*haben*) grumble (**über** + *acc* about); **mit jdm s~n** scold s.o. □ *vt* scold; (*bezeichnen*) call
Schema *nt* **-s,-mata** model, pattern; (*Skizze*) diagram
Schemel *m* **-s,-** stool
Schenke *f* **-,-n** tavern
Schenkel *m* **-s,-** thigh; (*Geom*) side
schenken *vt* give [as a present]; **jdm Vertrauen/Glauben s~** trust/believe s.o.; **sich** (*dat*) **etw s~** give sth a miss
scheppern *vi* (*haben*) clank
Scherbe *f* **-,-n** [broken] piece
Schere *f* **-,-n** scissors *pl*; (*Techn*) shears *pl*; (*Hummer-*) claw. **s~n**[1]† *vt* shear; crop ⟨*Haar*⟩; clip ⟨*Hund*⟩
scheren[2] *vt* (*reg*) (*fam*) bother; **sich nicht s~ um** not care about; **scher dich zum Teufel!** go to hell!
Scherenschnitt *m* silhouette
Scherereien *fpl* (*fam*) trouble *sg*
Scherz *m* **-es,-e** joke; **im/zum S~** as a joke. **s~en** *vi* (*haben*) joke. **S~frage** *f* riddle. **s~haft** *a* humorous
scheu *a* shy, *adv* -ly; ⟨*Tier*⟩ timid; **s~ werden** ⟨*Pferd*:⟩ shy; **s~ machen** startle. **S~** *f* - shyness; timidity; (*Ehrfurcht*) awe
scheuchen *vt* shoo
scheuen *vt* be afraid of; (*meiden*) shun; **keine Mühe/Kosten s~** spare no effort/expense; **sich s~** be afraid (**vor** + *dat* of); shrink (**etw zu tun** from doing sth) □ *vi* (*haben*) ⟨*Pferd*:⟩ shy
Scheuer|lappen *m* floor-cloth. **s~n** *vt* scrub; (*mit Scheuerpulver*) scour; (*reiben*) rub; **[wund] s~n** chafe □ *vi* (*haben*) rub, chafe. **S~tuch** *nt* floor-cloth
Scheuklappen *fpl* blinkers
Scheune *f* **-,-n** barn
Scheusal *nt* **-s,-e** monster
scheußlich *a* horrible, *adv* -bly
Schi *m* **-s,-er** ski; **S~ fahren** *od* **laufen** ski
Schicht *f* **-,-en** layer; (*Geol*) stratum; (*Gesellschafts-*) class; (*Arbeits-*) shift. **S~arbeit** *f* shift work. **s~en** *vt* stack [up]
schick *a* stylish, *adv* -ly; ⟨*Frau*⟩ chic; (*fam: prima*) great. **S~** *m* **-[e]s** style
schicken *vt/i* (*haben*) send; **s~ nach** send for; **sich s~ in** (+ *acc*) resign oneself to
schicklich *a* fitting, proper
Schicksal *nt* **-s,-e** fate. **s~haft** *a* fateful. **S~sschlag** *m* misfortune
Schieb|edach *nt* (*Auto*) sun-roof. **s~en**† *vt* push; (*gleitend*) slide;

(*fam: handeln mit*) traffic in; **etw s~en auf** (+ *acc*) (*fig*) put sth down to; shift ⟨*Schuld, Verantwortung*⟩ on to □ *vi* (*haben*) push. **S~er** *m* **-s,-** slide; (*Person*) black marketeer. **S~etür** *f* sliding door. **S~ung** *f* **-,-en** (*fam*) illicit deal; (*Betrug*) rigging, fixing

Schieds|gericht *nt* panel of judges; (*Jur*) arbitration tribunal. **S~richter** *m* referee; (*Tennis*) umpire; (*Jur*) arbitrator

schief *a* crooked; (*unsymmetrisch*) lopsided; (*geneigt*) slanting, sloping; (*nicht senkrecht*) leaning; ⟨*Winkel*⟩ oblique; (*fig*) false; (*misstrauisch*) suspicious □ *adv* not straight; **jdn s~ ansehen** look at s.o. askance; **s~ gehen** (*fam*) go wrong

Schiefer *m* **-s** slate

schief|gehen† *vi sep* (*sein*) (NEW) **s~ gehen**, *s.* **schief**. **s~lachen (sich)** *vr sep* double up with laughter

schielen *vi* (*haben*) squint

Schienbein *nt* shin; (*Knochen*) shinbone

Schiene *f* **-,-n** rail; (*Gleit-*) runner; (*Med*) splint. **s~n** *vt* (*Med*) put in a splint

schier1 *adv* almost

schier2 *a* pure; ⟨*Fleisch*⟩ lean

Schieß|bude *f* shooting-gallery. **s~en**† *vt* shoot; fire ⟨*Kugel*⟩; score ⟨*Tor*⟩ □ *vi* (*haben*) shoot, fire (**auf** + *acc* at) □ *vi* (*sein*) shoot [along]; (*strömen*) gush; **in die Höhe s~en** shoot up. **S~erei** *f* **-,-en** shooting. **S~scheibe** *f* target. **S~stand** *m* shooting-range

Schifahr|en *nt* skiing. **S~er(in)** *m(f)* skier

Schiff *nt* **-[e]s,-e** ship; (*Kirchen-*) nave; (*Seiten-*) aisle

Schiffahrt *f* (NEW) **Schifffahrt**

schiff|bar *a* navigable. **S~bau** *m* shipbuilding. **S~bruch** *m* shipwreck. **s~brüchig** *a* shipwrecked. **S~chen** *nt* **-s,-** small boat; (*Tex*) shuttle. **S~er** *m* **-s,-** skipper. **S~fahrt** *f* shipping

Schikan|e *f* **-,-n** harassment; **mit allen S~en** (*fam*) with every refinement. **s~ieren** *vt* harass; (*tyrannisieren*) bully

Schi|laufen *nt* **-s** skiing. **S~läufer(in)** *m(f)* **-s,-** (*f* **-,-nen**) skier

Schild1 *m* **-[e]s,-e** shield; **etw im S~e führen** (*fam*) be up to sth

Schild2 *nt* **-[e]s,-er** sign; (*Namens-, Nummern-*) plate; (*Mützen-*) badge; (*Etikett*) label

Schilddrüse *f* thyroid [gland]

schilder|n *vt* describe. **S~ung** *f* **-,-en** description

Schild|kröte *f* tortoise; (*See-*) turtle. **S~patt** *nt* **-[e]s** tortoiseshell

Schilf *nt* **-[e]s** reeds *pl*

schillern *vi* (*haben*) shimmer

Schimmel *m* **-s,-** mould; (*Pferd*) white horse. **s~ig** *a* mouldy. **s~n** *vi* (*haben/sein*) go mouldy

Schimmer *m* **-s** gleam; (*Spur*) glimmer. **s~n** *vi* (*haben*) gleam

Schimpanse *m* **-n,-n** chimpanzee

schimpf|en *vi* (*haben*) grumble (**mit** at; **über** + *acc* about); scold (**mit jdm** s.o.) □ *vt* call. **S~name** *m* term of abuse. **S~wort** *nt* (*pl* **-wörter**) swear-word; (*Beleidigung*) insult

schind|en† *vt* work *or* drive hard; (*quälen*) ill-treat; **sich s~en** slave [away]; **Eindruck s~en** (*fam*) try to impress. **S~er** *m* **-s,-** slave-driver. **S~erei** *f* **-** slave-driving; (*Plackerei*) hard slog

Schinken *m* **-s,-** ham. **S~speck** *m* bacon

Schippe *f* **-,-n** shovel. **s~n** *vt* shovel

Schirm *m* **-[e]s,-e** umbrella; (*Sonnen-*) sunshade; (*Lampen-*) shade; (*Augen-*) visor; (*Mützen-*) peak; (*Ofen-, Bild-*) screen; (*fig: Schutz*) shield. **S~herr** *m* patron. **S~herrschaft** *f* patronage. **S~mütze** *f* peaked cap

schizophren *a* schizophrenic. **S~ie** *f* - schizophrenia

Schlacht *f* -,-en battle

schlachten *vt* slaughter, kill

Schlachter, Schlächter *m* -s,- (*NGer*) butcher

Schlacht|feld *nt* battlefield. **S~haus** *nt*, **S~hof** *m* abattoir. **S~platte** *f* plate of assorted cooked meats and sausages. **S~schiff** *nt* battleship

Schlacke *f* -,-n slag

Schlaf *m* -[e]s sleep; **im S~** in one's sleep. **S~anzug** *m* pyjamas *pl*, (*Amer*) pajamas *pl*. **S~couch** *f* sofa bed

Schläfe *f* -,-n (*Anat*) temple

schlafen† *vi* (*haben*) sleep; (*fam: nicht aufpassen*) be asleep; **s~ gehen** go to bed; **er schläft noch** he is still asleep. **S~szeit** *f* bedtime

Schläfer(in) *m* **-s,-** (*f* **-,-nen**) sleeper

schlaff *a* limp, *adv* -ly; ⟨*Seil*⟩ slack; ⟨*Muskel*⟩ flabby

Schlaf|lied *nt* lullaby. **s~los** *a* sleepless. **S~losigkeit** *f* - insomnia. **S~mittel** *nt* sleeping drug

schläfrig *a* sleepy, *adv* -ily

Schlaf|saal *m* dormitory. **S~sack** *m* sleeping-bag. **S~tablette** *f* sleeping-pill. **s~trunken** *a* [still] half asleep. **S~wagen** *m* sleeping-car, sleeper. **s~wandeln** *vi* (*haben/sein*) sleep-walk. **S~zimmer** *nt* bedroom

Schlag *m* **-[e]s,¨e** blow; (*Faust-*) punch; (*Herz-, Puls-, Trommel-*) beat; (*einer Uhr*) chime; (*Glocken-, Gong- & Med*) stroke; (*elektrischer*) shock; (*Portion*) helping; (*Art*) type; (*Aust*) whipped cream; **S¨e bekommen** get a beating; **S~ auf S~** in rapid succession. **S~ader** *f* artery. **S~anfall** *m* stroke. **s~artig** *a* sudden, *adv* -ly. **S~baum** *m* barrier

Schlägel *m* **-s,-** mallet; (*Trommel-*) stick

schlagen† *vt* hit, strike; (*fällen*) fell; knock ⟨*Loch, Nagel*⟩ (**in** + *acc* into); (*prügeln, besiegen*) beat; (*Culin*) whisk ⟨*Eiweiß*⟩; whip ⟨*Sahne*⟩; (*legen*) throw; (*wickeln*) wrap; (*hinzufügen*) add (**zu** to); **sich s~** fight; **sich geschlagen geben** admit defeat □ *vi* (*haben*) beat; ⟨*Tür:*⟩ bang; ⟨*Uhr:*⟩ strike; (*melodisch*) chime; **mit den Flügeln s~** flap its wings; **um sich s~** lash out; **es schlug sechs** the clock struck six □ *vi* (*sein*) **in etw** (*acc*) **s~** ⟨*Blitz, Kugel:*⟩ strike sth; **s~ an** (+ *acc*) knock against; **nach jdm s~** (*fig*) take after s.o. **s~d** *a* (*fig*) conclusive, *adv* -ly

Schlager *m* **-s,-** popular song; (*Erfolg*) hit

Schläger *m* **-s,-** racket; (*Tischtennis-*) bat; (*Golf-*) club; (*Hockey-*) stick; (*fam: Raufbold*) thug. **S~ei** *f* -,-en fight, brawl

schlag|fertig *a* quick-witted. **S~instrument** *nt* percussion instrument. **S~loch** *nt* pot-hole. **S~sahne** *f* whipped cream; (*ungeschlagen*) whipping cream. **S~seite** *f* (*Naut*) list. **S~stock** *m* truncheon. **S~wort** *nt* (*pl* **-worte**) slogan. **S~zeile** *f* headline. **S~zeug** *nt* (*Mus*) percussion. **S~zeuger** *m* **-s,-** percussionist; (*in Band*) drummer

schlaksig *a* gangling

Schlamassel *m & nt* **-s** (*fam*) mess

Schlamm *m* **-[e]s** mud. **s~ig** *a* muddy

Schlamp|e *f* -,-n (*fam*) slut. **s~en** *vi* (*haben*) (*fam*) be sloppy (**bei** in). **S~erei** *f* **-,-en** sloppiness; (*Unordnung*) mess. **s~ig** *a* slovenly; ⟨*Arbeit*⟩ sloppy □ *adv* in a slovenly way; sloppily

Schlange *f* **-,-n** snake; (*Menschen-, Auto-*) queue; **S~ stehen** queue, (*Amer*) stand in line

schlängeln (sich) *vr* wind; ⟨*Person:*⟩ weave (**durch** through)

Schlangen|biss (**Schlangenbiß**) *m* snakebite. **S~linie** *f* wavy line

schlank *a* slim. **S~heit** *f* - slimness. **S~heitskur** *f* slimming diet

schlapp *a* tired; (*schlaff*) limp, *adv* -ly. **S~e** *f* -,-**n** (*fam*) setback

schlau *a* clever, *adv* -ly; (*gerissen*) crafty, *adv* -ily; **ich werde nicht s~ daraus** I can't make head or tail of it

Schlauch *m* -**[e]s,Schläuche** tube; (*Wasser-*) hose[pipe]. **S~boot** *nt* rubber dinghy. **s~en** *vt* (*fam*) exhaust

Schlaufe *f* -,-**n** loop

schlecht *a* bad; (*böse*) wicked; (*unzulänglich*) poor; **s~ werden** go bad; ⟨*Wetter:*⟩ turn bad; **s~er werden** get worse; **s~ aussehen** look bad/⟨*Person:*⟩ unwell; **mir ist s~** I feel sick; **s~ machen** (*fam*) run down □ *adv* badly; poorly; (*kaum*) not really. **s~gehen**† *vi sep* (*sein*) (NEW) **s~ gehen**, *s.* **gehen**. **s~gelaunt** *a* (NEW) **s~ gelaunt**, *s.* **gelaunt**. **s~hin** *adv* quite simply. **S~igkeit** *f* - wickedness. **s~machen** *vt sep* (NEW) **s~ machen**, *s.* **schlecht**

schlecken *vt/i* (*haben*) lick (**an etw** *dat* sth); (*auf-*) lap up

Schlegel *m* -**s,**- (*SGer: Keule*) leg; (*Hühner-*) drumstick; (*Techn, Mus*) (NEW) **Schlägel**

schleichen† *vi* (*sein*) creep; (*langsam gehen/fahren*) crawl □ *vr* **sich s~** creep. **s~d** *a* creeping; ⟨*Krankheit*⟩ insidious

Schleier *m* -**s,**- veil; (*fig*) haze. **s~haft** *a* **es ist mir s~haft** (*fam*) it's a mystery to me

Schleife *f* -,-**n** bow; (*Fliege*) bow-tie; (*Biegung*) loop

schleifen[1] *v* (*reg*) □ *vt* drag; (*zerstören*) raze to the ground □ *vi* (*haben*) trail, drag

schleifen†[2] *vt* grind; (*schärfen*) sharpen; cut ⟨*Edelstein, Glas*⟩; (*drillen*) drill

Schleim *m* -**[e]s** slime; (*Anat*) mucus; (*Med*) phlegm. **s~ig** *a* slimy

schlemm|en *vi* (*haben*) feast □ *vt* feast on. **S~er** *m* -**s,**- gourmet

schlendern *vi* (*sein*) stroll

schlenkern *vt/i* (*haben*) swing; **s~ mit** swing; dangle ⟨*Beine*⟩

Schlepp|dampfer *m* tug. **S~e** *f* -,-**n** train. **s~en** *vt* drag; (*tragen*) carry; (*ziehen*) tow; **sich s~en** drag oneself; (*sich hinziehen*) drag on; **sich s~en mit** carry. **s~end** *a* slow, *adv* -ly. **S~er** *m* -**s,**- tug; (*Traktor*) tractor. **S~kahn** *m* barge. **S~lift** *m* T-bar lift. **S~tau** *nt* tow-rope; **ins S~tau nehmen** take in tow

Schleuder *f* -,-**n** catapult; (*Wäsche-*) spin-drier. **s~n** *vt* hurl; spin ⟨*Wäsche*⟩; extract ⟨*Honig*⟩ □ *vi* (*sein*) skid; **ins S~n geraten** skid. **S~preise** *mpl* knock-down prices. **S~sitz** *m* ejector seat

schleunigst *adv* hurriedly; (*sofort*) at once

Schleuse *f* -,-**n** lock; (*Sperre*) sluice[-gate]. **s~n** *vt* steer

Schliche *pl* tricks; **jdm auf die S~kommen** (*fam*) get on to s.o.

schlicht *a* plain, *adv* -ly; (*einfach*) simple, *adv* -ply

schlicht|en *vt* settle □ *vi* (*haben*) arbitrate. **S~ung** *f* - settlement; (*Jur*) arbitration

Schlick *m* -**[e]s** silt

Schließe *f* -,-**n** clasp; (*Schnalle*) buckle

schließen† *vt* close (*ab-*) lock; fasten ⟨*Kleid, Verschluss*⟩; (*stilllegen*) close down; (*beenden, folgern*) conclude; enter into ⟨*Vertrag*⟩; **sich s~** close; **in die Arme s~** embrace; **etw s~ an** (+ *acc*) connect sth to; **sich s~ an** (+ *acc*) follow □ *vi* (*haben*) close, (*den Betrieb einstellen*) close down; (*den Schlüssel drehen*) turn the key; (*enden, folgern*) conclude; **s~ lassen auf** (+ *acc*) suggest

Schließ|fach *nt* locker. **s~lich** *adv* finally, in the end; (*immerhin*) after all. **S~ung** *f* -,-en closure

Schliff *m* **-[e]s** cut; (*Schleifen*) cutting; (*fig*) polish; **der letzte S~** the finishing touches *pl*

schlimm *a* bad, *adv* -ly; **s~er werden** get worse; **nicht so s~!** it doesn't matter! **s~stenfalls** *adv* if the worst comes to the worst

Schlinge *f* **-,-n** loop; (*Henkers-*) noose; (*Med*) sling; (*Falle*) snare

Schlingel *m* **-s,-** (*fam*) rascal

schling|en† *vt* wind, wrap; tie ⟨*Knoten*⟩; **sich s~en um** coil around □ *vi* (*haben*) bolt one's food. **S~pflanze** *f* climber

Schlips *m* **-es,-e** tie

Schlitten *m* **-s,-** sledge; (*Rodel-*) toboggan; (*Pferde-*) sleigh; **S~ fahren** toboggan

schlittern *vi* (*haben/ sein*) slide

Schlittschuh *m* skate; **S~ laufen** skate. **S~läufer(in)** *m(f)* **-s,-** (*f* **-,-nen**) skater

Schlitz *m* **-es,-e** slit; (*für Münze*) slot; (*Jacken-*) vent; (*Hosen-*) flies *pl.* **s~en** *vt* slit

Schloss *nt* **-es,¨-er** (**Schloß** *nt* **-sses,¨sser**) lock; (*Vorhänge-*) padlock; (*Verschluss*) clasp; (*Gebäude*) castle; (*Palast*) palace

Schlosser *m* **-s,-** locksmith; (*Auto-*) mechanic; (*Maschinen-*) fitter

Schlot *m* **-[e]s,-e** chimney

schlottern *vi* (*haben*) shake, tremble; ⟨*Kleider:*⟩ hang loose

Schlucht *f* **-,-en** ravine, gorge

schluchz|en *vi* (*haben*) sob. **S~er** *m* **-s,-** sob

Schluck *m* **-[e]s,-e** mouthful; (*klein*) sip

Schluckauf *m* **-s** hiccups *pl*

schlucken *vt/i* (*haben*) swallow. **S~** *m* **-s** hiccups *pl*

schlud|ern *vi* (*haben*) be sloppy (**bei** in). **s~rig** *a* sloppy, *adv* -ily; ⟨*Arbeit*⟩ slipshod

Schlummer *m* **-s** slumber. **s~n** *vi* (*haben*) slumber

Schlund *m* **-[e]s** [back of the] throat; (*fig*) mouth

schlüpf|en *vi* (*sein*) slip; [**aus dem Ei**] **s~en** hatch. **S~er** *m* **-s,-** knickers *pl.* **s~rig** *a* slippery; (*anstößig*) smutty

schlurfen *vi* (*sein*) shuffle

schlürfen *vt/i* (*haben*) slurp

Schluss *m* **-es,¨-e** (**Schluß** *m* **-sses, ¨sse**) end; (*S~folgerung*) conclusion; **zum S~** finally; **S~ machen** stop (**mit etw** sth); finish (**mit jdm** with s.o.)

Schlüssel *m* **-s,-** key; (*Schrauben-*) spanner; (*Geheim-*) code; (*Mus*) clef. **S~bein** *nt* collar-bone. **S~bund** *m & nt* bunch of keys. **S~loch** *nt* keyhole. **S~ring** *m* key-ring

Schlussfolgerung (**Schlußfolgerung**) *f* conclusion

schlüssig *a* conclusive, *adv* -ly; **sich** (*dat*) **s~ werden** make up one's mind

Schluss|licht (**Schluß|licht**) *nt* rear-light. **S~verkauf** *m* [end of season] sale

Schmach *f* - disgrace

schmachten *vi* (*haben*) languish

schmächtig *a* slight

schmackhaft *a* tasty

schmal *a* narrow; (*dünn*) thin; (*schlank*) slender; (*karg*) meagre

schmälern *vt* diminish; (*herabsetzen*) belittle

Schmalz[1] *nt* **-es** lard; (*Ohren-*) wax

Schmalz[2] *m* **-es** (*fam*) schmaltz. **s~ig** *a* (*fam*) schmaltzy, slushy

schmarotz|en *vi* (*haben*) be parasitic (**auf** + *acc* on); ⟨*Person:*⟩ sponge (**bei** on). **S~er** *m* **-s,-** parasite; (*Person*) sponger

Schmarren *m* **-s,-** (*Aust*) pancake [torn into strips]; (*fam: Unsinn*) rubbish
schmatzen *vi* (*haben*) eat noisily
schmausen *vi* (*haben*) feast
schmecken *vi* (*haben*) taste (**nach** of); **[gut] s~** taste good; **hat es dir geschmeckt?** did you enjoy it? □ *vt* taste
Schmeichelei *f* **-,-en** flattery; (*Kompliment*) compliment
schmeichel|haft *a* complimentary, flattering. **s~n** *vi* (*haben*) (+ *dat*) flatter
schmeißen† *vt/i* (*haben*) **s~ [mit]** (*fam*) chuck
Schmeißfliege *f* bluebottle
schmelz|en† *vt/i* (*sein*) melt; smelt ⟨*Erze*⟩. **S~wasser** *nt* melted snow and ice
Schmerbauch *m* (*fam*) paunch
Schmerz *m* **-es,-en** pain; (*Kummer*) grief; **S~en haben** be in pain. **s~en** *vt* hurt; (*fig*) grieve □ *vi* (*haben*) hurt, be painful. **S~ensgeld** *nt* compensation for pain and suffering. **s~haft** *a* painful. **s~lich** *a* (*fig*) painful; (*traurig*) sad, *adv* -ly. **s~los** *a* painless, *adv* -ly. **s~stillend** *a* pain-killing; **s~stillendes Mittel** analgesic, pain-killer. **S~tablette** *f* pain-killer
Schmetterball *m* (*Tennis*) smash
Schmetterling *m* **-s,-e** butterfly
schmettern *vt* hurl; (*Tennis*) smash; (*singen*) sing; (*spielen*) blare out □ *vi* (*haben*) sound; ⟨*Trompeten:*⟩ blare
Schmied *m* **-[e]s,-e** blacksmith
Schmiede *f* **-,-n** forge. **S~eisen** *nt* wrought iron. **s~n** *vt* forge; (*fig*) hatch; **Pläne s~n** make plans
schmieg|en *vt* press; **sich s~en an** (+ *acc*) nestle *or* snuggle up to; ⟨*Kleid:*⟩ cling to. **s~sam** *a* supple
Schmier|e *f* **-,-n** grease; (*Schmutz*) mess. **s~en** *vt* lubricate; (*streichen*) spread; (*schlecht schreiben*) scrawl; (*sl: bestechen*) bribe □ *vi* (*haben*) smudge; (*schreiben*) scrawl. **S~fett** *nt* grease. **S~geld** *nt* (*fam*) bribe. **s~ig** *a* greasy; (*schmutzig*) grubby; (*anstößig*) smutty; ⟨*Person*⟩ slimy. **S~mittel** *nt* lubricant
Schminke *f* **-,-n** make-up. **s~n** *vt* make up; **sich s~n** put on make-up; **sich** (*dat*) **die Lippen s~n** put on lipstick
schmirgel|n *vt* sand down. **S~papier** *nt* emery-paper
schmökern *vt/i* (*haben*) (*fam*) read
schmollen *vi* (*haben*) sulk; (*s~d den Mund verziehen*) pout
schmor|en *vt/i* (*haben*) braise; (*fam: schwitzen*) roast. **S~topf** *m* casserole
Schmuck *m* **-[e]s** jewellery; (*Verzierung*) ornament, decoration
schmücken *vt* decorate, adorn; **sich s~** adorn oneself
schmuck|los *a* plain. **S~stück** *nt* piece of jewellery; (*fig*) jewel
schmuddelig *a* grubby
Schmuggel *m* **-s** smuggling. **s~n** *vt* smuggle. **S~ware** *f* contraband
Schmuggler *m* **-s,-** smuggler
schmunzeln *vi* (*haben*) smile
schmusen *vi* (*haben*) cuddle
Schmutz *m* **-es** dirt; **in den S~ziehen** (*fig*) denigrate. **s~en** *vi* (*haben*) get dirty. **S~fleck** *m* dirty mark. **s~ig** *a* dirty
Schnabel *m* **-s,⸗** beak, bill; (*eines Kruges*) lip; (*Tülle*) spout
Schnake *f* **-,-n** mosquito; (*Kohl-*) daddy-long-legs
Schnalle *f* **-,-n** buckle. **s~n** *vt* strap; (*zu-*) buckle; **den Gürtel enger s~n** tighten one's belt
schnalzen *vi* (*haben*) **mit der Zunge/den Fingern s~** click one's tongue/snap one's fingers
schnapp|en *vi* (*haben*) **s~en nach** snap at; gasp for ⟨*Luft*⟩ □ *vt* snatch, grab; (*fam: festnehmen*) nab. **S~schloss (S~schloß)** *nt*

spring lock. **S~schuss** (**S~schuß**) *m* snapshot

Schnaps *m* **-es,¨e** schnapps

schnarchen *vi* (*haben*) snore

schnarren *vi* (*haben*) rattle; ⟨*Klingel:*⟩ buzz

schnattern *vi* (*haben*) cackle

schnauben *vi* (*haben*) snort □ *vt* **sich** (*dat*) **die Nase s~** blow one's nose

schnaufen *vi* (*haben*) puff, pant

Schnauze *f* **-,-n** muzzle; (*eines Kruges*) lip; (*Tülle*) spout

schnäuzen (sich) *vr* blow one's nose

Schnecke *f* **-,-n** snail; (*Nackt-*) slug; (*Spirale*) scroll; (*Gebäck*) ≈ Chelsea bun. **S~nhaus** *nt* snail-shell

Schnee *m* **-s** snow; (*Eier-*) beaten egg-white. **S~ball** *m* snowball. **S~besen** *m* whisk. **S~brille** *f* snow-goggles *pl*. **S~fall** *m* snowfall. **S~flocke** *f* snowflake. **S~glöckchen** *nt* **-s,-** snowdrop. **S~kette** *f* snow chain. **S~mann** *m* (*pl* **-männer**) snowman. **S~pflug** *m* snowplough. **S~schläger** *m* whisk. **S~sturm** *m* snowstorm, blizzard. **S~wehe** *f* **-,-n** snowdrift

Schneid *m* **-[e]s** (*SGer*) courage

Schneide *f* **-,-n** [cutting] edge; (*Klinge*) blade

schneiden† *vt* cut; (*in Scheiben*) slice; (*kreuzen*) cross; (*nicht beachten*) cut dead; **Gesichter s~** pull faces; **sich s~** cut oneself; (*über-*) intersect; **sich** (*dat/acc*) **in den Finger s~** cut one's finger. **s~d** *a* cutting; (*kalt*) biting

Schneider *m* **-s,-** tailor. **S~in** *f* **-,-nen** dressmaker. **s~n** *vt* make ⟨*Anzug, Kostüm*⟩

Schneidezahn *m* incisor

schneidig *a* dashing, *adv* -ly

schneien *vi* (*haben*) snow; **es schneit** it is snowing

Schneise *f* **-,-n** path; (*Feuer-*) firebreak

schnell *a* quick; ⟨*Auto, Tempo*⟩ fast □ *adv* quickly; (*in s~em Tempo*) fast; (*bald*) soon; **mach s~!** hurry up! **s~en** *vi* (*sein*) **in die Höhe s~en** shoot up. **S~igkeit** *f* **-** rapidity; (*Tempo*) speed. **S~imbiss** (**S~imbiß**) *m* snack-bar. **S~kochtopf** *m* pressure-cooker. **S~reinigung** *f* express cleaners. **s~stens** *adv* as quickly as possible. **S~zug** *m* express [train]

schnetzeln *vt* cut into thin strips

schneuzen (sich) *vr* (NEW) **schnäuzen (sich)**

schnippen *vt* flick

schnippisch *a* pert, *adv* -ly

Schnipsel *m & nt* **-s,-** scrap

Schnitt *m* **-[e]s,-e** cut; (*Film-*) cutting; (*S~muster*) [paper] pattern; **im S~** (*durchschnittlich*) on average

Schnitte *f* **-,-n** slice [of bread]; (*belegt*) open sandwich

schnittig *a* stylish; (*stromlinienförmig*) streamlined

Schnitt|käse *m* hard cheese. **S~lauch** *m* chives *pl*. **S~muster** *nt* [paper] pattern. **S~punkt** *m* [point of] intersection. **S~wunde** *f* cut

Schnitzel *nt* **-s,-** scrap; (*Culin*) escalope. **s~n** *vt* shred

schnitz|en *vt/i* (*haben*) carve. **S~er** *m* **-s,-** carver; (*fam: Fehler*) blunder. **S~erei** *f* **-,-en** carving

schnodderig *a* (*fam*) brash

schnöde *a* despicable, *adv* -bly; (*verächtlich*) contemptuous, *adv* -ly

Schnorchel *m* **-s,-** snorkel

Schnörkel *m* **-s,-** flourish; (*Kunst*) scroll. **s~ig** *a* ornate

schnorren *vt/i* (*haben*) (*fam*) scrounge

schnüffeln *vi* (*haben*) sniff (**an etw** *dat* sth); (*fam: spionieren*) snoop [around]

Schnuller *m* **-s,-** [baby's] dummy, (*Amer*) pacifier

schnupf|en *vt* sniff; **Tabak s~en** take snuff. **S~en** *m* **-s,-** [head] cold. **S~tabak** *m* snuff

schnuppern *vt/i* (*haben*) sniff (**an etw** *dat* sth)

Schnur *f* **-,¨e** string; (*Kordel*) cord; (*Besatz-*) braid; (*Electr*) flex; **eine S~** a piece of string

Schnür|chen *nt* **-s,- wie am S~chen** (*fam*) like clockwork. **s~en** *vt* tie; lace [up] ⟨*Schuhe*⟩

schnurgerade *a & adv* dead straight

Schnurr|bart *m* moustache. **s~en** *vi* (*haben*) hum; ⟨*Katze:*⟩ purr

Schnür|schuh *m* lace-up shoe. **S~senkel** *m* [shoe-]lace

schnurstracks *adv* straight

Schock *m* **-[e]s,-s** shock. **s~en** *vt* (*fam*) shock; **geschockt sein** be shocked. **s~ieren** *vt* shock; **s~ierend** shocking

Schöffe *m* **-n,-n** lay judge

Schokolade *f* **-** chocolate

Scholle *f* **-,-n** clod [of earth]; (*Eis-*) [ice-]floe; (*Fisch*) plaice

schon *adv* already; (*allein*) just; (*sogar*) even; (*ohnehin*) anyway; **s~ einmal** before; (*jemals*) ever; **s~ immer/oft/wieder** always/often/again; **hast du ihn s~ gesehen?** have you seen him yet? **s~ der Gedanke daran** the mere thought of it; **s~ deshalb** for that reason alone; **das ist s~ möglich** that's quite possible; **ja s~, aber** well yes, but; **nun geh/komm s~!** go/come on then!

schön *a* beautiful; ⟨*Wetter*⟩ fine; (*angenehm, nett*) nice; (*gut*) good; (*fam: beträchtlich*) pretty; **s~en Dank!** thank you very much! **na s~** all right then □ *adv* beautifully; nicely; (*gut*) well; **s~ langsam** nice and slowly

schonen *vt* spare; (*gut behandeln*) look after; **sich s~** take things easy. **s~d** *a* gentle, *adv* -tly

Schönheit *f* **-,-en** beauty. **S~sfehler** *m* blemish. **S~skonkurrenz** *f*, **S~swettbewerb** *m* beauty contest

schönmachen *vt sep* smarten up; **sich s~** make oneself look nice

Schonung *f* **-,-en** gentle care; (*nach Krankheit*) rest; (*Baum-*) plantation. **s~slos** *a* ruthless, *adv* -ly

Schonzeit *f* close season

schöpf|en *vt* scoop [up]; ladle ⟨*Suppe*⟩; **Mut s~en** take heart; **frische Luft s~en** get some fresh air. **S~er** *m* **-s,-** creator; (*Kelle*) ladle. **s~erisch** *a* creative. **S~kelle** *f*. **S~löffel** *m* ladle. **S~ung** *f* **-,-en** creation

Schoppen *m* **-s,-** (*SGer*) ≈ pint

Schorf *m* **-[e]s** scab

Schornstein *m* chimney. **S~feger** *m* **-s,-** chimney-sweep

Schoß *m* **-es,¨e** lap; (*Frack-*) tail

Schössling (Schößling) *m* **-s,-e** (*Bot*) shoot

Schote *f* **-,-n** pod; (*Erbse*) pea

Schotte *m* **-n,-n** Scot, Scotsman

Schotter *m* **-s** gravel; (*für Gleise*) ballast

schott|isch *a* Scottish, Scots. **S~land** *nt* **-s** Scotland

schraffieren *vt* hatch

schräg *a* diagonal, *adv* -ly; (*geneigt*) sloping; **s~ halten** tilt. **S~e** *f* **-,-n** slope. **S~strich** *m* oblique stroke

Schramme *f* **-,-n** scratch. **s~n** *vt* scrape, scratch

Schrank *m* **-[e]s,¨e** cupboard; (*Kleider-*) wardrobe; (*Akten-, Glas-*) cabinet

Schranke *f* **-,-n** barrier

Schraube *f* **-,-n** screw; (*Schiffs-*) propeller. **s~n** *vt* screw; (*ab-*) unscrew; (*drehen*) turn; **sich in die Höhe s~n** spiral upwards. **S~nmutter** *f* nut. **S~nschlüssel** *m* spanner. **S~nzieher** *m* **-s,-** screwdriver

Schraubstock *m* vice

Schrebergarten *m* ≈ allotment
Schreck *m* **-[e]s,-e** fright; **jdm einen S~ einjagen** give s.o. a fright. **S~en** *m* **-s,-** fright; (*Entsetzen*) horror. **s~en** *vt* (*reg*) frighten; (*auf-*) startle □ *vi*† (*sein*) **in die Höhe s~en** start up
Schreck|gespenst *nt* spectre. **s~haft** *a* easily frightened; (*nervös*) jumpy. **s~lich** *a* terrible, *adv* -bly. **S~schuss (S~schuß)** *m* warning shot
Schrei *m* **-[e]s,-e** cry, shout; (*gellend*) scream; **der letzte S~** (*fam*) the latest thing
Schreib|block *m* writing-pad. **s~en**† *vt/i* (*haben*) write; (*auf der Maschine*) type; **richtig/falsch s~en** spell right/wrong; **sich s~en** ⟨*Wort:*⟩ be spelt; (*korrespondieren*) correspond; **krank s~en** (NEW) **krankschreiben**. **S~en** *nt* **-s,-** writing; (*Brief*) letter. **S~fehler** *m* spelling mistake. **S~heft** *nt* exercise book. **S~kraft** *f* clerical assistant; (*für Maschineschreiben*) typist. **S~maschine** *f* typewriter. **S~papier** *nt* writing-paper. **S~schrift** *f* script. **S~tisch** *m* desk. **S~ung** *f* **-,-en** spelling. **S~waren** *fpl* stationery *sg*. **S~weise** *f* spelling
schreien† *vt/i* (*haben*) cry; (*gellend*) scream; (*rufen, laut sprechen*) shout; **zum S~ sein** (*fam*) be a scream. **s~d** *a* (*fig*) glaring; (*grell*) garish
Schreiner *m* **-s,-** joiner
schreiten† *vi* (*sein*) walk
Schrift *f* **-,-en** writing; (*Druck-*) type; (*Abhandlung*) paper; **die Heilige S~** the Scriptures *pl*. **S~führer** *m* secretary. **s~lich** *a* written □ *adv* in writing. **S~sprache** *f* written language. **S~steller(in)** *m* **-s,-** (*f* **-,-nen**) writer. **S~stück** *nt* document. **S~zeichen** *nt* character
schrill *a* shrill, *adv* -y
Schritt *m* **-[e]s,-e** step; (*Entfernung*) pace; (*Gangart*) walk; (*der Hose*) crotch; **im S~** in step; (*langsam*) at walking pace; **S~ halten mit** (*fig*) keep pace with. **S~macher** *m* **-s,-** pace-maker. **s~weise** *adv* step by step
schroff *a* precipitous, *adv* -ly; (*abweisend*) brusque, *adv* -ly; (*unvermittelt*) abrupt, *adv* -ly; ⟨*Gegensatz*⟩ stark
schröpfen *vt* (*fam*) fleece
Schrot *m & nt* **-[e]s** coarse meal; (*Blei-*) small shot. **s~en** *vt* grind coarsely. **S~flinte** *f* shotgun
Schrott *m* **-[e]s** scrap[-metal]; **zu S~ fahren** (*fam*) write off. **S~platz** *m* scrap-yard. **s~reif** *a* ready for the scrap-heap
schrubb|en *vt/i* (*haben*) scrub. **S~er** *m* **-s,-** [long-handled] scrubbing-brush
Schrull|e *f* **-,-n** whim; **alte S~e** (*fam*) old crone. **s~ig** *a* cranky
schrumpfen *vi* (*sein*) shrink; ⟨*Obst:*⟩ shrivel
schrump[e]lig *a* wrinkled
Schrunde *f* **-,-n** crack; (*Spalte*) crevasse
Schub *m* **-[e]s,¨-e** (*Phys*) thrust; (*S~fach*) drawer; (*Menge*) batch. **S~fach** *nt* drawer. **S~karre** *f*, **S~karren** *m* wheelbarrow. **S~lade** *f* drawer
Schubs *m* **-es,-e** push, shove **s~en** *vt* push, shove
schüchtern *a* shy, *adv* -ly; (*zaghaft*) tentative, *adv* -ly. **S~heit** *f* - shyness
Schuft *m* **-[e]s,-e** (*pej*) swine. **s~en** *vi* (*haben*) (*fam*) slave away
Schuh *m* **-[e]s,-e** shoe. **S~anzieher** *m* **-s,-** shoehorn. **S~band** *nt* (*pl* **-bänder**) shoe-lace. **S~creme** *f* shoe-polish. **S~löffel** *m* shoehorn. **S~macher** *m* **-s,-** shoemaker; (*zum Flicken*) [shoe] mender. **S~werk** *nt* shoes *pl*

Schul|abgänger *m* **-s,-** school-leaver. **S~arbeiten, S~aufgaben** *fpl* homework *sg*. **S~buch** *nt* school-book

Schuld *f* **-,-en** guilt; (*Verantwortung*) blame; (*Geld-*) debt; **S~en machen** get into debt; **S~ haben** be to blame (**an** + *dat* for); **jdm S~ geben** blame s.o.; **sich** (*dat*) **etwas zu S~en kommen lassen** = **sich etwas zuschulden kommen lassen**, *s.* **zuschulden** □ **s~ sein** be to blame (**an** + *dat* for); **s~ haben/jdm s~ geben** (NEW) **S~ haben/jdm S~ geben**, *s.* **Schuld**. **s~en** *vt* owe

schuldig *a* guilty (*gen* of); (*gebührend*) due; **jdm etw s~ sein** owe s.o. sth. **S~keit** *f* - duty

schuld|los *a* innocent. **S~ner** *m* **-s,-** debtor. **S~spruch** *m* guilty verdict

Schule *f* **-,-n** school; **in der/die S~** at/to school. **s~n** *vt* train

Schüler|(in) *m* **-s,-** (*f* **-,-nen**) pupil. **S~lotse** *m* pupil acting as crossing warden

schul|frei *a* **s~freier Tag** day without school; **wir haben morgen s~frei** there's no school tomorrow. **S~hof** *m* [school] playground. **S~jahr** *nt* school year; (*Klasse*) form. **S~junge** *m* schoolboy. **S~kind** *nt* schoolchild. **S~leiter(in)** *m(f)* head [teacher]. **S~mädchen** *nt* schoolgirl. **S~stunde** *f* lesson

Schulter *f* **-,-n** shoulder. **S~blatt** *nt* shoulder-blade. **s~n** *vt* shoulder. **S~tuch** *nt* shawl

Schulung *f* - training

schummeln *vi* (*haben*) (*fam*) cheat

Schund *m* **-[e]s** trash. **S~roman** *m* trashy novel

Schuppe *f* **-,-n** scale; **S~n** *pl* dandruff *sg*. **s~n (sich)** *vr* flake [off]

Schuppen *m* **-s,-** shed

Schur *f* - shearing

Schür|eisen *nt* poker. **s~en** *vt* poke; (*fig*) stir up

schürf|en *vt* mine; **sich** (*dat*) **das Knie s~en** graze one's knee □ *vi* (*haben*) **s~en nach** prospect for. **S~wunde** *f* abrasion, graze

Schürhaken *m* poker

Schurke *m* **-n,-n** villain

Schürze *f* **-,-n** apron. **s~n** *vt* (*raffen*) gather [up]; tie ⟨*Knoten*⟩; purse ⟨*Lippen*⟩. **S~njäger** *m* (*fam*) womanizer

Schuss *m* **-es,¨-e** (**Schuß** *m* **-sses, ¨-sse**) shot; (*kleine Menge*) dash

Schüssel *f* **-,-n** bowl; (*TV*) dish

schusselig *a* (*fam*) scatter-brained

Schuss|fahrt (**Schußfahrt**) *f* (*Ski*) schuss. **S~waffe** *f* firearm

Schuster *m* **-s,-** = **Schuhmacher**

Schutt *m* **-[e]s** rubble. **S~abladeplatz** *m* rubbish dump

Schüttel|frost *m* shivering fit. **s~n** *vt* shake; **sich s~n** shake oneself/itself; (*vor Ekel*) shudder; **jdm die Hand s~n** shake s.o.'s hand

schütten *vt* pour; (*kippen*) tip; (*ver-*) spill □ *vi* (*haben*) **es schüttet** it is pouring [with rain]

Schutthaufen *m* pile of rubble

Schutz *m* **-es** protection; (*Zuflucht*) shelter; (*Techn*) guard; **S~ suchen** take refuge; **unter dem S~ der Dunkelheit** under cover of darkness. **S~anzug** *m* protective suit. **S~blech** *nt* mudguard. **S~brille** goggles *pl*

Schütze *m* **-n,-n** marksman; (*Tor-*) scorer; (*Astr*) Sagittarius; **guter S~** good shot

schützen *vt* protect/(*Zuflucht gewähren*) shelter (**vor** + *dat* from) □ *vi* (*haben*) give protection/shelter (**vor** + *dat* from). **s~d** *a* protective, *adv* -ly

Schützenfest *nt* fair with shooting competition

Schutz|engel *m* guardian angel. **S~heilige(r)** *m/f* patron saint

Schützling *m* **-s,-e** charge; (*Protegé*) protégé

schutz|los *a* defenceless, helpless. **S~mann** *m* (*pl* **-männer** & **-leute**) policeman. **S~umschlag** *m* dust-jacket

Schwaben *nt* **-s** Swabia

schwäbisch *a* Swabian

schwach *a* (**schwächer, schwächst**) weak, *adv* -ly; (*nicht gut; gering*) poor, *adv* -ly; (*leicht*) faint, *adv* -ly

Schwäche *f* **-,-n** weakness. **s~n** *vt* weaken

Schwach|heit *f* **-** weakness. **S~kopf** *m* (*fam*) idiot

schwäch|lich *a* delicate. **S~ling** *m* **-s,-e** weakling

Schwachsinn *m* mental deficiency. **s~ig** *a* mentally deficient; (*fam*) idiotic

Schwächung *f* **-** weakening

schwafeln (*fam*) *vi* (*haben*) waffle □ *vt* talk

Schwager *m* **-s,⁻** brother-in-law

Schwägerin *f* **-,-nen** sister-in-law

Schwalbe *f* **-,-n** swallow

Schwall *m* **-[e]s** torrent

Schwamm *m* **-[e]s,⁻e** sponge; (*SGer: Pilz*) fungus; (*essbar*) mushroom. **s~ig** *a* spongy; (*aufgedunsen*) bloated

Schwan *m* **-[e]s,⁻e** swan

schwanen *vi* (*haben*) (*fam*) **mir schwante, dass** I had a nasty feeling that

schwanger *a* pregnant

schwängern *vt* make pregnant

Schwangerschaft *f* **-,-en** pregnancy

Schwank *m* **-[e]s,⁻e** (*Theat*) farce

schwank|en *vi* (*haben*) sway; ⟨*Boot:*⟩ rock; (*sich ändern*) fluctuate; (*unentschieden sein*) be undecided □ (*sein*) stagger. **S~ung** *f* **-,-en** fluctuation

Schwanz *m* **-es,⁻e** tail

schwänzen *vt* (*fam*) skip; **die Schule s~** play truant

Schwarm *m* **-[e]s,⁻e** swarm; (*Fisch-*) shoal; (*fam: Liebe*) idol

schwärmen *vi* (*haben*) swarm; **s~ für** (*fam*) adore; (*verliebt sein*) have a crush on; **s~ von** (*fam*) rave about

Schwarte *f* **-,-n** (*Speck-*) rind; (*fam: Buch*) tome

schwarz *a* (**schwärzer, schwärzest**) black; (*fam: illegal*) illegal, *adv* -ly; **s~er Markt** black market; **s~ gekleidet** dressed in black; **s~ auf weiß** in black and white; **s~ sehen** (*fig*) be pessimistic; **ins S~e treffen** score a bull's-eye. **S~** *nt* **-[e]s,-** black. **S~arbeit** *f* moonlighting. **s~arbeiten** *vi sep* (*haben*) moonlight. **S~brot** *nt* black bread. **S~e(r)** *m/f* black

Schwärze *f* **-** blackness. **s~n** *vt* blacken

Schwarz|fahrer *m* fare-dodger. **S~handel** *m* black market (**mit** in). **S~händler** *m* black marketeer. **S~markt** *m* black market. **s~sehen**† *vi sep* (*haben*) watch television without a licence; (*fig*) (NEW) **s~ sehen**, *s.* **schwarz**. **S~wald** *m* Black Forest. **s~weiß** *a* black and white

Schwatz *m* **-es** (*fam*) chat

schwatzen, (*SGer*) **schwätzen** *vi* (*haben*) chat; (*klatschen*) gossip; (*Sch*) talk [in class] □ *vt* talk

schwatzhaft *a* garrulous

Schwebe *f* **- in der S~** (*fig*) undecided. **S~bahn** *f* cable railway. **s~n** *vi* (*haben*) float; (*fig*) be undecided; ⟨*Verfahren:*⟩ be pending; **in Gefahr s~n** be in danger □ (*sein*) float

Schwed|e *m* **-n,-n** Swede. **S~en** *nt* **-s** Sweden. **S~in** *f* **-,-nen** Swede. **s~isch** *a* Swedish

Schwefel *m* **-s** sulphur. **S~säure** *f* sulphuric acid

schweigen† *vi* (*haben*) be silent; **ganz zu s~ von** to say nothing of, let alone. **S~** *nt* **-s** silence; **zum S~ bringen** silence. **s~d** *a* silent, *adv* -ly

schweigsam *a* silent; (*wortkarg*) taciturn
Schwein *nt* **-[e]s,-e** pig; (*Culin*) pork; (*sl*) (*schmutziger Mensch*) dirty pig; (*Schuft*) swine; **S~haben** (*fam*) be lucky. **S~ebraten** *m* roast pork. **S~efleisch** *nt* pork. **S~ehund** *m* (*sl*) swine. **S~erei** *f* **-,-en** (*sl*) [dirty] mess; (*Gemeinheit*) dirty trick. **S~estall** *m* pigsty. **s~isch** *a* lewd. **S~sleder** *nt* pigskin
Schweiß *m* **-es** sweat
schweiß|en *vt* weld. **S~er** *m* **-s,-** welder
Schweiz (die) - Switzerland. **S~er** *a* & *m* **-s,-**, **S~erin** *f* **-,-nen** Swiss. **s~erisch** *a* Swiss
schwelen *vi* (*haben*) smoulder
schwelgen *vi* (*haben*) feast; **s~ in** (+ *dat*) wallow in
Schwelle *f* **-,-n** threshold; (*Eisenbahn-*) sleeper
schwell|en† *vi* (*sein*) swell. **S~ung** *f* **-,-en** swelling
Schwemme *f* **-,-n** watering-place; (*fig: Überangebot*) glut. **s~n** *vt* wash; **an Land s~n** wash up
Schwenk *m* **-[e]s** swing. **s~en** *vt* swing; (*schwingen*) wave; (*spülen*) rinse; **in Butter s~en** toss in butter □ *vi* (*sein*) turn
schwer *a* heavy; (*schwierig*) difficult; (*mühsam, streng*) hard; (*ernst*) serious; (*schlimm*) bad; **3 Pfund s~ sein** weigh 3 pounds □ *adv* heavily; with difficulty; (*mühsam, streng*) hard; (*schlimm, sehr*) badly, seriously; **s~ krank/verletzt** seriously ill/injured; **s~ arbeiten** work hard; **s~ hören** be hard of hearing; **etw s~ nehmen** take sth seriously; **jdm s~ fallen** be hard for s.o.; **es jdm s~ machen** make it *or* things difficult for s.o.; **sich s~ tun** have difficulty (**mit** with); **s~ zu sagen** difficult *or* hard to say
Schwere *f* - heaviness; (*Gewicht*) weight; (*Schwierigkeit*) difficulty; (*Ernst*) gravity. **S~losigkeit** *f* - weightlessness
schwer|fallen† *vi sep* (*sein*) (NEW) **s~ fallen**, *s.* **schwer**. **s~fällig** *a* ponderous, *adv* -ly; (*unbeholfen*) clumsy, *adv* -ily. **S~gewicht** *nt* heavyweight. **s~hörig** *a* **s~hörig sein** be hard of hearing. **S~kraft** *f* (*Phys*) gravity. **s~krank** *a* (NEW) **s~ krank**, *s.* **schwer**. **s~lich** *adv* hardly. **s~machen** *vt sep* (NEW) **s~ machen**, *s.* **schwer**. **s~mütig** *a* melancholic. **s~nehmen†** *vt sep* (NEW) **s~ nehmen**, *s.* **schwer**. **S~punkt** *m* centre of gravity; (*fig*) emphasis
Schwert *nt* **-[e]s,-er** sword. **S~lilie** *f* iris
schwer|tun† (sich) *vr sep* (NEW) **s~ tun (sich)**, *s.* **schwer**. **S~verbrecher** *m* serious offender. **s~verdaulich** *a* (NEW) **s~ verdaulich**, *s.* **verdaulich**. **s~verletzt** *a* (NEW) **s~ verletzt**, *s.* **schwer**. **s~wiegend** *a* weighty
Schwester *f* **-,-n** sister; (*Kranken-*) nurse. **s~lich** *a* sisterly
Schwieger|eltern *pl* parents-in-law. **S~mutter** *f* mother-in-law. **S~sohn** *m* son-in-law. **S~tochter** *f* daughter-in-law. **S~vater** *m* father-in-law
Schwiele *f* **-,-n** callus
schwierig *a* difficult. **S~keit** *f* **-,-en** difficulty
Schwimm|bad *nt* swimming-baths *pl*. **S~becken** *nt* swimming-pool. **s~en†** *vt/i* (*sein/haben*) swim; (*auf dem Wasser treiben*) float. **S~er** *m* **-s,-** swimmer; (*Techn*) float. **S~weste** *f* life-jacket
Schwindel *m* **-s** dizziness, vertigo; (*fam: Betrug*) fraud; (*Lüge*) lie. **S~anfall** *m* dizzy spell. **s~frei** *a* **s~frei sein** have a good head for heights. **s~n** *vi* (*haben*) (*lügen*) lie; **mir** *od* **mich s~t** I feel dizzy

schwinden† *vi* (*sein*) dwindle; (*vergehen*) fade; (*nachlassen*) fail
Schwindl|er *m* **-s,-** liar; (*Betrüger*) fraud, con-man. **s~ig** *a* dizzy; **mir ist** *od* **wird s~ig** I feel dizzy
schwing|en† *vi* (*haben*) swing; (*Phys*) oscillate; (*vibrieren*) vibrate □ *vt* swing; wave ⟨*Fahne*⟩; (*drohend*) brandish. **S~tür** *f* swing-door. **S~ung** *f* **-,-en** oscillation; vibration
Schwips *m* **-es,-e einen S~ haben** (*fam*) be tipsy
schwirren *vi* (*haben/sein*) buzz; (*surren*) whirr
Schwitz|e *f* **-,-n** (*Culin*) roux. **s~en** *vi* (*haben*) sweat; **ich s~e** *od* **mich s~t** I am hot □ *vt* (*Culin*) sweat
schwören† *vt/i* (*haben*) swear (**auf** + *acc* by); **Rache s~** swear revenge
schwul *a* (*fam: homosexuell*) gay
schwül *a* close. **S~e** *f* - closeness
schwülstig *a* bombastic, *adv* -ally
Schwung *m* **-[e]s,⸚e** swing; (*Bogen*) sweep; (*Schnelligkeit*) momentum; (*Kraft*) vigour; (*Feuer*) verve; (*fam: Anzahl*) batch; **in S~ kommen** gather momentum; (*fig*) get going. **s~haft** *a* brisk, *adv* -ly. **s~los** *a* dull. **s~voll** *a* vigorous, *adv* -ly; ⟨*Bogen, Linie*⟩ sweeping; (*mitreißend*) spirited, lively
Schwur *m* **-[e]s,⸚e** vow; (*Eid*) oath. **S~gericht** *nt* jury [court]
sechs *inv a*, **S~** *f* **-,-en** six; (*Sch*) ≈ fail mark. **s~eckig** *a* hexagonal. **s~te(r,s)** *a* sixth
sech|zehn *inv a* sixteen. **s~zehnte(r,s)** *a* sixteenth. **s~zig** *inv a* sixty. **s~zigste(r,s)** *a* sixtieth
sedieren *vt* sedate
See[1] *m* **-s,-n** /ˈzeːən/ lake
See[2] *f* - sea; **an die/der See** to/at the seaside; **auf See** at sea. **S~bad** *nt* seaside resort. **S~fahrt** *f* [sea] voyage; (*Schifffahrt*) navigation. **S~gang** *m* **schwerer S~gang** rough sea. **S~hund** *m* seal. **s~krank** *a* seasick
Seele *f* **-,-n** soul. **s~nruhig** *a* calm, *adv* -ly
seelisch *a* psychological, *adv* -ly; (*geistig*) mental, *adv* -ly
Seelsorger *m* **-s,-** pastor
See|luft *f* sea air. **S~macht** *f* maritime power. **S~mann** *m* (*pl* **-leute**) seaman, sailor. **S~not** *f* **in S~not** in distress. **S~räuber** *m* pirate. **S~reise** *f* [sea] voyage. **S~rose** *f* water-lily. **S~sack** *m* kitbag. **S~stern** *m* starfish. **S~tang** *m* seaweed. **s~tüchtig** *a* seaworthy. **S~weg** *m* sea route; **auf dem S~weg** by sea. **S~zunge** *f* sole
Segel *nt* **-s,-** sail. **S~boot** *nt* sailing-boat. **S~fliegen** *nt* gliding. **S~flieger** *m* glider pilot. **S~flugzeug** *nt* glider. **s~n** *vt/i* (*sein/haben*) sail. **S~schiff** *nt* sailing-ship. **S~sport** *m* sailing. **S~tuch** *nt* canvas
Segen *m* **-s** blessing. **s~sreich** *a* beneficial; (*gesegnet*) blessed
Segler *m* **-s,-** yachtsman
Segment *nt* **-[e]s,-e** segment
segnen *vt* bless; **gesegnet mit** blessed with
sehen† *vt* see; watch ⟨*Fernsehsendung*⟩; **jdn/etw wieder s~** see s.o./sth again; **sich s~ lassen** show oneself □ *vi* (*haben*) see; (*blicken*) look (**auf** + *acc* at); (*ragen*) show (**aus** above); **gut/schlecht s~** have good/bad eyesight; **vom S~ kennen** know by sight; **s~ nach** keep an eye on; (*betreuen*) look after; (*suchen*) look for; **darauf s~, dass** see [to it] that. **s~swert, s~swürdig** *a* worth seeing. **S~swürdigkeit** *f* **-,-en** sight
Sehkraft *f* sight, vision
Sehne *f* **-,-n** tendon; (*eines Bogens*) string
sehnen (sich) *vr* long (**nach** for)

sehnig *a* sinewy; (*zäh*) stringy
sehn|lich[st] *a* ⟨*Wunsch*⟩ dearest □ *adv* longingly. **S~sucht** *f* - longing (**nach** for). **s~süchtig** *a* longing, *adv* -ly; ⟨*Wunsch*⟩ dearest
sehr *adv* very; (*mit Verb*) very much; **so s~, dass** so much that
seicht *a* shallow
seid *s.* **sein**[1]; **ihr s~** you are
Seide *f* -,-n silk
Seidel *nt* -s,- beer-mug
seiden *a* silk ... **S~papier** *nt* tissue paper. **S~raupe** *f* silk-worm. **s~weich** *a* silky-soft
seidig *a* silky
Seife *f* -,-n soap. **S~npulver** *nt* soap powder. **S~nschaum** *m* lather
seifig *a* soapy
seihen *vt* strain
Seil *nt* **-[e]s,-e** rope; (*Draht-*) cable. **S~bahn** *f* cable railway. **s~springen**† *vi* (*sein*) (*inf & pp only*) skip. **S~tänzer(in)** *m(f)* tightrope walker
sein†[1] *vi* (*sein*) be; **er ist Lehrer** he is a teacher; **sei still!** be quiet! **mir ist kalt/schlecht** I am cold/feel sick; **wie dem auch sei** be that as it may; **etw s~ lassen** leave sth; (*aufhören mit*) stop sth □ *v aux* have; **angekommen/gestorben s~** have arrived/died; **er war/wäre gefallen** he had/would have fallen; **es ist/war viel zu tun/nichts zu sehen** there is/was a lot to be done/nothing to be seen
sein[2] *poss pron* his; (*Ding, Tier*) its; (*nach man*) one's; **sein Glück versuchen** try one's luck. **s~e(r,s)** *poss pron* his; (*nach man*) one's own; **das S~e** *od* **seine tun** do one's share. **s~erseits** *adv* for his part. **s~erzeit** *adv* in those days. **s~etwegen** *adv* for his sake; (*wegen ihm*) because of him, on his account. **s~etwillen** *adv* **um s~etwillen** for his sake. **s~ige** *poss pron* **der/die/das s~ige** his
seinlassen† *vt sep* (NEW) **sein lassen**, *s.* **sein**[1]
seins *poss pron* his; (*nach man*) one's own
seit *conj & prep* (+ *dat*) since; **s~wann?** since when? **s~ einiger Zeit** for some time [past]; **ich wohne s~ zehn Jahren hier** I've lived here for ten years. **s~dem** *conj* since □ *adv* since then
Seite *f* -,-n side; (*Buch-*) page; **S~an S~** side by side; **zur S~ legen/treten** put/step aside; **jds starke S~** s.o.'s strong point; **auf der einen/anderen S~** (*fig*) on the one/other hand; **von S~n (s~n)** (+ *gen*) = **vonseiten**
seitens *prep* (+ *gen*) on the part of
Seiten|schiff *nt* [side] aisle. **S~sprung** *m* infidelity; **einen S~sprung machen** be unfaithful. **S~stechen** *nt* -s (*Med*) stitch. **S~straße** *f* side-street. **S~streifen** *m* verge; (*Autobahn-*) hard shoulder
seither *adv* since then
seit|lich *a* side ... □ *adv* at/on the side; **s~lich von** to one side of □ *prep* (+ *gen*) to one side of. **s~wärts** *adv* on/to one side; (*zur Seite*) sideways
Sekret *nt* **-[e]s,-e** secretion
Sekret|är *m* **-s,-e** secretary; (*Schrank*) bureau. **S~ariat** *nt* **-[e]s,-e** secretary's office. **S~ärin** *f* **-,-nen** secretary
Sekt *m* **-[e]s** [German] sparkling wine
Sekte *f* -,-n sect
Sektion /ˈtsi̯oːn/ *f* **-,-en** section; (*Sezierung*) autopsy
Sektor *m* **-s,-en** /-ˈtoːrən/ sector
Sekundant *m* **-en,-en** (*Sport*) second
sekundär *a* secondary
Sekunde *f* -,-n second
selber *pron* (*fam*) = **selbst**
selbst *pron* oneself; **ich/du/er/sie s~** I myself/you yourself/ he

himself/she herself; **wir/ihr/sie s~** we ourselves/you yourselves/they themselves; **ich schneide mein Haar s~** I cut my own hair; **von s~** of one's own accord; (*automatisch*) automatically; **s~ gemacht** home-made □ *adv* even. **S~achtung** *f* self-esteem, self-respect

selbständig *a* = **selbstständig**. **S~keit** *f* - = **Selbstständigkeit**

Selbstaufopferung *f* self-sacrifice

Selbstbedienung *f* self-service **S~srestaurant** *nt* self-service restaurant, cafeteria

Selbst|befriedigung *f* masturbation. **S~beherrschung** *f* self-control. **S~bestimmung** *f* self-determination. **s~bewusst (s~bewußt)** *a* self-confident. **S~bewusstsein (S~bewußtsein)** *nt* self-confidence. **S~bildnis** *nt* self-portrait. **S~erhaltung** *f* self-preservation. **s~gefällig** *a* self-satisfied, smug, *adv* -ly. **s~gemacht** *a* (NEW) **s~ gemacht**, *s.* **selbst**. **s~gerecht** *a* self-righteous. **S~gespräch** *nt* soliloquy; **S~gespräche führen** talk to oneself. **s~haftend** *a* self-adhesive. **s~herrlich** *a* autocratic, *adv* -ally. **S~hilfe** *f* self-help. **s~klebend** *a* self-adhesive. **S~kostenpreis** *m* cost price. **S~laut** *m* vowel. **s~los** *a* selfless, *adv* -ly. **S~mitleid** *nt* self-pity. **S~mord** *m* suicide. **S~mörder(in)** *m(f)* suicide. **s~mörderisch** *a* suicidal. **S~porträt** *nt* self-portrait. **s~sicher** *a* self-assured. **S~sicherheit** *f* self-assurance. **s~ständig** *a* independent, *adv* -ly; self-employed ⟨*Handwerker*⟩; **sich s~ständig machen** set up on one's own. **S~ständigkeit** *f* - independence. **s~süchtig** *a* selfish, *adv* -ly. **S~tanken** *nt* self-service (*for petrol*). **s~tätig** *a* automatic, *adv* -ally. **S~versorgung** *f* self-catering

selbstverständlich *a* natural, *adv* -ly; **etw für s~ halten** take sth for granted; **das ist s~** that goes without saying; **s~!** of course! **S~keit** *f* - matter of course; **das ist eine S~keit** that goes without saying

Selbst|verteidigung *f* self-defence. **S~vertrauen** *nt* self-confidence. **S~verwaltung** *f* self-government. **s~zufrieden** *a* complacent, *adv* -ly

selig *a* blissfully happy; (*Relig*) blessed; (*verstorben*) late. **S~keit** *f* - bliss

Sellerie *m* **-s,-s** & *f* **-,-** celeriac; (*Stangen-*) celery

selten *a* rare □ *adv* rarely, seldom; (*besonders*) exceptionally. **S~heit** *f* **-,-en** rarity

Selterswasser *nt* seltzer [water]

seltsam *a* odd, *adv* -ly, strange, *adv* -ly. **s~erweise** *adv* oddly/strangely enough

Semester *nt* **-s,-** (*Univ*) semester

Semikolon *nt* **-s,-s** semicolon

Seminar *nt* **-s,-e** seminar; (*Institut*) department; (*Priester-*) seminary

Semmel *f* **-,-n** [bread] roll. **S~brösel** *pl* breadcrumbs

Senat *m* **-[e]s,-e** senate. **S~or** *m* **-s,-en** /-ˈtoːrən/ senator

senden†[1] *vt* send

sende|n[2] *vt* (*reg*) broadcast; (*über Funk*) transmit, send. **S~r** *m* **-s,-** [broadcasting] station; (*Anlage*) transmitter. **S~reihe** *f* series

Sendung *f* **-,-en** consignment, shipment; (*Auftrag*) mission; (*Radio, TV*) programme

Senf *m* **-s** mustard

sengend *a* scorching

senil *a* senile. **S~ität** *f* - senility

Senior *m* **-s,-en** /-ˈoːrən/ senior; **S~en** senior citizens. **S~enheim** *nt* old people's home.

S~enteller *m* senior citizen's menu
Senke *f* -,-**n** dip, hollow
Senkel *m* -**s**,- [shoe-]lace
senken *vt* lower; bring down ⟨*Fieber, Preise*⟩; bow ⟨*Kopf*⟩; **sich s~** come down, fall; (*absinken*) subside; (*abfallen*) slope down
senkrecht *a* vertical, *adv* -ly. **S~e** *f* -**n**,-**n** perpendicular
Sensation /-'tsi̯o:n/ *f* -,-**en** sensation. **s~ell** *a* sensational, *adv* -ly
Sense *f* -,-**n** scythe
sensib|el *a* sensitive, *adv* -ly. **S~ilität** *f* - sensitivity
sentimental *a* sentimental. **S~ität** *f* - sentimentality
separat *a* separate, *adv* -ly
September *m* -**s**,- September
Serenade *f* -,-**n** serenade
Serie /'ze:ri̯ə/ *f* -,-**n** series; (*Briefmarken*) set; (*Comm*) range. **S~nnummer** *f* serial number
seriös *a* respectable, *adv* -bly; (*zuverlässig*) reliable, *adv* -bly; (*ernstgemeint*) serious
Serpentine *f* -,-**n** winding road; (*Kehre*) hairpin bend
Serum *nt* -**s**,**Sera** serum
Service¹ /zɛr'vi:s/ *nt* -[**s**],- /-'vi:s[əs], -'vi:sə/ service, set
Service² /'zø:ɐ̯vɪs/ *m* & *nt* -**s** /-vɪs[əs]/ (*Comm, Tennis*) service
servier|en *vt/i* (*haben*) serve. **S~erin** *f* -,-**nen** waitress. **S~wagen** *m* trolley
Serviette *f* -,-**n** napkin, serviette
Servus *int* (*Aust*) cheerio; (*Begrüßung*) hallo
Sessel *m* -**s**,- armchair. **S~bahn** *f*, **S~lift** *m* chair-lift
sesshaft (**seßhaft**) *a* settled; **s~ werden** settle down
Set /zɛt/ *nt* & *m* -[**s**],-**s** set; (*Deckchen*) place-mat
setz|en *vt* put; (*abstellen*) set down; (*hin-*) sit down ⟨*Kind*⟩; move ⟨*Spielstein*⟩; (*pflanzen*) plant; (*schreiben, wetten*) put; **sich s~en** sit down; (*sinken*) settle □ *vi* (*sein*) leap □ *vi* (*haben*) **s~en auf** (+ *acc*) back. **S~ling** *m* -**s**,-**e** seedling
Seuche *f* -,-**n** epidemic
seufz|en *vi* (*haben*) sigh. **S~er** *m* -**s**,- sigh
Sex /zɛks/ *m* -[**es**] sex. **s~istisch** *a* sexist
Sexu|alität *f* - sexuality. **s~ell** *a* sexual, *adv* -ly
sexy /'zɛksi/ *inv a* sexy
sezieren *vt* dissect
Shampoo /ʃam'pu:/, **Shampoon** /ʃam'po:n/ *nt* -**s** shampoo
siamesisch *a* Siamese
sich *refl pron* oneself; (*mit er/sie/es*) himself/herself/itself; (*mit sie pl*) themselves; (*mit Sie*) yourself; (*pl*) yourselves; (*einander*) each other; **s~ kennen** know oneself/(*einander*) each other; **s~ waschen** have a wash; **s~** (*dat*) **die Zähne putzen/die Haare kämmen** clean one's teeth/comb one's hair; **s~** (*dat*) **das Bein brechen** break a leg; **s~ wundern/schämen** be surprised/ashamed; **s~ gut lesen/verkaufen** read/sell well; **von s~ aus** of one's own accord
Sichel *f* -,-**n** sickle
sicher *a* safe; (*gesichert*) secure; (*gewiss*) certain; (*zuverlässig*) reliable; sure ⟨*Urteil, Geschmack*⟩; steady ⟨*Hand*⟩; (*selbstbewusst*) self-confident; **sich** (*dat*) **etw** (*gen*) **s~ sein** be sure of sth; **bist du s~?** are you sure? □ *adv* safely; securely; certainly; reliably; self-confidently; (*wahrscheinlich*) most probably; **er kommt s~** he is sure to come; **s~!** certainly! **s~gehen**† *vi sep* (*sein*) (*fig*) be sure
Sicherheit *f* - safety; (*Pol, Psych, Comm*) security; (*Gewissheit*) certainty; (*Zuverlässigkeit*) reliability; (*des Urteils, Geschmacks*) surety; (*Selbstbewusstsein*) self-confidence. **S~sgurt** *m* safety-belt; (*Auto*) seat-belt. **s~shalber**

adv to be on the safe side. **S~snadel** *f* safety-pin

sicherlich *adv* certainly; (*wahrscheinlich*) most probably

sicher|n *vt* secure; (*garantieren*) safeguard; (*schützen*) protect; put the safety-catch on ⟨*Pistole*⟩; **sich** (*dat*) **etw s~n** secure sth. **s~stellen** *vt sep* safeguard; (*beschlagnahmen*) seize. **S~ung** *f* -,-en safeguard, protection; (*Gewehr-*) safety-catch; (*Electr*) fuse

Sicht *f* - view; (*S~weite*) visibility; **in S~ kommen** come into view; **auf lange S~** in the long term. **s~bar** *a* visible, *adv* -bly. **s~en** *vt* sight; (*durchsehen*) sift through. **s~lich** *a* obvious, *adv* -ly. **S~vermerk** *m* visa. **S~weite** *f* visibility; **in/außer S~weite** within/out of sight

sickern *vi* (*sein*) seep

sie *pron* (*nom*) (*sg*) she; (*Ding, Tier*) it; (*pl*) they; (*acc*) (*sg*) her; (*Ding, Tier*) it; (*pl*) them

Sie *pron* you; **gehen/warten Sie!** go/wait!

Sieb *nt* -[e]s,-e sieve; (*Tee-*) strainer. **s~en**[1] *vt* sieve, sift

sieben[2] *inv a*, **S~** *f* -,-en seven. **S~sachen** *fpl* (*fam*) belongings. **s~te(r,s)** *a* seventh

sieb|te(r,s) *a* seventh. **s~zehn** *inv a* seventeen. **s~zehnte(r,s)** *a* seventeenth. **s~zig** *inv a* seventy. **s~zigste(r,s)** *a* seventieth

siede|n† *vt/i* (*haben*) boil; **s~nd heiß** boiling hot. **S~punkt** *m* boiling point

Siedl|er *m* -s,- settler. **S~ung** *f* -,-en [housing] estate; (*Niederlassung*) settlement

Sieg *m* -[e]s,-e victory

Siegel *nt* -s,- seal. **S~ring** *m* signet-ring

sieg|en *vi* (*haben*) win. **S~er(in)** *m* -s,- (*f* -,-nen) winner. **s~reich** *a* victorious

siezen *vt* **jdn s~** call s.o. 'Sie'

Signal *nt* -s,-e signal. **s~isieren** *vt* signal

signieren *vt* sign

Silbe *f* -,-n syllable. **S~ntrennung** *f* word-division

Silber *nt* -s silver. **S~hochzeit** *f* silver wedding. **s~n** *a* silver. **S~papier** *nt* silver paper

Silhouette /zɪˈlu̯ɛtə/ *f* -,-n silhouette

Silizium *nt* -s silicon

Silo *m & nt* -s,-s silo

Silvester *nt* -s New Year's Eve

simpel *a* simple, *adv* -ply; (*einfältig*) simple-minded

Simplex *nt* -,-e simplex

Sims *m & nt* -es,-e ledge; (*Kamin-*) mantelpiece

Simul|ant *m* -en,-en malingerer. **s~ieren** *vt* feign; (*Techn*) simulate □ *vi* (*haben*) pretend; (*sich krank stellen*) malinger

simultan *a* simultaneous, *adv* -ly

sind *s.* **sein**[1]; **wir/sie s~** we/they are

Sinfonie *f* -,-n symphony

singen† *vt/i* (*haben*) sing

Singular *m* -s,-e singular

Singvogel *m* songbird

sinken† *vi* (*sein*) sink; (*nieder-*) drop; (*niedriger werden*) go down, fall; **den Mut s~ lassen** lose courage

Sinn *m* -[e]s,-e sense; (*Denken*) mind; (*Zweck*) point; **im S~ haben** have in mind; **in gewissem S~e** in a sense; **es hat keinen S~** it is pointless; **nicht bei S~en sein** be out of one's mind. **S~bild** *nt* symbol. **s~en**† *vi* (*haben*) think; **auf Rache s~en** plot one's revenge

sinnlich *a* sensory; (*sexuell*) sensual; ⟨*Genüsse*⟩ sensuous. **S~keit** *f* - sensuality; sensuousness

sinn|los *a* senseless, *adv* -ly; (*zwecklos*) pointless, *adv* -ly. **s~voll** *a* meaningful; (*vernünftig*) sensible, *adv* -bly

Sintflut *f* flood

Siphon /'zi:fõ/ *m* **-s,-s** siphon
Sipp|e *f* **-,-n** clan. **S~schaft** *f* - clan; (*Pack*) crowd
Sirene *f* **-,-n** siren
Sirup *m* **-s,-e** syrup; (*schwarzer*) treacle
Sitte *f* **-,-n** custom; **S~n** manners. **s~nlos** *a* immoral
sittlich *a* moral, *adv* -ly. **S~keit** *f* - morality. **S~keitsverbrecher** *m* sex offender
sittsam *a* well-behaved; (*züchtig*) demure, *adv* -ly
Situ|ation /-'tsio:n/ *f* **-,-en** situation. **s~iert** *a* **gut/schlecht s~iert** well/badly off
Sitz *m* **-es,-e** seat; (*Passform*) fit
sitzen† *vi* (*haben*) sit; (*sich befinden*) be; (*passen*) fit; (*fam: treffen*) hit home; **[im Gefängnis] s~** (*fam*) be in jail; **s~ bleiben** remain seated; (*fam*) (*Sch*) stay *or* be kept down; (*nicht heiraten*) be left on the shelf; **s~ bleiben auf** (+ *dat*) be left with; **jdn s~ lassen** let s.o. sit down; (*fam*) (*Sch*) keep s.o. down; (*nicht heiraten*) jilt s.o.; (*im Stich lassen*) leave s.o. in the lurch. **s~bleiben**† *vi sep* (*sein*) (NEW) **s~ bleiben**, *s.* **sitzen**. **s~d** *a* seated; ⟨*Tätigkeit*⟩ sedentary. **s~lassen**† *vt sep* (NEW) **s~ lassen**, *s.* **sitzen**
Sitz|gelegenheit *f* seat. **S~platz** *m* seat. **S~ung** *f* **-,-en** session
Sizilien /-iən/ *nt* **-s** Sicily
Skala *f* **-,-len** scale; (*Reihe*) range
Skalpell *nt* **-s,-e** scalpel
skalpieren *vt* scalp
Skandal *m* **-s,-e** scandal. **s~ös** *a* scandalous
skandieren *vt* scan ⟨*Verse*⟩; chant ⟨*Parolen*⟩
Skandinav|ien /-iən/ *nt* **-s** Scandinavia. **s~isch** *a* Scandinavian
Skat *m* **-s** skat
Skelett *nt* **-[e]s,-e** skeleton
Skep|sis *f* - scepticism. **s~tisch** *a* sceptical, *adv* -ly; (*misstrauisch*) doubtful, *adv* -ly
Ski /ʃi:/ *m* **-s,-er** ski; **Ski fahren** *od* **laufen** ski. **S~fahrer(in)**, **S~läufer(in)** *m(f)* **-s,-** (*f* **-,-nen**) skier. **S~sport** *m* skiing
Skizz|e *f* **-,-n** sketch. **s~enhaft** *a* sketchy, *adv* -ily. **s~ieren** *vt* sketch
Sklav|e *m* **-n,-n** slave. **S~erei** *f* - slavery. **S~in** *f* **-,-nen** slave. **s~isch** *a* slavish, *adv* -ly
Skorpion *m* **-s,-e** scorpion; (*Astr*) Scorpio
Skrupel *m* **-s,-** scruple. **s~los** *a* unscrupulous
Skulptur *f* **-,-en** sculpture
skurril *a* absurd, *adv* -ly
Slalom *m* **-s,-s** slalom
Slang /slɛŋ/ *m* **-s** slang
Slaw|e *m* **-n,-n**, **S~in** *f* **-,-nen** Slav. **s~isch** *a* Slav; (*Lang*) Slavonic
Slip *m* **-s,-s** briefs *pl*
Smaragd *m* **-[e]s,-e** emerald
Smoking *m* **-s,-s** dinner jacket, (*Amer*) tuxedo
Snob *m* **-s,-s** snob. **S~ismus** *m* - snobbery **s~istisch** *a* snobbish
so *adv* so; (*so sehr*) so much; (*auf diese Weise*) like this/that; (*solch*) such; (*fam: sowieso*) anyway; (*fam: umsonst*) free; (*fam: ungefähr*) about; **nicht so schnell/viel** not so fast/much; **so gut/bald wie** as good/soon as; **so ein Mann** a man like that; **so ein Zufall!** what a coincidence! **so nicht** not like that; **mir ist so, als ob** I feel as if; **so oder so** in any case; **eine Stunde oder so** an hour or so; **so um zehn Mark** (*fam*) about ten marks; **[es ist] gut so** that's fine; **so, das ist geschafft** there, that's done; **so?** really? **so kommt doch!** come on then! □ *conj* (*also*) so; (*dann*) then; **so gern ich auch käme** as much as I would like to come; **so dass (daß)** = **sodass**
sobald *conj* as soon as
Söckchen *nt* **-s,-** [ankle] sock
Socke *f* **-,-n** sock

Sockel *m* **-s,-** plinth, pedestal
Socken *m* **-s,-** sock
Soda *nt* **-s** soda
sodass *conj* so that
Sodawasser *nt* soda water
Sodbrennen *nt* **-s** heartburn
soeben *adv* just [now]
Sofa *nt* **-s,-s** settee, sofa
sofern *adv* provided [that]
sofort *adv* at once, immediately; (*auf der Stelle*) instantly. **s~ig** *a* immediate
Software /'zɔftvɛːɐ̯/ *f* **-** software
sogar *adv* even
sogenannt *a* so-called
sogleich *adv* at once
Sohle *f* **-,-n** sole; (*Tal-*) bottom
Sohn *m* **-[e]s,¨e** son
Sojabohne *f* soya bean
solange *conj* as long as
solch *inv pron* such; **s~ ein(e)** such a; **s~ einer/eine/eins** one/(*Person*) someone like that. **s~e(r,s)** *pron* such; **ein s~er Mann/eine s~e Frau** a man/woman like that; **ich habe s~e Angst** I am so afraid □ (*substantivisch*) **ein s~er/eine s~e/ein s~es** one/(*Person*) someone like that; **s~e** (*pl*) those; (*Leute*) people like that
Sold *m* **-[e]s** (*Mil*) pay
Soldat *m* **-en,-en** soldier
Söldner *m* **-s,-** mercenary
solidarisch *a* **s~e Handlung** act of solidarity; **sich s~ erklären** declare one's solidarity
Solidarität *f* **-** solidarity
solide *a* solid, *adv* -ly; (*haltbar*) sturdy, *adv* -ily; (*sicher*) sound, *adv* -ly; (*anständig*) respectable, *adv* -bly
Solist(in) *m* **-en,-en** (*f* **-,-nen**) soloist
Soll *nt* **-s** (*Comm*) debit; (*Produktions-*) quota
sollen† *v aux* **er soll warten** he is to wait; (*möge*) let him wait; **was soll ich machen?** what shall I do? **du sollst nicht lügen** you shouldn't tell lies; **du sollst nicht töten** (*liter*) thou shalt not kill; **ihr sollt jetzt still sein!** will you be quiet now! **du solltest dich schämen** you ought to *or* should be ashamed of yourself; **es hat nicht sein s~** it was not to be; **ich hätte es nicht tun s~** I ought not to *or* should not have done it; **er soll sehr nett/reich sein** he is supposed to be very nice/rich; **sollte es regnen, so** ... if it should rain then ...; **das soll man nicht [tun]** you're not supposed to [do that]; **soll ich [mal versuchen]?** shall I [try]? **soll er doch!** let him! **was soll's!** so what!
Solo *nt* **-s,-los & -li** solo. **s~** *adv* solo
somit *adv* therefore, so
Sommer *m* **-s,-** summer. **S~ferien** *pl* summer holidays. **s~lich** *a* summery; (*Sommer-*) summer ... □ *adv* **s~lich warm** as warm as summer. **S~schlussverkauf** (**S~schlußverkauf**) *m* summer sale. **S~sprossen** *fpl* freckles. **s~sprossig** *a* freckled
Sonate *f* **-,-n** sonata
Sonde *f* **-,-n** probe
Sonder|angebot *nt* special offer. **s~bar** *a* odd, *adv* -ly. **S~fahrt** *f* special excursion. **S~fall** *m* special case. **s~gleichen** *adv* **eine Gemeinheit/Grausamkeit s~gleichen** unparalleled meanness/cruelty. **s~lich** *a* particular, *adv* -ly; (*sonderbar*) odd, *adv* -ly. **S~ling** *m* **-s,-e** crank. **S~marke** *f* special stamp
sondern *conj* but; **nicht nur** ... **s~ auch** not only ... but also
Sonder|preis *m* special price. **S~schule** *f* special school. **S~zug** *m* special train
sondieren *vt* sound out
Sonett *nt* **-[e]s,-e** sonnet
Sonnabend *m* **-s,-e** Saturday. **s~s** *adv* on Saturdays

Sonne *f* -,-**n** sun. **s~n (sich)** *vr* sun oneself; (*fig*) bask (**in** + *dat* in)

Sonnen|aufgang *m* sunrise. **s~baden** *vi* (*haben*) sunbathe. **S~bank** *f* sun-bed. **S~blume** *f* sunflower. **S~brand** *m* sunburn. **S~brille** *f* sun-glasses *pl*. **S~energie** *f* solar energy. **S~finsternis** *f* solar eclipse. **S~milch** *f* sun-tan lotion. **S~öl** *nt* sun-tan oil. **S~schein** *m* sunshine. **S~schirm** *m* sunshade. **S~stich** *m* sunstroke. **S~uhr** *f* sundial. **S~untergang** *m* sunset. **S~wende** *f* solstice

sonnig *a* sunny

Sonntag *m* -**s,-e** Sunday. **s~s** *adv* on Sundays

sonst *adv* (*gewöhnlich*) usually; (*im Übrigen*) apart from that; (*andernfalls*) otherwise, or [else]; **wer/was/wie/wo s~?** who/what/how/where else? **s~ niemand/nichts** no one/nothing else; **s~ noch jemand/etwas?** anyone/anything else? **s~ noch Fragen?** any more questions? **s~ jemand** *od* **wer** someone/(*fragend, verneint*) anyone else; (*irgendjemand*) [just] anyone; **s~ wie** some/(*fragend, verneint*) any other way; **s~ wo** somewhere/(*fragend, verneint*) anywhere else; (*irgendwo*) [just] anywhere. **s~ig** *a* other. **s~jemand** *pron* (NEW) **s~ jemand**, *s.* **sonst**. **s~wer** *pron* (NEW) **s~ wer**, *s.* **sonst**. **s~wie** *adv* (NEW) **s~ wie**, *s.* **sonst**. **s~wo** *adv* (NEW) **s~ wo**, *s.* **sonst**

sooft *conj* whenever

Sopran *m* -**s,-e** soprano

Sorge *f* -,-**n** worry (**um** about); (*Fürsorge*) care; **in S~ sein** be worried; **sich** (*dat*) **S~n machen** worry; **keine S~!** don't worry! **s~n** *vi* (*haben*) **s~n für** look after, care for; (*vorsorgen*) provide for; (*sich kümmern*) see to; **dafür s~n, dass** see [to it] *or* make sure that □ *vr* **sich s~n** worry. **s~nfrei** *a* carefree. **s~nvoll** *a* worried, *adv* -ly. **S~recht** *nt* (*Jur*) custody

Sorg|falt *f* - care. **s~fältig** *a* careful, *adv* -ly. **s~los** *a* careless, *adv* -ly; (*unbekümmert*) carefree. **s~sam** *a* careful, *adv* -ly

Sorte *f* -,-**n** kind, sort; (*Comm*) brand

sort|ieren *vt* sort [out]; (*Comm*) grade. **S~iment** *nt* -**[e]s,-e** range

sosehr *conj* however much

Soße *f* -,-**n** sauce; (*Braten-*) gravy; (*Salat-*) dressing

Souffl|eur /zu'flø:ɐ̯/ *m* -**s,-e**, **S~euse** /-ø:zə/ *f* -,-**n** prompter. **s~ieren** *vi* (*haben*) prompt

Souvenir /zuvə'ni:ɐ̯/ *nt* -**s,-s** souvenir

souverän /zuvə'rɛ:n/ *a* sovereign; (*fig: überlegen*) expert *adv* -ly. **S~ität** *f* - sovereignty

soviel *conj* however much; **s~ ich weiß** as far as I know □ *adv* (NEW) **so viel**, *s.* **viel**

soweit *conj* as far as; (*insoweit*) [in] so far as □ *adv* (NEW) **so weit**, *s.* **weit**

sowenig *conj* however little □ *adv* (NEW) **so wenig**, *s.* **wenig**

sowie *conj* as well as; (*sobald*) as soon as

sowieso *adv* anyway, in any case

sowjet|isch *a* Soviet. **S~union** *f* - Soviet Union

sowohl *adv* **s~ ... als** *od* **wie auch** ...... as well as ...; **s~ er als auch seine Frau** both he and his wife

sozial *a* social, *adv* -ly; ⟨*Einstellung, Beruf*⟩ caring. **S~arbeit** *f* social work. **S~arbeiter(in)** *m(f)* social worker. **S~demokrat** *m* social democrat. **S~hilfe** *f* social security

Sozialis|mus *m* - socialism. **S~t** *m* -**en,-en** socialist. **s~tisch** *a* socialist

Sozial|versicherung *f* National Insurance. **S~wohnung** *f* ≈ council flat

Soziol|oge *m* **-n,-n** sociologist. **S~ogie** *f* - sociology

Sozius *m* **-,-se** (*Comm*) partner; (*Beifahrersitz*) pillion

sozusagen *adv* so to speak

Spachtel *m* **-s,-** & *f* **-,-n** spatula

Spagat *m* **-[e]s,-e** (*Aust*) string; **S~ machen** do the splits *pl*

Spaghetti, **Spagetti** *pl* spaghetti *sg*

spähen *vi* (*haben*) peer

Spalier *nt* **-s,-e** trellis; **S~ stehen** line the route

Spalt *m* **-[e]s,-e** crack; (*im Vorhang*) chink

Spalt|e *f* **-,-n** crack, crevice; (*Gletscher-*) crevasse; (*Druck-*) column; (*Orangen-*) segment. **s~en**† *vt* split; **sich s~en** split. **S~ung** *f* **-,-en** splitting; (*Kluft*) split; (*Phys*) fission

Span *m* **-[e]s,¨e** [wood] chip; (*Hobel-*) shaving

Spange *f* **-,-n** clasp; (*Haar-*) slide; (*Zahn-*) brace; (*Arm-*) bangle

Span|ien /-iən/ *nt* **-s** Spain. **S~ier** *m* **-s,-**, **S~ierin** *f* **-,-nen** Spaniard. **s~isch** *a* Spanish. **S~isch** *nt* **-[s]** (*Lang*) Spanish

Spann *m* **-[e]s** instep

Spanne *f* **-,-n** span; (*Zeit-*) space; (*Comm*) margin

spann|en *vt* stretch; put up ⟨*Leine*⟩; (*straffen*) tighten; (*an-*) harness (**an** + *acc* to); **den Hahn s~en** cock the gun; **sich s~en** tighten □ *vi* (*haben*) be too tight. **s~end** *a* exciting. **S~er** *m* **-s,-** (*fam*) Peeping Tom. **S~ung** *f* **-,-en** tension; (*Erwartung*) suspense; (*Electr*) voltage

Spar|buch *nt* savings book. **S~büchse** *f* money-box. **s~en** *vt/i* (*haben*) save; (*sparsam sein*) economize (**mit/an** + *dat* on); **sich** (*dat*) **die Mühe s~en** save oneself the trouble. **S~er** *m* **-s,-** saver

Spargel *m* **-s,-** asparagus

Spar|kasse *f* savings bank. **S~konto** *nt* deposit account

spärlich *a* sparse, *adv* -ly; (*dürftig*) meagre; (*knapp*) scanty, *adv* -ily

Sparren *m* **-s,-** rafter

sparsam *a* economical, *adv* -ly; ⟨*Person*⟩ thrifty. **S~keit** *f* - economy; thrift

Sparschwein *nt* piggy bank

spartanisch *a* Spartan

Sparte *f* **-,-n** branch; (*Zeitungs-*) section; (*Rubrik*) column

Spaß *m* **-es,¨e** fun; (*Scherz*) joke; **im/aus/zum S~** for fun; **S~ machen** be fun; ⟨*Person:*⟩ be joking; **es macht mir keinen S~** I don't enjoy it; **viel S~!** have a good time! **s~en** *vi* (*haben*) joke. **s~ig** *a* amusing, funny. **S~vogel** *m* joker

Spast|iker *m* **-s,-** spastic. **s~isch** *a* spastic

spät *a* & *adv* late; **wie s~ ist es?** what time is it? **zu s~** too late; **zu s~ kommen** be late. **s~abends** *adv* late at night

Spatel *m* **-s,-** & *f* **-,-n** spatula

Spaten *m* **-s,-** spade

später *a* later; (*zukünftig*) future □ *adv* later

spätestens *adv* at the latest

Spatz *m* **-en,-en** sparrow

Spätzle *pl* (*Culin*) noodles

spazieren *vi* (*sein*) stroll; **s~ gehen** go for a walk. **s~gehen**† *vi sep* (*sein*) (NEW) **s~ gehen**, *s.* **spazieren**

Spazier|gang *m* walk; **einen S~gang machen** go for a walk. **S~gänger(in)** *m* **-s,-** (*f* **-,-nen**) walker. **S~stock** *m* walking-stick

Specht *m* **-[e]s,-e** woodpecker

Speck *m* **-s** bacon; (*fam: Fettpolster*) fat. **s~ig** *a* greasy

Spedi|teur /ʃpediˈtøːɐ̯/ *m* **-s,-e** haulage/(*für Umzüge*) removals contractor. **S~tion** /-ˈtsi̯oːn/ *f*

-,-en carriage, haulage; (*Firma*) haulage/(*für Umzüge*) removals firm

Speer *m* **-[e]s,-e** spear; (*Sport*) javelin

Speiche *f* **-,-n** spoke

Speichel *m* **-s** saliva

Speicher *m* **-s,-** warehouse; (*dial: Dachboden*) attic; (*Computer*) memory. **s~n** *vt* store

speien† *vt* spit; (*erbrechen*) vomit

Speise *f* **-,-n** food; (*Gericht*) dish; (*Pudding*) blancmange. **S~eis** *nt* ice-cream. **S~kammer** *f* larder. **S~karte** *f* menu. **s~n** *vi* (*haben*) eat; **zu Abend s~n** have dinner □ *vt* feed. **S~röhre** *f* oesophagus. **S~saal** *m* dining-room. **S~wagen** *m* dining-car

Spektakel *m* **-s** (*fam*) noise

spektakulär *a* spectacular

Spektrum *nt* **-s,-tra** spectrum

Spekul|ant *m* **-en,-en** speculator. **S~ation** /-'tsi̯o:n/ *f* **-,-en** speculation. **s~ieren** *vi* (*haben*) speculate; **s~ieren auf** (+ *acc*) (*fam*) hope to get

Spelze *f* **-,-n** husk

spendabel *a* generous

Spende *f* **-,-n** donation. **s~n** *vt* donate; give ⟨*Blut, Schatten*⟩; **Beifall s~n** applaud. **S~r** *m* **-s,-** donor; (*Behälter*) dispenser

spendieren *vt* pay for; **jdm etw/ein Bier s~** treat s.o. to sth/stand s.o. a beer

Spengler *m* **-s,-** (*SGer*) plumber

Sperling *m* **-s,-e** sparrow

Sperre *f* **-,-n** barrier; (*Verbot*) ban; (*Comm*) embargo. **s~n** *vt* close; (*ver-*) block; (*verbieten*) ban; cut off ⟨*Strom, Telefon*⟩; stop ⟨*Scheck, Kredit*⟩; **s~n in** (+ *acc*) put in ⟨*Gefängnis, Käfig*⟩; **sich s~n** balk (**gegen** at); **gesperrt gedruckt** (*Typ*) spaced

Sperr|holz *nt* plywood. **s~ig** *a* bulky. **S~müll** *m* bulky refuse. **S~stunde** *f* closing time

Spesen *pl* expenses

spezial|isieren (sich) *vr* specialize (**auf** + *acc* in). **S~ist** *m* **-en,-en** specialist. **S~ität** *f* **-,-en** speciality

speziell *a* special, *adv* -ly

spezifisch *a* specific, *adv* -ally

Sphäre /'sfɛ:rə/ *f* **-,-n** sphere

spicken *vt* (*Culin*) lard; **gespickt mit** (*fig*) full of □ *vi* (*haben*) (*fam*) crib (**bei** from)

Spiegel *m* **-s,-** mirror; (*Wasser-, Alkohol-*) level. **S~bild** *nt* reflection. **S~ei** *nt* fried egg. **s~n** *vt* reflect; **sich s~n** be reflected □ *vi* (*haben*) reflect [the light]; (*glänzen*) gleam. **S~ung** *f* **-,-en** reflection

Spiel *nt* **-[e]s,-e** game; (*Spielen*) playing; (*Glücks-*) gambling; (*Schau-*) play; (*Satz*) set; **ein S~ Karten** a pack/(*Amer*) deck of cards; **auf dem S~ stehen** be at stake; **aufs S~ setzen** risk. **S~art** *f* variety. **S~automat** *m* fruit machine. **S~bank** *f* casino. **S~dose** *f* musical box. **s~en** *vt/i* (*haben*) play; (*im Glücksspiel*) gamble; (*vortäuschen*) act; ⟨*Roman:*⟩ be set (**in** + *dat* in); **s~en mit** (*fig*) toy with. **s~end** *a* (*mühelos*) effortless, *adv* -ly

Spieler|(in) *m* **-s,-** (*f* **-,-nen**) player; (*Glücks-*) gambler. **S~ei** *f* **-,-en** amusement; (*Kleinigkeit*) trifle

Spiel|feld *nt* field, pitch. **S~gefährte** *m*, **S~gefährtin** *f* playmate. **S~karte** *f* playing-card. **S~marke** *f* chip. **S~plan** *m* programme. **S~platz** *m* playground. **S~raum** *m* (*fig*) scope; (*Techn*) clearance. **S~regeln** *fpl* rules [of the game]. **S~sachen** *fpl* toys. **S~verderber** *m* **-s,-** spoilsport. **S~waren** *fpl* toys. **S~warengeschäft** *nt* toyshop. **S~zeug** *nt* toy; (*S~sachen*) toys *pl*

Spieß *m* **-es,-e** spear; (*Brat-*) spit; (*für Schaschlik*) skewer; (*Fleisch-*) kebab; **den S~ umkehren** turn the tables on s.o.

S~bürger *m* [petit] bourgeois. **s~bürgerlich** *a* bourgeois. **s~en** *vt* **etw auf etw** (*acc*) **s~en** spear sth with sth. **S~er** *m* **-s,-** [petit] bourgeois. **s~ig** *a* bourgeois. **S~ruten** *fpl* **S~ruten laufen** run the gauntlet
Spike[s]reifen /ˈʃpaik[s]-/ *m* studded tyre
Spinat *m* **-s** spinach
Spind *m & nt* **-[e]s,-e** locker
Spindel *f* **-,-n** spindle
Spinne *f* **-,-n** spider
spinn|en† *vt/i* (*haben*) spin; **er spinnt** (*fam*) he's crazy. **S~ennetz** *nt* spider's web. **S~[en]gewebe** *nt*, **S~webe** *f* **-,-n** cobweb
Spion *m* **-s,-e** spy
Spionage /ʃpioˈnaːʒə/ *f* **-** espionage, spying; **S~ treiben** spy. **S~abwehr** *f* counter-espionage
spionieren *vi* (*haben*) spy
Spionin *f* **-,-nen** [woman] spy
Spiral|e *f* **-,-n** spiral. **s~ig** *a* spiral
Spiritis|mus *m* **-** spiritualism. **s~tisch** *a* spiritualist
Spirituosen *pl* spirits
Spiritus *m* **-** alcohol; (*Brenn-*) methylated spirits *pl*. **S~kocher** *m* spirit stove
Spital *nt* **-s,¨er** (*Aust*) hospital
spitz *a* pointed; (*scharf*) sharp; (*schrill*) shrill; ⟨*Winkel*⟩ acute; **s~e Bemerkung** dig. **S~bube** *m* scoundrel; (*Schlingel*) rascal. **s~bübisch** *a* mischievous, *adv* -ly
Spitze *f* **-,-n** point; (*oberer Teil*) top; (*vorderer Teil*) front; (*Pfeil-, Finger-, Nasen-*) tip; (*Schuh-, Strumpf-*) toe; (*Zigarren-, Zigaretten-*) holder; (*Höchstleistung*) maximum; (*Tex*) lace; (*fam: Anspielung*) dig; **an der S~ liegen** be in the lead
Spitzel *m* **-s,-** informer
spitzen *vt* sharpen; purse ⟨*Lippen*⟩; prick up ⟨*Ohren*⟩; **sich s~ auf** (+ *acc*) (*fam*) look forward to. **S~geschwindigkeit** *f* top speed
spitz|findig *a* over-subtle. **S~hacke** *f* pickaxe. **S~name** *m* nickname
Spleen /ʃpliːn/ *m* **-s,-e** obsession; **einen S~ haben** be crazy. **s~ig** *a* eccentric
Splitter *m* **-s,-** splinter. **s~n** *vi* (*sein*) shatter. **s~[faser]nackt** *a* (*fam*) stark naked
sponsern *vt* sponsor
spontan *a* spontaneous, *adv* -ly
sporadisch *a* sporadic, *adv* -ally
Spore *f* **-,-n** (*Biol*) spore
Sporn *m* **-[e]s, Sporen** spur; **einem Pferd die Sporen geben** spur a horse
Sport *m* **-[e]s** sport; (*Hobby*) hobby. **S~art** *f* sport. **S~fest** *nt* sports day. **S~ler** *m* **-s,-** sportsman. **S~lerin** *f* **-,-nen** sportswoman. **s~lich** *a* sports ...; (*fair*) sporting, *adv* -ly; (*flott, schlank*) sporty. **S~platz** *m* sports ground. **S~verein** *m* sports club. **S~wagen** *m* sports car; (*Kinder-*) push-chair, (*Amer*) stroller
Spott *m* **-[e]s** mockery. **s~billig** *a & adv* dirt cheap
spötteln *vi* (*haben*) mock; **s~ über** (+ *acc*) poke fun at
spotten *vi* (*haben*) mock; **s~ über** (+ *acc*) make fun of; (*höhnend*) ridicule
spöttisch *a* mocking, *adv* -ly
Sprach|e *f* **-,-n** language; (*Sprechfähigkeit*) speech; **zur S~e bringen** bring up. **S~fehler** *m* speech defect. **S~labor** *nt* language laboratory. **s~lich** *a* linguistic, *adv* -ally. **s~los** *a* speechless
Spray /ʃpreː/ *nt & m* **-s,-s** spray. **S~dose** *f* aerosol [can]
Sprech|anlage *f* intercom. **S~chor** *m* chorus; **im S~chor rufen** chant

sprechen† *vi (haben)* speak/(*sich unterhalten*) talk (**über** + *acc*/**von** about/of); **Deutsch/Englisch s~** speak German/English □ *vt* speak; (*sagen, aufsagen*) say; pronounce ⟨*Urteil*⟩; **schuldig s~** find guilty; **jdn s~** speak to s.o.; **Herr X ist nicht zu s~** Mr X is not available
Sprecher(in) *m* **-s,-** (*f* **-,-nen**) speaker; (*Radio, TV*) announcer; (*Wortführer*) spokesman, *f* spokeswoman
Sprechstunde *f* consulting hours *pl*; (*Med*) surgery. **S~nhilfe** *f* (*Med*) receptionist
Sprechzimmer *nt* consulting room
spreizen *vt* spread
Sprengel *m* **-s,-** parish
spreng|en *vt* blow up; blast ⟨*Felsen*⟩; (*fig*) burst; (*begießen*) water; (*mit Sprenger*) sprinkle; dampen ⟨*Wäsche*⟩. **S~er** *m* **-s,-** sprinkler. **S~kopf** *m* warhead. **S~körper** *m* explosive device. **S~stoff** *m* explosive
Spreu *f* - chaff
Sprich|wort *nt* (*pl* **-wörter**) proverb. **s~wörtlich** *a* proverbial
sprießen† *vi* (*sein*) sprout
Springbrunnen *m* fountain
spring|en† *vi* (*sein*) jump; (*Schwimmsport*) dive; ⟨*Ball:*⟩ bounce; (*spritzen*) spurt; (*zer-*) break; (*rissig werden*) crack; (*SGer: laufen*) run. **S~er** *m* **-s,-** jumper; (*Kunst-*) diver; (*Schach*) knight. **S~reiten** *nt* show-jumping. **S~seil** *nt* skipping-rope
Sprint *m* **-s,-s** sprint
Sprit *m* **-s** (*fam*) petrol
Spritz|e *f* **-,-n** syringe; (*Injektion*) injection; (*Feuer-*) hose. **s~en** *vt* spray; (*be-, ver-*) splash; (*Culin*) pipe; (*Med*) inject □ *vi* (*haben*) splash; ⟨*Fett:*⟩ spit □ *vi* (*sein*) splash; (*hervor-*) spurt; (*fam: laufen*) dash. **S~er** *m* **-s,-** splash; (*Schuss*) dash. **s~ig** *a* lively; ⟨*Wein, Komödie*⟩ sparkling. **S~tour** *f* (*fam*) spin
spröde *a* brittle; (*trocken*) dry; (*rissig*) chapped; ⟨*Stimme*⟩ harsh; (*abweisend*) aloof
Spross *m* **-es,-e** (**Sproß** *m* **-sses, -sse**) shoot
Sprosse *f* **-,-n** rung. **S~nkohl** *m* (*Aust*) Brussels sprouts *pl*
Sprössling (**Sprößling**) *m* **-s,-e** (*fam*) offspring
Sprotte *f* **-,-n** sprat
Spruch *m* **-[e]s,¨-e** saying; (*Denk-*) motto; (*Zitat*) quotation. **S~band** *nt* (*pl* **-bänder**) banner
Sprudel *m* **-s,-** sparkling mineral water. **s~n** *vi* (*haben/sein*) bubble
Sprüh|dose *f* aerosol [can]. **s~en** *vt* spray □ *vi* (*sein*) ⟨*Funken:*⟩ fly; (*fig*) sparkle. **S~regen** *m* fine drizzle
Sprung *m* **-[e]s,¨-e** jump, leap; (*Schwimmsport*) dive; (*fam: Katzen-*) stone's throw; (*Riss*) crack; **auf einen S~** (*fam*) for a moment. **S~brett** *nt* springboard. **s~haft** *a* erratic; (*plötzlich*) sudden, *adv* -ly. **S~schanze** *f* ski-jump. **S~seil** *nt* skipping-rope
Spucke *f* - spit. **s~n** *vt/i* (*haben*) spit; (*sich übergeben*) be sick
Spuk *m* **-[e]s,-e** [ghostly] apparition. **s~en** *vi* (*haben*) ⟨*Geist:*⟩ walk; **in diesem Haus s~t es** this house is haunted
Spülbecken *nt* sink
Spule *f* **-,-n** spool
Spüle *f* **-,-n** sink unit; (*Becken*) sink
spulen *vt* spool
spül|en *vt* rinse; (*schwemmen*) wash; **Geschirr s~en** wash up □ *vi* (*haben*) flush [the toilet]. **S~kasten** *m* cistern. **S~mittel** *nt* washing-up liquid. **S~tuch** *nt* dishcloth
Spur *f* **-,-en** track; (*Fahr-*) lane; (*Fährte*) trail; (*Anzeichen*) trace;

(*Hinweis*) lead; **keine** *od* **nicht die S~** (*fam*) not in the least
spürbar *a* noticeable, *adv* -bly
spuren *vi* (*haben*) (*fam*) toe the line
spür|en *vt* feel; (*seelisch*) sense. **S~hund** *m* tracker dog
spurlos *adv* without trace
spurten *vi* (*sein*) put on a spurt; (*fam: laufen*) sprint
sputen (sich) *vr* hurry
Staat *m* **-[e]s,-en** state; (*Land*) country; (*Putz*) finery. **s~lich** *a* state ... □ *adv* by the state
Staatsangehörig|e(r) *m/f* national. **S~keit** *f* - nationality
Staats|anwalt *m* state prosecutor. **S~beamte(r)** *m* civil servant. **S~besuch** *m* state visit. **S~bürger(in)** *m(f)* national. **S~mann** *m* (*pl* **-männer**) statesman. **S~streich** *m* coup
Stab *m* **-[e]s,¨e** rod; (*Gitter-*) bar (*Sport*) baton; (*Mitarbeiter-*) team; (*Mil*) staff
Stäbchen *ntpl* chopsticks
Stabhochsprung *m* pole-vault
stabil *a* stable; (*gesund*) robust; (*solide*) sturdy, *adv* -ily. **s~isieren** *vt* stabilize; **sich s~isieren** stabilize. **S~ität** *f* - stability
Stachel *m* **-s,-** spine; (*Gift-*) sting; (*Spitze*) spike. **S~beere** *f* gooseberry. **S~draht** *m* barbed wire. **s~ig** *a* prickly. **S~schwein** *nt* porcupine
Stadion *nt* **-s,-ien** stadium
Stadium *nt* **-s,-ien** stage
Stadt *f* **-,¨e** town; (*Groß-*) city
Städt|chen *nt* **-s,-** small town. **s~isch** *a* urban; (*kommunal*) municipal
Stadt|mauer *f* city wall. **S~mitte** *f* town centre. **S~plan** *m* street map. **S~teil** *m* district. **S~zentrum** *nt* town centre
Staffel *f* **-,-n** team; (*S~lauf*) relay; (*Mil*) squadron
Staffelei *f* **-,-en** easel
Staffel|lauf *m* relay race. **s~n** *vt* stagger; (*abstufen*) grade
Stagn|ation /-ˈtsi̯oːn/ *f* - stagnation. **s~ieren** *vi* (*haben*) stagnate
Stahl *m* **-s** steel. **S~beton** *m* reinforced concrete
Stall *m* **-[e]s,¨e** stable; (*Kuh-*) shed; (*Schweine-*) sty; (*Hühner-*) coop; (*Kaninchen-*) hutch
Stamm *m* **-[e]s,¨e** trunk; (*Sippe*) tribe; (*Kern*) core; (*Wort-*) stem. **S~baum** *m* family tree; (*eines Tieres*) pedigree
stammeln *vt/i* (*haben*) stammer
stammen *vi* (*haben*) come/(*zeitlich*) date (**von/aus** from); **das Zitat stammt von Goethe** the quotation is from Goethe
Stamm|gast *m* regular. **S~halter** *m* son and heir
stämmig *a* sturdy
Stamm|kundschaft *f* regulars *pl*. **S~lokal** *nt* favourite pub. **S~tisch** *m* table reserved for the regulars; (*Treffen*) meeting of the regulars
stampf|en *vi* (*haben*) stamp; ⟨*Maschine:*⟩ pound; **mit den Füßen s~en** stamp one's feet □ *vi* (*sein*) tramp □ *vt* pound; mash ⟨*Kartoffeln*⟩. **S~kartoffeln** *fpl* mashed potatoes
Stand *m* **-[e]s,¨e** standing position; (*Zustand*) state; (*Spiel-*) score; (*Höhe*) level; (*gesellschaftlich*) class; (*Verkaufs-*) stall; (*Messe-*) stand; (*Taxi-*) rank; **auf den neuesten S~ bringen** update; **in S~ halten/setzen** = **instand halten/setzen**, *s.* **instand**; **im/außer S~e sein** = **imstande/außerstande sein**, *s.* **imstande, außerstande**; **zu S~e bringen/kommen** = **zustande bringen/kommen**, *s.* **zustande**
Standard *m* **-s,-s** standard. **s~isieren** *vt* standardize
Standarte *f* **-,-n** standard
Standbild *nt* statue

Ständchen *nt* **-s,-** serenade; **jdm ein S~ bringen** serenade s.o.
Ständer *m* **-s,-** stand; (*Geschirr-, Platten-*) rack; (*Kerzen-*) holder
Standes|amt *nt* registry office. **S~beamte(r)** *m* registrar. **S~unterschied** *m* class distinction
stand|haft *a* steadfast, *adv* -ly. **s~halten**† *vi sep* (*haben*) stand firm; **etw** (*dat*) **s~halten** stand up to sth
ständig *a* constant, *adv* -ly; (*fest*) permanent, *adv* -ly
Stand|licht *nt* sidelights *pl.* **S~ort** *m* position; (*Firmen-*) location; (*Mil*) garrison. **S~pauke** *f* (*fam*) dressing-down. **S~punkt** *m* point of view. **S~spur** *f* hard shoulder. **S~uhr** *f* grandfather clock
Stange *f* **-,-n** bar; (*Holz-*) pole; (*Gardinen-*) rail; (*Hühner-*) perch; (*Zimt-*) stick; **von der S~** (*fam*) off the peg
Stängel *m* **-s,-** stalk, stem
Stangen|bohne *f* runner bean. **S~brot** *nt* French bread
Stanniol *nt* **-s** tin foil. **S~papier** *nt* silver paper
stanzen *vt* stamp; (*aus-*) stamp out; punch ⟨*Loch*⟩
Stapel *m* **-s,-** stack, pile; **vom S~ laufen** be launched. **S~ lauf** *m* launch[ing]. **s~n** *vt* stack *or* pile up; **sich s~n** pile up
stapfen *vi* (*sein*) tramp, trudge
Star[1] *m* **-[e]s,-e** starling
Star[2] *m* **-[e]s** (*Med*) **[grauer] S~** cataract; **grüner S~** glaucoma
Star[3] *m* **-s,-s** (*Theat, Sport*) star
stark *a* (**stärker, stärkst**) strong; ⟨*Motor*⟩ powerful; ⟨*Verkehr, Regen*⟩ heavy; ⟨*Hitze, Kälte*⟩ severe; (*groß*) big; (*schlimm*) bad; (*dick*) thick; (*korpulent*) stout □ *adv* strongly; heavily; badly; (*sehr*) very much
Stärk|e *f* **-,-n** (*s.* **stark**) strength; power; thickness; stoutness; (*Größe*) size; (*Mais-, Wäsche-*) starch. **S~emehl** *nt* cornflour. **s~en** *vt* strengthen; starch ⟨*Wäsche*⟩; **sich s~en** fortify oneself. **S~ung** *f* **-,-en** strengthening; (*Erfrischung*) refreshment
starr *a* rigid, *adv* -ly; (*steif*) stiff, *adv* -ly; ⟨*Blick*⟩ fixed; (*unbeugsam*) inflexible, *adv* -bly
starren *vi* (*haben*) stare; **vor Schmutz s~** be filthy
starr|köpfig *a* stubborn. **S~sinn** *m* obstinacy. **s~sinnig** *a* obstinate, *adv* -ly
Start *m* **-s,-s** start; (*Aviat*) take-off. **S~bahn** *f* runway. **s~en** *vi* (*sein*) start; (*Aviat*) take off; (*aufbrechen*) set off; (*teilnehmen*) compete □ *vt* start; (*fig*) launch
Station /-ˈt͡sio:n/ *f* **-,-en** station; (*Haltestelle*) stop; (*Abschnitt*) stage; (*Med*) ward; **S~ machen** break one's journey; **bei freier S~** all found. **s~är** *adv* as an in-patient. **s~ieren** *vt* station
statisch *a* static
Statist(in) *m* **-en,-en** (*f* **-,-nen**) (*Theat*) extra
Statisti|k *f* **-,-en** statistics *sg*; (*Aufstellung*) statistics *pl.* **s~sch** *a* statistical, *adv* -ly
Stativ *nt* **-s,-e** (*Phot*) tripod
statt *prep* (+ *gen*) instead of; **an seiner s~** in his place; **an Kindes s~ annehmen** adopt; **s~ dessen** (NEW) **s~dessen** □ *conj* **s~ etw zu tun** instead of doing sth. **s~dessen** *adv* instead
Stätte *f* **-,-n** place
statt|finden† *vi sep* (*haben*) take place. **s~haft** *a* permitted
stattlich *a* imposing; (*beträchtlich*) considerable
Statue /ˈʃta:tu̯ə/ *f* **-,-n** statue
Statur *f* **-** build, stature
Status *m* **-** status. **S~symbol** *nt* status symbol
Statut *nt* **-[e]s,-en** statute
Stau *m* **-[e]s,-s** congestion; (*Auto*) [traffic] jam; (*Rück-*) tailback

Staub *m* **-[e]s** dust; **S~ wischen** dust; **S~ saugen** vacuum, hoover
Staubecken *nt* reservoir
staub|en *vi* (*haben*) raise dust; **es s~t** it's dusty. **s~ig** *a* dusty. **s~saugen** *vt/i* (*haben*) vacuum, hoover. **S~sauger** *m* vacuum cleaner, Hoover (P). **S~tuch** *nt* duster
Staudamm *m* dam
Staude *f* **-,-n** shrub
stauen *vt* dam up; **sich s~** accumulate; ⟨*Autos:*⟩ form a tailback
staunen *vi* (*haben*) be amazed *or* astonished. **S~** *nt* **-s** amazement, astonishment
Stau|see *m* reservoir. **S~ung** *f* **-,-en** congestion; (*Auto*) [traffic] jam
Steak /ʃteːk, steːk/ *nt* **-s,-s** steak
stechen† *vt* stick (**in** + *acc* in); (*verletzen*) prick; (*mit Messer*) stab; ⟨*Insekt:*⟩ sting; ⟨*Mücke:*⟩ bite; (*gravieren*) engrave □ *vi* (*haben*) prick; ⟨*Insekt:*⟩ sting; ⟨*Mücke:*⟩ bite; (*mit Stechuhr*) clock in/out; **in See s~** put to sea. **s~d** *a* stabbing; ⟨*Geruch*⟩ pungent
Stech|ginster *m* gorse. **S~kahn** *m* punt. **S~mücke** *f* mosquito. **S~palme** *f* holly. **S~uhr** *f* time clock
Steck|brief *m* 'wanted' poster. **S~dose** *f* socket. **s~en** *vt* put; (*mit Nadel, Reißzwecke*) pin; (*pflanzen*) plant □ *vi* (*haben*) be; (*fest-*) be stuck; **s~ bleiben** get stuck; **den Schlüssel s~ lassen** leave the key in the lock; **hinter etw** (*dat*) **s~en** (*fig*) be behind sth
Stecken *m* **-s,-** (*SGer*) stick
stecken|bleiben† *vi sep* (*sein*) (NEW) **s~ bleiben**, *s.* **stecken**. **s~lassen**† *vt sep* (NEW) **s~ lassen**, *s.* **stecken**. **S~pferd** *nt* hobby-horse
Steck|er *m* **-s,-** (*Electr*) plug. **S~ling** *m* **-s,-e** cutting. **S~nadel** *f* pin. **S~rübe** *f* swede
Steg *m* **-[e]s,-e** foot-bridge; (*Boots-*) landing-stage; (*Brillen-*) bridge. **S~reif** *m* **aus dem S~reif** extempore
stehen† *vi* (*haben*) stand; (*sich befinden*) be; (*still-*) be stationary; ⟨*Maschine, Uhr:*⟩ have stopped; **s~ bleiben** remain standing; ⟨*Gebäude:*⟩ be left standing; (*anhalten*) stop; ⟨*Motor:*⟩ stall; ⟨*Zeit:*⟩ stand still; **s~ lassen** leave [standing]; **sich** (*dat*) **einen Bart s~ lassen** grow a beard; **vor dem Ruin s~** face ruin; **zu jdm/etw s~** (*fig*) stand by s.o./sth; **gut s~** ⟨*Getreide, Aktien:*⟩ be doing well; ⟨*Chancen:*⟩ be good; **jdm [gut] s~** suit s.o.; **sich gut s~** be on good terms; **es steht 3 zu 1** the score is 3–1; **es steht schlecht um ihn** he is in a bad way. **S~** *nt* **-s** standing; **zum S~ bringen/kommen** bring/come to a standstill. **s~bleiben**† *vi sep* (*sein*) (NEW) **s~ bleiben**, *s.* **stehen**. **s~d** *a* standing; (*sich nicht bewegend*) stationary; ⟨*Gewässer*⟩ stagnant. **s~lassen**† *vt sep* (NEW) **s~ lassen**, *s.* **stehen**
Steh|lampe *f* standard lamp. **S~leiter** *f* step-ladder
stehlen† *vt/i* (*haben*) steal; **sich s~** steal, creep
Steh|platz *m* standing place. **S~vermögen** *nt* stamina, staying-power
steif *a* stiff, *adv* -ly. **S~heit** *f* - stiffness
Steig|bügel *m* stirrup. **S~eisen** *nt* crampon
steigen† *vi* (*sein*) climb; (*hochgehen*) rise, go up; ⟨*Schulden, Spannung:*⟩ mount; **s~ auf** (+ *acc*) climb on [to] ⟨*Stuhl*⟩; climb ⟨*Berg, Leiter*⟩; get on ⟨*Pferd, Fahrrad*⟩; **s~ in** (+ *acc*) climb into; get in ⟨*Auto*⟩; get on ⟨*Bus, Zug*⟩; **s~ aus** climb out of; get out

of ⟨*Bett, Auto*⟩; get off ⟨*Bus, Zug*⟩; **einen Drachen s~ lassen** fly a kite; **s~de Preise** rising prices

steiger|n *vt* increase; **sich s~n** increase; (*sich verbessern*) improve. **S~ung** *f* **-,-en** increase; improvement; (*Gram*) comparison

Steigung *f* **-,-en** gradient; (*Hang*) slope

steil *a* steep, *adv* -ly. **S~küste** *f* cliffs *pl*

Stein *m* **-[e]s,-e** stone; (*Ziegel-*) brick; (*Spiel-*) piece. **s~alt** *a* ancient. **S~bock** *m* ibex; (*Astr*) Capricorn. **S~bruch** *m* quarry. **S~garten** *m* rockery. **S~gut** *nt* earthenware. **s~hart** *a* rock-hard. **s~ig** *a* stony. **s~igen** *vt* stone. **S~kohle** *f* [hard] coal. **s~reich** *a* (*fam*) very rich. **S~schlag** *m* rock fall

Stelle *f* **-,-n** place; (*Fleck*) spot; (*Abschnitt*) passage; (*Stellung*) job, post; (*Büro*) office; (*Behörde*) authority; **kahle S~** bare patch; **auf der S~** immediately; **an deiner S~** in your place

stellen *vt* put; (*aufrecht*) stand; set ⟨*Wecker, Aufgabe*⟩; ask ⟨*Frage*⟩; make ⟨*Antrag, Forderung, Diagnose*⟩; **zur Verfügung s~** provide; **lauter/leiser s~** turn up/down; **kalt/warm s~** chill/keep hot; **sich s~** [go and] stand; give oneself up (**der Polizei** to the police); **sich tot/schlafend s~** pretend to be dead/asleep; **gut gestellt sein** be well off

Stellen|anzeige *f* job advertisement. **S~vermittlung** *f* employment agency. **s~weise** *adv* in places

Stellung *f* **-,-en** position; (*Arbeit*) job; **S~nehmen** make a statement (**zu** on). **s~slos** *a* jobless. **S~suche** *f* job-hunting

stellvertret|end *a* deputy ... □ *adv* as a deputy; **s~end für jdn** on s.o.'s behalf. **S~er** *m* deputy

Stellwerk *nt* signal-box

Stelzen *fpl* stilts. **s~** *vi* (*sein*) stalk

stemmen *vt* press; lift ⟨*Gewicht*⟩; **sich s~ gegen** brace oneself against

Stempel *m* **-s,-** stamp; (*Post-*) postmark; (*Präge-*) die; (*Feingehalts-*) hallmark. **s~n** *vt* stamp; hallmark ⟨*Silber*⟩; cancel ⟨*Marke*⟩

Stengel *m* **-s,-** (NEW) **Stängel**

Steno *f* **-** (*fam*) shorthand

Steno|gramm *nt* **-[e]s,-e** shorthand text. **S~graphie**, **S~grafie** *f* **-** shorthand. **s~graphieren**, **s~grafieren** *vt* take down in shorthand □ *vi* (*haben*) do shorthand. **S~typistin** *f* **-,-nen** shorthand typist

Steppdecke *f* quilt

Steppe *f* **-,-n** steppe

Stepptanz (**Steptanz**) *m* tap-dance

sterben† *vi* (*sein*) die (**an** + *dat* of); **im S~ liegen** be dying

sterblich *a* mortal. **S~e(r)** *m/f* mortal. **S~keit** *f* **-** mortality

stereo *adv* in stereo. **S~anlage** *f* stereo [system]

stereotyp *a* stereotyped

steril *a* sterile. **s~isieren** *vt* sterilize. **S~ität** *f* **-** sterility

Stern *m* **-[e]s,-e** star. **S~bild** *nt* constellation. **S~chen** *nt* **-s,-** asterisk. **S~kunde** *f* astronomy. **S~schnuppe** *f* **-,-n** shooting star. **S~warte** *f* **-,-n** observatory

stetig *a* steady, *adv* -ily

stets *adv* always

Steuer[1] *nt* **-s,-** steering-wheel; (*Naut*) helm; **am S~** at the wheel

Steuer[2] *f* **-,-n** tax

Steuer|bord *nt* **-[e]s** starboard [side]. **S~erklärung** *f* tax return. **s~frei** *a* & *adv* tax-free. **S~mann** *m* (*pl* **-leute**) helmsman; (*beim Rudern*) cox. **s~n** *vt* steer; (*Aviat*) pilot; (*Techn*) control □ *vi* (*haben*) be at the wheel/(*Naut*) helm □ (*sein*) head (**nach** for). **s~pflichtig** *a* taxable. **S~rad** *nt* steering-wheel.

S~ruder *nt* helm. **S~ung** *f* - steering; (*Techn*) controls *pl*. **S~zahler** *m* **-s,-** taxpayer

Stewardess /ˈstjuːɐdɛs/ *f* **-,-en** (**Stewardeß** *f* **-,-ssen**) air hostess, stewardess

Stich *m* **-[e]s,-e** prick; (*Messer-*) stab; (**S~***wunde*) stab wound; (*Bienen-*) sting; (*Mücken-*) bite; (*Schmerz*) stabbing pain; (*Näh-*) stitch; (*Kupfer-*) engraving; (*Kartenspiel*) trick; **S~ ins Rötliche** tinge of red; **jdn im S~ lassen** leave s.o. in the lurch; ⟨*Gedächtnis:*⟩ fail s.o. **s~eln** *vi* (*haben*) make snide remarks

Stich|flamme *f* jet of flame. **s~haltig** *a* valid. **S~probe** *f* spot check. **S~wort** *nt* (*pl* **-wörter**) headword; (*pl* **-worte**) (*Theat*) cue; **S~worte** notes

stick|en *vt/i* (*haben*) embroider. **S~erei** *f* - embroidery

stickig *a* stuffy

Stickstoff *m* nitrogen

Stiefbruder *m* stepbrother

Stiefel *m* **-s,-** boot

Stief|kind *nt* stepchild. **S~mutter** *f* stepmother. **S~mütterchen** *nt* **-s,-** pansy. **S~schwester** *f* stepsister. **S~sohn** *m* stepson. **S~tochter** *f* stepdaughter. **S~vater** *m* stepfather

Stiege *f* **-,-n** stairs *pl*

Stiel *m* **-[e]s,-e** handle; (*Blumen-, Gläser-*) stem; (*Blatt-*) stalk

Stier *m* **-[e]s,-e** bull; (*Astr*) Taurus

stieren *vi* (*haben*) stare

Stier|kampf *m* bullfight

Stift[1] *m* **-[e]s,-e** pin; (*Nagel*) tack; (*Blei-*) pencil; (*Farb-*) crayon

Stift[2] *nt* **-[e]s,-e** [endowed] foundation. **s~en** *vt* endow; (*spenden*) donate; create ⟨*Unheil, Verwirrung*⟩; bring about ⟨*Frieden*⟩. **S~er** *m* **-s,-** founder; (*Spender*) donor. **S~ung** *f* **-,-en** foundation; (*Spende*) donation

Stigma *nt* **-s** (*fig*) stigma

Stil *m* **-[e]s,-e** style; **in großem S~** in style. **s~isiert** *a* stylized. **s~istisch** *a* stylistic, *adv* -ally

still *a* quiet, *adv* -ly; (*reglos, ohne Kohlensäure*) still; (*heimlich*) secret, *adv* -ly; **der S~e Ozean** the Pacific; **im S~en (s~en)** secretly; (*bei sich*) inwardly. **S~e** *f* - quiet; (*Schweigen*) silence

Stilleben *nt* (NEW) **Stillleben**

stillegen *vt sep* (NEW) **stilllegen**

stillen *vt* satisfy; quench ⟨*Durst*⟩; stop ⟨*Schmerzen, Blutung*⟩; breast-feed ⟨*Kind*⟩

still|halten† *vi sep* (*haben*) keep still. **S~leben** *nt* still life. **s~legen** *vt sep* close down. **S~legung** *f* **-,-en** closure

Stillschweigen *nt* silence. **s~d** *a* silent, *adv* -ly; (*fig*) tacit, *adv* -ly

still|sitzen† *vi sep* (*haben*) sit still. **S~stand** *m* standstill; **zum S~stand bringen/kommen** stop. **s~stehen**† *vi sep* (*haben*) stand still; (*anhalten*) stop; ⟨*Verkehr:*⟩ be at a standstill

Stil|möbel *pl* reproduction furniture *sg*. **s~voll** *a* stylish, *adv* -ly

Stimm|bänder *ntpl* vocal cords. **s~berechtigt** *a* entitled to vote. **S~bruch** *m* **er ist im S~bruch** his voice is breaking

Stimme *f* **-,-n** voice; (*Wahl-*) vote

stimmen *vi* (*haben*) be right; (*wählen*) vote; **stimmt das?** is that right/(*wahr*) true? □ *vt* tune; **jdn traurig/fröhlich s~** make s.o. feel sad/happy

Stimm|enthaltung *f* abstention. **S~recht** *nt* right to vote

Stimmung *f* **-,-en** mood; (*Atmosphäre*) atmosphere. **s~svoll** *a* full of atmosphere

Stimmzettel *m* ballot-paper

stimulieren *vt* stimulate

stink|en† *vi* (*haben*) smell/(*stark*) stink (**nach** of). **S~tier** *nt* skunk

Stipendium *nt* **-s,-ien** scholarship; (*Beihilfe*) grant

Stirn *f* -,-en forehead; **die S~ bieten** (+ *dat*) (*fig*) defy. **S~runzeln** *nt* -s frown
stöbern *vi* (*haben*) rummage
stochern *vi* (*haben*) **s~ in** (+ *dat*) poke ⟨*Feuer*⟩; pick at ⟨*Essen*⟩; pick ⟨*Zähne*⟩
Stock1 *m* **-[e]s,⸚e** stick; (*Ski-*) pole; (*Bienen-*) hive; (*Rosen-*) bush; (*Reb-*) vine
Stock2 *m* **-[e]s,-** storey, floor. **S~bett** *nt* bunk-beds *pl.* **s~dunkel** *a* (*fam*) pitch-dark
stock|en *vi* (*haben*) stop; ⟨*Verkehr:*⟩ come to a standstill; ⟨*Person:*⟩ falter. **s~end** *a* hesitant, *adv* -ly. **s~taub** a (*fam*) stone-deaf. **S~ung** *f* **-,-en** hold-up
Stockwerk *nt* storey, floor
Stoff *m* **-[e]s,-e** substance; (*Tex*) fabric, material; (*Thema*) subject [matter]; (*Gesprächs-*) topic. **S~tier** *nt* soft toy. **S~wechsel** *m* metabolism
stöhnen *vi* (*haben*) groan, moan. **S~** *nt* **-s** groan, moan
stoisch *a* stoic, *adv* -ally
Stola *f* **-,-len** stole
Stollen *m* **-s,-** gallery; (*Kuchen*) stollen
stolpern *vi* (*sein*) stumble; **s~ über** (+ *acc*) trip over
stolz *a* proud (**auf** + *acc* of), *adv* -ly. **S~** *m* **-es** pride
stolzieren *vi* (*sein*) strut
stopfen *vt* stuff; (*stecken*) put; (*ausbessern*) darn □ *vi* (*haben*) be constipating; (*fam: essen*) guzzle
Stopp *m* **-s,-s** stop. **s~** *int* stop!
stoppel|ig *a* stubbly. **S~n** *fpl* stubble *sg*
stopp|en *vt* stop; (*Sport*) time □ *vi* (*haben*) stop. **S~schild** *nt* stop sign. **S~uhr** *f* stop-watch
Stöpsel *m* **-s,-** plug; (*Flaschen-*) stopper
Storch *m* **-[e]s,⸚e** stork
Store /ʃtoːɐ̯/ *m* **-s,-s** net curtain
stören *vt* disturb; disrupt ⟨*Rede, Sitzung*⟩; jam ⟨*Sender*⟩; (*missfallen*) bother; **stört es Sie, wenn ich rauche?** do you mind if I smoke? □ *vi* (*haben*) be a nuisance; **entschuldigen Sie, dass ich störe** I'm sorry to bother you
stornieren *vt* cancel
störrisch *a* stubborn, *adv* -ly
Störung *f* **-,-en** (*s.* **stören**) disturbance; disruption; (*Med*) trouble; (*Radio*) interference; **technische S~** technical fault
Stoß *m* **-es,⸚e** push, knock; (*mit Ellbogen*) dig; (*Hörner-*) butt; (*mit Waffe*) thrust; (*Schwimm-*) stroke; (*Ruck*) jolt; (*Erd-*) shock; (*Stapel*) stack, pile. **S~dämpfer** *m* **-s,-** shock absorber
stoßen† *vt* push, knock; (*mit Füßen*) kick; (*mit Kopf, Hörnern*) butt; (*an-*) poke, nudge; (*treiben*) thrust; **sich s~** knock oneself; **sich** (*dat*) **den Kopf s~** hit one's head □ *vi* (*haben*) push; **s~ an** (+ *acc*) knock against; (*angrenzen*) adjoin □ *vi* (*sein*) **s~ gegen** knock against; bump into ⟨*Tür*⟩; **s~ auf** (+ *acc*) bump into; (*entdecken*) come across; strike ⟨*Öl*⟩; (*fig*) meet with ⟨*Ablehnung*⟩
Stoß|stange *f* bumper. **S~verkehr** *m* rush-hour traffic. **S~zahn** *m* tusk. **S~zeit** *f* rush-hour
stottern *vt/i* (*haben*) stutter, stammer
Str. *abbr* (**Straße**) St
Straf|anstalt *f* prison. **S~arbeit** *f* (*Sch*) imposition. **s~bar** *a* punishable; **sich s~bar machen** commit an offence
Strafe *f* **-,-n** punishment; (*Jur & fig*) penalty; (*Geld-*) fine; (*Freiheits-*) sentence. **s~n** *vt* punish
straff *a* tight, taut. **s~en** *vt* tighten; **sich s~en** tighten
Strafgesetz *nt* criminal law
sträf|lich *a* criminal, *adv* -ly. **S~ling** *m* **-s,-e** prisoner
Straf|mandat *nt* (*Auto*) [parking/speeding] ticket. **S~porto** *nt*

excess postage. **S~predigt** *f* (*fam*) lecture. **S~raum** *m* penalty area. **S~stoss** (**S~stoß**) *m* penalty. **S~tat** *f* crime. **S~zettel** *m* (*fam*) = **S~mandat**

Strahl *m* **-[e]s,-en** ray; (*einer Taschenlampe*) beam; (*Wasser-*) jet. **s~en** *vi* (*haben*) shine; (*funkeln*) sparkle; (*lächeln*) beam. **S~enbehandlung** *f* radiotherapy. **s~end** *a* shining; sparkling; beaming; radiant ⟨*Schönheit*⟩. **S~entherapie** *f* radiotherapy. **S~ung** *f* - radiation

Strähn|e *f* **-,-n** strand. **s~ig** *a* straggly

stramm *a* tight, *adv* -ly; (*kräftig*) sturdy; (*gerade*) upright

Strampel|höschen /-sç-/ *nt* **-s,-** rompers *pl*. **s~n** *vi* (*haben*) ⟨*Baby:*⟩ kick

Strand *m* **-[e]s,⸚e** beach. **s~en** *vi* (*sein*) run aground; (*fig*) fail. **S~korb** *m* wicker beach-chair. **S~promenade** *f* promenade

Strang *m* **-[e]s,⸚e** rope

Strapaz|e *f* **-,-n** strain. **s~ieren** *vt* be hard on; tax ⟨*Nerven, Geduld*⟩. **s~ierfähig** *a* hard-wearing. **s~iös** *a* exhausting

Strass *m* **- & -es** (**Straß** *m* **- & -sses**) paste

Straße *f* **-,-n** road; (*in der Stadt auch*) street; (*Meeres-*) strait; **auf der S~** in the road/street. **S~nbahn** *f* tram, (*Amer*) streetcar. **S~nkarte** *f* road-map. **S~nlaterne** *f* street lamp. **S~nsperre** *f* road-block

Strat|egie *f* **-,-n** strategy. **s~egisch** *a* strategic, *adv* -ally

sträuben *vt* ruffle up ⟨*Federn*⟩; **sich s~** ⟨*Fell, Haar:*⟩ stand on end; (*fig*) resist

Strauch *m* **-[e]s, Sträucher** bush

straucheln *vi* (*sein*) stumble

Strauß[1] *m* **-es, Sträuße** bunch [of flowers]; (*Bukett*) bouquet

Strauß[2] *m* **-es,-e** ostrich

Strebe *f* **-,-n** brace, strut

streben *vi* (*haben*) strive (**nach** for) □ *vi* (*sein*) head (**nach/zu** for)

Streb|er *m* **-s,-** pushy person; (*Sch*) swot. **s~sam** *a* industrious

Strecke *f* **-,-n** stretch, section; (*Entfernung*) distance; (*Rail*) line; (*Route*) route

strecken *vt* stretch; (*aus-*) stretch out; (*gerade machen*) straighten; (*Culin*) thin down; **sich s~** stretch; (*sich aus-*) stretch out; **den Kopf aus dem Fenster s~** put one's head out of the window

Streich *m* **-[e]s,-e** prank, trick; **jdm einen S~ spielen** play a trick on s.o.

streicheln *vt* stroke

streichen† *vt* spread; (*weg-*) smooth; (*an-*) paint; (*aus-*) delete; (*kürzen*) cut □ *vi* (*haben*) **s~ über** (+ *acc*) stroke

Streicher *m* **-s,-** string-player; **die S~** the strings

Streichholz *nt* match. **S~schachtel** *f* matchbox

Streich|instrument *nt* stringed instrument. **S~käse** *m* cheese spread. **S~orchester** *nt* string orchestra. **S~ung** *f* **-,-en** deletion; (*Kürzung*) cut

Streife *f* **-,-n** patrol

streifen *vt* brush against; (*berühren*) touch; (*verletzen*) graze; (*fig*) touch on ⟨*Thema*⟩; (*ziehen*) slip (**über** + *acc* over); **mit dem Blick s~** glance at □ *vi* (*sein*) roam

Streifen *m* **-s,-** stripe; (*Licht-*) streak; (*auf der Fahrbahn*) line; (*schmales Stück*) strip

Streif|enwagen *m* patrol car. **s~ig** *a* streaky. **S~schuss** (**S~schuß**) *m* glancing shot; (*Wunde*) graze

Streik *m* **-s,-s** strike; **in den S~ treten** go on strike. **S~brecher** *m* strike-breaker, (*pej*) scab. **s~en** *vi* (*haben*) strike; (*fam*) refuse; (*versagen*) pack up. **S~ende(r)** *m* striker. **S~posten** *m* picket

Streit *m* **-[e]s,-e** quarrel; (*Auseinandersetzung*) dispute. **s~en**† *vr/i* (*haben*) **[sich] s~en** quarrel. **s~ig** *a* **jdm etw s~ig machen** dispute s.o.'s right to sth. **S~igkeiten** *fpl* quarrels. **S~kräfte** *fpl* armed forces. **s~süchtig** *a* quarrelsome

streng *a* strict; *adv* -ly; ⟨*Blick, Ton*⟩ stern, *adv* -ly; (*rau, nüchtern*) severe, *adv* -ly; ⟨*Geschmack*⟩ sharp; **s~ genommen** strictly speaking. **S~e** *f* - strictness; sternness; severity. **s~genommen** *adv* (NEW) **s~ genommen**, *s.* **streng**. **s~gläubig** *a* strict; (*orthodox*) orthodox. **s~stens** *adv* strictly

Stress *m* **-es,-e** (**Streß** *m* **-sses,-sse**) stress

stressig *a* (*fam*) stressful

streuen *vt* spread; (*ver-*) scatter; sprinkle ⟨*Zucker, Salz*⟩; **die Straßen s~** grit the roads

streunen *vi* (*sein*) roam; **s~der Hund** stray dog

Strich *m* **-[e]s,-e** line; (*Feder-, Pinsel-*) stroke; (*Morse-, Gedanken-*) dash; **gegen den S~** the wrong way; (*fig*) against the grain. **S~kode** *m* bar code. **S~punkt** *m* semicolon

Strick *m* **-[e]s,-e** cord; (*Seil*) rope; (*fam: Schlingel*) rascal

strick|en *vt/i* (*haben*) knit. **S~jacke** *f* cardigan. **S~leiter** *f* rope-ladder. **S~nadel** *f* knitting-needle. **S~waren** *fpl* knitwear *sg*. **S~zeug** *nt* knitting

striegeln *vt* groom

strikt *a* strict, *adv* -ly

strittig *a* contentious

Stroh *nt* **-[e]s** straw. **S~blumen** *fpl* everlasting flowers. **S~dach** *nt* thatched roof. **s~gedeckt** *a* thatched. **S~halm** *m* straw

Strolch *m* **-[e]s,-e** (*fam*) rascal

Strom *m* **-[e]s,¨e** river; (*Menschen-, Auto-, Blut-*) stream; (*Tränen-*) flood; (*Schwall*) torrent; (*Electr*) current, power; **gegen den S~** (*fig*) against the tide; **es regnet in Strömen** it is pouring with rain. **s~abwärts** *adv* downstream. **s~aufwärts** *adv* upstream

strömen *vi* (*sein*) flow; ⟨*Menschen, Blut:*⟩ stream, pour; **s~der Regen** pouring rain

Strom|kreis *m* circuit. **s~linienförmig** *a* streamlined. **S~sperre** *f* power cut

Strömung *f* **-,-en** current

Strophe *f* **-,-n** verse

strotzen *vi* (*haben*) be full (vor + *dat* of); **vor Gesundheit s~d** bursting with health

Strudel *m* **-s,-** whirlpool; (*SGer Culin*) strudel

Struktur *f* **-,-en** structure; (*Tex*) texture

Strumpf *m* **-[e]s,¨e** stocking; (*Knie-*) sock. **S~band** *nt* (*pl* **-bänder**) suspender, (*Amer*) garter. **S~bandgürtel** *m* suspender/(*Amer*) garter belt. **S~halter** *m* = **S~band. S~hose** *f* tights *pl*, (*Amer*) pantyhose

Strunk *m* **-[e]s,¨e** stalk; (*Baum-*) stump

struppig *a* shaggy

Stube *f* **-,-n** room. **s~nrein** *a* house-trained

Stuck *m* **-s** stucco

Stück *nt* **-[e]s,-e** piece; (*Zucker-*) lump; (*Seife*) tablet; (*Theater-*) play; (*Gegenstand*) item; (*Exemplar*) specimen; **20 S~ Vieh** 20 head of cattle; **ein S~** (*Entfernung*) some way; **aus freien S~en** voluntarily. **S~chen** *nt* **-s,-** [little] bit. **s~weise** *adv* bit by bit; (*einzeln*) singly

Student|(in) *m* **-en,-en** (*f* **-,-nen**) student. **s~isch** *a* student . . .

Studie /-i̯ə/ *f* **-,-n** study

studier|en *vt/i* (*haben*) study. **S~zimmer** *nt* study

Studio *nt* **-s,-s** studio

Studium *nt* **-s,-ien** studies *pl*

Stufe *f* -,-n step; (*Treppen-*) stair; (*Raketen-*) stage; (*Niveau*) level. **s~n** *vt* terrace; (*staffeln*) grade

Stuhl *m* -[e]s,⸚e chair; (*Med*) stools *pl*. **S~gang** *m* bowel movement

stülpen *vt* put (**über** + *acc* over)

stumm *a* dumb; (*schweigsam*) silent, *adv* -ly

Stummel *m* -s,- stump; (*Zigaretten-*) butt; (*Bleistift-*) stub

Stümper *m* -s,- bungler. **s~haft** *a* incompetent, *adv* -ly

stumpf *a* blunt; ⟨*Winkel*⟩ obtuse; (*glanzlos*) dull; (*fig*) apathetic, *adv* -ally. **S~** *m* -[e]s,⸚e stump

Stumpfsinn *m* apathy; (*Langweiligkeit*) tedium. **s~ig** *a* apathetic, *adv* -ally; (*langweilig*) tedious

Stunde *f* -,-n hour; (*Sch*) lesson

stunden *vt* **jdm eine Schuld s~** give s.o. time to pay a debt

Stunden|kilometer *mpl* kilometres per hour. **s~lang** *adv* for hours. **S~lohn** *m* hourly rate. **S~plan** *m* timetable. **s~weise** *adv* by the hour

stündlich *a & adv* hourly

Stups *m* -es,-e nudge; (*Schubs*) push. **s~en** *vt* nudge; (*schubsen*) push. **S~nase** *f* snub nose

stur *a* pigheaded; (*phlegmatisch*) stolid, *adv* -ly; (*unbeirrbar*) dogged, *adv* -ly

Sturm *m* -[e]s,⸚e gale; (*schwer*) storm; (*Mil*) assault

stürm|en *vi* (*haben*) ⟨*Wind:*⟩ blow hard; **es s~t** it's blowing a gale □ *vi* (*sein*) rush □ *vt* storm; (*bedrängen*) besiege. **S~er** *m* -s,- forward. **s~isch** *a* stormy; ⟨*Überfahrt*⟩ rough; (*fig*) tumultuous, *adv* -ly; (*ungestüm*) tempestuous, *adv* -ly

Sturz *m* -es,⸚e [heavy] fall; (*Preis-, Kurs-*) sharp drop; (*Pol*) overthrow

stürzen *vi* (*sein*) fall [heavily]; (*in die Tiefe*) plunge; ⟨*Preise, Kurse:*⟩ drop sharply; ⟨*Regierung:*⟩ fall; (*eilen*) rush □ *vt* throw; (*umkippen*) turn upside down; turn out ⟨*Speise, Kuchen*⟩; (*Pol*) overthrow, topple; **sich s~** throw oneself (**aus/in** + *acc* out of/into); **sich s~ auf** (+ *acc*) pounce on

Sturz|flug *m* (*Aviat*) dive. **S~helm** *m* crash-helmet

Stute *f* -,-n mare

Stütze *f* -,-n support; (*Kopf-, Arm-*) rest

stutzen *vi* (*haben*) stop short □ *vt* trim; (*Hort*) cut back; (*kupieren*) crop

stützen *vt* support; (*auf-*) rest; **sich s~ auf** (+ *acc*) lean on; (*beruhen*) be based on

Stutzer *m* -s,- dandy

stutzig *a* puzzled; (*misstrauisch*) suspicious

Stützpunkt *m* (*Mil*) base

Subjekt *nt* -[e]s,-e subject. **s~iv** *a* subjective, *adv* -ly

Subskription /-ˈtsi̯oːn/ *f* -,-en subscription

Substantiv *nt* -s,-e noun

Substanz *f* -,-en substance

subtil *a* subtle, *adv* -tly

subtra|hieren *vt* subtract. **S~ktion** /-ˈtsi̯oːn/ *f* -,-en subtraction

Subvention /-ˈtsi̯oːn/ *f* -,-en subsidy. **s~ieren** *vt* subsidize

subversiv *a* subversive

Such|e *f* - search; **auf der S~e nach** looking for. **s~en** *vt* look for; (*intensiv*) search for; seek ⟨*Hilfe, Rat*⟩; **'Zimmer gesucht'** 'room wanted' □ *vi* (*haben*) look, search (**nach** for). **S~er** *m* -s,- (*Phot*) viewfinder

Sucht *f* -,⸚e addiction; (*fig*) mania

süchtig *a* addicted. **S~e(r)** *m/f* addict

Süd *m* -[e]s south. **S~afrika** *nt* South Africa. **S~amerika** *nt* South America. **s~deutsch** *a* South German

Süden *m* -s south; **nach S~** south

Süd|frucht *f* tropical fruit. **s~lich** *a* southern; ⟨*Richtung*⟩ southerly □ *adv & prep* (+ *gen*) **s~lich [von] der Stadt** [to the] south of the town. **S~osten** *m* south-east. **S~pol** *m* South Pole. **s~wärts** *adv* southwards. **S~westen** *m* south-west

süffisant *a* smug, *adv* -ly

suggerieren *vt* suggest (*dat to*)

Suggest|ion /-'tjo:n/ *f* -,-en suggestion. **s~iv** *a* suggestive

Sühne *f* -,-n atonement; (*Strafe*) penalty. **s~n** *vt* atone for

Sultanine *f* -,-n sultana

Sülze *f* -,-n [meat] jelly; (*Schweinskopf-*) brawn

Summe *f* -,-n sum

summ|en *vi* (*haben*) hum; ⟨*Biene:*⟩ buzz □ *vt* hum. **S~er** *m* -s,- buzzer

summieren (sich) *vr* add up; (*sich häufen*) increase

Sumpf *m* -[e]s,-̈e marsh, swamp. **s~ig** *a* marshy

Sünd|e *f* -,-n sin. **S~enbock** *m* scapegoat. **S~er(in)** *m* -s,- (*f* -,-nen) sinner. **s~haft** *a* sinful. **s~igen** *vi* (*haben*) sin

super *inv a* (*fam*) great. **S~lativ** *m* -s,-e superlative. **S~markt** *m* supermarket

Suppe *f* -,-n soup. **S~nlöffel** *m* soup-spoon. **S~nteller** *m* soup-plate. **S~nwürfel** *m* stock cube

Surf|brett /'sø:ɐ̯f-/ *nt* surfboard. **S~en** *nt* -s surfing

surren *vi* (*haben*) whirr

süß *a* sweet, *adv* -ly. **S~e** *f* - sweetness. **s~en** *vt* sweeten. **S~igkeit** *f* -,-en sweet. **s~lich** *a* sweetish; (*fig*) sugary. **S~speise** *f* sweet. **S~stoff** *m* sweetener. **S~waren** *fpl* confectionery *sg*, sweets *pl*. **S~wasser-** *pref* freshwater ...

Sylvester *nt* -s = **Silvester**

Symbol *nt* -s,-e symbol. **S~ik** *f* - symbolism. **s~isch** *a* symbolic, *adv* -ally. **s~isieren** *vt* symbolize

Sym|metrie *f* - symmetry. **s~metrisch** *a* symmetrical, *adv* -ly

Sympathie *f* -,-n sympathy

sympath|isch *a* agreeable; ⟨*Person*⟩ likeable. **s~isieren** *vi* (*haben*) be sympathetic (mit to)

Symphonie *f* -,-n = **Sinfonie**

Symptom *nt* -s,-e symptom. **s~atisch** *a* symptomatic

Synagoge *f* -,-n synagogue

synchronisieren /zʏnkroni'zi:rən/ *vt* synchronize; dub ⟨*Film*⟩

Syndikat *nt* -[e]s,-e syndicate

Syndrom *nt* -s,-e syndrome

synonym *a* synonymous, *adv* -ly. **S~** *nt* -s,-e synonym

Syntax /'zʏntaks/ *f* - syntax

Synthe|se *f* -,-n synthesis. **S~tik** *nt* -s synthetic material. **s~tisch** *a* synthetic, *adv* -ally

Syrien /-i̯ən/ *nt* -s Syria

System *nt* -s,-e system. **s~atisch** *a* systematic, *adv* -ally

Szene *f* -,-n scene. **S~rie** *f* - scenery

T

Tabak *m* -s,-e tobacco

Tabelle *f* -,-n table; (*Sport*) league table

Tablett *nt* -[e]s,-s tray

Tablette *f* -,-n tablet

tabu *a* taboo. **T~** *nt* -s,-s taboo

Tacho *m* -s,-s, **Tachometer** *m & nt* speedometer

Tadel *m* -s,- reprimand; (*Kritik*) censure; (*Sch*) black mark. **t~los** *a* impeccable, *adv* -bly. **t~n** *vt* reprimand; censure. **t~nswert** *a* reprehensible

Tafel *f* -,-n (*Tisch, Tabelle*) table; (*Platte*) slab; (*Anschlag-, Hinweis-*) board; (*Gedenk-*) plaque; (*Schiefer-*) slate; (*Wand-*) blackboard; (*Bild-*) plate; (*Schokolade*) bar. **t~n** *vi* (*haben*) feast

Täfelung *f* - panelling

Tag *m* **-[e]s,-e** day; **Tag für Tag** day by day; **am T~e** in the daytime; **eines T~es** one day; **unter T~e** underground; **es wird Tag** it is getting light; **guten Tag!** good morning/afternoon!; **zu T~e treten** *od* **kommen/bringen** = **zutage treten** *od* **kommen/bringen**, *s.* **zutage**. **t~aus** *adv* **t~aus, t~ein** day in, day out

Tage|buch *nt* diary. **t~lang** *adv* for days

tagen *vi* (*haben*) meet; ⟨*Gericht:*⟩ sit; **es tagt** day is breaking

Tages|anbruch *m* daybreak. **T~ausflug** *m* day trip. **T~decke** *f* bedspread. **T~karte** *f* day ticket; (*Speise-*) menu of the day. **T~licht** *nt* daylight. **T~mutter** *f* child-minder. **T~ordnung** *f* agenda. **T~rückfahrkarte** *f* day return [ticket]. **T~zeit** *f* time of the day. **T~zeitung** *f* daily [news]paper

täglich *a & adv* daily; **zweimal t~** twice a day

tags *adv* by day; **t~ zuvor/darauf** the day before/after

tagsüber *adv* during the day

tag|täglich *a* daily □ *adv* every single day. **T~traum** *m* daydream. **T~undnachtgleiche** *f* **-,-n** equinox. **T~ung** *f* **-,-en** meeting; (*Konferenz*) conference

Taill|e /ˈtaljə/ *f* **-,-n** waist. **t~iert** /taˈjiːɐ̯t/ *a* fitted

Takt *m* **-[e]s,-e** tact; (*Mus*) bar; (*Tempo*) time; (*Rhythmus*) rhythm; **im T~** in time [to the music]. **T~gefühl** *nt* tact

Takt|ik *f* **-** tactics *pl*. **t~isch** *a* tactical, *adv* -ly

takt|los *a* tactless, *adv* -ly. **T~losigkeit** *f* **-** tactlessness. **T~stock** *m* baton. **t~voll** *a* tactful, *adv* -ly

Tal *nt* **-[e]s,-̈e** valley

Talar *m* **-s,-e** robe; (*Univ*) gown

Talent *nt* **-[e]s,-e** talent. **t~iert** *a* talented

Talg *m* **-s** tallow; (*Culin*) suet

Talsperre *f* dam

Tampon /tamˈpõː/ *m* **-s,-s** tampon

Tang *m* **-s** seaweed

Tangente *f* **-,-n** tangent; (*Straße*) bypass

Tank *m* **-s,-s** tank. **t~en** *vt* fill up with ⟨*Benzin*⟩ □ *vi* (*haben*) fill up with petrol; (*Aviat*) refuel; **ich muss t~en** I need petrol. **T~er** *m* **-s,-** tanker. **T~stelle** *f* petrol/(*Amer*) gas station. **T~wart** *m* **-[e]s,-e** petrol-pump attendant

Tanne *f* **-,-n** fir [tree]. **T~nbaum** *m* fir tree; (*Weihnachtsbaum*) Christmas tree. **T~nzapfen** *m* fir cone

Tante *f* **-,-n** aunt

Tantiemen /tanˈtjeːmən/ *pl* royalties

Tanz *m* **-es,-̈e** dance. **t~en** *vt/i* (*haben*) dance

Tänzer(in) *m* **-s,-** (*f* **-,-nen**) dancer

Tanz|lokal *nt* dance-hall. **T~musik** *f* dance music

Tapete *f* **-,-n** wallpaper. **T~nwechsel** *m* (*fam*) change of scene

tapezier|en *vt* paper. **T~er** *m* **-s,-** paperhanger, decorator

tapfer *a* brave, *adv* -ly. **T~keit** *f* **-** bravery

tappen *vi* (*sein*) walk hesitantly; (*greifen*) grope (**nach** for)

Tarif *m* **-s,-e** rate; (*Verzeichnis*) tariff

tarn|en *vt* disguise; (*Mil*) camouflage; **sich t~en** disguise/camouflage oneself. **T~ung** *f* **-** disguise; camouflage

Tasche *f* **-,-n** bag; (*Hosen-, Mantel-*) pocket. **T~nbuch** *nt* paper-back. **T~ndieb** *m* pick-pocket. **T~ngeld** *nt* pocket-money. **T~nlampe** *f* torch, (*Amer*) flashlight. **T~nmesser** *nt* penknife. **T~ntuch** *nt* handkerchief

Tasse *f* **-,-n** cup

Tastatur *f* **-,-en** keyboard

tast|bar *a* palpable. **T~e** *f* **-,-n** key; (*Druck-*) push-button. **t~en**

vi (*haben*) feel, grope (**nach** for) □ *vt* key in ⟨*Daten*⟩; **sich t~en** feel one's way (zu to). **t~end** *a* tentative, *adv* -ly

Tat *f* -,-en action; (*Helden-*) deed; (*Straf-*) crime; **in der Tat** indeed; **auf frischer Tat ertappt** caught in the act. **t~enlos** *adv* passively

Täter(in) *m* **-s,-** (*f* **-,-nen**) culprit; (*Jur*) offender

tätig *a* active, *adv* -ly; **t~ sein** work. **T~keit** *f* **-,-en** activity; (*Funktionieren*) action; (*Arbeit*) work, job

Tatkraft *f* energy

tätlich *a* physical, *adv* -ly; **t~werden** become violent. **T~keiten** *fpl* violence *sg*

Tatort *m* scene of the crime

tätowier|en *vt* tattoo. **T~ung** *f* **-,-en** tattooing; (*Bild*) tattoo

Tatsache *f* fact. **T~nbericht** *m* documentary

tatsächlich *a* actual, *adv* -ly

tätscheln *vt* pat

Tatze *f* **-,-n** paw

Tau¹ *m* **-[e]s** dew

Tau² *nt* **-[e]s,-e** rope

taub *a* deaf; (*gefühllos*) numb; ⟨*Nuss*⟩ empty; ⟨*Gestein*⟩ worthless

Taube *f* **-,-n** pigeon; (*Turtel-* & *fig*) dove. **T~nschlag** *m* pigeon-loft

Taub|heit *f* - deafness; (*Gefühllosigkeit*) numbness. **t~stumm** *a* deaf and dumb

tauch|en *vt* dip, plunge; (*unter-*) duck □ *vi* (*haben/sein*) dive/(*ein-*) plunge (**in** + *acc* into); (*auf-*) appear (**aus** out of). **T~er** *m* **-s,-** diver. **T~eranzug** *m* diving-suit. **T~sieder** *m* **-s,-** [small, portable] immersion heater

tauen *vi* (*sein*) melt, thaw □ *impers* **es taut** it is thawing

Tauf|becken *nt* font. **T~e** *f* **-,-n** christening, baptism. **t~en** *vt* christen, baptize. **T~pate** *m* godfather. **T~stein** *m* font

tauge|n *vi* (*haben*) **etwas/nichts t~n** **be good**/no good; **zu etw t~n/nicht t~n** be good/no good for sth. **T~nichts** *m* **-es,-e** good-for-nothing

tauglich *a* suitable; (*Mil*) fit. **T~keit** *f* - suitability; fitness

Taumel *m* **-s** daze; **wie im T~** in a daze. **t~n** *vi* (*sein*) stagger

Tausch *m* **-[e]s,-e** exchange, (*fam*) swap. **t~en** *vt* exchange/(*handeln*) barter (*gegen* for); **die Plätze t~en** change places □ *vi* (*haben*) swap (**mit etw** sth; **mit jdm** with s.o.)

täuschen *vt* deceive, fool; betray ⟨*Vertrauen*⟩; **sich t~** delude oneself; (*sich irren*) be mistaken □ *vi* (*haben*) be deceptive. **t~d** *a* deceptive; ⟨*Ähnlichkeit*⟩ striking

Tausch|geschäft *nt* exchange. **T~handel** *m* barter; (*T~geschäft*) exchange

Täuschung *f* **-,-en** deception; (*Irrtum*) mistake; (*Illusion*) delusion

tausend *inv a* one/a thousand. **T~** *nt* **-s,-e** thousand; **T~e** *od* **t~e von** thousands of. **T~füßler** *m* **-s,-** centipede. **t~ste(r, s)** *a* thousandth. **T~stel** *nt* **-s,-** thousandth

Tau|tropfen *m* dewdrop. **T~wetter** *nt* thaw. **T~ziehen** *nt* **-s** tug of war

Taxe *f* **-,-n** charge; (*Kur-*) tax; (*Taxi*) taxi

Taxi *nt* **-s,-s** taxi, cab

taxieren *vt* estimate/(*im Wert*) value (**auf** + *acc* at); (*fam: mustern*) size up

Taxi|fahrer *m* taxi driver. **T~stand** *m* taxi rank

Teakholz /ˈtiːk-/ *nt* teak

Team /tiːm/ *nt* **-s,-s** team

Techni|k *f* **-,-en** technology; (*Methode*) technique. **T~ker** *m* **-s,-** technician. **t~sch** *a* technical, *adv* -ly; (*technologisch*) technological, *adv* -ly; **T~sche Hochschule** Technical University

Techno|logie *f* **-,-n** technology. **t~logisch** *a* technological

Teckel *m* **-s,-** dachshund

Teddybär *m* teddy bear

Tee *m* **-s,-s** tea. **T~beutel** *m* tea-bag. **T~kanne** *f* teapot. **T~kessel** *m* kettle. **T~löffel** *m* teaspoon

Teer *m* **-s** tar. **t~en** *vt* tar

Tee|sieb *nt* tea-strainer. **T~tasse** *f* teacup. **T~wagen** *m* [tea] trolley

Teich *m* **-[e]s,-e** pond

Teig *m* **-[e]s,-e** pastry; (*Knet-*) dough; (*Rühr-*) mixture; (*Pfannkuchen-*) batter. **T~rolle** *f*, **T~roller** *m* rolling-pin. **T~waren** *fpl* pasta *sg*

Teil *m* **-[e]s,-e** part; (*Bestand-*) component; (*Jur*) party; **der vordere T~** the front part; **zum T~** partly; **zum großen/größten T~** for the most part □ *m & nt* **-[e]s** (*Anteil*) share; **sein[en] T~beitragen** do one's share; **ich für mein[en] T~** for my part □ *nt* **-[e]s,-e** part; (*Ersatz-*) spare part; (*Anbau-*) unit

teil|bar *a* divisible. **T~chen** *nt* **-s,-** particle. **t~en** *vt* divide; (*auf-*) share out; (*gemeinsam haben*) share; (*Pol*) partition ⟨*Land*⟩; **sich** (*dat*) **etw [mit jdm] t~en** share sth [with s.o.]; **sich t~en** divide; (*sich gabeln*) fork; ⟨*Vorhang:*⟩ open; ⟨*Meinungen:*⟩ differ □ *vi* (*haben*) share

teilhab|en† *vi sep* (*haben*) share (**an etw** *dat* sth). **T~er** *m* **-s,-** (*Comm*) partner

Teilnahm|e *f* - participation; (*innere*) interest; (*Mitgefühl*) sympathy. **t~slos** *a* apathetic, *adv* -ally

teilnehm|en† *vi sep* (*haben*) **t~en an** (+ *dat*) take part in; (*mitfühlen*) share [in]. **T~er(in)** *m* **-s,-** (*f* **-,-nen**) participant; (*an Wettbewerb*) competitor

teil|s *adv* partly. **T~ung** *f* **-,-en** division; (*Pol*) partition. **t~weise** *a* partial □ *adv* partially, partly; (*manchmal*) in some cases. **T~zahlung** *f* part-payment; (*Rate*) instalment. **T~zeitbeschäftigung** *f* part-time job

Teint /tɛ̃:/ *m* **-s,-s** complexion

Telefax *nt* fax

Telefon *nt* **-s,-e** [tele]phone. **T~anruf** *m*, **T~at** *nt* **-[e]s,-e** [tele]phone call. **T~buch** *nt* [tele]phone book. **t~ieren** *vi* (*haben*) [tele]phone

telefon|isch *a* [tele]phone ... □ *adv* by [tele]phone. **T~ist(in)** *m* **-en,-en** (*f* **-,-nen**) telephonist. **T~karte** *f* phone card. **T~nummer** *f* [tele]phone number. **T~zelle** *f* [tele]phone box

Telegraf *m* **-en,-en** telegraph. **T~enmast** *m* telegraph pole. **t~ieren** *vi* (*haben*) send a telegram. **t~isch** *a* telegraphic □ *adv* by telegram

Telegramm *nt* **-s,-e** telegram

Telegraph *m* **-en,-en** = **Telegraf**

Teleobjektiv *nt* telephoto lens

Telepathie *f* - telepathy

Telephon *nt* **-s,-e** = **Telefon**

Teleskop *nt* **-s,-e** telescope. **t~isch** *a* telescopic

Telex *nt* **-,-[e]** telex. **t~en** *vt* telex

Teller *m* **-s,-** plate

Tempel *m* **-s,-** temple

Temperament *nt* **-s,-e** temperament; (*Lebhaftigkeit*) vivacity. **t~los** *a* dull. **t~voll** *a* vivacious; ⟨*Pferd*⟩ spirited

Temperatur *f* **-,-en** temperature

Tempo *nt* **-s,-s** speed; (*Mus: pl* **-pi**) tempo; **T~ [T~]!** hurry up!

Tend|enz *f* **-,-en** trend; (*Neigung*) tendency. **t~ieren** *vi* (*haben*) tend (**zu** towards)

Tennis *nt* - tennis. **T~platz** *m* tennis-court. **T~schläger** *m* tennis-racket

Tenor *m* **-s,-̈e** (*Mus*) tenor

Teppich *m* **-s,e** carpet. **T~boden** *m* fitted carpet

Termin *m* **-s,-e** date; (*Arzt-*) appointment; **[letzter] T~** deadline. **T~kalender** *m* [appointments] diary
Terminologie *f* **-,-n** terminology
Terpentin *nt* **-s** turpentine
Terrain /tɛ'rɛ̃:/ *nt* **-s,-s** terrain
Terrasse *f* **-,-n** terrace
Terrier /'tɛri̯ɐ/ *m* **-s,-** terrier
Terrine *f* **-,-n** tureen
Territorium *nt* **-s,-ien** territory
Terror *m* **-s** terror. **t~isieren** *vt* terrorize. **T~ismus** *m* **-** terrorism. **T~ist** *m* **-en,-en** terrorist
Terzett *nt* **-[e]s,-e** [vocal] trio
Tesafilm (P) *m* ≈ Sellotape (P)
Test *m* **-[e]s,-s** & **-e** test
Testament *nt* **-[e]s,-e** will; **Altes/ Neues T~** Old/New Testament. **T~svollstrecker** *m* **-s,-** executor
testen *vt* test
Tetanus *m* **-** tetanus
teuer *a* expensive, *adv* -ly; (*lieb*) dear; **wie t~?** how much? **T~ung** *f* **-,-en** rise in prices
Teufel *m* **-s,-** devil; **zum T~!** (*sl*) damn [it]! **T~skreis** *m* vicious circle
teuflisch *a* fiendish
Text *m* **-[e]s,-e** text; (*Passage*) passage; (*Bild-*) caption; (*Lied-*) lyrics *pl*, words *pl*; (*Opern-*) libretto. **T~er** *m* **-s,-** copy-writer; (*Schlager-*) lyricist
Textilien /-i̯ən/ *pl* textiles; (*Textilwaren*) textile goods. **T~industrie** *f* textile industry
Textverarbeitungssystem *nt* word processor
TH *abbr* = Technische Hochschule
Theater *nt* **-s,-** theatre; (*fam: Getue*) fuss, to-do; **T~ spielen** act; (*fam*) put on an act. **T~kasse** *f* box-office. **T~stück** *nt* play
theatralisch *a* theatrical, *adv* -ly
Theke *f* **-,-n** bar; (*Ladentisch*) counter
Thema *nt* **-s,-men** subject; (*Mus*) theme
Themse *f* **-** Thames
Theologe *m* **-n,-n** theologian. **T~gie** *f* **-** theology
theoretisch *a* theoretical, *adv* -ly. **T~ie** *f* **-,-n** theory
Therapeut|(in) *m* **-en,-en** (*f* **-,-nen**) therapist. **t~isch** *a* therapeutic
Therapie *f* **-,-n** therapy
Thermalbad *nt* thermal bath; (*Ort*) thermal spa. **T~quelle** *f* thermal spring
Thermometer *nt* **-s,-** thermometer
Thermosflasche (P) *f* Thermos flask (P)
Thermostat *m* **-[e]s,-e** thermostat
These *f* **-,-n** thesis
Thrombose *f* **-,-n** thrombosis
Thron *m* **-[e]s,-e** throne. **t~en** *vi* (*haben*) sit [in state]. **T~folge** *f* succession. **T~folger** *m* **-s,-** heir to the throne
Thunfisch *m* tuna
Thymian *m* **-s** thyme
Tick *m* **-s,-s** (*fam*) quirk; **einen T~haben** be crazy
ticken *vi* (*haben*) tick
tief *a* deep; (*t~ liegend, niedrig*) low; (*t~gründig*) profound; **t~er Teller** soup-plate; **im t~sten Winter** in the depths of winter □ *adv* deep; low; (*sehr*) deeply, profoundly; ⟨*schlafen*⟩ soundly; **t~ greifend** (*fig*) radical, *adv* -ly; **t~ schürfend** (*fig*) profound. **T~** *nt* **-s,-s** (*Meteorol*) depression. **T~bau** *m* civil engineering. **T~e** *f* **-,-n** depth
Tiefebene *f* [lowland] plain. **T~garage** *f* underground car park. **t~gekühlt** *a* [deep-]frozen. **t~greifend** *a* (NEW) **t~ greifend**, s. **tief**. **t~gründig** *a* (*fig*) profound
Tiefkühlfach *nt* freezer compartment. **T~kost** *f* frozen food. **T~truhe** *f* deep-freeze

Tief|land *nt* lowlands *pl.* **T~punkt** *m* (*fig*) low. **t~schürfend** *a* (NEW) **t~ schürfend,** *s.* **tief. t~sinnig** (*fig*) profound; (*trübsinnig*) melancholy. **T~stand** *m* (*fig*) low

Tiefsttemperatur *f* minimum temperature

Tier *nt* **-[e]s,-e** animal. **T~arzt** *m*, **T~ärztin** *f* vet, veterinary surgeon. **T~garten** *m* zoo. **t~isch** *a* animal ...; (*fig: roh*) bestial. **T~kreis** *m* zodiac. **T~kreiszeichen** *nt* sign of the zodiac. **T~kunde** *f* zoology. **T~quälerei** *f* cruelty to animals

Tiger *m* **-s,-** tiger

tilgen *vt* pay off ⟨*Schuld*⟩; (*streichen*) delete; (*fig: auslöschen*) wipe out

Tinte *f* **-,-n** ink. **T~nfisch** *m* squid

Tipp (Tip) *m* **-s,-s** (*fam*) tip

tipp|en *vt* (*fam*) type □ *vi* (*haben*) (*berühren*) touch **(auf/an etw** *acc* sth); (*fam: Maschine schreiben*) type; **t~en auf** (+ *acc*) (*fam: wetten*) bet on. **T~fehler** *m* (*fam*) typing error. **T~schein** *m* pools/lottery coupon

tipptopp *a* (*fam*) immaculate, *adv* -ly

Tirol *nt* **-s** [the] Tyrol

Tisch *m* **-[e]s,-e** table; (*Schreib-*) desk; **nach T~** after the meal. **T~decke** *f* table-cloth. **T~gebet** *nt* grace. **T~ler** *m* **-s,-** joiner; (*Möbel-*) cabinet-maker. **T~rede** *f* after-dinner speech. **T~tennis** *nt* table tennis. **T~tuch** *nt* table-cloth

Titel *m* **-s,-** title. **T~rolle** *f* title-role

Toast /to:st/ *m* **-[e]s,-e** toast; (*Scheibe*) piece of toast; **einen T~ ausbringen** propose a toast **(auf** + *acc* to). **T~er** *m* **-s,-** toaster

tob|en *vi* (*haben*) rave; ⟨*Sturm:*⟩ rage; ⟨*Kinder:*⟩ play boisterously □ *vi* (*sein*) rush. **t~süchtig** *a* raving mad

Tochter *f* **-,¨** daughter. **T~gesellschaft** *f* subsidiary

Tod *m* **-es** death. **t~blass (t~blaß)** *a* deathly pale. **t~ernst** *a* deadly serious, *adv* -ly

Todes|angst *f* mortal fear. **T~anzeige** *f* death announcement; (*Zeitungs-*) obituary. **T~fall** *m* death. **T~opfer** *nt* fatality, casualty. **T~strafe** *f* death penalty. **T~urteil** *nt* death sentence

Tod|feind *m* mortal enemy. **t~krank** *a* dangerously ill

tödlich *a* fatal, *adv* -ly; ⟨*Gefahr*⟩ mortal, *adv* -ly; (*groß*) deadly; **t~gelangweilt** bored to death

tod|müde *a* dead tired. **t~sicher** *a* (*fam*) dead certain □ *adv* for sure. **T~sünde** *f* deadly sin. **t~unglücklich** *a* desperately unhappy

Toilette /tọa'lɛtə/ *f* **-,-n** toilet. **T~npapier** *nt* toilet paper

toler|ant *a* tolerant. **T~anz** *f* - tolerance. **t~ieren** *vt* tolerate

toll *a* crazy, mad; (*fam: prima*) fantastic; (*schlimm*) awful □ *adv* beautifully; (*sehr*) very; (*schlimm*) badly. **t~en** *vi* (*haben/sein*) romp. **t~kühn** *a* foolhardy. **t~patschig** *a* clumsy, *adv* -ily. **T~wut** *f* rabies. **t~wütig** *a* rabid

tolpatschig *a* (NEW) **tollpatschig**

Tölpel *m* **-s,-** fool

Tomate *f* **-,-n** tomato. **T~nmark** *nt* tomato purée

Tombola *f* **-,-s** raffle

Ton[1] *m* **-[e]s** clay

Ton[2] *m* **-[e]s,¨e** tone; (*Klang*) sound; (*Note*) note; (*Betonung*) stress; (*Farb-*) shade; **der gute Ton** (*fig*) good form. **T~abnehmer** *m* **-s,-** pick-up. **t~angebend** *a* (*fig*) leading. **T~art** *f* tone [of voice]; (*Mus*) key. **T~band** *nt* (*pl* **-bänder**) tape. **T~bandgerät** *nt* tape recorder

tönen *vi* (*haben*) sound □ *vt* tint

Ton|fall *m* tone [of voice]: (*Akzent*) intonation. **T~leiter** *f* scale. **t~los** *a* toneless, *adv* -ly
Tonne *f* -,-**n** barrel, cask: (*Müll-*) bin; (*Maß*) tonne, metric ton
Topf *m* -**[e]s,¨e** pot; (*Koch-*) pan
Topfen *m* -**s** (Aust) ≈ curd cheese
Töpfer|(in) *m* -**s,-** (*f* -,-**nen**) potter. **T~ei** *f* -,-**en** pottery
Töpferwaren *fpl* pottery *sg*
Topf|lappen *m* oven-cloth. **T~pflanze** *f* potted plant
Tor[1] *m* -**en,-en** fool
Tor[2] *nt* -**[e]s,-e** gate; (*Einfahrt*) gateway; (*Sport*) goal. **T~bogen** *m* archway
Torf *m* -**s** peat
Torheit *f* -,-**en** folly
Torhüter *m* -**s,-** goalkeeper
töricht *a* foolish, *adv* -ly
torkeln *vi* (*sein/habe*) stagger
Tornister *m* -**s,-** knapsack; (*Sch*) satchel
torp|edieren *vt* torpedo. **T~edo** *m* -**s,-s** torpedo
Torpfosten *m* goal-post
Torte *f* -,-**n** gateau; (*Obst-*) flan
Tortur *f* -,-**en** torture
Torwart *m* -**s,-e** goalkeeper
tosen *vi* (*haben*) roar; ⟨*Sturm:*⟩ rage
tot *a* dead; **tot geboren** stillborn; **sich tot stellen** pretend to be dead; **einen t~en** Punkt haben (*fig*) be at a low ebb
total *a* total, *adv* -ly. **t~itär** *a* totalitarian. **T~schaden** *m* ≈ write-off
Tote|(r) *m/f* dead man/woman; (*Todesopfer*) fatality; **die T~n** the dead *pl*
töten *vt* kill
toten|blass (**totenblaß**) *a* deathly pale. **T~gräber** *m* -**s,-** grave-digger. **T~kopf** *m* skull. **T~schein** *m* death certificate. **T~stille** *f* deathly silence
tot|fahren† *vt sep* run over and kill. **t~geboren** *a* (NEW) **tot geboren**, *s.* **tot**. **t~lachen (sich)** *vt sep* (*fam*) be in stitches

Toto *nt & m* -**s** football pools *pl*. **T~schein** *m* pools coupon
tot|schießen† *vt sep* shoot dead. **T~schlag** *m* (*Jur*) manslaughter. **t~schlagen**† *vt sep* kill. **t~schweigen**† *vt sep* (*fig*) hush up. **t~stellen (sich)** *vr sep* (NEW) **tot stellen (sich)**, *s.* **tot**
Tötung *f* -,-**en** killing; **fahrlässige T~** (*Jur*) manslaughter
Toup|et /tu'pe:/ *nt* -**s,-s** toupee. **t~ieren** *vt* back-comb
Tour /tu:ɐ̯/ *f* -,-**en** tour; (*Ausflug*) trip; (*Auto-*) drive; (*Rad-*) ride; (*Strecke*) distance; (*Techn*) revolution; (*fam: Weise*) way; **auf vollen T~en** at full speed; (*fam*) flat out
Touris|mus /tu'rɪsmʊs/ *m* - tourism. **T~t** *m* -**en,-en** tourist
Tournee /tʊr'ne:/ *f* -,-**n** tour
Trab *m* -**[e]s** trot
Trabant *m* -**en,-en** satellite
traben *vi* (*haben/sein*) trot
Tracht *f* -,-**en** [national] costume; **eine T~Prügel** a good hiding
trachten *vi* (*haben*) strive (**nach** for); **jdm nach dem Leben t~** be out to kill s.o
trächtig *a* pregnant
Tradition /-'tsi̯o:n/ *f* -,-**en** tradition. **t~ell** *a* traditional, *adv* -ly
Trafik *f* -,-**en** (*Aust*) tobacconist's
Trag|bahre *f* stretcher. **t~bar** *a* portable; ⟨*Kleidung*⟩ wearable; (*erträglich*) bearable
träge *a* sluggish, *adv* -ly; (*faul*) lazy, *adv* -ily; (*Phys*) inert
tragen† *vt* carry; (*an-/ aufhaben*) wear; (*fig*) bear □ *vi* (*haben*) carry; **gut t~** ⟨*Baum:*⟩ produce a good crop; **schwer t~** carry a heavy load; (*fig*) be deeply affected (**an** + *dat* by). **t~d** *a* (*Techn*) load-bearing; (*trächtig*) pregnant
Träger *m* -**s,-** porter; (*Inhaber*) bearer; (*eines Ordens*) holder; (*Bau-*) beam; (*Stahl-*) girder; (*Achsel-*) [shoulder] strap. **T~kleid** *nt* pinafore dress

Trag|etasche *f* carrier bag. **T~fläche** *f* (*Aviat*) wing; (*Naut*) hydrofoil. **T~flächenboot, T~flügelboot** *nt* hydrofoil

Trägheit *f* - sluggishness; (*Faulheit*) laziness; (*Phys*) inertia

Trag|ik *f* - tragedy. **t~isch** *a* tragic, *adv* -ally

Tragödie /-i̯ə/ *f* -,-n tragedy

Tragweite *f* range; (*fig*) consequence

Train|er /ˈtrɛːnɐ/ *m* -s,- trainer; (*Tennis-*) coach. **t~ieren** *vt/i* (*haben*) train

Training /ˈtrɛːnɪŋ/ *nt* -s training. **T~sanzug** *m* tracksuit. **T~sschuhe** *mpl* trainers

Trakt *m* -[e]s,-e section; (*Flügel*) wing

traktieren *vi* (*haben*) **mit Schlägen/Tritten t~** hit/kick

Traktor *m* -s,-en /-ˈtoːrən/ tractor

trampeln *vi* (*haben*) stamp one's feet □ *vi* (*sein*) trample (**auf** + *acc* on) □ *vt* trample

trampen /ˈtrɛmpən/ *vi* (*sein*) (*fam*) hitch-hike

Trance /ˈtrɑ̃ːsə/ *f* -,-n trance

Tranchier|messer /trɑ̃ˈʃiːɐ̯-/ *nt* carving-knife. **t~en** *vt* carve

Träne *f* -,-n tear. **t~n** *vi* (*haben*) water. **T~ngas** *nt* tear-gas

Tränke *f* -,-n watering-place; (*Trog*) drinking-trough. **t~n** *vt* water ⟨*Pferd*⟩; (*nässen*) soak (**mit** with)

Trans|aktion *f* transaction. **T~fer** *m* -s,-s transfer. **T~formator** *m* -s,-en /-ˈtoːrən/ transformer. **T~fusion** *f* -,-en [blood] transfusion

Transistor *m* -,-en /-ˈtoːrən/ transistor

Transit /tranˈziːt/ *m* -s transit

transitiv *a* transitive, *adv* -ly

Transparent *nt* -[e]s,-e banner; (*Bild*) transparency

transpirieren *vi* (*haben*) perspire

Transplantation /-ˈtsi̯oːn/ *f* -,-en transplant

Transport *m* -[e]s,-e transport; (*Güter-*) consignment. **t~ieren** *vt* transport. **T~mittel** *nt* means of transport

Trapez *nt* -es,-e trapeze; (*Geom*) trapezium

Tratsch *m* -[e]s (*fam*) gossip. **t~en** *vi* (*haben*) (*fam*) gossip

Tratte *f* -,-n (*Comm*) draft

Traube *f* -,-n bunch of grapes; (*Beere*) grape; (*fig*) cluster. **T~nzucker** *m* glucose

trauen *vi* (*haben*) (+ *dat*) trust; **ich traute kaum meinen Augen** I could hardly believe my eyes □ *vt* marry; **sich t~** dare (**etw zu tun** [to] do sth); venture (**in** + *acc*/**aus** into/out of)

Trauer *f* - mourning; (*Schmerz*) grief (**um** for); **T~ tragen** be [dressed] in mourning. **T~fall** *m* bereavement. **T~feier** *f* funeral service. **T~marsch** *m* funeral march. **t~n** *vi* (*haben*) grieve; **t~n um** mourn [for]. **T~spiel** *nt* tragedy. **T~weide** *f* weeping willow

traulich *a* cosy, *adv* -ily

Traum *m* -[e]s, **Träume** dream

Trau|ma *nt* -s,-men trauma. **t~matisch** *a* traumatic

träumen *vt/i* (*haben*) dream

traumhaft *a* dreamlike; (*schön*) fabulous, *adv* -ly

traurig *a* sad, *adv* -ly; (*erbärmlich*) sorry. **T~keit** *f* - sadness

Trau|ring *m* wedding-ring. **T~schein** *m* marriage certificate. **T~ung** *f* -,-en wedding [ceremony]

Treck *m* -s,-s trek

Trecker *m* -s,- tractor

Treff *nt* -s,-s (*Karten*) spades *pl*

treff|en† *vt* hit; ⟨*Blitz:*⟩ strike; (*fig: verletzen*) hurt; (*zusammenkommen mit*) meet; take ⟨*Maßnahme*⟩; **sich t~en** meet (**mit jdm** s.o.); **sich gut t~en** be convenient; **es**

traf sich, dass it so happened that; **es gut/schlecht t~en** be lucky/unlucky □ *vi* (*haben*) hit the target; **t~en auf** (+ *acc*) meet; (*fig*) meet with. **T~en** *nt* **-s,-** meeting. **t~end** *a* apt, *adv* -ly; ⟨*Ähnlichkeit*⟩ striking. **T~er** *m* **-s,-** hit; (*Los*) winner. **T~punkt** *m* meeting-place

treiben† *vt* drive; (*sich befassen mit*) do; carry on ⟨*Gewerbe*⟩; indulge in ⟨*Luxus*⟩; get up to ⟨*Unfug*⟩; **Handel t~** trade; **Blüten/Blätter t~** come into flower/leaf; **zur Eile t~** hurry [up]; **was treibt ihr da?** (*fam*) what are you up to? □ *vi* (*sein*) drift; (*schwimmen*) float □ *vi* (*haben*) (*Bot*) sprout. **T~** *nt* **-s** activity; (*Getriebe*) bustle

Treib|haus *nt* hothouse. **T~hauseffekt** *m* greenhouse effect. **T~holz** *nt* driftwood. **T~riemen** *m* transmission belt. **T~sand** *m* quicksand. **T~stoff** *m* fuel

Trend *m* **-s,-s** trend

trenn|bar *a* separable. **t~en** *vt* separate/(*abmachen*) detach (**von** from); divide, split ⟨*Wort*⟩; **sich t~en** separate; (*auseinander gehen*) part; **sich t~en von** leave; (*fortgeben*) part with. **T~ung** *f* **-,-en** separation; (*Silben-*) division. **T~ungsstrich** *m* hyphen. **T~wand** *f* partition

trepp|ab *adv* downstairs. **t~auf** *adv* upstairs

Treppe *f* **-,-n** stairs *pl*; (*Außen-*) steps *pl*; **eine T~** a flight of stairs/steps. **T~nflur** *m* landing. **T~ngeländer** *nt* banisters *pl*. **T~nhaus** *nt* stairwell. **T~nstufe** *f* stair, step

Tresor *m* **-s,-e** safe

Tresse *f* **-,-n** braid

Treteimer *m* pedal bin

treten† *vi* (*sein/haben*) step; (*versehentlich*) tread; (*ausschlagen*) kick (**nach** at); **in Verbindung t~** get in touch □ *vt* tread; (*mit Füßen*) kick

treu *a* faithful, *adv* -ly; (*fest*) loyal, *adv* -ly. **T~e** *f* - faithfulness; loyalty; (*eheliche*) fidelity. **T~händer** *m* **-s,-** trustee. **t~herzig** *a* trusting, *adv* -ly; (*arglos*) innocent, *adv* -ly. **t~los** *a* disloyal, *adv* -ly; (*untreu*) unfaithful

Tribüne *f* **-,-n** platform; (*Zuschauer-*) stand

Tribut *m* **-[e]s,-e** tribute; (*Opfer*) toll

Trichter *m* **-s,-** funnel; (*Bomben-*) crater

Trick *m* **-s,-s** trick. **T~film** *m* cartoon. **t~reich** *a* clever

Trieb *m* **-[e]s,-e** drive, urge; (*Instinkt*) instinct; (*Bot*) shoot. **T~täter, T~verbrecher** *m* sex offender. **T~werk** *nt* (*Aviat*) engine; (*Uhr-*) mechanism

trief|en† *vi* (*haben*) drip; (*nass sein*) be dripping (**von/vor** + *dat* with). **t~nass (t~naß)** *a* dripping wet

triftig *a* valid

Trigonometrie *f* - trigonometry

Trikot[1] /tri'ko:/ *m* **-s** (*Tex*) jersey

Trikot[2] *nt* **-s,-s** (*Sport*) jersey; (*Fußball-*) shirt

Trimester *nt* **-s,-** term

Trimm-dich *nt* **-s** keep-fit

trimmen *vt* trim; (*fam*) train; tune ⟨*Motor*⟩; **sich t~** keep fit

trink|bar *a* drinkable. **t~en**† *vt/i* (*haben*) drink. **T~er(in)** *m* **-s,-** (*f* **-,-nen**) alcoholic. **T~geld** *nt* tip. **T~halm** *m* [drinking-]straw. **T~spruch** *m* toast. **T~wasser** *nt* drinking-water

Trio *nt* **-s,-s** trio

trippeln *vi* (*sein*) trip along

trist *a* dreary

Tritt *m* **-[e]s,-e** step; (*Fuß-*) kick. **T~brett** *nt* step. **T~leiter** *f* step-ladder

Triumph *m* **-s,-e** triumph. **t~ieren** *vi* (*haben*) rejoice; **t~ieren über** (+ *acc*) triumph over. **t~ierend** *a* triumphant, *adv* -ly

trocken *a* dry, *adv* drily. **T~haube** *f* drier. **T~heit** *f* -,-en dryness; (*Dürre*) drought. **t~legen** *vt sep* change ⟨*Baby*⟩; drain ⟨*Sumpf*⟩. **T~milch** *f* powdered milk

trockn|en *vt/i* (*sein*) dry. **T~er** *m* -s,- drier

Troddel *f* -,-n tassel

Trödel *m* -s (*fam*) junk. **T~laden** *m* (*fam*) junk-shop. **T~markt** *m* (*fam*) flea market. **t~n** *vi* (*haben*) dawdle

Trödler *m* -s,- (*fam*) slowcoach; (*Händler*) junk-dealer

Trog *m* -[e]s,¨e trough

Trommel *f* -,-n drum. **T~fell** *nt* ear-drum. **t~n** *vi* (*haben*) drum

Trommler *m* -s,- drummer

Trompete *f* -,-n trumpet. **T~r** *m* -s,- trumpeter

Tropen *pl* tropics

Tropf *m* -[e]s,-e (*Med*) drip

tröpfeln *vt/i* (*sein/haben*) drip; **es tröpfelt** it's spitting with rain

tropfen *vt/i* (*sein/haben*) drip. **T~** *m* -s,- drop; (*fallend*) drip. **t~weise** *adv* drop by drop

tropf|nass (**tropfnaß**) *a* dripping wet. **T~stein** *m* stalagmite; (*hängend*) stalactite

Trophäe /tro'fɛːə/ *f* -,-n trophy

tropisch *a* tropical

Trost *m* -[e]s consolation, comfort

tröst|en *vt* console, comfort; **sich t~en** console oneself. **t~lich** *a* comforting

trost|los *a* desolate; (*elend*) wretched; (*reizlos*) dreary. **T~preis** *m* consolation prize. **t~reich** *a* comforting

Trott *m* -s amble; (*fig*) routine

Trottel *m* -s,- (*fam*) idiot

trotten *vi* (*sein*) traipse; ⟨*Tier:*⟩ amble

Trottoir /trɔ'to̯aːɐ̯/ *nt* -s,-s pavement, (*Amer*) sidewalk

trotz *prep* (+ *gen*) despite, in spite of. **T~** *m* -es defiance. **t~dem** *adv* nevertheless. **t~en** *vi* (*haben*) (+ *dat*) defy. **t~ig** *a* defiant, *adv* -ly; ⟨*Kind*⟩ stubborn

trübe *a* dull; ⟨*Licht*⟩ dim; ⟨*Flüssigkeit*⟩ cloudy; (*fig*) gloomy

Trubel *m* -s bustle

trüben *vt* dull; make cloudy ⟨*Flüssigkeit*⟩; (*fig*) spoil; strain ⟨*Verhältnis*⟩ **sich t~** ⟨*Flüssigkeit:*⟩ become cloudy; ⟨*Himmel:*⟩ cloud over; ⟨*Augen:*⟩ dim; ⟨*Verhältnis, Erinnerung:*⟩ deteriorate

Trüb|sal *f* - misery; **T~sal blasen** (*fam*) mope. **t~selig** *a* miserable; (*trübe*) gloomy, *adv* -ily. **T~sinn** *m* melancholy. **t~sinnig** *a* melancholy

Trugbild *nt* illusion

trüg|en† *vt* deceive □ *vi* (*haben*) be deceptive. **t~erisch** *a* false; (*täuschend*) deceptive

Trugschluss (**Trugschluß**) *m* fallacy

Truhe *f* -,-n chest

Trümmer *pl* rubble *sg*; (*T~teile*) wreckage *sg*, (*fig*) ruins. **T~haufen** *m* pile of rubble

Trumpf *m* -[e]s,¨e trump [card]; **T~ sein** be trumps. **t~en** *vi* (*haben*) play trumps

Trunk *m* -[e]s drink. **T~enbold** *m* -[e]s,-e drunkard. **T~enheit** *f* - drunkenness; **T~enheit am Steuer** drunken driving. **T~sucht** *f* alcoholism

Trupp *m* -s,-s group; (*Mil*) squad. **T~e** *f* -,-n (*Mil*) unit; (*Theat*) troupe; **T~en** troops

Truthahn *m* turkey

Tschech|e *m* -n,-n, **T~in** *f* -,-nen Czech. **t~isch** *a* Czech. **T~oslowakei (die)** - Czechoslovakia

tschüs, **tschüss** *int* bye, cheerio

Tuba *f* -,-ben (*Mus*) tuba

Tube *f* -,-n tube

Tuberkulose *f* - tuberculosis

Tuch[1] *nt* -[e]s,¨er cloth; (*Hals-, Kopf-*) scarf; (*Schulter-*) shawl

Tuch2 *nt* **-[e]s,-e** (*Stoff*) cloth
tüchtig *a* competent; (*reichlich, beträchtlich*) good; (*groß*) big □ *adv* competently; (*ausreichend*) well; ⟨*regnen, schneien*⟩ hard. **T~keit** *f* - competence
Tück|e *f* **-,-n** malice; **T~en haben** be temperamental; (*gefährlich sein*) be treacherous. **t~isch** *a* malicious, *adv* -ly; (*gefährlich*) treacherous
tüfteln *vi* (*haben*) (*fam*) fiddle (**an** + *dat* with); (*geistig*) puzzle (*an* + *dat* over)
Tugend *f* **-,en** virtue. **t~haft** *a* virtuous
Tülle *f* **-,-n** spout
Tulpe *f* **-,-n** tulip
tummeln (sich) *vr romp* [about]; (*sich beeilen*) hurry [up]
Tümmler *m* **-s,-** porpoise
Tumor *m* **-s,-en** /-'mo:rən/ tumour
Tümpel *m* **-[e]s,-** pond
Tumult *m* **-[e]s,-e** commotion; (*Aufruhr*) riot
tun† *vt* do; take ⟨*Schritt, Blick*⟩; work ⟨*Wunder*⟩; (*bringen*) put (**in** + *acc* into); **sich tun** happen; **jdm etwas tun** hurt s.o.; **viel zu tun haben** have a lot to do; **das tut man nicht** it isn't done; **das tut nichts** it doesn't matter □ *vi* (*haben*) act (**als ob** as if); **überrascht tun** pretend to be surprised; **er tut nur so** he's just pretending; **jdm/etw gut tun** do s.o./sth good; **zu tun haben** have things/work to do; **[es] zu tun haben mit** have to deal with; **[es] mit dem Herzen zu tun haben** have heart trouble. **Tun** *nt* **-s** actions *pl*
Tünche *f* **-,-n** whitewash; (*fig*) veneer. **t~n** *vt* whitewash
Tunesien /-iən/ *nt* **-s** Tunisia
Tunfisch *m* = **Thunfisch**
Tunke *f* **-,-n** sauce. **t~n** *vt/i* (*haben*) (*fam*) dip (**in** + *acc* into)
Tunnel *m* **-s,-** tunnel
tupf|en *vt* dab □ *vi* (*haben*) **t~en an/auf** (+ *acc*) touch. **T~en** *m* **-s,-** spot. **T~er** *m* **-s,-** spot; (*Med*) swab
Tür *f* **-,-en** door
Turban *m* **-s,-e** turban
Turbine *f* **-,-n** turbine
turbulen|t *a* turbulent. **T~z** *f* **-,-en** turbulence
Türk|e *m* **-n,-n** Turk. **T~ei (die)** - Turkey. **T~in** *f* **-,-nen** Turk
türkis *inv a* turquoise. **T~** *m* **-es,-e** turquoise
türkisch *a* Turkish
Turm *m* **-[e]s,¨e** tower; (*Schach*) rook, castle
Türm|chen *nt* **-s,-** turret. **t~en** *vt* pile [up]; **sich t~en** pile up □ *vi* (*sein*) (*fam*) escape
Turmspitze *f* spire
turn|en *vi* (*haben*) do gymnastics. **T~en** *nt* **-s** gymnastics *sg*; (*Sch*) physical education, (*fam*) gym. **T~er(in)** *m* **-s,-** (*f* **-,-nen**) gymnast. **T~halle** *f* gymnasium
Turnier *nt* **-s,-e** tournament; (*Reit-*) show
Turnschuhe *mpl* gym shoes; (*Trainingsschuhe*) trainers
Türschwelle *f* doorstep, threshold
Tusch *m* **-[e]s,-e** fanfare
Tusche *f* **-,-n** [drawing] ink; (*Wasserfarbe*) watercolour
tuscheln *vt/i* (*haben*) whisper
Tüte *f* **-,-n** bag; (*Comm*) packet; (*Eis-*) cornet; **in die T~ blasen** (*fam*) be breathalysed
tuten *vi* (*haben*) hoot; ⟨*Schiff:*⟩ sound its hooter; ⟨*Sirene:*⟩ sound
TÜV *m* - ≈ MOT [test]
Typ *m* **-s,-en** type; (*fam: Kerl*) bloke. **T~e** *f* **-,-n** type; (*fam: Person*) character
Typhus *m* - typhoid
typisch *a* typical, *adv* -ly (**für** of)
Typographie, **Typografie** *f* - typography
Typus *m* **-, Typen** type

Tyrann *m* **-en,-en** tyrant. **T~ei** *f* - tyranny. **t~isch** *a* tyrannical. **t~isieren** *vt* tyrannize

U

u.a. *abbr* **(unter anderem)** amongst other things
U-Bahn *f* underground, (*Amer*) subway
übel *a* bad; (*hässlich*) nasty, *adv* -ily; **mir ist/wird ü~** I feel sick; **etw ü~ nehmen** take sth amiss; **jdm etw ü~ nehmen** hold sth against s.o. **Ü~** *nt* **-s,-** evil. **Ü~keit** *f* - nausea. **ü~nehmen†** *vt sep* (NEW) **ü~ nehmen**, *s.* **übel**. **Ü~täter** *m* culprit
üben *vt/i* (*haben*) practise; **sich in etw** (*dat*) **ü~** practise sth
über *prep* (+ *dat/acc*) over; (*höher als*) above; (*betreffend*) about; ⟨*Buch, Vortrag*⟩ on; ⟨*Scheck, Rechnung*⟩ for; (*quer ü~*) across; **ü~ Köln fahren** go via Cologne; **ü~ Ostern** over Easter; **die Woche ü~** during the week; **heute ü~ eine Woche** a week today; **Fehler ü~ Fehler** mistake after mistake □ *adv* **ü~ und ü~** all over; **jdm ü~ sein** be better/(*stärker*) stronger than s.o. □ *a* (*fam*) **ü~ sein** be left over; **etw ü~ sein** be fed up with sth
überall *adv* everywhere
überanstrengen *vt insep* overtax; strain ⟨*Augen*⟩; **sich ü~** overexert oneself
überarbeit|en *vt insep* revise; **sich ü~en** overwork. **Ü~ung** *f* - revision; overwork
überaus *adv* extremely
überbewerten *vt insep* overrate
überbieten† *vt insep* outbid; (*fig*) outdo; (*übertreffen*) surpass
Überblick *m* overall view; (*Abriss*) summary
überblicken *vt insep* overlook; (*abschätzen*) assess
überbringen† *vt insep* deliver
überbrücken *vt insep* (*fig*) bridge
überdauern *vt insep* survive
überdenken† *vt insep* think over
überdies *adv* moreover
überdimensional *a* oversized
Überdosis *f* overdose
Überdruss *m* **-es** (**Überdruß** *m* **-sses**) surfeit; **bis zum Ü~** ad nauseam
überdrüssig *a* **ü~ sein/werden** be/grow tired (*gen* of)
übereignen *vt insep* transfer
übereilt *a* over-hasty, *adv* -ily
übereinander *adv* one on top of/above the other; ⟨*sprechen*⟩ about each other; **die Arme/Beine ü~ schlagen** fold one's arms/cross one's legs. **ü~schlagen†** *vt sep* (NEW) **ü~ schlagen**, *s.* **übereinander**
überein|kommen† *vi sep* (*sein*) agree. **Ü~kunft** *f* - agreement. **ü~stimmen** *vi sep* (*haben*) agree; ⟨*Zahlen:*⟩ tally; ⟨*Ansichten:*⟩ coincide; ⟨*Farben:*⟩ match. **Ü~stimmung** *f* agreement
überempfindlich *a* over-sensitive; (*Med*) hypersensitive
überfahren† *vt insep* run over
Überfahrt *f* crossing
Überfall *m* attack; (*Bank-*) raid
überfallen† *vt insep* attack; raid ⟨*Bank*⟩; (*bestürmen*) bombard (**mit** with); (*überkommen*) come over; (*fam: besuchen*) surprise
überfällig *a* overdue
überfliegen† *vt insep* fly over; (*lesen*) skim over
überflügeln *vt insep* outstrip
Überfluss (**Überfluß**) *m* abundance; (*Wohlstand*) affluence
überflüssig *a* superfluous
überfluten *vt insep* flood
überfordern *vt insep* overtax
überführ|en *vt insep* transfer; (*Jur*) convict (*gen* of). **Ü~ung** *f*

transfer; (*Straße*) flyover; (*Fußgänger-*) foot-bridge
überfüllt *a* overcrowded
Übergabe *f* (*s.* **übergeben**) handing over; transfer
Übergang *m* crossing; (*Wechsel*) transition. **Ü~sstadium** *nt* transitional stage
übergeben† *vt insep* hand over; (*übereignen*) transfer; **sich ü~** be sick
übergehen†[1] *vi sep* (*sein*) pass (**an** + *acc* to); (*überwechseln*) go over (**zu** to); (*werden zu*) turn (**in** + *acc* into); **zum Angriff ü~** start the attack
übergehen†[2] *vt insep* (*fig*) pass over; (*nicht beachten*) ignore; (*auslassen*) leave out
Übergewicht *nt* excess weight; (*fig*) predominance; **Ü~ haben** be overweight
übergießen† *vt insep* **mit Wasser ü~** pour water over
überglücklich *a* overjoyed
über|greifen† *vi sep* (*haben*) spread (**auf** + *acc* to). **Ü~griff** *m* infringement
über|groß *a* outsize; (*übertrieben*) exaggerated. **Ü~größe** *f* outsize
überhaben† *vt sep* have on; (*fam: satthaben*) be fed up with
überhand *adv* **ü~ nehmen** increase alarmingly. **ü~nehmen**† *vi sep* (*haben*) (NEW) **ü~ nehmen**, *s.* **überhand**
überhängen *v sep* □ *vi*† (*haben*) overhang □ *vt* (*reg*) **sich** (*dat*) **etw ü~** sling over one's shoulder ⟨*Gewehr*⟩; put round one's shoulders ⟨*Jacke*⟩
überhäufen *vt insep* inundate (**mit** with)
überhaupt *adv* (*im Allgemeinen*) altogether; (*eigentlich*) anyway; (*überdies*) besides; **ü~ nicht/nichts** not/nothing at all
überheblich *a* arrogant, *adv* -ly. **Ü~keit** *f* - arrogance
überholen *vt insep* overtake; (*reparieren*) overhaul. **ü~t** *a* outdated. **Ü~ung** *f* -,-**en** overhaul. **Ü~verbot** *nt* '**Ü~verbot**' 'no overtaking'
überhören *vt insep* fail to hear; (*nicht beachten*) ignore
überirdisch *a* supernatural
überkochen *vi sep* (*sein*) boil over
überladen† *vt insep* overload □ *a* over-ornate
überlassen† *vt insep* **jdm etw ü~** leave sth to s.o.; (*geben*) let s.o. have sth; **sich seinem Schmerz ü~** abandon oneself to one's grief; **sich** (*dat*) **selbst ü~ sein** be left to one's own devices
überlasten *vt insep* overload; overtax ⟨*Person*⟩
Überlauf *m* overflow
überlaufen†[1] *vi sep* (*sein*) overflow; (*Mil, Pol*) defect
überlaufen†[2] *vt insep* **jdn ü~** ⟨*Gefühl:*⟩ come over s.o. □ *a* overrun; ⟨*Kursus*⟩ over-subscribed
Überläufer *m* defector
überleben *vt/i insep* (*haben*) survive. **Ü~de(r)** *m/f* survivor
überlegen[1] *vt sep* put over
überlegen[2] *v insep* □ *vt* [**sich** *dat*] **ü~** think over, consider; **es sich** (*dat*) **anders ü~** change one's mind □ *vi* (*haben*) think, reflect; **ohne zu ü~** without thinking
überlegen[3] *a* superior; (*herablassend*) supercilious, *adv* -ly. **Ü~heit** *f* - superiority
Überlegung *f* -,-**en** reflection
überlieferIn *vt insep* hand down. **Ü~ung** *f* tradition
überlisten *vt insep* outwit
überm *prep* = **über dem**
Über|macht *f* superiority. **ü~mächtig** *a* superior; ⟨*Gefühl*⟩ overpowering
übermannen *vt insep* overcome
Über|maß *nt* excess. **ü~mäßig** *a* excessive, *adv* -ly
Übermensch *m* superman. **ü~lich** *a* superhuman

übermitteln *vt insep* convey; (*senden*) transmit
übermorgen *adv* the day after tomorrow
übermüdet *a* overtired
Über|mut *m* high spirits *pl.* **ü~mütig** *a* high-spirited □ *adv* in high spirits
übern *prep* = **über den**
übernächst|e(r,s) *a* next ... but one; **ü~es Jahr** the year after next
übernacht|en *vi insep* (*haben*) stay overnight. **Ü~ung** *f* -,-en overnight stay; **Ü~ung und Frühstück** bed and breakfast
Übernahme *f* - taking over; (*Comm*) take-over
übernatürlich *a* supernatural
übernehmen† *vt insep* take over; (*annehmen*) take on; **sich ü~** overdo things; (*finanziell*) overreach oneself
überprüf|en *vt insep* check. **Ü~ung** *f* check
überqueren *vt insep* cross
überragen *vt insep* tower above; (*fig*) surpass. **ü~d** *a* outstanding
überrasch|en *vt insep* surprise. **ü~end** *a* surprising, *adv* -ly; (*unerwartet*) unexpected, *adv* -ly. **Ü~ung** *f* -,-en surprise
überreden *vt insep* persuade
überreichen *vt insep* present
überreizt *a* overwrought
überrennen† *vt insep* overrun
Überreste *mpl* remains
überrumpeln *vt insep* take by surprise
übers *prep* = **über das**
Überschall- *pref* supersonic
überschatten *vt insep* overshadow
überschätzen *vt insep* overestimate
Überschlag *m* rough estimate; (*Sport*) somersault
überschlagen†[1] *vt sep* cross (*Beine*)
überschlagen†[2] *vt insep* estimate roughly; (*auslassen*) skip; **sich ü~** somersault; (*Ereignisse:*) happen fast □ *a* tepid
überschnappen *vi sep* (*sein*) (*fam*) go crazy
überschneiden† **(sich)** *vr insep* intersect, cross; (*zusammenfallen*) overlap
überschreiben† *vt insep* entitle; (*übertragen*) transfer
überschreiten† *vt insep* cross; (*fig*) exceed
Überschrift *f* heading; (*Zeitungs-*) headline
Über|schuss (Überschuß) *m* surplus. **ü~schüssig** *a* surplus
überschütten *vt insep* **ü~ mit** cover with; (*fig*) shower with
überschwänglich *a* effusive, *adv* -ly
überschwemm|en *vt insep* flood; (*fig*) inundate. **Ü~ung** *f* -,-en flood
überschwenglich *a* (NEW) **überschwänglich**
Übersee in/nach Ü~ overseas; **aus/von Ü~** from overseas. **Ü~dampfer** *m* ocean liner. **ü~isch** *a* overseas
übersehen† *vt insep* look out over; (*abschätzen*) assess; (*nicht sehen*) overlook, miss; (*ignorieren*) ignore
übersenden† *vt insep* send
übersetzen[1] *vi sep* (*haben/sein*) cross [over]
übersetz|en[2] *vt insep* translate. **Ü~er(in)** *m* -s,- (*f* -,-nen) translator. **Ü~ung** *f* -,-en translation
Übersicht *f* overall view; (*Abriss*) summary; (*Tabelle*) table. **ü~lich** *a* clear, *adv* -ly
übersied|eln *vi sep* (*sein*), **übersied|eln** *vi insep* (*sein*) move (**nach** to). **Ü~lung** *f* move
übersinnlich *a* supernatural
überspannt *a* exaggerated; (*verschroben*) eccentric

überspielen *vt insep* (*fig*) cover up; **auf Band ü~** tape
überspitzt *a* exaggerated
überspringen† *vt insep* jump [over]; (*auslassen*) skip
überstehen†¹ *vi sep* (*haben*) project, jut out
überstehen†² *vt insep* come through; get over ⟨*Krankheit*⟩; (*überleben*) survive
übersteigen† *vt insep* climb [over]; (*fig*) exceed
überstimmen *vt insep* outvote
überstreifen *vt sep* slip on
Überstunden *fpl* overtime *sg*; **Ü~ machen** work overtime
überstürz|en *vt insep* rush; **sich ü~en** ⟨*Ereignisse:*⟩ happen fast; ⟨*Worte:*⟩ tumble out. **ü~t** *a* hasty, *adv* -ily
übertölpeln *vt insep* dupe
übertönen *vt insep* drown [out]
übertrag|bar *a* transferable; (*Med*) infectious. **ü~en**† *vt insep* transfer; (*übergeben*) assign (*dat* to); (*Techn, Med*) transmit; (*Radio, TV*) broadcast; (*übersetzen*) translate; (*anwenden*) apply (**auf** + *acc* to) □ *a* transferred, figurative. **Ü~ung** *f* -,-en transfer; transmission; broadcast; translation, application
übertreffen† *vt insep* surpass; (*übersteigen*) exceed; **sich selbst ü~** excel oneself
übertreib|en† *vt insep* exaggerate; (*zu weit treiben*) overdo. **Ü~ung** *f* -,-en exaggeration
übertret|en¹† *vi sep* (*sein*) step over the line; (*Pol*) go over/(*Relig*) convert (**zu** to)
übertret|en†² *vt insep* infringe; break ⟨*Gesetz*⟩. **Ü~ung** *f* -,-en infringement; breach
übertrieben *a* exaggerated; (*übermäßig*) excessive, *adv* -ly
übervölkert *a* overpopulated
übervorteilen *vt insep* cheat
überwachen *vt insep* supervise; (*kontrollieren*) monitor; (*bespitzeln*) keep under surveillance
überwachsen *a* overgrown
überwältigen *vt insep* overpower; (*fig*) overwhelm. **ü~d** *a* overwhelming
überweis|en† *vt insep* transfer; refer ⟨*Patienten*⟩. **Ü~ung** *f* transfer; (*ärztliche*) referral
überwerfen†¹ *vt sep* throw on ⟨*Mantel*⟩
überwerfen†² **(sich)** *vr insep* fall out (**mit** with)
überwiegen† *v insep* □ *vi* (*haben*) predominate, □ *vt* outweigh. **ü~d** *a* predominant, *adv* -ly
überwind|en† *vt insep* overcome; **sich ü~en** force oneself. **Ü~ung** *f* effort
Überwurf *m* wrap; (*Bett-*) bedspread
Über|zahl *f* majority. **ü~zählig** *a* spare
überzeug|en *vt insep* convince; **sich [selbst] ü~en** satisfy oneself. **ü~end** *a* convincing, *adv* -ly. **Ü~ung** *f* -,-en conviction
überziehen†¹ *vt sep* put on
überziehen†² *vt insep* cover; overdraw ⟨*Konto*⟩
Überzug *m* cover; (*Schicht*) coating
üblich *a* usual; (*gebräuchlich*) customary
U-Boot *nt* submarine
übrig *a* remaining; (*andere*) other; **alles Ü~e (ü~e)** [all] the rest; **im Ü~en (ü~en)** besides; (*ansonsten*) apart from that; **ü~ sein** *od* **bleiben** be left [over]; **etw ü~ haben** *od* **behalten** have sth left [over]; **etw ü~ lassen** leave sth [over]; **uns blieb nichts anderes ü~** we had no choice. **ü~behalten**† *vt sep* (NEW) **ü~ behalten**, *s.* **übrig**. **ü~bleiben**† *vi sep* (*sein*) (NEW) **ü~ bleiben**, *s.* **übrig**. **ü~ens** *adv* by the way. **ü~lassen**† *vt sep* (NEW) **ü~ lassen**, *s.* **übrig**
Übung *f* -,-en exercise; (*Üben*) practice; **außer** *od* **aus der Ü~** out of practice

UdSSR *f* - USSR
Ufer *nt* **-s,-** shore; (*Fluss-*) bank
Uhr *f* **-,-en** clock; (*Armband-*) watch; (*Zähler*) meter; **um ein U~** at one o'clock; **wie viel U~ ist es?** what's the time? **U~armband** *nt* watch-strap. **U~macher** *m* **-s,-** watch and clockmaker. **U~werk** *nt* clock/watch mechanism. **U~zeiger** *m* [clock-/watch-]hand. **U~zeigersinn** *m* **im/entgegen dem U~zeigersinn** clockwise/anticlockwise. **U~zeit** *f* time
Uhu *m* **-s,-s** eagle owl
UKW *abbr* (*Ultrakurzwelle*) VHF
Ulk *m* **-s** fun; (*Streich*) trick. **u~en** *vi* (*haben*) joke. **u~ig** *a* funny; (*seltsam*) odd, *adv* -ly
Ulme *f* **-,-n** elm
Ultimatum *nt* **-s,-ten** ultimatum
Ultrakurzwelle *f* very high frequency
Ultraschall *m* ultrasound
ultraviolett *a* ultraviolet
um *prep* (+ *acc*) [a]round; (*Uhrzeit*) at; ⟨*bitten, kämpfen*⟩ for; ⟨*streiten*⟩ over; ⟨*sich sorgen*⟩ about; ⟨*betrügen*⟩ out of; (*bei Angabe einer Differenz*) by; **um [... herum]** around, [round] about; **Tag um Tag** day after day; **einen Tag um den andern** every other day; **um seinetwillen** for his sake □ *adv* (*ungefähr*) around, about; **um sein** (*fam*) be over; ⟨*Zeit*⟩ be up □ *conj* **um zu** to; (*Absicht*) [in order] to; **zu müde, um zu ...** too tired to ...; **um so besser** (NEW) **umso besser**, *s.* **umso**
umändern *vt sep* alter
umarbeiten *vt sep* alter; (*bearbeiten*) revise
umarm|en *vt insep* embrace, hug. **U~ung** *f* **-,-en** embrace, hug
Umbau *m* rebuilding; conversion (**zu** into). **u~en** *vt sep* rebuild; convert (**zu** into)
umbild|en *vt sep* change; (*umgestalten*) reorganize; reshuffle ⟨*Kabinett*⟩. **U~ung** *f* reorganization; (*Pol*) reshuffle
umbinden† *vt sep* put on
umblättern *v sep* □ *vt* turn [over] □ *vi* (*haben*) turn the page
umblicken (sich) *vr sep* look round; (*zurück*) look back
umbringen† *vt sep* kill; **sich u~** kill oneself
Umbruch *m* (*fig*) radical change
umbuchen *v sep* □ *vt* change; (*Comm*) transfer □ *vi* (*haben*) change one's booking
umdrehen *v sep* □ *vt* turn round/(*wenden*) over; turn ⟨*Schlüssel*⟩; (*umkrempeln*) turn inside out; **sich u~** turn round; (*im Liegen*) turn over □ *vi* (*haben/sein*) turn back
Umdrehung *f* turn; (*Motor-*) revolution
umeinander *adv* around each other; **sich u~ sorgen** worry about each other
umfahren†[1] *vt sep* run over
umfahren†[2] *vt insep* go round; bypass ⟨*Ort*⟩
umfallen† *vi sep* (*sein*) fall over; ⟨*Person:*⟩ fall down
Umfang *m* girth; (*Geom*) circumference; (*Größe*) size; (*Ausmaß*) extent; (*Mus*) range
umfangen† *vt insep* embrace; (*fig*) envelop
umfangreich *a* extensive; (*dick*) big
umfassen *vt insep* consist of, comprise; (*umgeben*) surround. **u~d** *a* comprehensive
Umfrage *f* survey, poll
umfüllen *vt sep* transfer
umfunktionieren *vt sep* convert
Umgang *m* [social] contact; (*Umgehen*) dealing (**mit** with): **U~ haben mit** associate with
umgänglich *a* sociable

Umgangs|formen *fpl* manners. **U~sprache** *f* colloquial language. **u~sprachlich** *a* colloquial, *adv* -ly

umgeb|en† *vt/i insep (haben)* surround □ *a* **u~en von** surrounded by. **U~ung** *f* -,-**en** surroundings *pl*

umgehen†[1] *vi sep (sein)* go round; **u~ mit** treat, handle; *(verkehren)* associate with; **in dem Schloss geht ein Gespenst um** the castle is haunted

umgehen†[2] *vt insep* avoid; *(nicht beachten)* evade; ⟨*Straße:*⟩ bypass

umgehend *a* immediate, *adv* -ly

Umgehungsstraße *f* bypass

umgekehrt *a* inverse; ⟨*Reihenfolge*⟩ reverse; **es war u~** it was the other way round □ *adv* conversely; **und u~** and vice versa

umgraben† *vt sep* dig [over]

umhaben† *vt sep* have on

Umhang *m* cloak

umhauen† *vt sep* knock down; *(fällen)* chop down

umher *adv* **weit u~** all around. **u~gehen**† *vi sep (sein)* walk about

umhören (sich) *vr sep* ask around

Umkehr *f* - turning back. **u~en** *v sep* □ *vi (sein)* turn back □ *vt* turn round; turn inside out ⟨*Tasche*⟩; *(fig)* reverse. **U~ung** *f* - reversal

umkippen *v sep* □ *vt* tip over; *(versehentlich)* knock over □ *vi (sein)* fall over; ⟨*Boot:*⟩ capsize; *(fam: ohnmächtig werden)* faint

Umkleide|kabine *f* changing-cubicle. **u~n (sich)** *vr sep* change. **U~raum** *m* changing-room

umknicken *v sep* □ *vt* bend; *(falten)* fold □ *vi (sein)* bend; *(mit dem Fuß)* go over on one's ankle

umkommen† *vi sep (sein)* perish; **u~ lassen** waste ⟨*Lebensmittel*⟩

Umkreis *m* surroundings *pl*; **im U~ von** within a radius of

umkreisen *vt insep* circle; *(Astr)* revolve around; ⟨*Satellit:*⟩ orbit

umkrempeln *vt sep* turn up; *(von innen nach außen)* turn inside out; *(ändern)* change radically

Umlauf *m* circulation; *(Astr)* revolution. **U~bahn** *f* orbit

Umlaut *m* umlaut

umlegen *vt sep* lay *or* put down; flatten ⟨*Getreide*⟩; turn down ⟨*Kragen*⟩; put on ⟨*Schal*⟩; throw ⟨*Hebel*⟩; *(verlegen)* transfer; *(fam: niederschlagen)* knock down; *(töten)* kill

umleit|en *vt sep* divert. **U~ung** *f* diversion

umliegend *a* surrounding

umpflanzen *vt sep* transplant

umrahmen *vt insep* frame

umranden *vt insep* edge

umräumen *vt sep* rearrange

umrechn|en *vt sep* convert. **U~ung** *f* conversion

umreißen†[1] *vt sep* tear down; knock down ⟨*Person*⟩

umreißen†[2] *vt insep* outline

umringen *vt insep* surround

Umriss (Umriß) *m* outline

umrühren *vt/i sep (haben)* stir

ums *pron* = **um das; u~ Leben kommen** lose one's life

Umsatz *m (Comm)* turnover

umschalten *vt/i sep (haben)* switch over; **auf Rot u~** ⟨*Ampel:*⟩ change to red

Umschau *f* **U~ halten nach** look out for. **u~en (sich)** *vr sep* look round/*(zurück)* back

Umschlag *m* cover; *(Schutz-)* jacket; *(Brief-)* envelope; *(Med)* compress; *(Hosen-)* turn-up; *(Wechsel)* change. **u~en**† *v sep* □ *vt* turn up; turn over ⟨*Seite*⟩; *(fällen)* chop down □ *vi (sein)* topple over; ⟨*Boot:*⟩ capsize; ⟨*Wetter:*⟩ change; ⟨*Wind:*⟩ veer

umschließen† *vt insep* enclose

umschnallen *vt sep* buckle on

umschreiben†[1] *vt sep* rewrite

umschreib|en² *vt insep* define; (*anders ausdrücken*) paraphrase. **U~ung** *f* definition; paraphrase
umschulen *vt sep* retrain; (*Sch*) transfer to another school
Umschweife *pl* **keine U~ machen** come straight out with it; **ohne U~** straight out
Umschwung *m* (*fig*) change; (*Pol*) U-turn
umsehen† **(sich)** *vr sep* look round; (*zurück*) look back; **sich u~ nach** look for
umsein† *vi sep* (*sein*) NEW **um sein**, *s.* **um**
umseitig *a & adv* overleaf
umsetzen *vt sep* move; (*umpflanzen*) transplant; (*Comm*) sell
Umsicht *f* circumspection. **u~ig** *a* circumspect, *adv* -ly
umsied|eln *v sep* □ *vt* resettle □ *vi* (*sein*) move. **U~lung** *f* resettlement
umso *conj* **~ besser/mehr** all the better/more; **je mehr, ~ besser** the more the better
umsonst *adv* in vain; (*grundlos*) without reason; (*gratis*) free
umspringen† *vi sep* (*sein*) change; ⟨*Wind:*⟩ veer; **übel u~ mit** treat badly
Umstand *m* circumstance; (*Tatsache*) fact; (*Aufwand*) fuss; (*Mühe*) trouble; **unter U~en** possibly; **U~e machen** make a fuss; **jdm U~e machen** put s.o. to trouble; **in andern U~en** pregnant
umständlich *a* laborious, *adv* -ly; (*kompliziert*) involved; ⟨*Person*⟩ fussy
Umstands|kleid *nt* maternity dress. **U~wort** *nt* (*pl* **-wörter**) adverb
umstehen† *vi insep* surround
Umstehende *pl* bystanders
umsteigen† *vi sep* (*sein*) change
umstellen¹ *vt insep* surround
umstell|en² *vt sep* rearrange; transpose ⟨*Wörter*⟩; (*anders einstellen*) reset; (*Techn*) convert; (*ändern*) change; **sich u~en** adjust. **U~ung** *f* rearrangement; transposition; resetting; conversion; change; adjustment
umstimmen *vt sep* **jdn u~** change s.o.'s mind
umstoßen† *vt sep* knock over; (*fig*) overturn; upset ⟨*Plan*⟩
umstritten *a* controversial; (*ungeklärt*) disputed
umstülpen *vt sep* turn upside down; (*von innen nach außen*) turn inside out
Um|sturz *m* coup. **u~stürzen** *v sep* □ *vt* overturn; (*Pol*) overthrow □ *vi* (*sein*) fall over
umtaufen *vt sep* rename
Umtausch *m* exchange. **u~en** *vt sep* change; exchange **(gegen** for)
umwälzend *a* revolutionary
umwandeln *vt sep* convert; (*fig*) transform
umwechseln *vt sep* change
Umweg *m* detour; **auf U~en** (*fig*) in a roundabout way
Umwelt *f* environment. **u~freundlich** *a* environmentally friendly. **U~schutz** *m* protection of the environment. **U~schützer** *m* environmentalist
umwenden† *vt sep* turn over; **sich u~** turn round
umwerfen† *vt sep* knock over; (*fig*) upset ⟨*Plan*⟩; (*fam*) bowl over ⟨*Person*⟩
umziehen† *v sep* □ *vi* (*sein*) move □ *vt* change; **sich u~** change
umzingeln *vt insep* surround
Umzug *m* move; (*Prozession*) procession
unabänderlich *a* irrevocable; ⟨*Tatsache*⟩ unalterable
unabhängig *a* independent, *adv* -ly; **u~ davon, ob** irrespective of whether. **U~keit** *f* - independence
unabkömmlich *pred a* busy

unablässig *a* incessant, *adv* -ly
unabsehbar *a* incalculable
unabsichtlich *a* unintentional, *adv* -ly
unachtsam *a* careless, *adv* -ly. **U~keit** *f* - carelessness
unangebracht *a* inappropriate
unangemeldet *a* unexpected, *adv* -ly
unangemessen *a* inappropriate, *adv* -ly
unangenehm *a* unpleasant, *adv* -ly; (*peinlich*) embarrassing
Unannehmlichkeiten *fpl* trouble *sg*
unansehnlich *a* shabby; ⟨*Person*⟩ plain
unanständig *a* indecent, *adv* -ly
unantastbar *a* inviolable
unappetitlich *a* unappetizing
Unart *f* -,-en bad habit. **u~ig** *a* naughty
unauffällig *a* inconspicuous, *adv* -ly, unobtrusive, *adv* -ly
unauffindbar *a* **u~ sein** be nowhere to be found
unaufgefordert *adv* without being asked
unauf|haltsam *a* inexorable, *adv* -bly. **u~hörlich** *a* incessant, *adv* -ly
unaufmerksam *a* inattentive
unaufrichtig *a* insincere
unausbleiblich *a* inevitable
unausgeglichen *a* unbalanced; ⟨*Person*⟩ unstable
unaus|löschlich *a* (*fig*) indelible, *adv* -bly. **u~sprechlich** *a* indescribable, *adv* -bly. **u~stehlich** *a* insufferable
unbarmherzig *a* merciless, *adv* -ly
unbeabsichtigt *a* unintentional, *adv* -ly
unbedacht *a* rash, *adv* -ly
unbedenklich *a* harmless □ *adv* without hesitation
unbedeutend *a* insignificant; (*geringfügig*) slight, *adv* -ly
unbedingt *a* absolute, *adv* -ly; **nicht u~** not necessarily
unbefangen *a* natural, *adv* -ly; (*unparteiisch*) impartial
unbefriedig|end *a* unsatisfactory. **u~t** *a* dissatisfied
unbefugt *a* unauthorized □ *adv* without authorization
unbegreiflich *a* incomprehensible
unbegrenzt *a* unlimited □ *adv* indefinitely
unbegründet *a* unfounded
Unbehag|en *nt* unease; (*körperlich*) discomfort. **u~lich** *a* uncomfortable, *adv* -bly
unbeholfen *a* awkward, *adv* -ly
unbekannt *a* unknown; (*nicht vertraut*) unfamiliar. **U~e(r)** *m/f* stranger
unbekümmert *a* unconcerned; (*unbeschwert*) carefree
unbeliebt *a* unpopular. **U~heit** *f* unpopularity
unbemannt *a* unmanned
unbemerkt *a & adv* unnoticed
unbenutzt *a* unused
unbequem *a* uncomfortable, *adv* -bly; (*lästig*) awkward
unberechenbar *a* unpredictable
unberechtigt *a* unjustified; (*unbefugt*) unauthorized
unberufen *int* touch wood!
unberührt *a* untouched; (*fig*) virgin; ⟨*Landschaft*⟩ unspoilt
unbescheiden *a* presumptuous
unbeschrankt *a* unguarded
unbeschränkt *a* unlimited □ *adv* without limit
unbeschreiblich *a* indescribable, *adv* -bly
unbeschwert *a* carefree
unbesiegbar *a* invincible
unbesiegt *a* undefeated
unbesonnen *a* rash, *adv* -ly
unbespielt *a* blank
unbeständig *a* inconsistent; ⟨*Wetter*⟩ unsettled
unbestechlich *a* incorruptible

unbestimmt *a* indefinite: ⟨*Alter*⟩ indeterminate; (*ungewiss*) uncertain; (*unklar*) vague □ *adv* vaguely
unbestreitbar *a* indisputable, *adv* -bly
unbestritten *a* undisputed □ *adv* indisputably
unbeteiligt *a* indifferent; **u~ an** (+ *dat*) not involved in
unbetont *a* unstressed
unbewacht *a* unguarded
unbewaffnet *a* unarmed
unbeweglich *a & adv* motionless, still
unbewohnt *a* uninhabited
unbewusst (**unbewußt**) *a* unconscious, *adv* -ly
unbezahlbar *a* priceless
unbezahlt *a* unpaid
unbrauchbar *a* useless
und *conj* and; **und so weiter** and so on; **nach und nach** bit by bit
Undank *m* ingratitude. **u~bar** *a* ungrateful; (*nicht lohnend*) thankless. **U~barkeit** *f* ingratitude
undefinierbar *a* indefinable
undenk|bar *a* unthinkable. **u~lich** *a* **seit u~lichen Zeiten** from time immemorial
undeutlich *a* indistinct, *adv* -ly; (*vage*) vague, *adv* -ly
undicht *a* leaking; **u~e Stelle** leak
Unding *nt* absurdity
undiplomatisch *a* undiplomatic. *adv* -ally
unduldsam *a* intolerant
undurch|dringlich *a* impenetrable; ⟨*Miene*⟩ inscrutable. **u~führbar** *a* impracticable
undurch|lässig *a* impermeable. **u~sichtig** *a* opaque; (*fig*) doubtful
uneben *a* uneven, *adv* -ly. **U~heit** *f* -,-en unevenness; (*Buckel*) bump
unecht *a* false; **u~er Schmuck/Pelz** imitation jewellery/fur
unehelich *a* illegitimate
unehr|enhaft *a* dishonourable, *adv* -bly. **u~lich** *a* dishonest, *adv* -ly. **U~lichkeit** *f* dishonesty
uneinig *a* (*fig*) divided; [**sich** (*dat*)] **u~ sein** disagree. **U~keit** *f* disagreement; (*Streit*) discord
uneins *a* **~ sein** be at odds
unempfindlich *a* insensitive (**gegen** to); (*widerstandsfähig*) tough; (*Med*) immune
unendlich *a* infinite, *adv* -ly (*endlos*) endless, *adv* -ly. **U~keit** *f* - infinity
unentbehrlich *a* indispensable
unentgeltlich *a* free, ⟨*Arbeit*⟩ unpaid □ *adv* free of charge; ⟨*arbeiten*⟩ without pay
unentschieden *a* undecided; (*Sport*) drawn; **u~ spielen** draw. **U~** *nt* -s,- draw
unentschlossen *a* indecisive; (*unentschieden*) undecided. **U~heit** *f* indecision
unentwegt *a* persistent *adv* -ly (*unaufhörlich*) incessant, *adv* -ly
unerbittlich *a* implacable, *adv* -bly; ⟨*Schicksal*⟩ inexorable
unerfahren *a* inexperienced. **U~heit** *f* - inexperience
unerfreulich *a* unpleasant, *adv* -ly
unergründlich *a* unfathomable
unerhört *a* enormous, *adv* -ly; (*empörend*) outrageous, *adv* -ly
unerklärlich *a* inexplicable
unerlässlich (**unerläßlich**) *a* essential
unerlaubt *a* unauthorized □ *adv* without permission
unermesslich (**unermeßlich**) *a* immense, *adv* -ly
unermüdlich *a* tireless, *adv* -ly
unersättlich *a* insatiable
unerschöpflich *a* inexhaustible
unerschütterlich *a* unshakeable
unerschwinglich *a* prohibitive
unersetzlich *a* irreplaceable; ⟨*Verlust*⟩ irreparable

unerträglich *a* unbearable, *adv* -bly
unerwartet *a* unexpected, *adv* -ly
unerwünscht *a* unwanted; ⟨*Besuch*⟩ unwelcome
unfähig *a* incompetent; **u~, etw zu tun** incapable of doing sth; (*nicht in der Lage*) unable to do sth. **U~keit** *f* incompetence; inability (**zu** to)
unfair *a* unfair, *adv* -ly
Unfall *m* accident. **U~flucht** *f* failure to stop after an accident. **U~station** *f* casualty department
unfassbar (**unfaßbar**) *a* incomprehensible; (*unglaublich*) unimaginable
unfehlbar *a* infallible. **U~keit** *f* - infallibility
unfolgsam *a* disobedient
unförmig *a* shapeless
unfreiwillig *a* involuntary, *adv* -ily; (*unbeabsichtigt*) unintentional, *adv* -ly
unfreundlich *a* unfriendly; (*unangenehm*) unpleasant, *adv* -ly. **U~keit** *f* unfriendliness; unpleasantness
Unfriede[n] *m* discord
unfruchtbar *a* infertile; (*fig*) unproductive. **U~keit** *f* infertility
Unfug *m* **-s** mischief; (**Unsinn**) nonsense
Ungar|(in) *m* **-n,-n** (*f* **-,-nen**) Hungarian. **u~isch** *a* Hungarian. **U~n** *nt* **-s** Hungary
ungastlich *a* inhospitable
ungeachtet *prep* (+ *gen*) in spite of; **dessen u~** notwithstanding [this]. **ungebärdig** *a* unruly. **ungebeugt** *a* (*Gram*) uninflected. **ungebraucht** *a* unused. **ungebührlich** *a* improper, *adv* -ly. **ungedeckt** *a* uncovered; (*Sport*) unmarked; ⟨*Tisch*⟩ unlaid
Ungeduld *f* impatience. **u~ig** *a* impatient, *adv* -ly
ungeeignet *a* unsuitable
ungefähr *a* approximate, *adv* -ly, rough, *adv* -ly
ungefährlich *a* harmless
ungehalten *a* angry, *adv* -ily
ungeheuer *a* enormous, *adv* -ly. **U~** *nt* **-s,-** monster
ungeheuerlich *a* outrageous
ungehobelt *a* uncouth
ungehörig *a* improper, *adv* -ly; (*frech*) impertinent, *adv* -ly
ungehorsam *a* disobedient. **U~** *m* disobedience
ungeklärt *a* unsolved; ⟨*Frage*⟩ unsettled; ⟨*Ursache*⟩ unknown
ungeladen *a* unloaded; ⟨*Gast*⟩ uninvited
ungelegen *a* inconvenient. **U~heiten** *fpl* trouble *sg*
ungelernt *a* unskilled. **ungemein** *a* tremendous, *adv* -ly
ungemütlich *a* uncomfortable, *adv* -bly; (*unangenehm*) unpleasant, *adv* -ly
ungenau *a* inaccurate, *adv* -ly; (*vage*) vague, *adv* -ly. **U~igkeit** *f* **-,-en** inaccuracy
ungeniert /ˈʊnʒeniːɐ̯t/ *a* uninhibited □ *adv* openly
ungenießbar *a* inedible; ⟨*Getränk*⟩ undrinkable. **ungenügend** *a* inadequate, *adv* -ly; (*Sch*) unsatisfactory. **ungepflegt** *a* neglected; ⟨*Person*⟩ unkempt. **ungerade** *a* ⟨*Zahl*⟩ odd
ungerecht *a* unjust, *adv* -ly. **U~igkeit** *f* **-,-en** injustice
ungern *adv* reluctantly
ungesalzen *a* unsalted
ungeschehen *a* **u~ machen** undo
Ungeschick|lichkeit *f* clumsiness. **u~t** *a* clumsy, *adv* -ily
ungeschminkt *a* without make-up; ⟨*Wahrheit*⟩ unvarnished. **ungeschrieben** *a* unwritten. **ungesehen** *a & adv* unseen. **ungesellig** *a* unsociable. **ungesetzlich** *a* illegal, *adv* -ly. **ungestört** *a* undisturbed. **ungestraft** *adv* with impunity. **ungestüm** *a*

impetuous, *adv* -ly. **ungesund** *a* unhealthy. **ungesüßt** *a* unsweetened. **ungetrübt** *a* perfect

Ungetüm *nt* **-s,-e** monster

ungewiss (**ungewiß**) *a* uncertain; **im Ungewissen (ungewissen) sein/lassen** be/leave in the dark. **U~heit** *f* uncertainty

ungewöhnlich *a* unusual, *adv* -ly. **ungewohnt** *a* unaccustomed; (*nicht vertraut*) unfamiliar. **ungewollt** *a* unintentional, *adv* -ly; ⟨*Schwangerschaft*⟩ unwanted

Ungeziefer *nt* **-s** vermin

ungezogen *a* naughty, *adv* -ily

ungezwungen *a* informal, *adv* -ly; (*natürlich*) natural, *adv* -ly

ungläubig *a* incredulous

unglaublich *a* incredible, *adv* -bly, unbelievable, *adv* -bly

ungleich *a* unequal, *adv* -ly; (*verschieden*) different. **U~heit** *f* - inequality. **u~mäßig** *a* uneven, *adv* -ly

Unglück *nt* **-s,-e** misfortune; (*Pech*) bad luck; (*Missgeschick*) mishap; (*Unfall*) accident; **U~ bringen** be unlucky. **u~lich** *a* unhappy, *adv* -ily; (*ungünstig*) unfortunate, *adv* -ly. **u~licherweise** *adv* unfortunately. **u~selig** *a* unfortunate. **U~sfall** *m* accident

ungültig *a* invalid; (*Jur*) void

ungünstig *a* unfavourable, *adv* -bly; (*unpassend*) inconvenient, *adv* -ly

ungut *a* ⟨*Gefühl*⟩ uneasy; **nichts für u~!** no offence!

unhandlich *a* unwieldy

Unheil *nt* **-s** disaster; **U~ anrichten** cause havoc

unheilbar *a* incurable, *adv* -bly

unheimlich *a* eerie; (*gruselig*) creepy; (*fam: groß*) terrific □ *adv* eerily; (*fam: sehr*) terribly

unhöflich *a* rude, *adv* -ly. **U~keit** *f* rudeness

unhörbar *a* inaudible, *adv* -bly

unhygienisch *a* unhygienic

Uni *f* **-,-s** (*fam*) university

uni /y'ni:/ *inv a* plain

Uniform *f* **-,-en** uniform

uninteress|ant *a* uninteresting. **u~iert** *a* uninterested; (*unbeteiligt*) disinterested

Union *f* **-,-en** union

universal *a* universal

universell *a* universal, *adv* -ly

Universität *f* **-,-en** university

Universum *nt* **-s** universe

unkennt|lich *a* unrecognizable. **U~nis** *f* ignorance

unklar *a* unclear; (*ungewiss*) uncertain; (*vage*) vague, *adv* -ly; **im U~en (u~en) sein/lassen** be/leave in the dark. **U~heit** *f* **-,-en** uncertainty

unklug *a* unwise, *adv* -ly

unkompliziert *a* uncomplicated

Unkosten *pl* expenses

Unkraut *nt* weed; (*coll*) weeds *pl*; **U~ jäten** weed. **U~vertilgungsmittel** *nt* weed-killer

unkultiviert *a* uncultured

unlängst *adv* recently

unlauter *a* dishonest; (*unfair*) unfair

unleserlich *a* illegible, *adv* -bly

unleugbar *a* undeniable, *adv* -bly

unlogisch *a* illogical, *adv* -ly

unlös|bar *a* (*fig*) insoluble. **u~lich** *a* (*Chem*) insoluble

unlustig *a* listless, *adv* -ly

unmäßig *a* excessive, *adv* -ly; (*äußerst*) extreme, *adv* -ly

Unmenge *f* enormous amount/(*Anzahl*) number

Unmensch *m* (*fam*) brute. **u~lich** *a* inhuman; (*entsetzlich*) appalling, *adv* -ly

unmerklich *a* imperceptible, *adv* -bly

unmissverständlich (**unmißverständlich**) *a* unambiguous, *adv* -ly; (*offen*) unequivocal, *adv* -ly

unmittelbar *a* immediate, *adv* -ly; (*direkt*) direct, *adv* -ly

unmöbliert *a* unfurnished

unmodern *a* old-fashioned
unmöglich *a* impossible, *adv* -bly. **U~keit** *f* - impossibility
Unmoral *f* immorality. **u~isch** *a* immoral, *adv* -ly
unmündig *a* under-age
Unmut *m* displeasure
unnachahmlich *a* inimitable
unnachgiebig *a* intransigent
unnatürlich *a* unnatural, *adv* -ly
unnormal *a* abnormal, *adv* -ly
unnötig *a* unnecessary, *adv* -ily
unnütz *a* useless □ *adv* needlessly
unord|entlich *a* untidy, *adv* -ily (*nachlässig*) sloppy, *adv* -ily. **U~nung** *f* disorder; (*Durcheinander*) muddle
unorganisiert *a* disorganized
unorthodox *a* unorthodox □ *adv* in an unorthodox manner
unparteiisch *a* impartial, *adv* -ly
unpassend *a* inappropriate, *adv* -ly; ⟨*Moment*⟩ inopportune
unpässlich (**unpäßlich**) *a* indisposed
unpersönlich *a* impersonal
unpraktisch *a* impractical
unpünktlich *a* unpunctual □ *adv* late
unrasiert *a* unshaven
Unrast *f* restlessness
unrealistisch *a* unrealistic, *adv* -ally
unrecht *a* wrong, *adv* -ly □ *n* **jdm u~ tun** do s.o. an injustice; **u~ haben/geben** (NEW) **U~ haben/geben**, *s.* **Unrecht**. **U~** *nt* wrong; **zu U~** wrongly; **U~ haben** be wrong; **jdm U~ geben** disagree with s.o. **u~mäßig** *a* unlawful, *adv* -ly
unregelmäßig *a* irregular, *adv* -ly. **U~keit** *f* irregularity
unreif *a* unripe; (*fig*) immature
unrein *a* impure; ⟨*Luft*⟩ polluted; ⟨*Haut*⟩ bad; **ins U~e (u~e) schreiben** make a rough draft of
unrentabel *a* unprofitable, *adv* -bly
unrichtig *a* incorrect
Unruh|e *f* -,-**n** restlessness; (*Erregung*) agitation; (*Besorgnis*) anxiety; **U~en** (*Pol*) unrest *sg*. **u~ig** *a* restless, *adv* -ly; ⟨*Meer*⟩ agitated; (*laut*) noisy, *adv* -ily; (*besorgt*) anxious, *adv* -ly
uns *pron* (*acc/dat of* **wir**) us; (*refl*) ourselves; (*einander*) each other; **ein Freund von uns** a friend of ours
unsagbar, **unsäglich** *a* indescribable, *adv* -bly
unsanft *a* rough, *adv* -ly
unsauber *a* dirty; (*nachlässig*) sloppy, *adv* -ily; (*unlauter*) dishonest, *adv* -ly
unschädlich *a* harmless
unscharf *a* blurred
unschätzbar *a* inestimable
unscheinbar *a* inconspicuous
unschicklich *a* improper, *adv* -ly
unschlagbar *a* unbeatable
unschlüssig *a* undecided
Unschuld *f* - innocence; (*Jungfräulichkeit*) virginity. **u~ig** *a* innocent, *adv* -ly
unselbstständig, **unselbständig** *a* dependent □ *adv* **u~ denken** not think for oneself
unser *poss pron* our. **u~e(r,s)** *poss pron* ours. **u~erseits** *adv* for our part. **u~twegen** *adv* for our sake; (*wegen uns*) because of us, on our account. **u~twillen** *adv* **um u~twillen** for our sake
unsicher *a* unsafe; (*ungewiss*) uncertain; (*nicht zuverlässig*) unreliable; ⟨*Schritte, Hand*⟩ unsteady; ⟨*Person*⟩ insecure □ *adv* unsteadily. **U~heit** *f* uncertainty; unreliability; insecurity
unsichtbar *a* invisible
Unsinn *m* nonsense. **u~ig** *a* nonsensical, absurd
Unsitt|e *f* bad habit. **u~lich** *a* indecent, *adv* -ly
unsportlich *a* not sporty; (*unfair*) unsporting, *adv* -ly
uns|re(r,s) *poss pron* = **unsere(r,s)**. **u~rige** *poss pron* **der/die/das u~rige** ours

unsterblich *a* immortal. **U~keit** *f* immortality
unstet *a* restless, *adv* -ly; (*unbeständig*) unstable
Unstimmigkeit *f* **-,-en** inconsistency; (*Streit*) difference
Unsumme *f* vast sum
unsymmetrisch *a* not symmetrical
unsympathisch *a* unpleasant; **er ist mir u~** I don't like him
untätig *a* idle, *adv* idly. **U~keit** *f* - idleness
untauglich *a* unsuitable; (*Mil*) unfit
unteilbar *a* indivisible
unten *adv* at the bottom; (*auf der Unterseite*) underneath; (*eine Treppe tiefer*) downstairs; (*im Text*) below; **hier/da u~** down here/there; **nach u~** down [-wards]; (*die Treppe hinunter*) downstairs; **siehe u~** see below
unter *prep* (+ *dat/acc*) under; (*niedriger als*) below; (*inmitten, zwischen*) among; **u~ anderem** among other things; **u~ der Woche** during the week; **u~ sich** by themselves; **u~ uns gesagt** between ourselves
Unter|arm *m* forearm. **U~bewusstsein** (**U~bewußtsein**) *nt* subconscious
unterbieten† *vt insep* undercut; beat ⟨*Rekord*⟩
unterbinden† *vt insep* stop
unterbleiben† *vi insep* (*sein*) cease; **es hat zu u~** it must stop
unterbrech|en† *vt insep* interrupt; break ⟨*Reise*⟩. **U~ung** *f* **-,-en** interruption, break
unterbreiten *vt insep* present
unterbringen† *vt sep* put; (*beherbergen*) put up
unterdessen *adv* in the meantime
unterdrück|en *vt insep* suppress; oppress ⟨*Volk*⟩. **U~ung** *f* - suppression; oppression
untere(r,s) *a* lower
untereinander *adv* one below the other; (*miteinander*) among ourselves/yourselves/themselves
unterernähr|t *a* undernourished. **U~ung** *f* malnutrition
Unterfangen *nt* **-s,-** venture
Unterführung *f* underpass; (*Fußgänger-*) subway
Untergang *m* (*Astr*) setting; (*Naut*) sinking; (*Zugrundegehen*) disappearance; (*der Welt*) end
Untergebene(r) *m/f* subordinate
untergehen† *vi sep* (*sein*) (*Astr*) set; (*versinken*) go under; ⟨*Schiff:*⟩ go down, sink; (*zugrunde gehen*) disappear; ⟨*Welt:*⟩ come to an end
untergeordnet *a* subordinate
Untergeschoss (**Untergeschoß**) *nt* basement
untergraben† *vt insep* (*fig*) undermine
Untergrund *m* foundation; (*Hintergrund*) background; (*Pol*) underground. **U~bahn** *f* underground [railway]. (*Amer*) subway
unterhaken *vt sep* **jdn u~** take s.o.'s arm; **untergehakt** arm in arm
unterhalb *adv & prep* (+ *gen*) below
Unterhalt *m* maintenance
unterhalt|en† *vt insep* maintain; (*ernähren*) support; (*betreiben*) run; (*erheitern*) entertain; **sich u~en** talk; (*sich vergnügen*) enjoy oneself. **u~sam** *a* entertaining. **U~ung** *f* **-,-en** maintenance; (*Gespräch*) conversation; (*Zeitvertreib*) entertainment
unterhandeln *vi insep* (*haben*) negotiate
Unter|haus *nt* (*Pol*) lower house; (*in UK*) House of Commons. **U~hemd** *nt* vest. **U~holz** *nt* undergrowth. **U~hose** *f* underpants *pl*. **u~irdisch** *a & adv* underground
unterjochen *vt insep* subjugate

Unterkiefer *m* lower jaw
unter|kommen† *vi sep (sein)* find accommodation; *(eine Stellung finden)* get a job. **u~kriegen** *vt sep (fam)* get down
Unterkunft *f* **-,-künfte** accommodation
Unterlage *f* pad; **U~n** papers
Unterlass (Unterlaß) *m* **ohne U~** incessantly
unterlass|en† *vt insep* **etw u~en** refrain from [doing] sth; **es u~en, etw zu tun** fail *or* omit to do sth. **U~ung** *f* **-,-en** omission
unterlaufen† *vi insep (sein)* occur; **mir ist ein Fehler u~** I made a mistake
unterlegen1 *vt sep* put underneath
unterlegen2 *a* inferior; *(Sport)* losing; **zahlenmäßig u~** outnumbered *(dat* by). **U~e(r)** *m/f* loser
Unterleib *m* abdomen
unterliegen† *vi insep (sein)* lose *(dat* to); *(unterworfen sein)* be subject *(dat* to)
Unterlippe *f* lower lip
unterm *prep* = **unter dem**
Untermiete *f* **zur U~ wohnen** be a lodger. **U~r(in)** *m(f)* lodger
unterminieren *vt insep* undermine
untern *prep* = **unter den**
unternehm|en† *vt insep* undertake; take ⟨*Schritte*⟩; **etw/nichts u~en** do sth/nothing. **U~en** *nt* **-s,-** undertaking, enterprise *(Betrieb)* concern. **u~end** *a* enterprising. **U~er** *m* **-s,-** employer; *(Bau-)* contractor; *(Industrieller)* industrialist. **U~ung** *f* **-,-en** undertaking; *(Comm)* venture. **u~ungslustig** *a* enterprising; *(abenteuerlustig)* adventurous
Unteroffizier *m* non-commissioned officer
unterordnen *vt sep* subordinate; **sich u~** accept a subordinate role
Unterredung *f* **-,-en** talk
Unterricht *m* **-[e]s** teaching; *(Privat-)* tuition; *(U~sstunden)* lessons *pl*; **U~ geben/nehmen** give/have lessons
unterrichten *vt/i insep (haben)* teach; *(informieren)* inform; **sich u~** inform oneself
Unterrock *m* slip
unters *prep* = **unter das**
untersagen *vt insep* forbid
Untersatz *m* mat; *(mit Füßen)* stand; *(Gläser-)* coaster
unterschätzen *vt insep* underestimate
unterscheid|en† *vt/i insep (haben)* distinguish; *(auseinander halten)* tell apart; **sich u~en** differ. **U~ung** *f* **-,-en** distinction
Unterschied *m* **-[e]s,-e** difference; *(Unterscheidung)* distinction; **im U~ zu ihm** unlike him. **u~lich** *a* different; *(wechselnd)* varying; **das ist u~lich** it varies. **u~slos** *a* equal, *adv* -ly
unterschlag|en† *vt insep* embezzle; *(verheimlichen)* suppress. **U~ung** *f* **-,-en** embezzlement; suppression
Unterschlupf *m* **-[e]s** shelter; *(Versteck)* hiding-place
unterschreiben† *vt/i insep (haben)* sign
Unter|schrift *f* signature; *(Bild-)* caption. **U~seeboot** *nt* submarine. **U~setzer** *m* **-s,-** = **Untersatz**
untersetzt *a* stocky
Unterstand *m* shelter
unterste(r,s) *a* lowest, bottom
unterstehen†1 *vi sep (haben)* shelter
unterstehen†2 *v insep* □ *vi (haben)* be answerable *(dat* to); *(unterliegen)* be subject *(dat* to) □ *vr* **sich u~** dare; **untersteh dich!** don't you dare!
unterstellen1 *vt sep* put underneath; *(abstellen)* store; **sich u~** shelter

unterstellen² *vt insep* place under the control (*dat* of); (*annehmen*) assume; (*fälschlich zuschreiben*) impute (*dat* to)
unterstreichen† *vt insep* underline
unterstütz|en *vt insep* support; (*helfen*) aid. **U~ung** *f* -,-en support; (*finanziell*) aid; (*regelmäßiger Betrag*) allowance; (*Arbeitslosen-*) benefit
untersuch|en *vt insep* examine; (*Jur*) investigate; (*prüfen*) test; (*überprüfen*) check; (*durchsuchen*) search. **U~ung** *f* -,-en examination; investigation; test; check; search. **U~ungshaft** *f* detention on remand; **in U~ungshaft** on remand. **U~ungsrichter** *m* examining magistrate
Untertan *m* **-s & -en,-en** subject
Untertasse *f* saucer
untertauchen *v sep* □ *vt* duck □ *vi* (*sein*) go under; (*fig*) disappear
Unterteil *nt* bottom (part)
unterteilen *vt insep* subdivide; (*aufteilen*) divide
Untertitel *m* subtitle
Unterton *m* undertone
untervermieten *vt/i insep* (*haben*) sublet
unterwandern *vt insep* infiltrate
Unterwäsche *f* underwear
Unterwasser- *pref* underwater
unterwegs *adv* on the way; (*außer Haus*) out; (*verreist*) away
unterweisen† *vt insep* instruct
Unterwelt *f* underworld
unterwerfen† *vt insep* subjugate; **sich u~** submit (*dat* to); **etw** (*dat*) **unterworfen sein** be subject to sth
unterwürfig *a* obsequious, *adv* -ly
unterzeichnen *vt insep* sign
unterziehen†¹ *vt sep* put on underneath; (*Culin*) fold in
unterziehen†² *vt insep* **etw einer Untersuchung/Überprüfung u~** examine/ check sth; **sich einer Operation/Prüfung u~** have an operation/take a test
Untier *nt* monster
untragbar *a* intolerable
untrennbar *a* inseparable
untreu *a* disloyal; (*in der Ehe*) unfaithful. **U~e** *f* disloyalty; infidelity
untröstlich *a* inconsolable
untrüglich *a* infallible
Untugend *f* bad habit
unüberlegt *a* rash, *adv* -ly
unüber|sehbar *a* obvious; (*groß*) immense. **u~troffen** *a* unsurpassed
unum|gänglich *a* absolutely necessary. **u~schränkt** *a* absolute. **u~wunden** *adv* frankly
ununterbrochen *a* incessant, *adv* -ly
unveränderlich *a* invariable; (*gleichbleibend*) unchanging
unverändert *a* unchanged
unverantwortlich *a* irresponsible, *adv* -bly
unverbesserlich *a* incorrigible
unverbindlich *a* non-committal; (*Comm*) not binding □ *adv* without obligation
unverblümt *a* blunt □ *adv* -ly
unverdaulich *a* indigestible
unver|einbar *a* incompatible. **u~gesslich** (**u~geßlich**) *a* unforgettable. **u~gleichlich** *a* incomparable
unver|hältnismäßig *adv* disproportionately. **u~heiratet** *a* unmarried. **u~hofft** *a* unexpected, *adv* -ly. **u~hohlen** *a* undisguised □ *adv* openly. **u~käuflich** *a* not for sale; ⟨*Muster*⟩ free
unverkennbar *a* unmistakable, *adv* -bly
unverletzt *a* unhurt
unvermeidlich *a* inevitable
unver|mindert *a & adv* undiminished. **u~mittelt** *a* abrupt, *adv* -ly. **u~mutet** *a* unexpected, *adv* -ly

Unver|nunft *f* folly. **u~nünftig** *a* foolish, *adv* -ly
unverschämt *a* insolent, *adv* -ly; (*fam: ungeheuer*) outrageous, *adv* -ly. **U~heit** *f* -,-en insolence
unver|sehens *adv* suddenly. **u~sehrt** *a* unhurt; (*unbeschädigt*) intact. **u~söhnlich** *a* irreconcilable; ⟨*Gegner*⟩ implacable
unverständ|lich *a* incomprehensible; (*undeutlich*) indistinct. **U~nis** *nt* lack of understanding
unverträglich *a* incompatible; ⟨*Person*⟩ quarrelsome; (*unbekömmlich*) indigestible
unverwandt *a* fixed, *adv* -ly
unver|wundbar *a* invulnerable. **u~wüstlich** *a* indestructible; ⟨*Person, Humor*⟩ irrepressible; ⟨*Gesundheit*⟩ robust. **u~zeihlich** *a* unforgivable
unverzüglich *a* immediate, *adv* -ly
unvollendet *a* unfinished
unvollkommen *a* imperfect; (*unvollständig*) incomplete. **U~heit** *f* -,-en imperfection
unvollständig *a* incomplete
unvor|bereitet *a* unprepared. **u~eingenommen** *a* unbiased. **u~hergesehen** *a* unforeseen
unvorsichtig *a* careless, *adv* -ly. **U~keit** *f* - carelessness
unvorstellbar *a* unimaginable, *adv* -bly
unvorteilhaft *a* unfavourable; (*nicht hübsch*) unattractive; ⟨*Kleid, Frisur*⟩ unflattering
unwahr *a* untrue. **U~heit** *f* -,-en untruth. **u~scheinlich** *a* unlikely; (*unglaublich*) improbable; (*fam: groß*) incredible, *adv* -bly
unweigerlich *a* inevitable, *adv* -bly
unweit *adv & prep* (+ *gen*) not far; **u~ vom Fluss** *od* **des Flusses** not far from the river
unwesentlich *a* unimportant □ *adv* slightly
Unwetter *nt* **-s,-** storm
unwichtig *a* unimportant
unwider|legbar *a* irrefutable. **u~ruflich** *a* irrevocable, *adv* -bly. **u~stehlich** *a* irresistible
Unwill|e *m* displeasure. **u~ig** *a* angry, *adv* -ily; (*widerwillig*) reluctant, *adv* -ly. **u~kürlich** *a* involuntary, *adv* -ily; (*instinktiv*) instinctive, *adv* -ly
unwirklich *a* unreal
unwirksam *a* ineffective
unwirsch *a* irritable, *adv* -bly
unwirtlich *a* inhospitable
unwirtschaftlich *a* uneconomic, *adv* -ally
unwissen|d *a* ignorant. **U~heit** *f* - ignorance
unwohl *a* unwell; (*unbehaglich*) uneasy. **U~sein** *nt* **-s** indisposition
unwürdig *a* unworthy (*gen* of); (*würdelos*) undignified
Unzahl *f* vast number. **unzählig** *a* innumerable, countless
unzerbrechlich *a* unbreakable
unzerstörbar *a* indestructible
unzertrennlich *a* inseparable
Unzucht *f* sexual offence; **gewerbsmäßige U~** prostitution
unzüchtig *a* indecent, *adv* -ly; ⟨*Schriften*⟩ obscene
unzufrieden *a* dissatisfied; (*innerlich*) discontented. **U~heit** *f* dissatisfaction; (*Pol*) discontent
unzulänglich *a* inadequate, *adv* -ly
unzulässig *a* inadmissible
unzumutbar *a* unreasonable
unzurechnungsfähig *a* insane. **U~keit** *f* insanity
unzusammenhängend *a* incoherent
unzutreffend *a* inapplicable; (*falsch*) incorrect
unzuverlässig *a* unreliable
unzweckmäßig *a* unsuitable, *adv* -bly
unzweideutig *a* unambiguous
unzweifelhaft *a* undoubted, *adv* -ly

üppig *a* luxuriant, *adv* -ly; (*überreichlich*) lavish, *adv* -ly; ⟨*Busen, Figur*⟩ voluptuous
uralt *a* ancient
Uran *nt* **-s** uranium
Uraufführung *f* first performance
urbar *a* **u~ machen** cultivate
Ureinwohner *mpl* native inhabitants
Urenkel *m* great-grandson; (*pl*) great-grandchildren
Urgroß|mutter *f* great-grandmother. **U~vater** *m* great-grandfather
Urheber *m* **-s,-** originator; (*Verfasser*) author. **U~recht** *nt* copyright
Urin *m* **-s,-e** urine
Urkunde *f* **-,-n** certificate; (*Dokument*) document
Urlaub *m* **-s** holiday; (*Mil, Admin*) leave; **auf U~** on holiday/leave; **U~ haben** be on holiday/leave. **U~er(in)** *m* **-s,-** (*f* **-,-nen**) holiday-maker. **U~sort** *m* holiday resort
Urne *f* **-,-n** urn; (*Wahl-*) ballot-box
Ursache *f* cause; (*Grund*) reason; **keine U~!** don't mention it!
Ursprung *m* origin
ursprünglich *a* original, *adv* -ly; (*anfänglich*) initial, *adv* -ly; (*natürlich*) natural
Urteil *nt* **-s,-e** judgement; (*Meinung*) opinion; (*U~sspruch*) verdict; (*Strafe*) sentence. **u~en** *vi* (*haben*) judge. **U~svermögen** *nt* [power of] judgement
Urwald *m* primeval forest; (*tropischer*) jungle
urwüchsig *a* natural; (*derb*) earthy
Urzeit *f* primeval times *pl*; **seit U~en** from time immemorial
USA *pl* USA *sg*
usw. *abbr* (**und so weiter**) etc.
Utensilien /-iən/ *ntpl* utensils
utopisch *a* Utopian

V

vage /ˈvaːgə/ *a* vague, *adv* -ly
Vakuum /ˈvaːkuʊm/ *nt* **-s** vacuum. **v~verpackt** *a* vacuum-packed
Vanille /vaˈnɪljə/ *f* - vanilla
vari|abel /vaˈri̯aːbəl/ *a* variable. **V~ante** *f* **-,-n** variant. **V~ation** /-ˈtsi̯oːn/ *f* **-,-en** variation. **v~ieren** *vt/i* (*haben*) vary
Vase /ˈvaːzə/ *f* **-,-n** vase
Vater *m* **-s,-̈** father. **V~land** *nt* fatherland
väterlich *a* paternal; (*fürsorglich*) fatherly. **v~erseits** *adv* on one's/the father's side
Vater|schaft *f* - fatherhood; (*Jur*) paternity. **V~unser** *nt* **-s,-** Lord's Prayer
Vati *m* **-s,-s** (*fam*) daddy
v. Chr. *abbr* (**vor Christus**) BC
Vegetar|ier(in) /vegeˈtaːri̯ɐ, -i̯ərɪn/ *m*(*f*) **-s,-** (*f* **-,-nen**) vegetarian. **v~isch** *a* vegetarian
Vegetation /vegetaˈtsi̯oːn/ *f* **-,-en** vegetation
Veilchen *nt* **-s,-n** violet
Vene /ˈveːnə/ *f* **-,-n** vein
Venedig /veˈneːdɪç/ *nt* **-s** Venice
Ventil /vɛnˈtiːl/ *nt* **-s,-e** valve. **V~ator** *m* **-s,-en** /-ˈtoːrən/ fan
verabred|en *vt* arrange; **sich [mit jdm] v~en** arrange to meet [s.o.]. **V~ung** *f* **-,-en** arrangement; (*Treffen*) appointment
verabreichen *vt* administer
verabscheuen *vt* detest, loathe
verabschieden *vt* say goodbye to; (*aus dem Dienst*) retire; pass ⟨*Gesetz*⟩; **sich v~** say goodbye
verachten *vt* despise. **v~swert** *a* contemptible
verächtlich *a* contemptuous, *adv* -ly; (*unwürdig*) contemptible
Verachtung *f* - contempt

verallgemeiner|n *vt/i* (*haben*) generalize. **V∼ung** *f* -,-**en** generalization
veralte|n *vi* (*sein*) become obsolete. **v∼t** *a* obsolete
Veranda /ve'randa/ *f* -,-**den** veranda
veränder|lich *a* changeable; (*Math*) variable. **v∼n** *vt* change; **sich v∼n** change; (*beruflich*) change one's job. **V∼ung** *f* change
verängstigt *a* frightened, scared
verankern *vt* anchor
veranlag|t *a* **künstlerisch/musikalisch v∼t sein** have an artistic/a musical bent; **praktisch v∼t** practically minded. **V∼ung** *f* -,-**en** disposition; (*Neigung*) tendency; (*künstlerisch*) bent
veranlass|en *vt* (*reg*) arrange for; (*einleiten*) institute; **jdn v∼en** prompt s.o. (**zu** to). **V∼ung** *f* - reason; **auf meine V∼ung** at my suggestion; (*Befehl*) on my orders
veranschaulichen *vt* illustrate
veranschlagen *vt* (*reg*) estimate
veranstalt|en *vt* organize; hold, give ⟨*Party*⟩; make ⟨*Lärm*⟩. **V∼er** *m* -**s**,- organizer. **V∼ung** *f* -,-**en** event
verantwort|en *vt* take responsibility for; **sich v∼en** answer (**für** for). **v∼lich** *a* responsible; **v∼lich machen** hold responsible. **V∼ung** *f* - responsibility. **v∼ungsbewusst** (**v∼ungsbewußt**) *a* responsible, *adv* -bly. **v∼ungslos** *a* irresponsible, *adv* -bly. **v∼ungsvoll** *a* responsible
verarbeiten *vt* use; (*Techn*) process; (*verdauen & fig*) digest; **v∼ zu** make into
verärgern *vt* annoy
verarmt *a* impoverished
verästeln (sich) *vr* branch out
verausgaben (sich) *vr* spend all one's money; (*körperlich*) wear oneself out
veräußern *vt* sell
Verb /vɛrp/ *nt* -**s**,-**en** verb. **v∼al** /vɛr'ba:l/ *a* verbal, *adv* -ly
Verband *m* -**[e]s**,**⸗e** association; (*Mil*) unit; (*Med*) bandage; (*Wund-*) dressing. **V∼szeug** *nt* first-aid kit
verbann|en *vt* exile; (*fig*) banish. **V∼ung** *f* - exile
verbarrikadieren *vt* barricade
verbeißen† *vt* suppress; **ich konnte mir kaum das Lachen v∼** I could hardly keep a straight face
verbergen† *vt* hide; **sich v∼** hide
verbesser|n *vt* improve; (*berichtigen*) correct. **V∼ung** *f* -,-**en** improvement; correction
verbeug|en (sich) *vr* bow. **V∼ung** *f* bow
verbeulen *vt* dent
verbiegen† *vt* bend; **sich v∼** bend
verbieten† *vt* forbid; (*Admin*) prohibit, ban
verbillig|en *vt* reduce [in price]. **v∼t** *a* reduced
verbinden† *vt* connect (**mit** to); (*zusammenfügen*) join; (*verknüpfen*) combine; (*in Verbindung bringen*) associate; (*Med*) bandage; dress ⟨*Wunde*⟩; **sich v∼** combine; (*sich zusammentun*) join together; **jdm die Augen v∼** blindfold s.o.; **jdm verbunden sein** (*fig*) be obliged to s.o.
verbindlich *a* friendly; (*bindend*) binding. **V∼keit** *f* -,-**en** friendliness; **V∼keiten** obligations; (*Comm*) liabilities
Verbindung *f* connection; (*Verknüpfung*) combination; (*Kontakt*) contact; (*Vereinigung*) association; **chemiche V∼** chemical compound; **in V∼ stehen/sich in V∼ setzen** be/get in touch
verbissen *a* grim, *adv* -ly; (*zäh*) dogged, *adv* -ly
verbitten† *vt* **sich** (*dat*) **etw v∼** not stand for sth
verbitter|n *vt* make bitter. **v∼t** *a* bitter. **V∼ung** *f* - bitterness

verblassen *vi* (*sein*) fade
verbläuen *vt* (*fam*) beat up
Verbleib *m* -s whereabouts *pl*. **v~en**† *vi* (*sein*) remain
verbleichen† *vi* (*sein*) fade
verbleit *a* ⟨*Benzin*⟩ leaded
verbleuen *vt* (NEW) **verbläuen**
verblüff|en *vt* amaze, astound. **V~ung** *f* - amazement
verblühen *vi* (*sein*) wither, fade
verbluten *vi* (*sein*) bleed to death
verborgen¹ *a* hidden
verborgen² *vt* lend
Verbot *nt* **-[e]s,-e** ban. **v~en** *a* forbidden; (*Admin*) prohibited; **'Rauchen v~en'** 'no smoking'
Verbrauch *m* **-[e]s** consumption. **v~en** *vt* use; consume ⟨*Lebensmittel*⟩; (*erschöpfen*) use up, exhaust. **V~er** *m* **-s,-** consumer. **v~t** *a* worn; ⟨*Luft*⟩ stale
verbrechen† *vt* (*fam*) perpetrate. **V~** *nt* **-s,-** crime
Verbrecher *m* **-s,-** criminal. **v~isch** a criminal
verbreit|en *vt* spread; **sich v~en** spread. **v~ern** *vt* widen; **sich v~ern** widen. **v~et** *a* widespread. **V~ung** *f* - spread; (*Verbreiten*) spreading
verbrenn|en† *vt/i* (*sein*) burn; cremate ⟨*Leiche*⟩. **V~ung** *f* **-,-en** burning; cremation; (*Wunde*) burn
verbringen† *vt* spend
verbrühen *vt* scald
verbuchen *vt* enter; (*fig*) notch up ⟨*Erfolg*⟩
verbünd|en (sich) *vr* form an alliance. **V~ete(r)** *m/f* ally
verbürgen *vt* guarantee; **sich v~ für** vouch for
verbüßen *vt* serve ⟨*Strafe*⟩
Verdacht *m* **-[e]s** suspicion; **in** *or* **im V~ haben** suspect
verdächtig *a* suspicious, *adv* -ly. **v~en** *vt* suspect (*gen* of). **V~te(r)** *m/f* suspect
verdamm|en *vt* condemn; (*Relig*) damn. **V~nis** *f* - damnation. **v~t** *a & adv* (*sl*) damned; **v~t!** damn!
verdampfen *vt/i* (*sein*) evaporate
verdanken *vt* **owe** ⟨*dat* to⟩
verdau|en *vt* digest. **v~lich** *a* digestible; **schwer v~lich** indigestible. **V~ung** *f* - digestion
Verdeck *nt* **-[e]s,-e** hood; (*Oberdeck*) top deck. **v~en** *vt* cover; (*verbergen*) hide, conceal
verdenken† *vt* **das kann man ihm nicht v~** you can't blame him for it
verderb|en† *vi* (*sein*) spoil; ⟨*Lebensmittel:*⟩ go bad □ *vt* spoil; (*zerstören*) ruin; (*moralisch*) corrupt; **ich habe mir den Magen verdorben** I have an upset stomach. **V~en** *nt* **-s** ruin. **v~lich** *a* perishable; (*schädlich*) pernicious
verdeutlichen *vt* make clear
verdichten *vt* compress; **sich v~** ⟨*Nebel:*⟩ thicken
verdien|en *vt/i* (*haben*) earn; (*fig*) deserve. **V~er** *m* **-s,-** wage-earner
Verdienst¹ *m* **-[e]s** earnings *pl*
Verdienst² *nt* **-[e]s,-e** merit
verdient *a* well-deserved; ⟨*Person*⟩ of outstanding merit. **v~ermaßen** *adv* deservedly
verdoppeln *vt* double; (*fig*) redouble; **sich v~** double
verdorben *a* spoilt, ruined; ⟨*Magen*⟩ upset; (*moralisch*) corrupt; (*verkommen*) depraved
verdorren *vi* (*sein*) wither
verdrängen *vt* force out; (*fig*) displace; (*psychisch*) repress
verdreh|en *vt* twist; roll ⟨*Augen*⟩; (*fig*) distort. **v~t** *a* (*fam*) crazy
verdreifachen *vt* treble, triple
verdreschen† *vt* (*fam*) thrash
verdrießlich *a* morose, *adv* -ly
verdrücken *vt* crumple; (*fam: essen*) polish off; **sich v~** (*fam*) slip away
Verdruss *m* **-es** (**Verdruß** *m* **-sses**) annoyance
verdunk|eln *vt* darken; black out ⟨*Zimmer*⟩; **sich v~eln** darken. **V~[e]lung** *f* - black-out

verdünnen *vt* dilute; **sich v~** taper off
verdunst|en *vi* (*sein*) evaporate. **V~ung** *f* - evaporation
verdursten *vi* (*sein*) die of thirst
verdutzt *a* baffled
veredeln *vt* refine; (*Hort*) graft
verehr|en *vt* revere; (*Relig*) worship; (*bewundern*) admire; (*schenken*) give. **V~er(in)** *m* **-s,-** (*f* **-,-nen**) admirer. **V~ung** *f* - veneration; worship; admiration
vereidigen *vt* swear in
Verein *m* **-s,-e** society; (*Sport-*) club
vereinbar *a* compatible. **v~en** *vt* arrange; **nicht zu v~en** incompatible. **V~ung** *f* **-,-en** agreement
vereinen *vt* unite; **sich v~** unite
vereinfachen *vt* simplify
vereinheitlichen *vt* standardize
vereinig|en *vt* unite; merge ⟨*Firmen*⟩; **wieder v~en** reunite; reunify ⟨*Land*⟩; **sich v~en** unite; **V~te Staaten [von Amerika]** United States *sg* [of America]. **V~ung** *f* **-,-en** union; (*Organisation*) organization
vereinsamt *a* lonely
vereinzelt *a* isolated □ *adv* occasionally
vereist *a* frozen; ⟨*Straße*⟩ icy
vereiteln *vt* foil, thwart
vereitert *a* septic
verenden *vi* (*sein*) die
verengen *vt* restrict; **sich v~** narrow; ⟨*Pupille:*⟩ contract
vererb|en *vt* leave (*dat* to); (*Biol & fig*) pass on (*dat* to). **V~ung** *f* - heredity
verewigen *vt* immortalize; **sich v~** (*fam*) leave one's mark
verfahren† *vi* (*sein*) proceed; **v~ mit** deal with □ *vr* **sich v~** lose one's way □ *a* muddled. **V~** *nt* **-s,-** procedure; (*Techn*) process; (*Jur*) proceedings *pl*
Verfall *m* decay; (*eines Gebäudes*) dilapidation; (*körperlich & fig*) decline; (*Ablauf*) expiry. **v~en**† *vi* (*sein*) decay; ⟨*Person, Sitten:*⟩ decline; (*ablaufen*) expire; **v~en in** (+ *acc*) lapse into; **v~en auf** (+ *acc*) hit on ⟨*Idee*⟩; **jdm/etw v~en sein** be under the spell of s.o./sth; be addicted to ⟨*Alkohol*⟩
verfälschen *vt* falsify; adulterate ⟨*Wein, Lebensmittel*⟩
verfänglich *a* awkward
verfärben (sich) *vr* change colour; ⟨*Stoff:*⟩ discolour
verfass|en *vt* write; (*Jur*) draw up; (*entwerfen*) draft. **V~er** *m* **-s,-** author. **V~ung** *f* (*Pol*) constitution; (*Zustand*) state
verfaulen *vi* (*sein*) rot, decay
verfechten† *vt* advocate
verfehlen *vt* miss
verfeinde|n (sich) *vr* become enemies; **v~t sein** be enemies
verfeinern *vt* refine; (*verbessern*) improve
verfilmen *vt* film
verfilzt *a* matted
verfliegen† *vi* (*sein*) evaporate; ⟨*Zeit:*⟩ fly
verflixt *a* (*fam*) awkward; (*verdammt*) blessed; **v~!** damn!
verfluch|en *vt* curse. **v~t** *a & adv* (*fam*) damned; **v~t!** damn!
verflüchtigen (sich) *vr* evaporate
verflüssigen *vt* liquefy
verfolg|en *vt* pursue; (*folgen*) follow; (*bedrängen*) pester; (*Pol*) persecute; **strafrechtlich v~en** prosecute. **V~er** *m* **-s,-** pursuer. **V~ung** *f* - pursuit; persecution
verfrachten *vt* ship
verfrüht *a* premature
verfügbar *a* available
verfüg|en *vt* order; (*Jur*) decree □ *vi* (*haben*) **v~en über** (+ *acc*) have at one's disposal. **V~ung** *f* **-,-en** order; (*Jur*) decree; **jdm zur V~ung stehen/stellen** be/place at s.o.'s disposal

verführ|en *vt* seduce; *(verlocken)* tempt. **V~er** *m* seducer. **v~erisch** *a* seductive; tempting. **V~ung** *f* seduction; temptation

vergammelt *a* rotten; ⟨*Gebäude*⟩ decayed; ⟨*Person*⟩ scruffy

vergangen *a* past; *(letzte)* last. **V~heit** *f* - past; *(Gram)* past tense

vergänglich *a* transitory

vergas|en *vt* gas. **V~er** *m* **-s,-** carburettor

vergeb|en† *vt* award (**an** + *dat* to); *(weggeben)* give away; *(verzeihen)* forgive. **v~ens** *adv* in vain. **v~lich** *a* futile, vain □ *adv* in vain. **V~ung** *f* - forgiveness

vergehen† *vi (sein)* pass; **v~ vor** (+ *dat*) nearly die of; **sich v~** violate (**gegen etw** sth); *(sexuell)* sexually assault (**an jdm** s.o.). **V~** *nt* **-s,-** offence

vergelt|en† *vt* repay. **V~ung** *f* - retaliation; *(Rache)* revenge. **V~ungsmaßnahme** *f* reprisal

vergessen† *vt* forget; *(liegen lassen)* leave behind. **V~heit** *f* - oblivion; **in V~heit geraten** be forgotten

vergesslich (vergeßlich) *a* forgetful. **V~keit** *f* - forgetfulness

vergeuden *vt* waste, squander

vergewaltig|en *vt* rape. **V~ung** *f* **-,-en** rape

vergewissern (sich) *vr* make sure (*gen* of)

vergießen† *vt* spill; shed ⟨*Tränen, Blut*⟩

vergift|en *vt* poison. **V~ung** *f* **-,-en** poisoning

Vergissmeinnicht (Vergißmeinnicht) *nt* **-[e]s,-[e]** forget-me-not

vergittert *a* barred

verglasen *vt* glaze

Vergleich *m* **-[e]s,-e** comparison; *(Jur)* settlement. **v~bar** *a* comparable. **v~en**† *vt* compare (**mit** with/to). **v~sweise** *adv* comparatively

vergnüg|en (sich) *vr* enjoy oneself. **V~en** *nt* **-s,-** pleasure; *(Spaß)* fun; **viel V~en!** have a good time! **v~lich** *a* enjoyable. **v~t** *a* cheerful, *adv* -ly; *(zufrieden)* happy, *adv* -ily; *(vergnüglich)* enjoyable. **V~ungen** *fpl* entertainments

vergolden *vt* gild; *(plattieren)* gold-plate

vergönnen *vt* grant

vergöttern *vt* idolize

vergraben† *vt* bury

vergreifen† **(sich)** *vr* **sich v~an** (+ *dat*) assault; *(stehlen)* steal

vergriffen *a* out of print

vergrößer|n *vt* enlarge; ⟨*Linse:*⟩ magnify; *(vermehren)* increase; *(erweitern)* extend; expand ⟨*Geschäft*⟩; **sich v~n** grow bigger; ⟨*Firma:*⟩ expand; *(zunehmen)* increase. **V~ung** *f* **-,-en** magnification; increase; expansion; *(Phot)* enlargement. **V~ungsglas** *nt* magnifying glass

Vergünstigung *f* **-,-en** privilege

vergüt|en *vt* pay for; **jdm etw v~en** reimburse s.o. for sth. **V~ung** *f* **-,-en** remuneration; *(Erstattung)* reimbursement

verhaft|en *vt* arrest. **V~ung** *f* **-,-en** arrest

verhalten† **(sich)** *vr* behave; *(handeln)* act; *(beschaffen sein)* be; **sich still v~** keep quiet. **V~** *nt* **-s** behaviour, conduct

Verhältnis *nt* **-ses,-se** relationship; *(Liebes-)* affair; *(Math)* ratio; **V~se** circumstances; *(Bedingungen)* conditions; **über seine V~se leben** live beyond one's means. **v~mäßig** *adv* comparatively, relatively

verhand|eln *vt* discuss; *(Jur)* try □ *vi (haben)* negotiate; **v~eln gegen** *(Jur)* try. **V~lung** *f (Jur)* trial; **V~lungen** negotiations

verhängen *vt* cover; *(fig)* impose

Verhängnis *nt* **-ses** fate, doom. **v~voll** *a* fatal, disastrous

verharmlosen *vt* play down
verharren *vi (haben)* remain
verhärten *vt/i (sein)* harden; **sich v~** harden
verhasst (verhaßt) *a* hated
verhätscheln *vt* spoil, pamper
verhauen† *vt (fam)* beat; make a mess of ⟨*Prüfung*⟩
verheerend *a* devastating; *(fam)* terrible
verhehlen *vt* conceal
verheilen *vi (sein)* heal
verheimlichen *vt* keep secret
verheirat|en (sich) *vr* get married (**mit** to); **sich wieder v~en** remarry. **v~et** *a* married
verhelfen† *vi (haben)* **jdm zu etw v~** help s.o. get sth
verherrlichen *vt* glorify
verhexen *vt* bewitch; **es ist wie verhext** *(fam)* there is a jinx on it
verhinder|n *vt* prevent; **v~t sein** be unable to come. **V~ung** *f* - prevention
verhöhnen *vt* deride
Verhör *nt* **-s,-e** interrogation; **ins V~ nehmen** interrogate. **v~en** *vt* interrogate; **sich v~en** mishear
verhüllen *vt* cover; *(fig)* disguise. **v~d** *a* euphemistic, *adv* -ally
verhungern *vi (sein)* starve
verhüt|en *vt* prevent. **V~ung** *f* - prevention. **V~ungsmittel** *nt* contraceptive
verhutzelt *a* wizened
verirren (sich) *vr* get lost
verjagen *vt* chase away
verjüngen *vt* rejuvenate; **sich v~** taper
verkalkt *a (fam)* senile
verkalkulieren (sich) *vr* miscalculate
Verkauf *m* sale; **zum V~** for sale. **v~en** *vt* sell; **zu v~en** for sale
Verkäufer(in) *m(f)* seller; *(im Geschäft)* shop assistant
Verkehr *m* **-s** traffic; *(Kontakt)* contact; *(Geschlechts-)* intercourse; **aus dem V~ ziehen** take out of circulation. **v~en** *vi (haben)* operate; ⟨*Bus, Zug:*⟩ run; *(Umgang haben)* associate, mix (**mit** with); *(Gast sein)* visit (**bei jdm** s.o.); frequent (**in einem Lokal** a restaurant); **brieflich v~en** correspond □ *vt* **ins Gegenteil v~en** turn round
Verkehrs|ampel *f* traffic lights *pl*. **V~büro** *nt* = **V~verein. V~funk** *m* [radio] traffic information. **V~unfall** *m* road accident. **V~verein** *m* tourist office. **V~zeichen** *nt* traffic sign
verkehrt *a* wrong, *adv* -ly; **v~ herum** *adv* the wrong way round; *(links)* inside out
verkennen† *vt* misjudge
verklagen *vt* sue (**auf** + *acc* for)
verkleid|en *vt* disguise; *(Techn)* line; **sich v~en** disguise oneself; *(für Kostümfest)* dress up. **V~ung** *f* -,-en disguise; *(Kostüm)* fancy dress; *(Techn)* lining
verkleiner|n *vt* reduce [in size]. **V~ung** *f* - reduction. **V~ungsform** *f* diminutive
verklemmt *a* jammed; *(psychisch)* inhibited
verkneifen† *vt* **sich** *(dat)* **etw v~** do without sth; *(verbeißen)* suppress sth
verknittern *vt/i (sein)* crumple
verknüpfen *vt* knot together; *(verbinden)* connect, link; *(zugleich tun)* combine
verkommen† *vi (sein)* be neglected; *(sittlich)* go to the bad; *(verfallen)* decay; ⟨*Haus:*⟩ fall into disrepair; ⟨*Gegend:*⟩ become rundown; ⟨*Lebensmittel:*⟩ go bad □ *a* neglected; *(sittlich)* depraved; ⟨*Haus*⟩ dilapidated; ⟨*Gegend*⟩ rundown
verkörper|n *vt* embody, personify. **V~ung** *f* -,-en embodiment, personification
verkraften *vt* cope with
verkrampft *a (fig)* tense
verkriechen† **(sich)** *vr* hide
verkrümmt *a* crooked, bent

verkrüppelt *a* crippled; ⟨*Glied*⟩ deformed
verkühl|en (sich) *vr* catch a chill. **V∼ung** *f* -,-en chill
verkümmer|n *vi (sein)* waste/ ⟨*Pflanze:*⟩ wither away. **v∼t** *a* stunted
verkünd|en *vt* announce; pronounce ⟨*Urteil*⟩. **v∼igen** *vt* announce; (*predigen*) preach
verkürzen *vt* shorten; (*verringern*) reduce; (*abbrechen*) cut short; while away ⟨*Zeit*⟩
verladen† *vt* load
Verlag *m* **-[e]s,-e** publishing firm
verlangen *vt* ask for; (*fordern*) demand; (*berechnen*) charge; **am Telefon verlangt werden** be wanted on the telephone. **V∼** *nt* **-s** desire; (*Bitte*) request; **auf V∼** on demand
verlänger|n *vt* extend; lengthen ⟨*Kleid*⟩; (*zeitlich*) prolong; renew ⟨*Pass, Vertrag*⟩; (*Culin*) thin down. **V∼ung** *f* **-,-en** extension; renewal. **V∼ungsschnur** *f* extension cable
verlangsamen *vt* slow down
Verlass (Verlaß) *m* **auf ihn ist kein V∼** you cannot rely on him
verlassen† *vt* leave; (*im Stich lassen*) desert; **sich v∼ auf** (+ *acc*) rely *or* depend on □ *a* deserted. **V∼heit** *f* - desolation
verlässlich (verläßlich) *a* reliable
Verlauf *m* course; **im V∼** (+ *gen*) in the course of. **v∼en**† *vi (sein)* run; (*ablaufen*) go; (*zerlaufen*) melt; **gut v∼en** go [off] well □ *vr* **sich v∼en** lose one's way; ⟨*Menge:*⟩ disperse; ⟨*Wasser:*⟩ drain away
verleben *vt* spend
verlegen *vt* move; (*verschieben*) postpone; (*vor-*) bring forward; (*verlieren*) mislay; (*versperren*) block; (*legen*) lay ⟨*Teppich, Rohre*⟩; (*veröffentlichen*) publish; **sich v∼ auf** (+ *acc*) take up ⟨*Beruf, Fach*⟩; resort to ⟨*Taktik, Bitten*⟩ □ *a* embarrassed; **nie v∼ um** never at a loss for. **V∼heit** *f* - embarrassment
Verleger *m* **-s,-** publisher
verleihen† *vt* lend; (*gegen Gebühr*) hire out; (*überreichen*) award, confer; (*fig*) give
verleiten *vt* induce/(*verlocken*) tempt (**zu** to)
verlernen *vt* forget
verlesen†[1] *vt* read out; **ich habe mich v∼** I misread it
verlesen†[2] *vt* sort out
verletz|en *vt* injure; (*kränken*) hurt; (*verstoßen gegen*) infringe; violate ⟨*Grenze*⟩. **v∼end** *a* hurtful, wounding. **v∼lich** *a* vulnerable. **V∼te(r)** *m/f* injured person; (*bei Unfall*) casualty. **V∼ung** *f* **-,-en** injury; (*Verstoß*) infringement; violation
verleugnen *vt* deny; disown ⟨*Freund*⟩
verleumd|en *vt* slander; (*schriftlich*) libel. **v∼erisch** *a* slanderous; libellous. **V∼ung** *f* **-,-en** slander; (*schriftlich*) libel
verlieben (sich) *vr* fall in love (**in** + *acc* with); **verliebt sein** be in love (**in** + *acc* with)
verlier|en† *vt* lose; shed ⟨*Laub*⟩; **sich v∼en** disappear; ⟨*Weg:*⟩ peter out □ *vi (haben)* lose (**an etw** *dat* sth). **V∼er** *m* **-s,-** loser
verlob|en (sich) *vr* get engaged (**mit** to); **v∼t sein** be engaged. **V∼te** *f* fiancée. **V∼te(r)** *m* fiancé. **V∼ung** *f* **-,-en** engagement
verlock|en *vt* tempt; **v∼end** tempting. **V∼ung** *f* **-,-en** temptation
verlogen *a* lying
verloren *a* lost; **v∼e Eier** poached eggs; **v∼ gehen** get lost. **v∼gehen**† *vi sep (sein)* (NEW) **v∼ gehen**, *s.* **verloren**
verlos|en *vt* raffle. **V∼ung** *f* **-,-en** raffle; (*Ziehung*) draw
verlottert *a* run-down; ⟨*Person*⟩ scruffy; (*sittlich*) dissolute

Verlust *m* **-[e]s,-e** loss
vermachen *vt* leave, bequeath
Vermächtnis *nt* **-ses,-se** legacy
vermähl|en (sich) *vr* marry. **V~ung** *f* **-,-en** marriage
vermehren *vt* increase; propagate ⟨*Pflanzen*⟩; **sich v~** increase; (*sich fortpflanzen*) breed, multiply
vermeiden† *vt* avoid
vermeintlich *a* supposed, *adv* -ly
Vermerk *m* **-[e]s,-e** note. **v~en** note [down]; **übel v~en** take amiss
vermess|en† *vt* measure; survey ⟨*Gelände*⟩ □ *a* presumptuous. **V~enheit** *f* **-** presumption. **V~ung** *f* measurement; (*Land-*) survey
vermiet|en *vt* let, rent [out]; hire out ⟨*Boot, Auto*⟩; **zu v~en** to let; ⟨*Boot:*⟩ for hire. **V~er** *m* landlord. **V~erin** *f* landlady
vermind|er|n *vt* reduce, lessen. **V~ung** *f* **-** reduction, decrease
vermischen *vt* mix; **sich v~** mix
vermissen *vt* miss
vermisst (vermißt) *a* missing. **V~e(r)** *m* missing person/(*Mil*) soldier
vermittel|n *vi* (*haben*) mediate □ *vt* arrange; (*beschaffen*) find; place ⟨*Arbeitskräfte*⟩; impart ⟨*Wissen*⟩; convey ⟨*Eindruck*⟩. **v~s** *prep* (+ *gen*) by means of
Vermittl|er *m* **-s,-** agent; (*Schlichter*) mediator. **V~ung** *f* **-,-en** arrangement; (*Agentur*) agency; (*Teleph*) exchange; (*Schlichtung*) mediation
vermögen† *vt* be able (**zu** to). **V~** *nt* **-s,-** fortune. **v~d** *a* wealthy
vermut|en *vt* suspect; (*glauben*) presume. **v~lich** *a* probable □ *adv* presumably. **V~ung** *f* **-,-en** supposition; (*Verdacht*) suspicion; (*Mutmaßung*) conjecture
vernachlässig|en *vt* neglect. **V~ung** *f* **-** neglect
vernehm|en† *vt* hear; (*verhören*) question; (*Jur*) examine. **V~ung** *f* **-,-en** questioning
verneig|en (sich) *vr* bow. **V~ung** *f* **-,-en** bow
verne|in|en *vt* answer in the negative; (*ablehnen*) reject. **v~end** *a* negative. **V~ung** *f* **-,-en** negative answer; (*Gram*) negative
vernicht|en *vt* destroy; (*ausrotten*) exterminate. **v~end** *a* devastating; ⟨*Niederlage*⟩ crushing. **V~ung** *f* **-** destruction; extermination
Vernunft *f* **-** reason; **V~ annehmen** see reason
vernünftig *a* reasonable, sensible; (*fam: ordentlich*) decent □ *adv* sensibly; (*fam*) properly
veröffentlich|en *vt* publish. **V~ung** *f* **-,-en** publication
verordn|en *vt* prescribe (*dat* for). **V~ung** *f* **-,-en** prescription; (*Verfügung*) decree
verpachten *vt* lease [out]
verpack|en *vt* pack; (*einwickeln*) wrap. **V~ung** *f* packaging; wrapping
verpassen *vt* miss; (*fam: geben*) give
verpfänden *vt* pawn
verpflanzen *vt* transplant
verpfleg|en *vt* feed: **sich selbst v~en** cater for oneself. **V~ung** *f* **-** board; (*Essen*) food; **Unterkunft und V~ung** board and lodging
verpflicht|en *vt* oblige; (*einstellen*) engage; (*Sport*) sign; **sich v~en** undertake/(*versprechen*) promise (**zu** to); (*vertraglich*) sign a contract; **jdm v~et sein be** indebted to s.o. **V~ung** *f* **-,-en** obligation, commitment
verpfuschen *vt* make a mess of
verpönt *a* **v~ sein** be frowned upon
verprügeln *vt* beat up, thrash
Verputz *m* **-es** plaster. **v~en** *vt* plaster; (*fam: essen*) polish off

Verrat *m* **-[e]s** betrayal, treachery. **v~en**† *vt* betray; give away ⟨*Geheimnis*⟩; (*fam: sagen*) tell; **sich v~en** give oneself away

Verräter *m* **-s,-** traitor. **v~isch** *a* treacherous; (*fig*) revealing

verräuchert *a* smoky

verrech|nen *vt* settle; clear ⟨*Scheck*⟩; **sich v~nen** make a mistake; (*fig*) miscalculate. **V~nungsscheck** *m* crossed cheque

verregnet *a* spoilt by rain; ⟨*Tag*⟩ rainy, wet

verreisen *vi* (*sein*) go away; **verreist sein** be away

verreißen† *vt* (*fam*) pan, slate

verrenken *vt* dislocate; **sich v~** contort oneself

verricht|en *vt* perform, do; say ⟨*Gebet*⟩. **V~ung** *f* **-,-en** task

verriegeln *vt* bolt

verringer|n *vt* reduce; **sich v~n** decrease. **V~ung** *f* **-** reduction; decrease

verrost|en *vi* (*sein*) rust. **v~et** *a* rusty

verrücken *vt* move

verrückt *a* crazy, mad; **v~ werden/machen** go/drive crazy. **V~e(r)** *m/f* lunatic. **V~heit** *f* **-,-en** madness; (*Torheit*) folly

Verruf *m* disrepute. **v~en** *a* disreputable

verrühren *vt* mix

verrunzelt *a* wrinkled

verrutschen *vt* (*sein*) slip

Vers /fɛrs/ *m* **-es,-e** verse

versag|en *vi* (*haben*) fail □ *vt* **jdm/sich etw v~en** deny s.o./oneself sth. **V~en** *nt* **-s,-** failure. **V~er** *m* **-s,-** failure

versalzen† *vt* put too much salt in/on; (*fig*) spoil

versamm|eln *vt* assemble; **sich v~eln** assemble, meet. **V~lung** *f* assembly, meeting

Versand *m* **-[e]s** dispatch. **V~haus** *nt* mail-order firm

versäum|en *vt* miss; lose ⟨*Zeit*⟩; (*unterlassen*) neglect; **[es] v~en, etw zu tun** fail *or* neglect to do sth. **V~nis** *nt* **-ses,-se** omission

verschaffen *vt* get; **sich** (*dat*) **v~** obtain; gain ⟨*Respekt*⟩

verschämt *a* bashful, *adv* -ly

verschandeln *vt* spoil

verschärfen *vt* intensify; tighten ⟨*Kontrolle*⟩; increase ⟨*Tempo*⟩; aggravate ⟨*Lage*⟩; **sich v~** intensify; increase; ⟨*Lage:*⟩ worsen

verschätzen (sich) *vr* **sich v~ in** (+ *dat*) misjudge

verschenken *vt* give away

verscheuchen *vt* shoo/(*jagen*) chase away

verschicken *vt* send; (*Comm*) dispatch

verschieb|en† *vt* move; (*aufschieben*) put off, postpone; (*sl: handeln mit*) traffic in; **sich v~en** move, shift; (*verrutschen*) slip; (*zeitlich*) be postponed. **V~ung** *f* shift; postponement

verschieden *a* different; **v~e** (*pl*) different; (*mehrere*) various; **V~es** (**v~es**) some things; (*dieses und jenes*) various things; **die v~sten Farben** a whole variety of colours; **das ist v~** it varies □ *adv* differently; **v~ groß/lang** of different sizes/lengths. **v~artig** *a* diverse. **V~heit** *f* **-** difference; (*Vielfalt*) diversity. **v~tlich** *adv* several times

verschimmel|n *vi* (*sein*) go mouldy. **v~t** *a* mouldy

verschlafen† *vi* (*haben*) oversleep □ *vt* sleep through ⟨*Tag*⟩; (*versäumen*) miss ⟨*Zug, Termin*⟩; **sich v~** oversleep □ *a* sleepy; **noch v~** still half asleep

Verschlag *m* **-[e]s,¨e** shed

verschlagen† *vt* lose ⟨*Seite*⟩; **jdm die Sprache/den Atem v~** leave s.o. speechless/take s.o.'s breath away; **nach X v~ werden** end up in X □ *a* sly, *adv* -ly

verschlechter|n *vt* make worse; **sich v~n** get worse, deteriorate. **V~ung** *f* -,-en deterioration
verschleiern *vt* veil; (*fig*) hide
Verschleiß *m* -es wear and tear; (*Verbrauch*) consumption. **v~en†** *vt/i* (*sein*) wear out
verschleppen *vt* carry off; (*entführen*) abduct; spread ⟨*Seuche*⟩; neglect ⟨*Krankheit*⟩; (*hinausziehen*) delay
verschleudern *vt* sell at a loss; (*verschwenden*) squander
verschließen† *vt* close; (*abschließen*) lock; (*einschließen*) lock up
verschlimmer|n *vt* make worse; aggravate ⟨*Lage*⟩; **sich v~n** get worse, deteriorate. **V~ung** *f* -,-en deterioration
verschlingen† *vt* intertwine; (*fressen*) devour; (*fig*) swallow
verschlissen *a* worn
verschlossen *a* reserved. **V~heit** *f* - reserve
verschlucken *vt* swallow; **sich v~** choke (**an** + *dat* on)
Verschluss *m* **-es,¨e (Verschluß** *m* **-sses,¨sse)** fastener, clasp; (*Fenster-*, *Koffer-*) catch; (*Flaschen-*) top; (*luftdicht*) seal; (*Phot*) shutter; **unter V~** under lock and key
verschlüsselt *a* coded
verschmähen *vt* spurn
verschmelzen† *vt/i* (*sein*) fuse
verschmerzen *vt* get over
verschmutz|en *vt* soil; pollute ⟨*Luft*⟩ □ *vi* (*sein*) get dirty. **V~ung** *f* - pollution
verschnaufen *vi/r* (*haben*) **[sich] v~** get one's breath
verschneit *a* snow-covered
verschnörkelt *a* ornate
verschnüren *vt* tie up
verschollen *a* missing
verschonen *vt* spare
verschönern *vt* brighten up; (*verbessern*) improve
verschossen *a* faded
verschrammt *a* scratched
verschränken *vt* cross
verschreiben† *vt* prescribe; **sich v~** make a slip of the pen
verschrie[e]n *a* notorious
verschroben *a* eccentric
verschrotten *vt* scrap
verschulden *vt* be to blame for. **V~** *nt* -s fault
verschuldet *a* **v~ sein** be in debt
verschütten *vt* spill; (*begraben*) bury
verschweigen† *vt* conceal, hide
verschwend|en *vt* waste. **v~erisch** *a* extravagant, *adv* -ly; (*üppig*) lavish, *adv* -ly. **V~ung** *f* - extravagance; (*Vergeudung*) waste
verschwiegen *a* discreet; ⟨*Ort*⟩ secluded. **V~heit** *f* - discretion
verschwimmen† *vi* (*sein*) become blurred
verschwinden† *vi* (*sein*) disappear; **[mal] v~** (*fam*) spend a penny. **V~** *nt* **-s** disappearance
verschwommen *a* blurred
verschwör|en† **(sich)** *vr* conspire. **V~ung** *f* -,-en conspiracy
versehen† *vt* perform; hold ⟨*Posten*⟩; keep ⟨*Haushalt*⟩; **v~ mit** provide with; **sich v~** make a mistake; **ehe man sich's versieht** before you know where you are. **V~** *nt* **-s,-** oversight; (*Fehler*) slip; **aus V~** by mistake. **v~tlich** *adv* by mistake
Versehrte(r) *m* disabled person
versenden† *vt* send [out]
versengen *vt* singe; (*stärker*) scorch
versenken *vt* sink; **sich v~ in** (+ *acc*) immerse oneself in
versessen *a* keen (**auf** + *acc* on)
versetz|en *vt* move; transfer ⟨*Person*⟩; (*Sch*) move up; (*verpfänden*) pawn; (*verkaufen*) sell; (*vermischen*) blend; (*antworten*) reply; **jdn v~en** (*fam: warten lassen*) stand s.o. up; **jdm einen Stoß/Schreck v~en** give s.o. a

push/fright; **jdm in Angst/Erstaunen v~en** frighten/astonish s.o.; **sich in jds Lage v~en** put oneself in s.o.'s place. **V~ung** *f* -,-**en** move; transfer; (*Sch*) move to a higher class

verseuch|en *vt* contaminate. **V~ung** *f* - contamination

versicher|n *vt* insure; (*bekräftigen*) affirm; **jdm v~n** assure s.o (**dass** that). **V~ung** *f* -,-**en** insurance; assurance

versiegeln *vt* seal

versiegen *vi* (*sein*) dry up

versiert /vɛr'ʒi:ɐ̯t/ *a* experienced

versilbert *a* silver-plated

versinken† (*sein*) sink; **in Gedanken versunken** lost in thought

Version /vɛr'zi̯o:n/ *f* -,-**en** version

Versmaß /'fɛrs-/ *nt* metre

versöhn|en *vt* reconcile; **sich v~en** become reconciled. **v~lich** *a* conciliatory. **V~ung** *f* -,-**en** reconciliation

versorg|en *vt* provide, supply (**mit** with); provide for ⟨*Familie*⟩; (*betreuen*) look after; keep ⟨*Haushalt*⟩. **V~ung** *f* - provision, supply; (*Betreuung*) care

verspät|en (sich) *vr* be late. **v~et** *a* late; ⟨*Zug*⟩ delayed; ⟨*Dank, Glückwunsch*⟩ belated □ *adv* late; belatedly. **V~ung** *f* - lateness; **V~ung haben** be late

versperren *vt* block; bar ⟨*Weg*⟩

verspiel|en *vt* gamble away; **sich v~en** play a wrong note. **v~t** *a* playful, *adv* -ly

verspotten *vt* mock, ridicule

versprech|en† *vt* promise; **sich v~en** make a slip of the tongue; **sich** (*dat*) **viel v~en von** have high hopes of; **ein viel v~ender Anfang** a promising start. **V~en** *nt* **-s,-** promise. **V~ungen** *fpl* promises

verspüren *vt* feel

verstaatlich|en *vt* nationalize. **V~ung** *f* - nationalization

Verstand *m* **-[e]s** mind; (*Vernunft*) reason; **den V~ verlieren** go out of one's mind. **v~esmäßig** *a* rational, *adv* -ly

verständig *a* sensible, *adv* -bly; (*klug*) intelligent, *adv* -ly. **v~en** *vt* notify, inform; **sich v~en** communicate; (*sich verständlich machen*) make oneself understood; (*sich einigen*) reach agreement. **V~ung** *f* - notification; communication; (*Einigung*) agreement

verständlich *a* comprehensible, *adv* -bly; (*deutlich*) clear, *adv* -ly; (*begreiflich*) understandable; **leicht v~** easily understood; **sich v~ machen** make oneself understood. **v~erweise** *adv* understandably

Verständnis *nt* **-ses** understanding. **v~los** *a* uncomprehending, *adv* -ly. **v~voll** *a* understanding, *adv* -ly

verstärk|en *vt* strengthen, reinforce; (*steigern*) intensify, increase; amplify ⟨*Ton*⟩; **sich v~en** intensify. **V~er** *m* **-s,-** amplifier. **V~ung** *f* reinforcement; increase; amplification; (*Truppen*) reinforcements *pl*

verstaubt *a* dusty

verstauchen *vt* sprain

verstauen *vt* stow

Versteck *nt* **-[e]s,-e** hiding-place; **V~ spielen** play hide-and-seek. **v~en** *vt* hide; **sich v~en** hide. **v~t** *a* hidden; (*heimlich*) secret; (*verstohlen*) furtive, *adv* -ly

verstehen† *vt* understand; (*können*) know; **falsch v~** misunderstand; **sich v~** understand one another; (*auskommen*) get on; **das versteht sich von selbst** that goes without saying

versteifen *vt* stiffen; **sich v~** stiffen; (*fig*) insist (**auf** + *acc* on)

versteiger|n *vt* auction. **V~ung** *f* auction

versteinert *a* fossilized

verstell|bar *a* adjustable. **v~en** *vt* adjust; (*versperren*) block; (*verändern*) disguise; **sich v~en** pretend. **V~ung** *f* - pretence

versteuern *vt* pay tax on

verstiegen *a* (*fig*) extravagant

verstimm|t *a* disgruntled; ⟨*Magen*⟩ upset; (*Mus*) out of tune. **V~ung** *f* - ill humour; (*Magen-*) upset

verstockt *a* stubborn, *adv* -ly

verstohlen *a* furtive, *adv* -ly

verstopf|en *vt* plug; (*versperren*) block; **v~t** blocked; ⟨*Person*⟩ constipated. **V~ung** *f* -,-**en** blockage; (*Med*) constipation

verstorben *a* late, deceased. **V~e(r)** *m/f* deceased

verstört *a* bewildered

Verstoß *m* infringement. **v~en†** *vt* disown □ *vi* (*haben*) **v~en gegen** contravene, infringe; offend against ⟨*Anstand*⟩

verstreichen† *vt* spread □ *vi* (*sein*) pass

verstreuen *vt* scatter

verstümmeln *vt* mutilate; garble ⟨*Text*⟩

verstummen *vi* (*sein*) fall silent; ⟨*Gespräch, Lärm:*⟩ cease

Versuch *m* -**[e]s,-e** attempt; (*Experiment*) experiment. **v~en** *vt/i* (*haben*) try; **sich v~en in** (+ *dat*) try one's hand at; **v~t sein** be tempted (**zu** to). **V~skaninchen** *nt* (*fig*) guinea-pig. **v~sweise** *adv* as an experiment. **V~ung** *f* -,-**en** temptation

versündigen (sich) *vr* sin (**an** + *dat* against)

vertagen *vt* adjourn; (*aufschieben*) postpone; **sich v~** adjourn

vertauschen *vt* exchange; (*verwechseln*) mix up

verteidig|en *vt* defend. **V~er** *m* -**s,-** defender; (*Jur*) defence counsel. **V~ung** *f* -,-**en** defence

verteil|en *vt* distribute; (*zuteilen*) allocate; (*ausgeben*) hand out; (*verstreichen*) spread; **sich v~en** spread out. **V~ung** *f* - distribution; allocation

vertief|en *vt* deepen; **v~t sein in** (+ *acc*) be engrossed in. **V~ung** *f* -,-**en** hollow, depression

vertikal /vɛrti'ka:l/ *a* vertical, *adv* -ly

vertilgen *vt* exterminate; kill [off] ⟨*Unkraut*⟩; (*fam: essen*) demolish

vertippen (sich) *vr* make a typing mistake

vertonen *vt* set to music

Vertrag *m* -**[e]s,¨e** contract; (*Pol*) treaty

vertragen† *vt* tolerate, stand; take ⟨*Kritik, Spaß*⟩; **sich v~** get on; (*passen*) go (**mit** with); **sich wieder v~** make it up □ *a* worn

vertraglich *a* contractual

verträglich *a* good-natured; (*bekömmlich*) digestible

vertrauen *vi* (*haben*) trust (**jdm/etw** s.o./sth; **auf** + *acc* in). **V~** *nt* -**s** trust, confidence (**zu** in); **im V~** in confidence. **V~smann** *m* (*pl* -**leute**) representative; (*Sprecher*) spokesman. **v~svoll** *a* trusting, *adv* -ly. **v~swürdig** *a* trustworthy

vertraulich *a* confidential, *adv* -ly; (*intim*) familiar, *adv* -ly

vertraut *a* intimate; (*bekannt*) familiar; **sich v~ machen mit** familiarize oneself with. **V~heit** *f* - intimacy; familiarity

vertreib|en† *vt* drive away; drive out ⟨*Feind*⟩; (*Comm*) sell; **sich** (*dat*) **die Zeit v~en** pass the time. **V~ung** *f* -,-**en** expulsion

vertret|en† *vt* represent; (*einspringen für*) stand in *or* deputize for; (*verfechten*) support; hold ⟨*Meinung*⟩; **sich** (*dat*) **den Fuß v~en** twist one's ankle; **sich** (*dat*) **die Beine v~en** stretch one's legs. **V~er** *m* -**s,-** representative; deputy; (*Arzt-*) locum; (*Verfechter*) supporter, advocate. **V~ung** *f* -,-**en** representation; (*Person*) deputy; (*eines Arztes*) locum; (*Handels-*) agency

Vertrieb *m* **-[e]s** (*Comm*) sale. **V~ene(r)** *m/f* displaced person
vertrocknen *vi* (*sein*) dry up
vertrösten *vt* **jdn auf später v~** put s.o. off until later
vertun† *vt* waste; **sich v~** (*fam*) make a mistake
vertuschen *vt* hush up
verübeln *vt* **jdm etw v~** hold sth against s.o.
verüben *vt* commit
verunglimpfen *vt* denigrate
verunglücken *vi* (*sein*) be involved in an accident; (*fam: missglücken*) go wrong; **tödlich v~** be killed in an accident
verunreinigen *vt* pollute; (*verseuchen*) contaminate; (*verschmutzen*) soil
verunstalten *vt* disfigure
veruntreu|en *vt* embezzle. **V~ung** *f* - embezzlement
verursachen *vt* cause
verurteil|en *vt* condemn; (*Jur*) convict (**wegen** of); sentence (**zum Tode** to death). **V~ung** *f* - condemnation; (*Jur*) conviction
vervielfachen *vt* multiply
vervielfältigen *vt* duplicate
vervollkommnen *vt* perfect
vervollständigen *vt* complete
verwachsen *a* deformed
verwählen (sich) *vr* misdial
verwahren *vt* keep; (*verstauen*) put away; **sich v~** (*fig*) protest
verwahrlost *a* neglected; ⟨*Haus*⟩ dilapidated; (*sittlich*) depraved
Verwahrung *f* - keeping; **in V~ nehmen** take into safe keeping
verwaist *a* orphaned
verwalt|en *vt* administer; (*leiten*) manage; govern ⟨*Land*⟩. **V~er** *m* **-s,-** administrator; manager. **V~ung** *f* **-,-en** administration; management; government
verwand|eln *vt* transform, change (**in** + *acc* into) **sich v~eln** change, turn (**in** + *acc* into). **V~lung** *f* transformation
verwandt *a* related (**mit** to). **V~e(r)** *m/f* relative. **V~schaft** *f* - relationship; (*Menschen*) relatives *pl*
verwarn|en *vt* warn, caution. **V~ung** *f* warning, caution
verwaschen *a* washed out, faded
verwechs|eln *vt* mix up, confuse; (*halten für*) mistake (**mit** for). **V~lung** *f* -,-en mix-up
verwegen *a* audacious, *adv* -ly
Verwehung *f* **-,-en** [snow-]drift
verweichlicht *a* (*fig*) soft
verweiger|n *vt/i* (*haben*) refuse (**jdm etw** s.o sth); **den Gehorsam v~n** refuse to obey. **V~ung** *f* refusal
verweilen *vi* (*haben*) stay
Verweis *m* **-es,-e** reference (**auf** + *acc* to); (*Tadel*) reprimand; **v~en†** *vt* refer (**auf/an** + *acc* to); (*tadeln*) reprimand; **von der Schule v~en** expel
verwelken *vi* (*sein*) wilt
verwend|en† *vt* use; spend ⟨*Zeit, Mühe*⟩. **V~ung** *f* use
verwerf|en† *vt* reject; **sich v~en** warp. **v~lich** *a* reprehensible
verwert|en *vt* utilize, use; (*Comm*) exploit. **V~ung** *f* - utilization; exploitation
verwesen *vi* (*sein*) decompose
verwick|eln *vt* involve (**in** + *acc* in); **sich v~eln** get tangled up; **in etw** (*acc*) **v~elt sein** (*fig*) be involved *or* mixed up in sth. **v~elt** *a* complicated
verwildert *a* wild; ⟨*Garten*⟩ overgrown; ⟨*Aussehen*⟩ unkempt
verwinden† *vt* (*fig*) get over
verwirken *vt* forfeit
verwirklichen *vt* realize; **sich v~** be realized
verwirr|en *vt* tangle up; (*fig*) confuse; **sich v~en** get tangled; (*fig*) become confused. **v~t** *a* confused. **V~ung** *f* - confusion
verwischen *vt* smudge
verwittert *a* weathered; ⟨*Gesicht*⟩ weather-beaten

verwitwet *a* widowed
verwöhn|en *vt* spoil. **v~t** *a* spoilt; (*anspruchsvoll*) discriminating
verworren *a* confused
verwund|bar *a* vulnerable. **v~en** *vt* wound
verwunder|lich *a* surprising. **v~n** *vt* surprise; **sich v~n** be surprised. **V~ung** *f* - surprise
Verwund|ete(r) *m* wounded soldier; **die V~eten** the wounded *pl*. **V~ung** *f* -,-en wound
verwünsch|en *vt* curse. **v~t** *a* confounded
verwüst|en *vt* devastate, ravage. **V~ung** *f* -,-en devastation
verzagen *vi* (*haben*) lose heart
verzählen (sich) *vr* miscount
verzärteln *vt* mollycoddle
verzaubern *vt* bewitch; (*fig*) enchant; **v~ in** (+ *acc*) turn into
Verzehr *m* -s consumption. **v~en** *vt* eat; (*aufbrauchen*) use up; **sich v~en** (*fig*) pine away
verzeich|nen *vt* list; (*registrieren*) register. **V~nis** *nt* **-ses, -se** list; (*Inhalts-*) index
verzeih|en† *vt* forgive; **v~en Sie!** excuse me! **V~ung** *f* - forgiveness; **um V~ung bitten** apologize; **V~ung!** sorry! (*bei Frage*) excuse me!
verzerren *vt* distort; contort ⟨*Gesicht*⟩; pull ⟨*Muskel*⟩
Verzicht *m* **-[e]s** renunciation (**auf** + *acc* of). **v~en** *vi* (*haben*) do without; **v~en auf** (+ *acc*) give up; renounce ⟨*Recht, Erbe*⟩
verziehen† *vt* pull out of shape; (*verwöhnen*) spoil; **sich v~** lose shape; ⟨*Holz:*⟩ warp; ⟨*Gesicht:*⟩ twist; (*verschwinden*) disappear; ⟨*Nebel:*⟩ disperse; ⟨*Gewitter:*⟩ pass; **das Gesicht v~** pull a face □ *vi* (*sein*) move [away]
verzier|en *vt* decorate. **V~ung** *f* -,-en decoration
verzinsen *vt* pay interest on
verzöger|n *vt* delay; (*verlangsamen*) slow down; **sich v~n** be delayed. **V~ung** *f* -,-en delay
verzollen *vt* pay duty on; **haben Sie etwas zu v~?** have you anything to declare?
verzück|t *a* ecstatic, *adv* -ally. **V~ung** *f* - rapture, ecstasy
Verzug *m* delay; **in V~** in arrears
verzweif|eln *vi* (*sein*) despair. **v~elt** *a* desperate, *adv* -ly; **v~elt sein** be in despair; (*ratlos*) be desperate. **V~lung** *f* - despair; (*Ratlosigkeit*) desperation
verzweigen (sich) *vr* branch [out]
verzwickt *a* (*fam*) tricky
Veto /ˈveːto/ *nt* **-s,-s** veto
Vetter *m* **-s,-n** cousin. **V~nwirtschaft** *f* nepotism
vgl. *abbr* (**vergleiche**) cf.
Viadukt /vi̯aˈdʊkt/ *nt* **-[e]s,-e** viaduct
vibrieren /viˈbriːrən/ *vi* (*haben*) vibrate
Video /ˈviːdeo/ *nt* **-s,-s** video. **V~kassette** *f* video cassette. **V~recorder** /-rəkɔrdɐ/ *m* **-s,-** video recorder
Vieh *nt* **-[e]s** livestock; (*Rinder*) cattle *pl*; (*fam: Tier*) creature. **v~isch** *a* brutal, *adv* -ly
viel *pron* a great deal/(*fam*) a lot of; (*pl*) many, (*fam*) a lot of; (*substantivisch*) **v~[es]** much, (*fam*) a lot; **nicht/so/wie/zu v~** not/so/how/too much/ (*pl*) many; **v~e** *pl* many; **das v~e Geld/Lesen** all that money/reading □ *adv* much, (*fam*) a lot; **v~ mehr/weniger** much more/less; **v~zu groß/klein/viel** much *or* far too big/small/much; **so v~ wie möglich** as much as possible; **so/zu v~ arbeiten** work so/too much
viel|deutig *a* ambiguous. **v~erlei** *inv a* many kinds of □ *pron* many things. **v~fach** *a* multiple □ *adv* many times; (*fam: oft*) frequently. **V~falt** *f* - diversity,

[great] variety. **v~fältig** *a* diverse, varied
vielleicht *adv* perhaps, maybe; (*fam: wirklich*) really
vielmals *adv* very much; **danke v~!** thank you very much!
viel|mehr *adv* rather; (*im Gegenteil*) on the contrary. **v~sagend** *a* (NEW) **v~ sagend**, *s.* **sagen**
vielseitig *a* varied; ⟨*Person*⟩ versatile □ *adv* **v~ begabt** versatile. **V~keit** *f* - versatility
vielversprechend *a* (NEW) **viel versprechend**, *s.* **versprechen**
vier *inv a*, **V~** *f* -,-en four; (*Sch*) ≈ fair. **V~eck** *nt* **-[e]s,-e** oblong, rectangle; (*Quadrat*) square. **v~eckig** *a* oblong, rectangular; square. **v~fach** *a* quadruple. **V~linge** *mpl* quadruplets
viertel /'fɪrtəl/ *inv a* quarter; **eine v~ Million** a quarter of a million; **um v~ neun** at [a] quarter past eight; **um drei v~ neun** at [a] quarter to nine; **eine v~ Stunde = eine Viertelstunde. V~** *nt* **-s,-** quarter; (*Wein*) quarter litre; **V~ vor/nach sechs** [a] quarter to/past six; **um V~/drei V~ neun** (NEW) **um v~/drei v~ neun**, *s.* **viertel**. **V~finale** *nt* quarter-final. **V~jahr** *nt* three months *pl*; (*Comm*) quarter. **v~jährlich** *a & adv* quarterly. **v~n** *vt* quarter. **V~note** *f* crotchet, (*Amer*) quarter note. **V~stunde** *f* quarter of an hour
vier|zehn /'fɪr-/ *inv a* fourteen. **v~zehnte(r,s)** *a* fourteenth. **v~zig** *inv a* forty. **v~zigste(r,s)** *a* fortieth
Villa /'vɪla/ *f* **-,-len** villa
violett /vio'lɛt/ *a* violet
Vio|line /vio'li:nə/ *f* **-,-n** violin. **V~linschlüssel** *m* treble clef. **V~loncello** /-lɔn'tʃɛlo/ *nt* cello
Virtuose /vɪr'tuo:zə/ *m* **-n,-n** virtuoso
Virus /'vi:rʊs/ *nt* **-,-ren** virus
Visier /vi'zi:ɐ/ *nt* **-s,-e** visor
Vision /vi'zio:n/ *f* **-,-en** vision
Visite /vi'zi:tə/ *f* **-,-n** round; **V~ machen** do one's round
visuell /vi'zuɛl/ *a* visual, *adv* -ly
Visum /'vi:zʊm/ *nt* **-s,-sa** visa
vital /vi'ta:l/ *a* vital; ⟨*Person*⟩ energetic. **V~ität** *f* - vitality
Vitamin /vita'mi:n/ *nt* **-s,-e** vitamin
Vitrine /vi'tri:nə/ *f* **-,-n** display cabinet/(*im Museum*) case
Vizepräsident /'fi:tsə-/ *m* vice president
Vogel *m* **-s,¨** bird; **einen V~ haben** (*fam*) have a screw loose. **V~scheuche** *f* **-,-n** scarecrow
Vokab|eln /vo'ka:bəln/ *fpl* vocabulary *sg*. **V~ular** *nt* **-s,-e** vocabulary
Vokal /vo'ka:l/ *m* **-s,-e** vowel
Volant /vo'lã:/ *m* **-s,-s** flounce; (*Auto*) steering-wheel
Volk *nt* **-[e]s,¨er** people *sg*; (*Bevölkerung*) people *pl*; (*Bienen-*) colony
Völker|kunde *f* ethnology. **V~mord** *m* genocide. **V~recht** *nt* international law
Volks|abstimmung *f* plebiscite. **V~fest** *nt* public festival. **V~hochschule** *f* adult education classes *pl*/(*Gebäude*) centre. **V~lied** *nt* folk-song. **V~tanz** *m* folk-dance. **v~tümlich** *a* popular. **V~wirt** *m* economist. **V~wirtschaft** *f* economics *sg*. **V~zählung** *f* [national] census
voll *a* full (**von** *od* **mit** of); ⟨*Haar*⟩ thick; ⟨*Erfolg, Ernst*⟩ complete; ⟨*Wahrheit*⟩ whole; **v~ machen** fill up; **v~ tanken** fill up with petrol; **die Uhr schlug v~** (*fam*) the clock struck the hour □ *adv* (*ganz*) completely; ⟨*arbeiten*⟩ full-time; ⟨*auszahlen*⟩ in full; **v~ und ganz** completely
vollauf *adv* fully, completely
Voll|beschäftigung *f* full employment. **V~blut** *nt* thoroughbred

vollbringen† *vt insep* accomplish work ⟨*Wunder*⟩
vollende|n *vt insep* complete. **v~t** *a* perfect, *adv* -ly; **v~te Gegenwart/Vergangenheit** perfect/pluperfect
vollends *adv* completely
Vollendung *f* completion; (*Vollkommenheit*) perfection
voller *inv a* full of; **v~ Angst/Freude** filled with fear/joy; **v~ Flecken** covered with stains
Völlerei *f* - gluttony
Volleyball /ˈvɔli-/ *m* volleyball
vollführen *vt insep* perform
vollfüllen *vt sep* fill up
Vollgas *nt* **V~ geben** put one's foot down; **mit V~** flat out
völlig *a* complete, *adv* -ly
volljährig *a* **v~ sein** (*Jur*) be of age. **V~keit** *f* - (*Jur*) majority
Vollkaskoversicherung *f* fully comprehensive insurance
vollkommen *a* perfect, *adv* -ly; (*völlig*) complete, *adv* -ly. **V~heit** *f* - perfection
Voll|kornbrot *nt* wholemeal bread. **V~macht** *f* -,-en authority; (*Jur*) power of attorney. **V~mond** *m* full moon. **V~pension** *f* full board. **v~schlank** *a* with a fuller figure
vollständig *a* complete, *adv* -ly
vollstrecken *vt insep* execute; carry out ⟨*Urteil*⟩
volltanken *vi sep* (*haben*)
(NEW) **voll tanken**, *s.* **voll**
Volltreffer *m* direct hit
vollzählig *a* complete; **sind wir v~?** are we all here?
vollziehen† *vt insep* carry out; perform ⟨*Handlung*⟩; consummate ⟨*Ehe*⟩; **sich v~** take place
Volt /vɔlt/ *nt* **-[s],-** volt
Volumen /voˈluːmən/ *nt* **-s,-** volume
vom *prep* = **von dem; vom Rauchen** from smoking
von *prep* (+ *dat*) of; (*über*) about; (*Ausgangspunkt, Ursache*) from; (*beim Passiv*) by; **Musik von Mozart** music by Mozart; **einer von euch** one of you; **von hier/heute an** from here/today; **von mir aus** I don't mind
voneinander *adv* from each other; ⟨*abhängig*⟩ on each other
vonseiten *prep* (+ *gen*) on the part of
vonstatten *adv* **v~ gehen** take place; **gut v~ gehen** go [off] well
vor *prep* (+ *dat/acc*) in front of; (*zeitlich, Reihenfolge*) before; (+ *dat*) (*bei Uhrzeit*) to; ⟨*warnen, sich fürchten/schämen*⟩ of; ⟨*schützen, davonlaufen*⟩ from; ⟨*Respekt haben*⟩ for; **vor Angst/Kälte zittern** tremble with fear/cold; **vor drei Tagen/Jahren** three days/years ago; **vor sich** (*acc*) **hin murmeln** mumble to oneself; **vor allen Dingen** above all □ *adv* forward; **vor und zurück** backwards and forwards
Vor|abend *m* eve. **V~ahnung** *f* premonition
voran *adv* at the front; (*voraus*) ahead; (*vorwärts*) forward. **v~gehen**† *vi sep* (*sein*) lead the way; (*Fortschritte machen*) make progress; **jdm/etw v~gehen** precede s.o./sth. **v~kommen**† *vi sep* (*sein*) make progress; (*fig*) get on
Vor|anschlag *m* estimate. **V~anzeige** *f* advance notice. **V~arbeit** *f* preliminary work. **V~arbeiter** *m* foreman
voraus *adv* ahead (*dat* of); (*vorn*) at the front; (*vorwärts*) forward □ **im Voraus (voraus)** in advance. **v~bezahlen** *vt sep* pay in advance. **v~gehen**† *vi sep* (*sein*) go on ahead; **jdm/etw v~gehen** precede s.o./sth. **V~sage** *f* -,-n prediction. **v~sagen** *vt sep* predict. **v~sehen**† *vt sep* foresee
voraussetz|en *vt sep* take for granted; (*erfordern*) require; **vorausgesetzt, dass** provided that.

V∼ung *f* **-,-en** assumption; (*Erfordernis*) prerequisite; **unter der V∼ung, dass** on condition that

Voraussicht *f* foresight; **aller V∼ nach** in all probability. **v∼lich** *a* anticipated, expected □ *adv* probably

Vorbehalt *m* **-[e]s,-e** reservation. **v∼en†** *vt sep* **sich** (*dat*) **v∼en** reserve ⟨*Recht*⟩; **jdm v∼en sein/bleiben** be left to s.o. **v∼los** *a* unreserved, *adv* -ly

vorbei *adv* past (**an jdm/etw** s.o./sth); (*zu Ende*) over. **v∼fahren†** *vi sep* (*sein*) drive/go past. **v∼gehen†** *vi sep* (*sein*) go past; (*verfehlen*) miss; (*vergehen*) pass; (*fam: besuchen*) drop in (**bei** on). **v∼kommen†** *vi sep* (*sein*) pass/(*v∼können*) get past (**an jdm/etw** s.o./sth); (*fam: besuchen*) drop in (**bei** on)

vorbereit|en *vt sep* prepare; prepare for ⟨*Reise*⟩; **sich v∼en** prepare [oneself] (**auf** + *acc* for). **V∼ung** *f* **-,-en** preparation

vorbestellen *vt sep* order/(*im Theater, Hotel*) book in advance

vorbestraft *a* **v∼ sein** have a [criminal] record

vorbeug|en *v sep* □ *vt* bend forward; **sich v∼en** bend *or* lean forward □ *vi* (*haben*) prevent (**etw** *dat* sth); **v∼end** preventive. **V∼ung** *f* - prevention

Vorbild *nt* model. **v∼lich** *a* exemplary, model □ *adv* in an exemplary manner

vorbringen† *vt sep* put forward; offer ⟨*Entschuldigung*⟩

vordatieren *vt sep* post-date

Vorder|bein *nt* foreleg. **v∼e(r,s)** *a* front. **V∼grund** *m* foreground. **V∼mann** *m* (*pl* **-männer**) person in front; **auf V∼mann bringen** (*fam*) lick into shape; (*aufräumen*) tidy up. **V∼rad** *nt* front wheel. **V∼seite** *f* front; (*einer Münze*) obverse. **v∼ste(r,s)** *a* front, first. **V∼teil** *nt* front

vor|drängeln (sich) *vr sep* (*fam*) jump the queue. **v∼drängen (sich)** *vr sep* push forward. **v∼dringen†** *vi sep* (*sein*) advance

vor|ehelich *a* pre-marital. **v∼eilig** *a* rash, *adv* -ly

voreingenommen *a* biased, prejudiced. **V∼heit** *f* - bias

vorenthalten† *vt sep* withhold

vorerst *adv* for the time being

Vorfahr *m* **-en,-en** ancestor

vorfahren† *vi sep* (*sein*) drive up; (*vorwärts-*) move forward; (*voraus-*) drive on ahead

Vorfahrt *f* right of way; **'V∼ beachten'** 'give way'. **V∼sstraße** *f* ≈ major road

Vorfall *m* incident. **v∼en†** *vi sep* (*sein*) happen

vorfinden† *vt sep* find

Vorfreude *f* [happy] anticipation

vorführ|en *vt sep* present, show; (*demonstrieren*) demonstrate; (*aufführen*) perform. **V∼ung** *f* presentation; demonstration; performance

Vor|gabe *f* (*Sport*) handicap. **V∼gang** *m* occurrence; (*Techn*) process. **V∼gänger(in)** *m* **-s,-** (*f* **-,-nen**) predecessor. **V∼garten** *m* front garden

vorgeben† *vt sep* pretend

vor|gefasst (**vor|gefaßt**) *a* preconceived. **v∼gefertigt** *a* prefabricated

vorgehen† *vi sep* (*sein*) go forward; (*voraus-*) go on ahead; ⟨*Uhr:*⟩ be fast; (*wichtig sein*) take precedence; (*verfahren*) act, proceed; (*geschehen*) happen, go on. **V∼** *nt* **-s** action

vor|geschichtlich *a* prehistoric. **V∼geschmack** *m* foretaste. **V∼gesetzte(r)** *m/f* superior. **v∼gestern** *adv* the day before yesterday; **v∼gestern Abend/Nacht** the evening/night before last

vorhaben† *vt sep* propose, intend (**zu** to); **etw v∼** have sth planned;

nichts v~ have no plans. V~ *nt* -s,- plan; (*Projekt*) project
vorhalt|en† *v sep* □ *vt* hold up; **jdm etw v~en** reproach s.o. for sth □ *vi* (*haben*) last. **V~ungen** *fpl* **jdm V~ungen machen** reproach s.o. (**wegen** for)
Vorhand *f* (*Sport*) forehand
vorhanden *a* existing; **v~ sein** exist; (*verfügbar sein*) be available. **V~sein** *nt* -s existence
Vorhang *m* curtain
Vorhängeschloss (**Vorhängeschloß**) *nt* padlock
vorher *adv* before[hand]
vorhergehend *a* previous
vorherig *a* prior; (*vorhergehend*) previous
Vorherrsch|aft *f* supremacy. **v~en** *vi sep* (*haben*) predominate. **v~end** *a* predominant
Vorher|sage *f* -,-n prediction: (*Wetter-*) forecast. **v~sagen** *vt sep* predict; forecast ⟨*Wetter*⟩. **v~sehen†** *vt sep* foresee
vorhin *adv* just now
vorige(r,s) *a* last, previous
Vor|kämpfer *m* (*fig*) champion. **V~kehrungen** *fpl* precautions. **V~kenntnisse** *fpl* previous knowledge *sg*
vorkommen† *vi sep* (*sein*) happen; (*vorhanden sein*) occur; (*nach vorn kommen*) come forward; (*hervorkommen*) come out; (*zu sehen sein*) show; **jdm bekannt/verdächtig v~** seem familiar/suspicious to s.o.; **sich** (*dat*) **dumm/alt v~** feel stupid/old. **V~** *nt* -s,- occurrence; (*Geol*) deposit
Vorkriegszeit *f* pre-war period
vorlad|en† *vt sep* (*Jur*) summons. **V~ung** *f* summons
Vorlage *f* model; (*Muster*) pattern; (*Gesetzes-*) bill
vorlassen† *vt sep* admit; **jdn v~** (*fam*) let s.o. pass; (*den Vortritt lassen*) let s.o. go first
Vor|lauf *m* (*Sport*) heat. **V~läufer** *m* forerunner. **v~läufig** *a* provisional, *adv* -ly; (*zunächst*) for the time being. **v~laut** *a* forward. **V~leben** *nt* past
vorleg|en *vt sep* put on ⟨*Kette*⟩; (*unterbreiten*) present; (*vorzeigen*) show; **jdm Fleisch v~en** serve s.o. with meat. **V~er** *m* -s,- mat; (*Bett-*) rug
vorles|en† *vt sep* read [out]; **jdm v~en** read to s.o. **V~ung** *f* lecture
vorletzt|e(r,s) *a* last ... but one; ⟨*Silbe*⟩ penultimate; **v~es Jahr** the year before last
vorlieb *adv* **v~ nehmen** make do (**mit** with). **v~nehmen†** *vt sep* (NEW) **v~ nehmen**, *s.* **vorlieb**
Vorliebe *f* preference
vorliegen† *vi sep* (*haben*) be present/(*verfügbar*) available; (*bestehen*) exist, be; **es muss ein Irrtum v~** there must be some mistake. **v~d** *a* present; ⟨*Frage*⟩ at issue
vorlügen† *vt sep* lie (*dat* to)
vorm *prep* = **vor dem**
vormachen *vt sep* put up; put on ⟨*Kette*⟩; push ⟨*Riegel*⟩; (*zeigen*) demonstrate; **jdm etwas v~** (*fam: täuschen*) kid s.o.
Vormacht *f* supremacy
vormals *adv* formerly
Vormarsch *m* (*Mil & fig*) advance
vormerken *vt sep* make a note of; (*reservieren*) reserve
Vormittag *m* morning; **gestern/heute V~** yesterday/this morning. **v~** *adv* **gestern/heute v~** (NEW) **gestern/heute V~**, *s.* **Vormittag**. **v~s** *adv* in the morning
Vormund *m* -[e]s,-munde & -münder guardian
vorn *adv* at the front; **nach v~** to the front; **von v~** from the front/(*vom Anfang*) beginning; **von v~ anfangen** start afresh
Vorname *m* first name

vorne *adv* = **vorn**
vornehm *a* distinguished; (*elegant*) smart, *adv* -ly
vornehmen† *vt sep* carry out; **sich** (*dat*) **v~, etw zu tun** plan/ (*beschließen*) resolve to do sth
vorn|herein *adv* **von v~herein** from the start. **v~über** *adv* forward
Vor|ort *m* suburb. **V~rang** *m* priority, precedence (**vor** + *dat* over). **V~rat** *m* **-[e]s,-e** supply, stock (**an** + *dat* of). **v~rätig** *a* available; **v~rätig haben** have in stock. **V~ratskammer** *f* larder. **V~raum** *m* ante-room. **V~recht** *nt* privilege. **V~richtung** *f* device
vorrücken *vt/i sep* (*sein*) move forward; (*Mil*) advance
Vorrunde *f* qualifying round
vors *prep* = **vor das**
vorsagen *vt/i sep* (*haben*) recite; **jdm [die Antwort] v~** tell s.o. the answer
Vor|satz *m* resolution. **v~sätzlich** *a* deliberate, *adv* -ly; (*Jur*) premeditated
Vorschau *f* preview; (*Film-*) trailer
Vorschein *m* **zum V~kommen** appear
vorschießen† *vt sep* advance ⟨*Geld*⟩
Vorschlag *m* suggestion, proposal. **v~en**† *vt sep* suggest, propose
vorschnell *a* rash, *adv* -ly
vorschreiben† *vt sep* lay down; dictate (*dat* to); **vorgeschriebene Dosis** prescribed dose
Vorschrift *f* regulation; (*Anweisung*) instruction; **jdm V~en machen** tell s.o. what to do; **Dienst nach V~** work to rule. **v~smäßig** *a* correct, *adv* -ly
Vorschule *f* nursery school
Vorschuss (Vorschuß) *m* advance
vorschützen *vt sep* plead [as an excuse]; feign ⟨*Krankheit*⟩
vorseh|en† *v sep* □ *vt* intend (**für/ als** for/as); (*planen*) plan; **sich v~en** be careful (**vor** + *dat* of) □ *vi* (*haben*) peep out. **V~ung** *f* - providence
vorsetzen *vt sep* move forward; **jdm etw v~** serve s.o. sth
Vorsicht *f* - care; (*bei Gefahr*) caution; **V~!** careful! (*auf Schild*) 'caution'. **v~ig** *a* careful, *adv* -ly; cautious, *adv* -ly. **v~shalber** *adv* to be on the safe side. **V~smaßnahme** *f* precaution
Vorsilbe *f* prefix
Vorsitz *m* chairmanship; **den V~ führen** be in the chair. **v~en**† *vi sep* (*haben*) preside (*dat* over). **V~ende(r)** *m/f* chairman
Vorsorge *f* **V~ treffen** take precautions; make provisions (**für** for). **v~n** *vi sep* (*haben*) provide (**für** for). **V~untersuchung** *f* check-up
vorsorglich *adv* as a precaution
Vorspeise *f* starter
Vorspiel *nt* prelude. **v~en** *v sep* □ *vt* perform/ (*Mus*) play (*dat* for) □ *vi* (*haben*) audition
vorsprechen† *v sep* □ *vt* recite; (*zum Nachsagen*) say (*dat* to) □ *vi* (*haben*) (*Theat*) audition; **bei jdm v~** call on s.o.
vorspringen† *vi sep* (*sein*) jut out; **v~des Kinn** prominent chin
Vor|sprung *m* projection; (*Fels-*) ledge; (*Vorteil*) lead (**vor** + *dat* over). **V~stadt** *f* suburb. **v~städtisch** *a* suburban. **V~stand** *m* board [of directors]; (*Vereins-*) committee; (*Partei-*) executive
vorsteh|en† *vi sep* (*haben*) project, protrude; **einer Abteilung v~en** be in charge of a department; **v~end** protruding; ⟨*Augen*⟩ bulging. **V~er** *m* **-s,-** head; (*Gemeinde-*) chairman

vorstell|bar *a* imaginable, conceivable. **v~en** *vt sep* put forward ⟨*Bein, Uhr*⟩; (*darstellen*) represent; (*bekanntmachen*) introduce; **sich v~en** introduce oneself; (*als Bewerber*) go for an interview; **sich** (*dat*) **etw v~en** imagine sth. **V~ung** *f* introduction; (*bei Bewerbung*) interview; (*Aufführung*) performance; (*Idee*) idea; (*Phantasie*) imagination. **V~ungsgespräch** *nt* interview. **V~ungskraft** *f* imagination

Vorstoß *m* advance

Vorstrafe *f* previous conviction

Vortag *m* day before

vortäuschen *vt sep* feign, fake

Vorteil *m* advantage. **v~haft** *a* advantageous, *adv* -ly; ⟨*Kleidung, Farbe*⟩ flattering

Vortrag *m* **-[e]s,¨e** talk; (*wissenschaftlich*) lecture; ⟨*Klavier-, Gedicht-*⟩ recital. **v~en**† *vt sep* perform; (*aufsagen*) recite; (*singen*) sing; (*darlegen*) present (*dat* to); express ⟨*Wunsch*⟩

vortrefflich *a* excellent, *adv* -ly

vortreten† *vi sep* (*sein*) step forward, (*hervor-*) protrude

Vortritt *m* precedence; **jdm den V~ lassen** let s.o. go first

vorüber *adv* **v~ sein** be over; **an etw** (*dat*) **v~** past sth. **v~gehen**† *vi sep* (*sein*) walk past; (*vergehen*) pass. **v~gehend** *a* temporary, *adv* -ily

Vor|urteil *nt* prejudice. **V~verkauf** *m* advance booking

vorverlegen *vt sep* bring forward

Vor|wahl[nummer] *f* dialling code. **V~wand** *m* **-[e]s,¨e** pretext; (*Ausrede*) excuse

vorwärts *adv* forward[s]; **v~ kommen** make progress; (*fig*) get on *or* ahead. **v~kommen**† *vi sep* (*sein*) (NEW) **v~ kommen**, *s.* **vorwärts**

vorweg *adv* beforehand; (*vorn*) in front; (*voraus*) ahead. **v~nehmen**† *vt sep* anticipate

vorweisen† *vt sep* show

vorwerfen† *vt sep* throw (*dat* to); **jdm etw v~** reproach s.o. with sth; (*beschuldigen*) accuse s.o. of sth

vorwiegend *adv* predominantly

Vorwort *nt* (*pl* **-worte**) preface

Vorwurf *m* reproach; **jdm Vorwürfe machen** reproach s.o. **v~svoll** *a* reproachful, *adv* -ly

Vorzeichen *nt* sign; (*fig*) omen

vorzeigen *vt sep* show

vorzeitig *a* premature, *adv* -ly

vorziehen† *vt sep* pull forward; draw ⟨*Vorhang*⟩; (*vorverlegen*) bring forward; (*lieber mögen*) prefer; (*bevorzugen*) favour

Vor|zimmer *nt* ante-room; (*Büro*) outer office. **V~zug** *m* preference; (*gute Eigenschaft*) merit, virtue; (*Vorteil*) advantage

vorzüglich *a* excellent, *adv* -ly

vorzugsweise *adv* preferably

vulgär /vʊl'gɛːɐ̯/ *a* vulgar □ *adv* in a vulgar way

Vulkan /vʊl'kaːn/ *m* **-s,-e** volcano

W

Waage *f* **-,-n** scales *pl*; (*Astr*) Libra. **w~recht** *a* horizontal, *adv* -ly

Wabe *f* **-,-n** honeycomb

wach *a* awake; (*aufgeweckt*) alert; **w~ werden** wake up

Wach|e *f* **-,-n** guard; (*Posten*) sentry; (*Dienst*) guard duty; (*Naut*) watch; (*Polizei-*) station; **W~e halten** keep watch; **W~e stehen** stand guard. **w~en** *vi* (*haben*) be awake; **w~en über** (+ *acc*) watch over. **W~hund** *m* guard-dog

Wacholder *m* **-s** juniper

Wachposten *m* sentry

Wachs *nt* **-es** wax

wachsam *a* vigilant, *adv* -ly. **W~keit** *f* - vigilance

wachsen†[1] *vi* (*sein*) grow

wachs|en[2] *vt* (*reg*) wax. **W~figur** *f* waxwork. **W~tuch** *nt* oil-cloth
Wachstum *nt* **-s** growth
Wächter *m* **-s,-** guard; (*Park-*) keeper; (*Parkplatz-*) attendant
Wacht|meister *m* [police] constable. **W~posten** *m* sentry
Wachturm *m* watch-tower
wackel|ig *a* wobbly; ⟨*Stuhl*⟩ rickety; ⟨*Person*⟩ shaky. **W~kontakt** *m* loose connection. **w~n** *vi* (*haben*) wobble; (*zittern*) shake □ *vi* (*sein*) totter
wacklig *a* = **wackelig**
Wade *f* **-,-n** (*Anat*) calf
Waffe *f* **-,-n** weapon; **W~n** arms
Waffel *f* **-,-n** waffle; (*Eis-*) wafer
Waffen|ruhe *f* cease-fire. **W~schein** *m* firearms licence. **W~stillstand** *m* armistice
Wagemut *m* daring. **w~ig** *a* daring, *adv* -ly
wagen *vt* risk; **es w~, etw zu tun** dare [to] do sth; **sich w~** (*gehen*) venture
Wagen *m* **-s,-** cart; (*Eisenbahn-*) carriage, coach; (*Güter-*) wagon; (*Kinder-*) pram; (*Auto*) car. **W~heber** *m* **-s,-** jack
Waggon /va'gõ:/ *m* **-s,-s** wagon
waghalsig *a* daring, *adv* -ly
Wagnis *nt* **-ses,-se** risk
Wagon /va'gõ:/ *m* **-s,-s** = **Waggon**
Wahl *f* **-,-en** choice; (*Pol, Admin*) election; (*geheime*) ballot; **zweite W~** (*Comm*) seconds *pl*
wähl|en *vt/i* (*haben*) choose; (*Pol, Admin*) elect; (*stimmen*) vote; (*Teleph*) dial; **jdn wieder w~en** re-elect s.o. **W~er(in)** *m* **-s,-** (*f* **-,-nen**) voter. **w~erisch** *a* choosy, fussy
Wahl|fach *nt* optional subject. **w~frei** *a* optional. **W~kampf** *m* election campaign. **W~kreis** *m* constituency. **W~lokal** *nt* polling-station. **w~los** *a* indiscriminate, *adv* -ly. **W~recht** *nt* [right to] vote
Wählscheibe *f* (*Teleph*) dial
Wahl|spruch *m* motto. **W~urne** *f* ballot-box
Wahn *m* **-[e]s** delusion; (*Manie*) mania
wähnen *vt* believe
Wahnsinn *m* madness. **w~ig** *a* mad, insane; (*fam: unsinnig*) crazy; (*fam: groß*) terrible; **w~ig werden** go mad □ *adv* (*fam*) terribly. **W~ige(r)** *m/f* maniac
wahr *a* true; (*echt*) real; **w~ werden** come true; **du kommst doch, nicht w~?** you are coming, aren't you?
wahren *vt* keep; (*verteidigen*) safeguard; **den Schein w~** keep up appearances
währen *vi* (*haben*) last
während *prep* (+ *gen*) during □ *conj* while; (*wohingegen*) whereas. **w~dessen** *adv* in the meantime
wahrhaben *vt* **etw nicht w~wollen** refuse to admit sth
wahrhaftig *adv* really, truly
Wahrheit *f* **-,-en** truth. **w~sgemäß** *a* truthful, *adv* -ly
wahrnehm|bar *a* perceptible. **w~en**† *vt sep* notice; (*nutzen*) take advantage of; exploit ⟨*Vorteil*⟩; look after ⟨*Interessen*⟩. **W~ung** *f* **-,-en** perception
wahrsag|en *v sep* □ *vt* predict □ *vi* (*haben*) **jdm w~en** tell s.o.'s fortune. **W~erin** *f* **-,-nen** fortune-teller
wahrscheinlich *a* probable, *adv* -bly. **W~keit** *f* - probability
Währung *f* **-,-en** currency
Wahrzeichen *nt* symbol
Waise *f* **-,-n** orphan. **W~nhaus** *nt* orphanage. **W~nkind** *nt* orphan
Wal *m* **-[e]s,-e** whale
Wald *m* **-[e]s,¨er** wood; (*groß*) forest. **w~ig** *a* wooded
Walis|er *m* **-s,-** Welshman. **w~isch** *a* Welsh
Wall *m* **-[e]s,¨e** mound; (*Mil*) rampart

Wallfahr|er(in) *m(f)* pilgrim. **W~t** *f* pilgrimage

Walnuss (Walnuß) *f* walnut

Walze *f* **-,-n** roller. **w~n** *vt* roll

wälzen *vt* roll; pore over ⟨*Bücher*⟩; mull over ⟨*Probleme*⟩; **sich w~** roll [about]; (*schlaflos*) toss and turn

Walzer *m* **-s,-** waltz

Wand *f* **-,¨e** wall; (*Trenn-*) partition; (*Seite*) side; (*Fels-*) face

Wandel *m* **-s** change. **w~bar** *a* changeable. **w~n** *vi* (*sein*) stroll □ *vr* **sich w~n** change

Wander|er *m* **-s,-**, **W~in** *f* **-,-nen** hiker, rambler. **w~n** *vi* (*sein*) hike, ramble; (*ziehen*) travel; (*gemächlich gehen*) wander; (*ziellos*) roam. **W~schaft** *f* **-** travels *pl*. **W~ung** *f* **-,-en** hike, ramble; (*länger*) walking tour. **W~weg** *m* footpath

Wandgemälde *nt* mural

Wandlung *f* **-,-en** change, transformation

Wand|malerei *f* mural. **W~tafel** *f* blackboard. **W~teppich** *m* tapestry

Wange *f* **-,-n** cheek

wank|elmütig *a* fickle. **w~en** *vi* (*haben*) sway; ⟨*Person:*⟩ stagger; (*fig*) waver □ *vi* (*sein*) stagger

wann *adv* when

Wanne *f* **-,-n** tub

Wanze *f* **-,-n** bug

Wappen *nt* **-s,-** coat of arms. **W~kunde** *f* heraldry

war, **wäre** *s.* **sein**[1]

Ware *f* **-,-n** article; (*Comm*) commodity; (*coll*) merchandise; **W~n** goods. **W~nhaus** *nt* department store. **W~nprobe** *f* sample. **W~nzeichen** *nt* trademark

warm *a* **(wärmer, wärmst)** warm; ⟨*Mahlzeit*⟩ hot; **w~ machen** heat □ *adv* warmly; **w~ essen** have a hot meal

Wärm|e *f* **-** warmth; (*Phys*) heat; **10 Grad W~e** 10 degrees above zero. **w~en** *vt* warm; heat ⟨*Essen, Wasser*⟩. **W~flasche** *f* hot-water bottle

warmherzig *a* warm-hearted

Warn|blinkanlage *f* hazard [warning] lights *pl*. **w~en** *vt/i* (*haben*) warn **(vor** + *dat* of). **W~ung** *f* **-,-en** warning

Warteliste *f* waiting list

warten *vi* (*haben*) wait **(auf** + *acc* for); **auf sich** (*acc*) **w~ lassen** take one's/its time □ *vt* service

Wärter(in) *m* **-s,-** (*f* **-,-nen**) keeper; (*Museums-*) attendant; (*Gefängnis-*) warder, (*Amer*) guard; (*Kranken-*) orderly

Warte|raum, W~saal *m* waiting-room. **W~zimmer** *nt* (*Med*) waiting-room

Wartung *f* **-** (*Techn*) service

warum *adv* why

Warze *f* **-,-n** wart

was *pron* what; **was für [ein]?** what kind of [a]? **was für ein Pech!** what bad luck! **das gefällt dir, was?** you like that, don't you? □ *rel pron* that; **alles, was ich brauche** all [that] I need □ *indef pron* (*fam: etwas*) something; (*fragend, verneint*) anything; **was zu essen** something to eat; **so was Ärgerliches!** what a nuisance! □ *adv* (*fam*) (*warum*) why; (*wie*) how

wasch|bar *a* washable. **W~becken** *nt* wash-basin. **W~beutel** *m* sponge-bag

Wäsche *f* **-** washing; (*Unter-*) underwear; **in der W~** in the wash

waschecht *a* colour-fast; (*fam*) genuine

Wäsche|klammer *f* clothes-peg. **W~leine** *f* clothes-line

waschen† *vt* wash; **sich w~** have a wash; **sich** (*dat*) **die Hände w~** wash one's hands; **W~ und Legen** shampoo and set □ *vi* (*haben*) do the washing

Wäscherei *f* **-,-en** laundry

Wäsche|schleuder *f* spin-drier. **W~trockner** *m* tumble-drier

Wasch|küche *f* laundry-room. **W~lappen** *m* face-flannel, (*Amer*) washcloth; (*fam: Feigling*) sissy. **W~maschine** *f* washing machine. **W~mittel** *nt* detergent. **W~pulver** *nt* washing-powder. **W~raum** *m* washroom. **W~salon** *m* launderette. **W~zettel** *m* blurb

Wasser *nt* **-s** water; (*Haar-*) lotion; **ins W~ fallen** (*fam*) fall through; **mir lief das W~ im Mund zusammen** my mouth was watering. **W~ball** *m* beachball; (*Spiel*) water polo. **w~dicht** *a* watertight; ⟨*Kleidung*⟩ waterproof. **W~fall** *m* waterfall. **W~farbe** *f* water-colour. **W~hahn** *m* tap, (*Amer*) faucet. **W~kasten** *m* cistern. **W~kraft** *f* water-power. **W~kraftwerk** *nt* hydroelectric power-station. **W~leitung** *f* water-main; **aus der W~leitung** from the tap. **W~mann** *m* (*Astr*) Aquarius

wässern *vt* soak; (*begießen*) water □ *vi* (*haben*) water

Wasser|scheide *f* watershed. **W~ski** *nt* **-s** water-skiing. **W~stoff** *m* hydrogen. **W~straße** *f* waterway. **W~-waage** *f* spirit-level. **W~werfer** *m* **-s,-** water-cannon. **W~zeichen** *nt* watermark

wässrig (**wäßrig**) *a* watery

waten *vi* (*sein*) wade

watscheln *vi* (*sein*) waddle

Watt[1] *nt* **-[e]s** mud-flats *pl*

Watt[2] *nt* **-s,-** (*Phys*) watt

Watt|e *f* - cotton wool. **w~iert** *a* padded; (*gesteppt*) quilted

WC /ve'tse:/ *nt* **-s,-s** WC

web|en *vt/i* (*haben*) weave. **W~er** *m* **-s,-** weaver. **W~stuhl** *m* loom

Wechsel *m* **-s,-** change; (*Tausch*) exchange; (*Comm*) bill of exchange. **W~geld** *nt* change. **w~haft** *a* changeable. **W~jahre** *npl* menopause *sg*. **W~kurs** *m* exchange rate. **w~n** *vt* change; (*tauschen*) exchange □ *vi* (*haben*) change; (*ab-*) alternate; (*verschieden sein*) vary. **w~nd** *a* changing; (*verschieden*) varying. **w~seitig** *a* mutual, *adv* -ly. **W~strom** *m* alternating current. **W~stube** *f* bureau de change. **w~weise** *adv* alternately. **W~wirkung** *f* interaction

weck|en *vt* wake [up]; (*fig*) awaken □ *vi* (*haben*) ⟨*Wecker:*⟩ go off. **W~er** *m* **-s,-** alarm [clock]

wedeln *vi* (*haben*) wave; **mit dem Schwanz w~** wag its tail

weder *conj* **w~ ... noch** neither ... nor

Weg *m* **-[e]s,-e** way; (*Fuß-*) path; (*Fahr-*) track; (*Gang*) errand; **auf dem Weg** on the way (**nach** to); **sich auf den Weg machen** set off; **im Weg sein** be in the way; **zu W~e bringen** = **zuwege bringen**, *s.* **zuwege**

weg *adv* away, off; (*verschwunden*) gone; **weg sein** be away; (*gegangen/verschwunden*) have gone; (*fam: schlafen*) be asleep; **Hände weg!** hands off! **w~bleiben**† *vi sep* (*sein*) stay away. **w~bringen**† *vt sep* take away

wegen *prep* (+ *gen*) because of; (*um ... willen*) for the sake of; (*bezüglich*) about

weg|fahren† *vi sep* (*sein*) go away; (*abfahren*) leave. **w~fallen**† *vi sep* (*sein*) be dropped/(*ausgelassen*) omitted; (*entfallen*) no longer apply; (*aufhören*) cease. **w~geben**† *vt sep* give away; send to the laundry ⟨*Wäsche*⟩. **w~gehen**† *vi sep* (*sein*) leave, go away; (*ausgehen*) go out; ⟨*Fleck:*⟩ come out. **w~jagen** *vt sep* chase away. **w~kommen**† *vi sep* (*sein*) get away; (*verloren gehen*) disappear; **schlecht w~kommen** (*fam*) get a raw deal. **w~lassen**† *vt sep* let go; (*auslassen*) omit. **w~laufen**† *vi sep* (*sein*) run away. **w~machen** *vt sep* remove.

w~nehmen† *vt sep* take away. **w~räumen** *vt sep* put away; (*entfernen*) clear away. **w~schicken** *vt sep* send away; (*abschicken*) send off. **w~tun**† *vt sep* put away; (*wegwerfen*) throw away

Wegweiser *m* **-s,-** signpost

weg|werfen† *vt sep* throw away. **w~ziehen**† *v sep* □ *vt* pull away □ *vi* (*sein*) move away

weh *a* sore; **weh tun** hurt; ⟨*Kopf, Rücken:*⟩ ache; **jdm weh tun** hurt s.o. □ *int* **oh weh!** oh dear!

wehe *int* alas; **w~ [dir/euch]!** (*drohend*) don't you dare!

wehen *vi* (*haben*) blow; (*flattern*) flutter □ *vt* blow

Wehen *fpl* contractions; **in den W~liegen** be in labour

weh|leidig *a* soft; (*weinerlich*) whining. **W~mut** *f* - wistfulness. **w~mütig** *a* wistful, *adv* -ly

Wehr[1] *nt* **-[e]s,-e** weir

Wehr[2] *f* **sich zur W~ setzen** resist. **W~dienst** *m* military service. **W~dienstverweigerer** *m* **-s,-** conscientious objector

wehren (sich) *vr* resist; (*gegen Anschuldigung*) protest; (*sich sträuben*) refuse

wehr|los *a* defenceless. **W~macht** *f* armed forces *pl*. **W~pflicht** *f* conscription

Weib *nt* **-[e]s,-er** woman; (*Ehe-*) wife. **W~chen** *nt* **-s,-** (*Zool*) female. **W~erheld** *m* womanizer. **w~isch** *a* effeminate. **w~lich** *a* feminine; (*Biol*) female. **W~lichkeit** *f* - femininity

weich *a* soft, *adv* -ly; (*gar*) done; ⟨*Ei*⟩ soft-boiled; ⟨*Mensch*⟩ soft-hearted; **w~ werden** (*fig*) relent

Weiche *f* **-,-n** (*Rail*) points *pl*

weichen[1] *vi* (*sein*) (*reg*) soak

weichen†[2] *vi* (*sein*) give way (*dat* to); **nicht von jds Seite w~** not leave s.o.'s side

Weich|heit *f* - softness. **w~herzig** *a* soft-hearted. **w~lich** *a* soft; ⟨*Charakter*⟩ weak. **W~spüler** *m* **-s,-** (*Tex*) conditioner. **W~tier** *nt* mollusc

Weide[1] *f* **-,-n** (*Bot*) willow

Weide[2] *f* **-,-n** pasture. **w~n** *vt/i* (*haben*) graze; **sich w~n an** (+ *dat*) enjoy; (*schadenfroh*) gloat over

weiger|n (sich) *vr* refuse. **W~ung** *f* **-,-en** refusal

Weihe *f* **-,-n** consecration; (*Priester-*) ordination. **w~n** *vt* consecrate; (*zum Priester*) ordain; dedicate ⟨*Kirche*⟩ (*dat* to)

Weiher *m* **-s,-** pond

Weihnacht|en *nt* **-s** & *pl* Christmas. **w~lich** *a* Christmassy. **W~sbaum** *m* Christmas tree. **W~sfest** *nt* Christmas. **W~slied** *nt* Christmas carol. **W~smann** *m* (*pl* **-männer**) Father Christmas. **W~stag** *m* **erster/zweiter W~stag** Christmas Day/Boxing Day

Weih|rauch *m* incense. **W~wasser** *nt* holy water

weil *conj* because; (*da*) since

Weile *f* - while

Wein *m* **-[e]s,-e** wine; (*Bot*) vines *pl*; (*Trauben*) grapes *pl*. **W~bau** *m* wine-growing. **W~beere** *f* grape. **W~berg** *m* vineyard. **W~brand** *m* **-[e]s** brandy

wein|en *vt/i* (*haben*) cry, weep. **w~erlich** *a* tearful, *adv* -ly

Wein|glas *nt* wineglass. **W~karte** *f* wine-list. **W~keller** *m* wine-cellar. **W~lese** *f* grape harvest. **W~liste** *f* wine-list. **W~probe** *f* wine-tasting. **W~rebe** *f*, **W~stock** *m* vine. **W~stube** *f* wine-bar. **W~traube** *f* bunch of grapes; (*W~beere*) grape

weise *a* wise, *adv* -ly

Weise *f* **-,-n** way; (*Melodie*) tune; **auf diese W~** in this way

weisen† *vt* show; **von sich w~** (*fig*) reject □ *vi* (*haben*) point (**auf** + *acc* at)

Weisheit *f* **-,-en** wisdom. **W~szahn** *m* wisdom tooth
weiß *a*, **W~** *nt* **-,-** white
weissag|en *vt/i insep (haben)* prophesy. **W~ung** *f* **-,-en** prophecy
Weiß|brot *nt* white bread. **W~e(r)** *m/f* white man/woman. **w~en** *vt* whitewash. **W~wein** *m* white wine
Weisung *f* **-,-en** instruction; (*Befehl*) order
weit *a* wide; (*ausgedehnt*) extensive; (*lang*) long □ *adv* widely; ⟨*offen, öffnen*⟩ wide; (*lang*) far; **von w~em** from a distance; **bei w~em** by far; **w~ und breit** far and wide; **ist es noch w~?** is it much further? **so w~ wie möglich** as far as possible; **ich bin so w~** I'm ready; **es ist so w~** the time has come; **zu w~ gehen** (*fig*) go too far; **w~ verbreitet** widespread; **w~ blickend** (*fig*) far-sighted; **w~ reichende Folgen** far-reaching consequences. **w~aus** *adv* far. **W~blick** *m* (*fig*) far-sightedness. **w~blickend** *a* = **w~ blickend**, *s.* **weit**
Weite *f* **-,-n** expanse; (*Entfernung*) distance; (*Größe*) width. **w~n** *vt* widen; stretch ⟨*Schuhe*⟩; **sich w~n** widen; stretch; ⟨*Pupille*⟩ dilate
weiter *a* further □ *adv* further; (*außerdem*) in addition; (*anschließend*) then; **etw w~tun** go on doing sth; **w~ nichts/niemand** nothing/no one else; **und so w~** and so on. **w~arbeiten** *vi sep (haben)* go on working
weiter|e(r,s) *a* further; **im w~en Sinne** in a wider sense; **ohne w~es** just like that; (*leicht*) easily; **bis auf w~es** until further notice; (*vorläufig*) for the time being
weiter|erzählen *vt sep* go on with; (*w~sagen*) repeat. **w~fahren†** *vi sep (sein)* go on. **w~geben†** *vt sep* pass on. **w~gehen†** *vi sep (sein)* go on. **w~hin** *adv* (*immer noch*) still; (*in Zukunft*) in future; (*außerdem*) furthermore; **etw w~hin tun** go on doing sth. **w~kommen†** *vi sep (sein)* get on. **w~machen** *vi sep (haben)* carry on. **w~sagen** *vt sep* pass on; (*verraten*) repeat
weit|gehend *a* extensive □ *adv* to a large extent. **w~hin** *adv* a long way; (*fig*) widely. **w~läufig** *a* spacious; (*entfernt*) distant, *adv* -ly; (*ausführlich*) lengthy, *adv* at length. **w~reichend** *a* = **w~ reichend**, *s.* **weit**. **w~schweifig** *a* long-winded. **w~sichtig** *a* long-sighted; (*fig*) far-sighted. **W~sprung** *m* long jump. **w~verbreitet** *a* = **w~ verbreitet**, *s.* **weit**
Weizen *m* **-s** wheat
welch *inv pron* what; **w~ ein(e)** what a. **w~e(r,s)** *pron* which; **um w~e Zeit?** at what time? □ *rel pron* which; (*Person*) who □ *indef pron* some; (*fragend*) any; **was für w~e?** what sort of?
welk *a* wilted; ⟨*Laub*⟩ dead. **w~en** *vi (haben)* wilt; (*fig*) fade
Wellblech *nt* corrugated iron
Well|e *f* **-,-n** wave; (*Techn*) shaft. **W~enlänge** *f* wavelength. **W~enlinie** *f* wavy line. **W~enreiten** *nt* surfing. **W~ensittich** *m* **-s,-e** budgerigar. **w~ig** *a* wavy
Welt *f* **-,-en** world; **auf der W~** in the world; **auf die** *od* **zur W~ kommen** be born. **W~all** *nt* universe. **w~berühmt** *a* world-famous. **w~fremd** *a* unworldly. **w~gewandt** *a* sophisticated. **W~kugel** *f* globe. **w~lich** *a* worldly; (*nicht geistlich*) secular
Weltmeister|(in) *m(f)* world champion. **W~schaft** *f* world championship
Weltraum *m* space. **W~fahrer** *m* astronaut
Welt|rekord *m* world record. **w~weit** *a & adv* world-wide

wẹm *pron* (*dat of* **wer**) to whom
wẹn *pron* (*acc of* **wer**) whom
Wẹnde *f* **-,-n** change. **W~kreis** *m* (*Geog*) tropic
Wẹndeltreppe *f* spiral staircase
wẹnden[1] *vt* (*reg*) turn; **sich zum Guten w~** take a turn for the better □ *vi* (*haben*) turn [round]
wẹnden†[2] (& *reg*) *vt* turn; **sich w~** turn; **sich an jdn w~** turn/(*schriftlich*) write to s.o.
Wẹnd|epunkt *m* (*fig*) turning-point. **w~ig** *a* nimble; ⟨*Auto*⟩ manœuvrable. **W~ung** *f* **-,-en** turn; (*Biegung*) bend; (*Veränderung*) change; **eine W~ung zum Besseren/Schlechteren** a turn for the better/worse
wẹnig *pron* little; (*pl*) few; **so/zu w~** so/too little/(*pl*) few; **w~e** *pl* few □ *adv* little; (*kaum*) not much; **so/zu w~ verdienen** earn so/too little; **so w~ wie möglich** as little as possible. **w~er** *pron* less; (*pl*) fewer; **immer w~er** less and less □ *adv* & *conj* less. **w~ste(r,s)** *pron* least; **am w~sten** least [of all]. **w~stens** *adv* at least
wẹnn *conj* if; (*sobald*) when; **immer w~** whenever; **w~ nicht** *od* **außer w~** unless; **w~ auch** even though
wẹr *pron* who; (*fam: jemand*) someone; (*fragend*) anyone; **ist da wer?** is anyone there?
Wẹrbe|agentur *f* advertising agency. **w~n**† *vt* recruit; attract ⟨*Kunden, Besucher*⟩ □ *vi* (*haben*) **w~n für** advertise; canvass for ⟨*Partei*⟩; **w~n um** try to attract ⟨*Besucher*⟩; court ⟨*Frau, Gunst*⟩. **W~spot** /-sp-/ *m* **-s,-s** commercial
Wẹrbung *f* **-** advertising
wẹrden† *vi* (*sein*) become; ⟨*müde, alt, länger*⟩ get, grow; ⟨*blind, wahnsinnig*⟩ go; **blass w~** turn pale; **krank w~** fall ill; **es wird warm/dunkel** it is getting warm/dark; **mir wurde schlecht/schwindlig** I felt sick/dizzy; **er will Lehrer w~** he wants to be a teacher; **was ist aus ihm geworden?** what has become of him? □ *v aux* (*Zukunft*) shall; **wir w~ sehen** we shall see; **es wird bald regnen** it's going to rain soon; **würden Sie so nett sein?** would you be so kind? □ (*Passiv; pp* **worden**) be; **geliebt/geboren w~** be loved/born; **es wurde gemunkelt** it was rumoured
wẹrfen† *vt* throw; cast ⟨*Blick, Schatten*⟩; **sich w~** ⟨*Holz:*⟩ warp □ *vi* (*haben*) **w~mit** throw
Wẹrft *f* **-,-en** shipyard
Wẹrk *nt* **-[e]s,-e** work; (*Fabrik*) works *sg*, factory; (*Trieb-*) mechanism. **W~en** *nt* **-s** (*Sch*) handicraft. **W~statt** *f* **-,¨en** workshop; (*Auto-*) garage; (*Künstler-*) studio. **W~tag** *m* weekday. **w~tags** *adv* on weekdays. **w~tätig** *a* working. **W~unterricht** *m* (*Sch*) handicraft
Wẹrkzeug *nt* tool; (*coll*) tools *pl*. **W~maschine** *f* machine tool
Wẹrmut *m* **-s** vermouth
wẹrt *a* **viel/50 Mark w~** worth a lot/50 marks; **nichts w~ sein** be worthless; **jds/etw** (*gen*) **w~ sein** be worthy of s.o./sth. **W~** *m* **-[e]s,-e** value; (*Nenn-*) denomination; **im W~ von** worth; **W~ legen auf** (+ *acc*) set great store by. **w~en** *vt* rate
Wẹrt|gegenstand *m* object of value; **W~gegenstände** valuables. **w~los** *a* worthless. **W~minderung** *f* depreciation. **W~papier** *nt* (*Comm*) security. **W~sachen** *fpl* valuables. **w~voll** *a* valuable
Wẹsen *nt* **-s,-** nature; (*Lebe-*) being; (*Mensch*) creature
wẹsentlich *a* essential; (*grundlegend*) fundamental; (*erheblich*) considerable; **im W~en (w~en)**

essentially □ *adv* considerably, much
weshalb *adv* why
Wespe *f* -,-n wasp
wessen *pron* (*gen of* **wer**) whose
westdeutsch *a* West German
Weste *f* -,-n waistcoat, (*Amer*) vest
Westen *m* -s west; **nach W~** west
Western *m* -[s],- western
Westfalen *nt* -s Westphalia
Westindien *nt* West Indies *pl*
west|lich *a* western; ⟨*Richtung*⟩ westerly □ *adv & prep* (+ *gen*) **w~lich [von] der Stadt** [to the] west of the town. **w~wärts** *adv* westwards
weswegen *adv* why
wett *a* **w~ sein** be quits
Wett|bewerb *m* -s,-e competition. **W~büro** *nt* betting shop
Wette *f* -,-n bet; **um die W~ laufen** race (**mit jdm** s.o.)
wetteifern *vi* (*haben*) compete
wetten *vt/i* (*haben*) bet (**auf** + *acc* on); **mit jdm w~** have a bet with s.o.
Wetter *nt* -s,- weather; (*Un-*) storm. **W~bericht** *m* weather report. **W~hahn** *m* weathercock. **W~lage** *f* weather conditions *pl*. **W~vorhersage** *f* weather forecast. **W~warte** *f* -,-n meteorological station
Wett|kampf *m* contest. **W~kämpfer(in)** *m(f)* competitor. **W~lauf** *m* race. **w~machen** *vt sep* make up for. **W~rennen** *nt* race. **W~streit** *m* contest
wetzen *vt* sharpen □ *vi* (*sein*) (*fam*) dash
Whisky *m* -s whisky
wichsen *vt* polish
wichtig *a* important; **w~ nehmen** take seriously. **W~keit** *f* - importance. **w~tuerisch** *a* self-important
Wicke *f* -,-n sweet pea
Wickel *m* -s,- compress
wick|eln *vt* wind; (*ein-*) wrap; (*bandagieren*) bandage; **ein Kind frisch w~eln** change a baby. **W~ler** *m* -s,- curler
Widder *m* -s,- ram; (*Astr*) Aries
wider *prep* (+ *acc*) against; (*entgegen*) contrary to; **w~ Willen** against one's will
widerfahren† *vi insep* (*sein*) **jdm w~** happen to s.o.
widerhallen *vi sep* (*haben*) echo
widerlegen *vt insep* refute
wider|lich *a* repulsive; (*unangenehm*) nasty, *adv* -ily. **w~rechtlich** *a* unlawful, *adv* -ly. **W~rede** *f* contradiction; **keine W~rede!** don't argue!
widerrufen† *vt/i insep* (*haben*) retract; revoke ⟨*Befehl*⟩
Widersacher *m* -s,- adversary
widersetzen (sich) *vr insep* resist (**jdm/etw** s.o./sth)
wider|sinnig *a* absurd. **w~spenstig** *a* unruly; (*störrisch*) stubborn
widerspiegeln *vt sep* reflect; **sich w~** be reflected
widersprechen† *vi insep* (*haben*) contradict (**jdm/etw** s.o./sth)
Wider|spruch *m* contradiction; (*Protest*) protest. **w~sprüchlich** *a* contradictory. **w~spruchslos** *adv* without protest
Widerstand *m* resistance; **W~ leisten** resist. **w~sfähig** *a* resistant; (*Bot*) hardy
widerstehen† *vi insep* (*haben*) resist (**jdm/etw** s.o/sth); (*anwidern*) be repugnant (**jdm** to *s.o.*)
widerstreben *vi insep* (*haben*) **es widerstrebt mir** I am reluctant (**zu** to). **W~** *nt* -s reluctance. **w~d** *a* reluctant, *adv* -ly
widerwärtig *a* disagreeable, unpleasant; (*ungünstig*) adverse
Widerwill|e *m* aversion, repugnance. **w~ig** *a* reluctant, *adv* -ly
widm|en *vt* dedicate (*dat* to); (*verwenden*) devote (*dat* to); **sich**

w~en (+ *dat*) devote oneself to. **W~ung** *f* -,-en dedication
widrig *a* adverse, unfavourable
wie *adv* how; **wie viel** how much/(*pl*) many; **um wie viel Uhr?** at what time? **wie viele?** how many? **wie ist Ihr Name?** what is your name? **wie ist das Wetter?** what is the weather like? □ *conj* as; (*gleich wie*) like; (*sowie*) as well as; (*als*) when, as; **genau wie du** just like you; **so gut/reich wie** as good/rich as; **nichts wie** nothing but; **größer wie ich** (*fam*) bigger than me
wieder *adv* again; **er ist w~ da** he is back; **jdn/etw w~ erkennen** recognize s.o./sth; **eine Tätigkeit w~ aufnehmen** resume an activity; **etw w~ verwenden/verwerten** reuse/recycle sth; **etw w~ gutmachen** make up for ⟨*Schaden*⟩; redress ⟨*Unrecht*⟩; (*bezahlen*) pay for sth
Wiederaufbau *m* reconstruction. **w~en** *vt sep* (NEW) **wieder aufbauen**, *s.* **aufbauen**
wieder|aufnehmen† *vt sep* (NEW) **w~ aufnehmen**, *s.* **wieder**. **W~aufrüstung** *f* rearmament
wieder|bekommen† *vt sep* get back. **w~beleben** *vt sep* (NEW) **w~ beleben**, *s.* **beleben**. **W~belebung** *f* - resuscitation. **w~bringen†** *vt sep* bring back. **w~erkennen†** *vt sep* (NEW) **w~ erkennen**, *s.* **wieder**. **W~gabe** *f* (*s.* **w~geben**) return; portrayal; rendering; reproduction. **w~geben†** *vt sep* give back, return; (*darstellen*) portray; (*ausdrücken, übersetzen*) render; (*zitieren*) quote; (*Techn*) reproduce. **W~geburt** *f* reincarnation
wiedergutmach|en *vt sep* (NEW) **w~ gutmachen**, *s.* **wieder**. **W~ung** *f* - reparation; (*Entschädigung*) compensation
wiederher|stellen *vt sep* re-establish; restore ⟨*Gebäude*⟩; restore to health ⟨*Kranke*⟩; **w~gestellt sein** be fully recovered. **W~stellung** *f* re-establishment; restoration; (*Genesung*) recovery
wiederholen[1] *vt sep* get back
wiederhol|en[2] *vt insep* repeat; (*Sch*) revise; **sich w~en** recur; ⟨*Person:*⟩ repeat oneself. **w~t** *a* repeated, *adv* -ly. **W~ung** *f* -,-en repetition; (*Sch*) revision
Wieder|hören *nt* **auf W~hören!** goodbye! **W~käuer** *m* -s,- ruminant. **W~kehr** *f* - return; (*W~holung*) recurrence. **w~kehren** *vi sep* (*sein*) return; (*sich wiederholen*) recur. **w~kommen†** *vi sep* (*sein*) come back
wiedersehen† *vt sep* (NEW) **wieder sehen**, *s.* **sehen**. **W~** *nt* -s,- reunion; **auf W~!** goodbye!
wiederum *adv* again; (*andererseits*) on the other hand
wiedervereinig|en *vt sep* (NEW) **wieder vereinigen**, *s.* **vereinigen**. **W~ung** *f* reunification
wieder|verheiraten (sich) *vr sep* (NEW) **w~ verheiraten (sich)**, *s.* **verheiraten**. **w~verwenden†** *vt sep* (NEW) **w~ verwenden**, *s.* **wieder**. **w~verwerten** *vt sep* (NEW) **w~ verwerten**, *s.* **wieder**. **w~wählen** *vt sep* (NEW) **w~ wählen**, *s.* **wählen**
Wiege *f* -,-n cradle
wiegen†[1] *vt/i* (*haben*) weigh
wiegen[2] *vt* (*reg*) rock; **sich w~** sway; (*schaukeln*) rock. **W~lied** *nt* lullaby
wiehern *vi* (*haben*) neigh
Wien *nt* -s Vienna. **W~er** *a* Viennese; **W~er Schnitzel** Wiener schnitzel □ *m* -s,- Viennese □ *f* -,- ≈ frankfurter. **w~erisch** *a* Viennese
Wiese *f* -,-n meadow
Wiesel *nt* -s,- weasel
wieso *adv* why

wieviel *pron* (NEW) **wie viel**, *s.* **wie**. **w~te(r,s)** *a* which; **der W~te ist heute?** what is the date today?
wieweit *adv* how far
wild *a* wild, *adv* -ly; ⟨*Stamm*⟩ savage; **w~er Streik** wildcat strike; **w~ wachsen** grow wild. **W~** *nt* **-[e]s** game; (*Rot-*) deer; (*Culin*) venison. **W~dieb** *m* poacher. **W~e(r)** *m/f* savage
Wilder|er *m* **-s,-** poacher. **w~n** *vt/i* (*haben*) poach
wildfremd *a* totally strange; **w~e Leute** total strangers
Wild|heger, **W~hüter** *m* **-s,-** gamekeeper. **W~leder** *nt* suede. **w~ledern** *a* suede. **W~nis** *f* **-** wilderness. **W~schwein** *nt* wild boar. **W~westfilm** *m* western
Wille *m* **-ns** will; **letzter W~** will; **seinen W~n durchsetzen** get one's [own] way; **mit W~n** intentionally
willen *prep* (+ *gen*) **um ... w~** for the sake of ...
Willens|kraft *f* will-power. **w~stark** *a* strong-willed
willig *a* willing, *adv* -ly
willkommen *a* welcome; **w~ heißen** welcome. **W~** *nt* **-s** welcome
willkürlich *a* arbitrary, *adv* -ily
wimmeln *vi* (*haben*) swarm
wimmern *vi* (*haben*) whimper
Wimpel *m* **-s,-** pennant
Wimper *f* **-,-n** [eye]lash; **nicht mit der W~ zucken** (*fam*) not bat an eyelid. **W~ntusche** *f* mascara
Wind *m* **-[e]s,-e** wind
Winde *f* **-,-n** (*Techn*) winch
Windel *f* **-,-n** nappy, (*Amer*) diaper
winden† *vt* wind; make ⟨*Kranz*⟩; **in die Höhe w~** winch up; **sich w~** wind (**um** round); (*sich krümmen*) writhe
Wind|hund *m* greyhound. **w~ig** *a* windy. **W~mühle** *f* windmill. **W~pocken** *fpl* chickenpox *sg*. **W~schutzscheibe** *f* windscreen, (*Amer*) windshield. **w~still** *a* calm. **W~stille** *f* calm. **W~stoß** *m* gust of wind. **W~surfen** *nt* windsurfing
Windung *f* **-,-en** bend; (*Spirale*) spiral
Wink *m* **-[e]s,-e** sign; (*Hinweis*) hint
Winkel *m* **-s,-** angle; (*Ecke*) corner. **W~messer** *m* **-s,-** protractor
winken *vi* (*haben*) wave; **jdm w~** wave/(*herbei-*) beckon to s.o.
winseln *vi* (*haben*) whine
Winter *m* **-s,-** winter. **w~lich** *a* wintry; (*Winter-*) winter ... **W~schlaf** *m* hibernation; **W~schlaf halten** hibernate. **W~sport** *m* winter sports *pl*
Winzer *m* **-s,-** winegrower
winzig *a* tiny, minute
Wipfel *m* **-s,-** [tree-]top
Wippe *f* **-,-n see-saw**. **w~n** *vi* (*haben*) bounce; (*auf Wippe*) play on the **see-saw**
wir *pron* **we; wir sind es** it's us
Wirbel *m* **-s,-** eddy; (*Drehung*) whirl; (*Trommel-*) roll; (*Anat*) vertebra; (*Haar-*) crown; (*Aufsehen*) fuss. **w~n** *vt/i* (*sein/haben*) whirl. **W~säule** *f* spine. **W~sturm** *m* cyclone. **W~tier** *nt* vertebrate. **W~wind** *m* whirlwind
wird *s.* **werden**
wirken *vi* (*haben*) have an effect (**auf** + *acc* on); (*zur Geltung kommen*) be effective; (*tätig sein*) work; (*scheinen*) seem □ *vt* (*Tex*) knit; **Wunder w~** work miracles
wirklich *a* real, *adv* -ly. **W~keit** *f* **-,-en** reality
wirksam *a* effective, *adv* -ly. **W~keit** *f* **-** effectiveness
Wirkung *f* **-,-en** effect. **w~slos** *a* ineffective, *adv* -ly. **w~svoll** *a* effective, *adv* -ly
wirr *a* tangled; ⟨*Haar*⟩ tousled; (*verwirrt, verworren*) confused. **W~warr** *m* **-s** tangle; (*fig*) confusion; (*von Stimmen*) hubbub

Wirt *m* **-[e]s,-e** landlord. **W~in** *f* **-,-nen** landlady

Wirtschaft *f* **-,-en** economy; (*Gast-*) restaurant; (*Kneipe*) pub. **w~en** *vi* (*haben*) manage one's finances; (*sich betätigen*) busy oneself; **sie kann nicht w~en** she's a bad manager. **W~erin** *f* **-,-nen** housekeeper. **w~lich** *a* economic, *adv* -ally; (*sparsam*) economical, *adv* -ly. **W~sgeld** *nt* housekeeping [money]. **W~s-prüfer** *m* auditor

Wirtshaus *nt* inn; (*Kneipe*) pub

Wisch *m* **-[e]s,-e** (*fam*) piece of paper

wisch|en *vt/i* (*haben*) wipe; wash ⟨*Fußboden*⟩ □ *vi* (*sein*) slip; ⟨*Maus:*⟩ scurry. **W~lappen** *m* cloth; (*Aufwisch-*) floor-cloth

wispern *vt/i* (*haben*) whisper

wissen† *vt/i* (*haben*) know; **weißt du noch?** do you remember? **ich wüsste gern...** I should like to know...; **nichts w~ wollen von** not want anything to do with. **W~** *nt* **-s** knowledge; **meines W~s** to my knowledge

Wissenschaft *f* **-,-en** science. **W~ler** *m* **-s,-** academic; (*Natur-*) scientist. **w~lich** *a* academic, *adv* -ally; scientific, *adv* -ally

wissen|swert *a* worth knowing. **w~tlich** *a* deliberate □ *adv* knowingly

witter|n *vt* scent; (*ahnen*) sense. **W~ung** *f* - scent; (*Wetter*) weather

Witwe *f* **-,-n** widow. **W~r** *m* **-s,-** widower

Witz *m* **-es,-e** joke; (*Geist*) wit. **W~bold** *m* **-[e]s,-e** joker. **w~ig** *a* funny; (*geistreich*) witty

wo *adv* where; (*als*) when; (*irgendwo*) somewhere; **wo immer** wherever □ *conj* seeing that; (*obwohl*) although; (*wenn*) if

woanders *adv* somewhere else

wobei *adv* how; (*relativ*) during the course of which

Woche *f* **-,-n** week. **W~nende** *nt* weekend. **W~nkarte** *f* weekly ticket. **w~nlang** *adv* for weeks. **W~ntag** *m* day of the week; (*Werktag*) weekday. **w~tags** *adv* on weekdays

wöchentlich *a & adv* weekly

Wodka *m* **-s** vodka

wodurch *adv* how; (*relativ*) through/(*Ursache*) by which; (*Folge*) as a result of which

wofür *adv* what ... for; (*relativ*) for which

Woge *f* **-,-n** wave

wogegen *adv* what... against; (*relativ*) against which □ *conj* whereas. **woher** *adv* where from; **woher weißt du das?** how do you know that? **wohin** *adv* where [to]; **wohin gehst du?** where are you going? **wohingegen** *conj* whereas

wohl *adv* well; (*vermutlich*) probably; (*etwa*) about; (*zwar*) perhaps; **w~ kaum** hardly; **w~ oder übel** willy-nilly; **sich w~ fühlen** feel well/(*behaglich*) comfortable; **jdm w~ tun** do s.o. good; **der ist w~ verrückt!** he must be mad! **W~** *nt* **-[e]s** welfare, well-being; **auf jds W~ trinken** drink s.o.'s health; **zum W~** (+ *gen*) for the good of; **zum W~!** cheers!

wohlauf *a* **w~sein** be well

Wohl|befinden *nt* well-being. **W~behagen** *nt* feeling of well-being. **w~behalten** *a* safe, *adv* -ly. **W~ergehen** *nt* **-s** welfare. **w~erzogen** *a* well brought-up

Wohlfahrt *f* - welfare. **W~sstaat** *m* Welfare State

Wohl|gefallen *nt* **-s** pleasure. **W~geruch** *m* fragrance. **w~gesinnt** *a* well disposed (*dat* towards). **w~habend** *a* prosperous, well-to-do. **w~ig** *a* comfortable, *adv* -bly. **w~klingend** *a* melodious. **w~riechend** *a* fragrant. **w~schmeckend** *a* tasty

Wohlstand *m* prosperity. **W~sgesellschaft** *f* affluent society

Wohltat *f* [act of] kindness; (*Annehmlichkeit*) treat; (*Genuss*) bliss

Wohltät|er *m* benefactor. **w~ig** *a* charitable

wohl|tuend *a* agreeable, *adv* -bly. **w~tun**† *vi sep* (*haben*) (NEW) **w~ tun**, *s.* **wohl**. **w~verdient** *a* well-deserved. **w~weislich** *adv* deliberately

Wohlwollen *nt* **-s** goodwill; (*Gunst*) favour. **w~d** *a* benevolent, *adv* -ly

Wohn|anhänger *m* = **Wohnwagen**. **W~block** *m* block of flats. **w~en** *vi* (*haben*) live; (*vorübergehend*) stay. **W~gegend** *f* residential area. **w~haft** *a* resident. **W~haus** *nt* [dwelling]-house. **W~heim** *nt* hostel; (*Alten-*) home. **w~lich** *a* comfortable, *adv* -bly. **W~mobil** *nt* **-s,-e** camper. **W~ort** *m* place of residence. **W~raum** *m* living space; (*Zimmer*) living-room. **W~sitz** *m* place of residence

Wohnung *f* **-,-en** flat, (*Amer*) apartment; (*Unterkunft*) accommodation. **W~snot** *f* housing shortage

Wohn|wagen *m* caravan, (*Amer*) trailer. **W~zimmer** *nt* living-room

wölb|en *vt* curve; arch ⟨*Rücken*⟩. **W~ung** *f* **-,-en** curve; (*Archit*) vault

Wolf *m* **-[e]s,¨e** wolf; (*Fleisch-*) mincer; (*Reiß-*) shredder

Wolk|e *f* **-,-n** cloud. **W~enbruch** *m* cloudburst. **W~enkratzer** *m* skyscraper. **w~enlos** *a* cloudless. **w~ig** *a* cloudy

Woll|decke *f* blanket. **W~e** *f* **-,-n** wool

wollen†[1] *vt/i* (*haben*) & *v aux* want; **etw tun w~** want to do sth; (*beabsichtigen*) be going to do sth; **ich will nach Hause** I want to go home; **wir wollten gerade gehen** we were just going; **ich wollte, ich könnte dir helfen** I wish I could help you; **der Motor will nicht anspringen** the engine won't start

woll|en[2] *a* woollen. **w~ig** *a* woolly. **W~sachen** *fpl* woollens

wollüstig *a* sensual, *adv* -ly

womit *adv* what ... with; (*relativ*) with which. **womöglich** *adv* possibly. **wonach** *adv* what ... after/⟨*suchen*⟩ for/⟨*riechen*⟩ of; (*relativ*) after/for/of which

Wonn|e *f* **-,-n** bliss; (*Freude*) joy. **w~ig** *a* sweet

woran *adv* what ... on/⟨*denken, sterben*⟩ of; (*relativ*) on/of which; **woran hast du ihn erkannt?** how did you recognize him?

worauf *adv* what ... on/⟨*warten*⟩ for; (*relativ*) on/for which; (*woraufhin*) whereupon. **woraufhin** *adv* whereupon. **woraus** *adv* what ... from; (*relativ*) from which. **worin** *adv* what ... in; (*relativ*) in which

Wort *nt* **-[e]s,¨er & -e** word; **jdm ins W~fallen** interrupt s.o.; **ein paar W~e sagen** say a few words. **w~brüchig** *a* **w~brüchig werden** break one's word

Wörterbuch *nt* dictionary

Wort|führer *m* spokesman. **w~getreu** *a* & *adv* word-for-word. **w~gewandt** *a* eloquent, *adv* -ly. **w~karg** *a* taciturn. **W~laut** *m* wording

wörtlich *a* literal, *adv* -ly; (*wortgetreu*) word-for-word

wort|los *a* silent □ *adv* without a word. **W~schatz** *m* vocabulary. **W~spiel** *nt* pun, play on words. **W~wechsel** *m* exchange of words; (*Streit*) argument. **w~wörtlich** *a* & *adv* = **wörtlich**

worüber *adv* what ... over/⟨*lachen, sprechen*⟩ about; (*relativ*) over/about which. **worum** *adv* what ... round/⟨*bitten, kämpfen*⟩

for; (*relativ*) round/for which; **worum geht es?** what is it about? **worunter** *adv* what ... under/ (*wozwischen*) among; (*relativ*) under/among which. **wovon** *adv* what ... from/⟨*sprechen*⟩ about; (*relativ*) from/about which. **wovor** *adv* what ... in front of; ⟨*sich fürchten*⟩ what ... of; (*relativ*) in front of which; of which. **wozu** *adv* what ... to/⟨*brauchen, benutzen*⟩ for; (*relativ*) to/for which; **wozu?** what for?

Wrack *nt* **-s,-s** wreck

wringen† *vt* wring

wucher|n *vi* (*haben/sein*) grow profusely. **W~preis** *m* extortionate price. **W~ung** *f* **-,-en** growth

Wuchs *m* **-es** growth; (*Gestalt*) stature

Wucht *f* **-** force. **w~en** *vt* heave. **w~ig** *a* massive

wühlen *vi* (*haben*) rummage; (*in der Erde*) burrow □ *vt* dig

Wulst *m* **-[e]s,¨e** bulge; (*Fett-*) roll. **w~ig** *a* bulging; ⟨*Lippen*⟩ thick

wund *a* sore; **w~ reiben** chafe; **sich w~ liegen** get bedsores. **W~brand** *m* gangrene

Wunde *f* **-,-n** wound

Wunder *nt* **-s,-** wonder, marvel; (*übernatürliches*) miracle; **kein W~!** no wonder! **w~bar** *a* miraculous; (*herrlich*) wonderful, *adv* -ly, marvellous, *adv* -ly. **W~kind** *nt* infant prodigy. **w~lich** *a* odd, *adv* -ly. **w~n** *vt* surprise; **sich w~n** be surprised (**über** + *acc* at). **w~schön** *a* beautiful, *adv* -ly. **w~voll** *a* wonderful, *adv* -ly

Wundstarrkrampf *m* tetenus

Wunsch *m* **-[e]s,¨e** wish; (*Verlangen*) desire; (*Bitte*) request

wünschen *vt* want; **sich** (*dat*) **etw w~** want sth; (*bitten um*) ask for sth; **jdm Glück/gute Nacht w~** wish s.o. luck/good night; **ich wünschte, ich könnte** ... I wish I could ...; **Sie w~?** can I help you? **zu w~ übrig lassen** leave something to be desired. **w~swert** *a* desirable

Wunsch|konzert *nt* musical request programme. **W~traum** *m* (*fig*) dream

wurde, würde *s.* **werden**

Würde *f* **-,-n** dignity; (*Ehrenrang*) honour. **w~los** *a* undignified. **W~nträger** *m* dignitary. **w~voll** *a* dignified □ *adv* with dignity

würdig *a* dignified; (*wert*) worthy. **w~en** *vt* recognize; (*schätzen*) appreciate; **keines Blickes w~en** not deign to look at

Wurf *m* **-[e]s,¨e** throw; (*Junge*) litter

Würfel *m* **-s,-** cube; (*Spiel-*) dice; (*Zucker-*) lump. **w~n** *vi* (*haben*) throw the dice; **w~n um** play dice for □ *vt* throw; (*in Würfel schneiden*) dice. **W~zucker** *m* cube sugar

Wurfgeschoss (Wurfgeschoß) *nt* missile

würgen *vt* choke □ *vi* (*haben*) retch; choke (**an** + *dat* on)

Wurm *m* **-[e]s,¨er** worm; (*Made*) maggot. **w~en** *vi* (*haben*) **jdn w~en** (*fam*) rankle [with s.o.]. **w~stichig** *a* worm-eaten

Wurst *f* **-,¨e** sausage; **das ist mir W~** (*fam*) I couldn't care less

Würstchen *nt* **-s,-** small sausage; **Frankfurter W~** frankfurter

Würze *f* **-,-n** spice; (*Aroma*) aroma

Wurzel *f* **-,-n** root; **W~n schlagen** take root. **w~n** *vi* (*haben*) root

würz|en *vt* season. **w~ig** *a* tasty; (*aromatisch*) aromatic; (*pikant*) spicy

wüst *a* chaotic; (*wirr*) tangled; (*öde*) desolate; (*wild*) wild, *adv* -ly; (*schlimm*) terrible, *adv* -bly

Wüste *f* **-,-n** desert

Wut *f* **-** rage, fury. **W~anfall** *m* fit of rage

wüten *vi* (*haben*) rage. **w~d** *a* furious, *adv* -ly; **w~d machen** infuriate

X

x /ɪks/ *inv a* (*Math*) x; (*fam*) umpteen. **X-Beine** *ntpl* knock-knees. **x-beinig, X-beinig** *a* knock-kneed. **x-beliebig** *a* (*fam*) any; **eine x-beliebige Zahl** any number [you like]. **x-mal** *adv* (*fam*) umpteen times; **zum x-ten Mal** for the umpteenth time

Y

Yoga /ˈjo:ga/ *m & nt* **-[s]** yoga

Z

Zack|e *f* **-,-n** point; (*Berg-*) peak; (*Gabel-*) prong. **z~ig** *a* jagged; (*gezackt*) serrated; (*fam: schneidig*) smart, *adv* -ly

zaghaft *a* timid, *adv* -ly; (*zögernd*) tentative, *adv* -ly

zäh *a* tough; (*hartnäckig*) tenacious, *adv* -ly; (*zähflüssig*) viscous; (*schleppend*) sluggish, *adv* -ly. **z~flüssig** *a* viscous; ⟨*Verkehr*⟩ slow-moving. **Z~igkeit** *f* - toughness; tenacity

Zahl *f* **-,-en** number; (*Ziffer, Betrag*) figure

zahl|bar *a* payable. **z~en** *vt/i* (*haben*) pay; (*bezahlen*) pay for; **bitte z~en!** the bill please!

zählen *vi* (*haben*) count; **z~ zu** (*fig*) be one/(*pl*) some of; **z~ auf** (+ *acc*) count on □ *vt* count; **z~ zu** add to; (*fig*) count among; **die Stadt zählt 5000 Einwohner** the town has 5000 inhabitants

zahlenmäßig *a* numerical, *adv* -ly

Zähler *m* **-s,-** meter

Zahl|grenze *f* fare-stage. **Z~karte** *f* paying-in slip. **z~los** *a* countless. **z~reich** *a* numerous; ⟨*Anzahl, Gruppe*⟩ large □ *adv* in large numbers. **Z~ung** *f* **-,-en** payment; **in Z~ung nehmen** take in part-exchange

Zählung *f* **-,-en** count

zahlungsunfähig *a* insolvent

Zahlwort *nt* (*pl* **-wörter**) numeral

zahm *a* tame

zähmen *vt* tame; (*fig*) restrain

Zahn *m* **-[e]s,⸚e** tooth; (*am Zahnrad*) cog. **Z~arzt** *m*, **Z~ärztin** *f* dentist. **Z~belag** *m* plaque. **Z~bürste** *f* toothbrush. **z~en** *vi* (*haben*) be teething. **Z~fleisch** *nt* gums *pl*. **z~los** *a* toothless. **Z~pasta** *f* **-,-en** toothpaste. **Z~rad** *nt* cog-wheel. **Z~schmelz** *m* enamel. **Z~schmerzen** *mpl* toothache *sg*. **Z~spange** *f* brace. **Z~stein** *m* tartar. **Z~stocher** *m* **-s,-** toothpick

Zange *f* **-,-n** pliers *pl*; (*Kneif-*) pincers *pl*; (*Kohlen-, Zucker-*) tongs *pl*; (*Geburts-*) forceps *pl*

Zank *m* **-[e]s** squabble. **z~en** *vr* **sich z~en** squabble □ *vi* (*haben*) scold (**mit jdm** s.o.)

zänkisch *a* quarrelsome

Zäpfchen *nt* **-s,-** (*Anat*) uvula; (*Med*) suppository

Zapfen *m* **-s,-** (*Bot*) cone; (*Stöpsel*) bung; (*Eis-*) icicle. **z~** *vt* tap, draw. **Z~streich** *m* (*Mil*) tattoo

Zapf|hahn *m* tap. **Z~säule** *f* petrol-pump

zappel|ig *a* fidgety; (*nervös*) jittery. **z~n** *vi* (*haben*) wriggle; ⟨*Kind:*⟩ fidget

zart *a* delicate, *adv* -ly; (*weich, zärtlich*) tender, *adv* -ly; (*sanft*) gentle, *adv* -ly. **Z~gefühl** *nt* tact. **Z~heit** *f* - delicacy; tenderness; gentleness

zärtlich *a* tender, *adv* -ly; (*liebevoll*) loving, *adv* -ly. **Z~keit** *f* **-,-en** tenderness; (*Liebkosung*) caress

Zauber *m* **-s** magic; (*Bann*) spell. **Z~er** *m* **-s,-** magician. **z~haft** *a* enchanting. **Z~künstler** *m* conjuror. **Z~kunststück** *nt* = **Z~trick. z~n** *vi* (*haben*) do magic; (*Zaubertricks ausführen*) do conjuring tricks □ *vt* produce as if by magic. **Z~stab** *m* magic wand. **Z~trick** *m* conjuring trick

zaudern *vi* (*haben*) delay; (*zögern*) hesitate

Zaum *m* **-[e]s,Zäume** bridle; **im Z~ halten** (*fig*) restrain

Zaun *m* **-[e]s,Zäune** fence. **Z~könig** *m* wren

z.B. *abbr* (**zum Beispiel**) e.g.

Zebra *nt* **-s,-s** zebra. **Z~streifen** *m* zebra crossing

Zeche *f* **-,-n** bill; (*Bergwerk*) pit

zechen *vi* (*haben*) (*fam*) drink

Zeder *f* **-,-n** cedar

Zeh *m* **-[e]s,-en** toe. **Z~e** *f* **-,-n** toe; (*Knoblauch-*) clove. **Z~ennagel** *m* toenail

zehn *inv a*, **Z~** *f* **-,-en** ten. **z~te(r, s)** *a* tenth. **Z~tel** *nt* **-s,-** tenth

Zeichen *nt* **-s,-** sign; (*Signal*) signal. **Z~setzung** *f* **-** punctuation. **Z~trickfilm** *m* cartoon [film]

zeichn|en *vt/i* (*haben*) draw; (*kenn-*) mark; (*unter-*) sign. **Z~er** *m* **-s,-** draughtsman. **Z~ung** *f* **-,-en** drawing; (*auf Fell*) markings *pl*

Zeige|finger *m* index finger. **z~n** *vt* show; **sich z~n** appear; (*sich herausstellen*) become clear; **das wird sich z~n** we shall see □ *vi* (*haben*) point (**auf** + *acc* to). **Z~r** *m* **-s,-** pointer; (*Uhr-*) hand

Zeile *f* **-,-n** line; (*Reihe*) row

zeit *prep* (+ *gen*) **z~ meines/seines Lebens** all my/his life

Zeit *f* **-,-en** time; **sich** (*dat*) **Z~ lassen** take one's time; **es hat Z~** theres's no hurry; **mit der Z~** in time; **in nächster Z~** in the near future; **die erste Z~** at first; **von Z~ zu Z~** from time to time; **zur Z~** (*rechtzeitig*) in time; (*derzeit*) (NEW) **zurzeit**; **eine Z~ lang** for a time *or* while; **[ach] du liebe Z~!** (*fam*) good heavens!

Zeit|alter *nt* age, era. **Z~arbeit** *f* temporary work. **Z~bombe** *f* time bomb. **z~gemäß** *a* modern, up-to-date. **Z~genosse** *m*, **Z~genossin** *f* contemporary. **z~genössisch** *a* contemporary. **z~ig** *a & adv* early. **Z~lang** *f* **eine Z~lang** (NEW) **eine Z~ lang**, *s.* **Zeit. z~lebens** *adv* all one's life

zeitlich *a* ⟨*Dauer*⟩ in time; ⟨*Folge*⟩ chronological. □ *adv* **z~ begrenzt** for a limited time

zeit|los *a* timeless. **Z~lupe** *f* slow motion. **Z~punkt** *m* time. **z~raubend** *a* timeconsuming. **Z~raum** *m* period. **Z~schrift** *f* magazine, periodical

Zeitung *f* **-,-en** newspaper. **Z~spapier** *nt* newspaper

Zeit|verschwendung *f* waste of time. **Z~vertreib** *m* pastime; **zum Z~vertreib** to pass the time. **z~weilig** *a* temporary □ *adv* temporarily; (*hin und wieder*) at times. **z~weise** *adv* at times. **Z~wort** *nt* (*pl* **-wörter**) verb. **Z~zünder** *m* time fuse

Zelle *f* **-,-n** cell; (*Telefon-*) box

Zelt *nt* **-[e]s,-e** tent; (*Fest-*) marquee. **z~en** *vi* (*haben*) camp. **Z~en** *nt* **-s** camping. **Z~plane** *f* tarpaulin. **Z~platz** *m* campsite

Zement *m* **-[e]s** cement. **z~ieren** *vt* cement

zen|sieren *vt* (*Sch*) mark; censor ⟨*Presse, Film*⟩. **Z~sur** *f* **-,-en** (*Sch*) mark, (*Amer*) grade; (*Presse-*) censorship

Zentimeter *m & nt* centimetre. **Z~maß** *nt* tape-measure

Zentner *m* **-s,-** [metric] hundredweight (*50 kg*)

zentral *a* central. *adv* -ly. **Z~e** *f* **-,-n** central office; (*Partei-*) headquarters *pl*; (*Teleph*) exchange. **Z~heizung** *f* central heating. **z~isieren** *vt* centralize

Zentrum *nt* **-s,-tren** centre

zerbrech|en† *vt/i* (*sein*) break; **sich** (*dat*) **den Kopf z~en** rack one's brains. **z~lich** *a* fragile

zerdrücken *vt* crush; mash ⟨*Kartoffeln*⟩

Zeremonie *f* **-,-n** ceremony

Zeremoniell *nt* **-s,-e** ceremonial. **z~** *a* ceremonial, *adv* -ly

Zerfall *m* disintegration; (*Verfall*) decay. **z~en**† *vi* (*sein*) disintegrate; (*verfallen*) decay; **in drei Teile z~en** be divided into three parts

zerfetzen *vt* tear to pieces

zerfließen† *vi* (*sein*) melt; ⟨*Tinte:*⟩ run

zergehen† *vi* (*sein*) melt; (*sich auflösen*) dissolve

zergliedern *vt* dissect

zerkleinern *vt* chop/(*schneiden*) cut up; (*mahlen*) grind

zerknirscht *a* contrite

zerknüllen *vt* crumple [up]

zerkratzen *vt* scratch

zerlassen† *vt* melt

zerlegen *vt* take to pieces, dismantle; (*zerschneiden*) cut up; (*tranchieren*) carve

zerlumpt *a* ragged

zermalmen *vt* crush

zermürb|en *vt* (*fig*) wear down. **Z~ungskrieg** *m* war of attrition

zerplatzen *vi* (*sein*) burst

zerquetschen *vt* squash; crush; mash ⟨*Kartoffeln*⟩

Zerrbild *nt* caricature

zerreißen† *vt* tear; (*in Stücke*) tear up; break ⟨*Faden, Seil*⟩ □ *vi* (*sein*) tear; break

zerren *vt* drag; pull ⟨*Muskel*⟩ □ *vi* (*haben*) pull (**an** + *dat* at)

zerrinnen† *vi* (*sein*) melt

zerrissen *a* torn

zerrütten *vt* ruin, wreck; shatter ⟨*Nerven*⟩; **zerrüttete Ehe** broken marriage

zerschlagen† *vt* smash; smash up ⟨*Möbel*⟩; **sich z~** (*fig*) fall through; ⟨*Hoffnung:*⟩ be dashed □ *a* (*erschöpft*) worn out

zerschmettern *vt/i* (*sein*) smash

zerschneiden† *vt* cut; (*in Stücke*) cut up

zersetzen *vt* corrode; undermine ⟨*Moral*⟩; **sich z~** decompose

zersplittern *vi* (*sein*) splinter; ⟨*Glas:*⟩ shatter □ *vt* shatter

zerspringen† *vi* (*sein*) shatter; (*bersten*) burst

Zerstäuber *m* **-s,-** atomizer

zerstör|en *vt* destroy; (*zunichte machen*) wreck. **Z~er** *m* **-s,-** destroyer. **Z~ung** *f* destruction

zerstreu|en *vt* scatter; disperse ⟨*Menge*⟩; dispel ⟨*Zweifel*⟩; **sich z~en** disperse; (*sich unterhalten*) amuse oneself. **z~t** *a* absent-minded, *adv* -ly. **Z~ung** *f* **-,-en** (*Unterhaltung*) entertainment

zerstückeln *vt* cut up into pieces

zerteilen *vt* divide up

Zertifikat *nt* **-[e]s,-e** certificate

zertreten† *vt* stamp on; (*zerdrücken*) crush

zertrümmern *vt* smash [up]; wreck ⟨*Gebäude, Stadt*⟩

zerzaus|en *vt* tousle. **z~t** *a* dishevelled; ⟨*Haar*⟩ tousled

Zettel *m* **-s,-** piece of paper; (*Notiz*) note; (*Bekanntmachung*) notice; (*Reklame-*) leaflet

Zeug *nt* **-s** (*fam*) stuff; (*Sachen*) things *pl*; (*Ausrüstung*) gear; **dummes Z~** nonsense; **das Z~ haben zu** have the makings of

Zeuge *m* **-n,-n** witness. **z~n** *vi* (*haben*) testify; **z~n von** (*fig*) show □ *vt* father. **Z~naussage** *f* testimony. **Z~nstand** *m* witness box/(*Amer*) stand

Zeugin *f* **-,-nen** witness

Zeugnis *nt* **-ses,-se** certificate; (*Sch*) report; (*Referenz*) reference; (*fig: Beweis*) evidence

Zickzack *m* **-[e]s,-e** zigzag
Ziege *f* **-,-n** goat
Ziegel *m* **-s,-** brick; (*Dach-*) tile. **Z~stein** *m* brick
ziehen† *vt* pull; (*sanfter; zücken; zeichnen*) draw; (*heraus-*) pull out; extract ⟨*Zahn*⟩; raise ⟨*Hut*⟩; put on ⟨*Bremse*⟩; move ⟨*Schachfigur*⟩; put up ⟨*Leine, Zaun*⟩; (*dehnen*) stretch; make ⟨*Grimasse, Scheitel*⟩; (*züchten*) breed; grow ⟨*Rosen, Gemüse*⟩; **nach sich z~** (*fig*) entail □ *vr* **sich z~** (*sich erstrecken*) run; (*sich verziehen*) warp □ *vi* (*haben*) pull (**an** + *dat* on/at); ⟨*Tee, Ofen:*⟩ draw; (*Culin*) simmer; **es zieht** there is a draught; **solche Filme z~ nicht mehr** films like that are no longer popular □ *vi* (*sein*) (*um-*) move (**nach** to); ⟨*Menge:*⟩ march; ⟨*Vögel:*⟩ migrate; ⟨*Wolken, Nebel:*⟩ drift. **Z~** *nt* **-s** ache
Ziehharmonika *f* accordion
Ziehung *f* **-,-en** draw
Ziel *nt* **-[e]s,-e** destination; (*Sport*) finish; (*Z~scheibe & Mil*) target; (*Zweck*) aim, goal. **z~bewusst** (**z~bewußt**) *a* purposeful, *adv* -ly. **z~en** *vi* (*haben*) aim (**auf** + *acc* at). **z~end** *a* (*Gram*) transitive. **z~los** *a* aimless, *adv* -ly. **Z~scheibe** *f* target; (*fig*) butt. **z~strebig** *a* single-minded, *adv* -ly
ziemen (sich) *vr* be seemly
ziemlich *a* (*fam*) fair □ *adv* rather, fairly; (*fast*) pretty well
Zier|de *f* **-,-n** ornament. **z~en** *vt* adorn; **sich z~en** make a fuss; (*sich bitten lassen*) need coaxing
zierlich *a* dainty, *adv* -ily; (*fein*) delicate, *adv* -ly; ⟨*Frau*⟩ petite
Ziffer *f* **-,-n** figure, digit; (*Zahlzeichen*) numeral. **Z~blatt** *nt* dial
zig *inv a* (*fam*) umpteen
Zigarette *f* **-,-n** cigarette
Zigarre *f* **-,-n** cigar
Zigeuner(in) *m* **-s,-** (*f* **-,-nen**) gypsy
Zimmer *nt* **-s,-** room. **Z~mädchen** *nt* chambermaid. **Z~mann** *m* (*pl* **-leute**) carpenter. **z~n** *vt* make □ *vi* (*haben*) do carpentry. **Z~nachweis** *m* accommodation bureau. **Z~pflanze** *f* house plant
zimperlich *a* squeamish; (*wehleidig*) soft; (*prüde*) prudish
Zimt *m* **-[e]s** cinnamon
Zink *nt* **-s** zinc
Zinke *f* **-,-n** prong; (*Kamm-*) tooth
Zinn *m* **-s** tin; (*Gefäße*) pewter
Zins|en *mpl* interest *sg*; **Z~en tragen** earn interest. **Z~eszins** *m* **-es,-en** compound interest. **Z~fuß, Z~satz** *m* interest rate
Zipfel *m* **-s,-** corner; (*Spitze*) point; (*Wurst-*) [tail-]end
zirka *adv* about
Zirkel *m* **-s,-** [pair of] compasses *pl*; (*Gruppe*) circle
Zirkul|ation /-ˈtsi̯oːn/ *f* **-** circulation. **z~ieren** *vi* (*sein*) circulate
Zirkus *m* **-,-se** circus
zirpen *vi* (*haben*) chirp
zischen *vi* (*haben*) hiss; ⟨*Fett:*⟩ sizzle □ *vt* hiss
Zit|at *nt* **-[e]s,-e** quotation. **z~ieren** *vt/i* (*haben*) quote; (*rufen*) summon
Zitr|onat *nt* **-[e]s** candied lemon-peel. **Z~one** *f* **-,-n** lemon. **Z~onenlimonade** *f* lemonade
zittern *vi* (*haben*) tremble; (*vor Kälte*) shiver; (*beben*) shake
zittrig *a* shaky, *adv* -ily
Zitze *f* **-,-n** teat
zivil *a* civilian; ⟨*Ehe, Recht, Luftfahrt*⟩ civil; (*mäßig*) reasonable. **Z~** *nt* **-s** civilian clothes *pl*. **Z~courage** /-kuraːʒə/ *f* **-** courage of one's convictions. **Z~dienst** *m* community service
Zivili|sation /-ˈtsi̯oːn/ *f* **-,-en** civilization. **z~sieren** *vt* civilize. **z~siert** *a* civilized □ *adv* in a civilized manner
Zivilist *m* **-en,-en** civilian

zögern *vi* (*haben*) hesitate. **Z~** *nt* **-s** hesitation. **z~d** *a* hesitant, *adv* -ly
Zoll[1] *m* **-[e]s,-** inch
Zoll[2] *m* **-[e]s,¨e** [customs] duty; (*Behörde*) customs *pl.* **Z~abfertigung** *f* customs clearance. **Z~beamte(r)** *m* customs officer. **z~frei** *a* & *adv* duty-free. **Z~kontrolle** *f* customs check
Zone *f* **-,-n** zone
Zoo *m* **-s,-s** zoo
Zoo|loge /tsoo'lo:gə/ *m* **-n,-n** zoologist. **Z~logie** *f* **-** zoology. **z~logisch** *a* zoological
Zopf *m* **-[e]s,¨e** plait
Zorn *m* **-[e]s** anger. **z~ig** *a* angry, *adv* -ily
zotig *a* smutty, dirty
zottig *a* shaggy
z.T. *abbr* (**zum Teil**) partly
zu *prep* (+ *dat*) to; (*dazu*) with; (*zeitlich, preislich*) at; (*Zweck*) for; (*über*) about; **zu ... hin** towards; **zu Hause** at home; **zu Fuß/Pferde** on foot/horseback; **zu beiden Seiten** on both sides; **zu Ostern** at Easter; **zu diesem Zweck** for this purpose; **zu meinem Erstaunen/Entsetzen** to my surprise/horror; **zu Dutzenden** by the dozen; **eine Marke zu 60 Pfennig** a 60-pfennig stamp; **das Stück zu zwei Mark** at two marks each; **wir waren zu dritt/viert** there were three/four of us; **es steht 5 zu 3** the score is 5–3; **zu etw werden** turn into sth □ *adv* (*allzu*) too; (*Richtung*) towards; (*geschlossen*) closed; (*an Schalter, Hahn*) off; **zu sein** be closed; **zu groß/viel/weit** too big/much/far; **nach dem Fluss zu** towards the river; **Augen zu!** close your eyes! **Tür zu!** shut the door! **nur zu!** go on! **macht zu!** (*fam*) hurry up! □ *conj* to; **etwas zu essen** something to eat; **nicht zu glauben** unbelievable; **zu erörternde Probleme** problems to be discussed
zualler|erst *adv* first of all. **z~letzt** *adv* last of all
Zubehör *nt* **-s** accessories *pl*
zubereit|en *vt sep* prepare. **Z~ung** *f* **-** preparation; (*in Rezept*) method
zubilligen *vt sep* grant
zubinden† *vt sep* tie [up]
zubring|en† *vt sep* spend. **Z~er** *m* **-s,-** access road; (*Bus*) shuttle
Zucchini /tsu'ki:ni/ *pl* courgettes
Zucht *f* **-,-en** breeding; (*Pflanzen-*) cultivation; (*Art, Rasse*) breed; (*von Pflanzen*) strain; (*Z~farm*) farm; (*Pferde-*) stud; (*Disziplin*) discipline
zücht|en *vt* breed; cultivate, grow ⟨*Rosen, Gemüse*⟩. **Z~er** *m* **-s,-** breeder; grower
Zuchthaus *nt* prison
züchtigen *vt* chastise
Züchtung *f* **-,-en** breeding; (*Pflanzen-*) cultivation; (*Art, Rasse*) breed; (*von Pflanzen*) strain
zucken *vi* (*haben*) twitch; (*sich z~d bewegen*) jerk; ⟨*Blitz:*⟩ flash; ⟨*Flamme:*⟩ flicker □ *vt* **die Achseln z~** shrug one's shoulders
zücken *vt* draw ⟨*Messer*⟩
Zucker *m* **-s** sugar. **Z~dose** *f* sugar basin. **Z~guss (Z~guß)** *m* icing. **z~krank** *a* diabetic. **Z~krankheit** *f* diabetes. **z~n** *vt* sugar. **Z~rohr** *nt* sugar cane. **Z~rübe** *f* sugar beet. **z~süß** *a* sweet; (*fig*) sugary. **Z~watte** *f* candyfloss. **Z~zange** *f* sugar tongs *pl*
zuckrig *a* sugary
zudecken *vt sep* cover up; (*im Bett*) tuck up; cover ⟨*Topf*⟩
zudem *adv* moreover
zudrehen *vt sep* turn off; **jdm den Rücken z~** turn one's back on s.o.
zudringlich *a* pushing, (*fam*) pushy

zudrücken *vt sep* press *or* push shut; close ⟨*Augen*⟩
zueinander *adv* to one another; **z~ passen** go together; **z~ halten** (*fig*) stick together. **z~halten**† *vi sep* (*haben*) (NEW) **z~ halten**, *s.* **zueinander**
zuerkennen† *vt sep* award (*dat* to)
zuerst *adv* first; (*anfangs*) at first; **mit dem Kopf z~** head first
zufahr|en† *vi sep* (*sein*) **z~en auf** (+ *acc*) drive towards. **Z~t** *f* access; (*Einfahrt*) drive
Zufall *m* chance; (*Zusammentreffen*) coincidence; **durch Z~** by chance/coincidence. **z~en**† *vi sep* (*sein*) close, shut; **jdm z~en** ⟨*Aufgabe:*⟩ fall/⟨*Erbe:*⟩ go to s.o.
zufällig *a* chance, accidental □ *adv* by chance; **ich war z~ da** I happened to be there
Zuflucht *f* refuge; (*Schutz*) shelter. **Z~sort** *m* refuge
zufolge *prep* (+ *dat*) according to
zufrieden *a* contented, *adv* -ly; (*befriedigt*) satisfied; **sich z~ geben** be satisfied; **jdn z~ lassen** leave s.o. in peace; **jdn z~ stellen** satisfy s.o.; **z~ stellend** satisfactory. **z~geben**† **(sich)** *vr sep* (NEW) **z~ geben (sich)**, *s.* **zufrieden**. **Z~heit** *f* - contentment; satisfaction. **z~lassen**† *vt sep* (NEW) **z~ lassen**, *s.* **zufrieden**. **z~stellen** *vt sep* (NEW) **z~ stellen**, *s.* **zufrieden**. **z~stellend** *a* (NEW) **z~ stellend**, *s.* **zufrieden**
zufrieren† *vi sep* (*sein*) freeze over
zufügen *vt sep* inflict (*dat* on); do ⟨*Unrecht*⟩ (*dat* to)
Zufuhr *f* - supply
zuführen *vt sep* □ *vt* supply □ *vi* (*haben*) **z~ auf** (+ *acc*) lead to
Zug *m* **-[e]s,¨e** train; (*Kolonne*) column; (*Um-*) procession; (*Mil*) platoon; (*Vogelschar*) flock; (*Ziehen, Zugkraft*) pull; (*Wandern, Ziehen*) migration; (*Schluck, Luft-*) draught; (*Atem-*) breath; (*beim Rauchen*) puff; (*Schach-*) move; (*beim Schwimmen, Rudern*) stroke; (*Gesichts-*) feature; (*Wesens-*) trait; **etw in vollen Zügen genießen** enjoy sth to the full; **in einem Zug[e]** at one go
Zugabe *f* (*Geschenk*) [free] gift; (*Mus*) encore
Zugang *m* access
zugänglich *a* accessible; ⟨*Mensch:*⟩ approachable; (*fig*) amenable (*dat*/**für** to)
Zugbrücke *f* drawbridge
zugeben† *vt sep* add; (*gestehen*) admit; (*erlauben*) allow. **zugegebenermaßen** *adv* admittedly
zugegen *a* **z~ sein** be present
zugehen† *vi sep* (*sein*) close; **jdm z~** be sent to s.o.; **z~ auf** (+ *acc*) go towards; **dem Ende z~** draw to a close; ⟨*Vorräte:*⟩ run low; **auf der Party ging es lebhaft zu** the party was pretty lively
Zugehörigkeit *f* - membership
Zügel *m* **-s,-** rein
zugelassen *a* registered
zügel|los *a* unrestrained, *adv* -ly; (*sittenlos*) licentious. **z~n** *vt* rein in; (*fig*) curb
Zuge|ständnis *nt* concession. **z~stehen**† *vt sep* grant
zugetan *a* fond (*dat* of)
zugig *a* draughty
zügig *a* quick, *adv* -ly
Zug|kraft *f* pull; (*fig*) attraction. **z~kräftig** *a* effective; (*anreizend*) popular; ⟨*Titel*⟩ catchy
zugleich *adv* at the same time
Zug|luft *f* draught. **Z~pferd** *nt* draught-horse; (*fam*) draw
zugreifen† *vi sep* (*haben*) grab it/them; (*bei Tisch*) help oneself; (*bei Angebot*) jump at it; (*helfen*) lend a hand
zugrunde *adv* **z~ richten** destroy; **z~ gehen** be destroyed; ⟨*Ehe:*⟩ founder; (*sterben*) die; **z~ liegen** form the basis (*dat* of)
zugucken *vi sep* (*haben*) = **zusehen**

zugunsten *prep* (+ *gen*) in favour of; ⟨*Sammlung*⟩ in aid of
zugute *adv* **jdm/etw z~ kommen** benefit s.o./sth; **jdm seine Jugend z~ halten** make allowances for s.o.'s youth
Zugvogel *m* migratory bird
zuhalten† *v sep* □ *vt* keep closed; (*bedecken*) cover; **sich** (*dat*) **die Nase z~** hold one's nose □ *vi* (*haben*) **z~ auf** (+ *acc*) head for
Zuhälter *m* **-s,-** pimp
zuhause *adv* = **zu Hause**, *s.* **Haus. Z~** *nt* **-s,-** home
zuhör|en *vi sep* (*haben*) listen (*dat* to). **Z~er(in)** *m(f)* listener
zujubeln *vi sep* (*haben*) **jdm z~** cheer s.o.
zukehren *vt sep* turn (*dat* to)
zukleben *vt sep* seal
zuknallen *vt/i sep* (*sein*) slam
zuknöpfen *vt sep* button up
zukommen† *vi sep* (*sein*) **z~ auf** (+ *acc*) come towards; (*sich nähern*) approach; **z~ lassen** send (**jdm** s.o.); devote ⟨*Pflege*⟩ (*dat* to); **jdm z~** be s.o.'s right
Zukunft *f* - future. **zukünftig** *a* future □ *adv* in future
zulächeln *vi sep* (*haben*) smile (*dat* at)
Zulage *f* **-,-n** extra allowance
zulangen *vi sep* (*haben*) help oneself; **tüchtig z~** tuck in
zulassen† *vt sep* allow, permit; (*teilnehmen lassen*) admit; (*Admin*) license, register; (*geschlossen lassen*) leave closed; leave unopened ⟨*Brief*⟩
zulässig *a* permissible
Zulassung *f* **-,-en** admission; registration; (*Lizenz*) licence
zulaufen† *vi sep* (*sein*) **z~en auf** (+ *acc*) run towards; **spitz z~en** taper to a point
zulegen *vt sep* add; **sich** (*dat*) **etw z~** get sth; grow ⟨*Bart*⟩
zuleide *adv* **jdm etwas z~ tun** hurt s.o.
zuletzt *adv* last; (*schließlich*) in the end; **nicht z~** not least
zuliebe *adv* **jdm/etw z~** for the sake of s.o./sth
zum *prep* = **zu dem; zum Spaß** for fun; **etw zum Lesen** sth to read
zumachen *v sep* □ *vt* close, shut; do up ⟨*Jacke*⟩; seal ⟨*Umschlag*⟩; turn off ⟨*Hahn*⟩; (*stilllegen*) close down □ *vi* (*haben*) close, shut; (*stillgelegt werden*) close down
zumal *adv* especially □ *conj* especially since
zumeist *adv* for the most part
zumindest *adv* at least
zumutbar *a* reasonable
zumute *adv* **mir ist traurig/elend z~** I feel sad/wretched; **mir ist nicht danach z~** I don't feel like it
zumut|en *vt sep* **jdm etw z~en** ask *or* expect sth of s.o.; **sich** (*dat*) **zu viel z~en** overdo things. **Z~ung** *f* - imposition; **eine Z~ung sein** be unreasonable
zunächst *adv* first [of all]; (*anfangs*) at first; (*vorläufig*) for the moment □ *prep* (+ *dat*) nearest to
Zunahme *f* **-,-n** increase
Zuname *m* surname
zünd|en *vt/i* (*haben*) ignite; **z~ende Rede** rousing speech. **Z~er** *m* **-s,-** detonator, fuse. **Z~holz** *nt* match. **Z~kerze** *f* sparking-plug. **Z~schlüssel** *m* ignition key. **Z~schnur** *f* fuse. **Z~ung** *f* **-,-en** ignition
zunehmen† *vi sep* (*haben*) increase (**an** + *dat* in); ⟨*Mond:*⟩ wax; (*an Gewicht*) put on weight. **z~d** *a* increasing, *adv* -ly
Zuneigung *f* - affection
Zunft *f* **-,⸚e** guild
zünftig *a* proper, *adv* -ly
Zunge *f* **-,-n** tongue. **Z~nbrecher** *m* tongue-twister
zunichte *a* **z~ machen** wreck; **z~ werden** come to nothing

zunicken *vi sep* (*haben*) nod (*dat* to)
zunutze *a* **sich** (*dat*) **etw z~ machen** make use of sth; (*ausnutzen*) take advantage of sth
zuoberst *adv* right at the top
zuordnen *vt sep* assign (*dat* to)
zupfen *vt/i* (*haben*) pluck (**an** + *dat* at); pull out ⟨*Unkraut*⟩
zur *prep* = **zu der; zur Schule/Arbeit** to school/work; **zur Zeit** at present
zurande *adv* **z~ kommen mit** (*fam*) cope with
zurate *adv* **z~ ziehen** consult
zurechnungsfähig *a* of sound mind
zurecht|finden† **(sich)** *vr sep* find one's way. **z~kommen**† *vi sep* (*sein*) cope (**mit** with); (*rechtzeitig kommen*) be in time. **z~legen** *vt sep* put out ready; **sich** (*dat*) **eine Ausrede z~legen** have an excuse all ready. **z~machen** *vt sep* get ready; **sich z~machen** get ready. **z~weisen**† *vt sep* reprimand. **Z~weisung** *f* reprimand
zureden *vi sep* (*haben*) **jdm z~** try to persuade s.o.
zurichten *vt sep* prepare; (*beschädigen*) damage; (*verletzen*) injure
zuriegeln *vt sep* bolt
zurück *adv* back; **Berlin, hin und z~** return to Berlin. **z~behalten**† *vt sep* keep back; be left with ⟨*Narbe*⟩. **z~bekommen**† *vt sep* get back; **20 Pfennig z~bekommen** get 20 pfennigs change. **z~bleiben**† *vi sep* (*sein*) stay behind; (*nicht mithalten*) lag behind. **z~blicken** *vi sep* (*haben*) look back. **z~bringen**† *vt sep* bring back; (*wieder hinbringen*) take back. **z~erobern** *vt sep* recapture; (*fig*) regain. **z~erstatten** *vt sep* refund. **z~fahren**† *v sep* □ *vt* drive back □ *vi* (*sein*) return, go back; (*im Auto*) drive back; (*z~weichen*) recoil. **z~finden**† *vi sep* (*haben*) find one's way back. **z~führen** *v sep* □ *vt* take back; (*fig*) attribute (**auf** + *acc* to) □ *vi* (*haben*) lead back. **z~geben**† *vt sep* give back, return. **z~geblieben** *a* retarded. **z~gehen**† *vi sep* (*sein*) go back, return; (*abnehmen*) go down; **z~gehen auf** (+ *acc*) (*fig*) go back to
zurückgezogen *a* secluded. **Z~heit** *f* - seclusion
zurückhalt|en† *vt sep* hold back; (*abhalten*) stop; **sich z~en** restrain oneself. **z~end** *a* reserved. **Z~ung** *f* - reserve
zurück|kehren *vi sep* (*sein*) return. **z~kommen**† *vi sep* (*sein*) come back, return; (*ankommen*) get back; **z~kommen auf** (+ *acc*) (*fig*) come back to. **z~lassen**† *vt sep* leave behind; (*z~kehren lassen*) allow back. **z~legen** *vt sep* put back; (*reservieren*) keep; (*sparen*) put by; cover ⟨*Strecke*⟩. **z~lehnen (sich)** *vr sep* lean back. **z~liegen**† *vi sep* (*haben*) be in the past; (*Sport*) be behind; **das liegt lange zurück** that was long ago. **z~melden (sich)** *vr sep* report back. **z~nehmen**† *vt sep* take back. **z~rufen**† *vt/i sep* (*haben*) call back. **z~scheuen** *vi sep* (*sein*) shrink (**vor** + *dat* from). **z~schicken** *vt sep* send back. **z~schlagen**† *v sep* □ *vi* (*haben*) hit back □ *vt* hit back; (*abwehren*) beat back; (*umschlagen*) turn back. **z~schneiden**† *vt sep* cut back. **z~schrecken**† *vi sep* (*sein*) shrink back, recoil; (*fig*) shrink (**vor** + *dat* from). **z~setzen** *v sep* □ *vt* put back; (*Auto*) reverse, back; (*herabsetzen*) reduce; (*fig*) neglect □ *vi* (*haben*) reverse, back. **z~stellen** *vt sep* put back; (*reservieren*) keep; (*fig*) put aside; (*aufschieben*) postpone. **z~stoßen**† *v sep* □ *vt* push back □ *vi* (*sein*) reverse, back. **z~treten**† *vi sep* (*sein*) step back;

(*vom Amt*) resign; (*verzichten*) withdraw. **z~weichen†** *vi sep* (*sein*) draw back; (*z~schrecken*) shrink back. **z~weisen†** *vt sep* turn away; (*fig*) reject. **z~werfen†** *vt* throw back; (*reflektieren*) reflect. **z~zahlen** *vt sep* pay back. **z~ziehen†** *vt sep* draw back; (*fig*) withdraw; **sich z~ziehen** withdraw; (*vom Beruf*) retire; (*Mil*) retreat

Zuruf *m* shout. **z~en†** *vt sep* shout (*dat* to)

zurzeit *adv* at present

Zusage *f* -,-n acceptance; (*Versprechen*) promise. **z~n** *v sep* □ *vt* promise □ *vi* (*haben*) accept; **jdm z~n** appeal to s.o.

zusammen *adv* together; (*insgesamt*) altogether; **z~ sein** be together. **Z~arbeit** *f* co-operation. **z~arbeiten** *vi sep* (*haben*) co-operate. **z~bauen** *vt sep* assemble. **z~beißen†** *vt sep* **die Zähne z~beißen** clench/(*fig*) grit one's teeth. **z~bleiben†** *vi sep* (*sein*) stay together. **z~brechen†** *vi sep* (*sein*) collapse. **z~bringen†** *vt sep* bring together; (*beschaffen*) raise. **Z~bruch** *m* collapse; (*Nerven- & fig*) breakdown. **z~fahren†** *vi sep* (*sein*) collide; (*z~zucken*) start. **z~fallen†** *vi sep* (*sein*) collapse; (*zeitlich*) coincide. **z~falten** *vt sep* fold up. **z~fassen** *vt sep* summarize, sum up. **Z~fassung** *f* summary. **z~fügen** *vt sep* fit together. **z~führen** *vt sep* bring together. **z~gehören** *vi sep* (*haben*) belong together; (*z~passen*) go together. **z~gesetzt** *a* (*Gram*) compound. **z~halten†** *v sep* □ *vt* hold together; (*beisammenhalten*) keep together □ *vi* (*haben*) (*fig*) stick together. **Z~hang** *m* connection; (*Kontext*) context. **z~hängen†** *vi sep* (*haben*) be connected. **z~hanglos** *a* incoherent, *adv* -ly. **z~klappen** *v sep* □ *vt* fold up □ *vi* (*sein*) collapse. **z~kommen†** *vi sep* (*sein*) meet; (*sich sammeln*) accumulate. **Z~kunft** *f* -,¨e meeting. **z~laufen†** *vi sep* (*sein*) gather; ⟨*Flüssigkeit:*⟩ collect; ⟨*Linien:*⟩ converge. **z~leben** *vi sep* (*haben*) live together. **z~legen** *v sep* □ *vt* put together; (*z~falten*) fold up; (*vereinigen*) amalgamate; pool ⟨*Geld*⟩ □ *vi* (*haben*) club together. **z~nehmen†** *vt sep* gather up; summon up ⟨*Mut*⟩; collect ⟨*Gedanken*⟩; **sich z~nehmen** pull oneself together. **z~passen** *vi sep* (*haben*) go together, match; ⟨*Personen:*⟩ be well matched. **Z~prall** *m* collision. **z~prallen** *vi sep* (*sein*) collide. **z~rechnen** *vt sep* add up. **z~reißen† (sich)** *vr sep* (*fam*) pull oneself together. **z~rollen** *vt sep* roll up; **sich z~rollen** curl up. **z~schlagen†** *vt sep* smash up; (*prügeln*) beat up. **z~schließen† (sich)** *vr sep* join together; ⟨*Firmen:*⟩ merge. **Z~schluss (Z~schluß)** *m* union; (*Comm*) merger. **z~schreiben†** *vt sep* write as one word

zusammensein† *vi sep* (*sein*) (NEW) **zusammen sein**, *s.* **zusammen. Z~** *nt* -s get-together

zusammensetz|en *vt sep* put together; (*Techn*) assemble; **sich z~en** sit [down] together; (*bestehen*) be made up (**aus** from). **Z~ung** *f* -,-en composition; (*Techn*) assembly; (*Wort*) compound

zusammen|stellen *vt sep* put together; (*gestalten*) compile. **Z~stoß** *m* collision; (*fig*) clash. **z~stoßen†** *vi sep* (*sein*) collide. **z~treffen†** *vi sep* (*sein*) meet; (*zeitlich*) coincide. **Z~treffen** *nt* meeting; coincidence. **z~zählen** *vt sep* add up. **z~ziehen†** *v sep* □ *vt* draw together; (*addieren*) add up; (*konzentrieren*) mass; **sich z~ziehen** contract; ⟨*Gewitter:*⟩ gather □ *vi* (*sein*) move in together; move in (**mit** with). **z~zucken** *vi sep (sein)* start; *(vor Schmerz)* wince

Zusatz *m* addition; *(Jur)* rider; *(Lebensmittel-)* additive. **Z~gerät** *nt* attachment. **zusätzlich** *a* additional □ *adv* in addition

zuschanden *adv* **z~ machen** ruin, wreck; **z~ werden** be wrecked *or* ruined; **z~ fahren** wreck

zuschau|en *vi sep (haben)* watch. **Z~er(in)** *m* **-s,-** *(f* **-,-nen)** spectator; *(TV)* viewer. **Z~erraum** *m* auditorium

zuschicken *vt sep* send *(dat* to)

Zuschlag *m* surcharge; *(D-Zug-)* supplement. **z~en**† *v sep* □ *vt* shut; *(heftig)* slam; *(bei Auktion)* knock down (**jdm** to s.o.) □ *vi (haben)* hit out; ⟨*Feind:*⟩ strike □ *vi (sein)* slam shut. **z~pflichtig** *a* ⟨*Zug*⟩ for which a supplement is payable

zuschließen† *v sep* □ *vt* lock □ *vi (haben)* lock up

zuschneiden† *vt sep* cut out; cut to size ⟨*Holz*⟩

zuschreiben† *vt sep* attribute *(dat* to); **jdm die Schuld z~** blame s.o.

Zuschrift *f* letter; *(auf Annonce)* reply

zuschulden *adv* **sich** *(dat)* **etwas z~ kommen lassen** do wrong

Zuschuss (**Zuschuß**) *m* contribution; *(staatlich)* subsidy

zusehen† *vi sep (haben)* watch; **z~, dass** see [to it] that

zusehends *adv* visibly

zusein† *vi sep (sein)* (NEW) **zu sein**, *s.* **zu**

zusenden† *vt sep* send *(dat* to)

zusetzen *v sep* □ *vt* add; *(einbüßen)* lose □ *vi (haben)* **jdm z~** pester s.o.; ⟨*Hitze:*⟩ take it out of s.o.

zusicher|n *vt sep* promise. **Z~ung** *f* promise.

Zuspätkommende(r) *m/f* latecomer

zuspielen *vt sep (Sport)* pass

zuspitzen (sich) *vr sep (fig)* become critical

zusprechen† *v sep* □ *vt* award (**jdm** s.o.); **jdm Trost/Mut z~** comfort/encourage s.o. □ *vi (haben)* **dem Essen z~** eat heartily

Zustand *m* condition, state

zustande *adv* **z~ bringen/kommen** bring/come about

zuständig *a* competent; *(verantwortlich)* responsible. **Z~keit** *f* - competence; responsibility

zustehen† *vi sep (haben)* **jdm z~** be s.o.'s right; ⟨*Urlaub:*⟩ be due to s.o.; **es steht ihm nicht zu** he is not entitled to it; *(gebührt)* it is not for him (**zu** to)

zusteigen† *vi sep (sein)* get on; **noch jemand zugestiegen?** tickets please; *(im Bus)* any more fares please?

zustell|en *vt sep* block; *(bringen)* deliver. **Z~ung** *f* delivery

zusteuern *v sep* □ *vi (sein)* head (**auf** + *acc* for) □ *vt* contribute

zustimm|en *vi sep (haben)* agree; *(billigen)* approve *(dat* of). **Z~ung** *f* consent; approval

zustoßen† *vi sep (sein)* happen *(dat* to)

Zustrom *m* influx

zutage *adv* **z~ treten** *od* **kommen/bringen** come/bring to light

Zutat *f (Culin)* ingredient

zuteil|en *vt sep* allocate; assign ⟨*Aufgabe*⟩. **Z~ung** *f* allocation

zutiefst *adv* deeply

zutragen† *vt sep* carry/*(fig)* report *(dat* to); **sich z~** happen

zutrau|en *vt sep* **jdm etw z~** believe s.o. capable of sth. **Z~en** *nt* **-s** confidence. **z~lich** *a* trusting, *adv* -ly; ⟨*Tier*⟩ friendly

zutreffen† *vi sep (haben)* be correct; **z~ auf** (+ *acc*) apply to. **z~d** *a* applicable (**auf** + *acc* to); *(richtig)* correct, *adv* -ly

zutrinken† *vi sep (haben)* **jdm z~** drink to s.o.
Zutritt *m* admittance
zuunterst *adv* right at the bottom
zuverlässig *a* reliable, *adv* -bly. **Z~keit** *f* - reliability
Zuversicht *f* - confidence. **z~lich** *a* confident, *adv* -ly
zuviel *pron & adv* (NEW) **zu viel**, *s.* **viel**
zuvor *adv* before; *(erst)* first
zuvorkommen† *vi sep (sein)* (+ *dat*) anticipate; **jdm z~** beat s.o. to it. **z~d** *a* obliging, *adv* -ly
Zuwachs *m* **-es** increase
zuwege *adv* **z~ bringen** achieve
zuweilen *adv* now and then
zuweisen† *vt sep* assign; *(zuteilen)* allocate
zuwend|en† *vt sep* turn (*dat* to); **sich z~en** (+ *dat*) turn to; *(fig)* devote oneself to. **Z~ung** *f* donation; *(Fürsorge)* care
zuwenig *pron & adv* (NEW) **zu wenig**, *s.* **wenig**
zuwerfen† *vt sep* slam ⟨*Tür*⟩; **jdm etw z~** throw s.o. sth; give s.o. ⟨*Blick, Lächeln*⟩
zuwider *adv* **jdm z~ sein** be repugnant to s.o. □ *prep* (+ *dat*) contrary to. **z~handeln** *vi sep (haben)* contravene (**etw** *dat* sth)
zuzahlen *vt sep* pay extra
zuziehen† *v sep* □ *vt* pull tight; draw ⟨*Vorhänge*⟩; *(hinzu-)* call in; **sich** *(dat)* **etw z~** contract ⟨*Krankheit*⟩; sustain ⟨*Verletzung*⟩; incur ⟨*Zorn*⟩ □ *vi (sein)* move into the area
zuzüglich *prep* (+ *gen*) plus
Zwang *m* **-[e]s,¨e** compulsion; *(Gewalt)* force; *(Verpflichtung)* obligation
zwängen *vt* squeeze
zwanglos *a* informal, *adv* -ly; ⟨*Benehmen*⟩ free and easy. **Z~igkeit** *f* - informality
Zwangs|jacke *f* straitjacket. **Z~lage** *f* predicament. **z~läufig** *a* inevitable, *adv* -bly
zwanzig *inv a* twenty. **z~ste(r,s)** *a* twentieth
zwar *adv* admittedly; **und z~** to be precise
Zweck *m* **-[e]s,-e** purpose; *(Sinn)* point; **es hat keinen Z~** there is no point. **z~dienlich** *a* appropriate; ⟨*Information*⟩ relevant. **z~los** *a* pointless. **z~mäßig** *a* suitable, *adv* -bly; *(praktisch)* functional, *adv* -ly. **z~s** *prep* (+ *gen*) for the purpose of
zwei *inv a*, **Z~** *f* **-,-en** two; *(Sch)* ≈ B. **Z~bettzimmer** *nt* twin-bedded room
zweideutig *a* ambiguous, *adv* -ly; *(schlüpfrig)* suggestive, *adv* -ly. **Z~keit** *f* **-,-en** ambiguity
zwei|erlei *inv a* two kinds of □ *pron* two things. **z~fach** *a* double
Zweifel *m* **-s,-** doubt. **z~haft** *a* doubtful; *(fragwürdig)* dubious. **z~los** *adv* undoubtedly. **z~n** *vi (haben)* doubt (**an etw** *dat* sth)
Zweig *m* **-[e]s,-e** branch. **Z~geschäft** *nt* branch. **Z~stelle** *f* branch [office]
Zwei|kampf *m* duel. **z~mal** *adv* twice. **z~reihig** *a* ⟨*Anzug*⟩ double-breasted. **z~sprachig** *a* bilingual
zweit *adv* **zu z~** in twos; **wir waren zu z~** there were two of us. **z~beste(r,s)** *a* second-best. **z~e(r,s)** *a* second
zwei|teilig *a* two-piece; ⟨*Film, Programm*⟩ two-part. **z~tens** *adv* secondly
zweitklassig *a* second-class
Zwerchfell *nt* diaphragm
Zwerg *m* **-[e]s,-e** dwarf
Zwetsch[g]e *f* **-,-n** quetsche
Zwickel *m* **-s,-** gusset
zwicken *vt/i (haben)* pinch
Zwieback *m* **-[e]s,¨e** rusk
Zwiebel *f* **-,-n** onion; *(Blumen-)*bulb
Zwielicht *nt* half-light; *(Dämmerlicht)* twilight. **z~ig** *a* shady

Zwie|spalt *m* conflict. **z~spältig** *a* conflicting. **Z~tracht** *f* - discord

Zwilling *m* **-s,-e** twin; **Z~e** (*Astr*) Gemini

zwingen† *vt* force; **sich z~** force oneself. **z~d** *a* compelling

Zwinger *m* **-s,-** run; (*Zucht-*) kennels *pl*

zwinkern *vi* (*haben*) blink; (*als Zeichen*) wink

Zwirn *m* **-[e]s** button thread

zwischen *prep* (+ *dat/acc*) between; (*unter*) among[st]. **Z~bemerkung** *f* interjection. **Z~ding** *nt* (*fam*) cross. **z~durch** *adv* in between; (*in der Z~zeit*) in the meantime; (*ab und zu*) now and again. **Z~fall** *m* incident. **Z~händler** *m* middleman. **Z~landung** *f* stopover. **Z~raum** *m* gap, space. **Z~ruf** *m* interjection. **Z~stecker** *m* adaptor. **Z~wand** *f* partition. **Z~zeit** *f* **in der Z~zeit** in the meantime

Zwist *m* **-[e]s,-e** discord; (*Streit*) feud. **Z~igkeiten** *fpl* quarrels

zwitschern *vi* (*haben*) chirp

zwo *inv a* two

zwölf *inv a* twelve. **z~te(r,s)** *a* twelfth

zwote(r,s) *a* second

Zyklus *m* **-,-klen** cycle

Zylind|er *m* **-s,-** cylinder; (*Hut*) top hat. **z~risch** *a* cylindrical

Zyn|iker *m* **-s,-** cynic. **z~isch** *a* cynical, *adv* -ly. **Z~ismus** *m* - cynicism

Zypern *nt* **-s** Cyprus

Zypresse *f* **-,-n** cypress

Zyste /ˈtsʏstə/ *f* **-,-n** cyst

A

a /ə, *betont* eɪ/ (*vor einem Vokal* **an**) *indef art* ein(e); (*each*) pro; **not a** kein(e)
aback /ə'bæk/ *adv* **be taken ~** verblüfft sein
abandon /ə'bændən/ *vt* verlassen; (*give up*) aufgeben □ *n* Hingabe *f*. **~ed** *a* verlassen; ⟨*behaviour*⟩ hemmungslos
abase /ə'beɪs/ *vt* demütigen
abashed /ə'bæʃt/ *a* beschämt, verlegen
abate /ə'beɪt/ *vi* nachlassen
abattoir /'æbətwɑ:(r)/ *n* Schlachthof *m*
abb|ey /'æbɪ/ *n* Abtei *f*. **~ot** /-ət/ *n* Abt *m*
abbreviat|e /ə'bri:vɪeɪt/ *vt* abkürzen. **~ion** /-'eɪʃn/ *n* Abkürzung *f*
abdicat|e /'æbdɪkeɪt/ *vi* abdanken. **~ion** /-'keɪʃn/ *n* Abdankung *f*
abdom|en /'æbdəmən/ *n* Unterleib *m*. **~inal** /-'dɒmɪnl/ *a* Unterleibs-
abduct /əb'dʌkt/ *vt* entführen. **~ion** /-ʌkʃn/ *n* Entführung *f*. **~or** *n* Entführer *m*
aberration /æbə'reɪʃn/ *n* Abweichung *f*; (*mental*) Verwirrung *f*
abet /ə'bet/ *vt* (*pt/pp* **abetted**) **aid and ~** (*Jur*) Beihilfe leisten (+ *dat*)
abeyance /ə'beɪəns/ *n* **in ~** [zeitweilig] außer Kraft; **fall into ~** außer Kraft kommen
abhor /əb'hɔ:(r)/ *vt* (*pt/pp* **abhorred**) verabscheuen. **~rence** /-'hɒrəns/ *n* Abscheu *f*. **~rent** /-'hɒrənt/ *a* abscheulich
abid|e /ə'baɪd/ *vt* (*pt/pp* **abided**) (*tolerate*) aushalten; ausstehen ⟨*person*⟩ □ *vi* **~e by** sich halten an (+ *acc*). **~ing** *a* bleibend
ability /ə'bɪlətɪ/ *n* Fähigkeit *f*; (*talent*) Begabung *f*
abject /'æbdʒekt/ *a* erbärmlich; (*humble*) demütig
ablaze /ə'bleɪz/ *a* in Flammen; **be ~** in Flammen stehen
able /'eɪbl/ *a* (**-r,-st**) fähig; **be ~ to do sth** etw tun können. **~-'bodied** *a* körperlich gesund; (*Mil*) tauglich
ably /'eɪblɪ/ *adv* gekonnt
abnormal /æb'nɔ:ml/ *a* anormal; (*Med*) abnorm. **~ity** /-'mælətɪ/ *n* Abnormität *f*. **~ly** *adv* ungewöhnlich
aboard /ə'bɔ:d/ *adv & prep* an Bord (+ *gen*)
abode /ə'bəʊd/ *n* Wohnsitz *m*
abol|ish /ə'bɒlɪʃ/ *vt* abschaffen. **~ition** /æbə'lɪʃn/ *n* Abschaffung *f*
abominable /ə'bɒmɪnəbl/ *a*, **-bly** *adv* abscheulich
abominate /ə'bɒmɪneɪt/ *vt* verabscheuen
aborigines /æbə'rɪdʒəni:z/ *npl* Ureinwohner *pl*
abort /ə'bɔ:t/ *vt* abtreiben. **~ion** /-ɔ:ʃn/ *n* Abtreibung *f*; **have an ~ion** eine Abtreibung vornehmen lassen. **~ive** /-tɪv/ *a* ⟨*attempt*⟩ vergeblich
abound /ə'baʊnd/ *vi* reichlich vorhanden sein; **~ in** reich sein an (+ *dat*)
about /ə'baʊt/ *adv* umher, herum; (*approximately*) ungefähr; **be ~** (*in circulation*)

umgehen; (*in existence*) vorhanden sein; **be up and ~** auf den Beinen sein; **be ~ to do sth** im Begriff sein, etw zu tun; **there are a lot ~** es gibt viele; **there was no one ~** es war kein Mensch da; **run/play ~** herumlaufen/-spielen □ *prep* um (+ *acc*) [... herum]; (*concerning*) über (+ *acc*); **what is it ~?** worum geht es? ⟨*book:*⟩ wovon handelt es? **I know nothing ~ it** ich weiß nichts davon; **talk/know ~** reden/wissen von

about: ~-'face *n*, **-'turn** *n* Kehrtwendung *f*

above /ə'bʌv/ *adv* oben □ *prep* über (+ *dat/acc*); **~ all** vor allem

above: ~-'board *a* legal. **~-mentioned** *a* oben erwähnt

abrasion /ə'breɪʒn/ *n* Schürfwunde *f*

abrasive /ə'breɪsɪv/ *a* Scheuer-; ⟨*remark*⟩ verletzend □ *n* Scheuermittel *nt*; (*Techn*) Schleifmittel *nt*

abreast /ə'brest/ *adv* nebeneinander; **keep ~ of** Schritt halten mit

abridge /ə'brɪdʒ/ *vt* kürzen

abroad /ə'brɔːd/ *adv* im Ausland; **go ~** ins Ausland fahren

abrupt /ə'brʌpt/ *a*, **-ly** *adv* abrupt; (*sudden*) plötzlich; (*curt*) schroff

abscess /'æbsɪs/ *n* Abszess *m*

abscond /əb'skɒnd/ *vi* entfliehen

absence /'æbsəns/ *n* Abwesenheit *f*

absent¹ /'æbsənt/ *a*, **-ly** *adv* abwesend; **be ~** fehlen

absent² /æb'sent/ *vt* **~ oneself** fernbleiben

absentee /æbsən'tiː/ *n* Abwesende(r) *m/f*

absent-minded /æbsənt'maɪndɪd/ *a*, **-ly** *adv* geistesabwesend; (*forgetful*) zerstreut

absolute /'æbsəluːt/ *a*, **-ly** *adv* absolut

absolution /æbsə'luːʃn/ *n* Absolution *f*

absolve /əb'zɒlv/ *vt* lossprechen

absorb /əb'sɔːb/ *vt* absorbieren, aufsaugen; **~ed in** vertieft in (+ *acc*). **~ent** /-ənt/ *a* saugfähig

absorption /əb'sɔːpʃn/ *n* Absorption *f*

abstain /əb'steɪn/ *vi* sich enthalten (**from** *gen*); **~ from voting** sich der Stimme enthalten

abstemious /əb'stiːmɪəs/ *a* enthaltsam

abstention /əb'stenʃn/ *n* (*Pol*) [Stimm]enthaltung *f*

abstinence /'æbstɪnəns/ *n* Enthaltsamkeit *f*

abstract /'æbstrækt/ *a* abstrakt □ *n* (*summary*) Abriss *m*

absurd /əb'sɜːd/ *a*, **-ly** *adv* absurd. **~ity** *n* Absurdität *f*

abundan|ce /ə'bʌndəns/ *n* Fülle *f* (**of** an + *dat*). **~t** *a* reichlich

abuse¹ /ə'bjuːz/ *vt* missbrauchen; (*insult*) beschimpfen

abus|e² /ə'bjuːs/ *n* Missbrauch *m*; (*insults*) Beschimpfungen *pl*. **~ive** /-ɪv/ ausfallend

abut /ə'bʌt/ *vi* (*pt/pp* **abutted**) angrenzen (**on to** an + *acc*)

abysmal /ə'bɪʒml/ *a* (*fam*) katastrophal

abyss /ə'bɪs/ *n* Abgrund *m*

academic /ækə'demɪk/ *a*, **-ally** *adv* akademisch □ *n* Akademiker(in) *m(f)*

academy /ə'kædəmɪ/ *n* Akademie *f*

accede /ək'siːd/ *vi* **~ to** zustimmen (+ *dat*); besteigen ⟨*throne*⟩

accelerat|e /ək'seləreɪt/ *vt* beschleunigen □ *vi* die Geschwindigkeit erhöhen. **~ion** /-'reɪʃn/ *n* Beschleunigung *f*. **~or** *n* (*Auto*) Gaspedal *nt*

accent¹ /'æksənt/ *n* Akzent *m*

accent² /æk'sent/ *vt* betonen

accentuate /ək'sentjʊeɪt/ *vt* betonen

accept /ək'sept/ *vt* annehmen; (*fig*) akzeptieren □ *vi* zusagen. **~able** /-əbl/ *a* annehmbar.

~ance *n* Annahme *f*; (*of invitation*) Zusage *f*
access /'ækses/ *n* Zugang *m*; (*road*) Zufahrt *f*. **~ible** /ək'sesəbl/ *a* zugänglich
accession /ək'seʃn/ *n* (*to throne*) Thronbesteigung *f*
accessor|y /ək'sesərɪ/ *n* (*Jur*) Mitschuldige(r) *m/f*; **~ies** *pl* (*fashion*) Accessoires *pl*; (*Techn*) Zubehör *nt*
accident /'æksɪdənt/ *n* Unfall *m*; (*chance*) Zufall *m*; **by ~** zufällig; (*unintentionally*) versehentlich. **~al** /-'dentl/ *a*, **-ly** *adv* zufällig; (*unintentional*) versehentlich
acclaim /ə'kleɪm/ *n* Beifall *m* □ *vt* feiern (**as** als)
acclimate /'æklɪmeɪt/ *vt* (*Amer*) = **acclimatize**
acclimatize /ə'klaɪmətaɪz/ *vt* **become ~d** sich akklimatisieren
accolade /'ækəleɪd/ *n* Auszeichnung *f*
accommodat|e /ə'kɒmədeɪt/ *vt* unterbringen; (*oblige*) entgegenkommen (+ *dat*). **~ing** *a* entgegenkommend. **~ion** /-'deɪʃn/ *n* (*rooms*) Unterkunft *f*
accompan|iment /ə'kʌmpənɪmənt/ *n* Begleitung *f*. **~ist** *n* (*Mus*) Begleiter(in) *m(f)*
accompany /ə'kʌmpənɪ/ *vt* (*pt/pp* **-ied**) begleiten
accomplice /ə'kʌmplɪs/ *n* Komplize/-zin *m/f*
accomplish /ə'kʌmplɪʃ/ *vt* erfüllen ⟨*task*⟩; (*achieve*) erreichen. **~ed** *a* fähig. **~ment** *n* Fertigkeit *f*; (*achievement*) Leistung *f*
accord /ə'kɔ:d/ *n* (*treaty*) Abkommen *nt*; **of one ~** einmütig; **of one's own ~** aus eigenem Antrieb □ *vt* gewähren. **~ance** *n* **in ~ance with** entsprechend (+ *dat*)
according /ə'kɔ:dɪŋ/ *adv* **~ to** nach (+ *dat*). **~ly** *adv* entsprechend
accordion /ə'kɔ:dɪən/ *n* Akkordeon *nt*
accost /ə'kɒst/ *vt* ansprechen
account /ə'kaʊnt/ *n* Konto *nt*; (*bill*) Rechnung *f*; (*description*) Darstellung *f*; (*report*) Bericht *m*; **~s** *pl* (*Comm*) Bücher *pl*; **on ~ of** wegen (+ *gen*); **on no ~** auf keinen Fall; **on this ~** deshalb; **on my ~** meinetwegen; **of no ~** ohne Bedeutung; **take into ~** in Betracht ziehen, berücksichtigen □ *vi* **~ for** Rechenschaft ablegen für; (*explain*) erklären
accountant /ə'kaʊntənt/ *n* Buchhalter(in) *m(f)*; (*chartered*) Wirtschaftsprüfer *m*; (*for tax*) Steuerberater *m*
accoutrements /ə'ku:trəmənts/ *npl* Ausrüstung *f*
accredited /ə'kredɪtɪd/ *a* akkreditiert
accrue /ə'kru:/ *vi* sich ansammeln
accumulat|e /ə'kju:mjʊleɪt/ *vt* ansammeln, anhäufen □ *vi* sich ansammeln, sich anhäufen. **~ion** /-'leɪʃn/ *n* Ansammlung *f*, Anhäufung *f*. **~or** *n* (*Electr*) Akkumulator *m*
accura|cy /'ækʊrəsɪ/ *n* Genauigkeit *f*. **~te** /-rət/ *a*, **-ly** *adv* genau
accusation /ækju:'zeɪʃn/ *n* Anklage *f*
accusative /ə'kju:zətɪv/ *a & n* **~ [case]** (*Gram*) Akkusativ *m*
accuse /ə'kju:z/ *vt* (*Jur*) anklagen (**of** *gen*); **~ s.o. of doing sth** jdn beschuldigen, etw getan zu haben. **~d** *n* **the ~d** der/die Angeklagte
accustom /ə'kʌstəm/ *vt* gewöhnen (**to** an + *dat*); **grow** *or* **get ~ed to** sich gewöhnen an (+ *acc*). **~ed** *a* gewohnt
ace /eɪs/ *n* (*Cards, Sport*) Ass *nt*
ache /eɪk/ *n* Schmerzen *pl* □ *vi* weh tun, schmerzen
achieve /ə'tʃi:v/ *vt* leisten; (*gain*) erzielen; (*reach*) erreichen. **~ment** *n* (*feat*) Leistung *f*
acid /'æsɪd/ *a* sauer; (*fig*) beißend □ *n* Säure *f*. **~ity** /ə'sɪdətɪ/ *n*

Säure *f*. **~'rain** *n* saurer Regen *m*

acknowledge /ək'nɒlɪdʒ/ *vt* anerkennen; (*admit*) zugeben; erwidern ⟨*greeting*⟩; **~ receipt of** den Empfang bestätigen (+ *gen*). **~ment** *n* Anerkennung *f*; (*of letter*) Empfangsbestätigung *f*

acne /'æknɪ/ *n* Akne *f*

acorn /'eɪkɔːn/ *n* Eichel *f*

acoustic /ə'kuːstɪk/ *a*, **-ally** *adv* akustisch. **~s** *npl* Akustik *f*

acquaint /ə'kweɪnt/ *vt* **~ s.o. with** jdn bekannt machen mit; **be ~ed with** kennen; vertraut sein mit ⟨*fact*⟩. **~ance** *n* Bekanntschaft *f*; (*person*) Bekannte(r) *m/f*; **make s.o.'s ~ance** jdn kennen lernen

acquiesce /ækwɪ'es/ *vi* einwilligen (**to** in + *acc*). **~nce** *n* Einwilligung *f*

acquire /ə'kwaɪə(r)/ *vt* erwerben

acquisit|ion /ækwɪ'zɪʃn/ *n* Erwerb *m*; (*thing*) Erwerbung *f*. **~ive** /æ'kwɪzətɪv/ *a* habgierig

acquit /ə'kwɪt/ *vt* (*pt/pp* **acquitted**) freisprechen; **~ oneself well** seiner Aufgabe gerecht werden. **~tal** *n* Freispruch *m*

acre /'eɪkə(r)/ *n* ≈ Morgen *m*

acrid /'ækrɪd/ *a* scharf

acrimon|ious /'ækrɪ'məʊnɪəs/ *a* bitter. **~y** /'ækrɪmənɪ/ *n* Bitterkeit *f*

acrobat /'ækrəbæt/ *n* Akrobat(in) *m*(*f*). **~ic** /-'bætrɪk/ *a* akrobatisch

across /ə'krɒs/ *adv* hinüber/herüber; (*wide*) breit; (*not lengthwise*) quer; (*in crossword*) waagerecht; **come ~ sth** auf etw (*acc*) stoßen; **go ~** hinübergehen; **bring ~** herüberbringen □ *prep* über (+ *acc*); (*crosswise*) quer über (+ *acc/dat*); (*on the other side of*) auf der anderen Seite (+ *gen*)

act /ækt/ *n* Tat *f*; (*action*) Handlung *f*; (*law*) Gesetz *nt*; (*Theat*) Akt *m*; (*Item*) Nummer *f*; **put on an ~** (*fam*) sich verstellen □ *vi* handeln; (*behave*) sich verhalten; (*Theat*) spielen; (*pretend*) sich verstellen; **~ as** fungieren als □ *vt* spielen ⟨*role*⟩. **~ing** *a* (*deputy*) stellvertretend □ *n* (*Theat*) Schauspielerei *f*. **~ing profession** *n* Schauspielerberuf *m*

action /'ækʃn/ *n* Handlung *f*; (*deed*) Tat *f*; (*Mil*) Einsatz *m*; (*Jur*) Klage *f*; (*effect*) Wirkung *f*; (*Techn*) Mechanismus *m*; **out of ~** ⟨*machine:*⟩ außer Betrieb; **take ~** handeln; **killed in ~** gefallen. **~ 'replay** *n* (*TV*) Wiederholung *f*

activate /'æktɪveɪt/ *vt* betätigen; (*Chem, Phys*) aktivieren

activ|e /'æktɪv/ *a*, **-ly** *adv* aktiv; **on ~e service** im Einsatz. **~ity** /-'tɪvətɪ/ *n* Aktivität *f*

act|or /'æktə(r)/ *n* Schauspieler *m*. **~ress** *n* Schauspielerin *f*

actual /'æktʃʊəl/ *a*, **-ly** *adv* eigentlich; (*real*) tatsächlich. **~ity** /-'ælətɪ/ *n* Wirklichkeit *f*

acumen /'ækjʊmən/ *n* Scharfsinn *m*

acupuncture /'ækjʊ-/ *n* Akupunktur *f*

acute /ə'kjuːt/ *a* scharf; ⟨*angle*⟩ spitz; ⟨*illness*⟩ akut. **~ly** *adv* sehr

ad /æd/ *n* (*fam*) = **advertisement**

AD *abbr* (**Anno Domini**) n.Chr.

adamant /'ædəmənt/ *a* **be ~ that** darauf bestehen, dass

adapt /ə'dæpt/ *vt* anpassen; bearbeiten ⟨*play*⟩ □ *vi* sich anpassen. **~ability** /-ə'bɪlətɪ/ *n* Anpassungsfähigkeit *f*. **~able** /-əbl/ *a* anpassungsfähig

adaptation /ædæp'teɪʃn/ *n* (*Theat*) Bearbeitung *f*

adapter, adaptor /ə'dæptə(r)/ *n* (*Techn*) Adapter *m*; (*Electr*) (*two-way*) Doppelstecker *m*

add /æd/ *vt* hinzufügen; (*Math*) addieren □ *vi* zusammenzählen, addieren; **~ to** hinzufügen zu; (*fig: increase*) steigern; (*compound*) verschlimmern. **~ up** *vt* zusammenzählen ⟨*figures*⟩ □ *vi* zusammenzählen, addieren; **~ up to** machen; **it doesn't ~ up** (*fig*) da stimmt etwas nicht

adder /'ædə(r)/ *n* Kreuzotter *f*

addict /'ædɪkt/ *n* Süchtige(r) *m/f*

addict|ed /ə'dɪktɪd/ *a* süchtig; **~ed to drugs** drogensüchtig. **~ion** /-ɪkʃn/ *n* Sucht *f*. **~ive** /-ɪv/ *a* **be ~ive** zur Süchtigkeit führen

addition /ə'dɪʃn/ *n* Hinzufügung *f*; (*Math*) Addition *f*; (*thing added*) Ergänzung *f*; **in ~** zusätzlich. **~al** *a*, **-ly** *adv* zusäzlich

additive /'ædɪtɪv/ *n* Zusatz *m*

address /ə'dres/ *n* Adresse *f*, Anschrift *f*; (*speech*) Ansprache *f*; **form of ~** Anrede *f* □ *vt* adressieren (**to** an + *acc*); (*speak to*) anreden ⟨*person*⟩; sprechen vor (+ *dat*) ⟨*meeting*⟩. **~ee** /ædre'si:/ *n* Empfänger *m*

adenoids /'ædənɔɪdz/ *npl* [Rachen]polypen *pl*

adept /'ædept/ *a* geschickt (**at** in + *dat*)

adequate /'ædɪkwət/ *a*, **-ly** *adv* ausreichend

adhere /əd'hɪə(r)/ *vi* kleben/(*fig*) festhalten (**to** an + *dat*). **~nce** *n* Festhalten *nt*

adhesive /əd'hi:sɪv/ *a* klebend □ *n* Klebstoff *m*

adjacent /ə'dʒeɪsnt/ *a* angrenzend

adjective /'ædʒɪktɪv/ *n* Adjektiv *nt*

adjoin /ə'dʒɔɪn/ *vt* angrenzen an (+ *acc*). **~ing** *a* angrenzend

adjourn /ə'dʒɜ:n/ *vt* vertagen (**until** auf + *acc*) □ *vi* sich vertagen. **~ment** *n* Vertagung *f*

adjudicate /ə'dʒu:dɪkeɪt/ *vi* entscheiden; (*in competition*) Preisrichter sein

adjust /ə'dʒʌst/ *vt* einstellen; (*alter*) verstellen □ *vi* sich anpassen (**to** *dat*). **~able** /-əbl/ *a* verstellbar. **~ment** *n* Einstellung *f*; Anpassung *f*

ad lib /æd'lɪb/ *adv* aus dem Stegreif □ *vi* (*pt/pp* **ad libbed**) (*fam*) improvisieren

administer /əd'mɪnɪstə(r)/ *vt* verwalten; verabreichen ⟨*medicine*⟩

administrat|ion /ədmɪnɪ'streɪʃn/ *n* Verwaltung *f*; (*Pol*) Regierung *f*. **~or** /əd'mɪnɪstreɪtə(r)/ *n* Verwaltungsbeamte(r) *m* /-beamtin *f*

admirable /'ædmərəbl/ *a* bewundernswert

admiral /'ædmərəl/ *n* Admiral *m*

admiration /ædmə'reɪʃn/ *n* Bewunderung *f*

admire /əd'maɪə(r)/ *vt* bewundern. **~r** *n* Verehrer(in) *m(f)*

admissable /əd'mɪsəbl/ *a* zulässig

admission /əd'mɪʃn/ *n* Eingeständnis *nt*; (*entry*) Eintritt *m*

admit /əd'mɪt/ *vt* (*pt/pp* **admitted**) (*let in*) hereinlassen; (*acknowledge*) zugeben; **~ to sth** etw zugeben. **~tance** *n* Eintritt *m*. **~tedly** *adv* zugegebenermaßen

admoni|sh /əd'mɒnɪʃ/ *vt* ermahnen. **~tion** /ædmə'nɪʃn/ *n* Ermahnung *f*

ado /ə'du:/ *n* **without more ~** ohne weiteres

adolescen|ce /ædə'lesns/ *n* Jugend *f*, Pubertät *f*. **~t** *a* Jugend-; ⟨*boy, girl*⟩ halbwüchsig □ *n* Jugendliche(r) *m/f*

adopt /ə'dɒpt/ *vt* adoptieren; ergreifen ⟨*measure*⟩; (*Pol*) annehmen ⟨*candidate*⟩. **~ion** /-ɒpʃn/ *n* Adoption. *f*. **~ive** /-ɪv/ *a* Adoptiv-

ador|able /ə'dɔ:rəbl/ *a* bezaubernd. **~ation** /ædə'reɪʃn/ *n* Anbetung *f*

adore /ə'dɔ:(r)/ *vt* (*worship*) anbeten; (*fam: like*) lieben

adorn /ə'dɔ:n/ *vt* schmücken. **~ment** *n* Schmuck *m*

adrenalin /ə'drenəlɪn/ *n* Adrenalin *nt*

Adriatic /eɪdrɪ'ætɪk/ *a & n* ~ **[Sea]** Adria *f*
adrift /ə'drɪft/ *a*, **be** ~ treiben; **come** ~ sich losreißen
adroit /ə'drɔɪt/ *a*, **-ly** *adv* gewandt, geschickt
adulation /ædjʊ'leɪʃn/ *n* Schwärmerei *f*
adult /'ædʌlt/ *n* Erwachsene(r) *m/f*
adulterate /ə'dʌltəreɪt/ *vt* verfälschen; panschen ⟨*wine*⟩
adultery /ə'dʌltərɪ/ *n* Ehebruch *m*
advance /əd'vɑ:ns/ *n* Fortschritt *m*; (*Mil*) Vorrücken *nt*; (*payment*) Vorschuss *m*; **in** ~ im Voraus □ *vi* vorankommen; (*Mil*) vorrücken; (*make progress*) Fortschritte machen □ *vt* fördern ⟨*cause*⟩; vorbringen ⟨*idea*⟩; vorschießen ⟨*money*⟩. ~ **booking** *n* Kartenvorverkauf *m*. ~**d** *a* fortgeschritten; (*progressive*) fortschrittlich. ~**ment** *n* Förderung *f*; (*promotion*) Beförderung *f*
advantage /əd'vɑ:ntɪdʒ/ *n* Vorteil *m*; **take** ~ **of** ausnutzen. ~**ous** /ædvən'teɪdʒəs/ *a* vorteilhaft
advent /'ædvent/ *n* Ankunft *f*; **A**~ (*season*) Advent *m*
adventur|e /əd'ventʃə(r)/ *n* Abenteuer *nt*. ~**er** *n* Abenteurer *m*. ~**ous** /-rəs/ *a* abenteuerlich; ⟨*person*⟩ abenteuerlustig
adverb /'ædvɜ:b/ *n* Adverb *nt*
adversary /'ædvəsərɪ/ *n* Widersacher *m*
advers|e /'ædvɜ:s/ *a* ungünstig. ~**ity** /əd'vɜ:sətɪ/ *n* Not *f*
advert /'ædvɜ:t/ *n* (*fam*) = **advertisement**
advertise /'ædvətaɪz/ *vt* Reklame machen für; (*by small ad*) inserieren □ *vi* Reklame machen; inserieren; ~ **for** per Anzeige suchen
advertisement /əd'vɜ:tɪsmənt/ *n* Anzeige *f*; (*publicity*) Reklame *f*; (*small ad*) Inserat *nt*
advertis|er /'ædvətaɪzə(r)/ *n* Inserent *m*. ~**ing** *n* Werbung *f* □ *attrib* Werbe-
advice /əd'vaɪs/ *n* Rat *m*. ~ **note** *n* Benachrichtigung *f*
advisable /əd'vaɪzəbl/ *a* ratsam
advis|e /əd'vaɪz/ *vt* raten (**s.o.** jdm); (*counsel*) beraten; (*inform*) benachrichtigen; ~**e s.o. against sth** jdm von etw abraten □ *vi* raten. ~**er** *n* Berater(in) *m(f)*. ~**ory** /-ərɪ/ *a* beratend
advocate[1] /'ædvəkət/ *n* [Rechts]-anwalt *m*/-anwältin *f*; (*supporter*) Befürworter *m*
advocate[2] /'ædvəkeɪt/ *vt* befürworten
aerial /'eərɪəl/ *a* Luft- □ *n* Antenne *f*
aerobics /eə'rəʊbɪks/ *n* Aerobic *nt*
aero|drome /'eərədrəʊm/ *n* Flugplatz *m*. ~**plane** *n* Flugzeug *nt*
aerosol /'eərəsɒl/ *n* Spraydose *f*
aesthetic /i:s'θetɪk/ *a* ästhetisch
afar /ə'fɑ:(r)/ *adv* **from** ~ aus der Ferne
affable /'æfəbl/ *a*, **-bly** *adv* freundlich
affair /ə'feə(r)/ *n* Angelegenheit *f*, Sache *f*; (*scandal*) Affäre *f*; **[love-]**~ [Liebes]verhältnis *nt*
affect /ə'fekt/ *vt* sich auswirken auf (+ *acc*); (*concern*) betreffen; (*move*) rühren; (*pretend*) vortäuschen. ~**ation** /æfek'teɪʃn/ *n* Affektiertheit *f*. ~**ed** *a* affektiert
affection /ə'fekʃn/ *n* Liebe *f*. ~**ate** /-ət/ *a*, **-ly** *adv* liebevoll
affiliated /ə'fɪlɪeɪtɪd/ *a* angeschlossen (**to** *dat*)
affinity /ə'fɪnətɪ/ *n* Ähnlichkeit *f*; (*attraction*) gegenseitige Anziehung *f*
affirm /ə'fɜ:m/ *vt* behaupten; (*Jur*) eidesstattlich erklären
affirmative /ə'fɜ:mətɪv/ *a* bejahend □ *n* Bejahung *f*
affix /ə'fɪks/ *vt* anbringen (**to** *dat*); (*stick*) aufkleben (**to** auf +

acc) setzen ⟨*signature*⟩ (**to** unter + *acc*)

afflict /ə'flɪkt/ *vt* **be ~ed with** behaftet sein mit. **~ion** /-ɪkʃn/ *n* Leiden *nt*

affluen|ce /'æfluəns/ *n* Reichtum *m*. **~t** *a* wohlhabend. **~t society** *n* Wohlstandsgesellschaft *f*

afford /ə'fɔ:d/ *vt* (*provide*) gewähren; **be able to ~ sth** sich (*dat*) etw leisten können. **~able** /-əbl/ *a* erschwinglich

affray /ə'freɪ/ *n* Schlägerei *f*

affront /ə'frʌnt/ *n* Beleidigung *f* □ *vt* beleidigen

afield /ə'fi:ld/ *adv* **further ~** weiter weg

afloat /ə'fləʊt/ *a* **be ~** ⟨*ship:*⟩ flott sein; **keep ~** ⟨*person:*⟩ sich über Wasser halten

afoot /ə'fʊt/ *a* im Gange

aforesaid /ə'fɔ:sed/ *a* (*Jur*) oben erwähnt

afraid /ə'freɪd/ *a* **be ~** Angst haben (**of** vor + *dat*); **I'm ~ not** leider nicht; **I'm ~ so** [ja] leider; **I'm ~ I can't help you** ich kann Ihnen leider nicht helfen

afresh /ə'freʃ/ *adv* von vorne

Africa /'æfrɪkə/ *n* Afrika *nt*. **~n** *a* afrikanisch □ *n* Afrikaner(in) *m(f)*

after /'ɑ:ftə(r)/ *adv* danach □ *prep* nach (+ *dat*); **~ that** danach; **~ all** schließlich; **the day ~ tomorrow** übermorgen; **be ~** aus sein auf (+ *acc*) □ *conj* nachdem

after: ~-effect *n* Nachwirkung *f*. **~math** /-mɑ:θ/ *n* Auswirkungen *pl*. **~'noon** *n* Nachmittag *m*; **good ~noon!** guten Tag! **~-sales service** *n* Kundendienst *m*. **~shave** *n* Rasierwasser *nt*. **~thought** *n* nachträglicher Einfall *m*. **~wards** *adv* nachher

again /ə'gen/ *adv* wieder; (*once more*) noch einmal; (*besides*) außerdem; **~ and ~** immer wieder

against /ə'genst/ *prep* gegen (+ *acc*)

age /eɪdʒ/ *n* Alter *nt*; (*era*) Zeitalter *nt*; **~s** (*fam*) ewig; **under ~** minderjährig; **of ~** volljährig; **two years of ~** zwei Jahre alt □ *v* (*pres p* **ageing**) □ *vt* älter machen □ *vi* altern; (*mature*) reifen

aged[1] /eɪdʒd/ *a* **~ two** zwei Jahre alt

aged[2] /'eɪdʒɪd/ *a* betagt □ *n* **the ~** *pl* die Alten

ageless /'eɪdʒlɪs/ *a* ewig jung

agency /'eɪdʒənsɪ/ *n* Agentur *f*; (*office*) Büro *nt*; **have the ~ for** die Vertretung haben für

agenda /ə'dʒendə/ *n* Tagesordnung *f*; **on the ~** auf dem Programm

agent /'eɪdʒənt/ *n* Agent(in) *m(f)*; (*Comm*) Vertreter(in) *m(f)*; (*substance*) Mittel *nt*

aggravat|e /'ægrəveɪt/ *vt* verschlimmern; (*fam: annoy*) ärgern. **~ion** /-'veɪʃn/ *n* (*fam*) Ärger *m*

aggregate /'ægrɪgət/ *a* gesamt □ *n* Gesamtzahl *f*; (*sum*) Gesamtsumme *f*

aggress|ion /ə'greʃn/ *n* Aggression *f*. **~ive** /-sɪv/ *a*, **-ly** *adv* aggressiv. **~iveness** *n* Aggressivität *f*. **~or** *n* Angreifer(in) *m(f)*

aggrieved /ə'gri:vd/ *a* verletzt

aggro /'ægrəʊ/ *n* (*fam*) Ärger *m*

aghast /ə'gɑ:st/ *a* entsetzt

agil|e /'ædʒaɪl/ *a* flink, behände; ⟨*mind*⟩ wendig. **~ity** /ə'dʒɪlətɪ/ *n* Flinkheit *f*, Behändigkeit *f*

agitat|e /'ædʒɪteɪt/ *vt* bewegen; (*shake*) schütteln □ *vi* (*fig*) **~ for** agitieren für. **~ed** *a*, **-ly** *adv* erregt. **~ion** /-'teɪʃn/ *n* Erregung *f*; (*Pol*) Agitation *f*. **~or** *n* Agitator *m*

agnostic /æg'nɒstɪk/ *n* Agnostiker *m*

ago /ə'gəʊ/ *adv* vor (+ *dat*); **a month ~** vor einem Monat; **a long time ~** vor langer Zeit; **how long ~ is it?** wie lange ist es her?

agog /ə'gɒg/ *a* gespannt

agoniz|e /'ægənaɪz/ *vi* [innerlich] ringen. **~ing** *a* qualvoll
agony /'ægənɪ/ *n* Qual *f*; **be in ~** furchtbare Schmerzen haben
agree /ə'gri:/ *vt* vereinbaren; (*admit*) zugeben; **~ to do sth** sich bereit erklären, etw zu tun □ *vi* ⟨*people, figures:*⟩ übereinstimmen; (*reach agreement*) sich einigen; (*get on*) gut miteinander auskommen; (*consent*) einwilligen (**to** in + *acc*); **I ~** der Meinung bin ich auch; **~ with s.o.** jdm zustimmen; ⟨*food:*⟩ jdm bekommen; **~ with sth** (*approve of*) mit etw einverstanden sein
agreeable /ə'gri:əbl/ *a* angenehm; **be ~** einverstanden sein (**to** mit)
agreed /ə'gri:d/ *a* vereinbart
agreement /ə'gri:mənt/ *n* Übereinstimmung *f*; (*consent*) Einwilligung *f*; (*contract*) Abkommen *nt*; **reach ~** sich einigen
agricultur|al /ægrɪ'kʌltʃərəl/ *a* landwirtschaftlich. **~e** /'ægrɪkʌltʃə(r)/ *n* Landwirtschaft *f*
aground /ə'graʊnd/ *a* gestrandet; **run ~** ⟨*ship:*⟩ stranden
ahead /ə'hed/ *adv* **straight ~** geradeaus; **be ~ of s.o./sth** vor jdm/etw sein; (*fig*) voraus sein; **draw ~** nach vorne ziehen; **go on ~** vorgehen; **get ~** vorankommen; **go ~!** (*fam*) bitte! **look/plan ~** vorausblicken/-planen
aid /eɪd/ *n* Hilfe *f*; (*financial*) Unterstützung *f*; **in ~ of** zugunsten (+ *gen*) □ *vt* helfen (+ *dat*)
aide /eɪd/ *n* Berater *m*
Aids /eɪdz/ *n* Aids *nt*
ail|ing /'eɪlɪŋ/ *a* kränkelnd. **~ment** *n* Leiden *nt*
aim /eɪm/ *n* Ziel *nt*; **take ~** zielen □ *vt* richten (**at** auf + *acc*); □ *vi* zielen (**at** auf + *acc*); **~ to do sth** beabsichtigen, etw zu tun. **~less** *a*, **-ly** *adv* ziellos
air /eə(r)/ *n* Luft *f*; (*tune*) Melodie *f*; (*expression*) Miene *f*; (*appearance*) Anschein *m*; **be on the ~** ⟨*programme:*⟩ gesendet werden; ⟨*person:*⟩ senden, auf Sendung sein; **put on ~s** vornehm tun; **by ~** auf dem Luftweg; (*airmail*) mit Luftpost □ *vt* lüften; vorbringen ⟨*views*⟩
air: ~-bed *n* Luftmatratze *f*. **~-conditioned** *a* klimatisiert. **~-conditioning** *n* Klimaanlage *f*. **~craft** *n* Flugzeug *nt*. **~fare** *n* Flugpreis *m*. **~field** *n* Flugplatz *m*. **~ force** *n* Luftwaffe *f*. **~ freshener** *n* Raumspray *nt*. **~gun** *n* Luftgewehr *nt*. **~ hostess** *n* Stewardess *f*. **~ letter** *n* Aerogramm *nt*. **~line** *n* Fluggesellschaft *f*. **~lock** *n* Luftblase *f*. **~mail** *n* Luftpost *f*. **~man** *n* Flieger *m*. **~plane** *n* (*Amer*) Flugzeug *nt*. **~ pocket** *n* Luftloch *nt*. **~port** *n* Flughafen *m*. **~-raid** *n* Luftangriff *m*. **~-raid shelter** *n* Luftschutzbunker *m*. **~ship** *n* Luftschiff *nt*. **~ ticket** *n* Flugschein *m*. **~tight** *a* luftdicht. **~ traffic** *n* Luftverkehr *m*. **~-traffic controller** *n* Fluglotse *m*. **~worthy** *a* flugtüchtig
airy /'eərɪ/ *a* (**ier,-iest**) luftig; ⟨*manner*⟩ nonchalant
aisle /aɪl/ *n* Gang *m*
ajar /ə'dʒɑ:(r)/ *a* angelehnt
akin /ə'kɪn/ *a* **~ to** verwandt mit; (*similar*) ähnlich (**to** *dat*)
alabaster /'æləbɑ:stə(r)/ *n* Alabaster *m*
alacrity /ə'lækrətɪ/ *n* Bereitfertigkeit *f*
alarm /əlɑ:m/ *n* Alarm *m*; (*device*) Alarmanlage *f*; (*clock*) Wecker *m*; (*fear*) Unruhe *f* □ *vt* erschrecken; alarmieren. **~ clock** *n* Wecker *m*
alas /ə'læs/ *int* ach!
album /'ælbəm/ *n* Album *nt*
alcohol /'ælkəhɒl/ *n* Alkohol *m*. **~ic** /-'hɒlɪk/ *a* alkoholisch □ *n* Alkoholiker(in) *m*(*f*). **~ism** *n* Alkoholismus *m*
alcove /'ælkəʊv/ *n* Nische *f*

alert /ə'lɜ:t/ *a* aufmerksam □ *n* Alarm *m*; **on the ~** auf der Hut □ *vt* alarmieren
algae /'ældʒi:/ *npl* Algen *pl*
algebra /'ældʒɪbrə/ *n* Algebra *f*
Algeria /æl'dʒɪərɪə/ *n* Algerien *nt*
alias /'eɪlɪəs/ *n* Deckname *m* □ *adv* alias
alibi /'ælɪbaɪ/ *n* Alibi *nt*
alien /'eɪlɪən/ *a* fremd □ *n* Ausländer(in) *m(f)*
alienat|e /'eɪlɪəneɪt/ *vt* entfremden. **~ion** /-'neɪʃn/ *n* Entfremdung *f*
alight[1] /ə'laɪt/ *vi* aussteigen (**from** aus); ⟨*bird:*⟩ sich niederlassen
alight[2] *a* **be ~** brennen; **set ~** anzünden
align /ə'laɪn/ *vt* ausrichten. **~ment** *n* Ausrichtung *f*; **out of ~ment** nicht richtig ausgerichtet
alike /ə'laɪk/ *a & adv* ähnlich; (*same*) gleich; **look ~** sich (*dat*) ähnlich sehen
alimony /'ælɪmənɪ/ *n* Unterhalt *m*
alive /ə'laɪv/ *a* lebendig; **be ~** leben; **be ~ with** wimmeln von
alkali /'ælkəlaɪ/ *n* Base *f*, Alkali *nt*
all /ɔ:l/ *a* alle *pl*; (*whole*) ganz; **~ [the] children** alle Kinder; **~ our children** alle unsere Kinder; **~ the others** alle anderen; **~ day** den ganzen Tag; **~ the wine** der ganze Wein; **for ~ that** (*nevertheless*) trotzdem; **in ~ innocence** in aller Unschuld □ *pron* alle *pl*; (*everything*) alles; **~ of you/-them** Sie/sie alle; **~ of the town** die ganze Stadt; **not at ~** gar nicht; **in ~** insgesamt; **~ in ~** alles in allem; **most of ~** am meisten; **once and for ~** ein für alle Mal □ *adv* ganz; **~ but** fast; **~ at once** auf einmal; **~ too soon** viel zu früh; **~ the same** (*nevertheless*) trotzdem; **~ the better** umso besser; **be ~ in** (*fam*) völlig erledigt sein; **four ~** (*Sport*) vier zu vier
allay /ə'leɪ/ *vt* zerstreuen
allegation /ælɪ'geɪʃn/ *n* Behauptung *f*
allege /ə'ledʒ/ *vt* behaupten. **~d** *a* **-ly** /-ɪdlɪ/ *adv* angeblich
allegiance /ə'li:dʒəns/ *n* Treue *f*
allegor|ical /ælɪ'gɒrɪkl/ *a* allegorisch. **~y** /'ælɪgərɪ/ *n* Allegorie *f*
allerg|ic /ə'lɜ:dʒɪk/ *a* allergisch (**to** gegen). **~y** /'ælədʒɪ/ *n* Allergie *f*
alleviate /ə'li:vɪeɪt/ *vt* lindern
alley /'ælɪ/ *n* Gasse *f*; (*for bowling*) Bahn *f*
alliance /ə'laɪəns/ *n* Verbindung *f*; (*Pol*) Bündnis *nt*
allied /'ælaɪd/ *a* alliiert; (*fig: related*) verwandt (**to** mit)
alligator /'ælɪgeɪtə(r)/ *n* Alligator *m*
allocat|e /'æləkeɪt/ *vt* zuteilen; (*share out*) verteilen. **~ion** /-'keɪʃn/ *n* Zuteilung *f*
allot /ə'lɒt/ *vt* (*pt/pp* **allotted**) zuteilen (**s.o.** jdm). **~ment** *n* ≈ Schrebergarten *m*
allow /ə'laʊ/ *vt* erlauben; (*give*) geben; (*grant*) gewähren; (*reckon*) rechnen; (*agree, admit*) zugeben; **~ for** berücksichtigen; **~ s.o. to do sth** jdm erlauben, etw zu tun; **be ~ed to do sth** etw tun dürfen
allowance /ə'laʊəns/ *n* [finanzielle] Unterstützung *f*; **~ for petrol** Benzingeld *nt*; **make ~s for** berücksichtigen
alloy /'ælɔɪ/ *n* Legierung *f*
allude /ə'lu:d/ *vi* anspielen (**to** auf + *acc*)
allure /æ'ljʊə(r)/ *n* Reiz *m*
allusion /ə'lu:ʒn/ *n* Anspielung *f*
ally[1] /'ælaɪ/ *n* Verbündete(r) *m/f*; **the Allies** *pl* die Alliierten
ally[2] /ə'laɪ/ *vt* (*pt/pp* **-ied**) verbinden; **~ oneself with** sich verbünden mit

almighty /ɔ:l'maɪtɪ/ *a* allmächtig; (*fam: big*) Riesen- □ *n* **the A** ~ der Allmächtige
almond /'ɑ:mənd/ *n* (*Bot*) Mandel *f*
almost /'ɔ:lməʊst/ *adv* fast, beinahe
alms /ɑ:mz/ *npl* (*liter*) Almosen *pl*
alone /ə'ləʊn/ *a* & *adv* allein; **leave me** ~ lass mich in Ruhe; **leave that** ~! lass die Finger davon! **let** ~ ganz zu schweigen von
along /ə'lɒŋ/ *prep* entlang (+ *acc*); ~ **the river** den Fluss entlang □ *adv* ~ **with** zusammen mit; **all** ~ die ganze Zeit; **come** ~ komm doch; **I'll bring it** ~ ich bringe es mit; **move** ~ weitergehen
along'side *adv* daneben □ *prep* neben (+ *dat*)
aloof /ə'lu:f/ *a* distanziert
aloud /ə'laʊd/ *adv* laut
alphabet /'ælfəbet/ *n* Alphabet *nt*. ~**ical** /-'betɪkl/ *a*, **-ly** *adv* alphabetisch
alpine /'ælpaɪn/ *a* alpin; **A**~ Alpen-
Alps /ælps/ *npl* Alpen *pl*
already /ɔ:l'redɪ/ *adv* schon
Alsace /æl'sæs/ *n* Elsass *nt*
Alsatian /æl'seɪʃn/ *n* (*dog*) [deutscher] Schäferhund *m*
also /'ɔ:lsəʊ/ *adv* auch
altar /'ɔ:ltə(r)/ *n* Altar *m*
alter /'ɔ:ltə(r)/ *vt* ändern □ *vi* sich verändern. ~**ation** /-'reɪʃn/ *n* Änderung *f*
alternate[1] /'ɔ:ltəneɪt/ *vi* [sich] abwechseln □ *vt* abwechseln
alternate[2] /ɔ:l'tɜ:nət/ *a*, **-ly** *adv* abwechselnd; (*Amer: alternative*) andere(r,s); **on** ~ **days** jeden zweiten Tag
'alternating current *n* Wechselstrom *m*
alternative /ɔ:l'tɜ:nətɪv/ *a* andere(r,s) □ *n* Alternative *f*. ~**ly** *adv* oder aber
although /ɔ:l'ðəʊ/ *conj* obgleich, obwohl
altitude /'æltɪtju:d/ *n* Höhe *f*
altogether /ɔ:ltə'geðə(r)/ *adv* insgesamt; (*on the whole*) alles in allem
altruistic /æltru:'ɪstɪk/ altruistisch
aluminium /æljʊ'mɪnɪəm/ *n*, (*Amer*) **aluminium** /ə'lu:mɪnəm/ *n* Aluminium *nt*
always /'ɔ:lweɪz/ *adv* immer
am /æm/ *see* **be**
a.m. *abbr* (**ante meridiem**) vormittags
amalgamate /ə'mælgəmeɪt/ *vt* vereinigen; (*Chem*) amalgamieren □ *vi* sich vereinigen; (*Chem*) sich amalgamieren
amass /ə'mæs/ *vt* anhäufen
amateur /'æmətə(r)/ *n* Amateur *m* □ *attrib* Amateur-; (*Theat*) Laien-. ~**ish** *a* laienhaft
amaze /ə'meɪz/ *vt* erstaunen. ~**d** *a* erstaunt. ~**ment** *n* Erstaunen *nt*
amazing /ə'meɪzɪŋ/ *a*, **-ly** *adv* erstaunlich
ambassador /æm'bæsədə(r)/ *n* Botschafter *m*
amber /'æmbə(r)/ *n* Bernstein *m* □ *a* (*colour*) gelb
ambidextrous /æmbɪ'dekstrəs/ *a* **be** ~ mit beiden Händen gleich geschickt sein
ambience /'æmbɪəns/ *n* Atmosphäre *f*
ambigu|ity /æmbɪ'gju:ətɪ/ *n* Zweideutigkeit *f*. ~**ous** /-'bɪgjʊəs/ *a* **-ly** *adv* zweideutig
ambiti|on /æm'bɪʃn/ *n* Ehrgeiz *m*; (*aim*) Ambition *f*. ~**ous** /-ʃəs/ *a* ehrgeizig
ambivalent /æm'bɪvələnt/ *a* zwiespältig; **be/feel** ~ im Zwiespalt sein
amble /'æmbl/ *vi* schlendern
ambulance /'æmbjʊləns/ *n* Krankenwagen *m*. ~ **man** *n* Sanitäter *m*

ambush /ˈæmbʊʃ/ *n* Hinterhalt *m* □ *vt* aus dem Hinterhalt überfallen
amen /ɑːˈmen/ *int* amen
amenable /əˈmiːnəbl/ *a* ~ **to** zugänglich (**to** *dat*)
amend /əˈmend/ *vt* ändern. **~ment** *n* Änderung *f*. **~s** *npl* **make ~s for sth** etw wieder gutmachen
amenities /əˈmiːnətɪz/ *npl* Einrichtungen *pl*
America /əˈmerɪkə/ *n* Amerika *nt*. **~n** *a* amerikanisch □ *n* Amerikaner(in) *m(f)*. **~nism** *n* Amerikanismus *m*
amiable /ˈeɪmɪəbl/ *a* nett
amicable /ˈæmɪkəbl/ *a*, **-bly** *adv* freundschaftlich; ⟨*agreement*⟩ gütlich
amid[st] /əˈmɪd[st]/ *prep* inmitten (+ *gen*)
amiss /əˈmɪs/ *a* **be ~** nicht stimmen □ *adv* **not come ~** nicht unangebracht sein; **take sth ~** etw ˈübel nehmen
ammonia /əˈməʊnɪə/ *n* Ammoniak *nt*
ammunition /æmjʊˈnɪʃn/ *n* Munition *f*
amnesia /æmˈniːzɪə/ *n* Amnesie *f*
amnesty /ˈæmnəstɪ/ *n* Amnestie *f*
among[st] /əˈmʌŋ[st]/ *prep* unter (+ *dat/acc*); **~ yourselves** untereinander
amoral /eɪˈmɒrəl/ *a* amoralisch
amorous /ˈæmərəs/ *a* zärtlich
amount /əˈmaʊnt/ *n* Menge *f*; (*sum of money*) Betrag *m*; (*total*) Gesamtsumme *f* □ *vi* **~ to** sich belaufen auf (+ *acc*); (*fig*) hinauslaufen auf (+ *acc*)
amp /æmp/ *n* Ampere *nt*
amphibi|an /æmˈfɪbɪən/ *n* Amphibie *f*. **~ous** /-ɪəs/ *a* amphibisch
amphitheatre /ˈæmfɪ-/ *n* Amphitheater *nt*
ample /ˈæmpl/ *a* (**-r,-st**), **-ly** *adv* reichlich; (*large*) füllig
amplif|ier /ˈæmplɪfaɪə(r)/ *n* Verstärker *m*. **~y** /-faɪ/ *vt* (*pt/pp* **-ied**) weiter ausführen; verstärken ⟨*sound*⟩
amputat|e /ˈæmpjʊteɪt/ *vt* amputieren. **~ion** /-ˈteɪʃn/ *n* Amputation *f*
amuse /əˈmjuːz/ *vt* amüsieren, belustigen; (*entertain*) unterhalten. **~ment** *n* Belustigung *f*; Unterhaltung *f*. **~ment arcade** *n* Spielhalle *f*
amusing /əˈmjuːzɪŋ/ *a* amüsant
an /ən, *betont* æn/ *see* **a**
anaem|ia /əˈniːmɪə/ *n* Blutarmut *f*, Anämie *f*. **~ic** *a* blutarm
anaesthesia /ænəsˈθiːzɪə/ *n* Betäubung *f*
anaesthetic /ænəsˈθetɪk/ *n* Narkosemittel *nt*, Betäubungsmittel *nt*; **under [an] ~** in Narkose; **give s.o. an ~** jdm eine Narkose geben
anaesthet|ist /əˈniːsθətɪst/ *n* Narkosearzt *m*. **~ize** /-taɪz/ *vt* betäuben
analog[ue] /ˈænəlɒg/ *a* Analog-
analogy /əˈnælədʒɪ/ *n* Analogie *f*
analyse /ˈænəlaɪz/ *vt* analysieren
analysis /əˈnæləsɪs/ *n* Analyse *f*
analyst /ˈænəlɪst/ *n* Chemiker(in) *m(f)*; (*Psych*) Analytiker *m*
analytical /ænəˈlɪtɪkl/ *a* analytisch
anarch|ist /ˈænəkɪst/ *n* Anarchist *m*. **~y** *n* Anarchie *f*
anathema /əˈnæθəmə/ *n* Gräuel *m*
anatom|ical /ænəˈtɒmɪkl/ *a*, **-ly** *adv* anatomisch. **~y** /əˈnætəmɪ/ *n* Anatomie *f*
ancest|or /ˈænsestə(r)/ *n* Vorfahr *m*. **~ry** *n* Abstammung *f*
anchor /ˈæŋkə(r)/ *n* Anker *m* □ *vi* ankern □ *vt* verankern
anchovy /ˈæntʃəvɪ/ *n* Sardelle *f*
ancient /ˈeɪnʃənt/ *a* alt

ancillary /æn'sɪlərɪ/ *a* Hilfs-

and /ənd, *betont* ænd/ *conj* und; **~ so on** und so weiter; **six hundred ~ two** sechshundertzwei; **more ~ more** immer mehr; **nice ~ warm** schön warm; **try ~ come** versuche zu kommen

anecdote /'ænɪkdəʊt/ *n* Anekdote *f*

anew /ə'nju:/ *adv* von neuem

angel /'eɪndʒl/ *n* Engel *m*. **~ic** /æn'dʒelɪk/ *a* engelhaft

anger /'æŋgə(r)/ *n* Zorn *m* □ *vt* zornig machen

angle[1] /'æŋgl/ *n* Winkel *m*; (*fig*) Standpunkt *m*; **at an ~** schräg

angle[2] *vi* angeln; **~ for** (*fig*) fischen nach. **~r** *n* Angler *m*

Anglican /'æŋglɪkən/ *a* anglikanisch □ *n* Anglikaner(in) *m(f)*

Anglo-Saxon /æŋgləʊ'sæksn/ *a* angelsächsich □ *n* Angelsächsisch *nt*

angry /'æŋgrɪ/ *a* **(-ier,-iest)**, **-ily** *adv* zornig; **be ~ with** böse sein auf (+ *acc*)

anguish /'æŋgwɪʃ/ *n* Qual *f*

angular /'æŋgjʊlə(r)/ *a* eckig; ⟨*features*⟩ kantig

animal /'ænɪml/ *n* Tier *nt* □ *a* tierisch

animate[1] /'ænɪmət/ *a* lebendig

animat|e[2] /'ænɪmeɪt/ *vt* beleben. **~ed** *a* lebhaft. **~ion** /-'meɪʃn/ *n* Lebhaftigkeit *f*

animosity /ænɪ'mɒsətɪ/ *n* Feindseligkeit *f*

aniseed /'ænɪsi:d/ *n* Anis *m*

ankle /'æŋkl/ *n* [Fuß]knöchel *m*

annex /ə'neks/ *vt* annektieren

annex[e] /'æneks/ *n* Nebengebäude *nt*; (*extension*) Anbau *m*

annihilat|e /ə'naɪəleɪt/ *vt* vernichten. **~ion** /-'leɪʃn/ *n* Vernichtung *f*

anniversary /ænɪ'vɜ:sərɪ/ *n* Jahrestag *m*

annotate /'ænəteɪt/ *vt* kommentieren

announce /ə'naʊns/ *vt* bekannt geben; (*over loudspeaker*) durchsagen; (*at reception*) ankündigen; (*Radio, TV*) ansagen; (*in newspaper*) anzeigen. **~ment** *n* Bekanntgabe *f*, Bekanntmachung *f*; Durchsage *f*; Ansage *f*; Anzeige *f*. **~r** *n* Ansager(in) *m(f)*

annoy /ə'nɔɪ/ *vt* ärgern; (*pester*) belästigen; **get ~ed** sich ärgern. **~ance** *n* Ärger *m*. **~ing** *a* ärgerlich

annual /'ænjʊəl/ *a*, **-ly** *adv* jährlich □ *n* (*Bot*) einjährige Pflanze *f*; (*book*) Jahresalbum *nt*

annuity /ə'nju:ətɪ/ *n* [Leib]rente *f*

annul /ə'nʌl/ *vt* (*pt/pp* **annulled**) annullieren

anoint /ə'nɔɪnt/ *vt* salben

anomaly /ə'nɒməlɪ/ *n* Anomalie *f*

anonymous /ə'nɒnɪməs/ *a*, **-ly** *adv* anonym

anorak /'ænəræk/ *n* Anorak *m*

anorexia /ænə'reksɪə/ *n* Magersucht *f*

another /ə'nʌðə(r)/ *a & pron* ein anderer/eine andere/ein anderes; (*additional*) noch ein(e); **~ [one]** noch einer/eine/eins; **~ day** an einem anderen Tag; **in ~ way** auf andere Weise; **~ time** ein andermal; **one ~** einander

answer /'ɑ:nsə(r)/ *n* Antwort *f*; (*solution*) Lösung *f* □ *vt* antworten (**s.o.** jdm); beantworten ⟨*question, letter*⟩; **~ the door/telephone** an die Tür/ans Telefon gehen □ *vi* antworten; (*Teleph*) sich melden; **~ back** eine freche Antwort geben; **~ for** verantwortlich sein für. **~able** /-əbl/ *a* verantwortlich. **~ing machine** *n* (*Teleph*) Anrufbeantworter *m*

ant /ænt/ *n* Ameise *f*

antagonis|m /æn'tægənɪzm/ *n* Antagonismus *m*. **~tic** /-'nɪstɪk/ *a* feindselig

antagonize /æn'tægənaɪz/ *vt* gegen sich aufbringen
Antarctic /ænt'ɑːktɪk/ *n* Antarktis *f*
antelope /'æntɪləʊp/ *n* Antilope *f*
antenatal /æntɪ'neɪtl/ *a* ~ **care** Schwangerschaftsfürsorge *f*
antenna /æn'tenə/ *n* Fühler *m*; (*Amer: aerial*) Antenne *f*
ante-room /'æntɪ-/ *n* Vorraum *m*
anthem /'ænθəm/ *n* Hymne *f*
anthology /æn'θɒlədʒɪ/ *n* Anthologie *f*
anthropology /ænθrə'pɒlədʒɪ/ *n* Anthropologie *f*
anti-'aircraft /æntɪ-/ *a* Flugabwehr-
antibiotic /æntɪbaɪ'ɒtɪk/ *n* Antibiotikum *nt*
'antibody *n* Antikörper *m*
anticipat|e /æn'tɪsɪpeɪt/ *vt* vorhersehen; (*forestall*) zuvorkommen (+ *dat*); (*expect*) erwarten. **~ion** /-'peɪʃn/ *n* Erwartung *f*
anti'climax *n* Enttäuschung *f*
anti'clockwise *a* & *adv* gegen den Uhrzeigersinn
antics /'æntɪks/ *npl* Mätzchen *pl*
anti'cyclone *n* Hochdruckgebiet *nt*
antidote /'æntɪdəʊt/ *n* Gegengift *nt*
'antifreeze *n* Frostschutzmittel *nt*
antipathy /æn'tɪpəθɪ/ *n* Abneigung *f*, Antipathie *f*
antiquarian /æntɪ'kweərɪən/ *a* antiquarisch. ~ **bookshop** *n* Antiquariat *nt*
antiquated /'æntɪkweɪtɪd/ *a* veraltet
antique /æn'tiːk/ *a* antik □ *n* Antiquität *f*. ~ **dealer** *n* Antiquitätenhändler *m*
antiquity /æn'tɪkwətɪ/ *n* Altertum *nt*
anti-Semitic /æntɪsɪ'mɪtɪk/ *a* antisemitisch
anti'septic *a* antiseptisch □ *n* Antiseptikum *nt*
anti'social *a* asozial; (*fam*) ungesellig
antithesis /æn'tɪθəsɪs/ *n* Gegensatz *m*
antlers /'æntləz/ *npl* Geweih *nt*
anus /'eɪnəs/ *n* After *m*
anvil /'ænvɪl/ *n* Amboss *m*
anxiety /æŋ'zaɪətɪ/ *n* Sorge *f*
anxious /'æŋkʃəs/ *a*, **-ly** *adv* ängstlich; (*worried*) besorgt; **be ~ to do sth** etw gerne machen wollen
any /'enɪ/ *a* irgendein(e); *pl* irgendwelche; (*every*) jede(r,s); *pl* alle; (*after negative*) kein(e); *pl* keine; **~ colour/number you like** eine beliebige Farbe/Zahl; **have you ~ wine/apples?** haben Sie Wein/Äpfel? **for ~ reason** aus irgendeinem Grund □ *pron* [irgend]einer/eine/eins; *pl* [irgend]welche; (*some*) welche(r,s); *pl* welche; (*all*) alle *pl*; (*negative*) keiner/keine/keins; *pl* keine; **I don't want ~ of it** ich will nichts davon; **there aren't ~** es gibt keine; **I need wine/apples/money—have we ~?** ich brauche Wein/Äpfel/Geld—haben wir welchen/welche/welches? □ *adv* noch; **~ quicker/slower** noch schneller/langsamer; **is it ~ better?** geht es etwas besser? **would you like ~ more?** möchten Sie noch [etwas]? **I can't eat ~ more** ich kann nichts mehr essen; **I can't go ~ further** ich kann nicht mehr weiter
'anybody *pron* [irgend]jemand; (*after negative*) niemand; **~ can do that** das kann jeder
'anyhow *adv* jedenfalls; (*nevertheless*) trotzdem; (*badly*) irgendwie
'anyone *pron* = **anybody**
'anything *pron* [irgend]etwas; (*after negative*) nichts; (*everything*) alles

'anyway *adv* jedenfalls; (*in any case*) sowieso
'anywhere *adv* irgendwo; (*after negative*) nirgendwo; ⟨*be, live*⟩ überall; **I'd go ~** ich würde überallhin gehen
apart /ə'pɑ:t/ *adv* auseinander; **live ~** getrennt leben; **~ from** abgesehen von
apartment /ə'pɑ:tmənt/ *n* Zimmer *nt*; (*Amer: flat*) Wohnung *f*
apathy /'æpəθɪ/ *n* Apathie *f*
ape /eɪp/ *n* [Menschen]affe *m* □ *vt* nachäffen
aperitif /ə'perəti:f/ *n* Aperitif *m*
aperture /'æpətʃə(r)/ *n* Öffnung *f*; (*Phot*) Blende *f*
apex /'eɪpeks/ *n* Spitze *f*; (*fig*) Gipfel *m*
apiece /ə'pi:s/ *adv* pro Person; (*thing*) pro Stück
apologetic /əpɒlə'dʒetɪk/ *a*, **-ally** *adv* entschuldigend; **be ~** sich entschuldigen
apologize /ə'pɒlədʒaɪz/ *vi* sich entschuldigen (**to** bei)
apology /ə'pɒlədʒɪ/ *n* Entschuldigung *f*
apostle /ə'pɒsl/ *n* Apostel *m*
apostrophe /ə'pɒstrəfɪ/ *n* Apostroph *m*
appal /ə'pɔ:l/ *vt* (*pt/pp* **appalled**) entsetzen. **~ling** *a* entsetzlich
apparatus /æpə'reɪtəs/ *n* Apparatur *f*; (*Sport*) Geräte *pl*; (*single piece*) Gerät *nt*
apparel /ə'pærəl/ *n* Kleidung *f*
apparent /ə'pærənt/ *a* offenbar; (*seeming*) scheinbar. **~ly** *adv* offenbar, anscheinend
apparition /æpə'rɪʃn/ *n* Erscheinung *f*
appeal /ə'pi:l/ *n* Appell *m*, Aufruf *m*; (*request*) Bitte *f*; (*attraction*) Reiz *m*; (*Jur*) Berufung *f* □ *vi* appellieren (**to** an + *acc*); (*ask*) bitten (**for** um); (*be attractive*) zusagen (**to** *dat*); (*Jur*) Berufung einlegen. **~ing** *a* ansprechend
appear /ə'pɪə(r)/ *vi* erscheinen; (*seem*) scheinen; (*Theat*) auftreten. **~ance** *n* Erscheinen *nt*; (*look*) Aussehen *nt*; **to all ~ances** allem Anschein nach
appease /ə'pi:z/ *vt* beschwichtigen
append /ə'pend/ *vt* nachtragen; setzen ⟨*signature*⟩ (**to** unter + *acc*). **~age** /-ɪdʒ/ *n* Anhängsel *nt*
appendicitis /əpendɪ'saɪtɪs/ *n* Blinddarmentzündung *f*
appendix /ə'pendɪks/ *n* (*pl* **-ices** /-ɪsi:z/) (*of book*) Anhang *m* □ (*pl* **-es**) (*Anat*) Blinddarm *m*
appertain /æpə'teɪn/ *vi* **~ to** betreffen
appetite /'æpɪtaɪt/ *n* Appetit *m*
appetizing /'æpɪtaɪzɪŋ/ *a* appetitlich
applau|d /ə'plɔ:d/ *vt/i* Beifall klatschen (+ *dat*). **~se** *n* Beifall *m*
apple /'æpl/ *n* Apfel *m*
appliance /ə'plaɪəns/ *n* Gerät *nt*
applicable /'æplɪkəbl/ *a* anwendbar (**to** auf + *acc*); (*on form*) **not ~** nicht zutreffend
applicant /'æplɪkənt/ *n* Bewerber(in) *m*(*f*)
application /æplɪ'keɪʃn/ *n* Anwendung *f*; (*request*) Antrag *m*; (*for job*) Bewerbung *f*; (*diligence*) Fleiß *m*
applied /ə'plaɪd/ *a* angewandt
apply /ə'plaɪ/ *vt* (*pt/pp* **-ied**) auftragen ⟨*paint*⟩; anwenden ⟨*force, rule*⟩ □ *vi* zutreffen (**to** auf + *acc*); **~ for** beantragen; sich bewerben um ⟨*job*⟩
appoint /ə'pɔɪnt/ *vt* ernennen; (*fix*) festlegen; **well ~ed** gut ausgestattet. **~ment** *n* Ernennung *f*; (*meeting*) Verabredung *f*; (*at doctor's, hairdresser's*) Termin *m*; (*job*) Posten *m*; **make an ~ment** sich anmelden
apposite /'æpəzɪt/ *a* treffend
appraise /ə'preɪz/ *vt* abschätzen

appreciable /ə'pri:ʃəbl/ *a* merklich; (*considerable*) beträchtlich
appreciat|e /ə'pri:ʃɪeɪt/ *vt* zu schätzen wissen; (*be grateful for*) dankbar sein für; (*enjoy*) schätzen; (*understand*) verstehen □ *vi* (*increase in value*) im Wert steigen. **~ion** /-'eɪʃn/ *n* (*gratitude*) Dankbarkeit *f*; **in ~ion** als Dank (**of** für). **~ive** /-ətɪv/ *a* dankbar
apprehend /æprɪ'hend/ *vt* festnehmen
apprehens|ion /æprɪ'henʃn/ *n* Festnahme *f*; (*fear*) Angst *f*. **~ive** /-sɪv/ *a* ängstlich
apprentice /ə'prentɪs/ *n* Lehrling *m*. **~ship** *n* Lehre *f*
approach /ə'prəʊtʃ/ *n* Näherkommen *nt*; (*of time*) Nahen *nt*; (*access*) Zugang *m*; (*road*) Zufahrt *f* □ *vi* sich nähern; ⟨*time:*⟩ nahen □ *vt* sich nähern (+ *dat*); (*with request*) herantreten an (+ *acc*); (*set about*) sich heranmachen an (+ *acc*). **~able** /-əbl/ *a* zugänglich
approbation /æprə'beɪʃn/ *n* Billigung *f*
appropriate[1] /ə'prəʊprɪət/ *a* angebracht, angemessen
appropriate[2] /ə'prəʊprɪeɪt/ *vt* sich (*dat*) aneignen
approval /ə'pru:vl/ *n* Billigung *f*; **on ~** zur Ansicht
approv|e /ə'pru:v/ *vt* billigen □ *vi* **~e of sth/s.o.** mit etw/jdm einverstanden sein. **~ing** *a*, **-ly** *adv* anerkennend
approximate[1] /ə'prɒksɪmeɪt/ *vi* **~ to** nahe kommen (+ *dat*)
approximate[2] /ə'prɒksɪmət/ *a* ungefähr. **~ly** *adv* ungefähr, etwa
approximation /əprɒksɪ'meɪʃn/ *n* Schätzung *f*
apricot /'eɪprɪkɒt/ *n* Aprikose *f*
April /'eɪprəl/ *n* April *m*; **make an ~ fool of** in den April schicken
apron /'eɪprən/ *n* Schürze *f*
apropos /'æprəpəʊ/ *adv* **~ [of]** betreffs (+ *gen*)
apt /æpt/ *a*, **-ly** *adv* passend; ⟨*pupil*⟩ begabt; **be ~ to do sth** dazu neigen, etw zu tun
aptitude /'æptɪtju:d/ *n* Begabung *f*
aqualung /'ækwəlʌŋ/ *n* Tauchgerät *nt*
aquarium /ə'kweərɪəm/ *n* Aquarium *nt*
Aquarius /ə'kweərɪəs/ *n* (*Astr*) Wassermann *m*
aquatic /ə'kwætɪk/ *a* Wasser-
Arab /'ærəb/ *a* arabisch □ *n* Araber(in) *m*(*f*). **~ian** /ə'reɪbɪən/ *a* arabisch
Arabic /'ærəbɪk/ *a* arabisch
arable /'ærəbl/ *a* **~ land** Ackerland *nt*
arbitrary /'ɑ:bɪtrərɪ/ *a*, **-ily** *adv* willkürlich
arbitrat|e /'ɑ:bɪtreɪt/ *vi* schlichten. **~ion** /-'treɪʃn/ *n* Schlichtung *f*
arc /ɑ:k/ *n* Bogen *m*
arcade /ɑ:'keɪd/ *n* Laubengang *m*; (*shops*) Einkaufspassage *f*
arch /ɑ:tʃ/ *n* Bogen *m*; (*of foot*) Gewölbe *nt* □ *vt* **~ its back** ⟨*cat:*⟩ einen Buckel machen
archaeological /ɑ:kɪə'lɒdʒɪkl/ *a* archäologisch
archaeolog|ist /ɑ:kɪ'ɒlədʒɪst/ *n* Archäologe *m*/-login *f*. **~y** *n* Archäologie *f*
archaic /ɑ:'keɪɪk/ *a* veraltet
arch'bishop /ɑ:tʃ-/ *n* Erzbischof *m*
arch-'enemy *n* Erzfeind *m*
archer /'ɑ:tʃə(r)/ *n* Bogenschütze *m*. **~y** *n* Bogenschießen *nt*
architect /'ɑ:kɪtekt/ *n* Architekt(in) *m*(*f*). **~ural** /ɑ:kɪ'tektʃərəl/ *a*, **-ly** *adv* architektonisch
architecture /'ɑ:kɪtektʃə(r)/ *n* Architektur *f*
archives /'ɑ:kaɪvz/ *npl* Archiv *nt*
archway /'ɑ:tʃweɪ/ *n* Torbogen *m*

Arctic /ˈɑːktɪk/ *a* arktisch □ *n* **the ~** die Arktis
ardent /ˈɑːdənt/ *a*, **-ly** *adv* leidenschaftlich
ardour /ˈɑːdə(r)/ *n* Leidenschaft *f*
arduous /ˈɑːdjʊəs/ *a* mühsam
are /ɑː(r)/ *see* **be**
area /ˈeərɪə/ *n* (*surface*) Fläche *f*; (*Geom*) Flächeninhalt *m*; (*region*) Gegend *f*; (*fig*) Gebiet *nt*. **~ code** *n* Vorwahlnummer *f*
arena /əˈriːnə/ *n* Arena *f*
aren't /ɑːnt/ = **are not**. *See* **be**
Argentina /ɑːdʒənˈtiːnə/ *n* Argentinien *nt*
Argentin|e /ˈɑːdʒəntaɪn/, **~ian** /-ˈtɪnɪən/ *a* argentinisch
argue /ˈɑːgjuː/ *vi* streiten (**about** über + *acc*); ⟨*two people:*⟩ sich streiten; (*debate*) diskutieren; **don't ~!** keine Widerrede! □ *vt* (*debate*) diskutieren; (*reason*) **~ that** argumentieren, dass
argument /ˈɑːgjʊmənt/ *n* Streit *m*, Auseinandersetzung *f*; (*reasoning*) Argument *nt*; **have an ~** sich streiten. **~ative** /-ˈmentətɪv/ *a* streitlustig
aria /ˈɑːrɪə/ *n* Arie *f*
arid /ˈærɪd/ *a* dürr
Aries /ˈeəriːz/ *n* (*Astr*) Widder *m*
arise /əˈraɪz/ *vi* (*pt* **arose**, *pp* **arisen**) sich ergeben (**from** aus)
aristocracy /ærɪˈstɒkrəsɪ/ *n* Aristokratie *f*
aristocrat /ˈærɪstəkræt/ *n* Aristokrat(in) *m(f)*. **~ic** /-ˈkrætɪk/ *a* aristokratisch
arithmetic /əˈrɪθmətɪk/ *n* Rechnen *nt*
ark /ɑːk/ *n* **Noah's A ~** die Arche Noah
arm /ɑːm/ *n* Arm *m*; (*of chair*) Armlehne *f*; **~s** *pl* (*weapons*) Waffen *pl*; (*Heraldry*) Wappen *nt*; **up in ~s** (*fam*) empört □ *vt* bewaffnen
armament /ˈɑːməmənt/ *n* Bewaffnung *f*; **~s** *pl* Waffen *pl*
ˈ**armchair** *n* Sessel *m*
armed /ɑːmd/ *a* bewaffnet; **~ forces** Streitkräfte *pl*
armistice /ˈɑːmɪstɪs/ *n* Waffenstillstand *m*
armour /ˈɑːmə(r)/ *n* Rüstung *f*. **~ed** *a* Panzer-
ˈ**armpit** *n* Achselhöhle *f*
army /ˈɑːmɪ/ *n* Heer *nt; (specific)* Armee *f*; **join the ~** zum Militär gehen
aroma /əˈrəʊmə/ *n* Aroma *nt*, Duft *m*. **~tic** /ærəˈmætɪk/ *a* aromatisch
arose /əˈrəʊz/ *see* **arise**
around /əˈraʊnd/ *adv* **[all] ~** rings herum; **he's not ~** er ist nicht da; **look/turn ~** sich umsehen/umdrehen; **travel ~** herumreisen □ *prep* um (+ *acc*) . . . herum (*approximately*) gegen
arouse /əˈraʊz/ *vt* aufwecken; (*excite*) erregen
arrange /əˈreɪndʒ/ *vt* arrangieren; anordnen ⟨*furniture, books*⟩; (*settle*) abmachen; **I have ~d to go there** ich habe abgemacht, dass ich dahingehe. **~ment** *n* Anordnung *f*; (*agreement*) Vereinbarung *f*; (*of flowers*) Gesteck *nt*; **make ~ments** Vorkehrungen treffen
arrears /əˈrɪəz/ *npl* Rückstände *pl*; **in ~** im Rückstand
arrest /əˈrest/ *n* Verhaftung *f*; **under ~** verhaftet □ *vt* verhaften
arrival /əˈraɪvl/ *n* Ankunft *f*; **new ~s** *pl* Neuankömmlinge *pl*
arrive /əˈraɪv/ *vi* ankommen; **~ at** (*fig*) gelangen zu
arrogan|ce /ˈærəgəns/ *n* Arroganz *f*. **~t** *a*, **-ly** *adv* arrogant
arrow /ˈærəʊ/ *n* Pfeil *m*
arse /ɑːs/ *n* (*vulg*) Arsch *m*
arsenic /ˈɑːsənɪk/ *n* Arsen *nt*
arson /ˈɑːsn/ *n* Brandstiftung *f*. **~ist** /-sənɪst/ *n* Brandstifter *m*
art /ɑːt/ *n* Kunst *f*; **work of ~** Kunstwerk *nt*; **~s and crafts** *pl*

Kunstgewerbe *nt*; **A~s** *pl* (*Univ*) Geisteswissenschaften *pl*
artery /ˈɑːtərɪ/ *n* Schlagader *f*, Arterie *f*
artful /ˈɑːtfl/ *a* gerissen
ˈart gallery *n* Kunstgalerie *f*
arthritis /ɑːˈθraɪtɪs/ *n* Arthritis *f*
artichoke /ˈɑːtɪtʃəʊk/ *n* Artischocke *f*
article /ˈɑːtɪkl/ *n* Artikel *m*; (*object*) Gegenstand *m*; **~ of clothing** Kleidungsstück *nt*
articulate[1] /ɑːˈtɪkjʊlət/ *a* deutlich; **be ~** sich gut ausdrücken können
articulate[2] /ɑːˈtɪkjʊleɪt/ *vt* aussprechen. **~d lorry** *n* Sattelzug *m*
artifice /ˈɑːtɪfɪs/ *n* Arglist *f*
artificial /ɑːtɪˈfɪʃl/ *a*, **-ly** *adv* künstlich
artillery /ɑːˈtɪlərɪ/ *n* Artillerie *f*
artist /ˈɑːtɪst/ *n* Künstler(in) *m(f)*
artiste /ɑːˈtiːst/ *n* (*Theat*) Artist(in) *m(f)*
artistic /ɑːˈtɪstɪk/ *a*, **-ally** *adv* künstlerisch
artless /ˈɑːtlɪs/ *a* unschuldig
as /æz/ *conj* (*because*) da; (*when*) als; (*while*) während □ *prep* als; **as a child/foreigner** als Kind/Ausländer □ *adv* **as well** auch; **as soon as** sobald; **as much as** so viel wie; **as quick as you** so schnell wie du; **as you know** wie Sie wissen; **as far as I'm concerned** was mich betrifft
asbestos /æzˈbestɒs/ *n* Asbest *m*
ascend /əˈsend/ *vi* [auf]steigen □ *vt* besteigen ⟨*throne*⟩
Ascension /əˈsenʃn/ *n* (*Relig*) [Christi] Himmelfahrt *f*
ascent /əˈsent/ *n* Aufstieg *m*
ascertain /æsəˈteɪn/ *vt* ermitteln
ascribe /əˈskraɪb/ *vt* zuschreiben (**to** *dat*)
ash[1] /æʃ/ *n* (*tree*) Esche *f*
ash[2] *n* Asche *f*
ashamed /əˈʃeɪmd/ *a* beschämt; **be ~** sich schämen (**of** über + *acc*)
ashore /əˈʃɔː(r)/ *adv* an Land
ash: ~tray *n* Aschenbecher *m*. **A~ ˈWednesday** *n* Aschermittwoch *m*
Asia /ˈeɪʃə/ *n* Asien *nt*. **~n** *a* asiatisch □ *n* Asiat(in) *m(f)*. **~tic** /eɪʃɪˈætɪk/ *a* asiatisch
aside /əˈsaɪd/ *adv* beiseite; **~ from** (*Amer*) außer (+ *dat*)
ask /ɑːsk/ *vt/i* **fragen**; stellen ⟨*question*⟩; (*invite*) einladen; **~ for** bitten um; verlangen ⟨*s.o.*⟩; **~ after** sich erkundigen nach; **~ s.o. in** jdn hereinbitten; **~ s.o. to do sth** jdn bitten, etw zu tun
askance /əˈskɑːns/ *adv* **look ~ at** schief ansehen
askew /əˈskjuː/ *a & adv* schief
asleep /əˈsliːp/ *a* **be ~** schlafen; **fall ~** einschlafen
asparagus /əˈspærəgəs/ *n* Spargel *m*
aspect /ˈæspekt/ *n* Aspekt *m*
aspersions /əˈspɜːʃnz/ *npl* **cast ~ on** schlecht machen
asphalt /ˈæsfælt/ *n* Asphalt *m*
asphyxia /æˈsfɪksɪə/ *n* Erstickung *f*. **~te** /æˈsfɪksɪeɪt/ *vt/i* ersticken. **~tion** /-ˈeɪʃn/ *n* Erstickung *f*
aspirations /æspəˈreɪʃnz/ *npl* Streben *nt*
aspire /əˈspaɪə(r)/ *vi* **~ to** streben nach
ass /æs/ *n* Esel *m*
assail /əˈseɪl/ *vt* bestürmen. **~ant** *n* Angreifer(in) *m(f)*
assassin /əˈsæsɪn/ *n* Mörder(in) *m(f)*. **~ate** *vt* ermorden. **~ation** /-ˈneɪʃn/ *n* [politischer] Mord *m*
assault /əˈsɔːlt/ *n* (*Mil*) Angriff *m*; (*Jur*) Körperverletzung *f* □ *vt* [tätlich] angreifen
assemble /əˈsembl/ *vi* sich versammeln □ *vt* versammeln; (*Techn*) montieren
assembly /əˈsemblɪ/ *n* Versammlung *f*; (*Sch*) Andacht *f*; (*Techn*) Montage *f*. **~ line** *n* Fließband *nt*

assent /ə'sent/ *n* Zustimmung *f* □ *vi* zustimmen (**to** *dat*)

assert /ə'sɜ:t/ *vt* behaupten; ~ **oneself** sich durchsetzen. **~ion** /-ɜ:ʃn/ *n* Behauptung *f*. **~ive** /-tɪv/ *a* **be ~ive** sich durchsetzen können

assess /ə'ses/ *vt* bewerten; (*fig & for tax purposes*) einschätzen: schätzen ⟨*value*⟩. **~ment** *n* Einschätzung *f*; (*of tax*) Steuerbescheid *m*

asset /'æset/ *n* Vorteil *m*; **~s** *pl* (*money*) Vermögen *nt*; (*Comm*) Aktiva *pl*

assiduous /ə'sɪdjʊəs/ *a*, **-ly** *adv* fleißig

assign /ə'saɪn/ *vt* zuweisen (**to** *dat*). **~ment** *n* (*task*) Aufgabe *f*

assimilate /ə'sɪmɪleɪt/ *vt* aufnehmen; (*integrate*) assimilieren

assist /ə'sɪst/ *vt/i* helfen (+ *dat*). **~ance** *n* Hilfe *f*. **~ant** *a* Hilfs- □ *n* Assistent(in) *m(f)*; (*in shop*) Verkäufer(in) *m(f)*

associat|e[1] /ə'səʊʃɪeɪt/ *vt* verbinden; (*Psych*) assoziieren □ *vi* ~ **with** verkehren mit. **~ion** /-'eɪʃn/ *n* Verband *m*. **A ~ion 'football** *n* Fußball *m*

associate[2] /ə'səʊʃɪət/ *a* assoziiert □ *n* Kollege *m*/-gin *f*

assort|ed /ə'sɔ:tɪd/ *a* gemischt. **~ment** *n* Mischung *f*

assum|e /ə'sju:m/ *vt* annehmen; übernehmen ⟨*office*⟩; **~ing that** angenommen, dass

assumption /ə'sʌmpʃn/ *n* Annahme *f*; **on the ~** in der Annahme (**that** dass)

assurance /ə'ʃʊərəns/ *n* Versicherung *f*; (*confidence*) Selbstsicherheit *f*

assure /ə'ʃʊə(r)/ *vt* versichern (**s.o.** jdm); **I ~ you [of that]** das versichere ich Ihnen. **~d** *a* sicher

asterisk /'æstərɪsk/ *n* Sternchen *nt*

astern /ə'stɜ:n/ *adv* achtern

asthma /'æsmə/ *n* Asthma *nt*. **~tic** /-'mætɪk/ *a* asthmatisch

astonish /ə'stɒnɪʃ/ *vt* erstaunen. **~ing** *a* erstaunlich. **~ment** *n* Erstaunen *nt*

astound /ə'staʊnd/ *vt* in Erstaunen setzen

astray /ə'streɪ/ *adv* **go ~** verloren gehen; ⟨*person:*⟩ sich verlaufen; (*fig*) vom rechten Weg abkommen; **lead ~** verleiten

astride /ə'straɪd/ *adv* rittlings □ *prep* rittlings auf (+ *dat/acc*)

astringent /ə'strɪndʒənt/ *a* adstringierend; (*fig*) beißend

astrolog|er /ə'strɒlədʒə(r)/ *n* Astrologe *m*/-gin *f*. **~y** *n* Astrologie *f*

astronaut /'æstrənɔ:t/ *n* Astronaut(in) *m(f)*

astronom|er /ə'strɒnəmə(r)/ *n* Astronom *m*. **~ical** /æstrə'nɒmɪkl/ *a* astronomisch. **~y** *n* Astronomie *f*

astute /ə'stju:t/ *a* scharfsinnig. **~ness** *n* Scharfsinn *m*

asylum /ə'saɪləm/ *n* Asyl *nt*; **[lunatic] ~** Irrenanstalt *f*

at /ət, *betont* æt/ *prep* an (+ *dat/acc*); (*with town*) in; (*price*) zu; (*speed*) mit; **at the station** am Bahnhof; **at the beginning/end** am Anfang/Ende; **at home** zu Hause; **at John's** bei John; **at work/the hairdresser's** bei der Arbeit/beim Friseur; **at school/the office** in der Schule/im Büro; **at a party/wedding** auf einer Party/Hochzeit; **at one o'clock** um ein Uhr; **at Christmas/Easter** zu Weihnachten/Ostern; **at the age of** im Alter von; **not at all** gar nicht; **at times** manchmal; **two at a time** zwei auf einmal; **good/bad at languages** gut/schlecht in Sprachen

ate /et/ *see* **eat**

atheist /'eɪθɪɪst/ *n* Atheist(in) *m(f)*

athlet|e /'æθli:t/ *n* Athlet(in) *m(f)*. **~ic** /-'letɪk/ *a* sportlich. **~ics** /-'letɪks/ *n* Leichtathletik *f*

Atlantic /ət'læntɪk/ *a & n* **the ~ [Ocean]** der Atlantik
atlas /'ætləs/ *n* Atlas *m*
atmospher|e /'ætməsfɪə(r)/ *n* Atmosphäre *f*. **~ic** /-'ferɪk/ *a* atmosphärisch
atom /'ætəm/ *n* Atom *nt*. **~ bomb** *n* Atombombe *f*
atomic /ə'tɒmɪk/ *a* Atom-
atone /ə'təʊn/ *vi* büßen **(for** für). **~ment** *n* Buße *f*
atrocious /ə'trəʊʃəs/ *a* abscheulich
atrocity /ə'trɒsətɪ/ *n* Gräueltat *f*
attach /ə'tætʃ/ *vt* befestigen **(to** an + *dat*); beimessen ⟨*importance*⟩ **(to** *dat*); **be ~ed to** (*fig*) hängen an (+ *dat*)
attaché /ə'tæʃeɪ/ *n* Attaché *m*. **~ case** *n* Aktenkoffer *m*
attachment /ə'tætʃmənt/ *n* Bindung *f*; (*tool*) Zubehörteil *nt*; (*additional*) Zusatzgerät *nt*
attack /ə'tæk/ *n* Angriff *m*; (*Med*) Anfall *m* □ *vt/i* angreifen. **~er** *n* Angreifer *m*
attain /ə'teɪn/ *vt* erreichen; (*get*) erlangen. **~able** /-əbl/ *a* erreichbar
attempt /ə'tempt/ *n* Versuch *m* □ *vt* versuchen
attend /ə'tend/ *vt* anwesend sein bei; (*go regularly to*) besuchen; (*take part in*) teilnehmen an (+ *dat*); (*accompany*) begleiten; ⟨*doctor:*⟩ behandeln □ *vi* anwesend sein; (*pay attention*) aufpassen; **~ to** sich kümmern um; (*in shop*) bedienen. **~ance** *n* Anwesenheit *f*; (*number*) Besucherzahl *f*. **~ant** *n* Wärter(in) *m(f)*; (*in car park*) Wächter *m*
attention /ə'tenʃn/ *n* Aufmerksamkeit *f*; **~!** (*Mil*) stillgestanden! **pay ~** aufpassen; **pay ~ to** beachten, achten auf (+ *acc*); **need ~** reparaturbedürftig sein; **for the ~ of** zu Händen von
attentive /ə'tentɪv/ *a*, **-ly** *adv* aufmerksam
attest /ə'test/ *vt/i* **~ [to]** bezeugen
attic /'ætɪk/ *n* Dachboden *m*
attire /ə'taɪə(r)/ *n* Kleidung *f* □ *vt* kleiden
attitude /'ætɪtju:d/ *n* Haltung *f*
attorney /ə'tɜ:nɪ/ *n* (*Amer: lawyer*) Rechtsanwalt *m*; **power of ~** Vollmacht *f*
attract /ə'trækt/ *vt* anziehen; erregen ⟨*attention*⟩; **~ s.o.'s attention** jds Aufmerksamkeit auf sich (*acc*) lenken. **~ion** /-ækʃn/ *n* Anziehungskraft *f*; (*charm*) Reiz *m*; (*thing*) Attraktion *f*. **~ive** /-tɪv/ *a*, **-ly** *adv* attraktiv
attribute¹ /'ætrɪbju:t/ *n* Attribut *nt*
attribut|e² /ə'trɪbju:t/ *vt* zuschreiben **(to** *dat*). **~ive** /-tɪv/ *a*, **-ly** *adv* attributiv
attrition /ə'trɪʃn/ *n* **war of ~** Zermürbungskrieg *m*
aubergine /'əʊbəʒi:n/ *n* Aubergine *f*
auburn /'ɔ:bən/ *a* kastanienbraun
auction /'ɔ:kʃn/ *n* Auktion *f* Versteigerung *f* □ *vt* versteigern. **~eer** /-ʃə'nɪə(r)/ *n* Auktionator *m*
audaci|ous /ɔ:'deɪʃəs/ *a*, **-ly** *adv* verwegen. **~ty** /-'dæsətɪ/ *n* Verwegenheit *f*; (*impudence*) Dreistigkeit *f*
audible /'ɔ:dəbl/ *a*, **-bly** *adv* hörbar
audience /'ɔ:dɪəns/ *n* Publikum *nt*; (*Theat, TV*) Zuschauer *pl*; (*Radio*) Zuhörer *pl*; (*meeting*) Audienz *f*
audio /'ɔ:dɪəʊ/: **~ typist** *n* Phonotypistin *f*. **~'visual** *a* audiovisuell
audit /'ɔ:dɪt/ *n* Bücherrevision *f* □ *vt* (*Comm*) prüfen
audition /ɔ:'dɪʃn/ *n* (*Theat*) Vorsprechen *nt*; (*Mus*) Vorspielen *nt* (*for singer*) Vorsingen *nt* □ *vi* vorsprechen; vorspielen; vorsingen

auditor /'ɔ:dɪtə(r)/ *n* Buchprüfer *m*
auditorium /ɔ:dɪ'tɔ:rɪəm/ *n* Zuschauerraum *m*
augment /ɔ:g'ment/ *vt* vergrößern
augur /'ɔ:gə(r)/ *vi* ~ **well/ill** etwas/nichts Gutes verheißen
august /ɔ:'gʌst/ *a* hoheitsvoll
August /'ɔ:gəst/ *n* August *m*
aunt /ɑ:nt/ *n* Tante *f*
au pair /əʊ'peə(r)/ *n* ~ **[girl]** Aupairmädchen *nt*
aura /'ɔ:rə/ *n* Fluidum *nt*
auspices /'ɔ:spɪsɪz/ *npl* (*protection*) Schirmherrschaft *f*
auspicious /ɔ:'spɪʃəs/ *a* günstig; ⟨*occasion*⟩ freudig
auster|e /ɒ'stɪə(r)/ *a* streng; (*simple*) nüchtern. ~**ity** /-terətɪ/ *n* Strenge *f*; (*hardship*) Entbehrung *f*
Australia /ɒ'streɪlɪə/ *n* Australien *nt*. ~**n** *a* australisch □ *n* Australier(in) *m(f)*
Austria /'ɒstrɪə/ *n* Österreich *nt* ~**n** *a* österreichisch □ *n* Österreicher(in) *m(f)*
authentic /ɔ:'θentɪk/ *a* echt, authentisch. ~**ate** *vt* beglaubigen. ~**ity** /-'tɪsətɪ/ *n* Echtheit *f*
author /'ɔ:θə(r)/ *n* Schriftsteller *m*, Autor *m*; (*of document*) Verfasser *m*
authoritarian /ɔ:θɒrɪ'teərɪən/ *a* autoritär
authoritative /ɔ:'θɒrɪtətɪv/ *a* maßgebend; **be** ~ Autorität haben
authority /ɔ:'θɒrətɪ/ *n* Autorität *f*; (*public*) Behörde *f*; **in** ~ verantwortlich
authorization /ɔ:θəraɪ'zeɪʃn/ *n* Ermächtigung *f*
authorize /'ɔ:θəraɪz/ *vt* ermächtigen ⟨*s.o.*⟩; genehmigen ⟨*sth*⟩
autobi'ography /ɔ:tə-/ *n* Autobiographie *f*
autocratic /ɔ:tə'krætɪk/ *a* autokratisch
autograph /'ɔ:tə-/ *n* Autogramm *nt*
automatic /ɔ:tə'mætɪk/ *a*, **-ally** *adv* automatisch □ *n* (*car*) Fahrzeug *nt* mit Automatikgetriebe; (*washing machine*) Waschautomat *m*
automation /ɔ:tə'meɪʃn/ *n* Automation *f*
automobile /'ɔ:təməbi:l/ *n* Auto *nt*
autonom|ous /ɔ:'tɒnəməs/ *a* autonom. ~**y** *n* Autonomie *f*
autopsy /'ɔ:tɒpsɪ/ *n* Autopsie *f*
autumn /'ɔ:təm/ *n* Herbst *m*. ~**al** /-'tʌmnl/ *a* herbstlich
auxiliary /ɔ:g'zɪlɪərɪ/ *a* Hilfs- □ *n* Helfer(in) *m(f)*, Hilfskraft *f*
avail /ə'veɪl/ *n* **to no** ~ vergeblich □ *vi* ~ **oneself of** Gebrauch machen von
available /ə'veɪləbl/ *a* verfügbar; (*obtainable*) erhältlich
avalanche /'ævəlɑ:nʃ/ *n* Lawine *f*
avaric|e /'ævərɪs/ *n* Habsucht *f*. ~**ious** /-'rɪʃəs/ *a* habgierig, habsüchtig
avenge /ə'vendʒ/ *vt* rächen
avenue /'ævənju:/ *n* Allee *f*
average /'ævərɪdʒ/ *a* Durchschnitts-, durchschnittlich □ *n* Durchschnitt *m*; **on** ~ im Durchschnitt, durchschnittlich □ *vt* durchschnittlich schaffen □ *vi* ~ **out at** im Durchschnitt ergeben
avers|e /ə'vɜ:s/ *a* **not be** ~**e to sth** etw (*dat*) nicht abgeneigt sein. ~**ion** /-ɜ:ʃn/ *n* Abneigung *f* (**to** gegen)
avert /ə'vɜ:t/ *vt* abwenden
aviary /'eɪvɪərɪ/ *n* Vogelhaus *nt*
aviation /eɪvɪ'eɪʃn/ *n* Luftfahrt *f*
avid /'ævɪd/ *a* gierig (**for** nach); (*keen*) eifrig
avocado /ævə'kɑ:dəʊ/ *n* Avocado *f*
avoid /ə'vɔɪd/ *vt* vermeiden; ~ **s.o.** jdm aus dem Weg gehen.

~able /-əbl/ *a* vermeidbar. **~ance** *n* Vermeidung *f*

await /ə'weɪt/ *vt* warten auf (+ *acc*)

awake /ə'weɪk/ *a* wach; **wide ~** hellwach □ *vi* (*pt* **awoke**, *pp* **awoken**) erwachen

awaken /ə'weɪkn/ *vt* wecken □ *vi* erwachen. **~ing** *n* Erwachen *nt*

award /ə'wɔ:d/ *n* Auszeichnung *f*; (*prize*) Preis *m* □ *vt* zuerkennen (**to s.o.** *dat*); verleihen ⟨*prize*⟩

aware /ə'weə(r)/ *a* **become ~** gewahr werden (**of** *gen*); **be ~ that** wissen, dass. **~ness** *n* Bewusstsein *nt*

awash /ə'wɒʃ/ *a* **be ~** unter Wasser stehen

away /ə'weɪ/ *adv* weg, fort; (*absent*) abwesend; **be ~** nicht da sein; **far ~** weit weg; **four kilometres ~** vier Kilometer entfernt; **play ~** (*Sport*) auswärts spielen; **go/stay ~** weggehen/-bleiben. **~ game** *n* Auswärtsspiel *nt*

awe /ɔ:/ *n* Ehrfurcht *f*

awful /'ɔ:fl/ *a*, **-ly** *adv* furchtbar

awhile /ə'waɪl/ *adv* eine Weile

awkward /'ɔ:kwəd/ *a* schwierig; (*clumsy*) ungeschickt; (*embarrassing*) peinlich; (*inconvenient*) ungünstig. **~ly** *adv* ungeschickt; (*embarrassedly*) verlegen

awning /'ɔ:nɪŋ/ *n* Markise *f*

awoke(n) /ə'wəʊk(n)/ *see* **awake**

awry /ə'raɪ/ *adv* schief

axe /æks/ *n* Axt *f* □ *vt* (*pres p* **axing**) streichen; (*dismiss*) entlassen

axis /'æksɪs/ *n* (*pl* **axes** /-si:z/) Achse *f*

axle /'æksl/ *n* (*Techn*) Achse *f*

ay[e] /aɪ/ *adv* ja □ *n* Jastimme *f*

B

B /bi:/ *n* (*Mus*) H *nt*

BA *abbr of* **Bachelor of Arts**

babble /'bæbl/ *vi* plappern; ⟨*stream:*⟩ plätschern

baboon /bə'bu:n/ *n* Pavian *m*

baby /'beɪbɪ/ *n* Baby *nt*; (*Amer, fam*) Schätzchen *nt*

baby: ~ carriage *n* (*Amer*) Kinderwagen *m*. **~ish** *a* kindisch. **~-minder** *n* Tagesmutter *f*. **~-sit** *vi* babysitten. **~-sitter** *n* Babysitter *m*

bachelor /'bætʃələ(r)/ *n* Junggeselle *m*; **B ~ of Arts/Science** Bakkalaureus Artium/Scientium

bacillus /bə'sɪləs/ *n* (*pl* **-lli**) Bazillus *m*

back /bæk/ *n* Rücken *m*; (*reverse*) Rückseite *f*; (*of chair*) Rückenlehne *f*; (*Sport*) Verteidiger *m*; **at/**(*Auto*) **in the ~** hinten; **on the ~** auf der Rückseite; **~ to front** verkehrt; **at the ~ of beyond** am Ende der Welt □ *a* Hinter- □ *adv* zurück; **~ here/there** hier/da hinten; **~ at home** zu Hause; **go/pay ~** zurückgehen/-zahlen □ *vt* (*support*) unterstützen; (*with money*) finanzieren; (*Auto*) zurücksetzen; (*Betting*) [Geld] setzen auf (+ *acc*); (*cover the back of*) mit einer Verstärkung versehen □ *vi* (*Auto*) zurücksetzen. **~ down** *vi* klein beigeben. **~ in** *vi* rückwärts hineinfahren. **~ out** *vi* rückwärts hinaus-/herausfahren; (*fig*) aussteigen (**of** aus). **~ up** *vt* unterstützen; (*confirm*) bestätigen □ *vi* (*Auto*) zurücksetzen

back: ~ache *n* Rückenschmerzen *pl*. **~biting** *n* gehässiges Gerede *nt*. **~bone** *n* Rückgrat *nt*. **~chat** *n* Widerrede *f*. **~-comb** *vt* toupieren. **~date** *vt* rückdatieren; **~dated to** rückwirkend von. **~'door** *n* Hintertür *f*

backer /'bækə(r)/ *n* Geldgeber *m*

back: ~'fire *vi* (*Auto*) fehlzünden; (*fig*) fehlschlagen. **~ground** *n* Hintergrund *m*; **family ~ground** Familienverhältnisse *pl*. **~hand** *n* (*Sport*) Rückhand *f*.

~'**handed** *a* ⟨*compliment*⟩ zweifelhaft. ~'**hander** *n* (*Sport*) Rückhandschlag *m*; (*fam: bribe*) Schmiergeld *nt*

backing /'bækɪŋ/ *n* (*support*) Unterstützung *f*; (*material*) Verstärkung *f*

back: ~**lash** *n* (*fig*) Gegenschlag *m*. ~**log** *n* Rückstand *m* (**of** an + *dat*). ~'**seat** *n* Rücksitz *m*. ~**side** *n* (*fam*) Hintern *m*. ~**stage** *adv* hinter der Bühne. ~**stroke** *n* Rückenschwimmen *nt*. ~**-up** *n* Unterstützung *f*; (*Amer: traffic jam*) Stau *m*

backward /'bækwəd/ *a* zurückgeblieben; ⟨*country*⟩ rückständig □ *adv* rückwärts. ~**s** rückwärts; ~**s and forwards** hin und her

back: ~**water** *n* (*fig*) unberührtes Fleckchen *nt*. ~'**yard** *n* Hinterhof *m*; **not in my** ~ **yard** (*fam*) nicht vor meiner Haustür

bacon /'beɪkn/ *n* [Schinken]speck *m*

bacteria /bæk'tɪərɪə/ *npl* Bakterien *pl*

bad /bæd/ *a* (**worse, worst**) schlecht; (*serious*) schwer, schlimm; (*naughty*) unartig; ~ **language** gemeine Ausdrucksweise *f*; **feel** ~ sich schlecht fühlen; (*feel guilty*) ein schlechtes Gewissen haben; **go** ~ schlecht werden

bade /bæd/ *see* **bid**[2]

badge /bædʒ/ *n* Abzeichen *nt*

badger /'bædʒə(r)/ *n* Dachs *m* □ *vt* plagen

badly /'bædlɪ/ *adv* schlecht; (*seriously*) schwer; ~ **off** schlecht gestellt; ~ **behaved** unerzogen; **want** ~ sich (*dat*) sehnsüchtig wünschen; **need** ~ dringend brauchen

bad-'mannered *a* mit schlechten Manieren

badminton /'bædmɪntən/ *n* Federball *m*

bad-'tempered *a* schlecht gelaunt

baffle /'bæfl/ *vt* verblüffen

bag /bæg/ *n* Tasche *f*; (*of paper*) Tüte *f*; (*pouch*) Beutel *m*; ~**s of** (*fam*) jede Menge □ *vt* (*fam: reserve*) in Beschlag nehmen

baggage /'bægɪdʒ/ *n* [Reise]gepäck *nt*

baggy /'bægɪ/ *a* ⟨*clothes*⟩ ausgebeult

'**bagpipes** *npl* Dudelsack *m*

bail /beɪl/ *n* Kaution *f*; **on** ~ gegen Kaution □ *vt* ~ **s.o. out** jdn gegen Kaution freibekommen; (*fig*) jdm aus der Patsche helfen. ~ **out** *vt* (*Naut*) ausschöpfen □ *vi* (*Aviat*) abspringen

bailiff /'beɪlɪf/ *n* Gerichtsvollzieher *m*; (*of estate*) Gutsverwalter *m*

bait /beɪt/ *n* Köder *m* □ *vt* mit einem Köder versehen; (*fig: torment*) reizen

bake /beɪk/ *vt/i* backen

baker /'beɪkə(r)/ *n* Bäcker *m*; ~**'s [shop]** Bäckerei *f*. ~**y** *n* Bäckerei *f*

baking /'beɪkɪŋ/ *n* Backen *nt*. ~**-powder** *n* Backpulver *nt*. ~**-tin** *n* Backform *f*

balance /'bæləns/ *n* (*equilibrium*) Gleichgewicht *nt*, Balance *f*; (*scales*) Waage *f*; (*Comm*) Saldo *m*; (*outstanding sum*) Restbetrag *m*; **[bank]** ~ Kontostand *m*; **in the** ~ (*fig*) in der Schwebe □ *vt* balancieren; (*equalize*) ausgleichen; (*Comm*) abschließen ⟨*books*⟩ □ *vi* balancieren; (*fig & Comm*) sich ausgleichen. ~**d** *a* ausgewogen. ~ **sheet** *n* Bilanz *f*

balcony /'bælkənɪ/ *n* Balkon *m*

bald /bɔːld/ *a* (**-er, -est**) kahl; ⟨*person*⟩ kahlköpfig; **go** ~ eine Glatze bekommen

balderdash /'bɔːldədæʃ/ *n* Unsinn *m*

bald|ing /'bɔːldɪŋ/ *a* **be** ~**ing** eine Glatze bekommen. ~**ly** *adv* unverblümt. ~**ness** *n* Kahlköpfigkeit *f*

bale /beɪl/ *n* Ballen *m*

baleful /ˈbeɪlfl/ *a*, **-ly** *adv* böse
balk /bɔ:lk/ *vt* vereiteln □ *vi* **~ at** zurückschrecken vor (+ *dat*)
Balkans /ˈbɔ:lknz/ *npl* Balkan *m*
ball¹ /bɔ:l/ *n* Ball *m*; (*Billiards, Croquet*) Kugel *f*; (*of yarn*) Knäuel *m & nt*; **on the ~** (*fam*) auf Draht
ball² *n* (*dance*) Ball *m*
ballad /ˈbæləd/ *n* Ballade *f*
ballast /ˈbæləst/ *n* Ballast *m*
ball-ˈbearing *n* Kugellager *nt*
ballerina /bæləˈri:nə/ *n* Ballerina *f*
ballet /ˈbæleɪ/ *m* Ballett *nt*. **~ dancer** *n* Balletttänzer(in) *m(f)*
ballistic /bəˈlɪstɪk/ *a* ballistisch. **~s** *n* Ballistik *f*
balloon /bəˈlu:n/ *n* Luftballon *m*; (*Aviat*) Ballon *m*
ballot /ˈbælət/ *n* [geheime] Wahl *f*; (*on issue*) [geheime] Abstimmung *f*. **~-box** *n* Wahlurne *f*. **~-paper** *n* Stimmzettel *m*
ball: ~-point [ˈpen] *n* Kugelschreiber *m*. **~room** *n* Ballsaal *m*
balm /bɑ:m/ *n* Balsam *m*
balmy /ˈbɑ:mɪ/ *a* (**-ier, -iest**) *a* sanft; (*fam: crazy*) verrückt
Baltic /ˈbɔ:ltɪk/ *a & n* **the ~ [Sea]** die Ostsee
balustrade /bæləˈstreɪd/ *n* Balustrade *f*
bamboo /bæmˈbu:/ *n* Bambus *m*
bamboozle /bæmˈbu:zl/ *vt* (*fam*) übers Ohr hauen
ban /bæn/ *n* Verbot *nt* □ *vt* (*pt/pp* **banned**) verbieten
banal /bəˈnɑ:l/ *a* banal. **~ity** /-ˈælətɪ/ *n* Banalität *f*
banana /bəˈnɑ:nə/ *n* Banane *f*
band /bænd/ *n* Band *nt*; (*stripe*) Streifen *m*; (*group*) Schar *f*; (*Mus*) Kapelle *f* □ *vi* **~ together** sich zusammenschließen
bandage /ˈbændɪdʒ/ *n* Verband *m*; (*for support*) Bandage *f* □ *vt* verbinden; bandagieren ⟨*limb*⟩
b. & b. *abbr of* **bed and breakfast**
bandit /ˈbændɪt/ *n* Bandit *m*
band: ~stand *n* Musikpavillon *m*. **~wagon** *n* **jump on the ~wagon** (*fig*) sich einer erfolgreichen Sache anschließen
bandy¹ /ˈbændɪ/ *vt* (*pt/pp* **-ied**) wechseln ⟨*words*⟩
bandy² *a* (**-ier, -iest**) **be ~** O-Beine haben. **~-legged** *a* O-beinig
bang /bæŋ/ *n* (*noise*) Knall *m*; (*blow*) Schlag *m* □ *adv* **go ~** knallen □ *int* bums! peng! □ *vt* knallen; (*shut noisily*) zuknallen; (*strike*) schlagen auf (+ *acc*); **~ one's head** sich (*dat*) den Kopf stoßen (**on** an + *acc*) □ *vi* schlagen; ⟨*door:*⟩ zuknallen
banger /ˈbæŋə(r)/ *n* (*firework*) Knallfrosch *m*; (*fam: sausage*) Wurst *f*; **old ~** (*fam: car*) Klapperkiste *f*
bangle /ˈbæŋgl/ *n* Armreifen *m*
banish /ˈbænɪʃ/ *vt* verbannen
banisters /ˈbænɪstəz/ *npl* [Treppen]geländer *nt*
banjo /ˈbændʒəʊ/ *n* Banjo *nt*
bank¹ /bæŋk/ *n* (*of river*) Ufer *nt*; (*slope*) Hang *m* □ *vi* (*Aviat*) in die Kurve gehen
bank² *n* Bank *f* □ *vt* einzahlen; **~ with** ein Konto haben bei. **~ on** *vt* sich verlassen auf (+ *acc*)
ˈbank account *n* Bankkonto *nt*
banker /ˈbæŋkə(r)/ *n* Bankier *m*
bank: ~ ˈholiday *n* gesetzlicher Feiertag *m*. **~ing** *n* Bankwesen *nt*. **~note** *n* Banknote *f*
bankrupt /ˈbæŋkrʌpt/ *a* bankrott; **go ~** Bankrott machen □ *n* Bankrotteur *m* □ *vt* Bankrott machen. **~cy** *n* Bankrott *m*
banner /ˈbænə(r)/ *n* Banner *nt*; (*carried by demonstrators*) Transparent *nt*, Spruchband *nt*
banns /bænz/ *npl* (*Relig*) Aufgebot *nt*
banquet /ˈbæŋkwɪt/ *n* Bankett *nt*
banter /ˈbæntə(r)/ *n* Spöttelei *f*
bap /bæp/ *n* weiches Brötchen *nt*
baptism /ˈbæptɪzm/ *n* Taufe *f*

Baptist /'bæptɪst/ *n* Baptist(in) *m(f)*
baptize /bæp'taɪz/ *vt* taufen
bar /bɑ:(r)/ *n* Stange *f*; (*of cage*) [Gitter]stab *m*; (*of gold*) Barren *m*; (*of chocolate*) Tafel *f*; (*of soap*) Stück *nt*; (*long*) Riegel *m*; (*café*) Bar *f*; (*counter*) Theke *f*; (*Mus*) Takt *m*; (*fig: obstacle*) Hindernis *nt*; **parallel ~s** (*Sport*) Barren *m*; **be called to the ~** (*Jur*) als plädierender Anwalt zugelassen werden; **behind ~s** (*fam*) hinter Gittern □ *vt* (*pt/pp* **barred**) versperren ⟨*way, door*⟩; ausschließen ⟨*person*⟩ □ *prep* außer; **~ none** ohne Ausnahme
barbarian /bɑ:'beərɪən/ *n* Barbar *m*
barbar|ic /bɑ:'bærɪk/ *a* barbarisch. **~ity** *n* Barbarei *f*. **~ous** /'bɑ:bərəs/ *a* barbarisch
barbecue /'bɑ:bɪkju:/ *n* Grill *m*; (*party*) Grillfest *nt* □ *vt* [im Freien] grillen
barbed /'bɑ:bd/ *a* **~ wire** Stacheldraht *m*
barber /'bɑ:bə(r)/ *n* [Herren]friseur *m*
barbiturate /bɑ:'bɪtjʊrət/ *n* Barbiturat *nt*
'bar code *n* Strichkode *m*
bare /beə(r)/ *a* (**-r, -st**) nackt, bloß; ⟨*tree*⟩ kahl; (*empty*) leer; (*mere*) bloß □ *vt* entblößen; fletschen ⟨*teeth*⟩
bare: ~back *adv* ohne Sattel. **~faced** *a* schamlos. **~foot** *adv* barfuß. **~'headed** *a* mit unbedecktem Kopf
barely /'beəlɪ/ *adv* kaum
bargain /'bɑ:gɪn/ *n* (*agreement*) Geschäft *nt*; (*good buy*) Gelegenheitskauf *m*; **into the ~** noch dazu; **make a ~** sich einigen □ *vi* handeln; (*haggle*) feilschen; **~ for** (*expect*) rechnen mit
barge /bɑ:dʒ/ *n* Lastkahn *m*; (*towed*) Schleppkahn *m* □ *vi* **~ in** (*fam*) hereinplatzen
baritone /'bærɪtəʊn/ *n* Bariton *m*
bark¹ /bɑ:k/ *n* (*of tree*) Rinde *f*
bark² *n* Bellen *nt* □ *vi* bellen
barley /'bɑ:lɪ/ *n* Gerste *f*
bar: ~maid *n* Schankmädchen *nt*. **~man** Barmann *m*
barmy /'bɑ:mɪ/ *a* (*fam*) verrückt
barn /bɑ:n/ *n* Scheune *f*
barometer /bə'rɒmɪtə(r)/ *n* Barometer *nt*
baron /'bærn/ *n* Baron *m*. **~ess** *n* Baronin *f*
baroque /bə'rɒk/ *a* barock □ *n* Barock *nt*
barracks /'bærəks/ *npl* Kaserne *f*
barrage /'bærɑ:ʒ/ *n* (*in river*) Wehr *nt*; (*Mil*) Sperrfeuer *nt*; (*fig*) Hagel *m*
barrel /'bærl/ *n* Fass *nt*; (*of gun*) Lauf *m*; (*of cannon*) Rohr *nt*. **~-organ** *n* Drehorgel *f*
barren /'bærn/ *a* unfruchtbar; ⟨*landscape*⟩ öde
barricade /bærɪ'keɪd/ *n* Barrikade *f* □ *vt* verbarrikadieren
barrier /'bærɪə(r)/ *n* Barriere *f*; (*across road*) Schranke *f*; (*Rail*) Sperre *f*; (*fig*) Hindernis *nt*
barring /'bɑ:rɪŋ/ *prep* **~ accidents** wenn alles gut geht
barrister /'bærɪstə(r)/ *n* [plädierender] Rechtsanwalt *m*
barrow /'bærəʊ/ *n* Karre *f*, Karren *m*. **~ boy** *n* Straßenhändler *m*
barter /'bɑ:tə(r)/ *vt* tauschen (**for** gegen)
base /beɪs/ *n* Fuß *m*; (*fig*) Basis *f*; (*Mil*) Stützpunkt *m* □ *a* gemein; ⟨*metal*⟩ unedel □ *vt* stützen (**on** auf + *acc*); **be ~d on** basieren auf (+ *dat*)
base: ~ball *n* Baseball *m*. **~less** *a* unbegründet. **~ment** *n* Kellergeschoss *nt*. **~ment flat** *n* Kellerwohnung *f*
bash /bæʃ/ *n* Schlag *m*; **have a ~!** (*fam*) probier es mal! □ *vt* hauen; (*dent*) einbeulen; **~ed in** verbeult

bashful /ˈbæʃfl/ *a*, **-ly** *adv* schüchtern
basic /ˈbeɪsɪk/ *a* Grund-; (*fundamental*) grundlegend; (*essential*) wesentlich; (*unadorned*) einfach; **the ~s** das Wesentliche. **~ally** *adv* grundsätzlich
basil /ˈbæzɪl/ *n* Basilikum *nt*
basilica /bəˈzɪlɪkə/ *n* Basilika *f*
basin /ˈbeɪsn/ *n* Becken *nt*; (*for washing*) Waschbecken *nt*; (*for food*) Schüssel *f*
basis /ˈbeɪsɪs/ *n* (*pl* **-ses** /-si:z/) Basis *f*
bask /bɑ:sk/ *vi* sich sonnen
basket /ˈbɑ:skɪt/ *n* Korb *m*. **~ball** *n* Basketball *m*
Basle /bɑ:l/ *n* Basel *nt*
bass /beɪs/ *a* Bass-; **~ voice** Bassstimme *f* □ *n* Bass *m*; (*person*) Bassist *m*
bassoon /bəˈsu:n/ *n* Fagott *nt*
bastard /ˈbɑ:stəd/ *n* (*sl*) Schuft *m*
baste[1] /beɪst/ *vt* (*sew*) heften
baste[2] *vt* (*Culin*) begießen
bastion /ˈbæstɪən/ *n* Bastion *f*
bat[1] /bæt/ *n* Schläger *m*; **off one's own ~** (*fam*) auf eigene Faust □ *vt* (*pt/pp* **batted**) schlagen; **not ~ an eyelid** (*fig*) nicht mit der Wimper zucken
bat[2] *n* (*Zool*) Fledermaus *f*
batch /bætʃ/ *n* (*of people*) Gruppe *f*; (*of papers*) Stoß *m*; (*of goods*) Sendung *f*; (*of bread*) Schub *m*
bated /ˈbeɪtɪd/ *a* **with ~ breath** mit angehaltenem Atem
bath /bɑ:θ/ *n* (*pl* **~s** /bɑ:ðz/) Bad *nt*; (*tub*) Badewanne *f*; **~s** *pl* Badeanstalt *f*; **have a ~** baden □ *vt/i* baden
bathe /beɪð/ *n* Bad *nt* □ *vt/i* baden. **~r** *n* Badende(r) *m/f*
bathing /ˈbeɪðɪŋ/ *n* Baden *nt*. **~-cap** *n* Bademütze *f*. **~-costume** *n* Badeanzug *m*
bath: ~-mat *n* Badematte *f*. **~robe** *n* (*Amer*) Bademantel *m*. **~room** *n* Badezimmer *nt*. **~-towel** *n* Badetuch *nt*
baton /ˈbætn/ *n* (*Mus*) Taktstock *m*; (*Mil*) Stab *m*
battalion /bəˈtælɪən/ *n* Bataillon *nt*
batten /ˈbætn/ *n* Latte *f*
batter /ˈbætə(r)/ *n* (*Culin*) flüssiger Teig *m* □ *vt* schlagen. **~ed** *a* ⟨*car*⟩ verbeult; ⟨*wife*⟩ misshandelt
battery /ˈbætərɪ/ *n* Batterie *f*
battle /ˈbætl/ *n* Schlacht *f*; (*fig*) Kampf *m* □ *vi* (*fig*) kämpfen (**for** um)
battle: ~axe *n* (*fam*) Drachen *m*. **~field** *n* Schlachtfeld *nt*. **~ship** *n* Schlachtschiff *nt*
batty /ˈbætɪ/ *a* (*fam*) verrückt
Bavaria /bəˈveərɪə/ *n* Bayern *nt*. **~n** *a* bayrisch □ *n* Bayer(in) *m(f)*
bawdy /ˈbɔ:dɪ/ *a* (**-ier, -iest**) derb
bawl /bɔ:l/ *vt/i* brüllen
bay[1] /beɪ/ *n* (*Geog*) Bucht *f*; (*Archit*) Erker *m*
bay[2] *n* **keep at ~** fern halten
bay[3] *n* (*horse*) Braune(r) *m*
bay[4] *n* (*Bot*) [echter] Lorbeer *m*. **~-leaf** *n* Lorbeerblatt *nt*
bayonet /ˈbeɪənet/ *n* Bajonett *nt*
bay 'window *n* Erkerfenster *nt*
bazaar /bəˈzɑ:(r)/ *n* Basar *m*
BC *abbr* (**before Christ**) v. Chr.
be /bi:/ *vi* (*pres* **am, are, is,** *pl* **are**; *pt* **was,** *pl* **were**; *pp* **been**) sein; (*lie*) liegen; (*stand*) stehen; (*cost*) kosten; **he is a teacher** er ist Lehrer; **be quiet!** sei still! **I am cold/hot** mir ist kalt/heiß; **how are you?** wie geht es Ihnen? **I am well** mir geht es gut; **there is/are** es gibt; **what do you want to be?** was willst du werden? **I have been to Vienna** ich bin in Wien gewesen; **has the postman been?** war der Briefträger schon da? **it's hot, isn't it?** es ist heiß, nicht [wahr]? **you are coming too, aren't you?** du kommst mit, nicht [wahr]? **it's yours, is it?** das gehört also Ihnen? **yes he is/I am** ja; (*negating previous statement*) doch; **three and three are**

six drei und drei macht sechs □ *v aux* ~ **reading/going** lesen/gehen; **I am coming/staying** ich komme/bleibe; **what is he doing?** was macht er? **I am being lazy** ich faulenze; **I was thinking of you** ich dachte an dich; **you were going to** . . . du wolltest . . .; **I am to stay** ich soll bleiben; **you are not to** . . . du darfst nicht . . .; **you are to do that immediately** das musst du sofort machen □ *passive* werden; **be attacked/deceived** überfallen/betrogen werden

beach /bi:tʃ/ *n* Strand *m*. ~**wear** *n* Strandkleidung *f*

beacon /ˈbi:kn/ *n* Leuchtfeuer *nt*; (*Naut, Aviat*) Bake *f*

bead /bi:d/ *n* Perle *f*

beak /bi:k/ *n* Schnabel *m*

beaker /ˈbi:kə(r)/ *n* Becher *m*

beam /bi:m/ *n* Balken *m*; (*of light*) Strahl *m* □ *vi* strahlen. ~**ing** *a* [freude]strahlend

bean /bi:n/ *n* Bohne *f*; **spill the** ~**s** (*fam*) alles ausplaudern

bear[1] /beə(r)/ *n* Bär *m*

bear[2] *vt/i* (*pt* **bore**, *pp* **borne**) tragen; (*endure*) ertragen; gebären ⟨*child*⟩; ~ **right** sich rechts halten. ~**able** /-əbl/ *a* erträglich

beard /bɪəd/ *n* Bart *m*. ~**ed** *a* bärtig

bearer /ˈbeərə(r)/ *n* Träger *m*; (*of news, cheque*) Überbringer *m*; (*of passport*) Inhaber(in) *m(f)*

bearing /ˈbeərɪŋ/ *n* Haltung *f*; (*Techn*) Lager *nt*; **have a** ~ **on** von Belang sein für; **get one's** ~**s** sich orientieren; **lose one's** ~**s** die Orientierung verlieren

beast /bi:st/ *n* Tier *nt*; (*fam: person*) Biest *nt*

beastly /ˈbi:stlɪ/ *a* (**-ier, -iest**) (*fam*) scheußlich; ⟨*person*⟩ gemein

beat /bi:t/ *n* Schlag *m*; (*of policeman*) Runde *f*; (*rhythm*) Takt *m* □ *vt/i* (*pt* **beat**, *pp* **beaten**) schlagen; (*thrash*) verprügeln; klopfen ⟨*carpet*⟩; (*hammer*) hämmern (**on** an + *acc*); ~ **a retreat** (*Mil*) sich zurückziehen; ~ **it!** (*fam*) hau ab! **it** ~**s me** (*fam*) das begreife ich nicht. ~ **up** *vt* zusammenschlagen

beat|en /ˈbi:tn/ *a* **off the** ~**en track** abseits. ~**ing** *n* Prügel *pl*

beautician /bju:ˈtɪʃn/ *n* Kosmetikerin *f*

beauti|ful /ˈbju:tɪfl/ *a*, **-ly** *adv* schön. ~**fy** /-faɪ/ *vt* (*pt/pp* **-ied**) verschönern

beauty /ˈbju:tɪ/ *n* Schönheit *f*. ~ **parlour** *n* Kosmetiksalon *m*. ~ **spot** *n* Schönheitsfleck *m*; (*place*) landschaftlich besonders reizvolles Fleckchen *nt*

beaver /ˈbi:və(r)/ *n* Biber *m*

became /bɪˈkeɪm/ *see* **become**

because /bɪˈkɒz/ *conj* weil □ *adv* ~ **of** wegen (+ *gen*)

beckon /ˈbekn/ *vt/i* ~ **[to]** herbeiwinken

becom|e /bɪˈkʌm/ *vt/i* (*pt* **became**, *pp* **become**) werden. ~**ing** *a* ⟨*clothes*⟩ kleidsam

bed /bed/ *n* Bett *nt*; (*layer*) Schicht *f*; (*of flowers*) Beet *nt*; **in** ~ im Bett; **go to** ~ ins *od* zu Bett gehen; ~ **and breakfast** Zimmer mit Frühstück. ~**clothes** *npl*, ~**ding** *n* Bettzeug *nt*

bedlam /ˈbedləm/ *n* Chaos *nt*

ˈ**bedpan** *n* Bettpfanne *f*

bedraggled /bɪˈdrægld/ *a* nass und verschmutzt

bed: ~**ridden** *a* bettlägerig. ~**room** *n* Schlafzimmer *nt*

ˈ**bedside** *n* **at his** ~ an seinem Bett. ~ ˈ**lamp** *n* Nachttischlampe *f*. ~ ˈ**rug** *n* Bettvorleger *m*. ~ ˈ**table** *n* Nachttisch *m*

bed: ~ˈ**sitter** *n*, ~-ˈ**sitting-room** *n* Wohnschlafzimmer *nt*. ~**spread** *n* Tagesdecke *f*. ~**time** *n* **at** ~**time** vor dem Schlafengehen

bee /bi:/ *n* Biene *f*

beech /bi:tʃ/ *n* Buche *f*

beef /biːf/ *n* Rindfleisch *nt*. **~burger** *n* Hamburger *m*

bee: ~hive *n* Bienenstock *m*. **~keeper** *n* Imker(in) *m(f)*. **~keeping** *n* Bienenzucht *f*. **~-line** *n* **make a ~-line for** (*fam*) zusteuern auf (+ *acc*)

been /biːn/ *see* **be**

beer /bɪə(r)/ *n* Bier *nt*

beet /biːt/ *n* (*Amer: beetroot*) rote Bete *f*; **[sugar] ~** Zuckerrübe *f*

beetle /'biːtl/ *n* Käfer *m*

'**beetroot** *n* rote Bete *f*

before /bɪ'fɔː(r)/ *prep* vor (+ *dat/acc*); **the day ~ yesterday** vorgestern; **~ long** bald □ *adv* vorher; (*already*) schon; **never ~** noch nie; **~ that** davor □ *conj* (*time*) ehe, bevor. **~hand** *adv* vorher, im Voraus

befriend /bɪ'frend/ *vt* sich anfreunden mit

beg /beg/ *v* (*pt/pp* **begged**) □ *vi* betteln □ *vt* (*entreat*) anflehen; (*ask*) bitten (**for** um)

began /bɪ'gæn/ *see* **begin**

beggar /'begə(r)/ *n* Bettler(in) *m(f)*; (*fam*) Kerl *m*

begin /bɪ'gɪn/ *vt/i* (*pt* **began**, *pp* **begun**, *pres p* **beginning**) anfangen, beginnen; **to ~ with** anfangs. **~ner** *n* Anfänger(in) *m(f)*. **~ning** *n* Anfang *m*, Beginn *m*

begonia /bɪ'gəʊnɪə/ *n* Begonie *f*

begrudge /bɪ'grʌdʒ/ *vt* **~ s.o. sth** jdm etw missgönnen

beguile /bl'gaɪl/ *vt* betören

begun /bɪ'gʌn/ *see* **begin**

behalf /bɪ'hɑːf/ *n* **on ~ of** im Namen von; **on my ~** meinetwegen

behave /bɪ'heɪv/ *vi* sich verhalten; **~ oneself** sich benehmen

behaviour /bɪ'heɪvjə(r)/ *n* Verhalten *nt*; **good/bad ~** gutes/schlechtes Benehmen *nt*; **~ pattern** Verhaltensweise *f*

behead /bɪ'hed/ *vt* enthaupten

beheld /bɪ'held/ *see* **behold**

behind /bɪ'haɪnd/ *prep* hinter (+ *dat/acc*); **be ~ sth** hinter etw (*dat*) stecken □ *adv* hinten; (*late*) im Rückstand; **a long way ~** weit zurück; **in the car ~** im Wagen dahinter □ *n* (*fam*) Hintern *m*. **~hand** *adv* im Rückstand

behold /bɪ'həʊld/ *vt* (*pt/pp* **beheld**) (*liter*) sehen

beholden /bɪ'həʊldn/ *a* verbunden (**to** *dat*)

beige /beɪʒ/ *a* beige

being /'biːɪŋ/ *n* Dasein *nt*; **living ~** Lebewesen *nt*; **come into ~** entstehen

belated /bɪ'leɪtɪd/ *a*, **-ly** *adv* verspätet

belch /beltʃ/ *vi* rülpsen □ *vt* **~ out** ausstoßen ⟨*smoke*⟩

belfry /'belfrɪ/ *n* Glockenstube *f*; (*tower*) Glockenturm *m*

Belgian /'beldʒən/ *a* belgisch □ *n* Belgier(in) *m(f)*

Belgium /'beldʒəm/ *n* Belgien *nt*

belief /bɪ'liːf/ *n* Glaube *m*

believable /bɪ'liːvəbl/ *a* glaubhaft

believe /bɪ'liːv/ *vt/i* glauben (**s.o.** jdm; **in** an + *acc*). **~r** *n* (*Relig*) Gläubige(r) *m/f*

belittle /bɪ'lɪtl/ *vt* herabsetzen

bell /bel/ *n* Glocke *f*; (*on door*) Klingel *f*

belligerent /bɪ'lɪdʒərənt/ *a* Krieg führend; (*aggressive*) streitlustig

bellow /'beləʊ/ *vt/i* brüllen

bellows /'beləʊz/ *npl* Blasebalg *m*

belly /'belɪ/ *n* Bauch *m*

belong /bɪ'lɒŋ/ *vi* gehören (**to** *dat*); (*be member*) angehören (**to** *dat*). **~ings** *npl* Sachen *pl*

beloved /bɪ'lʌvɪd/ *a* geliebt □ *n* Geliebte(r) *m/f*

below /bɪ'ləʊ/ *prep* unter (+ *dat/acc*) □ *adv* unten; (*Naut*) unter Deck

belt /belt/ *n* Gürtel *m*; (*area*) Zone *f*; (*Techn*) [Treib]riemen *m* □ *vi* (*fam: rush*) rasen □ *vt* (*fam: hit*) hauen

bemused /bɪ'mjuːzd/ *a* verwirrt

bench /bentʃ/ *n* Bank *f*; (*work-*) Werkbank *f*; **the B ~** (*Jur*) ≈ die Richter *pl*

bend /bend/ *n* Biegung *f*; (*in road*) Kurve *f*; **round the ~** (*fam*) verrückt □ *v* (*pt/pp* **bent**) □ *vt* biegen; beugen ⟨*arm, leg*⟩ □ *vi* sich bücken; ⟨*thing:*⟩ sich biegen; ⟨*road:*⟩ eine Biegung machen. **~ down** *vi* sich bücken. **~ over** *vi* sich vornüberbeugen

beneath /bɪ'ni:θ/ *prep* unter (+ *dat/acc*); **~ him** (*fig*) unter seiner Würde; **~ contempt** unter aller Würde □ *adv* darunter

benediction /benɪ'dɪkʃn/ *n* (*Relig*) Segen *m*

benefactor /'benɪfæktə(r)/ *n* Wohltäter(in) *m*(*f*)

beneficial /benɪ'fɪʃl/ *a* nützlich

beneficiary /benɪ'fɪʃərɪ/ *n* Begünstigte(r) *m/f*

benefit /'benɪfɪt/ *n* Vorteil *m*; (*allowance*) Unterstützung *f*; (*insurance*) Leistung *f*; **sickness ~** Krankengeld *nt* □ *v* (*pt/pp* **-fited**, *pres p* **-fiting**) □ *vt* nützen (+ *dat*) □ *vi* profitieren (**from** von)

benevolen|ce /bɪ'nevələns/ *n* Wohlwollen *nt*. **~t** *a*, **-ly** *adv* wohlwollend

benign /bɪ'naɪn/ *a*, **-ly** *adv* gütig; (*Med*) gutartig

bent /bent/ *see* **bend** □ *a* ⟨*person*⟩ gebeugt; (*distorted*) verbogen; (*fam: dishonest*) korrupt; **be ~ on doing sth** darauf erpicht sein, etw zu tun □ *n* Hang *m*, Neigung *f* (**for** zu); **artistic ~** künstlerische Ader *f*

be|queath /bɪ'kwi:ð/ *vt* vermachen (**to** *dat*). **~quest** /-'kwest/ *n* Vermächtnis *nt*

bereave|d /bɪ'ri:vd/ *n* **the ~d** *pl* die Hinterbliebenen. **~ment** *n* Trauerfall *m*; (*state*) Trauer *f*

bereft /bɪ'reft/ *a* **~ of** beraubt (+ *gen*)

beret /'bereɪ/ *n* Baskenmütze *f*

Berne /bɜ:n/ *n* Bern *nt*

berry /'berɪ/ *n* Beere *f*

berserk /bə'sɜ:k/ *a* **go ~** wild werden

berth /bɜ:θ/ *n* (*on ship*) [Schlaf]koje *f*; (*ship's anchorage*) Liegeplatz *m*; **give a wide ~ to** (*fam*) einen großen Bogen machen um □ *vi* anlegen

beseech /bɪ'si:tʃ/ *vt* (*pt/pp* **beseeched** *or* **besought**) anflehen

beside /bɪ'saɪd/ *prep* neben (+ *dat/acc*); **~ oneself** außer sich (*dat*)

besides /bɪ'saɪdz/ *prep* außer (+ *dat*) □ *adv* außerdem

besiege /bɪ'si:dʒ/ *vt* belagern

besought /bɪ'sɔ:t/ *see* **beseech**

bespoke /bɪ'spəʊk/ *a* ⟨*suit*⟩ maßgeschneidert

best /best/ *a* & *n* beste(r,s); **the ~** der/die/das Beste; **at ~** bestenfalls; **all the ~!** alles Gute! **do one's ~** sein Bestes tun; **the ~ part of a year** fast ein Jahr; **to the ~ of my knowledge** so viel ich weiß; **make the ~ of it** das Beste daraus machen □ *adv* am besten; **as ~ I could** so gut ich konnte. **~ 'man** *n* ≈ Trauzeuge *m*

bestow /bɪ'stəʊ/ *vt* schenken (**on** *dat*)

best'seller *n* Bestseller *m*

bet /bet/ *n* Wette *f* □ *v* (*pt/pp* **bet** *or* **betted**) □ *vt* **~ s.o. £5** mit jdm um £5 wetten □ *vi* wetten; **~ on** [Geld] setzen auf (+ *acc*)

betray /bɪ'treɪ/ *vt* verraten. **~al** *n* Verrat *m*

better /'betə(r)/ *a* besser; **get ~** sich bessern; (*after illness*) sich erholen □ *adv* besser; **~ off** besser dran; **~ not** lieber nicht; **all the ~** umso besser; **the sooner the ~** je eher, desto besser; **think ~ of sth** sich eines Besseren besinnen; **you'd ~ stay** du bleibst am besten hier □ *vt* verbessern; (*do better than*) übertreffen; **~ oneself** sich verbessern

'betting shop *n* Wettbüro *nt*

between /bɪ'twi:n/ *prep* zwischen (+ *dat/acc*); ~ **you and me** unter uns; ~ **us** (*together*) zusammen □ *adv* **[in]** ~ dazwischen
beverage /'bevərɪdʒ/ *n* Getränk *nt*
bevy /'bevɪ/ *n* Schar *f*
beware /bɪ'weə(r)/ *vi* sich in Acht nehmen (**of** vor + *dat*); ~ **of the dog!** Vorsicht, bissiger Hund!
bewilder /bɪ'wɪldə(r)/ *vt* verwirren. ~**ment** *n* Verwirrung *f*
bewitch /bɪ'wɪtʃ/ *vt* verzaubern; (*fig*) bezaubern
beyond /bɪ'jɒnd/ *prep* über (+ *acc*) ... hinaus; (*further*) weiter als; ~ **reach** außer Reichweite; ~ **doubt** ohne jeden Zweifel; **it's ~ me** (*fam*) das geht über meinen Horizont □ *adv* darüber hinaus
bias /'baɪəs/ *n* Voreingenommenheit *f*; (*preference*) Vorliebe *f*; (*Jur*) Befangenheit *f*; **cut on the ~** schräg geschnitten □ *vt* (*pt/pp* **biased**) (*influence*) beeinflussen. ~**ed** *a* voreingenommen; (*Jur*) befangen
bib /bɪb/ *n* Lätzchen *nt*
Bible /'baɪbl/ *n* Bibel *f*
biblical /'bɪblɪkl/ *a* biblisch
bibliography /bɪblɪ'ɒgrəfɪ/ *n* Bibliographie *f*
bicarbonate /baɪ'kɑ:bəneɪt/ *n* ~ **of soda** doppeltkohlensaures Natron *nt*
bicker /'bɪkə(r)/ *vi* sich zanken
bicycle /'baɪsɪkl/ *n* Fahrrad *nt* □ *vi* mit dem Rad fahren
bid[1] /bɪd/ *n* Gebot *nt*; (*attempt*) Versuch *m* □ *vt/i* (*pt/pp* **bid**, *pres p* **bidding**) bieten (**for** auf + *acc*); (*Cards*) reizen
bid[2] *vt* (*pt* **bade** *or* **bid**, *pp* **bidden** *or* **bid**, *pres p* **bidding**) (*liter*) heißen; ~ **s.o. welcome** jdn willkommen heißen
bidder /'bɪdə(r)/ *n* Bieter(in) *m(f)*
bide /baɪd/ *vt* ~ **one's time** den richtigen Moment abwarten
biennial /baɪ'enɪəl/ *a* zweijährlich; (*lasting two years*) zweijährig
bier /bɪə(r)/ *n* [Toten]bahre *f*
bifocals /baɪ'fəʊklz/ *npl* **[pair of]** ~ Bifokalbrille *f*
big /bɪg/ *a* (**bigger, biggest**) groß □ *adv* **talk** ~ (*fam*) angeben
bigam|ist /'bɪgəmɪst/ *n* Bigamist *m*. ~**y** *n* Bigamie *f*
big-'headed *a* (*fam*) eingebildet
bigot /'bɪgət/ *n* Eiferer *m*. ~**ed** *a* engstirnig
'**bigwig** *n* (*fam*) hohes Tier *nt*
bike /baɪk/ *n* (*fam*) [Fahr]rad *nt*
bikini /bɪ'ki:nɪ/ *n* Bikini *m*
bilberry /'bɪlbərɪ/ *n* Heidelbeere *f*
bile /baɪl/ *n* Galle *f*
bilingual /baɪ'lɪŋgwəl/ *a* zweisprachig
bilious /'bɪljəs/ *a* (*Med*) ~ **attack** verdorbener Magen *m*
bill[1] /bɪl/ *n* Rechnung *f*; (*poster*) Plakat *nt*; (*Pol*) Gesetzentwurf *m*; (*Amer: note*) Banknote *f*; ~ **of exchange** Wechsel *m* □ *vt* eine Rechnung schicken (+ *dat*)
bill[2] *n* (*break*) Schnabel *m*
billet /'bɪlɪt/ *n* (*Mil*) Quartier *nt* □ *vt* (*pt/pp* **billeted**) einquartieren (**on** bei)
'**billfold** *n* (*Amer*) Brieftasche *f*
billiards /'bɪljədz/ *n* Billard *nt*
billion /'bɪljən/ *n* (*thousand million*) Milliarde *f*; (*million million*) Billion *f*
billy-goat /'bɪlɪ-/ *n* Ziegenbock *m*
bin /bɪn/ *n* Mülleimer *m*; (*for bread*) Kasten *m*
bind /baɪnd/ *vt* (*pt/pp* **bound**) binden (**to** an + *acc*); (*bandage*) verbinden; (*Jur*) verpflichten; (*cover the edge of*) einfassen. ~**ing** *a* verbindlich □ *n* Einband *m*; (*braid*) Borte *f*; (*on ski*) Bindung *f*
binge /bɪndʒ/ *n* (*fam*) **go on the** ~ eine Sauftour machen

binoculars /bɪˈnɒkjʊləz/ *npl* **[pair of] ~** Fernglas *nt*

bio|ˈchemistry /baɪəʊ-/ *n* Biochemie *f*. **~degradable** /-dɪˈgreɪdəbl/ *a* biologisch abbaubar

biograph|er /baɪˈɒgrəfə(r)/ *n* Biograph(in) *m(f)*. **~y** *n* Biographie *f*

biological /baɪəˈlɒdʒɪkl/ *a* biologisch

biolog|ist /baɪˈɒlədʒɪst/ *n* Biologe *m*. **~y** *n* Biologie *f*

birch /bɜːtʃ/ *n* Birke *f*; (*whip*) Rute *f*

bird /bɜːd/ *n* Vogel *m*; (*fam: girl*) Mädchen *nt*; **kill two ~s with one stone** zwei Fliegen mit einer Klappe schlagen

Biro (P) /ˈbaɪrəʊ/ *n* Kugelschreiber *m*

birth /bɜːθ/ *n* Geburt *f*

birth: ~ certificate *n* Geburtsurkunde *f*. **~-control** *n* Geburtenregelung *f*. **~day** *n* Geburtstag *m*. **~mark** *n* Muttermal *nt*. **~-rate** *n* Geburtenziffer *f* **~right** *n* Geburtsrecht *nt*

biscuit /ˈbɪskɪt/ *n* Keks *m*

bisect /baɪˈsekt/ *vt* halbieren

bishop /ˈbɪʃəp/ *n* Bischof *m*; (*Chess*) Läufer *m*

bit[1] /bɪt/ *n* Stückchen *nt*; (*for horse*) Gebiss *nt*; (*Techn*) Bohreinsatz *m*; **a ~** ein bisschen; **~ by ~** nach und nach; **a ~ of bread** ein bisschen Brot; **do one's ~** sein Teil tun

bit[2] *see* **bite**

bitch /bɪtʃ/ *n* Hündin *f*; (*sl*) Luder *nt*. **~y** *a* gehässig

bit|e /baɪt/ *n* Biss *m*; **[insect] ~** Stich *m*; (*mouthful*) Bissen *m* □ *vt/i* (*pt* **bit**, *pp* **bitten**) beißen; ⟨*insect:*⟩ stechen; kauen ⟨*one's nails*⟩. **~ing** *a* beißend

bitten /ˈbɪtn/ *see* **bite**

bitter /ˈbɪtə(r)/ *a*, **-ly** *adv* bitter; **cry ~ly** bitterlich weinen; **~ly cold** bitterkalt □ *n* bitteres Bier *nt*. **~ness** *n* Bitterkeit *f*

bitty /ˈbɪtɪ/ *a* zusammengestoppelt

bizarre /bɪˈzɑː(r)/ *a* bizarr

blab /blæb/ *vi* (*pt/pp* **blabbed**) alles ausplaudern

black /blæk/ *a* (**-er, -est**) schwarz; **be ~ and blue** grün und blau sein □ *n* Schwarz *nt*; (*person*) Schwarze(r) *m/f* □ *vt* schwärzen; boykottieren ⟨*goods*⟩. **~ out** *vt* verdunkeln □ *vi* (*lose consciousness*) das Bewusstsein verlieren

black: ~berry *n* Brombeere *f*. **~bird** *n* Amsel *f*. **~board** *n* (*Sch*) [Wand]tafel *f*. **~ˈcurrant** *n* schwarze Johannisbeere *f*

blacken *vt/i* schwärzen

black: ~ ˈeye *n* blaues Auge *nt*. **B~ ˈForest** *n* Schwarzwald *m*. **~ ˈice** *n* Glatteis *nt*. **~leg** *n* Streikbrecher *m*. **~list** *vt* auf die schwarze Liste setzen. **~mail** *n* Erpressung *f* □ *vt* erpressen. **~mailer** *n* Erpresser(in) *m(f)*. **~ ˈmarket** *n* schwarzer Markt *m*. **~-out** *n* Verdunkelung *f*; **have a ~-out** (*Med*) das Bewusstsein verlieren. **~ ˈpudding** *n* Blutwurst *f*. **~smith** *n* [Huf]schmied *m*

bladder /ˈblædə(r)/ *n* (*Anat*) Blase *f*

blade /bleɪd/ *n* Klinge *f*; (*of grass*) Halm *m*

blame /bleɪm/ *n* Schuld *f* □ *vt* die Schuld geben (+ *dat*); **no one is to ~** keiner ist schuld daran. **~less** *a* schuldlos

blanch /blɑːntʃ/ *vi* blass werden □ *vt* (*Culin*) blanchieren

blancmange /bləˈmɒnʒ/ *n* Pudding *m*

bland /blænd/ *a* (**-er, -est**) mild

blank /blæŋk/ *a* leer; ⟨*look*⟩ ausdruckslos □ *n* Lücke *f*; (*cartridge*) Platzpatrone *f*. **~ ˈcheque** *n* Blankoscheck *m*

blanket /ˈblæŋkɪt/ *n* Decke *f*; **wet ~** (*fam*) Spielverderber(in) *m(f)*

blank ˈverse *n* Blankvers *m*

blare /bleə(r)/ *vt/i* schmettern

blasé /ˈblɑːzeɪ/ *a* blasiert

blaspheme /blæs'fi:m/ *vi* lästern
blasphem|ous /'blæsfəməs/ *a* [gottes]lästerlich. **~y** *n* [Gottes]-lästerung *f*
blast /blɑ:st/ *n* (*gust*) Luftstoß *m*; (*sound*) Schmettern *nt*; (*of horn*) Tuten *nt* □ *vt* sprengen □ *int* (*sl*) verdammt. **~ed** *a* (*sl*) verdammt
blast: ~-furnace *n* Hochofen *m*. **~-off** *n* (*of missile*) Start *m*
blatant /'bleɪtənt/ *a* offensichtlich
blaze /bleɪz/ *n* Feuer *nt* □ *vi* brennen
blazer /'bleɪzə(r)/ *n* Blazer *m*
bleach /bli:tʃ/ *n* Bleichmittel *nt* □ *vt/i* bleichen
bleak /bli:k/ *a* (**-er, -est**) öde; (*fig*) trostlos
bleary-eyed /'blɪərɪ-/ *a* mit trüben/(*on waking up*) verschlafenen Augen
bleat /bli:t/ *vi* blöken; ⟨*goat:*⟩ meckern
bleed /bli:d/ *v* (*pt/pp* **bled**) □ *vi* bluten □ *vt* entlüften ⟨*radiator*⟩
bleep /bli:p/ *n* Piepton *m* □ *vi* piepsen □ *vt* mit dem Piepser rufen. **~er** *n* Piepser *m*
blemish /'blemɪʃ/ *n* Makel *m*
blend /blend/ *n* Mischung *f* □ *vt* mischen □ *vi* sich vermischen. **~er** *n* (*Culin*) Mixer *m*
bless /bles/ *vt* segnen. **~ed** /'blesɪd/ *a* heilig; (*sl*) verflixt. **~ing** *n* Segen *m*
blew /blu:/ *see* **blow**[2]
blight /blaɪt/ *n* (*Bot*) Brand *m* □ *vt* (*spoil*) vereiteln
blind /blaɪnd/ *a* blind; ⟨*corner*⟩ unübersichtlich; **~ man/woman** Blinde(r) *m/f* □ *n* **[roller] ~** Rouleau *nt* □ *vt* blenden
blind: ~ 'alley *n* Sackgasse *f*. **~fold** *a & adv* mit verbundenen Augen □ *n* Augenbinde *f* □ *vt* die Augen verbinden (+ *dat*). **~ly** *adv* blindlings. **~ness** *n* Blindheit *f*
blink /blɪŋk/ *vi* blinzeln; ⟨*light:*⟩ blinken
blinkers /'blɪŋkəz/ *npl* Scheuklappen *pl*
bliss /blɪs/ *n* Glückseligkeit *f*. **~ful** *a* glücklich
blister /'blɪstə(r)/ *n* (*Med*) Blase *f* □ *vi* ⟨*paint:*⟩ Blasen werfen
blitz /blɪts/ *n* Luftangriff *m*; (*fam*) Großaktion *f*
blizzard /'blɪzəd/ *n* Schneesturm *m*
bloated /'bləʊtɪd/ *a* aufgedunsen
blob /blɒb/ *n* Klecks *m*
bloc /blɒk/ *n* (*Pol*) Block *m*
block /blɒk/ *n* Block *m*; (*of wood*) Klotz *m*; (*of flats*) [Wohn]block *m* □ *vt* blockieren. **~ up** *vt* zustopfen
blockade /blɒ'keɪd/ *n* Blockade *f* □ *vt* blockieren
blockage /'blɒkɪdʒ/ *n* Verstopfung *f*
block: ~head *n* (*fam*) Dummkopf *m*. **~ 'letters** *npl* Blockschrift *f*
bloke /bləʊk/ *n* (*fam*) Kerl *m*
blonde /blɒnd/ *a* blond □ *n* Blondine *f*
blood /blʌd/ *n* Blut *nt*
blood: ~ count *n* Blutbild *nt*. **~-curdling** *a* markerschütternd. **~ donor** *n* Blutspender *m*. **~ group** *n* Blutgruppe *f*. **~hound** *n* Bluthund *m*. **~-poisoning** *n* Blutvergiftung *f*. **~ pressure** *n* Blutdruck *m*. **~ relative** *n* Blutsverwandte(r) *m/f*. **~shed** *n* Blutvergießen *nt*. **~shot** *a* blutunterlaufen. **~ sports** *npl* Jagdsport *m*. **~-stained** *a* blutbefleckt. **~stream** *n* Blutbahn *f*. **~ test** *n* Blutprobe *f*. **~thirsty** *a* blutdürstig. **~ transfusion** *n* Blutübertragung *f*. **~ vessel** *n* Blutgefäß *nt*
bloody /'blʌdɪ/ *a* (**-ier, -iest**) blutig; (*sl*) verdammt. **~-'minded** *a* (*sl*) stur
bloom /blu:m/ *n* Blüte *f* □ *vi* blühen

bloom|er /'blu:mə(r)/ *n* (*fam*) Schnitzer *m*. **~ing** *a* (*fam*) verdammt

blossom /'blɒsəm/ *n* Blüte *f* □ *vi* blühen. **~ out** *vi* (*fig*) aufblühen

blot /blɒt/ *n* [Tinten]klecks *m*; (*fig*) Fleck *m* □ *vt* (*pt/pp* **blotted**) löschen. **~ out** *vt* (*fig*) auslöschen

blotch /blɒtʃ/ *n* Fleck *m*. **~y** *a* fleckig

'blotting-paper *n* Löschpapier *nt*

blouse /blaʊz/ *n* Bluse *f*

blow¹ /bləʊ/ *n* Schlag *m*

blow² *v* (*pt* **blew**, *pp* **blown**) □ *vt* blasen; (*fam; squander*) verpulvern; **~ one's nose** sich (*dat*) die Nase putzen □ *vi* blasen; ⟨*fuse:*⟩ durchbrennen. **~ away** *vt* wegblasen □ *vi* wegfliegen. **~ down** *vt* umwehen □ *vi* umfallen. **~ out** *vt* (*extinguish*) ausblasen. **~ over** *vi* umfallen; (*fig: die down*) vorübergehen. **~ up** *vt* (*inflate*) aufblasen; (*enlarge*) vergrößern; (*shatter by explosion*) sprengen □ *vi* explodieren

blow: ~-dry *vt* föhnen. **~fly** *n* Schmeißfliege *f*. **~lamp** *n* Lötlampe *f*

blown /bləʊn/ *see* **blow²**

'blowtorch *n* (*Amer*) Lötlampe *f*

blowy /'bləʊɪ/ *a* windig

bludgeon /'blʌdʒn/ *vt* (*fig*) zwingen

blue /blu:/ *a* (**-r, -st**) blau; **feel ~** deprimiert sein □ *n* Blau *nt*; **have the ~s** deprimiert sein; **out of the ~ aus** heiterem Himmel

blue: ~bell *n* Sternhyazinthe *f*. **~berry** *n* Heidelbeere *f*. **~bottle** *n* Schmeißfliege *f*. **~ film** *n* Pornofilm *m*. **~print** *n* (*fig*) Entwurf *m*

bluff /blʌf/ *n* Bluff *m* □ *vi* bluffen

blunder /'blʌndə(r)/ *n* Schnitzer *m* □ *vi* einen Schnitzer machen

blunt /blʌnt/ *a* stumpf; ⟨*person*⟩ geradeheraus. **~ly** *adv* unverblümt, geradeheraus

blur /blɜ:(r)/ *n* **it's all a ~** alles ist verschwommen □ *vt* (*pt/pp* **blurred**) verschwommen machen; **~red** verschwommen

blurb /blɜ:b/ *n* Klappentext *m*

blurt /blɜ:t/ *vt* **~ out** herausplatzen mit

blush /blʌʃ/ *n* Erröten *nt* □ *vi* erröten

bluster /'blʌstə(r)/ *n* Großtuerei *f*. **~y** *a* windig

boar /bɔ:(r)/ *n* Eber *m*

board /bɔ:d/ *n* Brett *nt*; (*for notices*) schwarzes Brett *nt*; (*committee*) Ausschuss *m*; (*of directors*) Vorstand *m*; **on ~** an Bord; **full ~** Vollpension *f*; **~ and lodging** Unterkunft und Verpflegung *pl*; **go by the ~** (*fam*) unter den Tisch fallen □ *vt* einsteigen in (+ *acc*); (*Naut, Aviat*) besteigen □ *vi* an Bord gehen; **~ with** in Pension wohnen bei. **~ up** *vt* mit Brettern verschlagen

boarder /'bɔ:də(r)/ *n* Pensionsgast *m*; (*Sch*) Internatsschüler(in) *m(f)*

board: ~-game *n* Brettspiel *nt*. **~ing-house** *n* Pension *f*. **~ing-school** *n* Internat *nt*

boast /bəʊst/ *vt* sich rühmen (+ *gen*) □ *vi* prahlen (**about** mit). **~ful** *a*, **-ly** *adv* prahlerisch

boat /bəʊt/ *n* Boot *nt*; (*ship*) Schiff *nt*. **-er** *n* (*hat*) flacher Strohhut *m*

bob /bɒb/ *n* Bubikopf *m* □ *vi* (*pt/pp* **bobbed**) (*curtsy*) knicksen; **~ up and down** sich auf und ab bewegen

bobbin /'bɒbɪn/ *n* Spule *f*

'bob-sleigh *n* Bob *m*

bode /bəʊd/ *vi* **~ well/ill** etwas/nichts Gutes verheißen

bodice /'bɒdɪs/ *n* Mieder *nt*

bodily /'bɒdɪlɪ/ *a* körperlich □ *adv* (*forcibly*) mit Gewalt

body /'bɒdɪ/ *n* Körper *m*; (*corpse*) Leiche *f*; (*corporation*) Körperschaft *f*; **the main ~** der Hauptanteil. **~guard** *n* Leibwächter *m*. **~work** *n* (*Auto*) Karosserie *f*

bog /bɒg/ *n* Sumpf *m* □ *vt* (*pt/pp* **bogged**) **get ~ged down** stecken bleiben

boggle /ˈbɒgl/ *vi* **the mind ~s** es ist kaum vorstellbar

bogus /ˈbəʊgəs/ *a* falsch

boil¹ /bɔɪl/ *n* Furunkel *m*

boil² *n* **bring/come to the ~** zum Kochen bringen/kommen □ *vt/i* kochen; **~ed potatoes** Salzkartoffeln *pl.* **~ down** *vi* (*fig*) hinauslaufen (**to** auf + *acc*). **~ over** *vi* überkochen. **~ up** *vt* aufkochen

boiler /ˈbɔɪlə(r)/ *n* Heizkessel *m.* **~suit** *n* Overall *m*

ˈ**boiling point** *n* Siedepunkt *m*

boisterous /ˈbɔɪstərəs/ *a* übermütig

bold /bəʊld/ *a* (**-er, -est**), **-ly** *adv* kühn; (*Typ*) fett. **~ness** *n* Kühnheit *f*

bollard /ˈbɒlɑːd/ *n* Poller *m*

bolster /ˈbəʊlstə(r)/ *n* Nackenrolle *f* □ *vt* **~ up** Mut machen (+ *dat*)

bolt /bəʊlt/ *n* Riegel *m*; (*Techn*) Bolzen *m*; **nuts and ~s** Schrauben und Muttern *pl* □ *vt* schrauben (**to** an + *acc*); verriegeln ⟨*door*⟩; hinunterschlingen ⟨*food*⟩ □ *vi* abhauen; ⟨*horse:*⟩ durchgehen □ *adv* **~ upright** *adv* kerzengerade

bomb /bɒm/ *n* Bombe *f* □ *vt* bombardieren

bombard /bɒmˈbɑːd/ *vt* beschießen; (*fig*) bombardieren

bombastic /bɒmˈbæstɪk/ *a* bombastisch

bomb|er /ˈbɒmə(r)/ *n* (*Aviat*) Bomber *m*; (*person*) Bombenleger(in) *m(f)*. **~shell** *n* **be a ~shell** (*fig*) wie eine Bombe einschlagen

bond /bɒnd/ *n* (*fig*) Band *nt*; (*Comm*) Obligation *f*; **be in ~** unter Zollverschluss stehen

bondage /ˈbɒbdɪdʒ/ *n* (*fig*) Sklaverei *f*

bone /bəʊn/ *n* Knochen *m*; (*of fish*) Gräte *f* □ *vt* von den Knochen lösen ⟨*meat*⟩; entgräten ⟨*fish*⟩. **~-ˈdry** *a* knochentrocken

bonfire /ˈbɒn-/ *n* Gartenfeuer *nt*; (*celebratory*) Freudenfeuer *nt*

bonnet /ˈbɒnɪt/ *n* Haube *f*

bonus /ˈbəʊnəs/ *n* Prämie *f*; (*gratuity*) Gratifikation *f*; (*fig*) Plus *nt*

bony /ˈbəʊnɪ/ *a* (**-ier, -iest**) knochig; ⟨*fish*⟩ grätig

boo /buː/ *int* buh! □ *vt* ausbuhen □ *vi* buhen

boob /buːb/ *n* (*fam: mistake*) Schnitzer *m* □ *vi* (*fam*) einen Schnitzer machen

book /bʊk/ *n* Buch *nt*; (*of tickets*) Heft *nt*; **keep the ~s** (*Comm*) die Bücher führen □ *vt/i* buchen; (*reserve*) [vor]bestellen; (*for offence*) aufschreiben. **~able** /-əbl/ *a* im Vorverkauf erhältlich

book: ~case *n* Bücherregal *nt.* **~-ends** *npl* Buchstützen *pl.* **~ing-office** *in* Fahrkartenschalter *m.* **~keeping** *n* Buchführung *f.* **~let** *n* Broschüre *f.* **~maker** *n* Buchmacher *m.* **~mark** *n* Lesezeichen *nt.* **~seller** *n* Buchhändler(in) *m(f)*. **~shop** *n* Buchhandlung *f.* **~stall** *n* Bücherstand *m.* **~worm** *n* Bücherwurm *m*

boom /buːm/ *n* (*Comm*) Hochkonjunktur *f*; (*upturn*) Aufschwung *m* □ *vi* dröhnen; (*fig*) blühen

boon /buːn/ *n* Segen *m*

boor /bʊə(r)/ *n* Flegel *m.* **~ish** *a* flegelhaft

boost /buːst/ *n* Auftrieb *m* □ *vt* Auftrieb geben (+ *dat*). **~er** *n* (*Med*) Nachimpfung *f*

boot /buːt/ *n* Stiefel *m*; (*Auto*) Kofferraum *m*

booth /buːð/ *n* Bude *f*; (*cubicle*) Kabine *f*

booty /ˈbuːtɪ/ *n* Beute *f*

booze /buːz/ *n* (*fam*) Alkohol *m* □ *vi* (*fam*) saufen

border /ˈbɔːdə(r)/ *n* Rand *m*; (*frontier*) Grenze *f*; (*in garden*) Rabatte *f* □ *vi* **~ on** grenzen an

(+ *acc*). **~line** *n* Grenzlinie *f*. **~line case** *n* Grenzfall *m*

bore¹ /bɔ:(r)/ *see* **bear**²

bore² *vt/i* (*Techn*) bohren

bor|e³ *n* (*of gun*) Kaliber *nt*; (*person*) langweiliger Mensch *m*; (*thing*) langweilige Sache *f* □ *vt* langweilen; **be ~ed** sich langweilen. **~edom** *n* Langeweile *f*. **~ing** *a* langweilig

born /bɔ:n/ *pp* **be ~** geboren werden □ *a* geboren

borne /bɔ:n/ *see* **bear**²

borough /'bʌrə/ *n* Stadtgemeinde *f*

borrow /'bɒrəʊ/ *vt* [sich (*dat*)] borgen *od* leihen (**from** von)

bosom /'bʊzm/ *n* Busen *m*

boss /bɒs/ *n* (*fam*) Chef *m* □ *vt* herumkommandieren. **~y** *a* herrschsüchtig

botanical /bə'tænɪkl/ *a* botanisch

botan|ist /'bɒtənɪst/ *n* Botaniker(in) *m*(*f*). **~y** *n* Botanik *f*

botch /bɒtʃ/ *vt* verpfuschen

both /bəʊθ/ *a & pron* beide; **~[of] the children** beide Kinder; **~ of them** beide [von ihnen] □ *adv* **~ men and women** sowohl Männer als auch Frauen

bother /'bɒðə(r)/ *n* Mühe *f*; (*minor trouble*) Ärger *m* □ *int* (*fam*) verflixt! □ *vt* belästigen; (*disturb*) stören □ *vi* sich kümmern (**about** um); **don't ~** nicht nötig

bottle /'bɒtl/ *n* Flasche *f* □ *vt* auf Flaschen abfüllen; (*preserve*) einmachen. **~ up** *vt* (*fig*) in sich (*dat*) aufstauen

bottle: ~-neck *n* (*fig*) Engpass *m*. **~-opener** *n* Flaschenöffner *m*

bottom /'bɒtəm/ *a* unterste(r,s) □ *n* (*of container*) Boden *m*; (*of river*) Grund *m*; (*of page, hill*) Fuß *m*; (*buttocks*) Hintern *m*; **at the ~** unten; **get to the ~ of sth** (*fig*) hinter etw (*acc*) kommen. **~less** *a* bodenlos

bough /baʊ/ *n* Ast *m*

bought /bɔ:t/ *see* **buy**

boulder /'bəʊldə(r)/ *n* Felsblock *m*

bounce /baʊns/ *vi* [auf]springen; ⟨*cheque:*⟩ (*fam*) nicht gedeckt sein □ *vt* aufspringen lassen ⟨*ball*⟩

bouncer /'baʊnsə(r)/ *n* (*fam*) Rausschmeißer *m*

bouncing /'baʊnsɪŋ/ *a* **~ baby** strammer Säugling *m*

bound¹ /baʊnd/ *n* Sprung *m* □ *vi* springen

bound² *see* **bind** □ *a* **~ for** ⟨*ship*⟩ mit Kurs auf (+ *acc*); **be ~ to do sth** etw bestimmt machen; (*obliged*) verpflichtet sein, etw zu machen

boundary /'baʊndərɪ/ *n* Grenze *f*

'**boundless** *a* grenzenlos

bounds /baʊndz/ *npl* (*fig*) Grenzen *pl*; **out of ~** verboten

bouquet /bʊ'keɪ/ *n* [Blumen]strauß *m*; (*of wine*) Bukett *nt*

bourgeois /'bʊəʒwɑ:/ *a* (*pej*) spießbürgerlich

bout /baʊt/ *n* (*Med*) Anfall *m*; (*Sport*) Kampf *m*

bow¹ /bəʊ/ *n* (*weapon & Mus*) Bogen *m*; (*knot*) Schleife *f*

bow² /baʊ/ *n* Verbeugung *f* □ *vi* sich verbeugen □ *vt* neigen ⟨*head*⟩

bow³ /baʊ/ *n* (*Naut*) Bug *m*

bowel /'baʊəl/ *n* Darm *m*; **~ movement** Stuhlgang *m*. **~s** *pl* Eingeweide *pl*; (*digestion*) Verdauung *f*

bowl¹ /bəʊl/ *n* Schüssel *f*; (*shallow*) Schale *f*; (*of pipe*) Kopf *m*; (*of spoon*) Schöpfteil *m*

bowl² *n* (*ball*) Kugel *f* □ *vt/i* werfen. **~ over** *vt* umwerfen

bow-legged /bəʊ'legd/ *a* O-beinig

bowler¹ /'bəʊlə(r)/ *n* (*Sport*) Werfer *m*

bowler² *n* **~ [hat]** Melone *f*

bowling /'bəʊlɪŋ/ *n* Kegeln *nt*. **~-alley** *n* Kegelbahn *f*

bowls /bəʊlz/ *n* Bowlsspiel *nt*

bow-'tie /bəʊ-/ *n* Fliege *f*

box[1] /bɒks/ *n* Schachtel *f*; (*wooden*) Kiste *f*; (*cardboard*) Karton *m*; (*Theat*) Loge *f*
box[2] *vt/i* (*Sport*) boxen; ~ **s.o.'s ears** jdn ohrfeigen
box|er /ˈbɒksə(r)/ *n* Boxer *m*. ~**ing** *n* Boxen *nt*. **B** ~**ing Day** *n* zweiter Weihnachtstag *m*
box: ~**-office** *n* (*Theat*) Kasse *f*. ~**-room** *n* Abstellraum *m*
boy /bɔɪ/ *n* Junge *m*
boycott /ˈbɔɪkɒt/ *n* Boykott *m* □ *vt* boykottieren
boy: ~**friend** *n* Freund *m*. ~**ish** *a* jungenhaft
bra /brɑː/ *n* BH *m*
brace /breɪs/ *n* Strebe *f*, Stütze *f*; (*dental*) Zahnspange *f*; ~**s** *npl* Hosenträger *mpl* □ *vt* ~ **oneself** sich stemmen (**against** gegen); (*fig*) sich gefasst machen (**for** auf + *acc*)
bracelet /ˈbreɪslɪt/ *n* Armband *nt*
bracing /ˈbreɪsɪŋ/ *a* stärkend
bracken /ˈbrækn/ *n* Farnkraut *nt*
bracket /ˈbrækɪt/ *n* Konsole *f*; (*group*) Gruppe *f*; (*Typ*) **round/square** ~**s** runde/eckige Klammern □ *vt* einklammern
brag /bræg/ *vi* (*pt/pp* **bragged**) prahlen (**about** mit)
braid /breɪd/ *n* Borte *f*
braille /breɪl/ *n* Blindenschrift *f*
brain /breɪn/ *n* Gehirn *nt*; ~**s** (*fig*) Intelligenz *f*
brain: ~**child** *n* geistiges Produkt *nt*. ~**less** *a* dumm. ~**wash** *vt* einer Gehirnwäsche unterziehen. ~**wave** *n* Geistesblitz *m*
brainy /ˈbreɪnɪ/ *a* (**-ier, -iest**) klug
braise /breɪz/ *vt* schmoren
brake /breɪk/ *n* Bremse *f* □ *vt/i* bremsen. ~**-light** *n* Bremslicht *nt*
bramble /ˈbræmbl/ *n* Brombeerstrauch *m*
bran /bræn/ *n* Kleie *f*
branch /brɑːntʃ/ *n* Ast *m*; (*fig*) Zweig *m*; (*Comm*) Zweigstelle *f*; (*shop*) Filiale *f* □ *vi* sich gabeln. ~ **off** *vi* abzweigen. ~ **out** *vi* ~ **out into** sich verlegen auf (+ *acc*)
brand /brænd/ *n* Marke *f*; (*on animal*) Brandzeichen *nt* □ *vt* mit dem Brandeisen zeichnen ⟨*animal*⟩; (*fig*) brandmarken als
brandish /ˈbrændɪʃ/ *vt* schwingen
brand-ˈnew *a* nagelneu
brandy /ˈbrændɪ/ *n* Weinbrand *m*
brash /bræʃ/ *a* nassforsch
brass /brɑːs/ *n* Messing *nt*; (*Mus*) Blech *nt*; **get down to** ~ **tacks** (*fam*) zur Sache kommen; **top** ~ (*fam*) hohe Tiere *pl*. ~ **band** *n* Blaskapelle *f*
brassiere /ˈbræzɪə(r)/ *n* Büstenhalter *m*
brassy /ˈbrɑːsɪ/ *a* (**-ier, -iest**) (*fam*) ordinär
brat /bræt/ *n* (*pej*) Balg *nt*
bravado /brəˈvɑːdəʊ/ *n* Forschheit *f*
brave /breɪv/ *a* (**-r, -st**), **-ly** *adv* tapfer □ *vt* die Stirn bieten (+ *dat*). ~**ry** /-ərɪ/ *n* Tapferkeit *f*
bravo /brɑːˈvəʊ/ *int* bravo!
brawl /brɔːl/ *n* Schlägerei *f* □ *vi* sich schlagen
brawn /brɔːn/ *n* (*Culin*) Sülze *f*
brawny /ˈbrɔːnɪ/ *a* muskulös
bray /breɪ/ *vi* iahen
brazen /ˈbreɪzn/ *a* unverschämt
brazier /ˈbreɪzɪə(r)/ *n* Kohlenbecken *nt*
Brazil /brəˈzɪl/ *n* Brasilien *nt*. ~**ian** *a* brasilianisch. ~ **nut** *n* Paranuss *f*
breach /briːtʃ/ *n* Bruch *m*; (*Mil & fig*) Bresche *f*; ~ **of contract** Vertragsbruch *m* □ *vt* durchbrechen; brechen ⟨*contract*⟩
bread /bred/ *n* Brot *nt*; **slice of** ~ **and butter** Butterbrot *nt*
bread: ~**crumbs** *npl* Brotkrümel *pl*; (*Culin*) Paniermehl *nt*. ~**line** *n* **be on the** ~**line** gerade genug zum Leben haben
breadth /bredθ/ *n* Breite *f*

ˈ**bread-winner** *n* Brotverdiener *m*

break /breɪk/ *n* Bruch *m*; (*interval*) Pause *f*; (*interruption*) Unterbrechung *f*; (*fam: chance*) Chance *f* □ *v* (*pt* **broke**, *pp* **broken**) □ *vt* brechen; (*smash*) zerbrechen; (*damage*) kaputtmachen (*fam*); (*interrupt*) unterbrechen; ~ **one's arm** sich (*dat*) den Arm brechen □ *vi* brechen; ⟨*day:*⟩ anbrechen; ⟨*storm:*⟩ losbrechen; ⟨*thing:*⟩ kaputtgehen (*fam*); ⟨*rope, thread:*⟩ reißen; ⟨*news:*⟩ bekannt werden; **his voice is ~ing** er ist im Stimmbruch. ~ **away** *vi* sich losreißen/(*fig*) sich absetzen (**from** von). ~ **down** *vi* zusammenbrechen; (*Techn*) eine Panne haben; ⟨*negotiations:*⟩ scheitern □ *vt* aufbrechen ⟨*door*⟩; aufgliedern ⟨*figures*⟩. ~ **in** *vi* einbrechen. ~ **off** *vt/i* abbrechen; lösen ⟨*engagement*⟩. ~ **out** *vi* ausbrechen. ~ **up** *vt* zerbrechen □ *vi* ⟨*crowd:*⟩ sich zerstreuen; ⟨*marriage, couple:*⟩ auseinander gehen; (*Sch*) Ferien bekommen

break|able /ˈbreɪkəbl/ *a* zerbrechlich. **~age** /-ɪdʒ/ *n* Bruch *m*. **~down** *n* (*Techn*) Panne *f*; (*Med*) Zusammenbruch *m*; (*of figures*) Aufgliederung *f*. **~er** *n* (*wave*) Brecher *m*

breakfast /ˈbrekfəst/ *n* Frühstück *nt*

break: ~through *n* Durchbruch *m*. **~water** *n* Buhne *f*

breast /brest/ *n* Brust *f*. **~bone** *n* Brustbein *nt*. **~-feed** *vt* stillen. **~-stroke** *n* Brustschwimmen *nt*

breath /breθ/ *n* Atem *m*; **out of ~** außer Atem; **under one's ~** vor sich (*acc*) hin

breathalyse /ˈbreθəlaɪz/ *vt* ins Röhrchen blasen lassen. **~r (P)** *n* Röhrchen *nt*. **~r test** *n* Alcotest (P) *m*

breathe /bri:ð/ *vt/i* atmen. ~ **in** *vt/i* einatmen. ~ **out** *vt/i* ausatmen

breath|er /ˈbri:ðə(r)/ *n* Atempause *f*. **~ing** *n* Atmen *nt*

breath /ˈbreθ-/: **~less** *a* atemlos. **~-taking** *a* atemberaubend. **~ test** *n* Alcotest (P) *m*

bred /bred/ *see* **breed**

breeches /ˈbrɪtʃɪz/ *npl* Kniehose *f*; (*for riding*) Reithose *f*

breed /bri:d/ *n* Rasse *f* □ *v* (*pt/pp* **bred**) □ *vt* züchten; (*give rise to*) erzeugen □ *vi* sich vermehren. **~er** *n* Züchter *m*. **~ing** *n* Zucht *f*; (*fig*) [gute] Lebensart *f*

breez|e /bri:z/ *n* Lüftchen *nt*; (*Naut*) Brise *f*. **~y** *a* [leicht] windig

brevity /ˈbrevətɪ/ *n* Kürze *f*

brew /bru:/ *n* Gebräu *nt* □ *vt* brauen; kochen ⟨*tea*⟩ □ *vi* (*fig*) sich zusammenbrauen. **~er** *n* Brauer *m*. **~ery** *n* Brauerei *f*

bribe /braɪb/ *n* (*money*) Bestechungsgeld *nt* □ *vt* bestechen. **~ry** /-ərɪ/ *n* Bestechung *f*

brick /brɪk/ *n* Ziegelstein *m*, Backstein *m* □ *vt* ~ **up** zumauern

ˈ**bricklayer** *n* Maurer *m*

bridal /ˈbraɪdl/ *a* Braut-

bride /braɪd/ *n* Braut *f*. **~groom** *n* Bräutigam *m*. **~smaid** *n* Brautjungfer *f*

bridge[1] /brɪdʒ/ *n* Brücke *f*; (*of nose*) Nasenrücken *m*; (*of spectacles*) Steg *m* □ *vt* (*fig*) überbrücken

bridge[2] *n* (*Cards*) Bridge *nt*

bridle /ˈbraɪdl/ *n* Zaum *m*. **~-path** *n* Reitweg *m*

brief[1] /bri:f/ *a* (**-er, -est**) kurz; **be ~** ⟨*person:*⟩ sich kurz fassen

brief[2] *n* Instruktionen *pl*; (*Jur: case*) Mandat *nt* □ *vt* Instruktionen geben (+ *dat*); (*Jur*) beauftragen. **~case** *n* Aktentasche *f*

brief|ing /ˈbri:fɪŋ/ *n* Informationsgespräch *nt*. **~ly** *adv* kurz. **~ness** *n* Kürze *f*

briefs /bri:fs/ *npl* Slip *m*
brigad|e /brɪˈgeɪd/ *n* Brigade *f*. **~ier** /-əˈdɪə(r)/ *n* Brigadegeneral *m*
bright /braɪt/ *a* (**-er, -est**), **-ly** *adv* hell; ⟨*day*⟩ heiter; **~ red** hellrot
bright|en /ˈbraɪtn/ *v* **~en [up]** □ *vt* aufheitern □ *vi* sich aufheitern. **~ness** *n* Helligkeit *f*
brilliance /ˈbrɪljəns/ *n* Glanz *m*; (*of person*) Genialität *f*
brilliant /ˈbrɪljənt/ *a*, **-ly** *adv* glänzend; ⟨*person*⟩ genial
brim /brɪm/ *n* Rand *m*; (*of hat*) Krempe *f* □ *vi* (*pt/pp* **brimmed**) **~ over** überfließen
brine /braɪn/ *n* Salzwasser *nt*; (*Culin*) [Salz]lake *f*
bring /brɪŋ/ *vt* (*pt/pp* **brought**) bringen; **~ them with you** bring sie mit; **I can't b~ myself to do it** ich bringe es nicht fertig. **~ about** *vt* verursachen. **~ along** *vt* mitbringen. **~ back** *vt* zurückbringen. **~ down** *vt* herunterbringen; senken ⟨*price*⟩. **~ off** *vt* vollbringen. **~ on** *vt* (*cause*) verursachen. **~ out** *vt* herausbringen. **~ round** *vt* vorbeibringen; (*persuade*) überreden; wieder zum Bewusstsein bringen ⟨*unconscious person*⟩. **~ up** *vt* heraufbringen; (*vomit*) erbrechen; aufziehen ⟨*children*⟩; erwähnen ⟨*question*⟩
brink /brɪŋk/ *n* Rand *m*
brisk /brɪsk/ *a* (**-er, -est,**), **-ly** *adv* lebhaft; (*quick*) schnell
brist|le /ˈbrɪsl/ *n* Borste *f*. **~ly** *a* borstig
Brit|ain /ˈbrɪtn/ *n* Großbritannien *nt*. **~ish** *a* britisch; **the ~ish** die Briten *pl*. **~on** *n* Brite *m*/Britin *f*
Brittany /ˈbrɪtənɪ/ *n* die Bretagne
brittle /ˈbrɪtl/ *a* brüchig, spröde
broach /brəʊtʃ/ *vt* anzapfen; anschneiden ⟨*subject*⟩
broad /brɔːd/ *a* (**-er, -est**) breit; ⟨*hint*⟩ deutlich; **in ~ daylight** am helllichten Tag. **~ beans** *npl* dicke Bohnen *pl*
ˈ**broadcast** *n* Sendung *f* □ *vt/i* (*pt/pp* **-cast**) senden. **~er** *n* Rundfunk- und Fernsehpersönlichkeit *f*. **~ing** *n* Funk und Fernsehen *pl*
broaden /ˈbrɔːdn/ *vt* verbreitern; (*fig*) erweitern □ *vi* sich verbreitern
broadly /ˈbrɔːdlɪ/ *adv* breit; **~ speaking** allgemein gesagt
broadˈ**minded** *a* tolerant
brocade /brəˈkeɪd/ *n* Brokat *m*
broccoli /ˈbrɒkəlɪ/ *n inv* Brokkoli *pl*
brochure /ˈbrəʊʃə(r)/ *n* Broschüre *f*
brogue /brəʊg/ *n* (*shoe*) Wanderschuh *m*; **Irish ~** irischer Akzent *m*
broke /brəʊk/ *see* **break** □ *a* (*fam*) pleite
broken /ˈbrəʊkn/ *see* **break** □ *a* zerbrochen, (*fam*) kaputt; **~ English** gebrochenes Englisch *nt*. **~-hearted** *a* untröstlich
broker /ˈbrəʊkə(r)/ *n* Makler *m*
brolly /ˈbrɒlɪ/ *n* (*fam*) Schirm *m*
bronchitis /brɒŋˈkaɪtɪs/ *n* Bronchitis *f*
bronze /brɒnz/ *n* Bronze *f*
brooch /brəʊtʃ/ *n* Brosche *f*
brood /bruːd/ *n* Brut *f* □ *vi* brüten; (*fig*) grübeln
brook[1] /brʊk/ *n* Bach *m*
brook[2] *vt* dulden
broom /bruːm/ *n* Besen *m*; (*Bot*) Ginster *m*. **~stick** *n* Besenstiel *m*
broth /brɒθ/ *n* Brühe *f*
brothel /ˈbrɒθl/ *n* Bordell *nt*
brother /ˈbrʌðə(r)/ *n* Bruder *m*
brother: ~-in-law *n* (*pl* **-s-in-law**) Schwager *m*. **~ly** *a* brüderlich
brought /brɔːt/ *see* **bring**
brow /braʊ/ *n* Augenbraue *f*; (*forehead*) Stirn *f*; (*of hill*) [Berg]kuppe *f*

ˈbrowbeat *vt* (*pt* **-beat**, *pp* **-beaten**) einschüchtern
brown /braʊn/ *a* (**-er, -est**) braun; **~ ˈpaper** Packpapier *nt* □ *n* Braun *nt* □ *vt* bräunen □ *vi* braun werden
Brownie /ˈbraʊnɪ/ *n* Wichtel *m*
browse /braʊz/ *vi* (*read*) schmökern; (*in shop*) sich umsehen
bruise /bruːz/ *n* blauer Fleck *m* □ *vt* beschädigen ⟨*fruit*⟩; **~ one's arm** sich (*dat*) den Arm quetschen
brunch /brʌntʃ/ *n* Brunch *m*
brunette /bruːˈnet/ *n* Brünette *f*
Brunswick /ˈbrʌnzwɪk/ *n* Braunschweig *nt*
brunt /brʌnt/ *n* **the ~ of** die volle Wucht (+ *gen*)
brush /brʌʃ/ *n* Bürste *f*; (*with handle*) Handfeger *m*; (*for paint, pastry*) Pinsel *m*; (*bushes*) Unterholz *nt*; (*fig: conflict*) Zusammenstoß *m* □ *vt* bürsten putzen ⟨*teeth*⟩; **~ against** streifen [gegen]; **~ aside** (*fig*) abtun. **~ off** *vt* abbürsten; (*reject*) zurückweisen. **~ up** *vt/i* (*fig*) **~ up [on]** auffrischen
brusque /brʊsk/ *a*, **-ly** *adv* brüsk
Brussels /ˈbrʌslz/ *n* Brüssel *nt*. **~ sprouts** *npl* Rosenkohl *m*
brutal /ˈbruːtl/ *a*, **-ly** *adv* brutal. **~ity** /-ˈtælətɪ/ *n* Brutalität *f*
brute /bruːt/ *n* Unmensch *m*. **~ force** *n* rohe Gewalt *f*
B.Sc. *abbr of* **Bachelor of Science**
bubble /ˈbʌbl/ *n* [Luft]blase *f* □ *vi* sprudeln
buck[1] /bʌk/ *n* (*deer & Gym*) Bock *m*; (*rabbit*) Rammler *m* □ *vi* ⟨*horse:*⟩ bocken. **~ up** *vi* (*fam*) sich aufheitern; (*hurry*) sich beeilen
buck[2] *n* (*Amer, fam*) Dollar *m*
buck[3] *n* **pass the ~** die Verantwortung abschieben
bucket /ˈbʌkɪt/ *n* Eimer *m*
buckle /ˈbʌkl/ *n* Schnalle *f* □ *vt* zuschnallen □ *vi* sich verbiegen
bud /bʌd/ *n* Knospe *f* □ *vi* (*pt/pp* **budded**) knospen
Buddhis|m /ˈbʊdɪzm/ *n* Buddhismus *m*. **~t** *a* buddhistisch □ *n* Buddhist(in) *m(f)*
buddy /ˈbʌdɪ/ *n* (*fam*) Freund *m*
budge /bʌdʒ/ *vt* bewegen □ *vi* sich [von der Stelle] rühren
budgerigar /ˈbʌdʒərɪgɑː(r)/ *n* Wellensittich *m*
budget /ˈbʌdʒɪt/ *n* Budget *nt*; (*Pol*) Haushaltsplan *m*; (*money available*) Etat *m* □ *vi* (*pt/pp* **budgeted**) **~ for sth etw** einkalkulieren
buff /bʌf/ *a* (*colour*) sandfarben □ *n* Sandfarbe *f*; (*Amer, fam*) Fan *m* □ *vt* polieren
buffalo /ˈbʌfələʊ/ *n* (*inv or pl* **-es**) Büffel *m*
buffer /ˈbʌfə(r)/ *n* (*Rail*) Puffer *m*; **old ~** (*fam*) alter Knacker *m*; **~ zone** Pufferzone *f*
buffet[1] /ˈbʊfeɪ/ *n* Büfett *nt*, (*on station*) Imbissstube *f*
buffet[2] /ˈbʌfɪt/ *vt* (*pt/pp* **buffeted**) hin und her werfen
buffoon /bəˈfuːn/ *n* Narr *m*
bug /bʌg/ *n* Wanze *f*; (*fam: virus*) Bazillus *m*; (*fam: device*) Abhörgerät *nt*, (*fam*) Wanze *f* □ *vt* (*pt/pp* **bugged**) (*fam*) verwanzen ⟨*room*⟩; abhören ⟨*telephone*⟩; (*Amer: annoy*) ärgern
buggy /ˈbʌgɪ/ *n* [Kinder]sportwagen *m*
bugle /ˈbjuːgl/ *n* Signalhorn *m*
build /bɪld/ *n* (*of person*) Körperbau *m* □ *vt/i* (*pt/pp* **built**) bauen. **~ on** *vt* anbauen (**to** an + *acc*). **~ up** *vt* aufbauen □ *vi* zunehmen; ⟨*traffic:*⟩ sich stauen
builder /ˈbɪldə(r)/ *n* Bauunternehmer *m*
building /ˈbɪldɪŋ/ *n* Gebäude *nt*. **~ site** *n* Baustelle *f*. **~ society** *n* Bausparkasse *f*

built /bɪlt/ *see* **build. ~-in** *a* eingebaut. **~-in 'cupboard** *n* Einbauschrank *m*. **~-up area** *n* bebautes Gebiet *nt*; (*Auto*) geschlossene Ortschaft *f*

bulb /bʌlb/ *n* [Blumen]zwiebel *f*; (*Electr*) [Glüh]birne *f*

bulbous /'bʌlbəs/ *a* bauchig

Bulgaria /bʌl'geərɪə/ *n* Bulgarien *nt*

bulg|e /bʌldʒ/ *n* Ausbauchung *f* □ *vi* sich ausbauchen. **~ing** *a* prall; ⟨*eyes*⟩ hervorquellend; **~ing with** prall gefüllt mit

bulk /bʌlk/ *n* Masse *f*; (*greater part*) Hauptteil *m*; **in ~** en gros; (*loose*) lose. **~y** *a* sperrig; (*large*) massig

bull /bʊl/ *n* Bulle *m*, Stier *m*

'bulldog *n* Bulldogge *f*

bulldozer /'bʊldəʊzə(r)/ *n* Planierraupe *f*

bullet /'bʊlɪt/ *n* Kugel *f*

bulletin /'bʊlɪtɪn/ *n* Bulletin *nt*

'bullet-proof *a* kugelsicher

'bullfight *n* Stierkampf *m*. **~er** *n* Stierkämpfer *m*

'bullfinch *n* Dompfaff *m*

bullion /'bʊlɪən/ *n* **gold ~** Barrengold *nt*

bullock /'bʊlək/ *n* Ochse *m*

bull: ~ring *n* Stierkampfarena *f*. **~'s-eye** *n* **score a ~'s-eye** ins Schwarze treffen

bully /'bʊlɪ/ *n* Tyrann *m* □ *vt* tyrannisieren

bum[1] /bʌm/ *n* (*sl*) Hintern *m*

bum[2] *n* (*Amer, fam*) Landstreicher *m*

bumble-bee /'bʌmbl-/ *n* Hummel *f*

bump /bʌmp/ *n* Bums *m*; (*swelling*) Beule *f*; (*in road*) holperige Stelle *f* □ *vt* stoßen; **~ into** stoßen gegen; (*meet*) zufällig treffen. **~ off** *vt* (*fam*) um die Ecke bringen

bumper /'bʌmpə(r)/ *a* Rekord- □ *n* (*Auto*) Stoßstange *f*

bumpkin /'bʌmpkɪn/ *n* **country ~** Tölpel *m*

bumptious /'bʌmpʃəs/ *a* aufgeblasen

bumpy /'bʌmpɪ/ *a* holperig

bun /bʌn/ *n* Milchbrötchen *nt*; (*hair*) [Haar]knoten *m*

bunch /bʌntʃ/ *n* (*of flowers*) Strauß *m*; (*of radishes, keys*) Bund *m*; (*of people*) Gruppe *f*; **~ of grapes** [ganze] Weintraube *f*

bundle /'bʌndl/ *n* Bündel *nt* □ *vt* **~ [up]** bündeln

bung /bʌŋ/ *vt* (*fam*) (*throw*) schmeißen. **~ up** *vt* (*fam*) verstopfen

bungalow /'bʌŋgələʊ/ *n* Bungalow *m*

bungle /'bʌŋgl/ *vt* verpfuschen

bunion /'bʌnjən/ *n* (*Med*) Ballen *m*

bunk /bʌŋk/ *n* [Schlaf]koje *f*. **~-beds** *npl* Etagenbett *nt*

bunker /'bʌŋkə(r)/ *n* Bunker *m*

bunkum /'bʌŋkəm/ *n* Quatsch *m*

bunny /'bʌnɪ/ *n* (*fam*) Kaninchen *nt*

buoy /bɔɪ/ *n* Boje *f*. **~ up** *vt* (*fig*) stärken

buoyan|cy /'bɔɪənsɪ/ *n* Auftrieb *m*. **~t** *a* **be ~t** schwimmen; ⟨*water:*⟩ gut tragen

burden /'bɜːdn/ *n* Last *f* □ *vt* belasten. **~some** /-səm/ *a* lästig

bureau /'bjʊərəʊ/ *n* (*pl* **-x** /-əʊz/ *or* **~s**) (*desk*) Sekretär *m*; (*office*) Büro *nt*

bureaucracy /bjʊə'rɒkrəsɪ/ *n* Bürokratie *f*

bureaucrat /'bjʊərəkræt/ *n* Bürokrat *m*. **~ic** /-'krætɪk/ *a* bürokratisch

burger /'bɜːgə(r)/ *n* Hamburger *m*

burglar /'bɜːglə(r)/ *n* Einbrecher *m*. **~ alarm** *n* Alarmanlage *f*

burglar|ize /'bɜːgləraɪz/ *vt* (*Amer*) einbrechen in (+ *acc*). **~y** *n* Einbruch *m*

burgle /'bɜːgl/ *vt* einbrechen in (+ *acc*); **they have been ~d** bei ihnen ist eingebrochen worden

Burgundy /ˈbɜːgəndɪ/ *n* Burgund *nt*; **b~** (*wine*) Burgunder *m*
burial /ˈberɪəl/ *n* Begräbnis *nt*
burlesque /bɜːˈlesk/ *n* Burleske *f*
burly /ˈbɜːlɪ/ *a* (**-ier, -iest**) stämmig
Burm|a /ˈbɜːmə/ *n* Birma *nt*. **~ese** /-ˈmiːz/ *a* birmanisch
burn /bɜːn/ *n* Verbrennung *f*; (*on skin*) **Brandwunde** *f*; (*on material*) **Brandstelle** *f* □ *v* (*pt/pp* **burnt** *or* **burned**) □ *vt* verbrennen □ *vi* brennen; ⟨*food:*⟩ anbrennen. **~ down** *vt/i* niederbrennen
burnish /ˈbɜːnɪʃ/ *vt* polieren
burnt /bɜːnt/ *see* **burn**
burp /bɜːp/ *vi* (*fam*) aufstoßen
burrow /ˈbʌrəʊ/ *n* Bau *m* □ *vi* wühlen
bursar /ˈbɜːsə(r)/ *n* Rechnungsführer *m*. **~y** *n* Stipendium *nt*
burst /bɜːst/ *n* Bruch *m*; (*surge*) Ausbruch *m* □ *v* (*pt/pp* **burst**) □ *vt* platzen machen □ *vi* platzen; ⟨*bud:*⟩ aufgehen; **~ into tears** in Tränen ausbrechen
bury /ˈberɪ/ *vt* (*pt/pp* **-ied**) begraben; (*hide*) vergraben
bus /bʌs/ *n* [Auto]bus *m* □ *vt/i* (*pt/pp* **bussed**) mit dem Bus fahren
bush /bʊʃ/ *n* Strauch *m*; (*land*) Busch *m*. **~y** *a* (**-ier, -iest**) buschig
busily /ˈbɪzɪlɪ/ *adv* eifrig
business /ˈbɪznɪs/ *n* Angelegenheit *f*; (*Comm*) Geschäft *nt*; **on ~** geschäftlich; **he has no ~** er hat kein Recht (**to** zu); **mind one's own ~** sich um seine eigenen Angelegenheiten kümmern; **that's none of your ~** das geht Sie nichts an. **~-like** *a* geschäftsmäßig. **~man** *n* Geschäftsmann *m*
busker /ˈbʌskə(r)/ *n* Straßenmusikant *m*
ˈ**bus-stop** *n* Bushaltestelle *f*
bust[1] /bʌst/ *n* Büste *f*. **~ size** *n* Oberweite *f*
bust[2] *a* (*fam*) kaputt; **go ~** Pleite gehen □ *v* (*pt/pp* **busted** *or* **bust**) (*fam*) □ *vt* kaputtmachen □ *vt* kaputtgehen
bustl|e /ˈbʌsl/ *n* Betrieb *m*, Getriebe *nt* □ *vi* **~e about** geschäftig hin und her laufen. **~ing** *a* belebt
ˈ**bust-up** *n* (*fam*) Streit *m*, Krach *m*
busy /ˈbɪzɪ/ *a* (**-ier, -iest**) beschäftigt; ⟨*day*⟩ voll; ⟨*street*⟩ belebt; (*with traffic*) stark befahren; (*Amer Teleph*) besetzt; **be ~** zu tun haben □ *vt* **~ oneself** sich beschäftigen (**with** mit)
ˈ**busybody** *n* Wichtigtuer(in) *m*(*f*)
but /bʌt, *unbetont* bət/ *conj* aber; (*after negative*) sondern □ *prep* außer (+ *dat*); **~ for** (*without*) ohne (+ *acc*); **the last ~ one** der/die/das vorletzte; **the next ~ one** der/die/das übernächste □ *adv* nur
butcher /ˈbʊtʃə(r)/ *n* Fleischer *m*, Metzger *m*; **~'s [shop]** Fleischerei *f*, Metzgerei *f* □ *vt* [ab]schlachten
butler /ˈbʌtlə(r)/ *n* Butler *m*
butt /bʌt/ *n* (*of gun*) [Gewehr]kolben *m*; (*fig: target*) Zielscheibe *f*; (*of cigarette*) Stummel *m*; (*for water*) Regentonne *f* □ *vt* mit dem Kopf stoßen □ *vi* **~ in** unterbrechen
butter /ˈbʌtə(r)/ *n* Butter *f* □ *vt* mit Butter bestreichen. **~ up** *vt* (*fam*) schmeicheln (+ *dat*)
butter: **~cup** *a* Butterblume *f*, Hahnenfuß *m*. **~fly** *n* Schmetterling *m*
buttocks /ˈbʌtəks/ *npl* Gesäß *nt*
button /ˈbʌtn/ *n* Knopf *m* □ *vt* **~ [up]** zuknöpfen □ *vi* geknöpft werden. **~hole** *n* Knopfloch *nt*
buttress /ˈbʌtrɪs/ *n* Strebepfeiler *m*; **flying ~** Strebebogen *m*
buxom /ˈbʌksəm/ *a* drall

buy /baɪ/ *n* Kauf *m* □ *vt* (*pt/pp* **bought**) kaufen. **~er** *n* Käufer(in) *m(f)*
buzz /bʌz/ *n* Summen *nt* □ *vi* summen. **~ off** *vi* (*fam*) abhauen
buzzard /ˈbʌzəd/ *n* Bussard *m*
buzzer /ˈbʌzə(r)/ *n* Summer *m*
by /baɪ/ *prep* (*close to*) bei (+ *dat*); (*next to*) neben (+ *dat/acc*); (*past*) an (+ *dat*) ... vorbei; (*to the extent of*) um (+ *acc*); (*at the latest*) bis; (*by means of*) durch; **by Mozart/Dickens** von Mozart/Dickens; **~ oneself** allein; **~ the sea** am Meer; **~ car/bus** mit dem Auto/Bus; **~ sea** mit dem Schiff; **~ day/night** bei Tag/Nacht; **~ the hour** pro Stunde; **~ the metre** meterweise; **six metres ~ four** sechs mal vier Meter; **win ~ a length** mit einer Länge Vorsprung gewinnen; **miss the train ~ a minute** den Zug um eine Minute verpassen □ *adv* **~ and ~** mit der Zeit; **~ and large** im Großen und Ganzen; **put ~** beiseite legen; **go/pass ~** vorbeigehen
bye /baɪ/ *int* (*fam*) tschüs
by: **~-election** *n* Nachwahl *f*. **~gone** *a* vergangen. **~-law** *n* Verordnung *f*. **~pass** *n* Umgehungsstraße *f*; (*Med*) Bypass *m* □ *vt* umfahren. **~-product** *n* Nebenprodukt *m*. **~-road** *n* Nebenstraße *f*. **~stander** *n* Zuschauer(in) *m(f)*
Byzantine /brˈzæntaɪn/ *a* byzantinisch

C

cab /kæb/ *n* Taxi *nt*; (*of lorry, train*) Führerhaus *nt*
cabaret /ˈkæbəreɪ/ *n* Kabarett *nt*
cabbage /ˈkæbɪdʒ/ *n* Kohl *m*
cabin /ˈkæbɪn/ *n* Kabine *f*; (*hut*) Hütte *f*
cabinet /ˈkæbɪnɪt/ *n* Schrank *m*; **[display] ~** Vitrine *f*; (*TV, Radio*) Gehäuse *nt*; **C~** (*Pol*) Kabinett *nt*. **~-maker** *n* Möbeltischler *m*
cable /ˈkeɪbl/ *n* Kabel *nt*; (*rope*) Tau *nt*. **~ ˈrailway** *n* Seilbahn *f*. **~ ˈtelevision** *n* Kabelfernsehen *nt*
cache /kæʃ/ *n* Versteck *nt*; **~ of arms** Waffenlager *nt*
cackle /ˈkækl/ *vi* gackern
cactus /ˈkæktəs/ *n* (*pl* **-ti** /-taɪ/ *or* **-tuses**) Kaktus *m*
caddie /ˈkædɪ/ *n* Caddie *m*
caddy /ˈkædɪ/ *n* **[tea-]~** Teedose *f*
cadet /kəˈdet/ *n* Kadett *m*
cadge /kædʒ/ *vt/i* (*fam*) schnorren
Caesarean /sɪˈzeərɪən/ *a* & *n* **~ [section]** Kaiserschnitt *m*
café /ˈkæfeɪ/ *n* Café *nt*
cafeteria /kæfəˈtɪərɪə/ *n* Selbstbedienungsrestaurant *nt*
caffeine /ˈkæfiːn/ *n* Koffein *nt*
cage /keɪdʒ/ *n* Käfig *m*
cagey /ˈkeɪdʒɪ/ *a* (*fam*) **be ~** mit der Sprache nicht herauswollen
cajole /kəˈdʒəʊl/ *vt* gut zureden (+ *dat*)
cake /keɪk/ *n* Kuchen *m*; (*of soap*) Stück *nt*. **~d** *a* verkrustet (**with** mit)
calamity /kəˈlæmətɪ/ *n* Katastrophe *f*
calcium /ˈkælsɪəm/ *n* Kalzium *nt*
calculat|e /ˈkælkjʊleɪt/ *vt* berechnen; (*estimate*) kalkulieren. **~ing** *a* (*fig*) berechnend. **~ion** /-ˈleɪʃn/ *n* Rechnung *f*, Kalkulation *f*. **~or** *n* Rechner *m*
calendar /ˈkælɪndə(r)/ *n* Kalender *m*
calf[1] /kɑːf/ *n* (*pl* **calves**) Kalb *nt*
calf[2] *n* (*pl* **calves**) (*Anat*) Wade *f*
calibre /ˈkælɪbə(r)/ *n* Kaliber *nt*
calico /ˈkælɪkəʊ/ *n* Kattun *m*
call /kɔːl/ *n* Ruf *m*; (*Teleph*) Anruf *m*; (*visit*) Besuch *m*; **be on ~** 〈*doctor:*〉 Bereitschaftsdienst haben

□ *vt* rufen; (*Teleph*) anrufen; (*wake*) wecken; ausrufen ⟨*strike*⟩ (*name*) nennen; **be ~ed** heißen □ *vi* rufen; **~ [in** *or* **round]** vorbeikommen. **~ back** *vt* zurückrufen □ *vi* noch einmal vorbeikommen. **~ for** *vt* rufen nach; (*demand*) verlangen; (*fetch*) abholen. **~ off** *vt* zurückrufen ⟨*dog*⟩; (*cancel*) absagen. **~ on** *vt* bitten (**for** um); (*appeal to*) appellieren an (+ *acc*); (*visit*) besuchen. **~ out** *vt* rufen; aufrufen ⟨*names*⟩ □ *vi* rufen. **~ up** *vt* (*Mil*) einberufen; (*Teleph*) anrufen

call: ~-box *n* Telefonzelle *f*. **~er** *n* Besucher *m*; (*Teleph*) Anrufer *m*. **~ing** *n* Berufung *f*

callous /ˈkæləs/ *a* gefühllos

'call-up *n* (*Mil*) Einberufung *f*

calm /kɑ:m/ *a* (**-er, -est**), **-ly** *adv* ruhig □ *n* Ruhe *f* □ *vt* **~ [down]** beruhigen □ *vi* **~ down** sich beruhigen. **~ness** *n* Ruhe *f*; (*of sea*) Stille *f*

calorie /ˈkælərɪ/ *n* Kalorie *f*

calves /kɑ:vz/ *npl see* **calf**[1] & [2]

camber /ˈkæmbə(r)/ *n* Wölbung *f*

came /keɪm/ *see* **come**

camel /ˈkæml/ *n* Kamel *nt*

camera /ˈkæmərə/ *n* Kamera *f*. **~man** *n* Kameramann *m*

camouflage /ˈkæməflɑ:ʒ/ *n* Tarnung *f* □ *vt* tarnen

camp /kæmp/ *n* Lager *nt* □ *vi* campen; (*Mil*) kampieren

campaign /kæmˈpeɪn/ *n* Feldzug *m*; (*Comm, Pol*) Kampagne *f* □ *vi* kämpfen; (*pol*) im Wahlkampf arbeiten

camp: ~-bed *n* Feldbett *nt*. **~er** *n* Camper *m*; (*Auto*) Wohnmobil *nt*. **~ing** *n* Camping *nt*. **~site** *n* Campingplatz *m*

campus /ˈkæmpəs/ *n* (*pl* **-puses**) (*Univ*) Campus *m*

can[1] /kæn/ *n* (*for petrol*) Kanister *m*; (*tin*) Dose *f*, Büchse *f*; **a ~ of beer** eine Dose Bier □ *vt* in Dosen *od* Büchsen konservieren

can[2] /kæn, *unbetont* kən/ *v aux* (*pres* **can**; *pt* **could**) können; **I cannot/can't go** ich kann nicht gehen; **he could not go** er konnte nicht gehen; **if I could go** wenn ich gehen könnte

Canad|a /ˈkænədə/ *n* Kanada *nt*. **~ian** /kəˈneɪdɪən/ *a* kanadisch □ *n* Kanadier(in) *m(f)*

canal /kəˈnæl/ *n* Kanal *m*

Canaries /kəˈneərɪz/ *npl* Kanarische Inseln *pl*

canary /kəˈneərɪ/ *n* Kanarienvogel *m*

cancel /ˈkænsl/ *vt/i* (*pt/pp* **cancelled**) absagen; entwerten ⟨*stamp*⟩; (*annul*) rückgängig machen; (*Comm*) stornieren; abbestellen ⟨*newspaper*⟩; **be ~led** ausfallen. **~lation** /-əˈleɪʃn/ *n* Absage *f*

cancer /ˈkænsə(r)/ *n*, & (*Astr*) **C~** Krebs *m*. **~ous** /-rəs/ *a* krebsig

candelabra /kændəˈlɑ:brə/ *n* Armleuchter *m*

candid /ˈkændɪd/ *a*, **-ly** *adv* offen

candidate /ˈkændɪdət/ *n* Kandidat(in) *m(f)*

candied /ˈkændɪd/ *a* kandiert

candle /ˈkændl/ *n* Kerze *f*. **~stick** *n* Kerzenständer *m*, Leuchter *m*

candour /ˈkændə(r)/ *n* Offenheit *f*

candy /ˈkændɪ/ *n* (*Amer*) Süßigkeiten *pl*; **[piece of] ~** Bonbon *m*. **~floss** /-flɒs/ *n* Zuckerwatte *f*

cane /keɪn/ *n* Rohr *nt*; (*stick*) Stock *m* □ *vt* mit dem Stock züchtigen

canine /ˈkeɪnaɪn/ *a* Hunde-. **~ tooth** *n* Eckzahn *m*

canister /ˈkænɪstə(r)/ *n* Blechdose *f*

cannabis /ˈkænəbɪs/ *n* Haschisch *nt*

canned /kænd/ *a* Dosen-, Büchsen-; **~ music** (*fam*) Musik *f* aus der Konserve

cannibal /ˈkænɪbl/ *n* Kannibale *m*. **~ism** /-bəlɪzm/ *n* Kannibalismus *m*

cannon /ˈkænən/ *n inv* Kanone *f*. **~ball** *n* Kanonenkugel *f*
cannot /ˈkænɒt/ *see* **can**[2]
canny /ˈkænɪ/ *a* schlau
canoe /kəˈnuː/ *n* Paddelboot *nt*; (*Sport*) Kanu *nt* □ *vi* paddeln; (*Sport*) Kanu fahren
canon /ˈkænən/ *n* Kanon *m*; (*person*) Kanonikus *m*. **~ize** /-aɪz/ *vt* kanonisieren
ˈ**can-opener** *n* Dosenöffner *m*, Büchsenöffner *m*
canopy /ˈkænəpɪ/ *n* Baldachin *m*
cant /kænt/ *n* Heuchelei *f*
can't /kɑːnt/ = **cannot.** *See* **can**[2]
cantankerous /kænˈtæŋkərəs/ *a* zänkisch
canteen /kænˈtiːn/ *n* Kantine *f*; **~ of cutlery** Besteckkasten *m*
canter /ˈkæntə(r)/ *n* Kanter *m* □ *vi* kantern
canvas /ˈkænvəs/ *n* Segeltuch *nt*; (*Art*) Leinwand *f*; (*painting*) Gemälde *nt*
canvass /ˈkænvəs/ *vi* um Stimmen werben
canyon /ˈkænjən/ *n* Cañon *m*
cap /kæp/ *n* Kappe *f*, Mütze *f*; (*nurse's*) Haube *f*; (*top, lid*) Verschluss *m* □ *vt* (*pt/pp* **capped**) (*fig*) übertreffen
capability /keɪpəˈbɪlətɪ/ *n* Fähigkeit *f*
capable /ˈkeɪpəbl/ *a*, **-bly** *adv* fähig; **be ~ of doing sth** fähig sein, etw zu tun
capacity /kəˈpæsətɪ/ *n* Fassungsvermögen *nt*; (*ability*) Fähigkeit *f*; **in my ~ as** in meiner Eigenschaft als
cape[1] /keɪp/ *n* (*cloak*) Cape *nt*
cape[2] *n* (*Geog*) Kap *nt*
caper[1] /ˈkeɪpə(r)/ *vi* herumspringen
caper[2] *n* (*Culin*) Kaper *f*
capital /ˈkæpɪtl/ *a* ⟨*letter*⟩ groß □ *n* (*town*) Hauptstadt *f*; (*money*) Kapital *nt*; (*letter*) Großbuchstabe *m*
capital|ism /ˈkæpɪtəlɪzm/ *n* Kapitalismus *m*. **~ist** /-ɪst/ *a* kapitalistisch □ *n* Kapitalist *m*. **~ize** /-aɪz/ *vi* **~ize on** (*fig*) Kapital schlagen aus. **~** ˈ**letter** *n* Großbuchstabe *m*. **~** ˈ**punishment** *n* Todesstrafe *f*
capitulat|e /kəˈpɪtjʊleɪt/ *vi* kapitulieren. **~ion** /-ˈleɪʃn/ *n* Kapitulation *f*
capricious /kəˈprɪʃəs/ *a* launisch
Capricorn /ˈkæprɪkɔːn/ *n* (*Astr*) Steinbock *m*
capsize /kæpˈsaɪz/ *vi* kentern □ *vt* zum Kentern bringen
capsule /ˈkæpsjʊl/ *n* Kapsel *f*
captain /ˈkæptɪn/ *n* Kapitän *m*; (*Mil*) Hauptmann *m* □ *vt* anführen ⟨*team*⟩
caption /ˈkæpʃn/ *n* Überschrift *f*; (*of illustration*) Bildtext *m*
captivate /ˈkæptɪveɪt/ *vt* bezaubern
captiv|e /ˈkæptɪv/ *a* **hold/take ~e** gefangen halten/nehmen □ *n* Gefangene(r) *m/f*. **~ity** /-ˈtɪvətɪ/ *n* Gefangenschaft *f*
capture /ˈkæptʃə(r)/ *n* Gefangennahme *f* □ *vt* gefangen nehmen; [ein]fangen ⟨*animal*⟩; (*Mil*) einnehmen ⟨*town*⟩
car /kɑː(r)/ *n* Auto *nt*, Wagen *m*; **by ~** mit dem Auto *od* Wagen
carafe /kəˈræf/ *n* Karaffe *f*
caramel /ˈkærəmel/ *n* Karamell *m*
carat /ˈkærət/ *n* Karat *nt*
caravan /ˈkærəvæn/ *n* Wohnwagen *m*; (*procession*) Karawane *f*
carbohydrate /kɑːbəˈhaɪdreɪt/ *n* Kohlenhydrat *nt*
carbon /ˈkɑːbən/ *n* Kohlenstoff *m*; (*paper*) Kohlepapier *nt*; (*copy*) Durchschlag *m*
carbon: ~ copy *n* Durchschlag *m*. **~ diˈoxide** *n* Kohlendioxid *nt*; (*in drink*) Kohlensäure *f*. **~ paper** *n* Kohlepapier *nt*

carburettor /kɑ:bjʊ'retə(r)/ *n* Vergaser *m*
carcass /'kɑ:kəs/ *n* Kadaver *m*
card /kɑ:d/ *n* Karte *f*
'cardboard *n* Pappe *f*, Karton *m*. **~ 'box** *n* Pappschachtel *f*; (*large*) [Papp]karton *m*
'card-game *n* Kartenspiel *nt*
cardiac /'kɑ:dɪæk/ *a* Herz-
cardigan /'kɑ:dɪgən/ *n* Strickjacke *f*
cardinal /'kɑ:dɪnl/ *a* Kardinal-; **~ number** Kardinalzahl *f* □ *n* (*Relig*) Kardinal *m*
card 'index *n* Kartei *f*
care /keə(r)/ *n* Sorgfalt *f*; (*caution*) Vorsicht *f*; (*protection*) Obhut *f*; (*looking after*) Pflege *f*; (*worry*) Sorge *f*; **~ of** (*on letter abbr* **c/o**) bei; **take ~** vorsichtig sein; **take into ~** in Pflege nehmen; **take ~ of** sich kümmern um □ *vi* **~ about** sich kümmern um; **~ for** (*like*) mögen; (*look after*) betreuen; **I don't ~** das ist mir gleich
career /kə'rɪə(r)/ *n* Laufbahn *f*; (*profession*) Beruf *m* □ *vi* rasen
care: ~free *a* sorglos. **~ful** *a*, **-ly** *adv* sorgfältig; (*cautious*) vorsichtig. **~less** *a*, **-ly** *adv* nachlässig. **~lessness** *n* Nachlässigkeit *f*
caress /kə'res/ *n* Liebkosung *f* □ *vt* liebkosen
'caretaker *n* Hausmeister *m*
'car ferry *n* Autofähre *f*
cargo /'kɑ:gəʊ/ *n* (*pl* **-es**) Ladung *f*
Caribbean /kærɪ'bi:ən/ *n* **the ~** die Karibik
caricature /'kærɪkətjʊə(r)/ *n* Karikatur *f* □ *vt* karikieren
caring /'keərɪŋ/ *a* ⟨*parent*⟩ liebevoll; ⟨*profession, attitude*⟩ sozial
carnage /'kɑ:nɪdʒ/ *n* Gemetzel *nt*
carnal /'kɑ:nl/ *a* fleischlich
carnation /kɑ:'neɪʃn/ *n* Nelke *f*
carnival /'kɑ:nɪvl/ *n* Karneval *m*
carnivorous /kɑ:'nɪvərəs/ *a* Fleisch fressend

carol /'kærl/ *n* **[Christmas] ~** Weihnachtslied *nt*
carp¹ /kɑ:p/ *n inv* Karpfen *m*
carp² *vi* nörgeln; **~ at** herumnörgeln an (+ *dat*)
'car park *n* Parkplatz *m*; (*multistorey*) Parkhaus *nt*; (*underground*) Tiefgarage *f*
carpent|er /'kɑ:pɪntə(r)/ *n* Zimmermann *m*; (*joiner*) Tischler *m*. **~ry** *n* Tischlerei *f*
carpet /'kɑ:pɪt/ *n* Teppich *m* □ *vt* mit Teppich auslegen
carriage /'kærɪdʒ/ *n* Kutsche *f*; (*Rail*) Wagen *m*; (*of goods*) Beförderung *f*; (*cost*) Frachtkosten *pl*; (*bearing*) Haltung *f*. **~way** *n* Fahrbahn *f*
carrier /'kærɪə(r)/ *n* Träger(in) *m*(*f*); (*Comm*) Spediteur *m*; **~ [bag]** Tragetasche *f*
carrot /'kærət/ *n* Möhre *f*, Karotte *f*
carry /'kærɪ/ *vt/i* (*pt/pp* **-ied**) tragen; **be carried away** (*fam*) hingerissen sein. **~ off** *vt* wegtragen; gewinnen ⟨*prize*⟩. **~ on** *vi* weitermachen; **~ on at** (*fam*) herumnörgeln an (+ *dat*); **~ on with** (*fam*) eine Affäre haben mit □ *vt* führen; (*continue*) fortführen. **~ out** *vt* hinaus-/heraustragen; (*perform*) ausführen
'carry-cot *n* Babytragetasche *f*
cart /kɑ:t/ *n* Karren *m*; **put the ~ before the horse** das Pferd beim Schwanz aufzäumen □ *vt* karren; (*fam: carry*) schleppen
cartilage /'kɑ:tɪlɪdʒ/ *n* (*Anat*) Knorpel *m*
carton /'kɑ:tn/ *n* [Papp]karton *m*; (*for drink*) Tüte *f*; (*of cream, yoghurt*) Becher *m*
cartoon /kɑ:'tu:n/ *n* Karikatur *f*; (*joke*) Witzzeichnung *f*; (*strip*) Comic Strips *pl*; (*film*) Zeichentrickfilm *m*; (*Art*) Karton *m*. **~ist** *n* Karikaturist *m*

cartridge /ˈkɑːtrɪdʒ/ *n* Patrone *f*; (*for film, typewriter ribbon*) Kassette *f*; (*of record player*) Tonabnehmer *m*
carve /kɑːv/ *vt* schnitzen; (*in stone*) hauen; (*Culin*) aufschneiden
carving /ˈkɑːvɪŋ/ *n* Schnitzerei *f*. **~-knife** *n* Tranchiermesser *nt*
ˈcar wash *n* Autowäsche *f*; (*place*) Autowaschanlage *f*
case[1] /keɪs/ *n* Fall *m*; **in any ~** auf jeden Fall; **just in ~** für alle Fälle; **in ~ he comes** falls er kommt
case[2] *n* Kasten *m*; (*crate*) Kiste *f*; (*for spectacles*) Etui *nt*; (*suitcase*) Koffer *m*; (*for display*) Vitrine *f*
cash /kæʃ/ *n* Bargeld *nt*; **pay [in] ~** [in] bar bezahlen; **~ on delivery** per Nachnahme □ *vt* einlösen ⟨*cheque*⟩. **~ desk** *n* Kasse *f*
cashier /kæˈʃɪə(r)/ *n* Kassierer(in) *m*(*f*)
ˈcash register *n* Registrierkasse *f*
casino /kəˈsiːnəʊ/ *n* Kasino *nt*
cask /kɑːsk/ *n* Fass *nt*
casket /ˈkɑːskɪt/ *n* Kasten *m*; (*Amer: coffin*) Sarg *m*
casserole /ˈkæsərəʊl/ *n* Schmortopf *m*; (*stew*) Eintopf *m*
cassette /kəˈset/ *n* Kassette *f*. **~ recorder** *n* Kassettenrecorder *m*
cast /kɑːst/ *n* (*throw*) Wurf *m*; (*mould*) Form *f*; (*model*) Abguss *m*; (*Theat*) Besetzung *f*; **[plaster] ~** (*Med*) Gipsverband *m* □ *vt* (*pt/pp* **cast**) (*throw*) werfen; (*shed*) abwerfen; abgeben ⟨*vote*⟩; gießen ⟨*metal*⟩; (*Theat*) besetzen ⟨*role*⟩; **~ a glance at** einen Blick werfen auf (+ *acc*). **~ off** *vi* (*Naut*) ablegen □ *vt* (*Knitting*) abketten. **~ on** *vt* (*Knitting*) anschlagen
castanets /kæstəˈnets/ *npl* Kastagnetten *pl*
castaway /ˈkɑːstəweɪ/ *n* Schiffbrüchige(r) *m/f*
caste /kɑːst/ *n* Kaste *f*
cast ˈiron *n* Gusseisen *nt*
cast-ˈiron *a* gusseisern
castle /ˈkɑːsl/ *n* Schloss *nt*; (*fortified*) Burg *f*; (*Chess*) Turm *m*
ˈcast-offs *npl* abgelegte Kleidung *f*
castor /ˈkɑːstə(r)/ *n* (*wheel*) [Lauf]rolle *f*
ˈcastor sugar *n* Streuzucker *m*
castrat|e /kæˈstreɪt/ *vt* kastrieren. **~ion** /-eɪʃn/ *n* Kastration *f*
casual /ˈkæʒʊəl/ *a*, **-ly** *adv* (*chance*) zufällig; (*offhand*) lässig; (*informal*) zwanglos; (*not permanent*) Gelegenheits-; **~ wear** Freizeitbekleidung *f*
casualty /ˈkæʒʊəltɪ/ *n* [Todes]-opfer *nt*; (*injured person*) Verletzte(r) *m/f*; **~ [department]** Unfallstation *f*
cat /kæt/ *n* Katze *f*
catalogue /ˈkætəlɒg/ *n* Katalog *m* □ *vt* katalogisieren
catalyst /ˈkætəlɪst/ *n* (*Chem & fig*) Katalysator *m*
catalytic /kætəˈlɪtɪk/ *a* **~ converter** (*Auto*) Katalysator *m*
catapult /ˈkætəpʌlt/ *n* Katapult *nt* □ *vt* katapultieren
cataract /ˈkætərækt/ *n* (*Med*) grauer Star *m*
catarrh /kəˈtɑː(r)/ *n* Katarrh *m*
catastroph|e /kəˈtæstrəfɪ/ *n* Katastrophe *f*. **~ic** /kætəˈstrɒfɪk/ *a* katastrophal
catch /kætʃ/ *n* (*of fish*) Fang *m*; (*fastener*) Verschluss *m*; (*on door*) Klinke *f*; (*fam: snag*) Haken *m* (*fam*) □ *v* (*pt/pp* **caught**) □ *vt* fangen; (*be in time for*) erreichen; (*travel by*) fahren mit; bekommen ⟨*illness*⟩; **~ a cold** sich erkälten; **~ sight of** erblicken; **~ s.o. stealing** jdn beim Stehlen erwischen; **~ one's finger in the door** sich (*dat*) den Finger in der Tür [ein]-klemmen □ *vi* (*burn*) anbrennen; (*get stuck*) klemmen. **~ on** *vi* (*fam*) (*understand*) kapieren; (*become popular*) sich durchsetzen.

~ up *vt* einholen □ *vi* aufholen; **~ up with** einholen ⟨*s.o.*⟩; nachholen ⟨*work*⟩
catching /ˈkætʃɪŋ/ *a* ansteckend
catch: ~-phrase *n*, **~word** *n* Schlagwort *nt*
catchy /ˈkætʃɪ/ *a* (**-ier, -iest**) einprägsam
catechism /ˈkætɪkɪzm/ *n* Katechismus *m*
categor|ical /kætɪˈgɒrɪkl/ *a*, **-ly** *adv* kategorisch. **~y** /ˈkætɪgərɪ/ *n* Kategorie *f*
cater /ˈkeɪtə(r)/ *vi* **~ for** beköstigen; ⟨*firm:*⟩ das Essen liefern für ⟨*party*⟩; (*fig*) eingestellt sein auf (+ *acc*). **~ing** *n* (*trade*) Gaststättengewerbe *nt*
caterpillar /ˈkætəpɪlə(r)/ *n* Raupe *f*
cathedral /kəˈθiːdrl/ *n* Dom *m*, Kathedrale *f*
Catholic /ˈkæθəlɪk/ *a* katholisch □ *n* Katholik(in) *m(f)*. **C ~ism** /kəˈθɒlɪsɪzm/ *n* Katholizismus *m*
catkin /ˈkætkɪn/ *n* (*Bot*) Kätzchen *nt*
cattle /ˈkætl/ *npl* Vieh *nt*
catty /ˈkætɪ/ *a* (**-ier, -iest**) boshaft
caught /kɔːt/ *see* **catch**
cauldron /ˈkɔːldrən/ *n* [großer] Kessel *m*
cauliflower /ˈkɒlɪ-/ *n* Blumenkohl *m*
cause /kɔːz/ *n* Ursache *f*; (*reason*) Grund *m*; **good ~** gute Sache *f* □ *vt* verursachen; **~ s.o. to do sth** jdn veranlassen, etw zu tun
'causeway *n* [Insel]damm *m*
caustic /ˈkɔːstɪk/ *a* ätzend; (*fig*) beißend
cauterize /ˈkɔːtəraɪz/ *vt* kauterisieren
caution /ˈkɔːʃn/ *n* Vorsicht *f*; (*warning*) Verwarnung *f* □ *vt* (*Jur*) verwarnen
cautious /ˈkɔːʃəs/ *a*, **-ly** *adv* vorsichtig
cavalry /ˈkævəlrɪ/ *n* Kavallerie *f*
cave /keɪv/ *n* Höhle *f* □ *vi* **~ in** einstürzen
cavern /ˈkævən/ *n* Höhle *f*
caviare /ˈkævɪɑː(r)/ *n* Kaviar *m*
caving /ˈkeɪvɪŋ/ *n* Höhlenforschung *f*
cavity /ˈkævətɪ/ *n* Hohlraum *m*; (*in tooth*) Loch *nt*
cavort /kəˈvɔːt/ *vi* tollen
cease /siːs/ *n* **without ~** unaufhörlich □ *vt/i* aufhören. **~-fire** *n* Waffenruhe *f*. **~less** *a*, **-ly** *adv* unaufhörlich
cedar /ˈsiːdə(r)/ *n* Zeder *f*
cede /siːd/ *vt* abtreten (**to an** + *acc*)
ceiling /ˈsiːlɪŋ/ *n* [Zimmer]decke *f*; (*fig*) oberste Grenze *f*
celebrat|e /ˈselɪbreɪt/ *vt/i* feiern. **~ed** *a* berühmt (**for** wegen). **~ion** /-ˈbreɪʃn/ *n* Feier *f*
celebrity /sɪˈlebrətɪ/ *n* Berühmtheit *f*
celery /ˈselərɪ/ *n* [Stangen]sellerie *m* & *f*
celiba|cy /ˈselɪbəsɪ/ *n* Zölibat *nt*. **~te** *a* **be ~te** im Zölibat leben
cell /sel/ *n* Zelle *f*
cellar /ˈselə(r)/ *n* Keller *m*
cellist /ˈtʃelɪst/ *n* Cellist(in) *m(f)*
cello /ˈtʃeləʊ/ *n* Cello *nt*
Celsius /ˈselsɪəs/ *a* Celsius
Celt /kelt/ *n* Kelte *m*/ Keltin *f*. **~ic** *a* keltisch
cement /sɪˈment/ *n* Zement *m*; (*adhesive*) Kitt *m* □ *vt* zementieren; (*stick*) kitten
cemetery /ˈsemətrɪ/ *n* Friedhof *m*
censor /ˈsensə(r)/ *n* Zensor *m* □ *vt* zensieren. **~ship** *n* Zensur *f*
censure /ˈsenʃə(r)/ *n* Tadel *m* □ *vt* tadeln
census /ˈsensəs/ *n* Volkszählung *f*
cent /sent/ *n* (*coin*) Cent *m*
centenary /senˈtiːnərɪ/ *n*, (*Amer*) **centennial** /senˈtenɪəl/ *n* Hundertjahrfeier *f*
center /ˈsentə(r)/ *n* (*Amer*) = **centre**

centi|grade /ˈsentɪ-/ *a* Celsius-; 5° ~ 5° Celsius. **~metre** *m* Zentimeter *m & nt*. **~pede** /-piːd/ *n* Tausendfüßler *m*

central /ˈsentrəl/ *a*, **-ly** *adv* zentral. ~ ˈ**heating** *n* Zentralheizung *f*. **~ize** *vt* zentralisieren. ~ **reserˈvation** *n* (*Auto*) Mittelstreifen *m*

centre /ˈsentə(r)/ *n* Zentrum *nt*; (*middle*) **Mitte** *f* □ *v* (*pt/pp* **centred**) □ *vt* zentrieren; ~ **on** (*fig*) sich drehen um. **~-ˈforward** *n* Mittelstürmer *m*

centrifugal /sentrɪˈfjuːgl/ *a* ~ **force** Fliehkraft *f*

century /ˈsentʃərɪ/ *n* Jahrhundert *nt*

ceramic /sɪˈræmɪk/ *a* Keramik-. **~s** *n* Keramik *f*

cereal /ˈsɪərɪəl/ *n* Getreide *nt*; (*breakfast food*) Frühstücksflocken *pl*

cerebral /ˈserɪbrl/ *a* Gehirn-

ceremon|ial /serɪˈməʊnɪəl/ *a*, **-ly** *adv* zeremoniell, feierlich □ *n* Zeremoniell *nt*. **~ious** /-ɪəs/ *a*, **-ly** *adv* formell

ceremony /ˈserɪmənɪ/ *n* Zeremonie *f*, Feier *f*; **without** ~ ohne weitere Umstände

certain /ˈsɜːtn/ *a* sicher; (*not named*) gewiss; **for** ~ mit Bestimmtheit; **make** ~ (*check*) sich vergewissern (**that** dass); (*ensure*) dafür sorgen (**that** dass); **he is ~ to win** er wird ganz bestimmt siegen. **~ly** *adv* bestimmt, sicher; **~ly not!** auf keinen Fall! **~ty** *n* Sicherheit *f*, Gewissheit *f*; **it's a ~ty** es ist sicher

certificate /səˈtɪfɪkət/ *n* Bescheinigung *f*; (*Jur*) Urkunde *f*; (*Sch*) Zeugnis *nt*

certify /ˈsɜːtɪfaɪ/ *vt* (*pt/pp* **-ied**) bescheinigen; (*declare insane*) für geisteskrank erklären

cessation /seˈseɪʃn/ *n* Ende *nt*

cesspool /ˈses-/ *n* Senkgrube *f*

cf. *abbr* (*compare*) vgl.

chafe /tʃeɪf/ *vt* wund reiben

chaff /tʃɑːf/ *n* Spreu *f*

chaffinch /ˈtʃæfɪntʃ/ *n* Buchfink *m*

chain /tʃeɪn/ *n* Kette *f* □ *vt* ketten (**to** an + *acc*). ~ **up** *vt* anketten

chain: ~ reˈaction *n* Kettenreaktion *f*. **~-smoker** *n* Kettenraucher *m*. ~ **store** *n* Kettenladen *m*

chair /tʃeə(r)/ *n* Stuhl *m*; (*Univ*) Lehrstuhl *m*; (*Adm*) Vorsitzende(r) *m/f* □ *vt* den Vorsitz führen bei. **~-lift** *n* Sessellift *m*. **~man** *n* Vorsitzende(r) *m/f*

chalet /ˈʃæleɪ/ *n* Chalet *nt*

chalice /ˈtʃælɪs/ *n* (*Relig*) Kelch *m*

chalk /tʃɔːk/ *n* Kreide *f*. **~y** *a* kreidig

challeng|e /ˈtʃælɪndʒ/ *n* Herausforderung *f*; (*Mil*) Anruf *m* □ *vt* herausfordern; (*Mil*) anrufen; (*fig*) anfechten ⟨*statement*⟩. **~er** *n* Herausforderer *m*. **~ing** *a* herausfordernd; (*demanding*) anspruchsvoll

chamber /ˈtʃeɪmbə(r)/ *n* Kammer *f*; **~s** *pl* (*Jur*) [Anwalts]büro *nt*; **C~ of Commerce** Handelskammer *f*

chamber: ~maid *n* Zimmermädchen *nt*. ~ **music** *n* Kammermusik *f*. **~-pot** *n* Nachttopf *m*

chamois[1] /ˈʃæmwɑː/ *n inv* (*animal*) Gämse *f*

chamois[2] /ˈʃæmɪ/ *n* **~[-leather]** Ledertuch *nt*

champagne /ʃæmˈpeɪn/ *n* Champagner *m*

champion /ˈtʃæmpɪən/ *n* (*Sport*) Meister(in) *m(f)*; (*of cause*) Verfechter *m* □ *vt* sich einsetzen für. **~ship** *n* (*Sport*) Meisterschaft *f*

chance /tʃɑːns/ *n* Zufall *m*; (*prospect*) Chancen *pl*; (*likelihood*) Aussicht *f*; (*opportunity*) Gelegenheit *f*; **by** ~ zufällig; **take a** ~ ein Risiko eingehen; **give s.o. a** ~ jdm eine Chance geben □ *attrib* zufällig □ *vt* ~ **it** es riskieren

chancellor /'tʃɑ:nsələ(r)/ *n* Kanzler *m*; (*Univ*) Rektor *m*; **C~ of the Exchequer** Schatzkanzler *m*

chancy /'tʃɑ:nsɪ/ *a* riskant

chandelier /ʃændə'lɪə(r)/ *n* Kronleuchter *m*

change /tʃeɪndʒ/ *n* Veränderung *f*; (*alteration*) Änderung *f*; (*money*) Wechselgeld *nt*; **for a ~** zur Abwechslung □ *vt* wechseln; (*alter*) ändern; (*exchange*) umtauschen (**for** gegen); (*transform*) verwandeln; trocken legen ⟨*baby*⟩; **~ one's clothes** sich umziehen; **~ trains** umsteigen □ *vi* sich verändern; (**~** *clothes*) sich umziehen; (**~** *trains*) umsteigen; **all ~!** alles aussteigen!

changeable /'tʃeɪndʒəbl/ *a* wechselhaft

'changing-room *n* Umkleideraum *m*

channel /'tʃænl/ *n* Rinne *f*; (*Radio, TV*) Kanal *m*; (*fig*) Weg *m*; **the [English] C~** der Ärmelkanal; **the C~ Islands** die Kanalinseln □ *vt* (*pt/pp* **channelled**) leiten; (*fig*) lenken

chant /tʃɑ:nt/ *n* liturgischer Gesang *m* □ *vt* singen; ⟨*demonstrators:*⟩ skandieren

chao|s /'keɪɒs/ *n* Chaos *nt*. **~tic** /-'ɒtɪk/ *a* chaotisch

chap /tʃæp/ *n* (*fam*) Kerl *m*

chapel /'tʃæpl/ *n* Kapelle *f*

chaperon /'ʃæpərəʊn/ *n* Anstandsdame *f* □ *vt* begleiten

chaplain /'tʃæplɪn/ *n* Geistliche(r) *m*

chapped /tʃæpt/ *a* ⟨*skin*⟩ aufgesprungen

chapter /'tʃæptə(r)/ *n* Kapitel *nt*

char¹ /tʃɑ:(r)/ *n* (*fam*) Putzfrau *f*

char² *vt* (*pt/pp* **charred**) (*burn*) verkohlen

character /'kærɪktə(r)/ *n* Charakter *m*; (*in novel, play*) Gestalt *f*; (*Typ*) Schriftzeichen *nt*; **out of ~** uncharakteristisch; **quite a ~** (*fam*) ein Original

characteristic /kærɪktə'rɪstɪk/ *a*, **-ally** *adv* charakteristisch (**of** für) □ *n* Merkmal *nt*

characterize /'kærɪktəraɪz/ *vt* charakterisieren

charade /ʃə'rɑ:d/ *n* Scharade *f*

charcoal /'tʃɑ:-/ *n* Holzkohle *f*

charge /tʃɑ:dʒ/ *n* (*price*) Gebühr *f*; (*Electr*) Ladung *f*; (*attack*) Angriff *m*; (*Jur*) Anklage *f*; **free of ~** kostenlos; **be in ~** verantwortlich sein (**of** für); **take ~** die Aufsicht übernehmen (**of** über + *acc*) □ *vt* berechnen ⟨*fee*⟩; (*Electr*) laden; (*attack*) angreifen; (*Jur*) anklagen (**with** *gen*); **~ s.o. for sth** jdm etw berechnen □ *vi* (*attack*) angreifen

chariot /'tʃærɪət/ *n* Wagen *m*

charisma /kə'rɪzmə/ *n* Charisma *nt*. **~tic** /kærɪz'mætɪk/ *a* charismatisch

charitable /'tʃærɪtəbl/ *a* wohltätig; (*kind*) wohlwollend

charity /'tʃærətɪ/ *n* Nächstenliebe *f*; (*organization*) wohltätige Einrichtung *f*; **for ~** für Wohltätigkeitszwecke; **live on ~** von Almosen leben

charlatan /'ʃɑ:lətən/ *n* Scharlatan *m*

charm /tʃɑ:m/ *n* Reiz *m*; (*of person*) Charme *f*; (*object*) Amulett *nt* □ *vt* bezaubern. **~ing** *a*, **-ly** *adv* reizend; ⟨*person, smile*⟩ charmant

chart /tʃɑ:t/ *n* Karte *f*; (*table*) Tabelle *f*

charter /'tʃɑ:tə(r)/ *n* **~ [flight]** Charterflug *m* □ *vt* chartern; **~ed accountant** Wirtschaftsprüfer(in) *m(f)*

charwoman /'tʃɑ:-/ *n* Putzfrau *f*

chase /tʃeɪs/ *n* Verfolgungsjagd *f* □ *vt* jagen, verfolgen. **~ away** *or* **off** *vt* wegjagen

chasm /'kæzm/ *n* Kluft *f*

chassis /'ʃæsɪ/ *n* (*pl* **chassis** /-sɪz/) Chassis *nt*

chaste /tʃeɪst/ *a* keusch

chastise /tʃæ'staɪz/ *vt* züchtigen

chastity /ˈtʃæstətɪ/ *n* Keuschheit *f*

chat /tʃæt/ *n* Plauderei *f*; **have a ~ with** plaudern mit □ *vi* (*pt/pp* **chatted**) plaudern. **~ show** *n* Talkshow *f*

chatter /ˈtʃætə(r)/ *n* Geschwätz *nt* □ *vi* schwatzen; ⟨*child:*⟩ plappern; ⟨*teeth:*⟩ klappern. **~box** *n* (*fam*) Plappermaul *nt*

chatty /ˈtʃætɪ/ *a* (**-ier, -iest**) geschwätzig

chauffeur /ˈʃəʊfə(r)/ *n* Chauffeur *m*

chauvin|ism /ˈʃəʊvɪnɪzm/ *n* Chauvinismus *m*. **~ist** *n* Chauvinist *m*; **male ~ist** (*fam*) Chauvi *m*

cheap /tʃi:p/ *a & adv* (**-er, -est**), **-ly** *adv* billig. **~en** *vt* entwürdigen; **~en oneself** sich erniedrigen

cheat /tʃi:t/ *n* Betrüger(in) *m(f)*; (*at games*) Mogler *m* □ *vt* betrügen □ *vi* (*at games*) mogeln (*fam*)

check¹ /tʃek/ *a* (*squared*) kariert □ *n* Karo *nt*

check² *n* Überprüfung *f*; (*inspection*) Kontrolle *f*; (*Chess*) Schach *nt*; (*Amer: bill*) Rechnung *f*; (*Amer: cheque*) Scheck *m*; (*Amer: tick*) Haken *m*; **keep a ~ on** kontrollieren □ *vt* [über]prüfen; (*inspect*) kontrollieren; (*restrain*) hemmen; (*stop*) aufhalten □ *vi* **[go and] ~** nachsehen. **~ in** *vi* sich anmelden; (*Aviat*) einchecken □ *vt* abfertigen; einchecken. **~ out** *vi* sich abmelden. **~ up** *vi* prüfen, kontrollieren; **~ up on** überprüfen

check|ed /tʃekt/ *a* kariert. **~ers** *n* (*Amer*) Damespiel *nt*

check: ~mate *int* schachmatt! **~-out** *n* Kasse *f*. **~room** *n* (*Amer*) Garderobe *f*. **~-up** *n* (*Med*) [Kontroll]untersuchung *f*

cheek /tʃi:k/ *n* Backe *f*; (*impudence*) Frechheit *f*. **~y** *a*, **-ily** *adv* frech

cheep /tʃi:p/ *vi* piepen

cheer /tʃɪə(r)/ *n* Beifallsruf *m*; **three ~s** ein dreifaches Hoch (**for** auf + *acc*); **~s!** prost! (*goodbye*) tschüs! □ *vt* zujubeln (+ *dat*) □ *vi* jubeln. **~ up** *vt* aufmuntern; aufheitern □ *vi* munterer werden. **~ful** *a*, **-ly** *adv* fröhlich. **~fulness** *n* Fröhlichkeit *f*

cheerio /tʃɪərɪˈəʊ/ *int* (*fam*) tschüs!

ˈcheerless *a* trostlos

cheese /tʃi:z/ *n* Käse *m*. **~cake** *n* Käsekuchen *m*

cheetah /ˈtʃi:tə/ *n* Gepard *m*

chef /ʃef/ *n* Koch *m*

chemical /ˈkemɪkl/ *a*, **-ly** *adv* chemisch □ *n* Chemikalie *f*

chemist /ˈkemɪst/ *n* (*pharmacist*) Apotheker(in) *m(f)*; (*scientist*) Chemiker(in) *m(f)*; **~'s [shop]** Drogerie *f*; (*dispensing*) Apotheke *f*. **~ry** *n* Chemie *f*

cheque /tʃek/ *n* Scheck *m*. **~-book** *n* Scheckbuch *nt*. **~ card** *n* Scheckkarte *f*

cherish /ˈtʃerɪʃ/ *vt* lieben; (*fig*) hegen

cherry /ˈtʃerɪ/ *n* Kirsche *f* □ *attrib* Kirsch-

cherub /ˈtʃerəb/ *n* Engelchen *nt*

chess /tʃes/ *n* Schach *nt*

chess: ~board *n* Schachbrett *nt*. **~-man** *n* Schachfigur *f*

chest /tʃest/ *n* Brust *f*; (*box*) Truhe *f*

chestnut /ˈtʃesnʌt/ *n* Esskastanie *f*, Marone *f*; (*horse-*) [Ross]kastanie *f*

chest of ˈdrawers *n* Kommode *f*

chew /tʃu:/ *vt* kauen. **~ing-gum** *n* Kaugummi *m*

chic /ʃi:k/ *a* schick

chick /tʃɪk/ *n* Küken *nt*

chicken /ˈtʃɪkɪn/ *n* Huhn *nt* □ *attrib* Hühner- □ *a* (*fam*) feige □ *vi* **~ out** (*fam*) kneifen. **~pox** *n* Windpocken *pl*

chicory /ˈtʃɪkərɪ/ *n* Chicorée *f*; (*in coffee*) Zichorie *f*

chief /tʃi:f/ *a* Haupt- □ *n* Chef *m*; (*of tribe*) Häuptling *m*. **~ly** *adv* hauptsächlich
chilblain /'tʃɪlbleɪn/ *n* Frostbeule *f*
child /tʃaɪld/ *n* (*pl* **~ren**) Kind *nt*
child: ~birth *n* Geburt *f*. **~hood** *n* Kindheit *f*. **~ish** *a* kindisch. **~less** *a* kinderlos. **~like** *a* kindlich. **~-minder** *n* Tagesmutter *f*
children /'tʃɪldrən/ *npl see* **child**
Chile /'tʃɪlɪ/ *n* Chile *nt*
chill /tʃɪl/ *n* Kälte *f*; (*illness*) Erkältung *f* □ *vt* kühlen
chilli /'tʃɪlɪ/ *n* (*pl* **-es**) Chili *m*
chilly /'tʃɪlɪ/ *a* kühl; **I felt ~** mich fröstelte [es]
chime /tʃaɪm/ *vi* läuten; ⟨*clock:*⟩ schlagen
chimney /'tʃɪmnɪ/ *n* Schornstein *m*. **~-pot** *n* Schornsteinaufsatz *m*. **~-sweep** *n* Schornsteinfeger *m*
chimpanzee /tʃɪmpæn'zi:/ *n* Schimpanse *m*
chin /tʃɪn/ *n* Kinn *nt*
china /'tʃaɪnə/ *n* Porzellan *nt*
Chin|a *n* China *nt*. **~ese** /-'ni:z/ *a* chinesisch □ *n* (*Lang*) Chinesisch *nt*; **the ~ese** *pl* die Chinesen. **~ese 'lantern** *n* Lampion *m*
chink[1] /tʃɪŋk/ *n* (*slit*) Ritze *f*
chink[2] *n* Geklirr *nt* □ *vi* klirren; ⟨*coins:*⟩ klimpern
chip /tʃɪp/ *n* (*fragment*) Span *m*; (*in china, paintwork*) angeschlagene Stelle *f*; (*Computing, Gambling*) Chip *m*; **~s** *pl* (*Culin*) Pommes frites *pl*; (*Amer: crisps*) Chips *pl* □ *vt* (*pt/pp* **chipped**) (*damage*) anschlagen. **~ped** *a* angeschlagen
chiropod|ist /kɪ'rɒpədɪst/ *n* Fußpfleger(in) *m*(*f*). **~y** *n* Fußpflege *f*
chirp /tʃɜ:p/ *vi* zwitschern; ⟨*cricket:*⟩ zirpen. **~y** *a* (*fam*) munter
chisel /'tʃɪzl/ *n* Meißel *m* □ *vt/i* (*pt/pp* **chiselled**) meißeln
chit /tʃɪt/ *n* Zettel *m*
chival|rous /'ʃɪvlrəs/ *a*, **-ly** *adv* ritterlich. **~ry** *n* Ritterlichkeit *f*
chives /tʃaɪvz/ *npl* Schnittlauch *m*
chlorine /'klɔ:ri:n/ *n* Chlor *nt*
chloroform /'klɒrəfɔ:m/ *n* Chloroform *nt*
chocolate /'tʃɒkələt/ *n* Schokolade *f*; (*sweet*) Praline *f*
choice /tʃɔɪs/ *n* Wahl *f*; (*variety*) Auswahl *f* □ *a* auserlesen
choir /'kwaɪə(r)/ *n* Chor *m*. **~boy** *n* Chorknabe *m*
choke /tʃəʊk/ *n* (*Auto*) Choke *m* □ *vt* würgen; (*to death*) erwürgen □ *vi* sich verschlucken; **~ on** [fast] ersticken an (+ *dat*)
cholera /'kɒlərə/ *n* Cholera *f*
cholesterol /kə'lestərɒl/ *n* Cholesterin *nt*
choose /tʃu:z/ *vt/i* (*pt* **chose**, *pp* **chosen**) wählen; (*select*) sich (*dat*) aussuchen; **~ to do/go** [freiwillig] tun/gehen; **as you ~** wie Sie wollen
choos[e]y /'tʃu:zɪ/ *a* (*fam*) wählerisch
chop /tʃɒp/ *n* (*blow*) Hieb *m*; (*Culin*) Kotelett *nt* □ *vt* (*pt/pp* **chopped**) hacken. **~ down** *vt* abhacken; fällen ⟨*tree*⟩. **~ off** *vt* abhacken
chop|per /'tʃɒpə(r)/ *n* Beil *nt*; (*fam*) Hubschrauber *m*. **~py** *a* kabbelig
'chopsticks *npl* Essstäbchen *pl*
choral /'kɔ:rəl/ *a* Chor-; **~ society** Gesangverein *m*
chord /kɔ:d/ *n* (*Mus*) Akkord *m*
chore /tʃɔ:(r)/ *n* lästige Pflicht *f*; **[household] ~s** Hausarbeit *f*
choreography /kɒrɪ'ɒgrəfɪ/ *n* Choreographie *f*
chortle /'tʃɔ:tl/ *vi* [vor Lachen] glucksen
chorus /'kɔ:rəs/ *n* Chor *m*; (*of song*) Refrain *m*
chose, chosen /tʃəʊz, 'tʃəʊzn/ *see* **choose**
Christ /kraɪst/ *n* Christus *m*

christen /ˈkrɪsn/ *vt* taufen. **~ing** *n* Taufe *f*

Christian /ˈkrɪstʃən/ *a* christlich □ *n* Christ(in) *m(f)*. **~ity** /-stɪˈænətɪ/ *n* Christentum *nt*. **~ name** *n* Vorname *m*

Christmas /ˈkrɪsməs/ *n* Weihnachten *nt*. **~ card** *n* Weihnachtskarte *f*. **~ ˈDay** *n* erster Weihnachtstag *m*. **~ ˈEve** *n* Heiligabend *m*. **~ tree** *n* Weihnachtsbaum *m*

chrome /krəʊm/ *n*, **chromium** /ˈkrəʊmɪəm/ *n* Chrom *nt*

chromosome /ˈkrəʊməsəʊm/ *n* Chromosom *nt*

chronic /ˈkrɒnɪk/ *a* chronisch

chronicle /ˈkrɒnɪkl/ *n* Chronik *f*

chronological /krɒnəˈlɒdʒɪkl/ *a*, **-ly** *adv* chronologisch

chrysalis /ˈkrɪsəlɪs/ *n* Puppe *f*

chrysanthemum /krɪˈsænθəməm/ *n* Chrysantheme *f*

chubby /ˈtʃʌbɪ/ *a* **(-ier, -iest)** mollig

chuck /tʃʌk/ *vt* (*fam*) schmeißen. **~ out** *vt* (*fam*) rausschmeißen

chuckle /ˈtʃʌkl/ *vi* in sich (*acc*) hineinlachen

chum /tʃʌm/ *n* Freund(in) *m(f)*

chunk /tʃʌŋk/ *n* Stück *nt*

church /tʃɜːtʃ/ *n* Kirche *f*. **~yard** *n* Friedhof *m*

churlish /ˈtʃɜːlɪʃ/ *a* unhöflich

churn /tʃɜːn/ *n* Butterfass *nt*; (*for milk*) Milchkanne *f* □ *vt* **~ out** am laufenden Band produzieren

chute /ʃuːt/ *n* Rutsche *f*; (*for rubbish*) Müllschlucker *m*

CID *abbr* **(Criminal Investigation Department)** Kripo *f*

cider /ˈsaɪdə(r)/ *n* Apfelwein *m*

cigar /sɪˈgɑː(r)/ *n* Zigarre *f*

cigarette /sɪgəˈret/ *n* Zigarette *f*

cine-camera /ˈsɪnɪ-/ *n* Filmkamera *f*

cinema /ˈsɪnɪmə/ *n* Kino *nt*

cinnamon /ˈsɪnəmən/ *n* Zimt *m*

cipher /ˈsaɪfə(r)/ *n* (*code*) Chiffre *f*; (*numeral*) Ziffer *f*; (*fig*) Null *f*

circle /ˈsɜːkl/ *n* Kreis *m*; (*Theat*) Rang *m* □ *vt* umkreisen □ *vi* kreisen

circuit /ˈsɜːkɪt/ *n* Runde *f*; (*racetrack*) Rennbahn *f*; (*Electr*) Stromkreis *m*. **~ous** /səˈkjuːɪtəs/ *a* **~ route** Umweg *m*

circular /ˈsɜːkjʊlə(r)/ *a* kreisförmig □ *n* Rundschreiben *nt*. **~ ˈsaw** *n* Kreissäge *f*. **~ ˈtour** *n* Rundfahrt *f*

circulat|e /ˈsɜːkjʊleɪt/ *vt* in Umlauf setzen □ *vi* zirkulieren. **~ion** /-ˈleɪʃn/ *n* Kreislauf *m*; (*of newspaper*) Auflage *f*

circumcis|e /ˈsɜːkəmsaɪz/ *vt* beschneiden. **~ion** /-ˈsɪʒn/ *n* Beschneidung *f*

circumference /ʃəˈkʌmfərəns/ *n* Umfang *m*

circumspect /ˈsɜːkəmspekt/ *a*, **-ly** *adv* umsichtig

circumstance /ˈsɜːkəmstəns/ *n* Umstand *m*; **~s** *pl* Umstände *pl*; (*financial*) Verhältnisse *pl*

circus /ˈsɜːkəs/ *n* Zirkus *m*

CIS *abbr* **(Commonwealth of Independent States)** GUS *f*

cistern /ˈsɪstən/ *n* (*tank*) Wasserbehälter *m*; (*of WC*) Spülkasten *m*

cite /saɪt/ *vt* zitieren

citizen /ˈsɪtɪzn/ *n* Bürger(in) *m(f)*. **~ship** *n* Staatsangehörigkeit *f*

citrus /ˈsɪtrəs/ *n* **~ [fruit]** Zitrusfrucht *f*

city /ˈsɪtɪ/ *n* [Groß]stadt *f*

civic /ˈsɪvɪk/ *a* Bürger-

civil /ˈʃɪvl/ *a* bürgerlich; ⟨*aviation, defence*⟩ zivil; (*polite*) höflich. **~ engiˈneering** *n* Hoch- und Tiefbau *m*

civilian /sɪˈvɪljən/ *a* Zivil-; **in ~ clothes** in Zivil □ *n* Zivilist *m*

civility /sɪˈvɪlətɪ/ *n* Höflichkeit *f*

civiliz|ation /sɪvəlaɪˈzeɪʃn/ *n* Zivilisation *f*. **~e** /ˈsɪvəlaɪz/ *vt* zivilisieren

civil: ~ **'servant** *n* Beamte(r) *m*/Beamtin *f*. **C~ 'Service** *n* Staatsdienst *m*
clad /klæd/ *a* gekleidet (**in** in + *acc*)
claim /kleɪm/ *n* Anspruch *m*; (*application*) Antrag *m*; (*demand*) Forderung *f*; (*assertion*) Behauptung *f* □ *vt* beanspruchen; (*apply for*) beantragen; (*demand*) fordern; (*assert*) behaupten; (*collect*) abholen. **ant** *n* Antragsteller *m*
clairvoyant /kleə'vɔɪənt/ *n* Hellseher(in) *m*(*f*)
clam /klæm/ *n* Klaffmuschel *f*
clamber /'klæmbə(r)/ *vi* klettern
clammy /'klæmɪ/ *a* (**-ier, -iest**) feucht
clamour /'klæmə(r)/ *n* Geschrei *nt* □ *vi* ~ **for** schreien nach
clamp /klæmp/ *n* Klammer *f* □ *vt* [ein]spannen □ *vi* (*fam*) ~ **down** durchgreifen; ~ **down on** vorgehen gegen
clan /klæn/ *n* Clan *m*
clandestine /klæn'destɪn/ *a* geheim
clang /klæŋ/ *n* Schmettern *nt*. **~er** *n* (*fam*) Schnitzer *m*
clank /klæŋk/ *vi* klirren
clap /klæp/ *n* **give s.o. a ~** jdm Beifall klatschen; ~ **of thunder** Donnerschlag *m* □ *vt/i* (*pt/pp* **clapped**) Beifall klatschen (+ *dat*); ~ **one's hands** [in die Hände] klatschen
claret /'klærət/ *n* roter Bordeaux *m*
clari|fication /klærɪfɪ'keɪʃn/ *n* Klärung *f*. **~fy** /'klærɪfaɪ/ *vt/i* (*pt/pp* **-ied**) klären
clarinet /klærɪ'net/ *n* Klarinette *f*
clarity /'klærətɪ/ *n* Klarheit *f*
clash /klæʃ/ *n* Geklirr *nt*; (*fig*) Konflikt *m* □ *vi* klirren; ⟨*colours*:⟩ sich beißen; ⟨*events*:⟩ ungünstig zusammenfallen
clasp /klɑ:sp/ *n* Verschluss *m* □ *vt* ergreifen; (*hold*) halten
class /klɑ:s/ *n* **Klasse** *f*; **travel first/second ~** erster/zweiter Klasse reisen □ *vt* einordnen
classic /'klæsɪk/ *a* klassisch □ *n* Klassiker *m*; **~s** *pl* (*Univ*) Altphilologie *f*. **~al** *a* klassisch
classi|fication /klæsɪfɪ'keɪʃn/ *n* Klassifikation *f*. **~fy** /'klæsɪfaɪ/ *vt* (*pt/pp* **-ied**) klassifizieren
'classroom *n* Klassenzimmer *nt*
classy /'klɑ:sɪ/ *a* (**-ier, -iest**) (*fam*) schick
clatter /'klætə(r)/ *n* Geklapper *nt* □ *vi* klappern
clause /klɔ:z/ *n* Klausel *f*; (*Gram*) Satzteil *m*
claustrophobia /klɔ:strə'fəʊbɪə/ *n* Klaustrophobie *f*, (*fam*) Platzangst *m*
claw /klɔ:/ *n* Kralle *f*; (*of bird of prey & Techn*) Klaue *f*; (*of crab, lobster*) Schere *f* □ *vt* kratzen
clay /kleɪ/ *n* Lehm *m*; (*pottery*) Ton *m*
clean /kli:n/ *a* (**-er, -est**) sauber □ *adv* glatt □ *vt* sauber machen; putzen ⟨*shoes, windows*⟩; ~ **one's teeth** sich (*dat*) die Zähne putzen; **have sth ~ed** etw reinigen lassen. ~ **up** *vt* sauber machen
cleaner /'kli:nə(r)/ *n* Putzfrau *f*; (*substance*) Reinigungsmittel *nt*; **[dry] ~'s** chemische Reinigung *f*
cleanliness /'klenlɪnɪs/ *n* Sauberkeit *f*
cleanse /klenz/ *vt* reinigen. **~r** *n* Reinigungsmittel *nt*
clean-shaven *a* glatt rasiert
cleansing cream /'klenz-/ *n* Reinigungscreme *f*
clear /klɪə(r)/ *a* (**-er, -est**), **-ly** *adv* klar; (*obvious*) eindeutig; (*distinct*) deutlich; ⟨*conscience*⟩ rein; (*without obstacles*) frei; **make sth ~** etw klarmachen (**to** *dat*) □ *adv* **stand ~** zurücktreten; **keep ~ of** aus dem Wege gehen (+ *dat*) □ *vt* räumen; abräumen ⟨*table*⟩; (*acquit*) freisprechen; (*authorize*) genehmigen; (*jump over*)

überspringen; ~ **one's throat** sich räuspern □ *vi* ⟨*fog:*⟩ sich auflösen. ~ **away** *vt* wegräumen. ~ **off** *vi* (*fam*) abhauen. ~ **out** *vt* ausräumen □ *vi* (*fam*) abhauen. ~ **up** *vt* (*tidy*) aufräumen; (*solve*) aufklären □ *vi* ⟨*weather:*⟩ sich aufklären

clearance /ˈklɪərəns/ *n* Räumung *f*; (*authorization*) Genehmigung *f*; (*customs*) [Zoll]abfertigung *f*; (*Techn*) Spielraum *m*. ~ **sale** *n* Räumungsverkauf *m*

clear|ing /ˈklɪərɪŋ/ *n* Lichtung *f*. ~ **way** *n* (*Auto*) Straße *f* mit Halteverbot

cleavage /ˈkliːvɪdʒ/ *n* Spaltung *f*; (*woman"s*) Dekolleté *nt*

clef /klef/ *n* Notenschlüssel *m*

cleft /kleft/ *n* Spalte *f*

clemen|cy /ˈklemənsɪ/ *n* Milde *f*. ~**t** *a* mild

clench /klentʃ/ *vt* ~ **one's fist** die Faust ballen; ~ **one's teeth** die Zähne zusammenbeißen

clergy /ˈklɜːdʒɪ/ *npl* Geistlichkeit *f*. ~**man** *n* Geistliche(r) *m*

cleric /ˈklerɪk/ *n* Geistliche(r) *m*. ~**al** *a* Schreib-; (*Relig*) geistlich

clerk /klɑːk/, *Amer*: /klɜːk/ *n* Büroangestellte(r) *m/f*; (*Amer: shop assistant*) Verkäufer(in) *m(f)*

clever /ˈklevə(r)/ *a* (**-er, -est**), -ly *adv* klug; (*skilful*) geschickt

cliché /ˈkliːʃeɪ/ *n* Klischee *nt*

click /klɪk/ *vi* klicken

client /ˈklaɪənt/ *n* Kunde *m*/ Kundin *f*; (*Jur*) Klient(in) *m(f)*

clientele /kliːɒnˈtel/ *n* Kundschaft *f*

cliff /klɪf/ *n* Kliff *nt*

climat|e /ˈklaɪmət/ *n* Klima *nt*. ~**ic** /-ˈmætɪk/ *a* klimatisch

climax /ˈklaɪmæks/ *n* Höhepunkt *m*

climb /klaɪm/ *n* Aufstieg *m* □ *vt* besteigen ⟨*mountain*⟩; steigen auf (+ *acc*) ⟨*ladder, tree*⟩ □ *vi* klettern; (*rise*) steigen; ⟨*road:*⟩ ansteigen. ~ **down** *vi* hinunter-/herunterklettern; (*from ladder, tree*) heruntersteigen; (*fam*) nachgeben

climber /ˈklaɪmə(r)/ *n* Bergsteiger *m*; (*plant*) Kletterpflanze *f*

clinch /klɪntʃ/ *vt* perfekt machen ⟨*deal*⟩ □ *vi* (*boxing*) clinchen

cling /klɪŋ/ *vi* (*pt/pp* **clung**) sich klammern (**to** an + *acc*); (*stick*) haften (**to** an + *dat*). ~ **film** *n* Sichtfolie *f* mit Hafteffekt

clinic /ˈklɪnɪk/ *n* Klinik *f*. ~**al** *a*, **-ly** *adv* klinisch

clink /klɪŋk/ *n* Klirren *nt*; (*fam: prison*) Knast *m* □ *vi* klirren

clip[1] /klɪp/ *n* Klammer *f*; (*jewellery*) Klipp *m* □ *vt* (*pt/pp* **clipped**) anklammern (**to** an + *acc*)

clip[2] *n* (*extract*) Ausschnitt *m* □ *vt* schneiden; knipsen ⟨*ticket*⟩. ~**board** *n* Klemmbrett *nt*. ~**pers** *npl* Schere *f*. ~**ping** *n* (*extract*) Ausschnitt *m*

clique /kliːk/ *n* Clique *f*

cloak /kləʊk/ *n* Umhang *m*. ~**room** *n* Garderobe *f*; (*toilet*) Toilette *f*

clobber /ˈklɒbə(r)/ *n* (*fam*) Zeug *nt* □ *vt* (*fam: hit, defeat*) schlagen

clock /klɒk/ *n* Uhr *f*; (*fam: speedometer*) Tacho *m* □ *vi* ~ **in/out** stechen

clock: ~ **tower** *n* Uhrenturm *m*. ~**wise** *a* & *adv* im Uhrzeigersinn. ~**work** *n* Uhrwerk *nt*; (*of toy*) Aufziehmechanismus *m*; **like** ~**work** (*fam*) wie am Schnürchen

clod /klɒd/ *n* Klumpen *m*

clog /klɒg/ *n* Holzschuh *m* □ *vt/i* (*pt/pp* **clogged**) ~ **[up]** verstopfen

cloister /ˈklɔɪstə(r)/ *n* Kreuzgang *m*

close[1] /kləʊs/ *a* (**-r, -st**) nah[e] (**to** *dat*); ⟨*friend*⟩ eng; ⟨*weather*⟩ schwül; **have a** ~ **shave** (*fam*) mit knapper Not davonkommen

□ *adv* nahe; ~ **by** nicht weit weg □ *n* (*street*) Sackgasse *f*

close² /kləʊz/ *n* Ende *nt*; **draw to a ~** sich dem Ende nähern □ *vt* zumachen, schließen; (*bring to an end*) beenden; sperren ⟨*road*⟩ □ *vi* sich schließen; ⟨*shop:*⟩ schließen, zumachen; (*end*) enden. **~ down** *vt* schließen; stilllegen ⟨*factory*⟩ □ *vi* schließen; ⟨*factory:*⟩ stillgelegt werden

closed 'shop /kləʊzd-/ *n* ≈ Gewerkschaftszwang *m*

closely /'kləʊslɪ/ *adv* eng, nah[e]; (*with attention*) genau

close season /'kləʊs-/ *n* Schonzeit *f*

closet /'klɒzɪt/ *n* (*Amer*) Schrank *m*

close-up /'kləʊs-/ *n* Nahaufnahme *f*

closure /'kləʊʒə(r)/ *n* Schließung *f*; (*of factory*) Stilllegung *f*; (*of road*) Sperrung *f*

clot /klɒt/ *n* [Blut]gerinnsel *nt*; (*fam: idiot*) Trottel *m* □ *vi* (*pt/pp* **clotted**) ⟨*blood:*⟩ gerinnen

cloth /klɒθ/ *n* Tuch *nt*

clothe /kləʊð/ *vt* kleiden

clothes /kləʊðz/ *npl* Kleider *pl*. **~-brush** *n* Kleiderbürste *f*. **~-line** *n* Wäscheleine *f*

clothing /'kləʊðɪŋ/ *n* Kleidung *f*

cloud /klaʊd/ *n* Wolke *f* □ *vi* **~ over** sich bewölken. **~burst** *n* Wolkenbruch *m*

cloudy /'klaʊdɪ/ *a* (**-ier, -iest**) wolkig, bewölkt; ⟨*liquid*⟩ trübe

clout /klaʊt/ *n* (*fam*) Schlag *m*; (*influence*) Einfluss *m* □ *vt* (*fam*) hauen

clove /kləʊv/ *n* [Gewürz]nelke *f*; **~ of garlic** Knoblauchzehe *f*

clover /'kləʊvə(r)/ *n* Klee *m*. **~ leaf** *n* Kleeblatt *nt*

clown /klaʊn/ *n* Clown *m* □ *vi* **~ [about]** herumalbern

club /klʌb/ *n* Klub *m*; (*weapon*) Keule *f*; (*Sport*) Schläger *m*; **~s** *pl* (*Cards*) Kreuz *nt*, Treff *nt* □ *v* (*pt/pp* **clubbed**) □ *vt* knüppeln □ *vi* **~ together** zusammenlegen

cluck /klʌk/ *vi* glucken

clue /klu:/ *n* Anhaltspunkt *m*; (*in crossword*) Frage *f*; **I haven't a ~** (*fam*) ich habe keine Ahnung

clump /klʌmp/ *n* Gruppe *f*

clumsiness /'klʌmzɪnɪs/ *n* Ungeschicklichkeit *f*

clumsy /'klʌmzɪ/ *a* (**-ier, -iest**), **-ily** *adv* ungeschickt; (*unwieldy*) unförmig

clung /klʌŋ/ *see* **cling**

cluster /'klʌstə(r)/ *n* Gruppe *f*; (*of flowers*) Büschel *nt* □ *vi* sich scharen (**round** um)

clutch /klʌtʃ/ *n* Griff *m*; (*Auto*) Kupplung *f*; **be in s.o.'s ~es** (*fam*) in jds Klauen sein □ *vt* festhalten; (*grab*) ergreifen □ *vi* **~ at** greifen nach

clutter /'klʌtə(r)/ *n* Kram *m* □ *vt* **~ [up]** vollstopfen

c/o *abbr* (**care of**) bei

coach /kəʊtʃ/ *n* [Reise]bus *m*; (*Rail*) Wagen *m*; (*horse-drawn*) Kutsche *f*; (*Sport*) Trainer *m* □ *vt* Nachhilfestunden geben (+ *dat*); (*Sport*) trainieren

coagulate /kəʊ'ægjʊleɪt/ *vi* gerinnen

coal /kəʊl/ *n* Kohle *f*

coalition /kəʊə'lɪʃn/ *n* Koalition *f*

'coal-mine *n* Kohlenbergwerk *nt*

coarse /kɔ:s/ *a* (**-r, -st**), **-ly** *adv* grob

coast /kəʊst/ *n* Küste *f* □ *vi* (*freewheel*) im Freilauf fahren; (*Auto*) im Leerlauf fahren. **~al** *a* Küsten-. **~er** *n* (*mat*) Untersatz *m*

coast: ~guard *n* Küstenwache *f*. **~line** *n* Küste *f*

coat /kəʊt/ *n* Mantel *m*; (*of animal*) Fell *nt*; (*of paint*) Anstrich *m*; **~ of arms** Wappen *nt* □ *vt* überziehen; (*with paint*) streichen. **~-hanger** *n* Kleiderbügel *m*. **~-hook** *n* Kleiderhaken *m*

coating /'kəʊtɪŋ/ *n* Überzug *m*, Schicht *f*; (*of paint*) Anstrich *m*
coax /kəʊks/ *vt* gut zureden (+ *dat*)
cob /kɒb/ *n* (*of corn*) [Mais]kolben *m*
cobble1 /'kɒbl/ *n* Kopfstein *m*; **~s** *pl* Kopfsteinpflaster *nt*
cobble2 *vt* flicken. **~r** *m* Schuster *m*
'cobblestones *npl* = **cobbles**
cobweb /'kɒb-/ *n* Spinnengewebe *nt*
cocaine /kə'keɪn/ *n* Kokain *nt*
cock /kɒk/ *n* Hahn *m*; (*any male bird*) Männchen *nt* □ *vt* ⟨*animal:*⟩ **its ~ ears** die Ohren spitzen; **~ the gun** den Hahn spannen. **~-and-'bull story** *n* (*fam*) Lügengeschichte *f*
cockerel /'kɒkərəl/ *n* [junger] Hahn *m*
cock-'eyed *a* (*fam*) schief; (*absurd*) verrückt
cockle /'kɒkl/ *n* Herzmuschel *f*
cockney /'kɒknɪ/ *n* (*dialect*) Cockney *nt*; (*person*) Cockney *m*
cock: ~pit *n* (*Aviat*) Cockpit *nt*. **~roach** /-rəʊtʃ/ *n* Küchenschabe *f*. **~tail** *n* Cocktail *m*. **~-up** *n* (*sl*) **make a ~-up** Mist bauen (**of** bei)
cocky /'kɒkɪ/ *a* (**-ier, -iest**) (*fam*) eingebildet
cocoa /'kəʊkəʊ/ *n* Kakao *m*
coconut /'kəʊkənʌt/ *n* Kokosnuß *f*
cocoon /kə'ku:n/ *n* Kokon *m*
cod /kɒd/ *n inv* Kabeljau *m*
COD *abbr* (**cash on delivery**) per Nachnahme
coddle /'kɒdl/ *vt* verhätscheln
code /kəʊd/ *n* Kode *m*; (*Computing*) Code *m*; (*set of rules*) Kodex *m*. **~d** *a* verschlüsselt
coedu'cational /kəʊ-/ *a* gemischt. **~ school** *n* Koedukationsschule *f*
coerc|e /kəʊ'ɜ:s/ *vt* zwingen. **~ion** /-'ɜ:ʃn/ *n* Zwang *m*
coe'xist *vi* koexistieren. **~ence** *n* Koexistenz *f*
coffee /'kɒfɪ/ *n* Kaffee *m*
coffee: ~-grinder *n* Kaffeemühle *f*. **~-pot** *n* Kaffeekanne *f*. **~-table** *n* Couchtisch *m*
coffin /'kɒfɪn/ *n* Sarg *m*
cog /kɒg/ *n* (*Techn*) Zahn *m*
cogent /'kəʊdʒənt/ *a* überzeugend
cog-wheel *n* Zahnrad *nt*
cohabit /kəʊ'hæbɪt/ *vi* (*Jur*) zusammenleben
coherent /kəʊ'hɪərənt/ *a* zusammenhängend; (*comprehensible*) verständlich
coil /kɔɪl/ *n* Rolle *f*; (*Electr*) Spule *f*; (*one ring*) Windung *f* □ *vt* **~[up]** zusammenrollen
coin /kɔɪn/ *n* Münze *f* □ *vt* prägen
coincide /kəʊɪn'saɪd/ *vi* zusammenfallen; (*agree*) übereinstimmen
coinciden|ce /kəʊ'ɪnsɪdəns/ *n* Zufall *m*. **~tal** /-'dentl/ *a*, **-ly** *adv* zufällig
coke /kəʊk/ *n* Koks *m*
Coke (P) *n* (*drink*) Cola *f*
colander /'kʌləndə(r)/ *n* (*Culin*) Durchschlag *m*
cold /kəʊld/ *a* (**-er, -est**) kalt; **I am** *or* **feel ~** mir ist kalt □ *n* Kälte *f*; (*Med*) Erkältung *f*
cold: ~-'blooded *a* kaltblütig. **~-'hearted** *a* kaltherzig. **~ly** *adv* (*fig*) kalt, kühl. **~ness** *n* Kälte *f*
coleslaw /'kəʊlslɔ:/ *n* Krautsalat *m*
colic /'kɒlɪk/ *n* Kolik *f*
collaborat|e /kə'læbəreɪt/ *vi* zusammenarbeiten (**with** mit); **~e on sth** mitarbeiten bei etw. **~ion** /-'reɪʃn/ *n* Zusammenarbeit *f*, Mitarbeit *f*; (*with enemy*) Kollaboration *f*. **~or** *n* Mitarbeiter(in) *m*(*f*); Kollaborateur *m*
collaps|e /kə'læps/ *n* Zusammenbruch *m*; Einsturz *m* □ *vi* zusammenbrechen; ⟨*roof, building:*⟩

einstürzen. **~ible** *a* zusammenklappbar

collar /ˈkɒlə(r)/ *n* Kragen *m*; (*for animal*) Halsband *nt*. **~-bone** *n* Schlüsselbein *nt*

colleague /ˈkɒli:g/ *n* Kollege *m*/Kollegin *f*

collect /kəˈlekt/ *vt* sammeln; (*fetch*) abholen; einsammeln ⟨*tickets*⟩; einziehen ⟨*taxes*⟩ □ *vi* sich [an]sammeln □ *adv* **call ~** (*Amer*) ein R-Gespräch führen. **~ed** /-ɪd/ *a* gesammelt; (*calm*) gefasst

collection /kəˈlekʃn/ *n* Sammlung *f*; (*in church*) Kollekte *f*; (*of post*) Leerung *f*; (*designer's*) Kollektion *f*

collective /kəˈlektɪv/ *a* gemeinsam; (*Pol*) kollektiv. **~ ˈnoun** *n* Kollektivum *nt*

collector /kəˈlektə(r)/ *n* Sammler(in) *m*(*f*)

college /ˈkɒlɪdʒ/ *n* College *nt*

collide /kəˈlaɪd/ *vi* zusammenstoßen

colliery /ˈkɒlɪərɪ/ *n* Kohlengrube *f*

collision /kəˈlɪʒn/ *n* Zusammenstoß *m*

colloquial /kəˈləʊkwɪəl/ *a*, **-ly** *adv* umgangssprachlich. **~ism** *n* umgangssprachlicher Ausdruck *m*

Cologne /kəˈləʊn/ *n* Köln *nt*

colon /ˈkəʊlən/ *n* Doppelpunkt *m*; (*Anat*) Dickdarm *m*

colonel /ˈkɜ:nl/ *n* Oberst *m*

colonial /kəˈləʊnɪəl/ *a* Kolonial-

colon|ize /ˈkɒlənaɪz/ *vt* kolonisieren. **~y** *n* Kolonie *f*

colossal /kəˈlɒsl/ *a* riesig

colour /ˈkʌlə(r)/ *n* Farbe *f*; (*complexion*) Gesichtsfarbe *f*; (*race*) Hautfarbe *f*; **~s** *pl* (*flag*) Fahne *f*; **off ~** (*fam*) nicht ganz auf der Höhe □ *vt* färben; **~ [in]** ausmalen □ *vi* (*blush*) erröten

colour: ~ bar *n* Rassenschranke *f*. **~-blind** *a* farbenblind. **~ed** *a* farbig □ *n* (*person*) Farbige(r) *m*/*f*. **~-fast** *a* farbecht. **~ film** *n* Farbfilm *m*. **~ful** *a* farbenfroh. **~less** *a* farblos. **~ photo[graph]** *n* Farbaufnahme *f*. **~ television** *n* Farbfernsehen *nt*

colt /kəʊlt/ *n* junger Hengst *m*

column /ˈkɒləm/ *n* Säule *f*; (*of soldiers, figures*) Kolonne *f*; (*Typ*) Spalte *f*; (*Journ*) Kolumne *f*. **~ist** /-nɪst/ *n* Kolumnist *m*

coma /ˈkəʊmə/ *n* Koma *nt*

comb /kəʊm/ *n* Kamm *m* □ *vt* kämmen; (*search*) absuchen; **~ one's hair** sich (*dat*) [die Haare] kämmen

combat /ˈkɒmbæt/ *n* Kampf *m* □ *vt* (*pt*/*pp* **combated**) bekämpfen

combination /kɒmbɪˈneɪʃn/ *n* Verbindung *f*; (*for lock*) Kombination *f*

combine[1] /kəmˈbaɪn/ *vt* verbinden □ *vi* sich verbinden; ⟨*people:*⟩ sich zusammenschließen

combine[2] /ˈkɒmbaɪn/ *n* (*Comm*) Konzern *m*. **~ [harvester]** *n* Mähdrescher *m*

combustion /kəmˈbʌstʃn/ *n* Verbrennung *f*

come /kʌm/ *vi* (*pt* **came**, *pp* **come**) kommen; (*reach*) reichen (**to** an + *acc*); **that ~s to £10** das macht £10; **~ into money** zu Geld kommen; **~ true** wahr werden; **~ in two sizes** in zwei Größen erhältlich sein; **the years to ~** die kommenden Jahre; **how ~?** (*fam*) wie das? **~ about** *vi* geschehen. **~ across** *vi* herüberkommen; (*fam*) klar werden □ *vt* stoßen auf (+ *acc*). **~ apart** *vi* sich auseinander nehmen lassen; (*accidentally*) auseinander gehen. **~ away** *vi* weggehen; ⟨*thing:*⟩ abgehen. **~ back** *vi* zurückkommen. **~ by** *vi* vorbeikommen □ *vt* (*obtain*) bekommen. **~ in** *vi* hereinkommen. **~ off** *vi* abgehen; (*take* *place*) stattfinden; (*succeed*) klappen (*fam*). ~ **out** *vi* herauskommen; ⟨*book:*⟩ erscheinen; ⟨*stain:*⟩ herausgehen. ~ **round** *vi* vorbeikommen; (*after fainting*) [wieder] zu sich kommen; (*change one's mind*) sich umstimmen lassen. ~ **to** *vi* [wieder] zu sich kommen. ~ **up** *vi* heraufkommen; ⟨*plant:*⟩ aufgehen; (*reach*) reichen (**to** bis); ~ **up with** sich (*dat*) einfallen lassen

'come-back *n* Comeback *nt*

comedian /kə'mi:dıən/ *n* Komiker *m*

'come-down *n* Rückschritt *m*

comedy /'kɒmədı/ *n* Komödie *f*

comet /'kɒmıt/ *n* Komet *m*

come-uppance /kʌm'ʌpəns/ *n* **get one's** ~ (*fam*) sein Fett abkriegen

comfort /'kʌmfət/ *n* Bequemlichkeit *f*; (*consolation*) Trost *m* □ *vt* trösten

comfortable /'kʌmfətəbl/ *a*, **-bly** *adv* bequem

'comfort station *n* (*Amer*) öffentliche Toilette *f*

comfy /'kʌmfı/ *a* (*fam*) bequem

comic /'kɒmık/ *a* komisch □ *n* Komiker *m*; (*periodical*) Comic-Heft *nt*. ~**al** *a*, **-ly** *adv* komisch. ~ **strip** *n* Comic Strips *pl*

coming /'kʌmıŋ/ *a* kommend □ *n* Kommen *nt*; ~**s and goings** Kommen und Gehen *nt*

comma /'kɒmə/ *n* Komma *nt*

command /kə'mɑ:nd/ *n* Befehl *m*; (*Mil*) Kommando *nt*; (*mastery*) Beherrschung *f* □ *vt* befehlen (+ *dat*); kommandieren ⟨*army*⟩

commandeer /kɒmən'dıə(r)/ *vt* beschlagnahmen

command|er /kə'mɑ:ndə(r)/ *n* Befehlshaber *m*; (*of unit*) Kommandeur *m*; (*of ship*) Kommandant *m*. ~**ing** *a* ⟨*view*⟩ beherrschend. ~**ing officer** *n* Befehlshaber *m*. ~**ment** *n* Gebot *nt*

commemorat|e /kə'meməreıt/ *vt* gedenken (+ *gen*). ~**ion** /-'reıʃn/ *n* Gedenken *nt*. ~**ive** /-ətıv/ *a* Gedenk-

commence /kə'mens/ *vt/i* anfangen, beginnen. ~**ment** *n* Anfang *m*, Beginn *m*

commend /kə'mend/ *vt* loben; (*recommend*) empfehlen (**to** *dat*). ~**able** /-əbl/ *a* lobenswert. ~**ation** /kɒmen'deıʃn/ *n* Lob *nt*

commensurate /kə'menʃərət/ *a* angemessen; **be** ~ **with** entsprechen (+ *dat*)

comment /'kɒment/ *n* Bemerkung *f*; **no** ~! kein Kommentar! □ *vi* sich äußern (**on** zu); ~ **on** (*Journ*) kommentieren

commentary /'kɒməntrı/ *n* Kommentar *m*; **[running]** ~ (*Radio, TV*) Reportage *f*

commentator /'kɒmənteıtə(r)/ *n* Kommentator *m*; (*Sport*) Reporter *m*

commerce /'kɒm3:s/ *n* Handel *m*

commercial /kə'm3:ʃl/ *a*, **-ly** *adv* kommerziell □ *n* (*Radio, TV*) Werbespot *m*. ~**ize** *vt* kommerzialisieren

commiserate /kə'mızəreıt/ *vi* sein Mitleid ausdrücken (**with** *dat*)

commission /kə'mıʃn/ *n* (*order for work*) Auftrag *m*; (*body of people*) Kommission *f*; (*payment*) Provision *f*; (*Mil*) [Offiziers]patent *nt*; **out of** ~ außer Betrieb □ *vt* beauftragen ⟨*s.o.*⟩; in Auftrag geben ⟨*thing*⟩; (*Mil*) zum Offizier ernennen

commissionaire /kəmıʃə'neə(r)/ *n* Portier *m*

commissioner /kə'mıʃənə(r)/ *n* Kommissar *m*; ~ **for oaths** Notar *m*

commit /kə'mıt/ *vt* (*pt/pp* **committed**) begehen; (*entrust*) anvertrauen (**to** *dat*); (*consign*) einweisen (**to** in + *acc*); ~ **oneself** sich festlegen; (*involve oneself*) sich engagieren; ~ **sth to memory** sich (*dat*) **etw** einprägen. ~**ment** *n* Verpflichtung

f; (*involvement*) Engagement *nt*. **~ted** *a* engagiert
committee /kə'mɪtɪ/ *n* Ausschuss *m*, Komitee *nt*
commodity /kə'mɒdətɪ/ *n* Ware *f*
common /'kɒmən/ *a* (**-er, -est**) gemeinsam; (*frequent*) häufig; (*ordinary*) gewöhnlich; (*vulgar*) ordinär □ *n* Gemeindeland *nt*; **have in ~** gemeinsam haben; **House of C~s** Unterhaus *nt*. **~er** *n* Bürgerliche(r) *m/f*
common: ~'law *n* Gewohnheitsrecht *nt*. **~ly** *adv* allgemein. **C~ 'Market** *n* Gemeinsamer Markt *m*. **~place** *a* häufig. **~-room** *n* Aufenthaltsraum *m*. **~ 'sense** *n* gesunder Menschenverstand *m*
commotion /kə'məʊʃn/ *n* Tumult *m*
communal /'kɒmjʊnl/ *a* gemeinschaftlich
communicable /kə'mju:nɪkəbl/ *a* ⟨*disease*⟩ übertragbar
communicate /kə'mju:nɪkeɪt/ *vt* mitteilen (**to** *dat*); übertragen ⟨disease⟩ □ *vi* sich verständigen; (*be in touch*) Verbindung haben
communication /kəmju:nɪ'keɪʃn/ *n* Verständigung *f*; (*contact*) Verbindung *f*; (*of disease*) Übertragung *f*; (*message*) Mitteilung *f*; **~s** *pl* (*technology*) Nachrichtenwesen *nt*. **~ cord** *n* Notbremse *f*
communicative /kə'mju:nɪkətɪv/ *a* mitteilsam
Communion /kə'mju:nɪən/ *n* **[Holy] ~** das [heilige] Abendmahl; (*Roman Catholic*) die [heilige] Kommunion
communiqué /kə'mju:nɪkeɪ/ *n* Kommuniqué *nt*
Communis|m /'kɒmjʊnɪzm/ *n* Kommunismus *m*. **~t** /-ɪst/ *a* kommunistisch □ *n* Kommunist(in) *m(f)*
community /kə'mju:nətɪ/ *n* Gemeinschaft *f*; **local ~** Gemeinde *f*. **~ centre** *n* Gemeinschaftszentrum *nt*
commute /kə'mju:t/ *vi* pendeln □ *vt* (*Jur*) umwandeln. **~r** *n* Pendler(in) *m(f)*
compact[1] /kəm'pækt/ *a* kompakt
compact[2] /'kɒmpækt/ *n* Puderdose *f*. **~ disc** *n* CD *f*
companion /kəm'pænjən/ *n* Begleiter(in) *m(f)*. **~ship** *n* Gesellschaft *f*
company /'kʌmpənɪ/ *n* Gesellschaft *f*; (*firm*) Firma *f*; (*Mil*) Kompanie *f*; (*fam: guests*) Besuch *m*. **~ car** *n* Firmenwagen *m*
comparable /'kɒmpərəbl/ *a* vergleichbar
comparative /kəm'pærətɪv/ *a* vergleichend; (*relative*) relativ □ *n* (*Gram*) Komparativ *m*. **~ly** *adv* verhältnismäßig
compare /kəm'peə(r)/ *vt* vergleichen (**with/to** mit) □ *vi* sich vergleichen lassen
comparison /kəm'pærɪsn/ *n* Vergleich *m*
compartment /kəm'pɑ:tmənt/ *n* Fach *nt*; (*Rail*) Abteil *nt*
compass /'kʌmpəs/ *n* Kompass *m*. **~es** *npl* **pair of ~es** Zirkel *m*
compassion /kəm'pæʃn/ *n* Mitleid *nt*. **~ate** /-ʃənət/ *a* mitfühlend
compatible /kəm'pætəbl/ *a* vereinbar; ⟨*drugs*⟩ verträglich; (*Techn*) kompatibel; **be ~** ⟨*people:*⟩ [gut] zueinander passen
compatriot /kəm'pætrɪət/ *n* Landsmann *m* /-männin *f*
compel /kəm'pel/ *vt* (*pt/pp* **compelled**) zwingen
compensat|e /'kɒmpənseɪt/ *vt* entschädigen □ *vi* **~e for** (*fig*) ausgleichen. **~ion** /-'seɪʃn/ *n* Entschädigung *f*; (*fig*) Ausgleich *m*
compère /'kɒmpeə(r)/ *n* Conférencier *m*
compete /kəm'pi:t/ *vi* konkurrieren; (*take part*) teilnehmen (**in** an + *dat*)

competen|ce /ˈkɒmpɪtəns/ *n* Tüchtigkeit *f*; (*ability*) Fähigkeit *f*; (*Jur*) Kompetenz *f*. **~t** *a* tüchtig; fähig; (*Jur*) kompetent
competition /kɒmpəˈtɪʃn/ *n* Konkurrenz *f*; (*contest*) Wettbewerb *m*; (*in newspaper*) Preisausschreiben *nt*
competitive /kəmˈpetətɪv/ *a* (*Comm*) konkurrenzfähig
competitor /kəmˈpetɪtə(r)/ *n* Teilnehmer *m*; (*Comm*) Konkurrent *m*
compile /kəmˈpaɪl/ *vt* zusammenstellen; verfassen ⟨*dictionary*⟩
complacen|cy /kəmˈpleɪsənsɪ/ *n* Selbstzufriedenheit *f*. **~t** *a*, **-ly** *adv* selbstzufrieden
complain /kəmˈpleɪn/ *vi* klagen (**about/of** über + *acc*); (*formally*) sich beschweren. **~t** *n* Klage *f*; (*formal*) Beschwerde *f*; (*Med*) Leiden *nt*
complement[1] /ˈkɒmplɪmənt/ *n* Ergänzung *f*; **full ~** volle Anzahl *f*
complement[2] /ˈkɒmplɪment/ *vt* ergänzen; **~ each other** sich ergänzen. **~ary** /-ˈmentərɪ/ *a* sich ergänzend; **be ~ary** sich ergänzen
complete /kəmˈpliːt/ *a* vollständig; (*finished*) fertig; (*utter*) völlig □ *vt* vervollständigen; (*finish*) abschließen; (*fill in*) ausfüllen. **~ly** *adv* völlig
completion /kəmˈpliːʃn/ *n* Vervollständigung *f*; (*end*) Abschluss *m*
complex /ˈkɒmpleks/ *a* komplex □ *n* Komplex *m*
complexion /kəmˈplekʃn/ *n* Teint *m*; (*colour*) Gesichtsfarbe *f*; (*fig*) Aspekt *m*
complexity /kəmˈpleksətɪ/ *n* Komplexität *f*
compliance /kəmˈplaɪəns/ *n* Einverständnis *nt*; **in ~ with** gemäß (+ *dat*)
complicat|e /ˈkɒmplɪkeɪt/ *vt* komplizieren. **~ed** *a* kompliziert. **~ion** /-ˈkeɪʃn/ *n* Komplikation *f*
complicity /kəmˈplɪsətɪ/ *n* Mittäterschaft *f*
compliment /ˈkɒmplɪmənt/ *n* Kompliment *nt*; **~s** *pl* Grüße *pl* □ *vt* ein Kompliment machen (+ *dat*). **~ary** /-ˈmentərɪ/ *a* schmeichelhaft; (*given free*) Frei-
comply /kəmˈplaɪ/ *vi* (*pt/pp* **-ied**) **~ with** nachkommen (+ *dat*)
component /kəmˈpəʊnənt/ *a* & *n* **~ [part]** Bestandteil *m*, Teil *nt*
compose /kəmˈpəʊz/ *vt* verfassen; (*Mus*) komponieren; **~ oneself** sich fassen; **be ~d of** sich zusammensetzen aus. **~d** *a* (*calm*) gefasst. **~r** *n* Komponist *m*
composition /kɒmpəˈzɪʃn/ *n* Komposition *f*; (*essay*) Aufsatz *m*
compost /ˈkɒmpɒst/ *n* Kompost *m*
composure /kəmˈpəʊʒə(r)/ *n* Fassung *f*
compound[1] /kəmˈpaʊnd/ *vt* (*make worse*) verschlimmern
compound[2] /ˈkɒmpaʊnd/ *a* zusammengesetzt; ⟨*fracture*⟩ kompliziert □ *n* (*Chem*) Verbindung *f*; (*Gram*) Kompositum *nt*; (*enclosure*) Einfriedigung *f*. **~ 'interest** *n* Zinseszins *m*
comprehen|d /kɒmprɪˈhend/ *vt* begreifen, verstehen; (*include*) umfassen. **~sible** *a*, **-bly** *adv* verständlich. **~sion** /-ˈhenʃn/ *n* Verständnis *nt*
comprehensive /kɒmprɪˈhensɪv/ *a* & *n* umfassend; **~ [school]** Gesamtschule *f*. **~ insurance** *n* (*Auto*) Vollkaskoversicherung *f*
compress[1] /ˈkɒmpres/ *n* Kompresse *f*
compress[2] /kəmˈpres/ *vt* zusammenpressen; **~ed air** Druckluft *f*
comprise /kəmˈpraɪz/ *vt* umfassen, bestehen aus

compromise /ˈkɒmprəmaɪz/ *n* Kompromiss *m* □ *vt* kompromittieren ⟨*person*⟩ □ *vi* einen Kompromiss schließen
compuls|ion /kəmˈpʌlʃn/ *n* Zwang *m*. **~ive** /-sɪv/ *a* zwanghaft; **~ive eating** Esszwang *m*. **~ory** /-sərɪ/ *a* obligatorisch; **~ory subject** Pflichtfach *nt*
compunction /kəmˈpʌŋkʃn/ *n* Gewissensbisse *pl*
comput|er /kəmˈpju:tə(r)/ *n* Computer *m*. **~erize** *vt* computerisieren ⟨*data*⟩; auf Computer umstellen ⟨*firm*⟩. **~ing** *n* Computertechnik *f*
comrade /ˈkɒmreɪd/ *n* Kamerad *m*; (*Pol*) Genosse *m*/Genossin *f*. **~ship** *n* Kameradschaft *f*
con¹ /kɒn/ *see* **pro**
con² *n* (*fam*) Schwindel *m* □ *vt* (*pt/pp* **conned**) (*fam*) beschwindeln
concave /ˈkɒŋkeɪv/ *a* konkav
conceal /kənˈsi:l/ *vt* verstecken; (*keep secret*) verheimlichen
concede /kənˈsi:d/ *vt* zugeben; (*give up*) aufgeben
conceit /kənˈsi:t/ *n* Einbildung *f*. **~ed** *a* eingebildet
conceivable /kənˈsi:vəbl/ *a* denkbar
conceive /kənˈsi:v/ *vt* (*Biol*) empfangen; (*fig*) sich (*dat*) ausdenken □ *vi* schwanger werden. **~ of** (*fig*) sich (*dat*) vorstellen
concentrat|e /ˈkɒnsəntreɪt/ *vt* konzentrieren □ *vi* sich konzentrieren. **~ion** /-ˈtreɪʃn/ *n* Konzentration *f*. **~ion camp** *n* Konzentrationslager *nt*
concept /ˈkɒnsept/ *n* Begriff *m*. **~ion** /kənˈsepʃn/ *n* Empfängnis *f*; (*idea*) Vorstellung *f*
concern /kənˈsɜ:n/ *n* Angelegenheit *f*; (*worry*) Sorge *f*; (*Comm*) Unternehmen *nt* □ *vt* (*be about, affect*) betreffen; (*worry*) kümmern; **be ~ed about** besorgt sein um; **~ oneself with** sich beschäftigen mit; **as far as I am ~ed** was mich angeht *od* betrifft. **~ing** *prep* bezüglich (+ *gen*)
concert /ˈkɒnsət/ *n* Konzert *nt*; **in ~** im Chor. **~ed** /kənˈsɜ:tɪd/ *a* gemeinsam
concertina /kɒnsəˈti:nə/ *n* Konzertina *f*
ˈ**concertmaster** *n* (*Amer*) Konzertmeister *m*
concerto /kənˈtʃeətəʊ/ *n* Konzert *nt*
concession /kənˈseʃn/ *n* Zugeständnis *nt*; (*Comm*) Konzession *f*; (*reduction*) Ermäßigung *f*. **~ary** *a* (*reduced*) ermäßigt
conciliation /kənsɪlɪˈeɪʃn/ *n* Schlichtung *f*
concise /kənˈsaɪs/ *a*, **-ly** *adv* kurz
conclude /kənˈklu:d/ *vt/i* schließen
conclusion /kənˈklu:ʒn/ *n* Schluss *m*; **in ~** abschließend, zum Schluss
conclusive /kənˈklu:sɪv/ *a* schlüssig
concoct /kənˈkɒkt/ *vt* zusammenstellen; (*fig*) fabrizieren. **~ion** /-ɒkʃn/ *n* Zusammenstellung *f*; (*drink*) Gebräu *nt*
concourse /ˈkɒŋkɔ:s/ *a* Halle *f*
concrete /ˈkɒnkri:t/ *a* konkret □ *n* Beton *m* □ *vt* betonieren
concur /kənˈkɜ:(r)/ *vi* (*pt/pp* **concurred**) übereinstimmen
concurrently /kənˈkʌrəntlɪ/ *adv* gleichzeitig
concussion /kənˈkʌʃn/ *n* Gehirnerschütterung *f*
condemn /kənˈdem/ *vt* verurteilen; (*declare unfit*) für untauglich erklären. **~ation** /kɒndemˈneɪʃn/ *n* Verurteilung *f*
condensation /kɒndenˈseɪʃn/ *n* Kondensation *f*
condense /kənˈdens/ *vt* zusammenfassen; (*Phys*) kondensieren □ *vi* sich kondensieren. **~d milk** *n* Kondensmilch *f*
condescend /kɒndɪˈsend/ *vi* sich herablassen (**to** zu). **~ing** *a*, **-ly** *adv* herablassend

condiment /ˈkɒndɪmənt/ *n* Gewürz *nt*
condition /kənˈdɪʃn/ *n* Bedingung *f*; (*state*) Zustand *m*; **~s** *pl* Verhältnisse *pl*; **on ~ that** unter der Bedingung, dass □ *vt* (*Psych*) konditionieren. **~al** *a* bedingt; **be ~al on** abhängen von □ *n* (*Gram*) Konditional *m*. **~er** *n* Haarkur *f*; (*for fabrics*) Weichspüler *m*
condolences /kənˈdəʊlənsɪz/ *npl* Beileid *nt*
condom /ˈkɒndəm/ *n* Kondom *nt*
condominium /kɒndəˈmɪnɪəm/ *n* (*Amer*) ≈ Eigentumswohnung *f*
condone /kənˈdəʊn/ *vt* hinwegsehen über (+ *acc*)
conducive /kənˈdjuːsɪv/ *a* förderlich (**to** *dat*)
conduct[1] /ˈkɒndʌkt/ *n* Verhalten *nt*; (*Sch*) Betragen *nt*
conduct[2] /kənˈdʌkt/ *vt* führen; (*Phys*) leiten; (*Mus*) dirigieren. **~or** *n* Dirigent *m*; (*of bus*) Schaffner *m*; (*Phys*) Leiter *m*. **~ress** *n* Schaffnerin *f*
cone /kəʊn/ Kegel *m*; (*Bot*) Zapfen *m*; (*for ice-cream*) [Eis]tüte *f*; (*Auto*) Leitkegel *m*
confectioner /kənˈfekʃənə(r)/ *n* Konditor *m*. **~y** *n* Süßwaren *pl*
confederation /kənfedəˈreɪʃn/ *n* Bund *m*; (*Pol*) Konföderation *f*
confer /kənˈfɜː(r)/ *v* (*pt/pp* **conferred**) □ *vt* verleihen (**on** *dat*) □ *vi* sich beraten
conference /ˈkɒnfərəns/ *n* Konferenz *f*
confess /kənˈfes/ *vt/i* gestehen; (*Relig*) beichten. **~ion** /-eʃn/ *n* Geständnis *nt*; (*Relig*) Beichte *f*. **~ional** /-eʃənəl/ *n* Beichtstuhl *m*. **~or** *n* Beichtvater *m*
confetti /kənˈfetɪ/ *n* Konfetti *nt*
confide /kənˈfaɪd/ *vt* anvertrauen □ *vi* **~ in s.o.** sich jdm anvertrauen
confidence /ˈkɒnfɪdəns/ *n* (*trust*) Vertrauen *nt*; (*self-assurance*) Selbstvertrauen *nt*; (*secret*) Geheimnis *nt*; **in ~** im Vertrauen. **~ trick** *n* Schwindel *m*
confident /ˈkɒnfɪdənt/ *a*, **-ly** *adv* zuversichtlich; (*self-assured*) selbstsicher
confidential /kɒnfɪˈdenʃl/ *a*, **-ly** *adv* vertraulich
confine /kənˈfaɪn/ *vt* beschränken auf (+ *acc*); **be ~d to bed** das Bett hüten müssen. **~d** *a* (*narrow*) eng. **~ment** *n* Haft *f*
confines /ˈkɒnfaɪnz/ *npl* Grenzen *pl*
confirm /kənˈfɜːm/ *vt* bestätigen; (*Relig*) konfirmieren; (*Roman Catholic*) firmen. **~ation** /kɒnfəˈmeɪʃn/ *n* Bestätigung *f*; Konfirmation *f*; Firmung *f*. **~ed** *a* **~ed bachelor** eingefleischter Junggeselle *m*
confiscat|e /ˈkɒnfɪskeɪt/ *vt* beschlagnahmen. **~ion** /-ˈkeɪʃn/ *n* Beschlagnahme *f*
conflict[1] /ˈkɒnflɪkt/ *n* Konflikt *m*
conflict[2] /kənˈflɪkt/ *vi* im Widerspruch stehen (**with** zu). **~ing** *a* widersprüchlich
conform /kənˈfɔːm/ *vi* ⟨*person:*⟩ sich anpassen; ⟨*thing:*⟩ entsprechen (**to** *dat*). **~ist** *n* Konformist *m*
confounded /kənˈfaʊndɪd/ *a* (*fam*) verflixt
confront /kənˈfrʌnt/ *vt* konfrontieren. **~ation** /kɒnfrənˈteɪʃn/ *n* Konfrontation *f*
confus|e /kənˈfjuːz/ *vt* verwirren; (*mistake for*) verwechseln (**with** mit). **~ing** *a* verwirrend. **~ion** /-juːʒn/ *n* Verwirrung *f*; (*muddle*) Durcheinander *nt*
congeal /kənˈdʒiːl/ *vi* fest werden; ⟨*blood:*⟩ gerinnen
congenial /kənˈdʒiːnɪəl/ *a* angenehm
congenital /kənˈdʒenɪtl/ *a* angeboren
congest|ed /kənˈdʒestɪd/ *a* verstopft; (*with people*) überfüllt.

~ion /-estʃn/ *n* Verstopfung *f*; Überfüllung *f*
congratulat|e /kən'grætjʊleɪt/ *vt* gratulieren (+ *dat*) (**on** zu). **~ions** /-'leɪʃnz/ *npl* Glückwünsche *pl*; **~ions!** [ich] gratuliere!
congregat|e /'kɒŋgrɪgeɪt/ *vi* sich versammeln. **~ion** /-'geɪʃn/ *n* (*Relig*) Gemeinde *f*
congress /'kɒŋgres/ *n* Kongress *m*. **~man** *n* Kongressabgeordnete(r) *m*
conical /'kɒnɪkl/ *a* kegelförmig
conifer /'kɒnɪfə(r)/ *n* Nadelbaum *m*
conjecture /kən'dʒektʃə(r)/ *n* Mutmaßung *f* □ *vt/i* mutmaßen
conjugal /'kɒndʒʊgl/ *a* ehelich
conjugat|e /'kɒndʒʊgeɪt/ *vt* konjugieren. **~ion** /-'geɪʃn/ *n* Konjugation *f*
conjunction /kən'dʒʌŋkʃn/ *n* Konjunktion *f*; **in ~ with** zusammen mit
conjunctivitis /kəndʒʌŋktɪ'vaɪtɪs/ *n* Bindehautentzündung *f*
conjur|e /'kʌndʒə(r)/ *vi* zaubern □ *vt* **~e up** heraufbeschwören. **~or** *n* Zauberkünstler *m*
conk /kɒŋk/ *vi* **~ out** (*fam*) ⟨*machine:*⟩ kaputtgehen; ⟨*person:*⟩ zusammenklappen
conker /'kɒŋkə(r)/ *n* (*fam*) Kastanie *f*
'con-man *n* (*fam*) Schwindler *m*
connect /kə'nekt/ *vt* verbinden (**to** mit); (*Electr*) anschließen (**to** an + *acc*) □ *vi* verbunden sein; ⟨*train:*⟩ Anschluss haben (**with** an + *acc*); **be ~ed with** zu tun haben mit; (*be related to*) verwandt sein mit
connection /kə'nekʃn/ *n* Verbindung *f*; (*Rail, Electr*) Anschluss *m*; **in ~ with** in Zusammenhang mit. **~s** *npl* Beziehungen *pl*
conniv|ance /kə'naɪvəns/ *n* stillschweigende Duldung *f*. **~e** *vi* **~e at** stillschweigend dulden
connoisseur /kɒnə'sɜ:(r)/ *n* Kenner *m*
connotation /kɒnə'teɪʃn/ *n* Assoziation *f*
conquer /'kɒŋkə(r)/ *vt* erobern; (*fig*) besiegen. **~or** *n* Eroberer *m*
conquest /'kɒŋkwest/ *n* Eroberung *f*
conscience /'kɒnʃəns/ *n* Gewissen *nt*
conscientious /kɒnʃɪ'enʃəs/ *a*, **-ly** *adv* gewissenhaft. **~ ob'jector** *n* Kriegsdienstverweigerer *m*
conscious /'kɒnʃəs/ *a*, **-ly** *adv* bewusst; **[fully] ~** bei [vollem] Bewusstsein; **be/become ~ of sth** sich (*dat*) etw (*gen*) bewusst sein/werden. **~ness** *n* Bewusstsein *nt*
conscript[1] /'kɒnskrɪpt/ *n* Einberufene(r) *m*
conscript[2] /kən'skrɪpt/ *vt* einberufen. **~ion** /-ɪpʃn/ *n* allgemeine Wehrpflicht *f*.
consecrat|e /'kɒnsɪkreɪt/ *vt* weihen; einweihen ⟨*church*⟩. **~ion** /-'kreɪʃn/ *n* Weihe *f*; Einweihung *f*
consecutive /kən'sekjʊtɪv/ *a* aufeinander folgend. **-ly** *adv* fortlaufend
consensus /kən'sensəs/ *n* Übereinstimmung *f*
consent /kən'sent/ *n* Einwilligung *f*, Zustimmung *f* □ *vi* einwilligen (**to** in + *acc*), zustimmen (**to** *dat*)
consequen|ce /'kɒnsɪkwəns/ *n* Folge *f*; (*importance*) Bedeutung *f*. **~t** *a* daraus folgend. **~tly** *adv* folglich
conservation /kɒnsə'veɪʃn/ *n* Erhaltung *f*, Bewahrung *f*. **~ist** *n* Umweltschützer *m*
conservative /kən'sɜ:vətɪv/ *a* konservativ; ⟨*estimate*⟩ vorsichtig. **C~** (*Pol*) *a* konservativ □ *n* Konservative(r) *m/f*
conservatory /kən'sɜ:vətrɪ/ *n* Wintergarten *m*

conserve /kən'sɜ:v/ *vt* erhalten, bewahren; sparen ⟨*energy*⟩

consider /kən'sɪdə(r)/ *vt* erwägen; (*think over*) sich (*dat*) überlegen; (*take into account*) berücksichtigen; (*regard as*) betrachten als; **~ doing sth** erwägen, etw zu tun. **~able** /-əbl/ *a*, **-bly** *adv* erheblich

consider|ate /kən'sɪdərət/ *a*, **-ly** *adv* rücksichtsvoll. **~ation** /-'reɪʃn/ *n* Erwägung *f*; (*thoughtfulness*) Rücksicht *f*; (*payment*) Entgelt *nt*; **take into ~ation** berücksichtigen. **~ing** *prep* wenn man bedenkt (**that** dass); **~ing the circumstances** unter den Umständen

consign /kən'saɪn/ *vt* übergeben (**to** *dat*). **~ment** *n* Lieferung *f*

consist /kən'sɪst/ *vi* **~ of** bestehen aus

consisten|cy /kən'sɪstənsɪ/ *n* Konsequenz *f*; (*density*) Konsistenz *f*. **~t** *a* konsequent; (*unchanging*) gleichbleibend; **be ~t with** entsprechen (+ *dat*). **~tly** *adv* konsequent; (*constantly*) ständig

consolation /kɒnsə'leɪʃn/ *n* Trost *m*. **~ prize** *n* Trostpreis *m*

console /kən'səʊl/ *vt* trösten

consolidate /kən'sɒlɪdeɪt/ *vt* konsolidieren

consonant /'kɒnsənənt/ *n* Konsonant *m*

consort /'kɒnsɔ:t/ *n* Gemahl(in) *m*(*f*)

conspicuous /kən'spɪkjʊəs/ *a* auffällig

conspiracy /kən'spɪrəsɪ/ *n* Verschwörung *f*

conspire /kən'spaɪə(r)/ *vi* sich verschwören

constable /'kʌnstəbl/ *n* Polizist *m*

constant /'kɒnstənt/ *a*, **-ly** *adv* beständig; (*continuous*) ständig

constellation /kɒnstə'leɪʃn/ *n* Sternbild *nt*

consternation /kɒnstə'neɪʃn/ *n* Bestürzung *f*

constipat|ed /'kɒnstɪpeɪtɪd/ *a* verstopft. **~ion** /-'peɪʃn/ *n* Verstopfung *f*

constituency /kən'stɪtjʊənsɪ/ *n* Wahlkreis *m*

constituent /kən'stɪtjʊənt/ *n* Bestandteil *m*; (*Pol*) Wähler(in) *m*(*f*)

constitut|e /'kɒnstɪtju:t/ *vt* bilden. **~ion** /-'tju:ʃn/ *n* (*Pol*) Verfassung *f*; (*of person*) Konstitution *f*. **~ional** /-'tju:ʃənl/ *a* Verfassungs- □ *n* Verdauungsspaziergang *m*

constrain /kən'streɪn/ *vt* zwingen. **~t** *n* Zwang *m*; (*restriction*) Beschränkung *f*; (*strained manner*) Gezwungenheit *f*

constrict /kən'strɪkt/ *vt* einengen

construct /kən'strʌkt/ *vt* bauen. **~ion** /-ʌkʃn/ *n* Bau *m*; (*Gram*) Konstruktion *f*; (*interpretation*) Deutung *f*; **under ~ion** im Bau. **~ive** /-ɪv/ *a* konstruktiv

construe /kən'stru:/ *vt* deuten

consul /'kɒnsl/ *n* Konsul *m*. **~ate** /'kɒnsjʊlət/ *n* Konsulat *nt*

consult /kən'sʌlt/ *vt* [um Rat] fragen; konsultieren ⟨*doctor*⟩; nachschlagen in (+ *dat*) ⟨*book*⟩. **~ant** *n* Berater *m*; (*Med*) Chefarzt *m*. **~ation** /kɒnsl'teɪʃn/ *n* Beratung *f*; (*Med*) Konsultation *f*

consume /kɒn'sju:m/ *vt* verzehren; (*use*) verbrauchen. **~r** *n* Verbraucher *m*. **~r goods** *npl* Konsumgüter *pl*

consummat|e /'kɒnsəmeɪt/ *vt* vollziehen. **~ion** /-'meɪʃn/ *n* Vollzug *m*

consumption /kən'sʌmpʃn/ *n* Konsum *m*; (*use*) Verbrauch *m*

contact /'kɒntækt/ *n* Kontakt *m*; (*person*) Kontaktperson *f* □ *vt* sich in Verbindung setzen mit. **~ 'lenses** *npl* Kontaktlinsen *pl*

contagious /kən'teɪdʒəs/ *a* direkt übertragbar

contain /kən'teɪn/ *vt* enthalten; (*control*) beherrschen. **~er** *n* Behälter *m*; (*Comm*) Container *m*

contaminat|e /kən'tæmɪneɪt/ *vt* verseuchen. **~ion** /-'neɪʃn/ *n* Verseuchung *f*

contemplat|e /'kɒntəmpleɪt/ *vt* betrachten; (*meditate*) nachdenken über (+ *acc*); **~e doing sth** daran denken, **etw** zu tun. **~ion** /-'pleɪʃn/ *n* Betrachtung *f*; Nachdenken *nt*

contemporary /kən'tempərərɪ/ *a* zeitgenössisch □ *n* Zeitgenosse *m*/ -genossin *f*

contempt /kən'tempt/ *n* Verachtung *f*; **beneath ~** verabscheuungswürdig; **~ of court** Missachtung *f* des Gerichts. **~ible** /-əbl/ *a* verachtenswert. **~uous** /-tjʊəs/ *a*, **-ly** *adv* verächtlich

contend /kən'tend/ *vi* kämpfen (**with** mit) □ *vt* (*assert*) behaupten. **~er** *n* Bewerber(in) *m(f)*; (*Sport*) Wettkämpfer(in) *m(f)*

content[1] /'kɒntent/ *n* & **contents** *pl* Inhalt *m*

content[2] /kən'tent/ *a* zufrieden □ *n* **to one's heart's ~** nach Herzenslust □ *vt* **~ oneself** sich begnügen (**with** mit). **~ed** *a*, **-ly** *adv* zufrieden

contention /kən'tenʃn/ *n* (*assertion*) Behauptung *f*

contentment /kən'tentmənt/ *n* Zufriedenheit *f*

contest[1] /'kɒntest/ *n* Kampf *m*; (*competition*) Wettbewerb *m*

contest[2] /kən'test/ *vt* (*dispute*) bestreiten; (*Jur*) anfechten; (*Pol*) kandidieren in (+ *dat*). **~ant** *n* Teilnehmer *m*

context /'kɒntekst/ *n* Zusammenhang *m*

continent /'kɒntɪnənt/ *n* Kontinent *m*

continental /kɒntɪ'nentl/ *a* Kontinental-. **~ breakfast** *n* kleines Frühstück *nt*. **~ quilt** *n* Daunendecke *f*

contingen|cy /kən'tɪndʒənsɪ/ *n* Eventualität *f*. **~t** *a* **be ~t upon** abhängen von □ *n* (*Mil*) Kontingent *nt*

continual /kən'tɪnjʊəl/ *a*, **-ly** *adv* dauernd

continuation /kəntɪnjʊ'eɪʃn/ *n* Fortsetzung *f*

continue /kən'tɪnju:/ *vt* fortsetzen; **~ doing** *or* **to do sth** fortfahren, **etw** zu tun; **to be ~d** Fortsetzung folgt □ *vi* weitergehen; (*doing sth*) weitermachen; (*speaking*) fortfahren; ⟨*weather:*⟩ anhalten

continuity /kɒntɪ'nju:ətɪ/ *n* Kontinuität *f*

continuous /kən'tɪnjʊəs/ *a*, **-ly** *adv* anhaltend, ununterbrochen

contort /kən'tɔ:t/ *vt* verzerren. **~ion** /-ɔ:ʃn/ *n* Verzerrung *f*

contour /'kɒntʊə(r)/ *n* Kontur *f*; (*line*) Höhenlinie *f*

contraband /'kɒntrəbænd/ *n* Schmuggelware *f*

contracep|tion /kɒntrə'sepʃn/ *n* Empfängnisverhütung *f*. **~tive** /-tɪv/ *a* empfängnisverhütend □ *n* Empfängnisverhütungsmittel *nt*

contract[1] /'kɒntrækt/ *n* Vertrag *m*

contract[2] /kən'trækt/ *vi* sich zusammenziehen □ *vt* zusammenziehen; sich (*dat*) zuziehen ⟨*illness*⟩. **~ion** /-ækʃn/ *n* Zusammenziehung *f*; (*abbreviation*) Abkürzung *f*; (*in childbirth*) Wehe *f*. **~or** *n* Unternehmer *m*

contradict /kɒntrə'dɪkt/ *vt* widersprechen (+ *dat*). **~ion** /-ɪkʃn/ *n* Widerspruch *m*. **~ory** /-ərɪ/ *a* widersprüchlich

contra-flow /'kɒntrə-/ *n* Umleitung *f* [auf die entgegengesetzte Fahrbahn]

contralto /kən'træltəʊ/ *n* Alt *m*; (*singer*) Altistin *f*

contraption /kən'træpʃn/ *n* (*fam*) Apparat *m*

contrary¹ /'kɒntrərɪ/ *a & adv* entgegengesetzt; ~ **to** entgegen (+ *dat*) □ *n* Gegenteil *nt*; **on the** ~ im Gegenteil

contrary² /kən'treərɪ/ *a* widerspenstig

contrast¹ /'kɒntrɑ:st/ *n* Kontrast *m*

contrast² /kən'trɑ:st/ *vt* gegenüberstellen (**with** *dat*) □ *vi* einen Kontrast bilden (**with** zu). ~**ing** *a* gegensätzlich; ⟨*colour*⟩ Kontrast-

contraven|e /kɒntrə'vi:n/ *vt* verstoßen gegen. ~**tion** /-'venʃn/ *n* Verstoß *m* (**of** gegen)

contribut|e /kən'trɪbju:t/ *vt/i* beitragen; beisteuern ⟨*money*⟩; (*donate*) spenden. ~**ion** /kɒntrɪ'bju:ʃn/ *n* Beitrag *m*; (*donation*) Spende *f*. ~**or** *n* Beitragende(r) *m/f*

contrite /kən'traɪt/ *a* reuig

contrivance /kən'traɪvəns/ *n* Vorrichtung *f*

contrive /kən'traɪv/ *vt* verfertigen; ~ **to do sth** es fertig bringen, etw zu tun

control /kən'trəʊl/ *n* Kontrolle *f*; (*mastery*) Beherrschung *f*; (*Techn*) Regler *m*; ~**s** *pl* (*of car, plane*) Steuerung *f*; **get out of** ~ außer Kontrolle geraten □ *vt* (*pt/pp* **controlled**) kontrollieren; (*restrain*) unter Kontrolle halten; ~ **oneself** sich beherrschen

controvers|ial /kɒntrə'vɜ:ʃl/ *a* umstritten. ~**y** /'kɒntrəvɜ:ʃɪ/ *n* Kontroverse *f*

conundrum /kə'nʌndrəm/ *n* Rätsel *nt*

conurbation /kɒnɜ:'beɪʃn/ *n* Ballungsgebiet *nt*

convalesce /kɒnvə'les/ *vi* sich erholen. ~**nce** *n* Erholung *f*

convalescent /kɒnvə'lesnt/ *a* **be** ~ noch erholungsbedürftig sein. ~ **home** *n* Erholungsheim *nt*

convector /kən'vektə(r)/ *n* ~ **[heater]** Konvektor *m*

convene /kən'vi:n/ *vt* einberufen □ *v* sich versammeln

convenience /kən'vi:nɪəns/ *n* Bequemlichkeit *f*; **[public]** ~ öffentliche Toilette *f*; **with all modern** ~**s** mit allem Komfort

convenient /kən'vi:nɪənt/ *a*, **-ly** *adv* günstig; **be** ~ **for s.o.** jdm gelegen sein *od* jdm passen; **if it is** ~ **[for you]** wenn es Ihnen passt

convent /'kɒnvənt/ *n* [Nonnen]-kloster *nt*

convention /kən'venʃn/ *n* (*custom*) Brauch *m*, Sitte *f*; (*agreement*) Konvention *f*; (*assembly*) Tagung *f*. ~**al** *a*, **-ly** *adv* konventionell

converge /kən'vɜ:dʒ/ *vi* zusammenlaufen

conversant /kən'vɜ:sənt/ *a* ~ **with** vertraut mit

conversation /kɒnvə'seɪʃn/ *n* Gespräch *nt*; (*Sch*) Konversation *f*

converse¹ /kən'vɜ:s/ *vi* sich unterhalten

converse² /'kɒnvɜ:s/ *n* Gegenteil *nt*. ~**ly** *adv* umgekehrt

conversion /kən'vɜ:ʃn/ *n* Umbau *m*; (*Relig*) Bekehrung *f*; (*calculation*) Umrechnung *f*

convert¹ /'kɒnvɜ:t/ *n* Bekehrte(r) *m/f*, Konvertit *m*

convert² /kən'vɜ:t/ *vt* bekehren ⟨*person*⟩; (*change*) umwandeln (**into** in + *acc*); umbauen ⟨*building*⟩; (*calculate*) umrechnen; (*Techn*) umstellen. ~**ible** /-əbl/ *a* verwandelbar □ *n* (*Auto*) Kabriolett *nt*

convex /'kɒnveks/ *a* konvex

convey /kən'veɪ/ *vt* befördern; vermitteln ⟨*idea, message*⟩. ~**ance** *n* Beförderung *f*; (*vehicle*) Beförderungsmittel *nt*. ~**or belt** *n* Förderband *nt*

convict¹ /'kɒnvɪkt/ *n* Sträfling *m*

convict² /kən'vɪkt/ *vt* verurteilen (of wegen). **~ion** /-ɪkʃn/ *n* Verurteilung *f*; (*belief*) Überzeugung *f*; **previous ~ion** Vorstrafe *f*
convinc|e /kən'vɪns/ *vt* überzeugen. **~ing** *a*, **-ly** *adv* überzeugend
convivial /kən'vɪvɪəl/ *a* gesellig
convoluted /'kɒnvəlu:tɪd/ *a* verschlungen; (*fig*) verwickelt
convoy /'kɒnvɔɪ/ *n* Konvoi *m*
convuls|e /kən'vʌls/ *vt* **be ~ed** sich krümmen (**with** vor + *dat*). **~ion** /-ʌlʃn/ *n* Krampf *m*
coo /ku:/ *vi* gurren
cook /kʊk/ *n* Koch *m*/ Köchin *f* □ *vt/i* kochen; **is it ~ed?** ist es gar? **~ the books** (*fam*) die Bilanz frisieren. **~book** *n* (*Amer*) Kochbuch *nt*
cooker /'kʊkə(r)/ *n* [Koch]herd *m*; (*apple*) Kochapfel *m*. **~y** *n* Kochen *nt*. **~y book** *n* Kochbuch *nt*
cookie /'kʊkɪ/ *n* (*Amer*) Keks *m*
cool /ku:l/ *a* (**-er, -est**), **-ly** *adv* kühlen □ *n* Kühle *f* □ *vt* kühlen □ *vi* abkühlen. **~-box** *n* Kühlbox *f*. **~ness** *n* Kühle *f*
coop /ku:p/ *n* [Hühner]stall *m* □ *vt* **~ up** einsperren
co-operat|e /kəʊ'ɒpəreɪt/ *vi* zusammenarbeiten. **~ion** /-'reɪʃn/ *n* Kooperation *f*
co-operative /kəʊ'ɒpərətɪv/ *a* hilfsbereit □ *n* Genossenschaft *f*
co-opt /kəʊ'ɒpt/ *vt* hinzuwählen
co-ordinat|e /kəʊ'ɔ:dɪneɪt/ *vt* koordinieren. **~ion** /-'neɪʃn/ *n* Koordination *f*
cop /kɒp/ *n* (*fam*) Polizist *m*
cope /kəʊp/ *vi* (*fam*) zurechtkommen; **~ with** fertig werden mit
copious /'kəʊpɪəs/ *a* reichlich
copper¹ /'kɒpə(r)/ *n* Kupfer *nt*; **~s** *pl* Kleingeld *nt* □ *a* kupfern
copper² *n* (*fam*) Polizist *m*
copper 'beech *n* Blutbuche *f*
coppice /'kɒpɪs/ *n*, **copse** /kɒps/ *n* Gehölz *nt*
copulate /'kɒpjʊleɪt/ *vi* sich begatten
copy /'kɒpɪ/ *n* Kopie *f*; (*book*) Exemplar *nt* □ *vt* (*pt/pp* **-ied**) kopieren; (*imitate*) nachahmen; (*Sch*) abschreiben
copy: ~right *n* Copyright *nt*. **~-writer** *n* Texter *m*
coral /'kɒrl/ *n* Koralle *f*
cord /kɔ:d/ *n* Schnur *f*; (*fabric*) Cordsamt *m*; **~s** *pl* Cordhose *f*
cordial /'kɔ:dɪəl/ *a*, **-ly** *adv* herzlich □ *n* Fruchtsirup *m*
cordon /'kɔ:dn/ *n* Kordon *m* □ *vt* **~ off** absperren
corduroy /'kɔ:dərɔɪ/ *n* Cordsamt *m*
core /kɔ:(r)/ *n* Kern *m*; (*of apple, pear*) Kernegehäuse *nt*
cork /kɔ:k/ *n* Kork *m*; (*for bottle*) Korken *m*. **~screw** *n* Korkenzieher *m*
corn¹ /kɔ:n/ *n* Korn *nt*; (*Amer: maize*) Mais *m*
corn² *n* (*Med*) Hühnerauge *nt*
cornea /'kɔ:nɪə/ *n* Hornhaut *f*
corned beef /kɔ:nd'bi:f/ *n* Cornedbeef *nt*
corner /'kɔ:nə(r)/ *n* Ecke *f*; (*bend*) Kurve *f*; (*football*) Eckball *m* □ *vt* (*fig*) in die Enge treiben; (*Comm*) monopolisieren ⟨*market*⟩. **~-stone** *n* Eckstein *m*
cornet /'kɔ:nɪt/ *n* (*Mus*) Kornett *nt*; (*for ice-cream*) [Eis]tüte *f*
corn: ~flour *n*, (*Amer*) **~starch** *n* Stärkemehl *nt*
corny /'kɔ:nɪ/ *a* (*fam*) abgedroschen
coronary /'kɒrənərɪ/ *a* & *n* **~ [thrombosis]** Koronarthrombose *f*
coronation /kɒrə'neɪʃn/ *n* Krönung *f*
coroner /'kɒrənə(r)/ *n* Beamte(r) *m*, der verdächtige Todesfälle untersucht
coronet /'kɒrənet/ *n* Adelskrone *f*

corporal1 /ˈkɔːpərəl/ *n* (*Mil*) Stabsunteroffizier *m*

corporal2 *a* körperlich; ~ **punishment** körperliche Züchtigung *f*

corporate /ˈkɔːpərət/ *a* gemeinschaftlich

corporation /kɔːpəˈreɪʃn/ *n* Körperschaft *f*; (*of town*) Stadtverwaltung *f*

corps /kɔː(r)/ *n* (*pl* **corps** /kɔːz/) Korps *nt*

corpse /kɔːps/ *n* Leiche *f*

corpulent /ˈkɔːpjʊlənt/ *a* korpulent

corpuscle /ˈkɔːpʌsl/ *n* Blutkörperchen *nt*

correct /kəˈrekt/ *a*, **-ly** *adv* richtig; (*proper*) korrekt □ *vt* verbessern; (*Sch, Typ*) korrigieren. ~**ion** /-ekʃn/ *n* Verbesserung *f*; (*Typ*) Korrektur *f*

correlation /kɒrəˈleɪʃn/ *n* Wechselbeziehung *f*

correspond /kɒrɪˈspɒnd/ *vi* entsprechen (**to** *dat*); ⟨*two things:*⟩ sich entsprechen; (*write*) korrespondieren. ~**ence** *n* Briefwechsel *m*; (*Comm*) Korrespondenz *f*. ~**ent** *n* Korrespondent(in) *m(f)*. ~**ing** *a*, **-ly** *adv* entsprechend

corridor /ˈkɒrɪdɔː(r)/ *n* Gang *m*; (*Pol, Aviat*) Korridor *m*

corroborate /kəˈrɒbəreɪt/ *vt* bestätigen

corro|de /kəˈrəʊd/ *vt* zerfressen □ *vi* rosten. ~**sion** /-ˈrəʊʒn/ *n* Korrosion *f*

corrugated /ˈkɒrəgeɪtɪd/ *a* gewellt. ~ **iron** *n* Wellblech *nt*

corrupt /kəˈrʌpt/ *a* korrupt □ *vt* korrumpieren; (*spoil*) verderben. ~**ion** /-ʌpʃn/ *n* Korruption *f*

corset /ˈkɔːsɪt/ *n* & **-s** *pl* Korsett *nt*

Corsica /ˈkɔːsɪkə/ *n* Korsika *nt*

cortège /kɔːˈteɪʒ/ *n* **[funeral]** ~ Leichenzug *m*

cosh /kɒʃ/ *n* Totschläger *m*

cosmetic /kɒzˈmetɪk/ *a* kosmetisch □ *n* ~**s** *pl* Kosmetika *pl*

cosmic /ˈkɒzmɪk/ *a* kosmisch

cosmonaut /ˈkɒzmənɔːt/ *n* Kosmonaut(in) *m(f)*

cosmopolitan /kɒzməˈpɒlɪtən/ *a* kosmopolitisch

cosmos /ˈkɒzmɒs/ *n* Kosmos *m*

cosset /ˈkɒsɪt/ *vt* verhätscheln

cost /kɒst/ *n* Kosten *pl*; ~**s** *pl* (*Jur*) Kosten; **at all** ~**s** um jeden Preis; **I learnt to my** ~**es** ist mich teuer zu stehen gekommen □ *vt* (*pt/pp* **cost**) kosten; **it** ~ **me £20** es hat mich £20 gekostet □ *vt* (*pt/pp* **costed**) ~ **[out]** die Kosten kalkulieren für

costly /ˈkɒstlɪ/ *a* (**-ier, -iest**) teuer

cost: ~ **of ˈliving** *n* Lebenshaltungskosten *pl*. ~ **price** *n* Selbstkostenpreis *m*

costume /ˈkɒstjuːm/ *n* Kostüm *nt*; (*national*) Tracht *f*. ~ **jewellery** *n* Modeschmuck *m*

cosy /ˈkəʊzɪ/ *a* (**-ier, -iest**) gemütlich □ *n* (*tea-, egg-*) Wärmer *m*

cot /kɒt/ *n* Kinderbett *nt*; (*Amer: camp-bed*) Feldbett *nt*

cottage /ˈkɒtɪdʒ/ *n* Häuschen *nt*. ~ ˈ**cheese** *n* Hüttenkäse *m*

cotton /ˈkɒtn/ *n* Baumwolle *f*; (*thread*) Nähgarn *nt* □ *a* baumwollen □ *vi* ~ **on** (*fam*) kapieren

cotton ˈwool *n* Watte *f*

couch /kaʊtʃ/ *n* Liege *f*

couchette /kuːˈʃet/ *n* (*Rail*) Liegeplatz *m*

cough /kɒf/ *n* Husten *m* □ *vi* husten. ~ **up** *vt/i* husten; (*fam: pay*) blechen

ˈ**cough mixture** *n* Hustensaft *m*

could /kʊd, *unbetont* kəd/ *see* can²

council /ˈkaʊnsl/ *n* Rat *m*; (*Admin*) Stadtverwaltung *f*; (*rural*) Gemeindeverwaltung *f*. ~ **house** *n* ≈ Sozialwohnung *f*

councillor /ˈkaʊnsələ(r)/ *n* Stadtverordnete(r) *m/f*

ˈ**council tax** *n* Gemeindesteuer *f*

counsel /ˈkaʊnsl/ *n* Rat *m*; (*Jur*) Anwalt *m* □ *vt* (*pt/pp* **counselled**) beraten. **~lor** *n* Berater(in) *m*(*f*)
count¹ /kaʊnt/ *n* Graf *m*
count² *n* Zählung *f*; **keep ~** zählen □ *vt/i* zählen. **~ on** *vt* rechnen auf (+ *acc*)
countenance /ˈkaʊntənəns/ *n* Gesicht *nt* □ *vt* dulden
counter¹ /ˈkaʊntə(r)/ *n* (*in shop*) Ladentisch *m*; (*in bank*) Schalter *m*; (*in café*) Theke *f*; (*Games*) Spielmarke *f*
counter² *adv* **~ to** gegen (+ *acc*) □ *a* Gegen- □ *vt/i* kontern
counterˈact *vt* entgegenwirken (+ *dat*)
ˈcounter-attack *n* Gegenangriff *m*
counter-ˈespionage *n* Spionageabwehr *f*
ˈcounterfeit /-fɪt/ *a* gefälscht □ *n* Fälschung *f* □ *vt* fälschen
ˈcounterfoil *n* Kontrollabschnitt *m*
ˈcounterpart *n* Gegenstück *nt*
counter-proˈductive *a* **be ~** das Gegenteil bewirken
ˈcountersign *vt* gegenzeichnen
countess /ˈkaʊntɪs/ *n* Gräfin *f*
countless /ˈkaʊntlɪs/ *a* unzählig
countrified /ˈkʌntrɪfaɪd/ *a* ländlich
country /ˈkʌntrɪ/ *n* Land *nt*; (*native land*) Heimat *f*; (*countryside*) Landschaft *f*; **in the ~** auf dem Lande. **~man** *n* **[fellow] ~man** Landsmann *m*. **~side** *n* Landschaft *f*
county /ˈkaʊntɪ/ *n* Grafschaft *f*
coup /kuː/ *n* (*Pol*) Staatsstreich *m*
couple /ˈkʌpl/ *n* Paar *nt*; **a ~ of** (*two*) zwei □ *vt* verbinden; (*Rail*) koppeln
coupon /ˈkuːpɒn/ *n* Kupon *m*; (*voucher*) Gutschein *m*; (*entry form*) Schein *m*
courage /ˈkʌrɪdʒ/ *n* Mut *m*. **~ous** /kəˈreɪdʒəs/ *a*, **-ly** *adv* mutig
courgettes /kʊəˈʒets/ *npl* Zucchini *pl*
courier /ˈkʊrɪə(r)/ *n* Bote *m*; (*diplomatic*) Kurier *m*; (*for tourists*) Reiseleiter(in) *m*(*f*)
course /kɔːs/ *n* (*Naut, Sch*) Kurs *m*; (*Culin*) Gang *m*; (*for golf*) Platz *m*; **~ of treatment** (*Med*) Kur *f*; **of ~** natürlich, selbstverständlich; **in the ~ of** im Lauf[e] (+ *gen*)
court /kɔːt/ *n* Hof *m*; (*Sport*) Platz *m*; (*Jur*) Gericht *nt* □ *vt* werben um; herausfordern ⟨*danger*⟩
courteous /ˈkɜːtɪəs/ *a*, **-ly** *adv* höflich
courtesy /ˈkɜːtəsɪ/ *n* Höflichkeit *f*
court: ~ ˈmartial *n* (*pl* **~s martial**) Militärgericht *nt*. **~ shoes** *npl* Pumps *pl*. **~yard** *n* Hof *m*
cousin /ˈkʌzn/ *n* Vetter *m*, Cousin *m*; (*female*) Kusine *f*
cove /kəʊv/ *n* kleine Bucht *f*
cover /ˈkʌvə(r)/ *n* Decke *f*; (*of cushion*) Bezug *m*; (*of umbrella*) Hülle *f*; (*of typewriter*) Haube *f*; (*of book, lid*) Deckel *m*; (*of magazine*) Umschlag *m*; (*protection*) Deckung *f*, Schutz *m*; **take ~** Deckung nehmen; **under separate ~** mit getrennter Post □ *vt* bedecken; beziehen ⟨*cushion*⟩; decken ⟨*costs, needs*⟩; zurücklegen ⟨*distance*⟩; (*Journ*) berichten über (+ *acc*); (*insure*) versichern. **~ up** *vt* zudecken; (*fig*) vertuschen
coverage /ˈkʌvərɪdʒ/ *n* (*Journ*) Berichterstattung *f* (**of** über + *acc*)
cover: ~ charge *n* Gedeck *nt*. **~ing** *n* Decke *f*; (*for floor*) Belag *m*. **~-up** *n* Vertuschung *f*
covet /ˈkʌvɪt/ *vt* begehren
cow /kaʊ/ *n* Kuh *f*
coward /ˈkaʊəd/ *n* Feigling *m*. **~ice** /-ɪs/ *n* Feigheit *f*. **~ly** *a* feige
ˈcowboy *n* Cowboy *m*; (*fam*) unsolider Handwerker *m*

cower /ˈkaʊə(r)/ *vi* sich [ängstlich] ducken
ˈcowshed *n* Kuhstall *m*
cox /kɒks/ *n*, **coxswain** /ˈkɒksn/ *n* Steuermann *m*
coy /kɔɪ/ *a* (**-er, -est**) gespielt schüchtern
crab /kræb/ *n* Krabbe *f*. **~-apple** *n* Holzapfel *m*
crack /kræk/ *n* Riss *m*; (*in china, glass*) Sprung *m*; (*noise*) Knall *m*; (*fam: joke*) Witz *m*; (*fam: attempt*) Versuch *m* □ *a* (*fam*) erstklassig □ *vt* knacken ⟨*nut, code*⟩; einen Sprung machen in (+ *acc*) ⟨*china, glass*⟩; (*fam*) reißen ⟨*joke*⟩; (*fam*) lösen ⟨*problem*⟩ □ *vi* ⟨*china, glass:*⟩ springen; ⟨*whip:*⟩ knallen. **~ down** *vi* (*fam*) durchgreifen
cracked /krækt/ *a* gesprungen; ⟨*rib*⟩ angebrochen; (*fam: crazy*) verrückt
cracker /ˈkrækə(r)/ *n* (*biscuit*) Kräcker *m*; (*firework*) Knallkörper *m*; **[Christmas] ~** Knallbonbon *m*. **~s** *a* **be ~s** (*fam*) einen Knacks haben
crackle /ˈkrækl/ *vi* knistern
cradle /ˈkreɪdl/ *n* Wiege *f*
craft[1] /krɑːft/ *n inv* (*boat*) [Wasser]fahrzeug *nt*
craft[2] *n* Handwerk *nt*; (*technique*) Fertigkeit *f*. **~sman** *n* Handwerker *m*
crafty /ˈkrɑːftɪ/ *a* (**-ier, -iest**), **-ily** *adv* gerissen
crag /kræg/ *n* Felszacken *m*. **~gy** *a* felsig; ⟨*face*⟩ kantig
cram /kræm/ *v* (*pt/pp* **crammed**) □ *vt* hineinstopfen (**into** in + *acc*); vollstopfen (**with** mit) □ *vi* (*for exams*) pauken
cramp /kræmp/ *n* Krampf *m*. **~ed** *a* eng
crampon /ˈkræmpən/ *n* Steigeisen *nt*
cranberry /ˈkrænbərɪ/ *n* (*Culin*) Preiselbeere *f*
crane /kreɪn/ *n* Kran *m*; (*bird*) Kranich *m* □ *vt* **~ one's neck** den Hals recken
crank[1] /kræŋk/ *n* (*fam*) Exzentriker *m*
crank[2] *n* (*Techn*) Kurbel *f*. **~shaft** *n* Kurbelwelle *f*
cranky /ˈkræŋkɪ/ *a* exzentrisch; (*Amer: irritable*) reizbar
cranny /ˈkrænɪ/ *n* Ritze *f*
crash /kræʃ/ *n* (*noise*) Krach *m*; (*Auto*) Zusammenstoß *m*; (*Aviat*) Absturz *m* □ *vi* krachen (**into** gegen); ⟨*cars:*⟩ zusammenstoßen; ⟨*plane:*⟩ abstürzen □ *vt* einen Unfall haben mit ⟨*car*⟩
crash: ~ course *n* Schnellkurs *m*. **~-helmet** *n* Sturzhelm *m*. **~-landing** *n* Bruchlandung *f*
crate /kreɪt/ *n* Kiste *f*
crater /ˈkreɪtə(r)/ *n* Krater *m*
cravat /krəˈvæt/ *n* Halstuch *nt*
crav|e /kreɪv/ *vi* **~e for** sich sehnen nach. **~ing** *n* Gelüst *nt*
crawl /krɔːl/ *n* (*Swimming*) Kraul *nt*; **do the ~** kraulen; **at a ~** im Kriechtempo □ *vi* kriechen; ⟨*baby:*⟩ krabbeln; **~ with** wimmeln von. **~er lane** *n* (*Auto*) Kriechspur *f*
crayon /ˈkreɪən/ *n* Wachsstift *m*; (*pencil*) Buntstift *m*
craze /kreɪz/ *n* Mode *f*
crazy /ˈkreɪzɪ/ *a* (**-ier, -iest**) verrückt; **be ~ about** verrückt sein nach
creak /kriːk/ *n* Knarren *nt* □ *vi* knarren
cream /kriːm/ *n* Sahne *f*; (*Cosmetic, Med, Culin*) Creme *f* □ *a* (*colour*) cremefarben □ *vt* (*Culin*) cremig rühren. **~ ˈcheese** *n* ≈ **Quark** *m*. **~y** *a* sahnig; (*smooth*) cremig
crease /kriːs/ *n* Falte *f*; (*unwanted*) Knitterfalte *f* □ *vt* falten; (*accidentally*) zerknittern □ *vi* knittern. **~-resistant** *a* knitterfrei
creat|e /kriːˈeɪt/ *vt* schaffen. **~ion** /-ˈeɪʃn/ *n* Schöpfung *f*. **~ive** /-tɪv/ *a* schöpferisch. **~or** *n* Schöpfer *m*

creature /ˈkriːtʃə(r)/ *n* Geschöpf *nt*
crèche /kreʃ/ *n* Kinderkrippe *f*
credentials /krɪˈdenʃlz/ *npl* Beglaubigungsschreiben *nt*
credibility /kredəˈbɪlətɪ/ *n* Glaubwürdigkeit *f*
credible /ˈkredəbl/ *a* glaubwürdig
credit /ˈkredɪt/ *n* Kredit *m*; (*honour*) Ehre *f* □ *vt* glauben; **~ s.o. with sth** (*Comm*) jdm etw gutschreiben; (*fig*) jdm etw zuschreiben. **~able** /-əbl/ *a* lobenswert
credit: ~ card *n* Kreditkarte *f*. **~or** *n* Gläubiger *m*
creed /kriːd/ *n* Glaubensbekenntnis *nt*
creek /kriːk/ *n* enge Bucht *f*; (*Amer: stream*) Bach *m*
creep /kriːp/ *vi* (*pt/pp* **crept**) schleichen □ *n* (*fam*) fieser Kerl *m*; **it gives me the ~s** es ist mir unheimlich. **~er** *n* Kletterpflanze *f*. **~y** *a* gruselig
cremat|e /krɪˈmeɪt/ *vt* einäschern. **~ion** /-eɪʃn/ *n* Einäscherung *f*
crematorium /kreməˈtɔːrɪəm/ *n* Krematorium *nt*
crêpe /kreɪp/ *n* Krepp *m*. **~ paper** *n* Krepppapier *nt*
crept /krept/ *see* creep
crescent /ˈkresənt/ *n* Halbmond *m*
cress /kres/ *n* Kresse *f*
crest /krest/ *n* Kamm *m*; (*coat of arms*) Wappen *nt*
Crete /kriːt/ *n* Kreta *nt*
crevasse /krɪˈvæs/ *n* [Gletscher]spalte *f*
crevice /ˈkrevɪs/ *n* Spalte *f*
crew /kruː/ *n* Besatzung *f*; (*gang*) Bande *f*. **~ cut** *n* Bürstenschnitt *m*
crib[1] /krɪb/ *n* Krippe *f*
crib[2] *vt/i* (*pt/pp* **cribbed**) (*fam*) abschreiben
crick /krɪk/ *n* **~ in the neck** steifes Genick *nt*
cricket[1] /ˈkrɪkɪt/ *n* (*insect*) Grille *f*
cricket[2] *n* Kricket *nt*. **~er** *n* Kricketspieler *m*
crime /kraɪm/ *n* Verbrechen *nt*; (*rate*) Kriminalität *f*
criminal /ˈkrɪmɪnl/ *a* kriminell, verbrecherisch; ⟨*law, court*⟩ **Straf-** □ *n* Verbrecher *m*
crimson /ˈkrɪmzn/ *a* purpurrot
cringe /krɪndʒ/ *vi* sich [ängstlich] ducken
crinkle /ˈkrɪŋkl/ *vt/i* knittern
cripple /ˈkrɪpl/ *n* Krüppel *m* □ *vt* zum Krüppel machen; (*fig*) lahmlegen. **~d** *a* verkrüppelt
crisis /ˈkraɪsɪs/ *n* (*pl* **-ses** /-siːz/) Krise *f*
crisp /ˈkrɪsp/ *a* (**-er, -est**) knusprig. **~bread** *n* Knäckebrot *nt*. **~s** *npl* Chips *pl*
criss-cross /ˈkrɪs-/ *a* schräg gekreuzt
criterion /kraɪˈtɪərɪən/ *n* (*pl* **-ria** /-rɪə/) Kriterium *nt*
critic /ˈkrɪtɪk/ *n* Kritiker *m*. **~al** *a* kritisch. **~ally** *adv* kritisch; **~ally** ill schwer krank
criticism /ˈkrɪtɪsɪzm/ *n* Kritik *f*
criticize /ˈkrɪtɪsaɪz/ *vt* kritisieren
croak /krəʊk/ *vi* krächzen; ⟨*frog:*⟩ quaken
crochet /ˈkrəʊʃeɪ/ *n* Häkelarbeit *f* □ *vt/i* häkeln. **~-hook** *n* Häkelnadel *f*
crock /krɒk/ *n* (*fam*) **old ~** (*person*) Wrack *m*; (*car*) Klapperkiste *f*
crockery /ˈkrɒkərɪ/ *n* Geschirr *nt*
crocodile /ˈkrɒkədaɪl/ *n* Krokodil *nt*
crocus /ˈkrəʊkəs/ *n* (*pl* **-es**) Krokus *m*
crony /ˈkrəʊnɪ/ *n* Kumpel *m*
crook /krʊk/ *n* (*stick*) Stab *m*; (*fam: criminal*) Schwindler *m*, Gauner *m*
crooked /ˈkrʊkɪd/ *a* schief; (*bent*) krumm; (*fam: dishonest*) unehrlich

crop /krɒp/ *n* Feldfrucht *f*; (*harvest*) Ernte *f*; (*of bird*) Kropf *m* □ *v* (*pt/pp* **cropped**) □ *vt* stutzen □ *vi* **~ up** (*fam*) zur Sprache kommen; (*occur*) dazwischenkommen

croquet /ˈkrəʊkeɪ/ *n* Krocket *nt*

croquette /krəʊˈket/ *n* Krokette *f*

cross /krɒs/ *a*, **-ly** *adv* (*annoyed*) böse (**with** auf + *acc*); **talk at ~ purposes** aneinander vorbeireden □ *n* Kreuz *nt*; (*Bot, Zool*) Kreuzung *f*; **on the ~** schräg □ *vt* kreuzen ⟨*cheque, animals*⟩; überqueren ⟨*road*⟩; **~ oneself** sich bekreuzigen; **~ one's arms** die Arme verschränken; **~ one's legs** die Beine übereinander schlagen; **keep one's fingers ~ed for s.o.** jdm die Daumen drücken; **it ~ed my mind** es fiel mir ein □ *vi* (*go across*) hinübergehen/-fahren; ⟨*lines:*⟩ sich kreuzen. **~ out** *vt* durchstreichen

cross: ~bar *n* Querlatte *f*; (*on bicycle*) Stange *f*. **~-ˈcountry** *n* (*Sport*) Crosslauf *m*. **~-exˈamine** *vt* ins Kreuzverhör nehmen. **~-examiˈnation** *n* Kreuzverhör *nt*. **~-ˈeyed** *a* schielend; **be ~-eyed** schielen. **~fire** *n* Kreuzfeuer *nt*. **~ing** *n* Übergang *m*; (*sea journey*) Überfahrt *f*. **~-ˈreference** *n* Querverweis *m*. **~roads** *n* [Straßen]kreuzung *f*. **~-ˈsection** *n* Querschnitt *m*. **~-stitch** *n* Kreuzstich *m*. **~wise** *adv* quer. **~word** *n* **~word [puzzle]** Kreuzworträtsel *nt*

crotchet /ˈkrɒtʃɪt/ *n* Viertelnote *f*

crotchety /ˈkrɒtʃɪtɪ/ *a* griesgrämig

crouch /kraʊtʃ/ *vi* kauern

crow /krəʊ/ *n* Krähe *f*; **as the ~ flies** Luftlinie □ *vi* krähen. **~bar** *n* Brechstange *f*

crowd /kraʊd/ *n* [Menschen]menge *f* □ *vi* sich drängen. **~ed** /ˈkraʊdɪd/ *a* [gedrängt] voll

crown /kraʊn/ *n* Krone *f* □ *vt* krönen; überkronen ⟨*tooth*⟩

crucial /ˈkruːʃl/ *a* höchst wichtig; (*decisive*) entscheidend (**to** für)

crucifix /ˈkruːsɪfɪks/ *n* Kruzifix *nt*

crucif|ixion /kruːsɪˈfɪkʃn/ *n* Kreuzigung *f* **~y** /ˈkruːsɪfaɪ/ *vt* (*pt/pp* **-ied**) kreuzigen

crude /ˈkruːd/ *a* (**-r, -st**) (*raw*) roh

cruel /ˈkruːəl/ *a* (**crueller, cruellest**), **-ly** *adv* grausam (**to** gegen). **~ty** *n* Grausamkeit *f*; **~ty to animals** Tierquälerei *f*

cruis|e /kruːz/ *n* Kreuzfahrt *f* □ *vi* kreuzen; ⟨*car:*⟩ fahren. **~er** *n* (*Mil*) Kreuzer *m*; (*motor boat*) Kajütboot *nt*. **~ing speed** *n* Reisegeschwindigkeit *f*

crumb /krʌm/ *n* Krümel *m*

crumb|le /ˈkrʌmbl/ *vt/i* krümeln; (*collapse*) einstürzen. **~ly** *a* krümelig

crumple /ˈkrʌmpl/ *vt* zerknittern □ *vi* knittern

crunch /krʌntʃ/ *n* (*fam*) **when it comes to the ~** wenn es [wirklich] drauf ankommt □ *vt* mampfen □ *vi* knirschen

crusade /kruːˈseɪd/ *n* Kreuzzug *m*; (*fig*) Kampagne *f*. **~r** *n* Kreuzfahrer *m*; (*fig*) Kämpfer *m*

crush /krʌʃ/ *n* (*crowd*) Gedränge *nt* □ *vt* zerquetschen; zerknittern ⟨*clothes*⟩; (*fig: subdue*) niederschlagen

crust /krʌst/ *n* Kruste *f*

crutch /krʌtʃ/ *n* Krücke *f*

crux /krʌks/ *n* (*fig*) springender Punkt *m*

cry /kraɪ/ *n* Ruf *m*; (*shout*) Schrei *m*; **a far ~ from** (*fig*) weit entfernt von □ *vi* (*pt/pp* **cried**) (*weep*) weinen; ⟨*baby:*⟩ schreien; (*call*) rufen

crypt /krɪpt/ *n* Krypta *f*. **~ic** *a* rätselhaft

crystal /ˈkrɪstl/ *n* Kristall *m*; (*glass*) Kristall *nt*. **~lize** *vi* [sich] kristallisieren

cub /kʌb/ *n (Zool)* Junge(s) *nt*; **C~ [Scout]** Wölfling *m*
Cuba /'kju:bə/ *n* Kuba *nt*
cubby-hole /'kʌbɪ-/ *n* Fach *nt*
cub|e /kju:b/ *n* Würfel *m*. **~ic** *a* Kubik-
cubicle /'kju:bɪkl/ *n* Kabine *f*
cuckoo /'kʊku:/ *n* Kuckuck *m*. **~ clock** *n* Kuckucksuhr *f*
cucumber /'kju:kʌmbə(r)/ *n* Gurke *f*
cuddl|e /'kʌdl/ *vt* herzen □ *vi* **~e up to** sich kuscheln an (+ *acc*). **~y** *a* kuschelig. **~y 'toy** *n* Plüschtier *nt*
cudgel /'kʌdʒl/ *n* Knüppel *m*
cue¹ /kju:/ *n* Stichwort *nt*
cue² *n (Billiards)* Queue *nt*
cuff /kʌf/ *n* Manschette *f*; *(Amer: turn-up)* [Hosen]aufschlag *m*; *(blow)* Klaps *m*; **off the ~** *(fam)* aus dem Stegreif □ *vt* einen Klaps geben (+ *dat*). **~-link** *n* Manschettenknopf *m*
cul-de-sac /'kʌldəsæk/ *n* Sackgasse *f*
culinary /'kʌlɪnərɪ/ *a* kulinarisch
cull /kʌl/ *vt* pflücken ⟨*flowers*⟩; *(kill)* ausmerzen
culminat|e /'kʌlmɪneɪt/ *vi* gipfeln (**in** in + *dat*). **~ion** /-'neɪʃn/ *n* Gipfelpunkt *m*
culottes /kju:'lɒts/ *npl* Hosenrock *m*
culprit /'kʌlprɪt/ *n* Täter *m*
cult /kʌlt/ *n* Kult *m*
cultivate /'kʌltɪveɪt/ *vt* anbauen ⟨*crop*⟩; bebauen ⟨*land*⟩
cultural /'kʌltʃərəl/ *a* kulturell
culture /'kʌltʃə(r)/ *n* Kultur *f*. **~d** *a* kultiviert
cumbersome /'kʌmbəsəm/ *a* hinderlich; *(unwieldy)* unhandlich
cumulative /'kju:mjʊlətɪv/ *a* kumulativ
cunning /'kʌnɪŋ/ *a* listig □ *n* List *f*
cup /kʌp/ *n* Tasse *f*; *(prize)* Pokal *m*
cupboard /'kʌbəd/ *n* Schrank *m*
Cup 'Final *n* Pokalendspiel *nt*
Cupid /'kju:pɪd/ *n* Amor *m*
curable /'kjʊərəbl/ *a* heilbar
curate /'kjʊərət/ *n* Vikar *m*; *(Roman Catholic)* Kaplan *m*
curator /kjʊə'reɪtə(r)/ *n* Kustos *m*
curb /kɜ:b/ *vt* zügeln
curdle /'kɜ:dl/ *vi* gerinnen
cure /kjʊə(r)/ *n* [Heil]mittel *nt* □ *vt* heilen; *(salt)* pökeln; *(smoke)* räuchern; gerben ⟨*skin*⟩
curfew /'kɜ:fju:/ *n* Ausgangssperre *f*
curio /'kjʊərɪəʊ/ *n* Kuriosität *f*
curiosity /kjʊərɪ'ɒsətɪ/ *n* Neugier *f*; *(object)* Kuriosität *f*
curious /'kjʊərɪəs/ *a*, **-ly** *adv* neugierig; *(strange)* merkwürdig, seltsam
curl /kɜ:l/ *n* Locke *f* □ *vt* locken □ *vi* sich locken. **~ up** *vi* sich zusammenrollen
curler /'kɜ:lə(r)/ *n* Lockenwickler *m*
curly /'kɜ:lɪ/ *a* **(-ier, -iest)** lockig
currant /'kʌrənt/ *n (dried)* Korinthe *f*
currency /'kʌrənsɪ/ *n* Geläufigkeit *f*; *(money)* Währung *f*; **foreign ~** Devisen *pl*
current /'kʌrənt/ *a* augenblicklich, gegenwärtig; *(in general use)* geläufig, gebräuchlich □ *n* Strömung *f*; *(Electr)* Strom *m*. **~ affairs** *or* **events** *npl* Aktuelle(s) *nt*. **~ly** *adv* zurzeit
curriculum /kə'rɪkjʊləm/ *n* Lehrplan *m*. **~ vitae** /-'vi:taɪ/ *n* Lebenslauf *m*
curry /'kʌrɪ/ *n* Curry *nt* & *m*; *(meal)* Currygericht *nt* □ *vt* *(pt/pp* **-ied)** **~ favour** sich einschmeicheln (**with** bei)
curse /kɜ:s/ *n* Fluch *m* □ *vt* verfluchen □ *vi* fluchen
cursory /'kɜ:sərɪ/ *a* flüchtig
curt /kɜ:t/ *a*, **-ly** *adv* barsch

curtail /kɜ:ˈteɪl/ *vt* abkürzen
curtain /ˈkɜ:tn/ *n* Vorhang *m*
curtsy /ˈkɜ:tsɪ/ *n* Knicks *m* □ *vi* (*pt/pp* **-ied**) knicksen
curve /kɜ:v/ *n* Kurve *f* □ *vi* einen Bogen machen; **~ to the right/left** nach rechts/links biegen. **~d** *a* gebogen
cushion /ˈkʊʃn/ *n* Kissen *nt* □ *vt* dämpfen; (*protect*) beschützen
cushy /ˈkʊʃɪ/ *a* (**-ier, -iest**) (*fam*) bequem
custard /ˈkʌstəd/ *n* Vanillesoße *f*
custodian /kʌˈstəʊdɪən/ *n* Hüter *m*
custody /ˈkʌstədɪ/ *n* Obhut *f*; (*of child*) Sorgerecht *nt*; (*imprisonment*) Haft *f*
custom /ˈkʌstəm/ *n* Brauch *m*; (*habit*) Gewohnheit *f*; (*Comm*) Kundschaft *f*. **~ary** *a* üblich; (*habitual*) gewohnt. **~er** *n* Kunde *m*/Kundin *f*
customs /ˈkʌstəmz/ *npl* Zoll *m*. **~ officer** *n* Zollbeamte(r) *m*
cut /kʌt/ *n* Schnitt *m*; (*Med*) Schnittwunde *f*; (*reduction*) Kürzung *f*; (*in price*) Senkung *f*; **~ [of meat]** [Fleisch]stück *nt* □ *vt/i* (*pt/pp* **cut**, *pres p* **cutting**) schneiden; (*mow*) mähen; abheben ⟨*cards*⟩; (*reduce*) kürzen; senken ⟨*price*⟩; **~ one's finger** sich in den Finger schneiden; **~ s.o.'s hair** jdm die Haare schneiden; **~ short** abkürzen. **~ back** *vt* zurückschneiden; (*fig*) einschränken, kürzen. **~ down** *vt* fällen; (*fig*) einschränken. **~ off** *vt* abschneiden; (*disconnect*) abstellen; **be ~ off** (*Teleph*) unterbrochen werden. **~ out** *vt* ausschneiden; (*delete*) streichen; **be ~ out for** (*fam*) geeignet sein zu. **~ up** *vt* zerschneiden; (*slice*) aufschneiden
ˈcut-back *n* Kürzung *f*, Einschränkung *f*
cute /kju:t/ *a* (**-r, -st**) (*fam*) niedlich
cut ˈglass *n* Kristall *nt*
cuticle /ˈkju:tɪkl/ *n* Nagelhaut *f*
cutlery /ˈkʌtlərɪ/ *n* Besteck *nt*
cutlet /ˈkʌtlɪt/ *n* Kotelett *nt*
ˈcut-price *a* verbilligt
cutting /ˈkʌtɪŋ/ *a* ⟨*remark*⟩ bissig □ *n* (*from newspaper*) Ausschnitt *m*; (*of plant*) Ableger *m*
CV *abbr of* **curriculum vitae**
cyclamen /ˈsɪkləmən/ *n* Alpenveilchen *nt*
cycl|e /ˈsaɪkl/ *n* Zyklus *m*; (*bicycle*) [Fahr]rad *nt* □ *vi* mit dem Rad fahren. **~ing** *n* Radfahren *nt*. **~ist** *n* Radfahrer(in) *m(f)*
cyclone /ˈsaɪkləʊn/ *n* Wirbelsturm *m*
cylind|er /ˈsɪlɪndə(r)/ *n* Zylinder *m*. **~rical** /-ˈlɪndrɪkl/ *a* zylindrisch
cymbals /ˈsɪmblz/ *npl* (*Mus*) Becken *nt*
cynic /ˈsɪnɪk/ *n* Zyniker *m*. **~al** *a*, **-ly** *adv* zynisch. **~ism** /-sɪzm/ *n* Zynismus *m*
cypress /ˈsaɪprəs/ *n* Zypresse *f*
Cyprus /ˈsaɪprəs/ *n* Zypern *nt*
cyst /sɪst/ *n* Zyste *f*. **~itis** /-ˈtaɪtɪs/ *n* Blasenentzündung *f*
Czech /tʃek/ *a* tschechisch □ *n* Tscheche *m*/ Tschechin *f*
Czechoslovak /tʃekəˈsləʊvæk/ *a* tschechoslowakisch. **~ia** /-ˈvækɪə/ *n* die Tschechoslowakei. **~ian** /-ˈvækɪən/ *a* tschechoslowakisch

D

dab /dæb/ *n* Tupfer *m*; (*of butter*) Klecks *m*; **a ~ of** ein bisschen □ *vt* (*pt/pp* **dabbed**) abtupfen; betupfen (**with** mit)
dabble /ˈdæbl/ *vi* **~ in sth** (*fig*) sich nebenbei mit etw befassen
dachshund /ˈdækshʊnd/ *n* Dackel *m*
dad[dy] /ˈdæd[i]/ *n* (*fam*) Vati *m*

daddy-'long-legs *n* [Kohl]-schnake *f*; (*Amer: spider*) Weberknecht *m*
daffodil /'dæfədɪl/ *n* Osterglocke *f*, gelbe Narzisse *f*
daft /dɑ:ft/ *a* (**-er, -est**) dumm
dagger /'dægə(r)/ *n* Dolch *m*; (*Typ*) Kreuz *nt*; **be at ~s drawn** (*fam*) auf Kriegsfuß stehen
dahlia /'deɪlɪə/ *n* Dahlie *f*
daily /'deɪlɪ/ *a & adv* täglich □ *n* (*newspaper*) Tageszeitung *f*; (*fam: cleaner*) Putzfrau *f*
dainty /'deɪntɪ/ *a* (**-ier, -iest**) zierlich
dairy /'deərɪ/ *n* Molkerei *f*; (*shop*) Milchgeschäft *nt*. **~ cow** *n* Milchkuh *f*. **~ products** *pl* Milchprodukte *pl*
dais /'deɪɪs/ *n* Podium *nt*
daisy /'deɪzɪ/ *n* Gänseblümchen *nt*
dale /deɪl/ *n* (*liter*) Tal *nt*
dally /'dælɪ/ *vi* (*pt/pp* **-ied**) trödeln
dam /dæm/ *n* [Stau]damm *m* □ *vt* (*pt/pp* **dammed**) eindämmen
damag|e /'dæmɪdʒ/ *n* Schaden *m* (**to** an + *dat*); **~es** *pl* (*Jur*) Schadenersatz *m* □ *vt* beschädigen; (*fig*) beeinträchtigen. **~ing** *a* schädlich
damask /'dæməsk/ *n* Damast *m*
dame /deɪm/ *n* (*liter*) Dame *f*; (*Amer sl*) Weib *nt*
damn /dæm/ *a, int & adv* (*fam*) verdammt □ *n* **I don't care** *or* **give a ~** (*fam*) ich schere mich einen Dreck darum □ *vt* verdammen. **~ation** /-'neɪʃn/ *n* Verdammnis *f* □ *int* (*fam*) verdammt!
damp /dæmp/ *a* (**-er, -est**) feucht □ *n* Feuchtigkeit *f* □ *vt* = **dampen**
damp|en *vt* anfeuchten; (*fig*) dämpfen. **~ness** *n* Feuchtigkeit *f*
dance /dɑ:ns/ *n* Tanz *m*; (*function*) Tanzveranstaltung *f* □ *vt/i* tanzen. **~-hall** *n* Tanzlokal *nt*. **~ music** *n* Tanzmusik *f*
dancer /'dɑ:nsə(r)/ *n* Tänzer(in) *m(f)*
dandelion /'dændɪlaɪən/ *n* Löwenzahn *m*
dandruff /'dændrʌf/ *n* Schuppen *pl*
Dane /deɪn/ *n* Däne *m*/Dänin *f*; **Great ~** [deutsche] Dogge *f*
danger /'deɪndʒə(r)/ *n* Gefahr *f*; **in/out of ~** in/außer Gefahr. **~ous** /-rəs/ *a*, **-ly** *adv* gefährlich; **~ously ill** schwer erkrankt
dangle /'dæŋgl/ *vi* baumeln □ *vt* baumeln lassen
Danish /'deɪnɪʃ/ *a* dänisch. **~ 'pastry** *n* Hefeteilchen *nt*, Plunderstück *nt*
dank /dæŋk/ *a* (**-er, -est**) nasskalt
Danube /'dænju:b/ *n* Donau *f*
dare /deə(r)/ *n* Mutprobe *f* □ *vt/i* (*challenge*) herausfordern (**to** zu); **~ [to] do sth** [es] wagen, etw zu tun; **I ~ say!** das mag wohl sein! **~devil** *n* Draufgänger *m*
daring /'deərɪŋ/ *a* verwegen □ *n* Verwegenheit *f*
dark /dɑ:k/ *a* (**-er, -est**) dunkel; **~ blue/brown** dunkelblau/-braun; **~ horse** (*fig*) stilles Wasser *nt*; **keep sth ~** (*fig*) etw geheim halten □ *n* Dunkelheit *f*; **after ~** nach Einbruch der Dunkelheit; **in the ~** im Dunkeln; **keep in the ~** (*fig*) im Dunkeln lassen
dark|en /'dɑ:kn/ *vt* verdunkeln □ *vi* dunkler werden. **~ness** *n* Dunkelheit *f*
'dark-room *n* Dunkelkammer *f*
darling /'dɑ:lɪŋ/ *a* allerliebst □ *n* Liebling *m*
darn /dɑ:n/ *vt* stopfen. **~ing-needle** *n* Stopfnadel *f*
dart /dɑ:t/ *n* Pfeil *m*; (*Sewing*) Abnäher *m*; **~s** *sg* (*game*) [Wurf]pfeil *m* □ *vi* flitzen
dash /dæʃ/ *n* (*Typ*) Gedankenstrich *m*; (*in Morse*) Strich *m*; **a**

~ of milk ein Schuss Milch; **make a ~** losstürzen (**for** auf + *acc*) □ *vi* rennen □ *vt* schleudern. **~ off** *vi* losstürzen □ *vt* (*write quickly*) hinwerfen

'dashboard *n* Armaturenbrett *nt*

dashing /'dæʃɪŋ/ *a* schneidig

data /'deɪtə/ *npl & sg* Daten *pl.* **~ processing** *n* Datenverarbeitung *f*

date¹ /deɪt/ *n* (*fruit*) Dattel *f*

date² *n* Datum *nt*; (*fam*) Verabredung *f*; **to ~** bis heute; **out of ~** überholt; (*expired*) ungültig; **be up to ~** auf dem Laufenden sein □ *vt/i* datieren; (*Amer, fam: go out with*) ausgehen mit; **~ back to** zurückgehen auf (+ *acc*)

dated /'deɪtɪd/ *a* altmodisch

'date-line *n* Datumsgrenze *f*

dative /'deɪtɪv/ *a & n* (*Gram*) **~ [case]** Dativ *m*

daub /dɔ:b/ *vt* beschmieren (**with** mit); schmieren ⟨*paint*⟩

daughter /'dɔ:tə(r)/ *n* Tochter *f.* **~-in-law** *n* (*pl* **~s-in-law**) Schwiegertochter *f*

daunt /dɔ:nt/ *vt* entmutigen; **nothing ~ed** unverzagt. **~less** *a* furchtlos

dawdle /'dɔ:dl/ *vi* trödeln

dawn /dɔ:n/ *n* Morgendämmerung *f*; **at ~** bei Tagesanbruch □ *vi* anbrechen; **it ~ed on me** (*fig*) es ging mir auf

day /deɪ/ *n* Tag *m*; **~ by ~** Tag für Tag; **~ after ~** Tag um Tag; **these ~s** heutzutage; **in those ~s** zu der Zeit; **it's had its ~** (*fam*) es hat ausgedient

day: ~break *n* **at ~break** bei Tagesanbruch *m.* **~-dream** *n* Tagtraum *m* □ *vi* [mit offenen Augen] träumen. **~light** *n* Tageslicht *nt.* **~ re'turn** *n* (*ticket*) Tagesrückfahrkarte *f.* **~time** *n* **in the ~time** am Tage

daze /deɪz/ *n* **in a ~** wie benommen. **~d** *a* benommen

dazzle /'dæzl/ *vt* blenden

deacon /'di:kn/ *n* Diakon *m*

dead /ded/ *a* tot; ⟨*flower*⟩ verwelkt; (*numb*) taub; **~ body** Leiche *f*; **be ~ on time** auf die Minute pünktlich kommen; **~ centre** genau in der Mitte □ *adv* **~ tired** todmüde; **~ slow** sehr langsam; **stop ~** stehen bleiben □ *n* **the ~** *pl* die Toten; **in the ~ of night** mitten in der Nacht

deaden /'dedn/ *vt* dämpfen ⟨*sound*⟩; betäuben ⟨*pain*⟩

dead: ~ 'end *n* Sackgasse *f.* **~ 'heat** *n* totes Rennen *nt.* **~line** *n* [letzter] Termin *m.* **~lock** *n* **reach ~lock** (*fig*) sich festfahren

deadly /'dedlɪ/ *a* (**-ier, -iest**) tödlich; (*fam: dreary*) sterbenslangweilig; **~ sins** *pl* Todsünden *pl*

deaf /def/ *a* (**-er, -est**) taub; **~ and dumb** taubstumm. **~-aid** *n* Hörgerät *nt*

deaf|en /'defn/ *vt* betäuben; (*permanently*) taub machen. **~ening** *a* ohrenbetäubend. **~ness** *n* Taubheit *f*

deal /di:l/ *n* (*transaction*) Geschäft *nt*; **whose ~?** (*Cards*) wer gibt? **a good** *or* **great ~** eine Menge; **get a raw ~** (*fam*) schlecht wegkommen □ *v* (*pt/pp* **dealt** /delt/) □ *vt* (*Cards*) geben; **~ out** austeilen; **~ s.o. a blow** jdm einen Schlag versetzen □ *vi* **~ in** handeln mit; **~ with** zu tun haben mit; (*handle*) sich befassen mit; (*cope with*) fertig werden mit; (*be about*) handeln von; **that's been dealt with** das ist schon erledigt

deal|er /'di:lə(r)/ *n* Händler *m*; (*Cards*) Kartengeber *m.* **~ings** *npl* **have ~ings with** zu tun haben mit

dean /di:n/ *n* Dekan *m*

dear /dɪə(r)/ *a* (**-er, -est**) lieb; (*expensive*) teuer; (*in letter*) liebe(r,s)/ (*formal*) sehr geehrte(r,s) □ *n* Liebe(r) *m/f* □ *int* **oh ~!** oje! **~ly** *adv* ⟨*love*⟩ sehr; ⟨*pay*⟩ teuer

dearth /dɜ:θ/ *n* Mangel *m* (**of** an + *dat*)
death /deθ/ *n* Tod *m*; **three ~s** drei Todesfälle. **~ certificate** *n* Sterbeurkunde *f*. **~ duty** *n* Erbschaftssteuer *f*
deathly *a* **~ silence** Totenstille *f* □ *adv* **~ pale** totenblass
death: ~ penalty *n* Todesstrafe *f*. **~'s head** *n* Totenkopf *m*. **~-trap** *n* Todesfalle *f*
debar /dɪ'bɑ:(r)/ *vt* (*pt/pp* **debarred**) ausschließen
debase /dɪ'beɪs/ *vt* erniedrigen
debatable /dɪ'beɪtəbl/ *a* strittig
debate /dɪ'beɪt/ *n* Debatte *f* □ *vt/i* debattieren
debauchery /dɪ'bɔ:tʃərɪ/ *n* Ausschweifung *f*
debility /dɪ'bɪlətɪ/ *n* Entkräftung *f*
debit /'debɪt/ *n* Schuldbetrag *m*; **~ [side]** Soll *nt* □ *vt* (*pt/pp* **debited**) (*Comm*) belasten; abbuchen ⟨*sum*⟩
debris /'debri:/ *n* Trümmer *pl*
debt /det/ *n* Schuld *f*; **in ~** verschuldet. **~or** *n* Schuldner *m*
début /'deɪbu:/ *n* Debüt *nt*
decade /'dekeɪd/ *n* Jahrzehnt *nt*
decaden|ce /'dekədəns/ *n* Dekadenz *f*. **~t** *a* dekadent
decaffeinated /dɪ'kæfɪneɪtɪd/ *a* koffeinfrei
decant /dɪ'kænt/ *vt* umfüllen. **~er** *n* Karaffe *f*
decapitate /dɪ'kæpɪteɪt/ *vt* köpfen
decay /dɪ'keɪ/ *n* Verfall *m*; (*rot*) Verwesung *f*; (*of tooth*) Zahnfäule *f* □ *vi* verfallen; (*rot*) verwesen; ⟨*tooth:*⟩ schlecht werden
decease /dɪ'si:s/ *n* Ableben *nt*. **~d** *a* verstorben □ *n* **the ~d** der/die Verstorbene
deceit /dɪ'si:t/ *n* Täuschung *f*. **~ful** *a*, **-ly** *adv* unaufrichtig
deceive /dɪ'si:v/ *vt* täuschen; (*be unfaithful to*) betrügen
December /dɪ'sembə(r)/ *n* Dezember *m*
decency /'di:sənsɪ/ *n* Anstand *m*
decent /'di:sənt/ *a*, **-ly** *adv* anständig
decentralize /di:'sentrəlaɪz/ *vt* dezentralisieren
decept|ion /dɪ'sepʃn/ *n* Täuschung *f*; (*fraud*) Betrug *m*. **~ive** /-tɪv/ *a*, **-ly** *adv* täuschend
decibel /'desɪbel/ *n* Dezibel *nt*
decide /dɪ'saɪd/ *vt* entscheiden □ *vi* sich entscheiden (**on** für)
decided /dɪ'saɪdɪd/ *a*, **-ly** *adv* entschieden
deciduous /dɪ'sɪdjʊəs/ *a* **~ tree** Laubbaum *m*
decimal /'desɪml/ *a* Dezimal- □ *n* Dezimalzahl *f*. **~ 'point** *n* Komma *nt*. **~ system** *n* Dezimalsystem *nt*
decimate /'desɪmeɪt/ *vt* dezimieren
decipher /dɪ'saɪfə(r)/ *vt* entziffern
decision /dɪ'sɪʒn/ *n* Entscheidung *f*; (*firmness*) Entschlossenheit *f*
decisive /dɪ'saɪsɪv/ *a* ausschlaggebend; (*firm*) entschlossen
deck[1] /dek/ *vt* schmücken
deck[2] *n* (*Naut*) Deck *nt*; **on ~** an Deck; **top ~** (*of bus*) Oberdeck *nt*; **~ of cards** (*Amer*) [Karten]spiel *nt*. **~-chair** *n* Liegestuhl *m*
declaration /deklə'reɪʃn/ *n* Erklärung *f*
declare /dɪ'kleə(r)/ *vt* erklären; angeben ⟨*goods*⟩; **anything to ~?** etwas zu verzollen?
declension /dɪ'klenʃn/ *n* Deklination *f*
decline /dɪ'klaɪn/ *n* Rückgang *m*; (*in health*) Verfall *m* □ *vt* ablehnen; (*Gram*) deklinieren □ *vi* ablehnen; (*fall*) sinken; (*decrease*) nachlassen
decode /di:'kəʊd/ *vt* entschlüsseln

decompos|e /di:kəm'pəʊz/ *vi* sich zersetzen
décor /'deɪkɔ:(r)/ *n* Ausstattung *f*
decorat|e /'dekəreɪt/ *vt* (*adorn*) schmücken; verzieren ⟨*cake*⟩; (*paint*) streichen; (*wallpaper*) tapezieren; (*award medal to*) einen Orden verleihen (+ *dat*). **~ion** /-'reɪʃn/ *n* Verzierung *f*; (*medal*) Orden *m*; **~ions** *pl* Schumuck *m*. **~ive** /-rətɪv/ *a* dekorativ. **~or** *n* **painter and ~or** Maler und Tapezierer *m*
decorous /'dekərəs/ *a*, **-ly** *adv* schamhaft
decorum /dɪ'kɔ:rəm/ *n* Anstand *m*
decoy[1] /'di:kɔɪ/ *n* Lockvogel *m*
decoy[2] /dɪ'kɔɪ/ *vt* locken
decrease[1] /'di:kri:s/ *n* Verringerung *f*; (*in number*) Rückgang *m*; **be on the ~** zurückgehen
decrease[2] /dɪ'kri:s/ *vt* verringern; herabsetzen ⟨*price*⟩ □ *vi* sich veringern; ⟨*price:*⟩ sinken
decree /dɪ'kri:/ *n* Erlass *m* □ *vt* (*pt/pp* **decreed**) verordnen
decrepit /dɪ'krepɪt/ *a* altersschwach
dedicat|e /'dedɪkeɪt/ *vt* widmen; (*Relig*) weihen. **~ed** *a* hingebungsvoll; ⟨*person*⟩ aufopfernd. **~ion** /-'keɪʃn/ *n* Hingabe *f*; (*in book*) Widmung *f*
deduce /dɪ'dju:s/ *vt* folgern (**from** aus)
deduct /dɪ'dʌkt/ *vt* abziehen
deduction /dɪ'dʌkʃn/ *n* Abzug *m*; (*conclusion*) Folgerung *f*
deed /di:d/ *n* Tat *f*; (*Jur*) Urkunde *f*
deem /di:m/ *vt* halten für
deep /di:p/ *a* (**-er, -est**), **-ly** *adv* tief; **go off the ~ end** (*fam*) auf die Palme gehen □ *adv* tief
deepen /'di:pn/ *vt* vertiefen □ *vi* tiefer werden; (*fig*) sich vertiefen
deep-'freeze *n* Gefriertruhe *f*; (*upright*) Gefrierschrank *m*
deer /dɪə(r)/ *n inv* Hirsch *m*; (*roe*) Reh *nt*
deface /dɪ'feɪs/ *vt* beschädigen
defamat|ion /defə'meɪʃn/ *n* Verleumdung *f*. **~ory** /dɪ'fæmətərɪ/ *a* verleumderisch
default /dɪ'fɔ:lt/ *n* (*Jur*) Nichtzahlung *f*; (*failure to appear*) Nichterscheinen *nt*; **win by ~** (*Sport*) kampflos gewinnen □ *vi* nicht zahlen; nicht erscheinen
defeat /dɪ'fi:t/ *n* Niederlage *f*; (*defeating*) Besiegung *f*; (*rejection*) Ablehnung *f* □ *vt* besiegen; ablehnen; (*frustrate*) vereiteln
defect[1] /dɪ'fekt/ *vi* (*Pol*) überlaufen
defect[2] /'di:fekt/ *n* Fehler *m*; (*Techn*) Defekt *m*. **~ive** /dɪ'fektɪv/ *a* fehlerhaft; (*Techn*) defekt
defence /dɪ'fens/ *n* Verteidigung *f*. **~less** *a* wehrlos
defend /dɪ'fend/ *vt* verteidigen; (*justify*) rechtfertigen. **~ant** *n* (*Jur*) Beklagte(r) *m/f*; (*in criminal court*) Angeklagte(r) *m/f*
defensive /dɪ'fensɪv/ *a* defensiv □ *n* Defensive *f*
defer /dɪ'fɜ:(r)/ *vt* (*pt/pp* **deferred**) (*postpone*) aufschieben; **~ to s.o.** sich jdm fügen
deferen|ce /'defərəns/ *n* Ehrerbietung *f*. **~tial** /-'renʃl/ *a*, **-ly** *adv* ehrerbietig
defian|ce /dɪ'faɪəns/ *n* Trotz *m*; **in ~ce of** zum Trotz (+ *dat*). **~t** *a*, **-ly** *adv* aufsässig
deficien|cy /dɪ'fɪʃənsɪ/ *n* Mangel *m*. **~t** *a* mangelhaft; **he is ~t in** ... ihm mangelt es an ... (*dat*)
deficit /'defɪsɪt/ *n* Defizit *nt*
defile /dɪ'faɪl/ *vt* (*fig*) schänden
define /dɪ'faɪn/ *vt* bestimmen; definieren ⟨*word*⟩
definite /'defɪnɪt/ *a*, **-ly** *adv* bestimmt; (*certain*) sicher
definition /defɪ'nɪʃn/ *n* Definition *f*; (*Phot, TV*) Schärfe *f*
definitive /dɪ'fɪnətɪv/ *a* endgültig; (*authoritative*) maßgeblich

deflat|e /dɪˈfleɪt/ *vt* die Luft auslassen aus. **~ion** /-eɪʃn/ *n* (*Comm*) Deflation *f*
deflect /dɪˈflekt/ *vt* ablenken
deform|ed /dɪˈfɔːmd/ *a* missgebildet. **~ity** *n* Missbildung *f*
defraud /dɪˈfrɔːd/ *vt* betrügen (**of** um)
defray /dɪˈfreɪ/ *vt* bestreiten
defrost /diːˈfrɒst/ *vt* entfrosten; abtauen 〈*fridge*〉; auftauen 〈*food*〉
deft /deft/ *a* (**-er, -est**), **-ly** *adv* geschickt. **~ness** *n* Geschicklichkeit *f*
defunct /dɪˈfʌŋkt/ *a* aufgelöst; 〈*law*〉 außer Kraft gesetzt
defuse /diːˈfjuːz/ *vt* entschärfen
defy /dɪˈfaɪ/ *vt* (*pt/pp* **-ied**) trotzen (+ *dat*); widerstehen (+ *dat*) 〈*attempt*〉
degenerate[1] /dɪˈdʒenəreɪt/ *vi* degenerieren; **~ into** (*fig*) ausarten in (+ *acc*)
degenerate[2] /dɪˈdʒenərət/ *a* degeneriert
degrading /dɪˈgreɪdɪŋ/ *a* entwürdigend
degree /dɪˈgriː/ *n* Grad *m*; (*Univ*) akademischer Grad *m*; **20 ~s** 20 Grad
dehydrate /diːˈhaɪdreɪt/ *vt* Wasser entziehen (+ *dat*). **~d** /-ɪd/ *a* ausgetrocknet
de-ice /diːˈaɪs/ *vt* enteisen
deign /deɪn/ *vi* **~ to do sth** sich herablassen, etw zu tun
deity /ˈdiːɪtɪ/ *n* Gottheit *f*
dejected /dɪˈdʒektɪd/ *a*, **-ly** *adv* niedergeschlagen
delay /dɪˈleɪ/ *n* Verzögerung *f*; (*of train, aircraft*) Verspätung *f*; **without ~** unverzüglich □ *vt* aufhalten; (*postpone*) aufschieben; **be ~ed** 〈*person:*〉 aufgehalten werden; 〈*train, aircraft:*〉 Verspätung haben □ *vi* zögern
delegate[1] /ˈdelɪgət/ *n* Delegierte(r) *m/f*
delegat|e[2] /ˈdelɪgeɪt/ *vt* delegieren. **~ion** /-ˈgeɪʃn/ *n* Delegation *f*
delet|e /dɪˈliːt/ *vt* streichen. **~ion** /-iːʃn/ *n* Streichung *f*
deliberate[1] /dɪˈlɪbərət/ *a*, **-ly** *adv* absichtlich; (*slow*) bedächtig
deliberat|e[2] /dɪˈlɪbəreɪt/ *vt/i* überlegen. **~ion** /-ˈreɪʃn/ *n* Überlegung *f*; **with ~ion** mit Bedacht
delicacy /ˈdelɪkəsɪ/ *n* Feinheit *f*; Zartheit *f*; (*food*) Delikatesse *f*
delicate /ˈdelɪkət/ *a* fein; 〈*fabric, health*〉 zart; 〈*situation*〉 heikel; 〈*mechanism*〉 empfindlich
delicatessen /delɪkəˈtesn/ *n* Delikatessengeschäft *nt*
delicious /dɪˈlɪʃəs/ *a* köstlich
delight /dɪˈlaɪt/ *n* Freude *f* □ *vt* entzücken □ *vi* **~ in** sich erfreuen an (+ *dat*). **~ed** *a* hocherfreut; **be ~ed** sich sehr freuen. **~ful** *a* reizend
delinquen|cy /dɪˈlɪŋkwənsɪ/ *n* Kriminalität *f*. **~t** *a* straffällig □ *n* Straffällige(r) *m/f*
deli|rious /dɪˈlɪrɪəs/ *a* **be ~rious** im Delirium sein. **~rium** /-rɪəm/ *n* Delirium *nt*
deliver /dɪˈlɪvə(r)/ *vt* liefern; zustellen 〈*post, newspaper*〉; halten 〈*speech*〉; überbringen 〈*message*〉; versetzen 〈*blow*〉; (*set free*) befreien; **~ a baby** ein Kind zur Welt bringen. **~ance** *n* Erlösung *f*. **~y** *n* Lieferung *f*; (*of post*) Zustellung *f*; (*Med*) Entbindung *f*; **cash on ~y** per Nachnahme
delta /ˈdeltə/ *n* Delta *nt*
delude /dɪˈluːd/ *vt* täuschen; **~ oneself** sich (*dat*) Illusionen machen
deluge /ˈdeljuːdʒ/ *n* Flut *f*; (*heavy rain*) schwerer Guss *m* □ *vt* überschwemmen
delusion /dɪˈluːʒn/ *n* Täuschung *f*
de luxe /dəˈlʌks/ *a* Luxus-
delve /delv/ *vi* hineingreifen (**into** in + *acc*); (*fig*) eingehen (**into** auf + *acc*)

demand /dɪ'mɑ:nd/ *n* Forderung *f*; (*Comm*) Nachfrage *f*; **in ~** gefragt; **on ~** auf Verlangen □ *vt* verlangen, fordern (**of/from** von). **~ing** *a* anspruchsvoll
demarcation /di:mɑ:'keɪʃn/ *n* Abgrenzung *f*
demean /dɪ'mi:n/ *vt* **~ oneself** sich erniedrigen
demeanour /dɪ'mi:nə(r)/ *n* Verhalten *nt*
demented /dɪ'mentɪd/ *a* verrückt
demise /dɪ'maɪz/ *n* Tod *m*
demister /di:'mɪstə(r)/ *n* (*Auto*) Defroster *m*
demo /'deməʊ/ *n* (*pl* **~s**) (*fam*) Demonstration *f*
demobilize /di:'məʊbɪlaɪz/ *vt* (*Mil*) entlassen
democracy /dɪ'mɒkrəsɪ/ *n* Demokratie *f*
democrat /'deməkræt/ *n* Demokrat *m*. **~ic** /-'krætɪk/ *a*, **-ally** *adv* demokratisch
demo|lish /dɪ'mɒlɪʃ/ *vt* abbrechen; (*destroy*) zerstören. **~lition** /demə'lɪʃn/ *n* Abbruch *m*
demon /'di:mən/ *n* Dämon *m*
demonstrat|e /'demənstreɪt/ *vt* beweisen; vorführen ⟨*appliance*⟩ □ *vi* (*Pol*) demonstrieren. **~ion** /-'streɪʃn/ *n* Vorführung *f*; (*Pol*) Demonstration *f*
demonstrative /dɪ'mɒnstrətɪv/ *a* (*Gram*) demonstrativ; **be ~** seine Gefühle zeigen
demonstrator /'demənstreɪtə(r)/ *n* Vorführer *m*; (*Pol*) Demonstrant *m*
demoralize /dɪ'mɒrəlaɪz/ *vt* demoralisieren
demote /dɪ'məʊt/ *vt* degradieren
demure /dɪ'mjʊə(r)/ *a*, **-ly** *adv* sittsam
den /den/ *n* Höhle *f*; (*room*) Bude *f*
denial /dɪ'naɪəl/ *n* Leugnen *nt*; **official ~** Dementi *nt*
denigrate /'denɪgreɪt/ *vt* herabsetzen
denim /'denɪm/ *n* Jeansstoff *m*; **~s** *pl* Jeans *pl*
Denmark /'denmɑ:k/ *n* Dänemark *nt*
denomination /dɪnɒmɪ'neɪʃn/ *n* (*Relig*) Konfession *f*; (*money*) Nennwert *m*
denote /dɪ'nəʊt/ *vt* bezeichnen
denounce /dɪ'naʊns/ *vt* denunzieren; (*condemn*) verurteilen
dens|e /dens/ *a* (**-r, -st**), **-ly** *adv* dicht; (*fam: stupid*) blöd[e]. **~ity** *n* Dichte *f*
dent /dent/ *n* Delle *f*, Beule *f* □ *vt* einbeulen; **~ed** /-ɪd/ verbeult
dental /'dentl/ *a* Zahn-; ⟨*treatment*⟩ zahnärztlich. **~ floss** /flɒs/ *n* Zahnseide *f*. **~ surgeon** *n* Zahnarzt *m*
dentist /'dentɪst/ *n* Zahnarzt *m*/-ärztin *f*. **~ry** *n* Zahnmedizin *f*
denture /'dentʃə(r)/ *n* Zahnprothese *f*; **~s** *pl* künstliches Gebiss *nt*
denude /dɪ'nju:d/ *vt* entblößen
denunciation /dɪnʌnsɪ'eɪʃn/ *n* Denunziation *f*; (*condemnation*) Verurteilung *f*
deny /dɪ'naɪ/ *vt* (*pt/pp* **-ied**) leugnen; (*officially*) dementieren; **~ s.o. sth** jdm etw verweigern
deodorant /di:'əʊdərənt/ *n* Deodorant *nt*
depart /dɪ'pɑ:t/ *vi* abfahren; (*Aviat*) abfliegen; (*go away*) weggehen/-fahren; (*deviate*) abweichen (**from** von)
department /dɪ'pɑ:tmənt/ *n* Abteilung *f*; (*Pol*) Ministerium *nt*. **~ store** *n* Kaufhaus *nt*
departure /dɪ'pɑ:tʃə(r)/ *n* Abfahrt *f*; (*Aviat*) Abflug *m*; (*from rule*) Abweichung *f*; **new ~** Neuerung *f*
depend /dɪ'pend/ *vi* abhängen (**on** von); (*rely*) sich verlassen (**on** auf + *acc*); **it all ~s** das kommt darauf an. **~able** /-əbl/ *a* zuverlässig. **~ant** *n* Abhängige(r) *m/f*. **~ence** *n* Abhängigkeit *f*. **~ent** *a* abhängig (**on** von)

depict /dɪˈpɪkt/ *vt* darstellen
depilatory /dɪˈpɪlətərɪ/ *n* Enthaarungsmittel *nt*
deplete /dɪˈpliːt/ *vt* verringern
deplor|able /dɪˈplɔːrəbl/ *a* bedauerlich. **~e** *vt* bedauern
deploy /dɪˈplɔɪ/ *vt* (*Mil*) einsetzen □ *vi* sich aufstellen
depopulate /diːˈpɒpjʊleɪt/ *vt* entvölkern
deport /dɪˈpɔːt/ *vt* deportieren, ausweisen. **~ation** /diːpɔːˈteɪʃn/ *n* Ausweisung *f*
deportment /dɪˈpɔːtmənt/ *n* Haltung *f*
depose /dɪˈpəʊz/ *vt* absetzen
deposit /dɪˈpɒzɪt/ *n* Anzahlung *f*; (*against damage*) Kaution *f*; (*on bottle*) Pfand *nt*; (*sediment*) Bodensatz *m*; (*Geol*) Ablagerung *f* □ *vt* (*pt/pp* **deposited**) legen; (*for safety*) deponieren; (*Geol*) ablagern. **~ account** *n* Sparkonto *nt*
depot /ˈdepəʊ/ *n* Depot *nt*; (*Amer: railway station*) Bahnhof *m*
deprav|e /dɪˈpreɪv/ *vt* verderben. **~ed** *a* verkommen. **~ity** /-ˈprævətɪ/ *n* Verderbtheit *f*
deprecate /ˈdeprəkeɪt/ *vt* missbilligen
depreciat|e /dɪˈpriːʃɪeɪt/ *vi* an Wert verlieren. **~ion** /-ˈeɪʃn/ *n* Wertminderung *f*; (*Comm*) Abschreibung *f*
depress /dɪˈpres/ *vt* deprimieren; (*press down*) herunterdrücken. **~ed** *a* deprimiert; **~ed area** Notstandsgebiet *nt*. **~ing** *a* deprimierend. **~ion** /-eʃn/ *n* Vertiefung *f*; (*Med*) Depression *f*; (*Meteorol*) Tief *nt*
deprivation /deprɪˈveɪʃn/ *n* Entbehrung *f*
deprive /dɪˈpraɪv/ *vt* entziehen; **~ s.o. of sth** jdm etw entziehen. **~d** *a* benachteiligt
depth /depθ/ *n* Tiefe *f*; **in ~** gründlich; **in the ~s of winter** im tiefsten Winter
deputation /depjʊˈteɪʃn/ *n* Abordnung *f*
deputize /ˈdepjʊtaɪz/ *vi* **~ for** vertreten
deputy /ˈdepjʊtɪ/ *n* Stellvertreter *m* □ *attrib* stellvertretend
derail /dɪˈreɪl/ *vt* **be ~ed** entgleisen. **~ment** *n* Entgleisung *f*
deranged /dɪˈreɪndʒd/ *a* geistesgestört
derelict /ˈderəlɪkt/ *a* verfallen; (*abandoned*) verlassen
deri|de /dɪˈraɪd/ *vt* verhöhnen. **~sion** /-ˈrɪʒn/ *n* Hohn *m*
derisive /dɪˈraɪsɪv/ *a*, **-ly** *adv* höhnisch
derisory /dɪˈraɪsərɪ/ *a* höhnisch; ⟨*offer*⟩ lächerlich
derivation /derɪˈveɪʃn/ *n* Ableitung *f*
derivative /dɪˈrɪvətɪv/ *a* abgeleitet □ *n* Ableitung *f*
derive /dɪˈraɪv/ *vt/i* (*obtain*) gewinnen (**from** aus); **be ~d from** ⟨*word:*⟩ hergeleitet sein aus
dermatologist /dɜːməˈtɒlədʒɪst/ *n* Hautarzt *m* /-ärztin *f*
derogatory /dɪˈrɒgətrɪ/ *a* abfällig
derrick /ˈderɪk/ *n* Bohrturm *m*
derv /dɜːv/ *n* Diesel[kraftstoff] *m*
descend /dɪˈsend/ *vt/i* hinunter-/heruntergehen; ⟨*vehicle, lift:*⟩ hinunter-/herunterfahren; **be ~ed from** abstammen von. **~ant** *n* Nachkomme *m*
descent /dɪˈsent/ *n* Abstieg *m*; (*lineage*) Abstammung *f*
describe /dɪˈskraɪb/ *vt* beschreiben
descrip|tion /dɪˈskrɪpʃn/ *n* Beschreibung *f*; (*sort*) Art *f*. **~tive** /-tɪv/ *a* beschreibend; (*vivid*) anschaulich
desecrat|e /ˈdesɪkreɪt/ *vt* entweihen. **~ion** /-ˈkreɪʃn/ *n* Entweihung *f*
desert[1] /ˈdezət/ *n* Wüste *f* □ *a* Wüsten-; **~ island** verlassene Insel *f*
desert[2] /dɪˈzɜːt/ *vt* verlassen □ *vt* desertieren. **~ed** *a* verlassen.

~er *n* (*Mil*) Deserteur *m*. **~ion** /-ɜ:ʃn/ *n* Fahnenflucht *f*

deserts /dɪ'zɜ:ts/ *npl* **get one's ~** seinen verdienten Lohn bekommen

deserv|e /dɪ'zɜ:v/ *vt* verdienen. **~edly** /-ɪdlɪ/ *adv* verdientermaßen. **~ing** *a* verdienstvoll; **~ing cause** guter Zweck *m*

design /dɪ'zaɪn/ *n* Entwurf *m*; (*pattern*) Muster *nt*; (*construction*) Konstruktion *f*; (*aim*) Absicht *f* □ *vt* entwerfen; (*construct*) konstruieren; **be ~ed for** bestimmt sein für

designat|e /'dezɪgneɪt/ *vt* bezeichnen; (*appoint*) ernennen. **~ion** /-'neɪʃn/ *n* Bezeichnung *f*

designer /dɪ'zaɪnə(r)/ *n* Designer *m*; (*Techn*) Konstrukteur *m*; (*Theat*) Bühnenbildner *m*

desirable /dɪ'zaɪrəbl/ *a* wünschenswert; (*sexually*) begehrenswert

desire /dɪ'zaɪə(r)/ *n* Wunsch *m*; (*longing*) Verlangen *nt* (**for** nach); (*sexual*) Begierde *f* □ *vt* [sich (*dat*)] wünschen; (*sexually*) begehren

desk /desk/ *n* Schreibtisch *m*; (*Sch*) Pult *nt*; (*Comm*) Kasse *f*; (*in hotel*) Rezeption *f*

desolat|e /'desələt/ *a* trostlos. **~ion** /-'leɪʃn/ *n* Trostlosigkeit *f*

despair /dɪ'speə(r)/ *n* Verzweiflung *f*; **in ~** verzweifelt □ *vi* verzweifeln

desperat|e /'despərət/ *a*, **-ly** *adv* verzweifelt; (*urgent*) dringend; **be ~e** ⟨*criminal:*⟩ zum Äußersten entschlossen sein; **be ~e for** dringend brauchen. **~ion** /-'reɪʃn/ *n* Verzweiflung *f*; **in ~ion** aus Verzweiflung

despicable /dɪ'spɪkəbl/ *a* verachtenswert

despise /dɪ'spaɪz/ *vt* verachten

despite /dɪ'spaɪt/ *prep* trotz (+ *gen*)

despondent /dɪ'spɒndənt/ *a* niedergeschlagen

despot /'despɒt/ *n* Despot *m*

dessert /dɪ'zɜ:t/ *n* Dessert *nt*, Nachtisch *m*. **~ spoon** *n* Dessertlöffel *m*

destination /destɪ'neɪʃn/ *n* [Reise]ziel *nt*; (*of goods*) Bestimmungsort *m*

destine /'destɪn/ *vt* bestimmen

destiny /'destɪnɪ/ *n* Schicksal *nt*

destitute /'destɪtju:t/ *a* völlig mittellos

destroy /dɪ'strɔɪ/ *vt* zerstören; (*totally*) vernichten. **~er** *n* (*Naut*) Zerstörer *m*

destruc|tion /dɪ'strʌkʃn/ *n* Zerstörung *f*; Vernichtung *f*. **-tive** /-tɪv/ *a* zerstörerisch; (*fig*) destruktiv

detach /dɪ'tætʃ/ *vt* abnehmen; (*tear off*) abtrennen. **~able** /-əbl/ *a* abnehmbar. **~ed** *a* (*fig*) distanziert; **~ed house** Einzelhaus *nt*

detachment /dɪ'tætʃmənt/ *n* Distanz *f*; (*objectivity*) Abstand *m*; (*Mil*) Sonderkommando *nt*

detail /'di:teɪl/ *n* Einzelheit *f*, Detail *nt*; **in ~** ausführlich □ *vt* einzeln aufführen; (*Mil*) abkommandieren. **~ed** *a* ausführlich

detain /dɪ'teɪn/ *vt* aufhalten; ⟨*police:*⟩ in Haft behalten; (*take into custody*) in Haft nehmen. **~ee** /di:teɪ'ni:/ *n* Häftling *m*

detect /dɪ'tekt/ *vt* entdecken; (*perceive*) wahrnehmen. **~ion** /-ekʃn/ *n* Entdeckung *f*

detective /dɪ'tektɪv/ *n* Detektiv *m*. **~ story** *n* Detektivroman *m*

detector /dɪ'tektə(r)/ *n* Suchgerät *nt*; (*for metal*) Metalldetektor *m*

detention /dɪ'tenʃn/ *n* Haft *f*; (*Sch*) Nachsitzen *nt*

deter /dɪ'tɜ:(r)/ *vt* (*pt/pp* **deterred**) abschrecken; (*prevent*) abhalten

detergent /dɪ'tɜ:dʒənt/ *n* Waschmittel *nt*

deteriorat|e /dɪˈtɪərɪəreɪt/ *vi* sich verschlechtern. **~ion** /ˈ-reɪʃn/ *n* Verschlechterung *f*
determination /dɪtɜːmɪˈneɪʃn/ *n* Entschlossenheit *f*
determine /dɪˈtɜːmɪn/ *vt* bestimmen; **~ to** (*resolve*) sich entschließen zu. **~d** *a* entschlossen
deterrent /dɪˈterənt/ *n* Abschreckungsmittel *nt*
detest /dɪˈtest/ *vt* verabscheuen. **~able** /-əbl/ *a* abscheulich
detonat|e /ˈdetəneɪt/ *vt* zünden □ *vi* explodieren. **~or** *n* Zünder *m*
detour /ˈdiːtʊə(r)/ *n* Umweg *m*; (*for traffic*) Umleitung *f*
detract /dɪˈtrækt/ *vi* **~ from** beeinträchtigen
detriment /ˈdetrɪmənt/ *n* **to the ~** zum Schaden (**of** *gen*). **~al** /-ˈmentl/ *a* schädlich (**to** *dat*)
deuce /djuːs/ *n* (*Tennis*) Einstand *m*
devaluation /diːvæljʊˈeɪʃn/ *n* Abwertung *f*
deˈvalue *vt* abwerten ⟨*currency*⟩
devastat|e /ˈdevəsteɪt/ *vt* verwüsten. **~ed** /-ɪd/ *a* (*fam*) erschüttert. **~ing** *a* verheerend. **~ion** /-ˈsteɪʃn/ *n* Verwüstung *f*
develop /dɪˈveləp/ *vt* entwickeln; bekommen ⟨*illness*⟩; erschließen ⟨*area*⟩ □ *vi* sich entwickeln (**into** zu). **~er** *n* **[property] ~er** Bodenspekulant *m*
deˈveloping country *n* Entwicklungsland *nt*
development /dɪˈveləpmənt/ *n* Entwicklung *f*
deviant /ˈdiːvɪənt/ *a* abweichend
deviat|e /ˈdiːvɪeɪt/ *vi* abweichen. **~ion** /-ˈeɪʃn/ *n* Abweichung *f*
device /dɪˈvaɪs/ *n* Gerät *nt*; (*fig*) Mittel *nt*; **leave s.o. to his own ~s** jdn sich (*dat*) selbst überlassen
devil /ˈdevl/ *n* Teufel *m*. **~ish** *a* teuflisch
devious /ˈdiːvɪəs/ *a* verschlagen; **~ route** Umweg *m*
devise /dɪˈvaɪz/ *vt* sich (*dat*) ausdenken
devoid /dɪˈvɔɪd/ *a* **~ of** ohne
devolution /diːvəˈluːʃn/ *n* Dezentralisierung *f*; (*of power*) Übertragung *f*
devot|e /dɪˈvəʊt/ *vt* widmen (**to** *dat*). **~ed** *a*, **-ly** *adv* ergeben; ⟨*care*⟩ liebevoll; **be ~ed to s.o.** sehr an jdm hängen. **~ee** /devəˈtiː/ *n* Anhänger(in) *m(f)*
devotion /dɪˈvəʊʃn/ *n* Hingabe *f*; **~s** *pl* (*Relig*) Andacht *f*
devour /dɪˈvaʊə(r)/ *vt* verschlingen
devout /dɪˈvaʊt/ *a* fromm
dew /djuː/ *n* Tau *m*
dexterity /dekˈsterətɪ/ *n* Geschicklichkeit *f*
diabet|es /daɪəˈbiːtiːz/ *n* Zuckerkrankheit *f*. **~ic** /-ˈbetɪk/ *a* zuckerkrank □ *n* Zuckerkranke(r) *m/f*, Diabetiker(in) *m(f)*
diabolical /daɪəˈbɒlɪkl/ *a* teuflisch
diagnose /daɪəgˈnəʊz/ *vt* diagnostizieren
diagnosis /daɪəgˈnəʊsɪs/ *n* (*pl* **-oses** /-siːz/) Diagnose *f*
diagonal /daɪˈægənl/ *a*, **-ly** *adv* diagonal □ *n* Diagonale *f*
diagram /ˈdaɪəgræm/ *n* Diagramm *nt*
dial /ˈdaɪəl/ *n* (*of clock*) Zifferblatt *nt*; (*Techn*) Skala *f*; (*Teleph*) Wählscheibe *f* □ *vt/i* (*pt/pp* **dialled**) (*Teleph*) wählen; **~ direct** durchwählen
dialect /ˈdaɪəlekt/ *n* Dialekt *m*
dialling: ~ code *n* Vorwahlnummer *f*. **~ tone** *n* Amtszeichen *nt*
dialogue /ˈdaɪəlɒg/ *n* Dialog *m*
ˈdial tone *n* (*Amer, Teleph*) Amtszeichen *nt*
diameter /daɪˈæmɪtə(r)/ *n* Durchmesser *m*

diametrically /daɪəˈmetrɪkəlɪ/ *adv* ~ **opposed** genau entgegengesetzt (**to** *dat*)
diamond /ˈdaɪəmənd/ *n* Diamant *m*; (*cut*) Brillant *m*; (*shape*) Raute *f*; ~**s** *pl* (*Cards*) Karo *nt*
diaper /ˈdaɪəpə(r)/ *n* (*Amer*) Windel *f*
diaphragm /ˈdaɪəfræm/ *n* (*Anat*) Zwerchfell *nt*; (*Phot*) Blende *f*
diarrhoea /daɪəˈriːə/ *n* Durchfall *m*
diary /ˈdaɪərɪ/ *n* Tagebuch *nt*; (*for appointments*) [Termin]kalender *m*
dice /daɪs/ *n inv* Würfel *m* □ *vt* (*Culin*) in Würfel schneiden
dicey /ˈdaɪsɪ/ *a* (*fam*) riskant
dictat|e /dɪkˈteɪt/ *vt/i* diktieren. ~**ion** /-eɪʃn/ *n* Diktat *nt*
dictator /dɪkˈteɪtə(r)/ *n* Diktator *m*. ~**ial** /-təˈtɔːrɪəl/ *a* diktatorisch. ~**ship** *n* Diktatur *f*
diction /ˈdɪkʃn/ *n* Aussprache *f*
dictionary /ˈdɪkʃənrɪ/ *n* Wörterbuch *nt*
did /dɪd/ *see* **do**
didactic /dɪˈdæktɪk/ *a* didaktisch
diddle /ˈdɪdl/ *vt* (*fam*) übers Ohr hauen
didn't /ˈdɪdnt/ = **did not**
die[1] /daɪ/ *n* (*Techn*) Prägestempel *m*; (*metal mould*) Gussform *f*
die[2] *vi* (*pres p* **dying**) sterben (**of** an + *dat*); ⟨*plant, animal:*⟩ eingehen; ⟨*flower:*⟩ verwelken; **be dying to do sth** (*fam*) darauf brennen, etw zu tun; **be dying for sth** (*fam*) sich nach etw sehnen. ~ **down** *vi* nachlassen; ⟨*fire:*⟩ herunterbrennen. ~ **out** *vi* aussterben
diesel /ˈdiːzl/ *n* Diesel *m*. ~ **engine** *n* Dieselmotor *m*
diet /ˈdaɪət/ *n* Kost *f*; (*restricted*) Diät *f*; (*for slimming*) Schlankheitskur *f*; **be on a** ~ Diät leben; eine Schlankheitskur machen □ *vi* diät leben; eine Schlankheitskur machen
dietician /daɪəˈtɪʃn/ *n* Diätassistent(in) *m*(*f*)
differ /ˈdɪfə(r)/ *vi* sich unterscheiden; (*disagree*) verschiedener Meinung sein
differen|ce /ˈdɪfrəns/ *n* Unterschied *m*; (*disagreement*) Meinungsverschiedenheit *f*. ~**t** *a* andere(r,s); (*various*) verschiedene; **be** ~**t** anders sein (**from** als)
differential /dɪfəˈrenʃl/ *a* Differenzial- □ *n* Unterschied *m*; (*Techn*) Differenzial *nt*
differentiate /dɪfəˈrenʃɪeɪt/ *vt/i* unterscheiden (**between** zwischen + *dat*)
differently /ˈdɪfrəntlɪ/ *adv* anders
difficult /ˈdɪfɪkəlt/ *a* schwierig, schwer. ~**y** *n* Schwierigkeit *f*
diffiden|ce /ˈdɪfɪdəns/ *n* Zaghaftigkeit *f*. ~**t** *a* zaghaft
diffuse[1] /dɪˈfjuːs/ *a* ausgebreitet; (*wordy*) langatmig
diffuse[2] /dɪˈfjuːz/ *vt* (*Phys*) streuen
dig /dɪg/ *n* (*poke*) Stoß *m*; (*remark*) spitze Bemerkung *f*; (*Archaeol*) Ausgrabung *f*; ~**s** *pl* (*fam*) möbliertes Zimmer *nt* □ *vt/i* (*pt/pp* **dug**, *pres p* **digging**) graben; umgraben ⟨*garden*⟩; ~ **s.o. in the ribs** jdm einen Rippenstoß geben. ~ **out** *vt* ausgraben. ~ **up** *vt* ausgraben; umgraben ⟨*garden*⟩; aufreißen ⟨*street*⟩
digest[1] /ˈdaɪdʒest/ *n* Kurzfassung *f*
digest[2] /dɪˈdʒest/ *vt* verdauen. ~**ible** *a* verdaulich. ~**ion** /-estʃn/ *n* Verdauung *f*
digger /ˈdɪgə(r)/ *n* (*Techn*) Bagger *m*
digit /ˈdɪdʒɪt/ *n* Ziffer *f*; (*finger*) Finger *m*; (*toe*) Zehe *f*
digital /ˈdɪdʒɪtl/ *a* Digital-; ~ **clock** Digitaluhr *f*
dignified /ˈdɪgnɪfaɪd/ *a* würdevoll
dignitary /ˈdɪgnɪtərɪ/ *n* Würdenträger *m*

dignity /ˈdɪgnɪtɪ/ *n* Würde *f*
digress /daɪˈgres/ *vi* abschweifen **~ion** /-eʃn/ *n* Abschweifung *f*
dike /daɪk/ *n* Deich *m*; (*ditch*) Graben *m*
dilapidated /dɪˈlæpɪdeɪtɪd/ *a* baufällig
dilate /daɪˈleɪt/ *vt* erweitern □ *vi* sich erweitern
dilatory /ˈdɪlətərɪ/ *a* langsam
dilemma /dɪˈlemə/ *n* Dilemma *nt*
dilettante /dɪlɪˈtæntɪ/ *n* Dilettant(in) *m(f)*
diligen|ce /ˈdɪlɪdʒəns/ *n* Fleiß *m*. **~t** *a*, **-ly** *adv* fleißig
dill /dɪl/ *n* Dill *m*
dilly-dally /ˈdɪlɪdælɪ/ *vi* (*pt/pp* **-ied**) (*fam*) trödeln
dilute /daɪˈluːt/ *vt* verdünnen
dim /dɪm/ *a* (**dimmer, dimmest**). **-ly** *adv* (*weak*) schwach; (*dark*) trüb[e]; (*indistinct*) undeutlich; (*fam: stupid*) dumm, (*fam*) doof □ *v* (*pt/pp* **dimmed**) □ *vt* dämpfen □ *vi* schwächer werden
dime /daɪm/ *n* (*Amer*) Zehncentstück *nt*
dimension /daɪˈmenʃn/ *n* Dimension *f*; **~s** *pl* Maße *pl*
diminish /dɪˈmɪnɪʃ/ *vt* verringern □ *vi* sich verringern
diminutive /dɪˈmɪnjʊtɪv/ *a* winzig □ *n* Verkleinerungsform *f*
dimple /ˈdɪmpl/ *n* Grübchen *nt*
din /dɪn/ *n* Krach *m*, Getöse *nt*
dine /daɪn/ *vi* speisen. **~r** *n* Speisende(r) *m/f*; (*Amer: restaurant*) Esslokal *nt*
dinghy /ˈdɪŋgɪ/ *n* Dinghi *nt*; (*inflatable*) Schlauchboot *nt*
dingy /ˈdɪndʒɪ/ *a* (**-ier, -iest**) trübe
dining /ˈdaɪnɪŋ/: **~-car** *n* Speisewagen *m*. **~-room** *n* Esszimmer *nt*. **~-table** *n* Esstisch *m*
dinner /ˈdɪnə(r)/ *n* Abendessen *nt*; (*at midday*) Mittagessen *nt*; (*formal*) Essen *nt*. **~-jacket** *n* Smoking *m*
dinosaur /ˈdaɪnəsɔː(r)/ *n* Dinosaurier *m*
dint /dɪnt/ *n* **by ~ of** durch (+ *acc*)
diocese /ˈdaɪəsɪs/ *n* Diözese *f*
dip /dɪp/ *n* (*in ground*) Senke *f*; (*Culin*) Dip *m*; **go for a ~** kurz schwimmen gehen □ *v* (*pt/pp* **dipped**) *vt* [ein]tauchen; **~ one's headlights** (*Auto*) [die Scheinwerfer] abblenden □ *vi* sich senken
diphtheria /dɪfˈθɪərɪə/ *n* Diphtherie *f*
diphthong /ˈdɪfθɒŋ/ *n* Diphthong *m*
diploma /dɪˈpləʊmə/ *n* Diplom *nt*
diplomacy /dɪˈpləʊməsɪ/ *n* Diplomatie *f*
diplomat /ˈdɪpləmæt/ *n* Diplomat *m*. **~ic** /-ˈmætɪk/ *a*, **-ally** *adv* diplomatisch
'dip-stick *n* (*Auto*) Ölmessstab *m*
dire /ˈdaɪə(r)/ *a* (**-r, -st**) bitter; (*situation, consequences*) furchtbar
direct /dɪˈrekt/ *a & adv* direkt □ *vt* (*aim*) richten (**at** auf / (*fig*) an + *acc*); (*control*) leiten; (*order*) anweisen; **~ s.o.** (*show the way*) jdm den Weg sagen; **~ a film/play** bei einem Film/Theaterstück Regie führen. **~ 'current** *n* Gleichstrom *m*
direction /dɪˈrekʃn/ *n* Richtung *f*; (*control*) Leitung *f*; (*of play, film*) Regie *f*; **~s** *pl* Anweisungen *pl*; **~s for use** Gebrauchsanweisung *f*
directly /dɪˈrektlɪ/ *adv* direkt; (*at once*) sofort □ *conj* (*fam*) sobald
director /dɪˈrektə(r)/ *n* (*Comm*) Direktor *m*; (*of play, film*) Regisseur *m*
directory /dɪˈrektərɪ/ *n* Verzeichnis *nt*; (*Teleph*) Telefonbuch *nt*
dirt /dɜːt/ *n* Schmutz *m*; (*soil*) Erde *f*; **~ cheap** (*fam*) spottbillig

dirty /ˈdɜːtɪ/ *a* (**-ier, -iest**) schmutzig □ *vt* schmutzig machen

dis|aˈbility /dɪs-/ *n* Behinderung *f*. **~abled** /dɪˈseɪbld/ *a* [körper]behindert

disadˈvan|tage *n* Nachteil *m*; **at a ~tage** im Nachteil. **~taged** *a* benachteiligt. **~ˈtageous** *a* nachteilig

disafˈfected *a* unzufrieden; (*disloyal*) illoyal

disaˈgree *vi* nicht übereinstimmen (**with** mit); **I ~** ich bin anderer Meinung; **we ~** wir sind verschiedener Meinung; **oysters ~ with me** Austern bekommen mir nicht

disaˈgreeable *a* unangenehm

disaˈgreement *n* Meinungsverschiedenheit *f*

disapˈpear *vi* verschwinden. **~ance** *n* Verschwinden *nt*

disapˈpoint *vt* enttäuschen. **~ment** *n* Enttäuschung *f*

disapˈproval *n* Missbilligung *f*

disapˈprove *vi* dagegen sein; **~ of** missbilligen

disˈarm *vt* entwaffnen □ *vi* (*Mil*) abrüsten. **~ament** *n* Abrüstung *f*. **~ing** *a* entwaffnend

disarˈray *n* Unordnung *f*

disast|er /dɪˈzɑːstə(r)/ *n* Katastrophe *f*; (*accident*) Unglück *nt*. **~rous** /-rəs/ *a* katastrophal

disˈband *vt* auflösen □ *vi* sich auflösen

disbeˈlief *n* Ungläubigkeit *f*; **in ~** ungläubig

disc /dɪsk/ *n* Scheibe *f*; (*record*) [Schall]platte *f*; (*CD*) CD *f*

discard /dɪˈskɑːd/ *vt* ablegen; (*throw away*) wegwerfen

discern /dɪˈsɜːn/ *vt* wahrnehmen. **~ible** *a* wahrnehmbar. **~ing** *a* anspruchsvoll

ˈdischarge[1] *n* Ausstoßen *nt*; (*Naut, Electr*) Entladung *f*; (*dismissal*) Entlassung *f*; (*Jur*) Freispruch *m*; (*Med*) Ausfluss *m*

disˈcharge[2] *vt* ausstoßen; (*Naut, Electr*) entladen; (*dismiss*) entlassen; (*Jur*) freisprechen ⟨*accused*⟩; **~ a duty** sich einer Pflicht entledigen

disciple /dɪˈsaɪpl/ *n* Jünger *m*; (*fig*) Schüler *m*

disciplinary /ˈdɪsɪplɪnərɪ/ *a* disziplinarisch

discipline /ˈdɪsɪplɪn/ *n* Disziplin *f* □ *vt* Disziplin beibringen (+ *dat*); (*punish*) bestrafen

ˈdisc jockey *n* Diskjockey *m*

disˈclaim *vt* abstreiten. **~er** *n* Verzichterklärung *f*

disˈclos|e *vt* enthüllen. **~ure** *n* Enthüllung *f*

disco /ˈdɪskəʊ/ *n* (*fam*) Disko *f*

disˈcolour *vt* verfärben □ *vi* sich verfärben

disˈcomfort *n* Beschwerden *pl*; (*fig*) Unbehagen *nt*

disconcert /dɪskənˈsɜːt/ *vt* aus der Fassung bringen

disconˈnect *vt* trennen; (*Electr*) ausschalten; (*cut supply*) abstellen

disconsolate /dɪsˈkɒnsələt/ *a* untröstlich

disconˈtent *n* Unzufriedenheit *f*. **~ed** *a* unzufrieden

disconˈtinue *vt* einstellen; (*Comm*) nicht mehr herstellen

ˈdiscord *n* Zwietracht *f*; (*Mus & fig*) Missklang *m*. **~ant** /dɪˈskɔːdənt/ *a* **~ant note** Missklang *m*

discothèque /ˈdɪskətek/ *n* Diskothek *f*

ˈdiscount[1] *n* Rabatt *m*

disˈcount[2] *vt* außer Acht lassen

disˈcourage *vt* entmutigen; (*dissuade*) abraten (+ *dat*)

ˈdiscourse *n* Rede *f*

disˈcourteous *a*, **-ly** *adv* unhöflich

discover /dɪˈskʌvə(r)/ *vt* entdecken. **~y** *n* Entdeckung *f*

disˈcredit *n* Misskredit *m* □ *vt* in Misskredit bringen

discreet /dɪ'skri:t/ *a*, **-ly** *adv* diskret

discrepancy /dɪ'skrepənsɪ/ *n* Diskrepanz *f*

discretion /dɪ'skreʃn/ *n* Diskretion *f*; (*judgement*) Ermessen *nt*

discriminat|e /dɪ'skrɪmɪneɪt/ *vi* unterscheiden (**between** zwischen + *dat*); **~e against** diskriminieren. **~ing** *a* anspruchsvoll. **~ion** /-'neɪʃn/ *n* Diskriminierung *f*; (*quality*) Urteilskraft *f*

discus /'dɪskəs/ *n* Diskus *m*

discuss /dɪ'skʌs/ *vt* besprechen; (*examine critically*) diskutieren. **~ion** /-ʌʃn/ *n* Besprechung *f*; Diskussion *f*

disdain /dɪs'deɪn/ *n* Verachtung *f* □ *vt* verachten. **~ful** *a* verächtlich

disease /dɪ'zi:z/ *n* Krankheit *f*. **~d** *a* krank

disem'bark *vi* an Land gehen

disen'chant *vt* ernüchtern. **~ment** *n* Ernüchterung *f*

disen'gage *vt* losmachen; **~ the clutch** (*Auto*) auskuppeln

disen'tangle *vt* entwirren

dis'favour *n* Ungnade *f*; (*disapproval*) Missfallen *nt*

dis'figure *vt* entstellen

dis'gorge *vt* ausspeien

dis'grace *n* Schande *f*; **in ~** in Ungnade □ *vt* Schande machen (+ *dat*). **~ful** *a* schändlich

disgruntled /dɪs'grʌntld/ *a* verstimmt

disguise /dɪs'gaɪz/ *n* Verkleidung *f*; **in ~** verkleidet □ *vt* verkleiden; verstellen ⟨*voice*⟩; (*conceal*) verhehlen

disgust /dɪs'gʌst/ *n* Ekel *m*; **in ~** empört □ *vt* anekeln; (*appal*) empören. **~ing** *a* eklig; (*appalling*) abscheulich

dish /dɪʃ/ *n* Schüssel *f*; (*shallow*) Schale *f*; (*small*) Schälchen *nt*; (*food*) Gericht *nt*. **~ out** *vt* austeilen. **~ up** *vt* auftragen

'dishcloth *n* Spültuch *nt*

dis'hearten *vt* entmutigen. **~ing** *a* entmutigend

dishevelled /dɪ'ʃevld/ *a* zerzaust

dis'honest *a* **-ly** *adv* unehrlich. **~y** *n* Unehrlichkeit *f*

dis'honour *n* Schande *f* □ *vt* entehren; nicht honorieren ⟨*cheque*⟩. **~able** *a*, **-bly** *adv* unehrenhaft

'dishwasher *n* Geschirrspülmaschine *f*

disil'lusion *vt* ernüchtern. **~ment** *n* Ernüchterung *f*

disin'fect *vt* desinfizieren. **~ant** *n* Desinfektionsmittel *nt*

disin'herit *vt* enterben

dis'integrate *vi* zerfallen

dis'interested *a* unvoreingenommen; (*uninterested*) uninteressiert

dis'jointed *a* unzusammenhängend

disk /dɪsk/ *n* = **disc**

dis'like *n* Abneigung *f* □ *vt* nicht mögen

dislocate /'dɪsləkeɪt/ *vt* ausrenken; **~ one's shoulder** sich (*dat*) den Arm auskugeln

dis'lodge *vt* entfernen

dis'loyal *a*, **-ly** *adv* illoyal. **~ty** *n* Illoyalität *f*

dismal /'dɪzməl/ *a* trüb[e]; ⟨*person*⟩ trübselig; (*fam: poor*) kläglich

dismantle /dɪs'mæntl/ *vt* auseinander nehmen; (*take down*) abbauen

dis'may *n* Bestürzung *f*. **~ed** *a* bestürzt

dis'miss *vt* entlassen; (*reject*) zurückweisen. **~al** *n* Entlassung *f*; Zurückweisung *f*

dis'mount *vi* absteigen

diso'bedien|ce *n* Ungehorsam *m*. **~t** *a* ungehorsam

diso'bey *vt/i* nicht gehorchen (+ *dat*); nicht befolgen ⟨*rule*⟩

dis'order *n* Unordnung *f*; (*Med*) Störung *f*. **~ly** *a* unordentlich;

~ly conduct ungebührliches Benehmen *nt*
dis'organized *a* unorganisiert
dis'orientate *vt* verwirren; **be ~d** die Orientierung verloren haben
dis'own *vt* verleugnen
disparaging /dɪ'spærɪdʒɪŋ/ *a*, **-ly** *adv* abschätzig
disparity /dɪ'spærətɪ/ *n* Ungleichheit *f*
dispassionate /dɪ'spæʃənət/ *a*, **-ly** *adv* gelassen; (*impartial*) unparteiisch
dispatch /dɪ'spætʃ/ *n* (*Comm*) Versand *m*; (*Mil*) Nachricht *f*; (*report*) Bericht *m*; **with ~** prompt □ *vt* [ab]senden; (*deal with*) erledigen; (*kill*) töten. **~-rider** *n* Meldefahrer *m*
dispel /dɪ'spel/ *vt* (*pt/pp* **dispelled**) vertreiben
dispensable /dɪ'spensəbl/ *a* entbehrlich
dispensary /dɪ'spensərɪ/ *n* Apotheke *f*
dispense /dɪ'spens/ *vt* austeilen; **~ with** verzichten auf (+ *acc*). **~r** *n* Apotheker(in) *m(f)*; (*device*) Automat *m*
dispers|al /dɪ'spɜːsl/ *n* Zerstreuung *f*. **~e** /dɪ'spɜːs/ *vt* zerstreuen □ *vi* sich zerstreuen
dispirited /dɪ'spɪrɪtɪd/ *a* entmutigt
dis'place *vt* verschieben; **~d person** Vertriebene(r) *m/f*
display /dɪ'spleɪ/ *n* Ausstellung *f*; (*Comm*) Auslage *f*; (*performance*) Vorführung *f* □ *vt* zeigen; ausstellen ⟨*goods*⟩
dis'please *vt* missfallen (+ *dat*)
dis'pleasure *n* Missfallen *nt*
disposable /dɪ'spəʊzəbl/ *a* Wegwerf-; ⟨*income*⟩ verfügbar
disposal /dɪ'spəʊzl/ *n* Beseitigung *f*; **be at s.o.'s ~** jdm zur Verfügung stehen
dispose /dɪ'spəʊz/ *vi* **~ of** beseitigen; (*deal with*) erledigen; **be well ~d** wohlgesinnt sein (**to** *dat*)
disposition /dɪspə'zɪʃn/ *n* Veranlagung *f*; (*nature*) Wesensart *f*
disproportionate /dɪsprə'pɔːʃənət/ *a*, **-ly** *adv* unverhältnismäßig
dis'prove *vt* widerlegen
dispute /dɪ'spjuːt/ *n* Disput *m*; (*quarrel*) Streit *m* □ *vt* bestreiten
disqualifi'cation *n* Disqualifikation *f*
dis'qualify *vt* disqualifizieren; **~ s.o. from driving** jdm den Führerschein entziehen
disquieting /dɪs'kwaɪətɪŋ/ *a* beunruhigend
disre'gard *n* Nichtbeachtung *f* □ *vt* nicht beachten, ignorieren
disre'pair *n* **fall into ~** verfallen
dis'reputable *a* verrufen
disre'pute *n* Verruf *m*
disre'spect *n* Respektlosigkeit *f*. **~ful** *a*, **-ly** *adv* respektlos
disrupt /dɪs'rʌpt/ *vt* stören. **~ion** /-ʌpʃn/ *n* Störung *f*. **~ive** /-tɪv/ *a* störend
dissatis'faction *n* Unzufriedenheit *f*
dis'satisfied *a* unzufrieden
dissect /dɪ'sekt/ *vt* zergliedern; (*Med*) sezieren. **~ion** /-ekʃn/ *n* Zergliederung *f*; (*Med*) Sektion *f*
disseminat|e /dɪ'semɪneɪt/ *vt* verbreiten. **~ion** /-'neɪʃn/ *n* Verbreitung *f*
dissent /dɪ'sent/ *n* Nichtübereinstimmung *f* □ *vi* nicht übereinstimmen
dissertation /dɪsə'teɪʃn/ *n* Dissertation *f*
dis'service *n* schlechter Dienst *m*
dissident /'dɪsɪdənt/ *n* Dissident *m*
dis'similar *a* unähnlich (**to** *dat*)
dissociate /dɪ'səʊʃɪeɪt/ *vt* trennen; **~ oneself** sich distanzieren (**from** von)
dissolute /'dɪsəluːt/ *a* zügellos; ⟨*life*⟩ ausschweifend

dissolution /dɪsə'lu:ʃn/ *n* Auflösung *f*
dissolve /dɪ'zɒlv/ *vt* auflösen □ *vi* sich auflösen
dissuade /dɪ'sweɪd/ *vt* abbringen (**from** von)
distance /'dɪstəns/ *n* Entfernung *f*; **long/short ~** lange/kurze Strecke *f*; **in the/from a ~** in/aus der Ferne
distant /'dɪstənt/ *a* fern; (*aloof*) kühl; ⟨*relative*⟩ entfernt
dis'taste *n* Abneigung *f*. **~ful** *a* unangenehm
distend /dɪ'stend/ *vi* sich [auf]blähen
distil /dɪ'stɪl/ *vt* (*pt/pp* **distilled**) brennen; (*Chem*) destillieren. **~lation** /-'leɪʃn/ *n* Destillation *f*. **~lery** /-ərɪ/ *n* Brennerei *f*
distinct /dɪ'stɪŋkt/ *a* deutlich; (*different*) verschieden. **~ion** /-ɪŋkʃn/ *n* Unterschied *m*; (*Sch*) Auszeichnung *f*. **~ive** /-tɪv/ *a* kennzeichnend; (*unmistakable*) unverwechselbar. **~ly** *adv* deutlich
distinguish /dɪ'stɪŋgwɪʃ/ *vt/i* unterscheiden; (*make out*) erkennen; **~ oneself** sich auszeichnen. **~ed** *a* angesehen; ⟨*appearance*⟩ distinguiert
distort /dɪ'stɔ:t/ *vt* verzerren; (*fig*) verdrehen. **~ion** /-ɔ:ʃn/ *n* Verzerrung *f*; (*fig*) Verdrehung *f*
distract /dɪ'strækt/ *vt* ablenken. **~ed** /-ɪd/ *a* [völlig] aufgelöst. **~ion** /-ækʃn/ *n* Ablenkung *f*; (*despair*) Verzweiflung *f*
distraught /dɪ'strɔ:t/ *a* [völlig] aufgelöst
distress /dɪ'stres/ *n* Kummer *m*; (*pain*) Schmerz *m*; (*poverty, danger*) Not *f* □ *vt* Kummer/Schmerz bereiten (+ *dat*); (*sadden*) bekümmern; (*shock*) erschüttern. **~ing** *a* schmerzlich; (*shocking*) erschütternd. **~ signal** *n* Notsignal *nt*
distribut|e /dɪ'strɪbju:t/ *vt* verteilen; (*Comm*) vertreiben. **~ion** /-'bju:ʃn/ *n* Verteilung *f*; Vertrieb *m*. **~or** *n* Verteiler *m*
district /'dɪstrɪkt/ *n* Gegend *f*; (*Admin*) Bezirk *m*. **~ nurse** *n* Gemeindeschwester *f*
dis'trust *n* Misstrauen *nt* □ *vt* misstrauen (+ *dat*). **~ful** *a* misstrauisch
disturb /dɪ'stɜ:b/ *vt* stören; (*perturb*) beunruhigen; (*touch*) anrühren. **~ance** *n* Unruhe *f*; (*interruption*) Störung *f*. **~ed** *a* beunruhigt; **[mentally] ~ed** geistig gestört. **~ing** *a* beunruhigend
dis'used *a* stillgelegt; (*empty*) leer
ditch /dɪtʃ/ *n* Graben *m* □ *vt* (*fam: abandon*) fallen lassen ⟨*plan*⟩; wegschmeißen ⟨*thing*⟩
dither /'dɪðə(r)/ *vi* zaudern
ditto /'dɪtəʊ/ *n* dito; (*fam*) ebenfalls
divan /dɪ'væn/ *n* Polsterbett *nt*
dive /daɪv/ *n* [Kopf]sprung *m*; (*Aviat*) Sturzflug *m*; (*fam: place*) Spelunke *f* □ *vi* einen Kopfsprung machen; (*when in water*) tauchen; (*Aviat*) einen Sturzflug machen; (*fam: rush*) stürzen
diver /'daɪvə(r)/ *n* Taucher *m*; (*Sport*) [Kunst]springer *m*
diver|ge /daɪ'vɜ:dʒ/ *vi* auseinander gehen. **~gent** /-ənt/ *a* abweichend
diverse /daɪ'vɜ:s/ *a* verschieden
diversify /daɪ'vɜ:sɪfaɪ/ *vt/i* (*pt/pp* **-ied**) variieren; (*Comm*) diversifizieren
diversion /daɪ'vɜ:ʃn/ *n* Umleitung *f*; (*distraction*) Ablenkung *f*
diversity /daɪ'vɜ:sətɪ/ *n* Vielfalt *f*
divert /daɪ'vɜ:t/ *vt* umleiten; ablenken ⟨*attention*⟩; (*entertain*) unterhalten
divest /daɪ'vest/ *vt* sich entledigen (**of** + *gen*); (*fig*) entkleiden

divide /dɪˈvaɪd/ *vt* teilen; (*separate*) trennen; (*Math*) dividieren (**by** durch) □ *vi* sich teilen
dividend /ˈdɪvɪdend/ *n* Dividende *f*
divine /dɪˈvaɪn/ *a* göttlich
diving /ˈdaɪvɪŋ/ *n* (*Sport*) Kunstspringen *nt*. **~-board** *n* Sprungbrett *nt*. **~-suit** *n* Taucheranzug *m*
divinity /dɪˈvɪnətɪ/ *n* Göttlichkeit *f*; (*subject*) Theologie *f*
divisible /dɪˈvɪzɪbl/ *a* teilbar (**by** *durch*)
division /dɪˈvɪʒn/ *n* Teilung *f*; (*separation*) Trennung *f*; (*Math, Mil*) Division *f*; (*Parl*) Hammelsprung *m*; (*line*) Trennlinie *f*; (*group*) Abteilung *f*
divorce /dɪˈvɔːs/ *n* Scheidung *f* □ *vt* sich scheiden lassen von. **~d** *a* geschieden; **get ~d** sich scheiden lassen
divorcee /dɪvɔːˈsiː/ *n* Geschiedene(r) *m/f*
divulge /daɪˈvʌldʒ/ *vt* preisgeben
DIY *abbr of* **do-it-yourself**
dizziness /ˈdɪzɪnɪs/ *n* Schwindel *m*
dizzy /ˈdɪzɪ/ *a* (**-ier, -iest**) schwindlig; **I feel ~** mir ist schwindlig
do /duː/ *n* (*pl* **dos** *or* **do's**) (*fam*) Veranstaltung *f* □ *v* (*3 sg pres tense* **does**; *pt* **did**; *pp* **done**) □ *vt/i* tun, machen; (*be suitable*) passen; (*be enough*) reichen, genügen; (*cook*) kochen; (*clean*) putzen; (*Sch: study*) durchnehmen; (*fam: cheat*) beschwindeln (**out of** um); **do without** auskommen ohne; **do away with** abschaffen; **be done** (*Culin*) gar sein; **well done** gut gemacht! (*Culin*) gut durchgebraten; **done in** (*fam*) kaputt, fertig; **done for** (*fam*) verloren, erledigt; **do the flowers** die Blumen arrangieren; **do the potatoes** die Kartoffeln schälen; **do the washing up** abwaschen, spülen; **do one's hair** sich frisieren; **do well/badly** gut/schlecht abschneiden; **how is he doing?** wie geht es ihm? **this won't do** das geht nicht; **are you doing anything today?** haben Sie heute etwas vor? **I could do with a spanner** ich könnte einen Schraubenschlüssel gebrauchen □ *v aux* **do you speak German?** sprechen Sie Deutsch? **yes, I do** ja; (*emphatic*) doch; **no, I don't** nein; **I don't smoke** ich rauche nicht; **don't you/doesn't he?** nicht [wahr]? **so do I** ich auch; **do come in** kommen Sie doch herein; **how do you do?** guten Tag. **do in** *vt* (*fam*) um die Ecke bringen. **do up** *vt* (*fasten*) zumachen; (*renovate*) renovieren; (*wrap*) einpacken
docile /ˈdəʊsaɪl/ *a* fügsam
dock[1] /dɒk/ *n* (*Jur*) Anklagebank *f*
dock[2] *n* Dock *nt* □ *vi* anlegen, docken □ *vt* docken. **~er** *n* Hafenarbeiter *m*. **~yard** *n* Werft *f*
doctor /ˈdɒktə(r)/ *n* Arzt *m*/ Ärztin *f*; (*Univ*) Doktor *m* □ *vt* kastrieren; (*spay*) sterilisieren. **~ate** /-ət/ *n* Doktorwürde *f*
doctrine /ˈdɒktrɪn/ *n* Lehre *f*, Doktrin *f*
document /ˈdɒkjʊmənt/ *n* Dokument *nt*. **~ary** /-ˈmentərɪ/ *a* Dokumentar- □ *n* Dokumentarbericht *m*; (*film*) Dokumentarfilm *m*
doddery /ˈdɒdərɪ/ *a* (*fam*) tatterig
dodge /dɒdʒ/ *n* (*fam*) Trick *m*, Kniff *m* □ *vt/i* ausweichen (+ *dat*); **~ out of the way** zur Seite springen
dodgems /ˈdɒdʒəmz/ *npl* Autoskooter *pl*
dodgy /ˈdɒdʒɪ/ *a* (**-ier, -iest**) (*fam*) (*awkward*) knifflig; (*dubious*) zweifelhaft
doe /dəʊ/ *n* Ricke *f*; (*rabbit*) [Kaninchen]weibchen *nt*

does /dʌz/ *see* **do**
doesn't /'dʌznt/ = **does not**
dog /dɒg/ *n* Hund *m* □ *vt* (*pt/pp* **dogged**) verfolgen
dog: ~-biscuit *n* Hundekuchen *m*. **~-collar** *n* Hundehalsband *nt*; (*Relig, fam*) Kragen *m* eines Geistlichen. **~-eared** *a* **be ~-eared** Eselsohren haben
dogged /'dɒgɪd/ *a*, **-ly** *adv* beharrlich
dogma /'dɒgmə/ *n* Dogma *nt*. **~tic** /-'mætɪk/ *a* dogmatisch
'dogsbody *n* (*fam*) Mädchen *nt* für alles
doily /'dɔɪlɪ/ *n* Deckchen *nt*
do-it-yourself /du:ɪtjə'self/ *n* Heimwerken *nt*. **~ shop** *n* Heimwerkerladen *m*
doldrums /'dɒldrəmz/ *npl* **be in the ~** niedergeschlagen sein; ⟨*business*:⟩ daniederliegen
dole /dəʊl/ *n* (*fam*) Stempelgeld *nt*; **be on the ~** arbeitslos sein □ *vt* **~ out** austeilen
doleful /'dəʊlfl/ *a*, **-ly** *adv* trauervoll
doll /dɒl/ *n* Puppe *f* □ *vt* (*fam*) **~ oneself up** sich herausputzen
dollar /'dɒlə(r)/ *n* Dollar *m*
dollop /'dɒləp/ *n* (*fam*) Klecks *m*
dolphin /'dɒlfɪn/ *n* Delphin *m*
domain /də'meɪn/ *n* Gebiet *nt*
dome /dəʊm/ *n* Kuppel *m*
domestic /də'mestɪk/ *a* häuslich; (*Pol*) Innen-; (*Comm*) Binnen-. **~ animal** *n* Haustier *nt*
domesticated /də'mestɪkeɪtɪd/ *a* häuslich; ⟨*animal*⟩ zahm
domestic: ~ flight *n* Inlandflug *m*. **~ 'servant** Hausangestellte(r) *m/f*
dominant /'dɒmɪnənt/ *a* vorherrschend
dominat|e /'dɒmɪneɪt/ *vt* beherrschen □ *vi* dominieren; **~e over** beherrschen. **~ion** /-'neɪʃn/ *n* Vorherrschaft *f*
domineer /dɒmɪ'nɪə(r)/ *vi* **~ over** tyrannisieren. **~ing** *a* herrschsüchtig
dominion /də'mɪnjən/ *n* Herrschaft *f*
domino /'dɒmɪnəʊ/ *n* (*pl* **-es**) Dominostein *m*; **~es** *sg* (*game*) Domino *nt*
don[1] /dɒn/ *vt* (*pt/pp* **donned**) (*liter*) anziehen
don[2] *n* [Universitäts]dozent *m*
donat|e /dəʊ'neɪt/ *vt* spenden. **~ion** /-eɪʃn/ *n* Spende *f*
done /dʌn/ *see* **do**
donkey /'dɒŋkɪ/ *n* Esel *m*; **~'s years** (*fam*) eine Ewigkeit. **~-work** *n* Routinearbeit *f*
donor /'dəʊnə(r)/ *n* Spender(in) *m(f)*
don't /dəʊnt/ = **do not**
doodle /'du:dl/ *vi* kritzeln
doom /du:m/ *n* Schicksal *nt*; (*ruin*) Verhängnis *nt* □ *vt* **be ~ed to failure** zum Scheitern verurteilt sein
door /dɔ:(r)/ *n* Tür *f*; **out of ~s** im Freien
door: ~man *n* Portier *m*. **~mat** *n* [Fuß]abtreter *m*. **~step** *n* Türschwelle *f*; **on the ~step** vor der Tür. **~way** *n* Türöffnung *f*
dope /dəʊp/ *n* (*fam*) Drogen *pl*; (*fam: information*) Informationen *pl*; (*fam: idiot*) Trottel *m* □ *vt* betäuben; (*Sport*) dopen
dopey /'dəʊpɪ/ *a* (*fam*) benommen; (*stupid*) blöd[e]
dormant /'dɔ:mənt/ *a* ruhend
dormer /'dɔ:mə(r)/ *n* **~ [window]** Mansardenfenster *nt*
dormitory /'dɔ:mɪtərɪ/ *n* Schlafsaal *m*
dormouse /'dɔ:-/ *n* Haselmaus *f*
dosage /'dəʊsɪdʒ/ *n* Dosierung *f*
dose /dəʊs/ *n* Dosis *f*
doss /dɒs/ *vi* (*sl*) pennen. **~er** *n* Penner *m*. **~-house** *n* Penne *f*
dot /dɒt/ *n* Punkt *m*; **on the ~** pünktlich
dote /dəʊt/ *vi* **~ on** vernarrt sein in (+ *acc*)
dotted /'dɒtɪd/ *a* **~ line** punktierte Linie *f*; **be ~ with** bestreut sein mit

dotty /ˈdɒtɪ/ *a* (**-ier, -iest**) (*fam*) verdreht

double /ˈdʌbl/ *a & adv* doppelt; ⟨*bed, chin*⟩ Doppel-; ⟨*flower*⟩ gefüllt □ *n* das Doppelte; (*person*) Doppelgänger *m*; **~s** *pl* (*Tennis*) Doppel *nt*; **at the ~** im Laufschritt □ *vt* verdoppeln; (*fold*) falten □ *vi* sich verdoppeln. **~ back** *vi* zurückgehen. **~ up** *vi* sich krümmen (**with** vor + *dat*)

double: ~-ˈbass *n* Kontrabass *m*. **~-breasted** *a* zweireihig. **~-ˈcross** *vt* ein Doppelspiel treiben mit. **~-ˈdecker** *n* Doppeldecker *m*. **~ ˈDutch** *n* (*fam*) Kauderwelsch *nt*. **~ ˈglazing** *n* Doppelverglasung *f*. **~ ˈroom** *n* Doppelzimmer *nt*

doubly /ˈdʌblɪ/ *adv* doppelt

doubt /daʊt/ *n* Zweifel *m* □ *vt* bezweifeln. **~ful** *a*, **-ly** *adv* zweifelhaft; (*disbelieving*) skeptisch. **~less** *adv* zweifellos

dough /dəʊ/ *n* [fester] Teig *m*; (*fam: money*) Pinke *f*. **~nut** *n* Berliner [Pfannkuchen] *m*, Krapfen *m*

douse /daʊs/ *vt* übergießen; ausgießen ⟨*flames*⟩

dove /dʌv/ *n* Taube *f*. **~tail** *n* (*Techn*) Schwalbenschwanz *m*

dowdy /ˈdaʊdɪ/ *a* (**-ier, -iest**) unschick

down[1] /daʊn/ *n* (*feathers*) Daunen *pl*

down[2] *adv* unten; (*with movement*) nach unten; **go ~** hinuntergehen; **come ~** herunterkommen; **~ there** da unten; **£50 ~** £50 Anzahlung; **~!** (*to dog*) Platz! **~ with . . .!** nieder mit . . .! □ *prep* **~ the road/stairs** die Straße/Treppe hinunter; **~ the river** den Fluss abwärts; **be ~ the pub** (*fam*) in der Kneipe sein □ *vt* (*fam*) (*drink*) runterkippen; **~ tools** die Arbeit niederlegen

down: ~-and-ˈout *n* Penner *m*. **~cast** *a* niedergeschlagen. **~fall** *n* Sturz *m*; (*ruin*) Ruin *m*. **~ˈgrade** *vt* niedriger einstufen. **~-ˈhearted** *a* entmutigt. **~ˈhill** *adv* bergab. **~ payment** *n* Anzahlung *f*. **~pour** *n* Platzregen *m*. **~right** *a & adv* ausgesprochen. **~ˈstairs** *adv* unten; ⟨*go*⟩ nach unten □ *a* /ˈ--/ im Erdgeschoss. **~ˈstream** *adv* stromabwärts. **~-to-ˈearth** *a* sachlich. **~town** *adv* (*Amer*) im Stadtzentrum. **~trodden** *a* unterdrückt. **~ward** *a* nach unten; ⟨*slope*⟩ abfallend □ *adv* **~[s]** abwärts, nach unten

downy /ˈdaʊnɪ/ *a* (**-ier, -iest**) flaumig

dowry /ˈdaʊrɪ/ *n* Mitgift *f*

doze /dəʊz/ *n* Nickerchen *nt* □ *vi* dösen. **~ off** *vi* einnicken

dozen /ˈdʌzn/ *n* Dutzend *nt*

Dr *abbr of* **doctor**

draft[1] /drɑːft/ *n* Entwurf *m*; (*Comm*) Tratte *f*; (*Amer Mil*) Einberufung *f* □ *vt* entwerfen; (*Amer Mil*) einberufen

draft[2] *n* (*Amer*) = **draught**

drag /dræg/ *n* (*fam*) Klotz *m* am Bein; **in ~** (*fam*) ⟨*man*⟩ als Frau gekleidet □ *vt* (*pt/pp* **dragged**) schleppen; absuchen ⟨*river*⟩. **~ on** *vi* sich in die Länge ziehen

dragon /ˈdrægən/ *n* Drache *m*. **~-fly** *n* Libelle *f*

ˈdrag show *n* Transvestitenshow *f*

drain /dreɪn/ *n* Abfluss *m*; (*underground*) Kanal *m*; **the ~s** die Kanalisation □ *vt* entwässern ⟨*land*⟩; ablassen ⟨*liquid*⟩; das Wasser ablassen aus ⟨*tank*⟩; abgießen ⟨*vegetables*⟩; austrinken ⟨*glass*⟩ □ *vi* **~ [away]** ablaufen; **leave sth to ~** etw abtropfen lassen

drain|age /ˈdreɪnɪdʒ/ *n* Kanalisation *f*; (*of land*) Dränage *f*. **~ing board** *n* Abtropfbrett *nt*. **~-pipe** *n* Abflussrohr *nt*

drake /dreɪk/ *n* Enterich *m*

drama /ˈdrɑːmə/ *n* Drama *nt*; (*quality*) Dramatik *f*

dramatic /drəˈmætɪk/ *a*, **-ally** *adv* dramatisch
dramat|ist /ˈdræmətɪst/ *n* Dramatiker *m*. **~ize** *vt* für die Bühne bearbeiten; (*fig*) dramatisieren
drank /dræŋk/ *see* **drink**
drape /dreɪp/ *n* (*Amer*) Vorhang *m* □ *vt* drapieren
drastic /ˈdræstɪk/ *a*, **-ally** *adv* drastisch
draught /drɑːft/ *n* [Luft]zug *m*; **~s** *sg* (*game*) Damespiel *nt*; **there is a ~** es zieht
draught: ~ beer *n* Bier *nt* vom Fass. **~sman** *n* technischer Zeichner *m*
draughty /ˈdrɑːftɪ/ *a* zugig; **it's ~** es zieht
draw /drɔː/ *n* Attraktion *f*; (*Sport*) Unentschieden *nt*; (*in lottery*) Ziehung *f* □ *v* (*pt* **drew**, *pp* **drawn**) □ *vt* ziehen; (*attract*) anziehen; zeichnen ⟨*picture*⟩; abheben ⟨*money*⟩; holen ⟨*water*⟩; **~ the curtains** die Vorhänge zuziehen/ (*back*) aufziehen; **~ lots** losen (**for** um) □ *vi* ⟨*tea:*⟩ ziehen; (*Sport*) unentschieden spielen. **~ back** *vt* zurückziehen □ *vi* (*recoil*) zurückweichen. **~ in** *vt* einziehen □ *vi* einfahren; ⟨*days:*⟩ kürzer werden. **~ out** *vt* herausziehen; abheben ⟨*money*⟩ □ *vi* ausfahren; ⟨*days:*⟩ länger werden. **~ up** *vt* aufsetzen ⟨*document*⟩; herrücken ⟨*chair*⟩; **~ oneself up** sich aufrichten □ *vi* [an]halten
draw: ~back *n* Nachteil *m*. **~bridge** *n* Zugbrücke *f*
drawer /drɔː(r)/ *n* Schublade *f*
drawing /ˈdrɔːɪŋ/ *n* Zeichnung *f*
drawing: ~-board *n* Reißbrett *nt*. **~-pin** *n* Reißzwecke *f*. **~-room** *n* Wohnzimmer *nt*
drawl /drɔːl/ *n* schleppende Aussprache *f*
drawn /drɔːn/ *see* **draw**
dread /dred/ *n* Furcht *f* (**of** vor + *dat*) □ *vt* fürchten. **~ful** *a*, **-fully** *adv* fürchterlich

dream /driːm/ *n* Traum *m* □ *attrib* Traum- □ *vt/i* (*pt/pp* **dreamt** /dremt/ *or* **dreamed**) träumen (**about/of** von)
dreary /ˈdrɪərɪ/ *a* (**-ier, -iest**) trüb[e]; (*boring*) langweilig
dredge /dredʒ/ *vt/i* baggern. **~r** *n* [Nass]bagger *m*
dregs /dregz/ *npl* Bodensatz *m*
drench /drentʃ/ *vt* durchnässen
dress /dres/ *n* Kleid *nt*; (*clothing*) Kleidung *f* □ *vt* anziehen; (*decorate*) schmücken; (*Culin*) anmachen; (*Med*) verbinden; **~ oneself, get ~ed** sich anziehen □ *vi* sich anziehen. **~ up** *vi* sich schön anziehen; (*in disguise*) sich verkleiden (**as** als)
dress: ~ circle *n* (*Theat*) erster Rang *m*. **~er** *n* (*furniture*) Anrichte *f*; (*Amer: dressing-table*) Frisiertisch *m*
dressing *n* (*Culin*) Soße *f*; (*Med*) Verband *m*
dressing: ~ 'down *n* (*fam*) Standpauke *f*. **~-gown** *n* Morgenmantel *m*. **~-room** *n* Ankleidezimmer *nt*; (*Theat*) [Künstler]garderobe *f*. **~-table** *n* Frisiertisch *m*
dress: ~maker *n* Schneiderin *f*. **~making** *n* Damenschneiderei *f*. **~ rehearsal** *n* Generalprobe *f*
dressy /ˈdresɪ/ *a* (**-ier, -iest**) schick
drew /druː/ *see* **draw**
dribble /ˈdrɪbl/ *vi* sabbern; (*Sport*) dribbeln
dried /draɪd/ *a* getrocknet; **~ fruit** Dörrobst *nt*
drier /ˈdraɪə(r)/ *n* Trockner *m*
drift /drɪft/ *n* Abtrift *f*; (*of snow*) Schneewehe *f*; (*meaning*) Sinn *m* □ *vi* treiben; (*off course*) abtreiben; ⟨*snow:*⟩ Wehen bilden; (*fig*) ⟨*person:*⟩ sich treiben lassen; **~ apart** ⟨*persons:*⟩ sich auseinander leben. **~wood** *n* Treibholz *nt*

drill /drɪl/ *n* Bohrer *m*; (*Mil*) Drill *m* □ *vt/i* bohren (**for** nach); (*Mil*) drillen

drily /ˈdraɪlɪ/ *adv* trocken

drink /drɪŋk/ *n* Getränk *nt*; (*alcoholic*) Drink *m*; (*alcohol*) Alkohol *m*; **have a ~** etwas trinken □ *vt/i* (*pt* **drank**, *pp* **drunk**) trinken. **~ up** *vt/i* austrinken

drink|able /ˈdrɪŋkəbl/ *a* trinkbar. **~er** *n* Trinker *m*

ˈdrinking-water *n* Trinkwasser *nt*

drip /drɪp/ *n* Tropfen *nt*; (*drop*) Tropfen *m*; (*Med*) Tropf *m*; (*fam: person*) Niete *f* □ *vi* (*pt/pp* **dripped**) tropfen. **~-ˈdry** *a* bügelfrei. **~ping** *n* Schmalz *nt*

drive /draɪv/ *n* [Auto]fahrt *f*; (*entrance*) Einfahrt *f*; (*energy*) Elan *m*; (*Psych*) Trieb *m*; (*Pol*) Aktion *f*; (*Sport*) Treibschlag *m*; (*Techn*) Antrieb *m* □ *v* (*pt* **drove**, *pp* **driven**) □ *vt* treiben; fahren ⟨*car*⟩; (*Sport: hit*) schlagen; (*Techn*) antreiben; **~ s.o. mad** (*fam*) jdn verrückt machen; **what are you driving at?** (*fam*) worauf willst du hinaus? □ *vi* fahren. **~ away** *vt* vertreiben □ *vi* abfahren. **~ in** *vi* hinein-/hereinfahren. **~ off** *vt* vertreiben □ *vi* abfahren. **~ on** *vi* weiterfahren. **~ up** *vi* vorfahren

ˈdrive-in *a* **~ cinema** Autokino *nt*

drivel /ˈdrɪvl/ *n* (*fam*) Quatsch *m*

driven /ˈdrɪvn/ *see* **drive**

driver /ˈdraɪvə(r)/ *n* Fahrer(in) *m*(*f*); (*of train*) Lokführer *m*

driving /ˈdraɪvɪŋ/ *a* ⟨*rain*⟩ peitschend; ⟨*force*⟩ treibend

driving: ~ lesson *n* Fahrstunde *f*. **~ licence** *n* Führerschein *m*. **~ school** *n* Fahrschule *f*. **~ test** Fahrprüfung *f*; **take one's ~ test** den Führerschein machen

drizzle /ˈdrɪzl/ *n* Nieselregen *m* □ *vi* nieseln

drone /drəʊn/ *n* Drohne *f*; (*sound*) Brummen *nt*

droop /druːp/ *vi* herabhängen; ⟨*flowers:*⟩ die Köpfe hängen lassen

drop /drɒp/ *n* Tropfen *m*; (*fall*) Fall *m*; (*in price, temperature*) Rückgang *m* □ *v* (*pt/pp* **dropped**) □ *vt* fallen lassen; abwerfen ⟨*bomb*⟩; (*omit*) auslassen; (*give up*) aufgeben □ *vi* fallen; (*fall lower*) sinken; ⟨*wind:*⟩ nachlassen. **~ in** *vi* vorbeikommen. **~ off** *vt* absetzen ⟨*person*⟩ □ *vi* abfallen; (*fall asleep*) einschlafen. **~ out** *vi* herausfallen; (*give up*) aufgeben

ˈdrop-out *n* Aussteiger *m*

droppings /ˈdrɒpɪŋz/ *npl* Kot *m*

drought /draʊt/ *n* Dürre *f*

drove /drəʊv/ *see* **drive**

droves /drəʊvz/ *npl* **in ~** in Scharen

drown /draʊn/ *vi* ertrinken □ *vt* ertränken; übertönen ⟨*noise*⟩; **be ~ed** ertrinken

drowsy /ˈdraʊzɪ/ *a* schläfrig

drudgery /ˈdrʌdʒərɪ/ *n* Plackerei *f*

drug /drʌg/ *n* Droge *f* □ *vt* (*pt/pp* **drugged**) betäuben

drug: ~ addict *n* Drogenabhängige(r) *m*/*f*. **~gist** *n* (*Amer*) Apotheker *m*. **~store** *n* (*Amer*) Drogerie *f*; (*dispensing*) Apotheke *f*

drum /drʌm/ *n* Trommel *f*; (*for oil*) Tonne *f* □ *v* (*pt/pp* **drummed**) □ *vi* trommeln □ *vt* **~sth into s.o.** (*fam*) jdm etw einbläuen. **~mer** *n* Trommler *m*; (*in pop-group*) Schlagzeuger *m*. **~stick** *n* Trommelschlegel *m*; (*Culin*) Keule *f*

drunk /drʌŋk/ *see* **drink** □ *a* betrunken; **get ~** sich betrinken □ *n* Betrunkene(r) *m*

drunk|ard /ˈdrʌŋkəd/ *n* Trinker *m*. **~en** *a* betrunken; **~en driving** Trunkenheit *f* am Steuer

dry /draɪ/ *a* (**drier, driest**) trocken □ *vt/i* trocknen; **~ one's eyes** sich *dat* die Tränen abwischen. **~ up** *vi* austrocknen;

(*fig*) versiegen □ *vt* austrocknen; abtrocknen ⟨*dishes*⟩
dry: ~-'clean *vt* chemisch reinigen. **~-'cleaner's** *n* (*shop*) chemische Reinigung *f*. **~ness** *n* Trockenheit *f*
dual /'dju:əl/ *a* doppelt
dual: ~ 'carriageway *n* ≈ Schnellstraße *f*. **~-'purpose** *a* zweifach verwendbar
dub /dʌb/ *vt* (*pt/pp* **dubbed**) synchronisieren ⟨*film*⟩; kopieren ⟨*tape*⟩; (*name*) nennen
dubious /'dju:bɪəs/ *a* zweifelhaft; **be ~ about** Zweifel haben über (+ *acc*)
duchess /'dʌtʃɪs/ *n* Herzogin *f*
duck /dʌk/ *n* Ente *f* □ *vt* (*in water*) untertauchen; **~ one's head** den Kopf einziehen □ *vi* sich ducken. **~ling** *n* Entchen *nt*; (*Culin*) Ente *f*
duct /dʌkt/ *n* Rohr *nt*; (*Anat*) Gang *m*
dud /dʌd/ *a* (*fam*) nutzlos; ⟨*coin*⟩ falsch; ⟨*cheque*⟩ ungedeckt; (*forged*) gefälscht □ *n* (*fam*) (*banknote*) Blüte *f*; (*Mil: shell*) Blindgänger *m*
due /dju:/ *a* angemessen; **be ~** fällig sein; ⟨*baby:*⟩ erwartet werden; ⟨*train:*⟩ planmäßig ankommen; **~ to** (*owing to*) wegen (+ *gen*); **be ~ to** zurückzuführen sein auf (+ *acc*); **in ~ course** im Laufe der Zeit; ⟨*write*⟩ zu gegebener Zeit □ *adv* **~ west** genau westlich
duel /'dju:əl/ *n* Duell *nt*
dues /dju:z/ *npl* Gebühren *pl*
duet /dju:'et/ *n* Duo *nt*; (*vocal*) Duett *nt*
dug /dʌg/ *see* **dig**
duke /dju:k/ *n* Herzog *m*
dull /dʌl/ *a* (**-er, -est**) (*overcast, not bright*) trüb[e]; (*not shiny*) matt; ⟨*sound*⟩ dumpf; (*boring*) langweilig; (*stupid*) schwerfällig □ *vt* betäuben; abstumpfen ⟨*mind*⟩
duly /'dju:lɪ/ *adv* ordnungsgemäß
dumb /dʌm/ *a* (**-er, -est**) stumm; (*fam: stupid*) dumm. **~founded** *a* sprachlos
dummy /'dʌmɪ/ *n* (*tailor's*) [Schneider]puppe *f*; (*for baby*) Schnuller *m*; (*Comm*) Attrappe *f*
dump /dʌmp/ *n* Abfallhaufen *m*; (*for refuse*) Müllhalde *f*, Deponie *f*; (*fam: town*) Kaff *nt*; **be down in the ~s** (*fam*) deprimiert sein □ *vt* abladen; (*fam: put down*) hinwerfen (**on** auf + *acc*)
dumpling /'dʌmplɪŋ/ *n* Kloß *m*, Knödel *m*
dunce /dʌns/ *n* Dummkopf *m*
dune /dju:n/ *n* Düne *f*
dung /dʌŋ/ *n* Mist *m*
dungarees /dʌŋgə'ri:z/ *npl* Latzhose *f*
dungeon /'dʌndʒən/ *n* Verlies *nt*
dunk /dʌŋk/ *vt* eintunken
duo /'dju:əʊ/ *n* Paar *nt*; (*Mus*) Duo *nt*
dupe /dju:p/ *n* Betrogene(r) *m/f* □ *vt* betrügen
duplicate[1] /'dju:plɪkət/ *a* Zweit- □ *n* Doppel *nt*; (*document*) Duplikat *nt*; **in ~** in doppelter Ausfertigung *f*
duplicat|e[2] /'dju:plɪkeɪt/ *vt* kopieren; (*do twice*) zweimal machen. **~or** *n* Vervielfältigungsapparat *m*
durable /'djʊərəbl/ *a* haltbar
duration /djʊə'reɪʃn/ *n* Dauer *f*
duress /djʊə'res/ *n* Zwang *m*
during /'djʊərɪŋ/ *prep* während (+ *gen*)
dusk /dʌsk/ *n* [Abend]dämmerung *f*
dust /dʌst/ *n* Staub *m* □ *vt* abstauben; (*sprinkle*) bestäuben (**with** mit) □ *vi* Staub wischen
dust: ~bin *n* Mülltonne *f*. **~-cart** *n* Müllwagen *m*. **~er** *n* Staubtuch *nt*. **~-jacket** *n* Schutzumschlag *m*. **~man** *n* Müllmann *m*. **~pan** *n* Kehrschaufel *f*
dusty /'dʌstɪ/ *a* (**-ier, -iest**) staubig

Dutch /dʌtʃ/ *a* holländisch; **go ~** (*fam*) getrennte Kasse machen □ *n* (*Lang*) Holländisch *nt*; **the ~** *pl* die Holländer. **~man** *n* Holländer *m*
dutiable /ˈdjuːtɪəbl/ *a* zollpflichtig
dutiful /ˈdjuːtɪfl/ *a*, **-ly** *adv* pflichtbewusst; (*obedient*) gehorsam
duty /ˈdjuːtɪ/ *n* Pflicht *f*; (*task*) Aufgabe *f*; (*tax*) Zoll *m*; **be on ~** Dienst haben. **~-free** *a* zollfrei
duvet /ˈduːveɪ/ *n* Steppdecke *f*
dwarf /dwɔːf/ *n* (*pl* **-s** *or* **dwarves**) Zwerg *m*
dwell /dwel/ *vi* (*pt/pp* **dwelt**) (*liter*) wohnen; **~ on** (*fig*) verweilen bei. **~ing** *n* Wohnung *f*
dwindle /ˈdwɪndl/ *vi* abnehmen, schwinden
dye /daɪ/ *n* Farbstoff *m* □ *vt* (*pres p* **dyeing**) färben
dying /ˈdaɪɪŋ/ *see* **die**²
dynamic /daɪˈnæmɪk/ *a* dynamisch. **~s** *n* Dynamik *f*
dynamite /ˈdaɪnəmaɪt/ *n* Dynamit *nt*
dynamo /ˈdaɪnəməʊ/ *n* Dynamo *m*
dynasty /ˈdɪnəstɪ/ *n* Dynastie *f*
dysentery /ˈdɪsəntrɪ/ *n* Ruhr *f*
dyslex|ia /dɪsˈleksɪə/ *n* Legasthenie *f*. **~ic** *a* legasthenisch; **be ~ic** Legastheniker sein

E

each /iːtʃ/ *a & pron* jede(r,s); (*per*) je; **~ other** einander; **£1 ~** £1 pro Person; (*for thing*) pro Stück
eager /ˈiːgə(r)/ *a*, **-ly** *adv* eifrig; **be ~ to do sth** etw gerne machen wollen. **~ness** *n* Eifer *m*
eagle /ˈiːgl/ *n* Adler *m*
ear¹ /ɪə(r)/ *n* (*of corn*) Ähre *f*
ear² *n* Ohr *nt*. **~ache** *n* Ohrenschmerzen *pl*. **~-drum** *n* Trommelfell *nt*
earl /ɜːl/ *n* Graf *m*
early /ˈɜːlɪ/ *a & adv* (**-ier, -iest**) früh; ⟨*reply*⟩ baldig; **be ~** früh dran sein; **~ in the morning** früh am Morgen
ˈearmark *vt* **~ for** bestimmen für
earn /ɜːn/ *vt* verdienen
earnest /ˈɜːnɪst/ *a*, **-ly** *adv* ernsthaft □ *n* **in ~** im Ernst
earnings /ˈɜːnɪŋz/ *npl* Verdienst *m*
ear: ~phones *npl* Kopfhörer *pl*. **~-ring** *n* Ohrring *m*; (*clip-on*) Ohrklips *m*. **~shot** *n* **within/out of ~shot** in/außer Hörweite
earth /ɜːθ/ *n* Erde *f*; (*of fox*) Bau *m*; **where/what on ~?** wo/was in aller Welt? □ *vt* (*Electr*) erden
earthenware /ˈɜːθn-/ *n* Tonwaren *pl*
earthly /ˈɜːθlɪ/ *a* irdisch; **be no ~ use** (*fam*) völlig nutzlos sein
ˈearthquake *n* Erdbeben *nt*
earthy /ˈɜːθɪ/ *a* erdig; (*coarse*) derb
earwig /ˈɪəwɪg/ *n* Ohrwurm *m*
ease /iːz/ *n* Leichtigkeit *f*; **at ~!** (*Mil*) rührt euch! **be** *or* **feel ill at ~** ein ungutes Gefühl haben □ *vt* erleichtern; lindern ⟨*pain*⟩ □ *vi* ⟨*pain:*⟩ nachlassen; ⟨*situation:*⟩ sich entspannen
easel /ˈiːzl/ *n* Staffelei *f*
easily /ˈiːzɪlɪ/ *adv* leicht, mit Leichtigkeit
east /iːst/ *n* Osten *m*; **to the ~ of** östlich von □ *a* Ost-, ost- □ *adv* nach Osten
Easter /ˈiːstə(r)/ *n* Ostern *nt* □ *attrib* Oster-. **~ egg** *n* Osterei *nt*
east|erly /ˈiːstəlɪ/ *a* östlich. **~ern** *a* östlich. **~ward[s]** /-wəd[z]/ *adv* nach Osten
easy /ˈiːzɪ/ *a* (**-ier, -iest**) leicht; **take it ~** (*fam*) sich schonen; **take it ~!** beruhige dich! **go ~**

with (*fam*) sparsam umgehen mit

easy: ~ **chair** *n* Sessel *m*. ~'**going** *a* gelassen; **too ~going** lässig

eat /i:t/ *vt/i* (*pt* **ate**, *pp* **eaten**) essen; ⟨*animal:*⟩ fressen. ~ **up** *vt* aufessen

eat|able /'i:təbl/ *a* genießbar. **~er** *n* (*apple*) Essapfel *m*

eau-de-Cologne /əʊdəkə'ləʊn/ *n* Kölnisch Wasser *nt*

eaves /i:vz/ *npl* Dachüberhang *m*. **~drop** *vi* (*pt/pp* ~ **dropped**) [heimlich] lauschen; **~drop on** belauschen

ebb /eb/ *n* (*tide*) Ebbe *f*; **at a low** ~ (*fig*) auf einem Tiefstand □ *vi* zurückgehen; (*fig*) verebben

ebony /'ebənɪ/ *n* Ebenholz *nt*

ebullient /ɪ'bʌlɪənt/ *a* überschwänglich

EC *abbr* (**European Community**) EG *f*

eccentric /ɪk'sentrɪk/ *a* exzentrisch □ *n* Exzentriker *m*

ecclesiastical /ɪkli:zɪ'æstɪkl/ *a* kirchlich

echo /'ekəʊ/ *n* (*pl* **-es**) Echo *nt*, Widerhall *m* □ *v* (*pt/pp* **echoed**, *pres p* **echoing**) □ *vt* zurückwerfen; (*imitate*) nachsagen □ *vi* widerhallen (**with** von)

eclipse /ɪ'klɪps/ *n* (*Astr*) Finsternis *f* □ *vt* (*fig*) in den Schatten stellen

ecolog|ical /i:kə'lɒdʒɪkl/ *a* ökologisch. **~y** /i:'kɒlədʒɪ/ *n* Ökologie *f*

economic /i:kə'nɒmɪk/ *a* wirtschaftlich. **~al** *a* sparsam. **~ally** *adv* wirtschaftlich; (*thriftily*) sparsam. **~s** *n* Volkswirtschaft *f*

economist /ɪ'kɒnəmɪst/ *n* Volkswirt *m*; (*Univ*) Wirtschaftswissenschaftler *m*

economize /ɪ'kɒnəmaɪz/ *vi* sparen (**on** an + *dat*)

economy /ɪ'kɒnəmɪ/ *n* Wirtschaft *f*; (*thrift*) Sparsamkeit *f*

ecstasy /'ekstəsɪ/ *n* Ekstase *f*

ecstatic /ɪk'stætɪk/ *a*, **-ally** *adv* ekstatisch

ecu /'eɪkju:/ *n* Ecu *m*

ecumenical /i:kjʊ'menɪkl/ *a* ökumenisch

eczema /'eksɪmə/ *n* Ekzem *nt*

eddy /'edɪ/ *n* Wirbel *m*

edge /edʒ/ *n* Rand *m*; (*of table, lawn*) Kante *f*; (*of knife*) Schneide *f*; **on** ~ (*fam*) nervös; **have the** ~ **on** (*fam*) etwas besser sein als □ *vt* einfassen. ~ **forward** *vi* sich nach vorn schieben

edging /'edʒɪŋ/ *n* Einfassung *f*

edgy /'edʒɪ/ *a* (*fam*) nervös

edible /'edɪbl/ *a* essbar

edict /'i:dɪkt/ *n* Erlass *m*

edifice /'edɪfɪs/ *n* [großes] Gebäude *nt*

edify /'edɪfaɪ/ *vt* (*pt/pp* **-ied**) erbauen. **~ing** *a* erbaulich

edit /'edɪt/ *vt* (*pt/pp* **edited**) redigieren; herausgeben ⟨*anthology, dictionary*⟩; schneiden ⟨*film, tape*⟩

edition /ɪ'dɪʃn/ *n* Ausgabe *f*; (*impression*) Auflage *f*

editor /'edɪtə(r)/ *n* Redakteur *m*; (*of anthology, dictionary*) Herausgeber *m*; (*of newspaper*) Chefredakteur *m*; (*of film*) Cutter(in) *m(f)*

editorial /edɪ'tɔ:rɪəl/ *a* redaktionell, Redaktions- □ *n* (*Journ*) Leitartikel *m*

educate /'edjʊkeɪt/ *vt* erziehen; **be ~d at X** auf die X-Schule gehen. **~d** *a* gebildet

education /edjʊ'keɪʃn/ *n* Erziehung *f*; (*culture*) Bildung *f*. **~al** *a* pädagogisch; ⟨*visit*⟩ kulturell

eel /i:l/ *n* Aal *m*

eerie /'ɪərɪ/ *a* (**-ier, -iest**) unheimlich

effect /ɪ'fekt/ *n* Wirkung *f*, Effekt *m*; **in** ~ in Wirklichkeit; **take** ~ in Kraft treten □ *vt* bewirken

effective /ɪ'fektɪv/ *a*, **-ly** *adv* wirksam, effektiv; (*striking*) wirkungsvoll, effektvoll; (*actual*) tatsächlich. **~ness** *n* Wirksamkeit *f*

effeminate /ɪ'femɪnət/ *a* unmännlich
effervescent /efə'vesnt/ *a* sprudelnd
efficiency /ɪ'fɪʃənsɪ/ *n* Tüchtigkeit *f*; (*of machine, organization*) Leistungsfähigkeit *f*
efficient /ɪ'fɪʃənt/ *a* tüchtig; ⟨*machine, organization*⟩ leistungsfähig; ⟨*method*⟩ rationell. **~ly** *adv* gut; ⟨*function*⟩ rationell
effigy /'efɪdʒɪ/ *n* Bildnis *nt*
effort /'efət/ *n* Anstrengung *f*; **make an ~** sich (*dat*) Mühe geben. **~less** *a*, **-ly** *adv* mühelos
effrontery /ɪ'frʌntərɪ/ *n* Unverschämtheit *f*
effusive /ɪ'fju:sɪv/ *a*, **-ly** *adv* überschwänglich
e.g. *abbr* (**exempli gratia**) z.B.
egalitarian /ɪgælɪ'teərɪən/ *a* egalitär
egg¹ /eg/ *vt* **~on** (*fam*) anstacheln
egg² *n* Ei *nt*. **~-cup** *n* Eierbecher *m*. **~shell** *n* Eierschale *f*. **~-timer** *n* Eieruhr *f*
ego /'i:gəʊ/ *n* Ich *nt*. **~centric** /-'sentrɪk/ *a* egozentrisch. **~ism** *n* Egoismus *m*. **~ist** *n* Egoist *m*. **~tism** *n* Ichbezogenheit *f*. **~tist** *n* ichbezogener Mensch *m*
Egypt /'i:dʒɪpt/ *n* Ägypten *nt*. **~ian** /ɪ'dʒɪpʃn/ *a* ägyptisch □ *n* Ägypter(in) *m(f)*
eiderdown /'aɪdə-/ *n* (*quilt*) Daunendecke *f*
eigh|t /eɪt/ *a* acht □ *n* Acht *f*; (*boat*) Achter *m*. **~'teen** *a* achtzehn. **~'teenth** *a* achtzehnte(r,s)
eighth /eɪtθ/ *a* achte(r,s) □ *n* Achtel *nt*
eightieth /'eɪtɪɪθ/ *a* achtzigste(r,s)
eighty /'eɪtɪ/ *a* achtzig
either /'aɪðə(r)/ *a & pron* **~ [of them]** einer von [den] beiden; (*both*) beide; **on ~ side** auf beiden Seiten □ *adv* **I don't ~** ich auch nicht □ *conj* **~ ... or** entweder ... oder
eject /ɪ'dʒekt/ *vt* hinauswerfen
eke /i:k/ *vt* **~ out** strecken; (*increase*) ergänzen; **~ out a living** sich kümmerlich durchschlagen
elaborate¹ /ɪ'læbərət/ *a*, **-ly** *adv* kunstvoll; (*fig*) kompliziert
elaborate² /ɪ'læbəreɪt/ *vi* ausführlicher sein; **~ on** näher ausführen
elapse /ɪ'læps/ *vi* vergehen
elastic /ɪ'læstɪk/ *a* elastisch □ *n* Gummiband *nt*. **~ 'band** *n* Gummiband *nt*
elasticity /ɪlæs'tɪsətɪ/ *n* Elastizität *f*
elated /ɪ'leɪtɪd/ *a* überglücklich
elbow /'elbəʊ/ *n* Ellbogen *m*
elder¹ /'eldə(r)/ *n* Holunder *m*
eld|er² *a* ältere(r,s) □ *n* **the ~er** der/die Ältere. **~erly** *a* alt. **~est** *a* älteste(r,s) □ *n* **the ~est** der/die Älteste
elect /ɪ'lekt/ *a* **the president ~** der designierte Präsident □ *vt* wählen; **~ to do sth** sich dafür entscheiden, etw zu tun. **~ion** /-ekʃn/ *n* Wahl *f*
elector /ɪ'lektə(r)/ *n* Wähler(in) *m(f)*. **~al** *a* Wahl-; **~al roll** Wählerverzeichnis *nt*. **~ ate** /-rət/ *n* Wählerschaft *f*
electric /ɪ'lektrɪk/ *a*, **-ally** *adv* elektrisch
electrical /ɪ'lektrɪkl/ *a* elektrisch; **~ engineering** Elektrotechnik *f*
electric: ~ 'blanket *n* Heizdecke *f*. **~ 'fire** *n* elektrischer Heizofen *m*
electrician /ɪlek'trɪʃn/ *n* Elektriker *m*
electricity /ɪlek'trɪsətɪ/ *n* Elektrizität *f*; (*supply*) Strom *m*
electrify /ɪ'lektrɪfaɪ/ *vt* (*pt/pp* **-ied**) elektrifizieren. **~ing** *a* (*fig*) elektrisierend
electrocute /ɪ'lektrəkju:t/ *vt* durch einen elektrischen Schlag töten; (*execute*) auf dem elektrischen Stuhl hinrichten

electrode /ɪ'lektrəʊd/ *n* Elektrode *f*
electron /ɪ'lektrɒn/ *n* Elektron *nt*
electronic /ɪlek'trɒnɪk/ *a* elektronisch. **~s** *n* Elektronik *f*
elegance /'elɪgəns/ *n* Eleganz *f*
elegant /'elɪgənt/ *a*, **-ly** *adv* elegant
elegy /'elɪdʒɪ/ *n* Elegie *f*
element /'elɪmənt/ *n* Element *nt*. **~ary** /-'mentərɪ/ *a* elementar
elephant /'elɪfənt/ *n* Elefant *m*
elevat|e /'elɪveɪt/ *vt* heben; (*fig*) erheben. **~ion** /-'veɪʃn/ *n* Erhebung *f*
elevator /'elɪveɪtə(r)/ *n* (*Amer*) Aufzug *m*, Fahrstuhl *m*
eleven /ɪ'levn/ *a* elf □ *n* Elf *f*. **~th** *a* elfte(r,s); **at the ~th hour** (*fam*) in letzter Minute
elf /elf/ *n* (*pl* **elves**) Elfe *f*
elicit /ɪ'lɪsɪt/ *vt* herausbekommen
eligible /'elɪdʒəbl/ *a* berechtigt; **~ young man** gute Partie *f*
eliminate /ɪ'lɪmɪneɪt/ *vt* ausschalten; (*excrete*) ausscheiden
élite /eɪ'li:t/ *n* Elite *f*
ellip|se /ɪ'lɪps/ *n* Ellipse *f*. **~tical** *a* elliptisch
elm /elm/ *n* Ulme *f*
elocution /elə'kju:ʃn/ *n* Sprecherziehung *f*
elongate /'i:lɒŋgeɪt/ *vt* verlängern
elope /ɪ'ləʊp/ *vi* durchbrennen (*fam*)
eloquen|ce /'eləkwəns/ *n* Beredsamkeit *f*. **~t** *a*, **~ly** *adv* beredt
else /els/ *adv* sonst; **who ~?** wer sonst? **nothing ~** sonst nichts; **or ~** oder; (*otherwise*) sonst; **someone/somewhere ~** jemand/irgendwo anders; **anyone ~** jeder andere; (*as question*) sonst noch jemand? **anything ~** alles andere; (*as question*) sonst noch etwas? **~where** *adv* woanders
elucidate /ɪ'lu:sɪdeɪt/ *vt* erläutern
elude /ɪ'lu:d/ *vt* entkommen (+ *dat*); (*avoid*) ausweichen (+ *dat*)
elusive /ɪ'lu:sɪv/ *a* **be ~** schwer zu fassen sein
emaciated /ɪ'meɪsɪeɪtɪd/ *a* abgezehrt
emanate /'eməneɪt/ *vi* ausgehen (**from** von)
emancipat|ed /ɪ'mænsɪpeɪtɪd/ *a* emanzipiert. **~ion** /-'peɪʃn/ *n* Emanzipation *f*; (*of slaves*) Freilassung *f*
embalm /ɪm'bɑ:m/ *vt* einbalsamieren
embankment /ɪm'bæŋkmənt/ *n* Böschung *f*; (*of railway*) Bahndamm *m*
embargo /em'bɑ:gəʊ/ *n* (*pl* **-es**) Embargo *nt*
embark /ɪm'bɑ:k/ *vi* sich einschiffen; **~ on** anfangen mit. **~ation** /embɑ:'keɪʃn/ *n* Einschiffung *f*
embarrass /ɪm'bærəs/ *vt* in Verlegenheit bringen. **~ed** *a* verlegen. **~ing** *a* peinlich. **~ment** *n* Verlegenheit *f*
embassy /'embəsɪ/ *n* Botschaft *f*
embedded /ɪm'bedɪd/ *a* **be deeply ~ in** tief stecken in (+ *dat*)
embellish /ɪm'belɪʃ/ *vt* verzieren; (*fig*) ausschmücken
embers /'embəz/ *npl* Glut *f*
embezzle /ɪm'bezl/ *vt* unterschlagen. **~ment** *n* Unterschlagung *f*
embitter /ɪm'bɪtə(r)/ *vt* verbittern
emblem /'embləm/ *n* Emblem *nt*
embodiment /ɪm'bɒdɪmənt/ *n* Verkörperung *f*
embody /ɪm'bɒdɪ/ *vt* (*pt/pp* **-ied**) verkörpern; (*include*) enthalten
emboss /ɪm'bɒs/ *vt* prägen
embrace /ɪm'breɪs/ *n* Umarmung *f* □ *vt* umarmen; (*fig*) umfassen □ *vi* sich umarmen
embroider /ɪm'brɔɪdə(r)/ *vt* besticken; sticken (*design*); (*fig*)

ausschmücken □ *vi* sticken. **~y** *n* Stickerei *f*

embroil /ɪm'brɔɪl/ *vt* **become ~ed in sth** in etw (*acc*) verwickelt werden

embryo /'embrɪəʊ/ *n* Embryo *m*

emerald /'emərəld/ *n* Smaragd *m*

emer|ge /ɪ'mɜ:dʒ/ *vi* auftauchen (**from** aus); (*become known*) sich herausstellen; (*come into being*) entstehen. **~gence** /-əns/ *n* Auftauchen *nt*; Entstehung *f*

emergency /ɪ'mɜ:dʒənsɪ/ *n* Notfall *m*; **in an ~** im Notfall. **~ exit** *n* Notausgang *m*

emery-paper /'emərɪ-/ *n* Schmirgelpapier *nt*

emigrant /'emɪgrənt/ *n* Auswanderer *m*

emigrat|e /'emɪgreɪt/ *vi* auswandern. **~ion** /-'greɪʃn/ *n* Auswanderung *f*

eminent /'emɪnənt/ *a*, **-ly** *adv* eminent

emission /ɪ'mɪʃn/ *n* Ausstrahlung *f*; (*of pollutant*) Emission *f*

emit /ɪ'mɪt/ *vt* (*pt/pp* **emitted**) ausstrahlen ⟨*light, heat*⟩; ausstoßen ⟨*smoke, fumes, cry*⟩

emotion /ɪ'məʊʃn/ *n* Gefühl *nt*. **~al** *a* emotional; **become ~al** sich erregen

emotive /ɪ'məʊtɪv/ *a* emotional

empath|ize /'empəθaɪz/ *vi* **~ize with s.o.** sich in jdn einfühlen. **~y** *n* Einfühlungsvermögen *nt*

emperor /'empərə(r)/ *n* Kaiser *m*

emphasis /'emfəsɪs/ *n* Betonung *f*

emphasize /'emfəsaɪz/ *vt* betonen

emphatic /ɪm'fætɪk/ *a*, **-ally** *adv* nachdrücklich

empire /'empaɪə(r)/ *n* Reich *nt*

empirical /em'pɪrɪkl/ *a* empirisch

employ /ɪm'plɔɪ/ *vt* beschäftigen; (*appoint*) einstellen; (*fig*) anwenden. **~ee** /emplɔɪ'i:/ *n* Beschäftigte(r) *m/f*; (*in contrast to employer*) Arbeitnehmer *m*. **~er** *n* Arbeitgeber *m*. **~ment** *n* Beschäftigung *f*; (*work*) Arbeit *f*. **~ment agency** *n* Stellenvermittlung *f*

empower /ɪm'paʊə(r)/ *vt* ermächtigen

empress /'emprɪs/ *n* Kaiserin *f*

empties /'emptɪz/ *npl* leere Flaschen *pl*

emptiness /'emptɪnɪs/ *n* Leere *f*

empty /'emptɪ/ *a* leer □ *vt* leeren; ausleeren ⟨*container*⟩ □ *vi* sich leeren

emulate /'emjʊleɪt/ *vt* nacheifern (+ *dat*)

emulsion /ɪ'mʌlʃn/ *n* Emulsion *f*

enable /ɪ'neɪbl/ *vt* **~ s.o. to** es jdm möglich machen, zu

enact /ɪ'nækt/ *vt* (*Theat*) aufführen

enamel /ɪ'næml/ *n* Email *nt*; (*on teeth*) Zahnschmelz *m*; (*paint*) Lack *m* □ *vt* (*pt/pp* **enamelled**) emaillieren

enamoured /ɪ'næməd/ *a* **be ~ of** sehr angetan sein von

enchant /ɪn'tʃɑ:nt/ *vt* bezaubern. **~ing** *a* bezaubernd. **~ment** *n* Zauber *m*

encircle /ɪn'sɜ:kl/ *vt* einkreisen

enclave /'enkleɪv/ *n* Enklave *f*

enclos|e /ɪn'kləʊz/ *vt* einschließen; (*in letter*) beilegen (**with** *dat*). **~ure** /-ʒə(r)/ *n* (*at zoo*) Gehege *nt*; (*in letter*) Anlage *f*

encompass /ɪn'kʌmpəs/ *vt* umfassen

encore /'ɒŋkɔ:(r)/ *n* Zugabe *f* □ *int* bravo!

encounter /ɪn'kaʊntə(r)/ *n* Begegnung *f*; (*battle*) Zusammenstoß *m* □ *vt* begegnen (+ *dat*); (*fig*) stoßen auf (+ *acc*)

encourag|e /ɪn'kʌrɪdʒ/ *vt* ermutigen; (*promote*) fördern. **~ement** *n* Ermutigung *f*. **~ing** *a* ermutigend

encroach /ɪn'krəʊtʃ/ *vi* **~ on** eindringen in (+ *acc*) ⟨*land*⟩; beanspruchen ⟨*time*⟩

encumb|er /ɪn'kʌmbə(r)/ *vt* belasten (**with** mit). **~rance** /-rəns/ *n* Belastung *f*

encyclopaed|ia /ɪnsaɪklə'pi:dɪə/ *n* Enzyklopädie *f*, Lexikon *nt*. **~ic** *a* enzyklopädisch

end /end/ *n* Ende *nt*; (*purpose*) Zweck *m*; **in the ~** schließlich; **at the ~ of May** Ende Mai; **on ~** hochkant; **for days on ~** tagelang; **make ~s meet** (*fam*) [gerade] auskommen; **no ~ of** (*fam*) unheimlich viel(e) □ *vt* beenden □ *vi* enden; **~ up in** (*fam: arrive at*) landen in (+ *dat*)

endanger /ɪn'deɪndʒə(r)/ *vt* gefährden

endear|ing /ɪn'dɪərɪŋ/ *a* liebenswert. **~ment** *n* **term of ~ment** Kosewort *nt*

endeavour /ɪn'devə(r)/ *n* Bemühung *f* □ *vi* sich bemühen (**to** zu)

ending /'endɪŋ/ *n* Schluss *m*, Ende *nt*; (*Gram*) Endung *f*

endive /'endaɪv/ *n* Endivie *f*

endless /'endlɪs/ *a*, **-ly** *adv* endlos

endorse /en'dɔ:s/ *vt* (*Comm*) indossieren; (*confirm*) bestätigen. **~ment** *n* (*Comm*) Indossament *nt*; (*fig*) Bestätigung *f*; (*on driving licence*) Strafvermerk *m*

endow /ɪn'daʊ/ *vt* stiften; **be ~ed with** (*fig*) haben. **~ment** *n* Stiftung *f*

endur|able /ɪn'djʊərəbl/ *a* erträglich. **~ance** /-rəns/ *n* Durchhaltevermögen *nt*; **beyond ~ance** unerträglich

endur|e /ɪn'djʊə(r)/ *vt* ertragen □ *vi* [lange] bestehen. **~ing** *a* dauernd

enemy /'enəmɪ/ *n* Feind *m* □ *attrib* feindlich

energetic /enə'dʒetɪk/ *a* tatkräftig; **be ~** voller Energie sein

energy /'enədʒɪ/ *n* Energie *f*

enforce /ɪn'fɔ:s/ *vt* durchsetzen. **~d** *a* unfreiwillig

engage /ɪn'geɪdʒ/ *vt* einstellen ⟨*staff*⟩; (*Theat*) engagieren; (*Auto*) einlegen ⟨*gear*⟩ □ *vi* sich beteiligen (**in** an + *dat*); (*Techn*) ineinander greifen. **~d** *a* besetzt; ⟨*person*⟩ beschäftigt; (*to be married*) verlobt; **get ~d** sich verloben (**to** mit). **~ment** *n* Verlobung *f*; (*appointment*) Verabredung *f*; (*Mil*) Gefecht *nt*

engaging /ɪn'geɪdʒɪŋ/ *a* einnehmend

engender /ɪn'dʒendə(r)/ *vt* (*fig*) erzeugen

engine /'endʒɪn/ *n* Motor *m*; (*Naut*) Maschine *f*; (*Rail*) Lokomotive *f*; (*of jet-plane*) Triebwerk *nt*. **~-driver** *n* Lokomotivführer *m*

engineer /endʒɪ'nɪə(r)/ *n* Ingenieur *m*; (*service, installation*) Techniker *m*; (*Naut*) Maschinist *m*; (*Amer*) Lokomotivführer *m* □ *vt* (*fig*) organisieren. **~ing** *n* **[mechanical] ~ing** Maschinenbau *m*

England /'ɪŋglənd/ *n* England *nt*

English /'ɪŋglɪʃ/ *a* englisch; **the ~ Channel** der Ärmelkanal □ *n* (*Lang*) Englisch *nt*; **in ~** auf Englisch; **into ~** ins Englische; **the ~** *pl* die Engländer. **~man** *n* Engländer *m*. **~woman** *n* Engländerin *f*

engrav|e /ɪn'greɪv/ *vt* eingravieren. **~ing** *n* Stich *m*

engross /ɪn'grəʊs/ *vt* **be ~ed in** vertieft sein in (+ *acc*)

engulf /ɪn'gʌlf/ *vt* verschlingen

enhance /ɪn'hɑ:ns/ *vt* verschönern; (*fig*) steigern

enigma /ɪ'nɪgmə/ *n* Rätsel *nt*. **~tic** /enɪg'mætɪk/ *a* rätselhaft

enjoy /ɪn'dʒɔɪ/ *vt* genießen; **~ oneself** sich amüsieren; **~ cooking/painting** gern kochen/malen; **I ~ed it** es hat mir gut gefallen/ ⟨*food:*⟩ geschmeckt. **~able** /-əbl/ *a* angenehm, nett. **~ment** *n* Vergnügen *nt*

enlarge /ɪn'lɑ:dʒ/ *vt* vergrößern □ *vi* **~ upon** sich näher auslassen über (+ *acc*). **~ment** *n* Vergrößerung *f*

enlighten /ɪn'laɪtn/ *vt* aufklären. **~ment** *n* Aufklärung *f*

enlist /ɪn'lɪst/ *vt* (*Mil*) einziehen; **~ s.o.'s help** jdn zur Hilfe heranziehen □ *vi* (*Mil*) sich melden

enliven /ɪn'laɪvn/ *vt* beleben

enmity /'enmətɪ/ *n* Feindschaft *f*

enormity /ɪ'nɔ:mətɪ/ *n* Ungeheuerlichkeit *f*

enormous /ɪ'nɔ:məs/ *a*, **-ly** *adv* riesig

enough /ɪ'nʌf/ *a*, *adv* & *n* genug; **be ~** reichen; **funnily ~** komischerweise; **I've had ~!** (*fam*) jetzt reicht's mir aber!

enquir|e /ɪn'kwaɪə(r)/ *vi* sich erkundigen (**about** nach) □ *vt* sich **erkundigen nach. ~y** *n* Erkundigung *f*; (*investigation*) Untersuchung *f*

enrage /ɪn'reɪdʒ/ *vt* wütend machen

enrich /ɪn'rɪtʃ/ *vt* bereichern; (*improve*) anreichern

enrol /ɪn'rəʊl/ *v* (*pt/pp* **-rolled**) □ *vt* einschreiben □ *vi* sich einschreiben. **~ment** *n* Einschreibung *f*

ensemble /ɒn'sɒmbl/ *n* (*clothing & Mus*) Ensemble *nt*

ensign /'ensaɪn/ *n* Flagge *f*

enslave /ɪn'sleɪv/ *vt* versklaven

ensue /ɪn'sju:/ *vi* folgen; (*result*) sich ergeben (**from** aus)

ensure /ɪn'ʃʊə(r)/ *vt* sicherstellen; **~ that** dafür sorgen, dass

entail /ɪn'teɪl/ *vt* erforderlich machen; **what does it ~?** was ist damit verbunden?

entangle /ɪn'tæŋgl/ *vt* **get ~d** sich verfangen (**in** in + *dat*); (*fig*) sich verstricken (**in** in + *acc*)

enter /'entə(r)/ *vt* eintreten/ ⟨*vehicle:*⟩ einfahren in (+ *acc*); einreisen in (+ *acc*) ⟨*country*⟩; (*register*) eintragen; sich anmelden zu ⟨*competition*⟩ □ *vi* eintreten; ⟨*vehicle:*⟩ einfahren; (*Theat*) auftreten; (*register as competitor*) sich anmelden; (*take part*) sich beteiligen (**in** an + *dat*)

enterpris|e /'entəpraɪz/ *n* Unternehmen *nt*; (*quality*) Unternehmungsgeist *m*. **~ing** *a* unternehmend

entertain /entə'teɪn/ *vt* unterhalten; (*invite*) einladen; (*to meal*) bewirten ⟨*guest*⟩; (*fig*) in Erwägung ziehen □ *vi* unterhalten; (*have guests*) Gäste haben. **~er** *n* Unterhalter *m*. **~ment** *n* Unterhaltung *f*

enthral /ɪn'θrɔ:l/ *vt* (*pt/pp* **enthralled**) **be ~led** gefesselt sein (**by** von)

enthuse /ɪn'θju:z/ *vi* **~ over** schwärmen von

enthusias|m /ɪn'θju:zɪæzm/ *n* Begeisterung *f*. **~t** *n* Enthusiast *m*. **~tic** /-'æstɪk/ *a*, **-ally** *adv* begeistert

entice /ɪn'taɪs/ *vt* locken. **~ment** *n* Anreiz *m*

entire /ɪn'taɪə(r)/ *a* ganz. **~ly** *adv* ganz, völlig. **~ty** /-rətɪ/ *n* **in its ~ty** in seiner Gesamtheit

entitle /ɪn'taɪtl/ *vt* berechtigen; **~d** ... mit dem Titel ...; **be ~d to sth das** Recht auf etw (*acc*) haben. **~ment** *n* Berechtigung *f*; (*claim*) Anspruch *m* (**to auf** + *acc*)

entity /'entətɪ/ *n* Wesen *nt*

entomology /entə'mɒlədʒɪ/ *n* Entomologie *f*

entourage /'ɒntʊrɑ:ʒ/ *n* Gefolge *nt*

entrails /'entreɪlz/ *npl* Eingeweide *pl*

entrance[1] /ɪn'trɑ:ns/ *vt* bezaubern

entrance[2] /'entrəns/ *n* Eintritt *m*; (*Theat*) Auftritt *m*; (*way in*) Eingang *m*; (*for vehicle*) Einfahrt *f*. **~ examination** *n* Aufnahmeprüfung *f*. **~ fee** *n* Eintrittsgebühr *f*

entrant /ˈentrənt/ *n* Teilnehmer(in) *m(f)*
entreat /ɪnˈtriːt/ *vt* anflehen (**for** um)
entrench /ɪnˈtrentʃ/ *vt* **be ~ed in** verwurzelt sein in (+ *dat*)
entrust /ɪnˈtrʌst/ *vt* **~ s.o. with sth, ~ sth to s.o.** jdm etw anvertrauen
entry /ˈentrɪ/ *n* Eintritt *m*; (*into country*) Einreise *f*; (*on list*) Eintrag *m*; **no ~** Zutritt/ (*Auto*) Einfahrt verboten. **~ form** *n* Anmeldeformular *nt*. **~ visa** *n* Einreisevisum *nt*
enumerate /ɪˈnjuːməreɪt/ *vt* aufzählen
enunciate /ɪˈnʌnsɪeɪt/ *vt* [deutlich] aussprechen; (*state*) vorbringen
envelop /ɪnˈveləp/ *vt* (*pt/pp* **enveloped**) einhüllen
envelope /ˈenvələʊp/ *n* [Brief]umschlag *m*
enviable /ˈenvɪəbl/ *a* beneidenswert
envious /ˈenvɪəs/ *a*, **-ly** *adv* neidisch (**of** auf + *acc*)
environment /ɪnˈvaɪərənmənt/ *n* Umwelt *f*
environmental /ɪnvaɪərənˈmentl/ *a* Umwelt-. **~ist** *n* Umweltschützer *m*. **~ly** *adv* **~ly friendly** umweltfreundlich
envisage /ɪnˈvɪzɪdʒ/ *vt* sich (*dat*) vorstellen
envoy /ˈenvɔɪ/ *n* Gesandte(r) *m*
envy /ˈenvɪ/ *n* Neid *m* □ *vt* (*pt/pp* **-ied**) **~ s.o. sth** jdn um etw beneiden
enzyme /ˈenzaɪm/ *n* Enzym *nt*
epic /ˈepɪk/ *a* episch □ *n* Epos *nt*
epidemic /epɪˈdemɪk/ *n* Epidemie *f*
epilep|sy /ˈepɪlepsɪ/ *n* Epilepsie *f*. **~tic** /-ˈleptɪk/ *a* epileptisch □ *n* Epileptiker(in) *m(f)*
epilogue /ˈepɪlɒg/ *n* Epilog *m*
episode /ˈepɪsəʊd/ *n* Episode *f*; (*instalment*) Folge *f*
epistle /ɪˈpɪsl/ *n* (*liter*) Brief *m*
epitaph /ˈepɪtɑːf/ *n* Epitaph *nt*
epithet /ˈepɪθet/ *n* Beiname *m*
epitom|e /ɪˈpɪtəmɪ/ *n* Inbegriff *m*. **~ize** *vt* verkörpern
epoch /ˈiːpɒk/ *n* Epoche *f*. **~-making** *a* epochemachend
equal /ˈiːkwl/ *a* gleich (**to** *dat*); **be ~ to a task** einer Aufgabe gewachsen sein □ *n* Gleichgestellte(r) *m/f* □ *vt* (*pt/pp* **equalled**) gleichen (+ *dat*); (*fig*) gleichkommen (+ *dat*). **~ity** /ɪˈkwɒlətɪ/ *n* Gleichheit *f*
equalize /ˈiːkwəlaɪz/ *vt/i* ausgleichen. **~r** *n* (*Sport*) Ausgleich[streffer] *m*
equally /ˈiːkwəlɪ/ *adv* gleich; ⟨*divide*⟩ gleichmäßig; (*just as*) genauso
equanimity /ekwəˈnɪmətɪ/ *n* Gleichmut *f*
equat|e /ɪˈkweɪt/ *vt* gleichsetzen (**with** mit). **~ion** /-eɪʒn/ *n* (*Math*) Gleichung *f*
equator /ɪˈkweɪtə(r)/ *n* Äquator *m*. **~ial** /ekwəˈtɔːrɪəl/ *a* Äquator-
equestrian /ɪˈkwestrɪən/ *a* Reit-
equilibrium /iːkwɪˈlɪbrɪəm/ *n* Gleichgewicht *nt*
equinox /ˈiːkwɪnɒks/ *n* Tagundnachtgleiche *f*
equip /ɪˈkwɪp/ *vt* (*pt/pp* **equipped**) ausrüsten; (*furnish*) ausstatten. **~ment** *n* Ausrüstung *f*; Ausstattung *f*
equitable /ˈekwɪtəbl/ *a* gerecht
equity /ˈekwətɪ/ *n* Gerechtigkeit *f*
equivalent /ɪˈkwɪvələnt/ *a* gleichwertig; (*corresponding*) entsprechend □ *n* Äquivalent *nt*; (*value*) Gegenwert *m*; (*counterpart*) Gegenstück *nt*
equivocal /ɪˈkwɪvəkl/ *a* zweideutig
era /ˈɪərə/ *n* Ära *f*, Zeitalter *nt*
eradicate /ɪˈrædɪkeɪt/ *vt* ausrotten

erase /ɪ'reɪz/ *vt* ausradieren; (*from tape*) löschen; (*fig*) auslöschen. **~r** *n* Radiergummi *m*

erect /ɪ'rekt/ *a* aufrecht □ *vt* errichten. **~ion** /-ekʃn/ *n* Errichtung *f*; (*building*) Bau *m*; (*Biol*) Erektion *f*

ermine /'ɜ:mɪn/ *n* Hermelin *m*

ero|de /ɪ'rəʊd/ *vt* ⟨*water*:⟩ auswaschen; ⟨*acid*:⟩ angreifen. **~sion** /-əʊʒn/ *n* Erosion *f*

erotic /ɪ'rɒtɪk/ *a* erotisch. **~ism** /-tɪsɪzm/ *n* Erotik *f*

err /ɜ:(r)/ *vi* sich irren; (*sin*) sündigen

errand /'erənd/ *n* Botengang *m*

erratic /ɪ'rætɪk/ *a* unregelmäßig; ⟨*person*⟩ unberechenbar

erroneous /ɪ'rəʊnɪəs/ *a* falsch; ⟨*belief, assumption*⟩ irrig. **~ly** *adv* fälschlich; irrigerweise

error /'erə(r)/ *n* Irrtum *m*; (*mistake*) Fehler *m*; **in ~** irrtümlicherweise

erudit|e /'erʊdaɪt/ *a* gelehrt. **~ion** /-'dɪʃn/ *n* Gelehrsamkeit *f*

erupt /ɪ'rʌpt/ *vi* ausbrechen. **~ion** /-ʌpʃn/ *n* Ausbruch *m*

escalat|e /'eskəleɪt/ *vt/i* eskalieren. **~ion** /-'leɪʃn/ *n* Eskalation *f*. **~or** *n* Rolltreppe *f*

escapade /'eskəpeɪd/ *n* Eskapade *f*

escape /ɪ'skeɪp/ *n* Flucht *f*; (*from prison*) Ausbruch *m*; **have a narrow ~** gerade noch davonkommen □ *vi* flüchten; ⟨*prisoner*:⟩ ausbrechen; entkommen (**from** aus; **from s.o.** jdm); ⟨*gas*:⟩ entweichen □ *vt* **~ notice** unbemerkt bleiben; **the name ~s me** der Name entfällt mir

escapism /ɪ'skeɪpɪzm/ *n* Flucht *f* vor der Wirklichkeit, Eskapismus *m*

escort[1] /'eskɔ:t/ *n* (*of person*) Begleiter *m*; (*Mil*) Eskorte *f*; **under ~** unter Bewachung

escort[2] /ɪ'skɔ:t/ *vt* begleiten; (*Mil*) eskortieren

Eskimo /'eskɪməʊ/ *n* Eskimo *m*

esoteric /esə'terɪk/ *a* esoterisch

especial /ɪ'speʃl/ *a* besondere(r,s). **~ly** *adv* besonders

espionage /'espɪənɑ:ʒ/ *n* Spionage *f*

essay /'eseɪ/ *n* Aufsatz *m*

essence /'esns/ *n* Wesen *nt*; (*Chem, Culin*) Essenz *f*; **in ~** im Wesentlichen

essential /ɪ'senʃl/ *a* wesentlich; (*indispensable*) unentbehrlich □ *n* **the ~s** das Wesentliche; (*items*) das Nötigste. **~ly** *adv* im Wesentlichen

establish /ɪ'stæblɪʃ/ *vt* gründen; (*form*) bilden; (*prove*) beweisen. **~ment** *n* (*firm*) Unternehmen *nt*

estate /ɪ'steɪt/ *n* Gut *nt*; (*possessions*) Besitz *m*; (*after death*) Nachlass *m*; (*housing*) [Wohn]siedlung *f*. **~ agent** *n* Immobilienmakler *m*. **~ car** *n* Kombi[wagen] *m*

esteem /ɪ'sti:m/ *n* Achtung *f* □ *vt* hochschätzen

estimate[1] /'estɪmət/ *n* Schätzung *f*; (*Comm*) [Kosten]voranschlag *m*; **at a rough ~** grob geschätzt

estimat|e[2] /'estɪmeɪt/ *vt* schätzen. **~ion** /-'meɪʃn/ *n* Einschätzung *f*; (*esteem*) Achtung *f*; **in my ~ion** meiner Meinung nach

estuary /'estjʊərɪ/ *n* Mündung *f*

etc. /et'setərə/ *abbr* (**et cetera**) und so weiter, usw.

etching /'etʃɪŋ/ *n* Radierung *f*

eternal /ɪ'tɜ:nl/ *a*, **-ly** *adv* ewig

eternity /ɪ'θɜ:nətɪ/ *n* Ewigkeit *f*

ether /'i:θə(r)/ *n* Äther *m*

ethic /'eθɪk/ *n* Ethik *f*. **~al** *a* ethisch; (*morally correct*) moralisch einwandfrei. **~s** *n* Ethik *f*

Ethiopia /i:θɪ'əʊpɪə/ *n* Äthiopien *nt*

ethnic /'eθnɪk/ *a* ethnisch

etiquette /'etɪket/ *n* Etikette *f*

etymology /etɪ'mɒlədʒɪ/ *n* Etymologie *f*

eucalyptus /ju:kə'lɪptəs/ *n* Eukalyptus *m*
eulogy /'ju:lədʒɪ/ *n* Lobrede *f*
euphemis|m /'ju:fəmɪzm/ *n* Euphemismus *m*. **~tic** /-'mɪstɪk/ *a*, **-ally** *adv* verhüllend
euphoria /ju:'fɔ:rɪə/ *n* Euphorie *f*
Euro /'jʊərəʊ/ *n* Euro *m*. **~cheque** *n* Euroscheck *m*. **~passport** *n* Europaß *m*
Europe /'jʊərəp/ *n* Europa *nt*
European /jʊərə'pi:ən/ *a* europäisch; ~ **Community** Europäische Gemeinschaft *f* □ *n* Europäer(in) *m(f)*
evacuat|e /ɪ'vækjʊeɪt/ *vt* evakuieren; räumen ⟨*building, area*⟩. **~ion** /-'eɪʃn/ *n* Evakuierung *f*; Räumung *f*
evade /ɪ'veɪd/ *vt* sich entziehen (+ *dat*); hinterziehen ⟨*taxes*⟩; ~ **the issue** ausweichen
evaluate /ɪ'væljʊeɪt/ *vt* einschätzen
evange|lical /i:væn'dʒelɪkl/ *a* evangelisch. **~list** /ɪ'vændʒəlɪst/ *n* Evangelist *m*
evaporat|e /ɪ'væpəreɪt/ *vi* verdunsten; **~ed milk** Kondensmilch *f*, Dosenmilch *f*. **~ion** /-'reɪʃn/ *n* Verdampfung *f*
evasion /ɪ'veɪʒn/ *n* Ausweichen *nt*; ~ **of taxes** Steuerhinterziehung *f*
evasive /ɪ'veɪsɪv/ *a*, **-ly** *adv* ausweichend; **be** ~ ausweichen
eve /i:v/ *n* (*liter*) Vorabend *m*
even /'i:vn/ *a* (*level*) eben; (*same, equal*) gleich; (*regular*) gleichmäßig; ⟨*number*⟩ gerade; **get** ~ **with** (*fam*) es jdm heimzahlen □ *adv* sogar, selbst; ~ **so** trotzdem; **not** ~ nicht einmal □ *vt* ~ **the score** ausgleichen. ~ **up** *vt* ausgleichen □ *vi* sich ausgleichen
evening /'i:vnɪŋ/ *n* Abend *m*; **this** ~ heute Abend; **in the** ~ abends, am Abend. ~ **class** *n* Abendkurs *m*
evenly /'i:vnlɪ/ *adv* gleichmäßig
event /ɪ'vent/ *n* Ereignis *nt*; (*function*) Veranstaltung *f*; (*Sport*) Wettbewerb *m*; **in the** ~ **of** im Falle (+ *gen*); **in the** ~ wie es sich ergab. **~ful** *a* ereignisreich
eventual /ɪ'ventjʊəl/ *a* **his** ~ **success** der Erfolg, der ihm schließlich zuteil wurde. **~ity** /-'ælətɪ/ *n* Eventualität *f*, Fall *m*. **~ly** *adv* schließlich
ever /'evə(r)/ *adv* je[mals]; **not** ~ nie; **for** ~ für immer; **hardly** ~ fast nie; ~ **since** seitdem; ~ **so** (*fam*) sehr, furchtbar (*fam*)
'evergreen *n* immergrüner Strauch *m*/ (*tree*) Baum *m*
ever'lasting *a* ewig
every /'evrɪ/ *a* jede(r,s); ~ **one** jede(r,s) Einzelne; ~ **other day** jeden zweiten Tag
every: ~body *pron* jeder[mann]; alle *pl*. **~day** *a* alltäglich. ~ **one** *pron* jeder[mann]; alle *pl*. **~thing** *pron* alles. **~where** *adv* überall
evict /ɪ'vɪkt/ *vt* [aus der Wohnung] hinausweisen. **~ion** /-ɪkʃn/ *n* Ausweisung *f*
eviden|ce /'evɪdəns/ *n* Beweise *pl*; (*Jur*) Beweismaterial *nt*; (*testimony*) Aussage *f*; **give ~ce** aussagen. **~t** *a*, **-ly** *adv* offensichtlich
evil /'i:vl/ *a* böse □ *n* Böse *nt*
evocative /ɪ'vɒkətɪv/ *a* **be** ~ **of** heraufbeschwören
evoke /ɪ'vəʊk/ *vt* heraufbeschwören
evolution /i:və'lu:ʃn/ *n* Evolution *f*
evolve /ɪ'vɒlv/ *vt* entwickeln □ *vi* sich entwickeln
ewe /ju:/ *n* Schaf *nt*
exacerbate /ek'sæsəbeɪt/ *vt* verschlimmern; verschärfen ⟨*situation*⟩
exact /ɪg'zækt/ *a*, **-ly** *adv* genau; **not ~ly** nicht gerade □ *vt* erzwingen. **~ing** *a* anspruchs-

voll. **~itude** /-ɪtju:d/ *n*, **~ness** *n* Genauigkeit *f*

exaggerat|e /ɪg'zædʒəreɪt/ *vt/i* übertreiben. **~ion** /-'reɪʃn/ *n* Übertreibung *f*

exalt /ɪg'zɔ:lt/ *vt* erheben; (*praise*) preisen

exam /ɪg'zæm/ *n* (*fam*) Prüfung *f*

examination /ɪgzæmɪ'neɪʃn/ *n* Untersuchung *f*; (*Sch*) Prüfung *f*

examine /ɪg'zæmɪn/ *vt* untersuchen; (*Sch*) prüfen; (*Jur*) verhören. **~r** *n* (*Sch*) Prüfer *m*

example /ɪg'zɑ:mpl/ *n* Beispiel *nt* (**of** für); **for ~** zum Beispiel; **make an ~ of** ein Exempel statuieren an (+ *dat*)

exasperat|e /ɪg'zæspəreɪt/ *vt* zur Verzweiflung treiben. **~ion** /-'reɪʃn/ *n* Verzweiflung *f*

excavat|e /'ekskəveɪt/ *vt* ausschachten; (*Archaeol*) ausgraben. **~ion** /-'veɪʃn/ *n* Ausgrabung *f*

exceed /ɪk'si:d/ *vt* übersteigen. **~ingly** *adv* äußerst

excel /ɪk'sel/ *v* (*pt/pp* **excelled**) *vi* sich auszeichnen □ *vt* **~ oneself** sich selbst übertreffen

excellen|ce /'eksələns/ *n* Vorzüglichkeit *f*. **E ~cy** *n* (*title*) Exzellenz *f*. **~t** *a*, **-ly** *adv* ausgezeichnet, vorzüglich

except /ɪk'sept/ *prep* außer (+ *dat*); **~ for** abgesehen von □ *vt* ausnehmen. **~ing** *prep* außer (+ *dat*)

exception /ɪk'sepʃn/ *n* Ausnahme *f*; **take ~ to** Anstoß nehmen an (+ *dat*). **~al** *a*, **-ly** *adv* außergewöhnlich

excerpt /'eksɜ:pt/ *n* Auszug *m*

excess /ɪk'ses/ *n* Übermaß *nt* (**of** an + *dat*); (*surplus*) Überschuss *m*; **~es** *pl* Exzesse *pl*; **in ~ of** über (+ *dat*)

excess 'fare /'ekses-/ *n* Nachlösegebühr *f*

excessive /ɪk'sesɪv/ *a*, **-ly** *adv* übermäßig

exchange /ɪks'tʃeɪndʒ/ *n* Austausch *m*; (*Teleph*) Fernsprechamt *nt*; (*Comm*) [Geld]wechsel *m*; **[stock] ~** Börse *f*; **in ~** dafür □ *vt* austauschen (**for** gegen); tauschen ⟨*places, greetings, money*⟩. **~ rate** *n* Wechselkurs *m*

exchequer /ɪks'tʃekə(r)/ *n* (*Pol*) Staatskasse *f*

excise[1] /'eksaɪz/ *n* **~ duty** Verbrauchssteuer *f*

excise[2] /ek'saɪz/ *vt* herausschneiden

excitable /ɪk'saɪtəbl/ *a* [leicht] erregbar

excit|e /ɪk'saɪt/ *vt* aufregen; (*cause*) erregen. **~ed** *a*, **-ly** *adv* aufgeregt; **get ~ed** sich aufregen. **~ement** *n* Aufregung *f*; Erregung *f*. **~ing** *a* aufregend; ⟨*story*⟩ spannend

exclaim /ɪk'skleɪm/ *vt/i* ausrufen

exclamation /ekskla'meɪʃn/ *n* Ausruf *m*. **~ mark** *n*, (*Amer*) **~ point** *n* Ausrufezeichen *nt*

exclu|de /ɪk'sklu:d/ *vt* ausschließen. **~ding** *prep* ausschließlich (+ *gen*). **~sion** /-ʒn/ *n* Ausschluss *m*

exclusive /ɪk'sklu:sɪv/ *a*, **-ly** *adv* ausschließlich; (*select*) exklusiv; **~ of** ausschließlich (+ *gen*)

excommunicate /ekskə'mju:nɪkeɪt/ *vt* exkommunizieren

excrement /'ekskrɪmənt/ *n* Kot *m*

excrete /ɪk'skri:t/ *vt* ausscheiden

excruciating /ɪk'skru:ʃieɪtɪŋ/ *a* grässlich

excursion /ɪk'skɜ:ʃn/ *n* Ausflug *m*

excusable /ɪk'skju:zəbl/ *a* entschuldbar

excuse[1] /ɪk'skju:s/ *n* Entschuldigung *f*; (*pretext*) Ausrede *f*

excuse[2] /ɪk'skju:z/ *vt* entschuldigen; **~ from** freistellen von; **~ me!** Entschuldigung!

ex-di'rectory *a* **be ~** nicht im Telefonbuch stehen

execute /ˈeksɪkjuːt/ *vt* ausführen; (*put to death*) hinrichten
execution /eksɪˈkjuːʃn/ *n* (*see* **execute**) Ausführung *f*; Hinrichtung *f*. **~er** *n* Scharfrichter *m*
executive /ɪgˈzekjʊtɪv/ *a* leitend □ *n* leitende(r) Angestellte(r) *m/f*; (*Pol*) Exekutive *f*
executor /ɪgˈzekjʊtə(r)/ *n* (*Jur*) Testamentsvollstrecker *m*
exemplary /ɪgˈzemplərɪ/ *a* beispielhaft; (*as a warning*) exemplarisch
exemplify /ɪgˈzemplɪfaɪ/ *vt* (*pt/pp* **-ied**) veranschaulichen
exempt /ɪgˈzempt/ *a* befreit □ *vt* befreien (**from** von). **~ion** /-empʃn/ *n* Befreiung *f*
exercise /ˈeksəsaɪz/ *n* Übung *f*; **physical ~** körperliche Bewegung *f*; **take ~** sich bewegen □ *vt* (*use*) ausüben; bewegen ⟨*horse*⟩; spazieren führen ⟨*dog*⟩ □ *vi* sich bewegen. **~ book** *n* [Schul]heft *nt*
exert /ɪgˈzɜːt/ *vt* ausüben; **~ oneself** sich anstrengen. **~ion** /-ɜːʃn/ *n* Anstrengung *f*
exhale /eksˈheɪl/ *vt/i* ausatmen
exhaust /ɪgˈzɔːst/ *n* (*Auto*) Auspuff *m*; (*pipe*) Auspuffrohr *nt*; (*fumes*) Abgase *pl* □ *vt* erschöpfen. **~ed** *a* erschöpft. **~ing** *a* anstrengend. **~ion** /-ɔːstʃn/ *n* Erschöpfung *f*. **~ive** /-ɪv/ *a* (*fig*) erschöpfend
exhibit /ɪgˈzɪbɪt/ *n* Ausstellungsstück *nt*; (*Jur*) Beweisstück *nt* □ *vt* ausstellen; (*fig*) zeigen
exhibition /eksɪˈbɪʃn/ *n* Ausstellung *f*; (*Univ*) Stipendium *nt*. **~ist** *n* Exhibitionist(in) *m(f)*
exhibitor /ɪgˈzɪbɪtə(r)/ *n* Aussteller *m*
exhilerat|ed /ɪgˈzɪləreɪtɪd/ *a* beschwingt. **~ing** *a* berauschend. **~ion** /-ˈreɪʃn/ *n* Hochgefühl *nt*
exhort /ɪgˈzɔːt/ *vt* ermahnen
exhume /ɪgˈzjuːm/ *vt* exhumieren
exile /ˈeksaɪl/ *n* Exil *nt*; (*person*) im Exil Lebende(r) *m/f* □ *vt* ins Exil schicken
exist /ɪgˈzɪst/ *vi* bestehen, existieren. **~ence** /-əns/ *n* Existenz *f*; **be in ~ence** existieren
exit /ˈeksɪt/ *n* Ausgang *m*; (*Auto*) Ausfahrt *f*; (*Theat*) Abgang *m* □ *vi* (*Theat*) abgehen. **~ visa** *n* Ausreisevisum *nt*
exonerate /ɪgˈzɒnəreɪt/ *vt* entlasten
exorbitant /ɪgˈzɔːbɪtənt/ *a* übermäßig hoch
exorcize /ˈeksɔːsaɪz/ *vt* austreiben
exotic /ɪgˈzɒtɪk/ *a* exotisch
expand /ɪkˈspænd/ *vt* ausdehnen; (*explain better*) weiter ausführen □ *vi* sich ausdehnen; (*Comm*) expandieren; **~ on** (*fig*) weiter ausführen
expans|e /ɪkˈspæns/ *n* Weite *f*. **~ion** /-ænʃn/ *n* Ausdehnung *f*; (*Techn, Pol, Comm*) Expansion *f*. **~ive** /-ɪv/ *a* mitteilsam
expatriate /eksˈpætrɪət/ *n* **be an ~** im Ausland leben
expect /ɪkˈspekt/ *vt* erwarten; (*suppose*) annehmen; **I ~ so** wahrscheinlich; **we ~ to arrive on Monday** wir rechnen damit, dass wir am Montag ankommen
expectan|cy /ɪkˈspektənsɪ/ *n* Erwartung *f*. **~t** *a*, **-ly** *adv* erwartungsvoll; **~t mother** werdende Mutter *f*
expectation /ekspekˈteɪʃn/ *n* Erwartung *f*; **~ of life** Lebenserwartung *f*
expedient /ɪkˈspiːdɪənt/ *a* zweckdienlich
expedite /ˈekspɪdaɪt/ *vt* beschleunigen
expedition /ekspɪˈdɪʃn/ *n* Expedition *f*. **~ary** *a* (*Mil*) Expeditions-
expel /ɪkˈspel/ *vt* (*pt/pp* **expelled**) ausweisen (**from** aus); (*from

school) von der Schule verweisen

expend /ɪk'spend/ *vt* aufwenden. **~able** /-əbl/ *a* entbehrlich

expenditure /ɪk'spendɪtʃə(r)/ *n* Ausgaben *pl*

expense /ɪk'spens/ *n* Kosten *pl*; **business ~s** *pl* Spesen *pl*; **at my ~** auf meine Kosten; **at the ~ of** (*fig*) auf Kosten (+ *gen*)

expensive /ɪk'spensɪv/ *a*, **-ly** *adv* teuer

experience /ɪk'spɪərɪəns/ *n* Erfahrung *f*; (*event*) Erlebnis *nt* □ *vt* erleben. **~d** *a* erfahren

experiment /ɪk'sperɪmənt/ *n* Versuch *m*, Experiment *nt* □ /-ment/ *vi* experimentieren. **~al** /-'mentl/ *a* experimentell

expert /'ekspɜ:t/ *a*, **-ly** *adv* fachmännisch □ *n* Fachmann *m*, Experte *m*

expertise /ekspɜ:'ti:z/ *n* Sachkenntnis *f*; (*skill*) Geschick *nt*

expire /ɪk'spaɪə(r)/ *vi* ablaufen

expiry /ɪk'spaɪərɪ/ *n* Ablauf *m*. **~ date** *n* Verfallsdatum *nt*

explain /ɪk'spleɪn/ *vt* erklären

explana|tion /eksplə'neɪʃn/ *n* Erklärung *f*. **~tory** /ɪk'splænətərɪ/ *a* erklärend

expletive /ɪk'spli:tɪv/ *n* Kraftausdruck *m*

explicit /ɪk'splɪsɪt/ *a*, **-ly** *adv* deutlich

explode /ɪk'spləʊd/ *vi* explodieren □ *vt* zur Explosion bringen

exploit[1] /'eksplɔɪt/ *n* [Helden]tat *f*

exploit[2] /ɪk'splɔɪt/ *vt* ausbeuten. **~ation** /eksplɔɪ'teɪʃn/ *n* Ausbeutung *f*

explora|tion /eksplə'reɪʃn/ *n* Erforschung *f*. **~tory** /ɪk'splɒrətərɪ/ *a* Probe-

explore /ɪk'splɔ:(r)/ *vt* erforschen. **~r** *n* Forschungsreisende(r) *m*

explos|ion /ɪk'spləʊʒn/ *n* Explosion *f*. **~ive** /-sɪv/ *a* explosiv □ *n* Sprengstoff *m*

exponent /ɪk'spəʊnənt/ *n* Vertreter *m*

export[1] /'ekspɔ:t/ *n* Export *m*, Ausfuhr *f*

export[2] /ɪk'spɔ:t/ *vt* exportieren, ausführen. **~er** *n* Exporteur *m*

expos|e /ɪk'spəʊz/ *vt* freilegen; (*to danger*) aussetzen (**to** *dat*); (*reveal*) aufdecken; (*Phot*) belichten. **~ure** /-ʒə(r)/ *n* Aussetzung *f*; (*Med*) Unterkühlung *f*; (*Phot*) Belichtung *f*; **24 ~ures** 24 Aufnahmen

expound /ɪk'spaʊnd/ *vt* erläutern

express /ɪk'spres/ *a* ausdrücklich; ⟨*purpose*⟩ fest □ *adv* ⟨*send*⟩ per Eilpost □ *n* (*train*) Schnellzug *m* □ *vt* ausdrücken; **~ oneself** sich ausdrücken. **~ion** /-ʃn/ *n* Ausdruck *m*. **~ive** /-ɪv/ *a* ausdrucksvoll. **~ly** *adv* ausdrücklich

expulsion /ɪk'spʌlʃn/ *n* Ausweisung *f*; (*Sch*) Verweisung *f* von der Schule

expurgate /'ekspəgeɪt/ *vt* zensieren

exquisite /ek'skwɪzɪt/ *a* erlesen

ex-'serviceman *n* Veteran *m*

extempore /ɪk'stempərɪ/ *adv* ⟨*speak*⟩ aus dem Stegreif

extend /ɪk'stend/ *vt* verlängern; (*stretch out*) ausstrecken; (*enlarge*) vergrößern □ *vi* sich ausdehnen; ⟨*table:*⟩ sich ausziehen lassen

extension /ɪk'stenʃn/ *n* Verlängerung *f*; (*to house*) Anbau *m*; (*Teleph*) Nebenanschluss *m*; **~ 7** Apparat 7

extensive /ɪk'stensɪv/ *a* weit; (*fig*) umfassend. **~ly** *adv* viel

extent /ɪk'stent/ *n* Ausdehnung *f*; (*scope*) Ausmaß *nt*, Umfang *m*; **to a certain ~** in gewissem Maße

extenuating /ɪk'stenjʊeɪtɪŋ/ *a* mildernd

exterior /ɪk'stɪərɪə(r)/ *a* äußere(r,s) □ *n* **the ~ das** Äußere

exterminat|e /ɪk'stɜ:mɪneɪt/ *vt* ausrotten. **~ion** /-'neɪʃn/ *n* Ausrottung *f*
external /ɪk'stɜ:nl/ *a* äußere(r,s); **for ~ use only** (*Med*) nur äußerlich. **~ly** *adv* äußerlich
extinct /ɪk'stɪŋkt/ *a* ausgestorben; ⟨*volcano*⟩ erloschen. **~ion** /-ɪŋkʃn/ *n* Aussterben *nt*
extinguish /ɪk'stɪŋgwɪʃ/ *vt* löschen. **~er** *n* Feuerlöscher *m*
extol /ɪk'stəʊl/ *vt* (*pt/pp* **extolled**) preisen
extort /ɪk'stɔ:t/ *vt* erpressen. **~ion** /-ɔ:ʃn/ *n* Erpressung *f*
extortionate /ɪk'stɔ:ʃənət/ *a* übermäßig hoch
extra /'ekstrə/ *a* zusätzlich □ *adv* extra; (*especially*) besonders; **~ strong** extrastark □ *n* (*Theat*) Statist(in) *m*(*f*); **~s** *pl* Nebenkosten *pl*; (*Auto*) Extras *pl*
extract[1] /'ekstrækt/ *n* Auszug *m*; (*Culin*) Extrakt *m*
extract[2] /ɪk'strækt/ *vt* herausziehen; ziehen ⟨*tooth*⟩; (*fig*) erzwingen. **~or [fan]** *n* Entlüfter *m*
extradit|e /'ekstrədaɪt/ *vt* (*Jur*) ausliefern. **~ion** /-'dɪʃn/ *n* (*Jur*) Auslieferung *f*
extra'marital *a* außerehelich
extraordinary /ɪk'strɔ:dɪnərɪ/ *a*, **-ily** *adv* außerordentlich; (*strange*) seltsam
extravagan|ce /ɪk'strævəgəns/ *n* Verschwendung *f*; **an ~ce** ein Luxus *m*. **~t** *a* verschwenderisch; (*exaggerated*) extravagant
extrem|e /ɪk'stri:m/ *a* äußerste(r,s); (*fig*) extrem □ *n* Extrem *nt*; **in the ~e** im höchsten Grade. **~ely** *adv* äußerst. **~ist** *n* Extremist *m*
extremit|y /ɪk'stremətɪ/ *n* (*distress*) Not *f*; **the ~ies** *pl* die Extremitäten *pl*
extricate /'ekstrɪkeɪt/ *vt* befreien
extrovert /'ekstrəvɜ:t/ *n* extravertierter Mensch *m*
exuberant /ɪg'zju:bərənt/ *a* überglücklich
exude /ɪg'zju:d/ *vt* absondern; (*fig*) ausstrahlen
exult /ɪg'zʌlt/ *vi* frohlocken
eye /aɪ/ *n* Auge *nt*; (*of needle*) Öhr *nt*; (*for hook*) Öse *f*; **keep an ~ on** aufpassen auf (+ *acc*); **see ~ to ~** einer Meinung sein □ *vt* (*pt/pp* **eyed**, *pres p* **ey[e]ing**) ansehen
eye: ~ball *n* Augapfel *m*. **~ brow** *n* Augenbraue *f*. **~lash** *n* Wimper *f*. **~let** /-lɪt/ *n* Öse *f*. **~lid** *n* Augenlid *nt*. **~-shadow** *n* Lidschatten *m*. **~sight** *n* Sehkraft *f*. **~sore** *n* (*fam*) Schandfleck *m*. **~-tooth** *n* Eckzahn *m*. **~witness** *n* Augenzeuge *m*

F

fable /'feɪbl/ *n* Fabel *f*
fabric /'fæbrɪk/ *n* Stoff *m*; (*fig*) Gefüge *nt*
fabrication /fæbrɪ'keɪʃn/ *n* Erfindung *f*
fabulous /'fæbjʊləs/ *a* (*fam*) phantastisch
façade /fə'sɑ:d/ *n* Fassade *f*
face /feɪs/ *n* Gesicht *nt*; (*grimace*) Grimasse *f*; (*surface*) Fläche *f*; (*of clock*) Zifferblatt *nt*; **pull ~s** Gesichter schneiden; **in the ~ of** angesichts (+ *gen*); **on the ~ of it** allem Anschein nach □ *vt/i* gegenüberstehen (+ *dat*); **~ north** ⟨*house:*⟩ nach Norden liegen; **~ me!** sieh mich an! **~ the fact that** sich damit abfinden, dass; **~ up to s.o.** jdm die Stirn bieten
face: ~-flannel *n* Waschlappen *m*. **~less** *a* anonym. **~-lift** *n* Gesichtsstraffung *f*
facet /'fæsɪt/ *n* Facette *f*; (*fig*) Aspekt *m*
facetious /fə'si:ʃəs/ *a*, **-ly** *adv* spöttisch
'face value *n* Nennwert *m*

facial /ˈfeɪʃl/ *a* Gesichts-
facile /ˈfæsaɪl/ *a* oberflächlich
facilitate /fəˈsɪlɪteɪt/ *vt* erleichtern
facilit|y /fəˈsɪlətɪ/ *n* Leichtigkeit *f*; (*skill*) Gewandtheit *f*; **~ies** *pl* Einrichtungen *pl*
facing /ˈfeɪsɪŋ/ *n* Besatz *m*
facsimile /fækˈsɪməlɪ/ *n* Faksimile *nt*
fact /fækt/ *n* Tatsache *f*; **in ~** tatsächlich; (*actually*) eigentlich
faction /ˈfækʃn/ *n* Gruppe *f*
factor /ˈfæktə(r)/ *n* Faktor *m*
factory /ˈfæktərɪ/ *n* Fabrik *f*
factual /ˈfæktʃʊəl/ *a*, **-ly** *adv* sachlich
faculty /ˈfækəltɪ/ *n* Fähigkeit *f*; (*Univ*) Fakultät *f*
fad /fæd/ *n* Fimmel *m*
fade /feɪd/ *vi* verblassen; ⟨*material*:⟩ verbleichen; ⟨*sound*:⟩ abklingen; ⟨*flower*:⟩ verwelken. **~ in/out** *vt* (*Radio, TV*) ein-/ausblenden
fag /fæg/ *n* (*chore*) Plage *f*; (*fam: cigarette*) Zigarette *f*; (*Amer sl*) Homosexuelle(r) *m*
fagged /fægd/ *a* **~ out** (*fam*) völlig erledigt
Fahrenheit /ˈfærənhaɪt/ *a* Fahrenheit
fail /feɪl/ *n* **without ~** unbedingt □ *vi* ⟨*attempt*:⟩ scheitern; (*grow weak*) nachlassen; (*break down*) versagen; (*in exam*) durchfallen; **~ to do sth** etw nicht tun; **he ~ed to break the record** es gelang ihm nicht, den Rekord zu brechen □ *vt* nicht bestehen ⟨*exam*⟩; durchfallen lassen ⟨*candidate*⟩; (*disappoint*) enttäuschen; **words ~ me** ich weiß nicht, was ich sagen soll
failing /ˈfeɪlɪŋ/ *n* Fehler *m* □ *prep* **~ that** andernfalls
failure /ˈfeɪljə(r)/ *n* Misserfolg *m*; (*breakdown*) Versagen *nt*; (*person*) Versager *m*
faint /feɪnt/ *a* (**-er, -est**), **-ly** *adv* schwach; **I feel ~** mir ist schwach □ *n* Ohnmacht *f* □ *vi* ohnmächtig werden
faint: ~-ˈhearted *a* zaghaft. **~ness** *n* Schwäche *f*
fair[1] /feə(r)/ *n* Jahrmarkt *m*; (*Comm*) Messe *f*
fair[2] *a* (**-er, -est**) ⟨*hair*⟩ blond; ⟨*skin*⟩ hell; ⟨*weather*⟩ heiter; (*just*) gerecht, fair; (*quite good*) ziemlich gut; (*Sch*) genügend; **a ~ amount** ziemlich viel □ *adv* **play ~** fair sein. **~ly** *adv* gerecht; (*rather*) ziemlich. **~ness** *n* Blondheit *f*; Helle *f*; Gerechtigkeit *f*; (*Sport*) Fairness *f*
fairy /ˈfeərɪ/ *n* Elfe *f*; **good/wicked ~** gute/böse Fee *f*. **~ story, ~-tale** *n* Märchen *nt*
faith /feɪθ/ *n* Glaube *m*; (*trust*) Vertrauen *nt* (**in** zu); **in good ~** in gutem Glauben
faithful /ˈfeɪθfl/ *a*, **-ly** *adv* treu; (*exact*) genau; **Yours ~ly** Hochachtungsvoll. **~ness** *n* Treue *f*; Genauigkeit *f*
ˈfaith-healer *n* Gesundbeter(in) *m(f)*
fake /feɪk/ *a* falsch □ *n* Fälschung *f*; (*person*) Schwindler *m* □ *vt* fälschen; (*pretend*) vortäuschen
falcon /ˈfɔːlkən/ *n* Falke *m*
fall /fɔːl/ *n* Fall *m*; (*heavy*) Sturz *m*; (*in prices*) Fallen *nt*; (*Amer: autumn*) Herbst *m*; **have a ~** fallen □ *vi* (*pt* **fell**, *pp* **fallen**) fallen; (*heavily*) stürzen; ⟨*night*:⟩ anbrechen; **~in love** sich verlieben; **~ back on** zurückgreifen auf (+ *acc*); **~ for s.o.** (*fam*) sich in jdn verlieben; **~ for sth** (*fam*) auf etw (*acc*) hereinfallen. **~ about** *vi* (*with laughter*) sich [vor Lachen] kringeln. **~ down** *vi* umfallen; ⟨*thing*:⟩ herunterfallen; ⟨*building*:⟩ einstürzen. **~ in** *vi* hineinfallen; (*collapse*) einfallen; (*Mil*) antreten; **~ in with** sich anschließen (+ *dat*). **~ off** *vi*

herunterfallen; (*diminish*) abnehmen. ~ **out** *vi* herausfallen; ⟨*hair:*⟩ ausfallen; (*quarrel*) sich überwerfen. ~ **over** *vi* hinfallen. ~ **through** *vi* durchfallen; ⟨*plan:*⟩ ins Wasser fallen

fallacy /ˈfæləsɪ/ *n* Irrtum *m*

fallible /ˈfæləbl/ *a* fehlbar

ˈfall-out *n* [radioaktiver] Niederschlag *m*

fallow /ˈfæləʊ/ *a* **lie** ~ brachliegen

false /fɔːls/ *a* falsch; (*artificial*) künstlich; ~ **start** (*Sport*) Fehlstart *m*. ~**hood** *n* Unwahrheit *f*. ~**ly** *adv* falsch. ~**ness** *n* Falschheit *f*

false ˈteeth *npl* [künstliches] Gebiss *nt*

falsify /ˈfɔːlsɪfaɪ/ *vt* (*pt/pp* **-ied**) fälschen; (*misrepresent*) verfälschen

falter /ˈfɔːltə(r)/ *vi* zögern; (*stumble*) straucheln

fame /feɪm/ *n* Ruhm *m*. ~**d** *a* berühmt

familiar /fəˈmɪljə(r)/ *a* vertraut; (*known*) bekannt; **too** ~ familiär. ~**ity** /-lɪˈærətɪ/ *n* Vertrautheit *f*. ~**ize** *vt* vertraut machen (**with** mit)

family /ˈfæməlɪ/ *n* Familie *f*

family: ~ **alˈlowance** *n* Kindergeld *nt*. ~ **ˈdoctor** *n* Hausarzt *m*. ~ **ˈlife** *n* Familienleben *nt*. ~ **ˈplanning** *n* Familienplanung *f*. ~ **ˈtree** *n* Stammbaum *m*

famine /ˈfæmɪn/ *n* Hungersnot *f*

famished /ˈfæmɪʃt/ *a* sehr hungrig

famous /ˈfeɪməs/ *a* berühmt

fan[1] /fæn/ *n* Fächer *m*; (*Techn*) Ventilator *m* □ *v* (*pt/pp* **fanned**) □ *vt* fächeln; ~ **oneself** sich fächeln □ *vi* ~ **out** sich fächerförmig ausbreiten

fan[2] *n* (*admirer*) Fan *m*

fanatic /fəˈnætɪk/ *n* Fanatiker *m*. ~**al** *a*, **-ly** *adv* fanatisch. ~**ism** /-sɪzm/ *n* Fanatismus *m*

ˈfan belt *n* Keilriemen *m*

fanciful /ˈfænsɪfl/ *a* phantastisch; (*imaginative*) phantasiereich

fancy /ˈfænsɪ/ *n* Phantasie *f*; **have a** ~ **to** Lust haben, zu; **I have taken a real** ~ **to him** er hat es mir angetan □ *a* ausgefallen; ~ **cakes and biscuits** Feingebäck *nt* □ *vt* (*believe*) meinen; (*imagine*) sich (*dat*) einbilden; (*fam: want*) Lust haben auf (+ *acc*); ~ **that!** stell dir vor! (*really*) tatsächlich! ~ **ˈdress** *n* Kostüm *nt*

fanfare /ˈfænfeə(r)/ *n* Fanfare *f*

fang /fæŋ/ *n* Fangzahn *m*; (*of snake*) Giftzahn *m*

fan: ~ **heater** *n* Heizlüfter *m*. ~**light** *n* Oberlicht *nt*

fantas|ize /ˈfæntəsaɪz/ *vi* phantasieren. ~**tic** /-ˈtæstɪk/ *a* phantastisch. ~**y** *n* Phantasie *f*; (*Mus*) Fantasie *f*

far /fɑː(r)/ *adv* weit; (*much*) viel; **by** ~ bei weitem; ~ **away** weit weg; **as** ~ **as I know** soviel ich weiß; **as** ~ **as the church** bis zur Kirche □ *a* **at the** ~ **end** am anderen Ende; **the F**~ **East** der Ferne Osten

farc|e /fɑːs/ *n* Farce *f*. ~**ical** *a* lächerlich

fare /feə(r)/ *n* Fahrpreis *m*; (*money*) Fahrgeld *nt*; (*food*) Kost *f*; **air** ~ Flugpreis *m*. ~**-dodger** /-dɒdʒə(r)/ *n* Schwarzfahrer *m*

farewell /feəˈwel/ *int* (*liter*) lebe wohl! □ *n* Lebewohl *nt*; ~ **dinner** Abschiedsessen *nt*

far-ˈfetched *a* weit hergeholt; **be** ~ an den Haaren herbeigezogen sein

farm /fɑːm/ *n* Bauernhof *m* □ *vi* Landwirtschaft betreiben □ *vt* bewirtschaften ⟨*land*⟩. ~**er** *n* Landwirt *m*

farm: ~**house** *n* Bauernhaus *nt*. ~**ing** *n* Landwirtschaft *f*. ~**yard** *n* Hof *m*

far: ~-'**reaching** *a* weit reichend. ~-'**sighted** *a* (*fig*) umsichtig; (*Amer: long-sighted*) weitsichtig
fart /fɑ:t/ *n* (*vulg*) Furz *m* □ *vi* (*vulg*) furzen
farther /'fɑ:ðə(r)/ *adv* weiter; ~ **off** weiter entfernt □ *a* **at the** ~ **end** am anderen Ende
fascinat|e /'fæsɪneɪt/ *vt* faszinieren. ~**ing** *a* faszinierend. ~**ion** /-'neɪʃn/ *n* Faszination *f*
fascis|m /'fæʃɪzm/ *n* Faschismus *m*. ~**t** *n* Faschist *m* □ *a* faschistisch
fashion /'fæʃn/ *n* Mode *f*; (*manner*) Art *f* □ *vt* machen; (*mould*) formen. ~**able** /-əbl/ *a*, -**bly** *adv* modisch; **be** ~**able** Mode sein
fast[1] /fɑ:st/ *a & adv* (-**er**, -**est**) schnell; (*firm*) fest; ⟨*colour*⟩ waschecht; **be** ~ ⟨*clock:*⟩ vorgehen; **be** ~ **asleep** fest schlafen
fast[2] *n* Fasten *nt* □ *vi* fasten
'**fastback** *n* (*Auto*) Fließheck *nt*
fasten /'fɑ:sn/ *vt* zumachen; (*fix*) befestigen (**to an** + *dat*); ~ **one's seatbelt** sich anschnallen. ~**er** *n*, ~**ing** *n* Verschluss *m*
fastidious /fə'stɪdɪəs/ *a* wählerisch; (*particular*) penibel
fat /fæt/ *a* (**fatter, fattest**) dick; ⟨*meat*⟩ fett □ *n* Fett *nt*
fatal /'feɪtl/ *a* tödlich; ⟨*error*⟩ verhängnisvoll. ~**ism** /-təlɪzm/ *n* Fatalismus *m*. ~**ist** /-təlist/ *n* Fatalist *m*. ~**ity** /fə'tæləti/ *n* Todesopfer *nt*. ~**ly** /-təlɪ/ *adv* tödlich
fate /feɪt/ *n* Schicksal *nt*. ~**ful** *a* verhängnisvoll
'**fat-head** *n* (*fam*) Dummkopf *m*
father /'fɑ:ðə(r)/ *n* Vater *m*; **F** ~ **Christmas** der Weihnachtsmann □ *vt* zeugen
father: ~**hood** *n* Vaterschaft *f*. ~-**in-law** *n* (*pl* ~**s-in-law**) Schwiegervater *m*. ~**ly** *a* väterlich
fathom /'fæðəm/ *n* (*Naut*) Faden *m* □ *vt* verstehen; ~ **out** ergründen
fatigue /fə'ti:g/ *n* Ermüdung *f* □ *vt* ermüden
fatten /'fætn/ *vt* mästen ⟨*animal*⟩. ~**ing** *a* **cream is** ~**ing** Sahne macht dick
fatty /'fætɪ/ *a* fett; ⟨*foods*⟩ fetthaltig
fatuous /'fætjʊəs/ *a*, -**ly** *adv* albern
faucet /fɔ:sɪt/ *n* (*Amer*) Wasserhahn *m*
fault /fɔ:lt/ *n* Fehler *m*; (*Techn*) Defekt *m*; (*Geol*) Verwerfung *f*; **at** ~ im Unrecht; **find** ~ **with** etwas auszusetzen haben an (+ *dat*); **it's your** ~ du bist schuld □ *vt* etwas auszusetzen haben an (+ *dat*). ~**less** *a*, -**ly** *adv* fehlerfrei
faulty /'fɔ:ltɪ/ *a* fehlerhaft
fauna /'fɔ:nə/ *n* Fauna *f*
favour /'feɪvə(r)/ *n* Gunst *f*; **I am in** ~ ich bin dafür; **do s.o. a** ~ jdm einen Gefallen tun □ *vt* begünstigen; (*prefer*) bevorzugen. ~**able** /-əbl/ *a*, -**bly** *adv* günstig; ⟨*reply*⟩ positiv
favourit|e /'feɪvərɪt/ *a* Lieblings- □ *n* Liebling *m*; (*Sport*) Favorit(in) *m*(*f*). ~**ism** *n* Bevorzugung *f*
fawn[1] /fɔ:n/ *a* rehbraun □ *n* Hirschkalb *nt*
fawn[2] *vi* sich einschmeicheln (**on** bei)
fax /fæks/ *n* Fax *nt* □ *vt* faxen (**s.o.** jdm). ~ **machine** *n* Faxgerät *nt*
fear /fɪə(r)/ *n* Furcht *f*, Angst *f* (**of** vor + *dat*); **no** ~! (*fam*) keine Angst! □ *vt/i* fürchten
fear|ful /'fɪəfl/ *a* besorgt; (*awful*) furchtbar. ~**less** *a*, -**ly** *adv* furchtlos. ~**some** /-səm/ *a* Furcht erregend
feas|ibility /fi:zə'bɪlətɪ/ *n* Durchführbarkeit *f*. ~**ible** *a* durchführbar; (*possible*) möglich
feast /fi:st/ *n* Festmahl *nt*; (*Relig*) Fest *nt* □ *vi* ~ **[on]** schmausen
feat /fi:t/ *n* Leistung *f*

feather /ˈfeðə(r)/ *n* Feder *f*
feature /ˈfiːtʃə(r)/ *n* Gesichtszug *m*; (*quality*) Merkmal *nt*; (*Journ*) Feature *nt* □ *vt* darstellen; ⟨*film:*⟩ in der Hauptrolle zeigen. ~ **film** *n* Hauptfilm *m*
February /ˈfebrʊərɪ/ *n* Februar *m*
feckless /ˈfeklɪs/ *a* verantwortungslos
fed /fed/ *see* **feed** □ *a* **be ~ up** (*fam*) die Nase voll haben (**with** von)
federal /ˈfedərəl/ *a* Bundes-
federation /fedəˈreɪʃn/ *n* Föderation *f*
fee /fiː/ *n* Gebühr *f*; (*professional*) Honorar *nt*
feeble /ˈfiːbl/ *a* (**-r, -st**), **-bly** *adv* schwach
feed /fiːd/ *n* Futter *nt*; (*for baby*) Essen *nt* □ *v* (*pt/pp* **fed**) □ *vt* füttern; (*support*) ernähren; (*into machine*) eingeben; speisen ⟨*computer*⟩ □ *vi* sich ernähren (**on** von)
ˈ**feedback** *n* Feedback *nt*
feel /fiːl/ *v* (*pt/pp* **felt**) □ *vt* fühlen; (*experience*) empfinden; (*think*) meinen □ *vi* sich fühlen; ~ **soft/hard** sich weich/hart anfühlen; **I ~ hot/ill** mir ist heiß/schlecht; **I don't ~ like it** ich habe keine Lust dazu. **~er** *n* Fühler *m*. **~ing** *n* Gefühl *nt*; **no hard ~ings** nichts für ungut
feet /fiːt/ *see* **foot**
feign /feɪn/ *vt* vortäuschen
feint /feɪnt/ *n* Finte *f*
feline /ˈfiːlaɪn/ *a* Katzen-; (*catlike*) katzenartig
fell1 /fel/ *vt* fällen
fell2 *see* **fall**
fellow /ˈfeləʊ/ *n* (*of society*) Mitglied *nt*; (*fam: man*) Kerl *m*
fellow: **~ˈcountryman** *n* Landsmann *m*. **~ men** *pl* Mitmenschen *pl*. **~ship** *n* Kameradschaft *f*; (*group*) Gesellschaft *f*
felony /ˈfelənɪ/ *n* Verbrechen *nt*
felt1 /felt/ *see* **feel**
felt2 *n* Filz *m*. **~[-tipped]** ˈ**pen** *n* Filzstift *m*
female /ˈfiːmeɪl/ *a* weiblich □ *nt* Weibchen *nt*; (*pej: woman*) Weib *nt*
femin|ine /ˈfemɪnɪn/ *a* weiblich □ *n* (*Gram*) Femininum *nt*. **~inity** /-ˈnɪnətɪ/ *n* Weiblichkeit *f*. **~ist** *a* feministisch □ *n* Feminist(in) *m*(*f*)
fenc|e /fens/ *n* Zaun *m*; (*fam: person*) Hehler *m* □ *vi* (*Sport*) fechten □ *vt* **~e in** einzäunen. **~er** *n* Fechter *m*. **~ing** *n* Zaun *m*; (*Sport*) Fechten *nt*
fend /fend/ *vi* ~ **for oneself** sich allein durchschlagen. ~ **off** *vt* abwehren
fender /ˈfendə(r)/ *n* Kaminvorsetzer *m*; (*Naut*) Fender *m*; (*Amer: wing*) Kotflügel *m*
fennel /ˈfenl/ *n* Fenchel *m*
ferment1 /ˈfɜːment/ *n* Erregung *f*
ferment2 /fəˈment/ *vi* gären □ *vt* gären lassen. **~ation** /fɜːmenˈteɪʃn/ *n* Gärung *f*
fern /fɜːn/ *n* Farn *m*
feroc|ious /fəˈrəʊʃəs/ *a* wild. **~ity** /-ˈrɒsətɪ/ *n* Wildheit *f*
ferret /ˈferɪt/ *n* Frettchen *nt*
ferry /ˈferɪ/ *n* Fähre *f* □ *vt* ~ **[across]** übersetzen
fertil|e /ˈfɜːtaɪl/ *a* fruchtbar. **~ity** /fɜːˈtɪlətɪ/ *n* Fruchtbarkeit *f*
fertilize /ˈfɜːtəlaɪz/ *vt* befruchten; düngen ⟨*land*⟩. **~r** *n* Dünger *m*
fervent /ˈfɜːvənt/ *a* leidenschaftlich
fervour /ˈfɜːvə(r)/ *n* Leidenschaft *f*
fester /ˈfestə(r)/ *vi* eitern
festival /ˈfestɪvl/ *n* Fest *nt*; (*Mus, Theat*) Festspiele *pl*
festiv|e /ˈfestɪv/ *a* festlich; **~e season** Festzeit. *f*. **~ities** /feˈstɪvətɪz/ *npl* Feierlichkeiten *pl*
festoon /feˈstuːn/ *vt* behängen (**with** mit)

fetch /fetʃ/ *vt* holen; (*collect*) abholen; (*be sold for*) einbringen
fetching /ˈfetʃɪŋ/ *a* anziehend
fête /feɪt/ *n* Fest *nt* □ *vt* feiern
fetish /ˈfetɪʃ/ *n* Fetisch *m*
fetter /ˈfetə(r)/ *vt* fesseln
fettle /ˈfetl/ *n* **in fine ~** in bester Form
feud /fju:d/ *n* Fehde *f*
feudal /ˈfju:dl/ *a* Feudal-
fever /ˈfi:və(r)/ *n* Fieber *nt*. **~ish** *a* fiebrig; (*fig*) fieberhaft
few /fju:/ *a* (**-er, -est**) wenige; **every ~ days** alle paar Tage □ *n* **a ~** ein paar; **quite a ~** ziemlich viele
fiancé /fɪˈɒnseɪ/ *n* Verlobte(r) *m*. **fiancée** *n* Verlobte *f*
fiasco /fɪˈæskəʊ/ *n* Fiasko *nt*
fib /fɪb/ *n* kleine Lüge; **tell a ~** schwindeln
fibre /ˈfaɪbə(r)/ *n* Faser *f*
fickle /ˈfɪkl/ *a* unbeständig
fiction /ˈfɪkʃn/ *n* Erfindung *f*; **[works of] ~** Erzählungsliteratur *f*. **~al** *a* erfunden
fictitious /fɪkˈtɪʃəs/ *a* [frei] erfunden
fiddle /ˈfɪdl/ *n* (*fam*) Geige *f*; (*cheating*) Schwindel *m* □ *vi* herumspielen (**with** mit) □ *vt* (*fam*) frisieren ⟨*accounts*⟩; (*arrange*) arrangieren
fiddly /ˈfɪdlɪ/ *a* knifflig
fidelity /fɪˈdelətɪ/ *n* Treue *f*
fidget /ˈfɪdʒɪt/ *vi* zappeln. **~y** *a* zappelig
field /fi:ld/ *n* Feld *nt*; (*meadow*) Wiese *f*; (*subject*) Gebiet *nt*
field: ~ events *npl* Sprung- und Wurfdisziplinen *pl*. **~-glasses** *npl* Feldstecher *m*. **F~ 'Marshal** *n* Feldmarschall *m*. **~work** *n* Feldforschung *f*
fiend /fi:nd/ *n* Teufel *m*. **~ish** *a* teuflisch
fierce /fɪəs/ *a* (**-r, -st**), **-ly** *adv* wild; (*fig*) heftig. **~ness** *n* Wildheit *f*; (*fig*) Heftigkeit *f*
fiery /ˈfaɪərɪ/ *a* (**-ier, -iest**) feurig
fifteen /fɪfˈti:n/ *a* fünfzehn □ *n* Fünfzehn *f*. **~th** *a* fünfzehnte(r,s)
fifth /fɪfθ/ *a* fünfte(r,s)
fiftieth /ˈfɪftɪɪθ/ *a* fünfzigste(r,s)
fifty /ˈfɪftɪ/ *a* fünfzig
fig /fɪg/ *n* Feige *f*
fight /faɪt/ *n* Kampf *m*; (*brawl*) Schlägerei *f*; (*between children, dogs*) Rauferei *f* □ *v* (*pt/pp* **fought**) □ *vt* kämpfen gegen; (*fig*) bekämpfen □ *vi* kämpfen; (*brawl*) sich schlagen; ⟨*children, dogs:*⟩ sich raufen. **~er** *n* Kämpfer *m*; (*Aviat*) Jagdflugzeug *nt*. **~ing** *n* Kampf *m*
figment /ˈfɪgmənt/ *n* **~ of the imagination** Hirngespinst *nt*
figurative /ˈfɪgjərətɪv/ *a*, **-ly** *adv* bildlich, übertragen
figure /ˈfɪgə(r)/ *n* (*digit*) Ziffer *f*; (*number*) Zahl *f*; (*sum*) Summe *f*; (*carving, sculpture, woman's*) Figur *f*; (*form*) Gestalt *f*; (*illustration*) Abbildung *f*; **~ of speech** Redefigur *f*; **good at ~s** gut im Rechnen □ *vi* (*appear*) erscheinen □ *vt* (*Amer: think*) glauben. **~ out** *vt* ausrechnen
figure: ~-head *n* Galionsfigur *f*; (*fig*) Repräsentationsfigur *f*. **~ skating** *n* Eiskunstlauf *m*
filament /ˈfɪləmənt/ *n* Faden *m*; (*Electr*) Glühfaden *m*
filch /fɪltʃ/ *vt* (*fam*) klauen
file[1] /faɪl/ *n* Akte *f*; (*for documents*) [Akten]ordner *m* □ *vt* ablegen ⟨*documents*⟩; (*Jur*) einreichen
file[2] *n* (*line*) Reihe *f*; **in single ~** im Gänsemarsch
file[3] *n* (*Techn*) Feile *f* □ *vt* feilen
filigree /ˈfɪlɪgri:/ *n* Filigran *nt*
filings /ˈfaɪlɪŋz/ *npl* Feilspäne *pl*
fill /fɪl/ *n* **eat one's ~** sich satt essen □ *vt* füllen; plombieren ⟨*tooth*⟩ □ *vi* sich füllen. **~ in** *vt* auffüllen; ausfüllen ⟨*form*⟩. **~ out** *vt* ausfüllen ⟨*form*⟩. **~ up** *vi* sich füllen □ *vt* vollfüllen; (*Auto*) volltanken; ausfüllen ⟨*form*⟩

fillet /ˈfɪlɪt/ *n* Filet *nt* □ *vt* (*pt/pp* **filleted**) entgräten
filling /ˈfɪlɪŋ/ *n* Füllung *f*; (*of tooth*) Plombe *f*. **~ station** *n* Tankstelle *f*
filly /ˈfɪlɪ/ *n* junge Stute *f*
film /fɪlm/ *n* Film *m*; (*Culin*) **[cling] ~** Klarsichtfolie *f* □ *vt/i* filmen; verfilmen ⟨*book*⟩. **~ star** *n* Filmstar *m*
filter /ˈfɪltə(r)/ *n* Filter *m* □ *vt* filtern. **~ through** *vi* durchsickern. **~ tip** *n* Filter *m*; (*cigarette*) Filterzigarette *f*
filth /fɪlθ/ *n* Dreck *m*. **~y** *a* (**-ier, -iest**) dreckig
fin /fɪn/ *n* Flosse *f*
final /ˈfaɪnl/ *a* letzte(r,s); (*conclusive*) endgültig; **~ result** Endresultat *nt* □ *n* (*Sport*) Finale *nt*, Endspiel *nt*; **~s** *pl* (*Univ*) Abschlussprüfung *f*
finale /fɪˈnɑːlɪ/ *n* Finale *nt*
final|ist /ˈfaɪnəlɪst/ *n* Finalist(in) *m(f)*. **~ity** /-ˈnælətɪ/ *n* Endgültigkeit *f*
final|ize /ˈfaɪnəlaɪz/ *vt* endgültig festlegen. **~ly** *adv* schließlich
finance /faɪˈnæns/ *n* Finanz *f* □ *vt* finanzieren
financial /faɪˈnænʃl/ *a*, **-ly** *adv* finanziell
finch /fɪntʃ/ *n* Fink *m*
find /faɪnd/ *n* Fund *m* □ *vt* (*pt/pp* **found**) finden; (*establish*) feststellen; **go and ~** holen; **try to ~** suchen; **~ guilty** (*Jur*) schuldig sprechen. **~ out** *vt* herausfinden; (*learn*) erfahren □ *vi* (*enquire*) sich erkundigen
findings /ˈfaɪndɪŋz/ *npl* Ergebnisse *pl*
fine[1] /faɪn/ *n* Geldstrafe *f* □ *vt* zu einer Geldstrafe verurteilen
fine[2] *a* (**-r, -st,**) **-ly** *adv* fein; ⟨*weather*⟩ schön; **he's ~** es geht ihm gut □ *adv* gut; **cut it ~** (*fam*) sich (*dat*) wenig Zeit lassen. **~ arts** *npl* schöne Künste *pl*
finery /ˈfaɪnərɪ/ *n* Putz *m*, Staat *m*
finesse /fɪˈnes/ *n* Gewandtheit *f*
finger /ˈfɪŋgə(r)/ *n* Finger *m* □ *vt* anfassen
finger: ~-mark *n* Fingerabdruck *m*. **~-nail** *n* Fingernagel *m*. **~print** *n* Fingerabdruck *m*. **~tip** *n* Fingerspitze *f*; **have sth at one's ~tips** etw im kleinen Finger haben
finicky /ˈfɪnɪkɪ/ *a* knifflig; (*choosy*) wählerisch
finish /ˈfɪnɪʃ/ *n* Schluss *m*; (*Sport*) Finish *nt*; (*line*) Ziel *nt*; (*of product*) Ausführung *f* □ *vt* beenden; (*use up*) aufbrauchen; **~ one's drink** austrinken; **~ reading** zu Ende lesen □ *vi* fertig werden; ⟨*performance:*⟩ zu Ende sein; ⟨*runner:*⟩ durchs Ziel gehen
finite /ˈfaɪnaɪt/ *a* begrenzt
Finland /ˈfɪnlənd/ *n* Finnland *nt*
Finn /fɪn/ *n* Finne *m*/ Finnin *f*. **~ish** *a* finnisch
fiord /fjɔːd/ *n* Fjord *m*
fir /fɜː(r)/ *n* Tanne *f*
fire /ˈfaɪə(r)/ *n* Feuer *nt*; (*forest, house*) Brand *m*; **be on ~** brennen; **catch ~** Feuer fangen; **set ~ to** anzünden; ⟨*arsonist:*⟩ in Brand stecken; **under ~** unter Beschuss □ *vt* brennen ⟨*pottery*⟩; abfeuern ⟨*shot*⟩; schießen mit ⟨*gun*⟩; (*fam: dismiss*) feuern □ *vi* schießen (**at** auf + *acc*); ⟨*engine:*⟩ anspringen
fire: ~ alarm *n* Feueralarm *m*; (*apparatus*) Feuermelder *m*. **~arm** *n* Schusswaffe *f*. **~ brigade** *n* Feuerwehr *f*. **~-engine** *n* Löschfahrzeug *nt*. **~-escape** *n* Feuertreppe *f*. **~ extinguisher** *n* Feuerlöscher *m*. **~man** *n* Feuerwehrmann *m*. **~place** *n* Kamin *m*. **~side** *n* **by** *or* **at the ~side** am Kamin. **~ station** *n* Feuerwache *f*. **~wood** *n* Brennholz *nt*. **~work** *n* Feuerwerkskörper *m*; **~works** *pl* (*display*) Feuerwerk *nt*
ˈ**firing squad** *n* Erschießungskommando *nt*

firm[1] /fɜːm/ *n* Firma *f*

firm[2] *a* (**-er, -est**), **-ly** *adv* fest; (*resolute*) entschlossen; (*strict*) streng

first /fɜːst/ *a & n* erste(r,s); **at ~** zuerst; **who's ~?** wer ist der Erste? **at ~ sight** auf den ersten Blick; **for the ~ time** zum ersten Mal; **from the ~** von Anfang an □ *adv* zuerst; (*firstly*) erstens

first: ~ 'aid *n* erste Hilfe. **~-'aid kit** *n* Verbandkasten *m*. **~-class** *a* erstklassig; (*Rail*) erster Klasse □ /-'-/ *adv* ⟨*travel*⟩ erster Klasse. **~ e'dition** *n* Erstausgabe *f*. **~ 'floor** *n* erster Stock; (*Amer: groundfloor*) Erdgeschoss *nt*. **~ly** *adv* erstens. **~name** *n* Vorname *m*. **~-rate** *a* erstklassig

fish /fɪʃ/ *n* Fisch *m* □ *vt/i* fischen; (*with rod*) angeln. **~ out** *vt* herausfischen

fish: ~bone *n* Gräte *f*. **~erman** *n* Fischer *m*. **~-farm** *n* Fischzucht *f*. **~ 'finger** *n* Fischstäbchen *nt*

fishing /'fɪʃɪŋ/ *n* Fischerei *f*. **~ boat** *n* Fischerboot *nt*. **~-rod** *n* Angel[rute] *f*

fish: ~monger /-mʌŋgə(r)/ *n* Fischhändler *m*. **~-slice** *n* Fischheber *m*. **~y** *a* Fisch-; (*fam: suspicious*) verdächtig

fission /'fɪʃn/ *n* (*Phys*) Spaltung *f*

fist /fɪst/ *n* Faust *f*

fit[1] /fɪt/ *n* (*attack*) Anfall *m*

fit[2] *a* (**fitter, fittest**) (*suitable*) geeignet; (*healthy*) gesund; (*Sport*) fit; **~ to eat** essbar; **keep ~** sich fit halten; **see ~** es für angebracht halten (**to** zu)

fit[3] *n* (*of clothes*) Sitz *m*; **be a good ~** gut passen □ *v* (*pt/pp* **fitted**) □ *vi* (*be the right size*) passen □ *vt* anbringen (**to** an + *dat*); (*install*) einbauen; ⟨*clothes:*⟩ passen (+ *dat*); **~ with** versehen mit. **~ in** *vi* hineinpassen; (*adapt*) sich einfügen (**with** in + *acc*) □ *vt* (*accommodate*) unterbringen

fit|ful /'fɪtfl/ *a*, **-ly** *adv* ⟨*sleep*⟩ unruhig. **~ment** *n* Einrichtungsgegenstand *m*; (*attachment*) Zusatzgeränt *nt*. **~ness** *n* Eignung *f*; **[physical] ~ness** Gesundheit *f*; (*Sport*) Fitness *f*. **~ted** *a* eingebaut; ⟨*garment*⟩ tailliert

fitted: ~ 'carpet *n* Teppichboden *m*. **~ 'cupboard** *n* Einbauschrank *m*. **~ 'kitchen** *n* Einbauküche *f*. **~ 'sheet** *n* Spannlaken *nt*

fitter /'fɪtə(r)/ *n* Monteur *m*

fitting /'fɪtɪŋ/ *a* passend □ *n* (*of clothes*) Anprobe *f*; (*of shoes*) Weite *f*; (*Techn*) Zubehörteil *nt*; **~s** *pl* Zubehör *nt*. **~ room** *n* Anprobekabine *f*

five /faɪv/ *a* fünf □ *n* Fünf *f*. **~r** *n* Fünfpfundschein *m*

fix /fɪks/ *n* (*sl: drugs*) Fix *m*; **be in a ~** (*fam*) in der Klemme sitzen □ *vt* befestigen (**to** an + *dat*); (*arrange*) festlegen; (*repair*) reparieren; (*Phot*) fixieren; **~ a meal** (*Amer*) Essen machen

fixation /fɪk'seɪʃn/ *n* Fixierung *f*

fixed /'fɪkst/ *a* fest

fixture /'fɪkstʃə(r)/ *n* (*Sport*) Veranstaltung *f*; **~s and fittings** zu einer Wohnung gehörende Einrichtungen *pl*

fizz /fɪz/ *vi* sprudeln

fizzle /'fɪzl/ *vi* **~ out** verpuffen

fizzy /'fɪzɪ/ *a* sprudelnd. **~ drink** *n* Brause[limonade] *f*

flabbergasted /'flæbəgɑːstɪd/ *a* **be ~** platt sein (*fam*)

flabby /'flæbɪ/ *a* schlaff

flag[1] /flæg/ *n* Fahne *f*; (*Naut*) Flagge *f* □ *vt* (*pt/pp* **flagged**) **~ down** anhalten ⟨*taxi*⟩

flag[2] *vi* (*pt/pp* **flagged**) ermüden

flagon /'flægən/ *n* Krug *m*

'flag-pole *n* Fahnenstange *f*

flagrant /'fleɪgrənt/ *a* flagrant

'flagstone *n* [Pflaster]platte *f*

flair /fleə(r)/ *n* Begabung *f*

flake /fleɪk/ *n* Flocke *f* □ *vi* **~ [off]** abblättern

flaky /ˈfleɪkɪ/ *a* blättrig. **~ pastry** *n* Blätterteig *m*
flamboyant /flæmˈbɔɪənt/ *a* extravagant
flame /fleɪm/ *n* Flamme *f*
flammable /ˈflæməbl/ *a* feuergefährlich
flan /flæn/ *n* **[fruit] ~** Obsttorte *f*
flank /flæŋk/ *n* Flanke *f* □ *vt* flankieren
flannel /ˈflænl/ *n* Flanell *m*; ⟨*for washing*⟩ Waschlappen *m*
flannelette /flænəˈlet/ *n* (*Tex*) Biber *m*
flap /flæp/ *n* Klappe *f*; **in a ~** (*fam*) aufgeregt □ *v* (*pt/pp* **flapped**) *vi* flattern; (*fam*) sich aufregen □ *vt* **~ its wings** mit den Flügeln schlagen
flare /fleə(r)/ *n* Leuchtsignal *nt*. □ *vi* **~ up** auflodern; (*fam: get angry*) aufbrausen. **~d** *a* ⟨*garment*⟩ ausgestellt
flash /flæʃ/ *n* Blitz *m*; **in a ~** (*fam*) im Nu □ *vi* blitzen; (*repeatedly*) blinken; **~ past** vorbeirasen □ *vt* aufleuchten lassen; **~ one's headlights** die Lichthupe betätigen
flash: ~back *n* Rückblende *f*. **~bulb** *n* (*Phot*) Blitzbirne *f*. **~er** *n* (*Auto*) Blinker *m*. **~light** *n* (*Phot*) Blitzlicht *nt*; (*Amer: torch*) Taschenlampe *f*. **~y** a auffällig
flask /flɑːsk/ *n* Flasche *f*; (*Chem*) Kolben *m*; (*vacuum* **~**) Thermosflasche (P) *f*
flat /flæt/ *a* (**flatter, flattest**) flach; ⟨*surface*⟩ eben; ⟨*refusal*⟩ glatt; ⟨*beer*⟩ schal; ⟨*battery*⟩ verbraucht/ (*Auto*) leer; ⟨*tyre*⟩ platt; (*Mus*) **A ~** As *nt*; **B ~** B *nt* □ *n* Wohnung *f*; (*Mus*) Erniedrigungszeichen *nt*; (*fam: puncture*) Reifenpanne *f*
flat: ~ ˈfeet *npl* Plattfüße *pl*. **~fish** *n* Plattfisch *m*. **~ly** *adv* ⟨*refuse*⟩ glatt. **~ rate** *n* Einheitspreis *m*
flatten /ˈflætn/ *vt* platt drücken
flatter /ˈflætə(r)/ *vt* schmeicheln (+ *dat*). **~y** *n* Schmeichelei *f*
flat ˈtyre *n* Reifenpanne *f*
flatulence /flætjʊləns/ *n* Blähungen *pl*
flaunt /flɔːnt/ *vt* prunken mit
flautist /ˈflɔːtɪst/ *n* Flötist(in) *m(f)*
flavour /ˈfleɪvə(r)/ *n* Geschmack *m* □ *vt* abschmecken. **~ing** *n* Aroma *nt*
flaw /flɔː/ *n* Fehler *m*. **~less** *a* tadellos; ⟨*complexion*⟩ makellos
flax /flæks/ *n* Flachs *m*. **~en** *a* flachsblond
flea /fliː/ *n* Floh *m*. **~ market** *n* Flohmarkt *m*
fleck /flek/ *n* Tupfen *m*
fled /fled/ *see* **flee**
flee /fliː/ *v* (*pt/pp* **fled**) □ *vi* fliehen (**from** vor + *dat*) □ *vt* flüchten aus
fleec|e /fliːs/ *n* Vlies *nt* □ *vt* (*fam*) schröpfen. **~y** *a* flauschig
fleet /fliːt/ *n* Flotte *f*; (*of cars*) Wagenpark *m*
fleeting /ˈfliːtɪŋ/ *a* flüchtig
Flemish /ˈflemɪʃ/ *a* flämisch
flesh /fleʃ/ *n* Fleisch *nt*; **in the ~** (*fam*) in Person. **~y** *a* fleischig
flew /fluː/ *see* **fly**[2]
flex[1] /fleks/ *vt* anspannen ⟨*muscle*⟩
flex[2] *n* (*Electr*) Schnur *f*
flexib|ility /fleksəˈbɪlətɪ/ *n* Biegsamkeit *f*; (*fig*) Flexibilität *f*. **~le** *a* biegsam; (*fig*) flexibel
ˈflexitime /ˈfleksɪ-/ *n* Gleitzeit *f*
flick /flɪk/ *vt* schnippen. **~ through** *vi* schnell durchblättern
flicker /ˈflɪkə(r)/ *vi* flackern
flier /ˈflaɪə(r)/ *n* = **flyer**
flight[1] /flaɪt/ *n* (*fleeing*) Flucht *f*; **take ~** die Flucht ergreifen
flight[2] *n* (*flying*) Flug *m*; **~ of stairs** Treppe *f*
flight: ~ path *n* Flugschneise *f*. **~ recorder** *n* Flugschreiber *m*

flighty /ˈflaɪtɪ/ *a* (**-ier, -iest**) flatterhaft
flimsy /ˈflɪmzɪ/ *a* (**-ier, -iest**) dünn; ⟨*excuse*⟩ fadenscheinig
flinch /flɪntʃ/ *vi* zurückzucken
fling /flɪŋ/ *n* **have a ~** (*fam*) sich austoben □ *vt* (*pt/pp* **flung**) schleudern
flint /flɪnt/ *n* Feuerstein *m*
flip /flɪp/ *vt/i* schnippen; **~ through** durchblättern
flippant /ˈflɪpənt/ *a*, **-ly** *adv* leichtfertig
flipper /ˈflɪpə(r)/ *n* Flosse *f*
flirt /flɜːt/ *n* kokette Frau *f* □ *vi* flirten
flirtat|ion /flɜːˈteɪʃn/ *n* Flirt *m*. **~ious** /-ʃəs/ *a* kokett
flit /flɪt/ *vi* (*pt/pp* **flitted**) flattern
float /fləʊt/ *n* Schwimmer *m*; (*in procession*) Festwagen *m*; (*money*) Wechselgeld *nt* □ *vi* ⟨*thing:*⟩ schwimmen; ⟨*person:*⟩ sich treiben lassen; (*in air*) schweben; (*Comm*) floaten
flock /flɒk/ *n* Herde *f*; (*of birds*) Schwarm *m* □ *vi* strömen
flog /flɒg/ *vt* (*pt/pp* **flogged**) auspeitschen; (*fam: sell*) verkloppen
flood /flʌd/ *n* Überschwemmung *f*; (*fig*) Flut *f*; **be in ~** ⟨*river:*⟩ Hochwasser führen □ *vt* überschwemmen □ *vi* ⟨*river:*⟩ über die Ufer treten
ˈ**floodlight** *n* Flutlicht *nt* □ *vt* (*pt/pp* **floodlit**) anstrahlen
floor /flɔː(r)/ *n* Fußboden *m*; (*storey*) Stock *m* □ *vt* (*baffle*) verblüffen
floor: ~ board *n* Dielenbrett *nt*. **~-cloth** *n* Scheuertuch *nt*. **~-polish** *n* Bohnerwachs *nt*. **~ show** *n* Kabarettvorstellung *f*
flop /flɒp/ *n* (*fam*) (*failure*) Reinfall *m*; (*Theat*) Durchfall *m* □ *vi* (*pt/pp* **flopped**) (*fam*) (*fail*) durchfallen; **~ down** sich plumpsen lassen
floppy /ˈflɒpɪ/ *a* schlapp. **~ ˈdisc** *n* Diskette *f*
flora /ˈflɔːrə/ *n* Flora *f*
floral /ˈflɔːrl/ *a* Blumen-
florid /ˈflɒrɪd/ *a* ⟨*complexion*⟩ gerötet; ⟨*style*⟩ blumig
florist /ˈflɒrɪst/ *n* Blumenhändler(in) *m*(*f*)
flounce /flaʊns/ *n* Volant *m* □ *vi* **~ out** hinausstolzieren
flounder[1] /ˈflaʊndə(r)/ *vi* zappeln
flounder[2] *n* (*fish*) Flunder *f*
flour /ˈflaʊə(r)/ *n* Mehl *nt*
flourish /ˈflʌrɪʃ/ *n* große Geste *f*; (*scroll*) Schnörkel *m* □ *vi* gedeihen; (*fig*) blühen □ *vt* schwenken
floury /ˈflaʊərɪ/ *a* mehlig
flout /flaʊt/ *vt* missachten
flow /fləʊ/ *n* Fluss *m*; (*of traffic, blood*) Strom *m* □ *vi* fließen
flower /ˈflaʊə(r)/ *n* Blume *f* □ *vi* blühen
flower: ~-bed *n* Blumenbeet *nt*. **~ed** *a* geblümt. **~pot** *n* Blumentopf *m*. **~y** *a* blumig
flown /fləʊn/ *see* **fly**[2]
flu /fluː/ *n* (*fam*) Grippe *f*
fluctuat|e /ˈflʌktjʊeɪt/ *vi* schwanken. **~ion** /-ˈeɪʃn/ *n* Schwankung *f*
fluent /ˈfluːənt/ *a*, **-ly** *adv* fließend
fluff /flʌf/ *n* Fusseln *pl*; (*down*) Flaum *m*. **~y** *a* (**-ier, -iest**) flauschig
fluid /ˈfluːɪd/ *a* flüssig, (*fig*) veränderlich □ *n* Flüssigkeit *f*
fluke /fluːk/ *n* [glücklicher] Zufall *m*
flung /flʌŋ/ *see* **fling**
flunk /flʌŋk/ *vt/i* (*Amer, fam*) durchfallen (*in* + *dat*)
fluorescent /flʊəˈresnt/ *a* fluoreszierend; **~ lighting** Neonbeleuchtung *f*
fluoride /ˈflʊəraɪd/ *n* Fluor *nt*
flurry /ˈflʌrɪ/ *n* (*snow*) Gestöber *nt*; (*fig*) Aufregung *f*
flush /flʌʃ/ *n* (*blush*) Erröten *nt* □ *vi* rot werden □ *vt* spülen □ *a* in einer Ebene (**with** mit); (*fam: affluent*) gut bei Kasse

flustered /ˈflʌstəd/ *a* nervös
flute /fluːt/ *n* Flöte *f*
flutter /ˈflʌtə(r)/ *n* Flattern *nt* □ *vi* flattern
flux /flʌks/ *n* **in a state of ~** im Fluss
fly1 /flaɪ/ *n* (*pl* **flies**) Fliege *f*
fly2 *v* (*pt* **flew**, *pp* **flown**) □ *vi* fliegen; ⟨*flag:*⟩ wehen; (*rush*) sausen □ *vt* fliegen; führen ⟨*flag*⟩
fly3 *n* & **flies** *pl* (*on trousers*) Hosenschlitz *m*
flyer /ˈflaɪə(r)/ *n* Flieger(in) *m(f)*; (*Amer: leaflet*) Flugblatt *nt*
flying: ~ 'buttress *n* Strebebogen *m*. **~ 'saucer** *n* fliegende Untertasse *f*. **~ 'visit** *n* Stippvisite *f*
fly: ~ leaf *n* Vorsatzblatt *nt*. **~over** *n* Überführung *f*
foal /fəʊl/ *n* Fohlen *nt*
foam /fəʊm/ *n* Schaum *m*; (*synthetic*) Schaumstoff *m* □ *vi* schäumen. **~ 'rubber** *n* Schaumgummi *m*
fob /fɒb/ *vt* (*pt/pp* **fobbed**) **~ sth off** etw andrehen (**on s.o.** jdm); **~ s.o. off** jdn abspeisen (**with** mit)
focal /ˈfəʊkl/ *n* Brenn-
focus /ˈfəʊkəs/ *n* Brennpunkt *m*; **in ~** scharf eingestellt □ *v* (*pt/pp* **focused** *or* **focussed**) □ *vt* einstellen (**on** auf + *acc*); (*fig*) konzentrieren (**on** auf + *acc*); □ *vi* (*fig*) sich konzentrieren (**on** auf + *acc*)
fodder /ˈfɒdə(r)/ *n* Futter *nt*
foe /fəʊ/ *n* Feind *m*
foetus /ˈfiːtəs/ *n* (*pl*-**tuses**) Fötus *m*
fog /fɒg/ *n* Nebel *m*
foggy /ˈfɒgɪ/ *a* (**foggier, foggiest**) neblig
'fog-horn *n* Nebelhorn *nt*
fogy /ˈfəʊgɪ/ *n* **old ~** alter Knacker *m*
foible /ˈfɔɪbl/ *n* Eigenart *f*
foil1 /fɔɪl/ *n* Folie *f*; (*Culin*) Alufolie *f*
foil2 *vt* (*thwart*) vereiteln
foil3 *n* (*Fencing*) Florett *nt*
foist /fɔɪst/ *vt* andrehen (**on s.o.** jdm)
fold1 /fəʊld/ *n* (*for sheep*) Pferch *m*
fold2 *n* Falte *f*; (*in paper*) Kniff *m* □ *vt* falten; **~ one's arms** die Arme verschränken □ *vi* sich falten lassen; (*fail*) eingehen. **~ up** *vt* zusammenfalten; zusammenklappen ⟨*chair*⟩ □ *vi* sich zusammenfalten/-klappen lassen; (*fam*) ⟨*business:*⟩ eingehen
fold|er /ˈfəʊldə(r)/ *n* Mappe *f*. **~ing** *a* Klapp-
foliage /ˈfəʊlɪɪdʒ/ *n* Blätter *pl*; (*of tree*) Laub *nt*
folk /fəʊk/ *npl* Leute *pl*
folk: ~-dance *n* Volkstanz *m*. **~lore** *n* Folklore *f*. **~-song** *n* Volkslied *nt*
follow /ˈfɒləʊ/ *vt/i* folgen (+ *dat*); (*pursue*) verfolgen; (*in vehicle*) nachfahren (+ *dat*); **~ suit** (*fig*) dasselbe tun. **~ up** *vt* nachgehen (+ *dat*)
follow|er /ˈfɒləʊə(r)/ *n* Anhänger(in) *m(f)*. **~ing** *a* folgend □ *n* Folgende(s) *nt*; (*supporters*) Anhängerschaft *f* □ *prep* im Anschluss an (+ *acc*)
folly /ˈfɒlɪ/ *n* Torheit *f*
fond /fɒnd/ *a* (**-er, -est**), **-ly** *adv* liebevoll; **be ~ of** gern haben; gern essen ⟨*food*⟩
fondle /ˈfɒndl/ *vt* liebkosen
fondness /ˈfɒndnɪs/ *n* Liebe *f* (**for** zu)
font /fɒnt/ *n* Taufstein *m*
food /fuːd/ *n* Essen *nt*; (*for animals*) Futter *nt*; (*groceries*) Lebensmittel *pl*
food: ~ mixer *n* Küchenmaschine *f*. **~ poisoning** *n* Lebensmittelvergiftung *f*. **~ processor** *n* Küchenmaschine *f*. **~ value** *n* Nährwert *m*
fool1 /fuːl/ *n* (*Culin*) Fruchtcreme *f*
fool2 *n* Narr *m*; **you are a ~** du bist dumm; **make a ~ of oneself**

sich lächerlich machen □ *vt* hereinlegen □ *vi* ~ **around** herumalbern

'fool|hardy *a* tollkühn. **~ish** *a*, **-ly** *adv* dumm. **~ishness** *n* Dummheit *f*. **~proof** *a* narrensicher

foot /fʊt/ *n* (*pl* **feet**) Fuß *m*; (*measure*) Fuß *m* (*30,48 cm*); (*of bed*) Fußende *nt*; **on ~** zu Fuß; **on one's feet** auf den Beinen; **put one's ~ in it** (*fam*) ins Fettnäpfchen treten

foot: ~-and-'mouth disease *n* Maul- und Klauenseuche *f*. **~ball** *n* Fußball *m*. **~baller** *n* Fußballspieler *m*. **~ball pools** *npl* Fußballtoto *nt*. **~-brake** *n* Fußbremse *f*. **~-bridge** *n* Fußgängerbrücke *f*. **~hills** *npl* Vorgebirge *nt*. **~hold** *n* Halt *m*. **~ing** *n* Halt *m*: (*fig*) Basis *f*. **~lights** *npl* Rampenlicht *nt*. **~man** *n* Lakai *m*. **~note** *n* Fußnote *f*. **~path** *n* Fußweg *m*. **~print** *n* Fußabdruck *m*. **~step** *n* Schritt *m*; **follow in s.o.'s ~steps** (*fig*) in jds Fußstapfen treten. **~stool** *n* Fußbank *f*. **~wear** *n* Schuhwerk *nt*

for /fə(r), *betont* fɔ:(r)/ *prep* für (+ *acc*); ⟨*send, long*⟩ nach; ⟨*ask, fight*⟩ um; **what ~?** wozu? **~ supper** zum Abendessen; **~ nothing** umsonst; **~ all that** trotz allem; **~ this reason** aus diesem Grund; **~ a month** einen Monat; **I have lived here ~ ten years** ich wohne seit zehn Jahren hier □ *conj* denn

forage /'fɒrɪdʒ/ *n* **Futter** *nt* □ *vi* **~ for** suchen nach

forbade /fə'bæd/ *see* **forbid**

forbear|ance /fɔ:'beərəns/ *n* Nachsicht *f*. **~ing** *a* nachsichtig

forbid /fə'bɪd/ *vt* (*pt* **forbade**, *pp* **forbidden**) verbieten (**s.o.** jdm). **~ding** *a* bedrohlich; (*stern*) streng

force /fɔ:s/ *n* Kraft *f*; (*of blow*) **Wucht** *f*; (*violence*) **Gewalt** *f*; **in ~** gültig; (*in large numbers*) in großer Zahl; **come into ~** in Kraft treten; **the ~s** *pl* die Streitkräfte *pl* □ *vt* **zwingen**; (*break open*) aufbrechen; **~ sth on s.o.** jdm etw aufrdrängen

forced /fɔ:st/ *a* **gezwungen**; **~ landing** Notlandung *f*

force: ~-'feed *vt* (*pt/pp* **-fed**) zwangsernähren. **~ful** *a*, **-ly** *adv* energisch

forceps /'fɔ:seps/ *n inv* Zange *f*

forcibl|e /'fɔ:səbl/ *a* gewaltsam. **~y** *adv* mit Gewalt

ford /fɔ:d/ *n* **Furt** *f* □ *vt* durchwaten; (*in vehicle*) durchfahren

fore /fɔ:(r)/ *a* vordere(r,s) □ *n* **to the ~** im Vordergrund

fore: ~arm *n* Unterarm *m*. **~boding** /-'bəʊdɪŋ/ *n* Vorahnung *f*. **~cast** *n* Voraussage *f*; (*for weather*) Vorhersage *f* □ *vt* (*pt/pp* **~cast**) voraussagen, vorhersagen. **~court** *n* Vorhof *m*. **~fathers** *npl* Vorfahren *pl*. **~finger** *n* Zeigefinger *m*. **~front** *n* **be in the ~front** führend sein. **~gone** *a* **be a ~gone conclusion** von vornherein feststehen. **~ground** *n* Vodergrund *m*. **~head** /'fɒrɪd/ *n* Stirn *f*. **~hand** *n* Vorhand *f*

foreign /'fɒrən/ *a* ausländisch; ⟨*country*⟩ fremd; **he is ~er** ist Ausländer. **~ currency** *n* Devisen *pl*. **~er** *n* Ausländer(in) *m(f)*. **~ language** *n* Fremdsprache *f*

Foreign: ~ Office *n* ≈ Außenministerium *nt*. **~ 'Secretary** *n* ≈ Außenminister *m*

fore: ~leg *n* Vorderbein *nt*. **~man** *n* Vorarbeiter *m*. **~most** *a* führend □ *adv* **first and ~most** zuallererst. **~name** *n* Vorname *m*

forensic /fə'rensɪk/ *a* **~ medicine** Gerichtsmedizin *f*

'forerunner *n* Voläufer *m*

fore'see *vt* (*pt* **-saw**, *pp* **-seen**) voraussehen, vorhersehen. **~able** /-əbl/ *a* **in the ~able future** in absehbarer Zeit

'foresight *n* Weitblick *m*
forest /'fɒrɪstrɪ/ *n* Wald *m*. **~er** *n* Förster *m*
fore'stall *vt* zuvorkommen (+ *dat*)
forestry /'fɒrɪstrɪ/ *n* Forstwirtschaft *f*
'foretaste *n* Vorgeschmack *m*
fore'tell *vt* (*pt/pp* **-told**) vorhersagen
forever /fə'revə(r)/ *adv* für immer
fore'warn *vt* vorher warnen
foreword /'fɔ:wɜ:d/ *n* Vorwort *nt*
forfeit /'fɔ:fɪt/ *n* (*in game*) Pfand *nt* □ *vt* verwirken
forgave /fə'geɪv/ *see* **forgive**
forge[1] /fɔ:dʒ/ *vi* **~ ahead** (*fig*) Fortschritte machen
forge[2] *n* Schmiede *f* □ *vt* schmieden; (*counterfeit*) fälschen. **~r** *n* Fälscher *m*. **~ry** *n* Fälschung *f*
forget /fə'get/ *vt/i* (*pt* **-got**, *pp* **-gotten**) vergessen; verlernen ⟨*language, skill*⟩. **~ful** *a* vergesslich. **~fulness** *n* Vergesslichkeit *f*. **~-me-not** *n* Vergissmeinnicht *nt*
forgive /fə'gɪv/ *vt* (*pt* **-gave**, *pp* **-given**) **~ s.o. for sth** jdm etw vergeben *od* verzeihen. **~ness** *n* Vergebung *f*, Verzeihung *f*
forgo /fɔ:'gəʊ/ *vt* (*pt* **-went**, *pp* **-gone**) verzichten auf (+ *acc*)
forgot(ten) /fə'gɒt(n)/ *see* **forget**
fork /fɔ:k/ *n* Gabel *f*; (*in road*) Gabelung *f* □ *vi* ⟨*road:*⟩ sich gabeln; **~ right** rechts abzweigen. **~ out** *vt* (*fam*) blechen
fork-lift 'truck *n* Gabelstapler *m*
forlorn /fə'lɔ:n/ *a* verlassen; ⟨*hope*⟩ schwach
form /fɔ:m/ *n* Form *f*; (*document*) Formular *nt*; (*bench*) Bank *f*; (*Sch*) Klasse *f* □ *vt* formen (**into** zu); (*create*) bilden □ *vi* sich bilden; ⟨*idea:*⟩ Gestalt annehmen
formal /'fɔ:ml/ *a*, **-ly** *adv* formell, förmlich. **~ity** /-'mælətɪ/ *n* Förmlichkeit *f*; (*requirement*) Formalität *f*
format /'fɔ:mæt/ *n* Format *nt*
formation /fɔ:'meɪʃn/ *n* Formation *f*
formative /'fɔ:mətɪv/ *a* **~ years** Entwicklungsjahre *pl*
former /'fɔmə(r)/ *a* ehemalig; **the ~** der/die/das Erstere. **~ly** *adv* früher
formidable /'fɔmɪdəbl/ *a* gewaltig
formula /'fɔ:mjʊlə/ *n* (*pl* **-ae** /-li:/ *or* **-s**) Formel *f*
formulate /'fɔ:mjʊleɪt/ *vt* formulieren
forsake /fə'seɪk/ *vt* (*pt* **-sook** /-sʊk/, *pp* **-saken**) verlassen
fort /fɔ:t/ *n* (*Mil*) Fort *nt*
forte /'fɔ:teɪ/ *n* Stärke *f*
forth /fɔ:θ/ *adv* **back and ~** hin und her; **and so ~** und so weiter
forth: ~'coming *a* bevorstehend; (*fam: communicative*) mitteilsam. **~right** *a* direkt. **~'with** *adv* umgehend
fortieth /'fɔ:tɪɪθ/ *a* vierzigste(r,s)
fortification /fɔ:tɪfɪ'keɪʃn/ *n* Befestigung *f*
fortify /'fɔ:tɪfaɪ/ *vt* (*pt/pp* **-ied**) befestigen; (*fig*) stärken
fortitude /'fɔ:tɪtju:d/ *n* Standhaftigkeit *f*
fortnight /'fɔ:t-/ *n* vierzehn Tage *pl*. **~ly** *a* vierzehntäglich □ *adv* alle vierzehn Tage
fortress /'fɔ:trɪs/ *n* Festung *f*
fortuitous /fɔ:'tju:ɪtəs/ *a*, **-ly** *adv* zufällig
fortunate /'fɔ:tʃʊnət/ *a* glücklich; **be ~** Glück haben. **~ly** *adv* glüklicherweise
fortune /'fɔ:tʃu:n/ *n* Glück *nt*; (*money*) Vermögen *nt*. **~-teller** *n* Wahrsagerin *f*
forty /'fɔ:tɪ/ *a* vierzig; **have ~ winks** (*fam*) ein Nickerchen machen □ *n* Vierzig *f*
forum /'fɔ:rəm/ *n* Forum *nt*

forward /ˈfɔːwəd/ *adv* vorwärts; (*to the front*) nach vorn □ *a* Vorwärts-; (*presumptuous*) anmaßend □ *n* (*Sport*) Stürmer *m* □ *vt* nachsenden ⟨*letter*⟩. **~s** *adv* vorwärts

fossil /ˈfɒsl/ *n* Fossil *nt*. **~ized** *a* versteinert

foster /ˈfɒstə(r)/ *vt* fördern; in Pflege nehmen ⟨*child*⟩. **~-child** *n* Pflegekind *nt*. **~-mother** *n* Pflegemutter *f*

fought /fɔːt/ *see* **fight**

foul /faʊl/ *a* (**-er, -est**) widerlich; ⟨*language*⟩ unflätig; **~ play** (*Jur*) Mord *m* □ *n* (*Sport*) Foul *nt* □ *vt* verschmutzen; (*obstruct*) blockieren; (*Sport*) foulen. **~-smelling** *a* übel riechend

found1 /faʊnd/ *see* **find**

found2 *vt* gründen

foundation /faʊnˈdeɪʃn/ *n* (*basis*) Gundlage *f*; (*charitable*) Stiftung *f*; **~s** *pl* Fundament *nt*. **~-stone** *n* Grundstein *m*

founder1 /ˈfaʊndə(r)/ *n* Gründer(in) *m(f)*

founder2 *vi* ⟨*ship*:⟩ sinken; (*fig*) scheitern

foundry /ˈfaʊndrɪ/ *n* Gießerei *f*

fountain /ˈfaʊntɪn/ *n* Brunnen *m*. **~-pen** *n* Füllfederhalter *m*

four /fɔː(r)/ *a* vier □ *n* Vier *f*

four: ~-ˈposter *n* Himmelbett *nt*. **~some** /ˈfɔːsəm/ *n* **in a ~some** zu viert. **~ˈteen** *a* vierzehn □ *n* Vierzehn *f*. **~ˈteenth** *a* vierzehnte(r,s)

fourth /fɔːθ/ *a* vierte(r,s)

fowl /faʊl/ *n* Geflügel *nt*

fox /fɒks/ *n* Fuchs *m* □ *vt* (*puzzle*) verblüffen

foyer /ˈfɔɪeɪ/ *n* Foyer *nt*; (*in hotel*) Empfangshalle *f*

fraction /ˈfrækʃn/ *n* Bruchteil *m*; (*Math*) Bruch *m*

fracture /ˈfræktʃə(r)/ *n* Bruch *m* □ *vt/i* brechen

fragile /ˈfrædʒaɪl/ *a* zerbrechlich

fragment /ˈfrægmənt/ *n* Bruchstück *nt*, Fragment *nt*. **~ary** *a* bruchstückhaft

fragran|ce /ˈfreɪgrəns/ *n* Duft *m*. **~t** *a* duftend

frail /freɪl/ *a* (**-er, -est**) gebrechlich

frame /freɪm/ *n* Rahmen *m*; (*of spectacles*) Gestell *nt*; (*Anat*) Körperbau *m*; **~ of mind** Gemütsverfassung *f* □ *vt* einrahmen; (*fig*) formulieren; (*sl*) ein Verbrechen anhängen (+ *dat*). **~work** *n* Gerüst *nt*; (*fig*) Gerippe *nt*

franc /fræŋk/ *n* (*French, Belgian*) Franc *m*; (*Swiss*) Franken *m*

France /frɑːns/ *n* Frankreich *nt*

franchise /ˈfræntʃaɪz/ *n* (*Pol*) Wahlrecht *nt*; (*Comm*) Franchise *nt*

frank1 /fræŋk/ *vt* frankieren

frank2 *a*, **-ly** *adv* offen

frankfurter /ˈfræŋkfɜːtə(r)/ *n* Frankfurter *f*

frantic /ˈfræntɪk/ *a*, **-ally** *adv* verzweifelt; **be ~** außer sich (*dat*) sein (**with** vor)

fraternal /frəˈtɜːnl/ *a* brüderlich

fraud /frɔːd/ *n* Betrug *m*; (*person*) Betrüger(in) *m(f)*. **~ulent** /-jʊlənt/ *a* betrügerisch

fraught /frɔːt/ *a* **~ with danger** gefahrvoll

fray1 /freɪ/ *n* Kampf *m*

fray2 *vi* ausfransen

freak /friːk/ *n* Missbildung *f*; (*person*) Missgeburt *f*; (*phenomenon*) Ausnahmeerscheinung *f* □ *a* anormal. **~ish** *a* anormal

freckle /ˈfrekl/ *n* Sommersprosse *f*. **~d** *a* sommersprossig

free /friː/ *a* (**freer, freest**) frei; ⟨*ticket, copy, time*⟩ Frei-; (*lavish*) freigebig; **~ [of charge]** kostenlos; **set ~** freilassen; (*rescue*) befreien; **you are ~ to** . . . es steht Ihnen frei, zu . . . □ *vt* (*pt/pp* **freed**) freilassen; (*rescue*) befreien; (*disentangle*) freibekommen

free: **~dom** *n* Freiheit *f*. **~hand** *adv* aus freier Hand. **~hold** *n* [freier] Grundbesitz *m*. **~ 'kick** *n* Freistoß *m*. **~lance** *a & adv* freiberuflich. **~ly** *adv* frei; (*voluntarily*) freiwillig; (*generously*) großzügig. **F~mason** *n* Freimaurer *m*. **F~masonry** *n* Freimaurerei *f*. **~-range** *a* **~-range eggs** Landeier *pl*. **~ 'sample** *n* Gratisprobe *f*. **~style** *n* Freistil *m*. **~way** *n* (*Amer*) Autobahn *f*. **~-'wheel** *vi* im Freilauf fahren

freez|e /fri:z/ *vt* (*pt* **froze**, *pp* **frozen**) einfrieren; stoppen ⟨*wages*⟩ □ *vi* gefrieren; **it's ~ing** es friert

freez|er /'fri:zə(r)/ *n* Gefriertruhe *f*; (*upright*) Gefrierschrank *m*. **~ing** *a* eiskalt □ *n* **below ~ing** unter Null

freight /freɪt/ *n* Fracht *f*. **~er** *n* Frachter *m*. **~ train** *n* (*Amer*) Güterzug *m*

French /frentʃ/ *a* französisch □ *n* (*Lang*) Französisch *nt*; **the ~** *pl* die Franzosen

French: **~ 'beans** *npl* grüne Bohnen *pl*. **~ 'bread** *n* Stangenbrot *nt*. **~'fries** *npl* Pommes frites *pl*. **~man** *n* Franzose *m*. **~ 'window** *n* Terrassentür *f*. **~woman** *n* Französin *f*

frenzied /'frenzɪd/ *a* rasend

frenzy /'frenzɪ/ *n* Raserei *f*

frequency /'fri:kwənsɪ/ *n* Häufigkeit *f*; (*Phys*) Frequenz *f*

frequent[1] /'fri:kwənt/ *a*, **-ly** *adv* häufig

frequent[2] /frɪ'kwent/ *vt* regelmäßig besuchen

fresco /'freskəʊ/ *n* Fresko *nt*

fresh /freʃ/ *a* (**-er, -est**), **-ly** *adv* frisch; (*new*) neu; (*Amer: cheeky*) frech

freshen /'freʃn/ *vi* ⟨*wind:*⟩ auffrischen. **~ up** *vt* auffrischen □ *vi* sich frisch machen

freshness /'freʃnɪs/ *n* Frische *f*

'freshwater *a* Süßwasser-

fret /fret/ *vi* (*pt/pp* **fretted**) sich grämen. **~ful** *a* weinerlich

'fretsaw *n* Laubsäge *f*

friar /'fraɪə(r)/ *n* Mönch *m*

friction /'frɪkʃn/ *n* Reibung *f*; (*fig*) Reibereien *pl*

Friday /'fraɪdeɪ/ *n* Freitag *m*

fridge /frɪdʒ/ *n* Kühlschrank *m*

fried /fraɪd/ *see* **fry**[2] □ *a* gebraten; **~ egg** Spiegelei *nt*

friend /frend/ *n* Freund(in) *m(f)*. **~liness** *n* Freundlichkeit *f*. **~ly** *a* (**-ier, -iest**) freundlich; **~ly with** befreundet mit. **~ship** *n* Freundschaft *f*

frieze /fri:z/ *n* Fries *m*

fright /fraɪt/ *n* Schreck *m*

frighten /'fraɪtn/ *vt* Angst machen (+ *dat*); (*startle*) erschrecken; **be ~ed** Angst haben (**of** vor + *dat*). **~ing** *a* Angst erregend

frightful /'fraɪtfl/ *a*, **-ly** *adv* schrecklich

frigid /'frɪdʒɪd/ *a* frostig; (*Psych*) frigide. **~ity** /-'dʒɪdətɪ/ *n* Frostigkeit *f*; Frigidität *f*

frill /frɪl/ *n* Rüsche *f*; (*paper*) Manschette *f*. **~y** *a* rüschenbesetzt

fringe /frɪndʒ/ *n* Fransen *pl*; (*of hair*) Pony *m*; (*fig: edge*) Rand *m*. **~ benefits** *npl* zusätzliche Leistungen *pl*

frisk /frɪsk/ *vi* herumspringen □ *vt* (*search*) durchsuchen, (*fam*) filzen

frisky /'frɪskɪ/ *a* (**-ier, -iest**) lebhaft

fritter /'frɪtə(r)/ *vt* **~ [away]** verplempern (*fam*)

frivol|ity /frɪ'vɒlətɪ/ *n* Frivolität *f*. **~ous** /'frɪvələs/ *a*, **-ly** *adv* frivol, leichtfertig

frizzy /'frɪzɪ/ *a* kraus

fro /frəʊ/ *see* **to**

frock /frɒk/ *n* Kleid *nt*

frog /frɒg/ *n* Frosch *m*. **~man** *n* Froschmann *m*. **~-spawn** *n* Froschlaich *m*

frolic /ˈfrɒlɪk/ *vi* (*pt/pp* **frolicked**) herumtollen
from /frɒm/ *prep* von (+ *dat*); (*out of*) aus (+ *dat*); (*according to*) nach (+ *dat*); ~ **Monday** ab Montag; ~ **that day** seit dem Tag
front /frʌnt/ *n* Vorderseite *f*; (*fig*) Fassade *f*; (*of garment*) Vorderteil *nt*; (*sea-*) Strandpromenade *f*; (*Mil, Pol, Meteorol*) Front *f*; **in** ~ **of** vor; **in** or **at the** ~ vorne; **to the** ~ nach vorne □ *a* vordere(r, s); ⟨*page, row*⟩ erste(r,s); ⟨*tooth, wheel*⟩ Vorder-
frontal /ˈfrʌntl/ *a* Frontal-
front: ~ ˈ**door** *n* Haustür *f*. ~ ˈ**garden** *n* Vorgarten *m*
frontier /ˈfrʌntɪə(r)/ *n* Grenze *f*
front-wheel ˈ**drive** *n* Vorderradantrieb *m*
frost /frɒst/ *n* Frost *m*; (*hoar-*) Raureif *m*; **ten degrees of** ~ zehn Grad Kälte. ~**bite** *n* Erfrierung *f*. ~**bitten** *a* erfroren
frost|ed /ˈfrɒstɪd/ *a* ~**ed glass** Mattglas *nt*. ~**ing** *n* (*Amer Culin*) Zuckerguss *m*. ~**y** *a*, **-ily** *adv* frostig
froth /frɒθ/ *n* Schaum *m* □ *vi* schäumen. ~**y** *a* schaumig
frown /fraʊn/ *n* Stirnrunzeln *nt* □ *vi* die Stirn runzeln; ~ **on** missbilligen
froze /frəʊz/ *see* **freeze**
frozen /ˈfrəʊzn/ *see* **freeze** □ *a* gefroren; (*Culin*) tiefgekühlt; **I'm** ~ (*fam*) mir ist eiskalt. ~ **food** *n* Tiefkühlkost *f*
frugal /ˈfruːgl/ *a*, **-ly** *adv* sparsam; ⟨*meal*⟩ frugal
fruit /fruːt/ *n* Frucht *f*; (*collectively*) Obst *nt*. ~ **cake** *n* englischer [Tee]kuchen *m*
fruit|erer /ˈfruːtərə(r)/ *n* Obsthändler *m*. ~**ful** *a* fruchtbar
fruition /fruːˈɪʃn/ *n* **come to** ~ sich verwirklichen
fruit: ~ **juice** *n* Obstsaft *m*. ~**less** *a*, **-ly** *adv* fruchtlos. ~ **machine** *n* Spielautomat *m*. ~ ˈ**salad** *n* Obstsalat *m*
fruity /ˈfruːtɪ/ *a* fruchtig
frumpy /ˈfrʌmpɪ/ *a* unmodisch
frustrat|e /frʌˈstreɪt/ *vt* vereiteln; (*psych*) frustrieren. ~**ing** *a* frustrierend. ~**ion** /-eɪʃn/ *n* Frustration *f*
fry[1] /fraɪ/ *n inv* **small** ~ (*fig*) kleine Fische *pl*
fry[2] *vt/i* (*pt/pp* **fried**) [in der Pfanne] braten. ~**ing-pan** *n* Bratpfanne *f*
fuck /fʌk/ *vt/i* (*vulg*) ficken. ~**ing** *a* (*vulg*) Scheiß-
fuddy-duddy /ˈfʌdɪdʌdɪ/ *n* (*fam*) verknöcherter Kerl *m*
fudge /fʌdʒ/ *n* weiche Karamellen *pl*
fuel /ˈfjuːəl/ *n* Brennstoff *m*; (*for car*) Kraftstoff *m*; (*for aircraft*) Treibstoff *m*
fugitive /ˈfjuːdʒətɪv/ *n* Flüchtling *m*
fugue /fjuːg/ *n* (*Mus*) Fuge *f*
fulfil /fʊlˈfɪl/ *vt* (*pt/pp* **-filled**) erfüllen. ~**ment** *n* Erfüllung *f*
full /fʊl/ *a & adv* (**-er, -est**) voll; (*detailed*) ausführlich; ⟨*skirt*⟩ weit; ~ **of** voll von (+ *dat*), voller (+ *gen*); **at** ~ **speed** in voller Fahrt □ *n* **in** ~ vollständig
full: ~ ˈ**moon** *n* Vollmond *m*. ~-**scale** *a* ⟨*model*⟩ in Originalgröße; ⟨*rescue, alert*⟩ groß angelegt. ~ ˈ**stop** *n* Punkt *m*. ~-**time** *a* ganztägig □ *adv* ganztags
fully /ˈfʊlɪ/ *adv* völlig; (*in detail*) ausführlich
fulsome /ˈfʊlsəm/ *a* übertrieben
fumble /ˈfʌmbl/ *vi* herumfummeln (**with** an + *dat*)
fume /fjuːm/ *vi* vor Wut schäumen
fumes /fjuːmz/ *npl* Dämpfe *pl*; (*from car*) Abgase *pl*
fumigate /ˈfjuːmɪgeɪt/ *vt* ausräuchern
fun /fʌn/ *n* Spaß *m*; **for** ~ aus *od* zum Spaß; **make** ~ **of** sich lustig machen über (+ *acc*); **have** ~**!** viel Spaß!

function /ˈfʌŋkʃn/ *n* Funktion *f*; (*event*) Veranstaltung *f* □ *vi* funktionieren; (*serve*) dienen (**as** als). **~al** *a* zweckmäßig

fund /fʌnd/ *n* Fonds *m*; (*fig*) Vorrat *m*; **~s** *pl* Geldmittel *pl* □ *vt* finanzieren

fundamental /fʌndəˈmentl/ *a* grundlegend; (*essential*) wesentlich

funeral /ˈfju:nərl/ *n* Beerdigung *f*; (*cremation*) Feuerbestattung *f*

funeral: **~ directors** *pl*, (*Amer*) **~ home** *n* Bestattungsinstitut *nt*. **~ march** *n* Trauermarsch *m*. **~ parlour** *n* (*Amer*) Bestattungsinstitut *nt*. **~ service** *n* Trauergottesdienst *m*

ˈfunfair *n* Jahrmarkt *m*, Kirmes *f*

fungus /ˈfʌŋgəs/ *n* (*pl* **-gi** /-gaɪ/) Pilz *m*

funicular /fju:ˈnɪkjʊlə(r)/ *n* Seilbahn *f*

funnel /ˈfʌnl/ *n* Trichter *m*; (*on ship, train*) Schornstein *m*

funnily /ˈfʌnɪlɪ/ *adv* komisch; **~ enough** komischerweise

funny /ˈfʌnɪ/ *a* (**-ier, -iest**) komisch. **~-bone** *n* (*fam*) Musikantenknochen *m*

fur /fɜ:(r)/ *n* Fell *nt*; (*for clothing*) Pelz *m*; (*in kettle*) Kesselstein *m*. **~ ˈcoat** *n* Pelzmantel *m*

furious /ˈfjʊərɪəs/ *a*, **-ly** *adv* wütend (**with auf** + *acc*)

furnace /ˈfɜ:nɪs/ *n* (*Techn*) Ofen *m*

furnish /ˈfɜ:nɪʃ/ *vt* einrichten; (*supply*) liefern. **~ed** *a* **~ed room** möbliertes Zimmer *nt*. **~ings** *npl* Einrichtungsgegenstände *pl*

furniture /ˈfɜ:nɪtʃə(r)/ *n* Möbel *pl*

furred /fɜ:d/ *a* ⟨*tongue*⟩ belegt

furrow /ˈfʌrəʊ/ *n* Furche *f*

furry /ˈfɜ:rɪ/ *a* ⟨*animal*⟩ Pelz-; ⟨*toy*⟩ Plüsch-

further /ˈfɜ:ðə(r)/ *a* weitere(r,s); **at the ~ end** am anderen Ende; **until ~ notice** bis auf weiteres □ *adv* weiter; **~ off** weiter entfernt □ *vt* fördern

further: **~ eduˈcation** *n* Weiterbildung *f*. **~ˈmore** *adv* überdies

furthest /ˈfɜ:ðɪst/ *a* am weitesten entfernt □ *adv* am weitesten

furtive /ˈfɜ:tɪv/ *a*, **-ly** *adv* verstohlen

fury /ˈfjʊərɪ/ *n* Wut *f*

fuse¹ /fju:z/ *n* (*of bomb*) Zünder *m*; (*cord*) Zündschnur *f*

fuse² *n* (*Electr*) Sicherung *f* □ *vt/i* verschmelzen; **the lights have ~d** die Sicherung [für das Licht] ist durchgebrannt. **~-box** *n* Sicherungskasten *m*

fuselage /ˈfju:zəlɑ:ʒ/ *n* (*Aviat*) Rumpf *m*

fusion /ˈfju:ʒn/ *n* Verschmelzung *f*, Fusion *f*

fuss /fʌs/ *n* Getue *nt*; **make a ~ of** verwöhnen; (*caress*) liebkosen □ *vi* Umstände machen

fussy /ˈfʌsɪ/ *a* (**-ier, -iest**) wählerisch; (*particular*) penibel

fusty /ˈfʌstɪ/ *a* moderig

futil|e /ˈfju:taɪl/ *a* zwecklos. **~ity** /-ˈtɪlətɪ/ *n* Zwecklosigkeit *f*

future /ˈfju:tʃə(r)/ *a* zukünftig □ *n* Zukunft *f*; (*Gram*) [erstes] Futur *nt*; **~ perfect** zweites Futur *nt*; **in ~** in Zukunft

futuristic /fju:tʃəˈrɪstɪk/ *a* futuristisch

fuzz /fʌz/ *n* **the ~** (*sl*) die Bullen *pl*

fuzzy /ˈfʌzɪ/ *a* (**-ier, -iest**) ⟨*hair*⟩ kraus; (*blurred*) verschwommen

G

gab /gæb/ *n* (*fam*) **have the gift of the ~** gut reden können

gabble /ˈgæbl/ *vi* schnell reden

gable /ˈgeɪbl/ *n* Giebel *m*

gad /gæd/ *vi* (*pt/pp* **gadded**) **~ about** dauernd ausgehen

gadget /ˈgædʒɪt/ *n* [kleines] Gerät *nt*
Gaelic /ˈgeɪlɪk/ *n* Gälisch *nt*
gaffe /gæf/ *n* Fauxpas *m*
gag /gæg/ *n* Knebel *m*; (*joke*) Witz *m*; (*Theat*) Gag *m* □ *vt* (*pt/pp* **gagged**) knebeln
gaiety /ˈgeɪətɪ/ *n* Fröhlichkeit *f*
gaily /ˈgeɪlɪ/ *adv* fröhlich
gain /geɪn/ *n* Gewinn *m*; (*increase*) Zunahme *f* □ *vt* gewinnen; (*obtain*) erlangen; **~ weight** zunehmen □ *vi* ⟨*clock:*⟩ vorgehen. **~ful** *a* **~ful employment** Erwerbstätigkeit *f*
gait /geɪt/ *n* Gang *m*
gala /ˈgɑːlə/ *n* Fest *nt*; **swimming ~** Schwimmfest *nt* □ *attrib* Gala-
galaxy /ˈgæləksɪ/ *n* Galaxie *f*; **the G~** die Milchstraße
gale /geɪl/ *n* Sturm *m*
gall /gɔːl/ *n* Galle *f*; (*impudence*) Frechheit *f*
gallant /ˈgælənt/ *a*, **-ly** *adv* tapfer; (*chivalrous*) galant. **~ry** *n* Tapferkeit *f*
ˈgall-bladder *n* Gallenblase *f*
gallery /ˈgælərɪ/ *n* Galerie *f*
galley /ˈgælɪ/ *n* (*ship's kitchen*) Kombüse *f*; **~ [proof]** [Druck]-fahne *f*
gallivant /ˈgælɪvænt/ *vi* (*fam*) ausgehen
gallon /ˈgælən/ *n* Gallone *f* (= *4,5 l; Amer = 3,785 l*)
gallop /ˈgæləp/ *n* Galopp *m* □ *vi* galoppieren
gallows /ˈgæləʊz/ *n* Galgen *m*
ˈgallstone *n* Gallenstein *m*
galore /gəˈlɔː(r)/ *adv* in Hülle und Fülle
galvanize /ˈgælvənaɪz/ *vt* galvanisieren
gambit /ˈgæmbɪt/ *n* Eröffnungsmanöver *nt*
gamble /ˈgæmbl/ *n* (*risk*) Risiko *nt* □ *vi* [um Geld] spielen; **~ on** (*rely*) sich verlassen auf (+ *acc*). **~r** *n* Spieler(in) *m*(*f*)
game /geɪm/ *n* Spiel *nt*; (*animals, birds*) Wild *nt*; **~s** (*Sch*) Sport *m* □ *a* (*brave*) tapfer; (*willing*) bereit (**for** zu). **~keeper** *n* Wildhüter *m*
gammon /ˈgæmən/ *n* [geräucherter] Schinken *m*
gamut /ˈgæmət/ *n* Skala *f*
gander /ˈgændə(r)/ *n* Gänserich *m*
gang /gæŋ/ *n* Bande *f*; (*of workmen*) Kolonne *f* □ *vi* **~ up** sich zusammenrotten (**on** gegen)
gangling /ˈgæŋglɪŋ/ *a* schlaksig
gangrene /ˈgæŋgriːn/ *n* Wundbrand *m*
gangster /ˈgæŋstə(r)/ *n* Gangster *m*
gangway /ˈgæŋweɪ/ *n* Gang *m*; (*Naut, Aviat*) Gangway *f*
gaol /dʒeɪl/ *n* Gefängnis *nt* □ *vt* ins Gefängnis sperren. **~er** *n* Gefängniswärter *m*
gap /gæp/ *n* Lücke *f*; (*interval*) Pause *f*; (*difference*) Unterschied *m*
gap|e /geɪp/ *vi* gaffen; **~e at** anstarren. **~ing** *a* klaffend
garage /ˈgærɑːʒ/ *n* Garage *f*; (*for repairs*) Werkstatt *f*; (*for petrol*) Tankstelle *f*
garb /gɑːb/ *n* Kleidung *f*
garbage /ˈgɑːbɪdʒ/ *n* Müll *m*. **~ can** *n* (*Amer*) Mülleimer *m*
garbled /ˈgɑːbld/ *a* verworren
garden /ˈgɑːdn/ *n* Garten *m*; **[public] ~s** *pl* [öffentliche] Anlagen *pl* □ *vi* im Garten arbeiten. **~er** *n* Gärtner(in) *m*(*f*). **~ing** *n* Gartenarbeit *f*
gargle /ˈgɑːgl/ *n* (*liquid*) Gurgelwasser *nt* □ *vi* gurgeln
gargoyle /ˈgɑːgɔɪl/ *n* Wasserspeier *m*
garish /ˈgeərɪʃ/ *a* grell
garland /ˈgɑːlənd/ *n* Girlande *f*
garlic /ˈgɑːlɪk/ *n* Knoblauch *m*
garment /ˈgɑːmənt/ *n* Kleidungsstück *nt*
garnet /ˈgɑːnɪt/ *n* Granat *m*

garnish /ˈgɑːnɪʃ/ *n* Garnierung *f* □ *vt* garnieren
garret /ˈgærɪt/ *n* Dachstube *f*
garrison /ˈgærɪsn/ *n* Garnison *f*
garrulous /ˈgærʊləs/ *a* geschwätzig
garter /ˈgɑːtə(r)/ *n* Strumpfband *nt*; (*Amer*: *suspender*) Strumpfhalter *m*
gas /gæs/ *n* Gas *nt*; (*Amer fam*: *petrol*) Benzin *nt* □ *v* (*pt/pp* **gassed**) □ *vt* vergasen □ *vi* (*fam*) schwatzen. **~ cooker** *n* Gasherd *m*. **~ ˈfire** *n* Gasofen *m*
gash /gæʃ/ *n* Schnitt *m*; (*wound*) klaffende Wunde *f* □ *vt* **~ one's arm** sich (*dat*) den Arm aufschlitzen
gasket /ˈgæskɪt/ *n* (*Techn*) Dichtung *f*
gas: ~ mask *n* Gasmaske *f*. **~-meter** *n* Gaszähler *m*
gasoline /ˈgæsəliːn/ *n* (*Amer*) Benzin *nt*
gasp /gɑːsp/ *vi* keuchen; (*in surprise*) hörbar die Luft einziehen
ˈgas station *n* (*Amer*) Tankstelle *f*
gastric /ˈgæstrɪk/ *a* Magen-. **~ ˈflu** *n* Darmgrippe *f*. **~ ˈulcer** *n* Magengeschwür *nt*
gastronomy /gæˈstrɒnəmɪ/ *n* Gastronomie *f*
gate /geɪt/ *n* Tor *nt*; (*to field*) Gatter *nt*; (*barrier*) Schranke *f*; (*at airport*) Flugsteig *m*
gâteau /ˈgætəʊ/ *n* Torte *f*
gate: ~crasher *n* ungeladener Gast *m*. **~way** *n* Tor *nt*
gather /ˈgæðə(r)/ *vt* sammeln; (*pick*) pflücken; (*conclude*) folgern (**from** aus); (*Sewing*) kräuseln; **~ speed** schneller werden □ *vi* sich versammeln; (*storm*:) sich zusammenziehen. **~ing** *n* **family ~ing** Familientreffen *nt*
gaudy /ˈgɔːdɪ/ *a* (**-ier, -iest**) knallig
gauge /geɪdʒ/ *n* Stärke *f*; (*Rail*) Spurweite *f*; (*device*) Messinstrument *nt* □ *vt* messen; (*estimate*) schätzen
gaunt /gɔːnt/ *a* hager
gauntlet /ˈgɔːntlɪt/ *n* **run the ~** Spießruten laufen
gauze /gɔːz/ *n* Gaze *f*
gave /geɪv/ see **give**
gawky /ˈgɔːkɪ/ *a* (**-ier, -iest**) schlaksig
gawp /gɔːp/ *vi* (*fam*) glotzen; **~ at** anglotzen
gay /geɪ/ *a* (**-er, -est**) fröhlich; (*fam*) homosexuell, (*fam*) schwul
gaze /geɪz/ *n* [langer] Blick *m* □ *vi* sehen; **~ at** ansehen
gazelle /gəˈzel/ *n* Gazelle *f*
GB *abbr* of **Great Britain**
gear /gɪə(r)/ *n* Ausrüstung *f*; (*Techn*) Getriebe *nt*; (*Auto*) Gang *m*; **in ~** mit eingelegtem Gang; **change ~** schalten □ *vt* anpassen (**to** *dat*)
gear: ~box *n* (*Auto*) Getriebe *nt*. **~-lever** *n*, (*Amer*) **~-shift** *n* Schalthebel *m*
geese /giːs/ see **goose**
geezer /ˈgiːzə(r)/ *n* (*sl*) Typ *m*
gel /dʒel/ *n* Gel *nt*
gelatine /ˈdʒelətɪn/ *n* Gelatine *f*
gelignite /ˈdʒelɪgnaɪt/ *n* Gelatinedynamit *nt*
gem /dʒem/ *n* Juwel *nt*
Gemini /ˈdʒemɪnaɪ/ *n* (*Astr*) Zwillinge *pl*
gender /ˈdʒendə(r)/ *n* (*Gram*) Geschlecht *nt*
gene /dʒiːn/ *n* Gen *nt*
genealogy /dʒiːnɪˈælədʒɪ/ *n* Genealogie *f*
general /ˈdʒenrəl/ *a* allgemein □ *n* General *m*; **in ~** im Allgemeinen. **~ eˈlection** *n* allgemeine Wahlen *pl*
generaliz|ation /dʒenrəlaɪˈzeɪʃn/ *n* Verallgemeinerung *f*. **~e** /ˈdʒenrəlaɪz/ *vi* verallgemeinern
generally /ˈdʒenrəlɪ/ *adv* im Allgemeinen

general prac'titioner *n* praktischer Arzt *m*
generate /'dʒenəreɪt/ *vt* erzeugen
generation /dʒenə'reɪʃn/ *n* Generation *f*
generator /'dʒenəreɪtə(r)/ *n* Generator *m*
generic /dʒɪ'nerɪk/ *a* ~ **term** Oberbegriff *m*
generosity /dʒenə'rɒsɪtɪ/ *n* Großzügigkeit *f*
generous /'dʒenərəs/ *a*, **-ly** *adv* großzügig
genetic /dʒɪ'netɪk/ *a* genetisch. ~ **engineering** *n* Gentechnologie *f*. **~s** *n* Genetik *f*
Geneva /dʒɪ'ni:və/ *n* Genf *nt*
genial /'dʒi:nɪəl/ *a*, **-ly** *adv* freundlich
genitals /'dʒenɪtlz/ *pl* [äußere] Geschlechtsteile *pl*
genitive /'dʒenɪtɪv/ *a* & *n* ~ **[case]** Genitiv *m*
genius /'dʒi:nɪəs/ *n* (*pl* **-uses**) Genie *nt*; (*quality*) Genialität *f*
genocide /'dʒenəsaɪd/ *n* Völkermord *m*
genre /'ʒɑ̃rə/ *n* Gattung *f*, Genre *nt*
gent /dʒent/ *n* (*fam*) Herr *m*; **the ~s** *sg* die Herrentoilette *f*
genteel /dʒen'ti:l/ *a* vornehm
gentle /'dʒentl/ *a* (**-r, -st**) sanft
gentleman /'dʒentlmən/ *n* Herr *m*; (*well-mannered*) Gentleman *m*
gent|leness /'dʒentlnɪs/ *n* Sanftheit *f*. **~ly** *adv* sanft
genuine /'dʒenjʊɪn/ *a* echt; (*sincere*) aufrichtig. **~ly** *adv* (*honestly*) ehrlich
genus /'dʒi:nəs/ *n* (*Biol*) Gattung *f*
geograph|ical /dʒɪə'græfɪkl/ *a*, **-ly** *adv* geographisch. **~y** /dʒɪ'ɒgrəfɪ/ *n* Geographie *f*, Erdkunde *f*
geological /dʒɪə'lɒdʒɪkl/ *a*, **-ly** *adv* geologisch
geolog|ist /dʒɪ'ɒlədʒɪst/ *n* Geologe *m*/-gin *f*. **~y** *n* Geologie *f*
geometr|ic(al) /dʒɪə'metrɪk(l)/ *a* geometrisch. **~y** /dʒɪ'ɒmətrɪ/ *n* Geometrie *f*
geranium /dʒə'reɪnɪəm/ *n* Geranie *f*
geriatric /dʒerɪ'ætrɪk/ *a* geriatrisch □ *n* geriatrischer Patient *m*. **~s** *n* Geriatrie *f*
germ /dʒɜ:m/ *n* Keim *m*; **~s** *pl* (*fam*) Bazillen *pl*
German /'dʒɜ:mən/ *a* deutsch □ *n* (*person*) Deutsche(r) *m/f*; (*Lang*) Deutsch *nt*; **in ~** auf Deutsch; **into ~** ins Deutsche
Germanic /dʒə'mænɪk/ *a* germanisch
German: ~ 'measles *n* Röteln *pl*. **~ 'shepherd [dog]** *n* [deutscher] Schäferhund *m*
Germany /'dʒɜ:mənɪ/ *n* Deutschland *nt*
germinate /'dʒɜ:mɪneɪt/ *vi* keimen
gesticulate /dʒe'stɪkjʊleɪt/ *vi* gestikulieren
gesture /'dʒestʃə(r)/ *n* Geste *f*
get /get/ *v* (*pt/pp* **got**, *pp Amer also* **gotten**, *pres p* **getting**) □ *vt* bekommen, (*fam*) kriegen; (*procure*) besorgen; (*buy*) kaufen; (*fetch*) holen; (*take*) bringen; (*on telephone*) erreichen; (*fam: understand*) kapieren; machen ⟨*meal*⟩; **~ s.o. to do sth** jdn dazu bringen, etw zu tun □ *vi* (*become*) werden; **~ to** kommen zu/nach ⟨*town*⟩; (*reach*) erreichen; **~ dressed** sich anziehen; **~ married** heiraten. **~ at** *vt* herankommen an (+ *acc*); **what are you ~ting at?** worauf willst du hinaus? **~ away** *vi* (*leave*) wegkommen; (*escape*) entkommen. **~ back** *vi* zurückkommen □ *vt* (*recover*) zurückbekommen; **one's own back** sich revanchieren. **~ by** *vi* vorbeikommen; (*manage*) sein Auskommen haben. **~ down** *vi* heruntersteigen; **~ down to** sich [heran]machen an

(+ *acc*) □ *vt* (*depress*) deprimieren. ~ **in** *vi* einsteigen □ *vt* (*fetch*) hereinholen. ~ **off** *vi* (*dismount*) absteigen; (*from bus*) aussteigen; (*leave*) wegkommen; (*Jur*) freigesprochen werden □ *vt* (*remove*) abbekommen. ~ **on** *vi* (*mount*) aufsteigen; (*to bus*) einsteigen; (*be on good terms*) gut auskommen (**with** mit); (*make progress*) Fortschritte machen; **how are you ~ting on?** wie geht's? ~ **out** *vi* herauskommen; (*of car*) aussteigen; ~ **out of** (*avoid doing*) sich drücken um □ *vt* herausholen; herausbekommen ⟨*cork, stain*⟩. ~ **over** *vi* hinübersteigen □ *vt* (*fig*) hinwegkommen über (+ *acc*). ~ **round** *vi* herumkommen; **I never ~ round to it** ich komme nie dazu □ *vt* herumkriegen; (*avoid*) umgehen. ~ **through** *vi* durchkommen. ~ **up** *vi* aufstehen

get: ~**away** *n* Flucht *f*. ~**-up** *n* Aufmachung *f*

geyser /'gi:zə(r)/ *n* Durchlauferhitzer *m*; (*Geol*) Geysir *m*

ghastly /'gɑ:stlɪ/ *a* (**-ier, -iest**) grässlich; (*pale*) blass

gherkin /'gɜ:kɪn/ *n* Essiggurke *f*

ghetto /'getəʊ/ *n* Getto *nt*

ghost /gəʊst/ *n* Geist *m*, Gespenst *nt*. ~**ly** *a* geisterhaft

ghoulish /'gu:lɪʃ/ *a* makaber

giant /'dʒaɪənt/ *n* Riese *m* □ *a* riesig

gibberish /'dʒɪbərɪʃ/ *n* Kauderwelsch *nt*

gibe /dʒaɪb/ *n* spöttische Bemerkung *f* □ *vi* spotten (**at** über + *acc*)

giblets /'dʒɪblɪts/ *npl* Geflügelklein *nt*

giddiness /'gɪdɪnɪs/ *n* Schwindel *m*

giddy /'gɪdɪ/ *a* (**-ier, -iest**) schwindlig; **I feel ~** mir ist schwindlig

gift /gɪft/ *n* Geschenk *nt*; (*to charity*) Gabe *f*; (*talent*) Begabung *f*. ~**ed** /-ɪd/ *a* begabt. ~**-wrap** *vt* als Geschenk einpacken

gig /gɪg/ *n* (*fam, Mus*) Gig *m*

gigantic /dʒaɪ'gæntɪk/ *a* riesig, riesengroß

giggle /'gɪgl/ *n* Kichern *nt* □ *vi* kichern

gild /gɪld/ *vt* vergolden

gills /gɪlz/ *npl* Kiemen *pl*

gilt /gɪlt/ *a* vergoldet □ *n* Vergoldung *f*. ~**-edged** *a* (*Comm*) mündelsicher

gimmick /'gɪmɪk/ *n* Trick *m*

gin /dʒɪn/ *n* Gin *m*

ginger /'dʒɪndʒə(r)/ *a* rotblond; ⟨*cat*⟩ rot □ *n* Ingwer *m*. ~**bread** *n* Pfefferkuchen *m*

gingerly /'dʒɪndʒəlɪ/ *adv* vorsichtig

gipsy /'dʒɪpsɪ/ *n* = **gypsy**

giraffe /dʒɪ'rɑ:f/ *n* Giraffe *f*

girder /'gɜ:də(r)/ *n* (*Techn*) Träger *m*

girdle /'gɜ:dl/ *n* Bindegürtel *m*; (*corset*) Hüfthalter *m*

girl /gɜ:l/ *n* Mädchen *nt*; (*young woman*) junge Frau *f*. ~**friend** *n* Freundin *f*. ~**ish** *a*, **-ly** *adv* mädchenhaft

giro /'dʒaɪərəʊ/ *n* Giro *nt*; (*cheque*) Postscheck *m*

girth /gɜ:θ/ *n* Umfang *m*; (*for horse*) Bauchgurt *m*

gist /dʒɪst/ *n* **the ~** das Wesentliche

give /gɪv/ *n* Elastizität *f* □ *v* (*pt* **gave**, *pp* **given**) □ *vt* geben/(*as present*) schenken (**to** *dat*); (*donate*) spenden; ⟨*lecture*⟩ halten; ⟨*one's name*⟩ angeben □ *vi* geben; (*yield*) nachgeben. ~ **away** *vt* verschenken; (*betray*) verraten; (*distribute*) verteilen; ~ **away the bride** ≈ Brautführer sein. ~ **back** *vt* zurückgeben. ~ **in** *vt* einreichen □ *vi* (*yield*) nachgeben. ~ **off** *vt* abgeben. ~ **up** *vt/i* aufgeben; ~ **oneself up** sich stellen.

~ **way** *vi* nachgeben; (*Auto*) die Vorfahrt beachten

given /ˈgɪvn/ *see* **give** □ *a* ~ **name** Vorname *m*

glacier /ˈglæsɪə(r)/ *n* Gletscher *m*

glad /glæd/ *a* froh (**of** über + *acc*). ~ **den** /ˈglædn/ *vt* erfreuen

glade /gleɪd/ *n* Lichtung *f*

gladly /ˈglædlɪ/ *adv* gern[e]

glamorous /ˈglæmərəs/ *a* glanzvoll; ⟨*film star*⟩ glamourös

glamour /ˈglæmə(r)/ *n* [betörender] Glanz *m*

glance /glɑ:ns/ *n* [flüchtiger] Blick *m* □ *vi* ~ **at** einen Blick werfen auf (+ *acc*). ~ **up** *vi* aufblicken

gland /glænd/ *n* Drüse *f*

glandular /ˈglændjʊlə(r)/ *a* Drüsen-

glare /gleə(r)/ *n* grelles Licht *nt*; (*look*) ärgerlicher Blick *m* □ *vi* ~ **at** böse ansehen

glaring /ˈgleərɪŋ/ *a* grell; ⟨*mistake*⟩ krass

glass /glɑ:s/ *n* Glas *nt*; (*mirror*) Spiegel *m*; ~**es** *pl* (*spectacles*) Brille *f*. ~**y** *a* glasig

glaze /gleɪz/ *n* Glasur *f* □ *vt* verglasen; (*Culin, Pottery*) glasieren

glazier /ˈgleɪzɪə(r)/ *n* Glaser *m*

gleam /gli:m/ *n* Schein *m* □ *vi* glänzen

glean /gli:n/ *vi* Ähren lesen □ *vt* (*learn*) erfahren

glee /gli:/ *n* Frohlocken *nt*. ~**ful** *a*, **-ly** *adv* frohlockend

glen /glen/ *n* [enges] Tal *nt*

glib /glɪb/ *a*, **-ly** *adv* (*pej*) gewandt

glid|e /glaɪd/ *vi* gleiten; (*through the air*) schweben. ~**er** *n* Segelflugzeug *nt*. ~**ing** *n* Segelfliegen *nt*

glimmer /ˈglɪmə(r)/ *n* Glimmen *nt* □ *vi* glimmen

glimpse /glɪmps/ *n* **catch a** ~ **of** flüchtig sehen □ *vt* flüchtig sehen

glint /glɪnt/ *n* Blitzen *nt* □ *vi* blitzen

glisten /ˈglɪsn/ *vi* glitzern

glitter /ˈglɪtə(r)/ *vi* glitzern

gloat /gləʊt/ *vi* schadenfroh sein; ~ **over** sich weiden an (+ *dat*)

global /ˈgləʊbl/ *a*, **-ly** *adv* global

globe /gləʊb/ *n* Kugel *f*; (*map*) Globus *m*

gloom /glu:m/ *n* Düsterkeit *f*; (*fig*) Pessimismus *m*

gloomy /ˈglu:mɪ/ *a* (**-ier, -iest**), **-ily** *adv* düster; (*fig*) perssimistisch

glorif|y /ˈglɔ:rɪfaɪ/ *vt* (*pt/pp* **-ied**) verherrlichen; **a** ~**ied waitress** eine bessere Kellnerin *f*

glorious /ˈglɔ:rɪəs/ *a* herrlich; ⟨*deed, hero*⟩ glorreich

glory /ˈglɔ:rɪ/ *n* Ruhm *m*; (*splendour*) **Pracht** *f* □ *vi* ~ **in** genießen

gloss /glɒs/ *n* Glanz *m* □ *a* Glanz □ *vi* ~ **over** beschönigen

glossary /ˈglɒsərɪ/ *n* Glossar *nt*

glossy /ˈglɒsɪ/ *a* (**-ier, -iest**) glänzend

glove /glʌv/ *n* Handschuh *m*. ~ **compartment** *n* (*Auto*) Handschuhfach *nt*

glow /gləʊ/ *n* Glut *f*; (*of candle*) Schein *m* □ *vi* glühen; ⟨*candle*:⟩ scheinen. ~**ing** *a* glühend; ⟨*account*⟩ begeistert

ˈglow-worm *n* Glühwürmchen *nt*

glucose /ˈglu:kəʊs/ *n* Traubenzucker *m*, Glukose *f*

glue /glu:/ *n* Klebstoff *m* □ *vt* (*pres p* **gluing**) kleben (**to** an + *acc*)

glum /glʌm/ *a* (**glummer, glummest**), **-ly** *adv* niedergeschlagen

glut /glʌt/ *n* Überfluss *m* (**of** an + *dat*); ~ **of fruit** Obstschwemme *f*

glutton /ˈglʌtən/ *n* Vielfraß *m*. ~**ous** /-əs/ *a* gefräßig. ~**y** *n* Gefräßigkeit *f*

gnarled /nɑ:ld/ *a* knorrig; ⟨*hands*⟩ knotig

gnash /næʃ/ *vt* ~ **one's teeth** mit den Zähnen knirschen

gnat /næt/ *n* Mücke *f*

gnaw /nɔː/ *vt/i* nagen (**at** an + *dat*)

gnome /nəʊm/ *n* Gnom *m*

go /gəʊ/ *n* (*pl* **goes**) Energie *f*; (*attempt*) Versuch *m*; **on the go** auf Trab; **at one go** auf einmal; **it's your go** du bist dran; **make a go of it** Erfolg haben □ *vi* (*pt* **went**, *pp* **gone**) gehen; (*in vehicle*) fahren; (*leave*) weggehen; (*on journey*) abfahren; ⟨*time*:⟩ vergehen; (*vanish*) verschwinden; (*fail*) versagen; (*become*) werden; (*belong*) kommen; **go swimming/shopping** schwimmen/einkaufen gehen; **where are you going**? wo gehst du hin? **it's all gone** es ist nichts mehr übrig; **I am not going to** ich werde es nicht tun; **'to go'** (*Amer*) 'zum Mitnehmen'. **go away** *vi* weggehen/-fahren. **go back** *vi* zurückgehen/-fahren. **go by** *vi* vorbeigehen/-fahren; ⟨*time*:⟩ vergehen. **go down** *vi* hinuntergehen/-fahren; ⟨*sun, ship*:⟩ untergehen; ⟨*prices*:⟩ fallen; ⟨*temperature, swelling*:⟩ zurückgehen. **go for** *vt* holen; (*fam: attack*) losgehen auf (+ *acc*). **go in** *vi* hineingehen/-fahren; **go in for** teilnehmen an (+ *dat*) ⟨*competition*⟩; (*take up*) sich verlegen auf (+ *acc*). **go off** *vi* weggehen/-fahren; ⟨*alarm*:⟩ klingeln; ⟨*gun, bomb*:⟩ losgehen; (*go bad*) schlecht werden; **go off well** gut verlaufen. **go on** *vi* weitergehen/-fahren; (*continue*) weitermachen; (*talking*) fortfahren; (*happen*) vorgehen; **go on at** (*fam*) herumnörgeln an (+ *dat*). **go out** *vi* ausgehen; (*leave*) hinausgehen/-fahren. **go over** *vi* hinübergehen/-fahren □ *vt* (*check*) durchgehen. **go round** *vi* herumgehen/-fahren; (*visit*) vorbeigehen; (*turn*) sich drehen; (*be enough*) reichen. **go through** *vi* durchgehen/-fahren □ *vt* (*suffer*) durchmachen; (*check*) durchgehen. **go under** *vi* untergehen; (*fail*) scheitern. **go up** *vi* hinaufgehen/-fahren; ⟨*lift*:⟩ hochfahren; ⟨*prices*:⟩ steigen. **go without** *vt* verzichten auf (+ *acc*) □ *vi* darauf verzichten

goad /gəʊd/ *vt* anstacheln (**into** zu); (*taunt*) reizen

'go-ahead *a* fortschrittlich; (*enterprising*) unternehmend □ *n* (*fig*) grünes Licht *nt*

goal /gəʊl/ *n* Ziel *nt*; (*sport*) Tor *nt*. **~keeper** *n* Torwart *m*. **~-post** *n* Torpfosten *m*

goat /gəʊt/ *n* Ziege *f*

gobble /'gɒbl/ *vt* hinunterschlingen

'go-between *n* Vermittler(in) *m*(*f*)

goblet /'gɒblɪt/ *n* Pokal *m*; (*glass*) Kelchglas *nt*

goblin /'gɒblɪn/ *n* Kobold *m*

God, god /gɒd/ *n* Gott *m*

god: ~child *n* Patenkind *nt*. **~-daughter** *n* Patentochter *f*. **~dess** *n* Göttin *f*. **~father** *n* Pate *m*. **G~-forsaken** *a* gottverlassen. **~mother** *n* Patin *f*. **~parents** *npl* Paten *pl*. **~send** *n* Segen *m*. **~son** *n* Patensohn *m*

goggle /'gɒgl/ *vi* (*fam*) **~ at** anglotzen. **~s** *npl* Schutzbrille *f*

going /'gəʊɪŋ/ *a* ⟨*price, rate*⟩ gängig; ⟨*concern*⟩ gut gehend □ *n* **it is hard ~** es ist schwierig; **while the ~ is good** solange es noch geht. **~s-'on** *npl* [seltsame] Vorgänge *pl*

gold /gəʊld/ *n* Gold *nt* □ *a* golden

golden /'gəʊldn/ *a* golden. **~ 'handshake** *n* hohe Abfindungssumme *f*. **~ 'wedding** *n* goldene Hochzeit *f*

gold: ~fish *n inv* Goldfisch *m*. **~-mine** *n* Goldgrube *f*. **~-plated** *a* vergoldet. **~smith** *n* Goldschmied *m*

golf /gɒlf/ *n* Golf *nt*

golf: ~-club *n* Golfklub *m*; (*implement*) Golfschläger *m*. **~-course**

n Golfplatz *m*. **~er** *m* Golfspieler(in) *m(f)*

gondo|la /ˈgɒndələ/ *n* Gondel *f*. **~lier** /-ˈlɪə(r)/ *n* Gondoliere *m*

gone /gɒn/ *see* **go**

gong /gɒŋ/ *n* Gong *m*

good /gʊd/ *a* (**better, best**) gut; (*well-behaved*) brav, artig; **~ at** gut in (+ *dat*); **a ~ deal** ziemlich viel; **as ~ as** so gut wie; (*almost*) fast; **~ morning/evening** guten Morgen/Abend; **~ afternoon** guten Tag; **~ night** gute Nacht □ *n* **the ~** das Gute; **for ~** für immer; **do ~** Gutes tun; **do s.o. ~** jdm gut tun; **it's no ~** es ist nutzlos; (*hopeless*) da ist nichts zu machen; **be up to no ~** nichts Gutes im Schilde führen

goodbye /gʊdˈbaɪ/ *int* auf Wiedersehen; (*Teleph, Radio*) auf Wiederhören

good: ~-for-nothing *a* nichtsnutzig □ *n* Taugenichts *m*. **G~ ˈFriday** *n* Karfreitag *m*. **~-ˈlooking** *a* gut aussehend. **~-ˈnatured** *a* gutmütig

goodness /ˈgʊdnɪs/ *n* Güte *f*; **my ~!** du meine Güte! **thank ~!** Gott sei Dank!

goods /gʊdz/ *npl* Waren *pl*. **~ train** *n* Güterzug *m*

goodˈwill *n* Wohlwollen *nt*; (*Comm*) Goodwill *m*

goody /ˈgʊdɪ/ *n* (*fam*) Gute(r) *m/f*. **~-goody** *n* Musterkind *nt*

gooey /ˈguːɪ/ *a* (*fam*) klebrig

goof /guːf/ *vi* (*fam*) einen Schnitzer machen

goose /guːs/ *n* (*pl* **geese**) Gans *f*

gooseberry /ˈgʊzbərɪ/ *n* Stachelbeere *f*

goose /guːs/: **~-flesh** *n*, **~-pimples** *npl* Gänsehaut *f*

gore[1] /gɔː(r)/ *n* Blut *nt*

gore[2] *vt* mit den Hörnern aufspießen

gorge /gɔːdʒ/ *n* (*Geog*) Schlucht *f* □ *vt* **~ oneself** sich vollessen

gorgeous /ˈgɔːdʒəs/ *a* prachtvoll; (*fam*) herrlich

gorilla /gəˈrɪlə/ *n* Gorilla *m*

gormless /ˈgɔːmlɪs/ *a* (*fam*) doof

gorse /gɔːs/ *n inv* Stechginster *m*

gory /ˈgɔːrɪ/ *a* (**-ier, -iest**) blutig; ⟨*story*⟩ blutrünstig

gosh /gɒʃ/ *int* (*fam*) Mensch!

go-ˈslow *n* Bummelstreik *m*

gospel /ˈgɒspl/ *n* Evangelium *nt*

gossip /ˈgɒsɪp/ *n* Klatsch *m*; (*person*) Klatschbase *f* □ *vi* klatschen. **~y** *a* geschwätzig

got /gɒt/ *see* **get; have ~** haben; **have ~ to** müssen; **have ~ to do sth** etw tun müssen

Gothic /ˈgɒθɪk/ *a* gotisch

gotten /ˈgɒtn/ *see* **get**

gouge /gaʊdʒ/ *vt* **~ out** aushöhlen

goulash /ˈguːlæʃ/ *n* Gulasch *nt*

gourmet /ˈgʊəmeɪ/ *n* Feinschmecker *m*

gout /gaʊt/ *n* Gicht *f*

govern /ˈgʌvn/ *vt/i* regieren; (*determine*) bestimmen. **~ess** *n* Gouvernante *f*

government /ˈgʌvnmənt/ *n* Regierung *f*. **~al** /-ˈmentl/ *a* Regierungs-

governor /ˈgʌvənə(r)/ *n* Gouverneur *m*; (*on board*) Vorstandsmitglied *nt*; (*of prison*) Direktor *m*; (*fam: boss*) Chef *m*

gown /gaʊn/ *n* [elegantes] Kleid *nt*; (*Univ, Jur*) Talar *m*

GP *abbr of* **general practitioner**

grab /græb/ *vt* (*pt/pp* **grabbed**) ergreifen; **~ [hold of]** packen

grace /greɪs/ *n* Anmut *f*; (*before meal*) Tischgebet *nt*; (*Relig*) Gnade *f*; **with good ~** mit Anstand; **say ~** [vor dem Essen] beten; **three days' ~** drei Tage Frist. **~ful** *a*, **-ly** *adv* anmutig

gracious /ˈgreɪʃəs/ *a* gnädig; (*elegant*) vornehm

grade /greɪd/ *n* Stufe *f*; (*Comm*) Güteklasse *f*; (*Sch*) Note *f*; (*Amer, Sch: class*) Klasse *f*; (*Amer*) =

gradient □ *vt* einstufen; (*Comm*) sortieren. **~ crossing** *n* (*Amer*) Bahanübergang *m*
gradient /ˈgreɪdɪənt/ *n* Steigung *f*; (*downward*) Gefälle *nt*
gradual /ˈgrædʒʊəl/ *a*, **-ly** *adv* allmählich
graduate[1] /ˈgrædʒʊət/ *n* Akademiker(in) *m*(*f*)
graduate[2] /ˈgrædʒʊeɪt/ *vi* (*Univ*) sein Examen machen. **~d** *a* abgestuft; ⟨*container*⟩ mit Maßeinteilung
graffiti /grəˈfiːtiː/ *npl* Graffiti *pl*
graft /grɑːft/ *n* (*Bot*) Pfropfreis *nt*; (*Med*) Transplantat *nt*; (*fam: hard work*) Plackerei *f* □ *vt* (*Bot*) aufpfropfen; (*Med*) übertragen
grain /greɪn/ *n* (*sand, salt, rice*) Korn *nt*; (*cereals*) Getreide *nt*; (*in wood*) Maserung *f*; **against the ~** (*fig*) gegen den Strich
gram /græm/ *n* Gramm *nt*
grammar /ˈgræmə(r)/ *n* Grammatik *f*. **~ school** *n* ≈ Gymnasium *nt*
grammatical /grəˈmætɪkl/ *a*, **-ly** *adv* grammatisch
granary /ˈgrænərɪ/ *n* Getreidespeicher *m*
grand /grænd/ *a* (**-er, -est**) großartig
grandad /ˈgrændæd/ *n* (*fam*) Opa *m*
ˈgrandchild *n* Enkelkind *nt*
ˈgranddaughter *n* Enkelin *f*
grandeur /ˈgrændʒə(r)/ *n* Pracht *f*
ˈgrandfather *n* Großvater *m*. **~ clock** *n* Standuhr *f*
grandiose /ˈgrændɪəʊs/ *a* grandios
grand: ~mother *n* Großmutter *f*. **~parents** *npl* Großeltern *pl*. **~ piˈano** *n* Flügel *m*. **~son** *n* Enkel *m*. **~stand** *n* Tribüne *f*
granite /ˈgrænɪt/ *n* Granit *m*
granny /ˈgrænɪ/ *n* (*fam*) Oma *f*
grant /grɑːnt/ *n* Subvention *f*; (*Univ*) Studienbeihilfe *f* □ *vt* gewähren; (*admit*) zugeben; **take sth for ~ed** etw als selbstverständlich hinnehmen
granular /ˈgrænjʊlə(r)/ *a* körnig
granulated /ˈgrænjʊleɪtɪd/ *a* **~ sugar** Kristallzucker *m*
granule /ˈgrænjuːl/ *n* Körnchen *nt*
grape /greɪp/ *n* [Wein]traube *f*; **bunch of ~s** [ganze] Weintraube *f*
grapefruit /ˈgreɪp-/ *n invar* Grapefruit *f*, Pampelmuse *f*
graph /grɑːf/ *n* Kurvendiagramm *nt*
graphic /ˈgræfɪk/ *a*, **-ally** *adv* grafisch; (*vivid*) anschaulich. **~s** *n* (*design*) grafische Gestaltung *f*
ˈgraph paper *n* Millimeterpapier *nt*
grapple /ˈgræpl/ *vi* ringen
grasp /grɑːsp/ *n* Griff *m* □ *vt* ergreifen; (*understand*) begreifen. **~ing** *a* habgierig
grass /grɑːs/ *n* Gras *nt*; (*lawn*) Rasen *m*; **at the ~ roots** an der Basis. **~hopper** *n* Heuschrecke *f*. **~land** *n* Weideland *nt*
grassy /ˈgrɑːsɪ/ *a* grasig
grate[1] /greɪt/ *n* Feuerrost *m*; (*hearth*) Kamin *m*
grate[2] *vt* (*Culin*) reiben; **~ one's teeth** mit den Zähnen knirschen
grateful /ˈgreɪtfl/ *a*, **-ly** *adv* dankbar (**to** *dat*)
grater /ˈgreɪtə(r)/ *n* (*Culin*) Reibe *f*
gratify /ˈgrætɪfaɪ/ *vt* (*pt/pp* **-ied**) befriedigen. **~ing** *a* erfreulich
grating /ˈgreɪtɪŋ/ *n* Gitter *nt*
gratis /ˈgrɑːtɪs/ *adv* gratis
gratitude /ˈgrætɪtjuːd/ *n* Dankbarkeit *f*
gratuitous /grəˈtjuːɪtəs/ *a* (*uncalled for*) überflüssig
gratuity /grəˈtjuːətɪ/ *n* (*tip*) Trinkgeld *nt*
grave[1] /greɪv/ *a* (**-r, -st**), **-ly** *adv* ernst; **~ly ill** schwer krank
grave[2] *n* Grab *nt*. **~-digger** *n* Totengräber *m*

gravel /'grævl/ *n* Kies *m*
grave: ~stone *n* Grabstein *m*. **~yard** *n* Friedhof *m*
gravitate /'grævɪteɪt/ *vi* gravitieren
gravity /'grævətɪ/ *n* Ernst *m*; (*force*) Schwerkraft *f*
gravy /'greɪvɪ/ *n* [Braten]soße *f*
gray /greɪ/ *a* (*Amer*) = **grey**
graze[1] /greɪz/ *vi* ⟨*animal:*⟩ weiden
graze[2] *n* Schürfwunde *f* □ *vt* ⟨*car*⟩ streifen; ⟨*knee*⟩ aufschürfen
grease /gri:s/ *n* Fett *nt*; (*lubricant*) Schmierfett *nt* □ *vt* einfetten; (*lubricate*) schmieren. **~-proof 'paper** *n* Pergamentpapier *nt*
greasy /'gri:sɪ/ *a* (**-ier, -iest**) fettig
great /greɪt/ *a* (**-er, -est**) groß; (*fam: marvellous*) großartig
great: ~-'aunt *n* Großtante *f*. **G~ 'Britain** *n* Großbritannien *nt*. **~-'grandchildren** *npl* Urenkel *pl*. **~-'grandfather** *n* Urgroßvater *m*. **~-'grandmother** *n* Urgroßmutter *f*
great|ly /'greɪtlɪ/ *adv* sehr. **~ness** *n* Größe *f*
great-'uncle *n* Großonkel *m*
Greece /gri:s/ *n* Griechenland *nt*
greed /gri:d/ *n* [Hab]gier *f*
greedy /'gri:dɪ/ *a* (**-ier, -iest**), **-ily** *adv* gierig; **don't be ~** sei nicht so unbescheiden
Greek /gri:k/ *a* griechisch □ *n* Grieche *m*/Griechin *f*; (*Lang*) Griechisch *nt*
green /gri:n/ *a* (**-er, -est**) grün; (*fig*) unerfahren □ *n* Grün *nt*; (*grass*) Wiese *f*; **~s** *pl* Kohl *m*; **the G~s** *pl* (*Pol*) die Grünen *pl*
greenery /'gri:nərɪ/ *n* Grün *nt*
'greenfly *n* Blattlaus *f*
greengage /'gri:ngeɪdʒ/ *n* Reneklode *f*
green: ~grocer *n* Obst- und Gemüsehändler *m*. **~house** *n* Gewächshaus *nt*. **~house effect** *n* Treibhauseffekt *m*
Greenland /'gri:nlənd/ *n* Grönland *nt*
greet /gri:t/ *vt* grüßen; (*welcome*) begrüßen. **~ing** *n* Gruß *m*; (*welcome*) Begrüßung *f*. **~ings card** *n* Glückwunschkarte *f*
gregarious /grɪ'geərɪəs/ *a* gesellig
grenade /grɪ'neɪd/ *n* Granate *f*
grew /gru:/ *see* **grow**
grey /greɪ/ *a* (**-er, -est**) grau □ *n* Grau *nt* □ *vi* grau werden. **~hound** *n* Windhund *m*
grid /grɪd/ *n* Gitter *nt*; (*on map*) Gitternetz *nt*; (*Electr*) Überlandleitungsnetz *nt*
grief /gri:f/ *n* Trauer *f*; **come to ~** scheitern
grievance /'gri:vəns/ *n* Beschwerde *f*
grieve /gri:v/ *vt* betrüben □ *vi* trauern (**for** um)
grievous /'gri:vəs/ *a*, **-ly** *adv* schwer
grill /grɪl/ *n* Gitter *nt*; (*Culin*) Grill *m*; **mixed ~** Gemischtes *nt* vom Grill □ *vt/i* grillen; (*interrogate*) [streng] verhören
grille /grɪl/ *n* Gitter *nt*
grim /grɪm/ *a* (**grimmer, grimmest**), **-ly** *adv* ernst; ⟨*determination*⟩ verbissen
grimace /grɪ'meɪs/ *n* Grimasse *f* □ *vi* Grimassen schneiden
grime /graɪm/ *n* Schmutz *m*
grimy /'graɪmɪ/ *a* (**-ier, -iest**) schmutzig
grin /grɪn/ *n* Grinsen *nt* □ *vi* (*pt/pp* **grinned**) grinsen
grind /graɪnd/ *n* (*fam: hard work*) Plackerei *f* □ *vt* (*pt/pp* **ground**) mahlen; (*smooth, sharpen*) schleifen; (*Amer: mince*) durchdrehen; **~ one's teeth** mit den Zähnen knirschen
grip /grɪp/ *n* Griff *m*; (*bag*) Reisetasche *f* □ *vt* (*pt/pp* **gripped**) ergreifen; (*hold*) festhalten; fesseln ⟨*interest*⟩
gripe /graɪp/ *vi* (*sl: grumble*) meckern
gripping /'grɪpɪŋ/ *a* fesselnd

grisly /'grɪzlɪ/ *a* (**-ier, -iest**) grausig
gristle /'grɪsl/ *n* Knorpel *m*
grit /grɪt/ *n* [grober] Sand *m*; (*for roads*) Streugut *nt*; (*courage*) Mut *m* □ *vt* (*pt/pp* **gritted**) streuen ⟨*road*⟩; ~ **one's teeth** die Zähne zusammenbeißen
grizzle /'grɪzl/ *vi* quengeln
groan /grəʊn/ *n* Stöhnen *nt* □ *vi* stöhnen
grocer /'grəʊsə(r)/ *n* Lebensmittelhändler *m*; **~'s [shop]** Lebensmittelgeschäft *nt*. **~ies** *npl* Lebensmittel *pl*
groggy /'grɒgɪ/ *a* schwach; (*unsteady*) wackelig [auf den Beinen]
groin /grɔɪn/ *n* (*Anat*) Leiste *f*
groom /gru:m/ *n* Bräutigam *m*; (*for horse*) Pferdepfleger(in) *m(f)* □ *vt* striegeln ⟨*horse*⟩
groove /gru:v/ *n* Rille *f*
grope /grəʊp/ *vi* tasten (**for** nach)
gross /grəʊs/ *a* (**-er, -est**) fett; (*coarse*) derb; (*glaring*) grob; (*Comm*) brutto; ⟨*salary, weight*⟩ Brutto- □ *n inv* Gros *nt*. **~ly** *adv* (*very*) sehr
grotesque /grəʊ'tesk/ *a*, **-ly** *adv* grotesk
grotto /'grɒtəʊ/ *n* (*pl* **-es**) Grotte *f*
grotty /'grɒtɪ/ *a*, (*fam*) mies
ground¹ /graʊnd/ *see* **grind**
ground² *n* Boden *m*; (*terrain*) Gelände *nt*; (*reason*) Grund *m*; (*Amer, Electr*) Erde *f*; **~s** *pl* (*park*) Anlagen *pl*; (*of coffee*) Satz *m* □ *vi* ⟨*ship:*⟩ auflaufen □ *vt* aus dem Verkehr ziehen ⟨*aircraft*⟩; (*Amer, Electr*) erden
ground: ~ floor *n* Erdgeschoss *nt*. **~ing** *n* Grundlage *f*. **~less** *a* grundlos. **~ 'meat** *n* Hackfleisch *nt*. **~sheet** *n* Bodenplane *f*. **~work** *n* Vorarbeiten *pl*
group /gru:p/ *n* Gruppe *f* □ *vt* gruppieren □ *vi* sich gruppieren
grouse¹ /graʊs/ *n inv* schottisches Moorschneehuhn *nt*
grouse² *vi* (*fam*) meckern
grovel /'grɒvl/ *vi* (*pt/pp* **grovelled**) kriechen. **~ling** *a* kriecherisch
grow /grəʊ/ *v* (*pt* **grew**, *pp* **grown**) □ *vi* wachsen; (*become*) werden; (*increase*) zunehmen □ *vt* anbauen; **~ one's hair** sich (*dat*) die Haare wachsen lassen. **~ up** *vi* aufwachsen; ⟨*town:*⟩ entstehen
growl /graʊl/ *n* Knurren *nt* □ *vi* knurren
grown /grəʊn/ *see* **grow**. **~-up** *a* erwachsen □ *n* Erwachsene(r) *m/f*
growth /grəʊθ/ *n* Wachstum *nt*; (*increase*) Zunahme *f*; (*Med*) Gewächs *nt*
grub /grʌb/ *n* (*larva*) Made *f*; (*fam: food*) Essen *nt*
grubby /'grʌbɪ/ *a* (**-ier, -iest**) schmuddelig
grudg|e /grʌdʒ/ *n* Groll *m*; **bear s.o. a ~e** einen Groll gegen jdn hegen □ *vt* **~e s.o. sth** jdm etw missgönnen. **~ing** *a*, **-ly** *adv* widerwillig
gruelling /'gru:əlɪŋ/ *a* strapaziös
gruesome /'gru:səm/ *a* grausig
gruff /grʌf/ *a*, **-ly** *adv* barsch
grumble /'grʌmbl/ *vi* schimpfen (**at** mit)
grumpy /'grʌmpɪ/ *a* (**-ier, -iest**) griesgrämig
grunt /grʌnt/ *n* Grunzen *nt* □ *vi* grunzen
guarant|ee /gærən'ti:/ *n* Garantie *f*; (*document*) Garantieschein *m* □ *vt* garantieren; garantieren für ⟨*quality, success*⟩; **be ~eed** ⟨*product:*⟩ Garantie haben. **~or** *n* Bürge *m*
guard /gɑ:d/ *n* Wache *f*; (*security*) Wächter *m*; (*on train*) ≈ Zugführer *m*; (*Techn*) Schutz *m*; **be on ~** Wache stehen; **on one's ~** auf der Hut □ *vt* bewachen; (*protect*) schützen □ *vi* **~ against** sich hüten vor (+ *dat*). **~-dog** *n* Wachhund *m*
guarded /'gɑ:dɪd/ *a* vorsichtig

guardian /'gɑːdɪən/ *n* Vormund *m*
guerrilla /gə'rɪlə/ *n* Guerillakämpfer *m*. ~ **warfare** *n* Partisanenkrieg *m*
guess /ges/ *n* Vermutung *f* □ *vt* erraten □ *vi* raten; (*Amer: believe*) glauben. ~**work** *n* Vermutung *f*
guest /gest/ *n* Gast *m*. ~**-house** *n* Pension *f*
guffaw /gʌ'fɔː/ *n* derbes Lachen *nt* □ *vi* derb lachen
guidance /'gaɪdəns/ *n* Führung *f*, Leitung *f*; (*advice*) Beratung *f*
guide /gaɪd/ *n* Führer(in) *m(f)*; (*book*) Führer *m*; **[Girl] G~** Pfadfinderin *f* □ *vt* führen, leiten. ~**book** *n* Führer *m*
guided /'gaɪdɪd/ *a* ~ **missile** Fernlenkgeschoss *nt*; ~ **tour** Führung *f*
guide: ~-dog *n* Blindenhund *m*. ~**lines** *npl* Richtlinien *pl*
guild /gɪld/ *n* Gilde *f*, Zunft *f*
guile /gaɪl/ *n* Arglist *f*
guillotine /'gɪlətiːn/ *n* Guillotine *f*; (*for paper*) Papierschneidemaschine *f*
guilt /gɪlt/ *n* Schuld *f*. ~**ily** *adv* schuldbewusst
guilty /'gɪltɪ/ *a* (**-ier, -iest**) *a* schuldig (**of** *gen*); ⟨*look*⟩ schuldbewusst; ⟨*conscience*⟩ schlecht
guinea-pig /'gɪnɪ-/ *n* Meerschweinchen *nt*; (*person*) Versuchskaninchen *nt*
guise /gaɪz/ *n* **in the ~ of** in Gestalt (+ *gen*)
guitar /gɪ'tɑː(r)/ *n* Gitarre *f*. ~**ist** *n* Gitarrist(in) *m(f)*
gulf /gʌlf/ *n* (*Geog*) Golf *m*; (*fig*) Kluft *f*
gull /gʌl/ *n* Möwe *f*
gullet /'gʌlɪt/ *n* Speiseröhre *f*; (*throat*) Kehle *f*
gullible /'gʌlɪbl/ *a* leichtgläubig
gully /'gʌlɪ/ *n* Schlucht *f*; (*drain*) Rinne *f*
gulp /gʌlp/ *n* Schluck *m* □ *vi* schlucken □ *vt* ~ **down** hinunterschlucken
gum[1] /gʌm/ *n* & **-s** *pl* (*Anat*) Zahnfleisch *nt*
gum[2] *n* Gummi[harz] *nt*; (*glue*) Klebstoff *m*; (*chewing-gum*) Kaugummi *m* □ *vt* (*pt/pp* **gummed**) kleben (**to** an + *acc*). ~**boot** *n* Gummistiefel *m*
gummed /gʌmd/ *see* **gum**[2] □ *a* ⟨*label*⟩ gummiert
gumption /'gʌmpʃn/ *n* (*fam*) Grips *m*
gun /gʌn/ *n* Schusswaffe *f*; (*pistol*) Pistole *f*; (*rifle*) Gewehr *nt*; (*cannon*) Geschütz *nt* □ *vt* (*pt/pp* **gunned**) ~ **down** niederschießen
gun: ~fire *n* Geschützfeuer *nt*. ~**man** bewaffneter Bandit *m*
gunner /'gʌnə(r)/ *n* Artillerist *m*
gun: ~powder *n* Schießpulver *nt*. ~**shot** *n* Schuss *m*
gurgle /'gɜːgl/ *vi* gluckern; (*of baby*) glucksen
gush /gʌʃ/ *vi* strömen; (*enthuse*) schwärmen (**over** von). ~ **out** *vi* herausströmen
gusset /'gʌsɪt/ *n* Zwickel *m*
gust /gʌst/ *n* (*of wind*) Windstoß *m*; (*Naut*) Bö *f*
gusto /'gʌstəʊ/ *n* **with** ~ mit Schwung
gusty /'gʌstɪ/ *a* böig
gut /gʌt/ *n* Darm *m*; ~**s** *pl* Eingeweide *pl*; (*fam: courage*) Schneid *m* □ *vt* (*pt/pp* **gutted**) (*Culin*) ausnehmen; ~**ted by fire** ausgebrannt
gutter /'gʌtə(r)/ *n* Rinnstein *m*; (*fig*) Gosse *f*; (*on roof*) Dachrinne *f*
guttural /'gʌtərl/ *a* guttural
guy /gaɪ/ *n* (*fam*) Kerl *m*
guzzle /'gʌzl/ *vt/i* schlingen; (*drink*) schlürfen
gym /dʒɪm/ *n* (*fam*) Turnhalle *f*; (*gymnastics*) Turnen *nt*
gymnasium /dʒɪm'neɪzɪəm/ *n* Turnhalle *f*
gymnast /'dʒɪmnæst/ *n* Turner(in) *m(f)*. ~**ics** /-'næstɪks/ *n* Turnen *nt*

gym: ~ **shoes** *pl* Turnschuhe *pl.* **~-slip** *n* (*Sch*) Trägerkleid *nt*
gynaecolog|ist /gaɪnɪ'kɒlədʒɪst/ *n* Frauenarzt *m* /-ärztin *f*. **~y** *n* Gynäkologie *f*
gypsy /'dʒɪpsɪ/ *n* Zigeuner(in) *m(f)*
gyrate /dʒaɪə'reɪt/ *vi* sich drehen

H

haberdashery /'hæbədæʃərɪ/ *n* Kurzwaren *pl*; (*Amer*) Herrenmoden *pl*
habit /'hæbɪt/ *n* Gewohnheit *f*; (*Relig: costume*) Ordenstracht *f*; **be in the ~** die Angewohnheit haben (**of** zu)
habitable /'hæbɪtəbl/ *a* bewohnbar
habitat /'hæbɪtæt/ *n* Habitat *nt*
habitation /hæbɪ'teɪʃn/ *n* **unfit for human ~** für Wohnzwecke ungeeignet
habitual /hə'bɪtjʊəl/ *a* gewohnt; (*inveterate*) gewohnheitsmäßig. **~ly** *adv* gewohnheitsmäßig; (*constantly*) ständig
hack1 /hæk/ *n* (*writer*) Schreiberling *m*; (*hired horse*) Mietpferd *nt*
hack2 *vt* hacken; **~ to pieces** zerhacken
hackneyed /'hæknɪd/ *a* abgedroschen
'hacksaw *n* Metallsäge *f*
had /hæd/ *see* **have**
haddock /'hædək/ *n inv* Schellfisch *m*
haemorrhage /'hemərɪdʒ/ *n* Blutung *f*
haemorrhoids /'hemərɔɪdz/ *npl* Hämorrhoiden *pl*
hag /hæg/ *n* **old ~** alte Hexe *f*
haggard /'hægəd/ *a* abgehärmt
haggle /'hægl/ *vi* feilschen (**over** um)
hail1 /heɪl/ *vt* begrüßen; herbeirufen ⟨*taxi*⟩ □ *vi* **~ from** kommen aus
hail2 *n* Hagel *m* □ *vi* hageln. **~stone** *n* Hagelkorn *nt*
hair /heə(r)/ *n* Haar *nt*; **wash one's ~** sich (*dat*) die Haare waschen
hair: **~brush** *n* Haarbürste *f*. **~cut** *n* Haarschnitt *m*; **have a ~cut** sich (*dat*) die Haare schneiden lassen. **~-do** *n* (*fam*) Frisur *f*. **~dresser** *n* Friseur *m*/Friseuse *f*. **~-drier** *n* Haartrockner *m*; (*hand-held*) Föhn *m*. **~-grip** *n* [Haar]klemme *f*. **~pin** *n* Haarnadel *f*. **~pin 'bend** *n* Haarnadelkurve *f*. **~-raising** *a* haarsträubend. **~-style** *n* Frisur *f*
hairy /'heərɪ/ *a* (**-ier, -iest**) behaart; (*excessively*) haarig; (*fam; frightening*) brenzlig
hake /heɪk/ *n inv* Seehecht *m*
hale /heɪl/ *a* **~ and hearty** gesund und munter
half /hɑːf/ *n* (*pl* **halves**) Hälfte *f*; **cut in ~** halbieren; **one and a ~** eineinhalb, anderthalb; **~ a dozen** ein halbes Dutzend; **~ an hour** eine halbe Stunde □ *a & adv* halb; **~ past two** halb drei; **[at] ~ price** zum halben Preis
half: **~-board** *n* Halbpension *f*. **~-caste** *n* Mischling *m*. **~-'hearted** *a* lustlos. **~-'hourly** *a & adv* halbstündlich. **~-'mast** *n* **at ~-mast** auf halbmast. **~-measure** *n* Halbheit *f*. **~-'term** *n* schulfreie Tage nach dem halben Trimester. **~-'timbered** *a* Fachwerk-. **~-'time** *n* (*Sport*) Halbzeit *f*. **~-'way** *a* **the ~-way mark/stage** die Hälfte □ *adv* auf halbem Weg; **get ~-way** den halben Weg zurücklegen; (*fig*) bis zur Hälfte kommen. **~-wit** *n* Idiot *m*
halibut /'hælɪbət/ *n inv* Heilbutt *m*
hall /hɔːl/ *n* Halle *f*; (*room*) Saal *m*; (*Sch*) Aula *f*; (*entrance*) Flur *m*; (*mansion*) Gutshaus *nt*; **~ of residence** (*Univ*) Studentenheim *nt*

'hallmark *n* [Feingehalts]stempel *m*; (*fig*) Kennzeichen *nt* (**of** für) □ *vt* stempeln
hallo /hə'ləʊ/ *int* [guten] Tag! (*fam*) hallo!
Hallowe'en /hæləʊ'i:n/ *n* der Tag vor Allerheiligen
hallucination /həlu:sɪ'neɪʃn/ *n* Halluzination *f*
halo /'heɪləʊ/ *n* (*pl* **-es**) Heiligenschein *m*; (*Astr*) Hof *m*
halt /hɔ:lt/ *n* Halt *m*; **come to a ~** stehen bleiben; ⟨*traffic:*⟩ zum Stillstand kommen □ *vi* Halt machen; **~!** halt! **~ing** *a, adv* **-ly** zögernd
halve /hɑ:v/ *vt* halbieren; (*reduce*) um die Hälfte reduzieren
ham /hæm/ *n* Schinken *m*
hamburger /'hæmbɜ:gə(r)/ *n* Hamburger *m*
hamlet /'hæmlɪt/ *n* Weiler *m*
hammer /'hæmə(r)/ *n* Hammer *m* □ *vt/i* hämmern (**at** an + *acc*)
hammock /'hæmək/ *n* Hängematte *f*
hamper[1] /'hæmpə(r)/ *n* Picknickkorb *m*; **[gift] ~** Geschenkkorb *m*
hamper[2] *vt* behindern
hamster /'hæmstə(r)/ *n* Hamster *m*
hand /hænd/ *n* Hand *f*; (*of clock*) Zeiger *m*; (*writing*) Handscrift *f*; (*worker*) Arbeiter(in) *m*(*f*); (*Cards*) Blatt *nt*; **all ~s** (*Naut*) alle Mann; **at ~** in der Nähe; **on the one/other ~** einer-/andererseits; **out of ~** außer Kontrolle; (*summarily*) kurzerhand; **in ~** unter Kontrolle; (*available*) verfügbar; **give s.o. a ~** jdm behilflich sein □ *vt* reichen (**to** *dat*). **~ in** *vt* abgeben. **~ out** *vt* austeilen. **~ over** *vt* überreichen
hand: ~bag *n* Handtasche *f*. **~book** *n* Handbuch *nt*. **~brake** *n* Handbremse *f*. **~cuffs** *npl* Handschellen *pl*. **~ful** *n* Handvoll *f*; **be [quite] a ~ful** (*fam*) nicht leicht zu haben sein
handicap /'hændɪkæp/ *n* Behinderung *f*; (*Sport & fig*) Handikap *nt*. **~ped** *a* **mentally/physically ~ped** geistig/körperlich behindert
handi|craft /'hændɪkrɑ:ft/ *n* Basteln *nt*; (*Sch*) Werken *nt*. **~work** *n* Werk *nt*
handkerchief /'hæŋkətʃɪf/ *n* (*pl* **~s & -chieves**) Taschentuch *nt*
handle /'hændl/ *n* Griff *m*; (*of door*) Klinke *f*; (*of cup*) Henkel *m*; (*of broom*) Steil *m*; **fly off the ~** (*fam*) aus der Haut fahren □ *vt* handhaben; (*treat*) umgehen mit; (*touch*) anfassen. **~bars** *npl* Lenkstange *f*
hand: ~-luggage *n* Handgepäck *nt*. **~made** *a* handgemacht. **~-out** *n* Prospekt *m*; (*money*) Unterstützung *f*. **~rail** *n* Handlauf *m*. **~shake** *n* Händerdruck *m*
handsome /'hænsəm/ *a* gut aussehend; (*generous*) großzügig; (*large*) beträchtlich
hand: ~stand *n* Handstand *m*. **~writing** *n* Handschrift *f*. **~-'written** *a* handgeschrieben
handy /'hændɪ/ *a* (**-ier, -iest**) handlich; ⟨*person*⟩ geschickt; **have/keep ~** griffbereit haben/halten. **~man** *n* **[home] ~man** Heimwerker *m*
hang /hæŋ/ *vt/i* (*pt/pp* **hung**) hängen; **~ wallpaper** tapezieren □ *vt* (*pt/pp* **hanged**) hängen ⟨*criminal*⟩; **~ oneself** sich erhängen □ *n* **get the ~ of it** (*fam*) den Dreh herauskriegen. **~ about** *vi* sich herumdrücken. **~ on** *vi* sich festhalten (**to** an + *dat*); (*fam: wait*) warten. **~ out** *vi* heraushängen; (*fam: live*) wohnen □ *vt* draußen aufhängen ⟨*washing*⟩. **~ up** *vt/i* aufhängen
hangar /'hæŋə(r)/ *n* Flugzeughalle *f*
hanger /'hæŋə(r)/ *n* [Kleider]bügel *m*
hang: ~-glider *n* Drachenflieger *m*. **~-gliding** *n* Drachenfliegen

nt. **~man** *n* Henker *m*. **~over** *n* (*fam*) Kater *m* (*fam*). **~-up** *n* (*fam*) Komplex *m*

hanker /ˈhæŋkə(r)/ *vi* **~ after sth** sich (*dat*) etw wünschen

hanky /ˈhæŋkɪ/ *n* (*fam*) Taschentuch *nt*

hanky-panky /hæŋkɪˈpæŋkɪ/ *n* (*fam*) Mauscheleien *pl*

haphazard /hæpˈhæzəd/ *a*, **-ly** *adv* planlos

happen /ˈhæpn/ *vi* geschehen, passieren; **as it ~s** zufälligerweise; **I ~ed to be there** ich war zufällig da; **what has ~ed to him?** was ist mit ihm los? (*become of*) was ist aus ihm geworden? **~ing** *n* Ereignis *nt*

happi|ly /ˈhæpɪlɪ/ *adv* glücklich; (*fortunately*) glücklicherweise. **~ness** *n* Glück *nt*

happy /ˈhæpɪ/ *a* (**-ier, -iest**) glücklich. **~-go-ˈlucky** *a* sorglos

harass /ˈhærəs/ *vt* schikanieren. **~ed** *a* abgehetzt. **~ment** *n* Schikane *f*; (*sexual*) Belästigung *f*

harbour /ˈhɑːbə(r)/ *n* Hafen *m* □ *vt* Unterschlupf gewähren (+ *dat*); hegen ⟨*grudge*⟩

hard /hɑːd/ *a* (**-er, -est**) hart; (*difficult*) schwer; **~ of hearing** schwerhörig □ *adv* hart; ⟨*work*⟩ schwer; ⟨*pull*⟩ kräftig; ⟨*rain, snow*⟩ stark; **think ~!** denk mal nach! **be ~ up** (*fam*) knapp bei Kasse sein; **be ~ done by** (*fam*) ungerecht behandelt werden

hard: ~back *n* gebundene Ausgabe *f*. **~board** *n* Hartfaserplatte *f*. **~-boiled** *a* hart gekocht

harden /ˈhɑːdn/ *vi* hart werden

hard-ˈhearted *a* hartherzig

hard|ly /ˈhɑːdlɪ/ *adv* kaum; **~ly ever** kaum [jemals]. **~ness** *n* Härte *f*. **~ship** *n* Not *f*

hard: ~ ˈshoulder *n* (*Auto*) Randstreifen *m*. **~ware** *n* Haushaltswaren *pl*; (*Computing*) Hardware *f*. **~-ˈwearing** *a* strapazierfähig. **~-ˈworking** *a* fleißig

hardy /ˈhɑːdɪ/ *a* (**-ier, -iest**) abgehärtet; ⟨*plant*⟩ winterhart

hare /heə(r)/ *n* Hase *m*. **~ˈlip** *n* Hasenscharte *f*

hark /hɑːk/ *vi* **~!** hört! **~ back** *vi* **~ back to** (*fig*) zurückkommen auf (+ *acc*)

harm /hɑːm/ *n* Schaden *m*; **out of ~'s way** in Sicherheit; **it won't do any ~** es kann nichts schaden □ *vt* **~ s.o.** jdm etwas antun. **~ful** *a* schädlich. **~less** *a* harmlos

harmonica /hɑːˈmɒnɪkə/ *n* Mundharmonika *f*

harmonious /hɑːˈməʊnɪəs/ *a*, **-ly** *adv* harmonisch

harmon|ize /ˈhɑːmənaɪz/ *vi* (*fig*) harmonieren. **~y** *n* Harmonie *f*

harness /ˈhɑːnɪs/ *n* Geschirr *nt*; (*of parachute*) Gurtwerk *nt* □ *vt* anschirren ⟨*horse*⟩; (*use*) nutzbar machen

harp /hɑːp/ *n* **Harfe** *f* □ *vi* **~ on [about]** (*fam*) herumreiten auf (+ *dat*). **~ist** *n* Harfenist(in) *m*(*f*)

harpoon /hɑːˈpuːn/ *n* Harpune *f*

harpsichord /ˈhɑːpsɪkɔːd/ *n* Cembalo *nt*

harrow /ˈhærəʊ/ *n* Egge *f*. **~ing** *a* grauenhaft

harsh /hɑːʃ/ *a* (**-er, -est**), **-ly** *adv* hart; ⟨*voice*⟩ rau; ⟨*light*⟩ grell. **~ness** *n* Härte *f*; Rauheit *f*

harvest /ˈhɑːvɪst/ *n* Ernte *f* □ *vt* ernten

has /hæz/ *see* **have**

hash /hæʃ/ *n* (*Culin*) Haschee *nt*; **make a ~ of** (*fam*) verpfuschen

hashish /ˈhæʃɪʃ/ *n* Haschisch *nt*

hassle /ˈhæsl/ *n* (*fam*) Ärger *m* □ *vt* schikanieren

hassock /ˈhæsək/ *n* Kniekissen *nt*

haste /heɪst/ *n* Eile *f*; **make ~** sich beeilen

hasten /ˈheɪsn/ *vi* sich beeilen (**to** zu); (*go quickly*) eilen □ *vt* beschleunigen

hasty /ˈheɪstɪ/ *a* (**-ier, -iest**), **-ily** *adv* hastig; ⟨*decision*⟩ voreilig

hat /hæt/ *n* Hut *m*; (*knitted*) Mütze *f*
hatch¹ /hætʃ/ *n* (*for food*) Durchreiche *f*; (*Naut*) Luke *f*
hatch² *vi* **~[out]** ausschlüpfen □ *vt* ausbrüten
'**hatchback** *n* (*Auto*) Modell *nt* mit Hecktür
hatchet /'hætʃɪt/ *n* Beil *nt*
hate /heɪt/ *n* Hass *m* □ *vt* hassen. **~ful** *a* abscheulich
hatred /'heɪtrɪd/ *n* Hass *m*
haughty /'hɔ:tɪ/ *a* (**-ier, -iest**), **-ily** *adv* hochmütig
haul /hɔ:l/ *n* (*fish*) Fang *m*; (*loot*) Beute *f* □ *vt/i* ziehen (**on** an + *dat*). **~age** /-ɪdʒ/ *n* Transport *m*. **~ier** /-ɪə(r)/ *n* Spediteur *m*
haunt /hɔ:nt/ *n* Lieblingsaufenthalt *m* □ *vt* umgehen in (+ *dat*); **this house is ~ed** in diesem Haus spukt es
have /hæv/ *vt* (*3 sg pres tense* **has**; *pt/pp* **had**) haben; bekommen ⟨*baby*⟩; holen ⟨*doctor*⟩; **~ a meal/drink** etwas essen/trinken; **~ lunch** zu Mittag essen; **~ a walk** spazieren gehen; **~ a dream** träumen; **~ a rest** sich ausruhen; **~ a swim** schwimmen; **~ sth done** etw machen lassen; **~ sth made** sich (*dat*) etw machen lassen; **~ to do sth** etw tun müssen; **~ it out with** zur Rede stellen; **so I ~!** tatsächlich! **he has [got] two houses** er hat zwei Häuser; **you have got the money, haven't you?** du hast das Geld, nicht [wahr]? □ *v aux* haben; (*with verbs of motion & some others*) sein; **I ~ seen him** ich habe ihn gesehen; **he has never been there** er ist nie da gewesen. **~ on** *vt* (*be wearing*) anhaben; (*dupe*) anführen
haven /'heɪvn/ *n* (*fig*) Zuflucht *f*
haversack /'hævə-/ *n* Rucksack *m*
havoc /'hævək/ *n* Verwüstung *f*; **play ~ with** (*fig*) völlig durcheinander bringen
haw /hɔ:/ *see* **hum**
hawk¹ /hɔ:k/ *n* Falke *m*
hawk² *vt* hausieren mit. **~er** *n* Hausierer *m*
hawthorn /'hɔ:-/ *n* Hagedorn *m*
hay /heɪ/ *n* Heu *nt*. **~ fever** *n* Heuschnupfen *m*. **~stack** *n* Heuschober *m*
'**haywire** *a* (*fam*) **go ~** verrückt spielen; ⟨*plans:*⟩ über den Haufen geworfen werden
hazard /'hæzəd/ *n* Gefahr *f*; (*risk*) Risiko *nt* □ *vt* riskieren. **~ous** /-əs/ *a* gefährlich; (*risky*) riskant. **~ [warning] lights** *npl* (*Auto*) Warnblinkanlage *f*
haze /'heɪz/ *n* Dunst *m*
hazel /'heɪzl/ *n* Haselbusch *m*. **~-nut** *n* Haselnuss *f*
hazy /'heɪzɪ/ *a* (**-ier, -iest**) dunstig; (*fig*) unklar
he /hi:/ *pron* er
head /hed/ *n* Kopf *m*; (*chief*) Oberhaupt *nt*; (*of firm*) Chef(in) *m(f)*; (*of school*) Schulleiter(in) *m(f)*; (*on beer*) Schaumkrone *f*; (*of bed*) Kopfende *nt*; **20 ~ of cattle** 20 Stück Vieh; **~ first** kopfüber □ *vt* anführen; (*Sport*) köpfen ⟨*ball*⟩ □ *vi* **~ for** zusteuern auf (+ *acc*). **~ache** *n* Kopfschmerzen *pl*. **~-dress** *n* Kopfschmuck *m*
head|er /'hedə(r)/ *n* Kopfball *m*; (*dive*) Kopfsprung *m*. **~ing** *n* Überschrift *f*
head: ~lamp *n* (*Auto*) Scheinwerfer *m*. **~land** *n* Landspitze *f*. **~light** *n* (*Auto*) Scheinwerfer *m*. **~line** *n* Schlagzeile *f*. **~long** *adv* kopfüber. **~'master** *n* Schulleiter *m*. **~'mistress** *n* Schulleiterin *f*. **~-on** *a & adv* frontal. **~phones** *npl* Kopfhörer *m*. **~quarters** *npl* Hauptquartier *nt*; (*Pol*) Zentrale *f*. **~-rest** *n* Kopfstütze *f*. **~room** *n* lichte Höhe *f*. **~scarf** *n* Kopftuch *nt*. **~strong** *a* eigenwillig. **~ 'waiter** *n* Oberkellner *m*. **~way** *n* **make ~way** Fortschritte machen. **~wind** *n*

Gegenwind *m*. **~word** *n* Stichwort *nt*
heady /ˈhedɪ/ *a* berauschend
heal /hiːl/ *vt/i* heilen
health /helθ/ *n* Gesundheit *f*
health: ~ farm *n* Schönheitsfarm *f*. **~ foods** *npl* Reformkost *f*. **~-food shop** *n* Reformhaus *nt*. **~ insurance** *n* Krankenversicherung *f*
healthy /ˈhelθɪ/ *a* (**-ier, -iest**), **-ily** *adv* gesund
heap /hiːp/ *n* Haufen *m*; **~s** (*fam*) jede Menge □ *vt* **~ [up]** häufen; **~ed teaspoon** gehäufter Teelöffel
hear /hɪə(r)/ *vt/i* (*pt/pp* **heard**) hören; **~,~!** hört, hört! **he would not ~ of it** er ließ es nicht zu
hearing /ˈhɪərɪŋ/ *n* Gehör *nt*; (*Jur*) Verhandlung *f*. **~-aid** *n* Hörgerät *nt*
ˈhearsay *n* **from ~** vom Hörensagen
hearse /hɜːs/ *n* Leichenwagen *m*
heart /hɑːt/ *n* Herz *nt*; (*courage*) Mut *m*; **~s** *pl* (*Cards*) Herz *nt*; **by ~** auswendig
heart: ~ache *n* Kummer *m*. **~ attack** *n* Herzanfall *m*. **~beat** *n* Herzschlag *m*. **~-break** *n* Leid *nt*. **~-breaking** *a* herzzerreißend. **~-broken** *a* untröstlich. **~burn** *n* Sodbrennen *nt*. **~en** *vt* ermutigen. **~felt** *a* herzlich[st]
hearth /hɑːθ/ *n* Herd *m*; (*fireplace*) Kamin *m*. **~rug** *n* Kaminvorleger *m*
heart|ily /ˈhɑːtɪlɪ/ *adv* herzlich; ⟨*eat*⟩ viel. **~less** *a*, **-ly** *adv* herzlos. **~y** *a* herzlich; ⟨*meal*⟩ groß; ⟨*person*⟩ burschikos
heat /hiːt/ *n* Hitze *f*; (*Sport*) Vorlauf *m* □ *vt* heiß machen; heizen ⟨*room*⟩. **~ed** *a* geheizt; ⟨*swimming pool*⟩ beheizt; ⟨*discussion*⟩ hitzig. **~er** *n* Heizgerät *nt*; (*Auto*) Heizanlage *f*
heath /hiːθ/ *n* Heide *f*
heathen /ˈhiːðn/ *a* heidnisch □ *n* Heide *m*/Heidin *f*
heather /ˈheðə(r)/ *n* Heidekraut *nt*
heating /ˈhiːtɪŋ/ *n* Heizung *f*
heat: ~-stroke *n* Hitzschlag *m*. **~wave** *n* Hitzewelle *f*
heave /hiːv/ *vt/i* ziehen; (*lift*) heben; (*fam: throw*) schmeißen; **~ a sigh** einen Seufzer ausstoßen
heaven /ˈhevn/ *n* Himmel *m*. **~ly** *a* himmlisch
heavy /ˈhevɪ/ *a* (**-ier, -iest**), **-ily** *adv* schwer; ⟨*traffic, rain*⟩ stark; ⟨*sleep*⟩ tief. **~weight** *n* Schwergewicht *nt*
Hebrew /ˈhiːbruː/ *a* hebräisch
heckle /ˈhekl/ *vt* [durch Zwischenrufe] unterbrechen. **~r** *n* Zwischenrufer *m*
hectic /ˈhektɪk/ *a* hektisch
hedge /hedʒ/ *n* Hecke *f* □ *vi* (*fig*) ausweichen. **~hog** *n* Igel *m*
heed /hiːd/ *n* **pay ~ to** Beachtung schenken (+ *dat*) □ *vt* beachten. **~less** *a* ungeachtet (**of** *gen*)
heel[1] /hiːl/ *n* Ferse *f*; (*of shoe*) Absatz *m*; **down at ~** heruntergekommen; **take to one's ~s** (*fam*) Fersengeld geben
heel[2] *vi* **~ over** (*Naut*) sich auf die Seite legen
hefty /ˈheftɪ/ *a* (**-ier, -iest**) kräftig; (*heavy*) schwer
heifer /ˈhefə(r)/ *n* Färse *f*
height /haɪt/ *n* Höhe *f*; (*of person*) Größe *f*. **~en** *vt* (*fig*) steigern
heir /eə(r)/ *n* Erbe *m*. **~ess** *n* Erbin *f*. **~loom** *n* Erbstück *nt*
held /held/ *see* **hold**[2]
helicopter /ˈhelɪkɒptə(r)/ *n* Hubschrauber *m*
hell /hel/ *n* Hölle *f*; **go to ~!** (*sl*) geh zum Teufel! □ *int* verdammt!
hello /həˈləʊ/ *int* [guten] Tag! (*fam*) hallo!
helm /helm/ *n* [Steuer]ruder *nt*; **at the ~** (*fig*) am Ruder
helmet /ˈhelmɪt/ *n* Helm *m*
help /help/ *n* Hilfe *f*; (*employees*) Hilfskräfte *pl*; **that's no ~** das nützt nichts □ *vt/i* helfen **(s.o.**

jdm); **~ oneself to sth** sich (*dat*) etw nehmen; **~ yourself** (*at table*) greif zu; **I could not ~ laughing** ich musste lachen; **it cannot be ~ed** es lässt sich nicht ändern; **I can't ~ it** ich kann nichts dafür

help|er /ˈhelpə(r)/ *n* Helfer(in) *m(f)*. **~ful** *a*, -ly *adv* hilfsbereit; ⟨*advice*⟩ nützlich. **~ing** *n* Portion *f*. **~less** *a*, **-ly** *adv* hilflos

helter-skelter /heltəˈskeltə(r)/ *adv* holterdiepolter □ *n* Rutschbahn *f*

hem /hem/ *n* Saum *m* □ *vt* (*pt/pp* **hemmed**) säumen; **~ in** umzingeln

hemisphere /ˈhemɪ-/ *n* Hemisphäre *f*

ˈhem-line *n* Rocklänge *f*

hemp /hemp/ *n* Hanf *m*

hen /hen/ *n* Henne *f*; (*any female bird*) Weibchen *nt*

hence /hens/ *adv* daher; **five years ~** in fünf Jahren. **~ˈforth** *adv* von nun an

henchman /ˈhentʃmən/ *n* (*pej*) Gefolgsmann *m*

ˈhenpecked *a* **~ husband** Pantoffelheld *m*

her /hɜː(r)/ *a* ihr □ *pron* (*acc*) sie; (*dat*) ihr; **I know ~** ich kenne sie; **give ~ the money** gib ihr das Geld

herald /ˈherəld/ *vt* verkünden. **~ry** *n* Wappenkunde *f*

herb /hɜːb/ *n* Kraut *nt*

herbaceous /hɜːˈbeɪʃəs/ *a* krautartig; **~ border** Staudenrabatte *f*

herd /hɜːd/ *n* Herde *f* □ *vt* (*tend*) hüten; (*drive*) treiben. **~ together** *vi* sich zusammendrängen □ *vt* zusammentreiben

here /hɪə(r)/ *adv* hier; (*to this place*) hierher; **in ~** hier drinnen; **come/bring ~** herkommen/herbringen. **~ˈafter** *adv* im Folgenden. **~ˈby** *adv* hiermit

heredit|ary /həˈredɪtərɪ/ *a* erblich. **~y** *n* Vererbung *f*

here|sy /ˈherəsɪ/ *n* Ketzerei *f*. **~tic** *n* Ketzer(in) *m(f)*

hereˈwith *adv* (*Comm*) beiliegend

heritage /ˈherɪtɪdʒ/ *n* Erbe *nt*

hermetic /hɜːˈmetɪk/ *a*, **-ally** *adv* hermetisch

hermit /ˈhɜːmɪt/ *n* Einsiedler *m*

hernia /ˈhɜːnɪə/ *n* Bruch *m*, Hernie *f*

hero /ˈhɪərəʊ/ *n* (*pl* **-es**) Held *m*

heroic /hɪˈrəʊɪk/ *a*, **-ally** *adv* heldenhaft

heroin /ˈherəʊɪn/ *n* Heroin *nt*

hero|ine /ˈherəʊɪn/ *n* Heldin *f*. **~ism** *n* Heldentum *nt*

heron /ˈhern/ *n* Reiher *m*

herring /ˈherɪŋ/ *n* Hering *m*; **red ~** (*fam*) falsche Spur *f*. **~bone** *n* (*pattern*) Fischgrätenmuster *nt*

hers /hɜːz/ *poss pron* ihre(r), ihrs; **a friend of ~** ein Freund von ihr; **that is ~** das gehört ihr

herˈself *pron* selbst; (*refl*) sich; **by ~** allein

hesitant /ˈhezɪtənt/ *a*, **-ly** *adv* zögernd

hesitat|e /ˈhezɪteɪt/ *vi* zögern. **~ion** /-ˈteɪʃn/ *n* Zögern *nt*; **without ~ion** ohne zu zögern

het /het/ *a* **~ up** (*fam*) aufgeregt

heteroˈsexual /hetərəʊ-/ *a* heterosexuell

hew /hjuː/ *vt* (*pt* **hewed**, *pp* **hewed** *or* **hewn**) hauen

hexagonal /hekˈsægənl/ *a* sechseckig

heyday /ˈheɪ-/ *n* Glanzzeit *f*

hi /haɪ/ *int* he! (*hallo*) Tag!

hiatus /haɪˈeɪtəs/ *n* (*pl* **-tuses**) Lücke *f*

hibernat|e /ˈhaɪbəneɪt/ *vi* Winterschlaf halten. **~ion** /-ˈneɪʃn/ *n* Winterschlaf *m*

hiccup /ˈhɪkʌp/ *n* Hick *m*; (*fam: hitch*) Panne *f*; **have the ~s** den Schluckauf haben □ *vi* hick machen

hid /hɪd/, **hidden** *see* **hide**[2]

hide[1] /haɪd/ *n* (*Comm*) Haut *f*; (*leather*) Leder *nt*

hide[2] *v* (*pt* **hid**, *pp* **hidden**) □ *vt* verstecken; (*keep secret*) verheimlichen □ *vi* sich verstecken. **~-and-'seek** *n* **play ~-and-seek** Versteck spielen

hideous /'hɪdɪəs/ *a*, **-ly** *adv* hässlich; (*horrible*) grässlich

'hide-out *n* Versteck *nt*

hiding[1] /'haɪdɪŋ/ *n* (*fam*) **give s.o. a ~** jdn verdreschen

hiding[2] *n* **go into ~** untertauchen

hierarchy /'haɪərɑ:kɪ/ *n* Hierarchie *f*

hieroglyphics /haɪərə'glɪfɪks/ *npl* Hieroglyphen *pl*

higgledy-piggledy /hɪgldɪ'pɪgldɪ/ *adv* kunterbunt durcheinander

high /haɪ/ *a* (**-er, -est**) hoch; *attrib* hohe(r,s); ⟨*meat*⟩ angegangen; ⟨*wind*⟩ stark; (*on drugs*) high; **it's ~ time** es ist höchste Zeit □ *adv* hoch; **~ and low** überall □ *n* Hoch *nt*; (*temperature*) Höchsttemperatur *f*

high: ~brow *a* intellektuell. **~chair** *n* Kinderhochstuhl *m*. **~'-handed** *a* selbstherrlich. **~-'heeled** *a* hochhackig. **~jump** *n* Hochsprung *m*

'highlight *n* (*fig*) Höhepunkt *m*; **~s** *pl* (*in hair*) helle Strähnen *pl* □ *vt* (*emphasize*) hervorheben

highly /'haɪlɪ/ *adv* hoch; **speak ~ of** loben; **think ~ of** sehr schätzen. **~-'strung** *a* nervös

Highness /'haɪnɪs/ *n* Hoheit *f*

high: ~-rise *a* **~-rise flats** *pl* Wohnturm *m*. **~ season** *n* Hochsaison *f*. **~ street** *n* Hauptstraße *f*. **~ 'tide** *n* Hochwasser *nt*. **~way** *n* **public ~way** öffentliche Straße

hijack /'haɪdʒæk/ *vt* entführen. **~er** *n* Entführer *m*

hike /haɪk/ *n* Wanderung *f* □ *vi* wandern. **~r** *n* Wanderer *m*

hilarious /hɪ'leərɪəs/ *a* sehr komisch

hill /hɪl/ *n* Berg *m*; (*mound*) Hügel *m*; (*slope*) Hang *m*

hill: ~-billy *n* (*Amer*) Hinterwäldler *m*. **~side** *n* Hang *m*. **~y** *a* hügelig

hilt /hɪlt/ *n* Griff *m*; **to the ~** (*fam*) voll und ganz

him /hɪm/ *pron* (*acc*) ihn; (*dat*) ihm; **I know ~** ich kenne ihn; **give ~ the money** gib ihm das Geld. **~'self** *pron* selbst; (*refl*) sich; **by ~self** allein

hind /haɪnd/ *a* Hinter-

hind|er /'hɪndə(r)/ *vt* hindern. **~rance** /-rəns/ *n* Hindernis *nt*

hindsight /'haɪnd-/ *n* **with ~** rückblickend

Hindu /'hɪndu:/ *n* Hindu *m* □ *a* Hindu-. **~ism** *n* Hinduismus *m*

hinge /hɪndʒ/ *n* Scharnier *nt*; (*on door*) Angel *f* □ *vi* **~ on** (*fig*) ankommen auf (+ *acc*)

hint /hɪnt/ *n* Wink *m*, Andeutung *f*; (*advice*) Hinweis *m*; (*trace*) Spur *f* □ *vi* **~ at** anspielen auf (+ *acc*)

hip /hɪp/ *n* Hüfte *f*

hippie /'hɪpɪ/ *n* Hippie *m*

hip 'pocket *n* Gesäßtasche *f*

hippopotamus /hɪpə'pɒtəməs/ *n* (*pl* **-muses** *or* **-mi** /-maɪ/) Nilpferd *nt*

hire /'haɪə(r)/ *vt* mieten ⟨*car*⟩; leihen ⟨*suit*⟩; einstellen ⟨*person*⟩; **~[out]** vermieten; verleihen □ *n* Mieten *nt*; Leihen *nt*. **~-car** *n* Leihwagen *m*

his /hɪz/ *a* sein □ *poss pron* seine(r), seins; **a friend of ~** ein Freund von ihm; **that is ~** das gehört ihm

hiss /hɪs/ *n* Zischen *nt* □ *vt/i* zischen

historian /hɪ'stɔ:rɪən/ *n* Historiker(in) *m(f)*

historic /hɪ'stɒrɪk/ *a* historisch. **~al** *a*, **-ly** *adv* geschichtlich, historisch

history /'hɪstərɪ/ *n* Geschichte *f*

hit /hɪt/ *n* (*blow*) Schlag *m*; (*fam: success*) Erfolg *m*; **direct ~** Volltreffer *m* □ *vt/i* (*pt/pp* **hit,** *pres p* **hitting**) schlagen; (*knock against, collide with, affect*) treffen; **~ the target** das Ziel treffen; **~ on** (*fig*) kommen auf (+ *acc*); **~ it off** gut auskommen (**with** mit); **~ one's head on sth** sich (*dat*) den Kopf an etw (*dat*) stoßen

hitch /hɪtʃ/ *n* Problem *nt*; **technical ~** Panne *f* □ *vt* festmachen (**to** an + *dat*); **~ up** hochziehen; **~ a lift** per Anhalter fahren, (*fam*) trampen. **~-hiker** *vi* per Anhalter fahren, (*fam*) trampen. **~-hiker** *n* Anhalter(in) *m(f)*

hither /ˈhɪðə(r)/ *adv* hierher; **~ and thither** hin und her. **~ˈto** *adv* bisher

hive /haɪv/ *n* Bienenstock *m*. **~ off** *vt* (*Comm*) abspalten

hoard /hɔːd/ *n* Hort *m* □ *vt* horten, hamstern

hoarding /ˈhɔːdɪŋ/ *n* Bauzaun *m*; (*with advertisements*) Reklamewand *f*

hoar-frost /ˈhɔː-/ *n* Raureif *m*

hoarse /hɔːs/ *a* (**-r, -st**), **-ly** *adv* heiser. **~ness** *n* Heiserkeit *f*

hoax /həʊks/ *n* übler Scherz *m*; (*false alarm*) blinder Alarm *m*

hob /hɒb/ *n* Kochmulde *f*

hobble /ˈhɒbl/ *vi* humpeln

hobby /ˈhɒbɪ/ *n* Hobby *nt*. **~-horse** *n* (*fig*) Lieblingsthema *nt*

hobnailed /ˈhɒb-/ *a* **~ boots** *pl* genagelte Schuhe *pl*

hock /hɒk/ *n* [weißer] Rheinwein *m*

hockey /ˈhɒkɪ/ *n* Hockey *nt*

hoe /həʊ/ *n* Hacke *f* □ *vt* (*pres p* **hoeing**) hacken

hog /hɒg/ *n* [Mast]schwein *nt* □ *vt* (*pt/pp* **hogged**) (*fam*) mit Beschlag belegen

hoist /hɔɪst/ *n* Lastenaufzug *m* □ *vt* hochziehen; hissen ⟨*flag*⟩

hold[1] /həʊld/ *n* (*Naut*) Laderaum *m*

hold[2] *n* Halt *m*; (*Sport*) Griff *m*; (*fig: influence*) Einfluss *m*; **get ~ of** fassen; (*fam: contact*) erreichen □ *v* (*pt/pp* **held**) □ *vt* halten; ⟨*container:*⟩ fassen; (*believe*) meinen; (*possess*) haben; anhalten ⟨*breath*⟩; **~ one's tongue** den Mund halten □ *vi* ⟨*rope:*⟩ halten; ⟨*weather:*⟩ sich halten; **not ~ with** (*fam*) nicht einverstanden sein mit. **~ back** *vt* zurückhalten □ *vi* zögern. **~ on** *vi* (*wait*) warten; (*on telephone*) am Apparat bleiben; **~ on to** (*keep*) behalten; (*cling to*) sich festhalten an (+ *dat*). **~ out** *vt* hinhalten □ *vi* (*resist*) aushalten. **~ up** *vt* hochhalten; (*delay*) aufhalten; (*rob*) überfallen

ˈhold|all *n* Reisetasche *f*. **~er** *n* Inhaber(in) *m(f)*; (*container*) Halter *m*. **~-up** *n* Verzögerung *f*; (*attack*) Überfall *m*

hole /həʊl/ *n* Loch *nt*

holiday /ˈhɒlədeɪ/ *n* Urlaub *m*; (*Sch*) Ferien *pl*; (*public*) Feiertag *m*; (*day off*) freier Tag *m*; **go on ~** in Urlaub fahren. **~-maker** *n* Urlauber(in) *m(f)*

holiness /ˈhəʊlɪnɪs/ *n* Heiligkeit *f*

Holland /ˈhɒlənd/ *n* Holland *nt*

hollow /ˈhɒləʊ/ *a* hohl; ⟨*promise*⟩ leer □ *n* Vertiefung *f*; (*in ground*) Mulde *f*. **~ out** *vt* aushöhlen

holly /ˈhɒlɪ/ *n* Stechpalme *f*

ˈhollyhock *n* Stockrose *f*

hologram /ˈhɒləgræm/ *n* Hologramm *nt*

holster /ˈhəʊlstə(r)/ *n* Pistolentasche *f*

holy /ˈhəʊlɪ/ *a* (**-ier, -est**) heilig. **H~ Ghost** *or* **Spirit** *n* Heiliger Geist *m*. **~ water** *n* Weihwasser *nt*. **H~ Week** *n* Karwoche *f*

homage /ˈhɒmɪdʒ/ *n* Huldigung *f*; **pay ~ to** huldigen (+ *dat*)

home /həʊm/ *n* Zuhause *nt* (*house*) Haus *nt*; (*institution*) Heim *nt*; (*native land*) Heimat *f*

□ *adv* **at ~** zu Hause; **come/go ~** nach Hause kommen/gehen

home: ~ ad'dress *n* Heimatanschrift *f*. **~ com'puter** *n* Heimcomputer *m*. **~ game** *n* Heimspiel *nt*. **~ help** *n* Haushaltshilfe *f*. **~land** *n* Heimatland *nt*. **~less** *a* obdachlos

homely /'həʊmlɪ/ *a* (**-ier, -iest**) *a* gemütlich; (*Amer: ugly*) unscheinbar

home: ~-'made *a* selbst gemacht. **H~ Office** *n* Innenministerium *nt*. **H~ 'Secretary** Innenminister *m*. **~sick** *a* **be ~sick** Heimweh haben (**for** nach). **~sickness** *n* Heimweh *nt*. **~ 'town** *n* Heimatstadt *f*. **~work** *n* (*Sch*) Hausaufgaben *pl*

homicide /'hɒmɪsaɪd/ *n* Totschlag *m*; (*murder*) Mord *m*

homoeopath|ic /həʊmɪə'pæθɪk/ *a* homöopathisch. **~y** /-'ɒpəθɪ/ *n* Homöopathie *f*

homogeneous /hɒmə'dʒi:nɪəs/ *a* homogen

homo'sexual *a* homosexuell □ *n* Homosexuelle(r) *m/f*

honest /'ɒnɪst/ *a*, **-ly** *adv* ehrlich. **~y** *n* Ehrlichkeit *f*

honey /'hʌnɪ/ *n* Honig *m* (*fam: darling*) Schatz *m*

honey: ~comb *n* Honigwabe *f*. **~moon** *n* Flitterwochen *pl*; (*journey*) Hochzeitsreise *f*. **~suckle** *n* Geißblatt *nt*

honk /hɒŋk/ *vi* hupen

honorary /'ɒnərərɪ/ *a* ehrenamtlich; ⟨*member, doctorate*⟩ Ehren-

honour /'ɒnə(r)/ *n* Ehre *f* □ *vt* ehren; honorieren ⟨*cheque*⟩. **~able** /-əbl/ *a*, **-bly** *adv* ehrenhaft

hood /hʊd/ *n* Kapuze *f*; (*of pram*) [Klapp]verdeck *nt*; (*over cooker*) Abzugshaube *f*; (*Auto, Amer*) Kühlerhaube *f*

hoodlum /'hu:dləm/ *n* Rowdy *m*

'hoodwink *vt* (*fam*) reinlegen

hoof /hu:f/ *n* (*pl* **~s** *or* **hooves**) Huf *m*

hook /hʊk/ *n* Haken *m*; **by ~ or by crook** mit allen Mitteln □ *vt* festhaken (**to** an + *acc*)

hook|ed /hʊkt/ *a* **~ed nose** Hakennase *f*; **~ed on** (*fam*) abhängig von; (*keen on*) besessen von. **~er** *n* (*Amer, sl*) Nutte *f*

hookey /'hʊkɪ/ *n* **play ~** (*Amer, fam*) schwänzen

hooligan /'hu:lɪgən/ *n* Rowdy *m*. **~ism** *n* Rowdytum *nt*

hoop /hu:p/ *n* Reifen *m*

hooray /hʊ'reɪ/ *int & n* = **hurrah**

hoot /hu:t/ *n* Ruf *m*; **~s of laughter** schallendes Gelächter *nt* □ *vi* ⟨*owl:*⟩ rufen; ⟨*car:*⟩ hupen; (*jeer*) johlen. **~er** *n* (*of factory*) Sirene *f*; (*Auto*) Hupe *f*

hoover /'hu:və(r)/ *n* **H~** (**P**) Staubsauger *m* □ *vt/i* [staub]saugen

hop¹ /hɒp/ *n*, & **~s** *pl* Hopfen *m*

hop² *n* Hüpfer *m*; **catch s.o. on the ~** (*fam*) jdm ungelegen kommen □ *vi* (*pt/pp* **hopped**) hüpfen; **~ it!** (*fam*) hau ab! **~ in** *vi* (*fam*) einsteigen. **~ out** *vi* (*fam*) aussteigen

hope /həʊp/ *n* Hoffnung *f*; (*prospect*) Aussicht *f* (**of** auf + *acc*) □ *vt/i* hoffen (**for** auf + acc); **I ~ so** hoffentlich

hope|ful /'həʊpfl/ *a* hoffnungsvoll; **be ~ful that** hoffen, dass. **~fully** *adv* hoffnungsvoll; (*it is hoped*) hoffentlich. **~less** *a*, **-ly** *adv* hoffnungslos; (*useless*) nutzlos; (*incompetent*) untauglich

horde /hɔ:d/ *n* Horde *f*

horizon /hə'raɪzn/ *n* Horizont *m*; **on the ~** am Horizont

horizontal /hɒrɪ'zɒntl/ *a*, **-ly** *adv* horizontal. **~ 'bar** *n* Reck *nt*

horn /hɔ:n/ *n* Horn *nt*; (*Auto*) Hupe *f*

hornet /'hɔ:nɪt/ *n* Hornisse *f*

horny /'hɔ:nɪ/ *a* schwielig

horoscope /ˈhɒrəskəʊp/ *n* Horoskop *nt*
horrible /ˈhɒrɪbl/ *a*, **-bly** *adv* schrecklich
horrid /ˈhɒrɪd/ *a* grässlich
horrific /həˈrɪfɪk/ *a* entsetzlich
horrify /ˈhɒrɪfaɪ/ *vt* (*pt/pp* **-ied**) entsetzen
horror /ˈhɒrə(r)/ *n* Entsetzen *nt*. **~ film** *n* Horrorfilm *m*
hors-d'œuvre /ɔːˈdɜːvr/ *n* Vorspeise *f*
horse /hɔːs/ *n* Pferd *nt*
horse: ~back *n* **on ~back** zu Pferde. **~-ˈchestnut** *n* [Ross]kastanie *f*. **~man** *n* Reiter *m*. **~play** *n* Toben *nt*. **~power** *n* Pferdestärke *f*. **~-racing** *n* Pferderennen *nt*. **~radish** *n* Meerrettich *m*. **~shoe** *n* Hufeisen *nt*
hortiˈcultural /hɔːtɪ-/ *a* Garten-
ˈhorticulture *n* Gartenbau *m*
hose /həʊz/ *n* (*pipe*) Schlauch *m* □ *vt* **~ down** abspritzen
hosiery /ˈhəʊʒərɪ/ *n* Strumpfwaren *pl*
hospice /ˈhɒspɪs/ *n* Heim *nt*; (*for the terminally ill*) Sterbeklinik *f*
hospitable /hɒˈspɪtəbl/ *a*, **-bly** *adv* gastfreundlich
hospital /ˈhɒspɪtl/ *n* Krankenhaus *nt*
hospitality /hɒspɪˈtælətɪ/ *n* Gastfreundschaft *f*
host[1] /həʊst/ *n* **a ~ of** eine Menge von
host[2] *n* Gastgeber *m*
host[3] *n* (*Relig*) Hostie *f*
hostage /ˈhɒstɪdʒ/ *n* Geisel *f*
hostel /ˈhɒstl/ *n* [Wohn]heim *nt*
hostess /ˈhəʊstɪs/ *n* Gastgeberin *f*
hostile /ˈhɒstaɪl/ *a* feindlich; (*unfriendly*) feindselig
hostilit|y /hɒˈstɪlətɪ/ *n* Feindschaft *f*; **~ies** *pl* Feindseligkeiten *pl*
hot /hɒt/ *a* (**hotter, hottest**) heiß; ⟨*meal*⟩ warm; (*spicy*) scharf; **I am** *or* **feel ~** mir ist heiß
ˈhotbed *n* (*fig*) Brutstätte *f*
hotchpotch /ˈhɒtʃpɒtʃ/ *n* Mischmasch *m*
hotel /həʊˈtel/ *n* Hotel *nt*. **~ier** /-ɪə(r)/ *n* Hotelier *m*
hot: ~head *n* Hitzkopf *m*. **~-ˈheaded** *a* hitzköpfig. **~house** *n* Treibhaus *nt*. **~ly** *adv* (*fig*) heiß, heftig. **~plate** *n* Tellerwärmer *m*; (*of cooker*) Kochplatte *f*. **~ tap** *n* Warmwasserhahn *m*. **~-tempered** *a* jähzornig. **~-ˈwater-bottle** *n* Wärmflasche *f*
hound /haʊnd/ *n* Jagdhund *m* □ *vt* (*fig*) verfolgen
hour /ˈaʊə(r)/ *n* Stunde *f*. **~ly** *a* & *adv* stündlich; **~ly pay** *or* **rate** Stundenlohn *m*
house[1] /haʊs/ *n* Haus *nt*; **at my ~** bei mir
house[2] /haʊz/ *vt* unterbringen
house /haʊs/: **~boat** *n* Hausboot *nt*. **~breaking** *n* Einbruch *m*. **~hold** *n* Haushalt *m*. **~holder** *n* Hausinhaber(in) *m(f)*. **~keeper** *n* Haushälterin *f*. **~keeping** *n* Hauswirtschaft *f*; (*money*) Haushaltsgeld *nt*. **~-plant** *n* Zimmerpflanze *f*. **~-trained** *a* stubenrein. **~-warming** *n* **have a ~-warming party** Einstand feiern. **~wife** *n* Hausfrau *f*. **~work** *n* Hausarbeit *f*
housing /ˈhaʊzɪŋ/ *n* Wohnungen *pl*; (*Techn*) Gehäuse *nt*. **~ estate** *n* Wohnsiedlung *f*
hovel /ˈhɒvl/ *n* elende Hütte *f*
hover /ˈhɒvə(r)/ *vi* schweben; (*be undecided*) schwanken; (*linger*) herumstehen. **~craft** *n* Luftkissenfahrzeug *nt*
how /haʊ/ *adv* wie; **~ do you do?** guten Tag! **~ many** wie viele; **~ much** wie viel; **and ~!** und ob!
howˈever *adv* (*in question*) wie; (*nevertheless*) jedoch, aber; **~ small** wie klein es auch sein mag
howl /haʊl/ *n* Heulen *nt* □ *vi* heulen; ⟨*baby:*⟩ brüllen. **~er** *n* (*fam*) Schnitzer *m*

hub /hʌb/ *n* Nabe *f*; (*fig*) Mittelpunkt *m*
hubbub /'hʌbʌb/ *n* Stimmengewirr *nt*
'**hub-cap** *n* Radkappe *f*
huddle /'hʌdl/ *vi* ~ **together** sich zusammendrängen
hue1 /hjuː/ *n* Farbe *f*
hue2 *n* ~ **and cry** Aufruhr *m*
huff /hʌf/ *n* **in a** ~ beleidigt
hug /hʌg/ *n* Umarmung *f* □ vt (*pt/pp* **hugged**) umarmen
huge /hjuːdʒ/ *a*, **-ly** *adv* riesig
hulking /'hʌlkɪŋ/ *a* (*fam*) ungeschlacht
hull /hʌl/ *n* (*Naut*) Rumpf *m*
hullo /hə'ləʊ/ *int* = **hallo**
hum /hʌm/ *n* Summen *nt*; Brummen *nt* □ *vt/i* (*pt/pp* **hummed**) summen; ⟨*motor:*⟩ brummen; ~ **and haw** nicht mit der Sprache herauswollen
human /'hjuːmən/ *a* menschlich □ *n* Mensch *m*. ~ '**being** *n* Mensch *m*
humane /hjuː'meɪn/ *a*, **-ly** *adv* human
humanitarian /hjuːmænɪ'teərɪən/ *a* humanitär
humanit|y /hjuː'mænətɪ/ *n* Menschheit *f*; ~**ies** *pl* (*Univ*) Geisteswissenschaften *pl*
humble /'hʌmbl/ *a* (**-r, -st**), **-bly** *adv* demütig □ *vt* demütigen
'**humdrum** *a* eintönig
humid /'hjuːmɪd/ *a* feucht. ~**ity** /-'mɪdətɪ/ *n* Feuchtigkeit *f*
humiliat|e /hjuː'mɪlɪeɪt/ *vt* demütigen. ~**ion** /-'eɪʃn/ *n* Demütigung *f*
humility /hjuː'mɪlətɪ/ *n* Demut *f*
'**humming-bird** *n* Kolibri *m*
humorous /'hjuːmərəs/ *a*, **-ly** *adv* humorvoll; ⟨*story*⟩ humoristisch
humour /'hjuːmə(r)/ *n* Humor *m*; (*mood*) Laune *f*; **have a sense of** ~ Humor haben □ *vt* ~ **s.o** jdm seinen Willen lassen
hump /hʌmp/ *n* Buckel *m*; (*of camel*) Höcker *m* □ *vt* schleppen
hunch /hʌntʃ/ *n* (*idea*) Ahnung *f*
'**hunch|back** *n* Bucklige(r) *m/f*. ~**ed** *a* ~**ed up** gebeugt
hundred /'hʌndrəd/ a **one/a** ~ [ein]hundert □ *n* Hundert *nt*; (*written figure*) Hundert *f*. ~**th** *a* hundertste(r,s) □ *n* Hunderstel *nt*. ~**weight** *n* ≈ Zentner *m*
hung /hʌŋ/ *see* **hang**
Hungarian /hʌŋ'geərɪən/ *a* ungarisch □ *n* Ungarn(in) *m(f)*
Hungary /'hʌŋgərɪ/ *n* Ungar *nt*
hunger /'hʌŋgə(r)/ *n* Hunger *m*. ~**-strike** *n* Hungerstreik *m*
hungry /'hʌŋgrɪ/ *a* (**-ier, -iest**), **-ily** *adv* hungrig; **be** ~ Hunger haben
hunk /hʌŋk/ *n* [großes] Stück *nt*
hunt /hʌnt/ *n* Jagd *f*; (*for criminal*) Fahndung *f* □ *vt/i* jagen; fahnden nach ⟨*criminal*⟩; ~ **for** suchen. ~**er** *n* Jäger *m*; (*horse*) Jagdpferd *nt*. ~**ing** *n* Jagd *f*
hurdle /'hɜːdl/ *n* (*Sport & fig*) Hürde *f*. ~**r** *n* Hürdenläufer(in) *m(f)*
hurl /hɜːl/ *vt* schleudern
hurrah /hʊ'rɑː/, **hurray** /hʊ'reɪ/ *int* hurra! □ *n* Hurra *nt*
hurricane /'hʌrɪkən/ *n* Orkan *m*
hurried /'hʌrɪd/ *a*, **-ly** *adv* eilig; (*superficial*) flüchtig
hurry /'hʌrɪ/ *n* Eile *f*; **be in a** ~ es eilig haben □ *vi* (*pt/pp* **-ied**) sich beeilen; (*go quickly*) eilen. ~ **up** *vi* sich beeilen □ *vt* antreiben
hurt /hɜːt/ *n* Schmerz *m* □ *vt/i* (*pt/pp* **hurt**) **weh** tun (+ *dat*); (*injure*) verletzen; (*offend*) kränken. ~**ful** *a* verletzend
hurtle /'hɜːtl/ *vi* ~ **along** rasen
husband /'hʌzbənd/ *n* [Ehe]mann *m*
hush /hʌʃ/ *n* Stille *f* □ *vt* ~ **up** vertuschen. ~**ed** *a* gedämpft. ~-'**hush** *a* (*fam*) streng geheim
husk /hʌsk/ *n* Spelze *f*
husky /'hʌskɪ/ *a* (**-ier, -iest**) heiser; (*burly*) Stämmig

hustle /ˈhʌsl/ *vt* drängen □ *n* Gedränge *nt*; **~ and bustle** geschäftiges Treiben *nt*
hut /hʌt/ *n* Hütte *f*
hutch /hʌtʃ/ *n* [Kaninchen]stall *m*
hybrid /ˈhaɪbrɪd/ *a* hybrid □ *n* Hybride *f*
hydrangea /haɪˈdreɪndʒə/ *n* Hortensie *f*
hydrant /ˈhaɪdrənt/ *n* **[fire] ~** Hydrant *m*
hydraulic /haɪˈdrɔːlɪk/ *a*, **-ally** *adv* hydraulisch
hydrochloric /haɪdrəˈklɔːrɪk/ *a* **~ acid** Salzsäure *f*
hydroeˈlectric /haɪdrəʊ-/ *a* hydroelektrisch. **~ power station** *n* Wasserkraftwerk *nt*
hydrofoil /ˈhaɪdrə-/ *n* Tragflügelboot *nt*
hydrogen /ˈhaɪdrədʒən/ *n* Wasserstoff *m*
hyena /haɪˈiːnə/ *n* Hyäne *f*
hygien|e /ˈhaɪdʒiːn/ *n* Hygiene *f*. **~ic** /haɪˈdʒiːnɪk/ *a*, **-ally** *adv* hygienisch
hymn /hɪm/ *n* Kirchenlied *nt*. **~-book** *n* Gesangbuch *nt*
hyphen /ˈhaɪfn/ *n* Bindestrich *m*. **~ate** *vt* mit Bindestrich schreiben
hypno|sis /hɪpˈnəʊsɪs/ *n* Hypnose *f*. **~tic** /-ˈnɒtɪk/ *a* hypnotisch
hypno|tism /ˈhɪpnətɪzm/ *n* Hypnotik *f*. **~tist** /-tɪst/ *n* Hypnotiseur *m*. **~tize** *vt* hypnotisieren
hypochondriac /haɪpəˈkɒndrɪæk/ *a* hypochondrisch □ *n* Hypochonder *m*
hypocrisy /hɪˈpɒkrəsɪ/ *n* Heuchelei *f*
hypocrit|e /ˈhɪpəkrɪt/ *n* Heuchler(in) *m(f)*. **~ical** /-ˈkrɪtɪkl/ *a*, **-ly** *adv* heuchlerisch
hypodermic /haɪpəˈdɜːmɪk/ *a* & *n* **~ [syringe]** Injektionsspritze *f*
hypothe|sis /haɪˈpɒθəsɪs/ *n* Hypothese *f*. **~tical** /-əˈθetɪkl/ *a*, **-ly** *adv* hypothetisch
hyster|ia /hɪˈstɪərɪə/ *n* Hysterie *f*. **~ical** /-ˈsterɪkl/ *a*, **-ly** *adv* hysterisch. **~ics** /hɪˈsterɪks/ *npl* hysterischer Anfall *m*

I

I /aɪ/ *pron* ich
ice /aɪs/ *n* Eis *nt* □ *vt* mit Zuckerguss überziehen ⟨*cake*⟩
ice: ~ age *n* Eiszeit *f*. **~-axe** *n* Eispickel *m*. **~berg** /-bɜːg/ *n* Eisberg *m*. **~box** *n* (*Amer*) Kühlschrank *m*. **~-ˈcream** *n* [Speise]eis *nt*. **~-ˈcream parlour** *n* Eisdiele *f*. **~-cube** *n* Eiswürfel *m*
Iceland /ˈaɪslənd/ *n* Island *nt*
ice: ~ˈlolly *n* Eis *nt* am Stiel. **~ rink** *n* Eisbahn *f*
icicle /ˈaɪsɪkl/ *n* Eiszapfen *m*
icing /ˈaɪsɪŋ/ *n* Zuckerguss *m*. **~ sugar** *n* Puderzucker *m*
icon /ˈaɪkɒn/ *n* Ikone *f*
icy /ˈaɪsɪ/ *a* (**-ier, -iest**), **-ily** *adv* eisig; ⟨*road*⟩ vereist
idea /aɪˈdɪə/ *n* Idee *f*; (*conception*) Vorstellung *f*; **I have no ~!** ich habe keine Ahnung!
ideal /aɪˈdɪəl/ *a* ideal □ *n* Ideal *nt*. **~ism** *n* Idealismus *m*. **~ist** *n* Idealist(in) *m(f)*. **~istic** /-ˈlɪstɪk/ *a* idealistisch. **~ize** *vt* idealisieren. **~ly** *adv* ideal; (*in ideal circumstances*) idealerweise
identical /aɪˈdentɪkl/ *a* identisch; ⟨*twins*⟩ eineiig
identi|fication /aɪdentɪfɪˈkeɪʃn/ *n* Identifizierung *f*; (*proof of identity*) Ausweispapiere *pl*. **~fy** /aɪˈdentɪfaɪ/ *vt* (*pt/pp* **-ied**) identifizieren
identity /aɪˈdentətɪ/ *n* Identität *f*. **~ card** *n* [Personal]ausweis *m*
ideolog|ical /aɪdɪəˈlɒdʒɪkl/ *a* ideologisch. **~y** /aɪdɪˈɒlədʒɪ/ *n* Ideologie *f*
idiom /ˈɪdɪəm/ *n* [feste] Redewendung *f*. **~atic** /-ˈmætɪk/ *a*, **-ally** *adv* idiomatisch

idiosyncrasy /ɪdɪəˈsɪŋkrəsɪ/ *n* Eigenart *f*
idiot /ˈɪdɪət/ *n* Idiot *m*. **~ic** /-ˈɒtɪk/ *a* idiotisch
idle /ˈaɪdl/ *a* (**-r, -st**), **-ly** *adv* untätig; (*lazy*) faul; (*empty*) leer; ⟨*machine*⟩ nicht in Betrieb □ *vi* faulenzen; ⟨*engine:*⟩ leer laufen. **~ness** *n* Untätigkeit *f*; Faulheit *f*
idol /ˈaɪdl/ *n* Idol *nt*. **~ize** /ˈaɪdəlaɪz/ *vt* vergöttern
idyllic /ɪˈdɪlɪk/ *a* idyllisch
i.e. *abbr* (**id est**) d.h.
if /ɪf/ *conj* wenn; (*whether*) ob; **as if** als ob
ignite /ɪgˈnaɪt/ *vt* entzünden □ *vi* sich entzünden
ignition /ɪgˈnɪʃn/ *n* (*Auto*) Zündung *f*. **~ key** *n* Zündschlüssel *m*
ignoramus /ɪgnəˈreɪməs/ *n* Ignorant *m*
ignoran|ce /ˈɪgnərəns/ *n* Unwissenheit *f*. **~t** *a* unwissend; (*rude*) ungehobelt
ignore /ɪgˈnɔː(r)/ *vt* ignorieren
ilk /ɪlk/ *n* (*fam*) **of that ~** von der Sorte
ill /ɪl/ *a* krank; (*bad*) schlecht; **feel ~ at ease** sich unbehaglich fühlen □ *adv* schlecht □ *n* Schlechte(s) *nt*; (*evil*) Übel *nt*. **~-advised** *a* unklug. **~-bred** *a* schlecht erzogen
illegal /ɪˈliːgl/ *a*, **-ly** *adv* illegal
illegible /ɪˈledʒəbl/ *a*, **-bly** *adv* unleserlich
illegitima|cy /ɪlɪˈdʒɪtɪməsɪ/ *n* Unehelichkeit *f*. **~te** /-mət/ *a* unehelich; ⟨*claim*⟩ unberechtigt
illicit /ɪˈlɪsɪt/ *a*, **-ly** *adv* illegal
illitera|cy /ɪˈlɪtərəsɪ/ *n* Analphabetentum *nt*. **~te** /-rət/ *a* **be ~te** nicht lesen und schreiben können □ *n* Analphabet(in) *m(f)*
illness /ˈɪlnɪs/ *n* Krankheit *f*
illogical /ɪˈlɒdʒɪkl/ *a*, **-ly** *adv* unlogisch
ill-treat /ɪlˈtriːt/ *vt* misshandeln. **~ment** *n* Misshandlung *f*
illuminat|e /ɪˈluːmɪneɪt/ *vt* beleuchten. **~ing** *a* aufschlussreich. **~ion** /-ˈneɪʃn/ *n* Beleuchtung *f*
illusion /ɪˈluːʒn/ *n* Illusion *f*; **be under the ~ that** sich (*dat*) einbilden, dass
illusory /ɪˈluːsərɪ/ *a* illusorisch
illustrat|e /ˈɪləstreɪt/ *vt* illustrieren. **~ion** /-ˈstreɪʃn/ *n* Illustration *f*
illustrious /ɪˈlʌstrɪəs/ *a* berühmt
image /ˈɪmɪdʒ/ *n* Bild *nt*; (*statue*) Standbild *nt*; (*figure*) Figur *f*; (*exact likeness*) Ebenbild *nt*; **[public] ~** Image *nt*
imagin|able /ɪˈmædʒɪnəbl/ *a* vorstellbar. **~ary** /-ərɪ/ *a* eingebildet
imaginat|ion /ɪmædʒɪˈneɪʃn/ *n* Phantasie *f*; (*fancy*) Einbildung *f*. **~ive** /ɪˈmædʒɪnətɪv/ *a*, **-ly** *adv* phantasievoll; (*full of ideas*) einfallsreich
imagine /ɪˈmædʒɪn/ *vt* sich (*dat*) vorstellen; (*wrongly*) sich (*dat*) einbilden
imˈbalance *n* Unausgeglichenheit *f*
imbecile /ˈɪmbəsiːl/ *n* Schwachsinnige(r) *m/f*; (*pej*) Idiot *m*
imbibe /ɪmˈbaɪb/ *vt* trinken; (*fig*) aufnehmen
imbue /ɪmˈbjuː/ *vt* **be ~d with** erfüllt sein von
imitat|e /ˈɪmɪteɪt/ *vt* nachahmen, imitieren. **~ion** /-ˈteɪʃn/ *n* Nachahmung *f*, Imitation *f*
immaculate /ɪˈmækjʊlət/ *a*, **-ly** *adv* tadellos; (*Relig*) unbefleckt
immaˈterial *a* (*unimportant*) unwichtig, unwesentlich
immaˈture *a* unreif
immediate /ɪˈmiːdɪət/ *a* sofortig; (*nearest*) nächste(r,s). **~ly** *adv* sofort; **~ly next to** unmittelbar neben □ *conj* sobald
immemorial /ɪməˈmɔːrɪəl/ *a* **from time ~** seit Urzeiten

immense /ɪ'mens/ *a*, **-ly** *adv* riesig; (*fam*) enorm; (*extreme*) äußerst

immers|e /ɪ'mɜ:s/ *vt* untertauchen; **be ~ed in** (*fig*) vertieft sein in (+ *acc*). **~ion** /-ɜ:ʃn/ *n* Untertauchen *nt*. **~ion heater** *n* Heißwasserbereiter *m*

immigrant /'ɪmɪgrənt/ *n* Einwanderer *m*

immigrat|e /'ɪmɪgreɪt/ *vi* einwandern. **~ion** /-'greɪʃn/ *n* Einwanderung *f*

imminent /'ɪmɪnənt/ *a* **be ~** unmittelbar bevorstehen

immobil|e /ɪ'məʊbaɪl/ *a* unbeweglich. **~ize** /-bəlaɪz/ *vt* (*fig*) lähmen; (*Med*) ruhigstellen

immoderate /ɪ'mɒdərət/ *a* übermäßig

immodest /ɪ'mɒdɪst/ *a* unbescheiden

immoral /ɪ'mɒrəl/ *a*, **-ly** *adv* unmoralisch. **~ity** /ɪmə'rælətɪ/ *n* Unmoral *f*

immortal /ɪ'mɔ:tl/ *a* unsterblich. **~ity** /-'tælətɪ/ *n* Unsterblichkeit *f*. **~ize** *vt* verewigen

immovable /ɪ'mu:vəbl/ *a* unbeweglich; (*fig*) fest

immune /ɪ'mju:n/ *a* immun (**to/from** gegen). **~ system** *n* Abwehrsystem *nt*

immunity /ɪ'mju:nətɪ/ *n* Immunität *f*

immunize /'ɪmjʊnaɪz/ *vt* immunisieren

imp /ɪmp/ *n* Kobold *m*

impact /'ɪmpækt/ *n* Aufprall *m*; (*collision*) Zusammenprall *m*; (*of bomb*) Einschlag *m*; (*fig*) Auswirkung *f*

impair /ɪm'peə(r)/ *vt* beeinträchtigen

impale /ɪm'peɪl/ *vt* aufspießen

impart /ɪm'pɑ:t/ *vt* übermitteln (**to** *dat*); vermitteln ⟨*knowledge*⟩

im'parti|al *a* unparteiisch. **~'ality** *n* Unparteilichkeit *f*

im'passable *a* unpassierbar

impasse /æm'pɑ:s/ *n* (*fig*) Sackgasse *f*

impassioned /ɪm'pæʃnd/ *a* leidenschaftlich

im'passive *a*, **-ly** *adv* unbeweglich

im'patien|ce *n* Ungeduld *f*. **~t** *a*, **-ly** *adv* ungeduldig

impeach /ɪm'pi:tʃ/ *vt* anklagen

impeccable /ɪm'pekəbl/ *a*, **-bly** *adv* tadellos

impede /ɪm'pi:d/ *vt* behindern

impediment /ɪm'pedɪmənt/ *n* Hindernis *nt*; (*in speech*) Sprachfehler *m*

impel /ɪm'pel/ *vt* (*pt/pp* **impelled**) treiben; **feel ~led** sich genötigt fühlen (**to** zu)

impending /ɪm'pendɪŋ/ *a* bevorstehend

impenetrable /ɪm'penɪtrəbl/ *a* undurchdringlich

imperative /ɪm'perətɪv/ *a* **be ~** dringend notwendig sein □ *n* (*Gram*) Imperativ *m*, Befehlsform *f*

imper'ceptible *a* nicht wahrnehmbar

im'perfect *a* unvollkommen; (*faulty*) fehlerhaft □ *n* (*Gram*) Imperfekt *nt*. **~ion** /-'fekʃn/ *n* Unvollkommenheit *f*; (*fault*) Fehler *m*

imperial /ɪm'pɪərɪəl/ *a* kaiserlich. **~ism** *n* Imperialismus *m*

imperil /ɪm'perəl/ *vt* (*pt/pp* **imperilled**) gefährden

imperious /ɪm'pɪərɪəs/ *a*, **-ly** *adv* herrisch

im'personal *a* unpersönlich

impersonat|e /ɪm'pɜ:səneɪt/ *vt* sich ausgeben als; (*Theat*) nachahmen, imitieren. **~or** *n* Imitator *m*

impertinen|ce /ɪm'pɜ:tɪnəns/ *n* Frechheit *f*. **~t** *a* frech

imperturbable /ɪmpə'tɜ:bəbl/ *a* unerschütterlich

impervious /ɪm'pɜ:vɪəs/ *a* **~ to** (*fig*) unempfänglich für

impetuous /ɪmˈpetjʊəs/ *a*, **-ly** *adv* ungestüm
impetus /ˈɪmpɪtəs/ *n* Schwung *m*
impish /ˈɪmpɪʃ/ *a* schelmisch
implacable /ɪmˈplækəbl/ *a* unerbittlich
imˈplant¹ *vt* einpflanzen
ˈimplant² *n* Implantat *nt*
implement¹ /ˈɪmplɪmənt/ *n* Gerät *nt*
implement² /ˈɪmplɪment/ *vt* ausführen
implicat|e /ˈɪmplɪkeɪt/ *vt* verwickeln. **~ion** /-ˈkeɪʃn/ *n* Verwicklung *f*; **~ions** *pl* Auswirkungen *pl*; **by ~ion** implizit
implicit /ɪmˈplɪsɪt/ *a*, **-ly** *adv* unausgesprochen; (*absolute*) unbedingt
implore /ɪmˈplɔ:(r)/ *vt* anflehen
imply /ɪmˈplaɪ/ *vt* (*pt/pp* **-ied**) andeuten; **what are you ~ing?** was wollen Sie damit sagen?
impoˈlite *a*, **-ly** *adv* unhöflich
import¹ /ˈɪmpɔ:t/ *n* Import *m*, Einfuhr *f*; (*importance*) Wichtigkeit *f*; (*meaning*) Bedeutung *f*
import² /ɪmˈpɔ:t/ *vt* importieren, einführen
importan|ce /ɪmˈpɔ:tns/ *n* Wichtigkeit *f*. **~t** *a* wichtig
importer /ɪmˈpɔ:tə(r)/ *n* Importeur *m*
impos|e /ɪmˈpəʊz/ *vt* auferlegen (**on** *dat*) □ *vi* sich aufdrängen (**on** *dat*). **~ing** *a* eindrucksvoll. **~ition** /ɪmpəˈzɪʃn/ *n* **be an ~ition** eine Zumutung sein
impossiˈbility *n* Unmöglichkeit *f*
imˈpossible *a*, **-bly** *adv* unmöglich
impostor /ɪmˈpɒstə(r)/ *n* Betrüger(in) *m(f)*
impoten|ce /ˈɪmpətəns/ *n* Machtlosigkeit *f*; (*Med*) Impotenz *f*. **~t** *a* machtlos; (*Med*) impotent
impound /ɪmˈpaʊnd/ *vt* beschlagnahmen
impoverished /ɪmˈpɒvərɪʃt/ *a* verarmt
imˈpracticable *a* undurchführbar
imˈpractical *a* unpraktisch
impreˈcise *a* ungenau
impregnable /ɪmˈpregnəbl/ *a* uneinnehmbar
impregnate /ˈɪmpregneɪt/ *vt* tränken; (*Biol*) befruchten
imˈpress *vt* beeindrucken; **~ sth [up]on s.o.** jdm etw einprägen
impression /ɪmˈpreʃn/ *n* Eindruck *m*; (*imitation*) Nachahmung *f*; (*imprint*) Abdruck *m*; (*edition*) Auflage *f*. **~ism** *n* Impressionismus *m*
impressive /ɪmˈpresɪv/ *a* eindrucksvoll
ˈimprint¹ *n* Abdruck *m*
imˈprint² *vt* prägen; (*fig*) einprägen (**on** *dat*)
imˈprison *vt* gefangen halten; (*put in prison*) ins Gefängnis sperren
imˈprobable *a* unwahrscheinlich
impromptu /ɪmˈprɒmptju:/ *a* improvisiert □ *adv* aus dem Stegreif
imˈproper *a*, **-ly** *adv* inkorrekt; (*indecent*) unanständig
improˈpriety *n* Unkorrektheit *f*
improve /ɪmˈpru:v/ *vt* verbessern; verschönern ⟨*appearance*⟩ □ *vi* sich bessern; **~ [up]on** übertreffen. **~ment** /-mənt/ *n* Verbesserung *f*; (*in health*) Besserung *f*
improvise /ˈɪmprəvaɪz/ *vt/i* improvisieren
imˈprudent *a* unklug
impuden|ce /ˈɪmpjʊdəns/ *n* Frechheit *f*. **~t** *a*, **-ly** *adv* frech
impuls|e /ˈɪmpʌls/ *n* Impuls *m*; **on [an] ~e** impulsiv. **~ive** /-ˈpʌlsɪv/ *a*, **-ly** *adv* impulsiv
impunity /ɪmˈpju:nətɪ/ *n* **with ~** ungestraft
imˈpur|e *a* unrein. **~ity** *n* Unreinheit *f*; **~ities** *pl* Verunreinigungen *pl*

impute /ɪm'pjuːt/ *vt* zuschreiben (**to** *dat*)
in /ɪn/ *prep* in (+ *dat*/(*into*) + *acc*); **sit in the garden** im Garten sitzen; **go in the garden** in den Garten gehen; **in May** im Mai; **in the summer/winter** im Sommer/Winter; **in 1992** [im Jahre] 1992; **in this heat** bei dieser Hitze; **in the rain/sun** im Regen/in der Sonne; **in the evening** am Abend; **in the sky** am Himmel; **in the world** auf der Welt; **in the street** auf der Straße; **deaf in one ear** auf einem Ohr taub; **in the army** beim Militär; **in English/German** auf Englisch/Deutsch; **in ink/pencil** mit Tinte/Bleistift; **in a soft/loud voice** mit leiser/lauter Stimme; **in doing this, he ...** indem er das tut/tat, ... er □ *adv* (*at home*) zu Hause; (*indoors*) drinnen; **he's not in yet** er ist noch nicht da; **all in** alles inbegriffen; (*fam: exhausted*) kaputt; **day in, day out** tagaus, tagein; **keep in with s.o.** sich mit jdm gut stellen; **have it in for s.o.** (*fam*) es auf jdn abgesehen haben; **let oneself in for sth** sich auf etw (*acc*) einlassen; **send/go in** hineinschicken/-gehen; **come/bring in** hereinkommen/-bringen □ *a* (*fam: in fashion*) in □ *n* **the ins and outs** alle Einzelheiten *pl*
ina'bility *n* Unfähigkeit *f*
inac'cessible *a* unzugänglich
in'accura|cy *n* Ungenauigkeit *f*. **~te** *a*, **-ly** *adv* ungenau
in'ac|tive *a* untätig. **~'tivity** *n* Untätigkeit *f*
in'adequate *a*, **-ly** *adv* unzulänglich; **feel ~** sich der Situation nicht gewachsen fühlen
inad'missable *a* unzulässig
inadvertently /ɪnəd'vɜːtəntlɪ/ *adv* versehentlich
inad'visable *a* nicht ratsam
inane /ɪ'neɪn/ *a*, **-ly** *adv* albern
in'animate *a* unbelebt
in'applicable *a* nicht zutreffend
inap'propriate *a* unangebracht
inar'ticulate *a* undeutlich; **be ~** sich nicht gut ausdrücken können
inat'tentive *a* unaufmerksam
in'audible *a*, **-bly** *adv* unhörbar
inaugural /ɪ'nɔːgjʊrl/ *a* Antritts-
inaugurat|e /ɪ'nɔːgjʊreɪt/ *vt* [feierlich] in sein Amt einführen. **~ion** /-'reɪʃn/ *n* Amtseinführung *f*
inau'spicious *a* ungünstig
inborn /'ɪnbɔːn/ *a* angeboren
inbred /ɪn'bred/ *a* angeboren
incalculable /ɪn'kælkjʊləbl/ *a* nicht berechenbar; (*fig*) unabsehbar
in'capable *a* unfähig; **be ~ of doing sth** nicht fähig sein, etw zu tun
incapacitate /ɪnkə'pæsɪteɪt/ *vt* unfähig machen
incarcerate /ɪn'kɑːsəreɪt/ *vt* einkerkern
incarnat|e /ɪn'kɑːnət/ *a* **the devil ~e** der leibhaftige Satan. **~ion** /-'neɪʃn/ *n* Inkarnation *f*
incendiary /ɪn'sendɪərɪ/ *a* & *n* **~ [bomb]** Brandbombe *f*
incense¹ /'ɪnsens/ *n* Weihrauch *m*
incense² /ɪn'sens/ *vt* wütend machen
incentive /ɪn'sentɪv/ *n* Anreiz *m*
inception /ɪn'sepʃn/ *n* Beginn *m*
incessant /ɪn'sesnt/ *a*, **-ly** *adv* unaufhörlich
incest /'ɪnsest/ *n* Inzest *m*, Blutschande *f*
inch /ɪntʃ/ *n* Zoll *m* □ *vi* **~ forward** sich ganz langsam vorwärts schieben
inciden|ce /'ɪnsɪdəns/ *n* Vorkommen *nt*. **~t** *n* Zwischenfall *m*
incidental /ɪnsɪ'dentl/ *a* nebensächlich; ⟨*remark*⟩ beiläufig; ⟨*expenses*⟩ Neben-. **~ly** *adv* übrigens
incinerat|e /ɪn'sɪnəreɪt/ *vt* verbrennen. **~or** *n* Verbrennungsofen *m*

incipient /ɪn'sɪpɪənt/ *a* angehend
incision /ɪn'sɪʒn/ *n* Einschnitt *m*
incisive /ɪn'saɪsɪv/ *a* scharfsinnig
incisor /ɪn'saɪzə(r)/ *n* Schneidezahn *m*
incite /ɪn'saɪt/ *vt* aufhetzen. **~ment** *n* Aufhetzung *f*
inci'vility *n* Unhöflichkeit *f*
in'clement *a* rau
inclination /ɪnklɪ'neɪʃn/ *n* Neigung *f*
incline[1] /ɪn'klaɪn/ *vt* neigen; **be ~d to do sth** dazu neigen, etw zu tun □ *vi* sich neigen
incline[2] /'ɪnklaɪn/ *n* Neigung *f*
inclu|de /ɪn'klu:d/ *vt* einschließen; (*contain*) enthalten; (*incorporate*) aufnehmen (**in** in + *acc*). **~ding** *prep* einschließlich (+ *gen*). **~sion** /-u:ʒn/ *n* Aufnahme *f*
inclusive /ɪn'klu:sɪv/ *a* Inklusiv-; **~ of** einschließlich (+ *gen*) □ *adv* inklusive
incognito /ɪnkɒg'ni:təʊ/ *adv* inkognito
inco'herent *a*, **-ly** *adv* zusammenhanglos; (*incomprehensible*) unverständlich
income /'ɪnkəm/ *n* Einkommen *nt*. **~ tax** *n* Einkommensteuer *f*
'incoming *a* ankommend; ⟨*mail, call*⟩ eingehend. **~ tide** *n* steigende Flut *f*
in'comparable *a* unvergleichlich
incom'patible *a* unvereinbar; **be ~** ⟨*people:*⟩ nicht zueinander passen
in'competen|ce *n* Unfähigkeit *f*. **~t** *a* unfähig
incom'plete *a* unvollständig
incompre'hensible *a* unverständlich
incon'ceivable *a* undenkbar
incon'clusive *a* nicht schlüssig
incongruous /ɪn'kɒŋgrʊəs/ *a* unpassend
inconsequential /ɪnkɒnsɪ'kwenʃl/ *a* unbedeutend
incon'siderate *a* rücksichtslos
incon'sistent *a*, **-ly** *adv* widersprüchlich; (*illogical*) inkonsequent; **be ~** nicht übereinstimmen
inconsolable /ɪnkən'səʊləbl/ *a* untröstlich
incon'spicuous *a* unauffällig
incontinen|ce /ɪn'kɒntɪnəns/ *n* Inkontinenz *f*. **~t** *a* inkontinent
incon'venien|ce *n* Unannehmlichkeit *f*; (*drawback*) Nachteil *m*; **put s.o. to ~ce** jdm Umstände machen. **~t** *a*, **-ly** *adv* ungünstig; **be ~t for s.o.** jdm nicht passen
incorporate /ɪn'kɔ:pəreɪt/ *vt* aufnehmen; (*contain*) enthalten
incor'rect *a*, **-ly** *adv* inkorrekt
incorrigible /ɪn'kɒrɪdʒəbl/ *a* unverbesserlich
incorruptible /ɪnkə'rʌptəbl/ *a* unbestechlich
increase[1] /'ɪnkri:s/ *n* Zunahme *f*; (*rise*) Erhöhung *f*; **be on the ~** zunehmen
increas|e[2] /ɪn'kri:s/ *vt* vergrößern; (*raise*) erhöhen □ *vi* zunehmen; (*rise*) sich erhöhen. **~ing** *a*, **-ly** *adv* zunehmend
in'credible *a*, **-bly** *adv* unglaublich
incredulous /ɪn'kredjʊləs/ *a* ungläubig
increment /'ɪnkrɪmənt/ *n* Gehaltszulage *f*
incriminate /ɪn'krɪmɪneɪt/ *vt* (*Jur*) belasten
incubat|e /'ɪŋkjʊbeɪt/ *vt* ausbrüten. **~ion** /-'beɪʃn/ *n* Ausbrüten *nt*. **~ion period** *n* (*Med*) Inkubationszeit *f*. **~or** *n* (*for baby*) Brutkasten *m*
inculcate /'ɪnkʌlkeɪt/ *vt* einprägen (**in** *dat*)
incumbent /ɪn'kʌmbənt/ *a* **be ~ on s.o.** jds Pflicht sein
incur /ɪn'kɜ:(r)/ *vt* (*pt/pp* **incurred**) sich (*dat*) zuziehen; machen ⟨*debts*⟩

in'curable *a*, **-bly** *adv* unheilbar
incursion /ɪn'kɜːʃn/ *n* Einfall *m*
indebted /ɪn'detɪd/ *a* verpflichtet (**to** *dat*)
in'decent *a*, **-ly** *adv* unanständig
inde'cision *n* Unentschlossenheit *f*
inde'cisive *a* ergebnislos; ⟨*person*⟩ unentschlossen
indeed /ɪn'diːd/ *adv* in der Tat, tatsächlich; **yes ~!** allerdings! **~ I am/do** oh doch! **very much ~** sehr; **thank you very much ~** vielen herzlichen Dank
indefatigable /ɪndɪ'fætɪgəbl/ *a* unermüdlich
in'definite *a* unbestimmt. **~ly** *adv* unbegrenzt; ⟨*postpone*⟩ auf unbestimmte Zeit
indelible /ɪn'delɪbl/ *a*, **-bly** *adv* nicht zu entfernen; (*fig*) unauslöschlich
indemni|fy /ɪn'demnɪfaɪ/ *vt* (*pt/pp* **-ied**) versichern; (*compensate*) entschädigen. **~ty** *n* Versicherung *f*; Entschädigung *f*
indent /ɪn'dent/ *vt* (*Typ*) einrücken. **~ation** /-'teɪʃn/ *n* Einrückung *f*; (*notch*) Kerbe *f*
inde'penden|ce *n* Unabhängigkeit *f*; (*self-reliance*) Selbstständigkeit *f*. **~t** *a*, **-ly** *adv* unabhängig; selbstständig
indescribable /ɪndɪ'skraɪbəbl/ *a*, **-bly** *adv* unbeschreiblich
indestructible /ɪndɪ'strʌktəbl/ *a* unzerstörbar
indeterminate /ɪndɪ'tɜːmɪnət/ *a* unbestimmt
index /'ɪndeks/ *n* Register *nt*
index: ~ card *n* Karteikarte *f*. **~ finger** *n* Zeigefinger *m*. **~-linked** *a* ⟨*pension*⟩ dynamisch
India /'ɪndɪə/ *n* Indien *nt*. **~n** *a* indisch; (*American*) indianisch □ *n* Inder(in) *m*(*f*); (*American*) Indianer(in) *m*(*f*)
Indian: ~ 'ink *n* Tusche *f*. **~ 'summer** *n* Nachsommer *m*
indicat|e /'ɪndɪkeɪt/ *vt* zeigen; (*point at*) zeigen auf (+ *acc*); (*hint*) andeuten; (*register*) anzeigen □ *vi* (*Auto*) blinken. **~ion** /-'keɪʃn/ *n* Anzeichen *nt*
indicative /ɪn'dɪkətɪv/ *a* **be ~ of** schließen lassen auf (+ *acc*) □ *n* (*Gram*) Indikativ *m*
indicator /'ɪndɪkeɪtə(r)/ *n* (*Auto*) Blinker *m*
indict /ɪn'daɪt/ *vt* anklagen. **~ment** *n* Anklage *f*
in'differen|ce *n* Gleichgültigkeit *f*. **~t** *a*, **-ly** *adv* gleichgültig; (*not good*) mittelmäßig
indigenous /ɪn'dɪdʒɪnəs/ *a* einheimisch
indi'gest|ible *a* unverdaulich; (*difficult to digest*) schwer verdaulich. **~ion** *n* Magenverstimmung *f*
indigna|nt /ɪn'dɪgnənt/ *a*, **-ly** *adv* entrüstet, empört. **~tion** /-'neɪʃn/ *n* Entrüstung *f*, Empörung *f*
in'dignity *n* Demütigung *f*
indi'rect *a*, **-ly** *adv* indirekt
indi'screet *a* indiskret
indis'cretion *n* Indiskretion *f*
indiscriminate /ɪndɪ'skrɪmɪnət/ *a*, **-ly** *adv* wahllos
indi'spensable *a* unentbehrlich
indisposed /ɪndɪ'spəʊzd/ *a* indisponiert
indisputable /ɪndɪ'spjuːtəbl/ *a*, **-bly** *adv* unbestreitbar
indi'stinct *a*, **-ly** *adv* undeutlich
indistinguishable /ɪndɪ'stɪŋgwɪʃəbl/ *a* **be ~** nicht zu unterscheiden sein; (*not visible*) nicht erkennbar sein
individual /ɪndɪ'vɪdjʊəl/ *a*, **-ly** *adv* individuell; (*single*) einzeln □ *n* Individuum *nt*. **~ity** /-'ælətɪ/ *n* Individualität *f*
indi'visible *a* unteilbar
indoctrinate /ɪn'dɒktrɪneɪt/ *vt* indoktrinieren
indolen|ce /'ɪndələns/ *n* Faulheit *f*. **~t** *a* faul

indomitable /ɪn'dɒmɪtəbl/ *a* unbeugsam

indoor /'ɪndɔ:(r)/ *a* Innen-; ⟨*clothes*⟩ Haus-; ⟨*plant*⟩ Zimmer-; (*Sport*) Hallen-. **~s** /-'dɔ:z/ *adv* im Haus, drinnen; **go ~s** ins Haus gehen

induce /ɪn'dju:s/ *vt* dazu bewegen (**to** zu); (*produce*) herbeiführen. **~ment** *n* (*incentive*) Anreiz *m*

indulge /ɪn'dʌldʒ/ *vt* frönen (+ *dat*); verwöhnen ⟨*child*⟩ □ *vi* **~ in** frönen (+ *dat*). **~nce** /-əns/ *n* Nachgiebigkeit *f*; (*leniency*) Nachsicht *f*. **~nt** *a* [zu] nachgiebig; nachsichtig

industrial /ɪn'dʌstrɪəl/ *a* Industrie-; **take ~ action** streiken. **~ist** *n* Industrielle(r) *m*. **~ized** *a* industrialisiert

industr|ious /ɪn'dʌstrɪəs/ *a*, **-ly** *adv* fleißig. **~y** /'ɪndəstrɪ/ *n* Industrie *f*; (*zeal*) Fleiß *m*

inebriated /ɪ'ni:brɪeɪtɪd/ *a* betrunken

in'edible *a* nicht essbar

inef'fective *a*, **-ly** *adv* unwirksam; ⟨*person*⟩ untauglich

ineffectual /ɪnɪ'fektʃʊəl/ *a* unwirksam; ⟨*person*⟩ untauglich

inef'ficient *a* unfähig; ⟨*organization*⟩ nicht leistungsfähig; ⟨*method*⟩ nicht rationell

in'eligible *a* nicht berechtigt

inept /ɪ'nept/ *a* ungeschickt

ine'quality *n* Ungleichheit *f*

inert /ɪ'nɜ:t/ *a* unbeweglich; (*Phys*) träge. **~ia** /ɪ'nɜ:ʃə/ *n* Trägheit *f*

inescapable /ɪnɪ'skeɪpəbl/ *a* unvermeidlich

inestimable /ɪn'estɪməbl/ *a* unschätzbar

inevitab|le /ɪn'evɪtəbl/ *a* unvermeidlich. **~ly** *adv* zwangsläufig

ine'xact *a* ungenau

inex'cusable *a* unverzeihlich

inexhaustible /ɪnɪg'zɔ:stəbl/ *a* unerschöpflich

inexorable /ɪn'eksərəbl/ *a* unerbittlich

inex'pensive *a*, **-ly** *adv* preiswert

inex'perience *n* Unerfahrenheit *f*. **~d** *a* unerfahren

inexplicable /ɪnɪk'splɪkəbl/ *a* unerklärlich

in'fallible *a* unfehlbar

infam|ous /'ɪnfəməs/ *a* niederträchtig; (*notorious*) berüchtigt. **~y** *n* Niederträchtigkeit *f*

infan|cy /'ɪnfənsɪ/ *n* frühe Kindheit *f*; (*fig*) Anfangsstadium *nt*. **~t** *n* Kleinkind *nt*. **~tile** *a* kindisch

infantry /'ɪnfəntrɪ/ *n* Infanterie *f*

infatuated /ɪn'fætʃʊeɪtɪd/ *a* vernarrt (**with** in + *acc*)

infect /ɪn'fekt/ *vt* anstecken, infizieren; **become ~ed** ⟨*wound:*⟩ sich infizieren. **~ion** /-'fekʃn/ *n* Infektion *f*. **~ious** /-'fekʃəs/ *a* ansteckend

infer /ɪn'fɜ:(r)/ *vt* (*pt/pp* **inferred**) folgern (**from** aus); (*imply*) andeuten. **~ence** /'ɪnfərəns/ *n* Folgerung *f*

inferior /ɪn'fɪərɪə(r)/ *a* minderwertig; (*in rank*) untergeordnet □ *n* Untergebene(r) *m/f*

inferiority /ɪnfɪərɪ'ɒrətɪ/ *n* Minderwertigkeit *f*. **~ complex** *n* Minderwertigkeitskomplex *m*

infern|al /ɪn'fɜ:nl/ *a* höllisch. **~o** *n* flammendes Inferno *nt*

in'fer|tile *a* unfruchtbar. **~'tility** *n* Unfruchtbarkeit *f*

infest /ɪn'fest/ *vt* **be ~ed with** befallen sein von; ⟨*place*⟩ verseucht sein mit

infi'delity *n* Untreue *f*

infighting /'ɪnfaɪtɪŋ/ *n* (*fig*) interne Machtkämpfe *pl*

infiltrate /'ɪnfɪltreɪt/ *vt* infiltrieren; (*Pol*) unterwandern

infinite /'ɪnfɪnət/ *a*, **-ly** *adv* unendlich

infinitesimal /ɪnfɪnɪ'tesɪml/ *a* unendlich klein

infinitive /ɪnˈfɪnətɪv/ *n* (*Gram*) Infinitiv *m*
infinity /ɪnˈfɪnətɪ/ *n* Unendlichkeit *f*
infirm /ɪnˈfɜːm/ *a* gebrechlich. **~ary** *n* Krankenhaus *nt*. **~ity** *n* Gebrechlichkeit *f*
inflame /ɪnˈfleɪm/ *vt* entzünden; **become ~d** sich entzünden. **~d** *a* entzündet
inˈflammable *a* feuergefährlich
inflammation /ɪnfləˈmeɪʃn/ *n* Entzündung *f*
inflammatory /ɪnˈflæmətrɪ/ *a* aufrührerisch
inflatable /ɪnˈfleɪtəbl/ *a* aufblasbar
inflat|e /ɪnˈfleɪt/ *vt* aufblasen; (*with pump*) aufpumpen. **~ion** /-eɪʃn/ *n* Inflation *f*. **~ionary** /-eɪʃənərɪ/ *a* inflationär
inˈflexible *a* starr; ⟨*person*⟩ unbeugsam
inflexion /ɪnˈflekʃn/ *n* Tonfall *m*; (*Gram*) Flexion *f*
inflict /ɪnˈflɪkt/ *vt* zufügen (**on** *dat*); versetzen ⟨*blow*⟩ (**on** *dat*)
influen|ce /ˈɪnflʊəns/ *n* Einfluss *m* □ *vt* beeinflussen. **~tial** /-ˈenʃl/ *a* einflussreich
influenza /ɪnflʊˈenzə/ *n* Grippe *f*
influx /ˈɪnflʌks/ *n* Zustrom *m*
inform /ɪnˈfɔːm/ *vt* benachrichtigen; (*officially*) informieren; **~ s.o. of sth** jdm etw mitteilen; **keep s.o. ~ed** jdn auf dem Laufenden halten □ *vi* **~ against** denunzieren
inˈfor|mal *a*, **-ly** *adv* zwanglos; (*unofficial*) inoffiziell. **~ˈmality** *n* Zwanglosigkeit *f*
informant /ɪnˈfɔːmənt/ *n* Gewährsmann *m*
informat|ion /ɪnfəˈmeɪʃn/ *n* Auskunft *f*; **a piece of ~ion** eine Auskunft. **~ive** /ɪnˈfɔːmətɪv/ *a* aufschlussreich; (*instructive*) lehrreich
informer /ɪnˈfɔːmə(r)/ *n* Spitzel *m*; (*Pol*) Denunziant *m*
infra-ˈred /ɪnfrə-/ *a* infrarot
inˈfrequent *a*, **-ly** *adv* selten
infringe /ɪnˈfrɪndʒ/ *vt/i* **~ [on]** verstoßen gegen. **~ment** *n* Verstoß *m*
infuriat|e /ɪnˈfjʊərɪeɪt/ *vt* wütend machen. **~ing** *a* ärgerlich; **he is ~ing** er kann einen zur Raserei bringen
infusion /ɪnˈfjuːʒn/ *n* Aufguss *m*
ingenious /ɪnˈdʒiːnɪəs/ *a* erfinderisch; ⟨*thing*⟩ raffiniert
ingenuity /ɪndʒɪˈnjuːətɪ/ *n* Geschicklichkeit *f*
ingenuous /ɪnˈdʒenjʊəs/ *a* unschuldig
ingot /ˈɪŋgət/ *n* Barren *m*
ingrained /ɪnˈgreɪnd/ *a* eingefleischt; **be ~** ⟨*dirt:*⟩ tief sitzen
ingratiate /ɪnˈgreɪʃɪeɪt/ *vt* **~ oneself** sich einschmeicheln (**with** bei)
inˈgratitude *n* Undankbarkeit *f*
ingredient /ɪnˈgriːdɪənt/ *n* (*Culin*) Zutat *f*
ingrowing /ˈɪngrəʊɪŋ/ *a* ⟨*nail*⟩ eingewachsen
inhabit /ɪnˈhæbɪt/ *vt* bewohnen. **~ant** *n* Einwohner(in) *m(f)*
inhale /ɪnˈheɪl/ *vt/i* einatmen; (*Med & when smoking*) inhalieren
inherent /ɪnˈhɪərənt/ *a* natürlich
inherit /ɪnˈherɪt/ *vt* erben. **~ance** /-əns/ *n* Erbschaft *f*, Erbe *nt*
inhibit /ɪnˈhɪbɪt/ *vt* hemmen. **~ed** *a* gehemmt. **~ion** /-ˈbɪʃn/ *n* Hemmung *f*
inhoˈspitable *a* ungastlich
inˈhuman *a* unmenschlich
inimitable /ɪˈnɪmɪtəbl/ *a* unnachahmlich
iniquitous /ɪˈnɪkwɪtəs/ *a* schändlich; (*unjust*) ungerecht
initial /ɪˈnɪʃl/ *a* anfänglich, Anfangs- □ *n* Anfangsbuchstabe *m*; **my ~s** meine Initialen □ *vt* (*pt/pp* **initialled**) abzeichnen; (*Pol*) paraphieren. **~ly** *adv* anfangs, am Anfang

initiat|e /ɪˈnɪʃɪeɪt/ *vt* einführen. **~ion** /-ˈeɪʃn/ *n* Einführung *f*
initiative /ɪˈnɪʃətɪv/ *n* Initiative *f*
inject /ɪnˈdʒekt/ *vt* einspritzen, injizieren. **~ion** /-ekʃn/ *n* Spritze *f*, Injektion *f*
injunction /ɪnˈdʒʌŋkʃn/ *n* gerichtliche Verfügung *f*
injur|e /ˈɪndʒə(r)/ *vt* verletzen. **~y** *n* Verletzung *f*
in'justice *n* Ungerechtigkeit *f*; **do s.o. an ~** jdm unrecht tun
ink /ɪŋk/ *n* Tinte *f*
inkling /ˈɪŋklɪŋ/ *n* Ahnung *f*
inlaid /ɪnˈleɪd/ *a* eingelegt
inland /ˈɪnlənd/ *a* Binnen- □ *adv* landeinwärts. **I ~ Revenue** *n* ≈ Finanzamt *nt*
in-laws /ˈɪnlɔːz/ *npl* (*fam*) Schwiegereltern *pl*
inlay /ˈɪnleɪ/ *n* Einlegearbeit *f*
inlet /ˈɪnlet/ *n* schmale Bucht *f*; (*Techn*) Zuleitung *f*
inmate /ˈɪnmeɪt/ *n* Insasse *m*
inn /ɪn/ *n* Gasthaus *nt*
innards /ˈɪnədz/ *npl* (*fam*) Eingeweide *pl*
innate /ɪˈneɪt/ *a* angeboren
inner /ˈɪnə(r)/ *a* innere(r,s). **~most** *a* innerste(r,s)
'innkeeper *n* Gastwirt *m*
innocen|ce /ˈɪnəsəns/ *n* Unschuld *f*. **~t** *a* unschuldig. **~tly** *adv* in aller Unschuld
innocuous /ɪˈnɒkjʊəs/ *a* harmlos
innovat|e /ˈɪnəveɪt/ *vi* neu einführen. **~ion** /-ˈveɪʃn/ *n* Neuerung *f*. **~or** *n* Neuerer *m*
innuendo /ɪnjuːˈendəʊ/ *n* (*pl* **-es**) [versteckte] Anspielung *f*
innumerable /ɪˈnjuːmərəbl/ *a* unzählig
inoculat|e /ɪˈnɒkjʊleɪt/ *vt* impfen. **~ion** /-ˈleɪʃn/ *n* Impfung *f*
inof'fensive *a* harmlos
in'operable *a* nicht operierbar
in'opportune *a* unpassend
inordinate /ɪˈnɔːdɪnət/ *a*, **-ly** *adv* übermäßig
inor'ganic *a* anorganisch
'in-patient *n* [stationär behandelter] Krankenhauspatient *m*
input /ˈɪnpʊt/ *n* Input *m & nt*
inquest /ˈɪnkwest/ *n* gerichtliche Untersuchung *f*
inquir|e /ɪnˈkwaɪə(r)/ *vi* sich erkundigen (**about** nach); **~e into** untersuchen □ *vt* sich erkundigen nach. **~y** *n* Erkundigung *f*; (*investigation*) Untersuchung *f*
inquisitive /ɪnˈkwɪzətɪv/ *a*, **-ly** *adv* neugierig
inroad /ˈɪnrəʊd/ *n* Einfall *m*; **make ~s into sth** etw angreifen
in'sane *a* geisteskrank; (*fig*) wahnsinnig
in'sanitary *a* unhygienisch
in'sanity *n* Geisteskrankheit *f*
insatiable /ɪnˈseɪʃəbl/ *a* unersättlich
inscri|be /ɪnˈskraɪb/ *vt* eingravieren. **~ption** /-ˈskrɪpʃn/ *n* Inschrift *f*
inscrutable /ɪnˈskruːtəbl/ *a* unergründlich; ⟨*expression*⟩ undurchdringlich
insect /ˈɪnsekt/ *n* Insekt *nt*. **~icide** /-ˈsektɪsaɪd/ *n* Insektenvertilgungsmittel *nt*
inse'cur|e *a* nicht sicher; (*fig*) unsicher. **~ity** *n* Unsicherheit *f*
insemination /ɪnsemɪˈneɪʃn/ *n* Besamung *f*; (*Med*) Befruchtung *f*
in'sensible *a* (*unconscious*) bewusstlos
in'sensitive *a* gefühllos; **~ to** unempfindlich gegen
in'separable *a* untrennbar; (*people*) unzertrennlich
insert[1] /ˈɪnsɜːt/ *n* Einsatz *m*
insert[2] /ɪnˈsɜːt/ *vt* einfügen, einsetzen; einstecken ⟨*key*⟩; einwerfen ⟨*coin*⟩. **~ion** /-ɜːʃn/ *n* (*insert*) Einsatz *m*; (*in text*) Einfügung *f*

inside /ɪn'saɪd/ *n* Innenseite *f*; (*of house*) Innere(s) *nt* □ *attrib* Innen- □ *adv* innen; (*indoors*) drinnen; **go ~** hineingehen; **come ~** hereinkommen; **~ out** links [herum]; **know sth ~ out** etw in- und auswendig kennen □ *prep* **~ [of]** in (+ *dat*/ (*into*) + *acc*)

insidious /ɪn'sɪdɪəs/ *a*, **-ly** *adv* heimtückisch

insight /'ɪnsaɪt/ *n* Einblick *m* (**into** in + *acc*); (*understanding*) Einsicht *f*

insignia /ɪn'sɪgnɪə/ *npl* Insignien *pl*

insig'nificant *a* unbedeutend

insin'cere *a* unaufrichtig

insinuat|e /ɪn'sɪnjʊeɪt/ *vt* andeuten. **~ion** /-'eɪʃn/ *n* Andeutung *f*

insipid /ɪn'sɪpɪd/ *a* fade

insist /ɪn'sɪst/ *vi* darauf bestehen; **~ on** bestehen auf (+ *dat*) □ *vt* **~ that** darauf bestehen, dass. **~ence** *n* Bestehen *nt*. **~ent** *a*, **-ly** *adv* beharrlich; **be ~ent** darauf bestehen

'insole *n* Einlegesohle *f*

insolen|ce /'ɪnsələns/ *n* Unverschämtheit *f*. **~t** *a*, **-ly** *adv* unverschämt

in'soluble *a* unlöslich; (*fig*) unlösbar

in'solvent *a* zahlungsunfähig

insomnia /ɪn'sɒmnɪə/ *n* Schlaflosigkeit *f*

inspect /ɪn'spekt/ *vt* inspizieren; (*test*) prüfen; kontrollieren ⟨*ticket*⟩. **~ion** /-ekʃn/ *n* Inspektion *f*. **~or** *n* Inspektor *m*; (*of tickets*) Kontrolleur *m*

inspiration /ɪnspə'reɪʃn/ *n* Inspiration *f*

inspire /ɪn'spaɪə(r)/ *vt* inspirieren; **~ sth in s.o.** jdm etw einflößen

insta'bility *n* Unbeständigkeit *f*; (*of person*) Labilität *f*

install /ɪn'stɔ:l/ *vt* installieren; [in ein Amt] einführen ⟨*person*⟩. **~ation** /-stə'leɪʃn/ *n* Installation *f*; Amtseinführung *f*

instalment /ɪn'stɔ:lmənt/ *n* (*Comm*) Rate *f*; (*of serial*) Fortsetzung *f*; (*Radio, TV*) Folge *f*

instance /'ɪnstəns/ *n* Fall *m*; (*example*) Beispiel *nt*; **in the first ~** zunächst; **for ~** zum Beispiel

instant /'ɪnstənt/ *a* sofortig; (*Culin*) Instant- □ *n* Augenblick *m*, Moment *m*. **~aneous** /-'teɪnɪəs/ *a* unverzüglich, unmittelbar; **death was ~aneous** der Tod trat sofort ein

instant 'coffee *n* Pulverkaffee *m*

instantly /'ɪnstəntlɪ/ *adv* sofort

instead /ɪn'sted/ *adv* statt dessen; **~ of** statt (+ *gen*), anstelle von; **~ of me** an meiner Stelle; **~ of going** anstatt zu gehen

'instep *n* Spann *m*, Rist *m*

instigat|e /'ɪnstɪgeɪt/ *vt* anstiften; einleiten ⟨*proceedings*⟩. **~ion** /-'geɪʃn/ *n* Anstiftung *f*; **at his ~ion** auf seine Veranlassung. **~or** *n* Anstifter(in) *m(f)*

instil /ɪn'stɪl/ *vt* (*pt/pp* **instilled**) einprägen (**into s.o.** jdm)

instinct /'ɪnstɪŋkt/ *n* Instinkt *m*. **~ive** /ɪn'stɪŋktɪv/ *a*, **-ly** *adv* instinktiv

institut|e /'ɪnstɪtju:t/ *n* Institut *nt* □ *vt* einführen; einleiten ⟨*search*⟩. **~ion** /-'tju:ʃn/ *n* Institution *f*; (*home*) Anstalt *f*

instruct /ɪn'strʌkt/ *vt* unterrichten; (*order*) anweisen. **~ion** /-ʌkʃn/ *n* Unterricht *m*; Anweisung *f*; **~ions** *pl* **for use** Gebrauchsanweisung *f*. **~ive** /-ɪv/ *a* lehrreich. **~or** *n* Lehrer(in) *m(f)*; (*Mil*) Ausbilder *m*

instrument /'ɪnstrʊmənt/ *n* Instrument *nt*. **~al** /-'mentl/ *a* Instrumental-; **be ~al in** eine entscheidende Rolle spielen bei

insu'bordi|nate *a* ungehorsam. **~nation** /-'neɪʃn/ *n* Ungehorsam *m*; (*Mil*) Insubordination *f*

in'sufferable *a* unerträglich

insuf'ficient *a*, **-ly** *adv* nicht genügend
insular /'ɪnsjʊlə(r)/ *a* (*fig*) engstirnig
insulat|e /'ɪnsjʊleɪt/ *vt* isolieren. **~ing tape** *n* Isolierband *nt*. **~ion** /-'leɪʃn/ *n* Isolierung *f*
insulin /'ɪnsjʊlɪn/ *n* Insulin *nt*
insult¹ /'ɪnsʌlt/ *n* Beleidigung *f*
insult² /ɪn'sʌlt/ *vt* beleidigen
insuperable /ɪn'su:pərəbl/ *a* unüberwindlich
insur|ance /ɪn'ʃʊərəns/ *n* Versicherung *f*. **~e** *vt* versichern
insurrection /ɪnsə'rekʃn/ *n* Aufstand *m*
intact /ɪn'tækt/ *a* unbeschädigt; (*complete*) vollständig
'intake *n* Aufnahme *f*
in'tangible *a* nicht greifbar
integral /'ɪntɪgrl/ *a* wesentlich
integrat|e /'ɪntɪgreɪt/ *vt* integrieren □ *vi* sich integrieren. **~ion** /-'greɪʃn/ *n* Integration *f*
integrity /ɪn'tegrətɪ/ *n* Integrität *f*
intellect /'ɪntəlekt/ *n* Intellekt *m*. **~ual** /-'lektjʊəl/ *a* intellektuell
intelligen|ce /ɪn'telɪdʒəns/ *n* Intelligenz *f*; (*Mil*) Nachrichtendienst *m*; (*information*) Meldungen *pl*. **~t** *a*, **-ly** *adv* intelligent
intelligentsia /ɪntelɪ'dʒentsɪə/ *n* Intelligenz *f*
intelligible /ɪn'telɪdʒəbl/ *a* verständlich
intend /ɪn'tend/ *vt* beabsichtigen; **be ~ed for** bestimmt sein für
intense /ɪn'tens/ *a* intensiv; ⟨*pain*⟩ stark. **~ly** *adv* äußerst; ⟨*study*⟩ intensiv
intensi|fication /ɪntensɪfɪ'keɪʃn/ *n* Intensivierung *f*. **~fy** /-'tensɪfaɪ/ *v* (*pt/pp* **-ied**) □ *vt* intensivieren □ *vi* zunehmen
intensity /ɪn'tensətɪ/ *n* Intensität *f*
intensive /ɪn'tensɪv/ *a*, **-ly** *adv* intensiv; **be in ~ care** auf der Intensivstation sein
intent /ɪn'tent/ *a*, **-ly** *adv* aufmerksam; **~ on** (*absorbed in*) vertieft in (+ *acc*); **be ~ on doing sth** fest entschlossen sein, etw zu tun □ *n* Absicht *f*; **to all ~s and purposes** im Grunde
intention /ɪn'tenʃn/ *n* Absicht *f*. **~al** *a*, **-ly** *adv* absichtlich
inter /ɪn'tɜ:(r)/ *vt* (*pt/pp* **interred**) bestatten
inter'action *n* Wechselwirkung *f*
intercede /ɪntə'si:d/ *vi* Fürsprache einlegen (**on behalf of** für)
intercept /ɪntə'sept/ *vt* abfangen
'interchange¹ *n* Austausch *m*; (*Auto*) Autobahnkreuz *nt*
inter'change² *vt* austauschen. **~able** *a* austauschbar
intercom /'ɪntəkɒm/ *n* [Gegen]sprechanlage *f*
'intercourse *n* Verkehr *m*; (*sexual*) Geschlechtsverkehr *m*
interest /'ɪntrəst/ *n* Interesse *nt*; (*Comm*) Zinsen *pl*; **have an ~** (*Comm*) beteiligt sein (**in** an + *dat*) □ *vt* interessieren; **be ~ed** sich interessieren (**in** für). **~ing** *a* interessant. **~ rate** *n* Zinssatz *m*
interfere /ɪntə'fɪə(r)/ *vi* sich einmischen. **~nce** /-əns/ *n* Einmischung *f*; (*Radio, TV*) Störung *f*
interim /'ɪntərɪm/ *a* Zwischen-; (*temporary*) vorläufig □ *n* **in the ~** in der Zwischenzeit
interior /ɪn'tɪərɪə(r)/ *a* innere(r,s), Innen- □ *n* Innere(s) *nt*
interject /ɪntə'dʒekt/ *vt* einwerfen. **~ion** /-ekʃn/ *n* Interjektion *f*; (*remark*) Einwurf *m*
inter'lock *vi* ineinander greifen
interloper /'ɪntələʊpə(r)/ *n* Eindringling *m*
interlude /'ɪntəlu:d/ *n* Pause *f*; (*performance*) Zwischenspiel *nt*
inter'marry *vi* untereinander heiraten; ⟨*different groups:*⟩ Mischehen schließen
intermediary /ɪntə'mi:dɪərɪ/ *n* Vermittler(in) *m*(*f*)

intermediate /ɪntəˈmiːdɪət/ *a* Zwischen-

interminable /ɪnˈtɜːmɪnəbl/ *a* endlos [lang]

intermission /ɪntəˈmɪʃn/ *n* Pause *f*

intermittent /ɪntəˈmɪtənt/ *a* in Abständen auftretend

intern /ɪnˈtɜːn/ *vt* internieren

internal /ɪnˈtɜːnl/ *a* innere(r,s); ⟨*matter, dispute*⟩ intern. **~ly** *adv* innerlich; ⟨*deal with*⟩ intern

interˈnational *a*, **-ly** *adv* international □ *n* Länderspiel *nt*; (*player*) Nationalspieler(in) *m(f)*

internist /ɪnˈtɜːnɪst/ *n* (*Amer*) Internist *m*

internment /ɪnˈtɜːnmənt/ *n* Internierung *f*

ˈinterplay *n* Wechselspiel *nt*

interpolate /ɪnˈtɜːpəleɪt/ *vt* einwerfen

interpret /ɪnˈtɜːprɪt/ *vt* interpretieren; auslegen ⟨*text*⟩; deuten ⟨*dream*⟩; (*translate*) dolmetschen □ *vi* dolmetschen. **~ation** /-ˈteɪʃn/ *n* Interpretation *f*. **~er** *n* Dolmetscher(in) *m(f)*

interreˈlated *a* verwandt; ⟨*facts*⟩ zusammenhängend

interrogat|e /ɪnˈterəgeɪt/ *vt* verhören. **~ion** /-ˈgeɪʃn/ *n* Verhör *nt*

interrogative /ɪntəˈrɒgətɪv/ *a* & *n* ~ **[pronoun]** Interrogativpronomen *nt*

interrupt /ɪntəˈrʌpt/ *vt/i* unterbrechen; **don't ~!** red nicht dazwischen! **~ion** /-ʌpʃn/ *n* Unterbrechung *f*

intersect /ɪntəˈsekt/ *vi* sich kreuzen; (*Geom*) sich schneiden. **~ion** /-ekʃn/ *n* Kreuzung *f*

interspersed /ɪntəˈspɜːst/ *a* ~ **with** durchsetzt mit

interˈtwine *vi* sich ineinander schlingen

interval /ˈɪntəvl/ *n* Abstand *m*; (*Theat*) Pause *f*; (*Mus*) Intervall *nt*; **at hourly ~s** alle Stunde; **bright ~s** *pl* Aufheiterungen *pl*

interven|e /ɪntəˈviːn/ *vi* eingreifen; (*occur*) dazwischenkommen. **~tion** /-ˈvenʃn/ *n* Eingreifen *nt*; (*Mil, Pol*) Intervention *f*

interview /ˈɪntəvjuː/ *n* (*Journ*) Interview *nt*; (*for job*) Vorstellungsgespräch *nt*; **go for an ~** sich vorstellen □ *vt* interviewen; ein Vorstellungsgespräch führen mit. **~er** *n* Interviewer(in) *m(f)*

intestine /ɪnˈtestɪn/ *n* Darm *m*

intimacy /ˈɪntɪməsɪ/ *n* Vertrautheit *f*; (*sexual*) Intimität *f*

intimate¹ /ˈɪntɪmət/ *a*, **-ly** *adv* vertraut; ⟨*friend*⟩ eng; (*sexually*) intim

intimate² /ˈɪntɪmeɪt/ *vt* zu verstehen geben; (*imply*) andeuten

intimidat|e /ɪnˈtɪmɪdeɪt/ *vt* einschüchtern. **~ion** /-ˈdeɪʃn/ *n* Einschüchterung *f*

into /ˈɪntə, *vor einem Vokal* ˈɪntʊ/ *prep* in (+ *acc*); **go ~ the house** ins Haus [hinein]gehen; **be ~** (*fam*) sich auskennen mit; **7 ~ 21** 21 [geteilt] durch 7

inˈtolerable *a* unerträglich

inˈtoleran|ce *n* Intoleranz *f*. **~t** *a* intolerant

intonation /ɪntəˈneɪʃn/ *n* Tonfall *m*

intoxicat|ed /ɪnˈtɒksɪkeɪtɪd/ *a* betrunken; (*fig*) berauscht. **~ion** /-ˈkeɪʃn/ *n* Rausch *m*

intractable /ɪnˈtræktəbl/ *a* widerspenstig; ⟨*problem*⟩ hartnäckig

intransigent /ɪnˈtrænsɪdʒənt/ *a* unnachgiebig

inˈtransitive *a*, **-ly** *adv* intransitiv

intravenous /ɪntrəˈviːnəs/ *a*, **-ly** *adv* intravenös

intrepid /ɪnˈtrepɪd/ *a* kühn, unerschrocken

intricate /ˈɪntrɪkət/ *a* kompliziert

intrigu|e /ɪnˈtriːg/ *n* Intrige *f* □ *vt* faszinieren □ *vi* intrigieren. **~ing** *a* faszinierend

intrinsic /ɪnˈtrɪnsɪk/ *a* ~ **value** Eigenwert *m*

introduce /ɪntrəˈdjuːs/ *vt* vorstellen; (*bring in, insert*) einführen

introduct|ion /ɪntrəˈdʌkʃn/ *n* Einführung *f*; (*to person*) Vorstellung *f*; (*to book*) Einleitung *f*. **~ory** /-tərɪ/ *a* einleitend

introspective /ɪntrəˈspektɪv/ *a* in sich (*acc*) gerichtet

introvert /ˈɪntrəvɜːt/ *n* introvertierter Mensch *m*

intru|de /ɪnˈtruːd/ *vi* stören. **~der** *n* Eindringling *m*. **~sion** /-uːʒn/ *n* Störung *f*

intuit|ion /ɪntjuːˈɪʃn/ *n* Intuition *f*. **~ive** /-ˈtjuːɪtɪv/ *a*, **-ly** *adv* intuitiv

inundate /ˈɪnəndeɪt/ *vt* überschwemmen

invade /ɪnˈveɪd/ *vt* einfallen in (+ *acc*). **~r** *n* Angreifer *m*

invalid1 /ˈɪnvəlɪd/ *n* Kranke(r) *m/f*

invalid2 /ɪnˈvælɪd/ *a* ungültig. **~ate** *vt* ungültig machen

inˈvaluable *a* unschätzbar; ⟨*person*⟩ unersetzlich

inˈvariab|le *a* unveränderlich. **~ly** *adv* immer

invasion /ɪnˈveɪʒn/ *n* Invasion *f*

invective /ɪnˈvektɪv/ *n* Beschimpfungen *pl*

invent /ɪnˈvent/ *vt* erfinden. **~ion** /-enʃn/ *n* Erfindung *f*. **~ive** /-tɪv/ *a* erfinderisch. **~or** *n* Erfinder *m*

inventory /ˈɪnvəntrɪ/ *n* Bestandsliste *f*; **make an** ~ ein Inventar aufstellen

inverse /ɪnˈvɜːs/ *a*, **-ly** *adv* umgekehrt □ *n* Gegenteil *nt*

invert /ɪnˈvɜːt/ *vt* umkehren. **~ed commas** *npl* Anführungszeichen *pl*

invest /ɪnˈvest/ *vt* investieren, anlegen; ~ **in** (*fam: buy*) sich (*dat*) zulegen

investigat|e /ɪnˈvestɪgeɪt/ *vt* untersuchen. **~ion** /-ˈgeɪʃn/ *n* Untersuchung *f*

invest|ment /ɪnˈvestmənt/ *n* Anlage *f*; **be a good ~ment** (*fig*) sich bezahlt machen. **~or** *n* Kapitalanleger *m*

inveterate /ɪnˈvetərət/ *a* Gewohnheits-; ⟨*liar*⟩ unverbesserlich

invidious /ɪnˈvɪdɪəs/ *a* unerfreulich; (*unfair*) ungerecht

invigilate /ɪnˈvɪdʒɪleɪt/ *vi* (*Sch*) Aufsicht führen

invigorate /ɪnˈvɪgəreɪt/ *vt* beleben

invincible /ɪnˈvɪnsəbl/ *a* unbesiegbar

inviolable /ɪnˈvaɪələbl/ *a* unantastbar

inˈvisible *a* unsichtbar. ~ **mending** *n* Kunststopfen *nt*

invitation /ɪnvɪˈteɪʃn/ *n* Einladung *f*

invit|e /ɪnˈvaɪt/ *vt* einladen. **~ing** *a* einladend

invoice /ˈɪnvɔɪs/ *n* Rechnung *f* □ *vt* ~ **s.o.** jdm eine Rechnung schicken

invoke /ɪnˈvəʊk/ *vt* anrufen

inˈvoluntary *a*, **-ily** *adv* unwillkürlich

involve /ɪnˈvɒlv/ *vt* beteiligen; (*affect*) betreffen; (*implicate*) verwickeln; (*entail*) mit sich bringen; (*mean*) bedeuten; **be ~d in** beteiligt sein an (+ *dat*); (*implicated*) verwickelt sein in (+ *acc*); **get ~d with s.o.** sich mit jdm einlassen. **~d** *a* kompliziert

inˈvulnerable *a* unverwundbar; ⟨*position*⟩ unangreifbar

inward /ˈɪnwəd/ *a* innere(r,s). **~ly** *adv* innerlich. **~s** *adv* nach innen

iodine /ˈaɪədiːn/ *n* Jod *nt*

iota /aɪˈəʊtə/ *n* Jota *nt*, (*fam*) Funke *m*

IOU *abbr* (**I owe you**) Schuldschein *m*

Iran /ɪˈrɑːn/ *n* der Iran

Iraq /ɪˈrɑːk/ *n* der Irak

irascible /ɪˈræsəbl/ *a* aufbrausend

irate /aɪ'reɪt/ *a* wütend
Ireland /'aɪələnd/ *n* Irland *nt*
iris /'aɪərɪs/ *n* (*Anat*) Regenbogenhaut *f*, Iris *f*; (*Bot*) Schwertlilie *f*
Irish /'aɪərɪʃ/ *a* irisch □ *n* **the ~** *pl* die Iren. **~man** *n* Ire *m*. **~woman** *n* Irin *f*
irk /ɜ:k/ *vt* ärgern. **~some** /-səm/ *a* lästig
iron /'aɪən/ *a* Eisen-; (*fig*) eisern □ *n* Eisen *nt*; (*appliance*) Bügeleisen *nt* □ *vt/i* bügeln. **~ out** *vt* ausbügeln
ironic[al] /aɪ'rɒnɪk[l]/ *a* ironisch
ironing /'aɪənɪŋ/ *n* Bügeln *nt*; (*articles*) Bügelwäsche *f*; **do the ~** bügeln. **~-board** *n* Bügelbrett *nt*
ironmonger /'-mʌŋgə(r)/ *n* **~'s [shop]** Haushaltswarengeschäft *nt*
irony /'aɪərənɪ/ *n* Ironie *f*
irradiate /ɪ'reɪdɪeɪt/ *vt* bestrahlen
irrational /ɪ'ræʃənl/ *a* irrational
irreconcilable /ɪ'rekənsaɪləbl/ *a* unversöhnlich
irrefutable /ɪrɪ'fju:təbl/ *a* unwiderlegbar
irregular /ɪ'regjʊlə(r)/ *a*, **-ly** *adv* unregelmäßig; (*against rules*) regelwidrig. **~ity** /-'lærətɪ/ *n* Unregelmäßigkeit *f*; Regelwidrigkeit *f*
irrelevant /ɪ'reləvənt/ *a* irrelevant
irreparable /ɪ'repərəbl/ *a* unersetzlich; **be ~** nicht wieder gutzumachen sein
irreplaceable /ɪrɪ'pleɪsəbl/ *a* unersetzlich
irrepressible /ɪrɪ'presəbl/ *a* unverwüstlich; **be ~** ⟨*person:*⟩ nicht unterzukriegen sein
irresistible /ɪrɪ'zɪstəbl/ *a* unwiderstehlich
irresolute /ɪ'rezəlu:t/ *a* unentschlossen
irrespective /ɪrɪ'spektɪv/ *a* **~ of** ungeachtet (+ *gen*)
irresponsible /ɪrɪ'spɒnsəbl/ *a*, **-bly** *adv* unverantwortlich; ⟨*person*⟩ verantwortungslos
irreverent /ɪ'revərənt/ *a*, **-ly** *adv* respektlos
irreversible /ɪrɪ'vɜ:səbl/ *a* unwiderruflich; (*Med*) irreversibel
irrevocable /ɪ'revəkəbl/ *a*, **-bly** *adv* unwiderruflich
irrigat|e /'ɪrɪgeɪt/ *vt* bewässern. **~ion** /-'geɪʃn/ *n* Bewässerung *f*
irritability /ɪrɪtə'bɪlətɪ/ *n* Gereiztheit *f*
irritable /'ɪrɪtəbl/ *a* reizbar
irritant /'ɪrɪtənt/ *n* Reizstoff *m*
irritat|e /'ɪrɪteɪt/ *vt* irritieren; (*Med*) reizen. **~ion** /-'teɪʃn/ *n* Ärger *m*; (*Med*) Reizung *f*
is /ɪz/ *see* **be**
Islam /'ɪzlɑ:m/ *n* der Islam. **~ic** /-'læmɪk/ *a* islamisch
island /'aɪlənd/ *n* Insel *f*. **~er** *n* Inselbewohner(in) *m(f)*
isle /aɪl/ *n* Insel *f*
isolat|e /'aɪsəleɪt/ *vt* isolieren. **~ed** *a* (*remote*) abgelegen; (*single*) einzeln. **~ion** /-'leɪʃn/ *n* Isoliertheit *f*; (*Med*) Isolierung *f*
Israel /'ɪzreɪl/ *n* Israel *nt*. **~i** /ɪz'reɪlɪ/ *a* israelisch □ *n* Israeli *m/f*
issue /'ɪʃu:/ *n* Frage *f*; (*outcome*) Ergebnis *nt*; (*of magazine, stamps*) Ausgabe *f*; (*offspring*) Nachkommen *pl*; **what is at ~?** worum geht es? **take ~ with s.o.** jdm widersprechen □ *vt* ausgeben; ausstellen ⟨*passport*⟩; erteilen ⟨*order*⟩; herausgeben ⟨*book*⟩; **be ~d with sth** etw erhalten □ *vi* **~ from** herausströmen aus
isthmus /'ɪsməs/ *n* (*pl* **-muses**) Landenge *f*
it /ɪt/ *pron* es; (*m*) er; (*f*) sie; (*as direct object*) es; (*m*) ihn; (*f*) sie; (*as indirect object*) ihm; (*f*) ihr; **it is raining** es regnet; **it's me** ich bin's; **who is it?** wer ist da? **of/from it** davon; **with it** damit; **out of it** daraus

Italian /ɪ'tæljən/ *a* italienisch □ *n* Italiener(in) *m(f)*; (*Lang*) Italienisch *nt*
italic /ɪ'tælɪk/ *a* kursiv. **∼s** *npl* Kursivschrift *f*; **in ∼s** kursiv
Italy /'ɪtəlɪ/ *n* Italien *nt*
itch /ɪtʃ/ *n* Juckreiz *m*; **I have an ∼** es juckt mich □ *vi* jucken; **I'm ∼ing** (*fam*) es juckt mich (**to** zu). **∼y** *a* **be ∼y** jucken
item /'aɪtəm/ *n* Gegenstand *m*; (*Comm*) Artikel *m*; (*on agenda*) Punkt *m*; (*on invoice*) Posten *m*; (*act*) Nummer *f*; **∼ [of news]** Nachricht *f*. **∼ize** *vt* einzeln aufführen; spezifizieren ⟨*bill*⟩
itinerant /aɪ'tɪnərənt/ *a* Wander-
itinerary /aɪ'tɪnərərɪ/ *n* [Reise]route *f*
its /ɪts/ *poss pron* sein; (*f*) ihr
it's = **it is, it has**
itself /ɪt'self/ *pron* selbst; (*refl*) sich; **by ∼** von selbst; (*alone*) allein
ivory /'aɪvərɪ/ *n* Elfenbein *nt* □ *attrib* Elfenbein-
ivy /'aɪvɪ/ *n* Efeu *m*

J

jab /dʒæb/ *n* Stoß *m*; (*fam: injection*) Spritze *f* □ *vt* (*pt/pp* **jabbed**) stoßen
jabber /'dʒæbə(r)/ *vi* plappern
jack /dʒæk/ *n* (*Auto*) Wagenheber *m*; (*Cards*) Bube *m* □ *vt* **∼ up** (*Auto*) aufbocken
jackdaw /'dʒækdɔː/ *n* Dohle *f*
jacket /'dʒækɪt/ *n* Jacke *f*; (*of book*) Schutzumschlag *m*. **∼ po'tato** *n* in der Schale gebackene Kartoffel *f*
'jackpot *n* **hit the ∼** das große Los ziehen
jade /dʒeɪd/ *n* Jade *m*
jaded /'dʒeɪdɪd/ *a* abgespannt
jagged /'dʒægɪd/ *a* zackig
jail /dʒeɪl/ = **gaol**
jalopy /dʒə'lɒpɪ/ *n* (*fam*) Klapperkiste *f*
jam[1] /dʒæm/ *n* Marmelade *f*
jam[2] *n* Gedränge *nt*; (*Auto*) Stau *m*; (*fam. difficulty*) Klemme *f* □ *v* (*pt/pp* **jammed**) □ *vt* klemmen (**in** in + *acc*); stören ⟨*broadcast*⟩ □ *vi* klemmen
Jamaica /dʒə'meɪkə/ *n* Jamaika *nt*
jangle /'dʒæŋgl/ *vi* klimpern □ *vt* klimpern mit
janitor /'dʒænɪtə(r)/ *n* Hausmeister *m*
January /'dʒænjʊərɪ/ *n* Januar *m*
Japan /dʒə'pæn/ *n* Japan *nt*. **∼ese** /dʒæpə'niːz/ *a* japanisch □ *n* Japaner(in) *m(f)*; (*Lang*) Japanisch *nt*
jar[1] /dʒɑː(r)/ *n* Glas *nt*; (*earthenware*) Topf *m*
jar[2] *v* (*pt/pp* **jarred**) *vi* stören □ *vt* erschüttern
jargon /'dʒɑːgən/ *n* Jargon *m*
jaundice /'dʒɔːndɪs/ *n* Gelbsucht *f*. **∼d** *a* (*fig*) zynisch
jaunt /dʒɔːnt/ *n* Ausflug *m*
jaunty /'dʒɔːntɪ/ *a* (**-ier, -iest**) **-ily** *adv* **keck**
javelin /'dʒævlɪn/ *n* Speer *m*
jaw /dʒɔː/ *n* Kiefer *m*; **∼s** *pl* Rachen *m* □ *vi* (*fam*) quatschen
jay /dʒeɪ/ *n* Eichelhäher *m*. **∼-walker** *n* achtloser Fußgänger *m*
jazz /dʒæz/ *n* Jazz *m*. **∼y** *a* knallig
jealous /'dʒeləs/ *a*, **-ly** *adv* eifersüchtig (**of** auf + *acc*). **∼y** *n* Eifersucht *f*
jeans /dʒiːnz/ *npl* Jeans *pl*
jeer /dʒɪə(r)/ *n* Johlen *nt* □ *vi* johlen; **∼ at** verhöhnen
jell /dʒeɪ/ *vi* gelieren
jelly /'dʒelɪ/ *n* Gelee *nt*; (*dessert*) Götterspeise *f*. **∼fish** *n* Qualle *f*
jemmy /'dʒemɪ/ *n* Brecheisen *nt*
jeopar|dize /'dʒepədaɪz/ *vt* gefährden. **∼dy** /-dɪ/ *n* **in ∼dy** gefährdet
jerk /dʒɜːk/ *n* Ruck *m* □ *vt* stoßen; (*pull*) reißen □ *vi* rucken; ⟨*limb,*

muscle:⟩ zucken. **~ily** *adv* ruckweise. **~y** *a* ruckartig

jersey /ˈdʒɜːzɪ/ *n* Pullover *m*; (*Sport*) Trikot *nt*; (*fabric*) Jersey *m*

jest /dʒest/ *n* Scherz *m*; **in ~** im Spaß □ *vi* scherzen

jet[1] /dʒet/ *n* (*Miner*) Jett *m*

jet[2] *n* (*of water*) [Wasser]strahl *m*; (*nozzle*) Düse *f*; (*plane*) Düsenflugzeug *nt*

jet: **~-ˈblack** *a* pechschwarz. **~lag** *n* Jet-lag *nt*. **~-proˈpelled** *a* mit Düsenantrieb

jettison /ˈdʒetɪsn/ *vt* über Bord werfen

jetty /ˈdʒetɪ/ *n* Landesteg *m*; (*breakwater*) Buhne *f*

Jew /dʒuː/ *n* Jude *m* /Jüdin *f*

jewel /ˈdʒuːəl/ *n* Edelstein *m*; (*fig*) Juwel *nt*. **~ler** *n* Juwelier *m*; **~ler's [shop]** Juweliergeschäft *nt*. **~lery** *n* Schmuck *m*

Jew|ess /ˈdʒuːɪs/ *n* Jüdin *f*. **~ish** *a* jüdisch

jib /dʒɪb/ *vi* (*pt/pp* **jibbed**) (*fig*) sich sträuben (**at** gegen)

jiffy /ˈdʒɪfɪ/ *n* (*fam*) **in a ~** in einem Augenblick

jigsaw /ˈdʒɪgsɔː/ *n* **~ [puzzle]** Puzzlespiel *nt*

jilt /dʒɪlt/ *vt* sitzen lassen

jingle /ˈdʒɪŋgl/ *n* (*rhyme*) Verschen *nt* □ *vi* klimpern □ *vt* klimpern mit

jinx /dʒɪŋks/ *n* (*fam*) **it's got a ~ on it** es ist verhext

jitter|s /ˈdʒɪtəz/ *npl* (*fam*) **have the ~s** nervös sein. **~y** *a* (*fam*) nervös

job /dʒɒb/ *n* Aufgabe *f*; (*post*) Stelle *f*, (*fam*) Job *m*; **be a ~** (*fam*) nicht leicht sein; **it's a good ~ that** es ist [nur] gut, dass. **~ centre** *n* Arbeitsvermittlungsstelle *f*. **~less** *a* arbeitslos

jockey /ˈdʒɒkɪ/ *n* Jockei *m*

jocular /ˈdʒɒkjʊlə(r)/ *a*, **-ly** *adv* spaßhaft

jog /ˈdʒɒg/ *n* Stoß *m*; **at a ~** im Dauerlauf □ *v* (*pt/pp* **jogged**) □ *vt* anstoßen; **~ s.o.'s memory** jds Gedächtnis nachhelfen □ *vi* (*Sport*) joggen. **~ging** *n* Jogging *nt*

john /dʒɒn/ *n* (*Amer, fam*) Klo *nt*

join /dʒɔɪn/ *n* Nahtstelle *f* □ *vt* verbinden (**to** mit); sich anschließen (+ *dat*) ⟨*person*⟩; (*become member of*) beitreten (+ *dat*); eintreten in (+ *acc*) ⟨*firm*⟩ □ *vi* ⟨*roads:*⟩ sich treffen. **~ in** *vi* mitmachen. **~ up** *vi* (*Mil*) Soldat werden □ *vt* zusammenfügen

joiner /ˈdʒɔɪnə(r)/ *n* Tischler *m*

joint /dʒɔɪnt/ *a*, **-ly** *adv* gemeinsam □ *n* Gelenk *nt*; (*in wood, brickwork*) Fuge *f*; (*Culin*) Braten *m*; (*fam: bar*) Lokal *nt*

joist /dʒɔɪst/ *n* Dielenbalken *m*

jok|e /dʒəʊk/ *n* Scherz *m*; (*funny story*) Witz *m*; (*trick*) Streich *m* □ *vi* scherzen. **~er** *n* Witzbold *m*; (*Cards*) Joker *m*. **~ing** *n* **~ing apart** Spaß beiseite. **~ingly** *adv* im Spaß

jollity /ˈdʒɒlətɪ/ *n* Lustigkeit *f*

jolly /ˈdʒɒlɪ/ *a* (**-ier**, **-iest**) lustig □ *adv* (*fam*) sehr

jolt /dʒəʊlt/ *n* Ruck *m* □ *vt* einen Ruck versetzen (+ *dat*) □ *vi* holpern

Jordan /ˈdʒɔːdn/ *n* Jordanien *nt*

jostle /ˈdʒɒsl/ *vt* anrempeln □ *vi* drängeln

jot /dʒɒt/ *n* Jota *nt* □ *vt* (*pt/pp* **jotted**) **~ [down]** sich (*dat*) notieren. **~ter** *n* Notizblock *m*

journal /ˈdʒɜːnl/ *n* Zeitschrift *f*; (*diary*) Tagebuch *nt*. **~ese** /-əˈliːz/ *n* Zeitungsjargon *m*. **~ism** *n* Journalismus *m*. **~ist** *n* Journalist(in) *m*(*f*)

journey /ˈdʒɜːnɪ/ *n* Reise *f*

jovial /ˈdʒəʊvɪəl/ *a* lustig

joy /dʒɔɪ/ *n* Freude *f*. **~ful** *a*, **-ly** *adv* freudig, froh. **~ride** *n* (*fam*) Spritztour *f* [im gestohlenen Auto]

jubil|ant /ˈdʒuːbɪlənt/ *a* überglücklich. **~ation** /-ˈleɪʃn/ *n* Jubel *m*
jubilee /ˈdʒuːbɪliː/ *n* Jubiläum *nt*
Judaism /ˈdʒuːdeɪɪzm/ *n* Judentum *nt*
judder /ˈdʒʌdə(r)/ *vi* rucken
judge /dʒʌdʒ/ *n* Richter *m*; (*of competition*) Preisrichter *m* □ *vt* beurteilen; (*estimate*) [ein]schätzen □ *vi* urteilen (**by** nach). **~ment** *n* Beurteilung *f*; (*Jur*) Urteil *nt*; (*fig*) Urteilsvermögen *nt*
judic|ial /dʒuːˈdɪʃl/ *a* gerichtlich. **~iary** /-ʃərɪ/ *n* Richterstand *m*. **~ious** /-ʃəs/ *a* klug
judo /ˈdʒuːdəʊ/ *n* Judo *nt*
jug /dʒʌg/ *n* Kanne *f*; (*small*) Kännchen *nt*; (*for water, wine*) Krug *m*
juggernaut /ˈdʒʌgənɔːt/ *n* (*fam*) Riesenlaster *m*
juggle /ˈdʒʌgl/ *vi* jonglieren. **~r** *n* Jongleur *m*
juice /dʒuːs/ *n* Saft *m*. **~ extractor** *n* Entsafter *m*
juicy /ˈdʒuːsɪ/ *a* (**-ier, -iest**) saftig; (*fam*) ⟨*story*⟩ pikant
juke-box /ˈdʒuːk-/ *n* Musikbox *f*
July /dʒʊˈlaɪ/ *n* Juli *m*
jumble /ˈdʒʌmbl/ *n* Durcheinander *nt* □ *vt* **~ [up]** durcheinander bringen. **~ sale** *n* [Wohltätigkeits]basar *m*
jumbo /ˈdʒʌmbəʊ/ *n* **~ [jet]** Jumbo[jet] *m*
jump /dʒʌmp/ *n* Sprung *m*; (*in prices*) Anstieg *m*; (*in horse racing*) Hindernis *nt* □ *vi* springen; (*start*) zusammenzucken; **make s.o. ~** jdn erschrecken; **~ at** (*fig*) sofort zugreifen bei ⟨*offer*⟩; **~ to conclusions** voreilige Schlüsse ziehen □ *vt* überspringen; **~ the gun** (*fig*) vorschnell handeln. **~ up** *vi* aufspringen
jumper /ˈdʒʌmpə(r)/ *n* Pullover *m*, Pulli *m*
jumpy /ˈdʒʌmpɪ/ *a* nervös
junction /ˈdʒʌŋkʃn/ *n* Kreuzung *f*; (*Rail*) Knotenpunkt *m*
juncture /ˈdʒʌŋktʃə(r)/ *n* **at this ~** zu diesem Zeitpunkt
June /dʒuːn/ *n* Juni *m*
jungle /ˈdʒʌŋgl/ *n* Dschungel *m*
junior /ˈdʒuːnɪə(r)/ *a* jünger; (*in rank*) untergeordnet; (*Sport*) Junioren- □ *n* Junior *m*. **~ school** *n* Grundschule *f*
juniper /ˈdʒuːnɪpə(r)/ *n* Wacholder *m*
junk /dʒʌŋk/ *n* Gerümpel *nt*, Trödel *m*
junkie /ˈdʒʌŋkɪ/ *n* (*sl*) Fixer *m*
ˈjunk-shop *n* Trödelladen *m*
juris|diction /dʒʊərɪsˈdɪkʃn/ *n* Gerichtsbarkeit *f*. **~ˈprudence** *n* Rechtswissenschaft *f*
juror /ˈdʒʊərə(r)/ *n* Geschworene(r) *m/f*
jury /ˈdʒʊərɪ/ *n* **the ~** die Geschworenen *pl*; (*for competition*) die Jury
just /dʒʌst/ *a* gerecht □ *adv* gerade; (*only*) nur; (*simply*) einfach; (*exactly*) genau; **~ as tall** ebenso groß; **~ listen!** hör doch mal! **I'm ~ going** ich gehe schon; **~ put it down** stell es nur hin
justice /ˈdʒʌstɪs/ *n* Gerechtigkeit *f*; **do ~ to** gerecht werden (+ *dat*); **J~ of the Peace** ≈ Friedensrichter *m*
justifiab|le /ˈdʒʌstɪfaɪəbl/ *a* berechtigt. **~ly** *adv* berechtigterweise
justi|fication /dʒʌstɪfɪˈkeɪʃn/ *n* Rechtfertigung *f*. **~fy** /ˈdʒʌstɪfaɪ/ *vt* (*pt/pp* **-ied**) rechtfertigen
justly /ˈdʒʌstlɪ/ *adv* zu Recht
jut /dʒʌt/ *vi* (*pt/pp* **jutted**) **~ out** vorstehen
juvenile /ˈdʒuːvənaɪl/ *a* jugendlich; (*childish*) kindisch □ *n* Jugendliche(r) *m/f*. **~ delinquency** *n* Jugendkriminalität *f*

juxtapose /dʒʌkstəˈpəʊz/ *vt* nebeneinander stellen

K

kangaroo /kæŋgəˈruː/ *n* Känguru *nt*

karate /kəˈrɑːtɪ/ *n* Karate *nt*

kebab /kɪˈbæb/ *n* (*Culin*) Spießchen *nt*

keel /kiːl/ *n* Kiel *m* □ *vi* ~ **over** umkippen; (*Naut*) kentern

keen /kiːn/ *a* (**-er, -est**) (*sharp*) scharf; (*intense*) groß; (*eager*) eifrig, begeistert; ~ **on** (*fam*) erpicht auf (+ *acc*); ~ **on s.o.** von jdm sehr angetan; **be ~ to do sth** etw gerne machen wollen. **~ly** *adv* tief. **~ness** *n* Eifer *m*, Begeisterung *f*

keep /kiːp/ *n* (*maintenance*) Unterhalt *m*; (*of castle*) Bergfried *m*; **for ~s** für immer □ *v* (*pt/pp* **kept**) □ *vt* behalten; (*store*) aufbewahren; (*not throw away*) aufheben; (*support*) unterhalten; (*detain*) aufhalten; freihalten ⟨*seat*⟩; halten ⟨*promise, animals*⟩; führen, haben ⟨*shop*⟩; einhalten ⟨*law, rules*⟩; ~ **sth hot** etw warm halten; ~ **s.o. from doing sth** jdn davon abhalten, etw zu tun; ~ **s.o. waiting** jdn warten lassen; ~ **sth to oneself** etw nicht weitersagen; **where do you ~ the sugar?** wo hast du den Zucker? □ *vi* (*remain*) bleiben; ⟨*food:*⟩ sich halten; ~ **left/right** sich links/rechts halten; ~ **doing sth** etw dauernd machen; ~ **on doing sth** etw weitermachen; ~ **in with** sich gut stellen mit. ~ **up** *vi* Schritt halten □ *vt* (*continue*) weitermachen

keep|er /ˈkiːpə(r)/ *n* Wärter(in) *m(f)*. **~ing** *n* Obhut *f*; **be in ~ing with** passen zu. ~ **sake** *n* Andenken *nt*

keg /keg/ *n* kleines Fass *nt*

kennel /ˈkenl/ *n* Hundehütte *f*; **~s** *pl* (*boarding*) Hundepension *f*; (*breeding*) Zwinger *m*

Kenya /ˈkenjə/ *n* Kenia *nt*

kept /kept/ *see* **keep**

kerb /kɜːb/ *n* Bordstein *m*

kernel /ˈkɜːnl/ *n* kern *m*

kerosene /ˈkerəsiːn/ *n* (*Amer*) Petroleum *nt*

ketchup /ˈketʃʌp/ *n* Ketschup *m*

kettle /ˈketl/ *n* [Wasser]kessel *m*; **put the ~ on** Wasser aufsetzen; **a pretty ~ of fish** (*fam*) eine schöne Bescherung *f*

key /kiː/ *n* Schlüssel *m*; (*Mus*) Tonart *f*; (*of piano, typewriter*) Taste *f* □ *vt* ~ **in** eintasten

key: ~board *n* Tastatur *f*; (*Mus*) Klaviatur *f*. **~boarder** *n* Taster(in) *m(f)*. **~hole** *n* Schlüsselloch *nt*. **~-ring** *n* Schlüsselring *m*

khaki /ˈkɑːkɪ/ *a* khakifarben □ *n* Khaki *nt*

kick /kɪk/ *n* [Fuß]tritt *m*; **for ~s** (*fam*) zum Spaß □ *vt* treten; **~ the bucket** (*fam*) abkratzen □ *vi* ⟨*animal*⟩ ausschlagen. **~-off** *n* (*Sport*) Anstoß *m*

kid /kɪd/ *n* Kitz *nt*; (*fam: child*) Kind *nt* □ *vt* (*pt/pp* **kidded**) (*fam*) ~ **s.o.** jdm etwas vormachen. ~ **gloves** *npl* Glacéhandschuhe *pl*

kidnap /ˈkɪdnæp/ *vt* (*pt/pp* **-napped**) entführen. **~per** *n* Entführer *m*. **~ping** *n* Entführung *f*

kidney /ˈkɪdnɪ/ *n* Niere *f*. ~ **machine** *n* künstliche Niere *f*

kill /kɪl/ *vt* töten; (*fam*) totschlagen ⟨*time*⟩; ~ **two birds with one stone** zwei Fliegen mit einer Klappe schlagen. **~er** *n* Mörder(in) *m(f)*. **~ing** *n* Tötung *f*; (*murder*) Mord *m*

ˈkilljoy *n* Spielverderber *m*

kiln /kɪln/ *n* Brennofen *m*

kilo /ˈkiːləʊ/ *n* Kilo *nt*

kilo /ˈkɪlə/: **~gram** *n* Kilogramm *nt*. **~hertz** /-hɜːts/ *n* Kilohertz *nt.* **~metre** *n* Kilometer *m.* **~watt** *n* Kilowatt *nt*

kilt /kɪlt/ *n* Schottenrock *m*

kin /kɪn/ *n* Verwandtschaft *f*; **next of ~** nächster Verwandter *m*/nächste Verwandte *f*

kind¹ /kaɪnd/ *n* Art *f*; (*brand, type*) Sorte *f*; **what ~ of car?** was fürein Auto? **~ of** (*fam*) irgendwie

kind² *a* (**-er, -est**) nett; **~ to animals** gut zu Tieren; **~ regards** herzliche Grüße

kindergarten /ˈkɪndəgɑ:tn/ *n* Vorschule *f*

kindle /ˈkɪndl/ *vt* anzünden

kind|ly /ˈkaɪndlɪ/ *a* (**-ier, -iest**) nett □ *adv* netterweise; (*if you please*) gefälligst. **~ness** *n* Güte *f*; (*favour*) Gefallen *m*

kindred /ˈkɪndrɪd/ *a* **~ spirit** Gleichgesinnte(r) *m/f*

kinetic /kɪˈnetɪk/ *a* kinetisch

king /kɪŋ/ *n* König *m*; (*Draughts*) Dame *f*. **~dom** *n* Königreich *nt*; (*fig & Relig*) Reich *nt*

king: ~fisher *n* Eisvogel *m.* **~-sized** *a* extragroß

kink /kɪŋk/ *n* Knick *m.* **~y** *a* (*fam*) pervers

kiosk /ˈki:ɒsk/ *n* Kiosk *m*

kip /kɪp/ *n* **have a ~** (*fam*) pennen □ *vi* (*pt/pp* **kipped**) (*fam*) pennen

kipper /ˈkɪpə(r)/ *n* Räucherhering *m*

kiss /kɪs/ *n* Kuss *m* □ *vt/i* küssen

kit /kɪt/ *n* Ausrüstung *f*; (*tools*) Werkzeug *nt*; (*construction* **~**) Bausatz *m* □ *vt* (*pt/pp* **kitted**) **~out** ausrüsten. **~bag** *n* Seesack *m*

kitchen /ˈkɪtʃɪn/ *n* Küche *f* □ *attrib* Küchen-. **~ette** /kɪtʃɪˈnet/ *n* Kochnische *f*

kitchen: ~ ˈgarden *n* Gemüsegarten *m.* **~ ˈsink** *n* Spülbecken *nt*

kite /kaɪt/ *n* Drachen *m*

kith /kɪθ/ *n* **with ~ and kin** mit der ganzen Verwandtschaft

kitten /ˈkɪtn/ *n* Kätzchen *nt*

kitty /ˈkɪtɪ/ *n* (*money*) [gemeinsame] Kasse *f*

kleptomaniac /kleptəˈmeɪnɪæk/ *n* Kleptomane *m*/ -manin *f*

knack /næk/ *n* Trick *m*, Dreh *m*

knapsack /ˈnæp-/ *n* Tornister *m*

knead /ni:d/ *vt* kneten

knee /ni:/ *n* Knie *nt.* **~cap** *n* Kniescheibe *f*

kneel /ni:l/ *vi* (*pt/pp* **knelt**) knien; **~ [down]** sich [nieder]-knien

knelt /nelt/ *see* **kneel**

knew /nju:/ *see* **know**

knickers /ˈnɪkəz/ *npl* Schlüpfer *m*

knick-knacks /ˈnɪknæks/ *npl* Nippsachen *pl*

knife /naɪf/ *n* (*pl* **knives**) Messer *nt* □ *vt* einen Messerstich versetzen (+ *dat*); (*to death*) erstechen

knight /naɪt/ *n* Ritter *m*; (*Chess*) Springer *m* □ *vt* adeln

knit /nɪt/ *vt/i* (*pt/pp* **knitted**) stricken; **~ one, purl one** eine rechts eine links; **~ one's brow** die Stirn runzeln. **~ting** *n* Stricken *nt*; (*work*) Strickzeug *nt.* **~ting-needle** *n* Stricknadel *f.* **~wear** *n* Strickwaren *pl*

knives /naɪvz/ *npl see* **knife**

knob /nɒb/ *n* Knopf *m*; (*on door*) Knauf *m*; (*small lump*) Beule *f*; (*small piece*) Stückchen *nt.* **~bly** *a* knorrig; (*bony*) knochig

knock /nɒk/ *n* Klopfen *nt*; (*blow*) Schlag *m*; **there was a ~ at the door** es klopfte □ *vt* anstoßen; (*at door*) klopfen an (+ *acc*); (*fam: criticize*) heruntermachen; **~ a hole in sth** ein Loch in etw (*acc*) schlagen; **~ one's head** sich (*dat*) den Kopf stoßen (**on** an + *dat*) □ *vi* klopfen. **~ about** *vt* schlagen □ *vi* (*fam*) herumkommen. **~ down** *vt* herunterwerfen; (*with fist*) niederschlagen; (*in car*) anfahren; (*demolish*) abreißen; (*fam: reduce*) herabsetzen. **~ off** *vt* herunterwerfen; (*fam: steal*) klauen; (*fam: complete quickly*) hinhauen □ *vi* (*fam: cease work*) Feierabend machen. **~ out** *vt* ausschlagen; (*make unconscious*) bewusstlos schlagen; (*Boxing*) k.o. schlagen. **~ over** *vt* umwerfen; (*in car*) anfahren

knock: ~-down *a* **~-down prices** Schleuderpreise *pl.* **~er** *n* Türklopfer *m.* **~-kneed** /-ˈni:d/ *a* X-beinig. **~-out** *n* (*Boxing*) K.o. *m*

knot /nɒt/ *n* Knoten *m* □ *vt* (*pt/pp* **knotted**) knoten

knotty /ˈnɒtɪ/ *a* (**-ier, -iest**) (*fam*) verwickelt

know /nəʊ/ *vt/i* (*pt* **knew**, *pp* **known**) wissen; kennen ⟨*person*⟩; können ⟨*language*⟩; **get to ~** kennen lernen □ *n* **in the ~** (*fam*) im Bild

know: ~-all *n* (*fam*) Alleswisser *m.* **~-how** *n* (*fam*) [Sach]-kenntnis *f.* **~ing** *a* wissend. **~ingly** *adv* wissend; (*intentionally*) wissentlich

knowledge /ˈnɒlɪdʒ/ *n* Kenntnis *f* (**of** von/*gen*); (*general*) Wissen *nt*; (*specialized*) Kenntnisse *pl.* **~able** /-əbl/ *a* **be ~able** viel wissen

known /nəʊn/ *see* **know** □ *a* bekannt

knuckle /ˈnʌkl/ *n* [Finger]knöchel *m*; (*Culin*) Hachse *f* □ *vi* **~ under** sich fügen; **~ down** sich dahinter klemmen

kosher /ˈkəʊʃə(r)/ *a* koscher

kowtow /kaʊˈtaʊ/ *vi* Kotau machen (**to** vor + *dat*)

kudos /ˈkju:dɒs/ *n* (*fam*) Prestige *nt*

L

lab /læb/ *n* (*fam*) Labor *nt*

label /ˈleɪbl/ *n* Etikett *nt* □ *vt* (*pt/pp* **labelled**) etikettieren

laboratory /ləˈbɒrətrɪ/ *n* Labor *nt*

laborious /ləˈbɔ:rɪəs/ *a*, **-ly** *adv* mühsam

labour /ˈleɪbə(r)/ *n* Arbeit *f*; (*workers*) Arbeitskräfte *pl*; (*Med*) Wehen *pl*; **L~** (*Pol*) die Labourpartei □ *attrib* Labour- □ *vi* arbeiten □ *vt* (*fig*) sich lange auslassen über (+ *acc*). **~er** *n* Arbeiter *m*

ˈlabour-saving *a* arbeitssparend

laburnum /ləˈbɜ:nəm/ *n* Goldregen *m*

labyrinth /ˈlæbərɪnθ/ *n* Labyrinth *nt*

lace /leɪs/ *n* Spitze *f*; (*of shoe*) Schnürsenkel *m* □ *vt* schnüren; **~d with rum** mit einem Schuss Rum

lacerate /ˈlæsəreɪt/ *vt* zerreißen

lack /læk/ *n* Mangel *m* (**of** an + *dat*) □ *vt* **I ~ the time** mir fehlt die Zeit □ *vi* **be ~ing** fehlen

lackadaisical /lækəˈdeɪzɪkl/ *a* lustlos

laconic /ləˈkɒnɪk/ *a*, **-ally** *adv* lakonisch

lacquer /ˈlækə(r)/ *n* Lack *m*; (*for hair*) [Haar]spray *m*

lad /læd/ *n* Junge *m*

ladder /ˈlædə(r)/ *n* Leiter *f*; (*in fabric*) Laufmasche *f*

laden /ˈleɪdn/ *a* beladen

ladle /ˈleɪdl/ *n* [Schöpf]kelle *f* □ *vt* schöpfen

lady /ˈleɪdɪ/ *n* Dame *f*; (*title*) Lady *f*

lady: ~bird *n*, (*Amer*) **~bug** *n* Marienkäfer *m.* **~like** *a* damenhaft

lag¹ /læg/ *vi* (*pt/pp* **lagged**) **~ behind** zurückbleiben; (*fig*) nachhinken

lag² *vt* (*pt/pp* **lagged**) unwickeln ⟨*pipes*⟩

lager /ˈlɑ:gə(r)/ *n* Lagerbier *nt*

lagoon /ləˈgu:n/ *n* Lagune *f*

laid /leɪd/ *see* **lay³**

lain /leɪn/ *see* **lie²**

lair /leə(r)/ *n* Lager *nt*
laity /ˈleɪətɪ/ *n* Laienstand *m*
lake /leɪk/ *n* See *m*
lamb /læm/ *n* Lamm *nt*
lame /leɪm/ *a* (**-r, -st**) lahm
lament /ləˈment/ *n* Klage *f*; (*song*) Klagelied *nt* □ *vt* beklagen □ *vi* klagen. **~able** /ˈlæməntəbl/ *a* beklagenswert
laminated /ˈlæmɪneɪtɪd/ *a* laminiert
lamp /læmp/ *n* Lampe *f*; (*in street*) Laterne *f*. **~post** *n* Laternenpfahl *m*. **~shade** *n* Lampenschirm *m*
lance /lɑːns/ *n* Lanze *f* □ *vt* (*Med*) aufschneiden. **~-ˈcorporal** *n* Gefreite(r) *m*
land /lænd/ *n* Land *nt*; **plot of ~** Grundstück *nt* □ *vt/i* landen; **~ s.o. with sth** (*fam*) jdm etw auf halsen
landing /ˈlændɪŋ/ *n* Landung *f*; (*top of stairs*) Treppenflur *m*. **~-stage** *n* Landesteg *m*
land: ~lady *n* Wirtin *f*. **~-locked** *a* **~-locked country** Binnenstaat *m*. **~lord** *n* Wirt *m*; (*of land*) Grundbesitzer *m*; (*of building*) Hausbesitzer *m*. **~mark** *n* Erkennungszeichen *nt*; (*fig*) Meilenstein *m*. **~owner** *n* Grundbesitzer *m*. **~scape** /-skeɪp/ *n* Landschaft *f*. **~slide** *n* Erdrutsch *m*
lane /leɪn/ *n* kleine Landstraße *f*; (*Auto*) Spur *f*; (*Sport*) Bahn *f*; **'get in ~'** (*Auto*) 'bitte einordnen'
language /ˈlæŋgwɪdʒ/ *n* Sprache *f*; (*speech, style*) Ausdrucksweise *f*. **~ laboratory** *n* Sprachlabor *nt*
languid /ˈlæŋgwɪd/ *a*, **-ly** *adv* träge
languish /ˈlæŋgwɪʃ/ *vi* schmachten
lank /læŋk/ *a* ⟨*hair*⟩ strähnig
lanky /ˈlæŋkɪ/ *a* (**-ier, -iest**) schlaksig
lantern /ˈlæntən/ *n* Laterne *f*
lap¹ /læp/ *n* Schoß *m*
lap² *n* (*Sport*) Runde *f*; (*of journey*) Etappe *f* □ *vi* (*pt/pp* **lapped**) plätschern (**against** gegen)
lap³ *vt* (*pt/pp* **lapped**) **~ up** aufschlecken
lapel /ləˈpel/ *n* Revers *nt*
lapse /læps/ *n* Fehler *m*; (*moral*) Fehltritt *m*; (*of time*) Zeitspanne *f* □ *vi* (*expire*) erlöschen; **~ into** verfallen in (+ *acc*)
larceny /ˈlɑːsənɪ/ *n* Diebstahl *m*
lard /lɑːd/ *n* [Schweine]schmalz *nt*
larder /ˈlɑːdə(r)/ *n* Speisekammer *f*
large /lɑːdʒ/ *a* (**-r, -st**) & *adv* groß; **by and ~** im Großen und Ganzen; **at ~** auf freiem Fuß; (*in general*) im Allgemeinen. **~ly** *adv* großenteils
lark¹ /lɑːk/ *n* (*bird*) Lerche *f*
lark² *n* (*joke*) Jux *m* □ *vi* **~ about** herumalbern
larva /ˈlɑːvə/ *n* (*pl* **-vae** /-viː/) Larve *f*
laryngitis /lærɪnˈdʒaɪtɪs/ *n* Kehlkopfentzündung *f*
larynx /ˈlærɪŋks/ *n* Kehlkopf *m*
lascivious /ləˈsɪvɪəs/ *a* lüstern
laser /ˈleɪzə(r)/ *n* Laser *m*
lash /læʃ/ *n* Peitschenhieb *m*; (*eyelash*) Wimper *f* □ *vt* peitschen; (*tie*) festbinden (**to** an + *acc*). **~ out** *vi* um sich schlagen; (*spend*) viel Geld ausgeben (**on** für)
lashings /ˈlæʃɪŋz/ *npl* **~ of** (*fam*) eine Riesenmenge von
lass /læs/ *n* Mädchen *nt*
lasso /ləˈsuː/ *n* Lasso *nt*
last¹ /lɑːst/ *n* (*for shoe*) Leisten *m*
last² *a* & *n* letzte(r,s); **~ night** heute *od* gestern Nacht; (*evening*) gestern Abend; **at ~** endlich; **the ~ time** das letzte Mal; **for the ~ time** zum letzten Mal; **the ~ but one** der/die/das vorletzte; **that's the ~ straw** (*fam*) das schlägt dem Fass den Boden aus □ *adv* zuletzt; (*last time*) das letzte Mal;

do sth ~ etw zuletzt *od* als Letztes machen; **he/she went ~** er/sie ging als Letzter/Letzte □ *vi* dauern; ⟨*weather:*⟩ sich halten; ⟨*relationship:*⟩ halten. **~ing** *a* dauershaft. **~ly** *adv* schließlich, zum Schluss

latch /lætʃ/ *n* [einfache] Klinke *f*; **on the ~** nicht verschlossen

late /leɪt/ *a & adv* (**-r, -st**) spät; (*delayed*) verspätet; (*deceased*) verstorben; **the ~st news** die neuesten Nachrichten; **stay up ~** bis spät aufbleiben; **of ~** in letzter Zeit; **arrive ~** zu spät ankommen; **I am ~** ich komme zu spät *od* habe mich verspätet; **the train is ~** der Zug hat Verspätung. **~comer** *n* Zuspätkommende(r) *m/f*. **~ly** *adv* in letzter Zeit. **~ness** *n* Zuspätkommen *nt*; (*delay*) Verspätung *f*

latent /'leɪtnt/ *a* latent

later /'leɪtə(r)/ *a & adv* später; **~ on** nachher

lateral /'lætərəl/ *a* seitlich

lathe /leɪð/ *n* Drehbank *f*

lather /'lɑːðə(r)/ *n* [Seifen]-schaum *m* □ *vt* einseifen □ *vi* schäumen

Latin /'lætɪn/ *a* lateinisch □ *n* Latein *nt*. **~ A'merica** *n* Lateinamerika *nt*

latitude /'lætɪtjuːd/ *n* (*Geog*) Breite *f*; (*fig*) Freiheit *f*

latter /'lætə(r)/ *a & n* **the ~** der/die/das Letztere. **~ly** *adv* in letzter Zeit

lattice /'lætɪs/ *n* Gitter *nt*

Latvia /'lætvɪə/ *n* Lettland *nt*

laudable /'lɔːdəbl/ *a* lobenswert

laugh /lɑːf/ *n* Lachen *nt*; **with a ~** lachend □ *vi* lachen (**at/about** über + *acc*); **~ at s.o.** (*mock*) jdn auslachen. **~able** /-əbl/ *a* lachhaft, lächerlich. **~ing-stock** *n* Gegenstand *m* des Spottes

laughter /'lɑːftə(r)/ *n* Gelächter *nt*

launch[1] /lɔːntʃ/ *n* (*boat*) Barkasse *f*

launch[2] *n* Stapellauf *m*; (*of rocket*) Abschuss *m*; (*of product*) Lancierung *f* □ *vt* vom Stapel lassen ⟨*ship*⟩; zu Wasser lassen ⟨*lifeboat*⟩; abschießen ⟨*rocket*⟩; starten ⟨*attack*⟩; (*Comm*) lancieren ⟨*product*⟩

launder /'lɔːndə(r)/ *vt* waschen. **~ette** /-'dret/ *n* Münzwäscherei *f*

laundry /'lɔːndrɪ/ *n* Wäscherei *f*; (*clothes*) Wäsche *f*

laurel /'lɒrl/ *n* Lorbeer *m*

lava /'lɑːvə/ *n* Lava *f*

lavatory /'lævətrɪ/ *n* Toilette *f*

lavender /'lævəndə(r)/ *n* Lavendel *m*

lavish /'lævɪʃ/ *a*, **-ly** *adv* großzügig; (*wasteful*) verschwenderisch; **on a ~ scale** mit viel Aufwand □ *vt* **~ sth on s.o.** jdn mit etw überschütten

law /lɔː/ *n* Gesetz *nt*; (*system*) Recht *nt*; **study ~** Jura studieren; **~ and order** Recht und Ordnung

law: ~-abiding *a* gesetzestreu. **~court** *n* Gerichtshof *m*. **~ful** *a* rechtmäßig. **~less** *a* gesetzlos

lawn /lɔːn/ *n* Rasen *m*. **~-mower** *n* Rasenmäher *m*

'law suit *n* Prozess *m*

lawyer /'lɔːjə(r)/ *n* Rechtsanwalt *m* /-anwältin *f*

lax /læks/ *a* lax, locker

laxative /'læksətɪv/ *n* Abführmittel *nt*

laxity /'læksətɪ/ *n* Laxheit *f*

lay[1] /leɪ/ *a* Laien-

lay[2] *see* **lie**[2]

lay[3] *vt* (*pt/pp* **laid**) legen; decken ⟨*table*⟩; **~ a trap** eine Falle stellen. **~ down** *vt* hinlegen; festlegen ⟨*rules, conditions*⟩. **~ off** *vt* entlassen ⟨*workers*⟩ □ *vi* (*fam: stop*) aufhören. **~ out** *vt* hinlegen; aufbahren ⟨*corpse*⟩; anlegen ⟨*garden*⟩; (*Typ*) gestalten

lay: ~about *n* Faulenzer *m*. **~-by** *n* Parkbucht *f*; (*on motorway*) Rastplatz *m*

layer /ˈleɪə(r)/ *n* Schicht *f*
layette /leɪˈet/ *n* Babyausstattung *f*
lay: ~man *n* Laie *m*. **~out** *n* Anordnung *f*; (*design*) Gestaltung *f*; (*Typ*) Layout *nt*. **~ 'preacher** *n* Laienprediger *m*
laze /leɪz/ *vi* **~[about]** faulenzen
laziness /ˈleɪzɪnɪs/ *n* Faulheit *f*
lazy /ˈleɪzɪ/ *a* (**-ier, -iest**) faul. **~-bones** *n* Faulenzer *m*
lb /paʊnd/ *abbr* (**pound**) Pfd.
lead[1] /led/ *n* Blei *nt*; (*of pencil*) [Bleistift]mine *f*
lead[2] /li:d/ *n* Führung *f*; (*leash*) Leine *f*; (*flex*) Schnur *f*; (*clue*) Hinweis *m*, Spur *f*; (*Theat*) Hauptrolle *f*; (*distance ahead*) Vorsprung *m*; **be in the ~** in Führung liegen □ *vt/i* (*pt/pp* **led**) führen; leiten ⟨*team*⟩; (*induce*) bringen; (*at cards*) ausspielen; **~ the way** vorangehen; **~ up to sth** (*fig*) etw (*dat*) vorangehen. **~ away** *vt* wegführen
leaded /ˈledɪd/ *a* verbleit
leader /ˈli:də(r)/ *n* Führer *m*; (*of expedition, group*) Leiter(in) *m(f)*; (*of orchestra*) Konzertmeister *m*; (*in newspaper*) Leitartikel *m*. **~ship** *n* Führung *f*; Leitung *f*
leading /ˈli:dɪŋ/ *a* führend; **~ lady** Hauptdarstellerin *f*; **~ question** Suggestivfrage *f*
leaf /li:f/ *n* (*pl* **leaves**) Blatt *nt*; (*of table*) Ausziehplatte *f* □ *vi* **~ through sth** etw durchblättern. **~let** *n* Merkblatt *nt*; (*advertising*) Reklameblatt *nt*; (*political*) Flugblatt *nt*
league /li:g/ *n* Liga *f*; **be in ~ with** unter einer Decke stecken mit
leak /li:k/ *n* (*hole*) undichte Stelle *f*; (*Naut*) Leck *nt*; (*of gas*) Gasausfluss *m* □ *vi* undicht sein; ⟨*ship:*⟩ leck sein, lecken; ⟨*liquid:*⟩ auslaufen; ⟨*gas:*⟩ ausströmen □ *vt* auslaufen lassen; **~ sth to s.o.** (*fig*) jdm etw zuspielen. **~y** *a* undicht; (*Naut*) leck
lean[1] /li:n/ *a* (**-er, -est**) mager
lean[2] *v* (*pt/pp* **leaned** *or* **leant** /lent/) □ *vt* lehnen (**against/on** an + *acc*) □ *vi* ⟨*person*⟩ sich lehnen (**against/on** an + *acc*); (*not be straight*) sich neigen; **be ~ing against** lehnen an (+ *dat*); **~ on s.o.** (*depend*) bei jdm festen Halt finden. **~ back** *vi* sich zurücklehnen. **~ forward** *vi* sich vorbeugen. **~ out** *vi* sich hinauslehnen. **~ over** *vi* sich vorbeugen
leaning /ˈli:nɪŋ/ *a* schief □ *n* Neigung *f*
leap /li:p/ *n* Sprung *m* □ *vi* (*pt/pp* **leapt** /lept/ *or* **leaped**) springen; **he leapt at it** (*fam*) er griff sofort zu. **~-frog** *n* Bockspringen *nt*. **~ year** *n* Schaltjahr *nt*
learn /lɜ:n/ *vt/i* (*pt/pp* **learnt** *or* **learned**) lernen; (*hear*) erfahren; **~ to swim** schwimmen lernen
learn|ed /ˈlɜ:nɪd/ *a* gelehrt. **~er** *n* Anfänger *m*; **~er [driver]** Fahrschüler(in) *m(f)*. **~ing** *n* Gelehrsamkeit *f*
lease /li:s/ *n* Pacht *f*; (*contract*) Mietvertrag *m*; (*Comm*) Pachtvertrag *m* □ *vt* pachten; **~ [out]** verpachten
leash /li:ʃ/ *n* Leine *f*
least /li:st/ *a* geringste(r,s); **have ~ time** am wenigsten Zeit haben □ *n* **the ~** das wenigste; **at ~** wenigstens, mindestens; **not in the ~** nicht im Geringsten □ *adv* am wenigsten
leather /ˈleðə(r)/ *n* Leder *nt*. **~y** *a* ledern; (*tough*) zäh
leave /li:v/ *n* Erlaubnis *f*; (*holiday*) Urlaub *m*; **on ~** auf Urlaub; **take one's ~** sich verabschieden □ *v* (*pt/pp* **left**) □ *vt* lassen; (*go out of, abandon*) verlassen; (*forget*) liegen lassen; (*bequeath*) vermachen (**to** *dat*); **~ it to me!** überlassen Sie es mir! **there is nothing left** es ist nichts mehr übrig □ *vi* [weg]gehen/-fahren;

⟨*train, bus:*⟩ abfahren. ~ **behind** *vt* zurücklassen; (*forget*) liegen lassen. ~ **out** *vt* liegen lassen; (*leave outside*) draußen lassen; (*omit*) auslassen
leaves /li:vz/ *see* **leaf**
Lebanon /ˈlebənən/ *n* Libanon *m*
lecherous /ˈletʃərəs/ *a* lüstern
lectern /ˈlektən/ *n* [Lese]pult *nt*
lecture /ˈlektʃə(r)/ *n* Vortrag *m*; (*Univ*) Vorlesung *f*; (*reproof*) Strafpredigt *f* □ *vi* einen Vortrag/eine Vorlesung halten (**on** über + *acc*) □ *vt* ~ **s.o.** jdm eine Strafpredigt halten. ~**r** *n* Vortragende(r) *m/f*; (*Univ*) Dozent(in) *m(f)*
led /led/ *see* **lead**[2]
ledge /ledʒ/ *n* Leiste *f*; (*shelf, of window*) Sims *m*; (*in rock*) Vorsprung *m*
ledger /ˈledʒə(r)/ *n* Hauptbuch *nt*
lee /li:/ *n* (*Naut*) Lee *f*
leech /li:tʃ/ *n* Blutegel *m*
leek /li:k/ *n* Stange *f* Porree; ~**s** *pl* Porree *m*
leer /lɪə(r)/ *n* anzügliches Grinsen *nt* □ *vi* anzüglich grinsen
lee|ward /ˈli:wəd/ *adv* nach Lee. ~**way** *n* (*fig*) Spielraum *m*
left[1] /left/ *see* **leave**
left[2] *a* linke(r,s) □ *adv* links; ⟨*go*⟩ nach links □ *n* linke Seite *f*; **on the** ~ links; **from/to the** ~ von/nach links; **the** ~ (*Pol*) die Linke
left: ~-ˈ**handed** *a* linkshändig. ~-ˈ**luggage [office]** *n* Gepäckaufbewahrung *f*. ~**overs** *npl* Reste *pl*. ~-ˈ**wing** *a* (*Pol*) linke(r,s)
leg /leg/ *n* Bein *nt*; (*Culin*) Keule *f*; (*of journey*) Etappe *f*
legacy /ˈlegəsɪ/ *n* Vermächtnis *nt*, Erbschaft *f*
legal /ˈli:gl/ *a*, **-ly** *adv* gesetzlich; ⟨*matters*⟩ rechtlich; ⟨*department, position*⟩ Rechts-; **be** ~ [gesetzlich] erlaubt sein; **take** ~ **action** gerichtlich vorgehen
legality /lɪˈgælətɪ/ *n* Legalität *f*
legalize /ˈli:gəlaɪz/ *vt* legalisieren
legend /ˈledʒənd/ *n* Legende *f*. ~**ary** *a* legendär
legible /ˈledʒəbl/ *a*, **-bly** *adv* leserlich
legion /ˈli:dʒn/ *n* Legion *f*
legislat|e /ˈledʒɪsleɪt/ *vi* Gesetze erlassen. ~**ion** /-ˈleɪʃn/ *n* Gesetzgebung *f*; (*laws*) Gesetze *pl*
legislat|ive /ˈledʒɪslətɪv/ *a* gesetzgebend. ~**ure** /-leɪtʃə(r)/ *n* Legislative *f*
legitimate /lɪˈdʒɪtɪmət/ *a* rechtmäßig; (*justifiable*) berechtigt; ⟨*child*⟩ ehelich
leisure /ˈleʒə(r)/ *n* Freizeit *f*; **at your** ~ wenn Sie Zeit haben. ~**ly** *a* gemächlich
lemon /ˈlemən/ *n* Zitrone *f*. ~**ade** /-ˈneɪd/ *n* Zitronenlimonade *f*
lend /lend/ *vt* (*pt/pp* **lent**) leihen; ~ **s.o. sth** jdm etw leihen; ~ **a hand** (*fam*) helfen. ~**ing library** *n* Leihbücherei *f*
length /leŋθ/ *n* Länge *f*; (*piece*) Stück *nt*; (*of wallpaper*) Bahn *f*; (*of time*) Dauer *f*; **at** ~ ausführlich; (*at last*) endlich
length|en /ˈleŋθən/ *vt* länger machen □ *vi* länger werden. ~**ways** *adv* der Länge nach, längs
lengthy /ˈleŋθɪ/ *a* (**-ier, -iest**) langwierig
lenien|ce /ˈli:nɪəns/ *n* Nachsicht *f*. ~**t** *a*, **-ly** *adv* nachsichtig
lens /lenz/ *n* Linse *f*; (*Phot*) Objektiv *nt*; (*of spectacles*) Glas *nt*
lent /lent/ *see* **lend**
Lent *n* Fastenzeit *f*
lentil /ˈlentl/ *n* (*Bot*) Linse *f*
Leo /ˈli:əʊ/ *n* (*Astr*) Löwe *m*
leopard /ˈlepəd/ *n* Leopard *m*
leotard /ˈli:ətɑ:d/ *n* Trikot *nt*
leper /ˈlepə(r)/ *n* Leprakranke(r) *m/f*; *n* (*Bible & fig*) Aussätzige(r) *m/f*
leprosy /ˈleprəsɪ/ *n* Lepra *f*
lesbian /ˈlezbɪən/ *a* lesbisch □ *n* Lesbierin *f*

lesion /'li:ʒn/ *n* Verletzung *f*
less /les/ *a, adv, n & prep* weniger; **~ and ~** immer weniger; **not any the ~** um nichts weniger
lessen /'lesn/ *vt* verringern □ *vi* nachlassen; ⟨*value*:⟩ abnehmen
lesser /'lesə(r)/ *a* geringere(r,s)
lesson /'lesn/ *n* Stunde *f*; (*in textbook*) Lektion *f*; (*Relig*) Lesung *f*; **teach s.o. a ~** (*fig*) jdm eine Lehre erteilen
lest /lest/ *conj* (*liter*) damit . . . nicht
let /let/ *vt* (*pt/pp* **let**, *pres p* **letting**) lassen; (*rent*) vermieten; **~ alone** (*not to mention*) geschweige denn; '**~ to ~**' 'zu vermieten'; **~ us go** gehen wir; **~ me know** sagen Sie mir Bescheid; **~ him do it** lass ihn das machen; **just ~ him!** soll er doch! **~ s.o. sleep/win** jdn schlafen/gewinnen lassen; **~ oneself in for sth** (*fam*) sich (*dat*) etw einbrocken. **~ down** *vt* hinunter-/herunterlassen; (*lengthen*) länger machen; **~ s.o. down** (*fam*) jdn im Stich lassen; (*disappoint*) jdn enttäuschen. **~ in** *vt* hereinlassen. **~ off** *vt* abfeuern ⟨*gun*⟩; hochgehen lassen ⟨*firework, bomb*⟩; (*emit*) ausstoßen; (*excuse from*) befreien von; (*not punish*) frei ausgehen lassen. **~ out** *vt* hinaus-/herauslassen; (*make larger*) auslassen. **~ through** *vt* durchlassen. **~ up** *vi* (*fam*) nachlassen
'let-down *n* Enttäuschung *f*, (*fam*) Reinfall *m*
lethal /'li:θl/ *a* tödlich
letharg|ic /lɪ'θɑ:dʒɪk/ *a* lethargisch. **~y** /'leθədʒɪ/ *n* Lethargie *f*
letter /'letə(r)/ *n* Brief *m*; (*of alphabet*) Buchstabe *m*; **by ~** brieflich. **~-box** *n* Briefkasten *m*. **~-head** *n* Briefkopf *m*. **~ing** *n* Beschriftung *f*
lettuce /'letɪs/ *n* [Kopf]salat *m*
'let-up *n* (*fam*) Nachlassen *nt*
leukaemia /lu:'ki:mɪə/ *n* Leukämie *f*
level /'levl/ *a* eben; (*horizontal*) waagerecht; (*in height*) auf gleicher Höhe; ⟨*spoonful*⟩ gestrichen; **draw ~ with** gleichziehen mit; **one's ~ best** sein Möglichstes □ *n* Höhe *f*; (*fig*) Ebene *f*, Niveau *nt*; (*stage*) Stufe *f*; **on the ~** (*fam*) ehrlich □ *vt* (*pt/pp* **levelled**) einebnen; (*aim*) richten (**at** auf + *acc*)
level: ~ 'crossing *n* Bahnübergang *m*. **~-'headed** *a* vernünftig
lever /'li:və(r)/ *n* Hebel *m* □ *vt* **~ up** mit einem Hebel anheben. **~age** /-rɪdʒ/ *n* Hebelkraft *f*
levity /'levətɪ/ *n* Heiterkeit *f*; (*frivolity*) Leichtfertigkeit *f*
levy /'levɪ/ *vt* (*pt/pp* **levied**) erheben ⟨*tax*⟩
lewd /lju:d/ *a* (**-er, -est**) anstößig
liabilit|y /laɪə'bɪlətɪ/ *n* Haftung *f*; **~ies** *pl* Verbindlichkeiten *pl*
liable /'laɪəbl/ *a* haftbar; **be ~ to do sth** etw leicht tun können
liaise /lɪ'eɪz/ *vi* (*fam*) Verbindungsperson sein
liaison /lɪ'eɪzɒn/ *n* Verbindung *f*; (*affair*) Verhältnis *nt*
liar /'laɪə(r)/ *n* Lügner(in) *m(f)*
libel /'laɪbl/ *n* Verleumdung *f* □ *vt* (*pt/pp* **libelled**) verleumden. **~lous** *a* verleumderisch
liberal /'lɪbərl/ *a*, **-ly** *adv* tolerant; (*generous*) großzügig. **L~** *a* (*Pol*) liberal □ *n* Liberale(r) *m/f*
liberat|e /'lɪbəreɪt/ *vt* befreien. **~ed** *a* ⟨*woman*⟩ emanzipiert. **~ion** /-'reɪʃn/ *n* Befreiung *f*. **~or** *n* Befreier *m*
liberty /'lɪbətɪ/ *n* Freiheit *f*; **take the ~ of doing sth** sich (*dat*) erlauben, etw zu tun; **take liberties** sich (*dat*) Freiheiten erlauben
Libra /'li:brə/ *n* (*Astr*) Waage *f*
librarian /laɪ'breərɪən/ *n* Bibliothekar(in) *m(f)*
library /'laɪbrərɪ/ *n* Bibliothek *f*

Libya /ˈlɪbɪə/ *n* Libyen *nt*
lice /laɪs/ *see* **louse**
licence /ˈlaɪsns/ *n* Genehmigung *f*; (*Comm*) Lizenz *f*; (*for TV*) ≈ Fernsehgebühr *f*; (*for driving*) Führerschein *m*; (*for alcohol*) Schankkonzession *f*; (*freedom*) Freiheit *f*
license /ˈlaɪsns/ *vt* eine Genehmigung/(*Comm*) Lizenz erteilen (+ *dat*); **be ~d** ⟨*car:*⟩ zugelassen sein; ⟨*restaurant:*⟩ Schankkonzession haben. **~-plate** *n* Nummernschild *nt*
licentious /laɪˈsenʃəs/ *a* lasterhaft
lichen /ˈlaɪkən/ *n* (*Bot*) Flechte *f*
lick /lɪk/ *n* Lecken *nt*; **a ~ of paint** ein bisschen Farbe □ *vt* lecken; (*fam: defeat*) schlagen
lid /lɪd/ *n* Deckel *m*; (*of eye*) Lid *nt*
lie[1] /laɪ/ *n* Lüge *f*; **tell a ~** lügen □ *vi* (*pt/pp* **lied**, *pres p* **lying**) lügen; **~ to** belügen
lie[2] *vi* (*pt* **lay**, *pp* **lain**, *pres p* **lying**) liegen; **here ~s ...** hier ruht ... **~ down** *vi* sich hinlegen
Liège /lɪˈeɪʒ/ *n* Lüttich *nt*
ˈlie-in *n* **have a ~** [sich] ausschlafen
lieu /ljuː/ *n* **in ~ of** statt (+ *gen*)
lieutenant /lefˈtenənt/ *n* Oberleutnant *m*
life /laɪf/ *n* (*pl* **lives**) Leben *nt*; (*biography*) Biographie *f*; **lose one's ~** ums Leben kommen
life: ~belt *n* Rettungsring *m*. **~boat** *n* Rettungsboot *nt*. **~buoy** *n* Rettungsring *m*. **~-guard** *n* Lebensretter *m*. **~-jacket** *n* Schwimmweste *f*. **~less** *a* leblos. **~like** *a* naturgetreu. **~line** *n* Rettungsleine *f*. **~long** *a* lebenslang. **~ preserver** *n* (*Amer*) Rettungsring *m*. **~-size(d)** *a* ... in Lebensgröße. **~time** *n* Leben *nt*; **in s.o.'s ~time** zu jds Lebzeiten; **the chance of a ~time** eine einmalige Gelegenheit
lift /lɪft/ *n* Aufzug *m*, Lift *m*; **give s.o. a ~** jdn mitnehmen; **get a ~** mitgenommen werden □ *vt* heben; aufheben ⟨*restrictions*⟩ □ *vi* ⟨*fog:*⟩ sich lichten. **~ up** *vt* hochheben
ˈlift-off *n* Abheben *nt*
ligament /ˈlɪgəmənt/ *n* (*Anat*) Band *nt*
light[1] /laɪt/ *a* (**-er, -est**) (*not dark*) hell; **~ blue** hellblau □ *n* Licht *nt*; (*lamp*) Lampe *f*; **in the ~ of** (*fig*) angesichts (+ **gen**); **have you [got] a ~?** haben Sie Feuer? □ *vt* (*pt/pp* **lit** *or* **lighted**) anzünden ⟨*fire, cigarette*⟩; anmachen ⟨*lamp*⟩; (*illuminate*) beleuchten. **~ up** *vi* ⟨*face:*⟩ sich erhellen
light[2] *a* (**-er, -est**) (*not heavy*) leicht; **~ sentence** milde Strafe *f* □ *adv* **travel ~** mit wenig Gepäck reisen
ˈlight-bulb *n* Glühbirne *f*
lighten[1] /ˈlaɪtn/ *vt* heller machen □ *vi* heller werden
lighten[2] *vt* leichter machen ⟨*load*⟩
lighter /ˈlaɪtə(r)/ *n* Feuerzeug *nt*
light: ~-ˈheaded *a* benommen. **~-ˈhearted** *a* unbekümmert. **~house** *n* Leuchtturm *m*. **~ing** *n* Beleuchtung *f*. **~ly** *adv* leicht; (*casually*) leichthin; **get off ~ly** glimpflich davonkommen
lightning /ˈlaɪtnɪŋ/ *n* Blitz *m*. **~-conductor** *n* Blitzableiter *m*
ˈlightweight *a* leicht □ *n* (*Boxing*) Leichtgewicht *nt*
like[1] /laɪk/ *a* ähnlich; (*same*) gleich □ *prep* wie; (*similar to*) ähnlich (+ *dat*); **~ this** so; **a man ~ that** so ein Mann; **what's he ~?** wie ist er denn? □ *conj* (*fam: as*) wie; (*Amer: as if*) als ob
like[2] *vt* mögen; **I should/would ~** ich möchte; **I ~ the car** das Auto gefällt mir; **I ~ chocolate** ich esse gern Schokolade; **~ dancing/singing** gern tanzen/singen; **I ~ that!** (*fam*) das ist doch die Höhe! □ *n* **~s and dislikes** *pl* Vorlieben und Abneigungen *pl*

like|able /ˈlaɪkəbl/ *a* sympathisch. **~lihood** /-lɪhʊd/ *n* Wahrscheinlichkeit *f*. **~ly** *a* (-ier, -iest) & *adv* wahrscheinlich; **not ~ly!** (*fam*) auf gar keinen Fall!
ˈlike-minded *a* gleich gesinnt
liken /ˈlaɪkən/ *vt* vergleichen (**to** mit)
like|ness /ˈlaɪknɪs/ *n* Ähnlichkeit *f*. **~wise** *adv* ebenso
liking /ˈlaɪkɪŋ/ *n* Vorliebe *f*; **is it to your ~?** gefällt es Ihnen?
lilac /ˈlaɪlək/ *n* Flieder *m* □ *a* fliederfarben
lily /ˈlɪlɪ/ *n*. Lilie *f*. **~ of the valley** *n* Maiglöckchen *nt*
limb /lɪm/ *n* Glied *nt*
limber /ˈlɪmbə(r)/ *vi* **~ up** Lockerungsübungen machen
lime1 /laɪm/ *n* (*fruit*) Limone *f*; (*tree*) Linde *f*
lime2 *n* Kalk *m*. **~light** *n* **be in the ~light** im Rampenlicht stehen. **~stone** *n* Kalkstein *m*
limit /ˈlɪmɪt/ *n* Grenze *f*; (*limitation*) Beschränkung *f*; **that's the ~!** (*fam*) das ist doch die Höhe! □ *vt* beschränken (**to** auf + *acc*). **~ation** /-ˈteɪʃn/ *n* Beschränkung *f*; **~ed** *a* beschränkt; **~ed company** Gesellschaft *f* mit beschränkter Haftung
limousine /ˈlɪməziːn/ *n* Limousine *f*
limp1 /lɪmp/ *n* Hinken *nt*; **have a ~** hinken □ *vi* hinken
limp2 *a* (-er -est), -ly *adv* schlaff
limpet /ˈlɪmpɪt/ *n* **like a ~** (*fig*) wie eine Klette
limpid /ˈlɪmpɪd/ *a* klar
linctus /ˈlɪŋktəs/ *n* **[cough] ~** Hustensirup *m*
line1 /laɪn/ *n* Linie *f*; (*length of rope, cord*) Leine *f*; (*Teleph*) Leitung *f*; (*of writing*) Zeile *f*; (*row*) Reihe *f*; (*wrinkle*) Falte *f*; (*of business*) *f*; (*Amer: queue*) Schlange *f*; **in ~ with** gemäß (+ *dat*) □ *vt* säumen ⟨*street*⟩. **~ up** *vi* sich aufstellen □ *vt* aufstellen
line2 *vt* füttern ⟨*garment*⟩; (*Techn*) auskleiden
lineage /ˈlɪnɪɪdʒ/ *n* Herkunft *f*
linear /ˈlɪnɪə(r)/ *a* linear
lined1 /laɪnd/ *a* (*wrinkled*) faltig; ⟨*paper*⟩ liniert
lined2 *a* ⟨*garment*⟩ gefüttert
linen /ˈlɪnɪn/ *n* Leinen *nt*; (*articles*) Wäsche *f*
liner /ˈlaɪnə(r)/ *n* Passagierschiff *nt*
ˈlinesman *n* (*Sport*) Linienrichter *m*
linger /ˈlɪŋgə(r)/ *vi* [zurück]bleiben
lingerie /ˈlæʒərɪ/ *n* Damenunterwäsche *f*
linguist /ˈlɪŋgwɪst/ *n* Sprachkundige(r) *m/f*
linguistic /lɪŋˈgwɪstɪk/ *a*, **-ally** *adv* sprachlich. **~s** *n* Linguistik *f*
lining /ˈlaɪnɪŋ/ *n* (*of garment*) Futter *nt*; (*Techn*) Auskleidung *f*
link /lɪŋk/ *n* (*of chain*) Glied *nt* (*fig*) Verbidung *f* □ *vt* verbinden; **~ arms** sich unterhaken
links /lɪŋks/ *n or npl* Golfplatz *m*
lino /ˈlaɪnəʊ/ *n*, **linoleum** /lɪˈnəʊlɪəm/ *n* Linoleum *nt*
lint /lɪnt/ *n* Verbandstoff *m*
lion /ˈlaɪən/ *n* Löwe *m*; **~'s share** (*fig*) Löwenanteil *m*. **~ess** *n* Löwin *f*
lip /lɪp/ *n* Lippe *f*; (*edge*) Rand *m*; (*of jug*) Schnabel *m*
lip: ~-reading *n* Lippenlesen *nt*. **~-service** *n* **pay ~-service** ein Lippenbekenntnis ablegen (**to** zu). **~stick** *n* Lippenstift *m*
liquefy /ˈlɪkwɪfaɪ/ *vt* (*pt/pp* **-ied**) verflüssigen □ *vi* sich verflüssigen
liqueur /lɪˈkjʊə(r)/ *n* Likör *m*
liquid /ˈlɪkwɪd/ *n* Flüssigkeit *f* □ *a* flüssig
liquidat|e /ˈlɪkwɪdeɪt/ *vt* liquidieren. **~ion** /-ˈdeɪʃn/ *n* Liquidation *f*

liquidize /ˈlɪkwɪdaɪz/ *vt* [im Mixer] pürieren. **~r** *n* (*Culin*) Mixer *m*
liquor /ˈlɪkə(r)/ *n* Alkohol *m*; (*juice*) Flüssigkeit *f*
liquorice /ˈlɪkərɪs/ *n* Lakritze *f*
ˈliquor store *n* (*Amer*) Spirituosengeschäft *nt*
lisp /lɪsp/ *n* Lispeln *nt* □ *vt/i* lispeln
list[1] /lɪst/ *n* Liste *f* □ *vt* aufführen
list[2] *vi* ⟨*ship:*⟩ Schlagseite haben
listen /ˈlɪsn/ *vi* zuhören (**to** *dat*); **~ to the radio** Radio hören. **~er** *n* Zuhörer(in) *m(f)*; (*Radio*) Hörer(in) *m(f)*
listless /ˈlɪstlɪs/ *a*, **-ly** *adv* lustlos
lit /lɪt/ *see* **light**[1]
litany /ˈlɪtənɪ/ *n* Litanei *f*
literacy /ˈlɪtərəsɪ/ *n* Lese- und Schreibfertigkeit *f*
literal /ˈlɪtərl/ *a* wörtlich. **~ly** *adv* buchstäblich
literary /ˈlɪtərərɪ/ *a* literarisch
literate /ˈlɪtərət/ *a* **be ~** lesen und schreiben können
literature /ˈlɪtrətʃə(r)/ *n* Literatur *f*; (*fam*) Informationsmaterial *nt*
lithe /laɪð/ *a* geschmeidig
Lithuania /lɪθjʊˈeɪnɪə/ *n* Litauen *nt*
litigation /lɪtɪˈgeɪʃn/ *n* Rechtsstreit *m*
litre /ˈliːtə(r)/ *n* Liter *m & nt*
litter /ˈlɪtə(r)/ *n* Abfall *m*; (*Zool*) Wurf *m* □ *vt* **be ~ed with** übersät sein mit. **~-bin** *n* Abfalleimer *m*
little /ˈlɪtl/ *a* klein; (*not much*) wenig □ *adv & n* wenig; **a ~** ein bisschen/wenig; **~ by ~** nach und nach
liturgy /ˈlɪtədʒɪ/ *n* Liturgie *f*
live[1] /laɪv/ *a* lebendig; ⟨*ammunition*⟩ scharf; **~ broadcast** Live-Sendung *f*; **be ~** (*Electr*) unter Strom stehen □ *adv* (*Radio, TV*) live
live[2] /lɪv/ *vi* leben; (*reside*) wohnen; **~ up to** gerecht werden (+ *dat*). **~ on** *vt* leben von; (*eat*) sich ernähren von □ *vi* weiterleben
liveli|hood /ˈlaɪvlɪhʊd/ *n* Lebensunterhalt *m*. **~ness** *n* Lebendigkeit *f*
lively /ˈlaɪvlɪ/ *a* (**-ier, -iest**) lebhaft, lebendig
liven /ˈlaɪvn/ *v* **~ up** *vt* beleben □ *vi* lebhaft werden
liver /ˈlɪvə(r)/ *n* Leber *f*
lives /laɪvz/ *see* life
livestock /ˈlaɪv-/ *n* Vieh *nt*
livid /ˈlɪvɪd/ *a* (*fam*) wütend
living /ˈlɪvɪŋ/ *a* lebend □ *n* **earn one's ~** seinen Lebensunterhalt verdienen; **the ~** *pl* die Lebenden. **~-room** *n* Wohnzimmer *nt*
lizard /ˈlɪzəd/ *n* Eidechse *f*
load /ləʊd/ *n* Last *f*; (*quantity*) Ladung *f*; (*Electr*) Belastung *f*; **~s of** (*fam*) jede Menge □ *vt* laden ⟨*goods, gun*⟩; beladen ⟨*vehicle*⟩; **~ a camera** einen Film in eine Kamera einlegen. **~ed** *a* beladen; (*fam: rich*) steinreich; **~ed question** Fangfrage *f*
loaf[1] /ləʊf/ *n* (*pl* **loaves**) Brot *nt*
loaf[2] *vi* faulenzen
loan /ləʊn/ *n* Leihgabe *f*; (*money*) Darlehen *nt*; **on ~** geliehen □ *vt* leihen (*to dat*)
loath /ləʊθ/ *a* **be ~ to do sth** etw ungern tun
loath|e /ləʊð/ *vt* verabscheuen. **~ing** *n* Abscheu *m*. **~ some** *a* abscheulich
loaves /ləʊvz/ *see* **loaf**[1]
lobby /ˈlɒbɪ/ *n* Foyer *nt*; (*anteroom*) Vorraum *m*; (*Pol*) Lobby *f*
lobe /ləʊb/ *n* (*of ear*) Ohrläppchen *nt*
lobster /ˈlɒbstə(r)/ *n* Hummer *m*
local /ˈləʊkl/ *a* hiesig; ⟨*time, traffic*⟩ Orts-; **under ~ anaesthetic** unter örtlicher Betäubung; **I'm not ~** ich bin nicht von hier □ *n* Hiesige(r) *m/f*; (*fam: public house*) Stammkneipe *f*.

~ **au'thority** *n* Kommunalbehörde *f*. ~ **call** *n* (*Teleph*) Ortsgespräch *nt*
locality /ləʊ'kælətɪ/ *n* Gegend *f*
localized /'ləʊkəlaɪzd/ *a* lokalisiert
locally /'ləʊkəlɪ/ *adv* am Ort
locat|e /ləʊ'keɪt/ *vt* ausfindig machen; **be ~ed** sich befinden. **~ion** /-'keɪʃn/ *n* Lage *f*; **filmed on ~ion** als Außenaufnahme gedreht
lock[1] /lɒk/ *n* (*hair*) Strähne *f*
lock[2] *n* (*on door*) Schloss *nt*; (*on canal*) Schleuse *f* □ *vt* abschließen □ *vi* sich abschließen lassen. ~ **in** *vt* einschließen. ~ **out** *vt* ausschließen. ~ **up** *vt* abschließen; einsperren ⟨*person*⟩ □ *vi* zuschließen
locker /'lɒkə(r)/ *n* Schließfach *nt*; (*Mil*) Spind *m*; (*in hospital*) kleiner Schrank *m*
locket /'lɒkɪt/ *n* Medaillon *nt*
lock: ~-out *n* Aussperrung *f*. **~smith** *n* Schlosser *m*
locomotion /ləʊkə'məʊʃn/ *n* Fortbewegung *f*
locomotive /ləʊkə'məʊtɪv/ *n* Lokomotive *f*
locum /'ləʊkəm/ *n* Vertreter(in) *m(f)*
locust /'ləʊkəst/ *n* Heuschrecke *f*
lodge /lɒdʒ/ *n* (*porter's*) Pförtnerhaus *nt*; (*masonic*) Loge *f* □ *vt* (*submit*) einreichen; (*deposit*) deponieren □ *vi* zur Untermiete wohnen (**with** bei); (*become fixed*) stecken bleiben. **~r** *n* Untermieter(in) *m(f)*
lodging /'lɒdʒɪŋ/ *n* Unterkunft *f*; **~s** *npl* möbliertes Zimmer *nt*
loft /lɒft/ *n* Dachboden *m*
lofty /'lɒftɪ/ *a* (**-ier, -iest**) hoch; (*haughty*) hochmütig
log /lɒg/ *n* Baumstamm *m*; (*for fire*) [Holz]scheit *nt*; **sleep like a ~** (*fam*) wie ein Murmeltier schlafen
logarithm /'lɒgərɪðm/ *n* Logarithmus *m*
'log-book *n* (*Naut*) Logbuch *nt*
loggerheads /'lɒgə-/ *npl* **be at ~** (*fam*) sich in den Haaren liegen
logic /'lɒdʒɪk/ *n* Logik *f*. **~al** *a*, **-ly** *adv* logisch
logistics /lə'dʒɪstɪks/ *npl* Logistik *f*
logo /'ləʊgəʊ/ *n* Symbol *nt*, Logo *nt*
loin /lɔɪn/ *n* (*Culin*) Lende *f*
loiter /'lɔɪtə(r)/ *vi* herumlungern
loll /lɒl/ *vi* sich lümmeln
loll|ipop /'lɒlɪpɒp/ *n* Lutscher *m*. **~y** *n* Lutscher *m*; (*fam: money*) Moneten *pl*
London /'lʌndən/ *n* London *nt* □ *attrib* Londoner. **~er** *n* Londoner(in) *m(f)*
lone /ləʊn/ *a* einzeln. **~liness** *n* Einsamkeit *f*
lonely /'ləʊnlɪ/ *a* (**-ier, -iest**) einsam
lone|r /'ləʊnə(r)/ *n* Einzelgänger *m*. **~some** *a* einsam
long[1] /lɒŋ/ *a* (**-er** /'lɒŋgə(r)/, **-est** /'lɒŋgɪst/) lang; ⟨*journey*⟩ weit; **a ~ time** lange; **a ~ way** weit; **in the ~ run** auflange Sicht; (*in the end*) letzten Endes □ *adv* lange; **all day ~** den ganzen Tag; **not ~ ago** vor kurzem; **before ~** bald; **no ~er** nicht mehr; **as** *or* **so ~as** solange; **so ~!** (*fam*) tschüs! **will you be ~?** dauert es noch lange [bei dir]? **it won't take ~** es dauert nicht lange
long[2] *vi* **~ for** sich sehnen nach
long-'distance *a* Fern-; (*Sport*) Langstrecken-
longevity /lɒn'dʒevətɪ/ *n* Langlebigkeit *f*
'longhand *n* Langschrift *f*
longing /'lɒŋɪŋ/ *a*, **-ly** *adv* sehnsüchtig □ *n* Sehnsucht *f*
longitude /'lɒŋgɪtju:d/ *n* (*Geog*) Länge *f*
long: ~ jump *n* Weitsprung *m*. **~-life 'milk** *n* H-Milch *f*. **~-lived**

/-lɪvd/ *a* langlebig. **~-range** *a* (*Mil, Aviat*) Langstrecken-; ⟨*forecast*⟩ langfristig. **~-sighted** *a* weitsichtig. **~-sleeved** *a* langärmelig. **~-suffering** *a* langmütig. **~-term** *a* langfristig. **~ wave** *n* Langwelle *f*. **~-winded** /-ˈwɪndɪd/ *a* langatmig

loo /luː/ *n* (*fam*) Klo *nt*

look /lʊk/ *n* Blick *m*; (*appearance*) Aussehen *nt*; **[good] ~s** *pl* [gutes] Aussehen *nt*; **have a ~ at** sich (*dat*) ansehen; **go and have a ~** sieh mal nach □ *vi* sehen; (*search*) nachsehen; (*seem*) aussehen; **don't ~** sieh nicht hin; **~ here!** hören Sie mal! **~ at** ansehen; **~ for** suchen; **~ forward to** sich **freuen auf** (+ *acc*); **~ in on** vorbeischauen bei; **~ into** (*examine*) nachgehen (+ *dat*); **~ like** aussehen wie; **~ on to** ⟨*room:*⟩ gehen auf (+ *acc*). **~ after** *vt* betreuen. **~ down** *vi* hinuntersehen; **~ down on s.o.** (*fig*) auf jdn herabsehen. **~ out** *vi* hinaus-/heraussehen; (*take care*) aufpassen; **~ out for** Ausschau halten nach; **~ out!** Vorsicht! **~ round** *vi* sich umsehen. **~ up** *vi* aufblicken; **~ up to s.o.** (*fig*) zu jdm aufsehen □ *vt* nachshlagen ⟨*word*⟩

ˈlook-out *n* Wache *f*; (*prospect*) Aussicht *f*; **be on the ~ for** Ausschau halten nach

loom[1] /luːm/ *n* Webstuhl *m*

loom[2] *vi* auftauchen; (*fig*) sich abzeichnen

loony /ˈluːnɪ/ *a* (*fam*) verrückt

loop /luːp/ *n* Schlinge *f*; (*in road*) Schleife *f*; (*on garment*) Aufhänger *m* □ *vt* schlingen. **~hole** *n* Hintertürchen *nt*; (*in the law*) Lücke *f*

loose /luːs/ *a* (**-r, -st**), **-ly** *adv* lose; (*not tight enough*) locker; (*inexact*) frei; **be at a ~ end** nichts zu tun haben; **set ~** freilassen; **run ~** frei herumlaufen. **~ ˈchange** *n* Kleingeld *nt*. **~ ˈchippings** *npl* Rollsplit *m*

loosen /ˈluːsn/ *vt* lockern □ *vi* sich lockern

loot /luːt/ *n* Beute *f* □ *vt/i* plündern. **~er** *n* Plünderer *m*

lop /lɒp/ *vt* (*pt/pp* **lopped**) stutzen. **~ off** *vt* abhacken

lopˈsided *a* schief

loquacious /ləˈkweɪʃəs/ *a* redselig

lord /lɔːd/ *n* Herr *m*; (*title*) Lord *m*; **House of L~s** ≈ Oberhaus *nt*; **the L~'s Prayer** das Vaterunser; **good L~!** du liebe Zeit!

lore /lɔː(r)/ *n* Überlieferung *f*

lorry /ˈlɒrɪ/ *n* Last[kraft]wagen *m*

lose /luːz/ *v* (*pt/pp* **lost**) □ *vt* verlieren; (*miss*) verpassen □ *vi* verlieren; ⟨*clock:*⟩ nachgehen; **get lost** verloren gehen; ⟨*person*⟩ sich verlaufen. **~r** *n* Verlierer *m*

loss /lɒs/ *n* Verlust *m*; **be at a ~** nicht mehr weiter wissen; **be at a ~ for words** nicht wissen, was man sagen soll

lost /lɒst/ *see* **lose**. **~ ˈproperty office** *n* Fundbüro *nt*

lot[1] /lɒt/ Los *nt*; (*at auction*) Posten *m*; **draw ~s** losen (forum)

lot[2] *n* **the ~** alle; (*everything*) alles; **a ~ [of]** viel; (*many*) viele; **~s of** (*fam*) eine Menge; **it has changed a ~** es hat sich sehr verändert

lotion /ˈləʊʃn/ *n* Lotion *f*

lottery /ˈlɒtərɪ/ *n* Lotterie *f*. **~ ticket** *n* Los *nt*

loud /laʊd/ *a* (**-er, -est**), **-ly** *adv* laut; ⟨*colours*⟩ grell □ *adv* **[out] ~** laut. **~ˈhailer** *n* Megaphon *nt*. **~ˈspeaker** *n* Lautsprecher *m*

lounge /laʊndʒ/ *n* Wohnzimmer *nt*; (*in hotel*) Aufenthaltsraum *m*. □ *vi* sich lümmeln. **~ suit** *n* Straßenanzug *m*

louse /laʊs/ *n* (*pl* **lice**) Laus *f*

lousy /ˈlaʊzɪ/ *a* (**-ier, -iest**) (*fam*) lausig

lout /laʊt/ *n* Flegel *m*, Lümmel *m*. **~ish** *a* flegelhaft

lovable /ˈlʌvəbl/ *a* liebenswert

love /lʌv/ *n* Liebe *f*; (*Tennis*) null; **in ~** verliebt □ *vt* lieben; **~ doing sth** etw sehr gerne machen; **I ~ chocolate** ich esse sehr gerne Schokolade. **~-affair** *n* Liebesverhältnis *nt*. **~ letter** *n* Liebesbrief *m*
lovely /ˈlʌvlɪ/ *a* (**-ier, -iest**) schön; **we had a ~ time** es war sehr schön
lover /ˈlʌvə(r)/ *n* Liebhaber *m*
love: ~ song *n* Liebeslied *nt*. **~ story** *n* Liebesgeschichte *f*
loving /ˈlʌvɪŋ/ *a*, **-ly** *adv* liebevoll
low /ləʊ/ *a* (**-er, -est**) niedrig; ⟨*cloud, note*⟩ tief; ⟨*voice*⟩ leise; (*depressed*) niedergeschlagen □ *adv* niedrig; ⟨*fly, sing*⟩ tief; ⟨*speak*⟩ leise; **feel ~** deprimiert sein □ *n* (*Meteorol*) Tief *nt*; (*fig*) Tiefstand *m*
low: ~brow *a* geistig anspruchslos. **~-cut** *a* ⟨*dress*⟩ tief ausgeschnitten
lower /ˈləʊə(r)/ *a & adv see* **low** □ *vt* niedriger machen; (*let down*) herunterlassen; (*reduce*) senken; **~ oneself** sich herabwürdigen
low: ~-ˈfat *a* fettarm. **~-ˈgrade** *a* minderwertig. **~lands** /-ləndz/ *npl* Tiefland *nt*. **~ ˈtide** *n* Ebbe *f*
loyal /ˈlɔɪəl/ *a*, **-ly** *adv* treu. **~ty** *n* Treue *f*
lozenge /ˈlɒzɪndʒ/ *n* Pastille *f*
Ltd *abbr* (**Limited**) GmbH
lubricant /ˈluːbrɪkənt/ *n* Schmiermittel *nt*
lubricat|e /ˈluːbrɪkeɪt/ *vt* schmieren. **~ion** /-ˈkeɪʃn/ *n* Schmierung *f*
lucid /ˈluːsɪd/ *a* klar. **~ity** /-ˈsɪdətɪ/ *n* Klarheit *f*
luck /lʌk/ *n* Glück *nt*; **bad ~** Pech *nt*; **good ~!** viel Glück! **~ily** *adv* glücklicherweise, zum Glück
lucky /ˈlʌkɪ/ *a* (**-ier, -iest**) glücklich; ⟨*day, number*⟩ Glücks-; **be ~** Glück haben; ⟨*thing:*⟩ Glück bringen. **~ ˈcharm** *n* Amulett *nt*
lucrative /ˈluːkrətɪv/ *a* einträglich
ludicrous /ˈluːdɪkrəs/ *a* lächerlich
lug /lʌg/ *vt* (*pt/pp* **lugged**) (*fam*) schleppen
luggage /ˈlʌgɪdʒ/ *n* Gepäck *nt*
luggage: ~-rack *in* Gepäckablage *f*. **~ trolley** *n* Kofferkuli *m*. **~-van** *n* Gepäckwagen *m*
lugubrious /luːˈguːbrɪəs/ *a* traurig
lukewarm /ˈluːk-/ *a* lauwarm
lull /lʌl/ *n* Pause *f* □ *vt* **~ to sleep** einschläfern
lullaby /ˈlʌləbaɪ/ *n* Wiegenlied *nt*
lumbago /lʌmˈbeɪgəʊ/ *n* Hexenschuss *m*
lumber /ˈlʌmbə(r)/ *n* Gerümpel *nt*; (*Amer: timber*) Bauholz *nt* □ *vt* **~ s.o. with sth** jdm etw aufhalsen. **~jack** *n* (*Amer*) Holzfäller *m*
luminous /ˈluːmɪnəs/ *a* leuchtend; **be ~** leuchten
lump¹ /lʌmp/ *n* Klumpen *m*; (*of sugar*) Stück *nt*; (*swelling*) Beule *f*; (*in breast*) Knoten *m*; (*tumour*) Geschwulst *f*; **a ~ in one's throat** (*fam*) ein Kloß im Hals □ *vt* **~ together** zusammentun
lump² *vt* **~ it** (*fam*) sich damit abfinden
lump: ~ sugar *n* Würfelzucker *m*. **~ ˈsum** *n* Pauschalsumme *f*
lumpy /ˈlʌmpɪ/ *a* (**-ier, -iest**) klumpig
lunacy /ˈluːnəsɪ/ *n* Wahnsinn *m*
lunar /ˈluːnə(r)/ *a* Mond-
lunatic /ˈluːnətɪk/ *n* Wahnsinnige(r) *m/f*
lunch /lʌntʃ/ *n* Mittagessen *nt* □ *vi* zu Mittag essen
luncheon /ˈlʌntʃn/ *n* Mittagessen *nt*. **~ meat** *n* Frühstücksfleisch *nt*. **~ voucher** *n* Essensbon *m*
lunch: ~-hour *n* Mittagspause *f*. **~-time** *n* Mittagszeit *f*
lung /lʌŋ/ *n* Lungenflügel *m*; **~s** *pl* Lunge *f*. **~ cancer** *n* Lungenkrebs *m*

lunge /lʌndʒ/ *vi* sich stürzen (**at** auf + *acc*)
lurch[1] /lɜːtʃ/ *n* **leave in the ~** (*fam*) im Stich lassen
lurch[2] *vi* schleudern; ⟨*person:*⟩ torkeln
lure /ljʊə(r)/ *n* Lockung *f*; (*bait*) Köder *m* □ *vt* locken
lurid /ˈlʊərɪd/ *a* grell; (*sensational*) reißerisch
lurk /lɜːk/ *vi* lauern
luscious /ˈlʌʃəs/ *a* lecker, köstlich
lush /lʌʃ/ *a* üppig
lust /lʌst/ *n* Begierde *f* □ *vi* **~ after** gieren nach. **~ful** *a* lüstern
lustre /ˈlʌstə(r)/ *n* Glanz *m*
lusty /ˈlʌstɪ/ *a* (**-ier, -iest**) kräftig
lute /luːt/ *n* Laute *f*
luxuriant /lʌgˈʒʊərɪənt/ *a* üppig
luxurious /lʌgˈʒʊərɪəs/ *a*, **-ly** *adv* luxuriös
luxury /ˈlʌkʃərɪ/ *n* Luxus *m* □ *attrib* Luxus-
lying /ˈlaɪɪŋ/ *see* **lie**[1], **lie**[2]
lymph gland /ˈlɪmf-/ *n* Lymphdrüse *f*
lynch /lɪntʃ/ *vt* lynchen
lynx /lɪŋks/ *n* Luchs *m*
lyric /ˈlɪrɪk/ *a* lyrisch. **~al** *a* lyrisch; (*fam: enthusiastic*) schwärmerisch. **~ poetry** *n* Lyrik *f*. **~s** *npl* [Lied]text *m*

M

mac /mæk/ *n* (*fam*) Regenmantel *m*
macabre /məˈkɑːbr/ *a* makaber
macaroni /mækəˈrəʊnɪ/ *n* Makkaroni *pl*
macaroon /mækəˈruːn/ *n* Makrone *f*
mace[1] /meɪs/ *n* Amtsstab *m*
mace[2] *n* (*spice*) Muskatblüte *f*
machinations /mækɪˈneɪʃnz/ *pl* Machenschaften *pl*
machine /məˈʃiːn/ *n* Maschine *f* □ *vt* (*sew*) mit der Maschine nähen; (*Techn*) maschinell bearbeiten. **~-gun** *n* Maschinengewehr *nt*
machinery /məˈʃiːnərɪ/ *n* Maschinerie *f*
machine tool *n* Werkzeugmaschine *f*
machinist /məˈʃiːnɪst/ *n* Maschinist *m*; (*on sewing machine*) Maschinennäherin *f*
mackerel /ˈmækrl/ *n inv* Makrele *f*
mackintosh /ˈmækɪntoʃ/ *n* Regenmantel *m*
mad /mæd/ *a* (**madder, maddest**) verrückt; (*dog*) tollwütig; (*fam: angry*) böse (**at** auf + *acc*)
madam /ˈmædəm/ *n* gnädige Frau *f*
madden /ˈmædn/ *vt* (*make angry*) wütend machen
made /meɪd/ *see* **make**; **~ to measure** maßgeschneidert
Madeira cake /məˈdɪərə-/ *n* Sandkuchen *m*
mad|ly /ˈmædlɪ/ *adv* (*fam*) wahnsinnig. **~man** *n* Irre(r) *m*. **~ness** *n* Wahnsinn *m*
madonna /məˈdɒnə/ *n* Madonna *f*
magazine /mægəˈziːn/ *n* Zeitschrift *f*; (*Mil, Phot*) Magazin *nt*
maggot /ˈmægət/ *n* Made *f*. **~y** *a* madig
Magi /ˈmeɪdʒaɪ/ *npl* **the ~** die Heiligen Drei Könige
magic /ˈmædʒɪk/ *n* Zauber *m*; (*tricks*) Zauberkunst *f* □ *a* magisch; ⟨*word, wand, flute*⟩ Zauber-. **~al** *a* zauberhaft
magician /məˈdʒɪʃn/ *n* Zauberer *m*; (*entertainer*) Zauberkünstler *m*
magistrate /ˈmædʒɪstreɪt/ *n* ≈ Friedensrichter *m*
magnanim|ity /mægnəˈnɪmətɪ/ *n* Großmut *f*. **~ous** /-ˈnænɪməs/ *a* großmütig

magnesia /mæg'ni:ʃə/ *n* Magnesia *f*
magnet /'mægnɪt/ *n* Magnet *m*. **~ic** /-'netik/ *a* magnetisch. **~ism** *n* Magnetismus *m*. **~ize** *vt* magnetisieren
magnification /mægnɪfɪ'keɪʃn/ *n* Vergrößrung *f*
magnificen|ce /mæg'nɪfɪsəns/ *n* Großartigkeit *f*. **~t** *a*, **-ly** *adv* großartig
magnify /'mægnɪfaɪ/ *vt* (*pt/pp* **-ied**) vergrößern; (*exaggerate*) übertreiben. **~ing glass** *n* Vergrößerungsglas *nt*
magnitude /'mægnɪtju:d/ *n* Größe *f*; (*importance*) Bedeutung *f*
magpie /'mægpaɪ/ *n* Elster *f*
mahogany /mə'hɒgənɪ/ *n* Mahagoni *nt*
maid /meɪd/ *n* Dienstmädchen *nt*; (*liter: girl*) Maid *f*; **old ~** (*pej*) alte Jungfer *f*
maiden /'meɪdn/ *n* (*liter*) Maid *f* □ *a* ⟨*speech, voyage*⟩ Jungfern-. **~ 'aunt** *n* unverheiratete Tante *f*. **~ name** *n* Mädchenname *m*
mail¹ /meɪl/ *n* Kettenpanzer *m*
mail² *n* Post *f* □ *vt* mit der Post schicken; (*send off*) abschicken
mail: ~-bag *n* Postsack *m*. **~box** *n* (*Amer*) Briefkasten *m*. **~ing list** *n* Postversandliste *f*. **~man** *n* (*Amer*) Briefträger *m*. **~-order firm** *n* Versandhaus *nt*
maim /meɪm/ *vt* verstümmeln
main¹ /meɪn/ *n* (*water, gas, electricity*) Hauptleitung *f*
main² *a* Haupt- □ *n* **in the ~** im Großen und Ganzen
main: ~land /-lənd/ *n* Festland *nt*. **~ly** *adv* hauptsächlich. **~stay** *n* (*fig*) Stütze *f*. **~ street** *n* Hauptstraße *f*
maintain /meɪn'teɪn/ *vt* aufrechterhalten; (*keep in repair*) instand halten; (*support*) unterhalten; (*claim*) behaupten
maintenance /'meɪntənəns/ *n* Aufrechterhaltung *f*; (*care*) Instandhaltung *f*; (*allowance*) Unterhalt *m*
maisonette /meɪzə'net/ *n* Wohnung *f* [auf zwei Etagen]
maize /meɪz/ *n* Mais *m*
majestic /mə'dʒestɪk/ *a*, **-ally** *adv* majestätisch
majesty /'mædʒəstɪ/ *n* Majestät *f*
major /'meɪdʒə(r)/ *a* größer □ *n* (*Mil*) Major *m*; (*Mus*) Dur *nt* □ *vi* (*Amer*) **~ in** als Hauptfach studieren
Majorca /mə'jɔ:kə/ *n* Mallorca *nt*
majority /mə'dʒɒrətɪ/ *n* Mehrheit *f*; **in the ~** in der Mehrzahl
major road *n* Hauptverkehrsstraße *f*
make /meɪk/ *n* (*brand*) Marke *f* □ *v* (*pt/pp* **made**) □ *vt* machen; (*force*) zwingen; (*earn*) verdienen; halten ⟨*speech*⟩; treffen ⟨*decision*⟩; erreichen ⟨*destination*⟩ □ *vi* **~ as if to** Miene machen zu. **~ do** *vi* zurechtkommen (**with** mit). **~ for** *vi* zusteuern auf (+ *acc*). **~ off** *vi* sich davonmachen (**with** mit). **~ out** *vt* (*distinguish*) ausmachen; (*write out*) ausstellen; (*assert*) behaupten. **~ over** *vt* überschreiben (**to** auf + *acc*). **~ up** *vt* (*constitute*) bilden; (*invent*) erfinden; (*apply cosmetics to*) schminken; **~ up one's mind** sich entschließen □ *vi* sich versöhnen; **~ up for sth** etw wieder gutmachen; **~ up for lost time** verlorene Zeit aufholen
'make-believe *n* Phantasie *f*
maker /'meɪkə(r)/ *n* Hersteller *m*
make: ~shift *a* behelfsmäßig □ *n* Notbehelf *m*. **~-up** *n* Make-up *nt*
making /'meɪkɪŋ/ *n* **have the ~s of** das Zeug haben zu
maladjusted /mælə'dʒʌstɪd/ *a* verhaltensgestört
malaise /mə'leɪz/ *n* (*fig*) Unbehagen *nt*

male /meɪl/ *a* männlich □ *n* Mann *m*; (*animal*) Männchen *nt*. ~ **nurse** *n* Krankenpfleger *m*. ~ **voice** '**choir** *n* Männerchor *m*
malevolen|ce /mə'levələns/ *n* Bosheit *f*. ~**t** *a* boshaft
malfunction /mæl'fʌŋkʃn/ *n* technische Störung *f*; (*Med*) Funktionsstörung *f* □ *vi* nicht richtig funktionieren
malice /'mælɪs/ *n* Bosheit *f*; **bear s.o.** ~ einen Groll gegen jdn hegen
malicious /mə'lɪʃəs/ *a*, **-ly** *adv* böswillig
malign /mə'laɪŋ/ *vt* verleumden
malignan|cy /mə'lɪgnənsɪ/ *n* Bösartigkeit *f*. ~**t** *a* bösartig
malinger /mə'lɪŋgə(r)/ *vi* simulieren, sich krank stellen. ~**er** *n* Simulant *m*
malleable /'mælɪəbl/ *a* formbar
mallet /'mælɪt/ *n* Holzhammer *m*
malnu'trition /mæl-/ *n* Unterernährung *f*
mal'practice *n* Berufsvergehen *nt*
malt /mɔ:lt/ *n* Malz *nt*
mal'treat /mæl-/ *vt* misshandeln. ~**ment** *n* Misshandlung *f*
mammal /'mæml/ *n* Säugetier *nt*
mammoth /'mæməθ/ *a* riesig □ *n* Mammut *nt*
man /mæn/ *n* (*pl* **men**) Mann *m*; (*mankind*) der Mensch; (*chess*) Figur *f*; (*draughts*) Stein *m* □ *vt* (*pt/pp* **manned**) bemannen ⟨*ship*⟩; bedienen ⟨*pump*⟩; besetzen ⟨*counter*⟩
manacle /'mænəkl/ *vt* fesseln (**to** an + *acc*); ~ **d** in Handschellen
manage /'mænɪdʒ/ *vt* leiten; verwalten ⟨*estate*⟩; (*cope with*) fertig werden mit; ~ **to do sth** es schaffen, etw zu tun □ *vi* zurechtkommen; ~ **on** auskommen mit. ~**able** /-əbl/ *a* ⟨*tool*⟩ handlich; ⟨*person*⟩ fügsam. ~**ment** /-mənt/ *n* **the** ~**ment** die Geschäftsleitung *f*
manager /'mænɪdʒə(r)/ *n* Geschäftsführer *m*; (*of bank*) Direktor *m*; (*of estate*) Verwalter *m*; (*Sport*) [Chef]trainer *m*. ~**ess** *n* Geschäftsführerin *f*. ~**ial** /-'dʒɪərɪəl/ *a* ~**ial staff** Führungskräfte *pl*
managing /'mænɪdʒɪŋ/ *a* ~ **director** Generaldirektor *m*
mandarin /'mændərɪn/ *n* ~ **[orange]** Mandarine *f*
mandat|e /'mændeɪt/ *n* Mandat *nt*. ~**ory** /-dətrɪ/ *a* obligatorisch
mane /meɪn/ *n* Mähne *f*
manful /'mænfl/ *a*, **-ly** *adv* mannhaft
manger /'meɪndʒə(r)/ *n* Krippe *f*
mangle[1] /'mæŋgl/ *n* Wringmaschine *f*; (*for smoothing*) Mangel *f*
mangle[2] *vt* (*damage*) verstümmeln
mango /'mæŋgəʊ/ *n* (*pl* **-es**) Mango *f*
mangy /'meɪndʒɪ/ *a* ⟨*dog*⟩ räudig
man: ~'**handle** *vt* grob behandeln ⟨*person*⟩. ~**hole** *n* Kanalschacht *m*. ~**hole cover** *n* Kanaldeckel *m*. ~**hood** *n* Mannesalter *nt*; (*quality*) Männlichkeit *f*. ~**-hour** *n* Arbeitsstunde *f*. ~**-hunt** *n* Fahndung *f*
man|ia /'meɪnɪə/ *n* Manie *f*. ~**iac** /-ɪæk/ *n* Wahnsinnige(r) *m/f*
manicur|e /'mænɪkjʊə(r)/ *n* Maniküre *f* □ *vt* maniküren. ~**ist** *n* Maniküre *f*
manifest /'mænɪfest/ *a*, **-ly** *adv* offensichtlich □ *vt* ~ **itself** sich manifestieren
manifesto /mænɪ'festəʊ/ *n* Manifest *nt*
manifold /'mænɪfəʊld/ *a* mannigfaltig
manipulat|e /mə'nɪpjʊleɪt/ *vt* handhaben; (*pej*) manipulieren. ~**ion** /-'leɪʃn/ *n* Manipulation *f*
man'kind *n* die Menschheit
manly /'mænlɪ/ *a* männlich
'**man-made** *a* künstlich. ~ **fibre** *n* Kunstfaser *f*

manner /ˈmænə(r)/ *n* Weise *f*; (*kind, behaviour*) Art *f*; **in this ~** auf diese Weise; **[good/bad] ~s** [gute/schlechte] Manieren *pl*. **~ism** *n* Angewohnheit *f*
mannish /ˈmænɪʃ/ *a* männlich
manœuvrable /məˈnuːvrəbl/ *a* manövrierfähig
manœuvre /məˈnuːvə(r)/ *n* Manöver *nt* □ *vt/i* manövrieren
manor /ˈmænə(r)/ *n* Gutshof *m*; (*house*) Gutshaus *nt*
man: ~power *n* Arbeitskräfte *pl*. **~servant** *n* (*pl* **menservants**) Diener *m*
mansion /ˈmænʃn/ *n* Villa *f*
ˈmanslaughter *n* Totschlag *m*
mantelpiece /ˈmæntl-/ *n* Kaminsims *m & nt*
manual /ˈmænjʊəl/ *a* Hand- □ *n* Handbuch *nt*
manufacture /mænjʊˈfæktʃə(r)/ *vt* herstellen □ *n* Herstellung *f*. **~r** *n* Hersteller *m*
manure /məˈnjʊə(r)/ *n* Mist *m*
manuscript /ˈmænjʊskrɪpt/ *n* Manuskript *nt*
many /ˈmenɪ/ *a* viele; **~ a time** oft □ *n* **a good/great ~** sehr viele
map /mæp/ *n* Landkarte *f*; (*of town*) Stadtplan *m* □ *vt* (*pt/pp* **mapped**) **~ out** (*fig*) ausarbeiten
maple /ˈmeɪpl/ *n* Ahorn *m*
mar /mɑː(r)/ *vt* (*pt/pp* **marred**) verderben
marathon /ˈmærəθən/ *n* Marathon *m*
marauding /məˈrɔːdɪŋ/ *a* plündernd
marble /ˈmɑːbl/ *n* Marmor *m*; (*for game*) Murmel *f*
March /mɑːtʃ/ *n* März *m*
march *n* Marsch *m* □ *vi* marschieren □ *vt* marschieren lassen; **~ s.o. off** jdn abführen
mare /meə(r)/ *n* Stute *f*
margarine /mɑːdʒəˈriːn/ *n* Margarine *f*
margin /ˈmɑːdʒɪn/ *n* Rand *m*; (*leeway*) Spielraum *m*; (*Comm*) Spanne *f*. **~al** *a*, **-ly** *adv* geringfügig
marigold /ˈmærɪgəʊld/ *n* Ringelblume *f*
marijuana /mærɪˈhwɑːnə/ *n* Marihuana *nt*
marina /məˈriːnə/ *n* Jachthafen *m*
marinade /mærɪˈneɪd/ *n* Marinade *f* □ *vt* marinieren
marine /məˈriːn/ *a* Meeres- □ *n* Marine *f*; (*sailor*) Marineinfanterist *m*
marionette /mærɪəˈnet/ *n* Marionette *f*
marital /ˈmærɪtl/ *a* ehelich. **~ status** *n* Familienstand *m*
maritime /ˈmærɪtaɪm/ *a* See-
marjoram /ˈmɑːdʒərəm/ *n* Majoran *m*
mark[1] /mɑːk/ *n* (*currency*) Mark *f*
mark[2] *n* Fleck *m*; (*sign*) Zeichen *nt*; (*trace*) Spur *f*; (*target*) Ziel *nt*; (*Sch*) Note *f* □ *vt* markieren; (*spoil*) beschädigen; (*characterize*) kennzeichnen; (*Sch*) korrigieren; (*Sport*) decken; **~ time** (*Mil*) auf der Stelle treten; (*fig*) abwarten; **~ my words** das [eine] will ich dir sagen. **~ out** *vt* markieren
marked /mɑːkt/ *a*, **~ly** /-kɪdlɪ/ *adv* deutlich; (*pronounced*) ausgeprägt
marker /ˈmɑːkə(r)/ *n* Marke *f*; (*of exam*) Korrektor(in) *m(f)*
market /ˈmɑːkɪt/ *n* Markt *m* □ *vt* vertreiben; (*launch*) auf den Markt bringen. **~ing** *n* Marketing *nt*. **~ reˈsearch** *n* Marktforschung *f*
marking /ˈmɑːkɪŋ/ *n* Markierung *f*; (*on animal*) Zeichnung *f*
marksman /ˈmɑːksmən/ *n* Scharfschütze *m*
marmalade /ˈmɑːməleɪd/ *n* Orangenmarmelade *f*
marmot /ˈmɑːmət/ *n* Murmeltier *nt*

maroon /mə'ru:n/ *a* dunkelrot
marooned /mə'ru:nd/ *a* (*fig*) von der Außenweit abgeschnitten
marquee /mɑ:'ki:/ *n* Festzelt *nt*; (*Amer: awning*) Markise *f*
marquetry /'mɑ:kɪtrɪ/ *n* Einlegearbeit *f*
marquis /'mɑ:kwɪs/ *n* Marquis *m*
marriage /'mærɪdʒ/ *n* Ehe *f*; (*wedding*) Hochzeit *f*. **~able** /-əbl/ a heiratsfähig
married /'mærɪd/ *see* **marry** □ *a* verheiratet. **~ life** *n* Eheleben *nt*
marrow /'mærəʊ/ *n* (*Anat*) Mark *nt*; (*vegetable*) Kürbis *m*
marr|y /'mærɪ/ *vt/i* (*pt/pp* **married**) heiraten; (*unite*) trauen; **get ~ied** heiraten
marsh /mɑ:ʃ/ *n* Sumpf *m*
marshal /'mɑ:ʃl/ *n* Marschall *m*; (*steward*) Ordner *m* □ *vt* (*pt/pp* **marshalled**) (*Mil*) formieren; (*fig*) ordnen
marshy /'mɑ:ʃɪ/ *a* sumpfig
marsupial /mɑ:'su:pɪəl/ *n* Beuteltier *nt*
martial /'mɑ:ʃl/ *a* kriegerisch. **~ 'law** *n* Kriegsrecht *nt*
martyr /'mɑ:tə(r)/ *n* Märtyrer(in) *m(f)* □ *vt* zum Märtyrer machen. **~dom** /-dəm/ *n* Martyrium *nt*
marvel /'mɑ:vl/ *n* Wunder *nt* □ *vi* (*pt/pp* **marvelled**) staunen (**at** über + *acc*). **~lous** /-vələs/ a, **-ly** adv wunderbar
Marxis|m /'mɑ:ksɪzm/ *n* Marxismus *m*. **~t** *a* marxistisch □ *n* Marxist(in) *m(f)*
marzipan /'mɑ:zɪpæn/ *n* Marzipan *nt*
mascara /mæ'skɑ:rə/ *n* Wimperntusche *f*
mascot /'mæskət/ *n* Maskottchen *nt*
masculin|e /'mæskjʊlɪn/ *a* männlich □ *n* (*Gram*) Maskulinum *nt*. **~ity** /-'lɪnətɪ/ *n* Männlichkeit *f*
mash /mæʃ/ *n* (*fam, Culin*) Kartoffelpüree *nt* □ *vt* stampfen. **~ed potatoes** *npl* Kartoffelpüree *nt*
mask /mɑ:sk/ *n* Maske *f* □ *vt* maskieren
masochis|m /'mæsəkɪzm/ *n* Masochismus *m*. **~t** /-ɪst/ *n* Masochist *m*
mason /'meɪsn/ *n* Steinmetz *m*
Mason *n* Freimaurer *m*. **~ic** /mə'sɒnɪk/ *a* freimaurerisch
masonry /'meɪsnrɪ/ *n* Mauerwerk *nt*
masquerade /mæskə'reɪd/ *n* (*fig*) Maskerade *f* □ *vi* **~ as** (*pose*) sich ausgeben als
mass[1] /mæs/ *n* (*Relig*) Messe *f*
mass[2] *n* Masse *f* □ *vi* sich sammeln; (*Mil*) sich massieren
massacre /'mæsəkə(r)/ *n* Massaker *nt* □ *vt* niedermetzeln
massage /'mæsɑ:ʒ/ *n* Massage *f* □ *vt* massieren
masseu|r /mæ'sɜ:(r)/ *n* Masseur *m*. **~se** /-'sɜ:z/ *n* Masseuse *f*
massive /'mæsɪv/ *a* massiv; (*huge*) riesig
mass: ~ 'media *npl* Massenmedien *pl*. **~-pro'duce** *vt* in Massenproduktion herstellen. **~ pro'duction** *n* Massenproduktion *f*
mast /mɑ:st/ *n* Mast *m*
master /'mɑ:stə(r)/ *n* Herr *m*; (*teacher*) Lehrer *m*; (*craftsman, artist*) Meister *m*; (*of ship*) Kapitän *m* □ *vt* meistern; beherrschen ⟨*language*⟩
master: ~-key *n* Hauptschlüssel *m*. **~ly** *a* meisterhaft. **~-mind** *n* führender Kopf *m* □ *vt* der führende Kopf sein von. **~piece** *n* Meisterwerk *nt*. **~y** *n* (*of subject*) Beherrschung *f*
masturbat|e /'mæstəbeɪt/ *vi* masturbieren. **~ion** /-'beɪʃn/ *n* Masturbation *f*
mat /mæt/ *n* Matte *f*; (*on table*) Untersatz *m*

match[1] /mætʃ/ *n* Wettkampf *m*; (*in ball games*) Spiel *nt*; (*Tennis*) Match *nt*; (*marriage*) Heirat *f*; **be a good ~** ⟨*colours*:⟩ gut zusammenpassen; **be no ~ for s.o.** jdm nicht gewachsen sein □ *vt* (*equal*) gleichkommen (+ *dat*); (*be like*) passen zu; (*find sth similar*) etwas Passendes finden zu □ *vi* zusammenpassen

match[2] *n* Streichholz *nt*. **~box** *n* Streichholzschachtel *f*

matching /ˈmætʃɪŋ/ *a* [zusammen]passend

mate[1] /meɪt/ *n* Kumpel *m*; (*assistant*) Gehilfe *m*; (*Naut*) Maat *m*; (*Zool*) Männchen *nt*; (*female*) Weibchen *nt* □ *vi* sich paaren □ *vt* paaren

mate[2] *n* (*Chess*) Matt *nt*

material /məˈtɪərɪəl/ *n* Material *nt*; (*fabric*) Stoff *m*; **raw ~s** Rohstoffe *pl* □ *a* materiell

material|ism /məˈtɪərɪəlɪzm/ *n* Materialismus *m*. **~istic** /-ˈlɪstɪk/ *a* materialistisch. **~ize** /-laɪz/ *vi* sich verwirklichen

maternal /məˈtɜːnl/ *a* mütterlich

maternity /məˈtɜːnətɪ/ *n* Mutterschaft *f*. **~ clothes** *npl* Umstandskleidung *f*. **~ ward** *n* Entbindungsstation *f*

matey /ˈmeɪtɪ/ *a* (*fam*) freundlich

mathematic|al /mæθəˈmætɪkl/ *a*, **-ly** *adv* mathematisch. **~ian** /-məˈtɪʃn/ *n* Mathematiker(in) *m*(*f*)

mathematics /mæθəˈmætɪks/ *n* Mathematik *f*

maths /mæθs/ *n* (*fam*) Mathe *f*

matinée /ˈmætɪneɪ/ *n* (*Theat*) Nachmittagsvorstellung *f*

matriculat|e /məˈtrɪkjʊleɪt/ *vi* sich immatrikulieren. **~ion** /-ˈleɪʃn/ *n* Immatrikulation *f*

matrimon|ial /mætrɪˈməʊnɪəl/ *a* Ehe-. **~y** /ˈmætrɪmənɪ/ *n* Ehe *f*

matrix /ˈmeɪtrɪks/ *n* (*pl* **matrices** /-siːz/) *n* (*Techn: mould*) Matrize *f*

matron /ˈmeɪtrən/ *n* (*of hospital*) Oberin *f*; (*of school*) Hausmutter *f*. **~ly** *a* matronenhaft

matt /mæt/ *a* matt

matted /ˈmætɪd/ *a* verfilzt

matter /ˈmætə(r)/ *n* (*affair*) Sache *f*; (*pus*) Eiter *m*; (*Phys: substance*) Materie *f*; **money ~s** Geldangelegenheiten *pl*; **as a ~ of fact** eigentlich; **what is the ~?** was ist los? □ *vi* wichtig sein; **~ to s.o.** jdm etwas ausmachen; **it doesn't ~** es macht nichts. **~-of-fact** *a* sachlich

matting /ˈmætɪŋ/ *n* Matten *pl*

mattress /ˈmætrɪs/ *n* Matratze *f*

matur|e /məˈtjʊə(r)/ *a* reif; (*Comm*) fällig □ *vi* reifen; ⟨*person*:⟩ reifer werden; (*Comm*) fällig werden □ *vt* reifen lassen. **~ity** *n* Reife *f*; (*Comm*) Fälligkeit *f*

maul /mɔːl/ *vt* übel zurichten

Maundy /ˈmɔːndɪ/ *n* **~ Thursday** Gründonnerstag *m*

mauve /məʊv/ *a* lila

mawkish /ˈmɔːkɪʃ/ *a* rührselig

maxim /ˈmæksɪm/ *n* Maxime *f*

maximum /ˈmæksɪməm/ *a* maximal □ *n* (*pl* **-ima**) Maximum *nt*. **~ speed** *n* Höchstgeschwindigkeit *f*

may /meɪ/ *v aux* (*nur Präsens*) (*be allowed to*) dürfen; (*be possible*) können; **may I come in?** darf ich reinkommen? **may he succeed** möge es ihm gelingen; **I may as well stay** am besten bleibe ich hier; **it may be true** es könnte wahr sein

May *n* Mai *m*

maybe /ˈmeɪbiː/ *adv* vielleicht

ˈMay Day *n* der Erste Mai

mayonnaise /meɪəˈneɪz/ *n* Mayonnaise *f*

mayor /ˈmeə(r)/ *n* Bürgermeister *m*. **~ess** *n* Bürgermeisterin *f*; (*wife of mayor*) Frau Bürgermeister *f*

maze /meɪz/ *n* Irrgarten *m*; (*fig*) Labyrinth *nt*

me /miː/ *pron* (*acc*) mich; (*dat*) mir; **he knows ~** er kennt mich; **give ~ the money** gib mir das Geld; **it's ~** (*fam*) ich bin es
meadow /ˈmedəʊ/ *n* Wiese *f*
meagre /ˈmiːgə(r)/ *a* dürftig
meal¹ /miːl/ *n* Mahlzeit *f*; (*food*) Essen *nt*
meal² *n* (*grain*) Schrot *m*
mealy-mouthed /miːlɪˈmaʊðd/ *a* heuchlerisch
mean¹ /miːn/ *a* (**-er, -est**) geizig; (*unkind*) gemein; (*poor*) schäbig
mean² *a* mittlere(r,s) □ *n* (*average*) Durchschnitt *m*; **the golden ~** die goldene Mitte
mean³ *vt* (*pt/pp* **meant**) heißen; (*signify*) bedeuten; (*intend*) beabsichtigen; **I ~ it** das ist mein Ernst; **~ well** es gut meinen; **be meant for** ⟨*present*:⟩ bestimmt sein für; ⟨*remark*:⟩ gerichtet sein an (+ *acc*)
meander /mɪˈændə(r)/ *vi* sich schlängeln; ⟨*person*:⟩ schlendern
meaning /ˈmiːnɪŋ/ *n* Bedeutung *f*. **~ful** *a* bedeutungsvoll. **~less** *a* bedeutungslos
means /miːnz/ *n* Möglichkeit *f*, Mittel *nt*; **~ of transport** Verkehrsmittel *nt*; **by ~ of** durch; **by all ~!** aber natürlich! **by no ~** keineswegs □ *npl* (*resources*) [Geld]mittel *pl*. **~ test** *n* Bedürftigkeitsnachweis *m*
meant /ment/ *see* **mean³**
ˈmeantime *n* **in the ~** in der Zwischenzeit □ *adv* inzwischen
ˈmeanwhile *adv* inzwischen
measles /ˈmiːzlz/ *n* Masern *pl*
measly /ˈmiːzlɪ/ *a* (*fam*) mickerig
measurable /ˈmeʒərəbl/ *a* messbar
measure /ˈmeʒə(r)/ *n* Maß *nt*; (*action*) Maßnahme *f* □ *vt/i* messen; **~ up to** (*fig*) herankommen an (+ *acc*). **~d** *a* gemessen. **~ment** /-mənt/ *n* Maß *nt*
meat /miːt/ *n* Fleisch *nt*. **~ ball** *n* (*Culin*) Klops *m*. **~ loaf** *n* falscher Hase *m*
mechan|ic /mɪˈkænɪk/ *n* Mechaniker *m*. **~ical** *a*, **-ly** *adv* mechanisch. **~ical engineering** Maschinenbau *m*. **~ics** *n* Mechanik *f* □ *n pl* Mechanismus *m*
mechan|ism /ˈmekənɪzm/ *n* Mechanismus *m*. **~ize** *vt* mechanisieren
medal /ˈmedl/ *n* Orden *m*; (*Sport*) Medaille *f*
medallion /mɪˈdælɪən/ *n* Medaillon *nt*
medallist /ˈmedəlɪst/ *n* Medaillengewinner(in) *m(f)*
meddle /ˈmedl/ *vi* sich einmischen (**in** in + *acc*); (*tinker*) herumhantieren (**with** an + *acc*)
media /ˈmiːdɪə/ *see* **medium** □ *n pl* **the ~** die Medien *pl*
median /ˈmiːdɪən/ *a* **~ strip** (*Amer*) Mittelstreifen *m*
mediat|e /ˈmiːdɪeɪt/ *vi* vermitteln. **~or** *n* Vermittler(in) *m(f)*
medical /ˈmedɪkl/ *a* medizinisch; ⟨*treatment*⟩ ärztlich □ *n* ärztliche Untersuchung *f*. **~ insurance** *n* Krankenversicherung *f*. **~ student** *n* Medizinstudent *m*
medicat|ed /ˈmedɪkeɪtɪd/ *a* medizinisch. **~ion** /-ˈkeɪʃn/ *n* (*drugs*) Medikamente *pl*
medicinal /mɪˈdɪsɪnl/ *a* medizinisch; ⟨*plant*⟩ heilkräftig
medicine /ˈmedsən/ *n* Medizin *f*; (*preparation*) Medikament *nt*
medieval /medɪˈiːvl/ *a* mittelalterlich
mediocr|e /miːdɪˈəʊkə(r)/ *a* mittelmäßig. **~ity** /-ˈɒkrətɪ/ *n* Mittelmäßigkeit *f*
meditat|e /ˈmedɪteɪt/ *vi* nachdenken (**on** über + *acc*); (*Relig*) meditieren. **~ion** /-ˈteɪʃn/ *n* Meditation *f*
Mediterranean /medɪtəˈreɪnɪən/ *n* Mittelmeer *nt* □ *a* Mittelmeer-
medium /ˈmiːdɪəm/ *a* mittlere(r,s); ⟨*steak*⟩ medium; **of ~ size** von mittlerer Größe □ *n* (*pl* **media**) Medium *nt*; (*means*) Mittel *nt* □ (*pl* **-s**) (*person*) Medium *nt*

medium: ~**-sized** *a* mittelgroß. ~ **wave** *n* Mittelwelle *f*
medley /ˈmedlɪ/ *n* Gemisch *nt*; (*Mus*) Potpourri *nt*
meek /miːk/ *a* (**-er, -est**), **-ly** *adv* sanftmütig; (*unprotesting*) widerspruchslos
meet /miːt/ *v* (*pt/pp* **met**) □ *vt* treffen; (*by chance*) begegnen (+ *dat*); (*at station*) abholen; (*make the acquaintance of*) kennen lernen; stoßen auf (+ *acc*) ⟨*problem*⟩; bezahlen ⟨*bill*⟩; erfüllen ⟨*requirements*⟩ □ *vi* sich treffen; (*for the first time*) sich kennen lernen; ~ **with** stoßen auf (+ *acc*) ⟨*problem*⟩; sich treffen mit ⟨*person*⟩ □ *n* Jagdtreffen *nt*
meeting /ˈmiːtɪŋ/ *n* Treffen *nt*; (*by chance*) Begegnung *f*; (*discussion*) Besprechung *f*; (*of committee*) Sitzung *f*; (*large*) Versammlung *f*
megalomania /megələˈmeɪnɪə/ *n* Größenwahnsinn *m*
megaphone /ˈmegəfəʊn/ *n* Megaphon *nt*
melancholy /ˈmelənkəlɪ/ *a* melancholisch □ *n* Melancholie *f*
mellow /ˈmeləʊ/ *a*(**-er, -est**) ⟨*fruit*⟩ ausgereift; ⟨*sound, person*⟩ sanft □ *vi* reifer werden
melodic /mɪˈlɒdɪk/ *a* melodisch
melodious /mɪˈləʊdɪəs/ *a* melodiös
melodrama /ˈmelə-/ *n* Melodrama *nt*. ~**tic** /-drəˈmætɪk/ *a*, **-ally** *adv* melodramatisch
melody /ˈmelədɪ/ *n* Melodie *f*
melon /ˈmelən/ *n* Melone *f*
melt /melt/ *vt/i* schmelzen. ~ **down** *vt* einschmelzen. ~**ing-pot** *n* (*fig*) Schmelztiegel *m*
member /ˈmembə(r)/ *n* Mitglied *nt*; (*of family*) Angehörige(r) *m/f*; **M**~ **of Parliament** Abgeordnete(r) *m/f*. ~**ship** *n* Mitgliedschaft *f*; (*members*) Mitgliederzahl *f*
membrane /ˈmembreɪn/ *n* Membran *f*
memento /mɪˈmentəʊ/ *n* Andenken *nt*
memo /ˈmeməʊ/ *n* Mitteilung *f*
memoirs /ˈmemwɑːz/ *n pl* Memoiren *pl*
memorable /ˈmemərəbl/ *a* denkwürdig
memorandum /meməˈrændəm/ *n* Mitteilung *f*
memorial /mɪˈmɔːrɪəl/ *n* Denkmal *nt*. ~ **service** *n* Gedenkfeier *f*
memorize /ˈmeməraɪz/ *vt* sich (*dat*) einprägen
memory /ˈmemərɪ/ *n* Gedächtnis *nt*; (*thing remembered*) Erinnerung *f*; (*of computer*) Speicher *m*; **from** ~ auswendig; **in** ~ **of** zur Erinnerung an (+ *acc*)
men /men/ *see* **man**
menac|e /ˈmenɪs/ *n* Drohung *f*; (*nuisance*) Plage *f* □ *vt* bedrohen. ~**ing** *a*, ~**ly** *adv* drohend
mend /mend/ *vt* reparieren; (*patch*) flicken; ausbessern ⟨*clothes*⟩ □ *n* **on the** ~ auf dem Weg der Besserung
ˈ**menfolk** *n pl* Männer *pl*
menial /ˈmiːnɪəl/ *a* niedrig
meningitis /menɪnˈdʒaɪtɪs/ *n* Hirnhautentzündung *f*, Meningitis *f*
menopause /ˈmenə-/ *n* Wechseljahre *pl*
menstruat|e /ˈmenstrʊeɪt/ *vi* menstruieren. ~**ion** /-ˈeɪʃn/ *n* Menstruation *f*
mental /ˈmentl/ *a*, **-ly** *adv* geistig; (*fam: mad*) verrückt. ~ **aˈrithmetic** *n* Kopfrechnen *nt*. ~ ˈ**illness** *n* Geisteskrankheit *f*
mentality /menˈtælətɪ/ *n* Mentalität *f*
mention /ˈmenʃn/ *n* Erwähnung *f* □ *vt* erwähnen; **don't** ~ **it** keine Ursache; bitte
menu /ˈmenjuː/ *n* Speisekarte *f*
mercantile /ˈmɜːkəntaɪl/ *a* Handels-
mercenary /ˈmɜːsɪnərɪ/ *a* geldgierig □ *n* Söldner *m*

merchandise /ˈmɜːtʃəndaɪz/ *n* Ware *f*

merchant /ˈmɜːtʃənt/ *n* Kaufmann *m*; (*dealer*) Händler *m*. ~ **ˈnavy** *n* Handelsmarine *f*

merci|ful /ˈmɜːsɪfl/ *a* barmherzig. ~**fully** *adv* (*fam*) glücklicherweise. ~**less** *a*, **-ly** *adv* erbarmungslos

mercury /ˈmɜːkjʊrɪ/ *n* Quecksilber *nt*

mercy /ˈmɜːsɪ/ *n* Barmherzigkeit *f*, Gnade *f*; **be at s.o.'s** ~ jdm ausgeliefert sein

mere /mɪə(r)/ *a*, **-ly** *adv* bloß

merest /ˈmɪərɪst/ *a* kleinste(r,s)

merge /mɜːdʒ/ *vi* zusammenlaufen; (*Comm*) fusionieren □ *vt* (*Comm*) zusammenschließen

merger /ˈmɜːdʒə(r)/ *n* Fusion *f*

meridian /məˈrɪdɪən/ *n* Meridian *m*

meringue /məˈræŋ/ *n* Baiser *nt*

merit /ˈmerɪt/ *n* Verdienst *nt*; (*advantage*) Vorzug *m*; (*worth*) Wert *m* □ *vt* verdienen

mermaid /ˈmɜːmeɪd/ *n* Meerjungfrau *f*

merri|ly /ˈmerɪlɪ/ *adv* fröhlich. ~**ment** /-mənt/ *n* Fröhlichkeit *f*; (*laughter*) Gelächter *nt*

merry /ˈmerɪ/ *a* (**-ier, -iest**) fröhlich; ~ **Christmas!** fröhliche Weihnachten!

merry: ~**-go-round** *n* Karussell *nt*. ~**-making** *n* Feiern *nt*

mesh /meʃ/ *n* Masche *f*; (*size*) Maschenweite *f*; (*fig: network*) Netz *nt*

mesmerize /ˈmezməraɪz/ *vt* hypnotisieren. ~**d** *a* (*fig*) [wie] gebannt

mess /mes/ *n* Durcheinander *nt*; (*trouble*) Schwierigkeiten *pl*; (*something spilt*) Bescherung *f* (*fam*); (*Mil*) Messe *f*; **make a** ~ **of** (*botch*) verpfuschen □ *vt* ~ **up** in Unordnung bringen; (*botch*) verpfuschen □ *vi* ~ **about** herumalbern; (*tinker*) herumspielen (**with** mit)

message /ˈmesɪdʒ/ *n* Nachricht *f*; **give s.o. a** ~ jdm etwas ausrichten

messenger /ˈmesɪndʒə(r)/ *n* Bote *m*

Messiah /mɪˈsaɪə/ *n* Messias *m*

Messrs /ˈmesəz/ *n pl see* **Mr**; (*on letter*) ~ **Smith** Firma Smith

messy /ˈmesɪ/ *a* (**-ier, -iest**) schmutzig; (*untidy*) unordentlich

met /met/ *see* **meet**

metabolism /mɪˈtæbəlɪzm/ *n* Stoffwechsel *m*

metal /ˈmetl/ *n* Metall *nt* □ *a* Metall-. ~**lic** /mɪˈtælɪk/ *a* metallisch. ~**lurgy** /mɪˈtælədʒɪ/ *n* Metallurgie *f*

metamorphosis /metəˈmɔːfəsɪs/ *n* (*pl* **-phoses** /-siːz/) Metamorphose *f*

metaphor /ˈmetəfə(r)/ *n* Metapher *f*. ~**ical** /-ˈfɒrɪkl/ *a*, **-ly** *adv* metaphorisch

meteor /ˈmiːtɪə(r)/ *n* Meteor *m*. ~**ic** /-ˈɒrɪk/ *a* kometenhaft

meteorological /miːtɪərəˈlɒdʒɪkl/ *a* Wetter-

meteorolog|ist /miːtɪəˈrɒlədʒɪst/ *n* Meteorologe *m*/ -gin *f*. ~**y** *n* Meteorologie *f*

meter[1] /ˈmiːtə(r)/ *n* Zähler *m*

meter[2] *n* (*Amer*) = **metre**

method /ˈmeθəd/ *n* Methode *f*; (*Culin*) Zubereitung *f*

methodical /mɪˈθɒdɪkl/ *a*, **-ly** *adv* systematisch, methodisch

Methodist /ˈmeθədɪst/ *n* Methodist(in) *m(f)*

meths /meθs/ *n* (*fam*) Brennspiritus *m*

methylated /ˈmeθɪleɪtɪd/ *a* ~ **spirit[s]** Brennspiritus *m*

meticulous /mɪˈtɪkjʊləs/ *a*, **-ly** *adv* sehr genau

metre /ˈmiːtə(r)/ *n* Meter *m* & *n*; (*rhythm*) Versmaß *nt*

metric /ˈmetrɪk/ *a* metrisch

metropolis /mɪˈtrɒpəlɪs/ *n* Metropole *f*

metropolitan /metrə'pɒlɪtən/ *a* hauptstädtisch; (*international*) welstädtisch

mettle /'metl/ *n* Mut *m*

mew /mju:/ *n* Miau *nt* □ *vi* miauen

Mexican /'meksɪkən/ *a* mexikanisch □ *n* Mexikaner(in) *m(f)*. '**Mexico** *n* Mexiko *nt*

miaow /mɪ'aʊ/ *n* Miau *nt* □ *vi* miauen

mice /maɪs/ *see* **mouse**

microbe /'maɪkrəʊb/ *n* Mikrobe *f*

micro /'maɪkrəʊ/: **~chip** *n* Mikrochip *nt*. **~computer** *n* Mikrocomputer *m*. **~film** *n* Mikrofilm *m*. **~phone** *n* Mikrofon *nt*. **~processor** *n* Mikroprozessor *m*. **~scope** /-skəʊp/ *n* Mikroskop *nt*. **~scopic** /-'skɒpɪk/ *a* mikroskopisch. **~wave** *n* Mikrowelle *f*. **~wave [oven]** *n* Mikrowellenherd *m*

mid /mɪd/ *a* **~ May** Mitte Mai; **in ~ air** in der Luft

midday /mɪd'deɪ/ *n* Mittag *m*

middle /'mɪdl/ *a* mittlere(r,s); **the M~ Ages** das Mittelalter; **the class[es]** der Mittelstand; **the M~ East** der Nahe Osten □ *n* Mitte *f*; **in the ~ of the night** mitten in der Nacht

middle: ~-aged *a* mittleren Alters. **~-class** *a* bürgerlich. **~man** *n* (*Comm*) Zwischenhändler *m*

middling /'mɪdlɪŋ/ *a* mittelmäßig

midge /mɪdʒ/ *n* [kleine] Mücke *f*

midget /'mɪdʒɪt/ *n* Liliputaner(in) *m(f)*

Midlands /'mɪdləndz/ *npl* **the ~** Mittelengland *n*

'**midnight** *n* Mitternacht *f*

midriff /'mɪdrɪf/ *n* (*fam*) Taille *f*

midst /mɪdst/ *n* **in the ~ of** mitten in (+ *dat*); **in our ~** unter uns

mid: ~summer *n* Hochsommer *m*; (*solstice*) Sommersonnenwende *f*. **~way** *adv* auf halbem Wege. **~wife** *n* Hebamme *f*. **~wifery** /-wɪfrɪ/ *n* Geburtshilfe *f*. **~'winter** *n* Mitte *f* des Winters

might[1] /maɪt/ *v aux* **I ~** vielleicht; **it ~ be true** es könnte wahr sein; **I ~ as well stay** am besten bleibe ich hier; **he asked if he ~ go** er fragte, ob er gehen dürfte; **you ~ have drowned** du hättest ertrinken können

might[2] *n* Macht *f*

mighty /'maɪtɪ/ *a* (**-ier, -iest**) mächtig

migraine /'mi:greɪn/ *n* Migräne *f*

migrant /'maɪgrənt/ *a* Wander- □ *n* (*bird*) Zugvogel *m*

migrat|e /maɪ'greɪt/ *vi* abwandern; ⟨*birds:*⟩ ziehen. **~ion** /-'greɪʃn/ *n* Wanderung *f*; (*of birds*) Zug *m*

mike /maɪk/ *n* (*fam*) Mikrofon *nt*

mild /maɪld/ *a* (**-er, -est**) mild

mildew /'mɪldju:/ *n* Schimmel *m*; (*Bot*) Mehltau *m*

mild|ly /'maɪldlɪ/ *adv* leicht; **to put it ~ly** gelinde gesagt. **~ness** *n* Milde *f*

mile /maɪl/ *n* Meile *f* (= *1,6 km*); **~s too big** (*fam*) viel zu groß

mile|age /-ɪdʒ/ *n* Meilenzahl *f*; (*of car*) Meilenstand *m*. **~stone** *n* Meilenstein *m*

militant /'mɪlɪtənt/ *a* militant

military /'mɪlɪtrɪ/ *a* militärisch. **~ service** *n* Wehrdienst *m*

militate /'mɪlɪteɪt/ *vi* **~ against** sprechen gegen

militia /mɪ'lɪʃə/ *n* Miliz *f*

milk /mɪlk/ *n* Milch *f* □ *vt* melken

milk: ~man *n* Milchmann *m*. **~shake** *n* Milchmixgetränk *nt*. **~ tooth** *n* Milchzahn *m*

milky /'mɪlkɪ/ *a* (**-ier, -iest**) milchig. **M~ Way** *n* (*Astr*) Milchstraße *f*

mill /mɪl/ *n* Mühle *f*; (*factory*) Fabrik *f* □ *vt/i* mahlen; (*Techn*) fräsen. ~ **about,** ~ **around** *vi* umherlaufen

millenium /mɪˈlenɪəm/ *n* Jahrtausend *nt*

miller /ˈmɪlə(r)/ *n* Müller *m*

millet /ˈmɪlɪt/ *n* Hirse *f*

milli|gram /ˈmɪlɪ-/ *n* Milligramm *nt.* ~**metre** *n* Millimeter *m & nt*

milliner /ˈmɪlɪnə(r)/ *n* Modistin *f*; (*man*) Hutmacher *m.* ~**y** *n* Damenhüte *pl*

million /ˈmɪljən/ *n* Million *f*; **a** ~ **pounds** eine Million Pfund. ~**aire** /-ˈneə(r)/ *n* Millionär(in) *m(f)*

ˈ**millstone** *n* Mühlstein *m*

mime /maɪm/ *n* Pantomime *f* □ *vt* pantomimisch darstellen

mimic /ˈmɪmɪk/ *n* Imitator *m* □ *vt* (*pt/pp* **mimicked**) nachahmen. ~**ry** *n* Nachahmung *f*

mimosa /mɪˈməʊzə/ *n* Mimose *f*

mince /mɪns/ *n* Hackfleisch *nt* □ *vt* (*Culin*) durchdrehen; **not** ~ **words** kein Blatt vor den Mund nehmen

mince: ~**meat** *n* Masse *f* aus Korinthen, Zitronat *usw*; **make** ~ **meat of** (*fig*) vernichtend schlagen. ~ˈ**pie** *n* mit 'mincemeat' gefülltes Pastetchen *nt*

mincer /ˈmɪnsə(r)/ *n* Fleischwolf *m*

mind /maɪnd/ *n* Geist *m*; (*sanity*) Verstand *m*; **to my** ~ meiner Meinung nach; **give s.o. a piece of one's** ~ jdm gehörig die Meinung sagen; **make up one's** ~ sich entschließen; **be out of one's** ~ nicht bei Verstand sein; **have sth in** ~ etw im Sinn haben; **bear sth in** ~ an etw (*acc*) denken; **have a good** ~ **to** große Lust haben, zu; **I have changed my** ~ ich habe es mir anders überlegt □ *vt* aufpassen auf (+ *acc*); **I don't** ~ **the noise** der Lärm stört mich nicht; ~ **the step!** Achtung Stufe! □ *vi* (*care*) sich kümmern (**about** um); **I don't** ~ mir macht es nichts aus; **never** ~! macht nichts! **do you** ~ **if?** haben Sie etwas dagegen, wenn? ~ **out** *vi* aufpassen

mind|ful *a* ~**ful of** eingedenk (+ *gen*). ~**less** *a* geistlos

mine[1] /maɪn/ *poss pron* meine(r), meins; **a friend of** ~ ein Freund von mir; **that is** ~ das gehört mir

mine[2] *n* Bergwerk *nt*; (*explosive*) Mine *f* □ *vt* abbauen; (*Mil*) verminen. ~ **detector** *n* Minensuchgerät *nt.* ~**field** *n* Minenfeld *nt*

miner /ˈmaɪnə(r)/ *n* Bergarbeiter *m*

mineral /ˈmɪnərl/ *n* Mineral *nt.* ~**ogy** /-ˈrælədʒɪ/ *n* Mineralogie *f.* ~ **water** *n* Mineralwasser *nt*

minesweeper /ˈmaɪn-/ *n* Minenräumboot *nt*

mingle /ˈmɪŋgl/ *vi* ~ **with** sich mischen unter (+ *acc*)

miniature /ˈmɪnɪtʃə(r)/ *a* Klein- □ *n* Miniatur *f*

mini|bus /ˈmɪnɪ-/ *n* Kleinbus *m.* ~**cab** *n* Taxi *nt*

minim /ˈmɪnɪm/ *n* (*Mus*) halbe Note *f*

minim|al /ˈmɪnɪməl/ *a* minimal. ~**ize** *vt* auf ein Minimum reduzieren. ~**um** *n* (*pl* **-ima**) Minimum *nt* □ *a* Mindest-

mining /ˈmaɪnɪŋ/ *n* Bergbau *m*

miniskirt /ˈmɪnɪ-/ *n* Minirock *m*

minist|er /ˈmɪnɪstə(r)/ *n* Minister *m*; (*Relig*) Pastor *m.* ~**erial** /-ˈstɪərɪəl/ *a* ministeriell

ministry /ˈmɪnɪstrɪ/ *n* (*Pol*) Ministerium *nt*; **the** ~ (*Relig*) das geistliche Amt

mink /mɪŋk/ *n* Nerz *m*

minor /ˈmaɪnə(r)/ *a* kleiner; (*less important*) unbedeutend □ *n* Minderjährige(r) *m/f*; (*Mus*) Moll *nt*

minority /maɪˈnɒrətɪ/ *n* Minderheit *f*; (*age*) Minderjährigkeit *f*

minor road *n* Nebenstraße *f*

mint[1] /mɪnt/ *n* Münzstätte *f* □ *a* ⟨*stamp*⟩ postfrisch; **in** ~ **condition** wie neu □ *vt* prägen

mint[2] *n* (*herb*) Minze *f*; (*sweet*) Pfefferminzbonbon *m & nt*
minuet /mɪnjʊ'et/ *n* Menuett *nt*
minus /'maɪnəs/ *prep* minus, weniger; (*fam: without*) ohne □ *n* **~ [sign]** Minuszeichen *nt*
minute[1] /'mɪnɪt/ *n* Minute *f*; **in a ~** (*shortly*) gleich; **~s** *pl* (*of meeting*) Protokoll *nt*
minute[2] /maɪ'nju:t/ *a* winzig; (*precise*) genau
mirac|le /'mɪrəkl/ *n* Wunder *nt*. **~ulous** /-'rækjʊləs/ *a* wunderbar
mirage /'mɪrɑ:ʒ/ *n* Fata Morgana *f*
mire /'maɪə(r)/ *n* Morast *m*
mirror /'mɪrə(r)/ *n* Spiegel *m* □ *vt* widerspiegeln
mirth /mɜ:θ/ *n* Heiterkeit *f*
misad'venture /mɪs-/ *n* Missgeschick *nt*
misanthropist /mɪ'zænθrəpɪst/ *n* Menschenfeind *m*
misappre'hension *n* Missverständnis *nt*; **be under a ~** sich irren
misbe'hav|e *vi* sich schlecht benehmen. **~iour** *n* schlechtes Benehmen *nt*
mis'calcu|late *vt* falsch berechnen □ *vi* sich verrechnen. **~'lation** *n* Fehlkalkulation *f*
'miscarriage *n* Fehlgeburt *f*; **~ of justice** Justizirrtum *m*. **mis'carry** *vi* eine Fehlgeburt haben
miscellaneous /mɪsə'leɪnɪəs/ *a* vermischt
mischief /'mɪstʃɪf/ *n* Unfug *m*; (*harm*) Schaden *m*
mischievous /'mɪstʃɪvəs/ *a*, **-ly** *adv* schelmisch; (*malicious*) boshaft
miscon'ception *n* falsche Vorstellung *f*
mis'conduct *n* unkorrektes Verhalten *nt*; (*adultery*) Ehebruch *m*
miscon'strue *vt* missdeuten
mis'deed *n* Missetat *f*
misde'meanour *n* Missetat *f*
miser /'maɪzə(r)/ *n* Geizhals *m*
miserable /'mɪzrəbl/ *a*, **-bly** *adv* unglücklich; (*wretched*) elend
miserly /'maɪzəlɪ/ *adv* geizig
misery /'mɪzərɪ/ *n* Elend *nt*; (*fam: person*) Miesepeter *m*
mis'fire *vi* fehlzünden; (*go wrong*) fehlschlagen
'misfit *n* Außenseiter(in) *m*(*f*)
mis'fortune *n* Unglück *nt*
mis'givings *npl* Bedenken *pl*
mis'guided *a* töricht
mishap /'mɪshæp/ *n* Missgeschick *nt*
misin'form *vt* falsch unterrichten
misin'terpret *vt* missdeuten
mis'judge *vt* falsch beurteilen; (*estimate wrongly*) falsch einschätzen
mis'lay *vt* (*pt/pp* **-laid**) verlegen
mis'lead *vt* (*pt/pp* **-led**) irreführen. **~ing** *a* irreführend
mis'manage *vt* schlecht verwalten. **~ment** *n* Misswirtschaft *f*
misnomer /mɪs'nəʊmə(r)/ *n* Fehlbezeichnung *f*
'misprint *n* Druckfehler *m*
mis'quote *vt* falsch zitieren
misrepre'sent *vt* falsch darstellen
miss /mɪs/ *n* Fehltreffer *m* □ *vt* verpassen; (*fail to hit or find*) verfehlen; (*fail to attend*) versäumen; (*fail to notice*) übersehen; (*feel the loss of*) vermissen □ *vi* (*fail to hit*) nicht treffen. **~ out** *vt* auslassen
Miss *n* (*pl* **-es**) Fräulein *nt*
misshapen /mɪs'ʃeɪpən/ *a* missgestaltet
missile /'mɪsaɪl/ *n* [Wurf]geschoss *nt*; (*Mil*) Rakete *f*
missing /'mɪsɪŋ/ *a* fehlend (*lost*) verschwunden; (*Mil*) vermisst; **be ~** fehlen
mission /'mɪʃn/ *n* Auftrag *m*; (*Mil*) Einsatz *m*; (*Relig*) Mission *f*

missionary /ˈmɪʃənrɪ/ *n* Missionar(in) *m(f)*
mis'spell *vt* (*pt/pp* **-spelt** or **-spelled**) falsch schreiben
mist /mɪst/ *n* Dunst *m*; (*fog*) Nebel *m*; (*on window*) Beschlag *m* □ *vi* **~ up** beschlagen
mistake /mɪˈsteɪk/ *n* Fehler *m*; **by ~** aus Versehen □ *vt* (*pt* **mistook**, *pp* **mistaken**) missverstehen; **~ for** verwechseln mit
mistaken /mɪˈsteɪkən/ *a* falsch; **be ~** sich irren; **~ identity** Verwechslung *f*. **~ly** *adv* irrtümlicherweise
mistletoe /ˈmɪsltəʊ/ *n* Mistel *f*
mistress /ˈmɪstrɪs/ *n* Herrin *f*; (*teacher*) Lehrerin *f*; (*lover*) Geliebte *f*
mis'trust *n* Misstrauen *nt* □ *vt* misstrauen (+ *dat*)
misty /ˈmɪstɪ/ *a* (**-ier, -iest**) dunstig; (*foggy*) neblig; (*fig*) unklar
misunder'stand *vt* (*pt/pp* **-stood**) missverstehen. **~ing** *n* Missverständnis *nt*
misuse[1] /mɪsˈjuːz/ *vt* missbrauchen
misuse[2] /mɪsˈjuːs/ *n* Missbrauch *m*
mite /maɪt/ *n* (*Zool*) Milbe *f*; **little ~** (*child*) kleines Ding *nt*
mitigat|e /ˈmɪtɪgeɪt/ *vt* mildern. **~ing** *a* mildernd
mitten /ˈmɪtn/ *n* Fausthandschuh *m*
mix /mɪks/ *n* Mischung *f* □ *vt* mischen □ *vi* sich mischen; **~ with** (*associate with*) verkehren mit. **~ up** *vt* mischen; (*muddle*) durcheinander bringen; (*mistake for*) verwechseln (**with** mit)
mixed /mɪkst/ *a* gemischt; **be ~ up** durcheinander sein
mixer /ˈmɪksə(r)/ *n* Mischmaschine *f*; (*Culin*) Küchenmaschine *f*
mixture /ˈmɪkstʃə(r)/ *n* Mischung *f*; (*medicine*) Mixtur *f*; (*Culin*) Teig *m*
'mix-up *n* Durcheinander *nt*; (*confusion*) Verwirrung *f*; (*mistake*) Verwechslung *f*
moan /məʊn/ *n* Stöhnen *nt* □ *vi* stöhnen; (*complain*) jammern
moat /məʊt/ *n* Burggraben *m*
mob /mɒb/ *n* Horde *f*; (*rabble*) Pöbel *m*; (*fam: gang*) Bande *f* □ *vt* (*pt/pp* **mobbed**) herfallen über (+ *acc*); belagern ⟨*celebrity*⟩
mobile /ˈməʊbaɪl/ *a* beweglich □ *n* Mobile *nt*; (*telephone*) Handy *nt*. **~ 'home** *n* Wohnwagen *m*. **~ 'phone** *n* Mobiltelefon *nt*, Handy *nt*
mobility /məˈbɪlətɪ/ *n* Beweglichkeit *f*
mobi|lization /məʊbɪlaɪˈzeɪʃn/ *n* Mobilisierung *f*. **~lize** /ˈməʊbɪlaɪz/ *vt* mobilisieren
mocha /ˈmɒkə/ *n* Mokka *m*
mock /mɒk/ *a* Schein- □ *vt* verspotten. **~ery** *n* Spott *m*
'mock-up *n* Modell *nt*
modal /ˈməʊdl/ *a* **~ auxiliary** Modalverb *nt*
mode /məʊd/ *n* [Art und] Weise *f*; (*fashion*) Mode *f*
model /ˈmɒdl/ *n* Modell *nt*; (*example*) Vorbild *nt*; **[fashion] ~** Mannequin *nt* □ *a* Modell-; (*exemplary*) Muster- □ *v* (*pt/pp* **modelled**) □ *vt* formen, modellieren; vorführen ⟨*clothes*⟩ □ *vi* Mannequin sein; (*for artist*) Modell stehen
moderate[1] /ˈmɒdəreɪt/ *vt* mäßigen □ *vi* sich mäßigen
moderate[2] /ˈmɒdərət/ *a* mäßig; ⟨*opinion*⟩ gemäßigt □ *n* (*Pol*) Gemäßigte(r) *m/f*. **~ly** *adv* mäßig; (*fairly*) einigermaßen
moderation /mɒdəˈreɪʃn/ *n* Mäßigung *f*; **in ~** mit Maß[en]
modern /ˈmɒdn/ *a* modern. **~ize** *vt* modernisieren. **~ 'languages** *npl* neuere Sprachen *pl*
modest /ˈmɒdɪst/ *a* bescheiden; (*decorous*) schamhaft. **~y** *n* Bescheidenheit *f*

modicum /ˈmɒdɪkəm/ *n* **a ~ of** ein bisschen
modif|ication /mɒdɪfɪˈkeɪʃn/ *n* Abänderung *f*. **~y** /ˈmɒdɪfaɪ/ *vt* (*pt/pp* **-fied**) abändern
modulate /ˈmɒdjʊleɪt/ *vt/i* modulieren
moist /mɔɪst/ *a* (**-er**, **-est**) feucht
moisten /ˈmɔɪsn/ *vt* befeuchten
moistur|e /ˈmɔɪstʃə(r)/ *n* Feuchtigkeit *f*. **~izer** *n* Feuchtigkeitscreme *f*
molar /ˈməʊlə(r)/ *n* Backenzahn *m*
molasses /məˈlæsɪz/ *n* (*Amer*) Sirup *m*
mole[1] /məʊl/ *n* Leberfleck *m*
mole[2] *n* (*Zool*) Maulwurf *m*
mole[3] *n* (*breakwater*) Mole *f*
molecule /ˈmɒlɪkjuːl/ *n* Molekül *nt*
ˈ**molehill** *n* Maulwurfshaufen *m*
molest /məˈlest/ *vt* belästigen
mollify /ˈmɒlɪfaɪ/ *vt* (*pt/pp* **-ied**) besänftigen
mollusc /ˈmɒləsk/ *n* Weichtier *nt*
mollycoddle /ˈmɒlɪkɒdl/ *vt* verzärteln
molten /ˈməʊltən/ *a* geschmolzen
mom /mɒm/ *n* (*Amer fam*) Mutti *f*
moment /ˈməʊmənt/ *n* Moment *m*, Augenblick *m*; **at the ~** im Augenblick, augenblicklich. **~ary** *a* vorübergehend
momentous /məˈmentəs/ *a* bedeutsam
momentum /məˈmentəm/ *n* Schwung *m*
monarch /ˈmɒnək/ *n* Monarch(in) *m(f)*. **~y** *n* Monarchie *f*
monast|ery /ˈmɒnəstrɪ/ *n* Kloster *nt*. **~ic** /məˈnæstɪk/ *a* Kloster-
Monday /ˈmʌndeɪ/ *n* Montag *m*
money /ˈmʌnɪ/ *n* Geld *nt*
money: ~-box *n* Sparbüchse *f*. **~-lender** *n* Geldverleiher *m*. **~ order** *n* Zahlungsanweisung *f*
mongrel /ˈmʌŋgrəl/ *n* Promenadenmischung *f*
monitor /ˈmɒnɪtə(r)/ *n* (*Techn*) Monitor *m* □ *vt* überwachen ⟨*progress*⟩; abhören ⟨*broadcast*⟩
monk /mʌŋk/ *n* Mönch *m*
monkey /ˈmʌŋkɪ/ *n* Affe *m*. **~-nut** *n* Erdnuss *f*. **~-wrench** *n* (*Techn*) Engländer *m*
mono /ˈmɒnəʊ/ *n* Mono *nt*
monocle /ˈmɒnəkl/ *n* Monokel *nt*
monogram /ˈmɒnəgræm/ *n* Monogramm *nt*
monologue /ˈmɒnəlɒg/ *n* Monolog *m*
monopol|ize /məˈnɒpəlaɪz/ *vt* monopolisieren. **~y** *n* Monopol *nt*
monosyll|abic /mɒnəsɪˈlæbɪk/ *a* einsilbig. **~able** /ˈmɒnəsɪləbl/ *n* einsilbiges Wort *nt*
monotone /ˈmɒnətəʊn/ *n* **in a ~** mit monotoner Stimme
monoton|ous /məˈnɒtənəs/ *a*, **-ly** *adv* eintonig, monoton; (*tedious*) langweillig. **~y** *n* Eintönigkeit *f*, Monotonie *f*
monsoon /mɒnˈsuːn/ *n* Monsun *m*
monster /ˈmɒnstə(r)/ *n* Ungeheuer *nt*; (*cruel person*) Unmensch *m*
monstrosity /mɒnˈstrɒsətɪ/ *n* Monstrosität *f*
monstrous /ˈmɒnstrəs/ *a* ungeheuer; (*outrageous*) ungeheuerlich
montage /mɒnˈtɑːʒ/ *n* Montage *f*
month /mʌnθ/ *n* Monat *m*. **~ly** *a* & *adv* monatlich □ *n* (*periodical*) Monatszeitschrift *f*
monument /ˈmɒnjʊmənt/ *n* Denkmal *nt*. **~al** /-ˈmentl/ *a* (*fig*) monumental
moo /muː/ *n* Muh *nt* □ *vi* (*pt/pp* **mooed**) muhen
mooch /muːtʃ/ *vi* **~ about** (*fam*) herumschleichen
mood /muːd/ *n* Laune *f*; **be in a good/bad ~** gute/schlechte Laune haben

moody /ˈmuːdɪ/ *a* (**-ier, -iest**) launisch

moon /muːn/ *n* Mond *m*; **over the ~** (*fam*) überglücklich

moon: ~light *n* Mondschein *m*. **~lighting** *n* (*fam*) ≈ Schwarzarbeit *f*. **~lit** *a* mondhell

moor¹ /mʊə(r)/ *n* Moor *nt*

moor² *vt* (*Naut*) festmachen □ *vi* anlegen. **~ings** *npl* (*chains*) Verankerung *f*; (*place*) Anlegestelle *f*

moose /muːs/ *n* Elch *m*

moot /muːt/ *a* **it's a ~ point** darüber lässt sich streiten □ *vt* aufwerfen ‹*question*›

mop /mɒp/ *n* Mopp *m*; **~ of hair** Wuschelkopf *m* *vt* (*pt/pp* **mopped**) wischen. **~ up** *vt* aufwischen

mope /məʊp/ *vi* Trübsal blasen

moped /ˈməʊped/ *n* Moped *nt*

moral /ˈmɒrl/ *a*, **-ly** *adv* moralisch, sittlich; (*virtuous*) tugendhaft □ *n* Moral *f*; **~s** *pl* Moral *f*

morale /məˈrɑːl/ *n* Moral *f*

morality /məˈrælətɪ/ *n* Sittlichkeit *f*

moralize /ˈmɒrəlaɪz/ *vi* moralisieren

morbid /ˈmɔːbɪd/ *a* krankhaft; (*gloomy*) trübe

more /mɔː(r)/ *a*, *adv* & *n* mehr; (*in addition*) noch; **a few ~** noch ein paar; **any ~** noch etwas; **once ~** noch einmal; **~ or less** mehr oder weniger; **some ~ tea?** noch etwas Tee? **~ interesting** interessanter; **~ [and ~] quickly** [immer] schneller; **no ~, thank you**, nichts mehr, danke; **no ~ bread** kein Brot mehr; **no ~ apples** keine Äpfel mehr

moreover /mɔːˈrəʊvə(r)/ *adv* außerdem

morgue /mɔːg/ *n* Leichenschauhaus *nt*

moribund /ˈmɒrɪbʌnd/ *a* sterbend

morning /ˈmɔːnɪŋ/ *n* Morgen *m*; **in the ~** morgens, am Morgen; (*tomorrow*) morgen früh

Morocco /məˈrɒkəʊ/ *n* Marokko *nt*

moron /ˈmɔːrɒn/ *n* (*fam*) Idiot *m*

morose /məˈrəʊs/ *a*, **-ly** *adv* mürrisch

morphine /ˈmɔːfiːn/ *n* Morphium *nt*

Morse /mɔːs/ *n* **~ [code]** Morsealphabet *nt*

morsel /ˈmɔːsl/ *n* (*food*) Happen *m*

mortal /ˈmɔːtl/ *a* sterblich; (*fatal*) tödlich □ *n* Sterbliche(r) *m/f*. **~ity** /mɔːˈtælətɪ/ *n* Sterblichkeit *f*. **~ly** *adv* tödlich

mortar /ˈmɔːtə(r)/ *n* Mörtel *m*

mortgage /ˈmɔːgɪdʒ/ *n* Hypothek *f* □ *vt* hypothekarisch belasten

mortify /ˈmɔːtɪfaɪ/ *vt* (*pt/pp* **-ied**) demütigen

mortuary /ˈmɔːtjʊərɪ/ *n* Leichenhalle *f*; (*public*) Leichenschauhaus *nt*; (*Amer*: *undertaker's*) Bestattungsinstitut *nt*

mosaic /məʊˈzeɪɪk/ *n* Mosaik *nt*

Moscow /ˈmɒskəʊ/ *n* Moskau *nt*

Moselle /məʊˈzel/ *n* Mosel *f*; (*wine*) Moselwein *m*

mosque /mɒsk/ *n* Moschee *f*

mosquito /mɒsˈkiːtəʊ/ *n* (*pl* **-es**) [Stech]mücke *f*, Schnake *f*; (*tropical*) Moskito *m*

moss /mɒs/ *n* Moos *nt*. **~y** *a* moosig

most /məʊst/ *a* der/die/das meiste; (*majority*) die meisten; **for the ~ part** zum größten Teil □ *adv* am meisten; (*very*) höchst; **the ~ interesting day** der interessanteste Tag; **~ unlikely** höchst unwahrscheinlich □ *n* das meiste; **~ of them** die meisten [von ihnen]; **at [the] ~** höchstens; **~ of the time** die meiste Zeit. **~ly** *adv* meist

MOT *n* ≈ TÜV *m*

motel /məʊˈtel/ *n* Motel *nt*

moth /mɒθ/ *n* Nachtfalter *m*; **[clothes-] ~** Motte *f*
moth: ~ball *n* Mottenkugel *f*. **~-eaten** *a* mottenzerfressen
mother /ˈmʌðə(r)/ *n* Mutter *f*; **M~'s Day** Muttertag *m* □ *vt* bemuttern
mother: ~hood *n* Mutterschaft *f*. **~-in-law** *n* (*pl* **~s-in-law**) Schwiegermutter *f*. **~land** *n* Mutterland *nt*. **~ly** *a* mütterlich. **~-of-pearl** *n* Perlmutter *f*. **~-to-be** *n* werdende Mutter *f*. **~ tongue** *n* Muttersprache *f*
mothproof /ˈmɒθ-/ *a* mottenfest
motif /məʊˈtiːf/ *n* Motiv *nt*
motion /ˈməʊʃn/ *n* Bewegung *f*; (*proposal*) Antrag *m* □ *vt/i* **~ [to] s.o.** jdm ein Zeichen geben (**to** zu). **~less** *a*, **-ly** *adv* bewegungslos
motivat|e /ˈməʊtɪveɪt/ *vt* motivieren. **~ion** /-ˈveɪʃn/ *n* Motivation *f*
motive /ˈməʊtɪv/ *n* Motiv *nt*
motley /ˈmɒtlɪ/ *a* bunt
motor /ˈməʊtə(r)/ *n* Motor *m*; (*car*) Auto *nt* □ *a* Motor-; (*Anat*) motorisch □ *vi* [mit dem Auto] fahren
Motorail /ˈməʊtəreɪl/ *n* Autozug *m*
motor: ~ bike *n* (*fam*) Motorrad *nt*. **~ boat** *n* Motorboot *nt*. **~cade** /-keɪd/ *n* (*Amer*) Autokolonne *f*. **~ car** *n* Auto *nt*, Wagen *m*. **~ cycle** *n* Motorrad *nt*. **~-cyclist** *n* Motorradfahrer *m*. **~ing** *n* Autofahren *nt*. **~ist** *n* Autofahrer(in) *m(f)*. **~ize** *vt* motorisieren. **~ vehicle** *n* Kraftfahrzeug *nt*. **~way** *n* Autobahn *f*
mottled /ˈmɒtld/ *a* gesprenkelt
motto /ˈmɒtəʊ/ *n* (*pl* **-es**) Motto *nt*
mould¹ /məʊld/ *n* (*fungus*) Schimmel *m*
mould² *n* Form *f* □ *vt* formen (**into** zu). **~ing** *n* (*Archit*) Fries *m*
mouldy /ˈməʊldɪ/ *a* schimmelig; (*fam: worthless*) schäbig
moult /məʊlt/ *vi* ⟨*bird:*⟩ sich mausern; ⟨*animal:*⟩ sich haaren
mound /maʊnd/ *n* Hügel *m*; (*of stones*) Haufen *m*
mount¹ /maʊnt/ *n* Berg *m*
mount² *n* (*animal*) Reittier *nt*; (*of jewel*) Fassung *f*; (*of photo, picture*) Passepartout *nt* □ *vt* (*get on*) steigen auf (+ *acc*); (*on pedestal*) montieren auf (+ *acc*); besteigen ⟨*horse*⟩; fassen ⟨*jewel*⟩; aufziehen ⟨*photo, picture*⟩ □ *vi* aufsteigen; ⟨*tension:*⟩ steigen. **~ up** *vi* sich häufen; (*add up*) sich anhäufen
mountain /ˈmaʊntɪn/ *n* Berg *m*
mountaineer /maʊntɪˈnɪə(r)/ *n* Bergsteiger(in) *m(f)*. **~ing** *n* Bergsteigen *nt*
mountainous /ˈmaʊntɪnəs/ *a* bergig, gebirgig
mourn /mɔːn/ *vt* betrauern □ *vi* trauern (**for** um). **~er** *n* Trauernde(r) *m/f*. **~ful** *a*, **-ly** *adv* trauervoll. **~ing** *n* Trauer *f*
mouse /maʊs/ *n* (*pl* **mice**) Maus *f*. **~trap** *n* Mausefalle *f*
mousse /muːs/ *n* Schaum *m*; (*Culin*) Mousse *f*
moustache /məˈstɑːʃ/ *n* Schnurrbart *m*
mousy /ˈmaʊsɪ/ *a* graubraun; ⟨*person*⟩ farblos
mouth¹ /maʊð/ *vt* **~ sth** etw lautlos mit den Lippen sagen
mouth² /maʊθ/ *n* Mund *m*; (*of animal*) Maul *nt*; (*of river*) Mündung *f*
mouth: ~ful *n* Mundvoll *m*; (*bite*) Bissen *m*. **~-organ** *n* Mundharmonika *f*. **~piece** *n* Mundstück *nt*; (*fig: person*) Sprachrohr *nt*. **~wash** *n* Mundwasser *nt*
movable /ˈmuːvəbl/ *a* beweglich
move /muːv/ *n* Bewegung *f*; (*fig*) Schritt *m*; (*moving house*) Umzug *m*; (*in board-game*) Zug *m*; **on the ~** unterwegs; **get a ~ on** (*fam*) sich beeilen □ *vt* bewegen; (*emotionally*) rühren; (*move along*) rücken; (*in board-game*) ziehen;

(*take away*) wegnehmen; wegfahren ⟨*car*⟩; (*rearrange*) umstellen; (*transfer*) versetzen ⟨*person*⟩; verlegen ⟨*office*⟩; (*propose*) beantragen; **~ house** umziehen □ *vi* sich bewegen; (*move house*) umziehen; **don't ~!** stillhalten! (*stop*) stillstehen! **~ along** *vt/i* weiterrücken. **~ away** *vt/i* wegrücken; (*move house*) wegziehen. **~ forward** *vt/i* vorrücken; ⟨*vehicle*⟩ vorwärts fahren. **~ in** *vi* einziehen. **~ off** *vi* ⟨*vehicle:*⟩ losfahren. **~ out** *vi* ausziehen. **~ over** *vt/i* [zur Seite] rücken. **~ up** *vi* aufrücken

movement /ˈmu:vmənt/ *n* Bewegung *f*; (*Mus*) Satz *m*; (*of clock*) Uhrwerk *nt*

movie /ˈmu:vɪ/ *n* (*Amer*) Film *m*; **go to the ~s** ins Kino gehen

moving /ˈmu:vɪŋ/ *a* beweglich; (*touching*) rührend

mow /məʊ/ *vt* (*pt* **mowed**, *pp* **mown** *or* **mowed**) mähen. **~ down** *vt* (*destroy*) niedermähen

mower /ˈməʊə(r)/ *n* Rasenmähen *m*

MP *abbr see* **Member of Parliament**

Mr /ˈmɪstə(r)/ *n* (*pl* **Messrs**) Herr *m*

Mrs /ˈmɪsɪz/ *n* Frau *f*

Ms /mɪz/ *n* Frau *f*

much /mʌtʃ/ *a, adv & n* viel; **as ~ as** so viel wie; **very ~ loved/interested** sehr geliebt/interessiert

muck /mʌk/ *n* Mist *m*; (*fam: filth*) Dreck *m*. **~ about** *vi* herumalbern; (*tinker*) herumspielen (**with** mit). **~ in** *vt* (*fam*) mitmachen. **~ out** *vt* ausmisten. **~ up** *vt* (*fam*) vermasseln; (*make dirty*) schmutzig machen

mucky /ˈmʌkɪ/ *a* (**-ier, -iest**) dreckig

mucus /ˈmju:kəs/ *n* Schleim *m*

mud /mʌd/ *n* Schlamm *m*

muddle /ˈmʌdl/ *n* Durcheinander *nt*; (*confusion*) Verwirrung *f* □ *vt* **~ [up]** durcheinander bringen

muddy /ˈmʌdɪ/ *a* (**-ier, -iest**) schlammig; ⟨*shoes*⟩ schmutzig

ˈ**mudguard** *n* Kotflügel *m*; (*on bicycle*) Schutzblech *nt*

muesli /ˈmu:zlɪ/ *n* Müsli *nt*

muff /mʌf/ *n* Muff *m*

muffle /ˈmʌfl/ *vt* dämpfen ⟨*sound*⟩; **~ [up]** (*for warmth*) einhüllen (**in** in + *acc*)

muffler /ˈmʌflə(r)/ *n* Schal *m*; (*Amer, Auto*) Auspufftopf *m*

mufti /ˈmʌftɪ/ *n* **in ~** in Zivil

mug¹ /mʌg/ *n* Becher *m*; (*for beer*) Bierkrug *m*; (*fam: face*) Visage *f*; (*fam; simpleton*) Trottel *m*

mug² *vt* (*pt/pp* **mugged**) überfallen. **~ger** *n* Straßenräuber *m*. **~ging** *n* Straßenraub *m*

muggy /ˈmʌgɪ/ *a* (**-ier, -iest**) schwül

mule¹ /mju:l/ *n* Maultier *nt*

mule² *n* (*slipper*) Pantoffel *m*

mull /mʌl/ *vt* **~ over** nachdenken über (+ *acc*)

mulled /mʌld/ *a* **~ wine** Glühwein *m*

multi /ˈmʌltɪ/: **~coloured** *a* vielfarbig, bunt. **~lingual** /-ˈlɪŋgwəl/ *a* mehrsprachig. **~ˈnational** *a* multinational

multiple /ˈmʌltɪpl/ *a* vielfach; (*with pl*) mehrere □ *n* Vielfache(s) *nt*

multiplication /mʌltɪplɪˈkeɪʃn/ *n* Multiplikation *f*

multiply /ˈmʌltɪplaɪ/ *v* (*pt/pp* **-ied**) □ *vt* multiplizieren (**by** mit) □ *vi* sich vermehren

multistorey *a* **~ car park** Parkhaus *nt*

mum¹ /mʌm/ *a* **keep ~** (*fam*) den Mund halten

mum² *n* (*fam*) Mutti *f*

mumble /ˈmʌmbl/ *vt/i* murmeln

mummy¹ /ˈmʌmɪ/ *n* (*fam*) Mutti *f*

mummy² *n* (*Archaeol*) Mumie *f*

mumps /mʌmps/ *n* Mumps *m*
munch /mʌntʃ/ *vt/i* mampfen
mundane /mʌn'deɪn/ *a* banal; (*worldly*) weltlich
municipal /mju:'nɪsɪpl/ *a* städtisch
munitions /mju:'nɪʃnz/ *npl* Kriegsmaterial *nt*
mural /'mjʊərəl/ *n* Wandgemälde *nt*
murder /'mɜ:də(r)/ *n* Mord *m* □ *vt* ermorden; (*fam: ruin*) verhunzen. **~er** *n* Mörder *m*. **~ess** *n* Mörderin *f*. **~ous** /-rəs/ *a* mörderisch
murky /'mɜ:kɪ/ *a* (**-ier, -iest**) düster
murmur /'mɜ:mə(r)/ *n* Murmeln *nt* □ *vt/i* murmeln
muscle /'mʌsl/ *n* Muskel *m*
muscular /'mʌskjʊlə(r)/ *a* Muskel-; (*strong*) muskulös
muse /mju:z/ *vi* nachsinnen (**on** über + *acc*)
museum /mju:'zɪəm/ *n* Museum *nt*
mush /mʌʃ/ *n* Brei *m*
mushroom /'mʌʃrʊm/ *n* [essbarer] Pilz *m*, *esp* Champignon *m* □ *vi* (*fig*) wie Pilze aus dem Boden schießen
mushy /'mʌʃɪ/ *a* breiig
music /'mju:zɪk/ *n* Musik *f*; (*written*) Noten *pl*; **set to ~** vertonen
musical /'mju:zɪkl/ *a* musikalisch □ *n* Musical *nt*. **~ box** *n* Spieldose *f*. **~ instrument** *n* Musikinstrument *nt*
'music-hall *n* Varieté *nt*
musician /mju:'zɪʃn/ *n* Musiker(in) *m*(*f*)
'music-stand *n* Notenständer *m*
Muslim /'mʊzlɪm/ *a* mohammedanisch □ *n* Mohammedaner(in) *m*(*f*)
muslin /'mʌzlɪn/ *n* Musselin *m*
mussel /'mʌsl/ *n* [Mies]muschel *f*
must /mʌst/ *v aux* (*nur Präsens*) müssen; (*with negative*) dürfen □ *n* **a ~** (*fam*) ein Muss *nt*
mustard /'mʌstəd/ *n* Senf *m*
muster /'mʌstə(r)/ *vt* versammeln; aufbringen ⟨*strength*⟩ □ *vi* sich versammeln
musty /'mʌstɪ/ *a* (**-ier, -iest**) muffig
mutation /mju:'teɪʃn/ *n* Veränderung *f*; (*Biol*) Mutation *f*
mute /mju:t/ *a* stumm
muted /'mju:tɪd/ *a* gedämpft
mutilat|e /'mju:tɪleɪt/ *vt* verstümmeln. **~ion** /-'leɪʃn/ *n* Verstümmelung *f*
mutin|ous /'mju:tɪnəs/ *a* meuterisch. **~y** *n* Meuterei *f* □ *vi* (*pt/pp* **-ied**) meutern
mutter /'mʌtə(r)/ *n* Murmeln *nt* □ *vt/i* murmeln
mutton /'mʌtn/ *n* Hammelfleisch *nt*
mutual /'mju:tjʊəl/ *a* gegenseitig; (*fam: common*) gemeinsam. **~ly** *adv* gegenseitig
muzzle /'mʌzl/ *n* (*of animal*) Schnauze *f*; (*of firearm*) Mündung *f*; (*for dog*) Maulkorb *m* □ *vt* einen Maulkorb anlegen (+ *dat*)
my /maɪ/ *a* mein
myopic /maɪ'ɒpɪk/ *a* kurzsichtig
myself /maɪ'self/ *pron* selbst; (*refl*) mich; **by ~** allein; **I thought to ~** ich habe mir gedacht
mysterious /mɪ'stɪərɪəs/ *a*, **-ly** *adv* geheimnisvoll; (*puzzling*) mysteriös, rätselhaft
mystery /'mɪstərɪ/ *n* Geheimnis *nt*; (*puzzle*) Rätsel *nt*; **~ [story]** Krimi *m*
mysti|c[al] /'mɪstɪk[l]/ *a* mystisch. **~cism** /-sɪzm/ *n* Mystik *f*
mystification /mɪstɪfɪ'keɪʃn/ *n* Verwunderung *f*
mystified /'mɪstɪfaɪd/ *a* **be ~** vor einem Rätsel stehen
mystique /mɪ'sti:k/ *n* geheimnisvoller Zauber *m*
myth /mɪθ/ *n* Mythos *m*; (*fam: untruth*) Märchen *nt*. **~ical** *a* mythisch; (*fig*) erfunden

mythology /mɪˈθɒlədʒɪ/ *n* Mythologie *f*

N

nab /næb/ *vt* (*pt/pp* **nabbed**) (*fam*) erwischen
nag¹ /næg/ *n* (*horse*) Gaul *m*
nag² *vt/i* (*pp/pp* **nagged**) herumnörgeln (**s.o.** an jdm). **~ging** *a* ⟨*pain*⟩ nagend □ *n* Nörgelei *f*
nail /neɪl/ *n* (*Anat, Techn*) Nagel *m*; **on the ~** (*fam*) sofort □ *vt* nageln (**to** an + *acc*). **~ down** *vt* festnageln; (*close*) zunageln
nail: ~-brush *n* Nagelbürste *f*. **~-file** *n* Nagelfeile *f*. **~ polish** *n* Nagellack *m*. **~ scissors** *npl* Nagelschere *f*. **~ varnish** *n* Nagellack *m*
naïve /naɪˈiːv/ *a*, **-ly** *adv* naiv. **~ty** /-ətɪ/ *n* Naivität *f*
naked /ˈneɪkɪd/ *a* nackt; ⟨*flame*⟩ offen; **with the ~ eye** mit bloßem Auge. **~ness** *n* Nacktheit *f*
name /neɪm/ *n* Name *m*; (*reputation*) Ruf *m*; **by ~** dem Namen nach; **by the ~ of** namens; **call s.o. ~s** (*fam*) jdn beschimpfen □ *vt* nennen; (*give a name to*) einen Namen geben (+ *dat*); (*announce publicly*) den Namen bekannt geben von. **~less** *a* namenlos. **~ly** *adv* nämlich
name: ~-plate *n* Namensschild *nt*. **~sake** *n* Namensvetter *m*/Namensschwester *f*
nanny /ˈnænɪ/ *n* Kindermädchen *nt*. **~-goat** *n* Ziege *f*
nap /næp/ *n* Nickerchen *nt*; **have a ~** ein Nickerchen machen □ *vi* **catch s.o. ~ping** jdn überrumpeln
nape /neɪp/ *n* **~ [of the neck]** Nacken *m*
napkin /ˈnæpkɪn/ *n* Serviette *f*; (*for baby*) Windel *f*
nappy /ˈnæpɪ/ *n* Windel *f*
narcotic /nɑːˈkɒtɪk/ *a* betäubend □ *n* Narkotikum *nt*; (*drug*) Rauschgift *nt*
narrat|e /nəˈreɪt/ *vt* erzählen. **~ion** /-eɪʃn/ *n* Erzählung *f*
narrative /ˈnærətɪv/ *a* erzählend □ *n* Erzählung *f*
narrator /nəˈreɪtə(r)/ *n* Erzähler(in) *m(f)*
narrow /ˈnærəʊ/ *a* (**-er, -est**) schmal; (*restricted*) eng; ⟨*margin, majority*⟩ knapp; (*fig*) beschränkt; **have a ~ escape**, *adv* **~ly escape** mit knapper Not davonkommen □ *vi* sich verengen. **~-ˈminded** *a* engstirnig
nasal /ˈneɪzl/ *a* nasal; (*Med & Anat*) Nasen-
nastily /ˈnɑːstɪlɪ/ *adv* boshaft
nasturtium /nəˈstɜːʃəm/ *n* Kapuzinerkresse *f*
nasty /ˈnɑːstɪ/ *a* (**-ier, -iest**) übel; (*unpleasant*) unangenehm; (*unkind*) boshaft; (*serious*) schlimm; **turn ~** gemein werden
nation /ˈneɪʃn/ *n* Nation *f*; (*people*) Volk *nt*
national /ˈnæʃənl/ *a* national; ⟨*newspaper*⟩ überregional; ⟨*campaign*⟩ landesweit □ *n* Staatsbürger(in) *m(f)*
national: ~ ˈanthem *n* Nationalhymne *f*. **N~ ˈHealth Service** *n* staatlicher Gesundheitsdienst *m*. **N~ Inˈsurance** *n* Sozialversicherung *f*
nationalism /ˈnæʃənəlɪzm/ *n* Nationalismus *m*
nationality /næʃəˈnælətɪ/ *n* Staatsangehörigkeit *f*
national|ization /næʃənəlaɪˈzeɪʃn/ *n* Verstaatlichung *f*. **~ize** /ˈnæʃənəlaɪz/ *vt* verstaatlichen. **~ly** /ˈnæʃənəlɪ/ *adv* landesweit
ˈnation-wide *a* landesweit
native /ˈneɪtɪv/ *a* einheimisch; (*innate*) angeboren □ *n* Eingeborene(r) *m/f*; (*local inhabitant*) Einheimische(r) *m/f*; **a ~ of Vienna** ein gebürtiger Wiener

native: ~ **'land** *n* Heimatland *nt.* ~ **'language** *n* Muttersprache *f*
Nativity /nəˈtɪvətɪ/ *n* **the** ~ Christi Geburt *f.* ~ **play** *n* Krippenspiel *nt*
natter /ˈnætə(r)/ *n* **have a** ~ (*fam*) einen Schwatz halten □ *vi* (*fam*) schwatzen
natural /ˈnætʃrəl/ *a*, **-ly** *adv* natürlich; ~**[-coloured]** naturfarben
natural: ~ **'gas** *n* Erdgas *nt.* ~ **'history** *n* Naturkunde *f*
naturalist /ˈnætʃrəlɪst/ *n* Naturforscher *m*
natural|ization /nætʃrəlaɪˈzeɪʃn/ *n* Einbürgerung *f.* ~**ize** /ˈnætʃrəlaɪz/ *vt* einbürgern
nature /ˈneɪtʃə(r)/ *n* Natur *f*; (*kind*) Art *f*; **by** ~ von Natur aus. ~ **reserve** *n* Naturschutzgebiet *nt*
naturism /ˈneɪtʃərɪzm/ *n* Freikörperkultur *f*
naught /nɔːt/ *n* = **nought**
naughty /ˈnɔːtɪ/ *a* (**-ier, -iest**), **-ily** *adv* unartig; (*slightly indecent*) gewagt
nausea /ˈnɔːzɪə/ *n* Übelkeit *f*
nause|ate /ˈnɔːzɪeɪt/ *vt* anekeln. ~**ating** *a* ekelhaft. ~**ous** /-ɪəs/ *a* **I feel** ~**ous** mir ist übel
nautical /ˈnɔːtɪkl/ *a* nautisch. ~ **mile** *n* Seemeile *f*
naval /ˈneɪvl/ *a* Marine-
nave /neɪv/ *n* Kirchenschiff *nt*
navel /ˈneɪvl/ *n* Nabel *m*
navigable /ˈnævɪgəbl/ *a* schiffbar
navigat|e /ˈnævɪgeɪt/ *vi* navigieren □ *vt* befahren ⟨*river*⟩. ~**ion** /-ˈgeɪʃn/ *n* Navigation *f.* ~**or** *n* Navigator *m*
navvy /ˈnævɪ/ *n* Straßenarbeiter *m*
navy /ˈneɪvɪ/ *n* [Kriegs]marine *f* □ *a* ~ **[blue]** marineblau
near /nɪə(r)/ *a* (**-er, -est**) nah[e]; **the** ~**est bank** die nächste Bank □ *adv* nahe; ~**by** nicht weit weg; ~ **at hand** in der Nähe; **draw** ~ sich nähern □ *prep* nahe an (+ *dat/acc*); in der Nähe von; ~ **to tears** den Tränen nahe; **go** ~ **[to] sth** nahe an etw (*acc*) herangehen □ *vt* sich nähern (+ *dat*)
near: ~**by** *a* nahe gelegen, nahe liegend. ~**ly** *adv* fast, beinahe; **not** ~**ly** bei weitem nicht. ~**ness** *n* Nähe *f.* ~ **side** *n* Beifahrerseite *f.* ~**-sighted** *a* (*Amer*) kurzsichtig
neat /niːt/ *a* (**-er, -est**), **-ly** *adv* adrett; (*tidy*) ordentlich; (*clever*) geschickt; (*undiluted*) pur. ~**ness** *n* Ordentlichkeit *f*
necessarily /ˈnesəserəlɪ/ *adv* notwendigerweise; **not** ~ nicht unbedingt
necessary /ˈnesəsərɪ/ *a* nötig, notwending
necessit|ate /nɪˈsesɪteɪt/ *vt* notwendig machen. ~**y** *n* Notwendigkeit *f*; **she works from** ~**y** sie arbeitet, weil sie es nötig hat
neck /nek/ *n* Hals *m*; ~ **and** ~ Kopf an Kopf
necklace /ˈneklɪs/ *n* Halskette *f*
neck: ~**line** *n* Halsausschnitt *m.* ~**tie** *n* Schlips *m*
nectar /ˈnektə(r)/ *n* Nektar *m*
née /neɪ/ *a* ~ **Brett** geborene Brett
need /niːd/ *n* Bedürfnis *nt*; (*misfortune*) Not *f*; **be in** ~ Not leiden; **be in** ~ **of** brauchen; **in case of** ~ notfalls; **if** ~ **be** wenn nötig; **there is a** ~ **for** es besteht ein Bedarf an (+ *dat*); **there is no** ~ **for that** das ist nicht nötig; **there is no** ~ **for you to go** du brauchst nicht zu gehen □ *vt* brauchen; **you** ~ **not go** du brauchst nicht zu gehen; ~ **I come?** muss ich kommen? **I** ~ **to know** ich muss es wissen; **it** ~**s to be done** es muss gemacht werden
needle /ˈniːdl/ *n* Nadel *f* □ *vt* (*annoy*) ärgern

needless /ˈniːdlɪs/ *a*, **-ly** *adv* unnötig; **~ to say** selbstverständlich, natürlich
ˈneedlework *n* Nadelarbeit *f*
needy /ˈniːdɪ/ *a* (**-ier, -iest**) bedürftig
negation /nɪˈgeɪʃn/ *n* Verneinung *f*
negative /ˈnegətɪv/ *a* negativ □ *n* Verneinung *f*; (*photo*) Negativ *nt*
neglect /nɪˈglekt/ *n* Vernachlässigung *f*; **state of ~** verwahrloster Zustand *m* □ *vt* vernachlässigen; (*omit*) versäumen (**to** zu). **~ed** *a* verwahrlost. **~ful** *a* nachlässig; **be ~ful of** vernachlässigen
negligen|ce /ˈneglɪdʒəns/ *n* Nachlässigkeit *f*; (*Jur*) Fahrlässigkeit *f*. **~t** *a*, **-ly** *adv* nachlässig; (*Jur*) fahrlässig
negligible /ˈneglɪdʒəbl/ *a* unbedeutend
negotiable /nɪˈgəʊʃəbl/ *a* ⟨*road*⟩ befahrbar; (*Comm*) unverbindlich; **not ~** nicht übertragbar
negotiat|e /nɪˈgəʊʃɪeɪt/ *vt* aushandeln; (*Auto*) nehmen ⟨*bend*⟩ □ *vi* verhandeln. **~ion** /-ˈeɪʃn/ *n* Verhandlung *f*. **~or** *n* Unterhändler(in) *m(f)*
Negro /ˈniːgrəʊ/ *a* Neger- □ *n* (*pl* **-es**) Neger *m*
neigh /neɪ/ *vi* wiehern
neighbour /ˈneɪbə(r)/ *n* Nachbar(in) *m(f)*. **~hood** *n* Nachbarschaft *f*; **in the ~hood of** in der Nähe von; (*fig*) um ... herum. **~ing** *a* Nachbar-. **~ly** *a* [gut]nachbarlich
neither /ˈnaɪðə(r)/ *a* & *pron* keine(r, s) [von beiden] □ *adv* **~... nor** weder ... noch □ *conj* auch nicht
neon /ˈniːɒn/ *n* Neon *nt*. **~ light** *n* Neonlicht *nt*
nephew /ˈnevjuː/ *n* Neffe *m*
nepotism /ˈnepətɪzm/ *n* Vetternwirtschaft *f*
nerve /nɜːv/ *n* Nerv *m*; (*fam: courage*) Mut *m*; (*fam: impudence*) Frechheit *f*; **lose one's ~** den Mut verlieren. **~-racking** *a* nervenaufreibend
nervous /ˈnɜːvəs/ *a*, **-ly** *adv* (*afraid*) ängstlich; (*highly strung*) nervös; (*Anat, Med*) Nerven-; **be ~** Angst haben. **~ ˈbreakdown** *n* Nervenzusammenbruch *m*. **~ness** Ängstlichkeit *f*; (*Med*) Nervosität *f*
nervy /ˈnɜːvɪ/ *a* (**-ier, -iest**) nervös; (*Amer: impudent*) frech
nest /nest/ *n* Nest *nt* □ *vi* nisten. **~-egg** *n* Notgroschen *m*
nestle /ˈnesl/ *vi* sich schmiegen (**against** an + *acc*)
net[1] /net/ *n* Netz *nt*; (*curtain*) Store *m* □ *vt* (*pt/pp* **netted**) (*catch*) [mit dem Netz] fangen
net[2] *a* netto; ⟨*salary, weight*⟩ Netto- □ *vt* (*pt/pp* **netted**) netto einnehmen; (*yield*) einbringen
ˈnetball *n* ≈ Korbball *m*
Netherlands /ˈneðələndz/ *npl* **the ~** die Niederlande *pl*
netting /ˈnetɪŋ/ *n* **[wire] ~** Maschendraht *m*
nettle /ˈnetl/ *n* Nessel *f*
ˈnetwork *n* Netz *nt*
neuralgia /njʊəˈrældʒə/ *n* Neuralgie *f*
neurolog|ist /njʊəˈrɒlədʒɪst/ *n* Neurologe *m*/ -gin *f*. **~y** *n* Neurologie *f*
neur|osis /njʊəˈrəʊsɪs/ *n* (*pl* **-oses** /-siːz/) Neurose *f*. **~otic** /-ˈrɒtɪk/ *a* neurotisch
neuter /ˈnjuːtə(r)/ *a* (*Gram*) sächlich □ *n* (*Gram*) Neutrum *nt* □ *vt* kastrieren; (*spay*) sterilisieren
neutral /ˈnjuːtrl/ *a* neutral □ *n* **in ~** (*Auto*) im Leerlauf. **~ity** /-ˈtrælətɪ/ *n* Neutralität *f*. **~ize** *vt* neutralisieren
never /ˈnevə(r)/ *adv* nie, niemals; (*fam: not*) nicht; **~ mind** macht nichts; **well I ~!** ja so was! **~-ending** *a* endlos
nevertheless /nevəðəˈles/ *adv* dennoch, trotzdem
new /njuː/ *a* (**-er, -est**) neu

new: ~born *a* neugeboren. **~comer** *n* Neuankömmling *m*. **~fangled** /-'fæŋgld/ *a* (*pej*) neumodisch. **~-laid** *a* frisch gelegt

'newly *adv* frisch. **~-weds** *npl* Jungverheiratete *pl*

new: ~ 'moon *n* Neumond *m*. **~ness** *n* Neuheit *f*

news /nju:z/ *n* Nachricht *f*; (*Radio, TV*) Nachrichten *pl*; **piece of ~** Neuigkeit *f*

news: ~agent *n* Zeitungshändler *m*. **~ bulletin** *n* Nachrichtensendung *f*. **~caster** *n* Nachrichtensprecher(in) *m(f)*. **~flash** *n* Kurzmeldung *f*. **~letter** *n* Mitteilungsblatt *nt*. **~paper** *n* Zeitung *f*; (*material*) Zeitungspapier *nt*. **~reader** *n* Nachrichtensprecher(in) *m(f)*

newt /nju:t/ *n* Molch *m*

New: ~ Year's 'Day *n* Neujahr *nt*. **~ Year's 'Eve** *n* Silvester *nt*. **~ Zealand** /'zi:lənd/ *n* Neuseeland *nt*

next /nekst/ *a* & *n* nächste(r, s); **who's ~?** wer kommt als Nächster dran? **the ~ best** das nächstbeste; **~ door** nebenan; **my ~ of kin** mein nächster Verwandter; **~ to nothing** fast gar nichts; **the week after ~** übernächste Woche □ *adv* als Nächstes; **~ to** neben

NHS *abbr see* National Health Service

nib /nɪb/ *n* Feder *f*

nibble /'nɪbl/ *vt/i* knabbern **(at** an + *dat*)

nice /naɪs/ *a* **(-r, -st)** nett; ⟨*day, weather*⟩ schön; ⟨*food*⟩ gut; ⟨*distinction*⟩ fein. **~ly** *adv* nett; (*well*) gut. **~ties** /'naɪsətɪz/ *npl* Feinheiten *pl*

niche /ni:ʃ/ *n* Nische *f*; (*fig*) Platz *m*

nick /nɪk/ *n* Kerbe *f*; (*fam: prison*) Knast *m*; (*fam: police station*) Revier *nt*; **in the ~ of time** (*fam*) gerade noch rechtzeitig; **in good ~** (*fam*) in gutem Zustand □ *vt* einkerben; (*steal*) klauen; (*fam: arrest*) schnappen

nickel /'nɪkl/ *n* Nickel *nt*; (*Amer*) Fünfcentstück *nt*

'nickname *n* Spitzname *m*

nicotine /'nɪkəti:n/ *n* Nikotin *nt*

niece /ni:s/ *n* Nichte *f*

Nigeria /naɪ'dʒɪərɪə/ *n* Nigeria *nt*. **~n** *a* nigerianisch □ *n* Nigerianer(in) *m(f)*

niggardly /'nɪgədlɪ/ *a* knauserig

niggling /'nɪglɪŋ/ *a* gering; (*petty*) kleinlich; ⟨*pain*⟩ quälend

night /naɪt/ *n* Nacht *f*; (*evening*) Abend *m*; **at ~** nachts; **Monday ~** Montag Nacht/Abend

night: ~cap *n* Schlafmütze *f*; (*drink*) Schlaftrunk *m*. **~-club** *n* Nachtklub *m*. **~-dress** *n* Nachthemd *nt*. **~fall** *n* **at ~fall** bei Einbruch der Dunkelheit. **~-gown** *n*, (*fam*) **~ie** /'naɪtɪ/ *n* Nachthemd *nt*

nightingale /'naɪtɪŋgeɪl/ *n* Nachtigall *f*

night: ~-life *n* Nachtleben *nt*. **~ly** *a* nächtlich □ *adv* jede Nacht. **~mare** *n* Alptraum *m*. **~shade** *n* (*Bot*) **deadly ~shade** Tollkirsche *f*. **~-time** *n* **at ~-time** bei Nacht. **~-'watchman** *n* Nachtwächter *m*

nil /nɪl/ *n* null

nimble /'nɪmbl/ *a* **(-r, -st)**, **-bly** *adv* flink

nine /naɪn/ *a* neun □ *n* Neun *f*. **~'teen** *a* neunzehn. **~'teenth** *a* neunzehnte(r, s)

ninetieth /'naɪntɪɪθ/ *a* neunzigste(r, s)

ninety /'naɪntɪ/ *a* neunzig

ninth /naɪnθ/ *a* neunte(r, s)

nip /nɪp/ *n* Kniff *m*; (*bite*) Biss *m* □ *vt* kneifen; (*bite*) beißen; **~ in the bud** (*fig*) im Keim ersticken □ *vi* (*fam: run*) laufen

nipple /'nɪpl/ *n* Brustwarze *f*; (*Amer: on bottle*) Sauger *m*

nippy /'nɪpɪ/ *a* **(-ier, -iest)** (*fam*) (*cold*) frisch; (*quick*) flink

nitrate /ˈnaɪtreɪt/ *n* Nitrat *nt*
nitrogen /ˈnaɪtrədʒən/ *n* Stickstoff *m*
nitwit /ˈnɪtwɪt/ *n* (*fam*) Dummkopf *m*
no /nəʊ/ *adv* nein □ *n* (*pl* **noes**) Nein *nt* □ *a* kein(e); (*pl*) keine; **in no time** [sehr] schnell; **no parking/smoking** Parken/Rauchen verboten; **no one** = **nobody**
nobility /nəʊˈbɪlətɪ/ *n* Adel *m*
noble /ˈnəʊbl/ *a* (**-r, -st**) edel; (*aristocratic*) adlig. **~man** *n* Adlige(r) *m*
nobody /ˈnəʊbədɪ/ *pron* niemand, keiner; **he knows ~** er kennt niemanden *od* keinen □ *n* **a ~** ein Niemand *m*
nocturnal /nɒkˈtɜːnl/ *a* nächtlich; ⟨*animal, bird*⟩ Nacht-
nod /nɒd/ *n* Nicken *nt* □ *v* (*pt/pp* **nodded**) □ *vi* nicken □ *vt* **~ one's head** mit dem Kopf nicken. **~ off** *vi* einnicken
nodule /ˈnɒdjuːl/ *n* Knötchen *nt*
noise /nɔɪz/ *n* Geräusch *nt*; (*loud*) Lärm *m*. **~less** *a*, **-ly** *adv* geräuschlos
noisy /ˈnɔɪzɪ/ *a* (**-ier, -iest**), **-ily** *adv* laut; ⟨*eater*⟩ geräuschvoll
nomad /ˈnəʊmæd/ *n* Nomade *m*. **~ic** /-ˈmædɪk/ *a* nomadisch; ⟨*life, tribe*⟩ Nomaden-
nominal /ˈnɒmɪnl/ *a*, **-ly** *adv* nominell
nominat|e /ˈnɒmɪneɪt/ *vt* nominieren, aufstellen; (*appoint*) ernennen. **~ion** /-ˈneɪʃn/ *n* Nominierung *f*; Ernennung *f*
nominative /ˈnɒmɪnətɪv/ *a* & *n* (*Gram*) **~[case]** Nominativ *m*
nonchalant /ˈnɒnʃələnt/ *a*, **-ly** *adv* nonchalant; ⟨*gesture*⟩ lässig
non-comˈmissioned /nɒn-/ *a* **~ officer** Unteroffizier *m*
non-comˈmittal *a* unverbindlich; **be ~** sich nicht festlegen
nondescript /ˈnɒndɪskrɪpt/ *a* unbestimmbar; ⟨*person*⟩ unscheinbar
none /nʌn/ *pron* keine(r)/keins; **~ of us** keiner von uns; **~ of it/this** nichts davon □ *adv* **~ too** nicht gerade; **~ too soon** [um] keine Minute zu früh; **~ the wiser** um nichts klüger; **~ the less** dennoch
nonentity /nɒˈnentətɪ/ *n* Null *f*
non-exˈistent *a* nicht vorhanden; **be ~** nicht vorhanden sein
non-ˈfiction *n* Sachliteratur *f*
non-ˈiron *a* bügelfrei
nonplussed /nɒnˈplʌst/ *a* verblüfft
nonsens|e /ˈnɒnsəns/ *n* Unsinn *m*. **~ical** /ˈ-sensɪkl/ *a* unsinnig
non-ˈsmoker *n* Nichtraucher *m*; (*compartment*) Nichtraucherabteil *nt*
non-ˈstop *adv* ununterbrochen; ⟨*fly*⟩ nonstop; **~ ˈflight** Nonstopflug *m*
non-ˈswimmer *n* Nichtschwimmer *m*
non-ˈviolent *a* gewaltlos
noodles /ˈnuːdlz/ *npl* Bandnudeln *pl*
nook /nʊk/ *n* Eckchen *nt*, Winkel *m*
noon /nuːn/ *n* Mittag *m*; **at ~** um 12 Uhr mittags
noose /nuːs/ *n* Schlinge *f*
nor /nɔː(r)/ *adv* noch □ *conj* auch nicht
Nordic /ˈnɔːdɪk/ *a* nordisch
norm /nɔːm/ *n* Norm *f*
normal /ˈnɔːml/ *a* normal. **~ity** /-ˈmælətɪ/ *n* Normalität *f*. **~ly** *adv* normal; (*usually*) normalerweise
north /nɔːθ/ *n* Norden *m*; **to the ~ of** nördlich von □ *a* Nord-, nord- □ *adv* nach Norden
north: N~ America *n* Nordamerika *nt*. **~-east** *a* Nordost- □ *n* Nordosten *m*
norther|ly /ˈnɔːðəlɪ/ *a* nördlich. **~n** *a* nördlich. **N~n Ireland** *n* Nordirland *nt*

north: N~ 'Pole *n* Nordpol *m*. **N~ 'Sea** *n* Nordsee *f*. **~ward[s]** /-wəd[z]/ *adv* nach Norden. **~-west** *a* Nordwest- □ *n* Nordwesten *m*

Nor|way /'nɔːweɪ/ *n* Norwegen *nt*. **~wegian** /-'wiːdʒn/ *a* norwegisch □ *n* Norweger(in) *m(f)*

nose /nəʊz/ *n* Nase *f* □ *vi* **~ about** herumschnüffeln

nose: ~bleed *n* Nasenbluten *nt*. **~dive** *n* (*Aviat*) Sturzflug *m*

nostalg|ia /nɒ'stældʒɪə/ *n* Nostalgie *f*. **~ic** *a* nostalgisch

nostril /'nɒstrəl/ *n* Nasenloch *nt*; (*of horse*) Nüster *f*

nosy /'nəʊzɪ/ *a* (**-ier, -iest**) (*fam*) neugierig

not /nɒt/ *adv* nicht; **~ a** kein(e); **if ~** wenn nicht; **~ at all** gar nicht; **~ a bit** kein bisschen; **~ even** nicht mal; **~ yet** noch nicht; **he is ~ a German** er ist kein Deutscher

notab|le /'nəʊtəbl/ a bedeutend; (*remarkable*) bemerkenswert. **~ly** *adv* insbesondere

notary /'nəʊtərɪ/ *n* **~ 'public** ≈ Notar *m*

notation /nəʊ'teɪʃn/ *n* Notation *f*; (*Mus*) Notenschrift *f*

notch /nɒtʃ/ *n* Kerbe *f*. **~ up** *vt* (*score*) erzielen

note /nəʊt/ *n* (*written comment*) Notiz *f*, Anmerkung *f*; (*short letter*) Briefchen *nt*, Zettel *m*; (*bank ~*) Banknote *f*, Schein *m*; (*Mus*) Note *f*; (*sound*) Ton *m*; (*on piano*) Taste *f*; **eighth/quarter ~** (*Amer*) Achtel-/Viertelnote *f*; **half/whole ~** (*Amer*) halbe/ganze Note *f*; **of ~** von Bedeutung; **make a ~ of** notieren □ *vt* beachten; (*notice*) bemerken (**that** dass). **~ down** *vt* notieren

'notebook *n* Notizbuch *nt*

noted /'nəʊtɪd/ *a* bekannt (**for** für)

note: ~paper *n* Briefpapier *nt*. **~worthy** *a* beachtenswert

nothing /'nʌθɪŋ/ *n, ron & adv* nichts; **for ~** umsonst; **~ but** nichts als; **~ much** nicht viel; **~ interesting** nichts Interessantes; **it's ~ to do with you** das geht dich nichts an

notice /'nəʊtɪs/ *n* (*on board*) Anschlag *m*, Bekanntmachung *f*; (*announcement*) Anzeige *f*; (*review*) Kritik *f*; (*termination of lease, employment*) Kündigung *f*; **[advance] ~** Bescheid *m*; **give [in one's] ~** kündigen; **give s.o. ~** jdm kündigen; **take no ~ of** keine Notiz nehmen von; **take no ~!** ignoriere es! □ *vt* bemerken. **~able** /-əbl/, *a*, **-bly** *adv* merklich. **~-board** *n* Anschlagbrett *nt*

noti|fication /nəʊtɪfɪ'keɪʃn/ *n* Benachrichtigung *f*. **~fy** /'nəʊtɪfaɪ/ *vt* (*pt/pp* **-ied**) benachrichtigen

notion /'nəʊʃn/ *n* Idee *f*; **~s** *pl* (*Amer: haberdashery*) Kurzwaren *pl*

notorious /nəʊ'tɔːrɪəs/ *a* berüchtigt

notwith'standing *prep* trotz (+ *gen*) □ *adv* trotzdem, dennoch

nought /nɔːt/ *n* Null *f*

noun /naʊn/ *n* Substantiv *nt*

nourish /'nʌrɪʃ/ *vt* nähren. **~ing** *a* nahrhaft. **~ment** *n* Nahrung *f*

novel /'nɒvl/ *a* neu[artig] □ *n* Roman *m*. **~ist** *n* Romanschriftsteller(in) *m(f)*. **~ty** *n* Neuheit *f*; **~ties** *pl* kleine Geschenkartikel *pl*

November /nəʊ'vembə(r)/ *n* November *m*

novice /'nɒvɪs/ *n* Neuling *m*; (*Relig*) Novize *m*/Novizin *f*

now /naʊ/ *adv & conj* jetzt; **~ [that]** jetzt, wo; **just ~** gerade, eben; **right ~** sofort; **~ and again** hin und wieder; **now, now!** na, na!

'nowadays *adv* heutzutage

nowhere /'nəʊ-/ *adv* nirgendwo, nirgends

noxious /'nɒkʃəs/ *a* schädlich

nozzle /ˈnɒzl/ *n* Düse *f*
nuance /ˈnju:ɑ̃s/ *n* Nuance *f*
nuclear /ˈnju:klɪə(r)/ *a* Kern-. **~ deˈterrent** *n* nukleares Abschreckungsmittel *nt*
nucleus /ˈnju:klɪəs/ *n* (*pl* **-lei** /-lɪaɪ/) Kern *m*
nude /nju:d/ *a* nackt □ *n* (*Art*) Akt *m*; **in the ~** nackt
nudge /nʌdʒ/ *n* Stups *m* □ *vt* stupsen
nud|ist /ˈnju:dɪst/ *n* Nudist *m*. **~ity** *n* Nacktheit *f*
nugget /ˈnʌgɪt/ *n* [Gold]klumpen *m*
nuisance /ˈnju:sns/ *n* Ärgernis *nt*; (*pest*) Plage *f*; **be a ~** ärgerlich sein; ⟨*person:*⟩ lästig sein; **what a ~!** wie ärgerlich!
null /nʌl/ *a* **~ and void** null und nichtig. **~ify** /ˈnʌlɪfaɪ/ *vt* (*pt/pp* **-ied**) für nichtig erklären
numb /nʌm/ *a* gefühllos, taub; **~ with cold** taub vor Kälte □ *vt* betäuben
number /ˈnʌmbə(r)/ *n* Nummer *f*; (*amount*) Anzahl *f*; (*Math*) Zahl *f* □ *vt* nummerieren; (*include*) zählen (**among** zu). **~-plate** *n* Nummernschild *nt*
numeral /ˈnju:mərl/ *n* Ziffer *f*
numerate /ˈnju:mərət/ *a* **be ~** rechnen können
numerical /nju:ˈmerɪkl/ *a*, **-ly** *adv* numerisch; **in ~ order** zahlenmäßig geordnet
numerous /ˈnju:mərəs/ *a* zahlreich
nun /nʌn/ *n* Nonne *f*
nuptial /ˈnʌpʃl/ *a* Hochzeits-. **~s** *npl* (*Amer*) Hochzeit *f*
nurse /nɜ:s/ *n* [Kranken]schwester *f*; (*male*) Krankenpfleger *m*; **children's ~** Kindermädchen *nt* □ *vt* pflegen. **~maid** *n* Kindermädchen *nt*
nursery /ˈnɜ:sərɪ/ *n* Kinderzimmer *nt*; (*Hort*) Gärtnerei *f*; **[day] ~** Kindertagesstätte *f*. **~ rhyme** *n* Kinderreim *m*. **~ school** *n* Kindergarten *m*
nursing /ˈnɜ:sɪŋ/ *n* Krankenpflege *f*. **~ home** *n* Pflegeheim *nt*
nurture /ˈnɜ:tʃə(r)/ *vt* nähren; (*fig*) hegen
nut /nʌt/ *n* Nuss *f*; (*Techn*) [Schrauben]mutter *f*; (*fam: head*) Birne *f* (*fam*); **be ~s** (*fam*) spinnen (*fam*). **~crackers** *npl* Nussknacker *m*. **~meg** *n* Muskat *m*
nutrient /ˈnju:trɪənt/ *n* Nährstoff *m*
nutrit|ion /nju:ˈtrɪʃn/ *n* Ernährung *f*. **~ious** /-ʃəs/ *a* nahrhaft
ˈnutshell *n* Nussschale *f*; **in a ~** (*fig*) kurz gesagt
nuzzle /ˈnʌzl/ *vt* beschnüffeln
nylon /ˈnaɪlɒn/ *n* Nylon *nt*; **~s** *pl* Nylonstrümpfe *pl*
nymph /nɪmf/ *n* Nymphe *f*

O

O /əʊ/ *n* (*Teleph*) null
oaf /əʊf/ *n* (*pl* **oafs**) Trottel *m*
oak /əʊk/ *n* Eiche *f* □ *attrib* Eichen-
OAP *abbr* (**old-age pensioner**) Rentner(in) *m*(*f*)
oar /ɔ:(r)/ *n* Ruder *nt*. **~sman** *n* Ruderer *m*
oasis /əʊˈeɪsɪs/ *n* (*pl* **oases** /-si:z/) Oase *f*
oath /əʊθ/ *n* Eid *m*; (*swear-word*) Fluch *m*
oatmeal /ˈəʊt-/ *n* Hafermehl *nt*
oats /əʊts/ *npl* Hafer *m*; (*Culin*) **[rolled] ~** Haferflocken *pl*
obedien|ce /əˈbi:dɪəns/ *n* Gehorsam *m*. **~t** *a*, **-ly** *adv* gehorsam
obes|e /əʊˈbi:s/ *a* fettleibig. **~ity** *n* Fettleibigkeit *f*
obey /əˈbeɪ/ *vt/i* gehorchen (+ *dat*); befolgen ⟨*instructions, rules*⟩

obituary /ə'bɪtjʊərɪ/ *n* Nachruf *m*; (*notice*) Todesanzeige *f*
object[1] /'ɒbdʒɪkt/ *n* Gegenstand *m*; (*aim*) Zweck *m*; (*intention*) Absicht *f*; (*Gram*) Objekt *nt*; **money is no ~** Geld spielt keine Rolle
object[2] /əb'dʒekt/ *vi* Einspruch erheben (**to** gegen); (*be against*) etwas dagegen haben
objection /əb'dʒekʃn/ *n* Einwand *m*; **have no ~** nichts dagegen haben. **~able** /-əbl/ *a* anstößig; ⟨*person*⟩ unangenehm
objectiv|e /əb'dʒektɪv/ *a*, **-ly** *adv* objektiv □ *n* Ziel *nt*. **~ity** /-'tɪvətɪ/ *n* Objektivität *f*
objector /əb'dʒektə(r)/ *n* Gegner *m*
obligation /ɒblɪ'geɪʃn/ *n* Pflicht *f*; **be under an ~** verpflichtet sein; **without ~** unverbindlich
obligatory /ə'blɪgətrɪ/ *a* obligatorisch; **be ~** Vorschrift sein
oblig|e /ə'blaɪdʒ/ *vt* verpflichten; (*compel*) zwingen; (*do a small service*) einen Gefallen tun (+ *dat*); **much ~ed!** vielen Dank! **~ing** *a* entgegenkommend
oblique /ə'bli:k/ *a* schräg; ⟨*angle*⟩ schief; (*fig*) indirekt. **~ stroke** *n* Schrägstrich *m*
obliterate /ə'blɪtəreɪt/ *vt* auslöschen
oblivion /ə'blɪvɪən/ *n* Vergessenheit *f*
oblivious /ə'blɪvɪəs/ *a* **be ~** sich (*dat*) nicht bewusst sein (**of** *or* **to** *gen*)
oblong /'ɒblɒŋ/ *a* rechteckig □ *n* Rechteck *nt*
obnoxious /əb'nɒkʃəs/ *a* widerlich
oboe /'əʊbəʊ/ *n* Oboe *f*
obscen|e /əb'si:n/ *a* obszön; (*atrocious*) abscheulich. **~ity** /-'senətɪ/ *n* Obszönität *f*; Abscheulichkeit *f*
obscur|e /əb'skjʊə(r)/ *a* dunkel; (*unknown*) unbekannt □ *vt* verdecken; (*confuse*) verwischen. **~ity** *n* Dunkelheit *f*; Unbekanntheit *f*
obsequious /əb'si:kwɪəs/ *a* unterwürfig
observa|nce /əb'zɜ:vns/ *n* (*of custom*) Einhaltung *f*. **~nt** *a* aufmerksam. **~tion** /ɒbzə'veɪʃn/ *n* Beobachtung *f*; (*remark*) Bemerkung *f*
observatory /əb'zɜ:vətrɪ/ *n* Sternwarte *f*; (*weather*) Wetterwarte *f*
observe /əb'zɜ:v/ *vt* beobachten; (*say, notice*) bemerken; (*keep, celebrate*) feiern; (*obey*) einhalten. **~r** *n* Beobachter *m*
obsess /əb'ses/ *vt* **be ~ed by** besessen sein von. **~ion** /-eʃn/ *n* Besessenheit *f*; (*persistent idea*) fixe Idee *f*. **~ive** /-ɪv/ *a*, **-ly** *adv* zwanghaft
obsolete /'ɒbsəli:t/ *a* veraltet
obstacle /'ɒbstəkl/ *n* Hindernis *nt*
obstetrician /ɒbstə'trɪʃn/ *n* Geburtshelfer *m*. **obstetrics** /-'stetrɪks/ *n* Geburtshilfe *f*
obstina|cy /'ɒbstɪnəsɪ/ *n* Starrsinn *m*. **~te** /-nət/ *a*, **-ly** *adv* starrsinnig; ⟨*refusal*⟩ hartnäckig
obstreperous /əb'strepərəs/ *a* widerspenstig
obstruct /əb'strʌkt/ *vt* blockieren; (*hinder*) behindern. **~ion** /-ʌkʃn/ *n* Blockierung *f*; Behinderung *f*; (*obstacle*) Hindernis *nt*. **~ive** /-ɪv/ *a* **be ~ive** Schwierigkeiten bereiten
obtain /əb'teɪn/ *vt* erhalten, bekommen □ *vi* gelten. **~able** /-əbl/ *a* erhältlich
obtrusive /əb'tru:sɪv/ *a* aufdringlich; ⟨*thing*⟩ auffällig
obtuse /əb'tju:s/ *a* (*Geom*) stumpf; (*stupid*) begriffsstutzig
obviate /'ɒbvɪeɪt/ *vt* beseitigen
obvious /'ɒbvɪəs/ *a*, **-ly** *adv* offensichtlich, offenbar
occasion /ə'keɪʒn/ *n* Gelegenheit *f*; (*time*) Mal *nt*; (*event*) Ereignis *nt*; (*cause*) Anlass *m*, Grund *m*; **on ~** gelegentlich, hin und wieder;

on the ~ of anlässlich (+ *gen*) □ *vt* veranlassen
occasional /əˈkeɪʒənl/ *a* gelegentlich; **he has the ~ glass of wine** er trinkt gelegentlich ein Glas Wein. **~ly** *adv* gelegentlich, hin und wieder
occult /ɒˈkʌlt/ *a* okkult
occupant /ˈɒkjʊpənt/ *n* Bewohner(in) *m(f)*; (*of vehicle*) Insasse *m*
occupation /ɒkjʊˈpeɪʃn/ *n* Beschäftigung *f*; (*job*) Beruf *m*; (*Mil*) Besetzung *f*; (*period*) Besatzung *f*. **~al** *a* Berufs-. **~al therapy** *n* Beschäftigungstherapie *f*
occupier /ˈɒkjʊpaɪə(r)/ *n* Bewohner(in) *m(f)*
occupy /ˈɒkjʊpaɪ/ *vt* (*pt/pp* **occupied**) besetzen ⟨*seat*, (*Mil*) *country*⟩; einnehmen ⟨*space*⟩; in Anspruch nehmen ⟨*time*⟩; (*live in*) bewohnen; (*fig*) bekleiden ⟨*office*⟩; (*keep busy*) beschäftigen; **~ oneself** sich beschäftigen
occur /əˈkɜː(r)/ *vi* (*pt/pp* **occurred**) geschehen; (*exist*) vorkommen, auftreten; **it ~red to me that** es fiel mir ein, dass. **occurrence** /əˈkʌrəns/ *n* Auftreten *nt*; (*event*) Ereignis *nt*
ocean /ˈəʊʃn/ *n* Ozean *m*
o'clock /əˈklɒk/ *adv* **[at] 7 ~** [um] 7 Uhr
octagonal /ɒkˈtægənl/ *a* achteckig
octave /ˈɒktɪv/ *n* (*Mus*) Oktave *f*
October /ɒkˈtəʊbə(r)/ *n* Oktober *m*
octopus /ˈɒktəpəs/ *n* (*pl* **-puses**) Tintenfisch *m*
odd /ɒd/ *a* (**-ier, -est**) seltsam, merkwürdig; ⟨*number*⟩ ungerade; (*not of set*) einzeln; **forty ~** über vierzig; **~ jobs** Gelegenheitsarbeiten *pl*; **the ~ one out** die Ausnahme; **at ~ moments** zwischendurch; **have the ~ glass of wine** gelegentlich ein Glas Wein trinken
odd|ity /ˈɒdɪtɪ/ *n* Kuriosität *f*. **~ly** *adv* merkwürdig; **~ly enough** merkwürdigerweise. **~ment** *n* (*of fabric*) Rest *m*
odds /ɒdz/ *npl* (*chances*) Chancen *pl*; **at ~** uneinig; **~ and ends** Kleinkram *m*; **it makes no ~** es spielt keine Rolle
ode /əʊd/ *n* Ode *f*
odious /ˈəʊdɪəs/ *a* widerlich, abscheulich
odour /ˈəʊdə(r)/ *n* Geruch *m*. **~less** *a* geruchlos
oesophagus /iːˈsɒfəgəs/ *n* Speiseröhre *f*
of /ɒv, *unbetont* əv/ *prep* von (+ *dat*); (*made of*) aus (+ *dat*); **the two of us** wir zwei; **a child of three** ein dreijähriges Kind; **the fourth of January** der vierte Januar; **a pound of butter** ein Pfund Butter; **a cup of tea/coffee** eine Tasse Tee/Kaffee; **a bottle of wine** eine Flasche Wein; **half of it** die Hälfte davon; **the whole of the room** das ganze Zimmer
off /ɒf/ *prep* von (+ *dat*); **£10 ~ the price** £10 Nachlass; **~ the coast** vor der Küste; **get ~ the ladder/bus** von der Leiter/aus dem Bus steigen; **take/leave the lid ~ the saucepan** den Topf abdecken/nicht zudecken □ *adv* weg; ⟨*button, lid, handle*⟩ ab; ⟨*light*⟩ aus; ⟨*brake*⟩ los; ⟨*machine*⟩ abgeschaltet; ⟨*tap*⟩ zu; (*on appliance*) **'off'** 'aus'; **2 kilometres ~** 2 Kilometer entfernt; **a long way ~** weit weg; (*time*) noch lange hin; **~ and on** hin und wieder; **with his hat/coat ~** ohne Hut/Mantel; **with the light/lid ~** ohne Licht/Deckel; **20% ~** 20% Nachlass; **be ~** (*leave*) [weg]gehen; (*Sport*) starten; ⟨*food:*⟩ schlecht/(*all gone*) alle sein; **be better/worse ~** besser/schlechter dran sein; **be well ~** gut dran sein; (*financially*) wohlhabend sein; **have a day ~**

einen freien Tag haben; **go/drive** ~ weggehen/-fahren; **turn/take sth** ~ etw abdrehen/-nehmen
offal /'ɒfl/ *n* (*Culin*) Innereien *pl*
offence /ə'fens/ *n* (*illegal act*) Vergehen *nt*; **give/take** ~ Anstoß erregen/nehmen (**at** an + *dat*)
offend /ə'fend/ *vt* beleidigen. ~**er** *n* (*Jur*) Straftäter *m*
offensive /ə'fensɪv/ *a* anstößig; (*Mil, Sport*) offensiv □ *n* Offensive *f*
offer /'ɒfə(r)/ *n* Angebot *nt*; **on special** ~ im Sonderangebot □ *vt* anbieten (**to** *dat*); leisten ⟨*resistance*⟩; ~ **s.o. sth** jdm etw anbieten; ~ **to do sth** sich anbieten, etw zu tun. ~**ing** *n* Gabe *f*
off'hand *a* brüsk; (*casual*) lässig □ *adv* so ohne weiteres
office /'ɒfɪs/ *n* Büro *nt*; (*post*) Amt *nt*; **in** ~ im Amt; ~ **hours** *pl* Dienststunden *pl*
officer /'ɒfɪsə(r)/ *n* Offizier *m*; (*official*) Beamte(r) *m*/ Beamtin *f*; (*police*) Polizeibeamte(r) *m*/ -beamtin *f*
official /ə'fɪʃl/ *a* offiziell, amtlich □ *n* Beamte(r) *m*/ Beamtin *f*; (*Sport*) Funktionär *m*. ~**ly** *adv* offiziell
officiate /ə'fɪʃɪeɪt/ *vi* amtieren
officious /ə'fɪʃəs/ *a*, **-ly** *adv* übereifrig
'offing *n* **in the** ~ in Aussicht
'off-licence *n* Wein- und Spirituosenhandlung *f*
off-'load *vt* ausladen
'off-putting *a* (*fam*) abstoßend
off'set *vt* (*pt/pp* **-set**, *pres p* **-setting**) ausgleichen
'offshoot *n* Schössling *m*; (*fig*) Zweig *m*
'offshore *a* offshore-. ~ **rig** *n* Bohrinsel *f*
off'side *a* (*Sport*) abseits
'offspring *n* Nachwuchs *m*
off'stage *adv* hinter den Kulissen
off-'white *a* fast weiß

often /'ɒfn/ *adv* oft; **every so** ~ von Zeit zu Zeit
ogle /'əʊgl/ *vt* beäugeln
ogre /'əʊgə(r)/ *n* Menschenfresser *m*
oh /əʊ/ *int* oh! ach! **oh dear**! o weh!
oil /ɔɪl/ *n* Öl *nt*; (*petroleum*) Erdöl *nt* □ *vt* ölen
oil: ~**cloth** *n* Wachstuch *nt*. ~**field** *n* Ölfeld *nt*. ~**-painting** *n* Ölgemälde *nt*. ~ **refinery** *n* [Erd]ölraffinerie *f*. ~**skins** *npl* Ölzeug *nt*. ~**-slick** *n* Ölteppich *m*. ~**-tanker** *n* Öltanker *m*. ~ **well** *n* Ölquelle *f*
oily /'ɔɪlɪ/ *a* (**-ier, -iest**) ölig
ointment /'ɔɪntmənt/ *n* Salbe *f*
OK /əʊ'keɪ/ *a & int* (*fam*) in Ordnung; okay □ *adv* (*well*) gut □ *vt* (*auch* **okay**) (*pt/pp* **okayed**) genehmigen
old /əʊld/ *a* (**-er, -est**) alt; (*former*) ehemalig
old: ~ **'age** *n* Alter *nt*. ~**-age 'pensioner** *n* Rentner(in) *m*(*f*). ~ **boy** *n* ehemaliger Schüler. ~**-'fashioned** *a* altmodisch. ~ **girl** ehemalige Schülerin *f*. ~ **'maid** *n* alte Jungfer *f*
olive /'ɒlɪv/ *n* Olive *f*; (*colour*) Oliv *nt* □ *a* olivgrün. ~ **branch** *n* Ölzweig *m*; (*fig*) Friedensangebot *nt*. ~ **'oil** *n* Olivenöl *nt*
Olympic /ə'lɪmpɪk/ *a* olympisch □ *n* **the** ~**s** die Olympischen Spiele *pl*
omelette /'ɒmlɪt/ *n* Omelett *nt*
omen /'əʊmən/ *n* Omen *nt*
ominous /'ɒmɪnəs/ *a* bedrohlich
omission /ə'mɪʃn/ *n* Auslassung *f*; (*failure to do*) Unterlassung *f*
omit /ə'mɪt/ *vt* (*pt/pp* **omitted**) auslassen; ~ **to do sth** es unterlassen, etw zu tun
omnipotent /ɒm'nɪpətənt/ *a* allmächtig
on /ɒn/ *prep* auf (+ *dat*/(*on to*) + *acc*); (*on vertical surface*) an (+ *dat*/(*on to*) + *acc*); (*about*) über

(+ *acc*); **on Monday** [am] Montag; **on Mondays** montags; **on the first of May** am ersten Mai; **on arriving** als ich ankam; **on one's finger** am Finger; **on the right/left** rechts/links; **on the Rhine/Thames** am Rhein/an der Themse; **on the radio/television** im Radio/Fernsehen; **on the bus/train** im Bus/Zug; **go on the bus/train** mit dem Bus/Zug fahren; **get on the bus/train** in den Bus/Zug einsteigen; **on me** (*with me*) bei mir; **it's on me** (*fam*) das spendiere ich □ *adv* (*further on*) weiter; (*switched on*) an; ⟨*brake*⟩ angezogen; ⟨*machine*⟩ angeschaltet; (*on appliance*) **'on'** 'ein'; **with/without his hat/coat on** mit/ohne Hut/Mantel; **with/without the lid on** mit/ohne Deckel; **be on** ⟨*film:*⟩ laufen; ⟨*event:*⟩ stattfinden; **be on at** (*fam*) bedrängen (**zu** to); **it's not on** (*fam*) das geht nicht; **on and on** immer weiter; **on and off** hin und wieder; **and so on** und so weiter; **later on** später; **move/drive on** weitergehen/-fahren; **stick/sew on** ankleben/-nähen

once /wʌns/ *adv* einmal; (*formerly*) früher; **at ~** sofort; (*at the same time*) gleichzeitig; **~ and for all** ein für alle Mal □ *conj* wenn; (*with past tense*) als. **~-over** *n* (*fam*) **give s.o./sth the ~-over** sich (*dat*) jdn/etw kurz ansehen

'oncoming *a* **~ traffic** Gegenverkehr *m*

one /wʌn/ *a* ein(e); (*only*) einzig; **not ~** kein(e); **~ day/evening** eines Tages/Abends □ *n* Eins *f* □ *pron* eine(r)/eins; (*impersonal*) man; **which ~** welche(r,s); **~ another** einander; **~ by ~** einzeln; **~ never knows** man kann nie wissen

one: ~-eyed *a* einäugig. **~-parent 'family** *n* Einelternfamilie *f*.

~'self *pron* selbst; (*refl*) sich; **by ~self** allein. **~-sided** *a* einseitig. **~-way** *a* ⟨*street*⟩ Einbahn-; ⟨*ticket*⟩ einfach

onion /'ʌnjən/ *n* Zwiebel *f*

'onlooker *n* Zuschauer(in) *m(f)*

only /'əʊnlɪ/ *a* einzige(r,s); **an ~ child** ein Einzelkind *nt* □ *adv & conj* nur; **~ just** gerade erst; (*barely*) gerade noch

'onset *n* Beginn *m*; (*of winter*) Einsetzen *nt*

onslaught /'ɒnslɔ:t/ *n* heftiger Angriff *m*

onus /'əʊnəs/ *n* **the ~ is on me** es liegt an mir (**to** zu)

onward[s] /'ɒnwəd[z]/ *adv* vorwärts; **from then ~** von der Zeit an

ooze /u:z/ *vi* sickern

opal /'əʊpl/ *n* Opal *m*

opaque /əʊ'peɪk/ *a* undurchsichtig

open /'əʊpən/ *a*, **-ly** *adv* offen; **be ~** ⟨*shop:*⟩ geöffnet sein; **in the ~ air** im Freien □ *n* **in the ~** im Freien □ *vt* öffnen, aufmachen; (*start, set up*) eröffnen □ *vi* sich öffnen; ⟨*flower:*⟩ aufgehen; ⟨*shop:*⟩ öffnen, aufmachen; (*be started*) eröffnet werden. **~ up** *vt* öffnen, aufmachen; (*fig*) eröffnen □ *vi* sich öffnen; (*fig*) sich eröffnen

open: ~-air 'swimming pool *n* Freibad *nt*. **~ day** *n* Tag *m* der offenen Tür

opener /'əʊpənə(r)/ *n* Öffner *m*

opening /'əʊpənɪŋ/ *n* Öffnung *f*; (*beginning*) Eröffnung *f*; (*job*) Einstiegsmöglichkeit *f*. **~ hours** *npl* Öffnungszeiten *pl*

open: ~-'minded *a* aufgeschlossen. **~-plan** *a* **~-plan office** Großraumbüro *nt*. **~ 'sandwich** *n* belegtes Brot *nt*

opera /'ɒpərə/ *n* Oper *f*

operable /'ɒpərəbl/ *a* operierbar

opera: ~-glasses *npl* Opernglas *nt*. **~-house** *n* Opernhaus *nt*. **~-singer** *n* Opernsänger(in) *m(f)*

operate /ˈɒpəreɪt/ *vt* bedienen ⟨*machine, lift*⟩; betätigen ⟨*lever, brake*⟩; (*fig: run*) betreiben □ *vi* (*Techn*) funktionieren; (*be in action*) in Betrieb sein; (*Mil & fig*) operieren; **~ [on]** (*Med*) operieren
operatic /ɒpəˈrætɪk/ *a* Opern-
operation /ɒpəˈreɪʃn/ *n* (*see* **operate**) Bedienung *f*; Betätigung *f*; Operation *f*; **in ~** (*Techn*) in Betrieb; **come into ~** (*fig*) in Kraft treten; **have an ~** (*Med*) operiert werden. **~al** *a* **be ~al** in Betrieb sein; ⟨*law:*⟩ in Kraft sein
operative /ˈɒpərətɪv/ *a* wirksam
operator /ˈɒpəreɪtə(r)/ *n* (*user*) Bedienungsperson *f*; (*Teleph*) Vermittlung *f*
operetta /ɒpəˈretə/ *n* Operette *f*
opinion /əˈpɪnjən/ *n* Meinung *f*; **in my ~** meiner Meinung nach. **~ated** *a* rechthaberisch
opium /ˈəʊpɪəm/ *n* Opium *nt*
opponent /əˈpəʊnənt/ *n* Gegner(in) *m(f)*
opportun|e /ˈɒpətjuːn/ *a* günstig. **~ist** /-ˈtjuːnɪst/ *a* opportunistisch □ *n* Opportunist *m*
opportunity /ɒpəˈtjuːnətɪ/ *n* Gelegenheit *f*
oppos|e /əˈpəʊz/ *vt* Widerstand leisten (+ *dat*); (*argue against*) sprechen gegen; **be ~ed to sth** gegen etw sein; **as ~ed to** im Gegensatz zu. **~ing** *a* gegnerisch; (*opposite*) entgegengesetzt
opposite /ˈɒpəzɪt/ *a* entgegengesetzt; ⟨*house, side*⟩ gegenüberliegend; **~ number** (*fig*) Gegenstück *nt*; **the ~ sex** das andere Geschlecht □ *n* Gegenteil *nt* □ *adv* gegenüber □ *prep* gegenüber (+ *dat*)
opposition /ɒpəˈzɪʃn/ *n* Widerstand *m*; (*pol*) Opposition *f*
oppress /əˈpres/ *vt* unterdrücken. **~ion** /-eʃn/ *n* Unterdrücken *f*. **~ive** /-ɪv/ *a* tyrannisch; ⟨*heat*⟩ drückend. **~or** *n* Unterdrücker *m*
opt /ɒpt/ *vi* **~ for** sich entscheiden für; **~ out** ausscheiden (**of** aus)
optical /ˈɒptɪkl/ *a* optisch; **~ illusion** optische Täuschung *f*
optician /ɒpˈtɪʃn/ *n* Optiker *m*
optics /ˈɒptɪks/ *n* Optik *f*
optimis|m /ˈɒptɪmɪzm/ *n* Optimismus *m*. **~t** /-mɪst/ *n* Optimist *m*. **~tic** /-ˈmɪstɪk/ *a*, **-ally** *adv* optimistisch
optimum /ˈɒptɪməm/ *a* optimal □ *n* (*pl* **-ima**) Optimum *nt*
option /ˈɒpʃn/ *n* Wahl *f*; (*Comm*) Option *f*. **~al** *a* auf Wunsch erhältlich; ⟨*subject*⟩ wahlfrei; **~al extras** *pl* Extras *pl*
opu|lence /ˈɒpjʊləns/ *n* Prunk *m*; (*wealth*) Reichtum *m*. **~lent** *a* prunkvoll; (*wealthy*) sehr reich
or /ɔː(r)/ *conj* oder; (*after negative*) noch; **or [else]** sonst; **in a year or two** in ein bis zwei Jahren
oracle /ˈɒrəkl/ *n* Orakel *nt*
oral /ˈɔːrl/ *a*, **-ly** *adv* mündlich; (*Med*) oral □ *n* (*fam*) Mündliche(s) *nt*
orange /ˈɒrɪndʒ/ *n* Apfelsine *f*, Orange *f*; (*colour*) Orange *nt* □ *a* orangefarben. **~ade** /-ˈdʒeɪd/ *n* Orangeade *f*
oration /əˈreɪʃn/ *n* Rede *f*
orator /ˈɒrətə(r)/ *n* Redner *m*
oratorio /ɒrəˈtɔːrɪəʊ/ *n* Oratorium *nt*
oratory /ˈɒrətərɪ/ *n* Redekunst *f*
orbit /ˈɔːbɪt/ *n* Umlaufbahn *f* □ *vt* umkreisen. **~al** *a* **~al road** Ringstraße *f*
orchard /ˈɔːtʃəd/ *n* Obstgarten *m*
orches|tra /ˈɔːkɪstrə/ *n* Orchester *nt*. **~tral** /-ˈkestrəl/ *a* Orchester-. **~trate** *vt* orchestrieren
orchid /ˈɔːkɪd/ *n* Orchidee *f*
ordain /ɔːˈdeɪn/ *vt* bestimmen; (*Relig*) ordinieren
ordeal /ɔːˈdiːl/ *n* (*fig*) Qual *f*
order /ˈɔːdə(r)/ *n* Ordnung *f*; (*sequence*) Reihenfolge *f*; (*condition*) Zustand *m*; (*command*) Befehl *m*;

(*in restaurant*) Bestellung *f*; (*Comm*) Auftrag *m*; (*Relig, medal*) Orden *m*; **out of ~** ⟨*machine*⟩ außer Betrieb; **in ~ that** damit; **in ~ to help** um zu helfen; **take holy ~s** Geistlicher werden □ *vt* (*put in ~*) ordnen; (*command*) befehlen (+ *dat*); (*Comm, in restaurant*) bestellen; (*prescribe*) verordnen

orderly /'ɔ:dəlɪ/ *a* ordentlich; (*not unruly*) friedlich □ *n* (*Mil, Med*) Sanitäter *m*

ordinary /'ɔ:dɪnərɪ/ *a* gewöhnlich, normal; ⟨*meeting*⟩ ordentlich

ordination /ɔ:dɪ'neɪʃn/ *n* (*Relig*) Ordination *f*

ore /ɔ:(r)/ *n* Erz *nt*

organ /'ɔ:gən/ *n* (*Biol & fig*) Organ *nt*; (*Mus*) Orgel *f*

organic /ɔ:'gænɪk/ *a*, **-ally** *adv* organisch; (*without chemicals*) biodynamisch; ⟨*crop*⟩ biologisch angebaut; ⟨*food*⟩ Bio-; **~ally grown** biologisch angebaut. **~ farm** *n* Biohof *m*. **~ farming** *n* biologischer Anbau *m*

organism /'ɔ:gənɪzm/ *n* Organismus *m*

organist /'ɔ:gənɪst/ *n* Organist *m*

organization /ɔ:gənaɪ'zeɪʃn/ *n* Organisation *f*

organize /'ɔ:gənaɪz/ *vt* organisieren; veranstalten ⟨*event*⟩. **~r** *n* Organisator *m*; Veranstalter *m*

orgasm /'ɔ:gæzm/ *n* Orgasmus *m*

orgy /'ɔ:dʒɪ/ *n* Orgie *f*

Orient /'ɔ:rɪənt/ *n* Orient *m*. **o~al** /-'entl/ *a* orientalisch; **~al carpet** Orientteppich *m* □ *n* Orientale *m*/Orientalin *f*

orient|ate /'ɔ:rɪənteɪt/ *vt* **~ate oneself** sich orientieren. **~ation** /-'teɪʃn/ *n* Orientierung *f*

orifice /'ɒrɪfɪs/ *n* Öffnung *f*

origin /'ɒrɪdʒɪn/ *n* Ursprung *m*; (*of person, goods*) Herkunft *f*

original /ə'rɪdʒənl/ *a* ursprünglich; (*not copied*) original; (*new*) originell □ *n* Original *nt*. **~ity** /-'nælətɪ/ *n* Originalität *f*. **~ly** *adv* ursprünglich

originat|e /ə'rɪdʒɪneɪt/ *vi* entstehen □ *vt* hervorbringen. **~or** *n* Urheber *m*

ornament /'ɔ:nəmənt/ *n* Ziergegenstand *m*; (*decoration*) Verzierung *f*. **~al** /-'mentl/ *a* dekorativ. **~ation** /-'teɪʃn/ *n* Verzierung *f*

ornate /ɔ:'neɪt/ *a* reich verziert

ornithology /ɔ:nɪ'θɒlədʒɪ/ *n* Vogelkunde *f*

orphan /'ɔ:fn/ *n* Waisenkind *nt*, Waise *f* □ *vt* zur Waise machen; **~ed** verwaist. **~age** /-ɪdʒ/ *n* Waisenhaus *nt*

orthodox /'ɔ:θədɒks/ *a* orthodox

orthography /ɔ:'θɒgrəfɪ/ *n* Rechtschreibung *f*

orthopaedic /ɔ:θə'pi:dɪk/ *a* orthopädisch

oscillate /'ɒsɪleɪt/ *vi* schwingen

ostensible /ɒ'stensəbl/ *a*, **-bly** *adv* angeblich

ostentat|tion /ɒsten'teɪʃn/ *n* Protzerei *f* (*fam*). **~ious** /-ʃəs/ *a* protzig (*fam*)

osteopath /'ɒstɪəpæθ/ *n* Osteopath *m*

ostracize /'ɒstrəsaɪz/ *vt* ächten

ostrich /'ɒstrɪtʃ/ *n* Strauß *m*

other /'ʌðə(r)/ *a, pron & n* andere(r,s); **the ~ [one]** der/die/das andere; **the ~ two** die zwei anderen; **two ~s** zwei andere; (*more*) noch zwei; **no ~s** sonst keine; **any ~ questions?** sonst noch Fragen? **every ~ day** jeden zweiten Tag; **the ~ day** neulich; **the ~ evening** neulich abends; **someone/something or ~** irgendjemand/-etwas □ *adv* anders; **~ than him** außer ihm; **somehow/somewhere or ~** irgendwie/irgendwo

'otherwise *adv* sonst; (*differently*) anders

otter /'ɒtə(r)/ *n* Otter *m*

ouch /aʊtʃ/ *int* autsch
ought /ɔːt/ *v aux* **I/we ~ to stay** ich sollte/wir sollten eigentlich bleiben; **he ~ not to have done it** er hätte es nicht machen sollen; **that ~ to be enough** das sollte eigentlich genügen
ounce /aʊns/ *n* Unze *f* (*28, 35 g*)
our /ˈaʊə(r)/ *a* unser
ours /ˈaʊəz/ *poss pron* unsere(r,s); **a friend of ~** ein Freund von uns; **that is ~** das gehört uns
ourselves /aʊəˈselvz/ *pron* selbst; (*refl*) uns; **by ~** allein
oust /aʊst/ *vt* entfernen
out /aʊt/ *adv* (*not at home*) weg; (*outside*) draußen; (*not alight*) aus; (*unconscious*) bewusstlos; **be ~** ⟨*sun:*⟩ scheinen; ⟨*flower*⟩ blühen; ⟨*workers*⟩ streiken; ⟨*calculation:*⟩ nicht stimmen; (*Sport*) aus sein; (*fig: not feasible*) nicht infrage kommen; **~ and about** unterwegs; **have it ~ with s.o.** (*fam*) jdn zur Rede stellen; **get ~!** (*fam*) raus! **~ with it!** (*fam*) heraus damit! **go/send ~** hinausgehen/-schicken; **come/bring ~** herauskommen/-bringen □ *prep* **~ of** aus (+ *dat*); **go ~ of the door** zur Tür hinausgehen; **be ~ of bed/ the room** nicht im Bett/im Zimmer sein; **~ of breath/danger** außer Atem/Gefahr; **~ of work** arbeitslos; **nine ~ of ten** neun von zehn; **be ~ of sugar/bread** keinen Zucker/kein Brot mehr haben □ *prep* aus (+ *dat*); **go ~ the door** zur Tür hinausgehen
outˈbid *vt* (*pt/pp* **-bid**, *pres p* **-bidding**) überbieten
ˈoutboard *a* **~ motor** Außenbordmotor *m*
ˈoutbreak *n* Ausbruch *m*
ˈoutbuilding *n* Nebengebäude *nt*
ˈoutburst *n* Ausbruch *m*
ˈoutcast *n* Ausgestoßene(r) *m/f*
ˈoutcome *n* Ergebnis *nt*
ˈoutcry *n* Aufschrei *m* [der Entrüstung]
outˈdated *a* überholt
outˈdo *vt* (*pt* **-did**, *pp* **-done**) übertreffen, übertrumpfen
ˈoutdoor *a* ⟨*life, sports*⟩ im Freien; **~ shoes** *pl* Straßenschuhe *pl*; **~ swimming pool** Freibad *nt*
outˈdoors *adv* draußen; **go ~** nach draußen gehen
ˈouter *a* äußere(r,s)
ˈoutfit *n* Ausstattung *f*; (*clothes*) Ensemble *nt*; (*fam: organization*) Betrieb *m*; (*fam*) Laden *m*. **~ter** *n* **men's ~ter's** Herrenbekleidungsgeschäft *nt*
ˈoutgoing *a* ausscheidend; ⟨*mail*⟩ ausgehend; (*sociable*) kontaktfreudig. **~s** *npl* Ausgaben *pl*
outˈgrow *vi* (*pt* **-grew**, *pp* **-grown**) herauswachsen aus
ˈouthouse *n* Nebengebäude *nt*
outing /ˈaʊtɪŋ/ *n* Ausflug *m*
outlandish /aʊtˈlændɪʃ/ *a* ungewöhnlich
ˈoutlaw *n* Geächtete(r) *m/f* □ *vt* ächten
ˈoutlay *n* Auslagen *pl*
ˈoutlet *n* Abzug *m*; (*for water*) Abfluss *m*; (*fig*) Ventil *nt*; (*Comm*) Absatzmöglichkeit *f*
ˈoutline *n* Umriss *m*; (*summary*) kurze Darstellung *f* □ *vt* umreißen
outˈlive *vt* überleben
ˈoutlook *n* Aussicht *f*; (*future prospect*) Aussichten *pl*; (*attitude*) Einstellung *f*
ˈoutlying *a* entlegen; **~ areas** *pl* Außengebiete *pl*
outˈmoded *a* überholt
outˈnumber *vt* zahlenmäßig überlegen sein (+ *dat*)
ˈout-patient *n* ambulanter Patient *m*; **~s' department** Ambulanz *f*
ˈoutpost *n* Vorposten *m*
ˈoutput *n* Leistung *f*; Produktion *f*
ˈoutrage *n* Gräueltat *f*; (*fig*) Skandal *m*; (*indignation*) Empörung *f*

□ *vt* empören. **~ous** /-'reɪdʒəs/ *a* empörend

'outright1 *a* völlig, total; ⟨*refusal*⟩ glatt

out'right2 *adv* ganz; (*at once*) sofort; (*frankly*) offen

'outset *n* Anfang *m*; **from the ~** von Anfang an

'outside1 *a* äußere(r,s); **~ wall** Außenwand *f* □ *n* Außenseite *f*; **from the ~** von außen; **at the ~** höchstens

out'side2 *adv* außen; (*out of doors*) draußen; **go ~** nach draußen gehen □ *prep* außerhalb (+ *gen*); (*in front of*) vor (+ *dat/acc*)

out'sider *n* Außenseiter *m*

'outsize *a* übergroß

'outskirts *npl* Rand *m*

out'spoken *a* offen; **be ~** kein Blatt vor den Mund nehmen

out'standing *a* hervorragend; (*conspicuous*) bemerkenswert; (*not settled*) unerledigt; (*Comm*) ausstehend

'outstretched *a* ausgestreckt

out'strip *vt* (*pt/pp* **-stripped**) davonlaufen (+ *dat*); (*fig*) übertreffen

out'vote *vt* überstimmen

'outward /-wəd/ *a* äußerlich; **~ journey** Hinreise *f* □ *adv* nach außen; **be ~ bound** ⟨*ship:*⟩ auslaufen. **~ly** *adv* nach außen hin, äußerlich. **~s** *adv* nach außen

out'weigh *vt* überwiegen

out'wit *vt* (*pt/pp* **-witted**) überlisten

oval /'əʊvl/ *a* oval □ *n* Oval *nt*

ovary /'əʊvərɪ/ *n* (*Anat*) Eierstock *m*

ovation /əʊ'veɪʃn/ *n* Ovation *f*

oven /'ʌvn/ *n* Backofen *m*. **~-ready** *a* bratfertig

over /'əʊvə(r)/ *prep* über (+ *acc/dat*); **~ dinner** beim Essen; **~ the weekend** übers Wochenende; **~ the phone** am Telefon; **~ the page** auf der nächsten Seite; **all ~ Germany** in ganz Deutschland; ⟨*travel*⟩ durch ganz Deutschland; **all ~ the place** (*fam*) überall □ *adv* (*remaining*) übrig; (*ended*) zu Ende; **~ again** noch einmal; **~ and ~** immer wieder; **~ here/there** hier/da drüben; **all ~** (*everywhere*) überall; **it's all ~** es ist vorbei; **I ache all ~** mir tut alles weh; **go/drive ~** hinübergehen/-fahren; **come/bring ~** herüberkommen/-bringen; **turn ~** herumdrehen

overall1 /'əʊvərɔːl/ *n* Kittel *m*; **~s** *pl* Overall *m*

overall2 /əʊvər'ɔːl/ *a* gesamt; (*general*) allgemein □ *adv* insgesamt

over'awe *vt* (*fig*) überwältigen

over'balance *vi* das Gleichgewicht verlieren

over'bearing *a* herrisch

'overboard *adv* (*Naut*) über Bord

'overcast *a* bedeckt

over'charge *vt* **~ s.o.** jdm zu viel berechnen □ *vi* zu viel verlangen

'overcoat *n* Mantel *m*

over'come *vt* (*pt* **-came**, *pp* **-come**) überwinden; **be ~ by** überwältigt werden von

over'crowded *a* überfüllt

over'do *vt* (*pt* **-did**, *pp* **-done**) übertreiben; (*cook too long*) zu lange kochen; **~ it** (*fam: do too much*) sich übernehmen

'overdose *n* Überdosis *f*

'overdraft *n* [Konto]überziehung *f*; **have an ~** sein Konto überzogen haben

over'draw *vt* (*pt* **-drew**, *pp* **-drawn**) (*Comm*) überziehen

over'due *a* überfällig

over'estimate *vt* überschätzen

'overflow1 *n* Überschuss *m*; (*outlet*) Überlauf *m*

over'flow2 *vi* überlaufen

over'grown *a* ⟨*garden*⟩ überwachsen

'overhang1 *n* Überhang *m*

over'hang2 *vt/i* (*pt/pp* **-hung**) überhängen (über + *acc*)

'overhaul[1] *n* Überholung *f*
over'haul[2] *vt* (*Techn*) überholen
over'head[1] *adv* oben
'overhead[2] *a* Ober-; (*ceiling*) Decken-. **~s** *npl* allgemeine Unkosten *pl*
over'hear *vt* (*pt/pp* **-heard**) mit anhören ⟨*conversation*⟩; **I overheard him saying it** ich hörte zufällig, wie er das sagte
over'heat *vi* zu heiß werden □ *vt* zu stark erhitzen
over'joyed *a* überglücklich
'overland *a & adv* /--'-/ auf dem Landweg; **~ route** Landroute *f*
over'lap *v* (*pt/pp* **-lapped**) □ *vi* sich überschneiden □ *vt* überlappen
over'leaf *adv* umseitig
over'load *vt* überladen; (*Electr*) überlasten
'overlook[1] *n* (*Amer*) Aussichtspunkt *m*
over'look[2] *vt* überblicken; (*fail to see, ignore*) übersehen
overly /'əʊvəlɪ/ *adv* übermäßig
over'night[1] *adv* über Nacht; **stay ~** übernachten
'overnight[2] *a* Nacht-; **~ stay** Übernachtung *f*
'overpass *n* Überführung *f*
over'pay *vt* (*pt/pp* **-paid**) überbezahlen
over'populated *a* übervölkert
over'power *vt* überwältigen. **~ing** *a* überwältigend
over'priced *a* zu teuer
overpro'duce *vt* überproduzieren
over'rate *vt* überschätzen. **~d** *a* überbewertet
over'reach *vt* **~ oneself** sich übernehmen
overre'act *vi* überreagieren. **~ion** *n* Überreaktion *f*
over'rid|e *vt* (*pt* **-rode**, *pp* **-ridden**) sich hinwegsetzen über (+ *acc*). **~ing** *a* Haupt-
over'rule *vt* ablehnen; **we were ~d** wir wurden überstimmt
over'run *vt* (*pt* **-ran**, *pp* **-run**, *pres p* **-running**) überrennen; überschreiten ⟨*time*⟩; **be ~ with** überlaufen sein von
over'seas[1] *adv* in Übersee; **go ~** nach Übersee gehen
'overseas[2] *a* Übersee-
over'see *vt* (*pt* **-saw**, *pp* **-seen**) beaufsichtigen
'overseer /-sɪə(r)/ *n* Aufseher *m*
over'shadow *vt* überschatten
over'shoot *vt* (*pt/pp* **-shot**) hinausschießen über (+ *acc*)
'oversight *n* Versehen *nt*
over'sleep *vi* (*pt/pp* **-slept**) [sich] verschlafen
over'step *vt* (*pt/pp* **-stepped**) überschreiten
over'strain *vt* überanstrengen
overt /əʊ'vɜːt/ *a* offen
over'tak|e *vt/i* (*pt* **-took**, *pp* **-taken**) überholen. **~ing** *n* Überholen *nt*; **no ~ing** Überholverbot *nt*
over'tax *vt* zu hoch besteuern; (*fig*) überfordern
'overthrow[1] *n* (*Pol*) Sturz *m*
over'throw[2] *vt* (*pt* **-threw**, *pp* **-thrown**) (*Pol*) stürzen
'overtime *n* Überstunden *pl* □ *adv* **work ~** Überstunden machen
over'tired *a* übermüdet
'overtone *n* (*fig*) Unterton *m*
overture /'əʊvətjʊə(r)/ *n* (*Mus*) Ouvertüre *f*; **~s** *pl* (*fig*) Annäherungsversuche *pl*
over'turn *vt* umstoßen □ *vi* umkippen
over'weight *a* übergewichtig; **be ~** Übergewicht haben
overwhelm /-'welm/ *vt* überwältigen. **~ing** *a* überwältigend
over'work *n* Überarbeitung *f* □ *vt* überfordern □ *vi* sich überarbeiten
over'wrought *a* überreizt
ovulation /ɒvjʊ'leɪʃn/ *n* Eisprung *m*

ow|e /əʊ/ *vt* schulden/ (*fig*) verdanken (**[to]** **s.o.** jdm); **~e s.o. sth** jdm etw schuldig sein; **be ~ing** ⟨*money:*⟩ ausstehen. **'~ing to** *prep* wegen (+ *gen*)

owl /aʊl/ *n* Eule *f*

own¹ /əʊn/ *a & pron* eigen; **it's my ~** es gehört mir; **a car of my ~** mein eigenes Auto; **on one's ~** allein; **hold one's ~** sich behaupten; **get one's ~ back** (*fam*) sich revanchieren

own² *vt* besitzen; (*confess*) zugeben; **I don't ~ it** es gehört mir nicht. **~ up** *vi* es zugeben

owner /'əʊnə(r)/ *n* Eigentümer(in) *m(f)*, Besitzer(in) *m(f)*; (*of shop*) Inhaber(in) *m(f)*. **~ship** *n* Besitz *m*

ox /ɒks/ *n* (*pl* **oxen**) Ochse *m*

oxide /'ɒksaɪd/ *n* Oxid *nt*

oxygen /'ɒksɪdʒən/ *n* Sauerstoff *m*

oyster /'ɔɪstə(r)/ *n* Auster *f*

ozone /'əʊzəʊn/ *n* Ozon *nt*. **~-'friendly** *a* ≈ ohne FCKW. **~ layer** *n* Ozonschicht *f*

P

pace /peɪs/ *n* Schritt *m*; (*speed*) Tempo *nt*; **keep ~ with** Schritt halten mit □ *vi* **~ up and down** auf und ab gehen. **~-maker** *n* (*Sport & Med*) Schrittmacher *m*

Pacific /pə'sɪfɪk/ *a & n* **the ~ [Ocean]** der Pazifik

pacifier /'pæsɪfaɪə(r)/ *n* (*Amer*) Schnuller *m*

pacifist /'pæsɪfɪst/ *n* Pazifist *m*

pacify /'pæsɪfaɪ/ *vt* (*pt/pp* **-ied**) beruhigen

pack /pæk/ *n* Packung *f*; (*Mil*) Tornister *m*; (*of cards*) [Karten]-spiel *nt*; (*gang*) Bande *f*; (*of hounds*) Meute *f*; (*of wolves*) Rudel *nt*; **a ~ of lies** ein Haufen Lügen □ *vt/i* packen; einpacken ⟨*article*⟩; **be ~ed** (*crowded*) [gedrängt] voll sein; **send s.o. ~ing** (*fam*) jdn wegschicken. **~ up** *vt* einpacken □ *vi* (*fam*) ⟨*machine:*⟩ kaputtgehen; ⟨*person:*⟩ einpacken (*fam*)

package /'pækɪdʒ/ *n* Paket *nt* □ *vt* verpacken. **~ holiday** *n* Pauschalreise *f*

packed 'lunch *n* Lunchpaket *nt*

packet /'pækɪt/ *n* Päckchen *nt*; **cost a ~** (*fam*) einen Haufen Geld kosten

packing /'pækɪŋ/ *n* Verpackung *f*

pact /pækt/ *n* Pakt *m*

pad¹ /pæd/ *n* Polster *nt*; (*for writing*) [Schreib]block *m*; (*fam: home*) Wohnung *f* □ *vt* (*pt/pp* **padded**) polstern

pad² *vi* (*pt/pp* **padded**) tappen

padding /'pædɪŋ/ *n* Polsterung *f*; (*in written work*) Füllwerk *nt*

paddle¹ /'pædl/ *n* Paddel *nt* □ *vt* (*row*) paddeln

paddle² *vi* waten

paddock /'pædək/ *n* Koppel *f*

padlock /'pædlɒk/ *n* Vorhängeschloss *nt* □ *vt* mit einem Vorhängeschloss verschließen

paediatrician /pi:dɪə'trɪʃn/ *n* Kinderarzt *m* /-ärztin *f*

pagan /'peɪgən/ *a* heidnisch □ *n* Heide *m*/Heidin *f*

page¹ /peɪdʒ/ *n* Seite *f*

page² *n* (*boy*) Page *m* □ *vt* ausrufen ⟨*person*⟩

pageant /'pædʒənt/ *n* Festzug *m*. **~ry** *n* Prunk *m*

paid /'peɪd/ *see* **pay** □ *a* bezahlt; **put ~ to** (*fam*) zunichte machen

pail /peɪl/ *n* Eimer *m*

pain /peɪn/ *n* Schmerz *m*; **be in ~** Schmerzen haben; **take ~s** sich (*dat*) Mühe geben; **~ in the neck** (*fam*) Nervensäge *f* □ *vt* (*fig*) schmerzen

pain: ~ful *a* schmerzhaft; (*fig*) schmerzlich. **~-killer** *n*

schmerzstillendes Mittel *nt*. ~**less** *a*, **-ly** *adv* schmerzlos
painstaking /'peɪnzteɪkɪŋ/ *a* sorgfältig
paint /peɪnt/ *n* Farbe *f* □ *vt/i* streichen; ⟨*artist:*⟩ malen. ~**brush** *n* Pinsel *m*. ~**er** *n* Maler *m*; (*decorator*) Anstreicher *m*. ~**ing** *n* Malerei *f*; (*picture*) Gemälde *nt*
pair /peə(r)/ *n* Paar *nt*; ~ **of trousers** Hose*f*; ~ **of scissors** Schere *f* □ *vt* paaren □ *vi* ~ **off** Paare bilden
pajamas /pə'dʒɑːməz/ *n pl* (*Amer*) Schlafanzug *m*
Pakistan /pɑːkɪ'stɑːn/ *n* Pakistan *nt*. ~**i** *a* pakistanisch □ *n* Pakistaner(in) *m(f)*
pal /pæl/ *n* Freund(in) *m(f)*
palace /'pælɪs/ *n* Palast *m*
palatable /'pælətəbl/ *a* schmackhaft
palate /'pælət/ *n* Gaumen *m*
palatial /pə'leɪʃl/ *a* palastartig
palaver /pə'lɑːvə(r)/ *n* (*fam: fuss*) Theater *nt* (*fam*)
pale1 /peɪl/ *n* (*stake*) Pfahl *m*; **beyond the** ~ (*fam*) unmöglich
pale2 *a* (**-r, -st**) blass □ *vi* blass werden. ~**ness** *n* Blässe *f*
Palestin|e /'pælɪstaɪn/ *n* Palästina *nt*. ~**ian** /pælə'stɪnɪən/ *a* palästinensisch □ *n* Palästinenser(in) *m(f)*
palette /'pælɪt/ *n* Palette *f*
pall /pɔːl/ *n* Sargtuch *nt*; (*fig*) Decke *f* □ *vi* an Reiz verlieren
pall|id /'pælɪd/ *a* bleich. ~**or** *n* Blässe *f*
palm /pɑːm/ *n* Handfläche *f*; (*tree, symbol*) Palme *f* □ *vt* ~ **sth off on s.o.** jdm etw andrehen. **P**~ **'Sunday** *n* Palmsonntag *m*
palpable /'pælpəbl/ *a* tastbar; (*perceptible*) spürbar
palpitat|e /'pælpɪteɪt/ *vi* klopfen. ~**ions** /-'teɪʃnz/ *npl* Herzklopfen *nt*
paltry /'pɔːltrɪ/ *a* (**-ier, -iest**) armselig
pamper /'pæmpə(r)/ *vt* verwöhnen
pamphlet /'pæmflɪt/ *n* Broschüre *f*
pan /pæn/ *n* Pfanne *f*; (*saucepan*) Topf *m*; (*of scales*) Schale *f* □ *vt* (*pt/pp* **panned**) (*fam*) verreißen
panacea /pænə'siːə/ *n* Allheilmittel *nt*
panache /pə'næʃ/ *n* Schwung *m*
'pancake *n* Pfannkuchen *m*
pancreas /'pæŋkrɪəs/ *n* Bauchspeicheldrüse *f*
panda /'pændə/ *n* Panda *m*. ~ **car** *n* Streifenwagen *m*
pandemonium /pændɪ'məʊnɪəm/ *n* Höllenlärm *m*
pander /'pændə(r)/ *vi* ~ **to s.o.** jdm zu sehr nachgeben
pane /peɪn/ *n* [Glas]scheibe *f*
panel /'pænl/ *n* Tafel *f*, Platte *f*; ~ **of experts** Expertenrunde *f*; ~ **of judges** Jury *f*. ~**ling** *n* Täfelung *f*
pang /pæŋ/ *n* ~**s of hunger** Hungergefühl *nt*; ~**s of conscience** Gewissensbisse *pl*
panic /'pænɪk/ *n* Panik *f* □ *vi* (*pt/pp* **panicked**) in Panik geraten. ~**-stricken** *a* von Panik ergriffen
panoram|a /pænə'rɑːmə/ *n* Panorama *nt*. ~**ic** /-'ræmɪk/ *a* Panorama-
pansy /'pænzɪ/ *n* Stiefmütterchen *nt*
pant /pænt/ *vi* keuchen; ⟨*dog:*⟩ hecheln
pantechnicon /pæn'teknɪkən/ *n* Möbelwagen *m*
panther /'pænθə(r)/ *n* Panther *m*
panties /'pæntɪz/ *npl* [Damen]slip *m*
pantomime /'pæntəmaɪm/ *n* [zu Weihnachten aufgeführte] Märchenvorstellung *f*
pantry /'pæntrɪ/ *n* Speisekammer *f*
pants /pænts/ *npl* Unterhose *f*; (*woman's*) Schlüpfer *m*; (*trousers*) Hose *f*

'pantyhose *n* (*Amer*) Strumpfhose *f*

papal /'peɪpl/ *a* päpstlich

paper /'peɪpə(r)/ *n* Papier *nt*; (*wall*~) Tapete *f*; (*newspaper*) Zeitung *f*; (*exam*~) Testbogen *m*; (*exam*) Klausur *f*; (*treatise*) Referat *nt*; **~s** *pl* (*documents*) Unterlagen *pl*; (*for identification*) [Ausweis]papiere *pl*; **on ~** schriftlich □ *vt* tapezieren

paper: ~back *n* Taschenbuch *nt*. **~-clip** *n* Büroklammer *f*. **~-knife** *n* Brieföffner *m*. **~weight** *n* Briefbeschwerer *m*. **~work** *n* Schreibarbeit *f*

par /pɑ:(r)/ *n* (*Golf*) Par *nt*; **on a ~** gleichwertig (**with** *dat*); **feel below ~** sich nicht ganz auf der Höhe fühlen

parable /'pærəbl/ *n* Gleichnis *nt*

parachut|e /'pærəʃu:t/ *n* Fallschirm *m* □ *vi* [mit dem Fallschirm] abspringen. **~ist** *n* Fallschirmspringer *m*

parade /pə'reɪd/ *n* Parade *f*; (*procession*) Festzug *m* □ *vi* marschieren □ *vt* (*show off*) zur Schau stellen

paradise /'pærədaɪs/ *n* Paradies *nt*

paradox /'pærədɒks/ *n* Paradox *nt*. **~ical** /-'dɒksɪkl/ paradox

paraffin /'pærəfɪn/ *n* Paraffin *nt*

paragon /'pærəgən/ *n* **~ of virtue** Ausbund *m* der Tugend

paragraph /'pærəgrɑ:f/ *n* Absatz *m*

parallel /'pærəlel/ *a* & *adv* parallel □ *n* (*Geog*) Breitenkreis *m*; (*fig*) Parallele *f*

paralyse /'pærəlaɪz/ *vt* lähmen; (*fig*) lahmlegen

paralysis /pə'ræləsɪs/ *n* (*pl* **-ses** /-si:z/) Lähmung *f*

paramount /'pærəmaʊnt/ *a* überragend; **be ~** vorgehen

paranoid /'pærənɔɪd/ *a* [krankhaft] misstrauisch

parapet /'pærəpɪt/ *n* Brüstung *f*

paraphernalia /pærəfə'neɪlɪə/ *n* Kram *m*

paraphrase /'pærəfreɪz/ *n* Umschreibung *f* □ *vt* umschreiben

paraplegic /pærə'pli:dʒɪk/ *a* querschnittsgelähmt □ *n* Querschnittsgelähmte(r) *m/f*

parasite /'pærəsaɪt/ *n* Parasit *m*, Schmarotzer *m*

parasol /'pærəsɒl/ *n* Sonnenschirm *m*

paratrooper /'pærətru:pə(r)/ *n* Fallschirmjäger *m*

parcel /'pɑ:sl/ *n* Paket *nt*

parch /pɑ:tʃ/ *vt* austrocknen; **be ~ed** ⟨*person:*⟩ einen furchtbaren Durst haben

parchment /'pɑ:tʃmənt/ *n* Pergament *nt*

pardon /'pɑ:dn/ *n* Verzeihung *f*; (*Jur*) Begnadigung *f*; **~?** (*fam*) bitte? **I beg your ~** wie bitte? (*sorry*) Verzeihung! □ *vt* verzeihen; (*Jur*) begnadigen

pare /peə(r)/ *vt* (*peel*) schälen

parent /'peərənt/ *n* Elternteil *m*; **~s** *pl* Eltern *pl*. **~al** /pə'rentl/ *a* elterlich

parenthesis /pə'renθəsɪs/ *n* (*pl* **-ses** /-si:z/) Klammer *f*

parish /'pærɪʃ/ *n* Gemeinde *f*. **~ioner** /pə'rɪʃənə(r)/ *n* Gemeindemitglied *nt*

parity /'pærətɪ/ *n* Gleichheit *f*

park /pɑ:k/ *n* Park *m* □ *vt/i* parken

parking /'pɑ:kɪŋ/ *n* Parken *nt*; **'no ~'** 'Parken verboten'. **~-lot** *n* (*Amer*) Parkplatz *m*. **~-meter** *n* Parkuhr *f*. **~ space** *n* Parkplatz *m*

parliament /'pɑ:ləmənt/ *n* Parlament *nt*. **~ary** /-'mentərɪ/ *a* parlamentarisch

parlour /'pɑ:lə(r)/ *n* Wohnzimmer *nt*

parochial /pə'rəʊkɪəl/ *a* Gemeinde-; (*fig*) beschränkt

parody /ˈpærədɪ/ *n* Parodie *f* □ *vt* (*pt/pp* **-ied**) parodieren
parole /pəˈrəʊl/ *n* **on ~** auf Bewährung
paroxysm /ˈpærəksɪzm/ *n* Anfall *m*
parquet /ˈpɑːkeɪ/ *n* **~ floor** Parkett *nt*
parrot /ˈpærət/ *n* Papagei *m*
parry /ˈpærɪ/ *vt* (*pt/pp* **-ied**) abwehren ⟨*blow*⟩; (*Fencing*) parieren
parsimonious /pɑːsɪˈməʊnɪəs/ *a* geizig
parsley /ˈpɑːslɪ/ *n* Petersilie *f*
parsnip /ˈpɑːsnɪp/ *n* Pastinake *f*
parson /ˈpɑːsn/ *n* Pfarrer *m*
part /pɑːt/ *n* Teil *m*; (*Techn*) Teil *nt*; (*area*) Gegend *f*; (*Theat*) Rolle *f*; (*Mus*) Part *m*; **spare ~** Ersatzteil *nt*; **for my ~** meinerseits; **on the ~ of** vonseiten (+ *gen*); **take s.o.'s ~** für jdn Partei ergreifen; **take ~ in** teilnehmen an (+ *dat*) □ *adv* teils □ *vt* trennen; scheiteln ⟨*hair*⟩ □ *vi* ⟨*people*:⟩ sich trennen; **~ with** sich trennen von
partake /pɑːˈteɪk/ *vt* (*pt* **-took**, *pp* **-taken**) teilnehmen; **~ of** (*eat*) zu sich nehmen
part-exˈchange *n* **take in ~** in Zahlung nehmen
partial /ˈpɑːʃl/ *a* Teil-; **be ~ to** mögen. **~ity** /pɑːʃɪˈælətɪ/ *n* Voreingenommenheit *f*; (*liking*) Vorliebe *f*. **-ly** *adv* teilweise
particip|ant /pɑːˈtɪsɪpənt/ *n* Teilnehmer(in) *m(f)*. **~ate** /-peɪt/ *vi* teilnehmen (**in** an + *dat*). **~ation** /-ˈpeɪʃn/ *n* Teilnahme *f*
participle /ˈpɑːtɪsɪpl/ *n* Partizip *nt*; **present/past ~** erstes/zweites Partizip *nt*
particle /ˈpɑːtɪkl/ *n* Körnchen *nt*; (*Phys*) Partikel *nt*; (*Gram*) Partikel *f*
particular /pəˈtɪkjʊlə(r)/ *a* besondere(r,s); (*precise*) genau; (*fastidious*) penibel; **in ~** besonders. **~ly** *adv* besonders. **~s** *npl* nähere Angaben *pl*

parting /ˈpɑːtɪŋ/ *n* Abschied *m*; (*in hair*) Scheitel *m* □ *attrib* Abschieds-
partition /pɑːˈtɪʃn/ *n* Trennwand *f*; (*Pol*) Teilung *f* □ *vt* teilen. **~ off** *vt* abtrennen
partly /ˈpɑːtlɪ/ *adv* teilweise
partner /ˈpɑːtnə(r)/ *n* Partner(in) *m(f)*; (*Comm*) Teilhaber *m*. **~ship** *n* Partnerschaft *f*; (*Comm*) Teilhaberschaft *f*
partridge /ˈpɑːtrɪdʒ/ *n* Rebhuhn *nt*
part-ˈtime *a & adv* Teilzeit-; **be** *or* **work ~** Teilzeitarbeit machen
party /ˈpɑːtɪ/ *n* Party *f*, Fest *nt*; (*group*) Gruppe *f*; (*Pol*, *Jur*) Partei *f*; **be ~ to** sich beteiligen an (+ *dat*)
ˈ**party line**[1] *n* (*Teleph*) Gemeinschaftsanschluss *m*
party ˈline[2] *n* (*Pol*) Parteilinie *f*
pass /pɑːs/ *n* Ausweis *m*; (*Geog*, *Sport*) Pass *m*; (*Sch*) ≈ ausreichend; **get a ~** bestehen □ *vt* vorbeigehen/-fahren an (+ *dat*); (*overtake*) überholen; (*hand*) reichen; (*Sport*) abgeben, abspielen; (*approve*) annehmen; (*exceed*) übersteigen; bestehen ⟨*exam*⟩; machen ⟨*remark*⟩; fällen ⟨*judgement*⟩; (*Jur*) verhängen ⟨*sentence*⟩; **~ water** Wasser lassen; **~ the time** sich (*dat*) die Zeit vertreiben; **~ sth off as sth** etw als etw ausgeben; **~ one's hand over sth** mit der Hand über etw (*acc*) fahren □ *vi* vorbeigehen/-fahren; (*get by*) vorbeikommen; (*overtake*) überholen; ⟨*time*:⟩ vergehen; (*in exam*) bestehen; **let sth ~** (*fig*) etw übergehen; **[I] ~!** [ich] passe! **~ away** *vi* sterben. **~ down** *vt* herunterreichen; (*fig*) weitergeben. **~ out** *vi* ohnmächtig werden. **~ round** *vt* herumreichen. **~ up** *vt* heraufreichen; (*fam: miss*) vorübergehen lassen
passable /ˈpɑːsəbl/ *a* ⟨*road*⟩ befahrbar; (*satisfactory*) passabel

passage /ˈpæsɪdʒ/ *n* Durchgang *m*; (*corridor*) Gang *m*; (*voyage*) Überfahrt *f*; (*in book*) Passage *f*
passenger /ˈpæsɪndʒə(r)/ *n* Fahrgast *m*; (*Naut, Aviat*) Passagier *m*; (*in car*) Mitfahrer *m*. **~ seat** *n* Beifahrersitz *m*
passer-by /pɑːsəˈbaɪ/ *n* (*pl* **-s-by**) Passant(in) *m*(*f*)
ˈ**passing place** *n* Ausweichstelle *f*
passion /ˈpæʃn/ *n* Leidenschaft *f*. **~ate** /-ət/ *a*, **-ly** *adv* leidenschaftlich
passive /ˈpæsɪv/ *a* passiv □ *n* Passiv *nt*
Passover /ˈpɑːsəʊvə(r)/ *n* Passah *nt*
pass: **~port** *n* [Reise]pass *m*. **~word** *n* Kennwort *nt*; (*Mil*) Losung *f*
past /pɑːst/ *a* vergangene(r,s); (*former*) ehemalig; **in the ~ few days** in den letzten paar Tagen; **that's all ~** das ist jetzt vorbei □ *n* Vergangenheit *f* □ *prep* an (+ *dat*) . . . vorbei; (*after*) nach; **at ten ~ two** um zehn nach zwei □ *adv* vorbei; **go/come ~** vorbeigehen/-kommen
pasta /ˈpæstə/ *n* Nudeln *pl*
paste /peɪst/ *n* Brei *m*; (*dough*) Teig *m*; (*fish-, meat-*) Paste *f*; (*adhesive*) Kleister *m*; (*jewellery*) Strass *m* □ *vt* kleistern
pastel /ˈpæstl/ *n* Pastellfarbe *f*; (*crayon*) Pastellstift *m*; (*drawing*) Pastell *nt* □ *attrib* Pastell-
pasteurize /ˈpɑːstʃəraɪz/ *vt* pasteurisieren
pastille /ˈpæstɪl/ *n* Pastille *f*
pastime /ˈpɑːstaɪm/ *n* Zeitvertreib *m*
pastoral /ˈpɑːstərl/ *a* ländlich; ⟨*care*⟩ seelsorgerisch
pastr|y /ˈpeɪstrɪ/ *n* Teig *m*; **cakes and ~ies** Kuchen und Gebäck
pasture /ˈpɑːstʃə(r)/ *n* Weide *f*
pasty[1] /ˈpæstɪ/ *n* Pastete *f*
pasty[2] /ˈpeɪstɪ/ *a* blass, (*fam*) käsig
pat /pæt/ *n* Klaps *m*; (*of butter*) Stückchen *nt* □ *adv* **have sth off ~** etw aus dem Effeff können □ *vt* (*pt/pp* **patted**) tätscheln; **~ s.o. on the back** jdm auf die Schulter klopfen
patch /pætʃ/ *n* Flicken *m*; (*spot*) Fleck *m*; **not a ~ on** (*fam*) gar nicht zu vergleichen mit □ *vt* flicken. **~ up** *vt* [zusammen]flicken; beilegen ⟨*quarrel*⟩
patchy /ˈpætʃɪ/ *a* ungleichmäßig
pâté /ˈpæteɪ/ *n* Pastete *f*
patent /ˈpeɪtnt/ *a*, **-ly** *adv* offensichtlich □ *n* Patent *nt* □ *vt* patentieren. **~ leather** *n* Lackleder *nt*
patern|al /pəˈtɜːnl/ *a* väterlich. **~ity** *n* Vaterschaft *f*
path /pɑːθ/ *n* (*pl* **~s** /pɑːðz/) [Fuß]weg *m*, Pfad *m*; (*orbit, track*) Bahn *f*; (*fig*) Weg *m*
pathetic /pəˈθetɪk/ *a* mitleiderregend; ⟨*attempt*⟩ erbärmlich
patholog|ical /pæθəˈlɒdʒɪkl/ *a* pathologisch. **~ist** /pəˈθɒlədʒɪst/ *n* Pathologe *m*
pathos /ˈpeɪθɒs/ *n* Rührseligkeit *f*
patience /ˈpeɪʃns/ *n* Geduld *f*; (*game*) Patience *f*
patient /ˈpeɪʃnt/ *a*, **-ly** *adv* geduldig □ *n* Patient(in) *m*(*f*)
patio /ˈpætɪəʊ/ *n* Terrasse *f*
patriot /ˈpætrɪət/ *n* Patriot(in) *m*(*f*). **~ic** /-ˈɒtɪk/ *a* patriotisch. **~ism** *n* Patriotismus *m*
Patrol /pəˈtrəʊl/ *n* Patrouille *f* □ *vt/i* patrouillieren [in (+ *dat*)]; ⟨*police:*⟩ auf Streife gehen/fahren [in (+ *dat*)]. **~ car** *n* Streifenwagen *m*
patron /ˈpeɪtrən/ *n* Gönner *m*; (*of charity*) Schirmherr *m*; (*of the arts*) Mäzen *m*; (*customer*) Kunde *m*/Kundin *f*; (*Theat*) Besucher *m*. **~age** /ˈpætrənɪdʒ/ *n* Schirmherrschaft *f*

patroniz|e /ˈpætrənaɪz/ *vt* (*fig*) herablassend behandeln. **~ing** *a*, **-ly** *adv* gönnerhaft

patter¹ /ˈpætə(r)/ *n* Getrippel *nt*; (*of rain*) Plätschern *nt* □ *vi* trippeln; plätschern

patter² *n* (*speech*) Gerede *nt*

pattern /ˈpætn/ *n* Muster *nt*

paunch /pɔːntʃ/ *n* [Schmer]-bauch *m*

pauper /ˈpɔːpə(r)/ *n* Arme(r) *m/f*

pause /pɔːz/ *n* Pause *f* □ *vi* innehalten

pave /peɪv/ *vt* pflastern; **~ the way** den Weg bereiten (**for** *dat*). **~ment** *n* Bürgersteig *m*

pavilion /pəˈvɪljən/ *n* Pavillon *m*; (*Sport*) Klubhaus *nt*

paw /pɔː/ *n* Pfote *f*; (*of large animal*) Pranke *f*, Tatze *f*

pawn¹ /pɔːn/ *n* (*Chess*) Bauer *m*; (*fig*) Schachfigur *f*

pawn² *vt* verpfänden □ *n* **in ~** verpfändet. **~ broker** *n* Pfandleiher *m*. **~shop** *n* Pfandhaus *nt*

pay /peɪ/ *n* Lohn *m*; (*salary*) Gehalt *nt*; **be in the ~ of** bezahlt werden von □ *v* (*pt/pp* **paid**) □ *vt* bezahlen; zahlen ⟨*money*⟩; **~ s.o. a visit** jdm einen Besuch abstatten; **~ s.o. a compliment** jdm ein Kompliment machen □ *vi* zahlen; (*be profitable*) sich bezahlt machen; (*fig*) sich lohnen; **~ for sth** etw bezahlen. **~ back** *vt* zurückzahlen. **~ in** *vt* einzahlen. **~ off** *vt* abzahlen ⟨*debt*⟩ □ *vi* (*fig*) sich auszahlen. **~ up** *vi* zahlen

payable /ˈpeɪəbl/ *a* zahlbar; **make ~ to** ausstellen auf (+ *acc*)

payee /peɪˈiː/ *n* [Zahlungs]-empfänger *m*

payment /ˈpeɪmənt/ *n* Bezahlung *f*; (*amount*) Zahlung *f*

pay: ~ packet *n* Lohntüte *f*. **~ phone** *n* Münzfernsprecher *m*

pea /piː/ *n* Erbse *f*

peace /piːs/ *n* Frieden *m*; **for my ~ of mind** zu meiner eigenen Beruhigung

peace|able /ˈpiːsəbl/ *a* friedlich. **~ful** *a*, **-ly** *adv* friedlich. **~maker** *n* Friedensstifter *m*

peach /piːtʃ/ *n* Pfirsich *m*

peacock /ˈpiːkɒk/ *n* Pfau *m*

peak /piːk/ *n* Gipfel *m*; (*fig*) Höhepunkt *m*. **~ed 'cap** *n* Schirmmütze *f*. **~ hours** *npl* Hauptbelastungszeit *f*; (*for traffic*) Hauptverkehrszeit *f*

peaky /ˈpiːkɪ/ *a* kränklich

peal /piːl/ *n* (*of bells*) Glockengeläut *nt*; **~s of laughter** schallendes Gelächter *nt*

'peanut *n* Erdnuss *f*; **for ~s** (*fam*) für einen Apfel und ein Ei

pear /peə(r)/ *n* Birne *f*

pearl /pɜːl/ *n* Perle *f*

peasant /ˈpeznt/ *n* Bauer *m*

peat /piːt/ *n* Torf *m*

pebble /ˈpebl/ *n* Kieselstein *m*

peck /pek/ *n* Schnabelhieb *m*; (*kiss*) flüchtiger Kuss *m* □ *vt/i* picken/(*nip*) hacken (**at** nach). **~ing order** *n* Hackordnung *f*

peckish /ˈpekɪʃ/ *a* **be ~** (*fam*) Hunger haben

peculiar /pɪˈkjuːlɪə(r)/ *a* eigenartig, seltsam; **~ to** eigentümlich (+ *dat*). **~ity** /-ˈærətɪ/ *n* Eigenart *f*

pedal /ˈpedl/ *n* Pedal *nt* □ *vt* fahren ⟨*bicycle*⟩ □ *vi* treten. **~ bin** *n* Treteimer *m*

pedantic /pɪˈdæntɪk/ *a*, **-ally** *adv* pedantisch

peddle /ˈpedl/ *vt* handeln mit

pedestal /ˈpedɪstl/ *n* Sockel *m*

pedestrian /pɪˈdestrɪən/ *n* Fußgänger(in) *m(f)* □ *a* (*fig*) prosaisch. **~ 'crossing** *n* Fußgängerüberweg *m*. **~ 'precinct** *n* Fußgängerzone *f*

pedicure /ˈpedɪkjʊə(r)/ *n* Pediküre *f*

pedigree /ˈpedɪgriː/ *n* Stammbaum *m* □ *attrib* ⟨*animal*⟩ Rasse-

pedlar /ˈpedlə(r)/ *n* Hausierer *m*

pee /pi:/ *vi* (*pt/pp* **peed**) (*fam*) pinkeln
peek /pi:k/ *vi* (*fam*) gucken
peel /pi:l/ *n* Schale *f* □ *vt* schälen; □ *vi* ⟨*skin:*⟩ sich schälen; ⟨*paint:*⟩ abblättern. **~ings** *npl* Schalen *pl*
peep /pi:p/ *n* kurzer Blick *m* □ *vi* gucken. **~-hole** *n* Guckloch *nt*. **P~ing 'Tom** *n* (*fam*) Spanner *m*
peer[1] /pɪə(r)/ *vi* **~ at** forschend ansehen
peer[2] *n* Peer *m*; **his ~s** *pl* seinesgleichen
peev|ed /pi:vd/ *a* (*fam*) ärgerlich. **~ish** *a* reizbar
peg /peg/ *n* (*hook*) Haken *m*; (*for tent*) Pflock *m*, Hering *m*; (*for clothes*) [Wäsche]klammer *f*; **off the ~** (*fam*) von der Strange □ *vt* (*pt/pp* **pegged**) anpflocken; anklammern ⟨*washing*⟩
pejorative /pɪ'dʒɒrətɪv/ *a*, **-ly** *adv* abwertend
pelican /'pelɪkən/ *n* Pelikan *m*
pellet /'pelɪt/ *n* Kügelchen *nt*
pelt[1] /pelt/ *n* (*skin*) Pelz *m*, Fell *nt*
pelt[2] *vt* bewerfen □ *vi* (*fam: run fast*) rasen; **~ [down]** ⟨*rain:*⟩ [hernieder]prasseln
pelvis /'pelvɪs/ *n* (*Anat*) Becken *nt*
pen[1] /pen/ *n* (*for animals*) Hürde *f*
pen[2] *n* Federhalter *m*; (*ball-point*) Kugelschreiber *m*
penal /'pi:nl/ *a* Straf-. **~ize** *vt* bestrafen; (*fig*) benachteiligen
penalty /'penltɪ/ *n* Strafe *f*; (*fine*) Geldstrafe *f*; (*Sport*) Strafstoß *m*; (*Football*) Elfmeter *m*
penance /'penəns/ *n* Buße *f*
pence /pens/ *see* **penny**
pencil /'pensɪl/ *n* Bleistift *m* □ *vt* (*pt/pp* **pencilled**) mit Bleistift schreiben. **~-sharpener** *n* Bleistiftspitzer *m*
pendant /'pendənt/ *n* Anhänger *m*
pending /'pendɪŋ/ *a* unerledigt □ *prep* bis zu
pendulum /'pendjʊləm/ *n* Pendel *nt*
penetrat|e /'penɪtreɪt/ *vt* durchdringen; **~e [into]** eindringen in (+ *acc*). **~ing** *a* durchdringend. **~ion** /-'treɪʃn/ *n* Durchdringen *nt*
'penfriend *n* Brieffreund(in) *m*(*f*)
penguin /'peŋgwɪn/ *n* Pinguin *m*
penicillin /penɪ'sɪlɪn/ *n* Penizillin *nt*
peninsula /pə'nɪnsʊlə/ *n* Halbinsel *f*
penis /'pi:nɪs/ *n* Penis *m*
peniten|ce /'penɪtəns/ *n* Reue *f*. **~t** *a* reuig □ *n* Büßer *m*
penitentiary /penɪ'tenʃərɪ/ *n* (*Amer*) Gefängnis *nt*
pen: ~knife *n* Taschenmesser *nt*. **~-name** *n* Pseudonym *nt*
pennant /'penənt/ *n* Wimpel *m*
penniless /'penɪlɪs/ *a* mittellos
penny /'penɪ/ *n* (*pl* **pence**; *single coins* **pennies**) Penny *m*; (*Amer*) Centstück *nt*; **spend a ~** (*fam*) mal verschwinden; **the ~'s dropped** (*fam*) der Groschen ist gefallen
pension /'penʃn/ *n* Rente *f*; (*of civil servant*) Pension *f*. **~er** *n* Rentner(in) *m*(*f*); Pensionär(in) *m*(*f*)
pensive /'pensɪv/ *a* nachdenklich
Pentecost /'pentɪkɒst/ *n* Pfingsten *nt*
pent-up /'pentʌp/ *a* angestaut
penultimate /pe'nʌltɪmət/ *a* vorletzte(r,s)
penury /'penjʊrɪ/ *n* Armut *f*
peony /'pɪənɪ/ *n* Pfingstrose *f*
people /'pi:pl/ *npl* Leute *pl*, Menschen *pl*; (*citizens*) Bevölkerung *f*; **the ~** das Volk; **English ~** die Engländer; **~ say** man sagt; **for four ~** für vier Personen □ *vt* bevölkern
pep /pep/ *n* (*fam*) Schwung *m*
pepper /'pepə(r)/ *n* Pfeffer *m*; (*vegetable*) Paprika *m* □ *vt* (*Culin*) pfeffern

pepper: ~**corn** *n* Pfefferkorn *nt.* ~**mint** *n* Pfefferminz *nt;* (*Bot*) Pfefferminze *f.* ~**pot** *n* Pfefferstreuer *m*

per /pɜ:(r)/ *prep* pro; ~ **cent** Prozent *nt*

perceive /pəˈsi:v/ *vt* wahrnehmen

percentage /pəˈsentɪdʒ/ *n* Prozentsatz *m;* (*part*) Teil *m*

perceptible /pəˈseptəbl/ *a* wahrnehmbar

percept|ion /pəˈsepʃn/ *n* Wahrnehmung *f.* ~**ive** /-tɪv/ *a* feinsinnig

perch1 /pɜ:tʃ/ *n* Stange *f* □ *vi* ⟨*bird*:⟩ sich niederlassen

perch2 *n inv* (*fish*) Barsch *m*

percolat|e /ˈpɜ:kəleɪt/ *vi* durchsickern. ~**or** *n* Kaffeemaschine *f*

percussion /pəˈkʌʃn/ *n* Schlagzeug *nt.* ~ **instrument** *n* Schlaginstrument *nt*

peremptory /pəˈremptərɪ/ *a* herrisch

perennial /pəˈrenɪəl/ *a* ⟨*problem*⟩ immer wiederkehrend □ *n* (*Bot*) mehrjährige Pflanze *f*

perfect1 /ˈpɜ:fɪkt/ *a* perfekt, vollkommen; (*fam: utter*) völlig □ *n* (*Gram*) Perfekt *nt*

perfect2 /pəˈfekt/ *vt* vervollkommnen. ~**ion** /-ekʃn/ *n* Vollkommenheit *f;* **to** ~**ion** perfekt

perfectly /ˈpɜ:fɪktlɪ/ *adv* perfekt; (*completely*) vollkommen, völlig

perforate /ˈpɜ:fəreɪt/ *vt* perforieren; (*make a hole in*) durchlöchern. ~**d** *a* perforiert

perform /pəˈfɔ:m/ *vt* ausführen; erfüllen ⟨*duty*⟩; (*Theat*) aufführen ⟨*play*⟩; spielen ⟨*role*⟩ □ *vi* (*Theat*) auftreten; (*Techn*) laufen. ~**ance** *n* Aufführung *f;* (*at theatre, cinema*) Vorstellung *f;* (*Techn*) Leistung *f.* ~**er** *n* Künstler(in) *m(f)*

perfume /ˈpɜ:fju:m/ *n* Parfüm *nt;* (*smell*) Duft *m*

perfunctory /pəˈfʌŋktərɪ/ *a* flüchtig

perhaps /pəˈhæps/ *adv* vielleicht

peril /ˈperəl/ *n* Gefahr *f.* ~**ous** /-əs/ *a* gefährlich

perimeter /pəˈrɪmɪtə(r)/ *n* [äußere] Grenze *f;* (*Geom*) Umfang *m*

period /ˈpɪərɪəd/ *n* Periode *f;* (*Sch*) Stunde *f;* (*full stop*) Punkt *m* □ *attrib* ⟨*costume*⟩ zeitgenössisch; ⟨*furniture*⟩ antik. ~**ic** /-ˈɒdɪk/ *a*, **-ally** *adv* periodisch. ~**ical** /-ˈɒdɪkl/ *n* Zeitschrift *f*

peripher|al /pəˈrɪfərl/ *a* nebensächlich. ~**y** *n* Peripherie *f*

periscope /ˈperɪskəʊp/ *n* Periskop *nt*

perish /ˈperɪʃ/ *vi* ⟨*rubber*:⟩ verrotten; ⟨*food*:⟩ verderben; (*die*) ums Leben kommen. ~**able** /-əbl/ *a* leicht verderblich. ~**ing** *a* (*fam: cold*) eiskalt

perjur|e /ˈpɜ:dʒə(r)/ *vt* ~**e oneself** einen Meineid leisten. ~**y** *n* Meineid *m*

perk1 /pɜ:k/ *n* (*fam*) [Sonder]vergünstigung *f*

perk2 *vi* ~ **up** munter werden

perky /ˈpɜ:kɪ/ *a* munter

perm /pɜ:m/ *n* Dauerwelle *f* □ *vt* ~ **s.o.'s hair** jdm eine Dauerwelle machen

permanent /ˈpɜ:mənənt/ *a* ständig; ⟨*job, address*⟩ fest. ~**ly** *adv* ständig; ⟨*work, live*⟩ dauernd, permanent; ⟨*employed*⟩ fest

permeable /ˈpɜ:mɪəbl/ *a* durchlässig

permeate /ˈpɜ:mɪeɪt/ *vt* durchdringen

permissible /pəˈmɪsəbl/ *a* erlaubt

permission /pəˈmɪʃn/ *n* Erlaubnis *f*

permissive /pəˈmɪsɪv/ *a* ⟨*society*⟩ permissiv

permit1 /pəˈmɪt/ *vt* (*pt/pp* **-mitted**) erlauben (**s.o.** jdm); ~ **me!** gestatten Sie!

permit2 /ˈpɜ:mɪt/ *n* Genehmigung *f*

pernicious /pəˈnɪʃəs/ *a* schädlich; (*Med*) perniziös
perpendicular /pɜːpənˈdɪkjʊlə(r)/ *a* senkrecht □ *n* Senkrechte *f*
perpetrat|e /ˈpɜːpɪtreɪt/ *vt* begehen. **~or** *n* Täter *m*
perpetual /pəˈpetjʊəl/ *a*, **-ly** *adv* ständig, dauernd
perpetuate /pəˈpetjʊeɪt/ *vt* bewahren; verewigen ⟨*error*⟩
perplex /pəˈpleks/ *vt* verblüffen. **~ed** *a* verblüfft. **~ity** *n* Verblüffung *f*
persecut|e /ˈpɜːsɪkjuːt/ *vt* verfolgen. **~ion** /-ˈkjuːʃn/ *n* Verfolgung *f*
perseverance /pɜːsɪˈvɪərəns/ *n* Ausdauer *f*
persever|e /pɜːsɪˈvɪə(r)/ *vi* beharrlich weitermachen. **~ing** *a* ausdauernd
Persia /ˈpɜːʃə/ *n* Persien *nt*
Persian /ˈpɜːʃn/ *a* persisch; ⟨*cat, carpet*⟩ Perser-
persist /pəˈsɪst/ *vi* beharrlich weitermachen; (*continue*) anhalten; ⟨*view:*⟩ weiter bestehen; **~ in doing sth** dabei bleiben, etw zu tun. **~ence** *n* Beharrlichkeit *f*. **~ent** *a*, **-ly** *adv* beharrlich; (*continuous*) anhaltend
person /ˈpɜːsn/ *n* Person *f*; **in ~** persönlich
personal /ˈpɜːsənl/ *a*, **-ly** *adv* persönlich. **~ ˈhygiene** *n* Körperpflege *f*
personality /pɜːsəˈnælətɪ/ *n* Persönlichkeit *f*
personify /pəˈsɒnɪfaɪ/ *vt* (*pt/pp* **-ied**) personifizieren, verkörpern
personnel /pɜːsəˈnel/ *n* Personal *nt*
perspective /pəˈspektɪv/ *n* Perspektive *f*
perspicacious /pɜːspɪˈkeɪʃəs/ *a* scharfsichtig
persp|iration /pɜːspɪˈreɪʃn/ *n* Schweiß *m*. **~ire** /-ˈspaɪə(r)/ *vi* schwitzen
persua|de /pəˈsweɪd/ *vt* überreden; (*convince*) überzeugen. **~sion** /-eɪʒn/ *n* Überredung *f*; (*powers of ~sion*) Überredungskunst *f*; (*belief*) Glaubensrichtung *f*
persuasive /pəˈsweɪsɪv/ *a*, **-ly** *adv* beredsam; (*convincing*) überzeugend
pert /pɜːt/ *a*, **-ly** *adv* kess
pertain /pəˈteɪn/ *vi* **~ to** betreffen; (*belong*) gehören zu
pertinent /ˈpɜːtɪnənt/ *a* relevant (**to** für)
perturb /pəˈtɜːb/ *vt* beunruhigen
peruse /pəˈruːz/ *vt* lesen
perva|de /pəˈveɪd/ *vt* durchdringen. **~sive** /-sɪv/ *a* durchdringend
pervers|e /pəˈvɜːs/ *a* eigensinnig. **~ion** /-ɜːʃn/ *n* Perversion *f*
pervert¹ /pəˈvɜːt/ *vt* verdrehen; verführen ⟨*person*⟩
pervert² /ˈpɜːvɜːt/ *n* Perverse(r) *m*
perverted /pəˈvɜːtɪd/ *a* abartig
pessimis|m /ˈpesɪmɪzm/ *n* Pessimismus *m*. **~t** /-mɪst/ *n* Pessimist *m*. **~tic** /-ˈmɪstɪk/ *a*, **-ally** *adv* pessimistisch
pest /pest/ *n* Schädling *m*; (*fam: person*) Nervensäge *f*
pester /ˈpestə(r)/ *vt* belästigen; **~ s.o. for sth** jdm wegen etw in den Ohren liegen
pesticide /ˈpestɪsaɪd/ *n* Schädlingsbekämpfungsmittel *nt*
pet /pet/ *n* Haustier *nt*; (*favourite*) Liebling *m* □ *vt* (*pt/pp* **petted**) liebkosen
petal /ˈpetl/ *n* Blütenblatt *nt*
peter /ˈpiːtə(r)/ *vi* **~ out** allmählich aufhören; ⟨*stream:*⟩ versickern
petite /pəˈtiːt/ *a* klein und zierlich
petition /pəˈtɪʃn/ *n* Bittschrift *f* □ *vt* eine Bittschrift richten an (+ *acc*)
pet ˈname *n* Kosename *m*

petrif|y /ˈpetrɪfaɪ/ *vt/i* (*pt/pp* **-ied**) versteinern; **~ied** (*frightened*) vor Angst wie versteinert
petrol /ˈpetrl/ *n* Benzin *nt*
petroleum /pɪˈtrəʊlɪəm/ *n* Petroleum *nt*
petrol: ~-pump *n* Zapfsäule *f*. **~ station** *n* Tankstelle *f*. **~ tank** *n* Benzintank *m*
ˈpet shop *n* Tierhandlung *f*
petticoat /ˈpetɪkəʊt/ *n* Unterrock *m*
petty /ˈpetɪ/ *a* (**-ier, -iest**) kleinlich. **~ ˈcash** *n* Portokasse *f*
petulant /ˈpetjʊlənt/ *a* gekränkt
pew /pjuː/ *n* [Kirchen]bank *f*
pewter /ˈpjuːtə(r)/ *n* Zinn *nt*
phantom /ˈfæntəm/ *n* Gespenst *nt*
pharmaceutical /fɑːməˈsjuːtɪkl/ *a* pharmazeutisch
pharmac|ist /ˈfɑːməsɪst/ *n* Apotheker(in) *m(f)*. **~y** *n* Pharmazie *f*; (*shop*) Apotheke *f*
phase /feɪz/ *n* Phase *f* □ *vt* **~ in/out** allmählich einführen/abbauen
Ph.D. (*abbr of* **Doctor of Philosophy**) Dr. phil.
pheasant /ˈfeznt/ *n* Fasan *m*
phenomen|al /fɪˈnɒmɪnl/ *a* phänomenal. **~on** *n* (*pl* **-na**) Phänomen *nt*
phial /ˈfaɪəl/ *n* Fläschchen *nt*
philanderer /fɪˈlændərə(r)/ *n* Verführer *m*
philanthrop|ic /fɪlənˈθrɒpɪk/ *a* menschenfreundlich. **~ist** /fɪˈlænθrəpɪst/ *n* Philanthrop *m*
philately /fɪˈlætəlɪ/ *n* Philatelie *f*, Briefmarkenkunde *f*
philharmonic /fɪlɑːˈmɒnɪk/ *n* (*orchestra*) Philharmoniker *pl*
Philippines /ˈfɪlɪpiːnz/ *npl* Philippinen *pl*
philistine /ˈfɪlɪstaɪn/ *n* Banause *m*
philosoph|er /fɪˈlɒsəfə(r)/ *n* Philosoph *m*. **~ical** /fɪləˈsɒfɪkl/ *a*, **-ly** *adv* philosophisch. **~y** *n* Philosophie *f*
phlegm /flem/ *n* (*Med*) Schleim *m*
phlegmatic /flegˈmætɪk/ *a* phlegmatisch
phobia /ˈfəʊbɪə/ *n* Phobie *f*
phone /fəʊn/ *n* Telefon *nt*; **be on the ~** Telefon haben; (*be phoning*) telefonieren □ *vt* anrufen □ *vi* telefonieren. **~ back** *vt/i* zurückrufen. **~ book** *n* Telefonbuch *nt*. **~ box** *n* Telefonzelle *f*. **~ card** *n* Telefonkarte *f*. **~-in** *n* (*Radio*) Hörersendung *f*. **~ number** *n* Telefonnummer *f*
phonetic /fəˈnetɪk/ *a* phonetisch. **~s** *n* Phonetik *f*
phoney /ˈfəʊnɪ/ *a* (**-ier, -iest**) falsch; (*forged*) gefälscht
phosphorus /ˈfɒsfərəs/ *n* Phosphor *m*
photo /ˈfəʊtəʊ/ *n* Foto *nt*, Aufnahme *f*. **~copier** *n* Fotokopiergerät *nt*. **~copy** *n* Fotokopie *f* □ *vt* fotokopieren
photogenic /fəʊtəʊˈdʒenɪk/ *a* fotogen
photograph /ˈfəʊtəgrɑːf/ *n* Fotografie *f*, Aufnahme *f* □ *vt* fotografieren
photograph|er /fəˈtɒgrəfə(r)/ *n* Fotograf(in) *m(f)*. **~ic** /fəʊtəˈgræfɪk/ *a*, **-ally** *adv* fotografisch. **~y** *n* Fotografie *f*
phrase /freɪz/ *n* Redensart *f* □ *vt* formulieren. **~-book** *n* Sprachführer *m*
physical /ˈfɪzɪkl/ *a*, **-ly** *adv* körperlich; ⟨*geography, law*⟩ physikalisch. **~ eduˈcation** *n* Turnen *nt*
physician /fɪˈzɪʃn/ *n* Arzt *m*/ Ärztin *f*
physic|ist /ˈfɪzɪsɪst/ *n* Physiker(in) *m(f)*. **~s** *n* Physik *f*
physiology /fɪzɪˈɒlədʒɪ/ *n* Physiologie *f*
physioˈtherap|ist /fɪzɪəʊ-/ *n* Physiotherapeut(in) *m(f)*. **~y** *n* Physiotherapie *f*

physique /fɪ'zi:k/ *n* Körperbau *m*
pianist /'pɪənɪst/ *n* Klavierspieler(in) *m(f)*; (*professional*) Pianist(in) *m(f)*
piano /pɪ'ænəʊ/ *n* Klavier *nt*
pick[1] /pɪk/ *n* Spitzhacke *f*
pick[2] *n* Auslese *f*; **take one's ~** sich (*dat*) aussuchen □ *vt/i* (*pluck*) pflücken; (*select*) wählen, sich (*dat*) aussuchen; **~ and choose** wählerisch sein; **~ one's nose** in der Nase bohren; **~ a quarrel** einen Streit anfangen; **~ a hole in sth** ein Loch in etw (*acc*) machen; **~ holes in** (*fam*) kritisieren; **~ at one's food** im Essen herumstochern. **~ on** *vt* wählen; (*fam: find fault with*) herumhacken auf (+ *dat*). **~ up** *vt* in die Hand nehmen; (*off the ground*) aufheben; hochnehmen ⟨*baby*⟩; (*learn*) lernen; (*acquire*) erwerben; (*buy*) kaufen; (*Teleph*) abnehmen ⟨*receiver*⟩; auffangen ⟨*signal*⟩; (*collect*) abholen; aufnehmen ⟨*passengers*⟩; ⟨*police:*⟩ aufgreifen ⟨*criminal*⟩; sich holen ⟨*illness*⟩; (*fam*) aufgabeln ⟨*girl*⟩; **~ oneself up** aufstehen □ *vi* (*improve*) sich bessern
'**pickaxe** *n* Spitzhacke *f*
picket /'pɪkɪt/ *n* Streikposten *m* □ *vt* Streikposten aufstellen vor (+ *dat*). **~ line** *n* Streikpostenkette *f*
pickle /'pɪkl/ *n* (*Amer: gherkin*) Essiggurke *f*; **~s** *pl* [Mixed] Pickles *pl* □ *vt* einlegen
pick: ~pocket *n* Taschendieb *m*. **~-up** *n* (*truck*) Lieferwagen *m*; (*on record-player*) Tonabnehmer *m*
picnic /'pɪknɪk/ *n* Picknick *nt* □ *vi* (*pt/pp* **-nicked**) picknicken
pictorial /pɪk'tɔ:rɪəl/ *a* bildlich
picture /'pɪktʃə(r)/ *n* Bild *nt*; (*film*) Film *m*; **as pretty as a ~** bildhübsch; **put s.o. in the ~** (*fig*) jdn ins Bild setzen □ *vt* (*imagine*) sich (*dat*) vorstellen
picturesque /pɪktʃə'resk/ *a* malerisch
pie /paɪ/ *n* Pastete *f*; (*fruit*) Kuchen *m*
piece /pi:s/ *n* Stück *nt*; (*of set*) Teil *nt*; (*in game*) Stein *m*; (*Journ*) Artikel *m*; **a ~ of bread/paper** ein Stück Brot/Papier; **a ~ of news/advice** eine Nachricht/ein Rat; **take to ~s** auseinander nehmen □ *vt* **~ together** zusammensetzen; (*fig*) zusammenstückeln. **~meal** *adv* stückweise. **~-work** *n* Akkordarbeit *f*
pier /pɪə(r)/ *n* Pier *m*; (*pillar*) Pfeiler *m*
pierc|e /pɪəs/ *vt* durchstechen; **~e a hole in sth** ein Loch in etw (*acc*) stechen. **~ing** *a* durchdringend
piety /'paɪətɪ/ *n* Frömmigkeit *f*
piffle /'pɪfl/ *n* (*fam*) Quatsch *m*
pig /pɪg/ *n* Schwein *nt*
pigeon /'pɪdʒɪn/ *n* Taube *f*. **~-hole** *n* Fach *nt*
piggy /'pɪgɪ/ *n* (*fam*) Schweinchen *nt*. **~back** *n* **give s.o. a ~back** jdn huckepack tragen. **~ bank** *n* Sparschwein *nt*
pig'headed *a* (*fam*) starrköpfig
pigment /'pɪgmənt/ *n* Pigment *nt*. **~ation** /-men'teɪʃn/ *n* Pigmentierung *f*
pig: ~skin *n* Schweinsleder *nt*. **~sty** *n* Schweinestall *m*. **~tail** *n* (*fam*) Zopf *m*
pike /paɪk/ *n inv* (*fish*) Hecht *m*
pilchard /'pɪltʃəd/ *n* Sardine *f*
pile[1] /paɪl/ *n* (*of fabric*) Flor *m*
pile[2] *n* Haufen *m* □ *vt* **~ sth on to sth** etw auf etw (*acc*) häufen. **~ up** *vt* häufen □ *vi* sich häufen
piles /paɪlz/ *npl* Hämorrhoiden *pl*
'**pile-up** *n* Massenkarambolage *f*
pilfer /'pɪlfə(r)/ *vt/i* stehlen
pilgrim /'pɪlgrɪm/ *n* Pilger(in) *m(f)*. **~age** /-ɪdʒ/ *n* Pilgerfahrt *f*, Wallfahrt *f*
pill /pɪl/ *n* Pille *f*

pillage /ˈpɪlɪdʒ/ *vt* plündern
pillar /ˈpɪlə(r)/ *n* Säule *f*. **~-box** *n* Briefkasten *m*
pillion /ˈpɪljən/ *n* Sozius[sitz] *m*
pillory /ˈpɪlərɪ/ *n* Pranger *m* □ *vt* (*pt/pp* **-ied**) anprangern
pillow /ˈpɪləʊ/ *n* Kopfkissen *nt*. **~case** *n* Kopfkissenbezug *m*
pilot /ˈpaɪlət/ *n* Pilot *m*; (*Naut*) Lotse *m* □ *vt* fliegen ⟨*plane*⟩; lotsen ⟨*ship*⟩. **~-light** *n* Zündflamme *f*
pimp /pɪmp/ *n* Zuhälter *m*
pimple /ˈpɪmpl/ *n* Pickel *m*
pin /pɪn/ *n* Stecknadel *f*; (*Techn*) Bolzen *m*, Stift *m*; (*Med*) Nagel *m*; **I have ~s and needles in my leg** (*fam*) mein Bein ist eingeschlafen □ *vt* (*pt/pp* **pinned**) anstecken (**to/on** an + *acc*); (*sewing*) stecken; (*hold down*) festhalten; **~ sth on s.o.** (*fam*) jdm etw anhängen. **~ up** *vt* hochstecken; (*on wall*) anheften, anschlagen
pinafore /ˈpɪnəfɔː(r)/ *n* Schürze *f*. **~ dress** *n* Kleiderrock *m*
pincers /ˈpɪnsəz/ *npl* Kneifzange *f*; (*Zool*) Scheren *pl*
pinch /pɪntʃ/ *n* Kniff *m*; (*of salt*) Prise *f*; **at a ~** (*fam*) zur Not □ *vt* kneifen, zwicken; (*fam; steal*) klauen; **~ one's finger** sich (*dat*) den Finger klemmen □ *vi* ⟨*shoe:*⟩ drücken
ˈpincushion *n* Nadelkissen *nt*
pine[1] /paɪn/ *n* (*tree*) Kiefer *f*
pine[2] *vi* **~ for** sich sehnen nach; **~ away** sich verzehren
pineapple /ˈpaɪn-/ *n* Ananas *f*
ping /pɪŋ/ *n* Klingeln *nt*
ˈping-pong *n* Tischtennis *nt*
pink /pɪŋk/ *a* rosa
pinnacle /ˈpɪnəkl/ *n* Gipfel *m*; (*on roof*) Turmspitze *f*
pin: ~point *vt* genau festlegen. **~stripe** *n* Nadelstreifen *m*
pint /paɪnt/ *n* Pint *nt* (*0,571, Amer: 0,47 l*)
ˈpin-up *n* Pin-up-Girl *nt*
pioneer /paɪəˈnɪə(r)/ *n* Pionier *m* □ *vt* bahnbrechende Arbeit leisten für
pious /ˈpaɪəs/ *a*, **-ly** *adv* fromm
pip[1] /pɪp/ *n* (*seed*) Kern *m*
pip[2] *n* (*sound*) Tonsignal *nt*
pipe /paɪp/ *n* Pfeife *f*; (*for water, gas*) Rohr *nt* □ *vt* in Rohren leiten; (*Culin*) spritzen. **~ down** *vi* (*fam*) den Mund halten
pipe: ~-dream *n* Luftschloss *nt*. **~line** *n* Pipeline *f*; **in the ~line** (*fam*) in Vorbereitung
piper /ˈpaɪpə(r)/ *n* Pfeifer *m*
piping /ˈpaɪpɪŋ/ *a* **~ hot** kochend heiß
piquant /ˈpiːkənt/ *a* pikant
pique /piːk/ *n* **in a fit of ~** beleidigt
pirate /ˈpaɪərət/ *n* Pirat *m*
Pisces /ˈpaɪsiːz/ *n* (*Astr*) Fische *pl*
piss /pɪs/ *vi* (*sl*) pissen
pistol /ˈpɪstl/ *n* Pistole *f*
piston /ˈpɪstən/ *n* (*Techn*) Kolben *m*
pit /pɪt/ *n* Grube *f*; (*for orchestra*) Orchestergraben *m* □ *vt* (*pt/pp* **pitted**) (*fig*) messen (**against** mit)
pitch[1] /pɪtʃ/ *n* (*steepness*) Schräge *f*; (*of voice*) Stimmlage *f*; (*of sound*) [Ton]höhe *f*; (*Sport*) Feld *nt*; (*of street-trader*) Standplatz *m*; (*fig: degree*) Grad *m* □ *vt* werfen; aufschlagen ⟨*tent*⟩ □ *vi* fallen
pitch[2] *n* (*tar*) Pech *nt*. **~-ˈblack** *a* pechschwarz. **~-ˈdark** *a* stockdunkel
pitcher /ˈpɪtʃə(r)/ *n* Krug *m*
ˈpitchfork *n* Heugabel *f*
piteous /ˈpɪtɪəs/ *a* erbärmlich
ˈpitfall *n* (*fig*) Falle *f*
pith /pɪθ/ *n* (*Bot*) Mark *nt*; (*of orange*) weiße Haut *f*; (*fig*) Wesentliche(s) *nt*
pithy /ˈpɪθɪ/ *a* (**-ier, -iest**) (*fig*) prägnant
piti|ful /ˈpɪtɪfl/ *a* bedauernswert. **~less** *a* mitleidslos
pittance /ˈpɪtns/ *n* Hungerlohn *m*

pity /ˈpɪtɪ/ *n* Mitleid *nt*, Erbarmen *nt*; **[what a] ~!** [wie] schade! **take ~ on** sich erbarmen über (+ *acc*) □ *vt* bemitleiden

pivot /ˈpɪvət/ *n* Drehzapfen *m*; (*fig*) Angelpunkt *m* □ *vi* sich drehen (**on** um)

pixie /ˈpɪksɪ/ *n* Kobold *m*

pizza /ˈpiːtsə/ *n* Pizza *f*

placard /ˈplækɑːd/ *n* Plakat *nt*

placate /pləˈkeɪt/ *vt* beschwichtigen

place /pleɪs/ *n* Platz *m*; (*spot*) Stelle *f*; (*town, village*) Ort *m*; (*fam: house*) Haus *nt*; **out of ~** fehl am Platze; **take ~** stattfinden; **all over the ~** überall □ *vt* setzen; (*upright*) stellen; (*flat*) legen; (*remember*) unterbringen (*fam*); **~ an order** eine Bestellung aufgeben; **be ~d** (*in race*) sich platzieren. **~-mat** *n* Set *nt*

placid /ˈplæsɪd/ *a* gelassen

plagiar|ism /ˈpleɪdʒərɪzm/ *n* Plagiat *nt*. **~ize** *vt* plagiieren

plague /pleɪg/ *n* Pest *f* □ *vt* plagen

plaice /pleɪs/ *n inv* Scholle *f*

plain /pleɪn/ *a* (**-er, -est**) klar; (*simple*) einfach; (*not pretty*) nicht hübsch; (*not patterned*) einfarbig; ⟨*chocolate*⟩ zartbitter; **in ~ clothes** in Zivil □ *adv* (*simply*) einfach □ *n* Ebene *f*; (*Knitting*) linke Masche *f*. **~ly** *adv* klar, deutlich; (*simply*) einfach; (*obviously*) offensichtlich

plaintiff /ˈpleɪntɪf/ *n* (*Jur*) Kläger(in) *m(f)*

plaintive /ˈpleɪntɪv/ *a*, **-ly** *adv* klagend

plait /plæt/ *n* Zopf *m* □ *vt* flechten

plan /plæn/ *n* Plan *m* □ *vt* (*pt/pp* **planned**) planen; (*intend*) vorhaben

plane1 /pleɪn/ *n* (*tree*) Platane *f*

plane2 *n* Flugzeug *nt*; (*Geom & fig*) Ebene *f*

plane3 *n* (*Techn*) Hobel *m* □ *vt* hobeln

planet /ˈplænɪt/ *n* Planet *m*

plank /plæŋk/ *n* Brett *nt*; (*thick*) Planke *f*

planning /ˈplænɪŋ/ *n* Planung *f*. **~ permission** *n* Baugenehmigung *f*

plant /plɑːnt/ *n* Pflanze *f*; (*Techn*) Anlage *f*; (*factory*) Werk *nt* □ *vt* pflanzen; (*place in position*) setzen; **~ oneself in front of s.o.** sich vor jdn hinstellen. **~ation** /plænˈteɪʃn/ *n* Plantage *f*

plaque /plɑːk/ *n* [Gedenk]tafel *f*; (*on teeth*) Zahnbelag *m*

plasma /ˈplæzmə/ *n* Plasma *nt*

plaster /ˈplɑːstə(r)/ *n* Verputz *m*; (*sticking ~*) Pflaster *nt*; **~ [of Paris]** Gips *m* □ *vt* verputzen ⟨*wall*⟩; (*cover*) bedecken mit. **~ed** *a* (*sl*) besoffen. **~er** *n* Gipser *m*

plastic /ˈplæstɪk/ *n* Kunststoff *m*, Plastik *nt* □ *a* Kunststoff-, Plastik-; (*malleable*) formbar, plastisch

Plasticine (P) /ˈplæstɪsiːn/ *n* Knetmasse *f*

plastic ˈsurgery *n* plastische Chirurgie *f*

plate /pleɪt/ *n* Teller *m*; (*flat sheet*) Platte *f*; (*with name, number*) Schild *nt*; (*gold and silverware*) vergoldete/versilberte **Ware** *f*; (*in book*) Tafel *f* □ *vt* (*with gold*) vergolden; (*with silver*) versilbern

plateau /ˈplætəʊ/ *n* (*pl* **~x** /-əʊz/) Hochebene *f*

platform /ˈplætfɔːm/ *n* Plattform *f*; (*stage*) Podium *nt*; (*Rail*) Bahnsteig *m*; **~ 5** Gleis 5

platinum /ˈplætɪnəm/ *n* Platin *nt*

platitude /ˈplætɪtjuːd/ *n* Plattitüde *f*

platonic /pləˈtɒnɪk/ *a* platonisch

platoon /pləˈtuːn/ *n* (*Mil*) Zug *m*

platter /ˈplætə(r)/ *n* Platte *f*

plausible /ˈplɔːzəbl/ *a* plausibel

play /pleɪ/ *n* Spiel *nt*; [Theater]stück *nt*; (*Radio*) Hörspiel *nt*; (*TV*) Fernsehspiel *nt*; **~ on**

words Wortspiel *nt* □ *vt/i* spielen; ausspielen ⟨*card*⟩; ~ **safe** sichergehen. ~ **down** *vt* herunterspielen. ~ **up** *vi* (*fam*) Mätzchen machen

play: ~boy *n* Playboy *m*. **~er** *n* Spieler(in) *m(f)*. **~ful** *a*, **-ly** *adv* verspielt. **~ground** *n* Spielplatz *m*; (*Sch*) Schulhof *m*. **~group** *n* Kindergarten *m*

playing: ~-card *n* Spielkarte *f*. **~-field** *n* Sportplatz *m*

play: ~mate *n* Spielkamerad *m*. **~-pen** *n* Laufstall *m*, Laufgitter *nt*. **~thing** *n* Spielzeug *nt*. **~wright** /-raɪt/ *n* Dramatiker *m*

plc *abbr* (**public limited company**) ≈ GmbH

plea /pli:/ *n* Bitte *f*; **make a ~ for** bitten um

plead /pli:d/ *vt* vorschützen; (*Jur*) vertreten ⟨*case*⟩ □ *vi* flehen (**for** um); ~ **guilty** sich schuldig bekennen; ~ **with s.o.** jdn anflehen

pleasant /ˈplezənt/ *a* angenehm; ⟨*person*⟩ nett. **~ly** *adv* angenehm; ⟨*say, smile*⟩ freundlich

pleas|e /pli:z/ *adv* bitte □ *vt* gefallen (+ *dat*); **~e s.o.** jdm eine Freude machen; **~e oneself** tun, was man will. **~ed** *a* erfreut; **be ~ed with/about sth** sich über etw (*acc*) freuen. **~ing** *a* erfreulich

pleasurable /ˈpleʒərəbl/ *a* angenehm

pleasure /ˈpleʒə(r)/ *n* Vergnügen *nt*; (*joy*) Freude *f*; **with ~** gern[e]

pleat /pli:t/ *n* Falte *f* □ *vt* fälteln. **~ed ˈskirt** *n* Faltenrock *m*

plebiscite /ˈplebɪsɪt/ *n* Volksabstimmung *f*

pledge /pledʒ/ *n* Pfand *nt*; (*promise*) Versprechen *nt* □ *vt* verpfänden; versprechen

plentiful /ˈplentɪfl/ *a* reichlich; **be ~** reichlich vorhanden sein

plenty /ˈplentɪ/ *n* eine Menge; (*enough*) reichlich; ~ **of money/people** viel Geld/viele Leute

pleurisy /ˈplʊərəsɪ/ *n* Rippenfellentzündung *f*

pliable /ˈplaɪəbl/ *a* biegsam

pliers /ˈplaɪəz/ *npl* [Flach]zange *f*

plight /plaɪt/ *n* [Not]lage *f*

plimsolls /ˈplɪmsəlz/ *npl* Turnschuhe *pl*

plinth /plɪnθ/ *n* Sockel *m*

plod /plɒd/ *vi* (*pt/pp* **plodded**) trotten; (*work hard*) sich abmühen

plonk /plɒŋk/ *n* (*fam*) billiger Wein *m*

plot /plɒt/ *n* Komplott *nt*; (*of novel*) Handlung *f*; ~ **of land** Stück *nt* Land □ *vt* einzeichnen □ *vi* ein Komplott schmieden

plough /plaʊ/ *n* Pflug *m* □ *vt/i* pflügen. ~ **back** *vt* (*Comm*) wieder investieren

ploy /plɔɪ/ *n* (*fam*) Trick *m*

pluck /plʌk/ *n* Mut *m* □ *vt* zupfen; rupfen ⟨*bird*⟩; pflücken ⟨*flower*⟩; ~ **up courage** Mut fassen

plucky /ˈplʌkɪ/ *a* (**-ier, -iest**) tapfer, mutig

plug /plʌg/ *n* Stöpsel *m*; (*wood*) Zapfen *m*; (*cotton wool*) Bausch *m*; (*Electr*) Stecker *m*; (*Auto*) Zündkerze *f*; (*fam: advertisement*) Schleichwerbung *f* □ *vt* zustopfen; (*fam: advertise*) Schleichwerbung machen für. ~ **in** *vt* (*Electr*) einstecken

plum /plʌm/ *n* Pflaume *f*

plumage /ˈplu:mɪdʒ/ *n* Gefieder *nt*

plumb /plʌm/ *n* Lot *nt* □ *adv* lotrecht □ *vt* loten. ~ **in** *vt* installieren

plumb|er /ˈplʌmə(r)/ *n* Klempner *m*. **~ing** *n* Wasserleitungen *pl*

ˈplumb-line *n* [Blei]lot *nt*

plume /plu:m/ *n* Feder *f*

plummet /ˈplʌmɪt/ *vi* herunterstürzen

plump /plʌmp/ *a* (**-er, -est**) mollig, rundlich □ *vt* ~ **for** wählen

plunder /ˈplʌndə(r)/ *n* Beute *f* □ *vt* plündern
plunge /plʌndʒ/ *n* Sprung *m*; **take the ~** (*fam*) den Schritt wagen □ *vt/i* tauchen
plu'perfect /pluː-/ *n* Plusquamperfekt *nt*
plural /ˈplʊərl/ *a* pluralisch □ *n* Mehrzahl *f*, Plural *m*
plus /plʌs/ *prep* plus (+ *dat*) □ *a* Plus- □ *n* Pluszeichen *nt*; (*advantage*) Plus *nt*
plush[y] /ˈplʌʃ[ɪ]/ *a* luxuriös
ply /plaɪ/ *vt* (*pt/pp* **plied**) ausüben ⟨*trade*⟩; **~ s.o. with drink** jdm ein Glas nach dem anderen eingießen. **~wood** *n* Sperrholz *nt*
p.m. *adv* (*abbr of* **post meridiem**) nachmittags
pneumatic /njuːˈmætɪk/ *a* pneumatisch. **~ 'drill** *n* Pressluft-hammer *m*
pneumonia /njuːˈməʊnɪə/ *n* Lungenentzündung *f*
poach /pəʊtʃ/ *vt* (*Culin*) pochieren; (*steal*) wildern. **~er** *n* Wilddieb *m*
pocket /ˈpɒkɪt/ *n* Tasche *f*; **~ of resistance** Widerstandsnest *nt*; **be out of ~** [an einem Geschäft] verlieren □ *vt* einstecken. **~-book** *n* Notizbuch *nt*; (*wallet*) Brieftasche *f*. **~-money** *n* Taschengeld *nt*
pock-marked /ˈpɒk-/ *a* pockennarbig
pod /pɒd/ *n* Hülse *f*
podgy /ˈpɒdʒɪ/ *a* (**-ier, -iest**) dick
poem /ˈpəʊɪm/ *n* Gedicht *nt*
poet /ˈpəʊɪt/ *n* Dichter(in) *m*(*f*). **~ic** /-ˈetɪk/ *a* dichterisch
poetry /ˈpəʊɪtrɪ/ *n* Dichtung *f*
poignant /ˈpɔɪnjənt/ *a* ergreifend
point /pɔɪnt/ *n* Punkt *m*; (*sharp end*) Spitze *f*; (*meaning*) Sinn *m*; (*purpose*) Zweck *m*; (*Electr*) Steckdose *f*; **~s** *pl* (*Rail*) Weiche *f*; **~ of view** Standpunkt *m*; **good/bad ~s** gute/schlechte Seiten; **what is the ~?** wozu? **the ~ is** es geht darum; **I don't see the ~** das sehe ich nicht ein; **up to a ~** bis zu einem gewissen Grade; **be on the ~ of doing sth** im Begriff sein, etw zu tun □ *vt* richten (**at** auf + *acc*); ausfugen ⟨*brickwork*⟩ □ *vi* deuten (**at/to** auf + *acc*); (*with finger*) mit dem Finger zeigen. **~ out** *vt* zeigen auf (+ *acc*); **~ sth out to s.o.** jdn auf etw (*acc*) hinweisen
point-'blank *a* aus nächster Entfernung; (*fig*) rundweg
point|ed /ˈpɔɪntɪd/ *a* spitz; ⟨*question*⟩ gezielt. **~er** *n* (*hint*) Hinweis *m*. **~less** *a* zwecklos, sinnlos
poise /pɔɪz/ *n* Haltung *f*. **~d** *a* (*confident*) selbstsicher; **~d to** bereit zu
poison /ˈpɔɪzn/ *n* Gift *nt* □ *vt* vergiften. **~ous** *a* giftig
poke /pəʊk/ *n* Stoß *m* □ *vt* stoßen; schüren ⟨*fire*⟩; (*put*) stecken; **~ fun at** sich lustig machen über (+ *acc*)
poker¹ /ˈpəʊkə(r)/ *n* Schüreisen *nt*
poker² *n* (*Cards*) Poker *nt*
poky /ˈpəʊkɪ/ *a* (**-ier, -iest**) eng
Poland /ˈpəʊlənd/ *n* Polen *nt*
polar /ˈpəʊlə(r)/ *a* Polar-. **~'bear** *n* Eisbär *m*. **~ize** *vt* polarisieren
Pole /pəʊl/ *n* Pole *m*/Polin *f*
pole¹ *n* Stange *f*
pole² *n* (*Geog, Electr*) Pol *m*
'polecat *n* Iltis *m*
'pole-star *n* Polarstern *m*
'pole-vault *n* Stabhochsprung *m*
police /pəˈliːs/ *npl* Polizei *f* □ *vt* polizeilich kontrollieren
police: ~man *n* Polizist *m*. **~state** *n* Polizeistaat *m*. **~ station** *n* Polizeiwache *f*. **~woman** *n* Polizistin *f*
policy¹ /ˈpɒlɪsɪ/ *n* Politik *f*
policy² *n* (*insurance*) Police *f*
polio /ˈpəʊlɪəʊ/ *n* Kinderlähmung *f*
Polish /ˈpəʊlɪʃ/ *a* polnisch

polish /ˈpɒlɪʃ/ *n (shine)* Glanz *m*; (*for shoes*) [Schuh]creme *f*; (*for floor*) Bohnerwachs *m*; (*for furniture*) Politur *f*; (*for silver*) Putzmittel *nt*; (*for nails*) Lack *m*; (*fig*) Schliff *m* □ *vt* polieren; bohnern ⟨*floor*⟩. **~ off** *vt* (*fam*) verputzen ⟨*food*⟩; erledigen ⟨*task*⟩

polisher /ˈpɒlɪʃə(r)/ *n* (*machine*) Poliermaschine *f*; (*for floor*) Bohnermaschine *f*

polite /pəˈlaɪt/ *a*, **-ly** *adv* höflich. **~ness** *n* Höflichkeit *f*

politic /ˈpɒlɪtɪk/ *a* ratsam

politic|al /pəˈlɪtɪkl/ *a*, **-ly** *adv* politisch. **~ian** /pɒlɪˈtɪʃn/ *n* Politiker(in) *m*(*f*)

politics /ˈpɒlətɪks/ *n* Politik *f*

polka /ˈpɒlkə/ *n* Polka *f*

poll /pəʊl/ *n* Abstimmung *f*; (*election*) Wahl *f*; **[opinion] ~** [Meinungs]umfrage *f*; **go to the ~s** wählen □ *vt* erhalten ⟨*votes*⟩

pollen /ˈpɒlən/ *n* Blütenstaub *m*, Pollen *m*

polling /ˈpəʊlɪŋ/: **~-booth** *n* Wahlkabine *f*. **~-station** *n* Wahllokal *nt*

ˈpoll tax *n* Kopfsteuer *f*

pollutant /pəˈluːtənt/ *n* Schadstoff *m*

pollut|e /pəˈluːt/ *vt* verschmutzen. **~ion** /-uːʃn/ *n* Verschmutzung *f*

polo /ˈpəʊləʊ/ *n* Polo *nt*. **~-neck** *n* Rollkragen *m*. **~ shirt** *n* Polohemd *nt*

polyester /pɒlɪˈestə(r)/ *n* Polyester *m*

polystyrene /pɒlɪˈstaɪriːn/ *n* Polystyrol *nt*; (*for packing*) Styropor (P) *nt*

polytechnic /pɒlɪˈteknɪk/ *n* ≈ technische Hochschule *f*

polythene /ˈpɒlɪθiːn/ *n* Polyäthylen *nt*. **~ bag** *n* Plastiktüte *f*

polyunˈsaturated *a* mehrfach ungesättigt

pomegranate /ˈpɒmɪgrænɪt/ *n* Granatapfel *m*

pomp /pɒmp/ *n* Pomp *m*

pompon /ˈpɒmpɒn/ *n* Pompon *m*

pompous /ˈpɒmpəs/ *a*, **-ly** *adv* großspurig

pond /pɒnd/ *n* Teich *m*

ponder /ˈpɒndə(r)/ *vi* nachdenken

ponderous /ˈpɒndərəs/ *a* schwerfällig

pong /pɒŋ/ *n* (*fam*) Mief *m*

pony /ˈpəʊnɪ/ *n* Pony *nt*. **~-tail** *n* Pferdeschwanz *m*. **~-trekking** *n* Ponyreiten *nt*

poodle /ˈpuːdl/ *n* Pudel *m*

pool¹ /puːl/ *n* [Schwimm]becken *nt*; (*pond*) Teich *m*; (*of blood*) Lache *f*

pool² *n* (*common fund*) [gemeinsame] Kasse *f*; **~s** *pl* [Fußball]toto *nt* □ *vt* zusammenlegen

poor /pʊə(r)/ *a* (**-er, -est**) arm; (*not good*) schlecht; **in ~ health** nicht gesund □ *npl* **the ~** die Armen. **~ly** *a* **be ~ly** krank sein □ *adv* ärmlich; (*badly*) schlecht

pop¹ /pɒp/ *n* Knall *m*; (*drink*) Brause *f* □ *v* (*pt/pp* **popped**) □ *vt* (*fam: put*) stecken (**in** in + *acc*) □ *vi* knallen; (*burst*) platzen. **~ in** *vi* (*fam*) reinschauen. **~ out** *vi* (*fam*) kurz rausgehen

pop² *n* (*fam*) Popmusik *f*, Pop *m* □ *attrib* Pop-

ˈpopcorn *n* Puffmais *m*

pope /pəʊp/ *n* Papst *m*

poplar /ˈpɒplə(r)/ *n* Pappel *f*

poppy /ˈpɒpɪ/ *n* Mohn *m*

popular /ˈpɒpjʊlə(r)/ *a* beliebt, populär; ⟨*belief*⟩ volkstümlich. **~ity** /-ˈlærətɪ/ *n* Beliebtheit *f*, Popularität *f*

populat|e /ˈpɒpjʊleɪt/ *vt* bevölkern. **~ion** /-ˈleɪʃn/ *n* Bevölkerung *f*

porcelain /ˈpɔːsəlɪn/ *n* Porzellan *nt*

porch /pɔːtʃ/ *n* Vorbau *m*; (*Amer*) Veranda *f*

porcupine /ˈpɔːkjʊpaɪn/ *n* Stachelschwein *nt*

pore[1] /pɔ:(r)/ *n* Pore *f*
pore[2] *vi* ~ **over** studieren
pork /pɔ:k/ *n* Schweinefleisch *nt*
porn /pɔ:n/ *n* (*fam*) Porno *m*
pornograph|ic /pɔ:nəˈgræfɪk/ *a* pornographisch. **~y** /-ˈnɒgrəfɪ/ *n* Pornographie *f*
porous /ˈpɔ:rəs/ *a* porös
porpoise /ˈpɔ:pəs/ *n* Tümmler *m*
porridge /ˈpɒrɪdʒ/ *n* Haferbrei *m*
port[1] /pɔ:t/ *n* Hafen *m*; (*town*) Hafenstadt *f*
port[2] *n* (*Naut*) Backbord *nt*
port[3] *n* (*wine*) Portwein *m*
portable /ˈpɔ:təbl/ *a* tragbar
porter /ˈpɔ:tə(r)/ *n* Portier *m*; (*for luggage*) Gepäckträger *m*
portfolio /pɔ:tˈfəʊlɪəʊ/ *n* Mappe *f*; (*Comm*) Portefeuille *nt*
ˈ**porthole** *n* Bullauge *nt*
portion /ˈpɔ:ʃn/ *n* Portion *f*; (*part, share*) Teil *nt*
portly /ˈpɔ:tlɪ/ *a* (**-ier, -iest**) beleibt
portrait /ˈpɔ:trɪt/ *n* Porträt *nt*
portray /pɔ:ˈtreɪ/ *vt* darstellen. **~al** *n* Darstellung *f*
Portug|al /ˈpɔ:tjʊgl/ *n* Portugal *nt*. **~uese** /-ˈgi:z/ *a* portugiesisch □ *n* Portugiese *m*/-giesin *f*
pose /pəʊz/ *n* Pose *f* □ *vt* aufwerfen ⟨*problem*⟩; stellen ⟨*question*⟩ □ *vi* posieren; (*for painter*) Modell stehen; ~ **as** sich ausgeben als
posh /pɒʃ/ *a* (*fam*) feudal
position /pəˈzɪʃn/ *n* Platz *m*; (*posture*) Haltung *f*; (*job*) Stelle *f*; (*situation*) **Lage** *f*, Situation *f*; (*status*) Stellung *f* □ *vt* platzieren; ~ **oneself** sich stellen
positive /ˈpɒzətɪv/ *a*, **-ly** *adv* positiv; (*definite*) eindeutig; (*real*) ausgesprochen □ *n* Positiv *nt*
possess /pəˈzes/ *vt* besitzen. **~ion** /pəˈzeʃn/ *n* Besitz *m*; **~ions** *pl* Sachen *pl*
possess|ive /pəˈzesɪv/ *a* Possessiv-; **be ~ive** zu sehr an jdm hängen. **~or** *n* Besitzer *m*
possibility /pɒsəˈbɪlətɪ/ *n* Möglichkeit *f*
possib|le /ˈpɒsəbl/ *a* möglich. **~ly** *adv* möglicherweise; **not ~ly** unmöglich
post[1] /pəʊst/ *n* (*pole*) Pfosten *m* □ *vt* anschlagen ⟨*notice*⟩
post[2] *n* (*place of duty*) Posten *m*; (*job*) Stelle *f* □ *vt* postieren; (*transfer*) versetzen
post[3] *n* (*mail*) Post *f*; **by ~** mit der Post □ *vt* aufgeben ⟨*letter*⟩; (*send by ~*) mit der Post schicken; **keep s.o. ~ed** jdn auf dem Laufenden halten
postage /ˈpəʊstɪdʒ/ *n* Porto *nt*. **~stamp** *n* Briefmarke *f*
postal /ˈpəʊstl/ *a* Post-. ~ **order** *n* ≈ Geldanweisung *f*
post: **~-box** *n* Briefkasten *m*. **~card** *n* Postkarte *f*; (*picture*) Ansichtskarte *f*. **~code** *n* Postleitzahl *f*. **~-ˈdate** *vt* vordatieren
poster /ˈpəʊstə(r)/ *n* Plakat *nt*
posterior /pɒˈstɪərɪə(r)/ *a* hintere(r,s) □ *n* (*fam*) Hintern *m*
posterity /pɒˈsterətɪ/ *n* Nachwelt *f*
posthumous /ˈpɒstjʊməs/ *a*, **-ly** *adv* postum
post: **~man** *n* Briefträger *m*. **~mark** *n* Poststempel *m*
post-mortem /-ˈmɔ:təm/ *n* Obduktion *f*
ˈ**post office** *n* Post *f*
postpone /pəʊstˈpəʊn/ *vt* aufschieben; ~ **until** verschieben auf (+ *acc*). **~ment** *n* Verschiebung *f*
postscript /ˈpəʊstskrɪpt/ *n* Nachschrift *f*
posture /ˈpɒstʃə(r)/ *n* Haltung *f*
post-ˈwar *a* Nachkriegs-
posy /ˈpəʊzɪ/ *n* Sträußchen *nt*
pot /pɒt/ *n* Topf *m*; (*for tea, coffee*) Kanne *f*; **~s of money** (*fam*) eine Menge Geld; **go to ~** (*fam*) herunterkommen
potassium /pəˈtæsɪəm/ *n* Kalium *nt*

potato /pəˈteɪtəʊ/ *n* (*pl* **-es**) Kartoffel *f*

poten|cy /ˈpəʊtənsɪ/ *n* Stärke *f*. **~t** *a* stark

potential /pəˈtenʃl/ *a*, **-ly** *adv* potenziell □ *n* Potenzial *nt*

pot: **~-hole** *n* Höhle *f*; (*in road*) Schlagloch *nt*. **~-holer** *n* Höhlenforscher *m*. **~-shot** *n* **take a ~-shot at** schießen auf (+ *acc*)

potted /ˈpɒtɪd/ *a* eingemacht; (*shortened*) gekürzt. **~ ˈplant** *n* Topfpflanze *f*

potter[1] /ˈpɒtə(r)/ *vi* **~ [about]** herumwerkeln

potter[2] *n* Töpfer(in) *m(f)*. **~y** *n* Töpferei *f*; (*articles*) Töpferwaren *pl*

potty /ˈpɒtɪ/ *a* (**-ier, -iest**) (*fam*) verrückt □ *n* Töpfchen *nt*

pouch /paʊtʃ/ *n* Beutel *m*

pouffe /pu:f/ *n* Sitzkissen *nt*

poultry /ˈpəʊltrɪ/ *n* Geflügel *nt*

pounce /paʊns/ *vi* zuschlagen; **~ on** sich stürzen auf (+ *acc*)

pound[1] /paʊnd/ *n* (*money & 0,454 kg*) Pfund *nt*

pound[2] *vt* hämmern □ *vi* ⟨*heart:*⟩ hämmern; (*run heavily*) stampfen

pour /pɔ:(r)/ *vt* gießen; einschenken ⟨*drink*⟩ □ *vi* strömen; (*with rain*) gießen. **~ out** *vi* ausströmen □ *vt* ausschütten; einschenken ⟨*drink*⟩

pout /paʊt/ *vi* einen Schmollmund machen

poverty /ˈpɒvətɪ/ *n* Armut *f*

powder /ˈpaʊdə(r)/ *n* Pulver *nt*; (*cosmetic*) Puder *m* □ *vt* pudern. **~y** *a* pulverig

power /ˈpaʊə(r)/ *n* Macht *f*; (*strength*) Kraft *f*; (*Electr*) Strom *m*; (*nuclear*) Energie *f*; (*Math*) Potenz *f*. **~ cut** *n* Stromsperre *f*. **~ed** *a* betrieben (**by** mit); **~ed by electricity** mit Elektroantrieb. **~ful** *a* mächtig; (*strong*) stark. **~less** *a* machtlos. **~-station** *n* Kraftwerk *nt*

practicable /ˈpræktɪkəbl/ *a* durchführbar, praktikabel

practical /ˈpræktɪkl/ *a*, **-ly** *adv* praktisch. **~ ˈjoke** *n* Streich *m*

practice /ˈpræktɪs/ *n* Praxis *f*; (*custom*) Brauch *m*; (*habit*) Gewohnheit *f*; (*exercise*) Übung *f*; (*Sport*) Training *nt*; **in ~** (*in reality*) in der Praxis; **out of ~** außer Übung; **put into ~** ausführen

practise /ˈpræktɪs/ *vt* üben; (*carry out*) praktizieren; ausüben ⟨*profession*⟩ □ *vi* üben; ⟨*doctor:*⟩ praktizieren. **~d** *a* geübt

pragmatic /prægˈmætɪk/ *a*, **~ally** *adv* pragmatisch

praise /preɪz/ *n* Lob *nt* □ *vt* loben. **~worthy** *a* lobenswert

pram /præm/ *n* Kinderwagen *m*

prance /prɑ:ns/ *vi* herumhüpfen; ⟨*horse:*⟩ tänzeln

prank /præŋk/ *n* Streich *m*

prattle /ˈprætl/ *vi* plappern

prawn /prɔ:n/ *n* Garnele *f*, Krabbe *f*. **~ ˈcocktail** *n* Krabbencocktail *m*

pray /preɪ/ *vi* beten. **~er** /preə(r)/ *n* Gebet *nt*; **~ers** *pl* (*service*) Andacht *f*

preach /pri:tʃ/ *vt/i* predigen. **~er** *n* Prediger *m*

preamble /pri:ˈæmbl/ *n* Einleitung *f*

pre-arˈrange /pri:-/ *vt* im Voraus arrangieren

precarious /prɪˈkeərɪəs/ *a*, **-ly** *adv* unsicher

precaution /prɪˈkɔ:ʃn/ *n* Vorsichtsmaßnahme *f*; **as a ~** zur Vorsicht. **~ary** *a* Vorsichts-

precede /prɪˈsi:d/ *vt* vorangehen (+ *dat*)

preceden|ce /ˈpresɪdəns/ *n* Vorrang *m*. **~t** *n* Präzedenzfall *m*

preceding /prɪˈsi:dɪŋ/ *a* vorhergehend

precinct /ˈpri:sɪŋkt/ *n* Bereich *m*; (*traffic-free*) Fußgängerzone *f*; (*Amer: district*) Bezirk *m*

precious /ˈpreʃəs/ *a* kostbar; ⟨*style*⟩ preziös □ *adv* (*fam*) **~ little** recht wenig

precipice /ˈpresɪpɪs/ *n* Steilabfall *m*

precipitate1 /prɪˈsɪpɪtət/ *a* voreilig

precipitat|e2 /prɪˈsɪpɪteɪt/ *vt* schleudern; (*fig: accelerate*) beschleunigen. **~ion** /-ˈteɪʃn/ *n* (*Meteorol*) Niederschlag *m*

précis /ˈpreɪsi:/ *n* (*pl* **précis** /-si:z/) Zusammenfassung *f*

precis|e /prɪˈsaɪs/ *a*, **-ly** *adv* genau. **~ion** /-ˈsɪʒn/ *n* Genauigkeit *f*

preclude /prɪˈklu:d/ *vt* ausschließen

precocious /prɪˈkəʊʃəs/ *a* frühreif

pre|con'ceived /pri:-/ *a* vorgefasst. **~con'ception** *n* vorgefasste Meinung *f*

precursor /pri:ˈkɜ:sə(r)/ *n* Vorläufer *m*

predator /ˈpredətə(r)/ *n* Raubtier *nt*

predecessor /ˈpri:dɪsesə(r)/ *n* Vorgänger(in) *m(f)*

predicament /prɪˈdɪkəmənt/ *n* Zwangslage *f*

predicat|e /ˈpredɪkət/ *n* (*Gram*) Prädikat *nt*. **~ive** /prɪˈdɪkətɪv/ *a*, **-ly** *adv* prädikativ

predict /prɪˈdɪkt/ *vt* voraussagen. **~able** /-əbl/ *a* voraussehbar; ⟨*person*⟩ berechenbar. **~ion** /-ˈdɪkʃn/ *n* Voraussage *f*

pre'domin|ant /prɪ-/ *a* vorherrschend. **~antly** *adv* hauptsächlich, überwiegend. **~ate** *vi* vorherrschen

pre-'eminent /pri:-/ *a* hervorragend

pre-empt /pri:ˈempt/ *vt* zuvorkommen (+ *dat*)

preen /pri:n/ *vt* putzen; **~ oneself** (*fig*) selbstgefällig tun

pre|fab /ˈpri:fæb/ *n* (*fam*) [einfaches] Fertighaus *nt*. **~'fabricated** *a* vorgefertigt

preface /ˈprefɪs/ *n* Vorwort *nt*

prefect /ˈpri:fekt/ *n* Präfekt *m*

prefer /prɪˈfɜ:(r)/ *vt* (*pt/pp* **preferred**) vorziehen; **I ~ to walk** ich gehe lieber zu Fuß; **I ~ wine** ich trinke lieber Wein

prefera|ble /ˈprefərəbl/ *a* **be ~ble** vorzuziehen sein (**to** *dat*). **~bly** *adv* vorzugsweise

preferen|ce /ˈprefərəns/ *n* Vorzug *m*. **~tial** /-ˈrenʃl/ *a* bevorzugt

prefix /ˈpri:fɪks/ *n* Vorsilbe *f*

pregnan|cy /ˈpregnənsɪ/ *n* Schwangerschaft *f*. **~t** *a* schwanger; ⟨*animal*⟩ trächtig

prehi'storic /pri:-/ *a* prähistorisch

prejudice /ˈpredʒʊdɪs/ *n* Vorurteil *nt*; (*bias*) Voreingenommenheit *f* □ *vt* einnehmen (**against** gegen). **~d** *a* voreingenommen

preliminary /prɪˈlɪmɪnərɪ/ *a* Vor-

prelude /ˈprelju:d/ *n* Vorspiel *nt*

pre-'marital *a* vorehelich

premature /ˈpremətjʊə(r)/ *a* vorzeitig; ⟨*birth*⟩ Früh-. **~ly** *adv* zu früh

pre'meditated /pri:-/ *a* vorsätzlich

premier /ˈpremɪə(r)/ *a* führend □ *n* (*Pol*) Premier[minister] *m*

première /ˈpremɪeə(r)/ *n* Premiere *f*

premises /ˈpremɪsɪz/ *npl* Räumlichkeiten *pl*; **on the ~** im Haus

premiss /ˈpremɪs/ *n* Prämisse *f*

premium /ˈpri:mɪəm/ *n* Prämie *f*; **be at a ~** hoch im Kurs stehen

premonition /preməˈnɪʃn/ *n* Vorahnung *f*

preoccupied /prɪˈɒkjʊpaɪd/ *a* [in Gedanken] beschäftigt

prep /prep/ *n* (*Sch*) Hausaufgaben *pl*

pre-'packed /pri:-/ *a* abgepackt

preparation /prepəˈreɪʃn/ *n* Vorbereitung *f*; (*substance*) Präparat *nt*

preparatory /prɪ'pærətrɪ/ *a* Vor- □ *adv* ~ **to** vor (+ *dat*)
prepare /prɪ'peə(r)/ *vt* vorbereiten; anrichten ⟨*meal*⟩ □ *vi* sich vorbereiten (**for** auf + *acc*); **~d to** bereit zu
pre'pay /pri:-/ *vt* (*pt/pp* **-paid**) im Voraus bezahlen
preposition /prepə'zɪʃn/ *n* Präposition *f*
prepossessing /pri:pə'zesɪŋ/ *a* ansprechend
preposterous /prɪ'pɒstərəs/ *a* absurd
prerequisite /pri:'rekwɪzɪt/ *n* Voraussetzung *f*
prerogative /prɪ'rɒgətɪv/ *n* Vorrecht *nt*
Presbyterian /prezbɪ'tɪərɪən/ *a* presbyterianisch □ *n* Presbyterianer(in) *m(f)*
prescribe /prɪ'skraɪb/ *vt* vorschreiben; (*Med*) verschreiben
prescription /prɪ'skrɪpʃn/ *n* (*Med*) Rezept *nt*
presence /'prezns/ *n* Anwesenheit *f*, Gegenwart *f*; **~ of mind** Geistesgegenwart *f*
present1 /'preznt/ *a* gegenwärtig; **be ~** anwesend sein; (*occur*) vorkommen □ *n* Gegenwart *f*; (*Gram*) Präsens *nt*; **at ~** zurzeit; **for the ~** vorläufig
present2 *n* (*gift*) Geschenk *nt*
present3 /prɪ'zent/ *vt* überreichen; (*show*) zeigen; vorlegen ⟨*cheque*⟩; (*introduce*) vorstellen; **~ s.o. with sth** jdm etw überreichen. **~able** /-əbl/ *a* **be ~able** sich zeigen lassen können
presentation /prezn'teɪʃn/ *n* Überreichung *f*. **~ ceremony** *n* Verleihungszeremonie *f*
presently /'prezntlɪ/ *adv* nachher; (*Amer: now*) zurzeit
preservation /prezə'veɪʃn/ *n* Erhaltung *f*
preservative /prɪ'zɜ:vətɪv/ *n* Konservierungsmittel *nt*
preserve /prɪ'zɜ:v/ *vt* erhalten; (*Culin*) konservieren; (*bottle*) einmachen □ *n* (*Hunting & fig*) Revier *nt*; (*jam*) Konfitüre *f*
preside /prɪ'zaɪd/ *vi* den Vorsitz haben (**over** bei)
presidency /'prezɪdənsɪ/ *n* Präsidentschaft *f*
president /'prezɪdənt/ *n* Präsident *m*; (*Amer: chairman*) Vorsitzende(r) *m/f*. **~ial** /-'denʃl/ *a* Präsidenten-; ⟨*election*⟩ Präsidentschafts-
press /pres/ *n* Presse *f* □ *vt/i* drücken; drücken auf (+ *acc*) ⟨*button*⟩; pressen ⟨*flower*⟩; (*iron*) bügeln; (*urge*) bedrängen; **~ for** drängen auf (+ *acc*); **be ~ed for time** in Zeitdruck sein. **~ on** *vi* weitergehen/-fahren; (*fig*) weitermachen
press: ~ cutting *n* Zeitungsausschnitt *m*. **~ing** *a* dringend. **~-stud** *n* Druckknopf *m*. **~-up** *n* Liegestütz *m*
pressure /'preʃə(r)/ *n* Druck *m* □ *vt* = **pressurize. ~-cooker** *n* Schnellkochtopf *m*. **~ group** *n* Interessengruppe *f*
pressurize /'preʃəraɪz/ *vt* Druck ausüben auf (+ *acc*). **~d** *a* Druck-
prestig|e /pre'sti:ʒ/ *n* Prestige *nt*. **~ious** /-'stɪdʒəs/ *a* Prestige-
presumably /prɪ'zju:məblɪ/ *adv* vermutlich
presume /prɪ'zju:m/ *vt* vermuten; **~ to do sth** sich (*dat*) anmaßen, etw zu tun □ *vi* **~ on** ausnutzen
presumpt|ion /prɪ'zʌmpʃn/ *n* Vermutung *f*; (*boldness*) Anmaßung *f*. **~uous** /-'zʌmptjʊəs/ *a*, **-ly** *adv* anmaßend
presup'pose /pri:-/ *vt* voraussetzen
pretence /prɪ'tens/ *n* Verstellung *f*; (*pretext*) Vorwand *m*; **it's all ~** das ist alles gespielt
pretend /prɪ'tend/ *vt* (*claim*) vorgeben; **~ that** so tun, als ob; **~ to be** sich ausgeben als

pretentious /prɪˈtenʃəs/ *a* protzig
pretext /ˈpriːtekst/ *n* Vorwand *m*
pretty /ˈprɪtɪ/ *a* (**-ier, -iest**), **~ily** *adv* hübsch □ *adv* (*fam: fairly*) ziemlich
pretzel /ˈpretsl/ *n* Brezel *f*
prevail /prɪˈveɪl/ *vi* siegen; ⟨*custom:*⟩ vorherrschen; **~ on s.o. to do sth** jdn dazu bringen, etw zu tun
prevalen|ce /ˈprevələns/ *n* Häufigkeit *f*. **~t** *a* vorherrschend
prevent /prɪˈvent/ *vt* verhindern, verhüten; **~ s.o. [from] doing sth** jdn daran hindern, etw zu tun. **~able** /-əbl/ *a* vermeidbar. **~ion** /-enʃn/ *n* Verhinderung *f*, Verhütung *f*. **~ive** /-ɪv/ *a* vorbeugend
preview /ˈpriːvjuː/ *n* Voraufführung *f*
previous /ˈpriːvɪəs/ *a* vorhergehend; **~ to** vor (+ *dat*). **~ly** *adv* vorher, früher
pre-ˈwar /priː-/ *a* Vorkriegs-
prey /preɪ/ *n* Beute *f*; **bird of ~** Raubvogel *m* □ *vi* **~ on** Jagd machen auf (+ *acc*); **~ on s.o.'s mind** jdm schwer auf der Seele liegen
price /praɪs/ *n* Preis *m* □ *vt* (*Comm*) auszeichnen. **~less** *a* unschätzbar; (*fig*) unbezahlbar
prick /prɪk/ *n* Stich *m* □ *vt/i* stechen; **~ up one's ears** die Ohren spitzen
prickl|e /ˈprɪkl/ *n* Stachel *m*; (*thorn*) Dorn *m*. **~y** *a* stachelig; ⟨*sensation*⟩ stechend
pride /praɪd/ *n* Stolz *m*; (*arrogance*) Hochmut *m*; (*of lions*) Rudel *nt* □ *vt* **~ oneself on** stolz sein auf (+ *acc*)
priest /priːst/ *n* Priester *m*
prig /prɪg/ *n* Tugendbold *m*
prim /prɪm/ *a* (**primmer, primmest**) prüde
primarily /ˈpraɪmərɪlɪ/ *adv* hauptsächlich, in erster Linie
primary /ˈpraɪmərɪ/ *a* Haupt-. **~ school** *n* Grundschule *f*
prime[1] /praɪm/ *a* Haupt-; (*first-rate*) erstklassig □ *n* **be in one's ~** in den besten Jahren sein
prime[2] *vt* scharf machen ⟨*bomb*⟩; grundieren ⟨*surface*⟩; (*fig*) instruieren
Prime Minister /praɪˈmɪnɪstə(r)/ *n* Premierminister(in) *m(f)*
primeval /praɪˈmiːvl/ *a* Ur-
primitive /ˈprɪmɪtɪv/ *a* primitiv
primrose /ˈprɪmrəʊz/ *n* gelbe Schlüsselblume *f*
prince /prɪns/ *n* Prinz *m*
princess /prɪnˈses/ *n* Prinzessin *f*
principal /ˈprɪnsəpl/ *a* Haupt- □ *n* (*Sch*) Rektor(in) *m(f)*
principality /prɪnsɪˈpælətɪ/ *n* Fürstentum *nt*
principally /ˈprɪnsəplɪ/ *adv* hauptsächlich
principle /ˈprɪnsəpl/ *n* Prinzip *nt*, Grundsatz *m*; **in/on ~** im/aus Prinzip
print /prɪnt/ *n* Druck *m*; (*Phot*) Abzug *m*; **in ~** gedruckt; (*available*) erhältlich; **out of ~** vergriffen □ *vt* drucken; (*write in capitals*) in Druckschrift schreiben; (*Computing*) ausdrucken; (*Phot*) abziehen. **~ed matter** *n* Drucksache *f*
print|er /ˈprɪntə(r)/ *n* Drucker *m*. **~ing** *n* Druck *m*
ˈprintout *n* (*Computing*) Ausdruck *m*
prior /ˈpraɪə(r)/ *a* frühere(r,s); **~ to** vor (+ *dat*)
priority /praɪˈɒrətɪ/ *n* Priorität *f*, Vorrang *m*; (*matter*) vordringliche Sache *f*
prise /praɪz/ *vt* **~ open/up** aufstemmen/hochstemmen
prism /ˈprɪzm/ *n* Prisma *nt*
prison /ˈprɪzn/ *n* Gefängnis *nt*. **~er** *n* Gefangene(r) *m/f*
pristine /ˈprɪstiːn/ *a* tadellos

privacy /'prɪvəsɪ/ *n* Privatsphäre *f*; **have no ~** nie für sich sein
private /'praɪvət/ *a*, **-ly** *adv* privat; (*confidential*) vertraulich; ⟨*car, secretary, school*⟩ Privat- □ *n* (*Mil*) [einfacher] Soldat *m*; **in ~** privat; (*confidentially*) vertraulich
privation /praɪ'veɪʃn/ *n* Entbehrung *f*
privatize /'praɪvətaɪz/ *vt* privatisieren
privilege /'prɪvəlɪdʒ/ *n* Privileg *nt*. **~d** *a* privilegiert
privy /'prɪvɪ/ *a* **be ~ to** wissen
prize /praɪz/ *n* Preis *m* □ *vt* schätzen. **~-giving** *n* Preisverleihung *f*. **~-winner** *n* Preisgewinner(in) *m(f)*
pro /prəʊ/ *n* (*fam*) Profi *m*; **the ~s and cons** das Für und Wider
probability /prɒbə'bɪlətɪ/ *n* Wahrscheinlichkeit *f*
probable /'prɒbəbl/ *a*, **-bly** *adv* wahrscheinlich
probation /prə'beɪʃn/ *n* (*Jur*) Bewährung *f*. **~ary** *a* Probe-; **~ary period** Probezeit *f*
probe /prəʊb/ *n* Sonde *f*; (*fig: investigation*) Untersuchung *f* □ *vt/i* **~ [into]** untersuchen
problem /'prɒbləm/ *n* Problem *nt*; (*Math*) Textaufgabe *f*. **~atic** /-'mætɪk/ *a* problematisch
procedure /prə'si:dʒə(r)/ *n* Verfahren *nt*
proceed /prə'si:d/ *vi* gehen; (*in vehicle*) fahren; (*continue*) weitergehen/-fahren; (*speaking*) fortfahren; (*act*) verfahren □ *vt* **~ to do sth** anfangen, etw zu tun
proceedings /prə'si:dɪŋz/ *npl* Verfahren *nt*; (*Jur*) Prozess *m*
proceeds /'prəʊsi:dz/ *npl* Erlös *m*
process /'prəʊses/ *n* Prozess *m*; (*procedure*) Verfahren *nt*; **in the ~** dabei □ *vt* verarbeiten; (*Admin*) bearbeiten; (*Phot*) entwickeln
procession /prə'seʃn/ *n* Umzug *m*, Prozession *f*
proclaim /prə'kleɪm/ *vt* ausrufen
proclamation /prɒklə'meɪʃn/ *n* Proklamation *f*
procure /prə'kjʊə(r)/ *vt* beschaffen
prod /prɒd/ *n* Stoß *m* □ *vt* stoßen; (*fig*) einen Stoß geben (+ *dat*)
prodigal /'prɒdɪgl/ *a* verschwenderisch
prodigious /prə'dɪdʒəs/ *a* gewaltig
prodigy /'prɒdɪdʒɪ/ *n* **[infant] ~** Wunderkind *nt*
produce[1] /'prɒdju:s/ *n* landwirtschaftliche Erzeugnisse *pl*
produce[2] /prə'dju:s/ *vt* erzeugen, produzieren; (*manufacture*) herstellen; (*bring out*) hervorholen; (*cause*) hervorrufen; inszenieren. ⟨*play*⟩; (*Radio, TV*) redigieren. **~r** *n* Erzeuger *m*, Produzent *m*; Hersteller *m*; (*Theat*) Regisseur *m*; (*Radio, TV*) Redakteur(in) *m(f)*
product /'prɒdʌkt/ *n* Erzeugnis *nt*, Produkt *nt*. **~ion** /prə'dʌkʃn/ *n* Produktion *f*; (*Theat*) Inszenierung *f*
productiv|e /prə'dʌktɪv/ *a* produktiv; ⟨*land, talks*⟩ fruchtbar. **~ity** /-'tɪvətɪ/ *n* Produktivität *f*
profan|e /prə'feɪn/ *a* weltlich; (*blasphemous*) [gottes]lästerlich. **~ity** /-'fænətɪ/ *n* (*oath*) Fluch *m*
profess /prə'fes/ *vt* behaupten; bekennen ⟨*faith*⟩
profession /prə'feʃn/ *n* Beruf *m*. **~al** *a*, **-ly** *adv* beruflich; (*not amateur*) Berufs-; (*expert*) fachmännisch; (*Sport*) professionell □ *n* Fachmann *m*; (*Sport*) Profi *m*
professor /prə'fesə(r)/ *n* Professor *m*
proficien|cy /prə'fɪʃnsɪ/ *n* Können *nt*. **~t** *a* **be ~t in** beherrschen
profile /'prəʊfaɪl/ *n* Profil *nt*; (*character study*) Porträt *nt*
profit /'prɒfɪt/ *n* Gewinn *m*, Profit *m* □ *vi* **~ from** profitieren von.

~able /-əbl/ *a*, **-bly** *adv* gewinnbringend; (*fig*) nutzbringend
profound /prə'faund/ *a*, **-ly** *adv* tief
profus|e /prə'fju:s/ *a*, **-ly** *adv* üppig; (*fig*) überschwenglich. **~ion** /-ju:ʒn/ *n* **in ~ion** in großer Fülle
progeny /'prɒdʒənɪ/ *n* Nachkommenschaft *f*
program /'prəʊgræm/ *n* Programm *nt*; □ *vt* (*pt/pp* **programmed**) programmieren
programme /'prəʊgræm/ *n* Programm *nt*; (*Radio, TV*) Sendung *f*. **~r** *n* (*Computing*) Programmierer(in) *m*(*f*)
progress[1] /'prəʊgres/ *n* Vorankommen *nt*; (*fig*) Fortschritt *m*; **in ~** im Gange; **make ~** (*fig*) Fortschritte machen
progress[2] /prə'gres/ *vi* vorankommen; (*fig*) fortschreiten. **~ion** /-eʃn/ *n* Folge *f*; (*development*) Entwicklung *f*
progressive /prə'gresɪv/ *a* fortschrittlich; ⟨*disease*⟩ fortschreitend. **~ly** *adv* zunehmend
prohibit /prə'hɪbɪt/ *vt* verbieten (**s.o.** jdm). **~ive** /-ɪv/ *a* unerschwinglich
project[1] /'prɒdʒekt/ *n* Projekt *nt*; (*Sch*) Arbeit *f*
project[2] /prə'dʒekt/ *vt* projizieren ⟨*film*⟩; (*plan*) planen □ *vi* (*jut out*) vorstehen
projectile /prə'dʒektaɪl/ *n* Geschoss *nt*
projector /prə'dʒektə(r)/ *n* Projektor *m*
proletariat /prəʊlɪ'teərɪət/ *n* Proletariat *nt*
prolific /prə'lɪfɪk/ *a* fruchtbar; (*fig*) produktiv
prologue /'prəʊlɒg/ *n* Prolog *m*
prolong /prə'lɒŋ/ *vt* verlängern
promenade /prɒmə'nɑ:d/ *n* Promenade *f* □ *vi* spazieren gehen
prominent /'prɒmɪnənt/ *a* vorstehend; (*important*) prominent; (*conspicuous*) auffällig; ⟨*place*⟩ gut sichtbar
promiscu|ity /prɒmɪ'skju:ətɪ/ *n* Promiskuität *f*. **~ous** /prə'mɪskjʊəs/ *a* **be ~ous** häufig den Partner wechseln
promis|e /'prɒmɪs/ *n* Versprechen *nt* □ *vt/i* versprechen (**s.o.** jdm); **the P ~ed Land** das Gelobte Land. **~ing** *a* viel versprechend
promot|e /prə'məʊt/ *vt* befördern; (*advance*) fördern; (*publicize*) Reklame machen für; **be ~ed** (*Sport*) aufsteigen. **~ion** /-əʊʃn/ *n* Beförderung *f*; (*Sport*) Aufstieg *m*; (*Comm*) Reklame *f*
prompt /prɒmpt/ *a* prompt, unverzüglich; (*punctual*) pünktlich □ *adv* pünktlich □ *vt/i* veranlassen (**to** zu); (*Theat*) soufflieren (+ *dat*). **~er** *n* Souffleur *m*/Souffleuse *f*. **~ly** *adv* prompt
prone /prəʊn/ *a* **be** *or* **lie ~** auf dem Bauch liegen; **be ~ to** neigen zu; **be ~ to do sth** dazu neigen, etw zu tun
prong /prɒŋ/ *n* Zinke *f*
pronoun /'prəʊnaʊn/ *n* Fürwort *nt*, Pronomen *nt*
pronounce /prə'naʊns/ *vt* aussprechen; (*declare*) erklären. **~d** *a* ausgeprägt; (*noticeable*) deutlich. **~ment** *n* Erklärung *f*
pronunciation /prənʌnsɪ'eɪʃn/ *n* Aussprache *f*
proof /pru:f/ *n* Beweis *m*; (*Typ*) Korrekturbogen *m* □ *a* **~ against water/theft** wasserfest/diebessicher. **~-reader** *n* Korrektor *m*
prop[1] /prɒp/ *n* Stütze *f* □ *vt* (*pt/pp* **propped**) **~ open** offen halten; **~ against** (*lean*) lehnen an (+ *acc*). **~ up** *vt* stützen
prop[2] *n* (*Theat, fam*) Requisit *nt*
propaganda /prɒpə'gændə/ *n* Propaganda *f*
propagate /'prɒpəgeɪt/ *vt* vermehren; (*fig*) verbreiten, propagieren

propel /prə'pel/ *vt* (*pt/pp* **propelled**) [an]treiben. **~ler** *n* Propeller *m*. **~ling 'pencil** *n* Drehbleistift *m*

propensity /prə'pensətɪ/ *n* Neigung *f* (**for** zu)

proper /'prɒpə(r)/ *a*, **-ly** *adv* richtig; (*decent*) anständig. **~ 'name, ~ 'noun** *n* Eigenname *m*

property /'prɒpətɪ/ *n* Eigentum *nt*; (*quality*) Eigenschaft *f*; (*Theat*) Requisit *nt*; (*land*) [Grund]besitz *m*; (*house*) Haus *nt*. **~ market** *n* Immobilienmarkt *m*

prophecy /'prɒfəsɪ/ *n* Prophezeiung *f*

prophesy /'prɒfɪsaɪ/ *vt* (*pt/pp* **-ied**) prophezeien

prophet /'prɒfɪt/ *n* Prophet *m*. **~ic** /prə'fetɪk/ *a* prophetisch

proportion /prə'pɔːʃn/ *n* Verhältnis *nt*; (*share*) Teil *m*; **~s** *pl* Proportionen; (*dimensions*) Maße. **~al** *a*, **-ly** *adv* proportional

proposal /prə'pəʊzl/ *n* Vorschlag *m*; (*of marriage*) [Heirats]antrag *m*

propose /prə'pəʊz/ *vt* vorschlagen; (*intend*) vorhaben; einbringen ⟨*motion*⟩; ausbringen ⟨*toast*⟩ □ *vi* einen Heiratsantrag machen

proposition /prɒpə'zɪʃn/ *n* Vorschlag *m*

propound /prə'paʊnd/ *vt* darlegen

proprietor /prə'praɪətə(r)/ *n* Inhaber(in) *m(f)*

propriety /prə'praɪətɪ/ *n* Korrektheit *f*; (*decorum*) Anstand *m*

propulsion /prə'pʌlʃn/ *n* Antrieb *m*

prosaic /prə'zeɪɪk/ *a* prosaisch

prose /prəʊz/ *n* Prosa *f*

prosecut|e /'prɒsɪkjuːt/ *vt* strafrechtlich verfolgen. **~ion** /-'kjuːʃn/ *n* strafrechtliche Verfolgung *f*; **the ~ion** die Anklage. **~or** *n* **[Public] P~or** Staatsanwalt *m*

prospect[1] /'prɒspekt/ *n* Aussicht *f*

prospect[2] /prə'spekt/ *vi* suchen (**for** nach)

prospect|ive /prə'spektɪv/ *a* (*future*) zukünftig. **~or** *n* Prospektor *m*

prospectus /prə'spektəs/ *n* Prospekt *m*

prosper /'prɒspə(r)/ *vi* gedeihen, florieren; ⟨*person*⟩ Erfolg haben. **~ity** /-'sperətɪ/ *n* Wohlstand *m*

prosperous /'prɒspərəs/ *a* wohlhabend

prostitut|e /'prɒstɪtjuːt/ *n* Prostituierte *f*. **~ion** /-'tjuːʃn/ *n* Prostitution *f*

prostrate /'prɒstreɪt/ *a* ausgestreckt; **~ with grief** (*fig*) vor Kummer gebrochen

protagonist /prəʊ'tægənɪst/ *n* Kämpfer *m*; (*fig*) Protagonist *m*

protect /prə'tekt/ *vt* schützen (**from** vor + *dat*); beschützen ⟨*person*⟩. **~ion** /-ekʃn/ *n* Schutz *m*. **~ive** /-ɪv/ *a* Schutz-; (*fig*) beschützend. **~or** *n* Beschützer *m*

protégé /'prɒtɪʒeɪ/ *n* Schützling *m*, Protegé *m*

protein /'prəʊtiːn/ *n* Eiweiß *nt*

protest[1] /'prəʊtest/ *n* Protest *m*

protest[2] /prə'test/ *vi* protestieren

Protestant /'prɒtɪstənt/ *a* protestantisch, evangelisch □ *n* Protestant(in) *m(f)*, Evangelische(r) *m/f*

protester /prə'testə(r)/ *n* Protestierende(r) *m/f*

protocol /'prəʊtəkɒl/ *n* Protokoll *nt*

prototype /'prəʊtə-/ *n* Prototyp *m*

protract /prə'trækt/ *vt* verlängern. **~or** *n* Winkelmesser *m*

protrude /prə'truːd/ *vi* [her]vorstehen

proud /praʊd/ *a*, **-ly** *adv* stolz (**of** auf + *acc*)

prove /pruːv/ *vt* beweisen □ *vi* **~ to be** sich erweisen als

proverb /'prɒvɜ:b/ *n* Sprichwort *nt*. **~ial** /prə'vɜ:bɪəl/ *a* sprichwörtlich
provide /prə'vaɪd/ *vt* zur Verfügung stellen; spenden ⟨*shade*⟩; **~ s.o. with sth** jdn mit etw versorgen *od* versehen □ *vi* **~ for** sorgen für
provided /prə'vaɪdɪd/ *conj* **~ [that]** vorausgesetzt [dass]
providen|ce /'prɒvɪdəns/ *n* Vorsehung *f*. **~tial** /-'denʃl/ *a* **be ~tial** ein Glück sein
providing /prə'vaɪdɪŋ/ *conj* = **provided**
provinc|e /'prɒvɪns/ *n* Provinz *f*; (*fig*) Bereich *m*. **~ial** /prə'vɪnʃl/ *a* provinziell
provision /prə'vɪʒn/ *n* Versorgung *f* (*of* mit); **~s** *pl* Lebensmittel *pl*. **~al** *a*, **-ly** *adv* vorläufig
proviso /prə'vaɪzəʊ/ *n* Vorbehalt *m*
provocat|ion /prɒvə'keɪʃn/ *n* Provokation *f*. **~ive** /prə'vɒkətɪv/ *a*, **-ly** *adv* provozierend; (*sexually*) aufreizend
provoke /prə'vəʊk/ *vt* provozieren; (*cause*) hervorrufen
prow /praʊ/ *n* Bug *m*
prowess /'praʊɪs/ *n* Kraft *f*
prowl /praʊl/ *vi* herumschleichen □ *n* **be on the ~** herumschleichen
proximity /prɒk'sɪmətɪ/ *n* Nähe *f*
proxy /'prɒksɪ/ *n* Stellvertreter(in) *m(f)*; (*power*) Vollmacht *f*
prude /pru:d/ *n* **be a ~** prüde sein
pruden|ce /'pru:dns/ *n* Umsicht *f*. **~t** *a*, **-ly** *adv* umsichtig; (*wise*) klug
prudish /'pru:dɪʃ/ *a* prüde
prune¹ /pru:n/ *n* Backpflaume *f*
prune² *vt* beschneiden
pry /praɪ/ *vi* (*pt/pp* **pried**) neugierig sein
psalm /sɑ:m/ *n* Psalm *m*
pseudonym /'sju:dənɪm/ *n* Pseudonym *nt*
psychiatric /saɪkɪ'ætrɪk/ *a* psychiatrisch
psychiatr|ist /saɪ'kaɪətrɪst/ *n* Psychiater(*in*) *m(f)*. **~y** *n* Psychiatrie *f*
psychic /'saɪkɪk/ *a* übersinnlich; **I'm not ~** ich kann nicht hellsehen
psycho|'analyse /saɪkəʊ-/ *vt* psychoanalysieren. **~a'nalysis** *n* Psychoanalyse *f*. **~'analyst** Psychoanalytiker(in) *m(f)*
psychological /saɪkə'lɒdʒɪkl/ *a*, **-ly** *adv* psychologisch; ⟨illness⟩ psychisch
psycholog|ist /saɪ'kɒlədʒɪst/ *n* Psychologe *m*/ -login *f*. **~y** *n* Psychologie *f*
psychopath /'saɪkəpæθ/ *n* Psychopath(in) *m(f)*
P.T.O. *abbr* (**please turn over**) b.w
pub /pʌb/ *n* (*fam*) Kneipe *f*
puberty /'pju:bətɪ/ *n* Pubertät *f*
public /'pʌblɪk/ *a*, **-ly** *adv* öffentlich; **make ~** publik machen □ *n* **the ~** die Öffentlichkeit; **in ~** in aller Öffentlichkeit
publican /'pʌblɪkən/ *n* [Gast]wirt *m*
publication /pʌblɪ'keɪʃn/ *n* Veröffentlichung *f*
public: ~ con'venience *n* öffentliche Toilette *f*. **~ 'holiday** *n* gesetzlicher Feiertag *m*. **~ 'house** *n* [Gast]wirtschaft *f*
publicity /pʌb'lɪsətɪ/ *n* Publicity *f*; (*advertising*) Reklame *f*
publicize /'pʌblɪsaɪz/ *vt* Reklame machen für
public: ~ 'library *n* öffentliche Bücherei *f*. **~ 'school** *n* Privatschule *f*; (*Amer*) staatliche Schule *f*. **~-'spirited** *a* **be ~-spirited** Gemeinsinn haben. **~'transport** *n* öffentliche Verkehrsmittel *pl*
publish /'pʌblɪʃ/ *vt* veröffentlichen. **~er** *n* Verleger(in) *m(f)*; (*firm*) Verlag *m*. **~ing** *n* Verlagswesen *nt*

pucker /ˈpʌkə(r)/ *vt* kräuseln
pudding /ˈpʊdɪŋ/ *n* Pudding *m*; (*course*) Nachtisch *m*
puddle /ˈpʌdl/ *n* Pfütze *f*
puerile /ˈpjʊəraɪl/ *a* kindisch
puff /pʌf/ *n* (*of wind*) Hauch *m*; (*of smoke*) Wölkchen *nt*; (*for powder*) Quaste *f* □ *vt* blasen, pusten; **~ out** ausstoßen. □ *vi* keuchen; **~ at** paffen an (+ *dat*) ⟨*pipe*⟩. **~ed** *a* (*out of breath*) aus der Puste. **~ pastry** *n* Blätterteig *m*
puffy /ˈpʌfɪ/ *a* geschwollen
pugnacious /pʌgˈneɪʃəs/ *a*, **-ly** *adv* aggressiv
pull /pʊl/ *n* Zug *m*; (*jerk*) Ruck *m*; (*fam: influence*) Einfluss *m* □ *vt* ziehen; ziehen an (+ *dat*) ⟨*rope*⟩; **~ a muscle** sich (*dat*) einen Muskel zerren; **~ oneself together** sich zusammennehmen; **~ one's weight** tüchtig mitarbeiten; **~ s.o.'s leg** (*fam*) jdn auf den Arm nehmen. **~ down** *vt* herunterziehen; (*demolish*) abreißen. **~ in** *vt* hereinziehen □ *vi* (*Auto*) einscheren. **~ off** *vt* abziehen; (*fam*) schaffen. **~ out** *vt* herausziehen □ *vi* (*Auto*) ausscheren. **~ through** *vt* durchziehen □ *vi* (*recover*) durchkommen. **~ up** *vt* heraufziehen; ausziehen ⟨*plant*⟩; (*reprimand*) zurechtweisen □ *vi* (*Auto*) anhalten
pulley /ˈpʊlɪ/ *n* (*Techn*) Rolle *f*
pullover /ˈpʊləʊvə(r)/ *n* Pullover *m*
pulp /pʌlp/ *n* Brei *m*; (*of fruit*) [Frucht]fleisch *nt*
pulpit /ˈpʊlpɪt/ *n* Kanzel *f*
pulsate /pʌlˈseɪt/ *vi* pulsieren
pulse /pʌls/ *n* Puls *m*
pulses /ˈpʌlsɪz/ *npl* Hülsenfrüchte *pl*
pulverize /ˈpʌlvəraɪz/ *vt* pulverisieren
pumice /ˈpʌmɪs/ *n* Bimsstein *m*
pummel /ˈpʌml/ *vt* (*pt/pp* **pummelled**) mit den Fäusten bearbeiten
pump /pʌmp/ *n* Pumpe *f* □ *vt* pumpen; (*fam*) aushorchen. **~ up** *vt* hochpumpen; (*inflate*) aufpumpen
pumpkin /ˈpʌmpkɪn/ *n* Kürbis *m*
pun /pʌn/ *n* Wortspiel *nt*
punch[1] /pʌntʃ/ *n* Faustschlag *m*; (*device*) Locher *m* □ *vt* boxen; lochen ⟨*ticket*⟩; stanzen ⟨*hole*⟩
punch[2] *n* (*drink*) Bowle *f*
punch: ~ line *n* Pointe *f*. **~-up** *n* Schlägerei *f*
punctual /ˈpʌŋktjʊəl/ *a*, **-ly** *adv* pünktlich. **~ity** /-ˈælətɪ/ *n* Pünktlichkeit *f*
punctuat|e /ˈpʌŋktjʊeɪt/ *vt* mit Satzzeichen versehen. **~ion** /-ˈeɪʃn/ *n* Interpunktion *f*. **~ion mark** *n* Satzzeichen *nt*
puncture /ˈpʌŋktʃə(r)/ *n* Loch *nt*; (*tyre*) Reifenpanne *f* □ *vt* durchstechen
pundit /ˈpʌndɪt/ *n* Experte *m*
pungent /ˈpʌndʒənt/ *a* scharf
punish /ˈpʌnɪʃ/ *vt* bestrafen. **~able** /-əbl/ *a* strafbar. **~ment** *n* Strafe *f*
punitive /ˈpjuːnɪtɪv/ *a* Straf-
punnet /ˈpʌnɪt/ *n* Körbchen *nt*
punt /pʌnt/ *n* (*boat*) Stechkahn *m*
punter /ˈpʌntə(r)/ *n* (*gambler*) Wetter *m*; (*client*) Kunde *m*
puny /ˈpjuːnɪ/ *a* (**-ier, -iest**) mickerig
pup /pʌp/ *n* = **puppy**
pupil /ˈpjuːpl/ *n* Schüler(in) *m*(*f*); (*of eye*) Pupille *f*
puppet /ˈpʌpɪt/ *n* Puppe *f*; (*fig*) Marionette *f*
puppy /ˈpʌpɪ/ *n* junger Hund *m*
purchase /ˈpɜːtʃəs/ *n* Kauf *m*; (*leverage*) Hebelkraft *f* □ *vt* kaufen. **~r** *n* Käufer *m*
pure /pjʊə(r)/ *a* (**-r, -st,**) **-ly** *adv* rein
purée /ˈpjʊəreɪ/ *n* Püree *nt*, Brei *m*
purgatory /ˈpɜːgətrɪ/ *n* (*Relig*) Fegefeuer *nt*; (*fig*) Hölle *f*

purge /pɜ:dʒ/ *n* (*Pol*) Säuberungsaktion *f* □ *vt* reinigen; (*Pol*) säubern
puri|fication /pjʊərɪfɪ'keɪʃn/ *n* Reinigung *f*. **~fy** /'pjʊərɪfaɪ/ *vt* (*pt/pp* **-ied**) reinigen
puritanical /pjʊərɪ'tænɪkl/ *a* puritanisch
purity /'pjʊərɪtɪ/ *n* Reinheit *f*
purl /pɜ:l/ *n* (*Knitting*) linke Masche *f* □ *vt/i* links stricken
purple /'pɜ:pl/ *a* [dunkel]lila
purport /pə'pɔ:t/ *vt* vorgeben
purpose /'pɜ:pəs/ *n* Zweck *m*; (*intention*) Absicht *f*; (*determination*) Entschlossenheit *f*; **on ~** absichtlich; **to no ~** unnützerweise. **~ful** *a*, **-ly** *adv* entschlossen. **~ly** *adv* absichtlich
purr /pɜ:(r)/ *vi* schnurren
purse /pɜ:s/ *n* Portemonnaie *nt*; (*Amer: handbag*) Handtasche *f* □ *vt* schürzen ⟨*lips*⟩
pursue /pə'sju:/ *vt* verfolgen; (*fig*) nachgehen (+ *dat*). **~r** /-ə(r)/ *n* Verfolger *m*
pursuit /pə'sju:t/ *n* Verfolgung *f*; Jagd *f*; (*pastime*) Beschäftigung *f*; **in ~** hinterher
pus /pʌs/ *n* Eiter *m*
push /pʊʃ/ *n* Stoß *m*, (*fam*) Schubs *m*; **get the ~** (*fam*) hinausfliegen □ *vt/i* schieben; (*press*) drücken; (*roughly*) stoßen; **be ~ed for time** (*fam*) unter Zeitdruck stehen. **~ off** *vt* hinunterstoßen □ *vi* (*fam: leave*) abhauen. **~ on** *vi* (*continue*) weitergehen/-fahren; (*with activity*) weitermachen. **~ up** *vt* hochschieben; hochtreiben ⟨*price*⟩
push: ~-button *n* Druckknopf *m*. **~-chair** *n* [Kinder]sportwagen *m*. **~-over** *n* (*fam*) Kinderspiel *nt*. **~-up** *n* (*Amer*) Liegestütz *m*
pushy /'pʊʃɪ/ *a* (*fam*) aufdringlich
puss /pʊs/ *n*, **pussy** /'pʊsɪ/ *n* Mieze *f*
put /pʊt/ *vt* (*pt/pp* **put**, *pres p* **putting**) tun; (*place*) setzen; (*upright*) stellen; (*flat*) legen; (*express*) ausdrücken; (*say*) sagen; (*estimate*) schätzen (**at** auf + *acc*); **~ aside** *or* **by** beiseite legen; **~ one's foot down** (*fam*) energisch werden; (*Auto*) Gas geben □ *vi* **~ to sea** auslaufen □ *a* **stay ~** dableiben. **~ away** *vt* wegräumen. **~ back** *vt* wieder hinsetzen/-stellen/-legen; zurückstellen ⟨*clock*⟩. **~ down** *vt* hinsetzen/-stellen/-legen; (*suppress*) niederschlagen; (*kill*) töten; (*write*) niederschreiben; (*attribute*) zuschreiben (**to** *dat*). **~ forward** *vt* vorbringen; vorstellen ⟨*clock*⟩. **~ in** *vt* hineinsetzen/-stellen/-legen; (*insert*) einstecken; (*submit*) einreichen □ *vi* **~ in for** beantragen. **~ off** *vt* ausmachen ⟨*light*⟩; (*postpone*) verschieben; **~ s.o. off** jdn abbestellen; (*disconcert*) jdn aus der Fassung bringen; **~ s.o. off sth** jdm etw verleiden. **~ on** *vt* anziehen ⟨*clothes, brake*⟩; sich (*dat*) aufsetzen ⟨*hat*⟩; (*Culin*) aufsetzen; anmachen ⟨*light*⟩; aufführen ⟨*play*⟩; annehmen ⟨*accent*⟩; **~ on weight** zunehmen. **~ out** *vt* hinaussetzen/-stellen/-legen; ausmachen ⟨*fire, light*⟩; ausstrecken ⟨*hand*⟩; (*disconcert*) aus der Fassung bringen; **~ s.o./oneself out** jdm/sich Umstände machen. **~ through** *vt* durchstecken; (*Teleph*) verbinden (**to** mit). **~ up** *vt* errichten ⟨*building*⟩; aufschlagen ⟨*tent*⟩; aufspannen ⟨*umbrella*⟩; anschlagen ⟨*notice*⟩; erhöhen ⟨*price*⟩; unterbringen ⟨*guest*⟩; **~ s.o. up to sth** jdn zu etw anstiften □ *vi* (*at hotel*) absteigen in (+ *dat*); **~ up with sth** sich (*dat*) etw bieten lassen
putrefy /'pju:trɪfaɪ/ *vi* (*pt/pp* **-ied**) verwesen
putrid /'pju:trɪd/ faulig
putty /'pʌtɪ/ *n* Kitt *m*

put-up /ˈpʊtʌp/ *a* **a ~ job** ein abgekartetes Spiel *nt*
puzzl|e /ˈpʌzl/ *n* Rätsel *nt*; (*jigsaw*) Puzzlespiel *nt* □ *vt* **it ~es me** es ist mir rätselhaft □ *vi* **~e over** sich (*dat*) den Kopf zerbrechen über (+ *acc*). **~ing** *a* rätselhaft
pyjamas /pəˈdʒɑːməz/ *npl* Schlafanzug *m*
pylon /ˈpaɪlən/ *n* Mast *m*
pyramid /ˈpɪrəmɪd/ *n* Pyramide *f*
python /ˈpaɪθn/ *n* Pythonschlange *f*

Q

quack¹ /kwæk/ *n* Quaken *nt* □ *vi* quaken
quack² *n* (*doctor*) Quacksalber *m*
quad /kwɒd/ *n* (*fam: court*) Hof *m*; **~s** *pl* = **quadruplets**
quadrangle /ˈkwɒdræŋgl/ *n* Viereck *nt*; (*court*) Hof *m*
quadruped /ˈkwɒdrʊped/ *n* Vierfüßer *m*
quadruple /ˈkwɒdrʊpl/ *a* vierfach □ *vt* vervierfachen □ *vi* sich vervierfachen. **~ts** /-plɪts/ *npl* Vierlinge *pl*
quagmire /ˈkwɒgmaɪə(r)/ *n* Sumpf *m*
quaint /kweɪnt/ *a* (**-er, -est**) malerisch; (*odd*) putzig
quake /kweɪk/ *n* (*fam*) Erdbeben *nt* □ *vi* beben; (*with fear*) zittern
Quaker /ˈkweɪkə(r)/ *n* Quäker(in) *m*(*f*)
qualif|ication /kwɒlɪfɪˈkeɪʃn/ *n* Qualifikation *f*; (*reservation*) Einschränkung *f*. **~ied** /-faɪd/ *a* qualifiziert; (*trained*) ausgebildet; (*limited*) bedingt
qualify /ˈkwɒlɪfaɪ/ *v* (*pt/pp* **-ied**) □ *vt* qualifizieren; (*entitle*) berechtigen; (*limit*) einschränken □ *vi* sich qualifizieren
quality /ˈkwɒlətɪ/ *n* Qualität *f*; (*characteristic*) Eigenschaft *f*
qualm /kwɑːm/ *n* Bedenken *pl*
quandary /ˈkwɒndərɪ/ *n* Dilemma *nt*
quantity /ˈkwɒntətɪ/ *n* Quantität *f*, Menge *f*; **in ~** in großen Mengen
quarantine /ˈkwɒrəntiːn/ *n* Quarantäne *f*
quarrel /ˈkwɒrl/ *n* Streit *m* □ *vi* (*pt/pp* **quarrelled**) sich streiten. **~some** *a* streitsüchtig
quarry¹ /ˈkwɒrɪ/ *n* (*prey*) Beute *f*
quarry² *n* Steinbruch *m*
quart /kwɔːt/ *n* Quart *nt*
quarter /ˈkwɔːtə(r)/ *n* Viertel *nt*; (*of year*) Vierteljahr *nt*; (*Amer*) 25-Cent-Stück *nt*; **~s** *pl* Quartier *nt*; **at [a] ~ to six** um Viertel vor sechs; **from all ~s** aus allen Richtungen □ *vt* vierteln; (*Mil*) einquartieren (**on** bei). **~-ˈfinal** *n* Viertelfinale *nt*
quarterly /ˈkwɔːtəlɪ/ *a & adv* vierteljährlich
quartet /kwɔːˈtet/ *n* Quartett *nt*
quartz /kwɔːts/ *n* Quarz *m*. **~ watch** *n* Quarzuhr *f*
quash /kwɒʃ/ *vt* aufheben; niederschlagen ⟨*rebellion*⟩
quaver /ˈkweɪvə(r)/ *n* (*Mus*) Achtelnote *f* □ *vi* zittern
quay /kiː/ *n* Kai *m*
queasy /ˈkwiːzɪ/ *a* **I feel ~** mir ist übel
queen /kwiːn/ *n* Königin *f*; (*Cards, Chess*) Dame *f*
queer /kwɪə(r)/ *a* (**-er, -est**) eigenartig; (*dubious*) zweifelhaft; (*ill*) unwohl; (*fam: homosexual*) schwul □ *n* (*fam*) Schwule(r) *m*
quell /kwel/ *vt* unterdrücken
quench /kwentʃ/ *vt* löschen
query /ˈkwɪərɪ/ *n* Frage *f*; (*question mark*) Fragezeichen *nt* □ *vt* (*pt/pp* **-ied**) infrage stellen; reklamieren ⟨*bill*⟩
quest /kwest/ *n* Suche *f* (**for** nach)

question /ˈkwestʃn/ *n* Frage *f*; (*for discussion*) Thema *nt*; **out of the ~** ausgeschlossen; **without ~** ohne Frage; **the person in ~** die fragliche Person □ *vt* infrage stellen; **~ s.o.** jdn ausfragen; ⟨*police:*⟩ jdn verhören. **~able** /-əbl/ *a* zweifelhaft. **~ mark** *n* Fragezeichen *nt*
questionnaire /kwestʃəˈneə(r)/ *n* Fragebogen *m*
queue /kjuː/ *n* Schlange *f* □ *vi* **~ [up]** Schlange stehen, sich anstellen (**for** nach)
quibble /ˈkwɪbl/ *vi* Haarspalterei treiben
quick /kwɪk/ *a* (**-er, -est**), **-ly** *adv* schnell; **be ~!** mach schnell! **have a ~ meal** schnell etwas essen □ *adv* schnell □ *n* **cut to the ~** (*fig*) bis ins Mark getroffen. **~en** *vt* beschleunigen □ *vi* sich beschleunigen
quick: ~sand *n* Treibsand *m*. **~-tempered** *a* aufbrausend
quid /kwɪd/ *n inv* (*fam*) Pfund *nt*
quiet /ˈkwaɪət/ *a* (**-er, -est**), **-ly** *adv* still; (*calm*) ruhig; (*soft*) leise; **keep ~ about** (*fam*) nichts sagen von □ *n* Stille *f*; Ruhe *f*; **on the ~** heimlich
quiet|en /ˈkwaɪətn/ *vt* beruhigen □ *vi* **~en down** ruhig werden. **~ness** *n* (*see* **quiet**) Stille *f*; Ruhe *f*
quill /kwɪl/ *n* Feder *f*; (*spine*) Stachel *m*
quilt /kwɪlt/ *n* Steppdecke *f*. **~ed** *a* Stepp-
quince /kwɪns/ *n* Quitte *f*
quins /kwɪnz/ *npl* (*fam*) = **quintuplets**
quintet /kwɪnˈtet/ *n* Quintett *nt*
quintuplets /ˈkwɪntjʊplɪts/ *npl* Fünflinge *pl*
quip /kwɪp/ *n* Scherz *m* □ *vi* (*pt/pp* **quipped**) scherzen
quirk /kwɜːk/ *n* Eigenart *f*
quit /kwɪt/ *v* (*pt/pp* **quitted** or **quit**) □ *vt* verlassen; (*give up*) aufgeben; **~ doing sth** aufhören, etw zu tun □ *vi* gehen; **give s.o. notice to ~** jdm die Wohnung kündigen
quite /kwaɪt/ *adv* ganz; (*really*) wirklich; **~ [so]!** genau! **~ a few** ziemlich viele
quits /kwɪts/ *a* quitt
quiver /ˈkwɪvə(r)/ *vi* zittern
quiz /kwɪz/ *n* Quiz *nt* □ *vt* (*pt/pp* **quizzed**) ausfragen. **~zical** *a*, **-ly** *adv* fragend
quorum /ˈkwɔːrəm/ *n* **have a ~** beschlussfähig sein
quota /ˈkwəʊtə/ *n* Anteil *m*; (*Comm*) Kontingent *nt*
quotation /kwəʊˈteɪʃn/ *n* Zitat *nt*; (*price*) Kostenvoranschlag *m*; (*of shares*) Notierung *f*. **~ marks** *npl* Anführungszeichen *pl*
quote /kwəʊt/ *n* (*fam*) = **quotation; in ~s** in Anführungszeichen □ *vt/i* zitieren

R

rabbi /ˈræbaɪ/ *n* Rabbiner *m*; (*title*) Rabbi *m*
rabbit /ˈræbɪt/ *n* Kaninchen *nt*
rabble /ˈræbl/ *n* **the ~** der Pöbel
rabid /ˈræbɪd/ *a* fanatisch; ⟨*animal*⟩ tollwütig
rabies /ˈreɪbiːz/ *n* Tollwut *f*
race¹ /reɪs/ *n* Rasse *f*
race² *n* Rennen *nt*; (*fig*) Wettlauf *m* □ *vi* [am Rennen] teilnehmen; ⟨*athlete, horse:*⟩ laufen; (*fam: rush*) rasen □ *vt* um die Wette laufen mit; an einem Rennen teilnehmen lassen ⟨*horse*⟩
race: ~course *n* Rennbahn *f*. **~horse** *n* Rennpferd *nt*. **~-track** *n* Rennbahn *f*
racial /ˈreɪʃl/ *a*, **-ly** *adv* rassisch; ⟨*discrimination, minority*⟩ Rassen-
racing /ˈreɪsɪŋ/ *n* Rennsport *m*; (*horse-*) Pferderennen *nt*. **~ car** *n*

Rennwagen *m.* ~ **driver** *n* Rennfahrer *m*

racis|m /ˈreɪsɪzm/ *n* Rassismus *m.* ~**t** /-ɪst/ *a* rassistisch □ *n* Rassist *m*

rack¹ /ræk/ *n* Ständer *m*; (*for plates*) Gestell *nt* □ *vt* ~ **one's brains** sich (*dat*) den Kopf zerbrechen

rack² *n* **go to** ~ **and ruin** verfallen; (*fig*) herunterkommen

racket¹ /ˈrækɪt/ *n* (*Sport*) Schläger *m*

racket² *n* (*din*) Krach *m*; (*swindle*) Schwindelgeschäft *nt*

racy /ˈreɪsɪ/ *a* (**-ier, -iest**) schwungvoll; (*risqué*) gewagt

radar /ˈreɪdɑː(r)/ *n* Radar *m*

radian|ce /ˈreɪdɪəns/ *n* Strahlen *nt.* ~**t** *a*, **-ly** *adv* strahlend

radiat|e /ˈreɪdɪeɪt/ *vt* ausstrahlen □ *vi* ⟨*heat:*⟩ ausgestrahlt werden; ⟨*roads:*⟩ strahlenförmig ausgehen. ~**ion** /-ˈeɪʃn/ *n* Strahlung *f*

radiator /ˈreɪdɪeɪtə(r)/ *n* Heizkörper *m*; (*Auto*) Kühler *m*

radical /ˈrædɪkl/ *a*, **-ly** *adv* radikal □ *n* Radikale(r) *m/f*

radio /ˈreɪdɪəʊ/ *n* Radio *nt*; **by** ~ über Funk □ *vt* funken ⟨*message*⟩

radio|ˈactive *a* radioaktiv. ~**acˈtivity** *n* Radioaktivität *f*

radiography /reɪdɪˈɒgrəfɪ/ *n* Röntgenographie *f*

ˈradio ham *n* Hobbyfunker *m*

radioˈtherapy *n* Strahlenbehandlung *f*

radish /ˈrædɪʃ/ *n* Radieschen *nt*

radius /ˈreɪdɪəs/ *n* (*pl* **-dii** /-dɪaɪ/) Radius *m*, Halbmesser *m*

raffle /ˈræfl/ *n* Tombola *f* □ *vt* verlosen

raft /rɑːft/ *n* Floß *nt*

rafter /ˈrɑːftə(r)/ *n* Dachsparren *m*

rag¹ /ræg/ *n* Lumpen *m*; (*pej: newspaper*) Käseblatt *nt*; **in** ~**s** in Lumpen

rag² *vt* (*pt/pp* **ragged**) (*fam*) aufziehen

rage /reɪdʒ/ *n* Wut *f*; **all the** ~ (*fam*) der letzte Schrei □ *vi* rasen; ⟨*storm:*⟩ toben

ragged /ˈrægɪd/ *a* zerlumpt; ⟨*edge*⟩ ausgefranst

raid /reɪd/ *n* Überfall *m*; (*Mil*) Angriff *m*; (*police*) Razzia *f* □ *vt* überfallen; (*Mil*) angreifen; ⟨*police*⟩ eine Razzia durchführen in (+ *dat*); (*break in*) eindringen in (+ *acc*). ~**er** *n* Eindringling *m*; (*of bank*) Bankräuber *m*

rail /reɪl/ *n* Schiene *f*; (*pole*) Stange *f*; (*hand*~) Handlauf *m*; (*Naut*) Reling *f*; **by** ~ mit der Bahn

railings /ˈreɪlɪŋz/ *npl* Geländer *nt*

ˈrailroad *n* (*Amer*) = **railway**

ˈrailway *n* [Eisen]bahn *f.* ~**man** *n* Eisenbahner *m.* ~ **station** *n* Bahnhof *m*

rain /reɪn/ *n* Regen *m* □ *vi* regnen

rain: ~**bow** *n* Regenbogen *m.* ~**check** *n* (*Amer*) **take a** ~**check on** aufschieben. ~**coat** *n* Regenmantel *m.* ~**fall** *n* Niederschlag *m*

rainy /ˈreɪnɪ/ *a* (**-ier, -iest**) regnerisch

raise /reɪz/ *n* (*Amer*) Lohnerhöhung *f* □ *vt* erheben; (*upright*) aufrichten; (*make higher*) erhöhen; (*lift*) [hoch]heben; lüften ⟨*hat*⟩; aufziehen ⟨*children, animals*⟩; aufwerfen ⟨*question*⟩; aufbringen ⟨*money*⟩

raisin /ˈreɪzn/ *n* Rosine *f*

rake /reɪk/ *n* Harke *f*, Rechen *m* □ *vt* harken, rechen. ~ **up** *vt* zusammenharken; (*fam*) wieder aufrühren

ˈrake-off *n* (*fam*) Prozente *pl*

rally /ˈrælɪ/ *n* Versammlung *f*; (*Auto*) Rallye *f*; (*Tennis*) Ballwechsel *m* □ *vt* sammeln □ *vi* sich sammeln; (*recover strength*) sich erholen

ram /ræm/ *n* Schafbock *m*; (*Astr*) Widder *m* □ *vt* (*pt/pp* **rammed**) rammen

rambl|e /'ræmbl/ *n* Wanderung *f* □ *vi* wandern; (*in speech*) irrereden. **~er** *n* Wanderer *m*; (*rose*) Kletterrose *f*. **~ing** *a* weitschweifig, ⟨*club*⟩ Wander-

ramp /ræmp/ *n* Rampe *f*; (*Aviat*) Gangway *f*

rampage[1] /'ræmpeɪdʒ/ *n* **be/go on the ~** randalieren

rampage[2] /ræm'peɪdʒ/ *vi* randalieren

rampant /'ræmpənt/ *a* weit verbreitet; (*in heraldry*) aufgerichtet

rampart /'ræmpɑ:t/ *n* Wall *m*

ramshackle /'ræmʃækl/ *a* baufällig

ran /ræn/ *see* **run**

ranch /rɑ:ntʃ/ *n* Ranch *f*

rancid /'rænsɪd/ *a* ranzig

rancour /'ræŋkə(r)/ *n* Groll *m*

random /'rændəm/ *a* willkürlich; **a ~ sample** eine Stichprobe □ *n* **at ~** aufs Geratewohl; ⟨*choose*⟩ willkürlich

randy /'rændɪ/ *a* (**-ier, -iest**) (*fam*) geil

rang /ræŋ/ *see* **ring**[2]

range /reɪndʒ/ *n* Serie *f*, Reihe *f*; (*Comm*) Auswahl *f*, Angebot *nt* (**of** an + *dat*); (*of mountains*) Kette *f*; (*Mus*) Umfang *m*; (*distance*) Reichweite *f*; (*for shooting*) Schießplatz *m*; (*stove*) Kohlenherd *m*; **at a ~ of** auf eine Entfernung von □ *vi* reichen; **~ from ... to** gehen von ... bis. **~r** *n* Aufseher *m*

rank[1] /ræŋk/ *n* (*row*) Reihe *f*; (*Mil*) Rang *m*; (*social position*) Stand *m*; **the ~ and file** die breite Masse; **the ~s** *pl* die gemeinen Soldaten □ *vt/i* einstufen; **~ among** zählen zu

rank[2] *a* (*bad*) übel; ⟨*plants*⟩ üppig; (*fig*) krass

ransack /'rænsæk/ *vt* durchwühlen; (*pillage*) plündern

ransom /'rænsəm/ *n* Lösegeld *nt*; **hold s.o. to ~** Lösegeld für jdn fordern

rant /rænt/ *vi* rasen

rap /ræp/ *n* Klopfen *nt*; (*blow*) Schlag *m* □ *v* (*pt/pp* **rapped**) □ *vt* klopfen auf (+ *acc*) □ *vi* **~ at/on** klopfen an/auf (+ *acc*)

rape[1] /reɪp/ *n* (*Bot*) Raps *m*

rape[2] *n* Vergewaltigung *f* □ *vt* vergewaltigen

rapid /'ræpɪd/ *a*, **-ly** *adv* schnell. **~ity** /rə'pɪdətɪ/ *n* Schnelligkeit *f*

rapids /'ræpɪdz/ *npl* Stromschnellen *pl*

rapist /'reɪpɪst/ *n* Vergewaltiger *m*

rapport /ræ'pɔ:(r)/ *n* [innerer] Kontakt *m*

rapt /ræpt/ *a*, **-ly** *adv* gespannt; ⟨*look*⟩ andächtig; **~ in** versunken in (+ *acc*)

raptur|e /'ræptʃə(r)/ *n* Entzücken *nt*. **~ous** /-rəs/ *a*, **-ly** *adv* begeistert

rare[1] /reə(r)/ *a* (**-r, -st**), **-ly** *adv* selten

rare[2] *a* (*Culin*) englisch gebraten

rarefied /'reərɪfaɪd/ *a* dünn

rarity /'reərətɪ/ *n* Seltenheit *f*

rascal /'rɑ:skl/ *n* Schlingel *m*

rash[1] /ræʃ/ *n* (*Med*) Ausschlag *m*

rash[2] *a* (**-er, -est**), **-ly** *adv* voreilig

rasher /'ræʃə(r)/ *n* Speckscheibe *f*

rasp /rɑ:sp/ *n* Raspel *f*

raspberry /'rɑ:zbərɪ/ *n* Himbeere *f*

rat /ræt/ *n* Ratte *f*; (*fam: person*) Schuft *m*; **smell a ~** (*fam*) Lunte riechen

rate /reɪt/ *n* Rate *f*; (*speed*) Tempo *nt*; (*of payment*) Satz *m*; (*of exchange*) Kurs *m*; **~s** *pl* (*taxes*) ≈ Grundsteuer *f*; **at any ~** auf jeden Fall; **at this ~** auf diese Weise □ *vt* einschätzen; **~ among** zählen zu □ *vi* **~ as** gelten als

rather /'rɑ:ðə(r)/ *adv* lieber; (*fairly*) ziemlich; **~!** und ob!
rati|fication /rætɪfɪ'keɪʃn/ *n* Ratifizierung *f*. **~fy** /'rætɪfaɪ/ *vt* (*pt/pp* **-ied**) ratifizieren
rating /'reɪtɪŋ/ *n* Einschätzung *f*; (*class*) Klasse *f*; (*sailor*) [einfacher] Matrose *m*; **~s** *pl* (*Radio, TV*) ≈ Einschaltquote *f*
ratio /'reɪʃɪəʊ/ *n* Verhältnis *nt*
ration /'ræʃn/ *n* Ration *f* □ *vt* rationieren
rational /'ræʃənl/ *a*, **-ly** *adv* rational. **~ize** *vt/i* rationalisieren
'rat race *n* (*fam*) Konkurrenzkampf *m*
rattle /'rætl/ *n* Rasseln *nt*; (*of china, glass*) Klirren *nt*; (*of windows*) Klappern *nt*; (*toy*) Klapper *f* □ *vi* rasseln; klirren; klappern □ *vt* rasseln mit; (*shake*) schütteln. **~ off** *vt* herunterrasseln
'rattlesnake *n* Klapperschlange *f*
raucous /'rɔ:kəs/ *a* rau
ravage /'rævɪdʒ/ *vt* verwüsten, verheeren
rave /reɪv/ *vi* toben; **~ about** schwärmen von
raven /'reɪvn/ *n* Rabe *m*
ravenous /'rævənəs/ *a* heißhungrig
ravine /rə'vi:n/ *n* Schlucht *f*
raving /'reɪvɪŋ/ *a* **~ mad** (*fam*) total verrückt
ravishing /'rævɪʃɪŋ/ *a* hinreißend
raw /rɔ:/ *a* (**-er, -est**) roh; (*not processed*) Roh-; ⟨*skin*⟩ wund; ⟨*weather*⟩ nasskalt; (*inexperienced*) unerfahren; **get a ~ deal** (*fam*) schlecht wegkommen. **~ ma'terials** *npl* Rohstoffe *pl*
ray /reɪ/ *n* Strahl *m*; **~ of hope** Hoffnungsschimmer *m*
raze /reɪz/ *vt* **~ to the ground** dem Erdboden gleichmachen
razor /'reɪzə(r)/ *n* Rasierapparat *m*. **~ blade** *n* Rasierklinge *f*
re /ri:/ *prep* betreffs (+ *gen*)
reach /ri:tʃ/ *n* Reichweite *f*; (*of river*) Strecke *f*; **within/out of ~** in/außer Reichweite; **within easy ~** leicht erreichbar □ *vt* erreichen; (*arrive at*) ankommen in (+ *dat*); (**~** *as far as*) reichen bis zu; kommen zu ⟨*decision, conclusion*⟩; (*pass*) reichen □ *vi* reichen (**to** bis zu); **~ for** greifen nach; **I can't ~** ich komme nicht daran
re'act /rɪ-/ *vi* reagieren (**to** auf + *acc*)
re'action /rɪ-/ *n* Reaktion *f*. **~ary** *a* reaktionär
reactor /rɪ'æktə(r)/ *n* Reaktor *m*
read /ri:d/ *vt/i* (*pt/pp* **read** /red/) lesen; (*aloud*) vorlesen (**to** *dat*); (*Univ*) studieren; ablesen ⟨*meter*⟩. **~ out** *vt* vorlesen
readable /'ri:dəbl/ *a* lesbar
reader /'ri:də(r)/ *n* Leser(in) *m*(*f*); (*book*) Lesebuch *nt*
readi|ly /'redɪlɪ/ *adv* bereitwillig; (*easily*) leicht. **~ness** *n* Bereitschaft *f*; **in ~ness** bereit
reading /'ri:dɪŋ/ *n* Lesen *nt*; (*Pol, Relig*) Lesung *f*
rea'djust /ri:-/ *vt* neu einstellen □ *vi* sich umstellen (**to** auf + *acc*)
ready /'redɪ/ *a* (**-ier, -iest**) fertig; (*willing*) bereit; (*quick*) schnell; **get ~** sich fertig machen; (*prepare to*) sich bereitmachen
ready: ~-'made *a* fertig. **~ 'money** *n* Bargeld *nt*. **~-to-'wear** *a* Konfektions-
real /rɪəl/ *a* wirklich; (*genuine*) echt; (*actual*) eigentlich □ *adv* (*Amer, fam*) echt. **~ estate** *n* Immobilien *pl*
realis|m /'rɪəlɪzm/ *n* Realismus *m*. **~t** /-lɪst/ *n* Realist *m*. **~tic** /-'lɪstɪk/ *a*, **-ally** *adv* realistisch
reality /rɪ'ælətɪ/ *n* Wirklichkeit *f*, Realität *f*
realization /rɪəlaɪ'zeɪʃn/ *n* Erkenntnis *f*
realize /'rɪəlaɪz/ *vt* einsehen; (*become aware*) gewahr werden; verwirklichen ⟨*hopes, plans*⟩;

(*Comm*) realisieren; einbringen ⟨*price*⟩; **I didn't ~** das wusste ich nicht

really /'rɪəlɪ/ *adv* wirklich; (*actually*) eigentlich

realm /relm/ *n* Reich *nt*

realtor /'ri:əltə(r)/ *n* (*Amer*) Immobilienmakler *m*

reap /ri:p/ *vt* ernten

reap'pear /ri:-/ *vi* wiederkommen

rear[1] /rɪə(r)/ *a* Hinter-; (*Auto*) Heck- □ *n* **the ~** der hintere Teil; **from the ~** von hinten

rear[2] *vt* aufziehen □ *vi* **~ [up]** ⟨*horse:*⟩ sich aufbäumen

'rear-light *n* Rücklicht *nt*

re'arm /ri:-/ *vi* wieder aufrüsten

rear'range /ri:-/ *vt* umstellen

rear-view 'mirror *n* (*Auto*) Rückspiegel *m*

reason /'ri:zn/ *n* Grund *m*; (*good sense*) Vernunft *f*; (*ability to think*) Verstand *m*; **within ~** in vernünftigen Grenzen □ *vi* argumentieren; **~ with** vernünftig reden mit. **~able** /-əbl/ *a* vernünftig; (*not expensive*) preiswert. **~ably** /-əblɪ/ *adv* (*fairly*) ziemlich

reas'sur|ance /ri:-/ *n* Beruhigung *f*; Versicherung *f*. **~e** *vt* beruhigen; **~ e s.o. of sth** jdm etw (*gen*) versichern

rebate /'ri:beɪt/ *n* Rückzahlung *f*; (*discount*) Nachlass *m*

rebel[1] /'rebl/ *n* Rebell *m*

rebel[2] /rɪ'bel/ *vi* (*pt/pp* **rebelled**) rebellieren. **~lion** /-ɪən/ *n* Rebellion *f*. **~lious** /-ɪəs/ *a* rebellisch

re'bound[1] /rɪ-/ *vi* abprallen

'rebound[2] /ri:-/ *n* Rückprall *m*

rebuff /rɪ'bʌf/ *n* Abweisung *f* □ *vt* abweisen; eine Abfuhr erteilen (**s.o.** jdm)

re'build /ri:-/ *vt* (*pt/pp* **-built**) wieder aufbauen

rebuke /rɪ'bju:k/ *n* Tadel *m* □ *vt* tadeln

rebuttal /rɪ'bʌtl/ *n* Widerlegung *f*

re'call /rɪ-/ *n* Erinnerung *f*; **beyond ~** unwiderruflich □ *vt* zurückrufen; abberufen ⟨*diplomat*⟩; vorzeitig einberufen ⟨*parliament*⟩; (*remember*) sich erinnern an (+ *acc*)

recant /rɪ'kænt/ *vi* widerrufen

recap /'ri:kæp/ *vt/i* (*fam*) = **recapitulate**

recapitulate /ri:kə'pɪtjʊleɪt/ *vt/i* zusammenfassen; rekapitulieren

re'capture /ri:-/ *vt* wieder gefangen nehmen ⟨*person*⟩; wieder einfangen ⟨*animal*⟩

reced|e /rɪ'si:d/ *vi* zurückgehen. **~ing** *a* ⟨*forehead, chin*⟩ fliehend; **~ing hair** Stirnglatze *f*

receipt /rɪ'si:t/ *n* Quittung *f*; (*receiving*) Empfang *m*; **~s** *pl* (*Comm*) Einnahmen *pl*

receive /rɪ'si:v/ *vt* erhalten, bekommen; empfangen ⟨*guests*⟩. **~r** *n* (*Teleph*) Hörer *m*; (*Radio, TV*) Empfänger *m*; (*of stolen goods*) Hehler *m*

recent /'ri:sənt/ *a* kürzlich erfolgte(r,s). **~ly** *adv* in letzter Zeit; (*the other day*) kürzlich, vor kurzem

receptacle /rɪ'septəkl/ *n* Behälter *m*

reception /rɪ'sepʃn/ *n* Empfang *m*; **~ [desk]** (*in hotel*) Rezeption *f*. **~ist** *n* Empfangsdame *f*

receptive /rɪ'septɪv/ *a* aufnahmefähig; **~ to** empfänglich für

recess /rɪ'ses/ *n* Nische *f*; (*holiday*) Ferien *pl*; (*Amer, Sch*) Pause *f*

recession /rɪ'seʃn/ *n* Rezession *f*

re'charge /ri:-/ *vt* [wieder] aufladen

recipe /'resəpɪ/ *n* Rezept *nt*

recipient /rɪ'sɪpɪənt/ *n* Empfänger *m*

recipro|cal /rɪ'sɪprəkl/ *a* gegenseitig. **~cate** /-keɪt/ *vt* erwidern

recital /rɪ'saɪtl/ *n* (*of poetry songs*) Vortrag *m*; (*on piano*) Konzert *nt*
recite /rɪ'saɪt/ *vt* aufsagen; (*before audience*) vortragen; (*list*) aufzählen
reckless /'reklɪs/ *a*, **-ly** *adv* leichtsinnig; (*careless*) rücksichtslos. **~ness** *n* Leichtsinn *m*; Rücksichtslosigkeit *f*
reckon /'rekən/ *vt* rechnen; (*consider*) glauben □ *vi* **~ on/with** rechnen mit
re'claim /rɪ-/ *vt* zurückfordern; zurückgewinnen ⟨*land*⟩
reclin|e /rɪ'klaɪn/ *vi* liegen. **~ing seat** *n* Liegesitz *m*
recluse /rɪ'klu:s/ *n* Einsiedler(in) *m(f)*
recognition /rekəg'nɪʃn/ *n* Erkennen *nt*; (*acknowledgement*) Anerkennung *f*; **in ~** als Anerkennung (**of** *gen*); **be beyond ~** nicht wieder zu erkennen sein
recognize /'rekəgnaɪz/ *vt* erkennen; (*know again*) wieder erkennen; (*acknowledge*) anerkennen
re'coil /rɪ-/ *vi* zurückschnellen; (*in fear*) zurückschrecken
recollect /rekə'lekt/ *vt* sich erinnern an (+ *acc*). **~ion** /-ekʃn/ *n* Erinnerung *f*
recommend /rekə'mend/ *vt* empfehlen. **~ation** /-'deɪʃn/ *n* Empfehlung *f*
recompense /'rekəmpens/ *n* Entschädigung *f* □ *vt* entschädigen
recon|cile /'rekənsaɪl/ *vt* versöhnen; **~cile oneself to** sich abfinden mit. **~ciliation** /-sɪlɪ'eɪʃn/ *n* Versöhnung *f*
recon'dition /ri:-/ *vt* generalüberholen. **~ed engine** *n* Austauschmotor *m*
reconnaissance /rɪ'kɒnɪsns/ *n* (*Mil*) Aufklärung *f*
reconnoitre /rekə'nɔɪtə(r)/ *vi* (*pres p* **-tring**) auf Erkundung ausgehen
recon'sider /ri:-/ *vt* sich (*dat*) noch einmal überlegen
recon'struct /ri:-/ *vt* wieder aufbauen; rekonstruieren ⟨*crime*⟩. **~ion** *n* Wiederaufbau *m*; Rekonstruktion *f*
record[1] /rɪ'kɔ:d/ *vt* aufzeichnen; (*register*) registrieren; (*on tape*) aufnehmen
record[2] /'rekɔ:d/ *n* Aufzeichnung *f*; (*Jur*) Protokoll *nt*; (*Mus*) [Schall]platte *f*; (*Sport*) Rekord *m*; **~s** *pl* Unterlagen *pl*; **keep a ~ of** sich (*dat*) notieren; **off the ~** inoffiziell; **have a [criminal] ~** vorbestraft sein
recorder /rɪ'kɔ:də(r)/ *n* (*Mus*) Blockflöte *f*
recording /rɪ'kɔ:dɪŋ/ *n* Aufzeichnung *f*, Aufnahme *f*
'record-player *n* Plattenspieler *m*
recount /rɪ'kaʊnt/ *vt* erzählen
re-'count[1] /ri:-/ *vt* nachzählen
're-count[2] /ri:-/ *n* (*Pol*) Nachzählung *f*
recoup /rɪ'ku:p/ *vt* wieder einbringen; ausgleichen ⟨*losses*⟩
recourse /rɪ'kɔ:s/ *n* **have ~ to** Zuflucht nehmen zu
re-'cover /ri:-/ *vt* neu beziehen
recover /rɪ'kʌvə(r)/ *vt* zurückbekommen; bergen ⟨*wreck*⟩ □ *vi* sich erholen. **~y** *n* Wiedererlangung *f*; Bergung *f*; (*of health*) Erholung *f*
recreation /rekrɪ'eɪʃn/ *n* Erholung *f*; (*hobby*) Hobby *nt*. **~al** *a* Freizeit-; **be ~al** erholsam sein
recrimination /rɪkrɪmɪ'neɪʃn/ *n* Gegenbeschuldigung *f*
recruit /rɪ'kru:t/ *n* (*Mil*) Rekrut *m*; **new ~** (*member*) neues Mitglied *nt*; (*worker*) neuer Mitarbeiter *m* □ *vt* rekrutieren; anwerben ⟨*staff*⟩. **~ment** *n* Rekrutierung *f*; Anwerbung *f*
rectang|le /'rektæŋgl/ *n* Rechteck *nt*. **~ular** /-'tæŋgjʊlə(r)/ *a* rechteckig
rectify /'rektɪfaɪ/ *vt* (*pt/pp* **-ied**) berichtigen

rector /ˈrektə(r)/ *n* Pfarrer *m*; (*Univ*) Rektor *m*. **~y** *n* Pfarrhaus *nt*

recuperat|e /rɪˈkjuːpəreɪt/ *vi* sich erholen. **~ion** /-ˈreɪʃn/ *n* Erholung *f*

recur /rɪˈkɜː(r)/ *vi* (*pt/pp* **recurred**) sich wiederholen; ⟨*illness:*⟩ wiederkehren

recurren|ce /rɪˈkʌrəns/ *n* Wiederkehr *f*. **~t** *a* wiederkehrend

recycle /riːˈsaɪkl/ *vt* wieder verwerten. **~d paper** *n* Umweltschutzpapier *nt*

red /red/ *a* (**redder, reddest**) rot □ *n* Rot *nt*. **~ˈcurrant** *n* rote Johannisbeere *f*

redd|en /ˈredn/ *vt* röten □ *vi* rot werden. **~ish** *a* rötlich

reˈdecorate /riː-/ *vt* renovieren; (*paint*) neu streichen; (*wallpaper*) neu tapezieren

redeem /rɪˈdiːm/ *vt* einlösen; (*Relig*) erlösen

redemption /rɪˈdempʃn/ *n* Erlösung *f*

redeˈploy /riː-/ *vt* an anderer Stelle einsetzen

red: ~-haired *a* rothaarig. **~-ˈhanded** *a* **catch s.o. ~-handed** jdn auf frischer Tat ertappen. **~ ˈherring** *n* falsche Spur *f*. **~-hot** *a* glühend heiß. **R~ ˈIndian** *n* Indianer(in) *m(f)*

rediˈrect /riː-/ *vt* nachsenden ⟨*letter*⟩; umleiten ⟨*traffic*⟩

red: ~ ˈlight *n* (*Auto*) rote Ampel *f*. **~ness** *n* Röte *f*

reˈdo /riː-/ *vt* (*pt* **-did**, *pp* **-done**) noch einmal machen

reˈdouble /riː-/ *vt* verdoppeln

redress /rɪˈdres/ *n* Entschädigung *f* □ *vt* wieder gutmachen; wiederherstellen ⟨*balance*⟩

red ˈtape *n* (*fam*) Bürokratie *f*

reduc|e /rɪˈdjuːs/ *vt* verringern, vermindern; (*in size*) verkleinern; ermäßigen ⟨*costs*⟩; herabsetzen ⟨*price, goods*⟩; (*Culin*) einkochen lassen. **~tion** /-ˈdʌkʃn/ *n* Verringerung *f*; (*in price*) Ermäßigung *f*; (*in size*) Verkleinerung *f*

redundan|cy /rɪˈdʌndənsɪ/ *n* Beschäftigungslosigkeit *f*; (*payment*) Abfindung *f*. **~t** *a* überflüssig; **make ~t** entlassen; **be made ~t** beschäftigungslos werden

reed /riːd/ *n* [Schilf]rohr *nt*; **~s** *pl* Schilf *nt*

reef /riːf/ *n* Riff *nt*

reek /riːk/ *vi* riechen (**of** nach)

reel /riːl/ *n* Rolle *f*, Spule *f* □ *vi* (*stagger*) taumeln □ *vt* **~ off** (*fig*) herunterrasseln

refectory /rɪˈfektərɪ/ *n* Refektorium *nt*; (*Univ*) Mensa *f*

refer /rɪˈfɜː(r)/ *v* (*pt/pp* **referred**) □ *vt* verweisen (**to** an + *acc*); übergeben, weiterleiten ⟨*matter*⟩ (**to** an + *acc*) □ *vi* **~ to** sich beziehen auf (+ *acc*); (*mention*) erwähnen; (*concern*) betreffen; (*consult*) sich wenden an (+ *acc*); nachschlagen in (+ *dat*) ⟨*book*⟩; **are you ~ring to me?** meinen Sie mich?

referee /refəˈriː/ *n* Schiedsrichter *m*; (*Boxing*) Ringrichter *m*; (*for job*) Referenz *f* □ *vt/i* (*pt/pp* **refereed**) Schiedsrichter/Ringrichter sein (**bei**)

reference /ˈrefərəns/ *n* Erwähnung *f*; (*in book*) Verweis *m*; (*for job*) Referenz *f*; (*Comm*) **'your ~'** 'Ihr Zeichen'; **with ~ to** in Bezug auf (+ *acc*); (*in letter*) unter Bezugnahme auf (+ *acc*); **make [a] ~ to** erwähnen. **~ book** *n* Nachschlagewerk *nt*. **~ number** *n* Aktenzeichen *nt*

referendum /refəˈrendəm/ *n* Volksabstimmung *f*

reˈfill¹ /riː-/ *vt* nachfüllen

ˈrefill² /riː-/ *n* (*for pen*) Ersatzmine *f*

refine /rɪˈfaɪn/ *vt* raffinieren. **~d** *a* fein, vornehm. **~ment** *n* Vornehmheit *f*; (*Techn*) Verfeinerung *f*. **~ry** /-ərɪ/ *n* Raffinerie *f*

reflect /rɪ'flekt/ *vt* reflektieren; ⟨*mirror*:⟩ [wider]spiegeln; **be ~ed in** sich spiegeln in (+ *dat*) □ *vi* nachdenken (**on** über + *acc*); **~ badly upon s.o.** (*fig*) jdn in ein schlechtes Licht stellen. **~ion** /-ekʃn/ *n* Reflexion *f*; (*image*) Spiegelbild *nt*; **on ~ion** nach nochmaliger Überlegung. **~ive** /-ɪv/ *a*, **-ly** *adv* nachdenklich. **~or** *n* Rückstrahler *m*

reflex /'ri:fleks/ *n* Reflex *m* □ *attrib* Reflex-

reflexive /rɪ'fleksɪv/ *a* reflexiv

reform /rɪ'fɔ:m/ *n* Reform *f* □ *vt* reformieren □ *vi* sich bessern. **R~ation** /refə'meɪʃn/ *n* (*Relig*) Reformation *f*. **~er** *n* Reformer *m*; (*Relig*) Reformator *m*

refract /rɪ'frækt/ *vt* (*Phys*) brechen

refrain[1] /rɪ'freɪn/ *n* Refrain *m*

refrain[2] *vi* **~ from doing sth** etw nicht tun

refresh /rɪ'freʃ/ *vt* erfrischen. **~ing** *a* erfrischend. **~ments** *npl* Erfrischungen *pl*

refrigerat|e /rɪ'frɪdʒəreɪt/ *vt* kühlen. **~or** *n* Kühlschrank *m*

re'fuel /ri:-/ *vt/i* (*pt/pp* **-fuelled**) auftanken

refuge /'refju:dʒ/ *n* Zuflucht *f*; **take ~ in** Zuflucht nehmen in (+ *dat*)

refugee /refjʊ'dʒi:/ *n* Flüchtling *m*

'refund[1] /ri:-/ **get a ~** sein Geld zurückbekommen

re'fund[2] /rɪ-/ *vt* zurückerstatten

refurbish /ri:'fɜ:bɪʃ/ *vt* renovieren

refusal /rɪ'fju:zl/ *n* (*see* **refuse**[1]) Ablehnung *f*; Weigerung *f*

refuse[1] /rɪ'fju:z/ *vt* ablehnen; (*not grant*) verweigern; **~ to do sth** sich weigern, etw zu tun □ *vi* ablehnen; sich weigern

refuse[2] /'refju:s/ *n* Müll *m*, Abfall *m*. **~ collection** *n* Müllabfuhr *f*

refute /rɪ'fju:t/ *vt* widerlegen

re'gain /rɪ-/ *vt* wiedergewinnen

regal /'ri:gl/ *a*, **-ly** *adv* königlich

regalia /rɪ'geɪlɪə/ *npl* Insignien *pl*

regard /rɪ'gɑ:d/ *n* (*heed*) Rücksicht *f*; (*respect*) Achtung *f*; **~s** *pl* Grüße *pl*; **with ~ to** in Bezug auf (+ *acc*) □ *vt* ansehen, betrachten (**as** als); **as ~s** in Bezug auf (+ *acc*). **~ing** *prep* bezüglich (+ *gen*). **~less** *adv* ohne Rücksicht (**of** auf + *acc*)

regatta /rɪ'gætə/ *n* Regatta *f*

regenerate /rɪ'dʒenəreɪt/ *vt* regenerieren □ *vi* sich regenerieren

regime /reɪ'ʒi:m/ *n* Regime *nt*

regiment /'redʒɪmənt/ *n* Regiment *nt*. **~al** /-'mentl/ *a* Regiments-. **~ation** /-'teɪʃn/ *n* Reglementierung *f*

region /'ri:dʒən/ *n* Region *f*; **in the ~ of** (*fig*) ungefähr. **~al** *a*, **-ly** *adv* regional

register /'redʒɪstə(r)/ *n* Register *nt*; (*Sch*) Anwesenheitsliste *f* □ *vt* registrieren; (*report*) anmelden; einschreiben ⟨*letter*⟩; aufgeben ⟨*luggage*⟩ □ *vi* (*report*) sich anmelden; **it didn't ~** (*fig*) ich habe es nicht registriert

registrar /redʒɪ'strɑ:(r)/ *n* Standesbeamte(r) *m*

registration /redʒɪ'streɪʃn/ *n* Registrierung *f*; Anmeldung *f*. **~ number** *n* Autonummer *f*

registry office /'redʒɪstrɪ-/ *n* Standesamt *nt*

regret /rɪ'gret/ *n* Bedauern *nt* □ *vt* (*pt/pp* **regretted**) bedauern. **~fully** *adv* mit Bedauern

regrettab|le /rɪ'gretəbl/ *a* bedauerlich. **~ly** *adv* bedauerlicherweise

regular /'regjʊlə(r)/ *a*, **-ly** *adv* regelmäßig; (*usual*) üblich; (*Mil*) Berufs- □ *n* Berufssoldat *m*; (*in pub*) Stammgast *m*; (*in shop*) Stammkunde *m*. **~ity** /-'lærətɪ/ *n* Regelmäßigkeit *f*

regulat|e /ˈregjʊleɪt/ *vt* regulieren. **~ion** /-ˈleɪʃn/ *n* (*rule*) Vorschrift *f*

rehabilitat|e /riːhəˈbɪlɪteɪt/ *vt* rehabilitieren. **~ion** /-ˈteɪʃn/ *n* Rehabilitation *f*

rehears|al /rɪˈhɜːsl/ *n* (*Theat*) Probe *f*. **~e** *vt* proben

reign /reɪn/ *n* Herrschaft *f* □ *vi* herrschen, regieren

reimburse /riːɪmˈbɜːs/ *vt* **~ s.o. for sth** jdm etw zurückerstatten

rein /reɪn/ *n* Zügel *m*

reincarnation /riːɪnkɑːˈneɪʃn/ *f* **Reinkarnation** *f*, Wiedergeburt *f*

reindeer /ˈreɪndɪə(r)/ *n inv* Rentier *nt*

reinforce /riːɪnˈfɔːs/ *vt* verstärken. **~d** ˈ**concrete** *n* Stahlbeton *m*. **~ment** *n* Verstärkung *f*; **send ~ments** Verstärkung schicken

reinstate /riːɪnˈsteɪt/ *vt* wieder einstellen; (*to office*) wieder einsetzen

reiterate /riːˈɪtəreɪt/ *vt* wiederholen

reject /rɪˈdʒekt/ *vt* ablehnen. **~ion** /-ekʃn/ *n* Ablehnung *f*

rejects /ˈriːdʒekts/ *npl* (*Comm*) Ausschussware *f*

rejoic|e /rɪˈdʒɔɪs/ *vi* (*liter*) sich freuen. **~ing** *n* Freude *f*

re'join /rɪ-/ *vt* sich wieder anschließen (+ *dat*); wieder beitreten (+ *dat*) ⟨*club, party*⟩; (*answer*) erwidern

rejuvenate /rɪˈdʒuːvəneɪt/ *vt* verjüngen

relapse /rɪˈlæps/ *n* Rückfall *m* □ *vi* einen Rückfall erleiden

relate /rɪˈleɪt/ *vt* (*tell*) erzählen; (*connect*) verbinden □ *vi* zusammenhängen (**to** mit). **~d** *a* verwandt (**to** mit)

relation /rɪˈleɪʃn/ *n* Beziehung *f*; (*person*) Verwandte(r) *m/f*. **~ship** *n* Beziehung *f*; (*link*) Verbindung *f*; (*blood tie*) Verwandtschaft *f*; (*affair*) Verhältnis *nt*

relative /ˈrelətɪv/ *n* Verwandte(r) *m/f* □ *a* relativ; (*Gram*) Relativ-. **~ly** *adv* relativ, verhälnismäßig

relax /rɪˈlæks/ *vt* lockern, entspannen □ *vi* sich lockern, sich entspannen. **~ation** /-ˈseɪʃn/ *n* Entspannung *f*. **~ing** *a* entspannend

relay[1] /riːˈleɪ/ *vt* (*pt/pp* **-layed**) weitergeben; (*Radio, TV*) übertragen

relay[2] /ˈriːleɪ/ *n* (*Electr*) Relais *nt*; **work in ~s** sich bei der Arbeit ablösen. **~ [race]** *n* Staffel *f*

release /rɪˈliːs/ *n* Freilassung *f*, Entlassung *f*; (*Techn*) Auslöser *m* □ *vt* freilassen; (*let go of*) loslassen; (*Techn*) auslösen; veröffentlichen ⟨*information*⟩

relegate /ˈrelɪgeɪt/ *vt* verbannen; **be ~d** (*Sport*) absteigen

relent /rɪˈlent/ *vi* nachgeben. **~less** *a*, **-ly** *adv* erbarmungslos; (*unceasing*) unaufhörlich

relevan|ce /ˈreləvəns/ *n* Relevanz *f*. **~t** *a* relevant (**to** für)

reliab|ility /rɪlaɪəˈbɪlətɪ/ *n* Zuverlässigkeit *f*. **~le** /-ˈlaɪəbl/ *a*, **-ly** *adv* zuverlässig

relian|ce /rɪˈlaɪəns/ *n* Abhängigkeit *f* (**on** von). **~t** *a* angewiesen (**on** auf + *acc*)

relic /ˈrelɪk/ *n* Überbleibsel *nt*; (*Relig*) Reliquie *f*

relief /rɪˈliːf/ *n* Erleichterung *f*; (*assistance*) Hilfe *f*; (*distraction*) Abwechslung *f*; (*replacement*) Ablösung *f*; (*Art*) Relief *nt*; **in ~** im Relief. **~ map** *n* Reliefkarte *f*. **~ train** *n* Entlastungszug *m*

relieve /rɪˈliːv/ *vt* erleichtern; (*take over from*) ablösen; **~ of** entlasten von

religion /rɪˈlɪdʒən/ *n* Religion *f*

religious /rɪˈlɪdʒəs/ *a* religiös. **~ly** *adv* (*conscientiously*) gewissenhaft

relinquish /rɪˈlɪŋkwɪʃ/ *vt* loslassen; (*give up*) aufgeben

relish /ˈrelɪʃ/ *n* Genuss *m*; (*Culin*) Würze *f* □ *vt* genießen

relo'cate /ri:-/ *vt* verlegen
reluctan|ce /rɪ'lʌktəns/ *n* Widerstreben *nt*. **~t** *a* widerstrebend; **be ~t** zögern (**to** zu). **~tly** *adv* ungern, widerstrebend
rely /rɪ'laɪ/ *vi* (*pt/pp* **-ied**) **~ on** sich verlassen auf (+ *acc*); (*be dependent on*) angewiesen sein auf (+ *acc*)
remain /rɪ'meɪn/ *vi* bleiben; (*be left*) übrig bleiben. **~der** *n* Rest *m*. **~ing** *a* restlich. **~s** *npl* Reste *pl*; **[mortal] ~s** [sterbliche] Überreste *pl*
remand /rɪ'mɑ:nd/ *n* **on ~** in Untersuchungshaft □ *vt* **~ in custody** in Untersuchungshaft schicken
remark /rɪ'mɑ:k/ *n* Bemerkung *f* □ *vt* bemerken. **~able** /-əbl/ *a*, **-bly** *adv* bemerkenswert
re|marry /ri:-/ *vi* wieder heiraten
remedial /rɪ'mi:dɪəl/ *a* Hilfs-; (*Med*) Heil-
remedy /'remədɪ/ *n* [Heil]mittel *nt* (**for** gegen); (*fig*) Abhilfe *f* □ *vt* (*pt/pp* **-ied**) abhelfen (+ *dat*); beheben ⟨*fault*⟩
rememb|er /rɪ'membə(r)/ *vt* sich erinnern an (+ *acc*); **~er to do sth** daran denken, etw zu tun; **~er me to him** grüßen Sie ihn von mir □ *vi* sich erinnern. **~rance** *n* Erinnerung *f*
remind /rɪ'maɪnd/ *vt* erinnern (**of** an + *acc*). **~er** *n* Andenken *nt*; (*letter, warning*) Mahnung *f*
reminisce /remɪ'nɪs/ *vi* sich seinen Erinnerungen hingeben. **~nces** /-ənsɪs/ *npl* Erinnerungen *pl*. **~nt** *a* **be ~nt of** erinnern an (+ *acc*)
remiss /rɪ'mɪs/ *a* nachlässig
remission /rɪ'mɪʃn/ *n* Nachlass *m*; (*of sentence*) [Straf]erlass *m*; (*Med*) Remission *f*
remit /rɪ'mɪt/ *vt* (*pt/pp* **remitted**) überweisen ⟨*money*⟩. **~tance** *n* Überweisung *f*
remnant /'remnənt/ *n* Rest *m*
remonstrate /'remənstreɪt/ *vi* protestieren; **~ with s.o.** jdm Vorhaltungen machen
remorse /rɪ'mɔ:s/ *n* Reue *f*. **~ful** *a*, **-ly** *adv* reumütig. **~less** *a*, **-ly** *adv* unerbittlich
remote /rɪ'məʊt/ *a* fern; (*isolated*) abgelegen; (*slight*) gering. **~ con'trol** *n* Fernsteuerung *f*; (*for TV*) Fernbedienung *f*. **~-con'trolled** *a* ferngesteuert; fernbedient
remotely /rɪ'məʊtlɪ/ *adv* entfernt; **not ~** nicht im Entferntesten
re'movable /rɪ-/ *a* abnehmbar
removal /rɪ'mu:vl/ *n* Entfernung *f*; (*from house*) Umzug *m*. **~ van** *n* Möbelwagen *m*
remove /rɪ'mu:v/ *vt* entfernen; (*take off*) abnehmen; (*take out*) herausnehmen
remunerat|e /rɪ'mju:nəreɪt/ *vt* bezahlen. **~ion** /-'reɪʃn/ *n* Bezahlung *f*. **~ive** /-ətɪv/ *a* einträglich
render /'rendə(r)/ *vt* machen; erweisen ⟨*service*⟩; (*translate*) wiedergeben; (*Mus*) vortragen
renegade /'renɪgeɪd/ *n* Abtrünnige(r) *m/f*
renew /rɪ'nju:/ *vt* erneuern; verlängern ⟨*contract*⟩. **~al** *n* Erneuerung *f*; Verlängerung *f*
renounce /rɪ'naʊns/ *vt* verzichten auf (+ *acc*); (*Relig*) abschwören (+ *dat*)
renovat|e /'renəveɪt/ *vt* renovieren. **~ion** /-'veɪʃn/ *n* Renovierung *f*
renown /rɪ'naʊn/ *n* Ruf *m*. **~ed** *a* berühmt
rent /rent/ *n* Miete *f* □ *vt* mieten; (*hire*) leihen; **~ [out]** vermieten; verleihen. **~al** *n* Mietgebühr *f*; Leihgebühr *f*
renunciation /rɪnʌnsɪ'eɪʃn/ *n* Verzicht *m*
re'open /ri:-/ *vt/i* wieder aufmachen
re'organize /ri:-/ *vt* reorganisieren
rep /rep/ *n* (*fam*) Vertreter *m*

repair /rɪ'peə(r)/ *n* Reparatur *f*; **in good/bad ~** in gutem/ schlechtem Zustand □ *vt* reparieren
repartee /repɑ:'ti:/ *n* **piece of ~** schlagfertige Antwort *f*
repatriat|e /ri:'pætrɪeɪt/ *vt* repatriieren. **~ion** /-'eɪʃn/ *n* Repatriierung *f*
re'pay /ri:-/ *vt* (*pt/pp* **-paid**) zurückzahlen; **~ s.o. for sth** jdm etw zurückzahlen. **~ment** *n* Rückzahlung *f*
repeal /rɪ'pi:l/ *n* Aufhebung *f* □ *vt* aufheben
repeat /rɪ'pi:t/ *n* Wiederholung *f* □ *vt/i* wiederholen; **~ after me** sprechen Sie mir nach. **~ed** *a*, **-ly** *adv* wiederholt
repel /rɪ'pel/ *vt* (*pt/pp* **repelled**) abwehren; (*fig*) abstoßen. **~lent** *a* abstoßend
repent /rɪ'pent/ *vi* Reue zeigen. **~ance** *n* Reue *f*. **~ant** *a* reuig
repercussions /ri:pə'kʌʃnz/ *npl* Auswirkungen *pl*
repertoire /'repətwɑ:(r)/ *n* Repertoire *nt*
repertory /'repətrɪ/ *n* Repertoire *nt*
repetit|ion /repɪ'tɪʃn/ *n* Wiederholung *f*. **~ive** /rɪ'petɪtɪv/ *a* eintönig
re'place /rɪ-/ *vt* zurücktun; (*take the place of*) ersetzen; (*exchange*) austauschen, auswechseln. **~ment** *n* Ersatz *m*. **~ment part** *n* Ersatzteil *nt*
'replay /ri:-/ *n* (*Sport*) Wiederholungsspiel *nt*; **[action] ~** Wiederholung *f*
replenish /rɪ'plenɪʃ/ *vt* auffüllen (*stocks*); (*refill*) nachfüllen
replete /rɪ'pli:t/ *a* gesättigt
replica /'replɪkə/ *n* Nachbildung *f*
reply /rɪ'plaɪ/ *n* Antwort *f* (**to** auf + *acc*) □ *vt/i* (*pt/pp* **replied**) antworten
report /rɪ'pɔ:t/ *n* Bericht *m*; (*Sch*) Zeugnis *nt*; (*rumour*) Gerücht *nt*; (*of gun*) Knall *m* □ *vt* berichten; (*notify*) melden; **~ s.o. to the police** jdn anzeigen □ *vi* berichten (**on** über + *acc*); (*present oneself*) sich melden (**to** bei). **~er** *n* Reporter(in) *m*(*f*)
repose /rɪ'pəʊz/ *n* Ruhe *f*
repos'sess /ri:-/ *vt* wieder in Besitz nehmen
reprehensible /reprɪ'hensəbl/ *a* tadelnswert
represent /reprɪ'zent/ *vt* darstellen; (*act for*) vertreten, repräsentieren. **~ation** /-'teɪʃn/ *n* Darstellung *f*; **make ~ations to** vorstellig werden bei
representative /reprɪ'zentətɪv/ *a* repräsentativ (**of** für) □ *n* Bevollmächtigte(r) *m*/(*f*); (*Comm*) Vertreter(in) *m*(*f*); (*Amer, Pol*) Abgeordnete(r) *m*/*f*
repress /rɪ'pres/ *vt* unterdrücken. **~ion** /-eʃn/ *n* Unterdrückung *f*. **~ive** /-ɪv/ *a* repressiv
reprieve /rɪ'pri:v/ *n* Begnadigung *f*; (*postponement*) Strafaufschub *m*; (*fig*) Gnadenfrist *f* □ *vt* begnadigen
reprimand /'reprɪmɑ:nd/ *n* Tadel *m* □ *vt* tadeln
'reprint¹ /ri:-/ *n* Nachdruck *m*
re'print² /ri:-/ *vt* neu auflegen
reprisal /rɪ'praɪzl/ *n* Vergeltungsmaßnahme *f*
reproach /rɪ'prəʊtʃ/ *n* Vorwurf *m* □ *vt* Vorwürfe *pl* machen (+ *dat*). **~ful** *a*, **-ly** *adv* vorwurfsvoll
repro'duc|e /ri:-/ *vt* wiedergeben, reproduzieren □ *vi* sich fortpflanzen. **~tion** /-'dʌkʃn/ *n* Reproduktion *f*; (*Biol*) Fortpflanzung *f*. **~tion furniture** *n* Stilmöbel *pl*. **~tive** /-'dʌktɪv/ *a* Fortpflanzungs-
reprove /rɪ'pru:v/ *vt* tadeln
reptile /'reptaɪl/ *n* Reptil *nt*
republic /rɪ'pʌblɪk/ *n* Republik *f*. **~an** *a* republikanisch □ *n* Republikaner(in) *m*(*f*)
repudiate /rɪ'pju:dɪeɪt/ *vt* zurückweisen

repugnan|ce /rɪ'pʌgnəns/ *n* Widerwille *m*. **~t** *a* widerlich
repuls|e /rɪ'pʌls/ *vt* abwehren; (*fig*) abweisen. **~ion** /-ʌlʃn/ *n* Widerwille *m*. **~ive** /-ɪv/ *a* abstoßend, widerlich
reputable /'repjʊtəbl/ *a* ⟨*firm*⟩ von gutem Ruf; (*respectable*) anständig
reputation /repjʊ'teɪʃn/ *n* Ruf *m*
repute /rɪ'pju:t/ *n* Ruf *m*. **~d** /-ɪd/ *a*, **-ly** *adv* angeblich
request /rɪ'kwest/ *n* Bitte *f* □ *vt* bitten. **~ stop** *n* Bedarfshaltestelle *f*
require /rɪ'kwaɪə(r)/ *vt* (*need*) brauchen; (*demand*) erfordern; **be ~d to do sth** etw tun müssen. **~ment** *n* Bedürfnis *nt*; (*condition*) Erfordernis *nt*
requisite /'rekwɪzɪt/ *a* erforderlich □ *n* **toilet/travel ~s** *pl* Toiletten-/Reiseartikel *pl*
requisition /rekwɪ'zɪʃn/ *n* **~ [order]** Anforderung *f* □ *vt* anfordern
re'sale /ri:-/ *n* Weiterverkauf *m*
rescind /rɪ'sɪnd/ *vt* aufheben
rescue /'reskju:/ *n* Rettung *f* □ *vt* retten. **~r** *n* Retter *m*
research /rɪ'sɜ:tʃ/ *n* Forschung *f* □ *vt* erforschen; (*Journ*) recherchieren □ *vi* **~ into** erforschen. **~er** *n* Forscher *m*; (*Journ*) Rechercheur *m*
resem|blance /rɪ'zembləns/ *n* Ähnlichkeit *f*. **~ble** /-bl/ *vt* ähneln (+ *dat*)
resent /rɪ'zent/ *vt* übel nehmen; einen Groll hegen gegen ⟨*person*⟩. **~ful** *a*, **-ly** *adv* verbittert. **~ment** *n* Groll *m*
reservation /rezə'veɪʃn/ *n* Reservierung *f*; (*doubt*) Vorbehalt *m*; (*enclosure*) Reservat *nt*
reserve /rɪ'zɜ:v/ *n* Reserve *f*; (*for animals*) Reservat *nt*; (*Sport*) Reservespieler(in) *m*(*f*) □ *vt* reservieren; ⟨*client:*⟩ reservieren lassen; (*keep*) aufheben; sich (*dat*) vorbehalten ⟨*right*⟩. **~d** *a* reserviert
reservoir /'rezəvwɑ:(r)/ *n* Reservoir *nt*
re'shape /ri:-/ *vt* umformen
re'shuffle /ri:-/ *n* (*Pol*) umbildung *f* □ *vt* (*Pol*) umbilden
reside /rɪ'zaɪd/ *vi* wohnen
residence /'rezɪdəns/ *n* Wohnsitz *m*; (*official*) Residenz *f*; (*stay*) Aufenthalt *m*. **~ permit** *n* Aufenthaltsgenehmigung *f*
resident /'rezɪdənt/ *a* ansässig (**in** in + *dat*); ⟨*housekeeper, nurse*⟩ im Haus wohnend □ *n* Bewohner(in) *m*(*f*); (*of street*) Anwohner *m*. **~ial** /-'denʃl/ *a* Wohn-
residue /'rezɪdju:/ *n* Rest *m*; (*Chem*) Rückstand *m*
resign /rɪ'zaɪn/ *vt* **~ oneself to** sich abfinden mit □ *vi* kündigen; (*from public office*) zurücktreten. **~ation** /rezɪg'neɪʃn/ *n* Resignation *f*; (*from job*) Kündigung *f*; Rücktritt *m*. **~ed** *a*, **-ly** *adv* resigniert
resilient /rɪ'zɪlɪənt/ *a* federnd; (*fig*) widerstandsfähig
resin /'rezɪn/ *n* Harz *nt*
resist /rɪ'zɪst/ *vt/i* sich widersetzen (+ *dat*); (*fig*) widerstehen (+ *dat*). **~ance** *n* Widerstand *m*. **~ant** *a* widerstandsfähig
resolut|e /'rezəlu:t/ *a*, **-ly** *adv* entschlossen. **~ion** /-'lu:ʃn/ *n* Entschlossenheit *f*; (*intention*) Vorsatz *m*; (*Pol*) Resolution *f*
resolve /rɪ'zɒlv/ *n* Entschlossenheit *f*; (*decision*) Beschluss *m* □ *vt* beschließen; (*solve*) lösen. **~d** *a* entschlossen
resonan|ce /'rezənəns/ *n* Resonanz *f*. **~t** *a* klangvoll
resort /rɪ'zɔ:t/ *n* (*place*) Urlaubsort *m*; **as a last ~** wenn alles andere fehlschlägt □ *vi* **~ to** (*fig*) greifen zu
resound /rɪ'zaʊnd/ *vi* widerhallen. **~ing** *a* widerhallend; (*loud*) laut; (*notable*) groß

resource /rɪ'sɔ:s/ *n* **~s** *pl* Ressourcen *pl.* **~ful** *a* findig. **~fulness** *n* Findigkeit *f*

respect /rɪ'spekt/ *n* Respekt *m*, Achtung *f* (**for** vor + *dat*); (*aspect*) Hinsicht *f*; **with ~ to** in Bezug auf (+ *acc*) □ *vt* respektieren, achten

respectability /rɪspektə'bɪlətɪ/ *n* (*see* **respectable**) Ehrbarkeit *f*; Anständigkeit *f*

respect|able /rɪ'spektəbl/ *a*, **-bly** *adv* ehrbar; (*decent*) anständig; (*considerable*) ansehnlich. **~ful** *a*, **-ly** *adv* respektvoll

respective /rɪ'spektɪv/ *a* jeweilig. **~ly** *adv* beziehungsweise

respiration /respə'reɪʃn/ *n* Atmung *f*

respite /'respaɪt/ *n* [Ruhe]pause *f*; (*delay*) Aufschub *m*

resplendent /rɪ'splendənt/ *a* glänzend

respond /rɪ'spɒnd/ *vi* antworten; (*react*) reagieren (**to** auf + *acc*); ⟨*patient:*⟩ ansprechen (**to** auf + *acc*)

response /rɪ'spɒns/ *n* Antwort *f*; Reaktion *f*

responsibility /rɪspɒnsɪ'bɪlətɪ/ *n* Verantwortung *f*; (*duty*) Verpflichtung *f*

responsib|le /rɪ'spɒnsəbl/ *a* verantwortlich; (*trustworthy*) verantwortungsvoll. **~ly** *adv* verantwortungsbewusst

responsive /rɪ'spɒnsɪv/ *a* **be ~** reagieren

rest[1] /rest/ *n* Ruhe *f*; (*holiday*) Erholung *f*; (*interval & Mus*) Pause *f*; **have a ~** eine Pause machen; (*rest*) sich ausruhen □ *vt* ausruhen; (*lean*) lehnen (**on** an/auf + *acc*) □ *vi* ruhen; (*have a rest*) sich ausruhen

rest[2] *n* **the ~** der Rest; (*people*) die Übrigen *pl* □ *vi* **it ~s with you** es ist an Ihnen (**to** zu)

restaurant /'restərɒnt/ *n* Restaurant *nt*, Gaststätte *f*. **~ car** *n* Speisewagen *m*

restful /'restfl/ *a* erholsam

restitution /restɪ'tju:ʃn/ *n* Entschädigung *f*; (*return*) Rückgabe *f*

restive /'restɪv/ *a* unruhig

restless /'restlɪs/ *a*, **-ly** *adv* unruhig

restoration /restə'reɪʃn/ *n* (*of building*) Restaurierung *f*

restore /rɪ'stɔ:(r)/ *vt* wiederherstellen; restaurieren ⟨*building*⟩; (*give back*) zurückgeben

restrain /rɪ'streɪn/ *vt* zurückhalten; **~ oneself** sich beherrschen. **~ed** *a* zurückhaltend. **~t** *n* Zurückhaltung *f*

restrict /rɪ'strɪkt/ *vt* einschränken; **~ to** beschränken auf (+ *acc*). **~ion** /-ɪkʃn/ *n* Einschränkung *f*; Beschränkung *f*. **~ive** /-ɪv/ *a* einschränkend

'rest room *n* (*Amer*) Toilette *f*

result /rɪ'zʌlt/ *n* Ergebnis *nt*, Resultat *nt*; (*consequence*) Folge *f*; **as a ~** als Folge (**of** *gen*) □ *vi* sich ergeben (**from** aus); **~ in** enden in (+ *dat*); (*lead to*) führen zu

resume /rɪ'zju:m/ *vt* wieder aufnehmen; wieder einnehmen ⟨*seat*⟩ □ *vi* wieder beginnen

résumé /'rezʊmeɪ/ *n* Zusammenfassung *f*

resumption /rɪ'zʌmpʃn/ *n* Wiederaufnahme *f*

resurgence /rɪ'sɜ:dʒəns/ *n* Wiederaufleben *nt*

resurrect /rezə'rekt/ *vt* (*fig*) wieder beleben. **~ion** /-ekʃn/ *n* **the R ~ion** (*Relig*) die Auferstehung

resuscitat|e /rɪ'sʌsɪteɪt/ *vt* wieder beleben. **~ion** /-'teɪʃn/ *n* Wiederbelebung *f*

retail /'ri:teɪl/ *n* Einzelhandel *m* □ *a* Einzelhandels- □ *adv* im Einzelhandel □ *vt* im Einzelhandel verkaufen □ *vi* **~ at** im Einzelhandel kosten. **~er** *n* Einzelhändler *m*. **~ price** *n* Ladenpreis *m*

retain /rɪ'teɪn/ *vt* behalten

retaliat|e /rɪ'tælɪeɪt/ *vi* zurückschlagen. **~ion** /-'eɪʃn/ *n* Vergeltung *f*; **in ~ion** als Vergeltung
retarded /rɪ'tɑ:dɪd/ *a* zurückgeblieben
retentive /rɪ'tentɪv/ *a* ⟨*memory*⟩ gut
reticen|ce /'retɪsns/ *n* Zurückhaltung *f*. **~t** *a* zurückhaltend
retina /'retɪnə/ *n* Netzhaut *f*
retinue /'retɪnju:/ *n* Gefolge *nt*
retire /rɪ'taɪə(r)/ *vi* in den Ruhestand treten; (*withdraw*) sich zurückziehen. **~d** *a* im Ruhestand. **~ment** *n* Ruhestand *m*; **since my ~ment** seit ich nicht mehr arbeite
retiring /rɪ'taɪərɪŋ/ *a* zurückhaltend
retort /rɪ'tɔ:t/ *n* scharfe Erwiderung *f*; (*Chem*) Retorte *f* □ *vt* scharf erwidern
re'touch /ri:-/ *vt* (*Phot*) retuschieren
re'trace /rɪ-/ *vt* zurückverfolgen; **~ one's steps** denselben Weg zurückgehen
retract /rɪ'trækt/ *vt* einziehen; zurücknehmen ⟨*remark*⟩ □ *vi* widerrufen
re'train /ri:-/ *vt* umschulen □ *vi* umgeschult werden
retreat /rɪ'tri:t/ *n* Rückzug *m*; (*place*) Zufluchtsort *m* □ *vi* sich zurückziehen
re'trial /ri:-/ *n* Wiederaufnahmeverfahren *nt*
retribution /retrɪ'bju:ʃn/ *n* Vergeltung *f*
retrieve /rɪ'tri:v/ *vt* zurückholen; (*from wreckage*) bergen; (*Computing*) wieder auffinden; ⟨*dog:*⟩ apportieren
retrograde /'retrəgreɪd/ *a* rückschrittlich
retrospect /'retrəspekt/ *n* **in ~** rückblickend. **~ive** /-ɪv/ *a*, **-ly** *adv* rückwirkend; (*looking back*) rückblickend

return /rɪ'tɜ:n/ *n* Rückkehr *f*; (*giving back*) Rückgabe *f*; (*Comm*) Ertrag *m*; (*ticket*) Rückfahrkarte *f*; (*Aviat*) Rückflugschein *m*; **by ~ [of post]** postwendend; **in ~** dafür; **in ~ for** für; **many happy ~s!** herzlichen Glückwunsch zum Geburtstag! □ *vt* zurückgehen/-fahren; (*come back*) zurückkommen □ *vt* zurückgeben; (*put back*) zurückstellen/-legen; (*send back*) zurückschicken; (*elect*) wählen
return: ~ flight *n* Rückflug *m*. **~ match** *n* Rückspiel *nt*. **~ ticket** *n* Rückfahrkarte *f*; (*Aviat*) Rückflugschein *m*
reunion /ri:'ju:nɪən/ *n* Wiedervereinigung *f*; (*social gathering*) Treffen *nt*
reunite /ri:ju:'naɪt/ *vt* wieder vereinigen □ *vi* sich wieder vereinigen
re'us|able /ri:-/ *a* wieder verwendbar. **~e** *vt* wieder verwenden
rev /rev/ *n* (*Auto, fam*) Umdrehung *f* □ *vt/i* **~ [up]** den Motor auf Touren bringen
reveal /rɪ'vi:l/ *vt* zum Vorschein bringen; (*fig*) enthüllen. **~ing** *a* (*fig*) aufschlussreich
revel /'revl/ *vi* (*pt/pp* **revelled**) **~ in sth** etw genießen
revelation /revə'leɪʃn/ *n* Offenbarung *f*, Enthüllung *f*
revelry /'revlrɪ/ *n* Lustbarkeit *f*
revenge /rɪ'vendʒ/ *n* Rache *f*; (*fig & Sport*) Revanche *f* □ *vt* rächen
revenue /'revənju:/ *n* [Staats]einnahmen *pl*
reverberate /rɪ'vɜ:bəreɪt/ *vi* nachhallen
revere /rɪ'vɪə(r)/ *vt* verehren. **~nce** /'revərəns/ *n* Ehrfurcht *f*
Reverend /'revərənd/ *a* **the ~ X** Pfarrer X; (*Catholic*) Hochwürden X
reverent /'revərənt/ *a*, **-ly** *adv* ehrfürchtig

reverie /'revərɪ/ *n* Träumerei *f*
revers /rɪ'vɪə/ *n* (*pl* **revers** /-z/) Revers *nt*
reversal /rɪ'vɜ:sl/ *n* Umkehrung *f*
reverse /rɪ'vɜ:s/ *a* umgekehrt □ *n* Gegenteil *nt*; (*back*) Rückseite *f*; (*Auto*) Rückwärtsgang *m* □ *vt* umkehren; (*Auto*) zurücksetzen; **~ the charges** (*Teleph*) ein R-Gespräch führen □ *vi* zurücksetzen
revert /rɪ'vɜ:t/ *vi* **~ to** zurückfallen an (+ *acc*); zurückkommen auf (+ *acc*) ⟨*topic*⟩
review /rɪ'vju:/ *n* Rückblick *m* (**of** auf + *acc*); (*re-examination*) Überprüfung *f*; (*Mil*) Truppenschau *f*; (*of book, play*) Kritik *f*, Rezension *f* □ *vt* zurückblicken auf (+ *acc*); überprüfen ⟨*situation*⟩; (*Mil*) besichtigen; kritisieren, rezensieren ⟨*book, play*⟩. **~er** *n* Kritiker *m*, Rezensent *m*
revile /rɪ'vaɪl/ *vt* verunglimpfen
revis|e /rɪ'vaɪz/ *vt* revidieren; (*for exam*) wiederholen. **~ion** /-'vɪʒn/ *n* Revision *f*; Wiederholung *f*
revival /rɪ'vaɪvl/ *n* Wiederbelebung *f*
revive /rɪ'vaɪv/ *vt* wieder beleben; (*fig*) wieder aufleben lassen □ *vi* wieder aufleben
revoke /rɪ'vəʊk/ *vt* aufheben; widerrufen ⟨*command, decision*⟩
revolt /rɪ'vəʊlt/ *n* Aufstand *m* □ *vi* rebellieren □ *vt* anwidern. **~ing** *a* widerlich, eklig
revolution /revə'lu:ʃn/ *n* Revolution *f*; (*Auto*) Umdrehung *f*. **~ary** /-ərɪ/ *a* revolutionär. **~ize** *vt* revolutionieren
revolve /rɪ'vɒlv/ *vi* sich drehen; **~ around** kreisen um
revolv|er /rɪ'vɒlvə(r)/ *n* Revolver *m*. **~ing** *a* Dreh-
revue /rɪ'vju:/ *n* Revue *f*; (*satirical*) Kabarett *nt*
revulsion /rɪ'vʌlʃn/ *n* Abscheu *m*
reward /rɪ'wɔ:d/ *n* Belohnung *f* □ *vt* belohnen. **~ing** *a* lohnend
re'write /ri:-/ *vt* (*pt* **rewrote**, *pp* **rewritten**) noch einmal [neu] schreiben; (*alter*) umschreiben
rhapsody /'ræpsədɪ/ *n* Rhapsodie *f*
rhetoric /'retərɪk/ *n* Rhetorik *f* **~al** /rɪ'tɒrɪkl/ *a* rhetorisch
rheuma|tic /ru:'mætɪk/ *a* rheumatisch. **~tism** /'ru:mətɪzm/ *n* Rheumatismus *m*, Rheuma *nt*
Rhine /raɪn/ *n* Rhein *m*
rhinoceros /raɪ'nɒsərəs/ *n* Nashorn *nt*, Rhinozeros *nt*
rhubarb /'ru:bɑ:b/ *n* Rhabarber *m*
rhyme /raɪm/ *n* Reim *m* □ *vt* reimen □ *vi* sich reimen
rhythm /'rɪðm/ *n* Rhythmus *m*. **~ic[al]** *a*, **-ally** *adv* rhythmisch
rib /rɪb/ *n* Rippe *f* □ *vt* (*pt/pp* **ribbed**) (*fam*) aufziehen (*fam*)
ribald /'rɪbld/ *a* derb
ribbon /'rɪbən/ *n* Band *nt*; (*for typewriter*) Farbband *nt*; **in ~s** in Fetzen
rice /raɪs/ *n* Reis *m*
rich /rɪtʃ/ *a* (**-er, -est**), **-ly** *adv* reich; ⟨*food*⟩ gehaltvoll; (*heavy*) schwer □ *n* **the ~** *pl* die Reichen; **~es** *pl* Reichtum *m*
rickets /'rɪkɪts/ *n* Rachitis *f*
rickety /'rɪkətɪ/ *a* wackelig
ricochet /'rɪkəʃeɪ/ *vi* abprallen
rid /rɪd/ *vt* (*pt/pp* **rid**, *pres p* **ridding**) befreien (**of** von); **get ~ of** loswerden
riddance /'rɪdns/ *n* **good ~!** auf Nimmerwiedersehen!
ridden /'rɪdn/ *see* **ride**
riddle /'rɪdl/ *n* Rätsel *nt*
riddled /'rɪdld/ *a* **~ with** durchlöchert mit
ride /raɪd/ *n* Ritt *m*; (*in vehicle*) Fahrt *f*; **take s.o. for a ~** (*fam*) jdn reinlegen □ *v* (*pt* **rode**, *pp* **ridden**) □ *vt* reiten ⟨*horse*⟩; fahren mit ⟨*bicycle*⟩ □ *vi* reiten; (*in vehicle*) fahren. **~r** *n* Reiter(in) *m(f)*; (*on bicycle*) Fahrer(in) *m(f)*; (*in document*) Zusatzklausel *f*

ridge /rɪdʒ/ *n* Erhebung *f*; (*on roof*) First *m*; (*of mountain*) Grat *m*, Kamm *m*; (*of high pressure*) Hochdruckkeil *m*
ridicule /ˈrɪdɪkju:l/ *n* Spott *m* □ *vt* verspotten, spotten über (+ *acc*)
ridiculous /rɪˈdɪkjʊləs/ *a*, **-ly** *adv* lächerlich
riding /ˈraɪdɪŋ/ *n* Reiten *nt* □ *attrib* Reit-
rife /raɪf/ *a* **be ~** weit verbreitet sein
riff-raff /ˈrɪfræf/ *n* Gesindel *nt*
rifle /ˈraɪfl/ *n* Gewehr *nt* □ *vt* plündern; **~ through** durchwühlen
rift /rɪft/ *n* Spalt *m*; (*fig*) Riss *m*
rig¹ /rɪg/ *n* Ölbohrturm *m*; (*at sea*) Bohrinsel *f* □ *vt* (*pt/pp* **rigged**) **~ out** ausrüsten; **~ up** aufbauen
rig² *vt* (*pt/pp* **rigged**) manipulieren
right /raɪt/ *a* richtig; (*not left*) rechte(r,s); **be ~** ⟨*person:*⟩ Recht haben; ⟨*clock:*⟩ richtig gehen; **put ~** wieder in Ordnung bringen; (*fig*) richtig stellen; **that's ~!** das stimmt! □ *adv* richtig; (*directly*) direkt; (*completely*) ganz; (*not left*) rechts; ⟨*go*⟩ nach rechts; **~ away** sofort □ *n* Recht *nt*; (*not left*) rechte Seite *f*; **on the ~** rechts; **from/to the ~** von/nach rechts; **be in the ~** Recht haben; **by ~s** eigentlich; **the R~** (*Pol*) die Rechte. **~ angle** *n* rechter Winkel *m*
righteous /ˈraɪtʃəs/ *a* rechtschaffen
rightful /ˈraɪtfl/ *a*, **-ly** *adv* rechtmäßig
right: **~-ˈhanded** *a* rechtshändig. **~-hand ˈman** *n* (*fig*) rechte Hand *f*
rightly /ˈraɪtlɪ/ *adv* mit Recht
right: **~ of way** *n* Durchgangsrecht *nt*; (*path*) öffentlicher Fußweg *m*; (*Auto*) Vorfahrt *f*. **~-ˈwing** *a* (*Pol*) rechte(r,s)
rigid /ˈrɪdʒɪd/ *a* starr; (*strict*) streng. **~ity** /-ˈdʒɪdətɪ/ *n* Starrheit *f*; Strenge *f*
rigmarole /ˈrɪgmərəʊl/ *n* Geschwätz *nt*; (*procedure*) Prozedur *f*
rigorous /ˈrɪgərəs/ *a*, **-ly** *adv* streng
rigour /ˈrɪgə(r)/ *n* Strenge *f*
rile /raɪl/ *vt* (*fam*) ärgern
rim /rɪm/ *n* Rand *m*; (*of wheel*) Felge *f*
rind /raɪnd/ *n* (*on fruit*) Schale *f*; (*on cheese*) Rinde *f*; (*on bacon*) Schwarte *f*
ring¹ /rɪŋ/ *n* Ring *m*; (*for circus*) Manege *f*; **stand in a ~** im Kreis stehen □ *vt* umringen; **~ in red** rot einkreisen
ring² *n* Klingeln *nt*; **give s.o. a ~** (*Teleph*) jdn anrufen □ *v* (*pt* **rang**, *pp* **rung**) □ *vt* läuten; **~ [up]** (*Teleph*) anrufen □ *vi* läuten, klingeln. **~ back** *vt/i* (*Teleph*) zurückrufen. **~ off** *vi* (*Teleph*) auflegen
ring: **~leader** *n* Rädelsführer *m*. **~ road** *n* Umgehungsstraße *f*
rink /rɪŋk/ *n* Eisbahn *f*
rinse /rɪns/ *n* Spülung *f*; (*hair colour*) Tönung *f* □ *vt* spülen; tönen ⟨*hair*⟩. **~ off** *vt* abspülen
riot /ˈraɪət/ *n* Aufruhr *m*; **~s** *pl* Unruhen *pl*; **~ of colours** bunte Farbenpracht *f*; **run ~** randalieren □ *vi* randalieren. **~er** *n* Randalierer *m*. **~ous** /-əs/ *a* aufrührerisch; (*boisterous*) wild
rip /rɪp/ *n* Riss *m* □ *vt/i* (*pt/pp* **ripped**) zerreißen; **~ open** aufreißen. **~ off** *vt* (*fam*) neppen
ripe /raɪp/ *a* (**-r, -st**) reif
ripen /ˈraɪpn/ *vi* reifen □ *vt* reifen lassen
ripeness /ˈraɪpnɪs/ *n* Reife *f*
ˈrip-off *n* (*fam*) Nepp *m*
ripple /ˈrɪpl/ *n* kleine Welle *f* □ *vt* kräuseln □ *vi* sich kräuseln
rise /raɪz/ *n* Anstieg *m*; (*fig*) Aufstieg *m*; (*increase*) Zunahme *f*; (*in wages*) Lohnerhöhung *f*; (*in salary*) Gehaltserhöhung *f*; **give ~ to** Anlass geben zu □ *vi* (*pt* **rose**,

pp **risen**) steigen; ⟨*ground:*⟩ ansteigen; ⟨*sun, dough:*⟩ aufgehen; ⟨*river:*⟩ entspringen; (*get up*) aufstehen; (*fig*) aufsteigen (**to** zu); (*rebel*) sich erheben; ⟨*court:*⟩ sich vertagen. **~r** *n* **early ~r** Frühaufsteher *m*

rising /ˈraɪzɪŋ/ *a* steigend; ⟨*sun*⟩ aufgehend; **the ~ generation** die heranwachsende Generation □ *n* (*revolt*) Aufstand *m*

risk /rɪsk/ *n* Risiko *nt*; **at one's own ~** auf eigene Gefahr □ *vt* riskieren

risky /ˈrɪskɪ/ *a* (**-ier, -iest**) riskant

risqué /ˈrɪskeɪ/ *a* gewagt

rissole /ˈrɪsəʊl/ *n* Frikadelle *f*

rite /raɪt/ *n* Ritus *m*; **last ~s** Letzte Ölung *f*

ritual /ˈrɪtjʊəl/ *a* rituell □ *n* Ritual *nt*

rival /ˈraɪvl/ *a* rivalisierend □ *n* Rivale *m*/Rivalin *f*; **~s** *pl* (*Comm*) Konkurrenten *pl* □ *vt* (*pt/pp* **rivalled**) gleichkommen (+ *dat*); (*compete with*) rivalisieren mit. **~ry** *n* Rivalität *f*; (*Comm*) Konkurrenzkampf *m*

river /ˈrɪvə(r)/ *n* Fluss *m*. **~-bed** *n* Flussbett *nt*

rivet /ˈrɪvɪt/ *n* Niete *f* □ *vt* [ver]nieten; **~ed by** (*fig*) gefesselt von

road /rəʊd/ *n* Straße *f*; (*fig*) Weg *m*

road: ~-block *n* Straßensperre *f*. **~-hog** *n* (*fam*) Straßenschreck *m*. **~-map** *n* Straßenkarte *f*. **~ safety** *n* Verkehrssicherheit *f*. **~ sense** *n* Verkehrssinn *m*. **~side** *n* Straßenrand *m*. **~way** *n* Fahrbahn *f*. **~-works** *npl* Straßenarbeiten *pl*. **~worthy** *a* verkehrssicher

roam /rəʊm/ *vi* wandern

roar /rɔː(r)/ *n* Gebrüll *nt*; **~s of laughter** schallendes Gelächter *nt* □ *vi* brüllen; (*with laughter*) schallend lachen. **~ing** *a* ⟨*fire*⟩ prasselnd; **do a ~ing trade** (*fam*) ein Bombengeschäft machen

roast /rəʊst/ *a* gebraten, Brat-; **~ beef/pork** Rinder-/Schweinebraten *m* □ *n* Braten *m* □ *vt/i* braten; rösten ⟨*coffee, chestnuts*⟩

rob /rɒb/ *vt* (*pt/pp* **robbed**) berauben (**of** *gen*); ausrauben ⟨*bank*⟩. **~ber** *n* Räuber *m*. **~bery** *n* Raub *m*

robe /rəʊb/ *n* Robe *f*; (*Amer: bathrobe*) Bademantel *m*

robin /ˈrɒbɪn/ *n* Rotkehlchen *nt*

robot /ˈrəʊbɒt/ *n* Roboter *m*

robust /rəʊˈbʌst/ *a* robust

rock[1] /rɒk/ *n* Fels *m*; **stick of ~** Zuckerstange *f*; **on the ~s** ⟨*ship*⟩ aufgelaufen; ⟨*marriage*⟩ kaputt; ⟨*drink*⟩ mit Eis

rock[2] *vt/i* schaukeln

rock[3] *n* (*Mus*) Rock *m*

rock-ˈbottom *n* Tiefpunkt *m*

rockery /ˈrɒkərɪ/ *n* Steingarten *m*

rocket /ˈrɒkɪt/ *n* Rakete *f* □ *vi* in die Höhe schießen

rocking: ~-chair *n* Schaukelstuhl *m*. **~-horse** *n* Schaukelpferd *nt*

rocky /ˈrɒkɪ/ *a* (**-ier, -iest**) felsig; (*unsteady*) wackelig

rod /rɒd/ *n* Stab *m*; (*stick*) Rute *f*; (*for fishing*) Angel[rute] *f*

rode /rəʊd/ *see* **ride**

rodent /ˈrəʊdnt/ *n* Nagetier *nt*

roe[1] /rəʊ/ *n* Rogen *m*; (*soft*) Milch *f*

roe[2] *n* (*pl* **roe** *or* **roes**) **~[-deer]** Reh *nt*

rogue /rəʊg/ *n* Gauner *m*

role /rəʊl/ *n* Rolle *f*

roll /rəʊl/ *n* Rolle *f*; (*bread*) Brötchen *nt*; (*list*) Liste *f*; (*of drum*) Wirbel *m* □ *vi* rollen; **be ~ing in money** (*fam*) Geld wie Heu haben □ *vt* rollen; walzen ⟨*lawn*⟩; ausrollen ⟨*pastry*⟩. **~ over** *vi* sich auf die andere Seite rollen. **~ up** *vt* aufrollen; hochkrempeln ⟨*sleeves*⟩ □ *vi* (*fam*) auftauchen

'roll-call *n* Namensaufruf *m*; (*Mil*) Appell *m*
roller /'rəʊlə(r)/ *n* Rolle *f*; (*lawn, road*) Walze *f*; (*hair*) Lockenwickler *m*. **~ blind** *n* Rollo *nt*. **~-coaster** *n* Berg-und-Talbahn *f*. **~-skate** *n* Rollschuh *m*
'rolling-pin *n* Teigrolle *f*
Roman /'rəʊmən/ *a* römisch □ *n* Römer(in) *m(f)*
romance /rə'mæns/ *n* Romantik *f*; (*love-affair*) Romanze *f*; (*book*) Liebesgeschichte *f*
Romania /rəʊ'meɪnɪə/ *n* Rumänien *nt*. **~n** *a* rumänisch □ *n* Rumäne *m*/-nin *f*
romantic /rəʊ'mæntɪk/ *a*, **-ally** *adv* romantisch. **~ism** /-tɪsɪzm/ *n* Romantik *f*
Rome /rəʊm/ *n* Rom *nt*
romp /rɒmp/ *n* Tollen *nt* □ *vi* [herum]tollen. **~ers** *npl* Strampelhöschen *nt*
roof /ru:f/ *n* Dach *nt*; (*of mouth*) Gaumen *m* □ *vt* **~ over** überdachen. **~-rack** *n* Dachgepäckträger *m*. **~-top** *n* Dach *nt*
rook /rʊk/ *n* Saatkrähe *f*; (*Chess*) Turm *m* □ *vt* (*fam: swindle*) schröpfen
room /ru:m/ *n* Zimmer *nt*; (*for functions*) Saal *m*; (*space*) Platz *m*. **~y** *a* geräumig
roost /ru:st/ *n* Hühnerstange *f* □ *vi* schlafen
root¹ /ru:t/ *n* Wurzel *f*; **take ~** anwachsen □ *vi* Wurzeln schlagen. **~ out** *vt* (*fig*) ausrotten
root² *vi* **~ about** wühlen; **~ for s.o.** (*Amer, fam*) für jdn sein
rope /rəʊp/ *n* Seil *nt*; **know the ~s** (*fam*) sich auskennen. **~ in** *vt* (*fam*) einspannen
rope-'ladder *n* Strickleiter *f*
rosary /'rəʊzərɪ/ *n* Rosenkranz *m*
rose¹ /rəʊz/ *n* Rose *f*; (*of watering-can*) Brause *f*
rose² *see* **rise**
rosemary /'rəʊzmərɪ/ *n* Rosmarin *m*
rosette /rəʊ'zet/ *n* Rosette *f*
roster /'rɒstə(r)/ *n* Dienstplan *m*
rostrum /'rɒstrəm/ *n* Podest *nt*, Podium *nt*
rosy /'rəʊzɪ/ *a* (**-ier, -iest**) rosig
rot /rɒt/ *n* Fäulnis *f*; (*fam: nonsense*) Quatsch *m* □ *vi* (*pt/pp* **rotted**) [ver]faulen
rota /'rəʊtə/ *n* Dienstplan *m*
rotary /'rəʊtərɪ/ *a* Dreh-; (*Techn*) Rotations-
rotat|e /rəʊ'teɪt/ *vt* drehen; im Wechsel anbauen ⟨*crops*⟩ □ *vi* sich drehen; (*Techn*) rotieren. **~ion** /-eɪʃn/ *n* Drehung *f*; (*of crops*) Fruchtfolge *f*; **in ~ion** im Wechsel
rote /rəʊt/ *n* **by ~** auswendig
rotten /'rɒtn/ *a* faul; (*fam*) mies; ⟨*person*⟩ fies
rotund /rəʊ'tʌnd/ *a* rundlich
rough /rʌf/ *a* (**-er, -est**) rau; (*uneven*) uneben; (*coarse, not gentle*) grob; (*brutal*) roh; (*turbulent*) stürmisch; (*approximate*) ungefähr □ *adv* **sleep ~** im Freien übernachten; **play ~** holzen □ *n* **do sth in ~** etw ins Unreine schreiben □ *vt* **~ it** primitiv leben; **~ out** *vt* im Groben entwerfen
roughage /'rʌfɪdʒ/ *n* Ballaststoffe *pl*
rough 'draft *n* grober Entwurf *m*
rough|ly /'rʌflɪ/ *adv* (*see* **rough**) rau; grob; roh; ungefähr. **~ness** *n* Rauheit *f*
'rough paper *n* Konzeptpapier *nt*
round /raʊnd/ *a* (**-er, -est**) rund □ *n* Runde *f*; (*slice*) Scheibe *f*; **do one's ~s** seine Runde machen □ *prep* um (+ *acc*); **~ the clock** rund um die Uhr □ *adv* **all ~** ringsherum; **~ and ~** im Kreis; **ask s.o. ~** jdn einladen; **turn/look ~** sich umdrehen/umsehen □ *vt* biegen um ⟨*corner*⟩ □ *vi* **~ on s.o.** jdn anfahren. **~ off** *vt* abrunden. **~ up** *vt* aufrunden; zusammentreiben ⟨*animals*⟩; festnehmen ⟨*criminals*⟩

roundabout /ˈraʊndəbaʊt/ *a* ~ **route** Umweg *m* □ *n* Karussell *nt*; (*for traffic*) Kreisverkehr *m*
round: ~-**'shouldered** *a* mit einem runden Rücken. ~ **'trip** *n* Rundreise *f*
rous|e /raʊz/ *vt* wecken; (*fig*) erregen. ~**ing** *a* mitreißend
route /ru:t/ *n* Route *f*; (*of bus*) Linie *f*
routine /ru:ˈti:n/ *a*, **-ly** *adv* routinemäßig □ *n* Routine *f*; (*Theat*) Nummer *f*
roux /ru:/ *n* Mehlschwitze *f*
rove /rəʊv/ *vi* wandern
row[1] /rəʊ/ *n* (*line*) Reihe *f*; **in a** ~ (*one after the other*) nacheinander
row[2] *vt/i* rudern
row[3] /raʊ/ *n* (*fam*) Krach *m* □ *vi* (*fam*) sich streiten
rowan /ˈrəʊən/ *n* Eberesche *f*
rowdy /ˈraʊdɪ/ *a* (**-ier, -iest**) laut
rowing boat /ˈrəʊɪŋ-/ *n* Ruderboot *nt*
royal /rɔɪəl/ *a*, **-ly** *adv* königlich
royalt|y /ˈrɔɪəltɪ/ *n* Königtum *nt*; (*persons*) Mitglieder *pl* der königlichen Familie; **-ies** *pl* (*payments*) Tantiemen *pl*
rub /rʌb/ *n* **give sth a** ~ etw reiben/(*polish*) polieren □ *vt* (*pt/pp* **rubbed**) reiben; (*polish*) polieren; **don't** ~ **it in** (*fam*) reib es mir nicht unter die Nase. ~ **off** *vt* abreiben □ *vi* abgehen; ~ **off on** abfärben auf (+ *acc*). ~ **out** *vt* ausradieren
rubber /ˈrʌbə(r)/ *n* Gummi *m*; (*eraser*) Radiergummi *m*. ~ **band** *n* Gummiband *nt*. ~**y** *a* gummiartig
rubbish /ˈrʌbɪʃ/ *n* Abfall *m*, Müll *m*; (*fam: nonsense*) Quatsch *m*; (*fam: junk*) Plunder *m*, Kram *m* □ *vt* (*fam*) schlecht machen. ~ **bin** *n* Mülleimer *m*, Abfalleimer *m*. ~ **dump** *n* Abfallhaufen *m*; (*official*) Müllhalde *f*
rubble /ˈrʌbl/ *n* Trümmer *pl*, Schutt *m*
ruby /ˈru:bɪ/ *n* Rubin *m*
rucksack /ˈrʌksæk/ *n* Rucksack *m*
rudder /ˈrʌdə(r)/ *n* [Steuer]ruder *nt*
ruddy /ˈrʌdɪ/ *a* (**-ier, -iest**) rötlich; (*sl*) verdammt
rude /ru:d/ *a* (**-r, -st**), **-ly** *adv* unhöflich; (*improper*) unanständig. ~**ness** *n* Unhöflichkeit *f*
rudiment /ˈru:dɪmənt/ *n* ~**s** *pl* Anfangsgründe *pl*. ~**ary** /-ˈmentərɪ/ *a* elementar; (*Biol*) rudimentär
rueful /ˈru:fl/ *a*, **-ly** *adv* reumütig
ruffian /ˈrʌfɪən/ *n* Rüpel *m*
ruffle /ˈrʌfl/ *n* Rüsche *f* □ *vt* zerzausen
rug /rʌg/ *n* Vorleger *m*, [kleiner] Teppich *m*; (*blanket*) Decke *f*
rugged /ˈrʌgɪd/ *a* ⟨*coastline*⟩ zerklüftet
ruin /ˈru:ɪn/ *n* Ruine *f*; (*fig*) Ruin *m* □ *vt* ruinieren. ~**ous** /-əs/ *a* ruinös
rule /ru:l/ *n* Regel *f*; (*control*) Herrschaft *f*; (*government*) Regierung *f*; (*for measuring*) Lineal *nt*; **as a** ~ in der Regel □ *vt* regieren, herrschen über (+ *acc*); (*fig*) beherrschen; (*decide*) entscheiden; ziehen ⟨*line*⟩ □ *vi* regieren, herrschen. ~ **out** *vt* ausschließen
ruled /ru:ld/ *a* ⟨*paper*⟩ liniert
ruler /ˈru:lə(r)/ *n* Herrscher(in) *m*(*f*); (*measure*) Lineal *nt*
ruling /ˈru:lɪŋ/ *a* herrschend; ⟨*factor*⟩ entscheidend; (*Pol*) regierend □ *n* Entscheidung *f*
rum /rʌm/ *n* Rum *m*
rumble /ˈrʌmbl/ *n* Grollen *nt* □ *vi* grollen; ⟨*stomach:*⟩ knurren
ruminant /ˈru:mɪnənt/ *n* Wiederkäuer *m*
rummage /ˈrʌmɪdʒ/ *vi* wühlen; ~ **through** durchwühlen
rummy /ˈrʌmɪ/ *n* Rommé *nt*
rumour /ˈru:mə(r)/ *n* Gerücht *nt* □ *vt* **it is** ~**ed that** es geht das Gerücht, dass

rump /rʌmp/ *n* Hinterteil *nt*. **~ steak** *n* Rumpsteak *nt*
rumpus /ˈrʌmpəs/ *n* (*fam*) Spektakel *m*
run /rʌn/ *n* Lauf *m*; (*journey*) Fahrt *f*; (*series*) Serie *f*, Reihe *f*; (*Theat*) Laufzeit *f*; (*Skiing*) Abfahrt *f*; (*enclosure*) Auslauf *m*; (*Amer: ladder*) Laufmasche *f*; **at a ~** im Laufschritt; **~ of bad luck** Pechsträhne *f*; **be on the ~** flüchtig sein; **have the ~ of sth** etw zu seiner freien Verfügung haben; **in the long ~** auf lange Sicht □ *v* (*pt* **ran**, *pp* **run**, *pres p* **running**) □ *vi* laufen; (*flow*) fließen; ⟨*eyes:*⟩ tränen; ⟨*bus:*⟩ verkehren, fahren; ⟨*butter, ink:*⟩ zerfließen; ⟨*colours:*⟩ [ab]färben; (*in election*) kandidieren; **~ across s.o./sth** auf jdn/ etw stoßen □ *vt* laufen lassen; einlaufen lassen ⟨*bath*⟩; (*manage*) führen, leiten; (*drive*) fahren; eingehen ⟨*risk*⟩; (*Journ*) bringen ⟨*article*⟩; **~ one's hand over sth** mit der Hand über etw (*acc*) fahren. **~ away** *vi* weglaufen. **~ down** *vi* hinunter-/herunterlaufen; ⟨*clockwork:*⟩ ablaufen; ⟨*stocks:*⟩ sich verringern □ *vt* (*run over*) überfahren; (*reduce*) verringern; (*fam: criticize*) heruntermachen. **~ in** *vi* hinein-/hereinlaufen. **~ off** *vi* weglaufen □ *vt* abziehen ⟨*copies*⟩. **~ out** *vi* hinaus-/herauslaufen; ⟨*supplies, money:*⟩ ausgehen; **I've ~ out of sugar** Ich habe keinen Zucker mehr. **~ over** *vi* hinüber-/herüberlaufen; (*overflow*) überlaufen □ *vt* überfahren. **~ through** *vi* durchlaufen. **~ up** *vi* hinauf-/herauflaufen; (*towards*) hinlaufen □ *vt* machen ⟨*debts*⟩; auflaufen lassen ⟨*bill*⟩; (*sew*) schnell nähen
ˈrunaway *n* Ausreißer *m*
run-ˈdown *a* ⟨*area*⟩ verkommen
rung¹ /rʌŋ/ *n* (*of ladder*) Sprosse *f*
rung² *see* **ring²**
runner /ˈrʌnə(r)/ *n* Läufer *m*; (*Bot*) Ausläufer *m*; (*on sledge*) Kufe *f*. **~ bean** *n* Stangenbohne *f*. **~-up** *n* Zweite(r) *m/f*
running /ˈrʌnɪŋ/ *a* laufend; ⟨*water*⟩ fließend; **four times ~** viermal nacheinander □ *n* Laufen *nt*; (*management*) Führung *f*, Leitung *f*; **be/not be in the ~** eine/keine Chance haben. **~ ˈcommentary** *n* fortlaufender Kommentar *m*
runny /ˈrʌnɪ/ *a* flüssig
run: ~-of-the-ˈmill *a* gewöhnlich. **~-up** *n* (*Sport*) Anlauf *m*; (*to election*) Zeit *f* vor der Wahl. **~way** *n* Start- und Landebahn *f*, Piste *f*
rupture /ˈrʌptʃə(r)/ *n* Bruch *m* □ *vt/i* brechen; **~ oneself** sich (*dat*) einen Bruch heben
rural /ˈrʊərəl/ *a* ländlich
ruse /ru:z/ *n* List *f*
rush¹ /rʌʃ/ *n* (*Bot*) Binse *f*
rush² *n* Hetze *f*; **in a ~** in Eile □ *vi* sich hetzen; (*run*) rasen; ⟨*water:*⟩ rauschen □ *vt* hetzen, drängen; **~ s.o. to hospital** jdn schnellstens ins Krankenhaus bringen. **~-hour** *n* Hauptverkehrszeit *f*, Stoßzeit *f*
rusk /rʌsk/ *n* Zwieback *m*
Russia /ˈrʌʃə/ *n* Russland *nt*. **~n** *a* russisch □ *n* Russe *m*/Russin *f*; (*Lang*) Russisch *nt*
rust /rʌst/ *n* Rost *m* □ *vi* rosten
rustic /ˈrʌstɪk/ *a* bäuerlich; ⟨*furniture*⟩ rustikal
rustle /ˈrʌsl/ *vi* rascheln □ *vt* rascheln mit; (*Amer*) stehlen ⟨*cattle*⟩. **~ up** *vt* (*fam*) improvisieren
ˈrustproof *a* rostfrei
rusty /ˈrʌstɪ/ *a* (**-ier, -iest**) rostig
rut /rʌt/ *n* Furche *f*; **be in a ~** (*fam*) aus dem alten Trott nicht herauskommen
ruthless /ˈru:θlɪs/ *a*, **-ly** *adv* rück-

sichtslos. **~ness** *n* Rücksichtslosigkeit *f*

rye /raɪ/ *n* Roggen *m*

S

sabbath /ˈsæbəθ/ *n* Sabbat *m*

sabbatical /səˈbætɪkl/ *n* (*Univ*) Forschungsurlaub *m*

sabot|age /ˈsæbətɑːʒ/ *n* Sabotage *f* □ *vt* sabotieren. **~eur** /-ˈtɜː(r)/ *n* Saboteur *m*

sachet /ˈsæʃeɪ/ *n* Beutel *m*; (*scented*) Kissen *nt*

sack1 /sæk/ *vt* (*plunder*) plündern

sack2 *n* Sack *m*; **get the ~** (*fam*) rausgeschmissen werden □ *vt* (*fam*) rausschmeißen. **~ing** *n* Sackleinen *nt*; (*fam: dismissal*) Rausschmiss *m*

sacrament /ˈsækrəmənt/ *n* Sakrament *nt*

sacred /ˈseɪkrɪd/ *a* heilig

sacrifice /ˈsækrɪfaɪs/ *n* Opfer *nt* □ *vt* opfern

sacrilege /ˈsækrɪlɪdʒ/ *n* Sakrileg *nt*

sad /sæd/ *a* (**sadder, saddest**) traurig; ⟨*loss, death*⟩ schmerzlich. **~den** *vt* traurig machen

saddle /ˈsædl/ *n* Sattel *m* □ *vt* satteln; **~ s.o. with sth** (*fam*) jdm etw aufhalsen

sadis|m /ˈseɪdɪzm/ *n* Sadismus *m*. **~t** /-dɪst/ *n* Sadist *m*. **~tic** /səˈdɪstɪk/ *a*, **-ally** *adv* sadistisch

sad|ly /ˈsædlɪ/ *adv* traurig; (*unfortunately*) leider. **~ness** *n* Traurigkeit *f*

safe /seɪf/ *a* (**-r, -st**) sicher; ⟨*journey*⟩ gut; (*not dangerous*) ungefährlich; **~ and sound** gesund und wohlbehalten □ *n* Safe *m*. **~guard** *n* Schutz *m* □ *vt* schützen. **~ly** *adv* sicher; ⟨*arrive*⟩ gut

safety /ˈseɪftɪ/ *n* Sicherheit *f*. **~-belt** *n* Sicherheitsgurt *m*. **~-pin** *n* Sicherheitsnadel *f*. **~-valve** *n* [Sicherheits] ventil *nt*

sag /sæg/ *vi* (*pt/pp* **sagged**) durchhängen

saga /ˈsɑːgə/ *n* Saga *f*; (*fig*) Geschichte *f*

sage1 /seɪdʒ/ *n* (*herb*) Salbei *m*

sage2 *a* weise □ *n* Weise(r) *m*

Sagittarius /sædʒɪˈteərɪəs/ *n* (*Astr*) Schütze *m*

said /sed/ *see* **say**

sail /seɪl/ *n* Segel *nt*; (*trip*) Segelfahrt *f* □ *vi* segeln; (*on liner*) fahren; (*leave*) abfahren (**for** nach) □ *vt* segeln mit

ˈ**sailboard** *n* Surfbrett *nt*. **~ing** *n* Windsurfen *nt*

sailing /ˈseɪlɪŋ/ *n* Segelsport *m*. **~-boat** *n* Segelboot *nt*. **~-ship** *n* Segelschiff *nt*

sailor /ˈseɪlə(r)/ *n* Seemann *m*; (*in navy*) Matrose *m*

saint /seɪnt/ *n* Heilige(r) *m/f*. **~ly** *a* heilig

sake /seɪk/ *n* **for the ~ of ...** um ... (*gen*) willen; **for my/your ~** um meinet-/deinetwillen

salad /ˈsæləd/ *n* Salat *m*. **~ cream** *n* ≈ Mayonnaise *f*. **~-dressing** *n* Salatsoße *f*

salary /ˈsælərɪ/ *n* Gehalt *nt*

sale /seɪl/ *n* Verkauf *m*; (*event*) Basar *m*; (*at reduced prices*) Schlussverkauf *m*; **for ~** zu verkaufen

sales|man *n* Verkäufer *m*. **~woman** *n* Verkäuferin *f*

salient /ˈseɪlɪənt/ *a* wichtigste(r,s)

saliva /səˈlaɪvə/ *n* Speichel *m*

sallow /ˈsæləʊ/ *a* (**-er, -est**) bleich

salmon /ˈsæmən/ *n* Lachs *m*. **~-pink** *a* lachsrosa

saloon /səˈluːn/ *n* Salon *m*; (*Auto*) Limousine *f*; (*Amer: bar*) Wirtschaft *f*

salt /sɔːlt/ *n* Salz *nt* □ *a* salzig; ⟨*water, meat*⟩ Salz- □ *vt* salzen; (*cure*) pökeln; streuen ⟨*road*⟩. **~-cellar** *n* Salzfass *nt*. **~** ˈ**water** *n* Salzwasser *nt*. **~y** *a* salzig

salutary /ˈsæljʊtərɪ/ *a* heilsam
salute /səˈluːt/ *n* (*Mil*) Gruß *m* □ *vt/i* (*Mil*) grüßen
salvage /ˈsælvɪdʒ/ *n* (*Naut*) Bergung *f* □ *vt* bergen
salvation /sælˈveɪʃn/ *n* Rettung *f*; (*Relig*) Heil *nt*. **S~ ˈArmy** *n* Heilsarmee *f*
salvo /ˈsælvəʊ/ *n* Salve *f*
same /seɪm/ *a & pron* **the ~** der/die/das gleiche; (*pl*) die gleichen; (*identical*) der-/die-/dasselbe; (*pl*) dieselben □ *adv* **the ~** gleich; **all the ~** trotzdem; **the ~ to you** gleichfalls
sample /ˈsɑːmpl/ *n* Probe *f*; (*Comm*) Muster *nt* □ *vt* probieren, kosten
sanatorium /sænəˈtɔːrɪəm/ *n* Sanatorium *nt*
sanctify /ˈsæŋktɪfaɪ/ *vt* (*pt/pp* **-fied**) heiligen
sanctimonious /sæŋktɪˈməʊnɪəs/ *a*, **-ly** *adv* frömmlerisch
sanction /ˈsæŋkʃn/ *n* Sanktion *f* □ *vt* sanktionieren
sanctity /ˈsæŋktətɪ/ *n* Heiligkeit *f*
sanctuary /ˈsæŋktjʊərɪ/ *n* (*Relig*) Heiligtum *nt*; (*refuge*) Zuflucht *f*; (*for wildlife*) Tierschutzgebiet *nt*
sand /sænd/ *n* Sand *m* □ *vt* **~ [down]** [ab]schmirgeln
sandal /ˈsændl/ *n* Sandale *f*
sand: ~bank *n* Sandbank *f*. **~paper** *n* Sandpapier *nt* □ *vt* [ab]schmirgeln. **~-pit** *n* Sandkasten *m*
sandwich /ˈsænwɪdʒ/ *n* ≈ belegtes Brot *nt*; Sandwich *m* □ *vt* **~ed between** eingeklemmt zwischen
sandy /ˈsændɪ/ *a* (**-ier, -iest**) sandig; ⟨*beach, soil*⟩ Sand-; ⟨*hair*⟩ rotblond
sane /seɪn/ *a* (**-r, -st**) geistig normal; (*sensible*) vernünftig
sang /sæŋ/ *see* **sing**
sanitary /ˈsænɪtərɪ/ *a* hygienisch; ⟨*system*⟩ sanitär. **~ napkin** *n* (*Amer*), **~ towel** *n* [Damen]binde *f*
sanitation /sænɪˈteɪʃn/ *n* Kanalisation und Abfallbeseitigung *pl*
sanity /ˈsænətɪ/ *n* [gesunder] Verstand *m*
sank /sæŋk/ *see* **sink**
sap /sæp/ *n* (*Bot*) Saft *m* □ *vt* (*pt/pp* **sapped**) schwächen
sapphire /ˈsæfaɪə(r)/ *n* Saphir *m*
sarcas|m /ˈsɑːkæzm/ *n* Sarkasmus *m*. **~tic** /-ˈkæstɪk/ *a*, **-ally** *adv* sarkastisch
sardine /sɑːˈdiːn/ *n* Sardine *f*
Sardinia /sɑːˈdɪnɪə/ *n* Sardinien *nt*
sardonic /sɑːˈdɒnɪk/ *a*, **-ally** *adv* höhnisch; ⟨*smile*⟩ sardonisch
sash /sæʃ/ *n* Schärpe *f*
sat /sæt/ *see* **sit**
satanic /səˈtænɪk/ *a* satanisch
satchel /ˈsætʃl/ *n* Ranzen *m*
satellite /ˈsætəlaɪt/ *n* Satellit *m*. **~ dish** *n* Satellitenschüssel *f*. **~ television** *n* Satellitenfernsehen *nt*
satin /ˈsætɪn/ *n* Satin *m*
satire /ˈsætaɪə(r)/ *n* Satire *f*
satirical /səˈtɪrɪkl/ *a*, **-ly** *adv* satirisch
satir|ist /ˈsætərɪst/ *n* Satiriker(in) *m(f)*. **~ize** *vt* satirisch darstellen; ⟨*book:*⟩ eine Satire sein auf (+ *acc*)
satisfaction /sætɪsˈfækʃn/ *n* Befriedigung *f*; to **my ~** zu meiner Zufriedenheit
satisfactory /sætɪsˈfæktərɪ/ *a*, **-ily** *adv* zufrieden stellend
satisf|y /ˈsætɪsfaɪ/ *vt* (*pp/pp* **-fied**) befriedigen; zufrieden stellen ⟨*customer*⟩; (*convince*) überzeugen; **be ~ied** zufrieden sein. **~ying** *a* befriedigend; ⟨*meal*⟩ sättigend
saturat|e /ˈsætʃəreɪt/ *vt* durchtränken; (*Chem & fig*) sättigen. **~ed** *a* durchnässt; ⟨*fat*⟩ gesättigt

Saturday /ˈsætədeɪ/ *n* Samstag *m*, Sonnabend *m*
sauce /sɔːs/ *n* Soße *f*; (*cheek*) Frechheit *f*. **~pan** *n* Kochtopf *m*
saucer /ˈsɔːsə(r)/ *n* Untertasse *f*
saucy /ˈsɔːʃɪ/ *a* (**-ier, -iest**) frech
Saudi Arabia /saʊdɪəˈreɪbɪə/ *n* Saudi-Arabien *n*
sauna /ˈsɔːnə/ *n* Sauna *f*
saunter /ˈsɔːntə(r)/ *vi* schlendern
sausage /ˈsɒsɪdʒ/ *n* Wurst *f*
savage /ˈsævɪdʒ/ *a* wild; (*fierce*) scharf; (*brutal*) brutal □ *n* Wilde(r) *m/f* □ *vt* anfallen. **~ry** *n* Brutalität *f*
save /seɪv/ *n* (*Sport*) Abwehr *f* □ *vt* retten (**from** vor + *dat*); (*keep*) aufheben; (*not waste*) sparen; (*collect*) sammeln; (*avoid*) ersparen; (*Sport*) verhindern ⟨*goal*⟩ □ *vi* **~ [up]** sparen □ *prep* außer (+ *dat*), mit Ausnahme (+ *gen*)
saver /ˈseɪvə(r)/ *n* Sparer *m*
saving /ˈseɪvɪŋ/ *n* (*see* **save**) Rettung *f*; Sparen *nt*; Ersparnis *f*; **~s** *pl* (*money*) Ersparnisse *pl*. **~s account** *n* Sparkonto *nt*. **~s bank** *n* Sparkasse *f*
saviour /ˈseɪvjə(r)/ *n* Retter *m*
savour /ˈseɪvə(r)/ *n* Geschmack *m* □ *vt* auskosten. **~y** *a* herzhaft, würzig; (*fig*) angenehm
saw¹ /sɔː/ *see* **see**¹
saw² *n* Säge *f* □ *vt/i* (*pt* **sawed**, *pp* **sawn** *or* **sawed**) sägen. **~dust** *n* Sägemehl *nt*
saxophone /ˈsæksəfəʊn/ *n* Saxophon *nt*
say /seɪ/ *n* Mitspracherecht *nt*; **have one's ~** seine Meinung sagen □ *vt/i* (*pt/pp* **said**) sagen; sprechen ⟨*prayer*⟩; **that is to ~** das heißt; **that goes without ~ing** das versteht sich von selbst; **when all is said and done** letzten Endes; **I ~!** (*attracting attention*) hallo! **~ing** *n* Redensart *f*
scab /skæb/ *n* Schorf *m*; (*pej*) Streikbrecher *m*
scaffold /ˈskæfəld/ *n* Schafott *nt*. **~ing** *n* Gerüst *nt*
scald /skɔːld/ *vt* verbrühen
scale¹ /skeɪl/ *n* (*of fish*) Schuppe *f*
scale² *n* Skala *f*; (*Mus*) Tonleiter *f*; (*ratio*) Maßstab *m*; **on a grand ~** in großem Stil □ *vt* (*climb*) erklettern. **~ down** *vt* verkleinern
scales /skeɪlz/ *npl* (*for weighing*) Waage *f*
scalp /skælp/ *n* Kopfhaut *f* □ *vt* skalpieren
scalpel /ˈskælpl/ *n* Skalpell *nt*
scam /skæm/ *n* (*fam*) Schwindel *m*
scamper /ˈskæmpə(r)/ *vi* huschen
scan /skæn/ *n* (*Med*) Szintigramm *nt* □ *v* (*pt/pp* **scanned**) □ *vt* absuchen; (*quickly*) flüchtig ansehen; (*Med*) szintigraphisch untersuchen □ *vi* ⟨*poetry:*⟩ das richtige Versmaß haben
scandal /ˈskændl/ *n* Skandal *m*; (*gossip*) Skandalgeschichten *pl*. **~ize** /-dəlaɪz/ *vt* schockieren. **~ous** /-əs/ *a* skandalös
Scandinavia /skændɪˈneɪvɪə/ *n* Skandinavien *nt*. **~n** *a* skandinavisch □ *n* Skandinavier(in) *m(f)*
scant /skænt/ *a* wenig
scanty /ˈskæntɪ/ *a* (**-ier, -iest**), **-ily** *adv* spärlich; ⟨*clothing*⟩ knapp
scapegoat /ˈskeɪp-/ *n* Sündenbock *m*
scar /skɑː(r)/ *n* Narbe *f* □ *vt* (*pt/pp* **scarred**) eine Narbe hinterlassen auf (+ *dat*)
scarc|e /skeəs/ *a* (**-r, -st**) knapp; **make oneself ~e** (*fam*) sich aus dem Staub machen. **~ely** *adv* kaum. **~ity** *n* Knappheit *f*
scare /skeə(r)/ *n* Schreck *m*; (*panic*) [allgemeine] Panik *f*; (*bomb* **~**) Bombendrohung *f* □ *vt* Angst machen (+ **dat**); **be ~d** Angst haben (**of** vor + *dat*)
scarecrow *n* Vogelscheuche *f*
scarf /skɑːf/ *n* (*pl* **scarves**) Schal *m*; (*square*) Tuch *nt*

scarlet /'skɑ:lət/ *a* scharlachrot. **~ 'fever** *n* Scharlach *m*
scary /'skeərɪ/ *a* unheimlich
scathing /'skeɪðɪŋ/ *a* bissig
scatter /'skætə(r)/ *vt* verstreuen; (*disperse*) zerstreuen □ *vi* sich zerstreuen. **~-brained** *a* (*fam*) schusselig. **~ed** *a* verstreut; ⟨*showers*⟩ vereinzelt
scatty /'skætɪ/ *a* (**-ier, -iest**) (*fam*) verrückt
scavenge /'skævɪndʒ/ *vi* [im Abfall] Nahrung suchen; ⟨*animal:*⟩ Aas fressen. **~r** *n* Aasfresser *m*
scenario /sɪ'nɑ:rɪəʊ/ *n* Szenario *nt*
scene /si:n/ *n* Szene *f*; (*sight*) Anblick *m*; (*place of event*) Schauplatz *m*; **behind the ~s** hinter den Kulissen; **~ of the crime** Tatort *m*
scenery /'si:nərɪ/ *n* Landschaft *f*; (*Theat*) Szenerie *f*
scenic /'si:nɪk/ *a* landschaftlich schön; (*Theat*) Bühnen-
scent /sent/ *n* Duft *m*; (*trail*) Fährte *f*; (*perfume*) Parfüm *nt*. **~ed** *a* parfümiert
sceptic|al /'skeptɪkl/ *a*, **-ly** *adv* skeptisch. **~ism** /-tɪsɪzm/ *n* Skepsis *f*
schedule /'ʃedju:l/ *n* Programm *nt*; (*of work*) Zeitplan *m*; (*timetable*) Fahrplan *m*; **behind ~** im Rückstand; **according to ~** planmäßig □ *vt* planen. **~d flight** *n* Linienflug *m*
scheme /ski:m/ *n* Programm *nt*; (*plan*) Plan *m*; (*plot*) Komplott *nt* □ *vi* Ränke schmieden
schizophren|ia /skɪtsə'fri:nɪə/ *n* Schizophrenie *f*. **~ic** /-'frenɪk/ *a* schizophren
scholar /'skɒlə(r)/ *n* Gelehrte(r) *m/f*. **~ly** *a* gelehrt. **~ship** *n* Gelehrtheit *f*; (*grant*) Stipendium *nt*
school /sku:l/ *n* Schule *f*; (*Univ*) Fakultät *f* □ *vt* schulen; dressieren ⟨*animal*⟩
school: ~boy *n* Schüler *m*. **~girl** *n* Schülerin *f*. **~ing** *n* Schulbildung *f*. **~master** *n* Lehrer *m*. **~mistress** *n* Lehrerin *f*. **~-teacher** *n* Lehrer(in) *m(f)*
sciatica /saɪ'ætɪkə/ *n* Ischias *m*
scien|ce /'saɪəns/ *n* Wissenschaft *f*. **~tific** /-'tɪfɪk/ *a* wissenschaftlich. **~tist** *n* Wissenschaftler *m*
scintillating /'sɪntɪleɪtɪŋ/ *a* sprühend
scissors /'sɪzəz/ *npl* Schere *f*; **a pair of ~** eine Schere
scoff[1] /skɒf/ *vi* **~ at** spotten über (+ *acc*)
scoff[2] *vt* (*fam*) verschlingen
scold /skəʊld/ *vt* ausschimpfen
scoop /sku:p/ *n* Schaufel *f*; (*Culin*) Portionierer *m*; (*Journ*) Exklusivmeldung *f* □ *vt* **~ out** aushöhlen; (*remove*) auslöffeln; **~ up** schaufeln; schöpfen ⟨*liquid*⟩
scoot /sku:t/ *vi* (*fam*) rasen. **~er** *n* Roller *m*
scope /skəʊp/ *n* Bereich *m*; (*opportunity*) Möglichkeiten *pl*
scorch /skɔ:tʃ/ *vt* versengen. **~ing** *a* glühend heiß
score /skɔ:(r)/ *n* [Spiel]stand *m*; (*individual*) Punktzahl *f*; (*Mus*) Partitur *f*; (*Cinema*) Filmmusik *f*; **a ~ [of]** (*twenty*) zwanzig; **keep [the] ~** zählen; (*written*) aufschreiben; **on that ~** was das betrifft □ *vt* erzielen; schießen ⟨*goal*⟩; (*cut*) einritzen □ *vi* Punkte erzielen; (*Sport*) ein Tor schießen; (*keep score*) Punkte zählen. **~r** *n* Punktezähler *m*; (*of goals*) Torschütze *m*
scorn /skɔ:n/ *n* Verachtung *f* □ *vt* verachten. **~ful** *a*, **-ly** *adv* verächtlich
Scorpio /'skɔ:pɪəʊ/ *n* (*Astr*) Skorpion *m*
Scorpion /'skɔ:pɪən/ *n* Skorpion *m*
Scot /skɒt/ *n* Schotte *m*/Schottin *f*

Scotch /skɒtʃ/ *a* Schottisch □ *n* (*whisky*) Scotch *m*
scotch *vt* unterbinden
scot-'free *a* **get off ~** straffrei ausgehen
Scot|land /'skɒtlənd/ *n* Schottland *nt*. **~s, ~tish** *a* schottisch
scoundrel /'skaʊndrl/ *n* Schurke *m*
scour¹ /'skaʊə(r)/ *vt* (*search*) absuchen
scour² *vt* (*clean*) scheuern
scourge /skɜ:dʒ/ *n* Geißel *f*
scout /skaʊt/ *n* (*Mil*) Kundschafter *m* □ *vi* **~ for** Ausschau halten nach
Scout *n* **[Boy] ~** Pfadfinder *m*
scowl /skaʊl/ *n* böser Gesichtsausdruck *m* □ *vi* ein böses Gesicht machen
scraggy /'skrægɪ/ *a* (**-ier, -iest**) (*pej*) dürr, hager
scram /skræm/ *vi* (*fam*) abhauen
scramble /'skræmbl/ *n* Gerangel *nt* □ *vi* klettern; **~ for** sich drängen nach □ *vt* (*Teleph*) verschlüsseln. **~d 'egg[s]** *n[pl]* Rührei *nt*
scrap¹ /skræp/ *n* (*fam: flight*) Rauferei *f* □ *vi* sich raufen
scrap² *n* Stückchen *nt*; (*metal*) Schrott *m*; **~s** *pl* Reste; **not a ~** kein bisschen □ *vt* (*pt/pp* **scrapped**) aufgeben
'scrap-book *n* Sammelalbum *nt*
scrape /skreɪp/ *vt* schaben; (*clean*) abkratzen; (*damage*) [ver]schrammen. **~ through** *vi* gerade noch durchkommen. **~ together** *vt* zusammenkriegen
scraper /'skreɪpə(r)/ *n* Kratzer *m*
'scrap iron *n* Alteisen *nt*
scrappy /'skræpɪ/ *a* lückenhaft
'scrap-yard *n* Schrottplatz *m*
scratch /skrætʃ/ *n* Kratzer *m*; **start from ~** von vorne anfangen; **not be up to ~** zu wünschen übrig lassen □ *vt/i* kratzen; (*damage*) zerkratzen
scrawl /skrɔ:l/ *n* Gekrakel *nt* □ *vt/i* krakeln
scrawny /'skrɔ:nɪ/ *a* (**-ier, -iest**) (*pej*) dürr, hager
scream /skri:m/ *n* Schrei *m* □ *vt/i* schreien
screech /skri:tʃ/ *n* Kreischen *nt* □ *vt/i* kreischen
screen /skri:n/ *n* Schirm *m*; (*Cinema*) Leinwand *f*; (*TV*) Bildschirm *m* □ *vt* schützen; (*conceal*) verdecken; vorführen ⟨*film*⟩; (*examine*) überprüfen; (*Med*) untersuchen. **~ing** *n* (*Med*) Reihenuntersuchung *f*. **~play** *n* Drehbuch *nt*
screw /skru:/ *n* Schraube *f* □ *vt* schrauben. **~ up** *vt* festschrauben; (*crumple*) zusammenknüllen; zusammenkneifen ⟨*eyes*⟩; (*sl: bungle*) vermasseln; **~ up one's courage** seinen Mut zusammennehmen
'screwdriver *n* Schraubenzieher *m*
screwy /'skru:ɪ/ *a* (**-ier, -iest**) (*fam*) verrückt
scribble /'skrɪbl/ *n* Gekritzel *nt* □ *vt/i* kritzeln
script /skrɪpt/ *n* Schrift *f*; (*of speech, play*) Text *m*; (*Radio, TV*) Skript *nt*; (*of film*) Drehbuch *nt*
Scripture /'skrɪptʃə(r)/ *n* (*Sch*) Religion *f*; **the ~s** *pl* die Heilige Schrift *f*
scroll /skrəʊl/ *n* Schriftrolle *f*; (*decoration*) Volute *f*
scrounge /skraʊndʒ/ *vt/i* schnorren. **~r** *n* Schnorrer *m*
scrub¹ /skrʌb/ *n* (*land*) Buschland *nt*, Gestrüpp *nt*
scrub² *vt/i* (*pt/pp* **scrubbed**) schrubben; (*fam: cancel*) absagen; fallen lassen ⟨*plan*⟩
scruff /skrʌf/ *n* **by the ~ of the neck** beim Genick
scruffy /'skrʌfɪ/ *a* (**-ier, -iest**) vergammelt
scrum /skrʌm/ *n* Gedränge *nt*
scruple /'skru:pl/ *n* Skrupel *m*

scrupulous /ˈskruːpjʊləs/ *a*, **-ly** *adv* gewissenhaft
scrutin|ize /ˈskruːtɪnaɪz/ *vt* [genau] ansehen. **~y** *n* (*look*) prüfender Blick *m*
scuff /skʌf/ *vt* abstoßen
scuffle /ˈskʌfl/ *n* Handgemenge *nt*
scullery /ˈskʌlərɪ/ *n* Spülküche *f*
sculpt|or /ˈskʌlptə(r)/ *n* Bildhauer(in) *m*(*f*). **~ure** /-tʃə(r)/ *n* Bildhauerei *f*; (*piece of work*) Skulptur *f*, Plastik *f*
scum /skʌm/ *n* Schmutzschicht *f*; (*people*) Abschaum *m*
scurrilous /ˈskʌrɪləs/ *a* niederträchtig
scurry /ˈskʌrɪ/ *vi* (*pt/pp* **-ied**) huschen
scuttle[1] /ˈskʌtl/ *n* Kohleneimer *m*
scuttle[2] *vt* versenken ⟨*ship*⟩
scuttle[3] *vi* schnell krabbeln
scythe /saɪð/ *n* Sense *f*
sea /siː/ *n* Meer *nt*, See *f*; **at ~** auf See; **by ~** mit dem Schiff. **~board** *n* Küste *f*. **~food** *n* Meeresfrüchte *pl*. **~gull** *n* Möwe *f*
seal[1] /siːl/ *n* (*Zool*) Seehund *m*
seal[2] *n* Siegel *nt*; (*Techn*) Dichtung *f* □ *vt* versiegeln; (*Techn*) abdichten; (*fig*) besiegeln. **~ off** *vt* abriegeln
ˈsea-level *n* Meeresspiegel *m*
seam /siːm/ *n* Naht *f*; (*of coal*) Flöz *nt*
ˈseaman *n* Seemann *m*; (*sailor*) Matrose *m*
seamless /ˈsiːmlɪs/ *a* nahtlos
seance /ˈseɪɑːns/ *n* spiritistische Sitzung *f*
sea: ~plane *n* Wasserflugzeug *nt*. **~port** *n* Seehafen *m*
search /sɜːtʃ/ *n* Suche *f*; (*official*) Durchsuchung *f* □ *vt* durchsuchen; absuchen ⟨*area*⟩ □ *vi* suchen (**for** nach). **~ing** *a* prüfend, forschend
search: ~light *n* [Such]scheinwerfer *m*. **~-party** *n* Suchmannschaft *f*
sea: ~sick *a* seekrank. **~side** *n* **at/to the ~side** am/ans Meer
season /ˈsiːzn/ *n* Jahreszeit *f*; (*social, tourist, sporting*) Saison *f* □ *vt* (*flavour*) würzen. **~able** /-əbl/ *a* der Jahreszeit gemäß. **~al** *a* Saison-. **~ing** *n* Gewürze *pl*
ˈseason ticket *n* Dauerkarte *f*
seat /siːt/ *n* Sitz *m*; (*place*) Sitzplatz *m*; (*bottom*) Hintern *m*; **take a ~** Platz nehmen □ *vt* setzen; (*have seats for*) Sitzplätze bieten (+ *dat*); **remain ~ed** sitzen bleiben. **~-belt** *n* Sicherheitsgurt *m*; **fasten one's ~-belt** sich anschnallen
sea: ~weed *n* [See]tang *m*. **~worthy** *a* seetüchtig
secateurs /sekəˈtɜːz/ *npl* Gartenschere *f*
seclu|de /sɪˈkluːd/ *vt* absondern. **~ded** *a* abgelegen. **~sion** /-ʒn/ *n* Zurückgezogenheit *f*
second[1] /sɪˈkɒnd/ *vt* (*transfer*) [vorübergehend] versetzen
second[2] /ˈsekənd/ *a* zweite(r,s); **on ~ thoughts** nach weiterer Überlegung □ *n* Sekunde *f*; (*Sport*) Sekundant *m*; **~s** *pl* (*goods*) Waren zweiter Wahl; **the ~** der/die/das Zweite □ *adv* (*in race*) an zweiter Stelle □ *vt* unterstützen ⟨*proposal*⟩
secondary /ˈsekəndrɪ/ *a* zweitrangig; (*Phys*) Sekundär-. **~ school** *n* höhere Schule *f*
second: ~-best *a* zweitbeste(r,s). **~ ˈclass** *adv* ⟨*travel, send*⟩ zweiter Klasse. **~-class** *a* zweitklassig
ˈsecond hand *n* (*on clock*) Sekundenzeiger *m*
second-ˈhand *a* gebraucht □ *adv* aus zweiter Hand
secondly /ˈsekəndlɪ/ *adv* zweitens
second-ˈrate *a* zweitklassig
secrecy /ˈsiːkrəsɪ/ *n* Heimlichkeit *f*
secret /ˈsiːkrɪt/ *a* geheim; ⟨*agent, police*⟩ Geheim-; ⟨*drinker, lover*⟩ heimlich □ *n* Geheimnis *nt*

secretarial /sekrə'teərɪəl/ *a* Sekretärinnen-; ⟨*work, staff*⟩ Sekretariats-
secretary /'sekrətərɪ/ *n* Sekretär(in) *m(f)*
secret|e /sɪ'kri:t/ *vt* absondern. **~ion** /-i:ʃn/ *n* Absonderung *f*
secretive /'si:krətɪv/ *a* geheimtuerisch. **~ness** *n* Heimlichtuerei *f*
secretly /'si:krɪtlɪ/ *adv* heimlich
sect /sekt/ *n* Sekte *f*
section /'sekʃn/ *n* Teil *m*; (*of text*) Abschnitt *m*; (*of firm*) Abteilung *f*; (*of organization*) Sektion *f*
sector /'sektə(r)/ *n* Sektor *m*
secular /'sekjʊlə(r)/ *a* weltlich
secure /sɪ'kjʊə(r)/ *a*, **-ly** *adv* sicher; (*firm*) fest; (*emotionally*) geborgen □ *vt* sichern; (*fasten*) festmachen; (*obtain*) sich (*dat*) sichern
securit|y /sɪ'kjʊərətɪ/ *n* Sicherheit *f*; (*emotional*) Geborgenheit *f*; **~ies** *pl* Wertpapiere *pl*; (*Fin*) Effekten *pl*
sedan /sɪ'dæn/ *n* (*Amer*) Limousine *f*
sedate¹ /sɪ'deɪt/ *a*, **-ly** *adv* gesetzt
sedate² *vt* sedieren
sedation /sɪ'deɪʃn/ *n* Sedierung *f*; **be under ~** sediert sein
sedative /'sedətɪv/ *a* beruhigend □ *n* Beruhigungsmittel *nt*
sedentary /'sedəntərɪ/ *a* sitzend
sediment /'sedɪmənt/ *n* [Boden]satz *m*
seduce /sɪ'dju:s/ *vt* verführen
seduct|ion /sɪ'dʌkʃn/ *n* Verführung *f*. **~ive** /-tɪv/ *a*, **-ly** *adv* verführerisch
see¹ /si:/ *v* (*pt* **saw**, *pp* **seen**) □ *vt* sehen; (*understand*) einsehen; (*imagine*) sich (*dat*) vorstellen; (*escort*) begleiten; **go and ~** nachsehen; (*visit*) besuchen; **~ you later!** bis nachher! **~ing that** da □ *vi* sehen; (*check*) nachsehen; **~ about** sich kümmern um. **~ off** *vt* verabschieden; (*chase away*) vertreiben. **~ through** *vi* durchsehen □ *vt* (*fig*) **~ through s.o.** jdn durchschauen
see² *n* (*Relig*) Bistum *nt*
seed /si:d/ *n* Samen *m*; (*of grape*) Kern *m*; (*fig*) Saat *f*; (*Tennis*) gesetzter Spieler *m*; **go to ~** Samen bilden; (*fig*) herunterkommen. **~ed** *a* (*Tennis*) gesetzt. **~ling** *n* Sämling *m*
seedy /'si:dɪ/ *a* (**-ier, -iest**) schäbig; ⟨*area*⟩ heruntergekommen
seek /si:k/ *vt* (*pt/pp* **sought**) suchen
seem /si:m/ *vi* scheinen. **~ingly** *adv* scheinbar
seemly /'si:mlɪ/ *a* schicklich
seen /si:n/ *see* **see¹**
seep /si:p/ *vi* sickern
see-saw /'si:sɔ:/ *n* Wippe *f*
seethe /si:ð/ *vi* **~ with anger** vor Wut schäumen
'see-through *a* durchsichtig
segment /'segmənt/ *n* Teil *m*; (*of worm*) Segment *nt*; (*of orange*) Spalte *f*
segregat|e /'segrɪgeɪt/ *vt* trennen. **~ion** /-'geɪʃn/ *n* Trennung *f*
seize /si:z/ *vt* ergreifen; (*Jur*) beschlagnahmen; **~ s.o. by the arm** jdn am Arm packen. **~ up** *vi* (*Techn*) sich festfressen
seizure /'si:ʒə(r)/ *n* (*Jur*) Beschlagnahme *f*; (*Med*) Anfall *m*
seldom /'seldəm/ *adv* selten
select /sɪ'lekt/ *a* ausgewählt; (*exclusive*) exklusiv □ *vt* auswählen; aufstellen ⟨*team*⟩. **~ion** /-ekʃn/ *n* Auswahl *f*. **~ive** /-ɪv/ *a*, **-ly** *adv* selektiv; (*choosy*) wählerisch
self /self/ *n* (*pl* **selves**) Ich *nt*
self: ~-ad'dressed *a* adressiert. **~-ad'hesive** *a* selbstklebend. **~-as'surance** *n* Selbstsicherheit *f*. **~-as'sured** *a* selbstsicher. **~-'catering** *n* Selbstversorgung *f*. **~-'centred** *a* egozentrisch. **~-'confidence** *n* Selbstbewusstsein

nt, Selbstvertrauen *nt*. **~-'confident** *a* selbstbewusst. **~-'conscious** *a* befangen. **~-con'tained** *a* ⟨*flat*⟩ abgeschlossen. **~-con'trol** *n* Selbstbeherrschung *f*. **~-de'fence** *n* Selbstverteidigung *f*; (*Jur*) Notwehr *f*. **~-de'nial** *n* Selbstverleugnung *f*. **~-determi'nation** *n* Selbstbestimmung *f*. **~-em'ployed** selbstständig. **~-e'steem** *n* Selbstachtung *f*. **~-'evident** *a* offensichtlich. **~-'governing** *a* selbst verwaltet. **~-'help** *n* Selbsthilfe *f*. **~-in'dulgent** *a* maßlos. **~-'interest** *n* Eigennutz *m*

self|ish /'selfɪʃ/ *a*, **-ly** *adv* egoistisch, selbstsüchtig. **~less** *a*, **-ly** *adv* selbstlos

self: **~-'pity** *n* Selbstmitleid *nt*. **~-'portrait** *n* Selbstporträt *nt*. **~-pos'sessed** *a* selbstbeherrscht. **~-preser'vation** *n* Selbsterhaltung *f*. **~-re'spect** *n* Selbstachtung *f*. **~-'righteous** *a* selbstgerecht. **~-'sacrifice** *n* Selbstaufopferung *f*. **~-'satisfied** *a* selbstgefällig. **~-'service** *n* Selbstbedienung *f* □ *attrib* Selbstbedienungs-. **~-suf'ficient** *a* selbstständig. **~-'willed** *a* eigenwillig

sell /sel/ *v* (*pt/pp* **sold**) □ *vt* verkaufen; *be sold out* ausverkauft sein □ *vi* sich verkaufen. **~ off** *vt* verkaufen

seller /'selə(r)/ *n* Verkäufer *m*

Sellotape (P) /'seləʊ-/ *n* ≈ Tesafilm (P) *m*

'sell-out *n* **be a ~** ausverkauft sein; (*fam: betrayal*) Verrat sein

selves /selvz/ *see* **self**

semblance /'sembləns/ *n* Anschein *m*

semen /'si:mən/ *n* (*Anat*) Samen *m*

semester /sɪ'mestə(r)/ *n* (*Amer*) Semester *nt*

semi|breve /'semɪbri:v/ *n* (*Mus*) ganze Note *f*. **~circle** *n* Halbkreis *m*. **~'circular** *a* halbkreisförmig. **~'colon** *n* Semikolon *nt*. **~-de'tached** *a* & *n* **~-detached [house]** Doppelhaushälfte *f*. **~-'final** *n* Halbfinale *nt*

seminar /'semɪnɑ:(r)/ *n* Seminar *nt*. **-y** /-nərɪ/ *n* Priesterseminar *nt*

'semitone *n* (*Mus*) Halbton *m*

semolina /semə'li:nə/ *n* Grieß *m*

senat|e /'senət/ *n* Senat *m*. **~or** *n* Senator *m*

send /send/ *vt/i* (*pt/pp* **sent**) schicken; **~ one's regards** grüßen lassen; **~ for** kommen lassen ⟨*person*⟩; sich (*dat*) schicken lassen ⟨*thing*⟩. **~er** *n* Absender *m*. **~-off** *n* Verabschiedung *f*

senil|e /'si:naɪl/ *a* senil. **~ity** /sɪ'nɪlətɪ/ *n* Senilität *f*

senior /'si:nɪə(r)/ *a* älter; (*in rank*) höher □ *n* Ältere(r) *m/f*; (*in rank*) Vorgesetzte(r) *m/f*. **~ 'citizen** *n* Senior(in) *m(f)*

seniority /si:nɪ'ɒrətɪ/ *n* höheres Alter *nt*; (*in rank*) höherer Rang *m*

sensation /sen'seɪʃn/ *n* Sensation *f*; (*feeling*) Gefühl *nt*. **~al** *a*, **-ly** *adv* sensationell

sense /sens/ *n* Sinn *m*; (*feeling*) Gefühl *nt*; (*common* **~**) Verstand *m*; **in a ~** in gewisser Hinsicht; **make ~** Sinn ergeben □ *vt* spüren. **~less** *a*, **-ly** *adv* sinnlos; (*unconscious*) bewusstlos

sensible /'sensəbl/ *a*, **-bly** *adv* vernünftig; ⟨*suitable*⟩ zweckmäßig

sensitiv|e /'sensətɪv/ *a*, **-ly** *adv* empfindlich; (*understanding*) einfühlsam. **~ity** /-'tɪvətɪ/ *n* Empfindlichkeit *f*

sensory /'sensərɪ/ *a* Sinnes-

sensual /'sensjʊəl/ *a* sinnlich. **-ity** /-'ælətɪ/ *n* Sinnlichkeit *f*

sensuous /'sensjʊəs/ *a* sinnlich

sent /sent/ *see* **send**

sentence /'sentəns/ *n* Satz *m*; (*Jur*) Urteil *nt*; (*punishment*) Strafe *f* □ *vt* verurteilen

sentiment /'sentɪmənt/ *n* Gefühl *nt*; (*opinion*) Meinung *f*; (*sentimentality*) Sentimentalität *f* **~al** /-'mentl/ *a* sentimental. **~ality** /-'tæləti/ *n* Sentimentalität *f*
sentry /'sentrɪ/ *n* Wache *f*
separable /'sepərəbl/ *a* trennbar
separate¹ /'sepərət/ *a*, **-ly** *adv* getrennt, separat
separat|e² /'sepəreɪt/ *vt* trennen □ *vi* sich trennen. **~ion** /-'reɪʃn/ *n* Trennung *f*
September /sep'tembə(r)/ *n* September *m*
septic /'septɪk/ *a* vereitert; **go ~** vereitern
sequel /'si:kwl/ *n* Folge *f*; (*fig*) Nachspiel *nt*
sequence /'si:kwəns/ *n* Reihenfolge *f*
sequin /'si:kwɪn/ *n* Paillette *f*
serenade /serə'neɪd/ *n* Ständchen *nt* □ *vt* **~ s.o.** jdm ein Ständchen bringen
seren|e /sɪ'ri:n/ *a*, **-ly** *adv* gelassen. **~ity** /-'renəti/ *n* Gelassenheit *f*
sergeant /'sɑ:dʒənt/ *n* (*Mil*) Feldwebel *m*; (*in police*) Polizeimeister *m*
serial /'sɪərɪəl/ *n* Fortsetzungsgeschichte *f*; (*Radio, TV*) Serie *f*. **~ize** *vt* in Fortsetzungen veröffentlichen/(*Radio, TV*) senden
series /'sɪəri:z/ *n inv* Serie *f*
serious /'sɪərɪəs/ *a*, **-ly** *adv* ernst; ⟨*illness, error*⟩ schwer. **~ness** *n* Ernst *m*
sermon /'sɜ:mən/ *n* Predigt *f*
serpent /'sɜ:pənt/ *n* Schlange *f*
serrated /se'reɪtɪd/ *a* gezackt
serum /'sɪərəm/ *n* Serum *nt*
servant /'sɜ:vənt/ *n* Diener(in) *m(f)*
serve /sɜ:v/ *n* (*Tennis*) Aufschlag *m* □ *vt* dienen (+ *dat*); bedienen ⟨*customer, guest*⟩; servieren ⟨*food*⟩; (*Jur*) zustellen (**on s.o.** jdm); verbüßen ⟨*sentence*⟩; **~ its purpose** seinen Zweck erfüllen; **it ~s you right!** das geschieht dir recht! **~s two** für zwei Personen □ *vi* dienen; (*Tennis*) aufschlagen
service /'sɜ:vɪs/ *n* Dienst *m*; (*Relig*) Gottesdienst *m*; (*in shop, restaurant*) Bedienung *f*; (*transport*) Verbindung *f*; (*maintenance*) Wartung *f*; (*set of crockery*) Service *nt*; (*Tennis*) Aufschlag *m*; **~s** *pl* Dienstleistungen *pl*; (*on motorway*) Tankstelle und Raststätte *f*; **in the ~s** beim Militär; **be of ~** nützlich sein; **out of/in ~** ⟨*machine:*⟩ außer/ in Betrieb □ *vt* (*Techn*) warten. **~able** /-əbl/ *a* nützlich; (*durable*) haltbar
service: ~ area *n* Tankstelle und Raststätte *f*. **~ charge** *n* Bedienungszuschlag *m*. **~man** *n* Soldat *m*. **~ station** *n* Tankstelle *f*
serviette /sɜ:vɪ'et/ *n* Serviette *f*
servile /'sɜ:vaɪl/ *a* unterwürfig
session /'seʃn/ *n* Sitzung *f*; (*Univ*) Studienjahr *nt*
set /set/ *n* Satz *m*; (*of crockery*) Service *nt*; (*of cutlery*) Garnitur *f*; (*TV, Radio*) Apparat *m*; (*Math*) Menge *f*; (*Theat*) Bühnenbild *nt*; (*Cinema*) Szenenaufbau *m*; (*of people*) Kreis *m*; **shampoo and ~** Waschen und Legen □ *a* (*ready*) fertig, bereit; (*rigid*) fest; ⟨*book*⟩ vorgeschrieben; **be ~ on doing sth** entschlossen sein, etw zu tun; **be ~ in one's ways** in seinen Gewohnheiten festgefahren sein □ *v* (*pt/pp* **set**, *pres p* **setting**) □ *vt* setzen; (*adjust*) einstellen; stellen ⟨*task, alarm clock*⟩; festsetzen, festlegen ⟨*date, limit*⟩; aufgeben ⟨*homework*⟩; zusammenstellen ⟨*questions*⟩; [ein]fassen ⟨*gem*⟩; einrichten ⟨*bone*⟩; legen ⟨*hair*⟩; decken ⟨*table*⟩ □ *vi* ⟨*sun:*⟩ untergehen; (*become hard*) fest werden; **~ about sth** sich an etw (*acc*) machen; **~ about doing sth** sich daranmachen, etw zu tun. **~ back** *vt* zurücksetzen; (*hold up*)

aufhalten; (*fam: cost*) kosten. ~ **off** *vi* losgehen; (*in vehicle*) losfahren □ *vt* auslösen ⟨*alarm*⟩; explodieren lassen ⟨*bomb*⟩. ~ **out** *vi* losgehen; (*in vehicle*) losfahren; ~ **out to do sth** sich vornehmen, etw zu tun □ *vt* auslegen; (*state*) darlegen. ~ **up** *vt* aufbauen; (*fig*) gründen

set 'meal *n* Menü *nt*

settee /se'ti:/ *n* Sofa *nt*, Couch *f*

setting /'setɪŋ/ *n* Rahmen *m*; (*surroundings*) Umgebung *f*; (*of sun*) Untergang *m*; (*of jewel*) Fassung *f*

settle /'setl/ *vt* (*decide*) entscheiden; (*agree*) regeln; (*fix*) festsetzen; (*calm*) beruhigen; (*pay*) bezahlen □ *vi* sich niederlassen; ⟨*snow, dust:*⟩ liegen bleiben; (*subside*) sich senken; ⟨*sediment:*⟩ sich absetzen. ~ **down** *vi* sich beruhigen; (*permanently*) sesshaft werden. ~ **up** *vi* abrechnen

settlement /'setlmənt/ *n* (*see* **settle**) Entscheidung *f*; Regelung *f*; Bezahlung *f*; (*Jur*) Vergleich *m*; (*colony*) Siedlung *f*

settler /'setlə(r)/ *n* Siedler *m*

'set-to *n* (*fam*) Streit *m*

'set-up *n* System *nt*

seven /'sevn/ *a* sieben. ~**'teen** *a* siebzehn. ~**'teenth** *a* siebzehnte(r,s)

seventh /'sevnθ/ *a* siebte(r,s)

seventieth /'sevntɪɪθ/ *a* siebzigste(r,s)

seventy /'sevntɪ/ *a* siebzig

sever /'sevə(r)/ *vt* durchtrennen; abbrechen ⟨*relations*⟩

several /'sevrl/ *a & pron* mehrere, einige

sever|e /sɪ'vɪə(r)/ *a* (**-r, -st,**) **-ly** *adv* streng; ⟨*pain*⟩ stark; ⟨*illness*⟩ schwer. ~**ity** /-'verətɪ/ *n* Strenge *f*; Schwere *f*

sew /səʊ/ *vt/i* (*pt* **sewed**, *pp* **sewn** *or* **sewed**) nähen. ~ **up** *vt* zunähen

sewage /'su:ɪdʒ/ *n* Abwasser *nt*

sewer /'su:ə(r)/ *n* Abwasserkanal *m*

sewing /'səʊɪŋ/ *n* Nähen *nt*; (*work*) Näharbeit *f*. ~ **machine** *n* Nähmaschine *f*

sewn /səʊn/ *see* **sew**

sex /seks/ *n* Geschlecht *nt*; (*sexuality, intercourse*) Sex *m*. ~**ist** *a* sexistisch. ~ **offender** *n* Triebverbrecher *m*

sexual /'seksjʊəl/ *a*, **-ly** *adv* sexuell. ~ **'intercourse** *n* Geschlechtsverkehr *m*

sexuality /seksjʊ'ælətɪ/ *n* Sexualität *f*

sexy /'seksɪ/ *a* (**-ier, -iest**) sexy

shabby /'ʃæbɪ/ *a* (**-ier, -iest**), **-ily** *adv* schäbig

shack /ʃæk/ *n* Hütte *f*

shackles /'ʃæklz/ *npl* Fesseln *pl*

shade /ʃeɪd/ *n* Schatten *m*; (*of colour*) [Farb]ton *m*; (*for lamp*) [Lampen]schirm *m*; (*Amer: window-blind*) Jalousie *f* □ *vt* beschatten; (*draw lines on*) schattieren

shadow /'ʃædəʊ/ *n* Schatten *m* □ *vt* (*follow*) beschatten. ~**y** *a* schattenhaft

shady /'ʃeɪdɪ/ *a* (**-ier, -iest**) schattig; (*fam: disreputable*) zwielichtig

shaft /ʃɑ:ft/ *n* Schaft *m*; (*Techn*) Welle *f*; (*of light*) Strahl *m*; (*of lift*) Schacht *m*; ~**s** *pl* (*of cart*) Gabeldeichsel *f*

shaggy /'ʃægɪ/ *a* (**-ier, -iest**) zottig

shake /ʃeɪk/ *n* Schütteln *nt* □ *v* (*pt* **shook**, *pp* **shaken**) □ *vt* schütteln; (*cause to tremble, shock*) erschüttern; ~ **hands with s.o.** jdm die Hand geben □ *vi* wackeln; (*tremble*) zittern. ~ **off** *vt* abschütteln

shaky /'ʃeɪkɪ/ *a* (**-ier, -iest**) wackelig; ⟨*hand, voice*⟩ zittrig

shall /ʃæl/ *v aux* **I** ~ **go** ich werde gehen; **we** ~ **see** wir werden sehen; **what** ~ **I do?** was soll ich machen? **I'll come too,** ~ **I?** ich komme mit, ja? **thou shalt not kill** (*liter*) du sollst nicht töten

shallow /ˈʃæləʊ/ *a* (**-er, -est**) seicht; ⟨*dish*⟩ flach; (*fig*) oberflächlich

sham /ʃæm/ *a* unecht □ *n* Heuchelei *f*; (*person*) Heuchler(in) *m(f)* □ *vt* (*pt/pp* **shammed**) vortäuschen

shambles /ˈʃæmblz/ *n* Durcheinander *nt*

shame /ʃeɪm/ *n* Scham *f*; (*disgrace*) Schande *f*; **be a ~** schade sein; **what a ~!** wie schade! **~-faced** *a* betreten

shame|ful /ˈʃeɪmfl/ *a*, **-ly** *adv* schändlich. **~less** *a*, **-ly** *adv* schamlos

shampoo /ʃæmˈpuː/ *n* Shampoo *nt* □ *vt* schamponieren

shandy /ˈʃændɪ/ *n* Radler *m*

shan't /ʃɑːnt/ = **shall not**

shape /ʃeɪp/ *n* Form *f*; (*figure*) Gestalt *f*; **take ~** Gestalt annehmen □ *vt* formen (**into** zu) □ *vi* **~ up** sich entwickeln. **~less** *a* formlos; ⟨*clothing*⟩ unförmig

shapely /ˈʃeɪplɪ/ *a* (**-ier, -iest**) wohlgeformt

share /ʃeə(r)/ *n* [An]teil *m*; (*Comm*) Aktie *f* □ *vt/i* teilen. **~holder** *n* Aktionär(in) *m(f)*

shark /ʃɑːk/ *n* Hai[fisch] *m*

sharp /ʃɑːp/ *a* (**-er, -est**), **-ly** *adv* scharf; (*pointed*) spitz; (*severe*) heftig; (*sudden*) steil; (*alert*) clever; (*unscrupulous*) gerissen □ *adv* scharf; (*Mus*) zu hoch; **at six o'clock ~** Punkt sechs Uhr; **look ~!** beeil dich! □ *n* (*Mus*) Kreuz *nt*. **~en** *vt* schärfen; [an]spitzen ⟨*pencil*⟩

shatter /ˈʃætə(r)/ *vt* zertrümmern; (*fig*) zerstören; **be ~ed** ⟨*person:*⟩ erschüttert sein; (*fam: exhausted*) kaputt □ *vi* zersplittern

shave /ʃeɪv/ *n* Rasur *f*; **have a ~** sich rasieren □ *vt* rasieren □ *vi* sich rasieren. **~r** *n* Rasierapparat *m*

shaving /ˈʃeɪvɪŋ/ *n* Rasieren *nt*. **~-brush** *n* Rasierpinsel *m*

shawl /ʃɔːl/ *n* Schultertuch *nt*

she /ʃiː/ *pron* sie

sheaf /ʃiːf/ *n* (*pl* **sheaves**) Garbe *f*; (*of papers*) Bündel *nt*

shear /ʃɪə(r)/ *vt* (*pt* **sheared**, *pp* **shorn** *or* **sheared**) scheren

shears /ʃɪəz/ *npl* [große] Schere *f*

sheath /ʃiːθ/ *n* (*pl* **~s** /ʃiːðz/) Scheide *f*

sheaves /ʃiːvz/ *see* **sheaf**

shed¹ /ʃed/ *n* Schuppen *m*; (*for cattle*) Stall *m*

shed² *vt* (*pt/pp* **shed**, *pres p* **shedding**) verlieren; vergießen ⟨*blood, tears*⟩; **~ light on** Licht bringen in (+ *acc*)

sheen /ʃiːn/ *n* Glanz *m*

sheep /ʃiːp/ *n inv* Schaf *nt*. **~-dog** *n* Hütehund *m*

sheepish /ˈʃiːpɪʃ/ *a*, **-ly** *adv* verlegen

'sheepskin *n* Schaffell *nt*

sheer /ʃɪə(r)/ *a* rein; (*steep*) steil; (*transparent*) hauchdünn □ *adv* steil

sheet /ʃiːt/ *n* Laken *nt*, Betttuch *nt*; (*of paper*) Blatt *nt*; (*of glass, metal*) Platte *f*

sheikh /ʃeɪk/ *n* Scheich *m*

shelf /ʃelf/ *n* (*pl* **shelves**) Brett *nt*, Bord *nt*; (*set of shelves*) Regal *nt*

shell /ʃel/ *n* Schale *f*; (*of snail*) Haus *nt*; (*of tortoise*) Panzer *m*; (*on beach*) Muschel *f*; (*of unfinished building*) Rohbau *m*; (*Mil*) Granate *f* □ *vt* pellen; enthülsen ⟨*peas*⟩; (*Mil*) [mit Granaten] beschießen. **~ out** *vi* (*fam*) blechen

'shellfish *n inv* Schalentiere *pl*; (*Culin*) Meeresfrüchte *pl*

shelter /ˈʃeltə(r)/ *n* Schutz *m*; (*air-raid ~*) Luftschutzraum *m* □ *vt* schützen (**from** vor + *dat*) □ *vi* sich unterstellen. **~ed** *a* geschützt; ⟨*life*⟩ behütet

shelve /ʃelv/ *vt* auf Eis legen; (*abandon*) aufgeben □ *vi* ⟨*slope:*⟩ abfallen

shelves /ʃelvz/ *see* **shelf**
shelving /ˈʃelvɪŋ/ *n* (*shelves*) Regale *pl*
shepherd /ˈʃepəd/ *n* Schäfer *m*; (*Relig*) Hirte *m* □ *vt* führen. **~ess** *n* Schäferin *f*. **~'s pie** *n* Auflauf *m* aus mit Kartoffelbrei bedecktem Hackfleisch
sherry /ˈʃerɪ/ *n* Sherry *m*
shield /ʃi:ld/ *n* Schild *m*; (*for eyes*) Schirm *m*; (*Techn & fig*) Schutz *m* □ *vt* schützen (**from** vor + *dat*)
shift /ʃɪft/ *n* Verschiebung *f*; (*at work*) Schicht *f*; **make ~** sich (*dat*) behelfen (**with** mit) □ *vt* rücken; (*take away*) wegnehmen; (*rearrange*) umstellen; schieben ⟨*blame*⟩ (**on to** auf + *acc*) □ *vi* sich verschieben; (*fam; move quickly*) rasen
'shift work *n* Schichtarbeit *f*
shifty /ˈʃɪftɪ/ *a* (**-ier, -iest**) (*pej*) verschlagen
shilly-shally /ˈʃɪlɪʃælɪ/ *vi* fackeln (*fam*)
shimmer /ˈʃɪmə(r)/ *n* Schimmer *m* □ *vi* schimmern
shin /ʃɪn/ *n* Schienbein *nt*
shine /ʃaɪn/ *n* Glanz *m* □ *v* (*pt/pp* **shone**) □ *vi* leuchten; (*reflect light*) glänzen; ⟨*sun:*⟩ scheinen □ *vt* **~ a light on** beleuchten
shingle /ˈʃɪŋgl/ *n* (*pebbles*) Kiesel *pl*
shingles /ˈʃɪŋglz/ *n* (*Med*) Gürtelrose *f*
shiny /ˈʃaɪnɪ/ *a* (**-ier, -iest**) glänzend
ship /ʃɪp/ *n* Schiff *nt* □ *vt* (*pt/pp* **shipped**) verschiffen
ship: ~building *n* Schiffbau *m*. **~ment** *n* Sendung *f*. **~per** *n* Spediteur *m*. **~ping** *n* Versand *m*; (*traffic*) Schifffahrt *f*. **~shape** *a* & *adv* in Ordnung. **~wreck** *n* Schiffbruch *m*. **~wrecked** *a* schiffbrüchig. **~yard** *n* Werft *f*
shirk /ʃɜ:k/ *vt* sich drücken vor (+ *dat*). **~er** *n* Drückeberger *m*
shirt /ʃɜ:t/ *n* [Ober]hemd *nt*; (*for woman*) Hemdbluse *f*
shit /ʃɪt/ *n* (*vulg*) Scheiße *f* □ *vi* (*pt/pp* **shit**) (*vulg*) scheißen
shiver /ˈʃɪvə(r)/ *n* Schauder *m* □ *vi* zittern
shoal /ʃəʊl/ *n* (*of fish*) Schwarm *m*
shock /ʃɒk/ *n* Schock *m*; (*Electr*) Schlag *m*; (*impact*) Erschütterung *f* □ *vt* einen Schock versetzen (+ *dat*); (*scandalize*) schockieren. **~ing** *a* schockierend; (*fam: dreadful*) fürchterlich
shod /ʃɒd/ *see* **shoe**
shoddy /ˈʃɒdɪ/ *a* (**-ier, -iest**) minderwertig
shoe /ʃu:/ *n* Schuh *m*; (*of horse*) Hufeisen *nt* □ *vt* (*pt/pp* **shod**, *pres p* **shoeing**) beschlagen ⟨*horse*⟩
shoe: ~horn *n* Schuhanzieher *m*. **~-lace** *n* Schnürsenkel *m*. **~maker** *n* Schuhmacher *m*. **~-string** *n* **on a ~-string** (*fam*) mit ganz wenig Geld
shone /ʃɒn/ *see* **shine**
shoo /ʃu:/ *vt* scheuchen □ *int* sch!
shook /ʃʊk/ *see* **shake**
shoot /ʃu:t/ *n* (*Bot*) Trieb *m*; (*hunt*) Jagd *f* □ *v* (*pt/pp* **shot**) □ *vt* schießen; (*kill*) erschießen; drehen ⟨*film*⟩ □ *vi* schießen. **~ down** *vt* abschießen. **~ out** *vi* (*rush*) herausschießen. **~ up** *vi* (*grow*) in die Höhe schießen/⟨*prices:*⟩ schnellen
'shooting-range *n* Schießstand *m*
shop /ʃɒp/ *n* Laden *m*, Geschäft *nt*; (*workshop*) Werkstatt *f*; **talk ~** (*fam*) fachsimpeln □ *vi* (*pt/pp* **shopped**, *pres p* **shopping**) einkaufen; **go ~ping** einkaufen gehen
shop: ~ assistant *n* Verkäufer(in) *m*(*f*). **~keeper** *n* Ladenbesitzer(in) *m*(*f*). **~-lifter** *n* Ladendieb *m*. **~-lifting** *n* Ladendiebstahl *m*
shopping /ˈʃɒpɪŋ/ *n* Einkaufen *nt*; (*articles*) Einkäufe *pl*; **do the**

~ einkaufen. ~ **bag** *n* Einkaufstasche *f* ~ **centre** *n* Einkaufszentrum *nt*. ~ **trolley** *n* Einkaufswagen *m*

shop: ~ **'steward** *n* [gewerkschaftlicher] Vertrauensmann *m*. ~-**'window** *n* Schaufenster *nt*

shore /ʃɔ:(r)/ *n* Strand *m*; (*of lake*) Ufer *nt*

shorn /ʃɔ:n/ *see* **shear**

short /ʃɔ:t/ **(er, -est)** kurz; ⟨*person*⟩ klein; (*curt*) schroff; **a** ~ **time ago** vor kurzem; **be** ~ **of ...** zu wenig ... haben; **be in** ~ **supply** knapp sein □ *adv* kurz; (*abruptly*) plötzlich; (*curtly*) kurz angebunden; **in** ~ kurzum; ~ **of** (*except*) außer; **go** ~ Mangel leiden; **stop** ~ **of doing sth** davor zurückschrecken, etw zu tun

shortage /'ʃɔ:tɪdʒ/ *n* Mangel *m* **(of** an + *dat*); (*scarcity*) Knappheit *f*

short: ~**bread** *n* ≈ Mürbekekse *pl*. ~ **'circuit** *n* Kurzschluss *m*. ~**coming** *n* Fehler *m*. ~ **'cut** *n* Abkürzung *f*

shorten /'ʃɔ:tn/ *vt* [ab]kürzen; kürzer machen ⟨*garment*⟩

short: ~**hand** *n* Kurzschrift *f*, Stenographie *f*. ~-**'handed** *a* **be** ~-**handed** zu wenig Personal haben. ~**hand 'typist** *n* Stenotypistin *f*. ~ **list** *n* engere Auswahl *f*. ~-**lived** /-lɪvd/ *a* kurzlebig

short|ly /'ʃɔ:tlɪ/ *adv* in Kürze; ~**ly before/after** kurz vorher/danach. ~**ness** *n* Kürze *f*; (*of person*) Kleinheit *f*

shorts /ʃɔ:ts/ *npl* kurze Hose *f*, Shorts *pl*

short: ~-**'sighted** *a* kurzsichtig. ~-**sleeved** *a* kurzärmelig. ~-**'staffed** *a* **be** ~-**staffed** zu wenig Personal haben. ~ **'story** *n* Kurzgeschichte *f*. ~-**'tempered** *a* aufbrausend. ~-**term** *a* kurzfristig. ~ **wave** *n* Kurzwelle *f*

shot /ʃɒt/ *see* **shoot** □ *n* Schuss *m*; (*pellets*) Schrot *m*; (*person*) Schütze *m*; (*Phot*) Aufnahme *f*; (*injection*) Spritze *f*; (*fam: attempt*) Versuch *m*; **like a** ~ (*fam*) sofort. ~**gun** *n* Schrotflinte *f*. ~-**putting** *n* (*Sport*) Kugelstoßen *nt*

should /ʃʊd/ *v aux* **you** ~ **go** du solltest gehen; **I** ~ **have seen him** ich hätte ihn sehen sollen; **I** ~ **like** ich möchte; **this** ~ **be enough** das müsste eigentlich reichen; **if he** ~ **be there** falls er da sein sollte

shoulder /'ʃəʊldə(r)/ *n* Schulter *f* □ *vt* schultern; (*fig*) auf sich (*acc*) nehmen. ~-**blade** *n* Schulterblatt *nt*. ~-**strap** *n* Tragriemen *m*; (*on garment*) Träger *m*

shout /ʃaʊt/ *n* Schrei *m* □ *vt/i* schreien. ~ **down** *vt* niederschreien

shouting /'ʃaʊtɪŋ/ *n* Geschrei *nt*

shove /ʃʌv/ *n* Stoß *m*; (*fam*) Schubs *m* □ *vt* stoßen; (*fam*) schubsen; (*fam: put*) tun □ *vi* drängeln. ~ **off** *vi* (*fam*) abhauen

shovel /'ʃʌvl/ *n* Schaufel *f* □ *vt* (*pt/pp* **shovelled**) schaufeln

show /ʃəʊ/ *n* (*display*) Pracht *f*; (*exhibition*) Ausstellung *f*, Schau *f*; (*performance*) Vorstellung *f*; (*Theat, TV*) Show *f*; **on** ~ ausgestellt □ *v* (*pt* **showed**, *pp* **shown**) □ *vt* zeigen; (*put on display*) ausstellen; vorführen ⟨*film*⟩ □ *vi* sichtbar sein; ⟨*film:*⟩ gezeigt werden. ~ **in** *vt* hereinführen. ~ **off** *vi* (*fam*) angeben □ *vt* vorführen; (*flaunt*) angeben mit. ~ **up** *vi* [deutlich] zu sehen sein; (*fam: arrive*) auftauchen □ *vt* deutlich zeigen; (*fam: embarrass*) blamieren

'show-down *n* Entscheidungskampf *m*

shower /'ʃaʊə(r)/ *n* Dusche *f*; (*of rain*) Schauer *m*; **have a** ~ duschen □ *vt* ~ **with** überschütten mit □ *vi* duschen. ~**proof** *a* regendicht. ~**y** *a* regnerisch

'show-jumping *n* Springreiten *nt*

shown /ʃəʊn/ *see* **show**
show: ~-off *n* Angeber(in) *m(f)*. **~-piece** *n* Paradestück *nt*. **~room** *n* Ausstellungsraum *m*
showy /'ʃəʊɪ/ *a* protzig
shrank /ʃræŋk/ *see* **shrink**
shred /ʃred/ *n* Fetzen *m*; (*fig*) Spur *f* □ *vt* (*pt/pp* **shredded**) zerkleinern; (*Culin*) schnitzeln. **~der** *n* Reißwolf *m*; (*Culin*) Schnitzelwerk *nt*
shrewd /ʃru:d/ *a* (**-er, -est**), **-ly** *adv* klug. **~ness** *n* Klugheit *f*
shriek /ʃri:k/ *n* Schrei *m* □ *vt/i* schreien
shrift /ʃrɪft/ *n* **give s.o. short ~** jdn kurz abfertigen
shrill /ʃrɪl/ *a*, **-y** *adv* schrill
shrimp /ʃrɪmp/ *n* Garnele *f*, Krabbe *f*
shrine /ʃraɪn/ *n* Heiligtum *nt*
shrink /ʃrɪŋk/ *vi* (*pt* **shrank**, *pp* **shrunk**) schrumpfen; ⟨*garment:*⟩ einlaufen; (*draw back*) zurückschrecken (**from** vor + *dat*)
shrivel /'ʃrɪvl/ *vi* (*pt/pp* **shrivelled**) verschrumpeln
shroud /ʃraʊd/ *n* Leichentuch *nt*; (*fig*) Schleier *m*
Shrove /ʃrəʊv/ *n* **~ 'Tuesday** Fastnachtsdienstag *m*
shrub /ʃrʌb/ *n* Strauch *m*
shrug /ʃrʌg/ *n* Achselzucken *nt* □ *vt/i* (*pt/pp* **shrugged**) **~ [one's shoulders]** die Achseln zucken
shrunk /ʃrʌŋk/ *see* **shrink. ~en** *a* geschrumpft
shudder /'ʃʌdə(r)/ *n* Schauder *m* □ *vi* schaudern; (*tremble*) zittern
shuffle /'ʃʌfl/ *vi* schlurfen □ *vt* mischen ⟨*cards*⟩
shun /ʃʌn/ *vt* (*pt/pp* **shunned**) meiden
shunt /ʃʌnt/ *vt* rangieren
shush /ʃʊʃ/ *int* sch!
shut /ʃʌt/ *v* (*pt/pp* **shut**, *pres p* **shutting**) □ *vt* zumachen, schließen; **~ one's finger in the door** sich (*dat*) den Finger in der Tür einklemmen □ *vi* sich schließen; ⟨*shop:*⟩ schließen, zumachen. **~ down** *vt* schließen; stilllegen ⟨*factory*⟩ □ *vi* schließen; ⟨*factory:*⟩ stillgelegt werden. **~ up** *vt* abschließen; (*lock in*) einsperren □ *vi* (*fam*) den Mund halten
'shut-down *n* Stilllegung *f*
shutter /'ʃʌtə(r)/ *n* [Fenster]laden *m*; (*Phot*) Verschluss *m*
shuttle /'ʃʌtl/ *n* (*Tex*) Schiffchen *nt* □ *vi* pendeln
shuttle: ~cock *n* Federball *m*. **~ service** *n* Pendelverkehr *m*
shy /ʃaɪ/ *a* (**-er, -est**), **-ly** *adv* schüchtern; (*timid*) scheu □ *vi* (*pt/pp* **shied**) ⟨*horse:*⟩ scheuen. **~ness** *n* Schüchternheit *f*
Siamese /saɪə'mi:z/ *a* siamesisch
siblings /'sɪblɪŋz/ *npl* Geschwister *pl*
Sicily /'sɪsɪlɪ/ *n* Sizilien *nt*
sick /sɪk/ *a* krank; ⟨*humour*⟩ makaber; **be ~** (*vomit*) sich übergeben; **be ~ of sth** (*fam*) etw satt haben; **I feel ~** mir ist schlecht
sicken /'sɪkn/ *vt* anwidern □ *vi* **be ~ing for something** krank werden
sickle /'sɪkl/ *n* Sichel *f*
sick|ly /'sɪklɪ/ *a* (**-ier, -iest**) kränklich. **~ness** *n* Krankheit *f*; (*vomiting*) Erbrechen *nt*
'sick-room *n* Krankenzimmer *nt*
side /saɪd/ *n* Seite *f*; **on the ~** (*as sideline*) nebenbei; **~ by ~** nebeneinander; (*fig*) Seite an Seite; **take ~s** Partei ergreifen (**with** für); **to be on the safe ~** vorsichtshalber □ *attrib* Seiten- □ *vi* **~ with** Partei ergreifen für
side: ~board *n* Anrichte *f*. **~burns** *npl* Koteletten *pl*. **~-effect** *n* Nebenwirkung *f*. **~lights** *npl* Standlicht *nt*. **~line** *n* Nebenbeschäftigung *f*. **~-show** *n* Nebenattraktion *f*. **~-step** *vt* ausweichen (+ *dat*). **~-track** *vt* ablenken. **~walk** *n* (*Amer*) Bürgersteig *m*. **~ways** *adv* seitwärts

siding /ˈsaɪdɪŋ/ *n* Abstellgleis *nt*
sidle /ˈsaɪdl/ *vi* sich heranschleichen (**up to** an + *acc*)
siege /siːdʒ/ *n* Belagerung *f*; (*by police*) Umstellung *f*
sieve /sɪv/ *n* Sieb *nt* □ *vt* sieben
sift /sɪft/ *vt* sieben; (*fig*) durchsehen
sigh /saɪ/ *n* Seufzer *m* □ *vi* seufzen
sight /saɪt/ *n* Sicht *f*; (*faculty*) Sehvermögen *nt*; (*spectacle*) Anblick *m*; (*on gun*) Visier *nt*; **~s** *pl* Sehenswürdigkeiten *pl*; **at first ~** auf den ersten Blick; **within/out of ~** in/außer Sicht; **lose ~ of** aus dem Auge verlieren; **know by ~** vom Sehen kennen; **have bad ~** schlechte Augen haben □ *vt* sichten
ˈsightseeing *n* **go ~** die Sehenswürdigkeiten besichtigen
sign /saɪn/ *n* Zeichen *nt*; (*notice*) Schild *nt* □ *vt/i* unterschreiben; ⟨*author, artist:*⟩ signieren. **~ on** *vi* (*as unemployed*) sich arbeitslos melden; (*Mil*) sich verpflichten
signal /ˈsɪgnl/ *n* Signal *nt* □ *vt/i* (*pt/pp* **signalled**) signalisieren; **~ to s.o.** jdm ein Signal geben (**to** zu). **~-box** *n* Stellwerk *nt*
signature /ˈsɪgnətʃə(r)/ *n* Unterschrift *f*; (*of artist*) Signatur *f*. **~ tune** *n* Kennmelodie *f*
signet-ring /ˈsɪgnɪt-/ *n* Siegelring *m*
significan|ce /sɪgˈnɪfɪkəns/ *n* Bedeutung *f*. **~t** *a*, **-ly** *adv* bedeutungsvoll; (*important*) bedeutend
signify /ˈsɪgnɪfaɪ/ *vt* (*pt/pp* **-ied**) bedeuten
signpost /ˈsaɪn-/ *n* Wegweiser *m*
silence /ˈsaɪləns/ *n* Stille *f*; (*of person*) Schweigen *nt* □ *vt* zum Schweigen bringen. **~r** *n* (*on gun*) Schalldämpfer *m*; (*Auto*) Auspufftopf *m*
silent /ˈsaɪlənt/ *a*, **-ly** *adv* still; (*without speaking*) schweigend; **remain ~** schweigen. **~ film** *n* Stummfilm *m*
silhouette /sɪluːˈet/ *n* Silhouette *f*; (*picture*) Schattenriss *m* □ *vt* **be ~d** sich als Silhouette abheben
silicon /ˈsɪlɪkən/ *n* Silizium *nt*
silk /sɪlk/ *n* Seide *f* □ *attrib* Seiden-. **~worm** *n* Seidenraupe *f*
silky /ˈsɪlkɪ/ *a* (**-ier, -iest**) seidig
sill /ʃɪl/ *n* Sims *m & nt*
silly /ˈʃɪlɪ/ *a* (**-ier, -iest**) dumm, albern
silo /ˈsaɪləʊ/ *n* Silo *m*
silt /sɪlt/ *n* Schlick *m*
silver /ˈsɪlvə(r)/ *a* silbern; ⟨*coin, paper*⟩ Silber- □ *n* Silber *nt*
silver: ~-plated *a* versilbert. **~ware** *n* Silber *nt*. **~ ˈwedding** *n* Silberhochzeit *f*
similar /ˈsɪmɪlə(r)/ *a*, **-ly** *adv* ähnlich. **~ity** /-ˈlærətɪ/ *n* Ähnlichkeit *f*
simile /ˈsɪmɪlɪ/ *n* Vergleich *m*
simmer /ˈsɪmə(r)/ *vi* leise kochen, ziehen □ *vt* ziehen lassen
simple /ˈsɪmpl/ *a* (**-r, -st**) einfach; ⟨*person*⟩ einfältig. **~-ˈminded** *a* einfältig. **~ton** /ˈsɪmpltən/ *n* Einfaltspinsel *m*
simplicity /sɪmˈplɪsətɪ/ *n* Einfachheit *f*
simpli|fication /sɪmplɪfɪˈkeɪʃn/ *n* Vereinfachung *f*. **~fy** /ˈsɪmplɪfaɪ/ *vt* (*pt/pp* **-ied**) vereinfachen
simply /ˈsɪmplɪ/ *adv* einfach
simulat|e /ˈsɪmjʊleɪt/ *vt* vortäuschen; (*Techn*) simulieren. **~ion** /-ˈleɪʃn/ *n* Vortäuschung *f*; Simulation *f*
simultaneous /sɪmlˈteɪnɪəs/ *a*, **-ly** *adv* gleichzeitig; ⟨*interpreting*⟩ Simultan-
sin /sɪn/ *n* Sünde *f* □ *vi* (*pt/pp* **sinned**) sündigen
since /sɪns/ *prep* seit (+ *dat*) □ *adv* seitdem □ *conj* seit; (*because*) da
sincere /sɪnˈsɪə(r)/ a aufrichtig; (*heartfelt*) herzlich. **~ly** *adv* aufrichtig; **Yours ~ly** Mit freundlichen Grüßen

sincerity /sɪn'serətɪ/ *n* Aufrichtigkeit *f*
sinew /'sɪnju:/ *n* Sehne *f*
sinful /'sɪnfl/ *a* sündhaft
sing /sɪŋ/ *vt/i* (*pt* **sang**, *pp* **sung**) singen
singe /sɪndʒ/ *vt* (*pres p* **singeing**) versengen
singer /'sɪŋə(r)/ *n* Sänger(in) *m(f)*
single /'sɪŋgl/ *a* einzeln; (*one only*) einzig; (*unmarried*) ledig; ⟨*ticket*⟩ einfach; ⟨*room, bed*⟩ Einzel- □ *n* (*ticket*) einfache Fahrkarte *f*; (*record*) Single *f*; **~s** *pl* (*Tennis*) Einzel *nt* □ *vt* **~out** auswählen
single: **~-breasted** *a* einreihig. **~-handed** *a & adv* allein. **~-minded** *a* zielstrebig. **~ 'parent** *n* Alleinerziehende(r) *m/f*
singlet /'sɪŋglɪt/ *n* Unterhemd *nt*
singly /'sɪŋglɪ/ *adv* einzeln
singular /'sɪŋgjʊlə(r)/ *a* eigenartig; (*Gram*) im Singular □ *n* Singular *m*. **~ly** *adv* außerordentlich
sinister /'sɪnɪstə(r)/ *a* finster
sink /sɪŋk/ *n* Spülbecken *nt* □ *v* (*pt* **sank**, *pp* **sunk**) □ *vi* sinken □ *vt* versenken ⟨*ship*⟩; senken ⟨*shaft*⟩. **~ in** *vi* einsinken; (*fam: be understood*) kapiert werden
'sink unit *n* Spüle *f*
sinner /'sɪnə(r)/ *n* Sünder(in) *m(f)*
sinus /'saɪnəs/ *n* Nebenhöhle *f*
sip /sɪp/ *n* Schlückchen *nt* □ *vt* (*pt/pp* **sipped**) in kleinen Schlucken trinken
siphon /'saɪfn/ *n* (*bottle*) Siphon *m*. **~ off** *vt* mit einem Saugheber ablassen
sir /sɜ:(r)/ *n* mein Herr; **S~** (*title*) Sir; **Dear S~s** Sehr geehrte Herren
siren /'saɪrən/ *n* Sirene *f*
sissy /'sɪsɪ/ *n* Waschlappen *m*
sister /'sɪstə(r)/ *n* Schwester *f*; (*nurse*) Oberschwester *f*. **~-in-law** *n* (*pl* **~s-in-law**) Schwägerin *f*. **~ly** *a* schwesterlich
sit /sɪt/ *v* (*pt/pp* **sat**, *pres p* **sitting**) □ *vi* sitzen; (*sit down*) sich setzen; ⟨*committee:*⟩ tagen □ *vt* setzen; machen ⟨*exam*⟩. **~ back** *vi* sich zurücklehnen. **~ down** *vi* sich setzen. **~ up** *vi* [aufrecht] sitzen; (*rise*) sich aufsetzen; (*not slouch*) gerade sitzen; (*stay up*) aufbleiben
site /saɪt/ *n* Gelände *nt*; (*for camping*) Platz *m*; (*Archaeol*) Stätte *f* □ *vt* legen
sitting /'sɪtɪŋ/ *n* Sitzung *f*; (*for meals*) Schub *m*
situat|e /'sɪtjʊeɪt/ *vt* legen; **be ~ed** liegen. **~ion** /-'eɪʃn/ *n* Lage *f*; (*circumstances*) Situation *f*; (*job*) Stelle *f*
six /sɪks/ *a* sechs. **~teen** *a* sechzehn. **~teenth** *a* sechzehnte(r,s)
sixth /sɪksθ/ *a* sechste(r,s)
sixtieth /'sɪkstɪɪθ/ *a* sechzigste(r,s)
sixty /'sɪkstɪ/ *a* sechzig
size /saɪz/ *n* Größe *f* □ *vt* **~ up** (*fam*) taxieren
sizeable /'saɪzəbl/ *a* ziemlich groß
sizzle /'sɪzl/ *vi* brutzeln
skate¹ /skeɪt/ *n inv* (*fish*) Rochen *m*
skate² *n* Schlittschuh *m*; (*roller-*) Rollschuh *m* □ *vi* Schlittschuh/Rollschuh laufen. **~r** *n* Eisläufer(in) *m(f)*; Rollschuhläufer(in) *m(f)*
skating /'skeɪtɪŋ/ *n* Eislaufen *nt*. **~-rink** *n* Eisbahn *f*
skeleton /'skelɪtn/ *n* Skelett *nt*. **~ 'key** *n* Dietrich *m*. **~ 'staff** *n* Minimalbesetzung *f*
sketch /sketʃ/ *n* Skizze *f*; (*Theat*) Sketch *m* □ *vt* skizzieren
sketchy /'sketʃɪ/ *a* (**-ier, -iest**), **-ily** *adv* skizzenhaft
skew /skju:/ *n* **on the ~** schräg
skewer /'skjʊə(r)/ *n* [Brat]spieß *m*
ski /ski:/ *n* Ski *m* □ *vi* (*pt/pp* **skied**, *pres p* **skiing**) Ski fahren *or* laufen

skid /skɪd/ *n* Schleudern *nt* □ *vi* (*pt/pp* **skidded**) schleudern
skier /ˈskiːə(r)/ *n* Skiläufer(in) *m(f)*
skiing /ˈskiːɪŋ/ *n* Skilaufen *nt*
skilful /ˈskɪlfl/ *a*, **-ly** *adv* geschickt
skill /skɪl/ *n* Geschick *nt*. **~ed** *a* geschickt; (*trained*) ausgebildet
skim /skɪm/ *vt* (*pt/pp* **skimmed**) entrahmen ⟨*milk*⟩. **~ off** *vt* abschöpfen. **~ through** *vt* überfliegen
skimp /skɪmp/ *vt* sparen an (+ *dat*)
skimpy /ˈskɪmpɪ/ *a* (**-ier, -iest**) knapp
skin /skɪn/ *n* Haut *f*; (*on fruit*) Schale *f* □ *vt* (*pt/pp* **skinned**) häuten; schälen ⟨*fruit*⟩
skin: ~-deep *a* oberflächlich. **~-diving** *n* Sporttauchen *nt*
skinflint /ˈskɪnflɪnt/ *n* Geizhals *m*
skinny /ˈskɪnɪ/ *a* (**-ier, -iest**) dünn
skip[1] /skɪp/ *n* Container *m*
skip[2] *n* Hüpfer *m* □ *v* (*pt/pp* **skipped**) *vi* hüpfen; (*with rope*) seilspringen □ *vt* überspringen
skipper /ˈskɪpə(r)/ *n* Kapitän *m*
ˈskipping-rope *n* Sprungseil *nt*
skirmish /ˈskɜːmɪʃ/ *n* Gefecht *nt*
skirt /skɜːt/ *n* Rock *m* □ *vt* herumgehen um
skit /skɪt/ *n* parodistischer Sketch *m*
skittle /ˈskɪtl/ *n* Kegel *m*
skive /skaɪv/ *vi* (*fam*) blaumachen
skulk /skʌlk/ *vi* lauern
skull /skʌl/ *n* Schädel *m*
skunk /skʌŋk/ *n* Stinktier *nt*
sky /skaɪ/ *n* Himmel *m*. **~light** *n* Dachluke *f*. **~scraper** *n* Wolkenkratzer *m*
slab /slæb/ *n* Platte *f*; (*slice*) Scheibe *f*; (*of chocolate*) Tafel *f*
slack /slæk/ *a* (**-er, -est**) schlaff, locker; ⟨*person*⟩ nachlässig; (*Comm*) flau □ *vi* bummeln
slacken /ˈslækn/ *vi* sich lockern; (*diminish*) nachlassen; ⟨*speed:*⟩ sich verringern □ *vt* lockern; (*diminish*) verringern
slacks /slæks/ *npl* Hose *f*
slag /slæg/ *n* Schlacke *f*
slain /sleɪn/ *see* **slay**
slake /sleɪk/ *vt* löschen
slam /slæm/ *v* (*pt/pp* **slammed**) □ *vt* zuschlagen; (*put*) knallen (*fam*); (*fam: criticize*) verreißen □ *vi* zuschlagen
slander /ˈslɑːndə(r)/ *n* Verleumdung *f* □ *vt* verleumden. **~ous** /-rəs/ *a* verleumderisch
slang /slæŋ/ *n* Slang *m*. **~y** *a* salopp
slant /slɑːnt/ Schräge *f*; **on the ~** schräg □ *vt* abschrägen; (*fig*) färben ⟨*report*⟩ □ *vi* sich neigen
slap /slæp/ *n* Schlag *m* □ *vt* (*pt/pp* **slapped**) schlagen; (*put*) knallen (*fam*) □ *adv* direkt
slap: ~dash *a* (*fam*) schludrig. **~-up** *a* (*fam*) toll
slash /slæʃ/ *n* Schlitz *m* □ *vt* aufschlitzen; [drastisch] reduzieren ⟨*prices*⟩
slat /slæt/ *n* Latte *f*
slate /sleɪt/ *n* Schiefer *m* □ *vt* (*fam*) heruntermachen; verreißen ⟨*performance*⟩
slaughter /ˈslɔːtə(r)/ *n* Schlachten *nt*; (*massacre*) Gemetzel *nt* □ *vt* schlachten; abschlachten. **~house** *n* Schlachthaus *nt*
Slav /slɑːv/ *a* slawisch □ *n* Slawe *m*/ Slawin *f*
slave /sleɪv/ *n* Sklave *m*/ Sklavin *f* □ *vi* **~ [away]** schuften. **~-driver** *n* Leuteschinder *m*
slav|ery /ˈsleɪvərɪ/ *n* Sklaverei *f*. **~ish** *a*, **-ly** *adv* sklavisch
Slavonic /sləˈvɒnɪk/ *a* slawisch
slay /sleɪ/ *vt* (*pt* **slew**, *pp* **slain**) ermorden
sleazy /ˈsliːzɪ/ *a* (**-ier, -iest**) schäbig
sledge /sledʒ/ *n* Schlitten *m*. **~-hammer** *n* Vorschlaghammer *m*

sleek /sli:k/ *a* (**-er, -est**) seidig; (*well-fed*) wohlgenährt
sleep /sli:p/ *n* Schlaf *m*; **go to ~** einschlafen; **put to ~** einschläfern □ *v* (*pt/pp* **slept**) □ *vi* schlafen □ *vt* (*accommodate*) Unterkunft bieten für. **~er** *n* Schläfer(in) *m*(*f*); (*Rail*) Schlafwagen *m*; (*on track*) Schwelle *f*
sleeping: ~-bag *n* Schlafsack *m*. **~-car** *n* Schlafwagen *m*. **~-pill** *n* Schlaftablette *f*
sleep: ~less *a* schlaflos. **~-walking** *n* Schlafwandeln *nt*
sleepy /'sli:pɪ/ *a* (**-ier, -iest**), **-ily** *adv* schläfrig
sleet /sli:t/ *n* Schneeregen *m* □ *vi* **it is ~ing** es gibt Schneeregen
sleeve /sli:v/ *n* Ärmel *m*; (*for record*) Hülle *f*. **~less** *a* ärmellos
sleigh /sleɪ/ *n* [Pferde]schlitten *m*
sleight /slaɪt/ *n* **~ of hand** Taschenspielerei *f*
slender /'slendə(r)/ *a* schlank; (*fig*) gering
slept /slept/ *see* **sleep**
sleuth /slu:θ/ *n* Detektiv *m*
slew[1] /slu:/ *vi* schwenken
slew[2] *see* **slay**
slice /slaɪs/ *n* Scheibe *f* □ *vt* in Scheiben schneiden; **~d bread** Schnittbrot *nt*
slick /slɪk/ *a* clever □ *n* (*of oil*) Ölteppich *m*
slid|e /slaɪd/ *n* Rutschbahn *f*; (*for hair*) Spange *f*; (*Phot*) Dia *nt* □ *v* (*pt/pp* **slid**) □ *vi* rutschen □ *vt* schieben. **~ing** *a* gleitend; ⟨*door, seat*⟩ Schiebe-
slight /slaɪt/ *a* (**-er, -est**), **-ly** *adv* leicht; ⟨*importance*⟩ gering; ⟨*acquaintance*⟩ flüchtig; (*slender*) schlank; **not in the ~est** nicht im Geringsten; **~ly better** ein bisschen besser □ *vt* kränken, beleidigen □ *n* Beleidigung *f*
slim /slɪm/ *a* (**slimmer, slimmest**) schlank; ⟨*volume*⟩ schmal; (*fig*) gering □ *vi* eine Schlankheitskur machen
slim|e /slaɪm/ *n* Schleim *m*. **~y** *a* schleimig
sling /slɪŋ/ *n* (*Med*) Schlinge *f* □ *vt* (*pt/pp* **slung**) (*fam*) schmeißen
slip /slɪp/ *n* (*mistake*) Fehler *m*, (*fam*) Patzer *m*; (*petticoat*) Unterrock *m*; (*for pillow*) Bezug *m*; (*paper*) Zettel *m*; **give s.o. the ~** (*fam*) jdm entwischen; **~ of the tongue** Versprecher *m* □ *v* (*pt/pp* **slipped**) □ *vi* rutschen; (*fall*) ausrutschen; (*go quickly*) schlüpfen; (*decline*) nachlassen □ *vt* schieben; **~ s.o.'s mind** jdm entfallen. **~ away** *vi* sich fortschleichen; ⟨*time:*⟩ verfliegen. **~ up** *vi* (*fam*) einen Schnitzer machen
slipped 'disc *n* (*Med*) Bandscheibenvorfall *m*
slipper /'slɪpə(r)/ *n* Hausschuh *m*
slippery /'slɪpərɪ/ *a* glitschig; ⟨*surface*⟩ glatt
slipshod /'slɪpʃɒd/ *a* schludrig
'slip-up *n* (*fam*) Schnitzer *m*
slit /slɪt/ *n* Schlitz *m* □ *vt* (*pt/pp* **slit**) aufschlitzen
slither /'slɪðə(r)/ *vi* rutschen
sliver /'slɪvə(r)/ *n* Splitter *m*
slobber /'slɒbə(r)/ *vi* sabbern
slog /slɒg/ *n* **[hard] ~** Schinderei *f* □ *v* (*pt/pp* **slogged**) □ *vi* schuften □ *vt* schlagen
slogan /'sləʊgən/ *n* Schlagwort *nt*; (*advertising*) Werbespruch *m*
slop /slɒp/ *v* (*pt/pp* **slopped**) □ *vt* verschütten □ *vi* **~ over** überschwappen. **~s** *npl* Schmutzwasser *nt*
slop|e /sləʊp/ *n* Hang *m*; (*inclination*) Neigung *f* □ *vi* sich neigen. **~ing** *a* schräg
sloppy /'slɒpɪ/ *a* (**-ier, -iest**) schludrig; (*sentimental*) sentimental
slosh /slɒʃ/ *vi* (*fam*) platschen; ⟨*water:*⟩ schwappen □ *vt* (*fam: hit*) schlagen

slot /slɒt/ *n* Schlitz *m*; (*TV*) Sendezeit *f* □ *v* (*pt/pp* **slotted**) □ *vt* einfügen □ *vi* sich einfügen (**in** in + *acc*)
sloth /sləʊθ/ *n* Trägheit *f*
'slot-machine *n* Münzautomat *m*; (*for gambling*) Spielautomat *m*
slouch /slaʊtʃ/ *vi* sich schlecht halten
slovenly /'slʌvnlɪ/ *a* schlampig
slow /sləʊ/ *a* (**-er, -est**), **-ly** *adv* langsam; **be ~** ⟨*clock:*⟩ nachgehen; **in ~ motion** in Zeitlupe □ *adv* langsam □ *vt* verlangsamen □ *vi* **~ down, ~ up** langsamer werden
slow: ~coach *n* (*fam*) Trödler *m*. **~ness** *n* Langsamkeit *f*
sludge /slʌdʒ/ *n* Schlamm *m*
slug /slʌg/ *n* Nacktschnecke *f*
sluggish /'slʌgɪʃ/ *a*, **-ly** *adv* träge
sluice /slu:s/ *n* Schleuse *f*
slum /slʌm/ *n* (*house*) Elendsquartier *nt*; **~s** *pl* Elendsviertel *nt*
slumber /'slʌmbə(r)/ *n* Schlummer *m* □ *vi* schlummern
slump /slʌmp/ *n* Sturz *m* □ *vi* fallen; (*crumple*) zusammensacken; ⟨*prices:*⟩ stürzen; ⟨*sales:*⟩ zurückgehen
slung /slʌŋ/ *see* **sling**
slur /slɜ:(r)/ *n* (*discredit*) Schande *f* □ *vt* (*pt/pp* **slurred**) undeutlich sprechen
slurp /slɜ:p/ *vt/i* schlürfen
slush /slʌʃ/ *n* [Schnee]matsch *m*; (*fig*) Kitsch *m*. **~ fund** *n* Fonds *m* für Bestechungsgelder
slushy /'slʌʃɪ/ *a* matschig; (*sentimental*) kitschig
slut /slʌt/ *n* Schlampe *f* (*fam*)
sly /slaɪ/ *a* (**-er, -est**), **-ly** *adv* verschlagen □ *n* **on the ~** heimlich
smack¹ /smæk/ *n* Schlag *m*, Klaps *m* □ *vt* schlagen; **~ one's lips** mit den Lippen schmatzen □ *adv* (*fam*) direkt
smack² *vi* **~ of** (*fig*) riechen nach
small /smɔ:l/ *a* (**-er, -est**) klein; **in the ~ hours** in den frühen Morgenstunden □ *adv* **chop up ~** klein hacken □ *n* **~ of the back** Kreuz *nt*
small: ~ ads *npl* Kleinanzeigen *pl*. **~ 'change** *n* Kleingeld *nt*. **~-holding** *n* landwirtschaftlicher Kleinbetrieb *m*. **~pox** *n* Pocken *pl*. **~ talk** *n* leichte Konversation *f*
smarmy /'smɑ:mɪ/ *a* (**-ier, -iest**) (*fam*) ölig
smart /smɑ:t/ *a* (**-er, -est**), **-ly** *adv* schick; (*clever*) schlau, clever; (*brisk*) flott; (*Amer fam: cheeky*) frech □ *vi* brennen
smarten /'smɑ:tn/ *vt* **~ oneself up** mehr auf sein Äußeres achten
smash /smæʃ/ *n* Krach *m*; (*collision*) Zusammenstoß *m*; (*Tennis*) Schmetterball *m* □ *vt* zerschlagen; (*strike*) schlagen; (*Tennis*) schmettern □ *vi* zerschmettern; (*crash*) krachen (**into** gegen). **~ing** *a* (*fam*) toll
smattering /'smætərɪŋ/ *n* **a ~ of German** ein paar Brocken Deutsch
smear /smɪə(r)/ *n* verschmierter Fleck *m*; (*Med*) Abstrich *m*; (*fig*) Verleumdung *f* □ *vt* schmieren; (*coat*) beschmieren (**with** mit); (*fig*) verleumden □ *vi* schmieren
smell /smel/ *n* Geruch *m*; (*sense*) Geruchssinn *m* □ *v* (*pt/pp* **smelt** *or* **smelled**) □ *vt* riechen; (*sniff*) riechen an (+ *dat*) □ *vi* riechen (**of** nach)
smelly /'smelɪ/ *a* (**-ier, -iest**) übel riechend
smelt¹ /smelt/ *see* **smell**
smelt² *vt* schmelzen
smile /smaɪl/ *n* Lächeln *nt* □ *vi* lächeln; **~ at** anlächeln
smirk /smɜ:k/ *vi* feixen
smith /smɪθ/ *n* Schmied *m*
smithereens /smɪðə'ri:nz/ *npl* **smash to ~** in tausend Stücke schlagen

smitten /ˈsmɪtn/ *a* ~ **with** sehr angetan von
smock /smɒk/ *n* Kittel *m*
smog /smɒg/ *n* Smog *m*
smoke /sməʊk/ *n* Rauch *m* □ *vt/i* rauchen; (*Culin*) räuchern. ~**less** *a* rauchfrei; ⟨*fuel*⟩ rauchlos
smoker /ˈsməʊkə(r)/ *n* Raucher *m*; (*Rail*) Raucherabteil *nt*
ˈ**smoke-screen** *n* [künstliche] Nebelwand *f*
smoking /ˈsməʊkɪŋ/ *n* Rauchen *nt*; '**no** ~' 'Rauchen verboten'
smoky /ˈsməʊkɪ/ *a* (**-ier, -iest**) verraucht; ⟨*taste*⟩ rauchig
smooth /smu:ð/ *a* (**-er, -est**), **-ly** *adv* glatt □ *vt* glätten. ~ **out** *vt* glatt streichen
smother /ˈsmʌðə(r)/ *vt* ersticken; (*cover*) bedecken; (*suppress*) unterdrücken
smoulder /ˈsməʊldə(r)/ *vi* schwelen
smudge /smʌdʒ/ *n* Fleck *m* □ *vt* verwischen □ *vi* schmieren
smug /smʌg/ *a* (**smugger, smuggest**), **-ly** *adv* selbstgefällig
smuggl|e /ˈsmʌgl/ *vt* schmuggeln. ~**er** *n* Schmuggler *m*. ~**ing** *n* Schmuggel *m*
smut /smʌt/ *n* Rußflocke *f*; (*mark*) Rußfleck *m*; (*fig*) Schmutz *m*
smutty /ˈsmʌtɪ/ *a* (**-ier, -iest**) schmutzig
snack /snæk/ *n* Imbiss *m*. ~**-bar** *n* Imbissstube *f*
snag /snæg/ *n* Schwierigkeit *f*, (*fam*) Haken *m*
snail /sneɪl/ *n* Schnecke *f*; **at a** ~**'s pace** im Schneckentempo
snake /sneɪk/ *n* Schlange *f*
snap /snæp/ *n* Knacken *nt*; (*photo*) Schnappschuss *m* □ *attrib* ⟨*decision*⟩ plötzlich □ *v* (*pt/pp* **snapped**) □ *vi* [entzwei]brechen; ~ **at** (*bite*) schnappen nach; (*speak sharply*) [scharf] anfahren □ *vt* zerbrechen; (*say*) fauchen; (*Phot*) knipsen. ~ **up** *vt* wegschnappen
snappy /ˈsnæpɪ/ *a* (**-ier, -iest**) bissig; (*smart*) flott; **make it** ~! ein bisschen schnell!
ˈ**snapshot** *n* Schnappschuss *m*
snare /sneə(r)/ *n* Schlinge *f*
snarl /snɑ:l/ *vi* [mit gefletschten Zähnen] knurren
snatch /snætʃ/ *n* (*fragment*) Fetzen *pl*; (*theft*) Raub *m*; **make a** ~ **at** greifen nach □ *vt* schnappen; (*steal*) klauen; entführen ⟨*child*⟩; ~ **sth from s.o.** jdm etw entreißen
sneak /sni:k/ *n* (*fam*) Petze *f* □ *vi* schleichen; (*fam: tell tales*) petzen □ *vt* (*take*) mitgehen lassen □ *vi* ~ **in/out** sich hinein-/hinausschleichen
sneakers /ˈsni:kəz/ *npl* (*Amer*) Turnschuhe *pl*
sneaking /ˈsni:kɪŋ/ *a* heimlich; ⟨*suspicion*⟩ leise
sneaky /ˈsni:kɪ/ *a* hinterhältig
sneer /snɪə(r)/ *vi* höhnisch lächeln; (*mock*) spotten
sneeze /sni:z/ *n* Niesen *nt* □ *vi* niesen
snide /snaɪd/ *a* (*fam*) abfällig
sniff /snɪf/ *vi* schnüffeln □ *vt* schnüffeln an (+ *dat*); schnüffeln ⟨*glue*⟩
snigger /ˈsnɪgə(r)/ *vi* [boshaft] kichern
snip /snɪp/ *n* Schnitt *m*; (*fam: bargain*) günstiger Kauf *m* □ *vt/i* ~ **[at]** schnippeln an (+ *dat*)
snipe /snaɪp/ *vi* ~ **at** aus dem Hinterhalt schießen auf (+ *acc*); (*fig*) anschießen. ~**r** *n* Heckenschütze *m*
snippet /ˈsnɪpɪt/ *n* Schnipsel *m*; (*of information*) Bruchstück *nt*
snivel /ˈsnɪvl/ *vi* (*pt/pp* **snivelled**) flennen
snob /snɒb/ *n* Snob *m*. ~**bery** *n* Snobismus *m*. ~**bish** *a* snobistisch
snoop /snu:p/ *vi* (*fam*) schnüffeln

snooty /ˈsnu:tɪ/ *a* (*fam*) hochnäsig
snooze /snu:z/ *n* Nickerchen *nt* □ *vi* dösen
snore /snɔ:(r)/ *vi* schnarchen
snorkel /ˈsnɔ:kl/ *n* Schnorchel *m*
snort /snɔ:t/ *vi* schnauben
snout /snaʊt/ *n* Schnauze *f*
snow /snəʊ/ *n* Schnee *m* □ *vi* schneien; **~ed under with** (*fig*) überhäuft mit
snow: ~ball *n* Schneeball *m* □ *vi* lawinenartig anwachsen. **~drift** *n* Schneewehe *f*. **~drop** *n* Schneeglöckchen *nt*. **~fall** *n* Schneefall *m*. **~flake** *n* Schneeflocke *f*. **~ flurry** *n* Schneegestöber *nt*. **~man** *n* Schneemann *m*. **~plough** *n* Schneepflug *m*. **~storm** *n* Schneesturm *m*
snub /snʌb/ *n* Abfuhr *f* □ *vt* (*pt/pp* **snubbed**) brüskieren
ˈsnub-nosed *a* stupsnasig
snuff[1] /snʌf/ *n* Schnupftabak *m*
snuff[2] *vt* **~[out]** löschen
snuffle /ˈsnʌfl/ *vi* schnüffeln
snug /snʌg/ *a* (**snugger, snuggest**) behaglich, gemütlich
snuggle /ˈsnʌgl/ *vi* sich kuscheln (**up to** an + *acc*)
so /səʊ/ *adv* so; **not so fast** nicht so schnell; **so am I** ich auch; **so does he** er auch; **so I see** das sehe ich; **that is so** das stimmt; **so much the better** umso besser; **so it is** tatsächlich; **if so** wenn ja; **so as to** um zu; **so long**! (*fam*) tschüs! □ *pron* **I hope so** hoffentlich; **I think so** ich glaube schon; **I told you so** ich hab's dir gleich gesagt; **because I say so** weil ich es sage; **I'm afraid so** leider ja; **so saying/doing, he/she** ... indem er/sie das sagte/tat, ...; **an hour or so** eine Stunde oder so; **very much so** durchaus □ *conj* (*therefore*) also; **so that** damit; **so there**! fertig! **so what**! na und! **so you see** wie du siehst; **so where have you been?** wo warst du denn?
soak /səʊk/ *vt* nass machen; (*steep*) einweichen; (*fam: fleece*) schröpfen □ *vi* weichen; ⟨*liquid:*⟩ sickern. **~ up** *vt* aufsaugen
soaking /ˈsəʊkɪŋ/ *a* & *adv* **~ [wet]** patschnass (*fam*)
soap /səʊp/ *n* Seife *f*. **~ opera** *n* Seifenoper *f*. **~ powder** *n* Seifenpulver *nt*
soapy /ˈsəʊpɪ/ *a* (**-ier, -iest**) seifig
soar /sɔ:(r)/ *vi* aufsteigen; ⟨*prices:*⟩ in die Höhe schnellen
sob /sɒb/ *n* Schluchzer *m* □ *vi* (*pt/pp* **sobbed**) schluchzen
sober /ˈsəʊbə(r)/ *a*, **-ly** *adv* nüchtern; (*serious*) ernst; ⟨*colour*⟩ gedeckt. **~ up** *vi* nüchtern werden
ˈso-called *a* sogenannt
soccer /ˈsɒkə(r)/ *n* (*fam*) Fußball *m*
sociable /ˈsəʊʃəbl/ *a* gesellig
social /ˈsəʊʃl/ *a* gesellschaftlich; (*Admin, Pol, Zool*) sozial
socialis|m /ˈsəʊʃəlɪzm/ *n* Sozialismus *m*. **~t** /-ɪst/ *a* sozialistisch □ *n* Sozialist *m*
socialize /ˈsəʊʃəlaɪz/ *vi* [gesellschaftlich] verkehren
socially /ˈsəʊʃəlɪ/ *adv* gesellschaftlich; **know ~** privat kennen
social: ~ seˈcurity *n* Sozialhilfe *f*. **~ work** *n* Sozialarbeit *f*. **~ worker** *n* Sozialarbeiter(in) *m*(*f*)
society /səˈsaɪətɪ/ *n* Gesellschaft *f*; (*club*) Verein *m*
sociolog|ist /səʊsɪˈɒlədʒɪst/ *n* Soziologe *m*. **~y** *n* Soziologie *f*
sock[1] /sɒk/ *n* Socke *f*; (*knee-length*) Kniestrumpf *m*
sock[2] *n* (*fam*) Schlag *m* □ *vt* (*fam*) hauen
socket /ˈsɒkɪt/ *n* (*of eye*) Augenhöhle *f*; (*of joint*) Gelenkpfanne *f*; (*wall plug*) Steckdose *f*; (*for bulb*) Fassung *f*
soda /ˈsəʊdə/ *n* Soda *nt*; (*Amer*) Limonade *f*. **~ water** *n* Sodawasser *nt*

sodden /ˈsɒdn/ *a* durchnässt
sodium /ˈsəʊdɪəm/ *n* Natrium *nt*
sofa /ˈsəʊfə/ *n* Sofa *nt*. **~ bed** *n* Schlafcouch *f*
soft /sɒft/ *a* (**-er, -est**), **-ly** *adv* weich; (*quiet*) leise; (*gentle*) sanft; (*fam: silly*) dumm; **have a ~ spot for s.o.** jdn mögen. **~ drink** *n* alkoholfreies Getränk *nt*
soften /ˈsɒfn/ *vt* weich machen; (*fig*) mildern □ *vi* weich werden
soft: ~ toy *n* Stofftier *nt*. **~ware** *n* Software *f*
soggy /ˈsɒgɪ/ *a* (**-ier, -iest**) aufgeweicht
soil1 /sɔɪl/ *n* Erde *f*, Boden *m*
soil2 *vt* verschmutzen
solace /ˈsɒləs/ *n* Trost *m*
solar /ˈsəʊlə(r)/ *a* Sonnen-
sold /səʊld/ *see* **sell**
solder /ˈsəʊldə(r)/ *n* Lötmetall *nt* □ *vt* löten
soldier /ˈsəʊldʒə(r)/ *n* Soldat *m* □ *vi* **~ on** [unbeirrbar] weitermachen
sole1 /səʊl/ *n* Sohle *f*
sole2 *n* (*fish*) Seezunge *f*
sole3 *a* einzig. **~ly** *adv* einzig und allein
solemn /ˈsɒləm/ *a*, **-ly** *adv* feierlich; (*serious*) ernst. **~ity** /səˈlemnətɪ/ *n* Feierlichkeit *f*; Ernst *m*
solicit /səˈlɪsɪt/ *vt* bitten um □ *vi* ⟨*prostitute:*⟩ sich an Männer heranmachen
solicitor /səˈlɪsɪtə(r)/ *n* Rechtsanwalt *m*/-anwältin *f*
solicitous /səˈlɪsɪtəs/ *a* besorgt
solid /ˈsɒlɪd/ *a* fest; (*sturdy*) stabil; (*not hollow, of same substance*) massiv; (*unanimous*) einstimmig; (*complete*) ganz □ *n* (*Geom*) Körper *m*; **~s** *pl* (*food*) feste Nahrung *f*
solidarity /sɒlɪˈdærətɪ/ *n* Solidarität *f*
solidify /səˈlɪdɪfaɪ/ *vi* (*pt/pp* **-ied**) fest werden
soliloquy /səˈlɪləkwɪ/ *n* Selbstgespräch *nt*
solitary /ˈsɒlɪtərɪ/ *a* einsam; (*sole*) einzig. **~ conˈfinement** *n* Einzelhaft *f*
solitude /ˈsɒlɪtjuːd/ *n* Einsamkeit *f*
solo /ˈsəʊləʊ/ *n* Solo *nt* □ *a* Solo-; ⟨*flight*⟩ Allein- □ *adv* solo. **~ist** *n* Solist(in) *m*(*f*)
solstice /ˈsɒlstɪs/ *n* Sonnenwende *f*
soluble /ˈsɒljʊbl/ *a* löslich; (*solvable*) lösbar
solution /səˈluːʃn/ *n* Lösung *f*
solvable /ˈsɒlvəbl/ *a* lösbar
solve /sɒlv/ *vt* lösen
solvent /ˈsɒlvənt/ *a* zahlungsfähig; (*Chem*) lösend □ *n* Lösungsmittel *nt*
sombre /ˈsɒmbə(r)/ *a* dunkel; ⟨*mood*⟩ düster
some /sʌm/ *a & pron* etwas; (*a little*) ein bisschen; (*with pl noun*) einige; (*a few*) ein paar; (*certain*) manche(r,s); (*one or the other*) [irgend]ein; **~ day** eines Tages; **I want ~** ich möchte etwas/ (*pl*) welche; **will you have ~ wine?** möchten Sie Wein? **I need ~ money/books** ich brauche Geld/ Bücher; **do ~ shopping** einkaufen
some: ~body /-bədɪ/ *pron & n* jemand; (*emphatic*) irgendjemand. **~how** *adv* irgendwie. **~one** *pron & n* = **somebody**
somersault /ˈsʌməsɔːlt/ *n* Purzelbaum *m* (*fam*); (*Sport*) Salto *m*; **turn a ~** einen Purzelbaum schlagen/einen Salto springen
ˈ**something** *pron & adv* etwas; (*emphatic*) irgendetwas; **~ different** etwas anderes; **~ like** so etwas wie; **see ~ of s.o.** jdn mal sehen
some: ~time *adv* irgendwann □ *a* ehemalig. **~times** *adv* manchmal. **~what** *adv* ziemlich. **~where** *adv* irgendwo; ⟨*go*⟩ irgendwohin

son /sʌn/ *n* Sohn *m*
sonata /sə'nɑ:tə/ *n* Sonate *f*
song /sɒŋ/ *n* Lied *nt*. **~bird** *n* Singvogel *m*
sonic /'sɒnɪk/ *a* Schall-. **~ 'boom** *n* Überschallknall *m*
'son-in-law *n* (*pl* **~s-in-law**) Schwiegersohn *m*
soon /su:n/ *adv* (**-er, -est**) bald; (*quickly*) schnell; **too ~** zu früh; **as ~ as** sobald; **as ~ as possible** so bald wie möglich; **~er or later** früher oder später; **no ~er had I arrived than ...** kaum war ich angekommen, da ...; **I would ~er stay** ich würde lieber bleiben
soot /sʊt/ *n* Ruß *m*
sooth|e /su:ð/ *vt* beruhigen; lindern ⟨*pain*⟩. **~ing** *a*, **-ly** *adv* beruhigend; lindernd
sooty /'sʊtɪ/ *a* rußig
sop /sɒp/ *n* Beschwichtigungsmittel *nt*
sophisticated /sə'fɪstɪkeɪtɪd/ *a* weltgewandt; (*complex*) hoch entwickelt
soporific /sɒpə'rɪfɪk/ *a* einschläfernd
sopping /'sɒpɪŋ/ *a* & *adv* **~ [wet]** durchnässt
soppy /'sɒpɪ/ *a* (**-ier, -iest**) (*fam*) rührselig
soprano /sə'prɑ:nəʊ/ *n* Sopran *m*; (*woman*) Sopranistin *f*
sordid /'sɔ:dɪd/ *a* schmutzig
sore /sɔ:(r)/ *a* (**-r, -st**) wund; (*painful*) schmerzhaft; **have a ~ throat** Halsschmerzen haben □ *n* wunde Stelle *f*. **~ly** *adv* sehr
sorrow /'sɒrəʊ/ *n* Kummer *m*, Leid *nt*. **~ful** *a* traurig
sorry /'sɒrɪ/ *a* (**-ier, -iest**) (*sad*) traurig; (*wretched*) erbärmlich; **I am ~ es** tut mir Leid; **she is** *or* **feels ~ for him** er tut ihr Leid; **I am ~ to say** leider; **~!** Entschuldigung!
sort /sɔ:t/ *n* Art *f*; (*brand*) Sorte *f*; **he's a good ~** (*fam*) er ist in Ordnung; **be out of ~s** (*fam*) nicht auf der Höhe sein □ *vt* sortieren. **~ out** *vt* sortieren; (*fig*) klären
sought /sɔ:t/ *see* **seek**
soul /səʊl/ *n* Seele *f*. **~ful** *a* gefühlvoll
sound[1] /saʊnd/ *a* (**-er, -est**) gesund; (*sensible*) vernünftig; (*secure*) solide; (*thorough*) gehörig □ *adv* **be ~ asleep** fest schlafen
sound[2] *vt* (*Naut*) loten. **~ out** *vt* (*fig*) aushorchen
sound[3] *n* (*strait*) Meerenge *f*
sound[4] *n* Laut *m*; (*noise*) Geräusch *nt*; (*Phys*) Schall *m*; (*Radio, TV*) Ton *m*; (*of bells, music*) Klang *m*; **I don't like the ~ of it** (*fam*) das hört sich nicht gut an □ *vi* [er]tönen; (*seem*) sich anhören □ *vt* (*pronounce*) aussprechen; schlagen ⟨*alarm*⟩; (*Med*) abhorchen ⟨*chest*⟩. **~ barrier** *n* Schallmauer *f*. **~less** *a*, **-ly** *adv* lautlos
soundly /'saʊndlɪ/ *adv* solide; ⟨*sleep*⟩ fest; ⟨*defeat*⟩ vernichtend
'soundproof *a* schalldicht
soup /su:p/ *n* Suppe *f*. **~ed-up** *a* (*fam*) ⟨*engine*⟩ frisiert
soup: ~-plate *n* Suppenteller *m*. **~-spoon** *n* Suppenlöffel *m*
sour /'saʊə(r)/ *a* (**-er, -est**) sauer; (*bad-tempered*) griesgrämig, verdrießlich
source /sɔ:s/ *n* Quelle *f*
south /saʊθ/ *n* Süden *m*; **to the ~ of** südlich von □ *a* Süd-, süd- □ *adv* nach Süden
south: S~ 'Africa *n* Südafrika *nt*. **S~ A'merica** *n* Südamerika *nt*. **~-'east** *n* Südosten *m*
southerly /'sʌðəlɪ/ *a* südlich
southern /'sʌðən/ *a* südlich
South 'Pole *n* Südpol *m*
'southward[s] /-wəd[z]/ *adv* nach Süden
souvenir /su:və'nɪə(r)/ *n* Andenken *nt*, Souvenir *nt*

sovereign /ˈsɒvrɪn/ *a* souverän □ *n* Souverän *m*. **~ty** *n* Souveränität *f*
Soviet /ˈsəʊvɪət/ *a* sowjetisch; **~ Union** Sowjetunion *f*
sow[1] /saʊ/ *n* Sau *f*
sow[2] /səʊ/ *vt* (*pt* **sowed**, *pp* **sown** *or* **sowed**) säen
soya /ˈsɔɪə/ *n* **~ bean** Sojabohne *f*
spa /spɑː/ *n* Heilbad *nt*
space /speɪs/ *n* Raum *m*; (*gap*) Platz *m*; (*Astr*) Weltraum *m*; **leave/clear a ~** Platz lassen/schaffen □ *vt* **~ [out]** [in Abständen] verteilen
space: ~craft *n* Raumfahrzeug *nt*. **~ship** *n* Raumschiff *nt*
spacious /ˈspeɪʃəs/ *a* geräumig
spade /speɪd/ *n* Spaten *m*; (*for child*) Schaufel *f*; **~s** *pl* (*Cards*) Pik *nt*; **call a ~ a ~** das Kind beim rechten Namen nennen. **~work** *n* Vorarbeit *f*
Spain /speɪn/ *n* Spanien *nt*
span[1] /spæn/ *n* Spanne *f*; (*of arch*) Spannweite *f* □ *vt* (*pt/pp* **spanned**) überspannen; umspannen ⟨*time*⟩
span[2] *see* **spick**
Span|iard /ˈspænjəd/ *n* Spanier(in) *m*(*f*). **~ish** *a* spanisch □ *n* (*Lang*) Spanisch *nt*; **the ~ish** *pl* die Spanier
spank /spæŋk/ *vt* verhauen
spanner /ˈspænə(r)/ *n* Schraubenschlüssel *m*
spar /spɑː(r)/ *vi* (*pt/pp* **sparred**) (*Sport*) sparren; (*argue*) sich zanken
spare /speə(r)/ *a* (*surplus*) übrig; (*additional*) zusätzlich; ⟨*seat, time*⟩ frei; ⟨*room*⟩ Gäste-; ⟨*bed, cup*⟩ Extra- □ *n* (*part*) Ersatzteil *nt* □ *vt* ersparen; (*not hurt*) verschonen; (*do without*) entbehren; (*afford to give*) erübrigen; **to ~** (*surplus*) übrig. **~ ˈwheel** *n* Reserverad *nt*
sparing /ˈspeərɪŋ/ *a*, **-ly** *adv* sparsam
spark /spɑːk/ *n* Funke *nt* □ *vt* **~ off** zünden; (*fig*) auslösen. **~ing-plug** *n* (*Auto*) Zündkerze *f*
sparkl|e /ˈspɑːkl/ *n* Funkeln *nt* □ *vi* funkeln. **~ing** *a* funkelnd; ⟨*wine*⟩ Schaum-
sparrow /ˈspærəʊ/ *n* Spatz *m*
sparse /spɑːs/ *a* spärlich. **~ly** *adv* spärlich; ⟨*populated*⟩ dünn
Spartan /ˈspɑːtn/ *a* spartanisch
spasm /ˈspæzm/ *n* Anfall *m*; (*cramp*) Krampf *m*. **~odic** /-ˈmɒdɪk/ *a*, **-ally** *adv* sporadisch; (*Med*) krampfartig
spastic /ˈspæstɪk/ *a* spastisch [gelähmt] □ *n* Spastiker(in) *m*(*f*)
spat /spæt/ *see* **spit**[2]
spate /speɪt/ *n* Flut *f*; (*series*) Serie *f*; **be in full ~** Hochwasser führen
spatial /ˈspeɪʃl/ *a* räumlich
spatter /ˈspætə(r)/ *vt* spritzen; **~ with** bespritzen mit
spatula /ˈspætjʊlə/ *n* Spachtel *m*; (*Med*) Spatel *m*
spawn /spɔːn/ *n* Laich *m* □ *vi* laichen □ *vt* (*fig*) hervorbringen
spay /speɪ/ *vt* sterilisieren
speak /spiːk/ *v* (*pt* **spoke**, *pp* **spoken**) □ *vi* sprechen (**to** mit) **~ing!** (*Teleph*) am Apparat! □ *vt* sprechen; sagen ⟨*truth*⟩. **~ up** *vi* lauter sprechen; **~ up for oneself** seine Meinung äußern
speaker /ˈspiːkə(r)/ *n* Sprecher(in) *m*(*f*); (*in public*) Redner(in) *m*(*f*); (*loudspeaker*) Lautsprecher *m*
spear /spɪə(r)/ *n* Speer *m* □ *vt* aufspießen. **~head** *vt* (*fig*) anführen
spec /spek/ *n* **on ~** (*fam*) auf gut Glück
special /ˈspeʃl/ *a* besondere(r,s), speziell. **~ist** *n* Spezialist *m*; (*Med*) Facharzt *m*/-ärztin *f*. **~ity** /-ʃɪˈælətɪ/ *n* Spezialität *f*
special|ize /ˈspeʃəlaɪz/ *vi* sich spezialisieren (**in** auf + *acc*). **~ly** *adv* speziell; (*particularly*) besonders

species /'spi:ʃi:z/ *n* Art *f*
specific /spə'sɪfɪk/ *a* bestimmt; (*precise*) genau; (*Phys*) spezifisch. **~ally** *adv* ausdrücklich
specification /spesɪfɪ'keɪʃn/ *n* & **~s** *pl* genaue Angaben *pl*
specify /'spesɪfaɪ/ *vt* (*pt/pp* **-ied**) [genau] angeben
specimen /spesɪmən/ *n* Exemplar *nt*; (*sample*) Probe *f*; (*of urine*) Urinprobe *f*
speck /spek/ *n* Fleck *m*; (*particle*) Teilchen *nt*
speckled /'spekld/ *a* gesprenkelt
specs /speks/ *npl* (*fam*) Brille *f*
spectacle /'spektəkl/ *n* (*show*) Schauspiel *nt*; (*sight*) Anblick *m*. **~s** *npl* Brille *f*
spectacular /spek'tækjʊlə(r)/ *a* spektakulär
spectator /spek'teɪtə(r)/ *n* Zuschauer(in) *m(f)*
spectre /'spektə(r)/ *n* Gespenst *nt*; (*fig*) Schreckgespenst *nt*
spectrum /'spektrəm/ *n* (*pl* **-tra**) Spektrum *nt*
speculat|e /'spekjʊleɪt/ *vi* spekulieren. **~ion** /-'leɪʃn/ *n* Spekulation *f*. **~or** *n* Spekulant *m*
sped /sped/ *see* **speed**
speech /spi:tʃ/ *n* Sprache *f*; (*address*) Rede *f*. **~less** *a* sprachlos
speed /spi:d/ *n* Geschwindigkeit *f*; (*rapidity*) Schnelligkeit *f*; (*gear*) **Gang** *m*; **at ~** mit hoher Geschwindigkeit □ *vi* (*pt/pp* **sped**) schnell fahren □ (*pt/pp* **speeded**) (*go too fast*) zu schnell fahren. **~ up** (*pt/pp* **speeded up**) □ *vt* beschleunigen □ *vi* schneller werden; ⟨*vehicle:*⟩ schneller fahren
speed: ~boat *n* Rennboot *nt*. **~ing** *n* Geschwindigkeitsüberschreitung *f*. **~ limit** *n* Geschwindigkeitsbeschränkung *f*
speedometer /spi:'dɒmɪtə(r)/ *n* Tachometer *m*
speedy /'spi:dɪ/ *a* (**-ier, -iest**), **-ily** *adv* schnell
spell¹ /spel/ *n* Weile *f*; (*of weather*) Periode *f*
spell² *v* (*pt/pp* **spelled** or **spelt**) □ *vt* schreiben; (*aloud*) buchstabieren; (*fig: mean*) bedeuten □ *vi* richtig schreiben; (*aloud*) buchstabieren. **~ out** *vt* buchstabieren; (*fig*) genau erklären
spell³ *n* Zauber *m*; (*words*) Zauberspruch *m*. **~bound** *a* wie verzaubert
spelling /'spelɪŋ/ *n* Schreibweise *f*; (*orthography*) Rechtschreibung *f*
spelt /spelt/ *see* **spell**²
spend /spend/ *vt/i* (*pt/pp* **spent**) ausgeben; verbringen ⟨*time*⟩
spent /spent/ *see* **spend**
sperm /spɜ:m/ *n* Samen *m*
spew /spju:/ *vt* speien
spher|e /sfɪə(r)/ *n* Kugel *f*; (*fig*) Sphäre *f*. **~ical** /'sferɪkl/ *a* kugelförmig
spice /spaɪs/ *n* Gewürz *nt*; (*fig*) Würze *f*
spick /spɪk/ *a* **~ and span** blitzsauber
spicy /'spaɪsɪ/ *a* würzig, pikant
spider /'spaɪdə(r)/ *n* Spinne *f*
spik|e /spaɪk/ *n* Spitze *f*; (*Bot, Zool*) Stachel *m*; (*on shoe*) Spike *m*. **~y** *a* stachelig
spill /spɪl/ *v* (*pt/pp* **spilt** *or* **spilled**) □ *vt* verschütten; vergießen ⟨*blood*⟩ □ *vi* überlaufen
spin /spɪn/ *v* (*pt/pp* **spun**, *pres p* **spinning**) □ *vt* drehen; spinnen ⟨*wool*⟩; schleudern ⟨*washing*⟩ □ *vi* sich drehen. **~ out** *vt* in die Länge ziehen
spinach /'spɪnɪdz/ *n* Spinat *m*
spinal /'spaɪnl/ *a* Rückgrat-. **~ 'cord** *n* Rückenmark *nt*
spindl|e /'spɪndl/ *n* Spindel *f*. **~y** *a* spindeldürr
spin-'drier *n* Wäscheschleuder *f*
spine /spaɪn/ *n* Rückgrat *nt*; (*of book*) [Buch]rücken *m*; (*Bot, Zool*) Stachel *m*. **~less** *a* (*fig*) rückgratlos

spinning /ˈspɪnɪŋ/ *n* Spinnen *nt*. **~-wheel** *n* Spinnrad *nt*
ˈspin-off *n* Nebenprodukt *nt*
spinster /ˈspɪnstə(r)/ *n* ledige Frau *f*
spiral /ˈspaɪrl/ *a* spiralig □ *n* Spirale *f* □ *vi* (*pt/pp* **spiralled**) sich hochwinden; ⟨*smoke:*⟩ in einer Spirale aufsteigen. **~ ˈstaircase** *n* Wendeltreppe *f*
spire /ˈspaɪə(r)/ *n* Turmspitze *f*
spirit /ˈspɪrɪt/ *n* Geist *m*; (*courage*) Mut *m*; **~s** *pl* (*alcohol*) Spirituosen *pl*; **in high ~s** in gehobener Stimmung; **in low ~s** niedergedrückt. **~ away** *vt* verschwinden lassen
spirited /ˈspɪrɪtɪd/ *a* lebhaft; (*courageous*) beherzt
spirit: ~-level *n* Wasserwaage *f*. **~ stove** *n* Spirituskocher *m*
spiritual /ˈspɪrɪtjʊəl/ *a* geistig; (*Relig*) geistlich. **~ism** /-ɪzm/ *n* Spiritismus *m*. **~ist** /-ɪst/ *a* spiritistisch □ *n* Spiritist *m*
spit[1] /spɪt/ *n* (*for roasting*) [Brat]spieß *m*
spit[2] *n* Spucke *f* □ *vt/i* (*pt/pp* **spat**, *pres p* **spitting**) spucken; ⟨*cat:*⟩ fauchen; ⟨*fat:*⟩ spritzen; **it's ~ting with rain** es tröpfelt; **be the ~ting image of s.o.** jdm wie aus dem Gesicht geschnitten sein
spite /spaɪt/ *n* Boshaftigkeit *f*; **in ~ of** trotz (+ *gen*) □ *vt* ärgern. **~ful** *a*, **-ly** *adv* gehässig
spittle /ˈspɪtl/ *n* Spucke *f*
splash /splæʃ/ *n* Platschen *nt*; (*fam: drop*) Schuss *m*; **~ of colour** Farbfleck *m* □ *vt* spritzen; **~ s.o. with sth** jdn mit etw bespritzen □ *vi* spritzen. **~ about** *vi* planschen
spleen /spli:n/ *n* Milz *f*
splendid /ˈsplendɪd/ *a* herrlich, großartig
splendour /ˈsplendə(r)/ *n* Pracht *f*
splint /splɪnt/ *n* (*Med*) Schiene *f*
splinter /ˈsplɪntə(r)/ *n* Splitter *m* □ *vi* zersplittern
split /splɪt/ *n* Spaltung *f*; (*Pol*) Bruch *m*; (*tear*) Riss *m* □ *v* (*pt/pp* **split**, *pres p* **splitting**) □ *vt* spalten; (*share*) teilen; (*tear*) zerreißen; **~ one's sides** sich kaputtlachen □ *vi* sich spalten; (*tear*) zerreißen; **~ on s.o.** (*fam*) jdn verpfeifen. **~ up** *vt* aufteilen □ *vi* ⟨*couple:*⟩ sich trennen
splutter /ˈsplʌtə(r)/ *vi* prusten
spoil /spɔɪl/ *n* **~s** *pl* Beute *f* □ *v* (*pt/pp* **spoilt** *or* **spoiled**) □ *vt* verderben; verwöhnen ⟨*person*⟩ □ *vi* verderben. **~sport** *n* Spielverderber *m*
spoke[1] /spəʊk/ *n* Speiche *f*
spoke[2], **spoken** /ˈspəʊkn/ *see* **speak**
ˈspokesman *n* Sprecher *m*
sponge /spʌndʒ/ *n* Schwamm *m* □ *vt* abwaschen □ *vi* **~ on** schmarotzen bei. **~-bag** *n* Waschbeutel *m*. **~-cake** *n* Biskuitkuchen *m*
spong|er /ˈspʌndʒə(r)/ *n* Schmarotzer *m*. **~y** *a* schwammig
sponsor /ˈspɒnsə(r)/ *n* Sponsor *m*; (*god-parent*) Pate *m*/Patin *f*; (*for membership*) Bürge *m* □ *vt* sponsern; bürgen für
spontaneous /spɒnˈteɪnɪəs/ *a*, **-ly** *adv* spontan
spoof /spu:f/ *n* (*fam*) Parodie *f*
spooky /ˈspu:kɪ/ *a* (**-ier, -iest**) (*fam*) gespenstisch
spool /spu:l/ *n* Spule *f*
spoon /spu:n/ *n* Löffel *m* □ *vt* löffeln. **~-feed** *vt* (*pt/pp* **-fed**) (*fig*) alles vorkauen (+ *dat*). **~ful** *n* Löffel *m*
sporadic /spəˈrædɪk/ *a*, **-ally** *adv* sporadisch
sport /spɔ:t/ *n* Sport *m*; (*amusement*) Spaß *m* □ *vt* [stolz] tragen. **~ing** *a* sportlich; **a ~ing chance** eine faire Chance
sports: ~car *n* Sportwagen *m*. **~ coat** *n*, **~ jacket** *n* Sakko *m*. **~man** *n* Sportler *m*. **~woman** *n* Sportlerin *f*
sporty /ˈspɔ:tɪ/ *a* (**-ier, -iest**) sportlich

spot /spɒt/ *n* Fleck *m*; (*place*) Stelle *f* (*dot*) Punkt *m*; (*drop*) Tropfen *m*; (*pimple*) Pickel *m*; **~s** *pl* (*rash*) Ausschlag *m*; **a ~ of** (*fam*) ein bisschen; **on the ~** auf der Stelle; **be in a tight ~** (*fam*) in der Klemme sitzen □ *vt* (*pt/pp* **spotted**) entdecken

spot: ~ 'check *n* Stichprobe *f*. **~less** *a* makellos; (*fam: very clean*) blitzsauber. **~light** *n* Scheinwerfer *m*; (*fig*) Rampenlicht *nt*

spotted /'spɒtɪd/ *a* gepunktet

spotty /'spɒtɪ/ *a* (**-ier, -iest**) fleckig; (*pimply*) pickelig

spouse /spaʊz/ *n* Gatte *m*/Gattin *f*

spout /spaʊt/ *n* Schnabel *m*, Tülle *f* □ *vi* schießen (**from** aus)

sprain /spreɪn/ *n* Verstauchung *f* □ *vt* verstauchen

sprang /spræŋ/ *see* **spring²**

sprat /spræt/ *n* Sprotte *f*

sprawl /sprɔ:l/ *vi* sich ausstrecken; (*fall*) der Länge nach hinfallen

spray¹ /spreɪ/ *n* (*of flowers*) Strauß *m*

spray² *n* Sprühnebel *m*; (*from sea*) Gischt *m*; (*device*) Spritze *f*; (*container*) Sprühdose *f*; (*preparation*) Spray *nt* □ *vt* spritzen; (*with aerosol*) sprühen

spread /spred/ *n* Verbreitung *f*; (*paste*) Aufstrich *m*; (*fam: feast*) Festessen *nt* □ *v* (*pt/pp* **spread**) □ *vt* ausbreiten; streichen ⟨*butter, jam*⟩; bestreichen ⟨*bread, surface*⟩; streuen ⟨*sand, manure*⟩; verbreiten ⟨*news, disease*⟩; verteilen ⟨*payments*⟩ □ *vi* sich ausbreiten. **~ out** *vt* ausbreiten; (*space out*) verteilen □ *vi* sich verteilen

spree /spri:/ *n* (*fam*) **go on a shopping ~** groß einkaufen gehen

sprig /sprɪg/ *n* Zweig *m*

sprightly /'spraɪtlɪ/ *a* (**-ier, -iest**) rüstig

spring¹ /sprɪŋ/ *n* Frühling *m* □ *attrib* Frühlings-

spring² *n* (*jump*) Sprung *m*; (*water*) Quelle *f*; (*device*) Feder *f*; (*elasticity*) Elastizität *f* □ *v* (*pt* **sprang**, *pp* **sprung**) □ *vi* springen; (*arise*) entspringen (**from** *dat*) □ *vt* **~ sth on s.o.** jdn mit etw überfallen

spring: ~board *n* Sprungbrett *nt*. **~-'cleaning** *n* Frühjahrsputz *m*. **~time** *n* Frühling *m*

sprinkl|e /'sprɪŋkl/ *vt* sprengen; (*scatter*) streuen; bestreuen ⟨*surface*⟩. **~er** *n* Sprinkler *m*; (*Hort*) Sprenger *m*. **~ing** *n* dünne Schicht *f*

sprint /sprɪnt/ *n* Sprint *m* □ *vi* rennen; (*Sport*) sprinten. **~er** *n* Kurzstreckenläufer(in) *m(f)*

sprout /spraʊt/ *n* Trieb *m*; **[Brussels] ~s** *pl* Rosenkohl *m* □ *vi* sprießen

spruce /spru:s/ *a* gepflegt □ *n* Fichte *f*

sprung /sprʌŋ/ *see* **spring²** □ *a* gefedert

spry /spraɪ/ *a* (**-er, -est**) rüstig

spud /spʌd/ *n* (*fam*) Kartoffel *f*

spun /spʌn/ *see* **spin**

spur /spɜ:(r)/ *n* Sporn *m*; (*stimulus*) Ansporn *m*; (*road*) Nebenstraße *f*; **on the ~ of the moment** ganz spontan □ *vt* (*pt/pp* **spurred**) **~ [on]** (*fig*) anspornen

spurious /'spjʊərɪəs/ *a*, **-ly** *adv* falsch

spurn /spɜ:n/ *vt* verschmähen

spurt /spɜ:t/ *n* Strahl *m*; (*Sport*) Spurt *m*; **put on a ~** spurten □ *vi* spritzen

spy /spaɪ/ *n* Spion(in) *m(f)* □ *vi* spionieren; **~ on s.o.** jdm nachspionieren. □ *vt* (*fam: see*) sehen. **~ out** *vt* auskundschaften

spying /'spaɪɪŋ/ *n* Spionage *f*

squabble /'skwɒbl/ *n* Zank *m* □ *vi* sich zanken

squad /skwɒd/ *n* Gruppe *f*; (*Sport*) Mannschaft *f*

squadron /'skwɒdrən/ *n* (*Mil*) Geschwader *nt*

squalid /ˈskwɒlɪd/ *a*, **-ly** *adv* schmutzig
squall /skwɔːl/ *n* Bö *f* □ *vi* brüllen
squalor /ˈskwɒlə(r)/ *n* Schmutz *m*
squander /ˈskwɒndə(r)/ *vt* vergeuden
square /skweə(r)/ *a* quadratisch; ⟨*metre, mile*⟩ Quadrat-; ⟨*meal*⟩ anständig; **all** ~ (*fam*) quitt □ *n* Quadrat *nt*; (*area*) Platz *m*; (*on chessboard*) Feld *nt* □ *vt* (*settle*) klären; (*Math*) quadrieren □ *vi* (*agree*) übereinstimmen
squash /skwɒʃ/ *n* Gedränge *nt*; (*drink*) Fruchtsaftgetränk *nt*; (*Sport*) Squash *nt* □ *vt* zerquetschen; (*suppress*) niederschlagen. **~y** *a* weich
squat /skwɒt/ *a* gedrungen □ *n* (*fam*) besetztes Haus *nt* □ *vi* (*pt/pp* **squatted**) hocken; **~ in a house** ein Haus besetzen. **~ter** *n* Hausbesetzer *m*
squawk /skwɔːk/ *vi* krächzen
squeak /skwiːk/ *n* Quieken *nt*; (*of hinge, brakes*) Quietschen *nt* □ *vi* quieken; quietschen
squeal /skwiːl/ *n* Schrei *m*; (*screech*) Kreischen *nt* □ *vi* schreien; kreischen
squeamish /ˈskwiːmɪʃ/ *a* empfindlich
squeeze /skwiːz/ *n* Druck *m*; (*crush*) Gedränge *nt* □ *vt* drücken; (*to get juice*) ausdrücken; (*force*) zwängen; (*fam: extort*) herauspressen (**from** aus) □ *vi* **~ in/out** sich hinein-/hinauszwängen
squelch /skweltʃ/ *vi* quatschen
squid /skwɪd/ *n* Tintenfisch *m*
squiggle /ˈskwɪgl/ *n* Schnörkel *m*
squint /skwɪnt/ *n* Schielen *nt* □ *vi* schielen
squire /ˈskwaɪə(r)/ *n* Gutsherr *m*
squirm /skwɜːm/ *vi* sich winden
squirrel /ˈskwɪrl/ *n* Eichhörnchen *nt*
squirt /skwɜːt/ *n* Spritzer *m* □ *vt/i* spritzen
St *abbr* (**Saint**) St.; (**Street**) Str.
stab /stæb/ *n* Stich *m*; (*fam: attempt*) Versuch *m* □ *vt* (*pt/pp* **stabbed**) stechen; (*to death*) erstechen
stability /stəˈbɪlətɪ/ *n* Stabilität *f*
stabilize /ˈsteɪbɪlaɪz/ *vt* stabilisieren □ *vi* sich stabilisieren
stable¹ /ˈsteɪbl/ *a* (**-r, -st**) stabil
stable² *n* Stall *m*; (*establishment*) Reitstall *m*
stack /stæk/ *n* Stapel *m*; (*of chimney*) Schornstein *m*; (*fam: large quantity*) Haufen *m* □ *vt* stapeln
stadium /ˈsteɪdɪəm/ *n* Stadion *nt*
staff /stɑːf/ *n* (*stick & Mil*) Stab *m* □ (*& pl*) (*employees*) Personal *nt*; (*Sch*) Lehrkräfte *pl* □ *vt* mit Personal besetzen. **~-room** *n* (*Sch*) Lehrerzimmer *nt*
stag /stæg/ *n* Hirsch *m*
stage /steɪdʒ/ *n* Bühne *f*; (*in journey*) Etappe *f*; (*in process*) Stadium *nt*; **by** *or* **in ~s** in Etappen □ *vt* aufführen; (*arrange*) veranstalten
stage: ~ door *n* Bühneneingang *m*. **~ fright** *n* Lampenfieber *nt*
stagger /ˈstægə(r)/ *vi* taumeln □ *vt* staffeln ⟨*holidays*⟩; versetzt anordnen ⟨*seats*⟩; **I was ~ed** es hat mir die Sprache verschlagen. **~ing** *a* unglaublich
stagnant /ˈstægnənt/ *a* stehend; (*fig*) stagnierend
stagnat|e /stægˈneɪt/ *vi* (*fig*) stagnieren. **~ion** /-ˈneɪʃn/ *n* Stagnation *f*
staid /steɪd/ *a* gesetzt
stain /steɪn/ *n* Fleck *m*; (*for wood*) Beize *f* □ *vt* färben; beizen ⟨*wood*⟩; (*fig*) beflecken; **~ed glass** farbiges Glas *nt*. **~less** *a* fleckenlos; ⟨*steel*⟩ rostfrei. **~ remover** *n* Fleckentferner *m*
stair /steə(r)/ *n* Stufe *f*; **~s** *pl* Treppe *f*. **~case** *n* Treppe *f*
stake /steɪk/ *n* Pfahl *m*; (*wager*) Einsatz *m*; (*Comm*) Anteil *m*; **be at ~** auf dem Spiel stehen □ *vt* [an einem Pfahl] anbinden; (*wager*)

setzen; **~ a claim to sth** Anspruch auf etw (*acc*) erheben

stale /steɪl/ *a* (**-r, -st**) alt; ⟨*air*⟩ verbraucht. **~mate** *n* Patt *nt*

stalk¹ /stɔːk/ *n* Stiel *m*, Stängel *m*

stalk² *vt* pirschen auf (+ *acc*) □ *vi* stolzieren

stall /stɔːl/ *n* Stand *m*; **~s** *pl* (*Theat*) Parkett *nt* □ *vi* ⟨*engine:*⟩ stehen bleiben; (*fig*) ausweichen □ *vt* abwürgen ⟨*engine*⟩

stallion /ˈstæljən/ *n* Hengst *m*

stalwart /ˈstɔːlwət/ *a* treu □ *n* treuer Anhänger *m*

stamina /ˈstæmɪnə/ *n* Ausdauer *f*

stammer /ˈstæmə(r)/ *n* Stottern *nt* □ *vt/i* stottern

stamp /stæmp/ *n* Stempel *m*; (*postage* **~**) [Brief]marke *f* □ *vt* stempeln; (*impress*) prägen; (*put postage on*) frankieren; **~ one's feet** mit den Füßen stampfen □ *vi* stampfen. **~ out** *vt* [aus]stanzen; (*fig*) ausmerzen

stampede /stæmˈpiːd/ *n* wilde Flucht *f*; (*fam*) Ansturm *m* □ *vi* in Panik fliehen

stance /stɑːns/ *n* Haltung *f*

stand /stænd/ *n* Stand *m*; (*rack*) Ständer *m*; (*pedestal*) Sockel *m*; (*Sport*) Tribüne *f*; (*fig*) Einstellung *f* □ *v* (*pt/pp* **stood**) □ *vi* stehen; (*rise*) aufstehen; (*be candidate*) kandidieren; (*stay valid*) gültig bleiben; **~ still** stillstehen; **~ firm** (*fig*) festbleiben; **~ together** zusammenhalten; **~ to lose / gain** gewinnen / verlieren können; **~ to reason** logisch sein; **~ in for** vertreten; **~ for** (*mean*) bedeuten; **I won't ~ for that** das lasse ich mir nicht bieten □ *vt* stellen; (*withstand*) standhalten (+ *dat*); (*endure*) ertragen; vertragen ⟨*climate*⟩; (*put up with*) aushalten; haben ⟨*chance*⟩; **~ one's ground** nicht nachgeben; **~ the test of time** sich bewähren; **~ s.o. a beer** jdm ein Bier spendieren; **I can't ~ her** (*fam*) ich kann sie nicht ausstehen. **~ by** *vi* daneben stehen; (*be ready*) sich bereithalten □ *vt* **by s.o.** (*fig*) zu jdm stehen. **~ down** *vi* (*retire*) zurücktreten. **~ out** *vi* hervorstehen; (*fig*) herausragen. **~ up** *vi* aufstehen; **~ up for** eintreten für; **~ up to** sich wehren gegen

standard /ˈstændəd/ *a* Normal-; **be ~ practice** allgemein üblich sein □ *n* Maßstab *m*; (*Techn*) Norm *f*; (*level*) Niveau *nt*; (*flag*) Standarte *f*; **~s** *pl* (*morals*) Prinzipien *pl*; **~ of living** Lebensstandard *m*. **~ize** *vt* standardisieren; (*Techn*) normen

ˈstandard lamp *n* Stehlampe *f*

ˈstand-in *n* Ersatz *m*

standing /ˈstændɪŋ/ *a* (*erect*) stehend; (*permanent*) ständig □ *n* Rang *m*; (*duration*) Dauer *f*. **~ ˈorder** *n* Dauerauftrag *m*. **~-room** *n* Stehplätze *pl*

stand: ~-offish /stændˈɒfɪʃ/ *a* distanziert. **~point** *n* Standpunkt *m*. **~still** *n* Stillstand *m*; **come to a ~still** zum Stillstand kommen

stank /stæŋk/ *see* **stink**

staple¹ /ˈsteɪpl/ *a* Grund- □ *n* (*product*) Haupterzeugnis *nt*

staple² *n* Heftklammer *f* □ *vt* heften. **~r** *n* Heftmaschine *f*

star /stɑː(r)/ *n* Stern *m*; (*asterisk*) Sternchen *nt*; (*Theat, Sport*) Star *m* □ *vi* (*pt/pp* **starred**) die Hauptrolle spielen

starboard /ˈstɑːbəd/ *n* Steuerbord *nt*

starch /stɑːtʃ/ *n* Stärke *f* □ *vt* stärken. **~y** *a* stärkehaltig; (*fig*) steif

stare /steə(r)/ *n* Starren *nt* □ *vt* starren; **~ at** anstarren

ˈstarfish *n* Seestern *m*

stark /stɑːk/ *a* (**-er, -est**) scharf; ⟨*contrast*⟩ krass □ *adv* **~ naked** splitternackt

starling /ˈstɑːlɪŋ/ *n* Star *m*

ˈstarlit *a* sternhell

starry /ˈstɑːrɪ/ *a* sternklar

start /stɑ:t/ *n* Anfang *m*, Beginn *m*; (*departure*) Aufbruch *m*; (*Sport*) Start *m*; **from the ~** von Anfang an; **for a ~** erstens □ *vi* anfangen, beginnen; (*set out*) aufbrechen; ⟨*engine:*⟩ anspringen; (*Auto, Sport*) starten; (*jump*) aufschrecken; **to ~ with** zuerst □ *vt* anfangen, beginnen; (*cause*) verursachen; (*found*) gründen; starten ⟨*car, race*⟩; in Umlauf setzen ⟨*rumour*⟩. **~er** *n* (*Culin*) Vorspeise *f*; (*Auto, Sport*) Starter *m*. **~ing-point** *n* Ausgangspunkt *m*

startle /'stɑ:tl/ *vt* erschrecken

starvation /stɑ:'veɪʃn/ *n* Verhungern *nt*

starve /stɑ:v/ *vi* hungern; (*to death*) verhungern □ *vt* verhungern lassen

stash /stæʃ/ *vt* (*fam*) **~ [away]** beiseite schaffen

state /steɪt/ *n* Zustand *m*; (*grand style*) Prunk *m*; (*Pol*) Staat *m*; **~ of play** Spielstand *m*; **be in a ~** ⟨*person:*⟩ aufgeregt sein; **lie in ~** feierlich aufgebahrt sein □ *attrib* Staats-, staatlich □ *vt* erklären; (*specify*) angeben. **~-aided** *a* staatlich gefördert. **~less** *a* staatenlos

stately /'steɪtlɪ/ *a* (**-ier, -iest**) stattlich. **~ 'home** *n* Schloss *nt*

statement /'steɪtmənt/ *n* Erklärung *f*; (*Jur*) Aussage *f*; (*Banking*) Auszug *m*

'statesman *n* Staatsmann *m*

static /'stætɪk/ *a* statisch; **remain ~** unverändert bleiben

station /'steɪʃn/ *n* Bahnhof *m*; (*police*) Wache *f*; (*radio*) Sender *m*; (*space, weather*) Station *f*; (*Mil*) Posten *m*; (*status*) Rang *m* □ *vt* stationieren; (*post*) postieren. **~ary** /-ərɪ/ *a* stehend; **be ~ary** stehen

stationer /'steɪʃənə(r)/ *n* **~'s [shop]** Schreibwarengeschäft *nt*. **~y** *n* Briefpapier *nt*; (*writing-materials*) Schreibwaren *pl*

'station-wagon *n* (*Amer*) Kombi[wagen] *n*

statistic /stə'tɪstɪk/ *n* statistische Tatsache *f*. **~al** *a*, **-ly** *adv* statistisch. **~s** *n & pl* Statistik *f*

statue /'stætju:/ *n* Statue *f*

stature /'stætʃə(r)/ *n* Statur *f*; (*fig*) Format *nt*

status /'steɪtəs/ *n* Status *m*, Rang *m*. **~ symbol** *n* Statussymbol *nt*

statut|e /'stætju:t/ *n* Statut *nt*. **~ory** *a* gesetzlich

staunch /stɔ:ntʃ/ *a* (**-er, -est**), **-ly** *adv* treu

stave /steɪv/ *vt* **~ off** abwenden

stay /steɪ/ *n* Aufenthalt *m* □ *vi* bleiben; (*reside*) wohnen; **~ the night** übernachten; **~ put** dableiben □ *vt* **~ the course** durchhalten. **~ away** *vi* wegbleiben. **~ behind** *vi* zurückbleiben. **~ in** *vi* zu Hause bleiben; (*Sch*) nachsitzen. **~ up** *vi* oben bleiben; (*upright*) stehen bleiben; (*on wall*) hängen bleiben; ⟨*person:*⟩ aufbleiben

stead /sted/ *n* **in his ~** an seiner Stelle; **stand s.o. in good ~** jdm zustatten kommen. **~fast** *a*, **-ly** *adv* standhaft

steadily /'stedɪlɪ/ *adv* fest; (*continually*) stetig

steady /'stedɪ/ *a* (**-ier, -iest**) fest; (*not wobbly*) stabil; ⟨*hand*⟩ ruhig; (*regular*) regelmäßig; (*dependable*) zuverlässig

steak /steɪk/ *n* Steak *nt*

steal /sti:l/ *vt/i* (*pt* **stole**, *pp* **stolen**) stehlen (**from** *dat*). **~ in/out** *vi* sich hinein-/hinausstehlen

stealth /stelθ/ *n* Heimlichkeit *f*; **by ~** heimlich. **~y** *a* heimlich

steam /sti:m/ *n* Dampf *m*; **under one's own ~** (*fam*) aus eigener Kraft □ *vt* (*Culin*) dämpfen, dünsten □ *vi* dampfen. **~ up** *vi* beschlagen

'steam-engine *n* Dampfmaschine *f*; (*Rail*) Dampflokomotive *f*

steamer /'sti:mə(r)/ *n* Dampfer *m*

'**steamroller** *n* Dampfwalze *f*
steamy /'sti:mɪ/ *a* dampfig
steel /sti:l/ *n* Stahl *m* □ *vt* ~ **oneself** allen Mut zusammennehmen
steep[1] /sti:p/ *vt* (*soak*) einweichen
steep[2] *a*, **-ly** *adv* steil; (*fam: exorbitant*) gesalzen
steeple /'sti:pl/ *n* Kirchturm *m*. ~**chase** *n* Hindernisrennen *nt*
steer /stɪə(r)/ *vt/i* steuern; ~ **clear of s.o./sth** jdm/ etw aus dem Weg gehen. ~**ing** *n* (*Auto*) Steuerung *f*. ~**ing-wheel** *n* Lenkrad *nt*
stem[1] /stem/ *n* Stiel *m*; (*of word*) Stamm *m* □ *vi* (*pt/pp* **stemmed**) ~ **from** zurückzuführen sein auf (+ *acc*)
stem[2] *vt* (*pt/pp* **stemmed**) eindämmen; stillen ⟨*bleeding*⟩
stench /stentʃ/ *n* Gestank *m*
stencil /'stensl/ *n* Schablone *f*; (*for typing*) Matrize *f*
step /step/ *n* Schritt *m*; (*stair*) Stufe *f*; ~**s** *pl* (*ladder*) Trittleiter *f*; **in** ~ im Schritt; ~ **by** ~ Schritt für Schritt; **take** ~**s** (*fig*) Schritte unternehmen □ *vi* (*pt/pp* **stepped**) treten; ~ **in** (*fig*) eingreifen; ~ **into s.o.'s shoes** an jds Stelle treten; ~ **out of line** aus der Reihe tanzen. ~ **up** *vi* hinaufsteigen □ *vt* (*increase*) erhöhen, steigern; verstärken ⟨*efforts*⟩
step: ~**brother** *n* Stiefbruder *m*. ~**child** *n* Stiefkind *nt*. ~**daughter** *n* Stieftochter *f*. ~**father** *n* Stiefvater *m*. ~**-ladder** *n* Trittleiter *f*. ~**mother** *n* Stiefmutter *f*
'**stepping-stone** *n* Trittstein *m*; (*fig*) Sprungbrett *nt*
step: ~**sister** *n* Stiefschwester *f*. ~**son** *n* Stiefsohn *m*
stereo /'sterɪəʊ/ *n* Stereo *nt*; (*equipment*) Stereoanlage *f*; **in** ~ stereo. ~**phonic** /-'fɒnɪk/ *a* stereophon
stereotype /'sterɪətaɪp/ *n* stereotype Figur *f*. ~**d** *a* stereotyp
steril|e /'steraɪl/ *a* steril. ~**ity** /stə'rɪlətɪ/ *n* Sterilität *f*
steriliz|ation /sterəlaɪ'zeɪʃn/ *n* Sterilisation *f*. ~**e** *vt* sterilisieren
sterling /'stɜ:lɪŋ/ *a* Sterling-; (*fig*) gediegen □ *n* Sterling *m*
stern[1] /stɜ:n/ *a* (**-er, -est**), **-ly** *adv* streng
stern[2] *n* (*of boat*) Heck *nt*
stew /stju:/ *n* Eintopf *m*; **in a** ~ (*fam*) aufgeregt □ *vt/i* schmoren; ~**ed fruit** Kompott *nt*
steward /'stju:əd/ *n* Ordner *m*; (*on ship, aicraft*) **Steward** *m*. ~**ess** *n* Stewardess *f*
stick[1] /stɪk/ *n* Stock *m*; (*of chalk*) Stück *nt*; (*of rhubarb*) Stange *f*; (*Sport*) Schläger *m*
stick[2] *v* (*pt/pp* **stuck**) □ *vt* stecken; (*stab*) stechen; (*glue*) kleben; (*fam: put*) tun; (*fam: endure*) aushalten □ *vi* stecken; (*adhere*) kleben, haften (**to** an + *dat*); (*jam*) klemmen; ~ **to sth** (*fig*) bei etw bleiben; ~ **at it** (*fam*) dranbleiben; ~ **at nothing** (*fam*) vor nichts zurückschrecken; ~ **up for** (*fam*) eintreten für; **be stuck** nicht weiterkönnen; ⟨*vehicle:*⟩ festsitzen, festgefahren sein; ⟨*drawer:*⟩ klemmen; **be stuck with sth** (*fam*) etw am Hals haben. ~ **out** *vi* abstehen; (*project*) vorstehen □ *vt* (*fam*) hinausstrecken; herausstrecken ⟨*tongue*⟩
sticker /'stɪkə(r)/ *n* Aufkleber *m*
'**sticking plaster** *n* Heftpflaster *nt*
stickler /'stɪklə(r)/ *n* **be a** ~ **for** es sehr genau nehmen mit
sticky /'stɪkɪ/ *a* (**-ier, -iest**) klebrig; (*adhesive*) Klebe-
stiff /stɪf/ *a* (**-er, -est**), **-ly** *adv* steif; ⟨*brush*⟩ hart; ⟨*dough*⟩ fest; (*difficult*) schwierig; ⟨*penalty*⟩ schwer; **be bored** ~ (*fam*) sich zu Tode langweilen. ~**en** *vt* steif machen □ *vi* steif werden. ~**ness** *n* Steifheit *f*

stifl|e /'staɪfl/ *vt* ersticken; (*fig*) unterdrücken. **~ing** *a* **be ~ing** zum Ersticken sein
stigma /'stɪgmə/ *n* Stigma *nt*
stile /staɪl/ *n* Zauntritt *m*
stiletto /stɪ'letəʊ/ *n* Stilett *nt*; (*heel*) Bleistiftabsatz *m*
still[1] /stɪl/ *n* Destillierapparat *m*
still[2] *a* still; ⟨*drink*⟩ ohne Kohlensäure; **keep ~** stillhalten; **stand ~** stillstehen □ *n* Stille *f* □ *adv* noch; (*emphatic*) immer noch; (*nevertheless*) trotzdem; **~ not** immer noch nicht
'stillborn *a* tot geboren
still 'life *n* Stillleben *nt*
stilted /'stɪltɪd/ *a* gestelzt, geschraubt
stilts /stɪlts/ *npl* Stelzen *pl*
stimulant /'stɪmjʊlənt/ *n* Anregungsmittel *nt*
stimulat|e /'stɪmjʊleɪt/ *vt* anregen. **~ion** /-'leɪʃn/ *n* Anregung *f*
stimulus /'stɪmjʊləs/ *n* (*pl* **-li** /-laɪ/) Reiz *m*
sting /stɪŋ/ *n* Stich *m*; (*from nettle, jellyfish*) Brennen *nt*; (*organ*) Stachel *m* □ *v* (*pt/pp* **stung**) □ *vt* stechen □ *vi* brennen; ⟨*insect:*⟩ stechen. **~ing nettle** *n* Brennnessel *f*
stingy /'stɪndʒɪ/ *a* (**-ier, -iest**) geizig, (*fam*) knauserig
stink /stɪŋk/ *n* Gestank *m* □ *vi* (*pt* **stank**, *pp* **stunk**) stinken (**of** nach)
stint /stɪnt/ *n* Pensum *nt* □ *vi* **~ on** sparen an (+ *dat*)
stipulat|e /'stɪpjʊleɪt/ *vt* vorschreiben. **~ion** /-'leɪʃn/ *n* Bedingung *f*
stir /stɜ:(r)/ *n* (*commotion*) Aufregung *f* □ *v* (*pt/pp* **stirred**) *vt* rühren □ *vi* sich rühren
stirrup /'stɪrəp/ *n* Steigbügel *m*
stitch /stɪtʃ/ *n* Stich *m*; (*Knitting*) Masche *f*; (*pain*) Seitenstechen *nt*; **be in ~es** (*fam*) sich kaputtlachen □ *vt* nähen
stoat /stəʊt/ *n* Hermelin *nt*
stock /stɒk/ *n* Vorrat *m* (**of** an + *dat*); (*in shop*) [Waren]bestand *m*; (*livestock*) Vieh *nt*; (*lineage*) Abstammung *f*; (*Finance*) Wertpapiere *pl*; (*Culin*) Brühe *f*; (*plant*) Levkoje *f*; **in/out of ~** vorrätig/nicht vorrätig; **take ~** (*fig*) Bilanz ziehen □ *a* Standard- □ *vt* ⟨*shop:*⟩ führen; auffüllen ⟨*shelves*⟩. **~ up** *vi* sich eindecken (**with** mit)
stock: ~broker *n* Börsenmakler *m*. **~ cube** *n* Brühwürfel *m*. **S~ Exchange** *n* Börse *f*
stocking /'stɒkɪŋ/ *n* Strumpf *m*
stockist /'stɒkɪst/ *n* Händler *m*
stock: ~market *n* Börse *f*. **~pile** *vt* horten; anhäufen ⟨*weapons*⟩. **~-'still** *a* bewegungslos. **~-taking** *n* (*Comm*) Inventur *f*
stocky /'stɒkɪ/ *a* (**-ier, -iest**) untersetzt
stodgy /'stɒdʒɪ/ *a* pappig [und schwer verdaulich]
stoical /'stəʊɪkl/ *a*, **-ly** *adv* stoisch
stoke /stəʊk/ *vt* heizen
stole[1] /stəʊl/ *n* Stola *f*
stole[2], **stolen** /'stəʊlən/ *see* **steal**
stolid /'stɒlɪd/ *a*, **-ly** *adv* stur
stomach /'stʌmək/ *n* Magen *m* □ *vt* vertragen. **~-ache** *n* Magenschmerzen *pl*
stone /stəʊn/ *n* Stein *m*; (*weight*) 6,35kg □ *a* steinern; ⟨*wall, Age*⟩ Stein- □ *vt* mit Steinen bewerfen; entsteinen ⟨*fruit*⟩. **~-cold** *a* eiskalt. **~-'deaf** *n* (*fam*) stocktaub
stony /'stəʊnɪ/ *a* steinig
stood /stʊd/ *see* stand
stool /stu:l/ *n* Hocker *m*
stoop /stu:p/ *n* **walk with a ~** gebeugt gehen □ *vi* sich bücken; (*fig*) sich erniedrigen
stop /stɒp/ *n* Halt *m*; (*break*) Pause *f*; (*for bus*) Haltestelle *f*; (*for train*) Station *f*; (*Gram*) Punkt *m*; (*on organ*) Register *nt*; **come to a ~** stehen bleiben; **put a ~ to sth** etw unterbinden □ *v*

(*pt/pp* **stopped**) □ *vt* anhalten, stoppen; (*switch off*) abstellen; (*plug, block*) zustopfen; (*prevent*) verhindern; ~ **s.o. doing sth** jdn daran hindern, etw zu tun; ~ **doing sth** aufhören, etw zu tun; ~ **that!** hör auf damit! lass das sein! □ *vi* anhalten; (*cease*) aufhören; ⟨*clock:*⟩ stehen bleiben; (*fam: stay*) bleiben (**with** bei) □ *int* halt! stopp!

stop: ~**gap** *n* Notlösung *f*. ~**over** *n* Zwischenaufenthalt *m*; (*Aviat*) Zwischenlandung *f*

stoppage /ˈstɒpɪdʒ/ *n* Unterbrechung *f*; (*strike*) Streik *m*; (*deduction*) Abzug *m*

stopper /ˈstɒpə(r)/ *n* Stöpsel *m*

stop: ~**-press** *n* letzte Meldungen *pl*. ~**-watch** *n* Stoppuhr *f*

storage /ˈstɔːrɪdʒ/ *n* Aufbewahrung *f*; (*in warehouse*) Lagerung *f*; (*Computing*) Speicherung *f*

store /stɔː(r)/ *n* (*stock*) Vorrat *m*; (*shop*) Laden *m*; (*department* ~) Kaufhaus *nt*; (*depot*) Lager *nt*; **in** ~ auf Lager; **put in** ~ lagern; **set great** ~ **by** großen Wert legen auf (+ *acc*); **be in** ~ **for s.o.** (*fig*) jdm bevorstehen □ *vt* aufbewahren; (*in warehouse*) lagern; (*Computing*) speichern. ~**-room** *n* Lagerraum *m*

storey /ˈstɔːrɪ/ *n* Stockwerk *nt*

stork /stɔːk/ *n* Storch *m*

storm /stɔːm/ *n* Sturm *m*; (*with thunder*) Gewitter *nt* □ *vt/i* stürmen. ~**y** *a* stürmisch

story /ˈstɔːrɪ/ *n* Geschichte *f*; (*in newspaper*) Artikel *m*; (*fam: lie*) Märchen *nt*

stout /staʊt/ *a* (**-er, -est**) beleibt; (*strong*) fest

stove /stəʊv/ *n* Ofen *m*; (*for cooking*) Herd *m*

stow /stəʊ/ *vt* verstauen. ~**away** *n* blinder Passagier *m*

straddle /ˈstrædl/ *vt* rittlings sitzen auf (+ *dat*); (*standing*) mit gespreizten Beinen stehen über (*dat*)

straggl|e /ˈstrægl/ *vi* hinterherhinken. ~**er** *n* Nachzügler *m*. ~**y** *a* strähnig

straight /streɪt/ *a* (**-er, -est**) gerade; (*direct*) direkt; (*clear*) klar; ⟨*hair*⟩ glatt; ⟨*drink*⟩ pur; **be** ~ (*tidy*) in Ordnung sein □ *adv* gerade; (*directly*) direkt, geradewegs; (*clearly*) klar; ~ **away** sofort; ~ **on** *or* **ahead** geradeaus; ~ **out** (*fig*) geradeheraus; **go** ~ (*fam*) ein ehrliches Leben führen; **put sth** ~ etw in Ordnung bringen; **sit/stand up** ~ gerade sitzen/stehen

straighten /ˈstreɪtn/ *vt* gerade machen; (*put straight*) gerade richten □ *vi* gerade werden; ~ **[up]** ⟨*person:*⟩ sich aufrichten. ~ **out** *vt* gerade biegen

straightˈforward *a* offen; (*simple*) einfach

strain[1] /streɪn/ *n* Rasse *f*; (*Bot*) Sorte *f*; (*of virus*) Art *f*

strain[2] *n* Belastung *f*; ~**s** *pl* (*of music*) Klänge *pl* □ *vt* belasten; (*overexert*) überanstrengen; (*injure*) zerren ⟨*muscle*⟩; (*Culin*) durchseihen; abgießen ⟨*vegetables*⟩ □ *vi* sich anstrengen. ~**ed** *a* ⟨*relations*⟩ gespannt. ~**er** *n* Sieb *nt*

strait /streɪt/ *n* Meerenge *f*; **in dire** ~**s** in großen Nöten. ~**-jacket** *n* Zwangsjacke *f*. ~**-ˈlaced** *a* puritanisch

strand[1] /strænd/ *n* (*of thread*) Faden *m*; (*of beads*) Kette *f*; (*of hair*) Strähne *f*

strand[2] *vt* **be** ~**ed** festsitzen

strange /streɪndʒ/ *a* (**-r, -st**) fremd; (*odd*) seltsam, merkwürdig. ~**r** *n* Fremde(r) *m/f*

strangely /ˈstreɪndʒlɪ/ *adv* seltsam, merkwürdig; ~ **enough** seltsamerweise

strangle /ˈstræŋgl/ *vt* erwürgen; (*fig*) unterdrücken

strangulation /strængjʊˈleɪʃn/ *n* Erwürgen *nt*

strap /stræp/ *n* Riemen *m*; (*for safety*) Gurt *m*; (*to grasp in vehicle*) Halteriemen *m*; (*of watch*) Armband *nt*; (*shoulder-*) Träger *m* □ *vt* (*pt/pp* **strapped**) schnallen; ~ **in** *or* **down** festschnallen

strapping /'stræpɪŋ/ *a* stramm

strata /'strɑ:tə/ *npl see* **stratum**

stratagem /'strætədʒəm/ *n* Kriegslist *f*

strategic /strə'ti:dʒɪk/ *a*, **-ally** *adv* strategisch

strategy /'strætədʒɪ/ *n* Strategie *f*

stratum /'strɑ:təm/ *n* (*pl* **strata**) Schicht *f*

straw /strɔ:/ *n* Stroh *nt*; (*single piece, drinking*) Strohhalm *m*; **that's the last** ~ jetzt reicht's aber

strawberry /'strɔ:bərɪ/ *n* Erdbeere *f*

stray /streɪ/ *a* streunend □ *n* streunendes Tier *nt* □ *vi* sich verirren; (*deviate*) abweichen

streak /stri:k/ *n* Streifen *m*; (*in hair*) Strähne *f*; (*fig: trait*) Zug *m* □ *vi* flitzen. ~**y** *a* streifig; ⟨*bacon*⟩ durchwachsen

stream /stri:m/ *n* Bach *m*; (*flow*) Strom *m*; (*current*) Strömung *f*; (*Sch*) Parallelzug *m* □ *vi* strömen; ~ **in/out** hinaus-/herausströmen

streamer /'stri:mə(r)/ *n* Luftschlange *f*; (*flag*) Wimpel *m*

'streamline *vt* (*fig*) rationalisieren. ~**d** *a* stromlinienförmig

street /stri:t/ *n* Straße *f*. ~**car** *n* (*Amer*) Straßenbahn *f*. ~**lamp** *n* Straßenlaterne *f*

strength /streŋθ/ *n* Stärke *f*; (*power*) Kraft *f*; **on the** ~ **of** auf Grund (+ *gen*). ~**en** *vt* stärken; (*reinforce*) verstärken

strenuous /'strenjʊəs/ *a* anstrengend

stress /stres/ *n* (*emphasis*) Betonung *f*; (*strain*) Belastung *f*; (*mental*) Stress *m* □ *vt* betonen; (*put a strain on*) belasten. ~**ful** *a* stressig (*fam*)

stretch /stretʃ/ *n* (*of road*) Strecke *f*; (*elasticity*) Elastizität *f*; **at a** ~ ohne Unterbrechung; **a long** ~ eine lange Zeit; **have a** ~ sich strecken □ *vt* strecken; (*widen*) dehnen; (*spread*) ausbreiten; fordern ⟨*person*⟩; ~ **one's legs** sich (*dat*) die Beine vertreten □ *vt* sich erstrecken; (*become wider*) sich dehnen; ⟨*person:*⟩ sich strecken. ~**er** *n* **Tragbahre** *f*

strew /stru:/ *vt* (*pp* **strewn** *or* **strewed**) streuen

stricken /'strɪkn/ *a* betroffen; ~ **with** heimgesucht von

strict /strɪkt/ *a* (**-er**, **-est**), **-ly** *adv* streng; ~**ly speaking** streng genommen

stride /straɪd/ *n* [großer] Schritt *m*; **make great** ~**s** (*fig*) große Fortschritte machen; **take sth in one's** ~ mit etw gut fertig werden □ *vi* (*pt* **strode**, *pp* **stridden**) [mit großen Schritten] gehen

strident /'straɪdnt/ *a*, **-ly** *adv* schrill; ⟨*colour*⟩ grell

strife /straɪf/ *n* Streit *m*

strike /straɪk/ *n* Streik *m*; (*Mil*) Angriff *m*; **be on** ~ streiken □ *v* (*pt/pp* **struck**) □ *vt* schlagen; (*knock against, collide with*) treffen; prägen ⟨*coin*⟩; anzünden ⟨*match*⟩; stoßen auf (+ *acc*) ⟨*oil, gold*⟩; abbrechen ⟨*camp*⟩; (*delete*) streichen; (*impress*) beeindrucken; (*occur to*) einfallen (+ *dat*); (*Mil*) angreifen; ~ **s.o. a blow** jdm einen Schlag versetzen □ *vi* treffen; ⟨*lightning:*⟩ einschlagen; ⟨*clock:*⟩ schlagen; (*attack*) zuschlagen; ⟨*workers:*⟩ streiken; ~ **lucky** Glück haben. ~**-breaker** *n* Streikbrecher *m*

striker /'straɪkə(r)/ *n* Streikende(r) *m/f*

striking /'straɪkɪŋ/ *a* auffallend

string /strɪŋ/ *n* Schnur *f*; (*thin*) Bindfaden *m*; (*of musical instrument, racket*) Saite *f*; (*of bow*) Sehne *f*; (*of pearls*) Kette *f*; **the ~s** (*Mus*) die Streicher *pl*; **pull ~s** (*fam*) seine Beziehungen spielen lassen, Fäden ziehen □ *vt* (*pt/pp* **strung**) (*thread*) aufziehen ⟨*beads*⟩. **~ed** *a* (*Mus*) Saiten-; (*played with bow*) Streich-

stringent /ˈstrɪndʒnt/ *a* streng

strip /strɪp/ *n* Streifen *m* □ *v* (*pt/pp* **stripped**) □ *vt* ablösen; ausziehen ⟨*clothes*⟩; abziehen ⟨*bed*⟩; abbeizen ⟨*wood, furniture*⟩; auseinander nehmen ⟨*machine*⟩; (*deprive*) berauben (*of gen*); **~ sth off sth** etw von etw entfernen □ *vi* (*undress*) sich ausziehen. **~ club** *n* Stripteaselokal *nt*

stripe /straɪp/ *n* Streifen *m*. **~d** *a* gestreift

ˈstriplight *n* Neonröhre *f*

stripper /ˈstrɪpə(r)/ *n* Stripperin *f*; (*male*) Stripper *m*

strip-ˈtease *n* Striptease *m*

strive /straɪv/ *vi* (*pt* **strove**, *pp* striven) sich bemühen (**to** zu); **~ for** streben nach

strode /strəʊd/ *see* **stride**

stroke[1] /strəʊk/ *n* Schlag *m*; (*of pen*) Strich *m*; (*Swimming*) Zug *m*; (*style*) Stil *m*; (*Med*) Schlaganfall *m*; **~ of luck** Glücksfall *m*; **put s.o. off his ~** jdn aus dem Konzept bringen

stroke[2] □ *vt* streicheln

stroll /strəʊl/ *n* Spaziergang *m*, (*fam*) Bummel *m* □ *vi* spazieren, (*fam*) bummeln. **~er** *n* (*Amer: push-chair*) [Kinder]sportwagen *m*

strong /strɒŋ/ *a* (**-er** /-gə(r)/, **-est** /-gɪst/), **-ly** *adv* stark; (*powerful, healthy*) kräftig; (*severe*) streng; (*sturdy*) stabil; (*convincing*) gut

strong: ~-box *n* Geldkassette *f*. **~hold** *n* Festung *f*; (*fig*) Hochburg *f*. **~-ˈminded** *a* willensstark. **~-room** *n* Tresorraum *m*

stroppy /ˈstrɒpɪ/ *a* widerspenstig

strove /strəʊv/ *see* **strive**

struck /strʌk/ *see* **strike**

structural /ˈstrʌktʃərl/ *a*, **-ly** *adv* baulich

structure /ˈstrʌktʃə(r)/ *n* Struktur *f*; (*building*) Bau *m*

struggle /ˈstrʌgl/ *n* Kampf *m*; **with a ~** mit Mühe □ *vt* kämpfen; **~ for breath** nach Atem ringen; **~ to do sth** sich abmühen, etw zutun; **~ to one's feet** mühsam aufstehen

strum /strʌm/ *v* (*pt/pp* **strummed**) □ *vt* klimpern auf (+ *dat*) □ *vi* klimpern

strung /strʌŋ/ *see* **string**

strut[1] /strʌt/ *n* Strebe *f*

strut[2] *vi* (*pt/pp* **strutted**) stolzieren

stub /stʌb/ *n* Stummel *m*; (*counterfoil*) Abschnitt *m* □ *vt* (*pt/pp* **strubbed**) **~ one's toe** sich (*dat*) den Zeh stoßen (**on** an + *dat*). **~ out** *vt* ausdrücken ⟨*cigarette*⟩

stubb|le /ˈstʌbl/ *n* Stoppeln *pl*. **~ly** *a* stoppelig

stubborn /ˈstʌbən/ *a*, **-ly** *adv* starrsinnig; ⟨*refusal*⟩ hartnäckig

stubby /ˈstʌbɪ/ *a*, (**-ier**, **-iest**) kurz und dick

stucco /ˈstʌkəʊ/ *n* Stuck *m*

stuck /stʌk/ *see* **stick**[2]. **~-ˈup** *a* (*fam*) hochnäsig

stud[1] /stʌd/ *n* Nagel *m* (*on clothes*) Niete *f*; (*for collar*) Kragenknopf *m*; (*for ear*) Ohrstecker *m*

stud[2] *n* (*of horses*) Gestüt *nt*

student /ˈstju:dnt/ *n* Student(in) *m(f)*; (*Sch*) Schüler(in) *m(f)*. **~ nurse** *n* Lernschwester *f*

studied /ˈstʌdɪd/ *a* gewollt

studio /ˈstju:dɪəʊ/ *n* Studio *nt*; (*for artist*) Atelier *nt*

studious /ˈstju:dɪəs/ *a* lerneifrig; (*earnest*) ernsthaft

stud|y /ˈstʌdɪ/ *n* Studie *f*; (*room*) Studierzimmer *nt*; (*investigation*)

Untersuchung *f*; **~ies** *pl* Studium *nt* □ *v* (*pt/pp* **studied**) □ *vt* studieren; (*examine*) untersuchen □ *vi* lernen; (*at university*) studieren

stuff /stʌf/ *n* Stoff *m*; (*fam: things*) Zeug *nt* □ *vt* vollstopfen; (*with padding, Culin*) füllen; ausstopfen ⟨*animal*⟩; **~ sth into sth** etw in etw (*acc*) [hinein]stopfen. **~ing** *n* Füllung *f*

stuffy /ˈstʌfɪ/ *a* (**-ier, -iest**) stickig; (*old-fashioned*) spießig

stumbl|e /ˈstʌmbl/ *vi* stolpern; **~e across** zufällig stoßen auf (+ *acc*). **~ing-block** *n* Hindernis *nt*

stump /stʌmp/ *n* Stumpf *m* □ **~ up** *vt/i* (*fam*) blechen. **~ed** *a* (*fam*) überfragt

stun /stʌn/ *vt* (*pt/pp* **stunned**) betäuben; **~ned by** (*fig*) wie betäubt von

stung /stʌŋ/ *see* **sting**

stunk /stʌŋk/ *see* **stink**

stunning /ˈstʌnɪŋ/ *a* (*fam*) toll

stunt1 /stʌnt/ *n* (*fam*) Kunststück *nt*

stunt2 *vt* hemmen. **~ed** *a* verkümmert

stupendous /stju:ˈpendəs/ *a*, **-ly** *adv* enorm

stupid /ˈstju:pɪd/ *a* dumm. **~ity** /-ˈpɪdətɪ/ *n* Dummheit *f*. **~ly** *adv* dumm; **~ly [enough]** dummerweise

stupour /ˈstju:pə(r)/ *n* Benommenheit *f*

sturdy /ˈstɜ:dɪ/ *a* (**-ier, -iest**) stämmig; ⟨*furniture*⟩ stabil; ⟨*shoes*⟩ fest

stutter /ˈstʌtə(r)/ *n* Stottern *nt* □ *vt/i* stottern

sty1 /staɪ/ *n* (*pl* **sties**) Schweinestall *m*

sty2, **stye** *n* (*pl* **styes**) (*Med*) Gerstenkorn *nt*

style /staɪl/ *n* **Stil** *m*; (*fashion*) Mode *f*; (*sort*) Art *f*; (*hair~*) Frisur *f*; **in ~** in großem Stil

stylish /ˈstaɪlɪʃ/ *a*, **-ly** *adv* stilvoll

stylist /ˈstaɪlɪst/ *n* Friseur *m*/ Friseuse *f*. **~ic** /-ˈlɪstɪk/ *a*, **-ally** *adv* stilistisch

stylized /ˈstaɪlaɪzd/ *a* stilisiert

stylus /ˈstaɪləs/ *n* (*on record-player*) Nadel *f*

suave /swɑ:v/ *a* (*pej*) gewandt

subˈconscious /sʌb-/ *a*, **-ly** *adv* unterbewusst □ *n* Unterbewusstsein *nt*

subconˈtract *vt* [vertraglich] weitervergeben (**to an** + *acc*)

ˈsubdivi|de *vt* unterteilen. **~sion** *n* Unterteilung *f*

subdue /səbˈdju:/ *vt* unterwerfen; (*make quieter*) beruhigen. **~d** *a* gedämpft; ⟨*person*⟩ still

subject1 /ˈsʌbdʒɪkt/ *a* **be ~ to sth** etw (*dat*) unterworfen sein □ *n* Staatsbürger(in) *m*(*f*); (*of ruler*) Untertan *m*; (*theme*) Thema *nt*; (*of investigation*) Gegenstand *m*; (*Sch*) Fach *nt*; (*Gram*) Subjekt *nt*

subject2 /səbˈdʒekt/ *vt* unterwerfen (**to** *dat*); (*expose*) aussetzen (**to** *dat*)

subjective /səbˈdʒektɪv/ *a*, **-ly** *adv* subjektiv

subjugate /ˈsʌbdʒʊgeɪt/ *vt* unterjochen

subjunctive /səbˈdʒʌŋktɪv/ *n* Konjunktiv *m*

subˈlet *vt* (*pt/pp* **-let**) untervermieten

sublime /səˈblaɪm/ *a*, **-ly** *adv* erhaben

subliminal /sʌˈblɪmɪnl/ *a* unterschwellig

sub-maˈchine-gun *n* Maschinenpistole *f*

submaˈrine *n* Unterseeboot *nt*

submerge /səbˈmɜ:dʒ/ *vt* untertauchen; **be ~d** unter Wasser stehen □ *vi* tauchen

submiss|ion /səbˈmɪʃn/ *n* Unterwerfung *f*. **~ive** /-sɪv/ *a* gehorsam; (*pej*) unterwürfig

submit /səbˈmɪt/ *v* (*pt/pp* **-mitted**, *pres p* **-mitting**) □ *vt* vorlegen (**to** *dat*); (*hand in*) einreichen □ *vi* sich unterwerfen (**to** *dat*)

subordinate[1] /sə'bɔ:dɪnət/ *a* untergeordnet □ *n* Untergebene(r) *m/f*
subordinate[2] /sə'bɔ:dɪneɪt/ *vt* unterordnen (**to** *dat*)
subscribe /səb'skraɪb/ *vi* spenden; ~ **to** abonnieren ⟨*newspaper*⟩; (*fig*) sich anschließen (+ *dat*). ~**r** *n* Spender *m*; Abonnent *m*
subscription /səb'skrɪpʃn/ *n* (*to club*) [Mitglieds]beitrag *m*; (*to newspaper*) Abonnement *nt*; **by** ~ mit Spenden; ⟨*buy*⟩ im Abonnement
subsequent /'sʌbsɪkwənt/ *a*, **-ly** *adv* folgend; (*later*) später
subservient /səb'sɜ:vɪənt/ *a*, **-ly** *adv* untergeordnet; (*servile*) unterwürfig
subside /səb'saɪd/ *vi* sinken; ⟨*ground:*⟩ sich senken; ⟨*storm:*⟩ nachlassen
subsidiary /səb'sɪdɪərɪ/ *a* untergeordnet □ *n* Tochtergesellschaft *f*
subsid|ize /'sʌbsɪdaɪz/ *vt* subventionieren. ~**y** *n* Subvention *f*
subsist /səb'sɪst/ *vi* leben (**on** von). ~**ence** *n* Existenz *f*
substance /'sʌbstəns/ *n* Substanz *f*
sub'standard *a* unzulänglich; ⟨*goods*⟩ minderwertig
substantial /səb'stænʃl/ *a* solide; ⟨*meal*⟩ reichhaltig; (*considerable*) beträchtlich. ~**ly** *adv* solide; (*essentially*) im Wesentlichen
substantiate /səb'stænʃɪeɪt/ *vt* erhärten
substitut|e /'sʌbstɪtju:t/ *n* Ersatz *m*; (*Sport*) Ersatzspieler(in) *m(f)* □ *vt* ~**e A for B** B durch A ersetzen □ *vi* ~**e for s.o.** jdn vertreten. ~**ion** /-'tju:ʃn/ *n* Ersetzung *f*
subterfuge /'sʌbtəfju:dʒ/ *n* List *f*
subterranean /sʌbtə'reɪnɪən/ *a* unterirdisch
'subtitle *n* Untertitel *m*
subtle /'sʌtl/ *a* (**-r, -st**), **-tly** *adv* fein; (*fig*) subtil
subtract /səb'trækt/ *vt* abziehen, subtrahieren. ~**ion** /-ækʃn/ *n* Subtraktion *f*
suburb /'sʌbɜ:b/ *n* Vorort *m*; **in the** ~**s** am Stadtrand. ~**an** /sə'bɜ:bən/ *a* Vorort-; (*pej*) spießig. ~**ia** /sə'bɜ:bɪə/ *n* die Vororte *pl*
subversive /səb'vɜ:sɪv/ *a* subversiv
'subway *n* Unterführung *f*; (*Amer: railway*) U-Bahn *f*
succeed /sək'si:d/ *vi* Erfolg haben; ⟨*plan:*⟩ gelingen; (*follow*) nachfolgen (+ *dat*); **I** ~**ed** es ist mir gelungen; **he** ~**ed in escaping** es gelang ihm zu entkommen □ *vt* folgen (+ *dat*). ~**ing** *a* folgend
success /sək'ses/ *n* Erfolg *m*. ~**ful** *a*,**-ly** *adv* erfolgreich
succession /sək'seʃn/ *n* Folge *f*; (*series*) Serie *f*; (*to title, office*) Nachfolge *f*; (*to throne*) Thronfolge *f*; **in** ~ hintereinander
successive /sək'sesɪv/ *a* aufeinander folgend. ~**ly** *adv* hintereinander
successor /sək'sesə(r)/ *n* Nachfolger(in) *m(f)*
succinct /sək'sɪŋkt/ *a*,**-ly** *adv* prägnant
succulent /'ʃʌkjʊlənt/ *a* saftig
succumb /sə'kʌm/ *vi* erliegen (**to** *dat*)
such /sʌtʃ/ *a* solche(r,s); ~ **a book** ein solches *od* solch ein Buch; ~ **a thing** so etwas; ~ **a long time** so lange; **there is no** ~ **thing** das gibt es gar nicht; **there is no** ~ **person** eine solche Person gibt es nicht □ *pron* **as** ~ als solche(r,s); (*strictly speaking*) an sich; ~ **as** wie [zum Beispiel]; **and** ~ und dergleichen. ~**like** *pron* (*fam*) dergleichen
suck /ʃʌk/ *vt/i* saugen; lutschen ⟨*sweet*⟩. ~ **up** *vt* aufsaugen □ *vi* ~ **up to s.o.** (*fam*) sich bei jdm einschmeicheln

sucker /'ʃʌkə(r)/ *n* (*Bot*) Ausläufer *m*; (*fam: person*) Dumme(r) *m/f*
suckle /'ʃʌkl/ *vt* säugen
suction /'ʌkʃn/ *n* Saugwirkung *f*
sudden /'sʌdn/ *a*, **-ly** *adv* plötzlich; (*abrupt*) jäh □ *n* **all of a ~** auf einmal
sue /su:/ *vt* (*pres p* **suing**) verklagen (**for** auf + *acc*) □ *vi* klagen
suede /sweɪd/ *n* Wildleder *nt*
suet /'su:ɪt/ *n* [Nieren]talg *m*
suffer /'sʌfə(r)/ *vi* leiden (**from an** + *dat*) □ *vt* erleiden; (*tolerate*) dulden. **~ance** /-əns/ *n* **on ~ance** bloß geduldet. **~ing** *n* Leiden *nt*
suffice /sə'faɪs/ *vi* genügen
sufficient /sə'fɪʃnt/ *a*, **-ly** *adv* genug, genügend; **be ~** genügen
suffix /'sʌfɪks/ *n* Nachsilbe *f*
suffocat|e /'sʌfəkeɪt/ *vt/i* ersticken. **~ion** /-'keɪʃn/ *n* Ersticken *nt*
sugar /'ʃʊgə(r)/ *n* Zucker *m* □ *vt* zuckern; (*fig*) versüßen. **~ basin, ~-bowl** *n* Zuckerschale *f*. **~y** *a* süß; (*fig*) süßlich
suggest /sə'dʒest/ *vt* vorschlagen; (*indicate, insinuate*) andeuten. **~ion** /-estʃn/ *n* Vorschlag *m*; Andeutung *f*; (*trace*) Spur *f*. **~ive** /-ɪv/ *a*, **-ly** *adv* anzüglich; **be ~ive of** schließen lassen auf (+ *acc*)
suicidal /su:ɪ'saɪdl/ *a* selbstmörderisch
suicide /'su:ɪsaɪd/ *n* Selbstmord *m*
suit /su:t/ *n* Anzug *m*; (*woman's*) Kostüm *nt*; (*Cards*) Farbe *f*; (*Jur*) Prozess *m*; **follow ~** (*fig*) das Gleiche tun □ *vt* (*adapt*) anpassen (**to** *dat*); (*be convenient for*) passen (+ *dat*); (*go with*) passen zu; ⟨*clothing:*⟩ stehen (**s.o.** *jdm*); **be ~ed for** geeignet sein für; **~ yourself!** wie du willst!
suit|able /'su:təbl/ *a* geeignet; (*convenient*) passend; (*appropriate*) angemessen; (*for weather, activity*) zweckmäßig. **~ably** *adv* angemessen; zweckmäßig
'**suitcase** *n* Koffer *m*
suite /swi:t/ *n* Suite *f*; (*of furniture*) Garnitur *f*
sulk /sʌlk/ *vi* schmollen. **~y** *a* schmollend
sullen /'sʌlən/ *a*, **-ly** *adv* mürrisch
sulphur /'sʌlfə(r)/ *n* Schwefel *f*. **~ic** /-'fjʊərɪk/ *a* **~ic acid** Schwefelsäure *f*
sultana /sʌl'tɑ:nə/ *n* Sultanine *f*
sultry /'sʌltrɪ/ *a* (**-ier, -iest**) ⟨*weather*⟩ schwül
sum /sʌm/ *n* Summe *f*; (*Sch*) Rechenaufgabe *f* □ *vt/i* (*pt/pp* **summed**) **~ up** zusammenfassen; (*assess*) einschätzen
summar|ize /'sʌməraɪz/ *vt* zusammenfassen. **~y** *n* Zusammenfassung *f* □ *a*, **-ily** *adv* summarisch; ⟨*dismissal*⟩ fristlos
summer /'sʌmə(r)/ *n* Sommer *m*. **~-house** *n* [Garten]laube *f*. **~time** *n* Sommer *m*
summery /'sʌmərɪ/ *a* sommerlich
summit /'sʌmɪt/ *n* Gipfel *m*. **~ conference** *n* Gipfelkonferenz *f*
summon /'sʌmən/ *vt* rufen; holen ⟨*help*⟩; (*Jur*) vorladen. **~ up** *vt* aufbringen
summons /'sʌmənz/ *n* (*Jur*) Vorladung *f* □ *vt* vorladen
sump /sʌmp/ *n* (*Auto*) Ölwanne *f*
sumptuous /'sʌmptjʊəs/ a, **-ly** *adv* prunkvoll; ⟨*meal*⟩ üppig
sun /sʌn/ *n* Sonne *f* □ *vt* (*pt/pp* **sunned**) **~ oneself** sich sonnen
sun: ~bathe *vi* sich sonnen. **~-bed** *n* Sonnenbank *f*. **~burn** *n* Sonnenbrand *m*
sundae /'sʌndeɪ/ *n* Eisbecher *m*
Sunday /'sʌndeɪ/ *n* Sonntag *m*
'**sundial** *n* Sonnenuhr *f*
sundry /'sʌndrɪ/ a verschiedene *pl*; **all and ~** alle *pl*
'**sunflower** *n* Sonnenblume *f*
sung /sʌŋ/ *see* **sing**

'sun-glasses *npl* Sonnenbrille *f*
sunk /sʌŋk/ *see* **sink**
sunken /'sʌŋkn/ a gesunken; ⟨*eyes*⟩ eingefallen
sunny /'sʌnɪ/ *a* (**-ier, -iest**) sonnig
sun: ~rise *n* Sonnenaufgang *m*. **~-roof** *n* (*Auto*) Schiebedach *nt*. **~set** *n* Sonnenuntergang *m*. **~shade** *n* Sonnenschirm *m*. **~shine** *n* Sonnenschein *m*. **~stroke** *n* Sonnenstich *m*. **~-tan** *n* [Sonnen]bräune *f*. **~-tanned** *a* braun [gebrannt]. **~-tan oil** *n* Sonnenöl *nt*
super /'su:pə(r)/ a (*fam*) prima, toll
superb /sʊ'pɜ:b/ *a* erstklassig
supercilious /su:pə'sɪlɪəs/ *a* überlegen
superficial /su:pə'fɪʃl/ a, **-ly** *adv* oberflächlich
superfluous /sʊ'pɜ:flʊəs/ *a* überflüssig
super'human *a* übermenschlich
superintendent /su:pərɪn-'tendənt/ *n* (*of police*) Kommissar *m*
superior /su:'pɪərɪə(r)/ a überlegen; (*in rank*) höher □ *n* Vorgesetzte(r) *m/f*. **~ity** /-'ɒrətɪ/ *n* Überlegenheit *f*
superlative /su:'pɜ:lətɪv/ a unübertrefflich □ *n* Superlativ *m*
'superman *n* Übermensch *m*
'supermarket *n* Supermarkt *m*
super'natural *a* übernatürlich
'superpower *n* Supermacht *f*
supersede /su:pə'si:d/ *vt* ersetzen
super'sonic *a* Überschall-
superstiti|on /su:pə'stɪʃn/ *n* Aberglaube *m*. **~ous** /-'stɪʃəs/ *a*, **-ly** *adv* abergläubisch
supervis|e /'su:pəvaɪz/ *vt* beaufsichtigen; überwachen ⟨*work*⟩. **~ion** /-'vɪʒn/ *n* Aufsicht *f*; Überwachung *f*. **~or** *n* Aufseher(in) *m(f)*
supper /'sʌpə(r)/ *n* Abendessen *nt*
supple /'sʌpl/ *a* geschmeidig
supplement /'sʌplɪmənt/ *n* Ergänzung *f*; (*addition*) Zusatz *m*; (*to fare*) Zuschlag *m*; (*book*) Ergänzungsband *m*; (*to newspaper*) Beilage *f* □ *vt* ergänzen. **~ary** /-'mentərɪ/ a zusätzlich
supplier /sə'plaɪə(r)/ *n* Lieferant *m*
supply /sə'plaɪ/ *n* Vorrat *m*; **supplies** *pl* (*Mil*) Nachschub *m* □ *vt* (*pt/pp* **-ied**) liefern; **~ s.o. with sth** jdn mit etw versorgen
support /sə'pɔ:t/ *n* Stütze *f*; (*fig*) Unterstützung *f* □ *vt* stützen; (*bear weight of*) tragen; (*keep*) ernähren; (*give money to*) unterstützen; (*speak in favour of*) befürworten; (*Sport*) Fan sein von. **~er** *n* Anhänger(in) *m(f)*; (*Sport*) Fan *m*. **~ive** /-ɪv/ *a* be **~ive [to s.o.]** [jdm] eine große Stütze sein
suppose /sə'pəʊz/ *vt* annehmen; (*presume*) vermuten; (*imagine*) sich (*dat*) vorstellen; **be ~d to do sth** etw tun sollen; **not be ~d to** (*fam*) nicht dürfen; **I ~ so** vermutlich. **~dly** /-ɪdlɪ/ *adv* angeblich
supposition /sʌpə'zɪʃn/ *n* Vermutung *f*
suppository /sʌ'pɒzɪtrɪ/ *n* Zäpfchen *nt*
suppress /sə'pres/ *vt* unterdrücken. **~ion** /-eʃn/ *n* Unterdrückung *f*
supremacy /su:'preməsɪ/ *n* Vorherrschaft *f*
supreme /su:'pri:m/ *a* höchste(r,s); ⟨*court*⟩ oberste(r,s)
surcharge /'sɜ:tʃɑ:dʒ/ *n* Zuschlag *m*
sure /ʃʊə(r)/ *a* (-r, -st) sicher; **make ~** sich vergewissern (**of** *gen*); (*check*) nachprüfen; **be ~ to do it** sieh zu, dass du es tust □ *adv* (*Amer, fam*) klar; **~ enough** tatsächlich. **~ly** *adv* sicher; (*for emphasis*) doch; (*Amer: gladly*) gern
surety /'ʃʊərətɪ/ *n* Bürgschaft *f*; **stand ~ for** bürgen für

surf /'sɜ:f/ *n* Brandung *f*
surface /'sɜ:fɪs/ *n* Oberfläche *f* □ *vi* (*emerge*) auftauchen. ~ **mail** *n* **by ~ mail** auf dem Land-/Seeweg
'**surfboard** *n* Surfbrett *nt*
surfeit /'sɜ:fɪt/ *n* Übermaß *nt*;
surfing /'sɜ:fɪŋ/ *n* Surfen *nt*
surge /sɜ:dʒ/ *n* (*of sea*) Branden *nt*; (*fig*) Welle *f* □ *vi* branden; ~ **forward** nach vorn drängen
surgeon /'sɜ:dʒən/ *n* Chirurg(in) *m*(*f*)
surgery /'sɜ:dʒərɪ/ *n* Chirurgie *f*; (*place*) Praxis *f*; (*room*) Sprechzimmer *nt*; (*hours*) Sprechstunde *f*; **have ~** operiert werden
surgical /'sɜ:dʒɪkl/ *a*, **-ly** *adv* chirurgisch
surly /'sɜ:lɪ/ *a* (**-ier, -iest**) mürrisch
surmise /sə'maɪz/ *vt* mutmaßen
surmount /sə'maʊnt/ *vt* überwinden
surname /'sɜ:neɪm/ *n* Nachname *m*
surpass /sə'pɑ:s/ *vt* übertreffen
surplus /'sɜ:pləs/ *a* überschüssig; **be ~ to requirements** nicht benötigt werden □ *n* Überschuss *m* (**of** an + *dat*)
surpris|e /sə'praɪz/ *n* Überraschung *f* □ *vt* überraschen; **be ~ed** sich wundern (**at** über + *acc*). **~ing** *a*, **-ly** *adv* überraschend
surrender /sə'rendə(r)/ *n* Kapitulation *f* □ *vi* sich ergeben; (*Mil*) kapitulieren □ *vt* aufgeben
surreptitious /sʌrəp'tɪʃəs/ *a*, **-ly** *adv* heimlich, verstohlen
surrogate /'sʌrəgət/ *n* Ersatz *m*. ~ '**mother** *n* Leihmutter *f*
surround /sə'raʊnd/ *vt* umgeben; (*encircle*) umzingeln; **~ed by** umgeben von. **~ing** *a* umliegend. **~ings** *npl* Umgebung *f*
surveillance /sə'veɪləns/ *n* Überwachung *f*; **be under ~** überwacht werden
survey[1] /'sɜ:veɪ/ *n* Überblick *m*; (*poll*) Umfrage *f*; (*investigation*) Untersuchung *f*; (*of land*) Vermessung *f*; (*of house*) Gutachten *nt*
survey[2] /sə'veɪ/ *vt* betrachten; vermessen ⟨*land*⟩; begutachten ⟨*building*⟩. **~or** *n* Landvermesser *m*; Gutachter *m*
survival /sə'vaɪvl/ *n* Überleben *nt*; (*of tradition*) Fortbestand *m*
surviv|e /sə'vaɪv/ *vt* überleben □ *vi* überleben; ⟨*tradition*:⟩ erhalten bleiben. **~or** *n* Überlebende(r) *m/f*; **be a ~or** (*fam*) nicht unterzukriegen sein
susceptible /sə'septəbl/ *a* empfänglich/ (*Med*) anfällig (**to** für)
suspect[1] /sə'spekt/ *vt* verdächtigen; (*assume*) vermuten; **he ~s nothing** er ahnt nichts
suspect[2] /'sʌspekt/ *a* verdächtig □ *n* Verdächtige(r) *m/f*
suspend /sə'spend/ *vt* aufhängen; (*stop*) [vorläufig] einstellen; (*from duty*) vorläufig beurlauben. **~er belt** *n* Strumpfbandgürtel *m*. **~ders** *npl* Strumpfbänder *pl*; (*Amer: braces*) Hosenträger *pl*
suspense /sə'spens/ *n* Spannung *f*
suspension /sə'spenʃn/ *n* (*Auto*) Federung *f*. ~ **bridge** *n* Hängebrücke *f*
suspici|on /sə'spɪʃn/ *n* Verdacht *m*; (*mistrust*) Misstrauen *nt*; (*trace*) Spur *f*. **~ous** /-ɪʃəs/ *a*, **-ly** *adv* misstrauisch; (*arousing suspicion*) verdächtig
sustain /sə'steɪn/ *vt* tragen; (*fig*) aufrechterhalten; erhalten ⟨*life*⟩; erleiden ⟨*injury*⟩
sustenance /'sʌstɪnəns/ *n* Nahrung *f*
swab /swɒb/ *n* (*Med*) Tupfer *m*; (*specimen*) Abstrich *m*
swagger /'swægə(r)/ *vi* stolzieren

swallow[1] /ˈswɒləʊ/ *vt/i* schlucken. ~ **up** *vt* verschlucken; verschlingen ⟨*resources*⟩
swallow[2] *n* (*bird*) Schwalbe *f*
swam /swæm/ *see* **swim**
swamp /swɒmp/ *n* Sumpf *m* □ *vt* überschwemmen. ~**y** *a* sumpfig
swan /swɒn/ *n* Schwan *m*
swank /swæŋk/ *vi* (*fam*) angeben
swap /swɒp/ *n* (*fam*) Tausch *m* □ *vt/i* (*pt/pp* **swapped**) (*fam*) tauschen (**for** gegen)
swarm /swɔːm/ *n* Schwarm *m* □ *vi* schwärmen; **be** ~**ing with** wimmeln von
swarthy /ˈswɔːðɪ/ *a* (**-ier, -iest**) dunkel
swastika /ˈswɒstɪkə/ *n* Hakenkreuz *nt*
swat /swɒt/ *vt* (*pt/pp* **swatted**) totschlagen
sway /sweɪ/ *n* (*fig*) Herrschaft *f* □ *vi* schwanken; (*gently*) sich wiegen □ *vt* wiegen; (*influence*) beeinflussen
swear /sweə(r)/ *v* (*pt* **swore**, *pp* **sworn**) □ *vt* schwören □ *vi* schwören (**by** auf + *acc*); (*curse*) fluchen. ~**-word** *n* Kraftausdruck *m*
sweat /swet/ *n* Schweiß *m* □ *vi* schwitzen
sweater /ˈswetə(r)/ *n* Pullover *m*
sweaty /ˈswetɪ/ *a* verschwitzt
swede /swiːd/ *n* Kohlrübe *f*
Swed|e *n* Schwede *m* /-din *f*. ~**en** *n* Schweden *nt*. ~**ish** *a* schwedisch
sweep /swiːp/ *n* Schornsteinfeger *m*; (*curve*) Bogen *m*; (*movement*) ausholende Bewegung *f*; **make a clean** ~ (*fig*) gründlich aufräumen □ *v* (*pt/pp* **swept**) □ *vt* fegen, kehren □ *vi* (*go swiftly*) rauschen; ⟨*wind:*⟩ fegen. ~ **up** *vt* zusammenfegen/-kehren
sweeping /ˈswiːpɪŋ/ *a* ausholend; ⟨*statement*⟩ pauschal; ⟨*changes*⟩ weit reichend
sweet /swiːt/ *a* (**-er, -est**) süß; **have a** ~ **tooth** gern Süßes mögen □ *n* Bonbon *m & nt*; (*dessert*) Nachtisch *m*. ~ **corn** *n* [Zucker]mais *m*
sweeten /ˈswiːtn/ *vt* süßen. ~**er** *n* Süßstoff *m*; (*fam: bribe*) Schmiergeld *nt*
sweet: ~**heart** *n* Schatz *m*. ~**-shop** *n* Süßwarenladen *m*. ~**ness** *n* Süße *f*. ~ ˈ**pea** *n* Wicke *f*
swell /swel/ *n* Dünung *f* □ *v* (*pt* **swelled**, *pp* **swollen** *or* **swelled**) □ *vi* [an]schwellen; ⟨*sails:*⟩ sich blähen; ⟨*wood:*⟩ aufquellen □ *vt* anschwellen lassen; (*increase*) vergrößern. ~**ing** *n* Schwellung *f*
swelter /ˈsweltə(r)/ *vi* schwitzen
swept /swept/ *see* **sweep**
swerve /swɜːv/ *vi* einen Bogen machen
swift /swɪft/ *a* (**-er, -est**), **-ly** *adv* schnell
swig /swɪg/ *n* (*fam*) Schluck *m*, Zug *m* □ *vt* (*pt/pp* **swigged**) (*fam*) [herunter]kippen
swill /swɪl/ *n* (*for pigs*) Schweinefutter *nt* □ *vt* ~ **[out]** [aus]spülen
swim /swɪm/ *n* **have a** ~ schwimmen □ *vi* (**pt swam**, *pp* **swum**) schwimmen; **my head is** ~**ming** mir dreht sich der Kopf. ~**mer** *n* Schwimmer(in) *m*(*f*)
swimming /ˈswɪmɪŋ/ *n* Schwimmen *nt*. ~**-baths** *npl* Schwimmbad *nt*. ~**-pool** *n* Schwimmbecken *nt*; (*private*) Swimmingpool *m*
ˈ**swim-suit** *n* Badeanzug *m*
swindle /ˈswɪndl/ *n* Schwindel *m*, Betrug *m* □ *vt* betrügen. ~**r** *n* Schwindler *m*
swine /swaɪn/ *n* Schwein *nt*
swing /swɪŋ/ *n* Schwung *m*; (*shift*) Schwenk *m*; (*seat*) Schaukel *f*; **in full** ~ in vollem Gange □ (*pt/pp* **swung**) □ *vi* schwingen; (*on swing*) schaukeln; (*sway*) schwanken; (*dangle*) baumeln; (*turn*) schwenken □ *vt*

schwingen; (*influence*) beeinflussen. **~-'door** *n* Schwingtür *f*
swingeing /'swɪndʒɪŋ/ *a* hart; (*fig*) drastisch
swipe /swaɪp/ *n* (*fam*) Schlag *m* □ *vt* (*fam*) knallen; (*steal*) klauen
swirl /swɜ:l/ *n* Wirbel *m* □ *vt/i* wirbeln
swish /swɪʃ/ *a* (*fam*) schick □ *vi* zischen
Swiss /swɪs/ *a* Schweizer, schweizerisch □ *n* Schweizer(in) *m*(*f*); **the ~** *pl* die Schweizer. **~ 'roll** *n* Biskuitrolle *f*
switch /swɪtʃ/ *n* Schalter *m*; (*change*) Wechsel *m*; (*Amer, Rail*) Weiche *f* □ *vt* wechseln; (*exchange*) tauschen □ *vi* wechseln; **~ to** umstellen auf (+ *acc*). **~ off** *vt* ausschalten; abschalten ⟨*engine*⟩. **~ on** *vt* einschalten, anschalten
switch: ~back *n* Achterbahn *f*. **~board** *n* [Telefon]zentrale *f*
Switzerland /'swɪtsələnd/ *n* die Schweiz
swivel /'swɪvl/ *v* (*pt/pp* **swivelled**) □ *vt* drehen □ *vi* sich drehen
swollen /'swəʊlən/ *see* **swell** □ *a* geschwollen. **~-'headed** *a* eingebildet
swoop /swu:p/ *n* Sturzflug *m*; (*by police*) Razzia *f* □ *vi* **~ down** herabstoßen
sword /sɔ:d/ *n* Schwert *nt*
swore /swɔ:(r)/ *see* **swear**
sworn /swɔ:n/ *see* **swear**
swot /swɒt/ *n* (*fam*) Streber *m* □ *vt* (*pt/pp* **swotted**) (*fam*) büffeln
swum /swʌm/ *see* **swim**
swung /swʌŋ/ *see* **swing**
syllable /'sɪləbl/ *n* Silbe *f*
syllabus /'sɪləbəs/ *n* Lehrplan *m*; (*for exam*) Studienplan *m*
symbol /'sɪmbəl/ *n* Symbol *nt* (**of** für). **~ic** /-'bɒlɪk/ *a*, **-ally** *adv* symbolisch **~ism** /-ɪzm/ *n* Symbolik *f*. **~ize** *vt* symbolisieren
symmetr|ical /sɪ'metrɪkl/ *a*, **-ly** *adv* symmetrisch. **~y** /'sɪmətrɪ/ *n* Symmetrie *f*
sympathetic /sɪmpə'θetɪk/ *a*, **-ally** *adv* mitfühlend; (*likeable*) sympathisch
sympathize /'sɪmpəθaɪz/ *vi* mitfühlen. **~r** *n* (*Pol*) Sympathisant *m*
sympathy /'sɪmpəθɪ/ *n* Mitgefühl *nt*; (*condolences*) Beileid *nt*
symphony /'sɪmfənɪ/ *n* Sinfonie *f*
symptom /'sɪmptəm/ *n* Symptom *nt*. **~atic** /-'mætɪk/ *a* symptomatisch (**of** für)
synagogue /'sɪnəgɒg/ *n* Synagoge *f*
synchronize /'sɪŋkrənaɪz/ *vt* synchronisieren
syndicate /'sɪndɪkət/ *n* Syndikat *nt*
syndrome /'sɪndrəʊm/ *n* Syndrom *nt*
synonym /'sɪnənɪm/ *n* Synonym *nt*. **~ous** /-'nɒnɪməs/ *a*, **-ly** *adv* synonym
synopsis /sɪ'nɒpsɪs/ *n* (*pl* **-opses** /-si:z/) Zusammenfassung *f*; (*of opera, ballet*) Inhaltsangabe *f*
syntax /'sɪntæks/ *n* Syntax *f*
synthesis /'sɪnθəsɪs/ *n* (*pl* **-ses** /-si:z/) Synthese *f*
synthetic /sɪn'θetɪk/ *a* synthetisch □ *n* Kunststoff *m*
Syria /'sɪrɪə/ *n* Syrien *nt*
syringe /sɪ'rɪndʒ/ *n* Spritze *f* □ *vt* spritzen; ausspritzen ⟨*ears*⟩
syrup /'sɪrəp/ *n* Sirup *m*
system /'sɪstəm/ *n* System *nt*. **~atic** /-'mætɪk/ *a*, **-ally** *adv* systematisch

T

tab /tæb/ *n* (*projecting*) Zunge *f*; (*with name*) Namensschild *nt*; (*loop*) Aufhänger *m*; **keep ~s on**

(*fam*) [genau] beobachten; **pick up the ~** (*fam*) bezahlen
tabby /ˈtæbɪ/ *n* getigerte Katze *f*
table /ˈteɪbl/ *n* Tisch *m*; (*list*) Tabelle *f*; **at [the] ~** bei Tisch □ *vt* einbringen. **~-cloth** *n* Tischdecke *f*, Tischtuch *nt*. **~spoon** *n* Servierlöffel *m*
tablet /ˈtæblɪt/ *n* Tablette *f*; (*of soap*) Stück *nt*; (*slab*) Tafel *f*
ˈ**table tennis** *n* Tischtennis *nt*
tabloid /ˈtæblɔɪd/ *n* kleinformatige Zeitung *f*; (*pej*) Boulevardzeitung *f*
taboo /təˈbuː/ *a* tabu □ *n* Tabu *nt*
tacit /ˈtæsɪt/ *a*, **-ly** *adv* stillschweigend
taciturn /ˈtæsɪtɜːn/ *a* wortkarg
tack /tæk/ *n* (*nail*) Stift *m*; (*stitch*) Heftstich *m*; (*Naut & fig*) Kurs *m* □ *vt* festnageln; (*sew*) heften □ *vi* (*Naut*) kreuzen
tackle /ˈtækl/ *n* Ausrüstung *f* □ *vt* angehen
tacky /ˈtækɪ/ *a* klebrig
tact /tækt/ *n* Takt *m*, Taktgefühl *nt*. **~ful** *a*, **-ly** *adv* taktvoll
tactic|al /ˈtæktɪkl/ *a*, **-ly** *adv* taktisch. **~s** *npl* Taktik *f*
tactless /ˈtæktlɪs/ *a*, **-ly** *adv* taktlos. **~ness** *n* Taktlosigkeit *f*
tadpole /ˈtædpəʊl/ *n* Kaulquappe *f*
tag¹ /tæg/ *n* (*label*) Schild *nt* □ *vi* (*pt/pp* **tagged**) **~ along** mitkommen
tag² *n* (*game*) Fangen *nt*
tail /teɪl/ *n* Schwanz *m*; **~s** *pl* (*tailcoat*) Frack *m*; **heads or ~s?** Kopf oder Zahl? □ *vt* (*fam: follow*) beschatten □ *vi* **~ off** zurückgehen
tail: ~back *n* Rückstau *m*. **~coat** *n* Frack *m*. **~-end** *n* Ende *nt*. **~ light** *n* Rücklicht *nt*
tailor /ˈteɪlə(r)/ *n* Schneider *m*. **~-made** *a* maßgeschneidert
ˈ**tail wind** *n* Rückenwind *m*
taint /teɪnt/ *vt* verderben
take /teɪk/ *v* (*pt* **took**, *pp* **taken**) □ *vt* nehmen: (*with one*) mitnehmen; (*take to a place*) bringen; (*steal*) stehlen; (*win*) gewinnen; (*capture*) einnehmen; (*require*) brauchen; (*last*) dauern; (*teach*) geben; machen ⟨*exam, subject holiday, photograph*⟩; messen ⟨*pulse, temperature*⟩; **~ s.o. home** jdn nach Hause bringen; **~ sth to the cleaner's** etw in die Reinigung bringen; **~ s.o. prisoner** jdn gefangen nehmen; **be ~n ill** krank werden; **~ sth calmly** etw gelassen aufnehmen □ *vi* ⟨*plant:*⟩ angehen; **~ after s.o.** jdm nachschlagen; (*in looks*) jdm ähnlich sehen; **~ to** (*like*) mögen; (*as a habit*) sich (*dat*) angewöhnen. **~ away** *vt* wegbringen; (*remove*) wegnehmen; (*subtract*) abziehen; **'to ~ away'** 'zum Mitnehmen'. **~ back** *vt* zurücknehmen; (*return*) zurückbringen. **~ down** *vt* herunternehmen; (*remove*) abnehmen; (*write down*) aufschreiben. **~ in** *vt* hineinbringen; (*bring indoors*) hereinholen; (*to one's home*) aufnehmen; (*understand*) begreifen; (*deceive*) hereinlegen; (*make smaller*) enger machen. **~ off** *vt* abnehmen; ablegen ⟨*coat*⟩; sich (*dat*) ausziehen ⟨*clothes*⟩; (*deduct*) abziehen; (*mimic*) nachmachen; **~ time off** sich (*dat*) freinehmen; **~ oneself off** [fort]gehen □ *vi* (*Aviat*) starten. **~ on** *vt* annehmen; (*undertake*) übernehmen; (*engage*) einstellen; (*as opponent*) antreten gegen. **~ out** *vt* hinausbringen; (*for pleasure*) ausgehen mit; ausführen ⟨*dog*⟩; (*remove*) herausnehmen; (*withdraw*) abheben ⟨*money*⟩; (*from library*) ausleihen; **~ out a subscription to sth** etw abonnieren; **~ it out on s.o.** (*fam*) seinen Ärger an jdm auslassen. **~ over** *vt* hinüberbringen; übernehmen ⟨*firm, control*⟩ □ *vi* **~ over from s.o.** jdn ablösen. **~ up** *vt* hinaufbringen; annehmen ⟨*offer*⟩; ergreifen ⟨*profession*⟩; sich

(*dat*) zulegen ⟨*hobby*⟩; in Anspruch nehmen ⟨*time*⟩; einnehmen ⟨*space*⟩; aufreißen ⟨*floorboards*⟩; ~ **sth up with s.o.** mit jdm über etw (*acc*) sprechen □ *vi* ~ **up with s.o.** sich mit jdm einlassen
take: ~-away *n* Essen *nt* zum Mitnehmen; (*restaurant*) Restaurant *nt* mit Straßenverkauf. **~-off** *n* (*Aviat*) Start *m*, Abflug *m*. **~-over** *n* Übernahme *f*
takings /'teɪkɪŋz/ *npl* Einnahmen *pl*
talcum /'tælkəm/ *n* ~ **[powder]** Körperpuder *m*
tale /teɪl/ *n* Geschichte *f*
talent /'tælənt/ *n* Talent *nt*. **~ed** *a* talentiert
talk /tɔ:k/ *n* Gespräch *nt*; (*lecture*) Vortrag *m*; **make small ~** Konversation machen □ *vi* reden, sprechen (**to/with** mit) □ *vt* reden; ~ **s.o. into sth** jdn zu etw überreden. ~ **over** *vt* besprechen
talkative /'tɔ:kətɪv/ *a* gesprächig
'talking-to *n* Standpauke *f*
tall /tɔ:l/ *a* (**-er, -est**) groß; ⟨*building, tree*⟩ hoch; **that's a ~ order** das ist ziemlich viel verlangt. **~boy** *n* hohe Kommode *f*. ~ **'story** *n* übertriebene Geschichte *f*
tally /'tælɪ/ *n* **keep a ~ of** Buch führen über (+ *acc*) □ *vi* übereinstimmen
talon /'tælən/ *n* Klaue *f*
tambourine /tæmbə'ri:n/ *n* Tamburin *nt*
tame /teɪm/ *a* (**-r, -st**), **-ly** *adv* zahm; (*dull*) lahm (*fam*) □ *vt* zähmen. **~r** *n* Dompteur *m*
tamper /'tæmpə(r)/ *vi* ~ **with** sich (*dat*) zu schaffen machen an (+ *dat*)
tampon /'tæmpɒn/ *n* Tampon *m*
tan /tæn/ *a* gelbbraun □ *n* Gelbbraun *nt*; (*from sun*) Bräune *f* □ *v* (*pt/pp* **tanned**) □ *vt* gerben ⟨*hide*⟩ □ *vi* braun werden
tang /tæŋ/ *n* herber Geschmack *m*; (*smell*) herber Geruch *m*
tangent /'tændʒənt/ *n* Tangente *f*; **go off at a ~** (*fam*) vom Thema abschweifen
tangible /'tændʒɪbl/ *a* greifbar
tangle /'tæŋgl/ *n* Gewirr *nt*; (*in hair*) Verfilzung *f* □ *vt* ~ **[up]** verheddern □ *vi* sich verheddern
tango /'tæŋgəʊ/ *n* Tango *m*
tank /tæŋk/ *n* Tank *m*; (*Mil*) Panzer *m*
tankard /'tæŋkəd/ *n* Krug *m*
tanker /'tæŋkə(r)/ *n* Tanker *m*; (*lorry*) Tank[last]wagen *m*
tantaliz|e /'tæntəlaɪz/ *vt* quälen. **~ing** *a* verlockend
tantamount /'tæntəmaʊnt/ *a* **be ~ to** gleichbedeutend sein mit
tantrum /'tæntrəm/ *n* Wutanfall *m*
tap /tæp/ *n* Hahn *m*; (*knock*) Klopfen *nt*; **on ~** zur Verfügung □ *v* (*pt/pp* **tapped**) □ *vt* klopfen an (+ *acc*); anzapfen ⟨*barrel, tree*⟩; erschließen ⟨*resources*⟩; abhören ⟨*telephone*⟩ □ *vi* klopfen. **~-dance** *n* Stepp[tanz] *m* □ *vi* Stepp tanzen, steppen
tape /teɪp/ *n* Band *nt*; (*adhesive*) Klebstreifen *m*; (*for recording*) Tonband *nt* □ *vt* mit Klebstreifen zukleben; (*record*) auf Band aufnehmen
'tape-measure *n* Bandmaß *nt*
taper /'teɪpə(r)/ *n* dünne Wachskerze *f* □ *vi* sich verjüngen
'tape recorder *n* Tonbandgerät *nt*
tapestry /'tæpɪstrɪ/ *n* Gobelinstickerei *f*
'tapeworm *n* Bandwurm *m*
'tap water *n* Leitungswasser *nt*
tar /tɑ:(r)/ *n* Teer *m* □ *vt* (*pt/pp* **tarred**) teeren
tardy /'tɑ:dɪ/ *a* (**-ier, -iest**) langsam; (*late*) spät
target /'tɑ:gɪt/ *n* Ziel *nt*; (*board*) [Ziel]scheibe *f*
tariff /'tærɪf/ *n* Tarif *m*; (*duty*) Zoll *m*

tarnish /ˈtɑːnɪʃ/ *vi* anlaufen
tarpaulin /tɑːˈpɔːlɪn/ *n* Plane *f*
tarragon /ˈtærəgən/ *n* Estragon *m*
tart[1] /tɑːt/ *a* (**-er, -est**) sauer; (*fig*) scharf
tart[2] *n* ≈ Obstkuchen *m*; (*individual*) Törtchen *nt*; (*sl: prostitute*) Nutte *f* □ *vt* ~ **oneself up** (*fam*) sich auftakeln
tartan /ˈtɑːtn/ *n* Schottenmuster *nt*; (*cloth*) Schottenstoff *m* □ *attrib* schottisch kariert
tartar /ˈtɑːtə(r)/ *n* (*on teeth*) Zahnstein *m*
tartar ˈsauce /tɑːtə-/ *n* ≈ Remouladensoße *f*
task /tɑːsk/ *n* Aufgabe *f*; **take s.o. to** ~ jdm Vorhaltungen machen. ~ **force** *n* Sonderkommando *nt*
tassel /ˈtæsl/ *n* Quaste *f*
taste /teɪst/ *n* Geschmack *m*; (*sample*) Kostprobe *f* □ *vt* kosten, probieren; schmecken ⟨*flavour*⟩ □ *vi* schmecken (**of** nach). ~**ful** *a*, **-ly** *adv* (*fig*) geschmackvoll. ~**less** *a*, **-ly** *adv* geschmacklos
tasty /ˈteɪstɪ/ *a* (**-ier, -iest**) lecker, schmackhaft
tat /tæt/ *see* **tit**[2]
tatter|ed /ˈtætəd/ *a* zerlumpt; ⟨*pages*⟩ zerfleddert. ~**s** *npl* **in** ~**s** in Fetzen
tattoo[1] /təˈtuː/ *n* Tätowierung *f* □ *vt* tätowieren
tattoo[2] *n* (*Mil*) Zapfenstreich *m*
tatty /ˈtætɪ/ *a* (**-ier, -iest**) schäbig; ⟨*book*⟩ zerfleddert
taught /tɔːt/ *see* **teach**
taunt /tɔːnt/ *n* höhnische Bemerkung *f* □ *vt* verhöhnen
Taurus /ˈtɔːrəs/ *n* (*Astr*) Stier *m*
taut /tɔːt/ *a* straff
tavern /ˈtævən/ *n* (*liter*) Schenke *f*
tawdry /ˈtɔːdrɪ/ *a* (**-ier, -iest**) billig und geschmacklos
tawny /ˈtɔːnɪ/ *a* gelbbraun
tax /tæks/ *n* Steuer *f* □ *vt* besteuern; (*fig*) strapazieren; ~ **with** beschuldigen (+ *gen*). ~**able** /-əbl/ *a* steuerpflichtig. ~**ation** /-ˈseɪʃn/ *n* Besteuerung *f*. ~**-free** *a* steuerfrei
taxi /ˈtæksɪ/ *n* Taxi *nt* □ *vi* (*pt/pp* **taxied**, *pres p* **taxiing**) ⟨*aircraft:*⟩ rollen. ~ **driver** *n* Taxifahrer *m*. ~ **rank** *n* Taxistand *m*
ˈtaxpayer *n* Steuerzahler *m*
tea /tiː/ *n* Tee *m*. ~**-bag** *n* Teebeutel *m*. ~**-break** *n* Teepause *f*
teach /tiːtʃ/ *vt/i* (*pt/pp* **taught**) unterrichten; ~ **s.o. sth** jdm etw beibringen. ~**er** *n* Lehrer(in) *m*(*f*)
tea: ~**-cloth** *n* (*for drying*) Geschirrtuch *nt*. ~**cup** *n* Teetasse *f*
teak /tiːk/ *n* Teakholz *nt*
team /tiːm/ *n* Mannschaft *f*; (*fig*) Team *nt*; (*of animals*) Gespann *nt* □ *vi* ~ **up** sich zusammentun
ˈteam-work *n* Teamarbeit *f*
ˈteapot *n* Teekanne *f*
tear[1] /teə(r)/ *n* Riss *m* □ *v* (*pt* **tore**, *pp* **torn**) □ *vt* reißen; (*damage*) zerreißen; ~ **open** aufreißen; ~ **oneself away** sich losreißen □ *vi* [zer]reißen; (*run*) rasen. ~ **up** *vt* zerreißen
tear[2] /tɪə(r)/ *n* Träne *f*. ~**ful** *a* weinend. ~**fully** *adv* unter Tränen. ~**gas** *n* Tränengas *nt*
tease /tiːz/ *vt* necken
tea: ~**-set** *n* Teeservice *nt*. ~**shop** *n* Café *nt*. ~**spoon** *n* Teelöffel *m*. ~**-strainer** *n* Teesieb *nt*
teat /tiːt/ *n* Zitze *f*; (*on bottle*) Sauger *m*
ˈtea-towel *n* Geschirrtuch *nt*
technical /ˈteknɪkl/ *a* technisch; (*specialized*) fachlich. ~**ity** /-ˈkælətɪ/ *n* technisches Detail *nt*; (*Jur*) Formfehler *m*. ~**ly** *adv* technisch; (*strictly*) streng genommen. ~ **term** *n* Fachausdruck *m*
technician /tekˈnɪʃn/ *n* Techniker *m*
technique /tekˈniːk/ *n* Technik *f*

technological /teknəˈlɒdʒɪkl/ *a*, **-ly** *adv* technologisch
technology /tekˈnɒlədʒɪ/ *n* Technologie *f*
teddy /ˈtedɪ/ *n* ~ **[bear]** Teddybär *m*
tedious /ˈtiːdɪəs/ *a* langweilig
tedium /ˈtiːdɪəm/ *n* Langeweile *f*
teem /tiːm/ *vi (rain)* in Strömen gießen; **be ~ing with** *(full of)* wimmeln von
teenage /ˈtiːneɪdʒ/ *a* Teenager-; ~ **boy/girl** Junge *m*/Mädchen *nt* im Teenageralter. **~r** *n* Teenager *m*
teens /tiːnz/ *npl* **the** ~ die Teenagerjahre *pl*
teeny /ˈtiːnɪ/ *a* (**-ier, -iest**) winzig
teeter /ˈtiːtə(r)/ *vi* schwanken
teeth /tiːθ/ *see* **tooth**
teeth|e /tiːð/ *vi* zahnen. **~ing troubles** *npl (fig)* Anfangsschwierigkeiten *pl*
teetotal /tiːˈtəʊtl/ *a* abstinent. **~ler** *n* Abstinenzler *m*
telecommunications /telɪkəmjuːnɪˈkeɪʃnz/ *npl* Fernmeldewesen *nt*
telegram /ˈtelɪɡræm/ *n* Telegramm *nt*
telegraph /ˈtelɪɡrɑːf/ *n* Telegraf *m*. **~ic** /-ˈɡræfɪk/ *a* telegrafisch. **~ pole** *n* Telegrafenmast *m*
telepathy /tɪˈlepəθɪ/ *n* Telepathie *f*; **by** ~ telepathisch
telephone /ˈtelɪfəʊn/ *n* Telefon *nt*; **be on the** ~ Telefon haben; *(be telephoning)* telefonieren □ *vt* anrufen □ *vi* telefonieren
telephone: ~ **book** *n* Telefonbuch *nt*. ~ **booth** *n*, ~ **box** *n* Telefonzelle *f*. ~ **directory** *n* Telefonbuch *nt*. ~ **number** *n* Telefonnummer *f*
telephonist /tɪˈlefənɪst/ *n* Telefonist(in) *m(f)*
teleˈphoto /telɪ-/ *a* ~ **lens** Teleobjektiv *nt*
teleprinter /ˈtelɪ-/ *n* Fernschreiber *m*
telescop|e /ˈtelɪskəʊp/ *n* Teleskop *nt*, Fernrohr *nt*. **~ic** /-ˈskɒpɪk/ *a* teleskopisch; *(collapsible)* ausziehbar
televise /ˈtelɪvaɪz/ *vt* im Fernsehen übertragen
television /ˈtelɪvɪʒn/ *n* Fernsehen *nt*; **watch** ~ fernsehen. ~ **set** *n* Fernsehapparat *m*, Fernseher *m*
telex /ˈteleks/ *n* Telex *nt* □ *vt* telexen
tell /tel/ *vt/i* (*pt/pp* **told**) sagen (**s.o.** jdm); *(relate)* erzählen; *(know)* wissen; *(distinguish)* erkennen; ~ **the time** die Uhr lesen; **time will** ~ das wird man erst sehen; **his age is beginning to** ~ sein Alter macht sich bemerkbar; **don't ~ me** sag es mir nicht; **you musn't** ~ du darfst nichts sagen. ~ **off** *vt* ausschimpfen
teller /ˈtelə(r)/ *n (cashier)* Kassierer(in) *m(f)*
telly /ˈtelɪ/ *n (fam)* = **television**
temerity /tɪˈmerətɪ/ *n* Kühnheit *f*
temp /temp/ *n (fam)* Aushilfssekretärin *f*
temper /ˈtempə(r)/ *n (disposition)* Naturell *nt*; *(mood)* Laune *f*; *(anger)* Wut *f*; **lose one's** ~ wütend werden □ *vt (fig)* mäßigen
temperament /ˈtemprəmənt/ *n* Temperament *nt*. **~al** /-ˈmentl/ *a* temperamentvoll; *(moody)* launisch
temperance /ˈtempərəns/ *n* Mäßigung *f*; *(abstinence)* Abstinenz *f*
temperate /ˈtempərət/ *a* gemäßigt
temperature /ˈtemprətʃə(r)/ *n* Temperatur *f*; **have** *or* **run a** ~ Fieber haben
tempest /ˈtempɪst/ *n* Sturm *m*. **~uous** /-ˈpestjʊəs/ *a* stürmisch
template /ˈtemplɪt/ *n* Schablone *f*
temple[1] /ˈtempl/ *n* Tempel *m*

temple2 *n* (*Anat*) Schläfe *f*
tempo /ˈtempəʊ/ *n* Tempo *nt*
temporary /ˈtempərərɪ/ *a*, **-ily** *adv* vorübergehend; ⟨*measure, building*⟩ provisorisch
tempt /tempt/ *vt* verleiten; (*Relig*) versuchen; herausfordern ⟨*fate*⟩; (*entice*) [ver]locken; **be ~ed** versucht sein (**to** zu); **I am ~ed by it** es lockt mich. **~ation** /-ˈteɪʃn/ *n* Versuchung *f*. **~ing** *a* verlockend
ten /ten/ *a* zehn
tenable /ˈtenəbl/ *a* (*fig*) haltbar
tenaci|ous /tɪˈneɪʃəs/ *a*, **-ly** *adv* hartnäckig. **~ty** /-ˈnæsətɪ/ *n* Hartnäckigkeit *f*
tenant /ˈtenənt/ *n* Mieter(in) *m*(*f*); (*Comm*) Pächter(in) *m*(*f*)
tend1 /tend/ *vt* (*look after*) sich kümmern um
tend2 *vi* **~ to do sth** dazu neigen, etw zu tun
tendency /ˈtendənsɪ/ *n* Tendenz *f*; (*inclination*) Neigung *f*
tender1 /ˈtendə(r)/ *n* □ (*Comm*) Angebot *nt*; **legal ~** gesetzliches Zahlungsmittel *nt* □ *vt* anbieten; einreichen ⟨*resignation*⟩
tender2 *a* zart; (*loving*) zärtlich; (*painful*) empfindlich. **~ly** *adv* zärtlich. **~ness** *n* Zartheit *f*; Zärtlichkeit *f*
tendon /ˈtendən/ *n* Sehne *f*
tenement /ˈtenəmənt/ *n* Mietshaus *nt*
tenet /ˈtenɪt/ *n* Grundsatz *m*
tenner /ˈtenə(r)/ *n* (*fam*) Zehnpfundschein *m*
tennis /ˈtenɪs/ *n* Tennis *nt*. **~-court** *n* Tennisplatz *m*
tenor /ˈtenə(r)/ *n* Tenor *m*
tense1 /tens/ *n* (*Gram*) Zeit *f*
tense2 *a* (**-r, -st**) gespannt □ *vt* anspannen ⟨*muscle*⟩
tension /ˈtenʃn/ *n* Spannung *f*
tent /tent/ *n* Zelt *nt*
tentacle /ˈtentəkl/ *n* Fangarm *m*
tentative /ˈtentətɪv/ *a*, **-ly** *adv* vorläufig; (*hesitant*) zaghaft
tenterhooks /ˈtentəhʊks/ *npl* **be on ~** wie auf glühenden Kohlen sitzen
tenth /tenθ/ *a* zehnte(r,s) □ *n* Zehntel *nt*
tenuous /ˈtenjʊəs/ *a* (*fig*) schwach
tepid /ˈtepɪd/ *a* lauwarm
term /tɜːm/ *n* Zeitraum *m*; (*Sch*) ≈ Halbjahr *nt*; (*Univ*) ≈ Semester *nt*; (*expression*) Ausdruck *m*; **~s** *pl* (*conditions*) Bedingungen *pl*; **~ of office** Amtszeit *f*; **in the short/long ~** kurz-/langfristig; **be on good/bad ~s** gut/nicht gut miteinander auskommen; **come to ~s with** sich abfinden mit
terminal /ˈtɜːmɪnl/ *a* End-; (*Med*) unheilbar □ *n* (*Aviat*) Terminal *m*; (*of bus*) Endstation *f*; (*on battery*) Pol *m*; (*Computing*) Terminal *nt*
terminat|e /ˈtɜːmɪneɪt/ *vt* beenden; lösen ⟨*contract*⟩; unterbrechen ⟨*pregnancy*⟩ □ *vi* enden. **~ion** /-ˈneɪʃn/ *n* Beendigung *f*; (*Med*) Schwangerschaftsabbruch *m*
terminology /tɜːmɪˈnɒlədʒɪ/ *n* Terminologie *f*
terminus /ˈtɜːmɪnəs/ *n* (*pl* **-ni** /-naɪ/) Endstation *f*
terrace /ˈterəs/ *n* Terrasse *f*; (*houses*) Häuserreihe *f*; **the ~s** (*Sport*) die [Steh]ränge *pl*. **~d house** *n* Reihenhaus *nt*
terrain /teˈreɪn/ *n* Gelände *nt*
terrible /ˈterəbl/ *a*, **-bly** *adv* schrecklich
terrier /ˈterɪə(r)/ *n* Terrier *m*
terrific /təˈrɪfɪk/ *a* (*fam*) (*excellent*) sagenhaft; (*huge*) riesig
terri|fy /ˈterɪfaɪ/ *vt* (*pt/pp* **-ied**) Angst machen (+ *dat*); **be ~fied** Angst haben. **~fying** *a* Furcht erregend
territorial /terɪˈtɔːrɪəl/ *a* Territorial-
territory /ˈterɪtərɪ/ *n* Gebiet *nt*

terror /ˈterə(r)/ *n* [panische] Angst *f*; (*Pol*) Terror *m*. **~ism** /-ɪzm/ *n* Terrorismus *m*. **~ist** /-ɪst/ *n* Terrorist *m*. **~ize** *vt* terrorisieren

terse /tɜːs/ *a*, **-ly** *adv* kurz, knapp

test /test/ *n* Test *m*; (*Sch*) Klassenarbeit *f*; **put to the ~** auf die Probe stellen □ *vt* prüfen; (*examine*) untersuchen (for auf + *acc*)

testament /ˈtestəmənt/ *n* Testament *nt*; **Old/New T~** Altes/Neues Testament *nt*

testicle /ˈtestɪkl/ *n* Hoden *m*

testify /ˈtestɪfaɪ/ *v* (*pt/pp* **-ied**) □ *vt* beweisen; **~ that** bezeugen, dass □ *vi* aussagen; **~ to** bezeugen

testimonial /testɪˈməʊnɪəl/ *n* Zeugnis *nt*

testimony /ˈtestɪmənɪ/ *n* Aussage *f*

ˈtest-tube *n* Reagenzglas *nt*. **~ ˈbaby** *n* (*fam*) Retortenbaby *nt*

testy /ˈtestɪ/ *a* gereizt

tetanus /ˈtetənəs/ *n* Tetanus *m*

tetchy /ˈtetʃɪ/ *a* gereizt

tether /ˈteðə(r)/ *n* **be at the end of one's ~** am Ende seiner Kraft sein □ *vt* anbinden

text /tekst/ *n* Text *m*. **~book** *n* Lehrbuch *nt*

textile /ˈtekstaɪl/ *a* Textil- □ *n* **~s** *pl* Textilien *pl*

texture /ˈtekstʃə(r)/ *n* Beschaffenheit *f*; (*Tex*) Struktur *f*

Thai /taɪ/ *a* thailändisch. **~land** *n* Thailand *nt*

Thames /temz/ *n* Themse *f*

than /ðən, *betont* ðæn/ *conj* als; **older ~ me** älter als ich

thank /θæŋk/ *vt* danken (+ *dat*); **~ you [very much]** danke [schön]. **~ful** *a*, **-ly** *adv* dankbar. **~less** *a* undankbar

thanks /θæŋks/ *npl* Dank *m*; **~!** (*fam*) danke! **~ to** dank (+ *dat or gen*)

that /ðæt/ *a & pron* (*pl* **those**) der/die/das; (*pl*) die; **~ one** der/die/das da; **I'll take ~** ich nehme den/die/das; **I don't like those** die mag ich nicht; **~ is** das heißt; **is ~ you?** bist du es? **who is ~?** wer ist da? **with/after ~** damit/danach; **like ~** so; **a man like ~** so ein Mann; **~ is why** deshalb; **~'s it!** genau! **all ~ I know** alles was ich weiß; **the day ~ I saw him** an dem Tag, als ich ihn sah □ *adv* so; **~ good/hot** so gut/heiß □ *conj* dass

thatch /θætʃ/ *n* Strohdach *nt*. **~ed** *a* strohgedeckt

thaw /θɔː/ *n* Tauwetter *nt* □ *vt/i* auftauen; **it's ~ing** es taut

the /ðə, *vor einem Vokal* ðiː/ *def art* der/die/das; (*pl*) die; **play ~ piano/violin** Klavier/Geige spielen □ *adv* **~ more ~ better** je mehr, desto besser; **all ~ better** umso besser

theatre /ˈθɪətə(r)/ *n* Theater *nt*; (*Med*) Operationssaal *m*

theatrical /θɪˈætrɪkl/ *a* Theater-; (*showy*) theatralisch

theft /θeft/ *n* Diebstahl *m*

their /ðeə(r)/ *a* ihr

theirs /ðeəz/ *poss pron* ihre(r), ihrs; **a friend of ~** ein Freund von ihnen; **those are ~** die gehören ihnen

them /ðem/ *pron* (*acc*) sie; (*dat*) ihnen; **I know ~** ich kenne sie; **give ~ the money** gib ihnen das Geld

theme /θiːm/ *n* Thema *nt*

themˈselves *pron* selbst; (*refl*) sich; **by ~** allein

then /ðen/ *adv* dann; (*at that time in past*) damals; **by ~** bis dahin; **since ~** seitdem; **before ~** vorher; **from ~ on** von da an; **now and ~** dann und wann; **there and ~** auf der Stelle □ *a* damalig

theolog|ian /θɪəˈləʊdʒɪən/ *n* Theologe *m*. **~y** /-ˈɒlədʒɪ/ *n* Theologie *f*

theorem /ˈθɪərəm/ *n* Lehrsatz *m*
theoretical /θɪəˈretɪkl/ *a*, **-ly** *adv* theoretisch
theory /ˈθɪərɪ/ *n* Theorie *f*; **in ~** theoretisch
therapeutic /θerəˈpjuːtɪk/ *a* therapeutisch
therap|ist /ˈθerəpɪst/ *n* Therapeut(in) *m(f)*. **~y** *n* Therapie *f*
there /ðeə(r)/ *adv* da; (*with movement*) dahin, dorthin; **down/up ~** da unten/oben; **~ is/are** da ist/sind; (*in existence*) es gibt; **~ he/she is** da ist er/sie; **send/take ~** hinschicken/-bringen □ *int* **there, there!** nun, nun!
there: ~abouts *adv* da [in der Nähe]; **or ~abouts** (*roughly*) ungefähr. **~ˈafter** *adv* danach. **~by** *adv* dadurch. **~fore** /-fɔː(r)/ *adv* deshalb, also
thermal /ˈθɜːml/ *a* Thermal-; **~ ˈunderwear** *n* Thermowäsche *f*
thermometer /θəˈmɒmɪtə(r)/ *n* Thermometer *nt*
Thermos (P) /ˈθɜːməs/ *n* **~ [flask]** Thermosflasche (P) *f*
thermostat /ˈθɜːməstæt/ *n* Thermostat *m*
these /ðiːz/ *see* **this**
thesis /ˈθiːsɪs/ *n* (*pl* **-ses** /-siːz/) Dissertation *f*; (*proposition*) These *f*
they /ðeɪ/ *pron* sie; **~ say** (*generalizing*) man sagt
thick /θɪk/ *a* (**-er, -est**), **-ly** *adv* dick; (*dense*) dicht; ⟨*liquid*⟩ dickflüssig; (*fam: stupid*) dumm □ *adv* dick □ *n* **in the ~ of** mitten in (+ *dat*). **~en** *vt* dicker machen; eindicken ⟨*sauce*⟩ □ *vi* dicker werden; ⟨*fog:*⟩ dichter werden; ⟨*plot:*⟩ kompliziert werden. **~ness** *n* Dicke *f*; Dichte *f*; Dickflüssigkeit *f*
thick: ~set *a* untersetzt. **~-ˈskinned** *a* (*fam*) dickfellig
thief /θiːf/ *n* (*pl* **thieves**) Dieb(in) *m(f)*
thieving /ˈθiːvɪŋ/ *a* diebisch □ *n* Stehlen *nt*
thigh /θaɪ/ *n* Oberschenkel *m*
thimble /ˈθɪmbl/ *n* Fingerhut *m*
thin /θɪn/ *a* (**thinner, thinnest**), **-ly** *adv* dünn □ *adv* dünn □ *v* (*pt/pp* **thinned**) □ *vt* verdünnen ⟨*liquid*⟩ □ *vi* sich lichten. **~ out** *vt* ausdünnen
thing /θɪŋ/ *n* Ding *nt*; (*subject, affair*) Sache *f*; **~s** *pl* (*belongings*) Sachen *pl*; **for one ~** erstens; **the right ~** das Richtige; **just the ~!** genau das Richtige! **how are ~s?** wie geht's? **the latest ~** (*fam*) der letzte Schrei; **the best ~ would be** am besten wäre es
think /θɪŋk/ *vt/i* (*pt/pp* **thought**) denken (**about/of** an + *acc*); (*believe*) meinen; (*consider*) nachdenken; (*regard as*) halten für; **I ~ so** ich glaube schon; **what do you ~?** was meinen Sie? **what do you ~ of it?** was halten Sie davon? **~ better of it** es sich (*dat*) anders überlegen. **~ over** *vt* sich (*dat*) überlegen. **~ up** *vt* sich (*dat*) ausdenken
third /θɜːd/ *a* dritte(r,s) □ *n* Drittel *nt*. **~ly** *adv* drittens. **~-rate** *a* drittrangig
thirst /θɜːst/ *n* Durst *m*. **~y** *a*, **-ily** *adv* durstig; **be ~y** Durst haben
thirteen /θɜːˈtiːn/ *a* dreizehn. **~th** *a* dreizehnte(r,s)
thirtieth /ˈθɜːtɪɪθ/ *a* dreißigste(r,s)
thirty /ˈθɜːtɪ/ *a* dreißig
this /ðɪs/ *a* (*pl* **these**) diese(r,s); (*pl*) diese; **~ one** diese(r,s) da; **I'll take ~** ich nehme diesen/diese/dieses; **~ evening/morning** heute Abend/Morgen; **these days** heutzutage □ *pron* (*pl* **these**) das, dies[es]; (*pl*) die, diese; **~ and that** dies und das; **~ or that** dieses oder das da; **like ~** so; **~ is Peter** das ist Peter; (*Teleph*) hier [spricht] Peter; **who is ~?** wer ist das? (*Teleph, Amer*) wer ist am Apparat?
thistle /ˈθɪsl/ *n* Distel *f*

thorn /θɔ:n/ *n* Dorn *m*. **~y** *a* dornig

thorough /'θʌrə/ *a* gründlich

thorough: ~bred *n* reinrassiges Tier *nt*; (*horse*) Rassepferd *nt*. **~fare** *n* Durchfahrtsstraße *f*; **'no ~fare'** 'keine Durchfahrt'

thorough|ly /'θʌrəlɪ/ *adv* gründlich; (*completely*) völlig; (*extremely*) äußerst. **~ness** *n* Gründlichkeit *f*

those /ðəʊz/ *see* **that**

though /ðəʊ/ *conj* obgleich, obwohl; **as ~** als ob □ *adv* (*fam*) doch

thought /θɔ:t/ *see* **think** □ *n* Gedanke *m*; (*thinking*) Denken *nt*. **~ful** *a*, **-ly** *adv* nachdenklich; (*considerate*) rücksichtsvoll. **~less** *a*, **-ly** *adv* gedankenlos

thousand /'θaʊznd/ *a* **one/a ~** [ein]tausend □ *n* Tausend *nt*; **~s of** Tausende von. **~th** *a* tausendste(r,s) □ *n* Tausendstel *nt*

thrash /θræʃ/ *vt* verprügeln; (*defeat*) [vernichtend] schlagen. **~ about** *vi* sich herumwerfen; ⟨*fish:*⟩ zappeln. **~ out** *vt* ausdiskutieren

thread /θred/ *n* Faden *m*; (*of screw*) Gewinde *nt* □ *vt* einfädeln; auffädeln ⟨*beads*⟩; **~ one's way through** sich schlängeln durch. **~bare** *a* fadenscheinig

threat /θret/ *n* Drohung *f*; (*danger*) Bedrohung *f*

threaten /'θretn/ *vt* drohen (+ *dat*); (*with weapon*) bedrohen; **~ to do sth** drohen, etw zu tun; **~ s.o. with sth** jdm etw androhen □ *vi* drohen. **~ing** *a*, **-ly** *adv* drohend; (*ominous*) bedrohlich

three /θri:/ *a* drei. **~fold** *a* & *adv* dreifach. **~some** /-səm/ *n* Trio *nt*

thresh /θreʃ/ *vt* dreschen

threshold /'θreʃəʊld/ *n* Schwelle *f*

threw /θru:/ *see* **throw**

thrift /θrɪft/ *n* Sparsamkeit *f*. **~y** *a* sparsam

thrill /θrɪl/ *n* Erregung *f*; (*fam*) Nervenkitzel *m* □ *vt* (*excite*) erregen; **be ~ed with** sich sehr freuen über (+ *acc*). **~er** *n* Thriller *m*. **~ing** *a* erregend

thrive /θraɪv/ *vi* (*pt* **thrived** *or* **throve**, *pp* **thrived** *or* **thriven** /'θrɪvn/) gedeihen (**on** bei); ⟨*business:*⟩ florieren

throat /θrəʊt/ *n* Hals *m*; **sore ~** Halsschmerzen *pl*; **cut s.o.'s ~** jdm die Kehle durchschneiden

throb /θrɒb/ *n* Pochen *nt* □ *vi* (*pt/pp* **throbbed**) pochen; (*vibrate*) vibrieren

throes /θrəʊz/ *npl* **in the ~ of** (*fig*) mitten in (+ *dat*)

thrombosis /θrɒm'bəʊsɪs/ *n* Thrombose *f*

throne /θrəʊn/ *n* Thron *m*

throng /θrɒŋ/ *n* Menge *f*

throttle /'θrɒtl/ *vt* erdrosseln

through /θru:/ *prep* durch (+ *acc*); (*during*) während (+ *gen*); (*Amer: up to & including*) bis einschließlich □ *adv* durch; **all ~** die ganze Zeit; **~ and ~** durch und durch; **wet ~** durch und durch nass; **read sth ~** etw durchlesen; **let/walk ~** durchlassen/-gehen □ *a* ⟨*train*⟩ durchgehend; **be ~** (*finished*) fertig sein; (*Teleph*) durch sein

throughout /θru:'aʊt/ *prep* **~ the country** im ganzen Land; **~ the night** die Nacht durch □ *adv* ganz; (*time*) die ganze Zeit

throve /θrəʊv/ *see* **thrive**

throw /θrəʊ/ *n* Wurf *m* □ *vt* (*pt* **threw**, *pp* **thrown**) werfen; schütten ⟨*liquid*⟩; betätigen ⟨*switch*⟩; abwerfen ⟨*rider*⟩; (*fam: disconcert*) aus der Fassung bringen; (*fam*) geben ⟨*party*⟩; **~ sth to s.o.** jdm etw zuwerfen; **~ sth at s.o.** etw nach jdm werfen; (*pelt with*) jdn mit etw bewerfen. **~ away** *vt* wegwerfen. **~ out** *vt* hinauswerfen; (**~** *away*) wegwerfen; verwerfen ⟨*plan*⟩. **~ up**

vt hochwerfen □ *vi* (*fam*) sich übergeben
'throw-away *a* Wegwerf-
thrush /θrʌʃ/ *n* Drossel *f*
thrust /θrʌst/ *n* Stoß *m*; (*Phys*) Schub *m* □ *vt* (*pt/pp* **thrust**) stoßen; (*insert*) stecken; **~ [up]on** aufbürden (**s.o.** jdm)
thud /θʌd/ *n* dumpfer Schlag *m*
thug /θʌg/ *n* Schläger *m*
thumb /θʌm/ *n* Daumen *m*; **rule of ~** Faustregel *f*; **under s.o.'s ~** unter jds Fuchtel □ *vt* **~ a lift** (*fam*) per Anhalter fahren. **~-index** *n* Daumenregister *nt*. **~tack** *n* (*Amer*) Reißzwecke *f*
thump /θʌmp/ *n* Schlag *m*; (*noise*) dumpfer Schlag *m* □ *vt* schlagen □ *vi* hämmern (**on** an/auf + *acc*); ⟨*heart*:⟩ pochen
thunder /'θʌndə(r)/ *n* Donner *m* □ *vi* donnern. **~clap** *n* Donnerschlag *m*. **~storm** *n* Gewitter *nt*. **~y** *a* gewittrig
Thursday /'θɜːzdeɪ/ *n* Donnerstag *m*
thus /ðʌs/ *adv* so
thwart /θwɔːt/ *vt* vereiteln; **~ s.o.** jdm einen Strich durch die Rechnung machen
thyme /taɪm/ *n* Thymian *m*
thyroid /'θaɪrɔɪd/ *n* Schilddrüse *f*
tiara /tɪ'ɑːrə/ *n* Diadem *nt*
tick[1] /tɪk/ *n* **on~** (*fam*) auf Pump
tick[2] *n* (*sound*) Ticken *nt*; (*mark*) Häkchen *nt*; (*fam: instant*) Sekunde *f* □ *vi* ticken □ *vt* abhaken. **~ off** *vt* abhaken; (*fam*) rüffeln. **~ over** *vi* ⟨*engine*:⟩ im Leerlauf laufen
ticket /'tɪkɪt/ *n* Karte *f*; (*for bus, train*) Fahrschein *m*; (*Aviat*) Flugschein *m*; (*for lottery*) Los *nt*; (*for article deposited*) Schein *m*; (*label*) Schild *nt*; (*for library*) Lesekarte *f*; (*fine*) Strafzettel *m*. **~-collector** *n* Fahrkartenkontrolleur *m*. **~-office** *n* Fahrkartenschalter *m*; (*for entry*) Kasse *f*
tick|le /'tɪkl/ *n* Kitzeln *nt* □ *vt/i* kitzeln. **~lish** /'tɪklɪʃ/ *a* kitzlig
tidal /'taɪdl/ *a* ⟨*river, harbour*⟩ Tide-. **~ wave** *n* Flutwelle *f*
tiddly-winks /'tɪdlɪwɪŋks/ *n* Flohspiel *nt*
tide /taɪd/ *n* Gezeiten *pl*; (*of events*) Strom *m*; **the ~ is in/out** es ist Flut/Ebbe □ *vt* **~ s.o. over** jdm über die Runden helfen
tidiness /'taɪdɪnɪs/ *n* Ordentlichkeit *f*
tidy /'taɪdɪ/ *a* (**-ier, -iest**), **-ily** *adv* ordentlich □ *vt* **~ [up]** aufräumen; **~ oneself up** sich zurechtmachen
tie /taɪ/ *n* Krawatte *f*; Schlips *m*; (*cord*) Schnur *f*; (*fig: bond*) Band *nt*; (*restriction*) Bindung *f*; (*Sport*) Unentschieden *nt*; (*in competition*) Punktgleichheit *f* □ *v* (*pres p* **tying**) □ *vt* binden; machen ⟨*knot*⟩ □ *vi* (*Sport*) unentschieden spielen; (*have equal scores, votes*) punktgleich sein; **~ in with** passen zu. **~ up** *vt* festbinden; verschnüren ⟨*parcel*⟩; fesseln ⟨*person*⟩; **be ~d up** (*busy*) beschäftigt sein
tier /tɪə(r)/ *n* Stufe *f*; (*of cake*) Etage *f*; (*in stadium*) Rang *m*
tiff /tɪf/ *n* Streit *m*, (*fam*) Krach *m*
tiger /'taɪgə(r)/ *n* Tiger *m*
tight /taɪt/ *a* (**-er, -est**), **-ly** *adv* fest; (*taut*) straff; ⟨*clothes*⟩ eng; ⟨*control*⟩ streng; (*fam: drunk*) blau; **in a ~ corner** (*fam*) in der Klemme □ *adv* fest
tighten /'taɪtn/ *vt* fester ziehen; straffen ⟨*rope*⟩; anziehen ⟨*screw*⟩; verschärfen ⟨*control*⟩ □ *vi* sich spannen
tight: ~-'fisted *a* knauserig. **~rope** *n* Hochseil *nt*
tights /taɪts/ *npl* Strumpfhose *f*
tile /taɪl/ *n* Fliese *f*; (*on wall*) Kachel *f*; (*on roof*) [Dach]ziegel *m* □ *vt* mit Fliesen auslegen; kacheln ⟨*wall*⟩; decken ⟨*roof*⟩
till[1] /tɪl/ *prep & conj* = **until**

till² *n* Kasse *f*
tiller /ˈtɪlə(r)/ *n* Ruderpinne *f*
tilt /tɪlt/ *n* Neigung *f*; **at full ~** mit voller Wucht □ *vt* kippen; [zur Seite] neigen ⟨*head*⟩ □ *vi* sich neigen
timber /ˈtɪmbə(r)/ *n* [Nutz]holz *nt*
time /taɪm/ *n* Zeit *f*; (*occasion*) Mal *nt*; (*rhythm*) Takt *m*; **~s** (*Math*) mal; **at any ~** jederzeit; **this ~** dieses Mal, diesmal; **at ~s** manchmal; **~ and again** immer wieder; **two at a ~** zwei auf einmal; **on ~** pünktlich; **in ~** rechtzeitig; (*eventually*) mit der Zeit; **in no ~** im Handumdrehen; **in a year's ~** in einem Jahr; **behind ~** verspätet; **behind the ~s** rückständig; **for the ~ being** vorläufig; **what is the ~?** wie spät ist es? wie viel Uhr ist es? **by the ~ we arrive** bis wir ankommen; **did you have a nice ~?** hat es dir gut gefallen? **have a good ~!** viel Vergnügen! □ *vt* stoppen ⟨*race*⟩; **be well ~d** gut abgepaßt sein
time: ~ bomb *n* Zeitbombe *f*. **~lag** *n* Zeitdifferenz *f*. **~less** *a* zeitlos. **~ly** *a* rechtzeitig. **~switch** *n* Zeitschalter *m*. **~-table** *n* Fahrplan *m*; (*Sch*) Stundenplan *m*
timid /ˈtɪmɪd/ *a*, **-ly** *adv* scheu; (*hesitant*) zaghaft
timing /ˈtaɪmɪŋ/ *n* Wahl *f* des richtigen Zeitpunkts; (*Sport*, *Techn*) Timing *nt*
tin /tɪn/ *n* Zinn *nt*; (*container*) Dose *f* □ *vt* (*pt/pp* **tinned**) in Dosen *od* Büchsen konservieren. **~ foil** *n* Stanniol *nt*; (*Culin*) Alufolie *f*
tinge /tɪndʒ/ *n* Hauch *m* □ *vt* **~d with** mit einer Spur von
tingle /ˈtɪŋgl/ *vi* kribbeln
tinker /ˈtɪŋkə(r)/ *vi* herumbasteln (**with** an + *dat*)
tinkle /ˈtɪŋkl/ *n* Klingeln *nt* □ *vi* klingeln
tinned /tɪnd/ *a* Dosen-, Büchsen-
ˈtin opener *n* Dosen-/Büchsenöffner *m*
ˈtinpot *a* (*pej*) ⟨*firm*⟩ schäbig
tinsel /ˈtɪnsl/ *n* Lametta *nt*
tint /tɪnt/ *n* Farbton *m* □ *vt* tönen
tiny /ˈtaɪnɪ/ *a* (**-ier, -iest**) winzig
tip¹ /tɪp/ *n* Spitze *f*
tip² *n* (*money*) Trinkgeld *nt*; (*advice*) Rat *m*, (*fam*) Tipp *m*; (*for rubbish*) Müllhalde *f* □ *v* (*pt/pp* **tipped**) □ *vt* (*tilt*) kippen; (*reward*) Trinkgeld geben (**s.o.** jdm) □ *vi* kippen. **~ off** *vt* **~ s.o. off** jdm einen Hinweis geben. **~ out** *vt* auskippen. **~ over** *vt/i* umkippen
ˈtip-off *n* Hinweis *m*
tipped /tɪpt/ *a* Filter-
tipsy /ˈtɪpsɪ/ *a* (*fam*) beschwipst
tiptoe /ˈtɪptəʊ/ *n* **on ~** auf Zehenspitzen
tiptop /tɪpˈtɒp/ *a* (*fam*) erstklassig
tire /ˈtaɪə(r)/ *vt/i* ermüden. **~d** *a* müde; **be ~d of sth** etw satt haben; **~d out** [völlig] erschöpft. **~less** *a*, **-ly** *adv* unermüdlich. **~some** /-səm/ *a* lästig
tiring /ˈtaɪrɪŋ/ *a* ermüdend
tissue /ˈtɪʃuː/ *n* Gewebe *nt*; (*handkerchief*) Papiertaschentuch *nt*. **~-paper** *n* Seidenpapier *nt*
tit¹ /tɪt/ *n* (*bird*) Meise *f*
tit² *n* **~ for tat** wie du mir, so ich dir
ˈtitbit *n* Leckerbissen *m*
titilate /ˈtɪtɪleɪt/ *vt* erregen
title /ˈtaɪtl/ *n* Titel *m*. **~-role** *n* Titelrolle *f*
tittle-tattle /ˈtɪtltætl/ *n* Klatsch *m*
titular /ˈtɪtjʊlə(r)/ *a* nominell
to /tuː, *unbetont* tə/ *prep* zu (+ *dat*); (*with place, direction*) nach; (*to cinema, theatre*) in (+ *acc*); (*to wedding, party*) auf (+ *acc*); ⟨*address, send, fasten*⟩ an (+ *acc*); (*per*) pro; (*up to, until*) bis; **to the**

station zum Bahnhof; **to Germany/Switzerland** nach Deutschland/ in die Schweiz; **to the toilet/one's room** auf die Toilette/sein Zimmer; **to the office/an exhibition** ins Büro/ in eine Ausstellung; **to university** auf die Universität; **twenty/quarter to eight** zwanzig/Viertel vor acht; **5 to 6 pounds** 5 bis 6 Pfund; **to the end** bis zum Schluss; **to this day** bis heute; **to the best of my knowledge** nach meinem besten Wissen; **give/say sth to s.o.** jdm etw geben/sagen; **go/come to s.o.** zu jdm gehen/kommen; **I've never been to Berlin** ich war noch nie in Berlin; **there's nothing to it** es ist nichts dabei □ *verbal construction* **to go** gehen; **to stay** bleiben; **learn to swim** schwimmen lernen; **want to/have to go** gehen wollen/ müssen; **be easy/difficult to forget** leicht/schwer zu vergessen sein; **too ill/tired to go** zu krank/müde, um zu gehen; **he did it to annoy me** er tat es, um mich zu ärgern; **you have to** du musst; **I don't want to** ich will nicht; **I'd love to** gern; **I forgot to** ich habe es vergessen; **he wants to be a teacher** er will Lehrer werden; **live to be 90** 90 werden; **he was the last to arrive** er kam als Letzter; **to be honest** ehrlich gesagt □ *adv* **pull to** anlehnen; **to and fro** hin und her

toad /təʊd/ *n* Kröte *f*. **~stool** *n* Giftpilz *m*

toast /təʊst/ *n* Toast *m* □ *vt* toasten ⟨*bread*⟩; (*drink a ~ to*) trinken auf (+ *acc*). **~er** *n* Toaster *m*

tobacco /tə'bækəʊ/ *n* Tabak *m*. **~nist's [shop]** *n* Tabakladen *m*

toboggan /tə'bɒgən/ *n* Schlitten *m* □ *vi* Schlitten fahren

today /tə'deɪ/ *n & adv* heute; **~ week** heute in einer Woche; **~'s paper** die heutige Zeitung

toddler /'tɒdlə(r)/ *n* Kleinkind *nt*

to-do /tə'du:/ *n* (*fam*) Getue *nt*, Theater *nt*

toe /təʊ/ *n* Zeh *m*; (*of footwear*) Spitze *f* □ *vt* **~ the line** spuren. **~nail** *n* Zehennagel *m*

toffee /'tɒfɪ/ *n* Karamell *m & nt*

together /tə'geðə(r)/ *adv* zusammen; (*at the same time*) gleichzeitig

toil /tɔɪl/ *n* [harte] Arbeit *f* □ *vi* schwer arbeiten

toilet /'tɔɪlɪt/ *n* Toilette *f*. **~ bag** *n* Kulturbeutel *m*. **~ paper** *n* Toilettenpapier *nt*

toiletries /'tɔɪlɪtrɪz/ *npl* Toilettenartikel *pl*

toilet: ~ roll *n* Rolle *f* Toilettenpapier. **~ water** *n* Toilettenwasser *nt*

token /'təʊkən/ *n* Zeichen *nt*; (*counter*) Marke *f*; (*voucher*) Gutschein *m* □ *attrib* symbolisch

told /təʊld/ *see* **tell** □ *a* **all ~** insgesamt

tolerable /'tɒlərəbl/ *a*, **-bly** *adv* erträglich; (*not bad*) leidlich

toleran|ce /'tɒlərəns/ *n* Toleranz *f*. **~t** *a*, **-ly** *adv* tolerant

tolerate /'tɒləreɪt/ *vt* dulden, tolerieren; (*bear*) ertragen

toll[1] /təʊl/ *n* Gebühr *f*; (*for road*) Maut *f* (*Aust*); **death ~** Zahl *f* der Todesopfer; **take a heavy ~** einen hohen Tribut fordern

toll[2] *vi* läuten

tom /tɒm/ *n* (*cat*) Kater *m*

tomato /tə'mɑ:təʊ/ *n* (*pl* **-es**) Tomate *f*. **~ purée** *n* Tomatenmark *nt*

tomb /tu:m/ *n* Grabmal *nt*

tomboy /'tɒm-/ *n* Wildfang *m*

'tombstone *n* Grabstein *m*

'tom-cat *n* Kater *m*

tome /təʊm/ *n* dicker Band *m*

tomfoolery /tɒm'fu:lərɪ/ *n* Blödsinn *m*

tomorrow /tə'mɒrəʊ/ *n & adv* morgen; **~ morning** morgen früh; **the day after ~** übermorgen; **see you ~!** bis morgen!
ton /tʌn/ *n* Tonne *f*; **~s of** (*fam*) jede Menge
tone /təʊn/ *n* Ton *m*; (*colour*) Farbton *m* □ *vt* **~ down** dämpfen; (*fig*) mäßigen. **~ up** *vt* kräftigen; straffen ⟨*muscles*⟩
tongs /tɒŋz/ *npl* Zange *f*
tongue /tʌŋ/ *n* Zunge *f*; **~ in cheek** (*fam*) nicht ernst. **~-twister** *n* Zungenbrecher *m*
tonic /'tɒnɪk/ *n* Tonikum *nt*; (*for hair*) Haarwasser *nt*; (*fig*) Wohltat *f*; **~ [water]** Tonic *nt*
tonight /tə'naɪt/ *n & adv* heute Nacht; (*evening*) heute Abend
tonne /tʌn/ *n* Tonne *f*
tonsil /'tɒnsl/ *n* (*Anat*) Mandel *f*. **~litis** /-sə'laɪtɪs/ *n* Mandelentzündung *f*
too /tu:/ *adv* zu; (*also*) auch; **~ much/little** zu viel/zu wenig
took /tʊk/ *see* **take**
tool /tu:l/ *n* Werkzeug *nt*; (*for gardening*) Gerät *nt*
toot /tu:t/ *n* Hupsignal *nt* □ *vi* tuten; (*Auto*) hupen
tooth /tu:θ/ *n* (*pl* **teeth**) Zahn *m*
tooth: ~ache *n* Zahnschmerzen *pl*. **~brush** *n* Zahnbürste *f*. **~less** *a* zahnlos. **~paste** *n* Zahnpasta *f*. **~pick** *n* Zahnstocher *m*
top¹ /tɒp/ *n* (*toy*) Kreisel *m*
top² *n* oberer Teil *m*; (*apex*) Spitze *f*; (*summit*) Gipfel *m*; (*Sch*) Erste(r) *m/f*; (*top part or half*) Oberteil *nt*; (*head*) Kopfende *nt*; (*of road*) oberes Ende *nt*; (*upper surface*) Oberfläche *f*; (*lid*) Deckel *m*; (*of bottle*) Verschluss *m*; (*garment*) Top *nt*; **at the/on ~** oben; **on ~ of** oben auf (+ *dat/acc*); **on ~ of that** (*besides*) obendrein; **from ~ to bottom** von oben bis unten □ *a* oberste(r,s); (*highest*) höchste(r,s); (*best*) beste(r,s) □ *vt* (*pt/pp* **topped**) an erster Stelle stehen auf (+ *dat*) ⟨*list*⟩; (*exceed*) übersteigen; (*remove the ~ of*) die Spitze abschneiden von. **~ up** *vt* nachfüllen, auffüllen
top: ~ 'hat *n* Zylinder[hut] *m*. **~-heavy** *a* kopflastig
topic /'tɒpɪk/ *n* Thema *nt*. **~al** *a* aktuell
top: ~less *a & adv* oben ohne. **~most** *a* oberste(r,s)
topple /'tɒpl/ *vt/i* umstürzen. **~ off** *vi* stürzen
top-'secret *a* streng geheim
topsy-turvy /tɒpsɪ'tɜ:vɪ/ *adv* völlig durcheinander
torch /tɔ:tʃ/ *n* Taschenlampe *f*; (*flaming*) Fackel *f*
tore /tɔ:(r)/ *see* **tear¹**
torment¹ /'tɔ:ment/ *n* Qual *f*
torment² /tɔ:'ment/ *vt* quälen
torn /tɔ:n/ *see* **tear¹** □ *a* zerrissen
tornado /tɔ:'neɪdəʊ/ *n* (*pl* **-es**) Wirbelsturm *m*
torpedo /tɔ:'pi:dəʊ/ *n* (*pl* **-es**) Torpedo *m* □ *vt* torpedieren
torrent /'tɒrənt/ *n* reißender Strom *m*. **~ial** /tə'renʃl/ *a* ⟨*rain*⟩ wolkenbruchartig
torso /'tɔ:səʊ/ *n* Rumpf *m*; (*Art*) Torso *m*
tortoise /'tɔ:təs/ *n* Schildkröte *f*. **~shell** *n* Schildpatt *nt*
tortuous /'tɔ:tjʊəs/ *a* verschlungen; (*fig*) umständlich
torture /'tɔ:tʃə(r)/ *n* Folter *f*; (*fig*) Qual *f* □ *vt* foltern; (*fig*) quälen
toss /tɒs/ *vt* werfen; (*into the air*) hochwerfen; (*shake*) schütteln; (*unseat*) abwerfen; mischen ⟨*salad*⟩; wenden ⟨*pancake*⟩; **~ a coin** mit einer Münze losen □ *vi* **~ and turn** (*in bed*) sich [schlaflos] im Bett wälzen. **~ up** *vi* [mit einer Münze] losen
tot¹ /tɒt/ *n* kleines Kind *nt*; (*fam: of liquor*) Gläschen *nt*
tot² *vt* (*pt/pp* **totted**) **~ up** (*fam*) zusammenzählen
total /'təʊtl/ *a* gesamt; (*complete*) völlig, total □ *n* Gesamtzahl *f*; (*sum*) Gesamtsumme *f* □ *vt*

(*pt/pp* **totalled**) zusammenzählen; (*amount to*) sich belaufen auf (+ *acc*)

totalitarian /təʊtælɪ'teərɪən/ *a* totalitär

totally /'təʊtəlɪ/ *adv* völling, total

totter /'tɒtə(r)/ *vi* taumeln; (*rock*) schwanken. **~y** *a* wackelig

touch /tʌtʃ/ *n* Berührung *f*; (*sense*) Tastsinn *m*; (*Mus*) Anschlag *m*; (*contact*) Kontakt *m*; (*trace*) Spur *f*; (*fig*) Anflug *m*; **get/be in ~** sich in Verbindung setzen/in Verbindung stehen (**with** mit) □ *vt* berühren; (*get hold of*) anfassen; (*lightly*) tippen auf/an (+ *acc*); (*brush against*) streifen [gegen]; (*reach*) erreichen; (*equal*) herankommen an (+ *acc*); (*fig: move*) rühren; anrühren ⟨*food, subject*⟩; **don't ~ that!** fass das nicht an! □ *vi* sich berühren; **~ on** (*fig*) berühren. **~ down** *vi* (*Aviat*) landen. **~ up** *vt* ausbessern

touch|ing /'tʌtʃɪŋ/ *a* rührend. **~y** *a* empfindlich; ⟨*subject*⟩ heikel

tough /tʌf/ *a* (**-er, -est**) zäh; (*severe, harsh*) hart; (*difficult*) schwierig; (*durable*) strapazierfähig

toughen /'tʌfn/ *vt* härten; **~ up** abhärten

tour /tʊə(r)/ *n* Reise *f*, Tour *f*; (*of building, town*) Besichtigung *f*; (*Theat, Sport*) Tournee *f*; (*of duty*) Dienstzeit *f* □ *vt* fahren durch; besichtigen ⟨*building*⟩ □ *vi* herumreisen

touris|m /'tʊərɪzm/ *n* Tourismus *m*, Fremdenverkehr *m*. **~t** /-rɪst/ *n* Tourist(in) *m(f)* □ *attrib* Touristen-. **~t office** *n* Fremdenverkehrsbüro *nt*

tournament /'tʊənəmənt/ *n* Turnier *nt*

'tour operator *n* Reiseveranstalter *m*

tousle /'taʊzl/ *vt* zerzausen

tout /taʊt/ *n* Anreißer *m*; (*ticket ~*) Kartenschwarzhändler *m* □ *vi* **~ for customers** Kunden werben

tow /təʊ/ *n* **give s.o./a car a ~** jdn/ein Auto abschleppen; **'on ~'** 'wird geschleppt'; **in ~** (*fam*) im Schlepptau □ *vt* schleppen; ziehen ⟨*trailer*⟩. **~ away** *vt* abschleppen

toward[s] /tə'wɔ:d(z)/ *prep* zu (+ *dat*); (*with time*) gegen (+ *acc*); (*with respect to*) gegenüber (+ *dat*)

towel /'taʊəl/ *n* Handtuch *nt*. **~ling** *n* (*Tex*) Frottee *nt*

tower /'taʊə(r)/ *n* Turm *m* □ *vi* **~ above** überragen. **~ block** *n* Hochhaus *nt*. **~ing** *a* hoch aufragend

town /taʊn/ *n* Stadt *f*. **~ 'hall** *n* Rathaus *nt*

tow: ~-path *n* Treidelpfad *m*. **~-rope** *n* Abschleppseil *nt*

toxic /'tɒksɪk/ *a* giftig. **~ 'waste** *n* Giftmüll *m*

toxin /'tɒksɪn/ *n* Gift *nt*

toy /tɔɪ/ *n* Spielzeug *nt* □ *vi* **~ with** spielen mit; stochern in (+ *dat*) ⟨*food*⟩. **~shop** *n* Spielwarengeschäft *nt*

trac|e /treɪs/ *n* Spur *f* □ *vt* folgen (+ *dat*); (*find*) finden; (*draw*) zeichnen; (*with tracing-paper*) durchpausen. **~ing-paper** *n* Pauspapier *nt*

track /træk/ *n* Spur *f*; (*path*) [unbefestigter] Weg *m*; (*Sport*) Bahn *f*; (*Rail*) Gleis *nt*; **keep ~ of** im Auge behalten □ *vt* verfolgen. **~ down** *vt* aufspüren; (*find*) finden

'tracksuit *n* Trainingsanzug *m*

tract[1] /trækt/ *n* (*land*) Gebiet *nt*

tract[2] *n* (*pamphlet*) [Flug]schrift *f*

tractor /'træktə(r)/ *n* Traktor *m*

trade /treɪd/ *n* Handel *m*; (*line of business*) Gewerbe *nt*; (*business*) Geschäft *nt*; (*craft*) Handwerk *nt*; **by ~** von Beruf □ *vt* tauschen; **~**

in (*give in part exchange*) in Zahlung geben □ *vi* handeln (**in** mit)
'**trade mark** *n* Warenzeichen *nt*
trader /'treɪdə(r)/ *n* Händler *m*
trade: ~ '**union** *n* Gewerkschaft *f*. ~ '**unionist** *n* Gewerkschaftler(in) *m(f)*
trading /'treɪdɪŋ/ *n* Handel *m*. ~ **estate** *n* Gewerbegebiet *nt*. ~ **stamp** *n* Rabattmarke *f*
tradition /trə'dɪʃn/ *n* Tradition *f*. ~**al** *a*, **-ly** *adv* traditionell
traffic /'træfɪk/ *n* Verkehr *m*; (*trading*) Handel *m* □ *vi* handeln (**in** mit)
traffic: ~ **circle** *n* (*Amer*) Kreisverkehr *m*. ~ **jam** *n* [Verkehrs]stau *m*. ~ **lights** *npl* [Verkehrs]ampel *f*. ~ **warden** *n* ≈ Hilfspolizist *m*; (*woman*) Politesse *f*
tragedy /'trædʒədɪ/ *n* Tragödie *f*
tragic /'trædʒɪk/ *a*, **-ally** *adv* tragisch
trail /treɪl/ *n* Spur *f*; (*path*) Weg *m*, Pfad *m* □ *vi* schleifen; ⟨*plant:*⟩ sich ranken; ~ **[behind]** zurückbleiben; (*Sport*) zurückliegen □ *vt* verfolgen, folgen (+ *dat*); (*drag*) schleifen
trailer /'treɪlə(r)/ *n* (*Auto*) Anhänger *m*; (*Amer: caravan*) Wohnwagen *m*; (*film*) Vorschau *f*
train /treɪn/ *n* Zug *m*; (*of dress*) Schleppe *f*; ~ **of thought** Gedankengang *m* □ *vt* ausbilden; (*Sport*) trainieren; (*aim*) richten auf (+ *acc*); erziehen ⟨*child*⟩; abrichten/(*to do tricks*) dressieren ⟨*animal*⟩; ziehen ⟨*plant*⟩ □ *vi* eine Ausbildung machen; (*Sport*) trainieren. ~**ed** *a* ausgebildet
trainee /treɪ'ni:/ *n* Auszubildende(r) *m/f*; (*Techn*) Praktikant(in) *m(f)*
train|er /'treɪnə(r)/ *n* (*Sport*) Trainer *m*; (*in circus*) Dompteur *m*; ~**ers** *pl* Trainingsschuhe *pl*. ~**ing** *n* Ausbildung *f*; (*Sport*) Training *nt*; (*of animals*) Dressur *f*
traipse /treɪps/ *vi* (*fam*) latschen
trait /treɪt/ *n* Eigenschaft *f*
traitor /'treɪtə(r)/ *n* Verräter *m*
tram /træm/ *n* Straßenbahn *f*. ~-**lines** *npl* Straßenbahnschienen *pl*
tramp /træmp/ *n* Landstreicher *m*; (*hike*) Wanderung *f* □ *vi* stapfen; (*walk*) marschieren
trample /'træmpl/ *vt/i* trampeln (**on** auf + *acc*)
trampoline /'træmpəli:n/ *n* Trampolin *nt*
trance /trɑ:ns/ *n* Trance *f*
tranquil /'træŋkwɪl/ *a* ruhig. ~**lity** /-'kwɪlətɪ/ *n* Ruhe *f*
tranquillizer /'træŋkwɪlaɪzə(r)/ *n* Beruhigungsmittel *nt*
transact /træn'zækt/ *vt* abschließen. ~**ion** /-ækʃn/ *n* Transaktion *f*
transcend /træn'send/ *vt* übersteigen
transcript /'trænskrɪpt/ *n* Abschrift *f*; (*of official proceedings*) Protokoll *nt*. ~**ion** /-'skrɪpʃn/ *n* Abschrift *f*
transept /'trænsept/ *n* Querschiff *nt*
transfer¹ /'trænsfɜ:(r)/ *n* (*see* **transfer²**) Übertragung *f*; Verlegung *f*; Versetzung *f*; Überweisung *f*; (*Sport*) Transfer *m*; (*design*) Abziehbild *nt*
transfer² /træns'fɜ:(r)/ *v* (*pt/pp* **transferred**) □ *vt* übertragen; verlegen ⟨*firm, prisoners*⟩; versetzen ⟨*employee*⟩; überweisen ⟨*money*⟩; (*Sport*) transferieren □ *vi* [über]wechseln; (*when travelling*) umsteigen. ~**able** /-əbl/ *a* übertragbar
transform /træns'fɔ:m/ *vt* verwandeln. ~**ation** /-fə'meɪʃn/ *n* Verwandlung *f*. ~**er** *n* Transformator *m*
transfusion /træns'fju:ʒn/ *n* Transfusion *f*
transient /'trænzɪənt/ *a* kurzlebig; ⟨*life*⟩ kurz

transistor /træn'zɪstə(r)/ *n* Transistor *m*
transit /'trænsɪt/ *n* Transit *m*; (*of goods*) Transport *m*; **in ~** ⟨*goods*⟩ auf dem Transport
transition /træn'sɪʒn/ *n* Übergang *m*. **~al** *a* Übergangs-
transitive /'trænsɪtɪv/ *a*, **-ly** *adv* transitiv
transitory /'trænsɪtərɪ/ *a* vergänglich; ⟨*life*⟩ kurz
translat|e /træns'leɪt/ *vt* übersetzen. **~ion** /-'leɪʃn/ *n* Übersetzung *f*. **~or** *n* Übersetzer(in) *m(f)*
translucent /trænz'lu:snt/ *a* durchscheinend
transmission /trænz'mɪʃn/ *n* Übertragung *f*
transmit /trænz'mɪt/ *vt* (*pt/pp* **transmitted**) übertragen. **~ter** *n* Sender *m*
transparen|cy /træns'pærənsɪ/ *n* (*Phot*) Dia *nt*. **~t** *a* durchsichtig
transpire /træn'spaɪə(r)/ *vi* sich herausstellen; (*fam: happen*) passieren
transplant¹ /'trænsplɑ:nt/ *n* Verpflanzung *f*, Transplantation *f*
transplant² /træns'plɑ:nt/ *vt* umpflanzen; (*Med*) verpflanzen
transport¹ /'trænspɔ:t/ *n* Transport *m*
transport² /træn'spɔ:t/ *vt* transportieren. **~ation** /-'teɪʃn/ *n* Transport *m*
transpose /træns'pəʊz/ *vt* umstellen
transvestite /træns'vestaɪt/ *n* Transvestit *m*
trap /træp/ *n* Falle *f*; (*fam: mouth*) Klappe *f*; **pony and ~** Einspänner *m* □ *vt* (*pt/pp* **trapped**) [mit einer Falle] fangen; (*jam*) einklemmen; **be ~ped** festsitzen; (*shut in*) eingeschlossen sein; (*cut off*) abgeschnitten sein. **~'door** *n* Falltür *f*
trapeze /trə'pi:z/ *n* Trapez *nt*
trash /træʃ/ *n* Schund *m*; (*rubbish*) Abfall *m*; (*nonsense*) Quatsch *m*. **~can** *n* (*Amer*) Mülleimer *m*. **~y** *a* Schund-
trauma /'trɔ:mə/ *n* Trauma *nt*. **~tic** /-'mætɪk/ *a* traumatisch
travel /'trævl/ *n* Reisen *nt* □ *v* (*pt/pp* **travelled**) □ *vi* reisen; (*go in vehicle*) fahren; ⟨*light, sound:*⟩ sich fortpflanzen; (*Techn*) sich bewegen □ *vt* bereisen; fahren ⟨*distance*⟩. **~ agency** *n* Reisebüro *nt*. **~ agent** *n* Reisebürokaufmann *m*
traveller /'trævələ(r)/ *n* Reisende(r) *m/f*; (*Comm*) Vertreter *m*; **~s** *pl* (*gypsies*) Zigeuner *pl*. **~'s cheque** *n* Reisescheck *m*
trawler /'trɔ:lə(r)/ *n* Fischdampfer *m*
tray /treɪ/ *n* Tablett *nt*; (*for baking*) [Back]blech *nt*; (*for documents*) Ablagekorb *m*
treacher|ous /'tretʃərəs/ *a* treulos; (*dangerous, deceptive*) tückisch. **~y** *n* Verrat *m*
treacle /'tri:kl/ *n* Sirup *m*
tread /tred/ *n* Schritt *m*; (*step*) Stufe *f*; (*of tyre*) Profil *nt* □ *v* (*pt* **trod**, *pp* **trodden**) □ *vi* (*walk*) gehen; **~ on/in** treten auf/in (+ *acc*) □ *vt* treten
treason /'tri:zn/ *n* Verrat *m*
treasure /'treʒə(r)/ *n* Schatz *m* □ *vt* in Ehren halten. **~r** *n* Kassenwart *m*
treasury /'treʒərɪ/ *n* Schatzkammer *f*; **the T~** das Finanzministerium
treat /tri:t/ *n* [besonderes] Vergnügen *nt*; **give s.o. a ~** jdm etwas Besonderes bieten □ *vt* behandeln; **~ s.o. to sth** jdm etw spendieren
treatise /'tri:tɪz/ *n* Abhandlung *f*
treatment /'tri:tmənt/ *n* Behandlung *f*
treaty /'tri:tɪ/ *n* Vertrag *m*
treble /'trebl/ *a* dreifach; **~ the amount** dreimal so viel □ *n* (*Mus*) Diskant *m*; (*voice*) Sopran *m* □ *vt*

verdreifachen □ *vi* sich verdreifachen. **~ clef** *n* Violinschlüssel *m*

tree /tri:/ *n* Baum *m*

trek /trek/ *n* Marsch *m* □ *vi* (*pt/pp* **trekked**) latschen

trellis /ˈtrelɪs/ *n* Gitter *nt*

tremble /ˈtrembl/ *vi* zittern

tremendous /trɪˈmendəs/ *a*, **-ly** *adv* gewaltig; (*fam: excellent*) großartig

tremor /ˈtremə(r)/ *n* Zittern *nt*; **[earth] ~** Beben *nt*

trench /trentʃ/ *n* Graben *m*; (*Mil*) Schützengraben *m*

trend /trend/ *n* Tendenz *f*; (*fashion*) Trend *m*. **~y** *a* (**-ier, -iest**) (*fam*) modisch

trepidation /trepɪˈdeɪʃn/ *n* Beklommenheit *f*

trespass /ˈtrespəs/ *vi* **~ on** unerlaubt betreten. **~er** *n* Unbefugte(r) *m/f*

trial /ˈtraɪəl/ *n* (*Jur*) [Gerichts]verfahren *nt*, Prozess *m*; (*test*) Probe *f*; (*ordeal*) Prüfung *f*; **be on ~** auf Probe sein; (*Jur*) angeklagt sein (**for** wegen); **by ~ and error** durch Probieren

triang|le /ˈtraɪæŋgl/ *n* Dreieck *nt*; (*Mus*) Triangel *m*. **~ular** /-ˈæŋgjʊlə(r)/ *a* dreieckig

tribe /traɪb/ *n* Stamm *m*

tribulation /trɪbjʊˈleɪʃn/ *n* Kummer *m*

tribunal /traɪˈbju:nl/ *n* Schiedsgericht *nt*

tributary /ˈtrɪbjʊtərɪ/ *n* Nebenfluss *m*

tribute /ˈtrɪbju:t/ *n* Tribut *m*; **pay ~** Tribut zollen (**to** *dat*)

trice /traɪs/ *n* **in a ~** im Nu

trick /trɪk/ *n* Trick *m*; (*joke*) Streich *m*; (*Cards*) Stich *m*; (*feat of skill*) Kunststück *nt*; **that should do the ~** (*fam*) damit dürfte es klappen □ *vt* täuschen, (*fam*) hereinlegen

trickle /ˈtrɪkl/ *vi* rinnen

trick|ster /ˈtrɪkstə(r)/ *n* Schwindler *m*. **~y** *a* (**-ier, -iest**) *a* schwierig

tricycle /ˈtraɪsɪkl/ *n* Dreirad *nt*

tried /traɪd/ *see* **try**

trifl|e /ˈtraɪfl/ *n* Kleinigkeit *f*; (*Culin*) Trifle *nt*. **~ing** *a* unbedeutend

trigger /ˈtrɪgə(r)/ *n* Abzug *m*; (*fig*) Auslöser *m* □ *vt* **~ [off]** auslösen

trigonometry /trɪgəˈnɒmɪtrɪ/ *n* Trigonometrie *f*

trim /trɪm/ *a* (**trimmer, trimmest**) gepflegt □ *n* (*cut*) Nachschneiden *nt*; (*decoration*) Verzierung *f*; (*condition*) Zustand *m* □ *vt* schneiden; (*decorate*) besetzen; (*Naut*) trimmen. **~ming** *n* Besatz *m*; **~mings** *pl* (*accessories*) Zubehör *nt*; (*decorations*) Verzierungen *pl*; **with all the ~mings** mit allem Drum und Dran

Trinity /ˈtrɪnətɪ/ *n* **the [Holy] ~** die [Heilige] Dreieinigkeit *f*

trinket /ˈtrɪŋkɪt/ *n* Schmuckgegenstand *m*

trio /ˈtri:əʊ/ *n* Trio *nt*

trip /trɪp/ *n* Reise *f*; (*excursion*) Ausflug *m* □ *v* (*pt/pp* **tripped**) □ *vt* **~ s.o. up** jdm ein Bein stellen □ *vi* stolpern (**on/over** über + *acc*)

tripe /traɪp/ *n* Kaldaunen *pl*; (*nonsense*) Quatsch *m*

triple /ˈtrɪpl/ *a* dreifach □ *vt* verdreifachen □ *vi* sich verdreifachen

triplets /ˈtrɪplɪts/ *npl* Drillinge *pl*

triplicate /ˈtrɪplɪkət/ *n* **in ~** in dreifacher Ausfertigung

tripod /ˈtraɪpɒd/ *n* Stativ *nt*

tripper /ˈtrɪpə(r)/ *n* Ausflügler *m*

trite /traɪt/ *a* banal

triumph /ˈtraɪʌmf/ *n* Triumph *m* □ *vi* triumphieren (**over** über + *acc*). **~ant** /-ˈʌmfnt/ *a*, **-ly** *adv* triumphierend

trivial /ˈtrɪvɪəl/ *a* belanglos. **~ity** /-ˈælətɪ/ *n* Belanglosigkeit *f*

trod, **trodden** /trɒd, 'trɒdn/ *see* **tread**

trolley /'trɒlɪ/ *n* (*for serving food*) Servierwagen *m*; (*for shopping*) Einkaufswagen *m*; (*for luggage*) Kofferkuli *m*; (*Amer: tram*) Straßenbahn *f*. ~ **bus** *n* O-Bus *m*

trombone /trɒm'bəʊn/ *n* Posaune *f*

troop /tru:p/ *n* Schar *f*; ~**s** *pl* Truppen *pl* □ *vi* ~ **in/out** hinein-/hinausströmen

trophy /'trəʊfɪ/ *n* Trophäe *f*; (*in competition*) ≈ Pokal *m*

tropic /'trɒpɪk/ *n* Wendekreis *m*; ~**s** *pl* Tropen *pl*. ~**al** *a* tropisch; ⟨*fruit*⟩ Süd-

trot /trɒt/ *n* Trab *m* □ *vi* (*pt/pp* **trotted**) traben

trouble /'trʌbl/ *n* Ärger *m*; (*difficulties*) Schwierigkeiten *pl*; (*inconvenience*) Mühe *f*; (*conflict*) Unruhe *f*; (*Med*) Beschwerden *pl*; (*Techn*) Probleme *pl*; **get into** ~ Ärger bekommen; **take** ~ sich (*dat*) Mühe geben □ *vt* (*disturb*) stören; (*worry*) beunruhigen □ *vi* sich bemühen. ~**-maker** *n* Unruhestifter *m*. ~**some** /-səm/ *a* schwierig; ⟨*flies, cough*⟩ lästig

trough /trɒf/ *n* Trog *m*

trounce /traʊns/ *vt* vernichtend schlagen; (*thrash*) verprügeln

troupe /tru:p/ *n* Truppe *f*

trousers /'traʊzəz/ *npl* Hose *f*

trousseau /'tru:səʊ/ *n* Aussteuer *f*

trout /traʊt/ *n inv* Forelle *f*

trowel /'traʊəl/ *n* Kelle *f*; (*for gardening*) Pflanzkelle *f*

truant /'tru:ənt/ *n* **play** ~ die Schule schwänzen

truce /tru:s/ *n* Waffenstillstand *m*

truck /trʌk/ *n* Last[kraft]wagen *m*; (*Rail*) Güterwagen *m*

truculent /'trʌkjʊlənt/ *a* aufsässig

trudge /trʌdʒ/ *n* [mühseliger] Marsch *m* □ *vi* latschen

true /tru:/ *a* (**-r**, **-st**) wahr; (*loyal*) treu; (*genuine*) echt; **come** ~ in Erfüllung gehen; **is that** ~? stimmt das?

truism /'tru:ɪzm/ *n* Binsenwahrheit *f*

truly /'tru:lɪ/ *adv* wirklich; (*faithfully*) treu; **Yours** ~ Hochachtungsvoll

trump /trʌmp/ *n* (*Cards*) Trumpf *m* □ *vt* übertrumpfen. ~ **up** *vt* (*fam*) erfinden

trumpet /'trʌmpɪt/ *n* Trompete *f*. ~**er** *n* Trompeter *m*

truncheon /'trʌntʃn/ *n* Schlagstock *m*

trundle /'trʌndl/ *vt/i* rollen

trunk /trʌŋk/ *n* [Baum]stamm *m*; (*body*) Rumpf *m*; (*of elephant*) Rüssel *m*; (*for travelling*) [Übersee]koffer *m*; (*for storage*) Truhe *f*; (*Amer: of car*) Kofferraum *m*; ~**s** *pl* Badehose *f*

truss /trʌs/ *n* (*Med*) Bruchband *nt*

trust /trʌst/ *n* Vertrauen *nt*; (*group of companies*) Trust *m*; (*organization*) Treuhandgesellschaft *f*; (*charitable*) Stiftung *f* □ *vt* trauen (+ *dat*), vertrauen (+ *dat*); (*hope*) hoffen □ *vi* vertrauen (**in/to** auf + *acc*)

trustee /trʌs'ti:/ *n* Treuhänder *m*

'**trust|ful** /'trʌstfl/ *a*, **-ly** *adv* vertrauensvoll. ~**ing** *a* vertrauensvoll. ~**worthy** *a* vertrauenswürdig

truth /tru:θ/ *n* (*pl* **-s** /tru:ðz/) Wahrheit *f*. ~**ful** *a*, **-ly** *adv* ehrlich

try /traɪ/ *n* Versuch *m* □ *v* (*pt/pp* **tried**) □ *vt* versuchen; (*sample, taste*) probieren; (*be a strain on*) anstrengen; (*Jur*) vor Gericht stellen; verhandeln ⟨*case*⟩ □ *vi* versuchen; (*make an effort*) sich bemühen. ~ **on** *vt* anprobieren; aufprobieren ⟨*hat*⟩. ~ **out** *vt* ausprobieren

trying /'traɪɪŋ/ *a* schwierig

T-shirt /'ti:-/ *n* T-Shirt *nt*

tub /tʌb/ *n* Kübel *m*; (*carton*) Becher *m*; (*bath*) Wanne *f*
tuba /'tju:bə/ *n* (*Mus*) Tuba *f*
tubby /'tʌbɪ/ *a* (**-ier, -iest**) rundlich
tube /tju:b/ *n* Röhre *f*; (*pipe*) Rohr *nt*; (*flexible*) Schlauch *m*; (*of toothpaste*) Tube *f*; (*Rail, fam*) U-Bahn *f*
tuber /'tju:bə(r)/ *n* Knolle *f*
tuberculosis /tju:bɜ:kjʊ'ləʊsɪs/ *n* Tuberkulose *f*
tubing /'tju:bɪŋ/ *n* Schlauch *m*
tubular /'tju:bjʊlə(r)/ *a* röhrenförmig
tuck /tʌk/ *n* Saum *m*; (*decorative*) Biese *f* □ *vt* (*put*) stecken. ~ **in** *vt* hineinstecken; ~ **s.o. in** jdn zudecken □ *vi* (*fam: eat*) zulangen. ~ **up** *vt* hochkrempeln ⟨*sleeves*⟩; (*in bed*) zudecken
Tuesday /'tju:zdeɪ/ *n* Dienstag *m*
tuft /tʌft/ *n* Büschel *nt*
tug /tʌg/ *n* Ruck *m*; (*Naut*) Schleppdampfer *m* □ *v* (*pt/pp* **tugged**) □ *vt* ziehen □ *vi* zerren (**at** an + *dat*). ~ **of war** *n* Tauziehen *nt*
tuition /tju:'ɪʃn/ *n* Unterricht *m*
tulip /'tju:lɪp/ *n* Tulpe *f*
tumble /'tʌmbl/ *n* Sturz *m* □ *vi* fallen; ~ **to sth** (*fam*) etw kapieren. ~**down** *a* verfallen. ~-**drier** *n* Wäschetrockner *m*
tumbler /'tʌmblə(r)/ *n* Glas *nt*
tummy /'tʌmɪ/ *n* (*fam*) Magen *m*; (*abdomen*) Bauch *m*
tumour /'tju:mə(r)/ *n* Geschwulst *f*, Tumor *m*
tumult /'tju:mʌlt/ *n* Tumult *m*. ~**uous** /-'mʌltjʊəs/ *a* stürmisch
tuna /'tju:nə/ *n* Thunfisch *m*
tune /tju:n/ *n* Melodie *f*; **out of** ~ ⟨*instrument*⟩ verstimmt; **to the** ~ **of** (*fam*) in Höhe von □ *vt* stimmen; (*Techn*) einstellen. ~ **in** *vt* einstellen □ *vi* ~ **in to a station** einen Sender einstellen. ~ **up** *vi* (*Mus*) stimmen
tuneful /'tju:nfl/ *a* melodisch
tunic /'tju:nɪk/ *n* (*Mil*) Uniformjacke *f*; (*Sch*) Trägerkleid *nt*
Tunisia /tju:'nɪzɪə/ *n* Tunesien *nt*
tunnel /'tʌnl/ *n* Tunnel *m* □ *vi* (*pt/pp* **tunnelled**) einen Tunnel graben
turban /'tɜ:bən/ *n* Turban *m*
turbine /'tɜ:baɪn/ *n* Turbine *f*
turbot /'tɜ:bət/ *n* Steinbutt *m*
turbulen|ce /'tɜ:bjʊləns/ *n* Turbulenz *f*. ~**t** *a* stürmisch
tureen /tjʊə'ri:n/ *n* Terrine *f*
turf /tɜ:f/ *n* Rasen *m*; (*segment*) Rasenstück *nt*. ~ **out** *vt* (*fam*) rausschmeißen
'**turf accountant** *n* Buchmacher *m*
Turk /tɜ:k/ *n* Türke *m*/Türkin *f*
turkey /'tɜ:kɪ/ *n* Pute *f*, Truthahn *m*
Turk|ey *n* die Türkei. ~**ish** *a* türkisch
turmoil /'tɜ:mɔɪl/ *n* Aufruhr *m*; (*confusion*) Durcheinander *nt*
turn /tɜ:n/ *n* (*rotation*) Drehung *f*; (*in road*) Kurve *f*; (*change of direction*) Wende *f*; (*short walk*) Runde *f*; (*Theat*) Nummer *f*; (*fam: attack*) Anfall *m*; **do s.o. a good** ~ jdm einen guten Dienst erweisen; **take** ~**s** sich abwechseln; **in** ~ der Reihe nach; **out of** ~ außer der Reihe; **it's your** ~ du bist an der Reihe □ *vt* drehen; (~ *over*) wenden; (*reverse*) umdrehen; (*Techn*) drechseln ⟨*wood*⟩; ~ **the page** umblättern; ~ **the corner** um die Ecke biegen □ *vi* sich drehen; (~ *round*) sich umdrehen; ⟨*car:*⟩ wenden; ⟨*leaves:*⟩ sich färben: ⟨*weather:*⟩ umschlagen; (*become*) werden; ~ **right/left** nach rechts/links abbiegen; ~ **to s.o.** sich an jdn wenden; **have** ~**ed against s.o.** gegen jdn sein. ~ **away** *vt* abweisen □ *vi* sich abwenden. ~ **down** *vt* herunterschlagen ⟨*collar*⟩; herunterdrehen ⟨*heat, gas*⟩; leiser stellen ⟨*sound*⟩; (*reject*) ablehnen; abweisen ⟨*person*⟩. ~ **in**

vt einschlagen ⟨*edges*⟩ □ *vi* ⟨*car:*⟩ einbiegen; (*fam: go to bed*) ins Bett gehen. **~ off** *vt* zudrehen ⟨*tap*⟩; ausschalten ⟨*light, radio*⟩; abstellen ⟨*water, gas, engine, machine*⟩ □ *vi* abbiegen. **~ on** *vt* aufdrehen ⟨*tap*⟩; einschalten ⟨*light, radio*⟩; anstellen ⟨*water, gas, engine, machine*⟩. **~ out** *vt* (*expel*) vertreiben, (*fam*) hinauswerfen; ausschalten ⟨*light*⟩; abdrehen ⟨*gas*⟩; (*produce*) produzieren; (*empty*) ausleeren; [gründlich] aufräumen ⟨*room, cupboard*⟩ □ *vi* (*go out*) hinausgehen; (*transpire*) sich herausstellen; **~ out well/badly** gut/schlecht gehen. **~ over** *vt* umdrehen. **~ up** *vt* hochschlagen ⟨*collar*⟩; aufdrehen ⟨*heat, gas*⟩; lauter stellen ⟨*sound, radio*⟩ □ *vi* auftauchen

turning /ˈtɜːnɪŋ/ *n* Abzweigung *f*. **~-point** *n* Wendepunkt *m*

turnip /ˈtɜːnɪp/ *n* weiße Rübe *f*

turn: ~-out *n* (*of people*) Teilnahme *f*, Beteiligung *f*; (*of goods*) Produktion *f*. **~over** *n* (*Comm*) Umsatz *m*; (*of staff*) Personalwechsel *m*. **~pike** *n* (*Amer*) gebührenpflichtige Autobahn *f*. **~stile** *n* Drehkreuz *nt*. **~table** *n* Drehscheibe *f*; (*on record-player*) Plattenteller *m*. **~-up** *n* [Hosen]aufschlag *m*

turpentine /ˈtɜːpəntaɪn/ *n* Terpentin *nt*

turquoise /ˈtɜːkwɔɪz/ *a* türkis[farben] □ *n* (*gem*) Türkis *m*

turret /ˈtʌrɪt/ *n* Türmchen *nt*

turtle /ˈtɜːtl/ *n* Seeschildkröte *f*

tusk /tʌsk/ *n* Stoßzahn *m*

tussle /ˈtʌsl/ *n* Balgerei *f*; (*fig*) Streit *m* □ *vi* sich balgen

tutor /ˈtjuːtə(r)/ *n* [Privat]lehrer *m*

tuxedo /tʌkˈsiːdəʊ/ *n* (*Amer*) Smoking *m*

TV /tiːˈviː/ *abbr of* **television**

twaddle /ˈtwɒdl/ *n* Geschwätz *nt*

twang /twæŋ/ *n* (*in voice*) Näseln *nt* □ *vt* zupfen

tweed /twiːd/ *n* Tweed *m*

tweezers /ˈtwiːzəz/ *npl* Pinzette *f*

twelfth /twelfθ/ *a* zwölfter(r,s)

twelve /twelv/ *a* zwölf

twentieth /ˈtwentɪɪθ/ *a* zwanzigste(r,s)

twenty /ˈtwentɪ/ *a* zwanzig

twerp /twɜːp/ *n* (*fam*) Trottel *m*

twice /twaɪs/ *adv* zweimal

twiddle /ˈtwɪdl/ *vt* drehen an (+ *dat*)

twig[1] /twɪg/ *n* Zweig *m*

twig[2] *vt/i* (*pt/pp* **twigged**) (*fam*) kapieren

twilight /ˈtwaɪ-/ *n* Dämmerlicht *nt*

twin /twɪn/ *n* Zwilling *m* □ *attrib* Zwillings-. **~ beds** *npl* zwei Einzelbetten *pl*

twine /twaɪn/ *n* Bindfaden *m* □ *vi* sich winden; ⟨*plant:*⟩ sich ranken

twinge /twɪndʒ/ *n* Stechen *nt*; **~ of conscience** Gewissensbisse *pl*

twinkle /ˈtwɪŋkl/ *n* Funkeln *nt* □ *vi* funkeln

twin 'town *n* Partnerstadt *f*

twirl /twɜːl/ *vt/i* herumwirbeln

twist /twɪst/ *n* Drehung *f*; (*curve*) Kurve *f*; (*unexpected occurrence*) überraschende Wendung *f* □ *vt* drehen; (*distort*) verdrehen; (*fam: swindle*) beschummeln; **~ one's ankle** sich (*dat*) den Knöchel verrenken □ *vi* sich drehen; ⟨*road:*⟩ sich winden. **~er** *n* (*fam*) Schwindler *m*

twit /twɪt/ *n* (*fam*) Trottel *m*

twitch /twɪtʃ/ *n* Zucken *nt* □ *vi* zucken

twitter /ˈtwɪtə(r)/ *n* Zwitschern *nt* □ *vi* zwitschern

two /tuː/ *a* zwei

two: ~-faced *a* falsch. **~-piece** *a* zweiteilig. **~some** /-səm/ *n* Paar *nt*. **~-way** *a* **~-way traffic** Gegenverkehr *m*

tycoon /taɪˈkuːn/ *n* Magnat *m*

tying /ˈtaɪɪŋ/ *see* **tie**

type /taɪp/ *n* Art *f*, Sorte *f*; (*person*) Typ *m*; (*printing*) Type *f* □ *vt* mit der Maschine schreiben, (*fam*) tippen; **~d letter** maschinegeschriebener Brief □ *vi* Maschine schreiben, (*fam*) tippen. **~writer** *n* Schreibmaschine *f*. **~written** *a* maschinegeschrieben

typhoid /ˈtaɪfɔɪd/ *n* Typhus *m*

typical /ˈtɪpɪkl/ *a*, **-ly** *adv* typisch (of für)

typify /ˈtɪpɪfaɪ/ *vt* (*pt/pp* **-ied**) typisch sein für

typing /ˈtaɪpɪŋ/ *n* Maschineschreiben *nt*. **~ paper** *n* Schreibmaschinenpapier *nt*

typist /ˈtaɪpɪst/ *n* Schreibkraft *f*

typography /taɪˈpɒgrəfɪ/ *n* Typographie *f*

tyrannical /tɪˈrænɪkl/ *a* tyrannisch

tyranny /ˈtɪrənɪ/ *n* Tyrannei *f*

tyrant /ˈtaɪrənt/ *n* Tyrann *m*

tyre /ˈtaɪə(r)/ *n* Reifen *m*

U

ubiquitous /juːˈbɪkwɪtəs/ *a* allgegenwärtig; **be ~** überall zu finden sein

udder /ˈʌdə(r)/ *n* Euter *nt*

ugl|iness /ˈʌglɪnɪs/ *n* Hässlichkeit *f*. **~y** *a* (**-ier, -iest**) hässlich; (*nasty*) übel

UK *abbr see* **United Kingdom**

ulcer /ˈʌlsə(r)/ *n* Geschwür *nt*

ulterior /ʌlˈtɪərɪə(r)/ *a* **~ motive** Hintergedanke *m*

ultimate /ˈʌltɪmət/ *a* letzte(r,s); (*final*) endgültig; (*fundamental*) grundlegend, eigentlich. **~ly** *adv* schließlich

ultimatum /ʌltɪˈmeɪtəm/ *n* Ultimatum *nt*

ultrasound /ˈʌltrə-/ *n* (*Med*) Ultraschall *m*

ultraˈviolet *a* ultraviolett

umbilical /ʌmˈbɪlɪkl/ *a* **~ cord** Nabelschnur *f*

umbrella /ʌmˈbrelə/ *n* [Regen]schirm *m*

umpire /ˈʌmpaɪə(r)/ *n* Schiedsrichter *m* □ *vt/i* Schiedsrichter sein (bei)

umpteen /ʌmpˈtiːn/ *a* (*fam*) zig. **~th** *a* (*fam*) zigste(r,s); **for the ~th time** zum zigsten Mal

unˈable /ʌn-/ *a* **be ~ to do sth** etw nicht tun können

unaˈbridged *a* ungekürzt

unacˈcompanied *a* ohne Begleitung; ⟨*luggage*⟩ unbegleitet

unacˈcountab|le *a* unerklärlich. **~y** *adv* unerklärlicherweise

unacˈcustomed *a* ungewohnt; **be ~ to sth** etw nicht gewohnt sein

unaˈdulterated *a* unverfälscht, rein; (*utter*) völlig

unˈaided *a* ohne fremde Hilfe

unalloyed /ʌnəˈlɔɪd/ *a* (*fig*) ungetrübt

unanimity /juːnəˈnɪmətɪ/ *n* Einstimmigkeit *f*

unanimous /juːˈnænɪməs/ *a*, **-ly** *adv* einmütig; ⟨*vote, decision*⟩ einstimmig

unˈarmed *a* unbewaffnet; **~ combat** Kampf *m* ohne Waffen

unasˈsuming *a* bescheiden

unatˈtached *a* nicht befestigt; ⟨*person*⟩ ungebunden

unatˈtended *a* unbeaufsichtigt

unˈauthorized *a* unbefugt

unaˈvoidable *a* unvermeidlich

unaˈware *a* **be ~ of sth** sich (*dat*) etw (*gen*) nicht bewusst sein. **~s** /-eəz/ *adv* **catch s.o. ~s** jdn überraschen

unˈbalanced *a* unausgewogen; (*mentally*) unausgeglichen

unˈbearable *a*, **-bly** *adv* unerträglich

unbeat|able /ʌnˈbiːtəbl/ *a* unschlagbar. **~en** *a* ungeschlagen; ⟨*record*⟩ ungebrochen

unbeknown /ʌnbɪˈnəʊn/ *a* (*fam*) **~ to me** ohne mein Wissen

unbe'lievable *a* unglaublich
un'bend *vi* (*pt/pp* **-bent**) (*relax*) aus sich herausgehen
un'biased *a* unvoreingenommen
un'block *vt* frei machen
un'bolt *vt* aufriegeln
un'breakable *a* unzerbrechlich
unbridled /ʌn'braɪdld/ *a* ungezügelt
un'burden *vt* **~ oneself** (*fig*) sich aussprechen
un'button *vt* aufknöpfen
uncalled-for /ʌn'kɔ:ldfɔ:(r)/ *a* unangebracht
un'canny *a* unheimlich
un'ceasing *a* unaufhörlich
uncere'monious *a*, **-ly** *adv* formlos; (*abrupt*) brüsk
un'certain *a* (*doubtful*) ungewiss; ⟨*origins*⟩ unbestimmt; **be ~** nicht sicher sein; **in no ~ terms** ganz eindeutig. **~ty** *n* Ungewissheit *f*
un'changed *a* unverändert
un'charitable *a* lieblos
uncle /'ʌŋkl/ *n* Onkel *m*
un'comfortable *a*, **-bly** *adv* unbequem; **feel ~** (*fig*) sich nicht wohl fühlen
un'common *a* ungewöhnlich
un'compromising *a* kompromisslos
uncon'ditional *a*, **~ly** *adv* bedingungslos
un'conscious *a* bewusstlos; (*unintended*) unbewusst; **be ~ of sth** sich (*dat*) etw (*gen*) nicht bewusst sein. **~ly** *adv* unbewusst
uncon'ventional *a* unkonventionell
unco'operative *a* nicht hilfsbereit
un'cork *vt* entkorken
uncouth /ʌn'ku:θ/ *a* ungehobelt
un'cover *vt* aufdecken
unctuous /'ʌŋktjʊəs/ *a*, **-ly** *adv* salbungsvoll
unde'cided *a* unentschlossen; (*not settled*) nicht entschieden
undeniable /ʌndɪ'naɪəbl/ *a*, **-bly** *adv* unbestreitbar
under /'ʌndə(r)/ *prep* unter (+ *dat/acc*); **~ it** darunter; **~ there** da drunter; **~ repair** in Reparatur; **~ construction** im Bau; **~ age** minderjährig; **~ way** unterwegs; (*fig*) im Gange □ *adv* darunter
'undercarriage *n* (*Aviat*) Fahrwerk *nt*, Fahrgestell *nt*
'underclothes *npl* Unterwäsche *f*
under'cover *a* geheim
'undercurrent *n* Unterströmung *f*; (*fig*) Unterton *m*
under'cut *vt* (*pt/pp* **-cut**) (*Comm*) unterbieten
'underdog *n* Unterlegene(r) *m*
under'done *a* nicht gar; (*rare*) nicht durchgebraten
under'estimate *vt* unterschätzen
under'fed *a* unterernährt
under'foot *adv* am Boden; **trample ~** zertrampeln
under'go *vt* (*pt* **-went**, *pp* **-gone**) durchmachen; sich unterziehen (+ *dat*) ⟨*operation, treatment*⟩; **~ repairs** repariert werden
under'graduate *n* Student(in) *m(f)*
under'ground¹ *adv* unter der Erde; ⟨*mining*⟩ unter Tage
'underground² *a* unterirdisch; (*secret*) Untergrund- □ *n* (*railway*) U-Bahn *f*. **~ car park** *n* Tiefgarage *f*
'undergrowth *n* Unterholz *nt*
'underhand *a* hinterhältig
'underlay *n* Unterlage *f*
under'lie *vt* (*pt* **-lay**, *pp* **-lain**, *pres p* **-lying**) (*fig*) zugrunde liegen (+ *dat*)
under'line *vt* unterstreichen
underling /'ʌndəlɪŋ/ *n* (*pej*) Untergebene(r) *m/f*
under'lying *a* (*fig*) eigentlich
under'mine *vt* (*fig*) unterminieren, untergraben
underneath /ʌndə'ni:θ/ *prep* unter (+ *dat/acc*); **~ it** darunter □ *adv* darunter

'underpants *npl* Unterhose *f*
'underpass *n* Unterführung *f*
under'privileged *a* unterprivilegiert
under'rate *vt* unterschätzen
'underseal *n* (*Auto*) Unterbodenschutz *m*
'undershirt *n* (*Amer*) Unterhemd *nt*
understaffed /-'stɑ:ft/ *a* unterbesetzt
under'stand *vt/i* (*pt/pp* **-stood**) verstehen; **I ~ that ...** (*have heard*) ich habe gehört, dass ... **~able** /-əbl/ *a* verständlich. **~ably** /-əblɪ/ *adv* verständlicherweise
under'standing *a* verständnisvoll □ *n* Verständnis *int*; (*agreement*) Vereinbarung *f*; **reach an ~** sich verständigen; **on the ~ that** unter der Voraussetzung, dass
'understatement *n* Untertreibung *f*
'understudy *n* (*Theat*) Ersatzspieler(in) *m(f)*
under'take *vt* (*pt* **-took**, *pp* **-taken**) unternehmen; **~ to do sth** sich verpflichten, etw zu tun
'undertaker *n* Leichenbestatter *m*; **[firm of] ~s** Bestattungsinstitut *n*
under'taking *n* Unternehmen *nt*; (*promise*) Versprechen *nt*
'undertone *n* (*fig*) Unterton *m*; **in an ~** mit gedämpfter Stimme
under'value *vt* unterbewerten
'underwater¹ *a* Unterwasser-
under'water² *adv* unter Wasser
'underwear *n* Unterwäsche *f*
under'weight *a* untergewichtig; **be ~** Untergewicht haben
'underworld *n* Unterwelt *f*
'underwriter *n* Versicherer *m*
unde'sirable *a* unerwünscht
undies /'ʌndɪz/ *npl* (*fam*) [Damen]unterwäsche *f*
un'dignified *a* würdelos
un'do *vt* (*pt* **-did**, *pp* **-done**) aufmachen; (*fig*) ungeschehen machen; (*ruin*) zunichte machen
un'done *a* offen; (*not accomplished*) unerledigt
un'doubted *a* unzweifelhaft. **~ly** *adv* zweifellos
un'dress *vt* ausziehen; **get ~ed** sich ausziehen □ *vi* sich ausziehen
un'due *a* übermäßig
undulating /'ʌndjʊleɪtɪŋ/ *a* Wellen-; ⟨*country*⟩ wellig
und'uly *adv* übermäßig
un'dying *a* ewig
un'earth *vt* ausgraben; (*fig*) zutage bringen. **~ly** *a* unheimlich; **at an ~ly hour** (*fam*) in aller Herrgottsfrühe
un'eas|e *n* Unbehagen *nt*. **~y** *a* unbehaglich; **I feel ~y** mir ist unbehaglich zumute
un'eatable *a* ungenießbar
uneco'nomic *a*, **-ally** *adv* unwirtschaftlich
uneco'nomical *a* verschwenderisch
unem'ployed *a* arbeitslos □ *npl* **the ~** die Arbeitslosen
unem'ployment *n* Arbeitslosigkeit *f*. **~ benefit** *n* Arbeitslosenunterstützung *f*
un'ending *a* endlos
un'equal *a* unterschiedlich; ⟨*struggle*⟩ ungleich; **be ~ to a task** einer Aufgabe nicht gewachsen sein. **~ly** *adv* ungleichmäßig
unequivocal /ʌnɪ'kwɪvəkl/ *a*, **-ly** *adv* eindeutig
unerring /ʌn'ɜ:rɪŋ/ *a* unfehlbar
un'ethical *a* unmoralisch; **be ~** gegen das Berufsethos verstoßen
un'even *a* uneben; (*unequal*) ungleich; (*not regular*) ungleichmäßig; ⟨*number*⟩ ungerade. **~ly** *adv* ungleichmäßig
unex'pected *a*, **-ly** *adv* unerwartet
un'failing *a* nie versagend

un'fair *a*, **-ly** *adv* ungerecht, unfair. **~ness** *n* Ungerechtigkeit *f*
un'faithful *a* untreu
unfa'miliar *a* ungewohnt; (*unknown*) unbekannt
un'fasten *vt* aufmachen; (*detach*) losmachen
un'favourable *a* ungünstig
un'feeling *a* gefühllos
un'finished *a* unvollendet; ⟨*business*⟩ unerledigt
un'fit *a* ungeeignet; (*incompetent*) unfähig; (*Sport*) nicht fit; **~ for work** arbeitsunfähig
unflinching /ʌn'flɪntʃɪŋ/ *a* unerschrocken
un'fold *vt* auseinander falten, entfalten; (*spread out*) ausbreiten □ *vi* sich entfalten
unfore'seen *a* unvorhergesehen
unforgettable /ʌnfə'getəbl/ *a* unvergesslich
unforgivable /ʌnfə'gɪvəbl/ *a* unverzeihlich
un'fortunate *a* unglücklich; (*unfavourable*) ungünstig; (*regrettable*) bedauerlich; **be ~** ⟨*person:*⟩ Pech haben. **~ly** *adv* leider
un'founded *a* unbegründet
unfurl /ʌn'fɜ:l/ *vt* entrollen □ *vi* sich entrollen
un'furnished *a* unmöbliert
ungainly /ʌn'geɪnlɪ/ *a* unbeholfen
ungodly /ʌn'gɒdlɪ/ *a* gottlos; **at an ~ hour** (*fam*) in aller Herrgottsfrühe
un'grateful *a*, **-ly** *adv* undankbar
un'happi|ly *adv* unglücklich; (*unfortunately*) leider. **~ness** *n* Kummer *m*
un'happy *a* unglücklich; (*not content*) unzufrieden
un'harmed *a* unverletzt
un'healthy *a* ungesund
un'hook *vt* vom Haken nehmen; aufhaken ⟨*dress*⟩
un'hurt *a* unverletzt
unhy'gienic *a* unhygienisch
unicorn /'ju:nɪkɔ:n/ *n* Einhorn *nt*
unification /ju:nɪfɪ'keɪʃn/ *n* Einigung *f*
uniform /'ju:nɪfɔ:m/ *a*, **-ly** *adv* einheitlich □ *n* Uniform *f*
unify /'ju:nɪfaɪ/ *vt* (*pt/pp* **-ied**) einigen
uni'lateral /ju:nɪ-/ *a*, **-ly** *adv* einseitig
uni'maginable *a* unvorstellbar
unim'portant *a* unwichtig
unin'habited *a* unbewohnt
unin'tentional *a*, **-ly** *adv* unabsichtlich
union /'ju:nɪən/ *n* Vereinigung *f*; (*Pol*) Union *f*; (*trade* **~**) Gewerkschaft *f*. **~ist** *n* (*Pol*) Unionist *m*
unique /ju:'ni:k/ *a* einzigartig. **~ly** *adv* einmalig
unison /'ju:nɪsn/ *n* **in ~** einstimmig
unit /'ju:nɪt/ *n* Einheit *f*; (*Math*) Einer *m*; (*of furniture*) Teil *nt*, Element *nt*
unite /ju:'naɪt/ *vt* vereinigen □ *vi* sich vereinigen
united /ju:'naɪtɪd/ *a* einig. **U~ 'Kingdom** *n* Vereinigtes Königreich *nt*. **U~ 'Nations** *n* Vereinte Nationen *pl*. **U~ States [of America]** *n* Vereinigte Staaten *pl* [von Amerika]
unity /'ju:nətɪ/ *n* Einheit *f*; (*harmony*) Einigkeit *f*
universal /ju:nɪ'vɜ:sl/ *a*, **-ly** *adv* allgemein
universe /'ju:nɪvɜ:s/ *n* [Welt]all *nt*, Universum *nt*
university /ju:nɪ'vɜ:sətɪ/ *n* Universität *f* □ *attrib* Universitäts-
un'just *a*, **-ly** *adv* ungerecht
unkempt /ʌn'kempt/ *a* ungepflegt
un'kind *a*, **-ly** *adv* unfreundlich; (*harsh*) hässlich. **~ness** *n* Unfreundlichkeit *f*; Hässlichkeit *f*
un'known *a* unbekannt
un'lawful *a*, **-ly** *adv* gesetzwidrig
unleaded /ʌn'ledɪd/ *a* bleifrei
un'leash *vt* (*fig*) entfesseln

unless /ən'les/ *conj* wenn ... nicht; ~ **I am mistaken** wenn ich mich nicht irre
un'like *a* nicht ähnlich, unähnlich; (*not the same*) ungleich □ *prep* im Gegensatz zu (+ *dat*)
un'likely *a* unwahrscheinlich
un'limited *a* unbegrenzt
un'load *vt* entladen; ausladen ⟨*luggage*⟩
un'lock *vt* aufschließen
un'lucky *a* unglücklich; ⟨*day, number*⟩ Unglücks-; **be** ~ Pech haben; ⟨*thing:*⟩ Unglück bringen
un'manned *a* unbemannt
un'married *a* unverheiratet. ~ '**mother** *n* ledige Mutter *f*
un'mask *vt* (*fig*) entlarven
unmistakable /ʌnmɪ'steɪkəbl/ *a*, **-bly** *adv* unverkennbar
un'mitigated *a* vollkommen
un'natural *a*, **-ly** *adv* unnatürlich; (*not normal*) nicht normal
un'necessary *a*, **-ily** *adv* unnötig
un'noticed *a* unbemerkt
unob'tainable *a* nicht erhältlich
unob'trusive *a*, **-ly** *adv* unaufdringlich; ⟨*thing*⟩ unauffällig
unof'ficial *a*, **-ly** *adv* inoffiziell
un'pack *vt/i* auspacken
un'paid *a* unbezahlt
un'palatable *a* ungenießbar
un'paralleled *a* beispiellos
un'pick *vt* auftrennen
un'pleasant *a*, **-ly** *adv* unangenehm. ~**ness** *n* (*bad feeling*) Ärger *m*
un'plug *vt* (*pt/pp* **-plugged**) den Stecker herausziehen von
un'popular *a* unbeliebt
un'precedented *a* beispiellos
unpre'dictable *a* unberechenbar
unpre'meditated *a* nicht vorsätzlich
unpre'pared *a* nicht vorbereitet
unprepos'sessing *a* wenig attraktiv
unpre'tentious *a* bescheiden
un'principled *a* skrupellos
unpro'fessional *a* **be** ~ gegen das Berufsethos verstoßen; (*Sport*) unsportlich sein
un'profitable *a* unrentabel
un'qualified *a* unqualifiziert; (*fig: absolute*) uneingeschränkt
un'questionable *a* unbezweifelbar; ⟨*right*⟩ unbestreitbar
unravel /ʌn'rævl/ *vt* (*pt/pp* **-ravelled**) entwirren; (*Knitting*) aufziehen
un'real *a* unwirklich
un'reasonable *a* unvernünftig; **be** ~ zu viel verlangen
unre'lated *a* unzusammenhängend; **be** ~ nicht verwandt sein; ⟨*events:*⟩ nicht miteinander zusammenhängen
unre'liable *a* unzuverlässig
unrequited /ʌnrɪ'kwaɪtɪd/ *a* unerwidert
unreservedly /ʌnrɪ'zɜ:vɪdlɪ/ *adv* uneingeschränkt; (*frankly*) offen
un'rest *n* Unruhen *pl*
un'rivalled *a* unübertroffen
un'roll *vt* aufrollen □ *vi* sich aufrollen
unruly /ʌn'ru:lɪ/ *a* ungebärdig
un'safe *a* nicht sicher
un'said *a* ungesagt
un'salted *a* ungesalzen
unsatis'factory *a* unbefriedigend
un'savoury *a* unangenehm; (*fig*) unerfreulich
unscathed /ʌn'skeɪðd/ *a* unversehrt
un'screw *vt* abschrauben
un'scrupulous *a* skrupellos
un'seemly *a* unschicklich
un'selfish *a* selbstlos
un'settled *a* ungeklärt; ⟨*weather*⟩ unbeständig; ⟨*bill*⟩ unbezahlt
unshakeable /ʌn'ʃeɪkəbl/ *a* unerschütterlich
unshaven /ʌn'ʃeɪvn/ *a* unrasiert
unsightly /ʌn'saɪtlɪ/ *a* unansehnlich

un'skilled *a* ungelernt; ⟨*work*⟩ unqualifiziert
un'sociable *a* ungesellig
unso'phisticated *a* einfach
un'sound *a* krank, nicht gesund; ⟨*building*⟩ nicht sicher; ⟨*advice*⟩ unzuverlässig; ⟨*reasoning*⟩ nicht stichhaltig; **of ~ mind** unzurechnungsfähig
unspeakable /ʌn'spi:kəbl/ *a* unbeschreiblich
un'stable *a* nicht stabil; (*mentally*) labil
un'steady *a*, **-ily** *adv* unsicher; (*wobbly*) wackelig
un'stuck *a* **come ~** sich lösen; (*fam: fail*) scheitern
unsuc'cessful *a*, **-ly** *adv* erfolglos; **be ~** keinen Erfolg haben
un'suitable *a* ungeeignet; (*inappropriate*) unpassend; (*for weather, activity*) unzweckmäßig
unsu'specting *a* ahnungslos
un'sweetened *a* ungesüßt
unthinkable /ʌn'θɪŋkəbl/ *a* unvorstellbar
un'tidiness *n* Unordentlichkeit *f*
un'tidy *a*, **-ily** *adv* unordentlich
un'tie *vt* aufbinden; losbinden ⟨*person, boat, horse*⟩
until /ən'tɪl/ *prep* bis (+ *acc*); **not ~** erst; **~ the evening** bis zum Abend; **~ his arrival** bis zu seiner Ankunft □ *conj* bis; **not ~** erst wenn; (*in past*) erst als
untimely /ʌn'taɪmlɪ/ *a* ungelegen; (*premature*) vorzeitig
un'tiring *a* unermüdlich
un'told *a* unermesslich
unto'ward *a* ungünstig; (*unseemly*) ungehörig; **if nothing ~ happens** wenn nichts dazwischenkommt
un'true *a* unwahr; **that's ~** das ist nicht wahr
unused[1] /ʌn'ju:zd/ *a* unbenutzt; (*not utilized*) ungenutzt
unused[2] /ʌn'ju:st/ *a* **be ~ to sth** etw nicht gewohnt sein
un'usual *a*, **-ly** *adv* ungewöhnlich
un'veil *vt* enthüllen
un'versed *a* nicht bewandert (**in** in + *dat*)
un'wanted *a* unerwünscht
un'warranted *a* ungerechtfertigt
un'welcome *a* unwillkommen
un'well *a* **be** *or* **feel ~** sich nicht wohl fühlen
unwieldy /ʌn'wi:ldɪ/ *a* sperrig
un'willing *a*, **-ly** *adv* widerwillig; **be ~ to do sth** etw nicht tun wollen
un'wind *v* (*pt/pp* **unwound**) □ *vt* abwickeln □ *vi* sich abwickeln; (*fam: relax*) sich entspannen
un'wise *a*, **-ly** *adv* unklug
unwitting /ʌn'wɪtɪŋ/ *a*, **-ly** *adv* unwissentlich
un'worthy *a* unwürdig
un'wrap *vt* (*pt/pp* **-wrapped**) auswickeln; auspacken ⟨*present*⟩
un'written *a* ungeschrieben
up /ʌp/ *adv* oben; (*with movement*) nach oben; (*not in bed*) auf; ⟨*collar*⟩ hochgeklappt; ⟨*road*⟩ aufgerissen; ⟨*price*⟩ gestiegen; ⟨*curtains*⟩ aufgehängt; ⟨*shelves*⟩ angebracht; ⟨*notice*⟩ angeschlagen; ⟨*tent*⟩ aufgebaut; ⟨*building*⟩ gebaut; **be up for sale** zu verkaufen sein; **up there** da oben; **up to** (*as far as*) bis; **time's up** die Zeit ist um; **what's up?** (*fam*) was ist los? **what's he up to?** (*fam*) was hat er vor? **I don't feel up to it** ich fühle mich dem nicht gewachsen; **be one up on s.o.** (*fam*) jdm etwas voraushaben; **go up** hinaufgehen; **come up** heraufkommen □ *prep* **be up on sth** [oben] auf etw (*dat*) sein; **up the mountain** oben am Berg; (*movement*) den Berg hinauf; **be up the tree** oben im Baum sein; **up the road** die Straße entlang; **up the river** stromaufwärts; **go up the stairs** die Treppe hinaufgehen; **be up the pub** (*fam*) in der Kneipe sein
'upbringing *n* Erziehung *f*

up'date *vt* auf den neuesten Stand bringen
up'grade *vt* aufstufen
upheaval /ʌp'hi:vl/ *n* Unruhe *f*; *(Pol)* Umbruch *m*
up'hill *a (fig)* mühsam □ *adv* bergauf
up'hold *vt (pt/pp* **upheld***)* unterstützen; bestätigen ⟨*verdict*⟩
upholster /ʌp'həʊlstə(r)/ *vt* polstern. **~er** *n* Polsterer *m*. **~y** *n* Polsterung *f*
'upkeep *n* Unterhalt *m*
up-'market *a* anspruchsvoll
upon /ə'pɒn/ *prep* auf (+ *dat/acc*)
upper /'ʌpə(r)/ *a* obere(r,s); ⟨*deck, jaw, lip*⟩ Ober-; **have the ~ hand** die Oberhand haben □ *n (of shoe)* Obermaterial *nt*
upper: ~ circle *n* zweiter Rang *m*. **~ class** *n* Oberschicht *f*. **~most** *a* oberste(r,s)
'upright *a* aufrecht □ *n* Pfosten *m*
'uprising *n* Aufstand *m*
'uproar *n* Aufruhr *m*
up'root *vt* entwurzeln
up'set¹ *vt (pt/pp* **upset**, *pres p* **upsetting***)* umstoßen; *(spill)* verschütten; durcheinander bringen ⟨*plan*⟩; *(distress)* erschüttern; ⟨*food:*⟩ nicht bekommen (+ *dat*); **get ~ about sth** sich über etw *(acc)* aufregen; **be very ~** sehr bestürzt sein
'upset² *n* Aufregung *f*; **have a stomach ~** einen verdorbenen Magen haben
'upshot *n* Ergebnis *nt*
upside 'down *adv* verkehrt herum; **turn ~** umdrehen
up'stairs¹ *adv* oben; ⟨*go*⟩ nach oben
'upstairs² *a* im Obergeschoss
'upstart *n* Emporkömmling *m*
up'stream *adv* stromaufwärts
'upsurge *n* Zunahme *f*
'uptake *n* **slow on the ~** schwer von Begriff; **be quick on the ~** schnell begreifen
up'tight *a* nervös
'upturn *n* Aufschwung *m*
upward /'ʌpwəd/ *a* nach oben; ⟨*movement*⟩ Aufwärts-; **~ slope** Steigung *f* □ *adv* **~[s]** aufwärts, nach oben
uranium /jʊ'reɪnɪəm/ *n* Uran *nt*
urban /'ɜ:bən/ *a* städtisch
urbane /ɜ:'beɪn/ *a* weltmännisch
urge /ɜ:dʒ/ *n* Trieb *m*, Drang *m* □ *vt* drängen; **~ on** antreiben
urgen|cy /'ɜ:dʒənsɪ/ *n* Dringlichkeit *f*. **~t** *a*, **-ly** *adv* dringend
urinate /'jʊərɪneɪt/ *vi* urinieren
urine /'jʊərɪn/ *n* Urin *m*, Harn *m*
urn /ɜ:n/ *n* Urne *f*; *(for tea)* Teemaschine *f*
us /ʌs/ *pron* uns; **it's us** wir sind es
US[A] *abbr* USA *pl*
usable /'ju:zəbl/ *a* brauchbar
usage /'ju:zɪdʒ/ *n* Brauch *m*; *(of word)* [Sprach]gebrauch *m*
use¹ /ju:s/ *n (see* **use²***)* Benutzung *f*; Verwendung *f*; Gebrauch *m*; **be of ~** nützlich sein; **be of no ~** nichts nützen; **make ~ of** Gebrauch machen von; *(exploit)* ausnutzen; **it is no ~** es hat keinen Zweck; **what's the ~?** wozu?
use² /ju:z/ *vt* benutzen ⟨*implement, room, lift*⟩; verwenden ⟨*ingredient, method, book, money*⟩; gebrauchen ⟨*words, force, brains*⟩; **~ [up]** aufbrauchen
used¹ /ju:zd/ *a* benutzt; ⟨*car*⟩ Gebraucht-
used² /ju:st/ *pt* **be ~ to sth** an etw *(acc)* gewöhnt sein; **get ~ to** sich gewöhnen an (+ *acc*); **he ~ to say** er hat immer gesagt; **he ~ to live here** er hat früher hier gewohnt
useful /'ju:sfl/ *a* nützlich. **~ness** *n* Nützlichkeit *f*
useless /'ju:slɪs/ *a* nutzlos; *(not usable)* unbrauchbar; *(pointless)* zwecklos
user /'ju:zə(r)/ *n* Benutzer(in) *m(f)*. **~-'friendly** *a* benutzerfreundlich

usher /ˈʌʃə(r)/ *n* Platzanweiser *m*; (*in court*) Gerichtsdiener *m* □ *vt* ~ **in** hineinführen
usherette /ʌʃəˈret/ *n* Platzanweiserin *f*
USSR *abbr* UdSSR *f*
usual /ˈjuːʒʊəl/ *a* üblich. **~ly** *adv* gewöhnlich
usurp /juːˈzɜːp/ *vt* sich (*dat*) widerrechtlich aneignen
utensil /juːˈtensl/ *n* Gerät *nt*
uterus /ˈjuːtərəs/ *n* Gebärmutter *f*
utilitarian /juːtɪlɪˈteərɪən/ *a* zweckmäßig
utility /juːˈtɪlətɪ/ *a* Gebrauchs- □ *n* Nutzen *m*. **~ room** *n* ≈ Waschküche *f*
utiliz|ation /juːtɪlaɪˈzeɪʃn/ *n* Nutzung *f*. **~e** /ˈjuːtɪlaɪz/ *vt* nutzen
utmost /ˈʌtməʊst/ *a* äußerste(r,s), größte(r,s) □ *n* **do one's ~** sein Möglichstes tun
utter[1] /ˈʌtə(r)/ *a*, **-ly** *adv* völlig
utter[2] *vt* von sich geben ⟨*sigh, sound*⟩; sagen ⟨*word*⟩. **~ance** /-əns/ *n* Äußerung *f*
U-turn /ˈjuː-/ *n* (*fig*) Kehrtwendung *f*; **'no ~s'** (*Auto*) 'Wenden verboten'

V

vacan|cy /ˈveɪkənsɪ/ *n* (*job*) freie Stelle *f*; (*room*) freies Zimmer *nt*; **'no ~cies'** 'belegt'. **~t** *a* frei; ⟨*look*⟩ [gedanken]leer
vacate /vəˈkeɪt/ *vt* räumen
vacation /vəˈkeɪʃn/ *n* (*Univ* & *Amer*) Ferien *pl*
vaccinat|e /ˈvæksɪneɪt/ *vt* impfen. **~ion** /-ˈneɪʃn/ *n* Impfung *f*
vaccine /ˈvæksiːn/ *n* Impfstoff *m*
vacuum /ˈvækjʊəm/ *n* Vakuum *nt*, luftleerer Raum *m* □ *vt* saugen. **~ cleaner** *n* Staubsauger *m*. **~ flask** *n* Thermosflasche (P) *f*. **~-packed** *a* vakuumverpackt
vagaries /ˈveɪgərɪz/ *npl* Launen *pl*
vagina /vəˈdʒaɪnə/ *n* (*Anat*) Scheide *f*
vagrant /ˈveɪgrənt/ *n* Landstreicher *m*
vague /veɪg/ *a* **(-r,-st)**, **-ly** *adv* vage; ⟨*outline*⟩ verschwommen
vain /veɪn/ *a* **(-er,-est)** eitel; ⟨*hope, attempt*⟩ vergeblich; **in ~** vergeblich. **~ly** *adv* vergeblich
vale /veɪl/ *n* (*liter*) Tal *nt*
valet /ˈvæleɪ/ *n* Kammerdiener *m*
valiant /ˈvælɪənt/ *a*, **-ly** *adv* tapfer
valid /ˈvælɪd/ *a* gültig; ⟨*claim*⟩ berechtigt; ⟨*argument*⟩ stichhaltig; ⟨*reason*⟩ triftig. **~ate** *vt* (*confirm*) bestätigen. **~ity** /vəˈlɪdətɪ/ *n* Gültigkeit *f*
valley /ˈvælɪ/ *n* Tal *nt*
valour /ˈvælə(r)/ *n* Tapferkeit *f*
valuable /ˈvæljʊəbl/ *a* wertvoll. **~s** *npl* Wertsachen *pl*
valuation /væljʊˈeɪʃn/ *n* Schätzung *f*
value /ˈvæljuː/ *n* Wert *m*; (*usefulness*) Nutzen *m* □ *vt* schätzen. **~ added ˈtax** *n* Mehrwertsteuer *f*
valve /vælv/ *n* Ventil *nt*; (*Anat*) Klappe *f*; (*Electr*) Röhre *f*
vampire /ˈvæmpaɪə(r)/ *n* Vampir *m*
van /væn/ *n* Lieferwagen *m*
vandal /ˈvændl/ *n* Rowdy *n*. **~ism** /-ɪzm/ *n* mutwillige Zerstörung *f*. **~ize** *vt* demolieren
vanilla /vəˈnɪlə/ *n* Vanille *f*
vanish /ˈvænɪʃ/ *vi* verschwinden
vanity /ˈvænətɪ/ *n* Eitelkeit *f*. **~ bag** *n* Kosmetiktäschchen *nt*
vantage-point /ˈvɑːntɪdʒ-/ *n* Aussichtspunkt *m*
vapour /ˈveɪpə(r)/ *n* Dampf *m*
variable /ˈveərɪəbl/ *a* unbeständig; (*Math*) variabel; (*adjustable*) regulierbar
variance /ˈveərɪəns/ *n* **be at ~** nicht übereinstimmen
variant /ˈveərɪənt/ *n* Variante *f*

variation /veərɪ'eɪʃn/ *n* Variation *f*; (*difference*) Unterschied *m*
varicose /'værɪkəʊs/ *a* ~ **veins** Krampfadern *pl*
varied /'veərɪd/ *a* vielseitig; 〈*diet*:〉 abwechslungsreich
variety /və'raɪətɪ/ *n* Abwechslung *f*; (*quantity*) Vielfalt *f*; (*Comm*) Auswahl *f*; (*type*) Art *f*; (*Bot*) Abart *f*; (*Theat*) Varieté *nt*
various /'veərɪəs/ *a* verschieden. ~**ly** *adv* unterschiedlich
varnish /'vɑ:nɪʃ/ *n* Lack *m* □ *vt* lackieren
vary /'veərɪ/ *v* (*pt/pp* **-ied**) □ *vi* sich ändern; (*be different*) verschieden sein □ *vt* [ver]ändern; (*add variety to*) abwechslungsreicher gestalten. ~**ing** *a* wechselnd; (*different*) unterschiedlich
vase /vɑ:z/ *n* Vase *f*
vast /vɑ:st/ *a* riesig; 〈*expanse*〉 weit. ~**ly** *adv* gewaltig
vat /væt/ *n* Bottich *m*
VAT /vi:eɪ'ti:, væt/ *abbr* (**value added tax**) Mehrwertsteuer *f*, MwSt.
vault¹ /vɔ:lt/ *n* (*roof*) Gewölbe *nt*; (*in bank*) Tresor *m*; (*tomb*) Gruft *f*
vault² *n* Sprung *m* □ *vt/i* ~ **[over]** springen über (+ *acc*)
VDU *abbr* (**visual display unit**) Bildschirmgerät *nt*
veal /vi:l/ *n* Kalbfleisch *nt* □ *attrib* Kalbs-
veer /vɪə(r)/ *vi* sich drehen; (*Naut*) abdrehen; (*Auto*) ausscheren
vegetable /'vedʒtəbl/ *n* Gemüse *nt*; ~**s** *pl* Gemüse *nt* □ *attrib* Gemüse-; 〈*oil, fat*〉 Pflanzen-
vegetarian /vedʒɪ'teərɪən/ *a* vegetarisch □ *n* Vegetarier(in) *m(f)*
vegetat|e /'vedʒɪteɪt/ *vi* dahinvegetieren. ~**ion** /-'teɪʃn/ *n* Vegetation *f*
vehemen|ce /'vi:əməns/ *n* Heftigkeit *f*. ~**t** *a*, **-ly** *adv* heftig
vehicle /'vi:ɪkl/ *n* Fahrzeug *nt*; (*fig: medium*) Mittel *nt*
veil /veɪl/ *n* Schleier *m* □ *vt* verschleiern
vein /veɪn/ *n* Ader *f*; (*mood*) Stimmung *f*; (*manner*) Art *f*; ~**s and arteries** Venen und Arterien. ~**ed** *a* geädert
Velcro (P) /'velkrəʊ/ *n* ~ **fastening** Klettverschluss *m*
velocity /vɪ'lɒsətɪ/ *n* Geschwindigkeit *f*
velvet /'velvɪt/ *n* Samt *m*. ~**y** *a* samtig
vending-machine /'vendɪŋ-/ *n* [Verkaufs]automat *m*
vendor /'vendə(r)/ *n* Verkäufer(in) *m(f)*
veneer /və'nɪə(r)/ *n* Furnier *nt*; (*fig*) Tünche *f*. ~**ed** *a* furniert
venerable /'venərəbl/ *a* ehrwürdig
venereal /vɪ'nɪərɪəl/ *a* ~ **disease** Geschlechtskrankheit *f*
Venetian /və'ni:ʃn/ *a* venezianisch. **v**~ **blind** *n* Jalousie *f*
vengeance /'vendʒəns/ *n* Rache *f*; **with a** ~ (*fam*) gewaltig
Venice /'venɪs/ *n* Venedig *nt*
venison /'venɪsn/ *n* (*Culin*) Wild *nt*
venom /'venəm/ *n* Gift *nt*; (*fig*) Hass *m*. ~**ous** /-əs/ *a* giftig
vent¹ /vent/ *n* Öffnung *f*; (*fig*) Ventil *nt*; **give** ~ **to** Luft machen (+ *dat*) □ *vt* Luft machen (+ *dat*)
vent² *n* (*in jacket*) Schlitz *m*
ventilat|e /'ventɪleɪt/ *vt* belüften. ~**ion** /-'leɪʃn/ *n* Belüftung *f*; (*installation*) Lüftung *f*. ~**or** *n* Lüftungsvorrichtung *f*; (*Med*) Beatmungsgerät *nt*
ventriloquist /ven'trɪləkwɪst/ *n* Bauchredner *m*
venture /'ventʃə(r)/ *n* Unternehmung *f* □ *vt* wagen □ *vi* sich wagen
venue /'venju:/ *n* Treffpunkt *m*; (*for event*) Veranstaltungsort *m*
veranda /və'rændə/ *n* Veranda *f*

verb /vɜ:b/ *n* Verb *nt*. **~al** *a*, **-ly** *adv* mündlich; (*Gram*) verbal
verbatim /vɜ:ˈbeɪtɪm/ *a & adv* [wort]wörtlich
verbose /vɜ:ˈbəʊs/ *a* weitschweifig
verdict /ˈvɜ:dɪkt/ *n* Urteil *nt*
verge /vɜ:dʒ/ *n* Rand *m*; **be on the ~ of doing sth** im Begriff sein, etw zu tun □ *vi* **~ on** (*fig*) grenzen an (+ *acc*)
verger /ˈvɜ:dʒə(r)/ *n* Küster *m*
verify /ˈverɪfaɪ/ *vt* (*pt/pp* **-ied**) überprüfen; (*confirm*) bestätigen
vermin /ˈvɜ:mɪn/ *n* Ungeziefer *nt*
vermouth /ˈvɜ:məθ/ *n* Wermut *m*
vernacular /vəˈnækjʊlə(r)/ *n* Landessprache *f*
versatil|e /ˈvɜ:sətaɪl/ *a* vielseitig. **~ity** /-ˈtɪlətɪ/ *n* Vielseitigkeit *f*
verse /vɜ:s/ *n* Strophe *f*; (*of Bible*) Vers *m*; (*poetry*) Lyrik *f*
version /ˈvɜ:ʃn/ *n* Version *f*; (*translation*) Übersetzung *f*; (*model*) Modell *nt*
versus /ˈvɜ:səs/ *prep* gegen (+ *acc*)
vertebra /ˈvɜ:tɪbrə/ *n* (*pl* **-brae** /-bri:/) (*Anat*) Wirbel *m*
vertical /ˈvɜ:tɪkl/ *a*, **-ly** *adv* senkrecht □ *n* Senkrechte *f*
vertigo /ˈvɜ:tɪgəʊ/ *n* (*Med*) Schwindel *m*
verve /vɜ:v/ *n* Schwung *m*
very /ˈverɪ/ *adv* sehr; **~ much** sehr; (*quantity*) sehr viel; **~ little** sehr wenig; **~ probably** höchstwahrscheinlich; **at the ~ most** allerhöchstens □ *a* (*mere*) bloß; **the ~ first** der/die/das allererste; **the ~ thing** genau das Richtige; **at the ~ end/beginning** ganz am Ende/Anfang; **only a ~ little** nur ein ganz kleines bisschen
vessel /ˈvesl/ *n* Schiff *nt*; (*receptacle & Anat*) Gefäß *nt*
vest /vest/ *n* [Unter]hemd *nt*; (*Amer: waistcoat*) Weste *f* □ *vt* **~ sth in s.o.** jdm etw verleihen; **have a ~ed interest in sth** ein persönliches Interesse an etw (*dat*) haben
vestige /ˈvestɪdʒ/ *n* Spur *f*
vestment /ˈvestmənt/ *n* (*Relig*) Gewand *nt*
vestry /ˈvestrɪ/ *n* Sakristei *f*
vet /vet/ *n* Tierarzt *m* /-ärztin *f* □ *vt* (*pt/pp* **vetted**) überprüfen
veteran /ˈvetərən/ *n* Veteran *m*. **~ car** *n* Oldtimer *m*
veterinary /ˈvetərɪnərɪ/ *a* tierärztlich. **~ surgeon** *n* Tierarzt *m* / -ärztin *f*
veto /ˈvi:təʊ/ *n* (*pl* **-es**) Veto *nt* □ *vt* sein Veto einlegen gegen
vex /veks/ *vt* ärgern. **~ation** /-ˈseɪʃn/ *n* Ärger *m*. **~ed** *a* verärgert; **~ed question** viel diskutierte Frage *f*
VHF *abbr* (**very high frequency**) UKW
via /ˈvaɪə/ *prep* über (+ *acc*)
viable /ˈvaɪəbl/ *a* lebensfähig; (*fig*) realisierbar; ⟨*firm*⟩ rentabel
viaduct /ˈvaɪədʌkt/ *n* Viadukt *nt*
vibrant /ˈvaɪbrənt/ *a* (*fig*) lebhaft
vibrat|e /vaɪˈbreɪt/ *vi* vibrieren. **~ion** /-ˈbreɪʃn/ *n* Vibrieren *nt*
vicar /ˈvɪkə(r)/ *n* Pfarrer *m*. **~age** /-rɪdʒ/ *n* Pfarrhaus *nt*
vicarious /vɪˈkeərɪəs/ *a* nachempfunden
vice[1] /vaɪs/ *n* Laster *nt*
vice[2] *n* (*Techn*) Schraubstock *m*
vice ˈchairman *n* stellvertretender Vorsitzender *m*
vice ˈpresident *n* Vizepräsident *m*
vice versa /vaɪsɪˈvɜ:sə/ *adv* umgekehrt
vicinity /vɪˈsɪnətɪ/ *n* Umgebung *f*; **in the ~ of** in der Nähe von
vicious /ˈvɪʃəs/ *a*, **-ly** *adv* boshaft; ⟨*animal*⟩ bösartig. **~ ˈcircle** *n* Teufelskreis *m*
victim /ˈvɪktɪm/ *n* Opfer *nt*. **~ize** *vt* schikanieren
victor /ˈvɪktə(r)/ *n* Sieger *m*

victor|ious /vɪkˈtɔːrɪəs/ *a* siegreich. **~y** /ˈvɪktərɪ/ *n* Sieg *m*
video /ˈvɪdɪəʊ/ *n* Video *nt*; *(recorder)* Videorecorder *m* □ *attrib* Video- □ *vt* [auf Videoband] aufnehmen
video: ~ casˈsette *n* Videokassette *f*. **~ game** *n* Videospiel *nt*. **~ ˈnasty** *n* Horrorvideo *nt*. **~ recorder** *n* Videorecorder *m*
vie /vaɪ/ *vi* (*pres p* **vying**) wetteifern
Vienn|a /vɪˈenə/ *n* Wien *nt*. **~ese** /vɪəˈniːz/ *a* Wiener
view /vjuː/ *n* Sicht *f*; *(scene)* Aussicht *f*, Blick *m*; *(picture, opinion)* Ansicht *f*; **in my ~** meiner Ansicht nach; **in ~ of** angesichts (+ *gen*); **keep/have sth in ~** etw im Auge behalten/haben; **be on ~** besichtigt werden können □ *vt* sich (*dat*) ansehen; besichtigen ⟨*house*⟩; *(consider)* betrachten □ *vi* (*TV*) fernsehen. **~er** *n* (*TV*) Zuschauer(in) *m(f)*; (*Phot*) Diabetrachter *m*
view: ~finder *n* (*Phot*) Sucher *m*. **~point** *n* Standpunkt *m*
vigil /ˈvɪdʒɪl/ *n* Wache *f*
vigilan|ce /ˈvɪdʒɪləns/ *n* Wachsamkeit *f*. **~t** *a*, **-ly** *adv* wachsam
vigorous /ˈvɪgərəs/ *a*, **-ly** *adv* kräftig; *(fig)* heftig
vigour /ˈvɪgə(r)/ *n* Kraft *f*; *(fig)* Heftigkeit *f*
vile /vaɪl/ *a* abscheulich
villa /ˈvɪlə/ *n* *(for holidays)* Ferienhaus *nt*
village /ˈvɪlɪdʒ/ *n* Dorf *nt*. **~r** *n* Dorfbewohner(in) *m(f)*
villain /ˈvɪlən/ *n* Schurke *m*; *(in story)* Bösewicht *m*
vim /vɪm/ *n* *(fam)* Schwung *m*
vindicat|e /ˈvɪndɪkeɪt/ *vt* rechtfertigen. **~ion** /-ˈkeɪʃn/ *n* Rechtfertigung *f*
vindictive /vɪnˈdɪktɪv/ *a* nachtragend
vine /vaɪn/ *n* Weinrebe *f*
vinegar /ˈvɪnɪgə(r)/ *n* Essig *m*
vineyard /ˈvɪnjɑːd/ *n* Weinberg *m*
vintage /ˈvɪntɪdʒ/ *a* erlesen □ *n* *(year)* Jahrgang *m*. **~ ˈcar** *n* Oldtimer *m*
viola /vɪˈəʊlə/ *n* *(Mus)* Bratsche *f*
violat|e /ˈvaɪəleɪt/ *vt* verletzen; *(break)* brechen; *(disturb)* stören; *(defile)* schänden. **~ion** /-ˈleɪʃn/ *n* Verletzung *f*; Schändung *f*
violen|ce /ˈvaɪələns/ *n* Gewalt *f*; *(fig)* Heftigkeit *f*. **~t** *a* gewalttätig; *(fig)* heftig. **~tly** *adv* brutal; *(fig)* heftig
violet /ˈvaɪələt/ *a* violett □ *n* *(flower)* Veilchen *nt*
violin /vaɪəˈlɪn/ *n* Geige *f*, Violine *f*. **~ist** *n* Geiger(in) *m(f)*
VIP *abbr* (**very important person**) Prominente(r) *m/f*
viper /ˈvaɪpə(r)/ *n* Kreuzotter *f*; *(fig)* Schlange *f*
virgin /ˈvɜːdʒɪn/ *a* unberührt □ *n* Jungfrau *f*. **~ity** /-ˈdʒɪnətɪ/ *n* Unschuld *f*
Virgo /ˈvɜːgəʊ/ *n* *(Astr)* Jungfrau *f*
viril|e /ˈvɪraɪl/ *a* männlich. **~ity** /-ˈrɪlətɪ/ *n* Männlichkeit *f*
virtual /ˈvɜːtjʊəl/ *a* **a ~ …** praktisch ein … **~ly** *adv* praktisch
virtu|e /ˈvɜːtjuː/ *n* Tugend *f*; *(advantage)* Vorteil *m*; **by** *or* **in ~e of** auf Grund (+ *gen*)
virtuoso /vɜːtjʊˈəʊzəʊ/ *n* (*pl* **-si** /-ziː/) Virtuose *m*
virtuous /ˈvɜːtjʊəs/ *a* tugendhaft
virulent /ˈvɪrʊlənt/ *a* bösartig; ⟨*poison*⟩ stark; *(fig)* scharf
virus /ˈvaɪərəs/ *n* Virus *nt*
visa /ˈviːzə/ *n* Visum *nt*
vis-à-vis /viːzɑːˈviː/ *adv & prep* gegenüber (+ *dat*)
viscous /ˈvɪskəs/ *a* dickflüssig
visibility /vɪzəˈbɪlətɪ/ *n* Sichtbarkeit *f*; *(Meteorol)* Sichtweite *f*
visible /ˈvɪzəbl/ *a*, **-bly** *adv* sichtbar
vision /ˈvɪʒn/ *n* Vision *f*; *(sight)* Sehkraft *f*; *(foresight)* Weitblick *m*

visit /ˈvɪzɪt/ *n* Besuch *m* □ *vt* besuchen; besichtigen ⟨*town, building*⟩. **~ing hours** *npl* Besuchszeiten *pl*. **~or** *n* Besucher(in) *m(f)*; (*in hotel*) Gast *m*; **have ~ors** Besuch haben
visor /ˈvaɪzə(r)/ *n* Schirm *m*; (*on helmet*) Visier *nt*; (*Auto*) [Sonnen]blende *f*
vista /ˈvɪstə/ *n* Aussicht *f*
visual /ˈvɪzjʊəl/ *a*, **-ly** *adv* visuell; **~ly handicapped** sehbehindert. **~ aids** *npl* Anschauungsmaterial *nt*. **~ disˈplay unit** *n* Bildschirmgerät *nt*
visualize /ˈvɪzjʊəlaɪz/ *vt* sich (*dat*) vorstellen
vital /ˈvaɪtl/ *a* unbedingt notwendig; (*essential to life*) lebenswichtig. **~ity** /vaɪˈtælətɪ/ *n* Vitalität *f*. **~ly** /ˈvaɪtəlɪ/ *adv* äußerst
vitamin /ˈvɪtəmɪn/ *n* Vitamin *nt*
vitreous /ˈvɪtrɪəs/ *a* glasartig; ⟨*enamel*⟩ Glas-
vivaci|ous /vɪˈveɪʃəs/ *a*, **-ly** *adv* lebhaft. **~ty** /-ˈvæsətɪ/ *n* Lebhaftigkeit *f*
vivid /ˈvɪvɪd/ *a*, **-ly** *adv* lebhaft; ⟨*description*⟩ lebendig
vixen /ˈvɪksn/ *n* Füchsin *f*
vocabulary /vəˈkæbjʊlərɪ/ *n* Wortschatz *m*; (*list*) Vokabelverzeichnis *nt*; **learn ~** Vokabeln lernen
vocal /ˈvəʊkl/ *a*, **-ly** *adv* stimmlich; (*vociferous*) lautstark. **~ cords** *npl* Stimmbänder *pl*
vocalist /ˈvəʊkəlɪst/ *n* Sänger(in) *m(f)*
vocation /vəˈkeɪʃn/ *n* Berufung *f*. **~al** *a* Berufs-
vociferous /vəˈsɪfərəs/ *a* lautstark
vodka /ˈvɒdkə/ *n* Wodka *m*
vogue /vəʊg/ *n* Mode *f*; **in ~** in Mode
voice /vɔɪs/ *n* Stimme *f* □ *vt* zum Ausdruck bringen
void /vɔɪd/ *a* leer; (*not valid*) ungültig; **~ of** ohne □ *n* Leere *f*
volatile /ˈvɒlətaɪl/ *a* flüchtig; ⟨*person*⟩ sprunghaft
volcanic /vɒlˈkænɪk/ *a* vulkanisch
volcano /vɒlˈkeɪnəʊ/ *n* Vulkan *m*
volition /vəˈlɪʃn/ *n* **of one's own ~** aus eigenem Willen
volley /ˈvɒlɪ/ *n* (*of gunfire*) Salve *f*; (*Tennis*) Volley *m*
volt /vəʊlt/ *n* Volt *nt*. **~age** /-ɪdʒ/ *n* (*Electr*) Spannung *f*
voluble /ˈvɒljʊbl/ *a*, **-bly** *adv* redselig; ⟨*protest*⟩ wortreich
volume /ˈvɒljuːm/ *n* (*book*) Band *m*; (*Geom*) Rauminhalt *m*; (*amount*) Ausmaß *nt*; (*Radio, TV*) Lautstärke *f*. **~ control** *n* Lautstärkeregler *m*
voluntary /ˈvɒləntərɪ/ *a*, **-ily** *adv* freiwillig
volunteer /vɒlənˈtɪə(r)/ *n* Freiwillige(r) *m/f* □ *vt* anbieten; geben ⟨*information*⟩ □ *vi* sich freiwillig melden
voluptuous /vəˈlʌptjʊəs/ *a* sinnlich
vomit /ˈvɒmɪt/ *n* Erbrochene(s) *nt* □ *vt* erbrechen □ *vi* sich übergeben
voracious /vəˈreɪʃəs/ *a* gefräßig; ⟨*appetite*⟩ unbändig
vot|e /vəʊt/ *n* Stimme *f*; (*ballot*) Abstimmung *f*; (*right*) Wahlrecht *nt*; **take a ~e on** abstimmen über (+ *acc*) □ *vi* abstimmen; (*in election*) wählen □ *vt* **~e s.o. president** jdn zum Präsidenten wählen. **~er** *n* Wähler(in) *m(f)*
vouch /vaʊtʃ/ *vi* **~ for** sich verbürgen für. **~er** *n* Gutschein *m*
vow /vaʊ/ *n* Gelöbnis *nt*; (*Relig*) Gelübde *nt* □ *vt* geloben
vowel /ˈvaʊəl/ *n* Vokal *m*
voyage /ˈvɔɪɪdʒ/ *n* Seereise *f*; (*in space*) Reise *f*, Flug *m*
vulgar /ˈvʌlgə(r)/ *a* vulgär, ordinär. **~ity** /-ˈgærətɪ/ *n* Vulgarität *f*
vulnerable /ˈvʌlnərəbl/ *a* verwundbar

vulture /ˈvʌltʃə(r)/ *n* Geier *m*
vying /ˈvaɪɪŋ/ *see* vie

W

wad /wɒd/ *n* Bausch *m*; (*bundle*) Bündel *nt*. **~ding** *n* Wattierung *f*
waddle /ˈwɒdl/ *vi* watscheln
wade /weɪd/ *vi* waten; **~ through** (*fam*) sich durchackern durch ⟨*book*⟩
wafer /ˈweɪfə(r)/ *n* Waffel *f*; (*Relig*) Hostie *f*
waffle1 /ˈwɒfl/ *vi* (*fam*) schwafeln
waffle2 *n* (*Culin*) Waffel *f*
waft /wɒft/ *vt/i* wehen
wag /wæg/ *v* (*pt/pp* **wagged**) □ *vt* wedeln mit; **~ one's finger at s.o.** jdm mit dem Finger drohen □ *vi* wedeln
wage1 /weɪdʒ/ *vt* führen
wage2 *n*, & **~s** *pl* Lohn *m*. **~ packet** *n* Lohntüte *f*
wager /ˈweɪdʒə(r)/ *n* Wette *f*
waggle /ˈwægl/ *vt* wackeln mit □ *vi* wackeln
wagon /ˈwægən/ *n* Wagen *m*; (*Rail*) Waggon *m*
wail /weɪl/ *n* [klagender] Schrei *m* □ *vi* heulen; (*lament*) klagen
waist /weɪst/ *n* Taille *f*. **~coat** /ˈweɪskəʊt/ *n* Weste *f*. **~line** *n* Taille *f*
wait /weɪt/ *n* Wartezeit *f*; **lie in ~ for** auflauern (+ *dat*) □ *vi* warten (**for** auf + *acc*); (*at table*) servieren; **~ on** bedienen □ *vt* **~ one's turn** warten, bis man an der Reihe ist
waiter /ˈweɪtə(r)/ *n* Kellner *m*; **~!** Herr Ober!
waiting: ~-list *n* Warteliste *f*. **~-room** *n* Warteraum *m*; (*doctor's*) Wartezimmer *nt*
waitress /ˈweɪtrɪs/ *n* Kellnerin *f*
waive /weɪv/ *vt* verzichten auf (+ *acc*)
wake1 /weɪk/ *n* Totenwache *f* □ *v* (*pt* **woke**, *pp* **woken**) **~ [up]** □ *vt* [auf]wecken □ *vi* aufwachen
wake2 *n* (*Naut*) Kielwasser *nt*; **in the ~ of** im Gefolge (+ *gen*)
waken /ˈweɪkn/ *vt* [auf]wecken □ *vi* aufwachen
Wales /weɪlz/ *n* Wales *nt*
walk /wɔːk/ *n* Spaziergang *m*; (*gait*) Gang *m*; (*path*) Weg *m*; **go for a ~** spazieren gehen □ *vi* gehen; (*not ride*) laufen, zu Fuß gehen; (*ramble*) wandern; **learn to ~** laufen lernen □ *vt* ausführen ⟨*dog*⟩. **~ out** *vi* hinausgehen; ⟨*workers:*⟩ in den Streik treten; **~ out on s.o.** jdn verlassen
walker /ˈwɔːkə(r)/ *n* Spaziergänger(in) *m(f)*; (*rambler*) Wanderer *m*/Wanderin *f*
walking /ˈwɔːkɪŋ/ *n* Gehen *nt*; (*rambling*) Wandern *nt*. **~-stick** *n* Spazierstock *m*
walk: ~-out *n* Streik *m*. **~-over** *n* (*fig*) leichter Sieg *m*
wall /wɔːl/ *n* Wand *f*; (*external*) Mauer *f*; **go to the ~** (*fam*) eingehen; **drive s.o. up the ~** (*fam*) jdn auf die Palme bringen □ *vt* **~ up** zumauern
wallet /ˈwɒlɪt/ *n* Brieftasche *f*
ˈwallflower *n* Goldlack *m*
wallop /ˈwɒləp/ *n* (*fam*) Schlag *m* □ *vt* (*pt/pp* **walloped**) (*fam*) schlagen
wallow /ˈwɒləʊ/ *vi* sich wälzen; (*fig*) schwelgen
ˈwallpaper *n* Tapete *f* □ *vt* tapezieren
walnut /ˈwɔːlnʌt/ *n* Walnuss *f*
waltz /wɔːlts/ *n* Walzer *m* □ *vi* Walzer tanzen; **come ~ing up** (*fam*) angetanzt kommen
wan /wɒn/ *a* bleich
wand /wɒnd/ *n* Zauberstab *m*
wander /ˈwɒndə(r)/ *vi* umherwandern, (*fam*) bummeln; (*fig: digress*) abschweifen. **~ about** *vi* umherwandern. **~lust** *n* Fernweh *nt*

wane /weɪn/ *n* **be on the ~** schwinden; ⟨*moon:*⟩ abnehmen □ *vi* schwinden; abnehmen
wangle /ˈwæŋgl/ *vt* (*fam*) organisieren
want /wɒnt/ *n* Mangel *m* (**of** an + *dat*); (*hardship*) Not *f*; (*desire*) Bedürfnis *nt* □ *vt* wollen; (*need*) brauchen; **~ [to have] sth** etw haben wollen; **~ to do sth** etw tun wollen; **we ~ to stay** wir wollen bleiben; **I ~ you to go** ich will, dass du gehst; **it ~s painting** es müsste gestrichen werden; **you ~ to learn to swim** du solltest schwimmen lernen □ *vi* **he doesn't ~ for anything** ihm fehlt es an nichts. **~ed** *a* gesucht. **~ing** *a* **be ~ing** fehlen; **he is ~ing in** ihm fehlt es an (+ *dat*)
wanton /ˈwɒntən/ *a*, **-ly** *adv* mutwillig
war /wɔː(r)/ *n* Krieg *m*; **be at ~** sich im Krieg befinden
ward /wɔːd/ *n* [Kranken]saal *m*; (*unit*) Station *f*; (*of town*) Wahlbezirk *m*; (*child*) Mündel *nt* □ *vt* **~ off** abwehren
warden /ˈwɔːdn/ *n* Heimleiter(in) *m(f)*; (*of youth hostel*) Herbergsvater *m*; (*supervisor*) Aufseher(in) *m(f)*
warder /ˈwɔːdə(r)/ *n* Wärter(in) *m(f)*
wardrobe /ˈwɔːdrəʊb/ *n* Kleiderschrank *m*; (*clothes*) Garderobe *f*
warehouse /ˈweəhaʊs/ *n* Lager *nt*; (*building*) Lagerhaus *nt*
wares /weəz/ *npl* Waren *pl*
war: ~fare *n* Krieg *m*. **~head** *n* Sprengkopf *m*. **~like** *a* kriegerisch
warm /wɔːm/ *a* (**-er, -est**), **-ly** *adv* warm; ⟨*welcome*⟩ herzlich; **I am ~** mir ist warm □ *vt* wärmen. **~ up** *vt* aufwärmen □ *vi* warm werden; (*Sport*) sich aufwärmen. **~-hearted** *a* warmherzig
warmth /wɔːmθ/ *n* Wärme *f*
warn /wɔːn/ *vt* warnen (**of** vor + *dat*). **~ing** *n* Warnung *f*; (*advance notice*) Vorwarnung *f*; (*caution*) Verwarnung *f*
warp /wɔːp/ *vt* verbiegen □ *vi* sich verziehen
ˈwar-path *n* **on the ~** auf dem Kriegspfad
warrant /ˈwɒrənt/ *n* (*for arrest*) Haftbefehl *m*; (*for search*) Durchsuchungsbefehl *m* □ *vt* (*justify*) rechtfertigen; (*guarantee*) garantieren
warranty /ˈwɒrəntɪ/ *n* Garantie *f*
warrior /ˈwɒrɪə(r)/ *n* Krieger *m*
ˈwarship *n* Kriegsschiff *nt*
wart /wɔːt/ *n* Warze *f*
ˈwartime *n* Kriegszeit *f*
wary /ˈweərɪ/ *a* (**-ier, -iest**), **-ily** *adv* vorsichtig; (*suspicious*) misstrauisch
was /wɒz/ *see* **be**
wash /wɒʃ/ *n* Wäsche *f*; (*Naut*) Wellen *pl*; **have a ~** sich waschen □ *vt* waschen; spülen ⟨*dishes*⟩; aufwischen ⟨*floor*⟩; (*flow over*) bespülen; **~ one's hands** sich (*dat*) die Hände waschen □ *vi* sich waschen; ⟨*fabric:*⟩ sich waschen lassen. **~ out** *vt* auswaschen; ausspülen ⟨*mouth*⟩. **~ up** *vt* abwaschen, spülen □ *vi* sich waschen
washable /ˈwɒʃəbl/ *a* waschbar
wash: ~-basin *n* Waschbecken *nt*. **~ cloth** *n* (*Amer*) Waschlappen *m*
washed ˈout *a* (*faded*) verwaschen; (*tired*) abgespannt
washer /ˈwɒʃə(r)/ *n* (*Techn*) Dichtungsring *m*; (*machine*) Waschmaschine *f*
washing /ˈwɒʃɪŋ/ *n* Wäsche *f*. **~-machine** *n* Waschmaschine *f*. **~-powder** *n* Waschpulver *nt*. **~-ˈup** *n* Abwasch *m*; **do the ~-up** abwaschen, spülen. **~-ˈup liquid** *n* Spülmittel *nt*
wash: ~-out *n* Pleite *f*; (*person*) Niete *f*. **~-room** *n* Waschraum *m*

wasp /wɒsp/ *n* Wespe *f*
wastage /ˈweɪstɪdʒ/ *n* Schwund *m*
waste /weɪst/ *n* Verschwendung *f*; (*rubbish*) Abfall *m*; **~s** *pl* Öde *f*; **~ of time** Zeitverschwendung *f* □ *a* ⟨*product*⟩ Abfall-; **lay ~** verwüsten □ *vt* verschwenden □ *vi* **~ away** immer mehr abmagern
waste: ~-diˈsposal unit *n* Müllzerkleinerer *m*. **~ful** *a* verschwenderisch. **~land** *n* Ödland *nt*. **~ ˈpaper** *n* Altpapier *nt*. **~-ˈpaper basket** *n* Papierkorb *m*
watch /wɒtʃ/ *n* Wache *f*; (*timepiece*) [Armband]uhr *f*; **be on the ~** aufpassen □ *vt* beobachten; sich (*dat*) ansehen ⟨*film, match*⟩; (*be careful of, look after*) achten auf (+ *acc*); **~ television** fernsehen □ *vi* zusehen. **~ out** *vi* Ausschau halten (**for** nach); (*be careful*) aufpassen
watch: ~-dog *n* Wachhund *m*. **~ful** *a*, **-ly** *adv* wachsam. **~maker** *n* Uhrmacher *m*. **~man** *n* Wachmann *m*. **~-strap** *n* Uhrarmband *nt*. **~-tower** *n* Wachturm *m*. **~word** *n* Parole *f*
water /ˈwɔːtə(r)/ *n* Wasser *nt*; **~s** *pl* Gewässer *pl* □ *vt* gießen ⟨*garden, plant*⟩; (*dilute*) verdünnen; (*give drink to*) tränken □ *vi* ⟨*eyes:*⟩ tränen; **my mouth was ~ing** mir lief das Wasser im Munde zusammen. **~ down** *vt* verwässern
water: ~-colour *n* Wasserfarbe *f*; (*painting*) Aquarell *nt*. **~cress** *n* Brunnenkresse *f*. **~fall** *n* Wasserfall *m*
ˈwatering-can *n* Gießkanne *f*
water: ~-lily *n* Seerose *f*. **~-logged** *a* **be ~logged** ⟨*ground:*⟩ unter Wasser stehen. **~-main** *n* Hauptwasserleitung *f*. **~mark** *n* Wasserzeichen *nt*. **~ polo** *n* Wasserball *m*. **~-power** *n* Wasserkraft *f*. **~proof** *a* wasserdicht. **~shed** *n* Wasserscheide *f*; (*fig*) Wendepunkt *m*. **~-skiing** *n* Wasserskilaufen *nt*. **~tight** *a* wasserdicht. **~way** *n* Wasserstraße *f*
watery /ˈwɔːtərɪ/ *a* wässrig
watt /wɒt/ *n* Watt *nt*
wave /weɪv/ *n* Welle *f*; (*gesture*) Handbewegung *f*; (*as greeting*) Winken *nt* □ *vt* winken mit; (*brandish*) schwingen; (*threateningly*) drohen mit; wellen ⟨*hair*⟩; **~ one's hand** winken □ *vi* winken (**to** *dat*); ⟨*flag:*⟩ wehen. **~length** *n* Wellenlänge *f*
waver /ˈweɪvə(r)/ *vi* schwanken
wavy /ˈweɪvɪ/ *a* wellig
wax[1] /wæks/ *vi* ⟨*moon:*⟩ zunehmen; (*fig: become*) werden
wax[2] *n* Wachs *nt*; (*in ear*) Schmalz *nt* □ *vt* wachsen. **~works** *n* Wachsfigurenkabinett *nt*
way /weɪ/ *n* Weg *m*; (*direction*) Richtung *f*; (*respect*) Hinsicht *f*; (*manner*) Art *f*; (*method*) Art und Weise *f*; **~s** *pl* Gewohnheiten *pl*; **in the ~** im Weg; **on the ~** auf dem Weg (**to** nach/zu); (*under way*) unterwegs; **a little/long ~** ein kleines/ganzes Stück; **a long ~ off** weit weg; **this ~** hierher; (*like this*) so; **which ~** in welche Richtung; (*how*) wie; **by the ~** übrigens; **in some ~s** in gewisser Hinsicht; **either ~** so oder so; **in this ~** auf diese Weise; **in a ~** in gewisser Weise; **in a bad ~** ⟨*person*⟩ in schlechter Verfassung; **lead the ~** vorausgehen; **make ~** Platz machen (**for** *dat*); **'give ~'** (*Auto*) 'Vorfahrt beachten'; **go out of one's ~** (*fig*) sich (*dat*) besondere Mühe geben (**to** zu); **get one's [own] ~** seinen Willen durchsetzen □ *adv* weit; **~ behind** weit zurück. **~ ˈin** *n* Eingang *m*
wayˈlay *vt* (*pt/pp* **-laid**) überfallen; (*fam: intercept*) abfangen
way ˈout *n* Ausgang *m*; (*fig*) Ausweg *m*
way-ˈout *a* (*fam*) verrückt

wayward /'weɪwəd/ *a* eigenwillig

WC *abbr* WC *nt*

we /wi:/ *pron* wir

weak /wi:k/ *a* (**-er, -est**), **-ly** *adv* schwach; ⟨*liquid*⟩ dünn. **~en** *vt* schwächen □ *vi* schwächer werden. **~ling** *n* Schwächling *m*. **~ness** *n* Schwäche *f*

wealth /welθ/ *n* Reichtum *m*; (*fig*) Fülle *f* (**of** an + *dat*). **~y** *a* (**-ier, -iest**) reich

wean /wi:n/ *vt* entwöhnen

weapon /'wepən/ *n* Waffe *f*

wear /weə(r)/ *n* (*clothing*) Kleidung *f*; **~ and tear** Abnutzung *f*, Verschleiß *m* □ *v* (*pt* **wore**, *pp* **worn**) □ *vt* tragen; (*damage*) abnutzen; **~ a hole in sth** etw durchwetzen; **what shall I ~?** was soll ich anziehen? □ *vi* sich abnutzen; (*last*) halten. **~ off** *vi* abgehen; ⟨*effect:*⟩ nachlassen. **~ out** *vt* abnutzen; (*exhaust*) erschöpfen □ *vi* sich abnutzen

wearable /'weərəbl/ *a* tragbar

weary /'wɪərɪ/ *a* (**-ier, -iest**), **-ily** *adv* müde □ *v* (*pt/pp* **wearied**) □ *vt* ermüden □ *vi* **~ of sth** etw (*gen*) überdrüssig werden

weasel /'wi:zl/ *n* Wiesel *nt*

weather /'weðə(r)/ *n* Wetter *nt*; **in this ~** bei diesem Wetter; **under the ~** (*fam*) nicht ganz auf dem Posten □ *vt* abwettern ⟨*storm*⟩; (*fig*) überstehen

weather: ~-beaten *a* verwittert; wettergegerbt ⟨*face*⟩. **~cock** *n* Wetterhahn *m*. **~ forecast** *n* Wettervorhersage *f*. **~-vane** *n* Wetterfahne *f*

weave[1] /wi:v/ *vi* (*pt/pp* **weaved**) sich schlängeln (**through** durch)

weave[2] *n* (*Tex*) Bindung *f* □ *vt* (*pt* **wove**, *pp* **woven**) weben; (*plait*) flechten; (*fig*) einflechten (**in** in + *acc*). **~r** *n* Weber *m*

web /web/ *n* Netz *nt*. **~bed feet** *npl* Schwimmfüße *pl*

wed /wed/ *vt/i* (*pt/pp* **wedded**) heiraten. **~ding** *n* Hochzeit *f*; (*ceremony*) Trauung *f*

wedding: ~ day *n* Hochzeitstag *m*. **~ dress** *n* Hochzeitskleid *nt*. **~-ring** *n* Ehering *m*, Trauring *m*

wedge /wedʒ/ *n* Keil *m*; (*of cheese*) [keilförmiges] **Stück** *nt* □ *vt* festklemmen

wedlock /'wedlɒk/ *n* (*liter*) Ehe *f*; **in/out of ~** ehelich/unehelich

Wednesday /'wenzdeɪ/ *n* Mittwoch *m*

wee /wi:/ *a* (*fam*) klein □ *vi* Pipi machen

weed /wi:d/ *n* & **~s** *pl* Unkraut *nt* □ *vt/i* jäten. **~ out** *vt* (*fig*) aussieben

'weed-killer *n* Unkrautvertilgungsmittel *nt*

weedy /'wi:dɪ/ *a* (*fam*) spillerig

week /wi:k/ *n* **Woche** *f*. **~day** *n* Wochentag *m*. **~end** *n* Wochenende *nt*

weekly /'wi:klɪ/ *a* & *adv* wöchentlich □ *n* Wochenzeitschrift *f*

weep /wi:p/ *vi* (*pt/pp* **wept**) weinen. **~ing 'willow** *n* Trauerweide *f*

weigh /weɪ/ *vt/i* wiegen; **~ anchor** den Anker lichten. **~ down** *vt* (*fig*) niederdrücken. **~ up** *vt* (*fig*) abwägen

weight /weɪt/ *n* Gewicht *nt*; **put on/lose ~** zunehmen/abnehmen. **~ing** *n* (*allowance*) Zulage *f*

weight: ~lessness *n* Schwerelosigkeit *f*. **~-lifting** *n* Gewichtheben *nt*

weighty /'weɪtɪ/ *a* (**-ier, -iest**) schwer; (*important*) gewichtig

weir /wɪə(r)/ *n* **Wehr** *nt*.

weird /wɪəd/ *a* (**-er, -est**) unheimlich; (*bizarre*) bizarr

welcome /'welkəm/ *a* willkommen; **you're ~!** nichts zu danken! **you're ~ to have it** das können Sie gerne haben □ *n* Willkommen *nt* □ *vt* begrüßen

weld /weld/ *vt* schweißen. **~er** *n* Schweißer *m*
welfare /ˈwelfeə(r)/ *n* Wohl *nt*; (*Admin*) Fürsorge *f*. **W~ State** *n* Wohlfahrtsstaat *m*
well1 /wel/ *n* Brunnen *m*; (*oil* **~**) Quelle *f*; (*of staircase*) Treppenhaus *nt*
well2 *adv* (**better, best**) gut; **as ~** auch; **as ~ as** (*in addition*) sowohl ... als auch; **~ done!** gut gemacht! □ *a* gesund; **he is not ~** es geht ihm nicht gut; **get ~ soon!** gute Besserung! □ *int* nun, na
well: ~-behaved *a* artig. **~-being** *n* Wohl *nt*. **~-bred** *a* wohlerzogen. **~-heeled** *a* (*fam*) gut betucht
wellingtons /ˈwelɪŋtənz/ *npl* Gummistiefel *pl*
well: ~-known *a* bekannt. **~-meaning** *a* wohlmeinend. **~-meant** *a* gut gemeint. **~-off** *a* wohlhabend; **be ~-off** gut dran sein. **~-read** *a* belesen. **~-to-do** *a* wohlhabend
Welsh /welʃ/ *a* walisisch □ *n* (*Lang*) Walisisch *nt*; **the ~** *pl* die Waliser. **~ man** *n* Waliser *m*. **~ rabbit** *n* überbackenes Käsebrot *nt*
went /went/ *see* **go**
wept /wept/ *see* **weep**
were /wɜː(r)/ *see* **be**
west /west/ *n* Westen *m*; **to the ~ of** westlich von □ *a* West-, west- □ *adv* nach Westen; **go ~** (*fam*) flöten gehen. **~erly** *a* westlich. **~ern** *a* westlich □ *n* Western *m*
West: ~ 'Germany *n* Westdeutschland *nt*. **~ 'Indian** *a* westindisch □ *n* Westinder(in) *m(f)*. **~ 'Indies** /-ˈɪndɪz/ *npl* Westindische Inseln *pl*
'westward[s] /-wəd[z]/ *adv* nach Westen
wet /wet/ *a* (**wetter, wettest**) nass; ⟨*fam: person*⟩ weichlich, lasch; **'~ paint'** 'frisch gestrichen' □ *vt* (*pt/pp* **wet** or **wetted**) nass machen. **~ 'blanket** *n* Spaßverderber *m*
whack /wæk/ *n* (*fam*) Schlag *m* □ *vt* (*fam*) schlagen. **~ed** *a* (*fam*) kaputt
whale /weɪl/ *n* Wal *m*; **have a ~ of a time** (*fam*) sich toll amüsieren
wharf /wɔːf/ *n* Kai *m*
what /wɒt/ *pron & int* was; **~ for?** wozu? **~ is it like?** wie ist es? **~ is your name?** wie ist Ihr Name? **~ is the weather like?** wie ist das Wetter? **~'s he talking about?** wovon redet er? □ *a* welche(r,s); **~ kind of a** was für ein(e); **at ~ time?** um wie viel Uhr?
what'ever *a* [egal] welche(r,s) □ *pron* was ... auch; **~ is it?** was ist das bloß? **~ he does** was er auch tut; **~ happens** was auch geschieht; **nothing ~** überhaupt nichts
whatso'ever *pron & a* ≈ **whatever**
wheat /wiːt/ *n* Weizen *m*
wheedle /ˈwiːdl/ *vt* gut zureden (+ *dat*); **~ sth out of s.o.** jdm etw ablocken
wheel /wiːl/ *n* Rad *nt*; (*pottery*) Töpferscheibe *f*; (*steering* **~**) Lenkrad *nt*; **at the ~** am Steuer □ *vt* (*push*) schieben □ *vi* kehrtmachen; (*circle*) kreisen
wheel: ~barrow *n* Schubkarre *f*. **~chair** *n* Rollstuhl *m*. **~-clamp** *n* Parkkralle *f*
wheeze /wiːz/ *vi* keuchen
when /wen/ *adv* wann; **the day ~** der Tag, an dem □ *conj* wenn; (*in the past*) als; (*although*) wo ... doch; **~ swimming/reading** beim Schwimmen/Lesen
whence /wens/ *adv* (*liter*) woher
when'ever *conj & adv* [immer] wenn; (*at whatever time*) wann immer; **~ did it happen?** wann ist das bloß passiert?

where /weə(r)/ *adv & conj* wo; ~ **[to]** wohin; ~ **[from]** woher
whereabouts[1] /weərə'baʊts/ *adv* wo
'whereabouts[2] *n* Verbleib *m*; (*of person*) Aufenthaltsort *m*
where'as *conj* während; (*in contrast*) wohingegen
where'by *adv* wodurch
whereu'pon *adv* worauf[hin]
wher'ever *conj & adv* wo immer; (*to whatever place*) wohin immer; (*from whatever place*) woher immer; (*everywhere*) überall wo; ~ **is he?** wo ist er bloß? ~ **possible** wenn irgend möglich
whet /wet/ *vt* (*pt/pp* **whetted**) wetzen; anregen ⟨*appetite*⟩
whether /'weðə(r)/ *conj* ob
which /wɪtʃ/ *a & pron* welche(r,s); ~ **one** welche(r,s) □ *rel pron* der/die/das, (*pl*) die; (*after clause*) was; **after** ~ wonach; **on** ~ worauf
which'ever *a & pron* [egal] welche(r,s); ~ **it is** was es auch ist
whiff /wɪf/ *n* Hauch *m*
while /waɪl/ *n* Weile *f*; **a long** ~ lange; **be worth** ~ sich lohnen; **its worth my** ~ es lohnt sich für mich □ *conj* während; (*as long as*) solange; (*although*) obgleich □ *vt* ~ **away** sich (*dat*) vertreiben
whilst /waɪlst/ *conj* während
whim /wɪm/ *n* Laune *f*
whimper /'wɪmpə(r)/ *vi* wimmern; ⟨*dog:*⟩ winseln
whimsical /'wɪmzɪkl/ *a* skurril
whine /waɪn/ *n* Winseln *nt* □ *vi* winseln
whip /wɪp/ *n* Peitsche *f*; (*Pol*) Einpeitscher *m* □ *vt* (*pt/pp* **whipped**) peitschen; (*Culin*) schlagen; (*snatch*) reißen; (*fam: steal*) klauen. ~ **up** *vt* (*incite*) anheizen; (*fam*) schnell hinzaubern ⟨*meal*⟩. ~**ped 'cream** *n* Schlagsahne *f*
whirl /wɜːl/ *n* Wirbel *m*; **I am in a** ~ mir schwirrt der Kopf □ *vt/i* wirbeln. ~**pool** *n* Strudel *m*. ~**wind** *n* Wirbelwind *m*
whirr /wɜː(r)/ *vi* surren
whisk /wɪsk/ *n* (*Culin*) Schneebesen *m* □ *vt* (*Culin*) schlagen. ~ **away** *vt* wegreißen
whisker /'wɪskə(r)/ *n* Schnurrhaar *nt*; ~**s** *pl* (*on man's cheek*) Backenbart *m*
whisky /'wɪskɪ/ *n* Whisky *m*
whisper /'wɪspə(r)/ *n* Flüstern *nt*; (*rumour*) Gerücht *nt*; **in a** ~ im Flüsterton □ *vt/i* flüstern
whistle /'wɪsl/ *n* Pfiff *m*; (*instrument*) Pfeife *f* □ *vt/i* pfeifen
white /waɪt/ *a* (**-r, -st**) weiß □ *n* Weiß *nt*; (*of egg*) Eiweiß *nt*; (*person*) Weiße(r) *m/f*
white: ~ **'coffee** *n* Kaffee *m* mit Milch. ~**-'collar worker** *n* Angestellte(r) *m*. ~ **'lie** *n* Notlüge *f*
whiten /'waɪtn/ *vt* weiß machen □ *vi* weiß werden
whiteness /'waɪtnɪs/ *n* Weiß *nt*
'whitewash *n* Tünche *f*; (*fig*) Schönfärberei *f* □ *vt* tünchen
Whitsun /'wɪtsn/ *n* Pfingsten *nt*
whittle /'wɪtl/ *vt* ~ **down** reduzieren; kürzen ⟨*list*⟩
whiz[z] /wɪz/ *vi* (*pt/pp* **whizzed**) zischen. ~**-kid** *n* (*fam*) Senkrechtstarter *m*
who /huː/ *pron* wer; (*acc*) wen; (*dat*) wem □ *rel pron* der/die/das, (*pl*) die
who'ever *pron* wer [immer]; ~ **he is** wer er auch ist; ~ **is it?** wer ist das bloß?
whole /həʊl/ *a* ganz; ⟨*truth*⟩ voll □ *n* Ganze(s) *nt*; **as a** ~ als Ganzes; **on the** ~ im Großen und Ganzen; **the** ~ **lot** alle; (*everything*) alles; **the** ~ **of Germany** ganz Deutschland; **the** ~ **time** die ganze Zeit
whole: ~**food** *n* Vollwertkost *f*. ~**-'hearted** *a* rückhaltlos. ~**meal** *a* Vollkorn-
'wholesale *a* Großhandels- □ *adv* en gros; (*fig*) in Bausch und Bogen. ~**r** *n* Großhändler *m*

wholesome /ˈhəʊlsəm/ *a* gesund
wholly /ˈhəʊlɪ/ *adv* völlig
whom /hu:m/ *pron* wen; **to ~** wem □ *rel pron* den/die/das, (*pl*) die; (*dat*) dem/der/dem, (*pl*) denen
whooping cough /ˈhu:pɪŋ-/ *n* Keuchhusten *m*
whopping /ˈwɒpɪŋ/ *a* (*fam*) Riesen-
whore /hɔ:(r)/ *n* Hure *f*
whose /hu:z/ *pron* wessen; **~ is that?** wem gehört das? □ *rel pron* dessen/deren/dessen, (*pl*) deren
why /waɪ/ *adv* warum; (*for what purpose*) wozu; **that's ~** darum □ *int* na
wick /wɪk/ *n* Docht *m*
wicked /ˈwɪkɪd/ *a* böse; (*mischievous*) frech, boshaft
wicker /ˈwɪkə(r)/ *n* Korbgeflecht *nt* □ *attrib* Korb-
wide /waɪd/ *a* (**-r,-st**) weit; (*broad*) breit; (*fig*) groß; **be ~** (*far from target*) danebengehen □ *adv* weit; (*off target*) daneben; **~ awake** hellwach; **far and ~** weit und breit. **~ly** *adv* weit; ⟨*known, accepted*⟩ weithin; ⟨*differ*⟩ stark
widen /ˈwaɪdn/ *vt* verbreitern; (*fig*) erweitern □ *vi* sich verbreitern
ˈwidespread *a* weit verbreitet
widow /ˈwɪdəʊ/ *n* Witwe *f*. **~ed** *a* verwitwet. **~er** *n* Witwer *m*
width /wɪdθ/ *n* Weite *f*; (*breadth*) Breite *f*
wield /wi:ld/ *vt* schwingen; ausüben ⟨*power*⟩
wife /waɪf/ *n* (*pl* **wives**) [Ehe]frau *f*
wig /wɪg/ *n* Perücke *f*
wiggle /ˈwɪgl/ *vi* wackeln □ *vt* wackeln mit
wild /waɪld/ *a* (**-er, -est**), **-ly** *adv* wild; ⟨*animal*⟩ wild lebend; ⟨*flower*⟩ wild wachsend; (*furious*) wütend; **be ~ about** (*keen on*) wild sein auf (+ *acc*) □ *adv* wild; **run ~** frei herumlaufen □ *n* **in the ~** wild; **the ~s** *pl* die Wildnis *f*
ˈwildcat strike *n* wilder Streik *m*
wilderness /ˈwɪldənɪs/ *n* Wildnis *f*; (*desert*) Wüste *f*
wild: ~-ˈgoose chase *n* aussichtslose Suche *f*. **~life** *n* Tierwelt *f*
wilful /ˈwɪlfl/ *a*, **-ly** *adv* mutwillig; (*self-willed*) eigenwillig
will[1] /wɪl/ *v aux* wollen; (*forming future tense*) werden; **he ~ arrive tomorrow** er wird morgen kommen; **~ you go?** gehst du? **you ~ be back soon, won't you?** du kommst doch bald wieder, nicht? **he ~ be there, won't he?** er wird doch da sein? **she ~ be there by now** sie wird jetzt schon da sein; **~ you be quiet!** willst du wohl ruhig sein! **~ you have some wine?** möchten Sie Wein? **the engine won't start** der Motor will nicht anspringen
will[2] *n* Wille *m*; (*document*) Testament *nt*
willing /ˈwɪlɪŋ/ *a* willig; (*eager*) bereitwillig; **be ~** bereit sein. **~ly** *adv* bereitwillig; (*gladly*) gern. **~ness** *n* Bereitwilligkeit *f*
willow /ˈwɪləʊ/ *n* Weide *f*
ˈwill-power *n* Willenskraft *f*
willy-ˈnilly *adv* wohl oder übel
wilt /wɪlt/ *vi* welk werden, welken
wily /ˈwaɪlɪ/ *a* (**-ier, -iest**) listig
wimp /wɪmp/ *n* Schwächling *m*
win /wɪn/ *n* Sieg *m*; **have a ~** gewinnen □ *v* (*pt/pp* **won**; *pres p* **winning**) □ *vi* gewinnen; bekommen ⟨*scholarship*⟩ □ *vi* gewinnen; (*in battle*) siegen. **~ over** *vt* auf seine Seite bringen
wince /wɪns/ *vi* zusammenzucken
winch /wɪntʃ/ *n* Winde *f* □ *vt* **~ up** hochwinden
wind[1] /wɪnd/ *n* Wind *m*; (*breath*) Atem *m*; (*fam: flatulence*) Blähungen *pl*; **have the ~ up** (*fam*) Angst haben □ *vt* **~ s.o.** jdm den Atem nehmen

wind² /waɪnd/ *v* (*pt/pp* **wound**) □ *vt* (*wrap*) wickeln; (*move by turning*) kurbeln; aufziehen ⟨*clock*⟩ □ *vi* ⟨*road:*⟩ sich winden. **~ up** *vt* aufziehen ⟨*clock*⟩; schließen ⟨*proceedings*⟩
wind /wɪnd/: **~fall** *n* unerwarteter Glücksfall *m*; **~falls** *pl* (*fruit*) Fallobst *nt*. **~ instrument** *n* Blasinstrument *nt*. **~mill** *n* Windmühle *f*
window /ˈwɪndəʊ/ *n* Fenster *nt*; (*of shop*) Schaufenster *nt*
window: ~-box *n* Blumenkasten *m*. **~-cleaner** *n* Fensterputzer *m*. **~-dresser** *n* Schaufensterdekorateur(in) *m(f)*. **~-dressing** *n* Schaufensterdekoration *f*; (*fig*) Schönfärberei *f*. **~-pane** *n* Fensterscheibe *f*. **~-shopping** *n* Schaufensterbummel *m*. **~-sill** *n* Fensterbrett *nt*
ˈwindpipe *n* Luftröhre *f*
ˈwindscreen *n*, (*Amer*) **ˈwindshield** *n* Windschutzscheibe *f*. **~ washer** *n* Scheibenwaschanlage *f*. **~-wiper** *n* Scheibenwischer *m*
wind: ~ surfing *n* Windsurfen *nt*. **~swept** *a* windgepeitscht; ⟨*person*⟩ zersaust
windy /ˈwɪndɪ/ *a* (**-ier, -iest**) windig; **be ~** (*fam*) Angst haben
wine /waɪn/ *n* Wein *m*
wine: ~-bar *n* Weinstube *f*. **~glass** *n* Weinglas *nt*. **~-list** *n* Weinkarte *f*
winery /ˈwaɪnərɪ/ *n* (*Amer*) Weingut *nt*
ˈwine-tasting *n* Weinprobe *f*
wing /wɪŋ/ *n* Flügel *m*; (*Auto*) Kotflügel *m*; **~s** *pl* (*Theat*) Kulissen *pl*
wink /wɪŋk/ *n* Zwinkern *nt*; **not sleep a ~** kein Auge zutun □ *vi* zwinkern; ⟨*light:*⟩ blinken
winner /ˈwɪnə(r)/ *n* Gewinner(in) *m(f)*; (*Sport*) Sieger(in) *m(f)*
winning /ˈwɪnɪŋ/ *a* siegreich; ⟨*smile*⟩ gewinnend. **~-post** *n* Zielpfosten *m*. **~s** *npl* Gewinn *m*
wint|er /ˈwɪntə(r)/ *n* Winter *m*. **~ry** *a* winterlich
wipe /waɪp/ *n* **give sth a ~** etw abwischen □ *vt* abwischen; aufwischen ⟨*floor*⟩; (*dry*) abtrocknen. **~ off** *vt* abwischen; (*erase*) auslöschen. **~ out** *vt* (*cancel*) löschen; (*destroy*) ausrotten. **~ up** *vt* aufwischen; abtrocknen ⟨*dishes*⟩
wire /ˈwaɪə(r)/ *n* Draht *m*. **~-haired** *a* rauhaarig
wireless /ˈwaɪəlɪs/ *n* Radio *nt*
wire ˈnetting *n* Maschendraht *m*
wiring /ˈwaɪərɪŋ/ *n* [elektrische] Leitungen *pl*
wiry /ˈwaɪərɪ/ *a* (**-ier, -iest**) drahtig
wisdom /ˈwɪzdəm/ *n* Weisheit *f*; (*prudence*) Klugheit *f*. **~ tooth** *n* Weisheitszahn *m*
wise /waɪz/ *a* (**-r, -st**), **-ly** *adv* weise; (*prudent*) klug
wish /wɪʃ/ *n* Wunsch *m* □ *vt* wünschen; **~ s.o. well** jdm alles Gute wünschen; **I ~ you could stay** ich wünschte, du könntest hier bleiben □ *vi* sich (*dat*) etwas wünschen. **~ful** *a* **~ful thinking** Wunschdenken *nt*
wishy-washy /ˈwɪʃɪwɒʃɪ/ *a* labberig; ⟨*colour*⟩ verwaschen; ⟨*person*⟩ lasch
wisp /wɪsp/ *n* Büschel *nt*; (*of hair*) Strähne *f*; (*of smoke*) Fahne *f*
wisteria /wɪsˈtɪərɪə/ *n* Glyzinie *f*
wistful /ˈwɪstfl/ *a*, **-ly** *adv* wehmütig
wit /wɪt/ *n* Geist *m*, Witz *m*; (*intelligence*) Verstand *m*; (*person*) geistreicher Mensch *m*; **be at one's ~s' end** sich (*dat*) keinen Rat mehr wissen; **scared out of one's ~s** zu Tode erschrocken
witch /wɪtʃ/ *n* Hexe *f*. **~craft** *n* Hexerei *f*. **~-hunt** *n* Hexenjagd *f*
with /wɪð/ *prep* mit (+ *dat*); **~ fear/cold** vor Angst/Kälte; **~ it** damit; **I'm going ~ you** ich gehe mit; **take it ~ you** nimm es mit;

I haven't got it ~ me ich habe es nicht bei mir; **I'm not ~ you** (*fam*) ich komme nicht mit
with'draw *v* (*pt* **-drew**, *pp* **-drawn**) □ *vt* zurückziehen; abheben ⟨*money*⟩ □ *vi* sich zurückziehen. **~al** *n* Zurückziehen *nt*; (*of money*) Abhebung *f*; (*from drugs*) Entzug *m*. **~al symptoms** *npl* Entzugserscheinungen *pl*
with'drawn *see* **withdraw** □ *a* ⟨*person*⟩ verschlossen
wither /'wɪðə(r)/ *vi* [ver]welken
with'hold *vt* (*pt/pp* **-held**) vorenthalten (**from s.o.** jdm)
with'in *prep* innerhalb (+ *gen*); **~ the law** im Rahmen des Gesetzes □ *adv* innen
with'out *prep* ohne (+ *acc*); **~ my noticing it** ohne dass ich es merkte
with'stand *vt* (*pt/pp* **-stood**) standhalten (+ *dat*)
witness /'wɪtnɪs/ *n* Zeuge *m*/ Zeugin *f*; (*evidence*) Zeugnis *nt* □ *vt* Zeuge/Zeugin sein (+ *gen*); bestätigen ⟨*signature*⟩. **~-box** *n*, (*Amer*) **~-stand** *n* Zeugenstand *m*
witticism /'wɪtɪsɪzm/ *n* geistreicher Ausspruch *m*
wittingly /'wɪtɪŋlɪ/ *adv* wissentlich
witty /'wɪtɪ/ *a* (**-ier, -iest**) witzig, geistreich
wives /waɪvz/ *see* **wife**
wizard /'wɪzəd/ *n* Zauberer *m*. **~ry** *n* Zauberei *f*
wizened /'wɪznd/ *a* verhutzelt
wobb|le /'wɒbl/ *vi* wackeln. **~ly** *a* wackelig
woe /wəʊ/ *n* (*liter*) Jammer *m*; **~ is me!** wehe mir!
woke, woken /wəʊk, 'wəʊkn/ *see* **wake**[1]
wolf /wʊlf/ *n* (*pl* **wolves** /wʊlvz/) Wolf *m* □ *vt* **~ [down]** hinunterschlingen
woman /'wʊmən/ *n* (*pl* **women**) Frau *f*. **~izer** *n* Schürzenjäger *m*. **~ly** *a* fraulich
womb /wu:m/ *n* Gebärmutter *f*
women /'wɪmɪn/ *npl see* **woman**; **W~'s Libber** /'lɪbə(r)/ *n* Frauenrechtlerin *f*. **W~'s Liberation** *n* Frauenbewegung *f*
won /wʌn/ *see* **win**
wonder /'wʌndə(r)/ *n* Wunder *nt*; (*surprise*) Staunen *nt* □ *vt/i* sich fragen; (*be surprised*) sich wundern; **I ~** da frage ich mich; **I ~ whether she is ill** ob sie wohl krank ist? **~ful** *a*, **-ly** *adv* wunderbar
won't /wəʊnt/ = **will not**
woo /wu:/ *vt* (*liter*) werben um; (*fig*) umwerben
wood /wʊd/ *n* Holz *nt*; (*forest*) Wald *m*; **touch ~!** unberufen!
wood: ~cut *n* Holzschnitt *m*. **~ed** /-ɪd/ *a* bewaldet. **~en** *a* Holz-; (*fig*) hölzern. **~pecker** *n* Specht *m*. **~wind** *n* Holzbläser *pl*. **~work** *n* (*wooden parts*) Holzteile *pl*; (*craft*) Tischlerei *f*. **~worm** *n* Holzwurm *m*. **~y** *a* holzig
wool /wʊl/ *n* Wolle *f* □ *attrib* Woll-. **~len** *a* wollen. **~lens** *npl* Wollsachen *pl*
woolly /'wʊlɪ/ *a* (**-ier, -iest**) wollig; (*fig*) unklar
word /wɜ:d/ *n* Wort *nt*; (*news*) Nachricht *f*; **by ~ of mouth** mündlich; **have a ~ with** sprechen mit; **have ~s** einen Wortwechsel haben. **~ing** *n* Wortlaut *m*. **~ processor** *n* Textverarbeitungssystem *nt*
wore /wɔ:(r)/ *see* **wear**
work /wɜ:k/ *n* Arbeit *f*; (*Art, Literature*) Werk *nt*; **~s** *pl* (*factory, mechanism*) Werk *nt*; **at ~** bei der Arbeit; **out of ~** arbeitslos □ *vi* arbeiten; ⟨*machine, system:*⟩ funktionieren; (*have effect*) wirken; (*study*) lernen; **it won't ~** (*fig*) es klappt nicht □ *vt* arbeiten lassen; bedienen ⟨*machine*⟩; betätigen ⟨*lever*⟩; **~ one's way through sth** sich durch etw hindurcharbeiten. **~**

off *vt* abarbeiten. ~ **out** *vt* ausrechnen; (*solve*) lösen □ *vi* gut gehen, (*fam*) klappen. ~ **up** *vt* aufbauen; sich (*dat*) holen ⟨*appetite*⟩; **get ~ed up** sich aufregen

workable /ˈwɜːkəbl/ *a* (*feasible*) durchführbar

workaholic /wɜːkəˈhɒlɪk/ *n* arbeitswütiger Mensch *m*

worker /ˈwɜːkə(r)/ *n* Arbeiter(in) *m(f)*

working /ˈwɜːkɪŋ/ *a* berufstätig; ⟨*day, clothes*⟩ Arbeits-; **be in ~ order** funktionieren. ~ **class** *n* Arbeiterklasse *f*. **~-class** *a* Arbeiter-; **be ~-class** zur Arbeiterklasse gehören

work: **~man** *n* Arbeiter *m*; (*craftsman*) Handwerker *m*. **~manship** *n* Arbeit *f*. **~-out** *n* [Fitness]training *nt*. **~shop** *n* Werkstatt *f*

world /wɜːld/ *n* Welt *f*; **in the ~** auf der Welt; **a ~ of difference** ein himmelweiter Unterschied; **think the ~ of s.o.** große Stücke auf jdn halten. **~ly** *a* weltlich; ⟨*person*⟩ weltlich gesinnt. **~-wide** *a & adv* /-ˈ-/ weltweit

worm /wɜːm/ *n* Wurm *m* □ *vi* **~ one's way into s.o.'s confidence** sich in jds Vertrauen einschleichen. **~-eaten** *a* wurmstichig

worn /wɔːn/ *see* **wear** □ *a* abgetragen. **~-out** *a* abgetragen; ⟨*carpet*⟩ abgenutzt; ⟨*person*⟩ erschöpft

worried /ˈwʌrɪd/ *a* besorgt

worry /ˈwʌrɪ/ *n* Sorge *f* □ *v* (*pt/pp* **worried**) □ *vt* beunruhigen, Sorgen machen (+ *dat*); (*bother*) stören □ *vi* sich beunruhigen, sich (*dat*) Sorgen machen. **~ing** *a* beunruhigend

worse /wɜːs/ *a & adv* schlechter; (*more serious*) schlimmer □ *n* Schlechtere(s) *nt*; Schlimmere(s) *nt*

worsen /ˈwɜːsn/ *vt* verschlechtern □ *vi* sich verschlechtern

worship /ˈwɜːʃɪp/ *n* Anbetung *f*; (*service*) Gottesdienst *m*; **Your/His W~** Euer/Seine Ehren □ *v* (*pt/pp* **-shipped**) □ *vt* anbeten □ *vi* am Gottesdienst teilnehmen

worst /wɜːst/ *a* schlechteste(r,s); (*most serious*) schlimmste(r,s) □ *adv* am schlechtesten; am schlimmsten □ *n* **the ~** das Schlimmste; **get the ~ of it** den Kürzeren ziehen

worsted /ˈwʊstɪd/ *n* Kammgarn *m*

worth /wɜːθ/ *n* Wert *m*; **£10's ~ of petrol** Benzin für £10 □ *a* **be ~ £5** £5 wert sein; **be ~ it** (*fig*) sich lohnen. **~less** *a* wertlos. **~while** *a* lohnend

worthy /ˈwɜːðɪ/ *a* würdig

would /wʊd/ *v aux* **I ~ do it** ich würde es tun, ich täte es; **~ you go?** würdest du gehen? **he said he ~n't** er sagte, er würde es nicht tun; **what ~ you like?** was möchten Sie?

wound[1] /wuːnd/ *n* Wunde *f* □ *vt* verwunden

wound[2] /waʊnd/ *see* **wind**[2]

wove, woven /wəʊv, ˈwəʊvn/ *see* **weave**[2]

wrangle /ˈræŋgl/ *n* Streit *m* □ *vi* sich streiten

wrap /ræp/ *n* Umhang *m* □ *vt* (*pt/pp* **wrapped**) **~ [up]** wickeln; einpacken ⟨*present*⟩ □ *vi* **~ up warmly** sich warm einpacken; **be ~ped up in** (*fig*) aufgehen in (+ *dat*). **~per** *n* Hülle *f*. **~ping** *n* Verpackung *f*. **~ping paper** *n* Einwickelpapier *nt*

wrath /rɒθ/ *n* Zorn *m*

wreak /riːk/ *vt* **~ havoc** Verwüstungen anrichten

wreath /riːθ/ *n* (*pl* **~s** /-ðz/) Kranz *m*

wreck /rek/ *n* Wrack *nt* □ *vt* zerstören; zunichte machen ⟨*plans*⟩; zerrütten ⟨*marriage*⟩. **~age** /-ɪdʒ/ *n* Wrackteile *pl*; (*fig*) Trümmer *pl*

wren /ren/ *n* Zaunkönig *m*

wrench /rentʃ/ *n* Ruck *m*; (*tool*) Schraubenschlüssel *m*; **be a ~** (*fig*) weh tun □ *vt* reißen; **~sth from s.o.** jdm etw entreißen
wrest /rest/ *vt* entwinden (**from s.o.** jdm)
wrestl|e /'resl/ *vi* ringen. **~er** *n* Ringer *m*. **~ing** *n* Ringen *nt*
wretch /retʃ/ *n* Kreatur *f*. **~ed** /-ɪd/ *a* elend; (*very bad*) erbärmlich
wriggle /'rɪgl/ *n* Zappeln *nt* □ *vi* zappeln; (*move forward*) sich schlängeln; **~ out of sth** (*fam*) sich vor etw (*dat*) drücken
wring /rɪŋ/ *vt* (*pt/pp* **wrung**) wringen; (**~** *out*) auswringen; umdrehen ⟨*neck*⟩; ringen ⟨*hands*⟩; **be ~ing wet** tropfnass sein
wrinkle /'rɪŋkl/ *n* Falte *f*; (*on skin*) Runzel *f* □ *vt* kräuseln □ *vi* sich kräuseln, sich falten. **~d** *a* runzlig
wrist /rɪst/ *n* Handgelenk *nt*. **~-watch** *n* Armbanduhr *f*
writ /rɪt/ *n* (*Jur*) Verfügung *f*
write /raɪt/ *vt/i* (*pt* **wrote**, *pp* **written**, *pres p* **writing**) schreiben. **~ down** *vt* aufschreiben. **~ off** *vt* abschreiben; zu Schrott fahren ⟨*car*⟩
'write-off *n* ≈ Totalschaden *m*
writer /'raɪtə(r)/ *n* Schreiber(in) *m(f)*; (*author*) Schriftsteller(in) *m(f)*
'write-up *n* Bericht *m*; (*review*) Kritik *f*
writhe /raɪð/ *vi* sich winden
writing /'raɪtɪŋ/ *n* Schreiben *nt*; (*handwriting*) Schrift *f*; **in ~** schriftlich. **~-paper** *n* Schreibpapier *nt*
written /'rɪtn/ *see* **write**
wrong /rɒŋ/ *a*, **-ly** *adv* falsch; (*morally*) unrecht; (*not just*) ungerecht; **be ~** nicht stimmen; ⟨*person:*⟩ Unrecht haben; **what's ~?** was ist los? □ *adv* falsch; **go ~** ⟨*person:*⟩ etwas falsch machen; ⟨*machine:*⟩ kaputtgehen; ⟨*plan:*⟩ schief gehen □ *n* Unrecht *nt* □ *vt* Unrecht tun (+ *dat*). **~ful** *a* ungerechtfertigt. **~fully** *adv* ⟨*accuse*⟩ zu Unrecht
wrote /rəʊt/ *see* **write**
wrought 'iron /rɔ:t-/ *n* Schmiedeeisen *nt* □ *attrib* schmiedeeisern
wrung /rʌŋ/ *see* **wring**
wry /raɪ/ *a* (**-er, -est**) ironisch; ⟨*humour*⟩ trocken

X

xerox (P) /'zɪərɒks/ *vt* fotokopieren
Xmas /'krɪsməs, 'eksməs/ *n* (*fam*) Weihnachten *nt*
X-ray /'eks-/ *n* (*picture*) Röntgenaufnahme *f*; **~s** *pl* Röntgenstrahlen *pl*; **have an ~** geröntgt werden □ *vt* röntgen; durchleuchten ⟨*luggage*⟩

Y

yacht /jɒt/ *n* Jacht *f*; (*for racing*) Segelboot *nt*. **~ing** *n* Segeln *nt*
yank /jæŋk/ *vt* (*fam*) reißen
Yank *n* (*fam*) Amerikaner(in) *m(f)*, (*fam*) Ami *m*
yap /jæp/ *vi* (*pt/pp* **yapped**) ⟨*dog:*⟩ kläffen
yard[1] /jɑ:d/ *n* Hof *m*; (*for storage*) Lager *nt*
yard[2] *n* Yard *nt* (= *0,91 m*). **~stick** *n* (*fig*) Maßstab *m*
yarn /jɑ:n/ *n* Garn *nt*; (*fam: tale*) Geschichte *f*
yawn /jɔ:n/ *n* Gähnen *nt* □ *vi* gähnen. **~ing** *a* gähnend
year /jɪə(r)/ *n* Jahr *nt*; (*of wine*) Jahrgang *m*; **for ~s** jahrelang. **~-book** *n* Jahrbuch *nt*. **~ly** *a & adv* jährlich
yearn /jɜ:n/ *vi* sich sehnen (**for** nach). **~ing** *n* Sehnsucht *f*

yeast /ji:st/ *n* Hefe *f*
yell /jel/ *n* Schrei *m* □ *vi* schreien
yellow /'jeləʊ/ *a* gelb □ *n* Gelb *nt*. **~ish** *a* gelblich
yelp /jelp/ *vi* jaulen
yen /jen/ *n* Wunsch *m* (**for** nach)
yes /jes/ *adv* ja; (*contradicting*) doch □ *n* Ja *nt*
yesterday /'jestədeɪ/ *n & adv* gestern; **~'s paper** die gestrige Zeitung; **the day before ~** vorgestern
yet /jet/ *adv* noch; (*in question*) schon; (*nevertheless*) doch; **as ~** bisher; **not ~** noch nicht; **the best ~** das bisher beste □ *conj* doch
yew /ju:/ *n* Eibe *f*
Yiddish /'jɪdɪʃ/ *n* Jiddisch *nt*
yield /ji:ld/ *n* Ertrag *m* □ *vt* bringen; abwerfen (*profit*) □ *vi* nachgeben; (*Amer, Auto*) die Vorfahrt beachten
yodel /'jəʊdl/ *vi* (*pt/pp* **yodelled**) jodeln
yoga /'jəʊgə/ *n* Yoga *m*
yoghurt /'jɒgət/ *n* Joghurt *m*
yoke /jəʊk/ *n* Joch *nt*; (*of garment*) Passe *f*
yokel /'jəʊkl/ *n* Bauerntölpel *m*
yolk /jəʊk/ *n* Dotter *m*, Eigelb *nt*
yonder /'jɒndə(r)/ *adv* (*liter*) dort drüben
you /ju:/ *pron* du; (*acc*) dich; (*dat*) dir; (*pl*) ihr; (*acc, dat*) euch; (*formal*) (*nom & acc, sg & pl*) Sie; (*dat, sg & pl*) Ihnen; (*one*) man; (*acc*) einen; (*dat*) einem; **all of ~** ihr/Sie alle; **I know ~** ich kenne dich/euch/Sie; **I'll give ~ the money** ich gebe dir/euch/Ihnen das Geld; **it does ~ good** es tut einem gut; **it's bad for ~** es ist ungesund
young /jʌŋ/ *a* (**-er** /-gə(r)/, **-est** /-gɪst/) jung □ *npl* (*animals*) Junge *pl*; **the ~** die Jugend *f*. **~ster** *n* Jugendliche(r) *m/f*; (*child*) Kleine(r) *m/f*
your /jɔ:(r)/ *a* dein; (*pl*) euer; (*formal*) Ihr
yours /jɔ:z/ *poss pron* deine(r), deins; (*pl*) eure(r), euers; (*formal, sg & pl*) Ihre(r), Ihr[e]s; **a friend of ~** ein Freund von dir/Ihnen/euch; **that is ~** das gehört dir/Ihnen/euch
your'self *pron* (*pl* **-selves**) selbst; (*refl*) dich; (*dat*) dir; (*pl*) euch; (*formal*) sich; **by ~** allein
youth /ju:θ/ *n* (*pl* **youths** /-ðːz/) Jugend *f*; (*boy*) Jugendliche(r) *m*. **~ful** *a* jugendlich. **~ hostel** *n* Jugendherberge *f*
Yugoslav /'ju:gəslɑ:v/ *a* jugoslawisch. **~ia** /-'slɑ:vɪə/ *n* Jugoslawien *nt*

Z

zany /'zeɪnɪ/ *a* (**-ier, -iest**) närrisch, verrückt
zeal /zi:l/ *n* Eifer *m*
zealous /'zeləs/ *a*, **-ly** *adv* eifrig
zebra /'zebrə/ *n* Zebra *nt*. **~ 'crossing** *n* Zebrastreifen *m*
zenith /'zenɪθ/ *n* Zenit *m*; (*fig*) Gipfel *m*
zero /'zɪərəʊ/ *n* Null *f*
zest /zest/ *n* Begeisterung *f*
zigzag /'zɪgzæg/ *n* Zickzack *m* □ *vi* (*pt/pp* **-zagged**) im Zickzack laufen/ (*in vehicle*) fahren
zinc /zɪŋk/ *n* Zink *nt*
zip /zɪp/ *n* **~ [fastener]** Reißverschluss *m* □ *vt* **~ [up]** den Reißverschluss zuziehen an (+ *dat*)
'Zip code n (*Amer*) Postleitzahl *f*
zipper /'zɪpə(r)/ *n* Reißverschluss *m*
zither /'zɪðə(r)/ *n* Zither *f*
zodiac /'zəʊdɪæk/ *n* Tierkreis *m*
zombie /'zɒmbɪ/ *n* (*fam*) **like a ~** ganz benommen

zone /zəʊn/ *n* Zone *f*
zoo /zu:/ *n* Zoo *m*
zoological /zəʊə'lɒdʒɪkl/ *a* zoologisch
zoolog|ist /zəʊ'ɒlədʒɪst/ *n* Zoologe *m* /-gin *f*. **~y** – Zoologie *f*
zoom /zu:m/ *vi* sausen. **~ lens** *n* Zoomobjektiv *nt*

Phonetic symbols used for German words

a	Hand	hant
a:	Bahn	ba:n
ɐ	Ober	'o:bɐ
ɐ̯	Uhr	u:ɐ̯
ã	Conférencier	kõferã'si̯e:
ã:	Abonnement	abɔnə'mã:
ai̯	weit	vai̯t
au̯	Haut	hau̯t
b	Ball	bal
ç	ich	ɪç
d	dann	dan
dʒ	Gin	dʒɪn
e	Metall	me'tal
e:	Beet	be:t
ɛ	mästen	'mɛstən
ɛ:	wählen	'vɛ:lən
ɛ̃:	Cousin	ku'zɛ̃:
ə	Nase	'na:zə
f	Faß	fas
g	Gast	gast
h	haben	'ha:bən
i	Rivale	ri'va:lə
i:	viel	fi:l
i̯	Aktion	ak'tsi̯o:n
ɪ	Birke	'bɪrkə
j	ja	ja:
k	kalt	kalt
l	Last	last
m	Mast	mast
n	Naht	na:t
ŋ	lang	laŋ
o	Moral	mo'ra:l
o:	Boot	bo:t
o̯	Foyer	fo̯a'je:
õ	Konkurs	kõ'kʊrs
õ:	Ballon	ba'lõ:
ɔ	Post	pɔst
ø	Ökonom	øko'no:m
ø:	Öl	ø:l
œ	göttlich	'gœtlɪç
ɔy̯	heute	'hɔy̯tə
p	Pakt	pakt
r	Rast	rast
s	Hast	hast
ʃ	Schal	ʃa:l
t	Tal	ta:l
ts	Zahl	tsa:l
tʃ	Couch	kau̯tʃ
u	kulant	ku'lant
u:	Hut	hu:t
u̯	aktuell	ak'tu̯ɛl
ʊ	Pult	pʊlt
v	was	vas
x	Bach	bax
y	Physik	fy'zi:k
y:	Rübe	'ry:bə
y̆	Nuance	'ny̆ã:sə
ʏ	Fülle	'fʏlə
z	Nase	'na:zə
ʒ	Regime	re'ʒi:m

ʔ Glottal stop, e.g. Koordination /koʔɔrdina'tsi̯o:n/.
: Length sign after a vowel, e.g. Chrom /kro:m/.
' Stress mark before stressed syllable, e.g. Balkon /bal'kõ:/.

Die für das Englische verwendeten Zeichen der Lautschrift

ɑ:	barn	bɑ:n	l	lot	lɒt
ɑ̃	nuance	'nju:ɑ̃s	m	mat	mæt
æ	fat	fæt	n	not	nɒt
æ̃	lingerie	'læ̃ʒərɪ	ŋ	sing	sɪŋ
aɪ	fine	faɪn	ɒ	got	gɒt
aʊ	now	naʊ	ɔ:	paw	pɔ:
b	bat	bæt	ɔɪ	boil	bɔɪl
d	dog	dɒg	p	pet	pet
dʒ	jam	dʒæm	r	rat	ræt
e	met	met	s	sip	sɪp
eɪ	fate	feɪt	ʃ	ship	ʃɪp
eə	fairy	'feərɪ	t	tip	tɪp
əʊ	goat	gəʊt	tʃ	chin	tʃɪn
ə	ago	ə'geʊ	θ	thin	θɪn
ɜ:	fur	fɜ:(r)	ð	the	ðə
f	fat	fæt	u:	boot	bu:t
g	good	gʊd	ʊ	book	bʊk
h	hat	hæt	ʊə	tourism	'tʊərɪzm
ɪ	bit, happy	bɪt, 'hæpɪ	ʌ	dug	dʌg
ɪə	near	nɪə(r)	v	van	væn
i:	meet	mi:t	w	win	wɪn
j	yet	jet	z	zip	zɪp
k	kit	kɪt	ʒ	vision	'viʒn

: bezeichnet Länge des vorhergehenden Vokals, z. B. boot [bu:t].

' Betonung, steht unmittelbar vor einer betonten Silbe, z. B. ago [ə'gəʊ].

(r) Ein „r“ in runden Klammern wird nur gesprochen, wenn im Textzusammenhang ein Vokal unmittelbar folgt, z. B. fire /'faɪə(r); fire at /'faɪər æt/.

Guide to German pronunciation

Consonants are pronounced as in English with the following exceptions:

b	as	p	*at the end of a word or syllable*
d	as	t	
g	as	k	
ch	as in Scottish lo<u>ch</u> *after a, o, u, au*		
	like an exaggerated h as in <u>h</u>uge		*after i, e, ä, ö, ü, eu, ei*
-chs	as	x	(as in bo<u>x</u>)
-ig	as	-ich /ɪç/	*when a suffix*
j	as	y	(as in <u>y</u>es)
ps			the p is pronounced
pn			
qu	as	k+v	
s	as	z	(as in <u>z</u>ero) *at the beginning of a word*
	as	s	(as in bu<u>s</u>) *at the end of a word or syllable, before a consonant, or when doubled*
sch	as	sh	
sp	as	shp	*at the beginning of a word*
st	as	sht	
v	as	f	(as in <u>f</u>or)
	as	v	(as in <u>v</u>ery) *within a word*
w	as	v	(as in <u>v</u>ery)
z	as	ts	

Vowels are approximately as follows:

a	short	as	u	(as in b<u>u</u>t)
	long	as	a	(as in c<u>a</u>r)
e	short	as	e	(as in p<u>e</u>n)
	long	as	a	(as in p<u>a</u>per)
i	short	as	i	(as in b<u>i</u>t)
	long	as	ee	(as in qu<u>ee</u>n)
o	short	as	o	(as in h<u>o</u>t)
	long	as	o	(as in p<u>o</u>pe)
u	short	as	oo	(as in f<u>oo</u>t)
	long	as	oo	(as in b<u>oo</u>t)

Vowels are always short before a double consonant, and long when followed by an h or when double

ie is pronounced ee (as in k<u>ee</u>p)

Diphthongs

au	as	ow	(as in h<u>ow</u>)
ei ai	as	y	(as in m<u>y</u>)
eu äu	as	oy	(as in b<u>oy</u>)

German irregular verbs

1st, 2nd and 3rd person present are given after the infinitive, and past subjunctive after the past indicative, where there is a change of vowel or any other irregularity.

Compound verbs are only given if they do not take the same forms as the corresponding simple verb, e.g. *befehlen*, or if there is no corresponding simple verb, e.g. *bewegen*.

An asterisk (*) indicates a verb which is also conjugated regularly.

Infinitive Infinitiv	Past Tense Präteritum	Past Participle 2. Partizip
abwägen	wog (wöge) ab	abgewogen
ausbedingen	bedang (bedänge) aus	ausbedungen
*backen (du bäckst, er bäckt)	buk (büke)	gebacken
befehlen (du befiehlst, er befiehlt)	befahl (beföhle, befähle)	befohlen
beginnen	begann (begänne)	begonnen
beißen (du/er beißt)	biss (bisse)	gebissen
bergen (du birgst, er birgt)	barg (bärge)	geborgen
bersten (du/er birst)	barst (bärste)	geborsten
bewegen[2]	bewog (bewöge)	bewogen
biegen	bog (böge)	gebogen
bieten	bot (böte)	geboten
binden	band (bände)	gebunden
bitten	bat (bäte)	gebeten
blasen (du/er bläst)	blies	geblasen
bleiben	blieb	geblieben
*bleichen	blich	geblichen
braten (du brätst, er brät)	briet	gebraten
brechen (du brichst, er bricht)	brach (bräche)	gebrochen
brennen	brannte (brennte)	gebrannt
bringen	brachte (brächte)	gebracht
denken	dachte (dächte)	gedacht
dreschen (du drischst, er drischt)	drosch (drösche)	gedroschen

Infinitive Infinitiv	Past Tense Präteritum	Past Participle 2. Partizip
dringen	drang (dränge)	gedrungen
dürfen (ich/er darf, du darfst)	durfte (dürfte)	gedurft
empfehlen (du empfiehlst, er empfiehlt)	empfahl (empföhle)	empfohlen
erlöschen (du erlischst, er erlischt)	erlosch (erlösche)	erloschen
*erschallen	erscholl (erschölle)	erschollen
*erschrecken (du erschrickst, er erschrickt)	erschrak (erschräke)	erschrocken
erwägen	erwog (erwöge)	erwogen
essen (du/er isst)	aß (äße)	gegessen
fahren (du fährst, er fährt)	fuhr (führe)	gefahren
fallen (du fällst, er fällt)	fiel	gefallen
fangen (du fängst, er fängt)	fing	gefangen
fechten (du fichtst, er ficht)	focht (föchte)	gefochten
finden	fand (fände)	gefunden
flechten (du flichtst, er flicht)	flocht (flöchte)	geflochten
fliegen	flog (flöge)	geflogen
fliehen	floh (flöhe)	geflohen
fließen (du/er fließt)	floss (flösse)	geflossen
fressen (du/er frisst)	fraß (fräße)	gefressen
frieren	fror (fröre)	gefroren
*gären	gor (göre)	gegoren
gebären (du gebierst, sie gebiert)	gebar (gebäre)	geboren
geben (du gibst, er gibt)	gab (gäbe)	gegeben
gedeihen	gedieh	gediehen
gehen	ging	gegangen
gelingen	gelang (gelänge)	gelungen
gelten (du giltst, er gilt)	galt (gölte, gälte)	gegolten
genesen (du/er genest)	genas (genäse)	genesen
genießen (du/er genießt)	genoss (genösse)	genossen
geschehen (es geschieht)	geschah (geschähe)	geschehen
gewinnen	gewann (gewönne, gewänne)	gewonnen
gießen (du/er gießt)	goss (gösse)	gegossen
gleichen	glich	geglichen

Infinitive Infinitiv	Past Tense Präteritum	Past Participle 2. Partizip
gleiten	glitt	geglitten
glimmen	glomm (glömme)	geglommen
graben (du gräbst, er gräbt)	grub (grübe)	gegraben
greifen	griff	gegriffen
haben (du hast, er hat)	hatte (hätte)	gehabt
halten (du hältst, er hält)	hielt	gehalten
hängen[2]	hing	gehangen
hauen	haute	gehauen
heben	hob (höbe)	gehoben
heißen (du/er heißt)	hieß	geheißen
helfen (du hilfst, er hilft)	half (hülfe)	geholfen
kennen	kannte (kennte)	gekannt
klingen	klang (klänge)	geklungen
kneifen	kniff	gekniffen
kommen	kam (käme)	gekommen
können (ich/er kann, du kannst)	konnte (könnte)	gekonnt
kriechen	kroch (kröche)	gekrochen
laden (du lädst, er lädt)	lud (lüde)	geladen
lassen (du/er lässt)	ließ	gelassen
laufen (du läufst, er läuft)	lief	gelaufen
leiden	litt	gelitten
leihen	lieh	geliehen
lesen (du/er liest)	las (läse)	gelesen
liegen	lag (läge)	gelegen
lügen	log (löge)	gelogen
mahlen	mahlte	gemahlen
meiden	mied	gemieden
melken	molk (mölke)	gemolken
messen (du/er misst)	maß (mäße)	gemessen
misslingen	misslang (misslänge)	misslungen
mögen (ich/er mag, du magst)	mochte (möchte)	gemocht
müssen (ich/er muss, du musst)	musste (müsste)	gemusst
nehmen (du nimmst, er nimmt)	nahm (nähme)	genommen
nennen	nannte (nennte)	genannt
pfeifen	pfiff	gepfiffen
preisen (du/er preist)	pries	gepriesen
quellen (du quillst, er quillt)	quoll (quölle)	gequollen

Infinitive Infinitiv	Past Tense Präteritum	Past Participle 2. Partizip
raten (du rätst, er rät)	riet	geraten
reiben	rieb	gerieben
reißen (du/er reißt)	riss	gerissen
reiten	ritt	geritten
rennen	rannte (rennte)	gerannt
riechen	roch (röche)	gerochen
ringen	rang (ränge)	gerungen
rinnen	rann (ränne)	geronnen
rufen	rief	gerufen
*salzen (du/er salzt)	salzte	gesalzen
saufen (du säufst, er säuft)	soff (söffe)	gesoffen
*saugen	sog (söge)	gesogen
schaffen[1]	schuf (schüfe)	geschaffen
scheiden	schied	geschieden
scheinen	schien	geschienen
scheißen (du/er scheißt)	schiss	geschissen
schelten (du schiltst, er schilt)	schalt (schölte)	gescholten
scheren[1]	schor (schöre)	geschoren
schieben	schob (schöbe)	geschoben
schießen (du/er schießt)	schoss (schösse)	geschossen
schinden	schindete	geschunden
schlafen (du schläfst, er schläft)	schlief	geschlafen
schlagen (du schlägst, er schlägt)	schlug (schlüge)	geschlagen
schleichen	schlich	geschlichen
schleifen[2]	schliff	geschliffen
schließen (du/er schließt)	schloss (schlösse)	geschlossen
schlingen	schlang (schlänge)	geschlungen
schmeißen (du/er schmeißt)	schmiss (schmisse)	geschmissen
schmelzen (du/er schmilzt)	schmolz (schmölze)	geschmolzen
schneiden	schnitt	geschnitten
*schrecken (du schrickst, er schrickt)	schrak (schräke)	geschreckt
schreiben	schrieb	geschrieben
schreien	schrie	geschrie[e]n
schreiten	schritt	geschritten
schweigen	schwieg	geschwiegen
schwellen (du schwillst, er schwillt)	schwoll (schwölle)	geschwollen

Infinitive Infinitiv	Past Tense Präteritum	Past Participle 2. Partizip
schwimmen	schwamm (schwömme)	geschwommen
schwinden	schwand (schwände)	geschwunden
schwingen	schwang (schwänge)	geschwungen
schwören	schwor (schwüre)	geschworen
sehen (du siehst, er sieht)	sah (sähe)	gesehen
sein (ich bin, du bist, er ist, wir sind, ihr seid, sie sind)	war (wäre)	gewesen
senden[1]	sandte (sendete)	gesandt
sieden	sott (sötte)	gesotten
singen	sang (sänge)	gesungen
sinken	sank (sänke)	gesunken
sinnen	sann (sänne)	gesonnen
sitzen (du/er sitzt)	saß (säße)	gesessen
sollen (ich/er soll, du sollst)	sollte	gesollt
*spalten	spaltete	gespalten
speien	spie	gespie[e]n
spinnen	spann (spönne, spänne)	gesponnen
sprechen (du sprichst, er spricht)	sprach (spräche)	gesprochen
sprießen (du/er sprießt)	spross (sprösse)	gesprossen
springen	sprang (spränge)	gesprungen
stechen (du stichst, er sticht)	stach (stäche)	gestochen
stehen	stand (stünde, stände)	gestanden
stehlen (du stiehlst, er stiehlt)	stahl (stähle)	gestohlen
steigen	stieg	gestiegen
sterben (du stirbst, er stirbt)	starb (stürbe)	gestorben
stinken	stank (stänke)	gestunken
stoßen (du/er stößt)	stieß	gestoßen
streichen	strich	gestrichen
streiten	stritt	gestritten
tragen (du trägst, er trägt)	trug (trüge)	getragen
treffen (du triffst, er trifft)	traf (träfe)	getroffen
treiben	trieb	getrieben
treten (du trittst, er tritt)	trat (träte)	getreten
*triefen	troff (tröffe)	getroffen
trinken	trank (tränke)	getrunken

Infinitive Infinitiv	Past Tense Präteritum	Past Participle 2. Partizip
trügen	**trog (tröge)**	**getrogen**
tun (du tust, er tut)	**tat (täte)**	**getan**
verderben (du verdirbst, er verdirbt)	**verdarb (verdürbe)**	**verdorben**
vergessen (du/er vergisst)	**vergaß (vergäße)**	**vergessen**
verlieren	**verlor (verlöre)**	**verloren**
verschleißen (du/er verschleißt)	**verschliss**	**verschlissen**
verzeihen	**verzieh**	**verziehen**
wachsen[1] **(du/er wächst)**	**wuchs (wüchse)**	**gewachsen**
waschen (du wäschst, er wäscht)	**wusch (wüsche)**	**gewaschen**
weichen[2]	**wich**	**gewichen**
weisen (du/er weist)	**wies**	**gewiesen**
***wenden**[2]	**wandte (wendete)**	**gewandt**
werben (du wirbst, er wirbt)	**warb (würbe)**	**geworben**
werden (du wirst, er wird)	**wurde (würde)**	**geworden**
werfen (du wirfst, er wirft)	**warf (würfe)**	**geworfen**
wiegen[1]	**wog (wöge)**	**gewogen**
winden	**wand (wände)**	**gewunden**
wissen (ich/er weiß, du weißt)	**wusste (wüsste)**	**gewusst**
wollen (ich/er will, du willst)	**wollte**	**gewollt**
wringen	**wrang (wränge)**	**gewrungen**
ziehen	**zog (zöge)**	**gezogen**
zwingen	**zwang (zwänge)**	**gezwungen**